CW00430857

To dear Oliver

Let the architectural
discovery begin!

With love
    Catrin xx

THE BUILDINGS OF ENGLAND

FOUNDING EDITOR: NIKOLAUS PEVSNER

SOMERSET: NORTH AND BRISTOL

ANDREW FOYLE AND NIKOLAUS PEVSNER

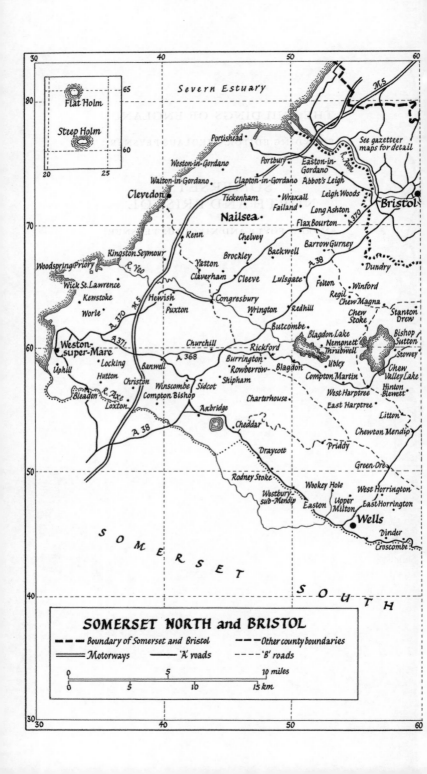

SOMERSET NORTH and BRISTOL

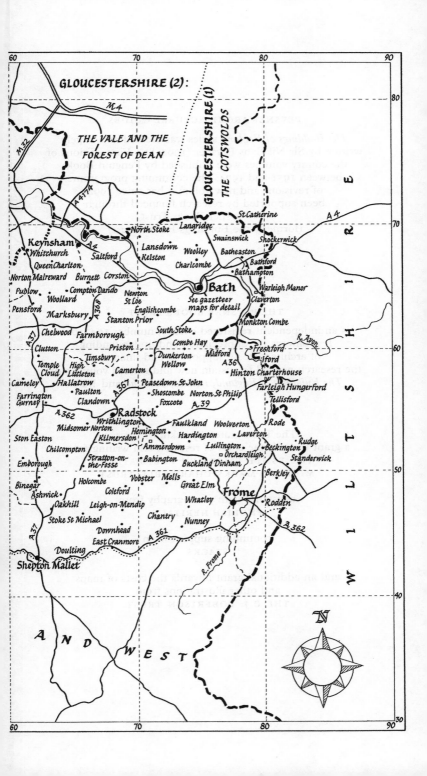

PEVSNER ARCHITECTURAL GUIDES

The Buildings of England series was created and largely
written by Sir Nikolaus Pevsner (1902–83). First editions of
the county volumes were published by Penguin Books
between 1951 and 1974. The continuing programme
of revisions and new volumes has since 1994
been supported by research financed through
the Pevsner Books Trust
(formerly the Buildings Books Trust)

THE PEVSNER BOOKS TRUST

is an independent registered charity, number 1042101.
It promotes the appreciation and understanding
of architecture by supporting and financing
the research needed to sustain new and revised volumes of
The Buildings of England, Ireland, Scotland and *Wales*

The Trust gratefully acknowledges
a grant towards the costs of research and writing from
THE ESMÉE FAIRBAIRN FOUNDATION
MICHAEL MARKS CHARITABLE TRUST

assistance with photography from
ENGLISH HERITAGE

continuing support from
STACKS

and an additional grant towards the costs of maps
and other illustrations from
THE C.J. ROBERTSON TRUST

Somerset: North and Bristol

BY

ANDREW FOYLE

AND

NIKOLAUS PEVSNER

WITH CONTRIBUTIONS FROM

MICHAEL FORSYTH

AND

STEPHEN BIRD

THE BUILDINGS OF ENGLAND

YALE UNIVERSITY PRESS
NEW HAVEN AND LONDON

YALE UNIVERSITY PRESS
NEW HAVEN AND LONDON
302 Temple Street, New Haven CT 06511
47 Bedford Square, London WC1B 3DP
www.pevsner.co.uk
www.lookingatbuildings.org
www.yalebooks.co.uk
www.yalebooks.com
for
THE BUILDINGS BOOKS TRUST

Published by Yale University Press 2011
2 4 6 8 10 9 7 5 3 1

ISBN 978 0 300 12658 7

Printed in China
through World Print
Set in Monotype Plantin

CONTENTS

LIST OF TEXT FIGURES AND MAPS

Every effort has been made to contact or trace all copyright holders. The publishers will be glad to make good any errors or omissions brought to our attention in future editions.

MAPS

PHOTOGRAPHIC ACKNOWLEDGEMENTS

We are grateful to English Heritage and its photographer James O. Davies for taking many of the photographs in this volume (© English Heritage Photo Library) and also to the sources of the remaining photographs as shown below. We are grateful for permission to reproduce them as appropriate.

Bath and North East Somerset Council: 5
James O. Davies: 122, 123, 124

MAP REFERENCES

The numbers printed in italic type in the margin against the place names in the gazetteer of the book indicate the position of the place in question on the index map (pp. ii–iii), which is divided into sections by the 10-km. reference lines of the National Grid. The reference given here omits the two initial letters which in a full grid reference refer to the 100-km. squares into which the county is divided. The first two numbers indicate the *western* boundary, and the last two the *southern* boundary, of the 10-km. square in which the place in question is situated. For example, Abbot's Leigh (reference 5070) will be found in the 10-km. square bounded by grid lines 50 (on the *west*) and 60, and 70 (on the *south*) and 80; Yatton (reference 4060) in the square bounded by the grid lines 40 (on the *west*) and 50, and 60 (on the *south*) and 70.

The map contains all those places, whether towns, villages, or isolated buildings, which are the subject of separate entries in the text.

EDITOR'S FOREWORD

This new edition replaces Nikolaus Pevsner's *North Somerset and Bristol* of 1958. The chief difference in scope from the old account concerns the division with the rest of Somerset, which now runs further N on the eastern side of the county, and also comes closer to the Mendip scarp just W of Wells. The former adjustment transfers sixteen entries in the 1958 edition to the forthcoming *Somerset: South and West* volume (Batcombe, Chesterblade, Cloford, East Cranmore, Gaer Hill, Marston Bigot, Milton Clevedon, Penselwood, South Brewham, Spargrove, Stavordale Priory, Wanstrow, Westcombe, West Cranmore, Witham Friary, Woodlands); the latter change does the same for Henton and Wookey. This new boundary has made possible a fuller treatment of much of Bristol and Bath, especially those suburbs and engulfed parishes which could be covered only briefly or not at all in the two paperback *City Guide* volumes, *Bath* by Michael Forsyth (2003), and *Bristol* by Andrew Foyle (2004). The present gazetteer descriptions of these cities are based on the texts of 2003 and 2004, which drew in turn on the first edition. For the rest of North Somerset, as well as for the companion volume, the starting point remains Pevsner's description as published in 1958.

ACKNOWLEDGEMENTS

The starting point for this book was Sir Nikolaus Pevsner's account published in 1958, based on his tours of the county in 1955 armed with sheaves of information compiled by Miss Schilling and Miss Mary Littlemore. There has been no intervening revision, and so this volume must bridge the yawning gap of fifty-five years. The exceptions are Bath and Bristol, where the *City Guides* of 2003 (by Michael Forsyth) and 2004 respectively have formed a basis for the new text, at least for the central areas; the acknowledgements already published in those books must here be taken as read. But those volumes in turn were based to a large degree on Pevsner's initial work, so it is to his characteristic insight and pan-European knowledge that the primary acknowledgement is due. The challenge has been to retain a sense of his original voice, while revising, updating and expanding the entire text, including the coverage of building types which were only just being considered proper subjects for architectural study in the 1950s, especially industrial and vernacular. In a few cases this has brought into the fold whole villages which were previously omitted, usually for lack of a church.

Except for adjustments s of Frome, detailed on p. 1, this volume retains much the same topographical southern boundary as its predecessor, including Bristol, Bath and Wells: respectively a major regional city, another which is in its entirety a World Heritage Site, and a third containing one of the finest concentrations of Gothic sculpture and architecture in Europe. Coverage elsewhere is necessarily abbreviated by comparison with recent revised volumes for certain less well-endowed counties: for this I can only apologize, and hope that the pen sketches of typical village buildings give some flavour of the riches awaiting the reader who ventures beyond the scope of the text.

Acknowledgement is due to the many who have made major contributions to the book, beginning with past and present staff at English Heritage who have provided consistent support: Elain Harwood enlightened me regarding the best of Somerset's C20 architecture; among many others, Nick Molyneux and Francis Kelly offered their expertise on various Bristol and Somerset buildings. Stephen Croad generously gave unrestricted access to his private studies at Taunton Museum and Record Office, saving me months of research and hundreds of miles of driving. Linda Monckton kindly lent her doctoral thesis on the local development of the Perpendicular style, which amplified the fine work of the late John Harvey (himself a resident of Frome).

James O. Davies took all the new photographs, with an astute eye for the most telling angle or intriguing detail.

The area covered by this volume is administered by several local authorities, most of whom have actively contributed to and supported the work. At Somerset County Council's Heritage Service, thanks are due to Russell Lilford, Tom Maybury, Bob Croft and the staff at the Somerset Studies Library, particularly David Bromwich. North Somerset through its Museum Service offered generous sponsorship in kind by facilitating access to archives covering Weston-super-Mare and the surrounding villages. The exceptional contribution of Chris Richards must be singled out here. The staff of the Record Offices and Archives at Bath, Taunton and Bristol were unfailingly helpful; the last especially for access to its significant material covering the work of Bristol architects beyond the city. Staff at the central and branch libraries of Bristol, Bath, Frome, Midsomer Norton, Nailsea, Clevedon, Weston-super-Mare and Wells responded patiently to my requests for obscure material from store, as did staff at Radstock Museum. Dan Brown kindly contributed his knowledge of Bath's archives of historic prints and photographs gained during the Bath in Time project. Other organizations providing support include the University of Bristol, through the History of Art department, libraries and Special Collections, and the University of the West of England, especially through the Regional History Centre.

Specialist contributors have added much to the text, in the well-established tradition of the Pevsner Guides. Michael Forsyth's text of *Bath* in the City Guide series (with Marion Harney) forms the basis of this shortened account, with their kind advice where additions were needed to cover the outer suburbs. Likewise, Bridget Cherry's contributions of Bristol Cathedral and St Mary Redcliffe from *Bristol* form the core of the new descriptions here. Eric Robinson wrote the succinct and very readable account of Somerset's Geology and Building Materials for the Introduction. Stephen Bird, head of Heritage Services at Bath and North East Somerset Council, wrote the surveys of Archaeology and the Roman period for the Introduction, and all the relevant gazetteer entries too. Geoffrey Fisher, formerly of the Conway Library at the Courtauld Institute of Art, kindly contributed material on C17 and C18 London sculptors, contributing some important new attributions for church monuments, indicated by (GF) in the gazetteer.

Contributions and corrections from many individual experts have been incorporated. Among them are Megan Aldrich, Anton Bantock, R. J. E. Bayliff, Douglas Bernhardt (on Manners of Bath), Geoff Brandwood, Alan Brooks (for his lifetime's study of stained glass), Desmond Donovan, Phil Draper, Julia Elton, Katherine Eustace, William Evans, Andy Foster, Amy Frost, the late Andor Gomme, Tom Harper, Clare Hickman, Mike Hooper, Antony Hotsom, Peter Howell, Jean Imray, Dr Roger Leech, Neil Marchant, David Martyn, George McHardy, David McLaughlin and Kay Ross, Julian Orbach, David Palliser, Stephen Price, Dr Aileen Reid, Anita Sims (on Ashton Court), Matthew

Slocombe of the SPAB, Cathryn Spence of the Building of Bath Museum, Matthew Williams and Diane Walker (on William Burges), Adam White, Lisa White of the Holburne Museum, and Dr Sarah Whittingham (on Sir George Oatley).

Local history societies flourish across the area, many publishing splendid local studies. Among the most helpful have been Brislington Conservation and History Society; Clevedon Civic Society and especially Jane Lilly; Chew Magna (Evelyn Burman); Fishponds Local History Society; the Frome Society (Alastair MacLeay, Michael McGarvie and John Peverley); Shepton Mallet History Society and Fred Davis MBE; Wells Civic Society; and the societies for Buckland Dinham (Jude Harris), Keynsham, Loxton and Portishead (John Rickard). Firms of architects who gave their time freely include Alec French Architects, especially David Mellor, NVB Architects (Mark Brierley), John Casselden, George Chedburn, Jeremy and Caroline Gould, Ivor Day Partnership, Aaron Evans of Aaron Evans Associates, Foster and Partners, Christopher Marsden-Smedley, the late Alan Rome, Alan and Ann Thomas, Caroe & Partners, especially Jerry Sampson, and Donald Insall Associates.

I am grateful as well to the Dean and Chapter of Wells and Dr Warwick Rodwell, to Philip Nokes and Nick Denison at the Old Deanery, to the Rev. Dr John Harding for his assistance at the Roman Catholic diocesan archive, and to Fr Aidan Bellenger, Dom Philip Jebb and Dr Simon Johnson at Downside Abbey. Quentin Alder, Lindsay Keniston and Felicia Smith of Arno's Vale Cemetery Trust were hugely helpful. Numerous custodians and owners of properties great and small were approached for access, sometimes necessarily without prior warning. Pevsner in 1958 alluded to one owner who refused; half a century on, in an increasingly suspicious world, many more than one refused or declined to respond to my requests. Even greater thanks are due then to the many who graciously offered free access and often generous hospitality too. Among them are Lord Hylton and the Hon. Andrew Jolliffe of Ammerdown, the Viscount Asquith at Mells Manor, Von Essen Hotels and the staff at Ston Easton Park, the National Trust, and David Fogden at Clevedon Court, Chris Crook at Woodspring Priory, Gerard and Julia Leighton at Hassage Manor, Michael and Hilly Cansdale, Andy Paterson, Vince and Gina Parker, Philip Binding, Isobel Squire, and Graham and Linda Bellamy.

This book could not have been produced without funding from the Pevsner Books Trust (formerly Buildings Books Trust), administered by Gavin Watson, or the support and patience of the team at Yale University Press. Sally Salvesen was the commissioning editor. Simon Bradley edited the book with his characteristic precision and lucidity, and with Charles O'Brien reviewed the text before copy editing. Sophie Kullmann managed the editing and early stages of production; Emily Winter designed the inset and saw the book through to publication. Sophie Sheldrake ably co-ordinated the text figure illustrations. Judith Wardman compiled the indexes.

Finally, in the established Pevsner tradition, I take full responsibility for any inadvertent errors or omissions, and appeal to readers to draw them to our attention for future revision.

INTRODUCTION

Somerset is a serene county, swept predominantly by westerly winds, and its proximity to the Bristol Channel coast ensures it is generally mild. The north of the county is our subject, and here the landscape varies in mood from the sublime crags and caves of Cheddar Gorge, the thin-soiled limestone plateaux of the Mendips and of the Cotswolds N of Bath, to the richly treed and folded agricultural land of the Chew Valley, and the coastal marshes E and N of Weston-super-Mare. The area covered is not a recognizable political entity, including as it does part of the present shire county of Somerset, the County of Bristol, and the unitary authorities of North Somerset and of Bath and North-East Somerset. The last three belonged to the former county of Avon, established in 1974, abolished 1996. However, the area is topographically coherent: our southern boundary is for over half of its length the steep escarpment of the Mendip Hills cutting SE across the county from Weston-super-Mare to Wells. The hills rise dramatically from the Somerset Levels almost in a single plane, to a height of just over 1,000 ft. From Wells the Mendips peter out into minor vales, their stopping point hardly discernible; here we take the road from Wells E to Frome as our boundary.* At the E end of the Mendips between Bath and Frome, hills and valleys cross in various directions, all green and all lovable. The N slope of Mendip drops steeply towards the Avon valley from Bath to Bristol. Here towns have spread, and industries too.

Bristol is a county of its own, with an estimated population in 2007 of c. 415,000. Bath has c. 84,000, Weston-super-Mare c. 72,000, and Frome c. 25,000. In the 1950s no other town had more than 15,000; today numerous towns (Clevedon, Portishead, Nailsea, etc.) exceed that, generally satellites of Bristol or Bath. Elsewhere one finds few large industrial and commercial buildings, and little council housing. Beyond the cities one thinks first of the churches, of the magnificence of the E.E. cathedral at Wells, then of the parish churches and especially their towers, for Somerset is the county of medieval towers *par excellence*. Numerous villages and towns abound still with agricultural and vernacular buildings, especially rich from the C17, a time of great wealth and rebuilding. Yet scattered throughout the county are many places with an urban character and an urban tradition, and

*To its S, the villages from West Cranmore to Stavordale, formerly included with North Somerset, will be treated in a revised South and West Somerset volume.

that is also a visual pleasure. One must also be reminded that towns, and even villages, often expanded in the post-medieval period under the impetus of crafts and industries, not agriculture. These included the weaving of woollen cloth (Shepton Mallet, Frome, Rode); the knitting of stockings (Wells); stone quarrying (around Bath, Downhead, Gurney Slade); lead and calamine extraction (Priddy, Shipham); brass and copper mills (Keynsham, Publow); paper making (Wookey Hole, Stoke Bottom, Stoke St Michael); iron tool making (Mells, etc.); milling gunpowder (Littleton, near Winford) and of course, coal mining. The Somerset coalfields stretched from Bristol in the N to Coleford and up to the walls of Downside Abbey in the S, with outliers, e.g. around Nailsea. Coal production in N Somerset peaked c. 1890–1920, with annual volumes of c. 1.2 million to 1.6 million tons; never more than a fraction of one per cent of national production. The last pit, at Writhlington, closed in 1973, and the scars inflicted by mining especially in that area have faded, leaving the intact Victorian mining town of Radstock as its legacy. Significant visible remains are included in the gazetteer.

GEOLOGY AND BUILDING STONES
BY ERIC ROBINSON

Of all the English counties, it is possible that Somerset contains the greatest diversity of distinct building stones of merit. As much would be evident to the user of this guide travelling from its villages and market towns, from churches or cathedrals to grand houses, observing and recalling colours and textures; in that simple process, everyone becomes a Somerset geologist. In a sense, this is appropriate: Forest Marble, Marlstone and Fullers' Earth are all names coined by quarrymen, masons or canal engineers within the county.

Most of the good building stones were recognized by the Romans and rediscovered by the Normans, so the history of use goes back many centuries. Stone, however, has always been weighty and difficult to transport along what were little better than farm tracks. For medieval and successive periods, there was therefore a close relationship between villages and their parish quarries. It was not until the coming of the canals that Bath stone, for example, could be delivered and used at Windsor Castle. Within less than a century, the railway network transformed all previous restrictions, and Somerset stones extended much further afield.

To these generalizations, however, there are several Somerset exceptions, and these follow from the navigable waterways of the Somerset Levels (S). The distinctive orange-yellow limestone, HAM HILL STONE, could be taken by what are now the rivers Parrett (S), Yeo (S), and Tone (S) to Bridgwater (S) and the sea, to be used at Bristol. The excellent limestone of Doulting near Shepton Mallet, on the opposite side of the Levels, also found its way well outside its quarry source (*see* p. 6). A final far-travelled Somerset stone was Dundry stone, a warm golden-brown limestone of Jurassic age, also as outlined below. These cases apart, vernacular Somerset remains a physical 'map' of the geology of the county.

In stone distribution of all different qualities, Somerset divides itself into six distinct geographical belts, each running E–W: the Avon Valley, the Mendip Hills, the Somerset Levels (s), the Quantock Hills (s), the Doniford Valley (s), and Exmoor and the Brendon Hills (s). Of these, the Mendips, the Quantocks, and

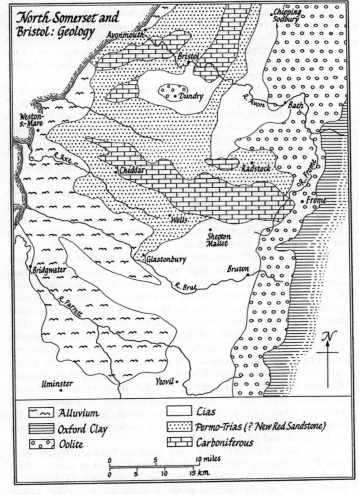

Geological map of North Somerset and Bristol

Exmoor and the Brendon Hills are all areas of older rocks, harder and less tractable to the mason, each with a vernacular architecture which is closer to that of Mid-Wales or the Pennines than to classical and ordered building.

The limestones of the Mendips (and the Avon Gorge) are brittle and splintery under the hammer, often giving a rubble walling to be disguised by render or stucco. Within the landscape of the Mendip Area of Outstanding Natural Beauty the stone expresses itself best in the myriads of dry-stone walls, which test the skills of wallers to standards which are justly famous. The Quantocks, and to a great extent Exmoor, present us with stones which are still older geologically (called Devonian from their relationship with the rocks of that county). They are slaty, gritty, or a strange mixed rock, a muddy sandstone, which carries the German miners' term, GREYWACKE. As quarried, the result is a slab stone which can be coursed in good walling. The good natural slates create roofs with low eaves. Windows tend to be small openings. All of this fits the weather and climate of what remain rugged upland moors.

The geology of the intervening areas, and the main subject of the present volume, could not be more different. Sandstones of the COAL MEASURES gave rise to the villages of the Radstock and Nailsea coalfields, and indeed to much of Bristol outside Clifton. Deep red and brown sandstones of the so-called NEW RED SANDSTONE create the colours and architecture of towns and villages fringing the Mendips, the Quantocks and Exmoor. Younger in time and overlying all these older rocks are JURASSIC LIMESTONES and MARLS which were formed when the entire county was flooded by a world-wide sub-tropical sea. From this succession come the warm golden coloured limestones, the best-known being the stone we call Bath stone. The several variants of this will be mentioned in due course.

As for the Bristol area, the city straddles what is an extension of the Mendip Hills, the high ground of Clifton and Durdham Down, and to the E, the lower-lying ground which was the Bristol Coalfield (Bedminster, Easton, St George and into S Gloucestershire). As explained above, the limestones of the higher ground have never been easy stone to quarry and dress for attractive buildings. Older Bristol buildings are more often of sandstones from the coal workings, actively quarried in Hanham (Gloucs.) and Fishponds. The stone is best seen in the deep cuttings which take the railway line from Temple Meads station to Bath, passing through St Anne's. There are up to 1,600 ft (500 metres) of what geologists term the PENNANT SANDSTONE, a major Bristol building stone of the C19, the stone texture often disguised by smooth render. It is a freestone, easy to dress either for houses or for dock and harbour walling.

Some RED SANDSTONES were quarried between Bedminster and Winterbourne (Gloucs.); these were formed of sandy debris eroded from the Mendip uplands at a later date (Triassic). A pebbly and much coarser-grained rock of a similar origin (mountain screes) was widely used in Bristol and the entire area of N Somerset and the Mendip fringes, known as DOLOMITIC CONGLOMERATE (it has a lime cement which includes the mineral dolomite). This was another building stone most often covered by a render, but it can be seen clearly in the chapel and domestic-range buildings of Tyntesfield Manor, Wraxall, where it is quarried within the estate. A variant occurs at Draycott on the S slope of Mendip, capable of being polished like marble; this DRAYCOTT STONE is seen e.g. at Ashton Court and Temple Meads station, Bristol.

In medieval Bristol, buildings of the quality of St Mary Redcliffe church and those of other major parishes required the supply of thousands of tons of best-quality DUNDRY FREESTONE. Quarried and indeed mined at the top of the hill S of Long Ashton (757 ft, 233 metres), this Jurassic limestone had a high reputation for decorative work far beyond Somerset; it could be sledged downhill to wharves on the Avon (and was shipped famously to Dublin, for the C12 Christ Church Cathedral there).

Moving E from Bristol up the Avon, we pass into country in which the building stones immediately shout of changes to the regional geology. This is the realm of BATH STONE and its near relatives. The history of Bath is closely involved with the exploitation of the golden-toned stone which carries its name abroad.* In 1727, Ralph Allen took an option to open a quarry on Combe Down high above the city. The stone had two main varieties. One was a limestone quite rich in fossil shells, giving a toughness and resistance to weathering which made it excellent for plinths and string courses in buildings. Quarrymen call this 'ragstone' from its roughness. The thicker bed units above the ragstone are of even-grained stone, easy to dress or carve with hand tools, and equally easy to detach from the quarry bed because of well-formed vertical cracks (joints). Several metres of this freestone are the valuable commercial Bath stone. The even-grained character of the freestone derives from the shell fragments that were rolled on the Jurassic sea floor, becoming coated with a thin skin of lime, and then bonded by a cement of lime to create the grainstone which geologists term 'oolite', from the Greek word for egg ('cod's roe' may be more descriptive). It is the quality of the Bath oolite that the stone can be dressed with the chisel and the steel comb tool of masons to give a perfectly smooth surface, ideal for the ashlar finishes of the typical Bath frontages. It is instructive, however, to seek out the gable-ends and back lanes to see how the same stone in irregular shaped pieces (rubble indeed) was bonded into sound if less attractive finishes. No waste!

In 1733 Allen set out to build himself an imposing Palladian villa, overlooking the city from the open space of Prior Park

p. 99

---

* Bath stone was specified by British architects asked to work in Cape Town and India, rather than struggle with local and untested alternatives. One C18 consignment for use at St Bartholomew's Hospital in London was taken by French privateers in the Channel, and now must grace some château in Normandy.

(*see* p. 200). Prior Park became the showpiece demonstrating Combe Down freestone. By means of a wooden railway, modelled by a Bristol engineer, *John Padmore*, upon the early colliery railways of NE England, vast tonnages of dressed stone were delivered down to the riverside wharves and stone yards to meet the needs of Nash and the Woods in their development of Bath as a spa city. Later quarries were at many sites in the Avon valley, Claverton, Bathford, and Limpley Stoke, extending into Wiltshire up to 8 m. E of Bath, but all is known as Bath stone. Barges on the Avon, and on the Kennet and Avon Canal, took the stone to distant market towns and great houses. The industry expanded in the C19, when *Brunel* brought his Great Western Railway through the city of Bath. The cutting of Box Tunnel for the railway (opened in 1841) extended quarrying eastwards when earlier sources were failing. It was Brunel's railway which took Bath stone into South Wales and up to London.

Bath stone was much promoted by William Smith, the canal builder and 'land improver' (1769–1839), often referred to as the Father of English Geology. He was the first to map stone outcrops around Bath, in an effort to encourage landowners to regard stone as a marketable resource. He demonstrated the result at the annual Bath and West Show (1798/9). Among other things, Smith sought to organize the naming and classification of the strata or stone beds. In his system, Bath stone was part of the Great Oolite. Other workable limestones at lower levels in the succession were, through co-operation with the French, with slight misfortune, named 'Inferior Oolite', a name which refers to their lower position rather than to quality.

This much immediately becomes evident when we discuss DOULTING STONE, a crystalline hard-wearing limestone quarried just E of Shepton Mallet. Used since Roman times, this was the principal stone of both Wells Cathedral and Glastonbury Abbey (S), ownership and exclusive use being disputed between the two at a critical period in the C12. Wells Cathedral's E end, cloisters and elaborate W front, richly carved and decorated, are testimony to the quality of Doulting stone as a freestone. Its niches and angles are ornamented with slender grey shafts of limestone, originally turned and polished from thin beds of Lias (*see also* below), a muddy dark limestone quarried to the W of the city (C19 replacements came from Kilkenny in southern Ireland).

10, 11,
16

The Doulting quarries were under Glastonbury's control by the time of the fire there in 1184, and their subsequent appropriation of all Doulting stone for rebuilding necessitated the introduction at Wells of brown-toned CHILCOTE STONE, a local form of the Dolomitic Conglomerate known as DOWNSIDE STONE which also occurs in and around Bristol. The wealth of chips of the older Mendip limestone, when polished, give this stone a 'marble' quality. Otherwise, this local stone was a substitute for the better-quality oolite.

Outside the limits of the Mendips, outcrops occur of the dark flaggy limestone, the LIAS or BLUE LIAS. That name may be a corruption of 'layers' in the vernacular of quarrymen in Somerset and Gloucestershire, but has passed into the universal language of geology, to be used as far afield as China.* From the shallow quarries, slabs several metres square could be levered from the bed to provide pavings that were much used for medieval churches, and the dark slabs which carry monumental brasses. As already noted, turned and polished Lias can provide shafts and columns, as seen in porches and screens. The variant WHITE LIAS is, however, much more the building stone of the Somerset Levels (s), e.g. Somerton, Huish Episcopi and Langport, or coastal sites such as Blue Anchor, s of Bridgwater Bay (s). Pockets also occur around Keynsham, where it is laden with ammonites.

THE PREHISTORIC AND ROMAN PERIODS
BY STEPHEN BIRD

North Somerset in Prehistory

The earliest human activity in the region is likely to have been in the LOWER PALAEOLITHIC, around half a million years ago. The period was characterized by successive glaciations which saw the advance and retreat of massive ice sheets across much of northern Europe. With so much sea water locked up in ice, today's Bristol Channel coastline would not have existed and, further s, Britain was still connected with continental Europe.

Although the glaciations may have stopped just short of N Somerset, they would have had a profound effect on the lives of the tiny nomadic bands of hunters. These people left no mark on the landscape; the only evidence for them takes the form of tools fashioned from flint and chert from Abbot's Leigh and the gravel terraces of the River Avon at Brislington and Kelston.

The cave and gorges of Mendip are likely to have attracted occupation from the earliest times. During the MIDDLE PALAEOLITHIC ice age of c. 75,000–80,000 B.C., people took shelter and laid hearths in Hyaena Den at Wookey, butchering and skinning their prey. The bones they left were the remains of mammoth, woolly rhinoceros, horse, reindeer and giant elk, all animals associated with a cold climate, although the large quantity of hyaena bones found suggests that these animals used the cave as a den during warmer periods, or 'interstadials'.

Between c. 20,000 and c. 12,000 B.C. the final glacial advance rendered the whole area a barren tundra. From around 12,000 B.C., however, the climate began to improve and the caves and rock shelters of Mendip were again occupied as modern man (*Homo sapiens sapiens*) arrived in southern Britain. In particular, Gough's (New) Cave in Cheddar Gorge on the s side of Mendip, and Aveline's Hole in Burrington Combe on the N side, are among the most important sites in Britain for the study of

3

*Dictionaries give an alternative etymology from the Old French *liais*.

UPPER PALAEOLITHIC human activity. Aveline's Hole was used as a refuge by hunters. The implements they left behind include a barbed antler harpoon head reminiscent of representations in the cave art of the Dordogne, a cultural link made plausible by the land bridge that still existed between Britain and Europe. Gough's Cave has yielded several thousand flint and chert artifacts.

By 7000 B.C. the ice sheets had retreated. The vast amounts of water released raised the sea level; the Bristol Channel was formed and Britain became an island. Pine and birch gave way to mixed forests of oak, elm and beech. In them people hunted, collected nuts, berries and tubers, and harpooned fish in the rivers using weapons tipped with small razor-sharp flint blades, or 'microliths'. Quantities of microliths dropped in the mud around the hot springs at Bath and scatters on the surrounding downland suggest seasonal patterns of behaviour, perhaps spending the winter in the shelter of river valleys and the summer on higher ground.

The NEOLITHIC PERIOD, when farming first started, began c. 4500 B.C., with more permanent settlements and the creation of megalithic burial sites and ceremonial monuments, in a gradual transition from a hunting and gathering economy to a more settled way of life. Early farmers cleared woodland and scrub to grow crops and build paddocks to keep cattle, pigs and perhaps goats and sheep, while hunter-gatherer bands continued their traditional practices in the forests around them. The earliest significant Neolithic DOMESTIC SITE in the area was found in 1953–5 close to fertile river gravels at Chew Park in the Chew valley, in advance of the creation of the reservoir there. Excavations revealed the post-holes of a circular hut c. 9 ft (3 metres) wide, and a refuse pit containing potsherds and evidence of flint-working. Middle Neolithic occupation debris and rubbish pits have been detected at Winscombe, Congresbury, Charmy Down (St Catherine) and, possibly, Camerton. Finds of quernstones indicate crop cultivation; animal bones are evidence of stock husbandry. Both activities required open land and, as the Neolithic period progressed, large areas of woodland were cleared. Stone axe-heads were imported from Wales, Cornwall and Cumbria, while flint for axe-heads came from the nearby Wessex and Marlborough downs. Both imports indicate the importance of the Avon valley and Bristol Channel as communication routes.

The earliest architectural structures in N Somerset date from the early to middle Neolithic. These CHAMBERED TOMBS belong to a broader 'Cotswold–Severn' tradition, and represent the communal burial places of the earliest farming communities. Many are badly damaged, others are known only from antiquarian records. Undoubtedly the finest example is Stoney Littleton long barrow, near Wellow: a trapezoid mound 98 ft (30 metres) long, originally flanked by ditches, with a recessed forecourt revetted with dry-stone walling, a monolithic entrance with a lintel, and a gallery with chambers from which human bones were recovered. Other remains of chambered tombs include those at Waterstone near Redhill, Felton Hill near Winford, Fairy's Toot near Nempnett Thrubwell, Giant's Grave near Holcombe and the Devil's Bed and Bolster near Beckington. Recent research has identified more possible tombs at Brean Down, Hengaston (Failand) and Bathford Hill. There are also remains of long barrows at Chewton Edge, Green Ore, Longwood and Pen Hill, not entered in the gazetteer. Three massive stones at Stanton Drew known as The Cove may have been the façade of a long barrow that pre-dated the stone circles by nearly 1,000 years.

Significant changes occurred in the third millennium B.C. Chambered tombs fell into disuse and were blocked up, and new ceremonial monuments appeared in the landscape. Several such impressive sites represent the LATE NEOLITHIC in our area. Most substantial of these, and a site of national significance, are the Stanton Drew STONE CIRCLES. This group of monuments comprises three depleted circles of different sizes, The Cove and a single standing stone, Hautville's Quoit, a few hundred yards to the N beyond the River Chew. The remains of avenues approaching two of the circles from the E can still be seen. The largest circle was over 100 yds (90 metres) across, one of the biggest in the country. In 1997 a geophysical survey of the largest stone circle revealed a ditch around it and a pattern of around 500 pits, each a metre or more across, laid out in nine concentric rings with a corridor to the centre. Circular ditched enclosures, or henges, of the Late Neolithic sometimes include stone circles and, occasionally, rings of pits, and there are striking comparisons between Stanton Drew and wooden temples detected at The Sanctuary near Avebury (Wilts.) and Woodhenge near Stonehenge. If the pits held timber uprights, they would have formed a structure up to 82 ft (25 metres) high and more than twice the size of its hitherto more famous counterparts. Whether part or all of it was roofed is unknown. Although we can only guess at its purpose, it is likely to have been a focus for ceremonial activities related to the solar and lunar calendars. What is clear, however, is that Stanton Drew represents the work and beliefs of a society that had the time, stability and cohesion to plan and construct a temple of this size and complexity. This was a society with growing wealth and broadening horizons, and which may have witnessed the passage up the Avon valley of bluestone monoliths from Preseli in West Wales, destined for another great West Country temple at Stonehenge.

On the higher ground of Mendip lie the Priddy Circles, four great henge monuments aligned roughly N–S, the northernmost incomplete, the others between 165 and 185 yds (151 and 169 metres) in diameter. Each has a single entrance and, unusually, the ditches all lie outside the bank, a characteristic only seen elsewhere in the earliest phase at Stonehenge. Also Late Neolithic is the much smaller henge of Gorsey Bigbury (Charterhouse) on Mendip plateau. Its rock-cut ditch contained parts of a human skeleton with personal possessions made of flint and pottery, possibly a ritual deposit.

The later third millennium B.C. is characterized by the appearance of new tool and weapon types, and a distinctive pottery 'beaker' of Continental origin. These may be linked to increased communication and, perhaps, population movements. Distinctive tanged-and-barbed flint arrowheads indicate a new emphasis on archery, with concentrations on the Failand Ridge and the downs around Bath suggesting considerable activity in upland areas. After a period of abandonment, Gorsey Bigbury was reoccupied by people who camped in the ditch, leaving fragments of nearly a hundred beakers behind them.

New styles of burial appear at the same time. A rock-cut cist lined with stone slabs at Corston contained the remains of a crouched male with a beaker in one grave, with an infant and two adolescents in another close by. At Black Down (*see* Charterhouse) near Burrington another beaker burial was found in a stone-lined cist beneath a round burial mound. The introduction of such mounds, or barrows, covering single inhumations and sometimes containing simple copper objects, is seen as a sign of an emerging élite associated with the spread of bronze-working, interpreted as warriors at the head of new tribal groupings, whose skills in metallurgy would have given them almost priest-like status.

The main evidence in the landscape for the early BRONZE AGE takes the form of ROUND BARROWS, mainly on higher ground, often in groups or linear cemeteries, as on Mendip. Some contained particularly rich burials, perhaps reflecting the proximity of the flowering 'Wessex Culture' centred on Salisbury Plain. The richest lie close to the major ceremonial centres of Stanton Drew, Priddy and Gorsey Bigbury, which were probably all still in use. Barrows at Camerton and Priddy contained grooved bronze daggers, while beads of amber, faience and shale have been found in numerous other Mendip barrows, fine imported materials used in items of personal adornment by high-ranking individuals. Other clusters of round barrows on Mendip are at Black Down and Beacon Batch (both in Charterhouse, p. 438).

The distribution of other Bronze Age finds shows concentrations in the Avon valley and its tributaries, indicating the value placed on good farmland and the importance of communication further afield. Additional evidence of influences from beyond the region comes in the form of seven foot-carvings and ten cup-marks incised on the inner face of a cist burial under a round barrow at Priddy, most closely associated with carvings on a megalithic tomb at Calderstones near Liverpool.

By the Middle Bronze Age, from around the middle of the second millennium B.C., the practice of barrow construction seems to have ceased. Domestic sites of this period are all but unknown, although stray finds of hoards of bronze objects indicate growing proficiency in bronze-working. Axe-heads, chisels and sickles show the continuing need for tree-felling, woodworking and agricultural tools. At the same time objects of personal adornment start to appear. The Monkswood Hoard, from the extreme NE of Somerset (*see* St Catherine), contained twisted torcs, bracelets and penannular arm-rings, perhaps of Irish influence. This hoard represents an 'ornament horizon' which can be identified across southern Britain.

The area around Bath was the focus for considerable Bronze Age activity. Numerous barrows stood on the surrounding hills, and one, on Lansdown, produced fragments of a gold-covered copper disc, now in the British Museum. It is tempting to associate this 'sundisc' with the hot springs in the valley below.

From about 800 B.C., concerns over rights of access to and use of land are reflected in the appearance of large defended enclosures, or HILL-FORTS. Although some are now thought to have origins in the later Bronze Age, hill-forts are the most prominent monuments of the IRON AGE in N Somerset and are found from the bluffs overlooking the Bristol Channel to the limestone hills of the eastern Mendips and the downs around Bath. They were constructed at different points during the first millennium B.C., were occupied for differing lengths of time, and may have been intended for different purposes. What they share, however, is the social cohesion and motivation that enabled and compelled communities to create defended settlements and refuges.

The hill-fort overlooking Weston-super-Mare at Worlebury, excavated in the mid to late C19, was one of the first in England to be examined in detail. A circuit of ditches and banks,

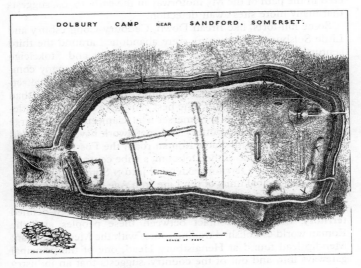

Churchill, Dolebury, hill-fort.
Engraving, 1883

complemented by steep hillsides and shore-line cliffs, was occupied over a long period by a settled agricultural population who
dug grain-storage pits into the rock. Its defences appear to have
been breached at some point during its occupation, leading to
p. 11   the massacre of at least eighteen individuals. Dolebury hill-fort
near Churchill had massive ramparts of stone, still standing over
20 ft (6 metres) high in places. In contrast, Bathampton Down's
low single circuit of rampart and ditch enclosing an area too large
to defend effectively may have served as little more than a live-
stock corral. Evidence of a building and 'celtic' field system
underlying the rampart indicates that the down was already occupied and cultivated and this may have resumed after the hill-fort
went out of use. Hill-forts like Banwell went through several
phases of development, while activity at other sites was short-
lived: the unfinished ramparts and absence of interior activity at
Burrington suggest that the site was never occupied. Examples
on the Mendips that are not entered in the gazetteer are Ben
Knoll, a fortified enclosure on Pen Hill, and Westbury Camp, an
irregular hexagon enclosing 6 acres and protected by a large ditch
and bank.

Hill-forts were probably built and used by the more dominant
communities, but other settlements are known. Field systems and
possible settlements associated with them suggest intensive
farming along the Failand Ridge. Unenclosed settlements, such
as at Pagan's Hill (*see* Chew Stoke) and in the Chew valley, are
harder to discern but may represent a large proportion of the
population for whom other evidence has not survived. Hut circles
are known at Portishead, Butcombe, Chew Park and Camerton,
and a hitherto unknown Iron Age cemetery at Christon, discovered in the path of the M5 motorway in the early 1970s, suggests
that many more sites await detection.

Some hill-forts, like Brean Down, Cadbury-Congresbury and
Little Solsbury (Batheaston), were abandoned around the third
century B.C., while others, such as Worlebury and Stokeleigh
Camp were strengthened. By the C1 B.C., however, many communities were abandoning their hill-forts in favour of large settlements located with good communications rather than
defensive qualities in mind. The best candidate for such a settlement, or 'oppidum', in N Somerset is at Camerton where large
quantities of Iron Age pottery and metalwork have been found
close to the line of the later Roman road, the Fosse Way. Finds
included many coins of the Dobunni, a tribe centred in Gloucestershire but whose territory extended into N Somerset.

How these tribal units of the Late Iron Age formed is unclear,
but by the C1 B.C. political power in southern England had coa-
lesced into a series of kingdoms, each with its own well-defined
territory. Increasing contact between these peoples and the
Roman world established trading routes with the Mediterranean;
Mendip lead found at Hengistbury Head, one of the principal
gateways into and out of the country, suggests that an industry
of more than local significance was already developing in the
Charterhouse area.

Roman North Somerset

The Roman invasion of A.D. 43 quickly occupied southern England as far W as the Bristol Channel. Control over the Iron Age population was exerted by a network of strategically sited timber FORTS and MILITARY ROADS. The Fosse Way, flanking the western extremity of the new province from the Humber to Lyme Bay, crossed the Avon downstream of the low-lying marshy area around Bath's hot springs, while another military road, reflecting the line of advance from the E, pushed down the Avon valley to the Bristol Channel. A fort probably stood in the Bathwick area, where other roads from the Cotswolds to the N and Poole Harbour to the S converged. An occupation-phase fort almost certainly stood at Camerton, where the Fosse Way passed close to the Iron Age settlement (*see* above), with another fort further S at Shepton Mallet. The Romans were doubtless aware of the rich galena deposits on Mendip and, as early as A.D. 49, a unit of the Second Legion Augusta was stationed at Charterhouse to oversee the extraction of lead and silver and its distribution within the province and across to the Continent.

The Boudiccan Revolt of A.D. 60 was followed by a period of reconciliation and regeneration. Much of the S of England was given over to civil administration. The N Somerset area was separated from the Dobunni to the N, who retained their tribal identity, and may have become part of a larger territory extending N of the Avon that was included in a newly created canton of the Belgae, with its administrative centre far to the S E at Winchester.

The abundance of natural resources in N Somerset was such that the area was retained under Imperial control to exploit them; the Romans had a large army to feed and many engineering and construction projects to oversee. In addition to the lead mines on Mendip, there is evidence for a major escalation of agricultural production in the Chew valley and for the reclamation of salt marshes on the Bristol Channel. A new interpretation of the Roman buildings at Gatcombe near Flax Bourton suggests that this and other nearby sites originally exploited and distributed local resources of lead, iron, coal and building stone. Quarries for oolitic limestone on the downs S of Bath may well have been run under similar arrangements from a station at Combe Down. In addition to new roads, flat-bottomed river craft on the Avon and keeled vessels on the Bristol Channel would have played a prominent role in the export of goods.

BATH, or Aquae Sulis – the waters of the Celtic goddess Sulis – was the only Roman town in N Somerset, although it was far from a normal town. Set in a bend of the River Avon and developed around the three hot springs, it took the form of a religious spa providing relief for the province's garrison and a destination for pilgrims from elsewhere in Britannia and the wider Empire.

Around A.D. 65, military engineers began the difficult process of capturing the largest of the hot springs in a polygonal lead-lined stone reservoir, allowing the surrounding marshy ground to dry out to enable the construction of a RELIGIOUS SPA. This

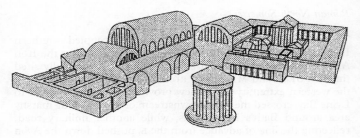

Reconstruction drawing of the Roman baths at Bath

sacred spring (as it is now known) became the focus around which the new establishment functioned; it supplied hot water to a sequence of immersion pools to the S, and served as a place of votive worship to the N where a temple dedicated to Sulis and Minerva, her nearest Roman equivalent, stood. Other monumental public buildings were constructed adjacent to the Baths and Temple. A Greek-style open circular temple or *tholos* stood to the E of the Temple and N of the Baths, possibly inspired by Hadrian's visit to Britain in A.D. 122. A theatre may have stood immediately N of the Temple, carved into the hillside, while shrines adorned the city's two smaller hot springs with at least one other bath house nearby.

In its earliest form the BATH HOUSE was simple in arrangement but massive in construction. A spacious entrance hall stood directly S of and overlooking the Sacred Spring and gave access to both a suite of steam rooms, heated from beneath by hypocausts, and to the main swimming bath, known today as the Great Bath, supplied with warm water directly from the Sacred Spring. The water was fed on to two smaller pools, both of which were filled in and replaced by another suite of artificially heated rooms in the early C2 and, during the next two centuries, as the Baths underwent numerous extensions and refinements.

N of the Sacred Spring, the TEMPLE of Sulis Minerva stood on a podium centrally positioned in a rectangular colonnaded precinct that incorporated the Sacred Spring in its SE corner. This was an imposing classical building whose Corinthian portico supported a pediment sporting an ornate array of motifs in relief with, at the centre of the tympanum, the fearsome so-called Gorgon's Head dominating the entrance and forecourt of the precinct. In the *cella,* accessible only to priests tending the perpetual flames, stood a lifesize gilded bronze cult statue of Minerva adorned by a high Corinthian helmet. Public ceremonies took place outside on the temple steps or in procession around the courtyard and temple augurs conducted animal sacrifices at a great altar.

It is clear that the Baths and Temple were intended to function together. Pilgrims seeking a cure might first petition the deity for help at the Sacred Spring, perhaps by throwing offerings into the water. These included coins, jewellery or other valuable or symbolic items, and messages to the goddess scratched on pewter tablets seeking help or retribution on others. They might also attend ceremonies in the Temple precinct before turning to the Baths to seek their cure in the healing waters.

In the CI and C2 Aquae Sulis had two distinct nuclei that performed very different rôles. The Baths and Temple complex were not part of a planned town involving other public buildings, shops and dwellings, although these were to come later. Unusually, the complex stood in semi-rural isolation with only timber buildings and metalled yards nearby that were needed for maintenance purposes. ½ m. to the N in Walcot, the other nucleus of well-built artisan and residential premises grew alongside the main road to the sanctuary. Doubtless it served both as a market for local people and the surrounding countryside as well as a source of labour and goods for the spa and its clientèle. By the C3 it had spread S along the road and merged with the nucleus around the springs. Further N, the town's cemetery lay astride the London Road.

The presumed walled area enclosing the hot springs and the major public buildings around them was just 24 acres, far smaller than conventional Romano-British cantonal capitals. Although Bath was an important spa with a thriving market centre at Walcot, the town itself lacked the critical mass and civic institutions to have performed this rôle.

In contrast with the classical thermal establishment of Aquae Sulis and its international clientèle, N Somerset was almost exclusively rural in nature, with few other urban centres. The early military station of Abonae at Sea Mills on the lower Avon became a port for the ferry crossing to South Wales. The elusive Traiectus ('crossing point') is known only from the C3 Antonine Itinerary, but probably lay close to the Somerdale area of Keynsham where an inscription of A.D. 155 may represent an official building. The majority of the Romano-British population lived on AGRICULTURAL SETTLEMENTS that have mostly escaped the archaeological record. Fieldwork in advance of the construction of the M5 motorway revealed many previously unknown sites, and it is reasonable to assume that the landscape was well populated with farming communities which retained their native character for much of the Roman period. On some farms, e.g. at Row of Ashes Farm, Butcombe, circular timber dwellings had been replaced by rectangular structures with stone footings by the end of the CI A.D. At Portishead and at Lower Common in Bath, traditional circular huts survived until the building of stone villas over them in the C3. Other villages specialized in industrial activities, such as the pewter-making settlements at Camerton and Lansdown.

An unusual characteristic of the Roman countryside in N Somerset is the absence of VILLAS prior to c. 270. Later in the C3 the flight of wealthy landowners from political turmoil in Gaul may have coincided with the sale of imperial estate lands, which could explain the sudden and dramatic appearance of so many villas in the fertile and attractive countryside of the Avon valley. By the C4 their concentration was as dense as anywhere else in the province. They introduced into the countryside a measure of capital and Romanization not previously seen. The great range of sizes reflects the differing wealth of the owners and, as is increasingly realized, very different functions. Prominent among them were great courtyard residences such as Keynsham and Wellow, fitted with intricate geometric and figure mosaics, painted wall plaster and window glass. At some villas the dwelling enclosed a space more suitable for a formal garden than a working farmyard; such establishments, e.g. Newton St Loe and Keynsham, were probably maintained as luxurious country houses by wealthy officials from Bath. This may help to explain the very close proximity of villas in some places, as at Bathford and Wellow, where one site might be a working estate and the other a dwelling or a residence for a nearby shrine.

Villa owners, who may often have been town-oriented people, surrounded themselves with the trappings of classical culture. Mosaics manufactured by schools at Cirencester and at Dorchester (Dorset) graced numerous villas, some illustrating scenes from classical mythology. It is likely that these floors were complemented by wall paintings; scraps of painted plaster have been found on many sites, but in too fragmentary a state to reconstruct the decorative panels. A glass bowl from Winthill villa, Banwell, is engraved in a mixture of Latin and Greek, 'Long life to you and yours; drink and good health to you.'

Many villas were farming estates geared to producing an agricultural surplus. Their concentration along the Avon valley highlights the importance of the river and connecting roads in the distribution of produce. Evidence from numerous villas points to cereals and cattle-raising as the principal components of the economy. Vegetables, fruit and nuts were also grown, probably only for winter feed and domestic consumption. Sheep were grazed on the grassy heights of Mendip and the downs around Bath. Loom-weights, shuttles and spindle-whorls indicate that wool was spun in the villas, although some was doubtless sent away to market. Fieldwork near Redhill in the Vale of Wrington has demonstrated a possible link between rural settlements on higher ground at Row of Ashes Farm and Scar's Farm and the Lye Hole villa in the valley below. It is also possible that some villas were tenurially related to others, and that a landowner based at one of the large ones oversaw satellite villas which contributed to the larger estate.

The villa-owning class may also be identified with a late Roman revival in pagan religion in the late C3, when numerous pagan TEMPLES appeared, often in hilltop locations. The extensive complex of an unknown cult (possibly Mercury), at Pagan's Hill, Chew Stoke, featured an octagonal temple building, a ceremonial well, priest's house and guest wing, all showing a high degree of planning that may have involved an architect from the Continent. At Henley Wood (Yatton) and Brean Down, E–W-aligned Romano-Celtic hilltop temples, consisting of a *cella* and two annexes, were part of a wider West Country tradition that extended to the addition of two late annexes to the Temple of Sulis Minerva at Bath.

Some scholars have suggested CHRISTIAN interpretations for some motifs on villa mosaics. Orpheus, for example, thought by some to have been associated with Christ, is featured in a mosaic at Newton St Loe. Peacocks and doves, possibly signifying Immortality and the Holy Spirit, are known at Keynsham and Wellow, and the cantharus, perhaps equated with the communion chalice, at Keynsham, Wellow and Brislington.

Through the late C3 and C4 Britain faced a growing threat from barbarian nations outside the Empire, and the Bristol Channel offered easy access for piratical raids from Ireland. The years 350–70 were a period of great unrest, and many villas around Bath were sacked and torched by Irish raiders. The massive wall around Gatcombe is thought to have been built as protection against these incursions. Some villas were abandoned, their owners perhaps seeking refuge in the towns. Much of the destruction has been attributed to the Barbarian Conspiracy of 367, but the available dating evidence is not sufficiently precise. Doubtless accidents also occurred, particularly in buildings of at least partial timber construction; at Star villa (Shipham), the house was burned down and reoccupied before finally being abandoned by c. 364. Chew Park appears to have been abandoned by c. 360, while the villa at Banwell was unoccupied beyond the mid C4. Evidence of raids is strong at two of the finer villas, both close to the river and thus quite vulnerable. The house at Brislington was destroyed by fire and four skulls were dumped in the well, while at Keynsham the roof of the hexagonal *triclinium* burned down and a wall collapsed, killing one occupant. Newton St Loe, the next attractive target upstream, seems to have escaped. Villas at Wellow and Combe Down suffered destruction by fire at some late date in the C4, perhaps during further barbarian raids. Other sites, such as Locking, Newton St Loe and Paulton, continued in use at least until coins went out of circulation by c. 400. Some communities may have raised their own forces in the absence of effective protection from the remnants of the Roman army, and late military buckles from Camerton and Hick's Gate near Keynsham suggest the presence of mercenaries.

In central Bath occupation continued well into the C5. The wall around the central area may belong to the later C4. Maintenance of the Temple of Sulis Minerva ceased in the late C4, and houses with hypocausts and mosaics were built over in the outer precinct. The Baths continued in use into the C5. Although central Bath was not completely abandoned, evidence of timber structures where once-grand public buildings had stood suggests a very different existence. To the N in the Walcot area, very late and possibly Christian burials, one in a plain lead coffin, suggest the presence of a community which would survive into the post-Roman era. To the S, the undefended town at Camerton may have continued in use well into the C5 and beyond.

The post-Roman period

It has long been accepted that, despite the withdrawal of
Roman administration, the story of society in the N Somerset
area is one of continuity rather than collapse. There is no evidence for massive depopulation caused by disease or war. Some
communities stayed where they were, others moved to new
centres. The settlement at Walcot in Bath became the nucleus of
a Christian settlement with a church at its heart. Other communities escaped to continue life in or close to the comparative
safety of Iron Age hill-forts. The best-known example is at
Cadbury-Congresbury, where finds dating from the late Roman
period to at least the C6 suggest a high-status settlement that may
have succeeded the defended villa site at Gatcombe as an emerging British political centre. A chain of elevated sites and hill-forts
E of Cadbury-Congresbury and parallel to the River Avon, such
as Pagan's Hill, Maes Knoll and Stantonbury, may be an early
sign of a new political unity in the N Somerset area, looking to
the river as its northern frontier.

Although these communities were no longer part of the Roman
Empire, they remained in contact with peoples far away. The
growing threat of the English in the E may have made the Bristol
Channel the preferred route for communication with the Continent and beyond. Rhenish glass of the C6–C7 and imports in
amphorae from North Africa and the eastern Mediterranean may
have been exchanged for Mendip lead.

It has been suggested that villa estates outlived the Roman
period to become territories controlled by local British leaders
from reoccupied hill-forts. These leaders may have been amongst
those whom Gildas said resisted the West Saxon advance from
the E at the Battle of Mount Badon in the late C5 or early C6.
This is often thought to have been fought on one of the hills overlooking Bath, although others have placed the battle as far away
as Dorset or Scotland.

In 577 the Saxons killed three kings at Dyrham N of the Avon
and captured their cities, of which Bath was one. The reference
to 'kings' and 'cities' may have been to magnify the significance
of the defeat, and a more realistic interpretation is that 'Bath' was
now a wider political territory around the former Roman town
and under the control of a local chieftain.

It is to this period that the WANSDYKE earthwork probably
belongs. With its bank to the N, it extends from Odd Down to
the S of Bath via Stantonbury hill-fort to Maes Knoll hill-fort,
and possibly beyond. It runs roughly parallel with the Avon,
cutting across the lines of the Fosse Way and other former Roman
roads. The monument is difficult to date, not least because it
seems to have been built over an extended period. Some suggest
that it was a boundary marked out by the communities in N Somerset in advance of the Battle of Mount Badon, while others
favour a post-Dyrham date in which the earthwork marks the
maximum extent of Saxon incursion. In either case, the picture
painted is of sub-Roman British communities working together
to resist a common enemy.

EARLY MEDIEVAL ARCHITECTURE

The scarcity of visible ANGLO-SAXON remains is surprising, given the abundant evidence in nearby Wiltshire and Gloucestershire. A palace complex has been excavated at Cheddar, but there are no structural survivals complete enough to allow more than tentative interpretation. One or two FONTS survive, notably that at Wells Cathedral with its arcaded sides, and (much less spectacular) a bulbous font at Shepton Mallet, perhaps early C11. Of greater importance is the fine early C11 SCULPTURE of the Harrowing of Hell at Bristol Cathedral. Elsewhere there are fragments of carving at Rowberrow (C10) and Langridge (early C11). The excavation of Keynsham Abbey has revealed numerous C8–C10 fragments, some of very fine quality. A C9 fragment at St John, Frome, probably from a monastic foundation there, exemplifies the carving style of the West Saxon lacertine group. Finally, the recently discovered Congresbury carvings parallel the crisp drapery folds and swirling movement of the Bristol piece; such large-scale carvings may have been more common in Wessex than the survivals indicate.

A survey of MONASTIC HOUSES in the N of Somerset begins with the Benedictines at Bath, where the huge Norman

Congresbury, Anglo-Saxon figures.
Drawing by Yvonne Beadnall, 2006

buildings were replaced by a very consistently designed early C16
church, one of the last to be built on such a scale (monastic buildings now lost). The small Benedictine community at Westbury-
on-Trym near Bristol (established by c. 803) was supplanted by
a secular college in the late C12, and again, rebuilding almost
obliterated the earlier buildings. There were Benedictine nuns
at Barrow Gurney, and perhaps at Chew Stoke. Augustinian
Canons were at Keynsham, the partial remains of their abbey
recently excavated, and at Woodspring, where the church partially survives by conversion to a house. There was a Charterhouse at Hinton, the second in Britain. From 1200 the Knights
Templar owned the manor of Cameley, which included Temple
Cloud, but any significant Templar building there has yet to be
uncovered. A powerful Augustinian Abbey at Bristol was founded
in 1140 under the patronage of the Gloucestershire family of
Berkeley. Numerous minor monastic foundations ringed the
centre of Bristol, many of c. 1200 or shortly after. Wells was never
a monastic community. Five miles to its s, the Benedictine abbey
of Glastonbury (outside the scope of this volume) was one of the
most powerful in England and naturally had significant influence
and land holdings in our area, e.g. Doulting, where it owned the
stone quarries and built a tithe barn.

For NORMAN ARCHITECTURE N Somerset is not rich. It
would no doubt be, if Wells and Bath had not so drastically
removed traces of their Norman cathedrals. So the best that
remains is at Bristol (*see* Bristol Introduction, p. 228). Quantita-
tively, not qualitatively, there is no shortage. DOORWAYS especially are quite numerous, and chancel arches too. There are all
the usual Norman motifs of abstract ornamentation, from simple
zigzag to bands of chevrons, lozenges formed by the meeting of
chevrons, crenellation, beading, and so on. Portbury has a fine
doorway with Greek-key motifs. Norman foliage is rare, decorative figurework too. Beakheads, the motif of a monster-head
biting into a roll moulding, occur at Lullington. The colonnettes
of doorways and chancel arches also carry their share of decoration, spiral fluting, diapering, etc. The splendidly bold twisted
piers of Compton Martin must in some remote way depend on
Durham (cf. especially Pittington, Co. Durham). Christon may
have had rich decoration before its overbearing Neo-Norman
restoration, while Kilmersdon retains a flavour of its former
riches with its sections of finely cut fish-scale frieze, figures and
abstract geometrical corbel table. CHANCEL ARCHES range from
the comparative simplicity of one order of colonnettes and one
chevron in the arch to three orders (Hemington) and barbari-
cally profuse decoration in the arches. A cruciform PLAN
with crossing tower and transepts was the standard for the bigger
Norman parish church (e.g. Frome, Queen Charlton,
Whitchurch, probably Axbridge); indications of this plan are
often discernible beneath later rebuildings (St Cuthbert, Wells).
Where there was no transept, a tower may yet be between
nave and chancel (Lullington, Uphill, Englishcombe, Christon,
etc.). Norman W towers are relatively rare (Beckington). Other

positions also existed, and it seems that from a N or S tower (e.g.
Loxton) we can conclude early origin, even if no actual motifs
are visible. VAULTING was rare in English parish churches
through the centuries. C12 rib-vaulting in N Somerset parish
churches survives only in the tower vault at Christon, and in the
chancel at Compton Martin. Here there are also aisles and a well-
preserved clerestory, not a frequent thing in Norman churches.
Lullington perhaps provides the best SCULPTURE, with the
figures in the tympanum and gable of the N door, the capitals of   6
the tower arches, etc.

   Three more points of detail must be mentioned. The first is
the survival of a large and extremely oddly detailed rose window
at Bristol (St James Priory, founded 1129), the second is the occa-   *p. 255*
sional segmental arches found in doorways (Chewton Mendip,
Loxton). The third is that occasionally a chancel arch on the nave
side is flanked by shallow arched recesses, probably for side
altars (Chewton Mendip, Compton Martin), as found in other
counties.

GOTHIC RELIGIOUS ARCHITECTURE

Early English to Decorated

The TRANSITIONAL style of the late C12, i.e. between Norman
and Early English, has some typical and recognizable motifs of
its own, such as waterleaf or trumpet capitals and the three-
dimensional chevron which stands at an angle of 45 or 90 degrees
to the wall. The pointed arch also occurs quite frequently in
contexts which still look entirely Norman. Of major buildings
Malmesbury used it in the 1160s, Worcester in the 1170s. In
Somerset it is, no doubt for sound structural reasons, specially
frequent where arches have to carry towers. In doorways it exists
in a depressed form with vertical pieces between abacus and arch
(which Wells favoured), or as a segmental arch as at Doulting.
Waterleaf capitals never became a fashion in the county
(Doulting), but the trumpet capital did, with good examples at
Shepton Mallet, Buckland Dinham, Clapton-in-Gordano and
Whitchurch. Its more generously three-dimensional character
corresponds to that of the three-dimensional chevrons frequent
in late Norman work, e.g. at Bristol Cathedral, and even found   7
hiding playfully in a welter of C13 stiff-leaf foliage in the N porch
at Wells.

   Stiff-leaf is the hallmark of the EARLY ENGLISH style. The
richness and yet the architectural discipline of these forms is the
happiest symbol of the C13. French crocket capitals are less
natural, French foliage capitals of the late C13 more natural.
Neither quite achieves the classic balance of style and nature of
the stiff-leaf capital. Stiff-leaf foliage was created as early as
c. 1185 (e.g. at St Mary's Chapel, Glastonbury, in SW Somerset)
but its development from timid beginnings to summery lushness

can be followed nowhere better than at Wells, beginning in the chancel *c.* 1180, and gradually carried on to the W parts of the nave. In one capital on the S side of the nave the Transitional trumpet form appears among the stiff-leaves, and it is worth considering whether the carver was not supplied by the hewer with a trumpet capital to work into. That might also explain the capitals in St Cuthbert at Wells, with trumpet and stiff-leaf side by side, and the same proximity at Shepton Mallet.

WELLS CATHEDRAL was rebuilt from *c.* 1175–80, and thus (with the concurrent rebuilding at Glastonbury after a disastrous fire in 1184) Somerset leaps into the forefront of architectural events in England. To summarize the dates, the eastern arm was completed as far W as the eastern aisles of the transepts by *c.* 1184, the transepts and crossing *c.* 1184–1205 (with two bays of the nave arcade), the N porch *c.* 1198–1207, and the nave as far W as the 'interdict break' by *c.* 1210. The lost E.E. cloister also began perhaps in the 1190s. Work on the western nave resumed in earnest *c.* 1219, and the plinth of the W front was laid out *c.* 1220, presumably to the design of the master mason *Adam Lock*. Work continued from 1229 under *Thomas Norreys*, with the nave completed to the base of the roof gable by *c.* 1239, when the church was consecrated. Work on the outer parts of the screen and the final placing of the W front sculpture was probably completed *c.* 1248. Wells still stands in its C13 glory, less interfered with than most cathedrals in England. Only the E.E. chancel was much altered in the C14, leaving just the arcade storey of the western three bays in its original state.

Wells was without doubt the first English building in which the pointed GOTHIC arch was accepted throughout and without exceptions; with Lincoln (begun ten years later), it is the earliest case in Europe of a national Gothic. The inspiration of its first architects was not the choir at Canterbury, which a Frenchman had begun rebuilding in 1175 in the French Gothic style, but West Country work done under the influence of Cistercian buildings, especially Malmesbury, *c.* 1160–70, and Worcester, *c.* 1175–85. Both used Gothic and Norman elements indiscriminately.

The elements which distinguish Wells from both Canterbury and Lincoln are the following: the use of pointed arches throughout, consistent emphasis on horizontals, oblong quadripartite vaults, piers of great breadth and excessive subdivision (twenty-four shafts), a triforium instead of a gallery, and this triforium detailed with un-French continuous mouldings instead of separate shafts, capitals and arches. These motifs come from varied sources, yet remarkably they are fused perfectly into an aesthetic whole. The continuous moulding is an English and more specifically a West Country speciality. Bristol has it in a purely Norman context (Chapter House), Malmesbury has it too, and Worcester. It also occurs in Somerset parish churches of the C12 (e.g. Frome). The idea of the arch on columns or pilasters is of Roman origin: two uprights carrying an arch, with capitals to express the change of function. That logic was controverted in England, where the whole was seen rather in terms of two lines bowing to

10, 11,
p. 649

16

20

each other and finally meeting. Also typical of Wells is the introduction of a triforium instead of the usual (French) gallery. But
the triforium existed also occasionally in Norman architecture,
especially in the Trinité at Caen (and at Worcester), and the character at Wells is emphatically more like Caen than like Chartres.
It is different with the oblong quadripartite vault of Wells. This
also was an innovation of Chartres (though Durham had had it
in England), and one that became *de rigueur* for High Gothic
architecture. The vault at Wells looks indeed French and not
English.

But in spite of that, Wells is wholly English too. To feel that
fully one has to experience it in the nave – and since a little of   12
the nave had to be built to abut the crossing, the internal elevations must have been designed perhaps *c.* 1195. Here the conventional Norman stress on the vertical (nave and gallery bound
together by one tall wall arch) was avoided, by a telling change
of detail. In the chancel and transept E and W walls the triforium
is in twins with the vaulting shafts for the high vault going up
between pair and pair. But in the end walls of the transepts,
where vaulting shafts are not required, the triforium is an uninterrupted band, and this principle was adopted for the nave too.
It is the essential and eminently English characteristic of Wells,
combining the verticality of Gothic with the down-to-earth security of horizontals. Nor does it give up a firm sense of enclosure.
The piers are so broad, the triforium openings so small, that wall
remains wall and never becomes that skeleton of thin verticals
which it is in C13 France. The foliage capitals in their generous   15
richness are without parallel on the Continent. The W front is a
rectangular screen in the English sense, with the towers pushed   10, 16
outside the line of the aisles, and with strongly developed buttresses giving room for more sculpture. Here there is another very
English attempt at marrying horizontal and vertical, though
admittedly less successful aesthetically than in the ample and balanced architecture of the nave. In the W front all is long gaunt
shafts and gabled niches for the iconographic scheme of statues,
dominated by the verticals of shafts and buttresses and the diagonals of the gables.

Nowhere else in England does so much C13 SCULPTURE   13, 14,
survive as at Wells. Pevsner, in disagreement with most other   17
commentators, saw it as significantly inferior to that of northern
French cathedrals, Winchester or Canterbury. The best has that
peculiarly English quality of long, close, rather hard, parallel folds
in the draperies. Recent evaluations show that the sculpture was
conceived primarily not as a sculpture gallery (i.e. in artistic
terms) but as a symbolic depiction of the history of the universe
from Creation to Second Coming.

Contemporary with the Wells W front are the Carthusian
remains at Hinton Charterhouse. Here the workmanship is very
good, perhaps amongst the best C13 WORK in the N of Somerset.
As for Bristol once again, the Elder Lady Chapel of the abbey
church (the present Cathedral) is of *c.* 1220–30, and the inner N
portal of St Mary Redcliffe is a proud display of *c.* 1215–20. But

they are referred to in the Bristol Introduction. What remains then? Some work by Wells Cathedral masons at St Cuthbert, Wells, the arcades at Queen Charlton and Tickenham, the s aisle at Portbury with sedilia and piscina, and the s porches at Compton Bishop and Tickenham. Arches on vertical springers have to be noted at Hemington and Great Elm, and one or two towers, e.g. an octagonal tower at Doulting.

PIER SHAPES of the C13 and early C14 are nowhere as elaborate as at Wells Cathedral, though at St Cuthbert in Wells a successful reduction is carried out. Circular piers, as used by the Normans, continue (e.g. at Hemington), octagonal piers are at Queen Charlton. The other designs are variations on the theme of the quatrefoil and the quatrefoil with diagonal shafts: plain quatrefoil (Chewton Mendip), quatrefoil with semi-octagonal foils (Frome), square with four demi-shafts (Norton St Philip), quatrefoil with four diagonal shafts (Chewton Mendip, Newton St Loe), quatrefoil with four semi-octagonal diagonal shafts (Congresbury), and so on. An alternative has the circular pier surrounded by four detached shafts, often of Blue Lias, e.g. at Hemington, where they face the cardinal points, or on the diagonals, e.g. at Congresbury. The double chamfer is the conventional E.E. arch moulding.

VAULTING received its most original and most English impetus in the first half of the C13 at Lincoln, with the introduction of the ridge rib and the tierceron. Both appear at Wells and in Somerset with some delay. At Wells the passage to the undercroft of the chapter house (c. 1260–70) is the first instance. This is followed later by the chapter-house lobby and staircase, and at about the same time, the vault of the Elder Lady Chapel at Bristol Cathedral. The chapel in the Bishop's Palace adds tiercerons, but that takes us to c. 1275–80 and a different style altogether.

TRACERY interested the Wells lodge little. At a time when bar tracery had already been introduced to Westminster from Reims, Wells kept to the lancet. Among the first examples of tracery is the doorway into the passage to the chapter-house undercroft. But the chapter-house stair at Wells still has fine plate-tracery displays of foiled circles in groups of three; only the sunk triangles in the spandrels hint at the existence of bar tracery. Other examples of plate tracery are St Cuthbert, Wells; of bar tracery, Orchardleigh and the E window of Bristol's Elder Lady Chapel.

No sooner, however, had this stage been reached in Somerset, and especially at Wells, than designers turned away from its harmoniousness and regularity in pursuit of the DECORATED style, a new ideal of complexity, intricacy, perhaps even perversity. In window tracery the classic French scheme of lancet lights with foiled circles is abandoned in favour of such motifs as pointed cusping, pointed trefoils in spandrels, and spheric triangles instead of circles. Then new combinations appear, no longer of quite such simplicity and logicality. For instance, where the early C13 had made a group of three or five isolated lancet windows, the late C13 preferred the three or five as lancet lights under one

arch (Bishop's Chapel, Wells, w window). The foremost examples of freer late C13 variations are at Wells: the Bishop's Chapel
c. 1285–90, and the Lady Chapel, of *c.* 1320. The Bishop's Chapel
belongs to a magnificent scheme of enlargement at the Palace for
Bishop Burnell. The Lady Chapel goes much further in novelty   22
and wilfulness. But from *c.* 1300 such an outburst of inventiveness takes place everywhere in the county that only a chart could
do justice to all the new forms. One is to make the outer lights
taller than the middle light and thus gain space for a somewhat
squeezed-in circle (Wrington), a spheric triangle or spheric quadrangle (Whitchurch). Alternatively the middle lancet is made
higher and three circles arranged above the three lights.
Intersection or Y-tracery can be combined with foiled circles
inserted in a few unexpected places (Yatton, St Mary Redcliffe
Bristol w windows, Wells Bishop's Palace Chapel E window).   21
About 1300–10, the ogee arch comes in (Wells chapter house;
Wells E transept and chancel aisles; Bristol Cathedral), and reticulation at once too. The most striking use of reticulation is as a
grille in the large oblong window of the chapel at Clevedon   27
Court, *c.* 1320. But flowing tracery of the fantastic kind so
favoured in Eastern England is rare in Somerset.

   C13 SPACE had possessed the same clarity as C13 decoration.
The early C14 marked a deeper change, of international importance, concerning the art of shaping space. Now space began to
flow, unexpected interpenetrations were sought, and effects
obtained which must have been disquieting to some and thrilling
to others. At Bristol the rebuilding of the E parts of the abbey   24
took place from 1298 to *c.* 1353. At Wells, the choir was remod-   20
elled from the retrochoir w *c.* 1325–40. That both Wells and
Bristol here worked in terms of the 'hall', with nave and aisles of
equal height, is telling.* The Lady Chapel, retrochoir and the
sensational strainer arches at Wells, and the rebuilt E end at   12
Bristol, are all conceived in terms of fluid open spaces and of surprising and ambiguous diagonal vistas. The arrangement of the
piers in the Wells retrochoir seems at first as arbitrary as the
arrangement of the bridges and transverse little vaults of the choir   23
aisles at Bristol. Above all it is this vaulting that establishes
Pevsner's claim that, for a moment, Bristol nurtured the most
advanced and original architecture in Europe. This is not now
accepted without argument, though neither has the claim been
demolished. The recent redating implies that the work was less
crucial than Pevsner believed for the transmission of ideas from
France; however, it takes up and reworks French *rayonnant*
themes with a curious, almost perverse inventiveness. In addition, contemporary metalwork and manuscript illustrations were
delightfully translated into ornamental stone details. The distinctive brilliance in the handling of space in the choir vaulting
is indisputable. The tiny skeletal vault outside the Berkeley   25
Chapel is further proof. Such a conceit, a rib-vault that reveals

---

*Pevsner pointed out that 150 years later, the hall-church became the leitmotif of
the most creative Late Gothic style on the Continent, the German *Sondergotik*.

rather than hides the prosaic flat ceiling above, 'may sound merely playful, [but] is in fact aesthetically of the greatest charm' (Pevsner).

The VAULTING at Wells and Bristol is no less enterprising. The lierne was introduced in England probably at the undercroft chapel of St Stephen at the Palace of Westminster, *c.* 1292–7. Wells Lady Chapel and the Bristol high vault are amongst the earliest to follow in the first decades of the C14. The lierne even more than the tierceron converts the surfaces of the vault into a linear pattern. The visible structural logic of the rib-vault in the French sense was here finally defeated. The cusping of ribs is first seen at Bristol Cathedral, second in the S aisle at St Mary Redcliffe, third in the chancel of Wells. It also appears in the Tewkesbury chancel in Gloucestershire. Three-dimensionally curved ribs were introduced in the S aisle at St Mary Redcliffe (and passed from there to Ottery St Mary, Devon). St Mary Redcliffe, one of the grandest parish churches in England, underwent a virtual rebuilding that was not completed until the Perp style was well established. The ambitious tower was begun in the late C13, and the glorious outer N porch *c.* 1320. It shares amply in all the Dec innovations: spatial enterprise (in the N porch), the ogee and the nodding ogee arch (which appeared a little earlier in the sedilia of the Wells Lady Chapel), and the lierne-vault. It shows the influence of St Augustine's Abbey, Bristol, although the differences (principally the dense knobbly foliage and the use of nodding ogee arches) suggest that other masons were responsible.

St Mary Redcliffe also has the finest SPIRE in N Somerset; it must have been complete *c.* 1330–40, with ballflower on the ribs and ogee-arched lucarnes. It was damaged by lightning in the mid C15 and rebuilt only in the C19. But in Somerset as a whole there are only twenty-two medieval spires (eighteen of stone, four of timber).*

Perpendicular churches

The PERPENDICULAR STYLE originated nationally *c.* 1335, with William Ramsey's chapter house and cloister at Old St Paul's Cathedral, London, and work at Gloucester Cathedral, probably also by Ramsey. The same spirit of verticality can already be sensed in the the choir and the E window at Wells, work of *c.* 1325–40; here are vertical mullions standing hard on arches or pushing up against arches. Among the earliest occurrences of the Perp style in Somerset must be the tracery on the ruined Choristers' House alongside the cloister, built in 1354. The upper W towers and the vaulting of the crossing remained to be done in the C15. At Bristol Cathedral the Perp style was explored briefly in the transepts, but initiative soon passed to the

*Nine survive in our area. At Bristol, St John and St Mary Redcliffe; elsewhere, Congresbury, Croscombe, Doulting, Frome, Whatley, Worle and Yatton (part dismantled).

rebuilding of St Mary Redcliffe. This change in significance from
the cathedral and the abbey church to the parish church is a
general characteristic of the later Middle Ages throughout
England and most of Europe. In Somerset, exceptions to this rule
include Bath Abbey church, rebuilt completely from 1499, and
the cloister and (much restored) upper parts of the Abbey gatehouse at Bristol. The c15–c16 remains at Woodspring Priory
include the tower, fan-vaulted crossing, and parts of the N aisle,
as well as the barn and infirmary.

Somerset is one of the richest counties in large and worthwhile
PERPENDICULAR PARISH CHURCHES, for the epoch was one of
great prosperity. By c. 1400, it has been calculated, Somerset produced about a quarter of the total woollens made in England.
Wells, Bath, and Frome were the centres. But small places like
Pensford, Beckington, Croscombe, Mells were also major pro-
ducers, their rise coinciding with the gradual diminution of
Bristol's weaving trade and its increasing importance as a centre
for dyeing and exporting the cloth. This wealth is reflected in the
rebuilding of churches, starting c. 1375–80. The major development in terms of PLANNING was the growing preference for W
towers over crossing towers. St Cuthbert at Wells is characteristic; the c13 crossing tower stood until 1561, and yet c. 1430 a
splendid W tower was built as well. The ideal new church, where
no compromise was necessary with earlier work, was simple: W
tower, nave and aisles, chancel and chancel chapels, all decked
out as lavishly as possible. Where pre-existing crossing towers
were kept, or built afresh, the problem of a W front proper arises:
Bath (with its delightful angels climbing ladders up and down
the buttresses), Yatton and perhaps Frome solved the problem
with a gabled W wall and large window between turrets, flanked
by the sloped ends of low aisles. Chancels were often given less
attention, owing to the rule that the patron (perhaps the rector
or lord of the manor) was responsible for the chancel, while the
parishioners paid for the W parts. So the W parts often display
the civic pride and prosperity of the parish, attributes less frequently of the patron; and Perp churches with older or stunted
chancels like, say, Leigh-on-Mendip are frequent. Distinctive
characteristics are high naves, often clerestoried, and long high
ranks of aisle windows.

Often the W TOWER dwarfs the rest of the church. For that
there is a purely aesthetic reason. The single tower (rather than
the grouped towers of the c12 and c13) was the greatest thrill for
the late Middle Ages, not only in Somerset but in England, and
much of Europe. Even so, amongst all English counties, Somerset remains the tower county *par excellence*, and there is much to
say about them.*

---

* Peter Poyntz-Wright's *Parish Church Towers of Somerset* (1981), the only major study
since Kenneth Wickham's book of 1952, has significant flaws and contains some
dates that are not supportable, differ from all other accounts, or contradict documentary evidence; however, they have been widely repeated. The best and essential
corrective is John Harvey's critique (*see* Further Reading).

39

37, 38,
p. 110

32

37

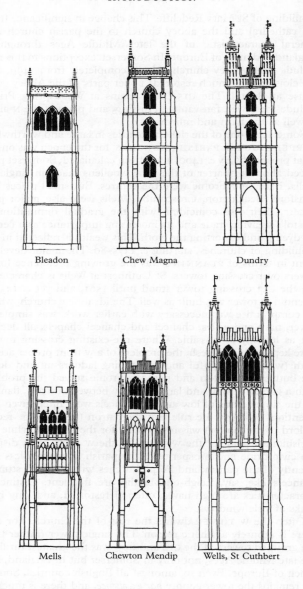

North Somerset Perpendicular church towers.
Elevation drawings, 1958

Bleadon Chew Magna Dundry

Mells Chewton Mendip Wells, St Cuthbert

Somerset towers as a rule are square in plan. They may be over crossings or to the W, N, or S. An oblong tower is a rarity; that over the crossing at Bath Abbey is dictated by the nave bays reusing Norman foundations. Spires generally were a C14 fashion; after 1400, a number of planned spires were abandoned (Shepton Mallet, of which a stub remains, and Cheddar and Banwell, which never got beyond the supporting squinches inside their towers). This is often attributed to the influence of the flat-topped W towers at Wells (the first built *c.* 1386–95), although the more general fashion must have played its part. Quite a number of flat-topped towers are strikingly tall. After the towers at Wells Cathedral and Bath Abbey (from 182 ft to 150 ft high, 55.5–*c.* 46 metres), the tallest in our volume are Chewton Mendip (126 ft, 38 metres), Wells, St Cuthbert (122 ft, 37 metres), Blagdon (116½ ft, 36.5 metres), Bristol, Temple Church (114 ft, just under 35 metres) and Wrington (113½ ft, 34.5 metres). The SW Somerset towers of the Vale of Taunton, it must be conceded, are as a group the finest masterpieces of Somerset tower design (e.g. Huish Episcopi, Ile Abbots, Kingsbury Episcopi, and of course Taunton itself). But they are not our concern.

Quite apart from height, immense energies were expended on the details of the towers in Somerset. Masons must have been asked by parishioners, on the strength of one tower, to design another, e.g. Chewton Mendip and Batcombe (SW Somerset). Which was designed first is unclear. In other cases masons must have travelled – the distances were not great – to see what one village was doing while they were working for another. Some towers betray the signs of such cherry-picking; the window arrangement from so-and-so, with the crown and pinnacles from such-and-such. But whatever inspiration or imitation did to form groups or types, there is not one amongst the fifty or so best towers which has not also its individual touches. It is precisely the individuality of the mason, told in the proportions he chooses or the detailing of buttresses and pinnacles, that is so fascinating to watch from place to place.

Pevsner's basic classification of Somerset towers is still a most useful system for analysis. The chief areas of concern are the North, from Bristol and Bath to the Mendips and Wells; and SW of the Mendips, not quite as far as Burnham. Designers focused mainly on the parts of the tower above the nave roof. The enrichments of W doorways and windows, diagonal or set-back buttresses, image niches or ornamental bands, must always be seen as a preparation for the upper part. For this upper part the chief aesthetic division is this: Class One, where the upper tower is ruled by descending mullions that integrate the bell-openings with blank panels below (known as the Long Panel motif), deriving from the towers at Wells; and Class Two, towers subdivided horizontally into stages, the usual form ever since the first Anglo-Saxon towers. The Long Panel type has relatively few descendants in N Somerset. Wrington, perhaps *c.* 1430, is the closest follower of the W towers at Wells, a variation of Evercreech (SW Somerset) and not an improvement. Two-thirds of the total

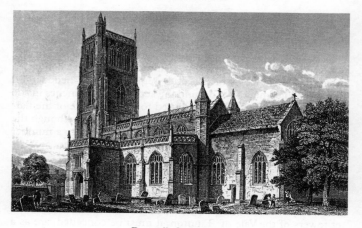

Banwell, St Andrew.
Engraving, 1829

32,
p. 28
height are left blank. St Cuthbert, Wells, on the other hand is a
decided improvement over the W towers of the cathedral. The
bell-openings here have three instead of two lights, and the mullions descend so precipitously that verticality in the design of a
tower could hardly go further. Here is an extreme statement, but
one that is wholly convincing.

We now turn to the far more numerous Class Two towers in
which design starts from the old convention of horizontal stages,
with less vertical linking. In Somerset this class consists of two
subspecies, the first of minor interest on the whole, the second
comprising the most spectacular of all English parish church
towers. The principle of the first was laid down at Shepton
Mallet, perhaps *c.* 1380; it stresses solid wall surfaces, has four
stages with no descending mullions, and three two-light bell-
openings, the outer two blank. This closed design achieves a sense
of noble calm without the aesthetic drama of Wells. It was
repeated in plenty of churches, such as Banwell, Cheddar and
Winscombe, and more simply (without shafts between the blank
windows and the bell-openings) at Axbridge and Bleadon.
Bleadon has only three stages, and three- or four-stage towers
p. 28 may have otherwise identical compositions. Admittedly even the
best designer could do little with a small two-stage tower, of
which there are plenty.

As well as these two classes, long panel and staged, dramatic
varieties of effect can be achieved depending on which 'lights' are
blank and which open. The simplest form, seen throughout
England, is one two-light window below, and one two-light bell-
opening above. In N Somerset this appears only in some minor
towers, e.g. Chew Stoke. Where money was available for a third
stage we get three vertical tiers each with one two-light opening
p. 28 (e.g. Batheaston, Chew Magna, Winford, Portishead). This can
look very stately, although there is no special subtlety about the

design, unless ornamentation was introduced – as at Publow, where a band of cusped diapers forms the transom in the third stage. Occasionally the bell-openings are expanded to three lights, as at Kilmersdon. All these examples are probably of the middle or late C15. 34,
p. 28
33

A second type has lower levels as before (one or two stages of two-light windows), but an expanded top stage with two two-light bell-openings. Here at once there is more variety. The lower part can be treated more or less openly to harmonize with the greater openness above. An important series in the w part of the Mendip range follows this plan: Backwell, Blagdon, Locking, Hutton and Banwell. As before, the same can of course be done in a four-stage tower, as at Temple Church, Bristol. Or the bell-openings can be expanded to three pairs of two, as at Shepton Mallet, Cheddar and Winscombe. Most of these examples seem to be earlier than the first type, that is, c. 1380–1440.

The third type has two three-light bell-openings, making the upper ensemble more and more sumptuous. Most are in sw Somerset; of the few successors in the N, Chewton Mendip, c. 1530s, has some w Somerset features. The sister towers of Mells and Leigh-on-Mendip, with three two-light openings repeated blank in the stage below, also share with the Vale of Taunton group their enrichment with ornament, though with greater emphasis on slenderness. To counterbalance that, there is some wall left above the blank lower windows and above the bell-openings. The result is particularly happy, classic and reposeful. Leigh is the most sophisticated Perp tower covered in this volume, with buttresses, battlements, and pinnacles all given a maximum of interest, the stages emphasized by stepped set-offs, and bands of quatrefoils in the parapet. 34,
p. 28
33

The stair-turret in Bristol and the N of Somerset often has a little spire, or Bristol spirelet, making it the chief, if asymmetrical, accent of the tower. Diagonal buttresses are often seen on small towers, and were the commonest form in the C14. By the C15 the Perp developments of the set-back buttress predominated, probably because they allowed such a delightful play of shafts and pinnacles in the upper parts. No two are alike in the ways in which buttresses turn into diagonal shafts, the angle of the tower is hidden or partially hidden by a diagonal plane laid from buttress to buttress, shafts detach themselves or are attached in relief to buttresses, pinnacles appear behind pinnacles, and so on. The crown may have four, eight, twelve or even twenty pinnacles (this last at Leigh-on-Mendip), and the main angle pinnacles may evolve from the buttresses or be quite independent of them. However it was done, it made a splendid final flourish. The danger of overplaying this magnificence is perhaps a trap fallen into at St Stephen, Bristol, and in the later addition at Dundry, where the towers have transparent crowns with battlements and big square pinnacles all in openwork. These derive from the much broader crossing tower of Gloucester Cathedral, which could bear such heavy emphasis, but here they overload the top, and upset the harmony between tower and crown. 31,
p. 28

The tower arch (i.e. inside, towards the nave), structurally very hard to alter without risking stability, is often the best indicator of the original date. However, the permutations of mouldings are numerous. Double or triple chamfers, popular in the late C13 and C14, carry on into the C15. Arches may be elaborately moulded with combinations of chamfers, hollows, casements (a deeply hollowed C-curve), ogees or serpentine (double wave) sections. These may or may not correspond to the arcade piers, and may like the latter have attached shafts too. Otherwise they can be panelled (e.g. St Cuthbert Wells, Wrington, Beckington, Compton Martin). To enhance the fine effect of the tall arch and also to strengthen the tower it is sometimes vaulted inside. Again no development can be traced. When the parish churches received their towers the tierceron-vault and the lierne-vault were both familiar. So both are found (tiercerons: Yatton, Churchill, etc.; liernes: Cheddar, Banwell, Winscombe – located close together). Fan-vaults in towers, a sign of a desire for costliness and splendour, were hardly attempted before the last quarter of the C15, and most belong to the C16. They appear at Mells, Beckington, Chewton Mendip, Wrington, and several other places. Under crossing towers they were built at Wells, at Axbridge, and at Woodspring Priory.

Towers and porches apart, VAULTING is unusual in English parish churches. Norman vaults have already been enumerated. There are more in the E.E. style. St Mary Redcliffe at Bristol is
39 our only example of the complete vaulting of a parish church. It
38 was begun before 1350. Bath has its magnificent fan-vaults of the early C16; but Bath was monastic. Parish churches with plenty of money liked to make something spectacular of PORCHES, a Dec tendency noted previously at St Mary Redcliffe. Yatton is perhaps
36 the most ornate, with its delicate net of Perp panelling including
35 S-curves. Mells, Doulting and Wellow feature a charming concave-sided gable. Porches may have tierceron-vaults (Keynsham, Chew Stoke), lierne-vaults (Yatton), or later fan-vaults (Doulting, Mells). They can also have a pointed tunnel-vault, with transverse ribs (Woolverton) or panels. This form was occasionally used in other parts of a church too, as in the early C14 N chancel chapel at Portbury, and in a chantry chapel at Backwell, probably derived from the form of a single Dec rib. The vestry (formerly the Chapel of St George) at Croscombe, by *John Carter* of Exeter, 1507–9, carries forward the same idea.

For naves and aisles the TIMBER ROOF remained the standard, and Somerset has some of the most beautiful. The county did not adopt the hammerbeam and double-hammerbeam roof (there is not a single example in the N, and few in the S). The two main types are the wagon roof, a general SW English type of
30 which, however, Somerset possesses the grandest of all: Shepton Mallet, *c.* 1510–20. The second type is so much a local speciality that it is in this volume called the Somerset roof. It is low-pitched, with tie-beams and kingposts and often tracery above the tie-beam, figures of angels against it and against the wall-plate, and ornamental panelling between the rafters and the

purlins. Again, the very best are in the s of the county; but in the
N we have Leigh-on-Mendip and St Cuthbert, Wells.

Battlements and pinnacles on aisles, clerestories, and especially
chantry chapels are rarer in Somerset than they are elsewhere.
Those on the splendid chantry aisle at Kilmersdon, c. 1445–65,
are of considerable interest. Somerset preferred the daintier motif
of the DECORATED PARAPET. The first type is the cusped triangle, which appears c. 1320 on the remodelled eastern arm at Wells   11
Cathedral, and developed into the triangle with trefoil, which
seems to spread from Yatton (c. 1454). Second, blank or pierced   36
arcading (e.g. St Cuthbert, Wells), sometimes developed in the   32
C15 as pierced panelled battlements (Tickenham, c. 1500). Third,
blank or pierced frieze of quatrefoils set upright or diagonally, i.e.
as cusped lozenges. This type only became fashionable c. 1500.

PIERS were widely standardized in Somerset. The most
common type has four shafts with four concave hollows in the
diagonals (sometimes with the refinement of a very slim attached
shaft in the centre of each hollow, e.g. St Stephen Bristol, Wring-   p. 269
ton, Yatton). The second type has wave mouldings in the diagonals, or even double waves (Axbridge, St Cuthbert Wells). Both
are frequent throughout the SW, and occur elsewhere in England.
The four-hollows standard has its sources far back; the middle
post of the N doorway at Wells Cathedral, c. 1230, has this moulding. Capitals are usually moulded, and often applied to the shafts
only, i.e. the hollows continue into the arches without capital or
abacus. Decoration on capitals is usually limited to a little foliage.
At Rode and Beckington in the E, the capitals have little leafy
crests above, a local variation. A very handsome enrichment is
the capital with demi-figures of angels on all sides (Shepton
Mallet, Axbridge); this occurs more commonly in SW Somerset.

Perp TRACERY is in general terms a reaction against the licence
of Dec. Windows are universally large. Ambitious parish churches
may have five lights all round (St Cuthbert, Wells). Bath Abbey   32, 37
has five lights in aisles and clerestory, and seven lights at the E
end. The E window and the end windows of the transepts are so
tall that they have three transoms. The feeling of airiness and spaciousness this lends to the interior is an essential part of English
Perp. But Perp tracery reveals a surprising repetition and lack of
inventiveness, making dating difficult. Here we shall use the basic
types delineated by John Harvey's article 'Somerset Perpendicular, the Dating Evidence' (see Further Reading).

The simplest and commonest form for two-light windows has
a single oculus or cell in the head, cusped in a variety of ways.
The oculus may be split by the continuation of the central
mullion to the head of the arch (a supermullion). With windows
of three lights or more, alternate tracery is the commonest, often   p. 37
seen in Bristol and often before 1400 (e.g. St Cuthbert, Wells);   32
here there are two or more tiers of cells (reticulation) in the
arch-head, the mullions at each tier standing on the point of the
arch below. These cells may be uncusped, cusped at the top only,
or (usually a late refinement) cusped top and bottom, adding
grace and liveliness (e.g. Wells Old Deanery, Wrington clerestory).

A subordinate mullion may be introduced to split each cell vertically. A further elaboration was the mullion with its base split to form an inverted Y, usually an indication of the late C15 or C16. By this device subordinate mullions could be made to straddle the spandrel between the arches of two lights below. Sub-reticulation is produced when a tracery cell is subdivided into three, not two, sub-panels, the third standing on top of the other two, thereby repeating the reticulation on a small scale. In windows of four or more lights, sub-arcuation is possible, where a main mullion splits at the springing point of the arch and throws a curve across to the side of the opening, producing two or more sub-lights. The usual arch form for early Perp tracery is two-centred. The ogee arch, a mainstay of Dec tracery, reappears in the rebuilding of Wells cloister from c. 1420, and from c. 1440 became the standard for Perp parish churches aspiring to some display. A large and well-developed Perp window with ogee lights is often the most useful dating clue available, as long as one can rule out Victorian interference. Five cusps rather than three is often a sign of expensive work. Ogee lights continue, in lower and flatter form, into the Tudor period. A seemingly unique little invention is the addition at Backwell tower of a quatrefoiled circle at the base of the main mullions. In bell-openings throughout the county we find what is known as SOMERSET TRACERY, where the lights are filled with a skin of stone given an all-over pattern of pierced quatrefoils or similar.

LABEL STOPS deserve note: headstops apart, labels over Perp arches might terminate with a horizontal bar, and occasionally a splayed or angled return. The square stop is common, but from c. 1440 the square could be set on the angle, known as a diamond stop bar. This form remained current until c. 1500–20. Circular label stops seem also to occur mainly in the later C15. The tower at Portishead displays both square and circular stops; the upper stages were evidently added somewhat later. Remarkably, Camerton's tower has large label stops including an elephant, a rhinoceros and a grinning cat.

Medieval sculpture and church furnishings

We deal first with FONTS. As in most counties, Norman fonts were preserved piously in churches where everything else was replaced and rebuilt. Somerset has many, some entirely plain, others enriched by a band of cable moulding or of saltire crosses, others with bold scalloping on the underside of the bowl: one scallop at Hinton Blewett; two at Leigh, three at Cameley and St John, Weston-super-Mare. More rarely one finds figure decoration as at Locking, with four thin figures joining hands around a square bowl, or intersected arches as at Lullington, the most ornate of all. As to the C13, Saltford has eight small carved heads; but more interesting are the few purely architectural fonts, those at Winscombe and Portishead like moulded capitals, and that at Wellow of an eight-lobed shape. The most noteworthy C14 font is at Orchardleigh, with small seated figures in sexfoils. There are innumerable Perp fonts, the standard pattern being octagonal with square or oblong panels on the bowl containing shields, quatrefoils etc. Sometimes the stem has slim cusped panels too. Occasionally demi-figures of angels carry the bowl (Axbridge, Doulting, Wrington, etc.) – just such angels as carry roof beams or appear on capitals. Another figured Perp font is at Nempnett Thrubwell, a naïve re-cutting of an earlier bowl.

Somerset is not a county of SCREENS like Devon and Cornwall or Suffolk and Norfolk. However some good wooden rood screens survive, mostly C15 or early C16, e.g. at Banwell (1521–4), Congresbury, Keynsham, Cheddar and Long Ashton. The tracery designs relate somewhat to windows, with e.g. narrow ogee-arched lights predominating at the end of the C15. Stone screens are plentiful at Wells, of standard design except for the screens of c. 1340–50 from transepts to choir aisles. These have to the l. and r. of the doorway a vertical frieze of pierced cusped lozenge-shapes, the same idea as in the S transept windows of St Mary Redcliffe and another proof of the close artistic relations in the C14 between Bristol and Wells. Another good stone screen, perhaps c. 1500, is at Kilmersdon, though seemingly imported from London.

PULPITS of wood cannot compare with Devon, but there is a fine series of about fifteen STONE PULPITS in and around the Mendips, among them Wick St Lawrence, Banwell, Bleadon, Brockley, Kewstoke and Hutton, probably all made by the same workshop. They are characterized by dainty details, panelled stems and bodies (sometimes built out from the side wall of the nave), and friezes of quatrefoils, fleurons and leaf trails. Cheddar's fine panelled pulpit has demi-angels beneath, as in the fonts mentioned above.

p. 90

BENCHES were introduced into churches generally from the C15 as an expression of the general late medieval desire for comfort in the church as well as at home, and an expression also of the growing importance of the sermon in services. Many are preserved in the S and W parts of Somerset, and have quite a county character, with densely carved tracery and iconographic figures, etc. However, the area of this volume has fewer, and those generally plainer. Clapton-in-Gordano has an unusually early set assigned to the C14, with finger-shaped tops, and a fairly complete C15 set with traceried end panels is at Leigh-on-Mendip. Other plainer collections with poppyheads etc. are at Banwell, Wellow, Cameley and Chelvey.

The MISERICORDS of the choir stalls of Wells of course are on quite a different plane. They date from c. 1330 and are no doubt the work of craftsmen of regional or national repute. The series is one of the most enjoyable in the country. Those at Bristol Cathedral are also fine and lively. Minor misericords are at Worle (early C16) and Weston-in-Gordano. One DOOR must not be overlooked, that of the late C13 into the Chapter House undercroft at Wells, with its decorative covering of split-curled iron hinges. That brings us to METALWORK, especially the iron railings of the Bekynton Tomb at Wells of c. 1452, and the similar railings at the castle chapel of Farleigh Hungerford, *c.* 1440. TILES are a rarity; the best are probably the early C14 floor in the NE transept at Wells Cathedral, from Bristol or the lower Severn. WALL PAINTING is represented by some C13 scrollwork at Cameley church, along with fragments from the succeeding two centuries, most notably the foot of a big St Christopher among crabs and fishes. Farleigh Hungerford and Nunney have figures of St George, the former *c.* 1440, and alongside it C15 blue-and-white damask-patterned window jambs.

Finally STAINED GLASS. The earliest in Somerset is foreign, the beautiful small C13 panels from Strasbourg at St Mary Walton, Clevedon. Wells Cathedral contains some of the best English glass of the early C14. In the Lady Chapel is jumbled glass of *c.* 1315–20, including some exquisite small pieces in the tracery heads, entirely in the style of contemporary illumination and still in rich yet translucent reds, blues, greens and yellows. Tickenham church has small figures of the same date and style, equally fine. Also at Wells is the Tree of Jesse in the great E window of *c.* 1340, its colouring rather less numinous than the earlier glass, with yellow and green predominating. The yellow may represent the earliest surviving use of silver-stain in England. The flanking lights in the clerestory with large figures of saints are also very fine. Village churches have plenty of bits, carefully listed by Canon Woodforde who could thus prove the existence of a Somerset school. Worth mentioning here, the tracery heads of *c.* 1375 at Compton Bishop, the window given *c.* 1490 by Prior Cantlow of Bath to St Catherine's, and three windows at Winscombe. Of these one is of about 1525, and contains some Italian Renaissance detail.

CHURCH MONUMENTS are of course more plentiful, but most of the EFFIGIES, principally of knights and ladies of the C13 and C14, are in too bad a condition to judge their aesthetic value, though quite often they must have been of good quality. An exception is the series of seven effigies of Saxon bishops in Wells Cathedral, five of *c.* 1200, two of *c.* 1230, created to underscore the translation of burials from the old Saxon church, reinforcing Wells's claim to the return of the bishopric from Bath. They are all well preserved and excellent, the earlier with vigorously characterized features and bold rounded draperies, the later far more realistic and also in higher relief – an object lesson in the change towards a greater consideration of nature during the first half of the C13. The slab for Bishop Bitton II †1274 at Wells and that to a knight at Chelvey, of *c.* 1260–80, are among the earliest INCISED SLABS in the country.

For the later Middle Ages it is advisable to look at monuments rather as architecture than as sculpture. There are, it is true, fine details in a number of monuments, such as the early C14 effigy of Bishop Marchia at Wells, the two early C15 alabaster panels of Annunciation and Trinity on the tomb of Thomas Boleyn at Wells, the brass of Philip Mede †1475 at St Mary Redcliffe (iconographically interesting because it consists no longer of cut-out figures but is a plate with kneeling figures engraved), the

SUPERMULLIONED
Cheddar N chapel
c. 1382

TWO-CENTRED
'BRISTOL' ALTERNATE
Wells, St Cuthbert s chapel
c. 1402

OGEE
ALTERNATE INVERTED CUSPS
Compton Martin, *c.* 1443
(Wells Cloister, *c.* 1420)

TWO-CENTRED
SUPERMULLIONED
Chew Magna, N aisle
c. 1448

Types of Perpendicular window tracery.
Drawings by J. H. Harvey, 1984

statuettes of mourners at St Stephen, Bristol (*c.* 1370) and Far-leigh Hungerford, and the alabaster effigy of William Canynges †1474 at St Mary Redcliffe, and so on. But if one thinks for a moment of the power to carve and the power to characterize in German and French late medieval monuments, one will realize how unrewarding as sculpture are the later bishops' tombs at Wells, and the tombs at Bristol Cathedral and St Mark's, Bristol.

The design of TOMB RECESSES on the other hand offers an interesting illustration of the development of architectural decoration, starting again from Bishop Marchia †1302, through those of the early C14 at Bristol Cathedral, ending with such elaborately

⁴⁰ Perp pieces as the Choke Monument †1486 at Long Ashton. It is only one step from these semi-architectural pieces to CHANTRY CHAPELS. We can see it taken in the Bekynton Tomb of before 1452 at Wells, an effigy on a stone table with a cadaver below, and to the E a wall with a coved top for an altar to be placed against it. There are two real chantry chapels at Wells, Bishop Bubwith's and Treasurer Sugar's of c. 1420 and c. 1480, although the latter follows the former design closely and was intended as its twin. Finally there are that to Prior Birde at Bath, begun 1515, the fan-vaulted Poyntz Chantry at St Mark, Bristol, of c. 1520, the size of a normal chapel added to a church.

SCULPTURE of course occurs frequently in conjunction with monuments. The earliest piece not in a strictly architectural context is the seated figure to the l. of the gateway of the former St Bartholomew's Hospital at Bristol, clearly work connected with the Wells W front. The most interesting piece of sculptural church furnishing is the two chipped-off reredoses at St Cuthbert, Wells, for one of which the contract of 1470 survives. It is hard to envisage their appearance, but the quality is obvious from the many good original bodies and heads which were reused as rubble and which are now in store. Otherwise there is the row of apostles in the W gable of Wells Cathedral, c. 1450–75. Minor sculpture occasionally survives outside in parish churches: the exceptionally good C15 Trinity group on the tower at Binegar, with a lesser parallel at Farrington Gurney, and the elegant Annunciation figures on the tower at Banwell. Similar figures at Cheddar are renewed, at Winscombe just the niches and the pot of lilies remain.

Medieval churchyard CROSSES are plentiful, or at least their broken or restored fragments. Perhaps the most imposing is at Chew Magna, probably C15, on an octagonal base of seven steps with panelled risers. Another good example is at Brislington, Bristol.

MEDIEVAL DOMESTIC BUILDINGS

Somerset is poor in CASTLES. Bristol had a large and well-developed castle begun shortly after the Conquest, and of national significance; it was through most of its life more effective as a symbolic royal stronghold than as a military defence. It was demolished c. 1655 (see p. 230), and all that can be seen now is some excavated masonry of the monumental Norman keep. Nunney and Farleigh Hungerford castles both have important late C14 characteristics: a regular geometrical plan, and four circular corner towers. However, they are otherwise quite dissimilar. Farleigh, which is in parts reduced to the wall bases only, encloses a large area, the towers were separated by long stretches of wall, and there was a gatehouse with its own rounded towers in the middle of one side. The inner courtyard had buildings in

16

p. 498

various positions. Nunney is much smaller and perhaps more impressive. It is just one tall solid block with the four towers attached to it. On the short sides they almost touch. Farleigh is of the type of Harlech, Nunney of a type more usual in the North of England (Langley, Northumberland). There are no other true castles in the N of the county with any significant structure surviving; FORTIFIED MANOR HOUSES rather than true castles can be found at Sutton Court (Stowey), where an early C14 tower and some embattled walls survive amid C19 embellishment, and at Newton St Loe, which has a complete but altered keep of c. 1290–1320.

The earliest DOMESTIC ARCHITECTURE other than castles is the altered Norman house, probably c. 1148, at Saltford, probably as good as the best in the country. Buttresses with many small steps on set-offs also appear in the Bishop's Palace at Wells, which Bishop Jocelyn began c. 1206–8 and completed perhaps in the 1220s. It must have been a noble building in its original form. It had a great hall on the upper floor with two-light windows with plate tracery, and a vaulted undercroft below. *Ferrey*'s alterations of 1846–7 unfortunately did much to reduce that nobility. The great hall added to the SW c. 1275–92 must have ranked among the proudest secular halls up to that time in England, being c. 115 ft by 60 ft (35 by 18.5 metres), with the very tall transomed windows with Geometrical tracery facing the cathedral giving some hint of its grandeur, while the plan-form is an early example of the convention of porch and cross-passage giving access to hall and service rooms. Domestic WALL PAINTING of c. 1200 occurs (though fragmentary) at Saltford Manor House, and fragments of a fine C15 scheme were recently discovered at the Bishop's Palace, Wells.

A surprising amount of domestic architecture c. 1300 to c. 1500 survives in N Somerset. The development of PLAN-FORMS is similar to the rest of Somerset, S Gloucestershire and W Dorset. The standard medieval form is the open-hearth hall, with an inner room beyond a screen in the better houses. More substantial houses had two or three rooms in line, i.e. the hall (and its inner room if it had one) then a cross-passage separating the service or lower-end room. West End Farm, near Winscombe, is probably a two-room plan of 1278–9. From the mid C16 began the gradual process of flooring-in halls to form an upper room, as happened at Brimbleworth Farm near Worle. The hall gained a chimneystack, often against the wall of the cross-passage, and a staircase might be inserted against the stack, winding up over the door from the passage, or in a stair-turret at the back. The asymmetrical three-room in-line plan survived well after 1650, when the symmetrical cross-passage plan took over.

Of PRIVATE HOUSES the most interesting remains of the early C14 are at Clevedon Court. It has the typical English plan with the porch entering a screens passage, the rear door opposite, the three doorways to kitchen, buttery and pantry leading off one side of the screens passage and the hall on the other, with its first-floor chapel over the oriel bay. The chapel windows have

28,
p. 572

18,
p. 679

27

Congresbury, St Andrew, vicarage.
Engraving, 1829

reticulated tracery which helps to date the buildings to *c.* 1320.
The hall was unfortunately re-roofed in the C18. OPEN-ROOFED
HALLS not subdivided horizontally survive at Tickenham Court
(*c.* 1471–6), Hutton Court, and the former Archdeaconry at
Wells, etc. The arch-braced collar-beam roof is the commonest
type, often with wind-braces. It survives in not a few places, e.g.
the Paltons' Manor House, Croscombe, C14; Seymour's Court
near Beckington, *c.* 1460–80; Tickenham Court, 1470s. Court
Farm, Portishead, has another, to a C15 upper hall, while the
second manor in that town, now The Grange, has a smoke-blackened roof indicating a ground-floor hall open to the roof and
without chimneys. In terms of plan, Congresbury Vicarage was
a special case, as the ground-floor chamber was semi-public.
Above was a private hall, with solar over the screens passage and
service room, leading to a study over the porch. This compact
plan with lower and upper halls was adopted elsewhere in the
C15, e.g. Gothelney Manor (SW Somerset), and Dunchideock,
Devon. A similar example, externally at least, is Yatton rectory,
although this has lost its service end, as has the Rib at Wells,
another good minor house, of *c.* 1470.

The separate GATEHOUSE comprises a special type, often as
part of the manor house. Wells has of course the best set, all
dating from the C15, though none of them among the best
English cathedral gatehouses. The turreted gatehouse at the
Bishop's Palace is of the mid C14; the C15 example at Newton St
Loe is splendidly vaulted in two bays. Another gatehouse to a
manor of the bishops of Wells has survived at Chew Magna.
MOATS survive rarely; apart from the obvious case of Wells, the
small manor house (now Moat Farm) at Bickfield, Compton
Martin, is perhaps the most complete.

p. 688

PORCHES are frequent survivals, ranging in height from two to five storeys. The tallest is the porch-tower at Birdcombe Court, Wraxall, with a tierceron-vault inside. Sometimes the CHAPEL is placed above the porch entrance, as was probably the case at Congresbury vicarage. More frequent in larger houses seems to have been a chapel wing or a detached chapel. No examples of the former arrangement seem to have survived in N Somerset, but a small C15 detached chapel exists at Lower Court, Long Ashton. STAIRCASES are as a rule of the spiral type. They are placed either by the side of the porch (Nailsea Court) or by the side of the back exit (the Old Rectory, Winford). Halls sometimes had a bay window or a square oriel bay, as seen e.g. at Clevedon Court, and the Old Manor House, Croscombe, with its fine vaulted ceiling. In other cases the oriel has disappeared, but the arch survives to indicate its position (Tower House, Wells, Tickenham Court, the Paltons' Manor House, Croscombe). Much decoration was applied to oriel windows at Wells (Bishop's Palace, Old Deanery, Vicars' Hall) and in a rather different context, at the George Inn, Norton St Philip, c. 1430. *pp. 683, 688*

WINDOWS range from two lights to as many as six. As a rule the hall windows are the largest, but parlour and solar may have windows of equal size. Large, regular fenestration almost as in a house of the C20 characterized the Tudor house at Bristol formerly inside the Assize Courts (demolished in 1961). The one remaining C15 window of the W front at Ashton Court is specially ornately traceried, and attractive enough to gain as companions several early C19 imitators. Inside the halls decoration in stone was concentrated on the CHIMNEYPIECE, and there are still several ornate examples preserved with leaves or tracery in the spandrels, such as those in the Bishop's Palace and the Deanery at Wells, and the one at Kingston Seymour which is all that survives of the C15 manor house. Big plain openings were commoner, as at Tickenham Court or, with a moulded arch, at Mells Manor. Contemporary polygonal chimneystacks and pots survive in the Vicars' Close at Wells, at Lyons Court, Whitchurch, and the Old Vicarage, Kilmersdon. Wooden SCREENS on the other hand seem to have been curiously utilitarian – see the examples in the Deanery and Bishop's Palace at Wells. There is little fine carving of Perp roof beams or wall panelling.

TIMBER FRAMING is not thought of as a Somerset tradition, and most of what survives seems to be urban rather than rural in character: the timber-framed house of c. 1500 in the Square at Axbridge and some lesser examples in the High Street to its W, 44 the C16 example (Church House) at Frome, and fragments surviving in Bath High Street. Much is obscured beneath later frontages, as in Wells High Street, and in Broad Street, Bristol. A fortunate survival is the George Inn at Norton St Philip, built in 43 the late C14 in connection with the cloth fairs; it has two stone canted bays, porch, and three oriels in the timber-framed upper storeys added c. 1430–1. At Mells a whole little street of cottages in terrace formation leads from the main road to the church, but curiously out of axis with the porch. URBAN BUILDING otherwise is confined to Bishop Bekynton's terrace of C15 houses along one side of the Market Place at Wells, a piece of Renaissance-inspired planning. Not unrelated is the perfectly planned street, Vicars' Close at Wells, which is the most interesting piece of secular medieval architecture in Somerset, built by Bishop Ralph of Shrewsbury in 1348–54 to provide separate houses and a hall for the vicars choral of the cathedral. Its apparent consistency was actually only achieved in the C15 when the houses were unified by Bishop Bubwith and then Bishop Bekynton. The model was probably a collegiate quadrangle. The houses had one large and one small room on the ground floor and the same on the upper floor, with a spiral staircase and privy. In the C15 the hall was enlarged too and several pretty oriel windows added.

An important survival is the impressive church house at Chew Magna, alongside the churchyard, reportedly of 1510. CHURCH HOUSES acted as a sort of community centre, where charity was dispensed and the church ale was brewed. Chew Magna's is unusually big, with an open timber roof. At least six others survive in our area, often converted after the Reformation as inns or parish poorhouses, e.g. Abbot's Leigh, Long Ashton. The best-documented is at Yatton (1471–3), though altered as almshouses in the C17 and C18.

Minor VERNACULAR building has been more comprehensively studied in the S of the county. However, medieval survivals are reasonably frequent in our area, often with later façades. For plan-forms, *see* above. Cruck construction is very rare, a matter of dozens being known compared to several hundred in the S of the county. Examples dated by dendrochronology include a true cruck roof at West End Farm, Winscombe (1278–9), the earliest vernacular building so far dated in Somerset; two base-cruck roofs at Wells (1314–15 and 1318–19); Cheddar (1341–2); Chew Stoke (1386); and Beckington (jointed cruck, 1391).

STONE BARNS are fine things in Somerset, much standardized in appearance, with their buttresses, their cross-archways, slit windows, and open timber roofs. That at Doulting, with a raised cruck roof, is of *c.* 1288–90, while the Bishop's Barn at Wells is C15, and only noticeably different in one or two details. The barn at Englishcombe is dated *c.* 1314–58. But more interesting is what little remains of the Canons' Barn at Wells; for this seems a building of the late C12 which had nave and aisles divided by tall plain stone pillars rounded at the corners. No other such building seems to survive anywhere.

TUDOR AND STUART BUILDING,
c. 1540 TO *c.* 1700

Churches and their furnishings

Our coverage of CHURCH ARCHITECTURE in the medieval period included everything up to *c.* 1540, for there is little real distinction in Perp pre- and post-1500. Rebuilding or new building faltered with the religious upheavals from the 1530s. Of the few later examples that can be identified, the addition of a N aisle at Hinton Blewett *c.* 1553 is the most significant; the masons, as one would expect, carried on in the late Perp style. The porch at East Harptree might be after 1540, and is an early use of brick in this region. There seems to be more C17 church work than has been recognized, mostly alterations rather than new buildings. Some of these may be evidence of a Gothic revival. But it is difficult to decide here; for if a church was to be built in the 1620s or 1630s, what other style than the Perp was available? Inigo Jones's London church work was the only pattern for a fully classical style, and the Elizabethan style had never established itself in ecclesiastical architecture. So at Corston (1622) and Marksbury (1634) we find alterations to the towers in bastardized Perp form; the repairs at Rodden with round-arched lights in square openings (1639–40); round-arched lights at Holcombe; and at Bath Abbey fan-vaulting inserted as late as the early C17. Pevsner saw Keynsham's w tower of 1634–55, and that at Norton St Philip (altered *c.* 1640), as cases of revival rather than survival, though it is not at all clear why. It seems nearly impossible to distinguish intention from the fabric alone, and additional evidence here is not available.

Renaissance FITTINGS began to appear *c.* 1530: see the little Italian ornaments in the glass at Winscombe, and on the basically Perp pulpit at Shepton Mallet. There is some Renaissance glass at Wells of 1507, but this is imported Flemish work. Of national interest is the stone pulpit at Wells Cathedral, given *c.* 1545 by Bishop William Knight (*c.* 1476–1547). This is not a piece of pretty Quattrocento decoration (which would still be quite up-to-date at that moment) but a heavy, serious piece with plain broad pilasters and a big cornice, a piece in which the Renaissance is taken up in earnest. It is amazingly early for such an attitude, but understandable once one takes into account Bishop Knight's Renaissance rebuilding of Horton Court, Gloucestershire *c.* 1521, his intimacy with the court of Henry VIII, and his visits to Italy. 41

Otherwise there are few datable fittings before 1600, and the progress of Renaissance motifs is best seen in MONUMENTS, which across the whole of Somerset seem specially late in adopting pilasters and columns, acanthus and arabesques. The earliest is the tomb of Bishop Bush †1558 at Bristol Cathedral; Ionic columns appear together with the late medieval tradition of the *gisant* or cadaver. That most curious of church effigies, the Hauteville monument at Chew Magna, may be an Elizabethan 50 attempt at reviving or reinterpreting the monument of a medieval knight. Meanwhile, monuments with Renaissance details appear at East Harptree †1568, Keynsham †1587, etc., in a Netherlandish-Elizabethan style, with two-arched canopy. Another group, of the late C16, impressive in its restraint, has no figures at all, just a reredos architecture with columns and ornament, as at St Mark, Bristol, †1590.

FURNISHINGS OF THE C17 are a richer field: the revival of enthusiasm seems to begin *c.* 1610, was perhaps encouraged by

William Laud as Bishop of Bath and Wells (1626–8), and again
when he became Archbishop of Canterbury in 1633. His insistence on orderly ritual resulted in many new altars, rails, screens
and pulpits. The finest ensemble in Somerset, and perhaps in
England, is at Croscombe (from 1616), possibly by *John Bolton*
who did similar work at Wadham College, Oxford, for the Somerset and Croscombe family of Bisse. It gives undoubtedly the
most complete picture of the c17 country church. Chelvey has a
fine manorial pew, probably 1621; St John, Bristol, has excellent
woodwork of *c.* 1630. Rodney Stoke has a pulpit, font cover, and
a screen dated 1625, still Perp in composition though with
bucolic Renaissance motifs (scrolls, acanthus, beasts) in round
arches of the type seen on so many pulpits. Above it are the
remains of a gallery front of the same style. An *ex situ* screen at
Keynsham may originally have been a chancel screen, and must
date from *c.* 1634. Benches are less frequent. Plain country
benches are hard to date from style alone. Those at Hemington
with heavy fleur-de-lys finials may be c17. Mells and Great Elm
have a more sophisticated type with semicircular tops to the
bench-ends, decorated with shells. In general the classical innovations seen in tombs of this date are slow to appear in other furnishings, the style remaining firmly Elizabethan and Jacobean,
with conventional motifs such as blank arches, Flemish strapwork, arabesques from France, etc. The only new ornamental
convention of the mid c17 is the kind of gristly cartouches that
replaced the late c16 leathery or fretwork forms, e.g. on the parclose screen at Keynsham. A grand door was given to Bath Abbey
in 1617. Examples of c17 metalwork are the two splendid sturdy
baluster-shaped lecterns, at St Mary Redcliffe of 1638, and at
Wells of 1661. The latter already has florid acanthus-leaf decoration, typical of the Restoration. But the most interesting embellishment of these years is in PLASTERWORK: the ceiling of
Axbridge church (1636) with its complex ribbed pattern in the
Elizabethan tradition. The use of Gothic cusping, more noticeable in the near-identical ceiling at East Brent (SW Somerset),
was unquestionably a self-conscious revival, perhaps referring
specifically to the c14 speciality of free-standing cusped ribs at
St Mary Redcliffe, and at Bristol and Wells cathedral choirs. It
ought to be understood in conjunction with the other instances
cited of a medieval revival at this time, and with domestic examples (e.g. Barrow Court). The folk-art painted chapel at Farleigh
Hungerford castle is another Renaissance conception – a religious
allegorical scheme – executed by local craftsmen, *c.* 1658–65.

MONUMENTS from the early c17 followed established types:
kneeling figures facing each other across a prayer-desk (Bath,
†1605; Barrow Gurney, †1616; Clapton-in-Gordano, †1672),
recumbent figures (the alabaster effigy at Rodney Stoke is specially good), or reclining figures (St Nicholas, Bristol, †1629).
Assuming money was available, the effigy would be set beneath
a columned canopy, either a coffered arch or a flat entablature
type, mostly with an achievement above. Among the most sumptuous are Joan Young, †1603 (Bristol Cathedral) and Sir George

52,
p. 482

49

Snygge, †1617 (St Stephen, Bristol) both attributed to *Samuel Baldwin*. Bishop Montague's tomb (†1618) at Bath is no longer in its original state. One late C16 and C17 group has a brass plate with kneeling figures, usually set in a stone frame. The type originates in the Mede plate of *c.* 1475 already mentioned. Examples are at Burnett (†1575), Croscombe (†1606 and †1625), Shepton Mallet (1649), etc. The standard C18 form, the hanging tablet, begins to appear in the early C17, usually as a framed or pilastered tablet with no pictorial image. From the 1630s big monuments achieved nationally a new freedom in their iconography, with livelier figures and new compositions; see the two frontal demi-figures at Rodney Stoke, †1657. The bust in an oval frame was favoured by London court sculptors; at Beckington is the wreathed bust of Samuel Danyel, attributed to *Thomas Stanton*, perhaps *c.* 1655. Another London conceit, in this case derived from Nicholas Stone, is the macabre fashion for shrouded figures rising from the tomb, e.g. Churchill (†1644), and Rodney Stoke (†1651). There too is the work of a stonemason who, down to the 1670s, turned out gaily coloured monuments with whole figures or three-quarter figures in niches and the paraphernalia of the Court style used with happy ignorance (Rodney Stoke, †1657, already noted; Keynsham, †1661; St Mark, Bristol, †1667; Axbridge, †1668 and †1670). A splendid double monument at Farleigh Hungerford, *c.* 1658–65, bears similarities to work attributed to *Thomas Burman* of London. The growing sophistication of small and large monuments in the late C17 can be sensed e.g. in the Carew tombs at Camerton, †1640 and †1683, and the Gore tablet at Barrow Gurney, †1662, attributed to *William Stanton*.

Domestic architecture

In DOMESTIC ARCHITECTURE the transition from Late Perp to Elizabethan is a story of the almost imperceptible gradations that occurred as the secular Renaissance takes precedence over a style based on church architecture. There are many fewer significant houses of this date N of the Mendip scarp than there are in the S, and none in the front rank, nationally speaking. Larger houses are frequently the product of local merchants spending their money on a place of retreat. Many were adapted from medieval religious buildings (e.g. Hinton Charterhouse, late C16, and Woodspring Priory). Windows of the early C16 often have individual lights with depressed arches; the full-blown ELIZABETHAN style discards this Gothic relic in favour of mullioned (and sometimes transomed) windows without any arches. Beckington Abbey has both types, from different phases. The Wake family at Clevedon Court made substantial changes *c.* 1570, remodelling the service wing, the solar and great chamber beyond the hall. Parts of this survive, with shouldered gables and mullioned-and-transomed lights. Mells Manor was expanded even more from the original small C15 house; in two phases in the later C16, with slim octagonal column-like buttresses at the angles. Likewise Nailsea Court, with a fireplace dated 1593, for Richard Cole of Bristol. Charlton House, Wraxall, gained the characteristic E-plan *c.* 1585–1610, although the porch was not central (evidence of the persistent tradition of the screens passage at the low end of the hall). By far the most complete Elizabethan house is the Red Lodge, Bristol, 1579–80, which borrows from the latest Renaissance ideas at Longleat, Wilts., and may indeed have been designed by *Robert Smythson*. It has a superbly carved and panelled Great Chamber with internal porch, and a thin-ribbed 'spider's web' ceiling with big moulded pendants. Rather similar to the Red Lodge house type is Beckington Castle, taller but essentially a compact square house perhaps *c.* 1540–70.

There is no break between the Elizabethan and JACOBEAN styles. St Catherine's Court N of Bath was enlarged, probably *c.* 1610, including the fine porch with canted angles, classical niches, Roman Doric doorcase etc. Barrow Court underwent its second post-Reformation remodelling *c.* 1602–40. Walton Castle, Clevedon, was built *c.* 1615–20 as an octagonal tower surrounded by an octagonal wall with angle turrets. It is not truly a castle, but a romantic or chivalric conceit, and such Elizabethan and Jacobean medievalism deserves special notice.

Urban TIMBER FRAMING survives in some quantity, mostly at Bristol. The difference from medieval work is the slightly more expansive breadth and regularity in the façades, the introduction of Renaissance motifs e.g. around doorcases, and the propensity for 'Ipswich' windows, i.e. with arched centres. The façade of the Crown Hotel in Wells Market Place is perhaps the best and closest example to Bristol work of the 1660s and 1670s, e.g. in King Street and St Thomas Street. One or two details of a house in Axbridge Square suggest the same idea.

PLASTERWORK underwent marked changes in the C17. The thin ribs of Elizabethan ceilings carry on, e.g. as late as 1639 at Chelwood, but broader flat ribs appear, and flat ovals with relief foliage, as at Chelvey Court. Seymour's Court, Beckington, has a big Ionic chimneypiece and an early to mid-C17 plaster ceiling with profuse quatrefoils, fruit etc., and rich frieze. The same moulds were used for a frieze at Laverton dated 1627, around a rich ceiling with an allegory of Vanity. Barrow Court has a magnificent ceiling and frieze with cusped Gothic panels amid curved ribs, another example of a Gothic Revival in the C17. The most sumptuous C17 work is perhaps the tunnel-vaulted ceiling with profuse strapwork etc. at Beckington Abbey, *c.* 1640. Several ceilings at Bristol show a fondness for flat grounds with isolated lozenges or quatrefoil motifs and floral infills, both attractive and economical.

Grand stone FIREPLACES form a special group in Bristol. The opening (often Tudor-arched) was framed with pilasters, paired half-columns or terms, and bordered with simple patterns of rosettes, dots or incised lines. Above was a broad frieze, richly carved with interlace, scrolled foliage, or occasionally with iconographic figures and emblems. Elaborate overmantels, sometimes ceiling-high, frequently combined strapwork with figures and emblems from Continental engravings. Similar examples in the countryside may come from Bristol workshops. Ornaments include cartouches of three-dimensional strapwork, caryatids, and scenes in relief. Examples are Barrow Court (allegories of Justice and Mercy, *c.* 1660), Abbey Church House, Bath; Laverton; and Gournay Court, West Harptree. At Charlton House, Wraxall, is a splendid Jacobean stone fireplace with colonnettes, caryatids and allegories of Charity and Justice.

The situation in provincial architecture in the second third of the C17 is an interesting one. The restrained Palladian CLASSICISM introduced into Court circles by Inigo Jones had little impact outside London. The only significant example in our area is Ashton Court, and specifically the SW wing remodelled by a Royalist courtier and M.P. in 1633–4. Its designer was obviously familiar with the Court style. He may have been the Bristol mason *Christopher Watts* (†1652), who was certainly involved in choosing the stone, and who seemingly worked at Sherborne Castle. The façade was treated not as a surface to be decorated; the skyline was not punctuated by gables but given a balustrade; and the upright windows had alternating triangular and segmental pediments, a hallmark of Palladianism. Yet this façade is not pure, for it was a remodelling of a possibly C16 wing, hence the irregular though rhythmic window spacing, and at the back truncated gables. There are horizontal oval attic windows too. Ashton Court remained without echo locally for more than thirty years. For this two reasons might be offered: first, the local craftsmen and builders had neither the skills nor the understanding necessary; more fundamentally, patrons perhaps saw London's classicism as irrelevant to local traditions.

Concurrently, however, began the infiltration of ARTISAN MANNERISM, that hybrid mix of classical and Italian Baroque details filtered through Low Countries printed sources. It appealed to tastes used to the visually overloaded Jacobean style, appearing first in details such as doorcases. At Barrow Court the entrance was dressed up perhaps *c.* 1630s, a hybrid of Tudor cambered opening with crude Ionic pilasters and a quite Baroque segmental pediment, all profusely ornamented with random Flemish-inspired strapwork and pure Italian grotesquerie. From *c.* 1660 start to appear such performances as the swan-necked pediments over the windows at Tilly Manor, West Harptree, and the porches of Chelvey Court, Wraxall Court, and Stoke House, Stoke Bishop, Bristol (1669). p. 409

A repertoire of essentially Jacobean motifs continued in domestic buildings throughout the C17, and in remoter places until deep into the C18. It is interesting to record mullioned windows with hoodmoulds as late as 1682 (Wells), and 1689 (Blagdon), and without hoodmoulds into the late C18 (Clapton-in-Gordano, 1766; High Littleton, 1777) and, exceptionally, as late as 1844 at Gurney Slade (i.e. not Tudor Revival). Alongside this appears the upright two-light mullioned window, both in the cottage and also in less visible places in major town houses (e.g. Dunkerton 1695, Newton St Loe 1698, Wells (Dr Morris's house)

1699, Oakhill 1723, Stanton Prior 1737). The standard classical
form until sashing came in is the upright window with a mullion-
and-transom cross. This had existed in Elizabethan and Jacobean
houses, but was not used systematically. Now we find it, e.g., at
Ashton Court, 1633–4 (later replaced by sashes), at Stanton Wick
Farm, Stanton Drew in 1666, and at Hassage in 1677. Concurrently the big segmental door pediment appears (Chelvey Court
and Barrow Court) and just before 1700 the shell-hood. There
are so many handsome and prosperous rural houses of the late
C17 that one will have to stand here for all: the broad and generous refronting of the Old Manor at Rudge, dated 1692, with a
simple doorcase with bolection surround and pediment, cross-
windows, continuous dripmoulds over them, and gabled attics.
A motif popular in the later C17 is the upright oval window keyed
into a rectangular panel (Farmborough 1667, Stoke House, Stoke
Bishop, Bristol 1669, Batheaston 1670, Hassage 1677, Old
Deanery Wells, Dunkerton 1695). Humbler URBAN VERNACU-
LAR BUILDINGS of this date are numerous in towns such as
Frome and Wells. Worth mentioning is the rear of No. 16 Stony
Street, Frome, 1688, which retains its cross-windows and decorative leadwork. At Bristol the Wren style in its most unpretentious form appears first in the Colston Almshouses of 1691, and
those of the Merchant Tailors (1701). The central entrance has a
shell-hood, a mark always of *c.* 1700, and the building material
is brick. CIVIC or PUBLIC BUILDINGS of the C17 outside Bristol
are virtually non-existent, among the few being small domestic-
looking almshouses at Waterlip, Downhead (1699) and Mells.

p. 517

54

   In the second half of the C17 great changes also took place in
INTERIOR DECORATION. A rare survival of mid-C17 taste in a
gentry house is the remarkable painted and panelled interiors at
Chelvey Court. The same house has a staircase balustrade of the
Jacobean type, with turned balusters of generous outline and
sturdy girth, perhaps *c.* 1640. The mid-century saw splat-
balusters, often heart-shaped and sloped to follow the rise of the
stairs, with stylized Ionic pilasters, as at Hassage Manor, 1677.
Contemporary with this were staircases with freely pierced flat
panels of scrolls, shields and fleur-de-lys, seen at Tilly Manor,
West Harptree, in 1659, at Farmborough in 1667, and at No. 8
High Street, Wells. Stoke House, Bristol (1669) still has flat balusters, but they are decorated with fruity garlands and swags.

LATER STUART AND GEORGIAN

Trends in Georgian architecture and planning

The C18 saw increasing ease of travel and communication, the
extension of literacy among the middle classes, and the embryonic professionalization of architecture. These in turn mark the
start of the decline for regional and local characteristics in building. But this is not to say that work by national figures became

common in Somerset. That began to happen, of course, at Bristol
and Bath: respectively the second city of England, and its first
spa town. In both, the start of the c18 is marked by regularized
TOWN PLANNING: at Bristol, with Queen Square laid out in   *p. 301*
1699, emulating the new squares of London's West End; and at
Bath with *John Wood the Elder*'s work at Queen Square from
1728, establishing Bath as the model of English c18 town planning. More is said on the planning of both cities in the gazetteer   70
introductions. Rural developments are somewhat different,
although the building evidence suggests that the c18 saw growth
and prosperity in many towns and villages.

The broad pattern of development established at Bath *c.* 1730
continued, guided by its peculiarly single purpose – the spa.
Bristol, by contrast, had always shown industrial, economic and
social diversity. It shunned the planned regularity of Bath –
squares were usually not square, often built up on three sides
only, and a terrace might peter out with one or two irregular
houses. Planning at Bristol and Clifton was piecemeal and small-
scale, for land ownership was fragmented among merchants and
farmers rather than aristocratic estates. Bath set its basements at
ground level, and built up the street on vaults; this happened at
Bristol only on hillsides, never between matching terraces on   2
level ground. Both cities had their spheres of influence in the hinterland, generally Bristol to the W and Bath to the E. But these
were not invariable: for instance, *Daniel Hague* of Bristol designed
additions to Mells Park, in the E of the county, in 1763.

The professionalization of architecture is an c18 conception,
with the Office of Works acting as the training ground for national
figures. Most of the names we shall come across worked region-
ally, and were trained in the building trades. In Bath, *John Wood
the Elder* was a carpenter, *Timothy Lightoler* a woodcarver and
joiner, *Thomas Warr Atwood* a plumber and glazier, and *John
Eveleigh* a builder. *George Townesend*, of the well-known family of
Oxford masons and familiar with classical architecture there,
settled in Bristol in the 1690s. The *Patys* of Bristol were a family
of builders, stonemasons, carvers and gilders. *William Paty*
(1758–1800) was the first local architect known to have had
formal training, at the Royal Academy schools, 1775–7. For
others, advice on designing, surveying and other practical matters
was provided by pattern books.

HOUSE BUILDING in the cities was often speculative, based on
the system normally used in London. Typically, landowner and
developer would agree a ninety-nine-year lease on a plot of land.
In return, the developer and his heirs made a fixed annual
payment, and when the lease expired the land and the houses on
it reverted to the landowner. To minimize financial exposure the
developer sub-let individual plots to builders who would agree
to build a house within a set time, for a peppercorn rent. To
finance the work, builders might borrow from banks, lawyers or
merchants, often in connected trades (timber merchants, brick-
yard owners, etc.). Façades were usually built to a uniform
design, provided by the developer or his architect. The builder

Clevedon.
Engraving, 1829

sold the house, the purchaser paying the developer a fixed annual
rent for the remainder of the lease. Many layers of sub-leases
might be agreed. Clifton and Bath experienced rushes of development mania from *c.* 1790, but the war with France of 1793 led
to high interest rates, loss of confidence and many bank failures
nationally. Builders, developers and architects were often bankrupted, leaving whole areas unfinished, e.g. the Bathwick estate
in Bath, Clifton, and St Paul's, Bristol. Confidence returned very
slowly from *c.* 1800, often with houses finished more cheaply (see
Windsor Terrace, Clifton, begun by *John Eveleigh*, whose com-
mitments at Bathwick led to bankruptcy).

Three SEASIDE RESORTS were established in the early C19,
despite their situation on the muddy reaches of the Severn
Estuary. The first, now the largest, was Weston-super-Mare,
which offered sea bathing by 1805. Clevedon can date its birth
as a resort precisely to 1821, when the Eltons began building
coastal villas; it has one of the least spoilt Early Victorian English
promenades. Lastly came Portishead; with no beach to speak of,
villas and a hotel were built on a low headland from 1828, by
George Dymond for Bristol Corporation. For Victorian seaside
developments, *see* p. 64.

Georgian domestic architecture

The most notable BAROQUE work in this volume is *Vanbrugh*'s
Kingsweston House, *c.* 1710–19, of monumental character
although in reality not a big house. The manor house at Bishopsworth, Bristol, has Kingsweston's arcaded chimneys in miniature, the only evidence of its direct influence. Near Bath and yet
not immediately dependent on it is Widcombe Manor – the very
fine main façade with giant Ionic pilasters and pediment added

2

59,
p. 406

58

1726–7, possibly by *Nathaniel Ireson*. To him are also attributed two wildly individualistic town houses, Rosewell House at Bath, and No. 59 Queen Charlotte Street, Bristol, with Borrominesque details filtered through the work of Thomas Archer. The free-and-easy Baroque of e.g. *Thomas Greenway* at Bath was quickly emulated in HOUSES OF THE RURAL GENTRY, such as Freshford Manor, also *Greenway*, c. 1719; and Eagle House, Batheaston, 1724–9. Underpinning this desire for display was the continued prosperity of the local cloth industry.* Sometimes the Anglo-Dutch style was preferred, with hipped roofs, sash windows, and stone or rendered walls usually standing in for the brick conventionally used elsewhere. Examples are the fine house of Dr Claver Morris at Wells, 1699, and Nunney Manor House, c. 1710–20. Both probably had sashes from the first. Also of c. 1710–20 are the handsome High Littleton House, with cross-windows, and the similar refacing of the Old Parsonage, Farrington Gurney, with some fully panelled rooms within. Large rural houses of unrendered brick are rare in the early C18: Newbury House, Coleford, is dated 1748. Good examples of plain Georgian gentry houses of c. 1720–40 are Babington, Berkley, Standerwick, etc.; generally with broad sashed ashlar fronts, and decoration limited perhaps to a little carving around the door, some plasterwork in the hall, and a good oak staircase.

It took the eminently urban and suburban style of PALLADI-ANISM longer to reach the countryside. The style was essentially a learned one, based on understanding and controlled revision of Italian Renaissance models; it did not lend itself to the practices of local masons building vernacular houses. It is seen in the 1740s and 1750s, for example, in the alterations to Ston Easton for the Hippisley family, with the sumptuous decoration of the Saloon, and at Titan Barrow, Bathford (1748), and Eagle House, Bathford (c. 1750), the latter two by the elder *Wood*. Titan Barrow has particularly festive yet refined decoration, such as Wood's favoured garlands between the capitals.

Neither Baroque or Palladian style ever fully displaced the local tradition. To follow their interactions, three country TOWNS at least are recommended: Wells for its handsome canons' houses in The Liberty, and the reserved Georgian of High Street, Chamberlain Street and New Street; Shepton Mallet and Frome for their early C18 Baroque merchants' houses (e.g. Melrose House, Frome) and for the weavers' suburb of Trinity. C18 industrial developments and housing are treated more fully on p. 59. *Thomas Prowse*'s pleasing design for The Cedars, Wells (1758–61), built for a sugar merchant, typifies the mid-sized Palladian town house; few similar houses are found beyond the towns. But nearly every village has its good house for a parson, doctor or prosperous merchant: e.g. The Cedars, Beckington; Webbsbrook House, Wrington; or Bourton House, Flax Bourton. A characteristic small FARMHOUSE evolved on Mendip, in the first half of the

*Defoe tells us that Bristol made druggets, Frome, Pensford, Norton St Philip and Shepton Mallet, finer cloths, Wells knitted stockings.

C18: symmetrical, with four mullioned windows ranged about a central door (e.g. Fosse Farm, Stoke St Michael, 1759). Often over the door is a small arched window (e.g. Bridge House, Temple Cloud). At the Dower House, Oakhill, this was developed into a Venetian window as local masons assimilated Palladianism.

COUNTRY HOUSES of the later C18 begin with Newton Park, by *Stiff Leadbetter*, c. 1762–5. Among the finest C18 houses in this volume, it is second-generation Palladian, a large villa rather than a mansion, reserved and extremely refined. The rectangular centre is relieved by canted or rounded bays in the centre, and on the entrance front by quadrants linked to pavilions. The plasterwork is particularly fine, an early example of NEOCLASSICAL motifs inspired by Stuart and Revett's *Antiquities of Athens*. Another large villa of almost square plan is Kelston Park (c. 1767–8, by the *younger Wood*), even plainer without. Shockerwick House, probably c. 1775–85, by *John Palmer* of Bath, represents the tail-end of Palladianism, with a tall central block with attached three-bay portico, rusticated ground floor, and originally single-storey wings with arched openings.

The Neoclassical refinement of Robert Adam is reflected at Combe Hay, where the S and E fronts were updated c. 1770–5; *George Steuart* has been suggested as architect. Bailbrook House, Batheaston (by *John Eveleigh*) is thoroughly Neoclassical in its lack of central emphasis (two equal blocks with central entrance in a single-storey link). Ammerdown House in Ammerdown, by *James Wyatt*, 1788–95, has flattened linear pilasters, semicircular recesses framing the Venetian windows, and delicate plasterwork by *Williams* of London. Claverton Manor, by *Jeffry Wyatt* (1819–20) has twinned segmental bows on the E front, a common device of houses after c. 1790. The single bow was favoured by *John Pinch* at e.g. Freshford Manor (c. 1796) and The Chantry at Chantry (1820–2). Babington House (enlarged c. 1790), Dinder House (c. 1802–3), and Merfield House, Rode (1810) use the same feature.

Unlike Palladianism, which seldom filtered down to houses smaller than those cited above, the sparseness of Neoclassical design was easily transposed to buildings of almost any size and type. If proof were needed of that, the little Neoclassical public swimming pool at Bathwick, Bath (*John Pinch*, 1815–17), with changing cubicles in curving wings, and entrance and attendant's house in the centre, provides it. It is the oldest survivor of its type in Britain.

Georgian INTERIORS were consistent. In all but the simplest houses the walls of the main rooms had timber mouldings implying the parts of a classical order, comprising dado (the pedestal), wall surface (the column shaft) and cornice (the entablature). Near-complete interiors are found scattered through N Somerset: Goldney House, Bristol has a fine mahogany-panelled parlour of c. 1722, and rooms of the 1730s survive at Redland Court; Melrose House, Frome has simpler panelled rooms with bolection-moulded chimneypieces, and, unusually, panels painted with snow scenes, landscapes and battles; while No. 22 Chamberlain Street, Wells, has a very richly carved and panelled parlour, *c.* 1720–40. From the mid C18, panelling was usually limited to the area below the dado, with plastered walls above. The formula sat equally happily in the village rectory and the smartest Bath terrace. The Cedars, Wells, has fine plasterwork of 80 the later C18. By then, standard components such as plasterwork, hob grates and composition ornaments allowed builders to produce quite high-status interiors. Fireplaces might be carved to reflect the usage of the room, e.g. wheatsheaves or grapes for dining rooms, musical depictions for parlours. Painted scenes covering an entire room survive at Phippens Farm, Butcombe, *c.* 1832.

The 1760s were the heyday of the playful Rococo GOTHICISM of Horace Walpole, which fulfilled the craving for lightness, liveliness and for English antique associations. Bath's first example was the Priory, Prior Park, by *Richard Jones*, *c.* 1740, then Ralph Allen's Sham Castle of 1762. Then came Midford Castle, *c.* 1775, 76 a tower-like Gothic house on a trefoil plan, with Rococo plasterwork perhaps by *Thomas Stocking*. Gothic was espoused (in Bristol especially) by middle-class merchants, often Quakers. Arno's Court, Brislington is a classical house dressed up with battlements and ogee hoods over the windows, but a fantastic Gothic of more than one mood pervades the gateway, the bathhouse (now at Portmeirion, Gwynedd) and the stables, all of 77 *c.* 1764. The architect was possibly *Thomas Paty*, whose firm produced a Gothic grotto and garden buildings at Goldney House, 78 Clifton, for another Quaker merchant. Probably at about the same date, the NW wing of Ashton Court, Long Ashton, was 45 Gothicized in forms favoured by the Patys. They may also have designed the Gothick W wing at Clevedon Court, demolished in the 1860s, but recorded in one or two telling sketches. In both cases the owners were not landed aristocracy but Bristol merchants made good. Stowey House, Stowey, deserves fuller investigation: a wing in the Bristol Gothick style added to an older range, with seemingly a *ferme ornée* nearby. Cameley House was romantically gothicized perhaps *c.* 1760, with ogee-headed windows and canted bays. In 1766 *Robert Mylne* designed Blaise Castle near Bristol, a triangular folly tower. It may have partaken in the symbolic significance of Gothick towers for Whig owners at this time, as proposed by David Lambert (cf. Henry Flitcroft's design of Alfred's Tower near Stourhead, Wilts., *c.* 1762). Finally *c.* 1803–5 the SE wing of Ashton Court was rebuilt in Tudor Gothic form, attributed to *James Foster* of Bristol. Was he also responsible for the fantastical Gothick plasterwork in the dining room? It is now in perilous disrepair, the fine bookcases broken and parts of the ceiling falling, despite being the finest example of its type and date in this volume.

In connection with these Romantic and Picturesque buildings, the *cottage orné* must also be mentioned. There are the sweet little lodge of *c.* 1790 on the Orchardleigh estate, and Priory Lodge, Chewton Mendip, with its rustic tree-trunk veranda.

87   Near Bristol is Blaise Hamlet (by *John Nash* assisted by *George Repton*, 1810–11), the most fanciful assembly of such cottages anywhere in England. Among its numerous offspring, the Bishop of Bath and Wells's three-room summerhouse at Banwell, 1827, was expanded to a *cottage orné* for summer retreat *c.* 1833, unfortunately since altered almost beyond recognition. *George Basevi* produced a charming *cottage orné* at Dinder rectory, 1827–9. ESTATE VILLAGES feature little in this volume, and before the C19, only The Folly at Chewton Mendip can be cited: a group of vernacular cottages with a modest display of datestones and decoration, mostly *c.* 1785. Industrial housing of the period is addressed below, p. 59.

66   PARKS AND GARDEN BUILDINGS are unusually well represented in N Somerset, especially in terms of buildings that do not belong to major country house estates. There is a fine group in the garden of Goldney House, Clifton, mostly of the 1760s. The grotto is especially good (the interior begun in the 1730s, set with shells gleaned from trading voyages, quartz and other stones); the little Gothick front was erected *c.* 1757, probably by *Thomas Paty*. A similar gazebo of *c.* 1760 is at Ham Green House, near Pill, and another in the terraced gardens at Clevedon Court. Here too is an interesting tower, seemingly an C18 remodelling of a medieval turret in the curtain wall. Antiquarian impulses perhaps also inspired the owners of The Pheasantry, Berkley, an Elizabethan lodge given a second storey in 1783, probably for use as a hunting lodge or belvedere. More Romantic in inspiration is *Jeffry Wyatt*'s Gloucester Lodge, Orchardleigh (*c.* 1815), a castle ruin purporting to be of 1434. Late Georgian parks can be seen at Orchardleigh, including a ruinous Roman Doric boathouse on the lake, at Ammerdown House, and at Pondsmead, Oakhill, a C19 house with rare surviving C18 grotto, tunnels and a hermit's cell. A grotto and temple garden at Mells Park survive in outline only. Early C19 Romantic landscapes exist (partially), at Brockley Hall, *c.* 1825, with Egyptian odalisque and sphinxes; at Hapsford House, Great Elm; and at Banwell, where the Bishop of Bath and Wells created a remarkable 1830s evocation of antediluvian history with bone caves, museum, folly tower etc.

      Now to the GREEK REVIVAL of the early C19, a style both demanding and scholarly. Most examples are urban, e.g. Bristol's Commercial Rooms (by *Busby*), the Old Council House and St George's church (both *Sir R. Smirke*) and at Bath, the former Masonic Lodge of 1819 (by *Wilkins*) and Partis College, Weston (by *Page*). Of COUNTRY HOUSES at this date, only one is pure Greek Revival, but that one outstanding: Leigh Court, Abbot's Leigh of 1814–17 (nominally by *Hopper*, but the design mostly

82   after *John Bennett*). It has exceptionally rich plasterwork, a palatial stair-hall, and a monumental arched Ionic lodge. Claverton Manor of 1819–20 (by *Wyatville*) is considerably less severe, its Greek Revival elements blended with Palladian ones in that hard-to-classify Regency manner. The odd Bunn Pillar at Frome is the only remnant of a scheme for a big Grecian development pro-

85   jected by a citizen with ambitions to outdo Bath. Beckford's

Tower, built above Bath by *Goodridge* for William Beckford's old age in 1825–6 is ponderously, funereally Greco-Egyptian, but very freely treated. The detailing is ahead of its time, with much that characterizes the change from Grecian to Victorian.

The TUDOR REVIVAL appears in N Somerset at a startlingly early date at Warleigh Manor, by *John Webb*, 1814–15. One does not expect a domestic Tudor Revival before *c.* 1825–30; examples begin to appear then, e.g. The Priory, Abbot's Leigh, by *Foster & Okely* of Bristol. Romantic CASTELLAR HOUSES in the C19 begin with Uphill Manor, where a small turreted villa of *c.* 1799 was robustly enlarged in the castle style by *Henry Rumley*, *c.* 1835. Against the nationalistic overtones of the Castle and Tudor styles, the Greek Revival quickly became a diminishing theme.

Georgian religious architecture

Many country PARISH CHURCHES were built or repaired in the early C18. A simple example is at Foxcote (1721). Towers were built or rebuilt at Clutton (Gothic Survival of 1726), Priston (1751) and Paulton, where a possibly medieval and certainly C17 structure was updated with ogee and quatrefoil motifs typical of the Georgian Gothic Revival (1757). Redland Chapel, Bristol (1740–3) was a family chapel for the owner of Redland Court, 60 designed probably by *Strahan* and completed by *Halfpenny*. The same relation exists between house and chapel at Babington (1748–50, possibly by *Thomas Paty*), also on a preaching-box plan 63 with cupola over the porch, and at Berkley, 1750–1, probably by *Thomas Prowse* (on a very interesting plan following Wren's St 62 Mary-at-Hill in London, and with fine stuccowork). It is the best surviving Georgian church in Somerset. The younger *Wood* possibly rebuilt Woolley church N of Bath in 1761, again plain Georgian with a modest cupola.

Of later Georgian parish churches, the finest in our area is Christ Church, Bristol, by *William Paty*, 1786–90, with its Neo- 75 classical plasterwork and spectacular vault of pendentive domes. The Church Building Acts of 1818 and 1824 funded some new churches in Bristol and Bath, but had little impact in the countryside, where Late Georgian church-building tended to result from manorial philanthropy. At Winford, the body of the church was replaced by *James Allen* of Bristol, 1796–7, looking like a Georgian Gothick chapel grafted onto a medieval tower. The classical nave and aisle at Locking (1814–16), *G. A. Underwood*'s bald Gothic at Timsbury, 1826, and rebuildings of the N chapel at Stratton-on-the-Fosse (1782), and of the tower at Marksbury (after 1780) might be noted too. The last classical church at Bristol was *C. R. Cockerell*'s Holy Trinity, Hotwells, of 1829–30: the first Gothic Revival ones were begun at Bristol in 1775–7 (still the insouciant Gothic of the C18), at Bath in 1798. The C19 tendency towards a more scholarly handling of Gothic materials is first seen at *Pinch*'s St Mary, Bathwick, of 1817–20. *Goodridge*, 88 the architect of Beckford's house, could be as fanciful and crazy

as the best: his church at Combe Down of 1835 has absurd polygonal spires, as does his remarkable and wilful, though most like-
able, invention – Christ Church, Rode, of 1822–4.

CHURCH FITTINGS must have been numerous, but relatively
little has survived successive restorations. There is a fine WEST
GALLERY on Doric pilasters at St Thomas, Bristol (1728–32),
and others, humbler but pleasing, at Cameley, Emborough,
Winford and Holcombe old church, with its pews, hat rails, royal
arms of George II, and charming balustraded musicians' gallery.
At Axbridge is a very pretty embroidered altar cover worked
by *Abigail Prowse*, daughter of the Bishop of Bath and Wells,
c. 1710–20; it is an invaluable depiction of the way an C18 communion table was furnished. Of course C18 sanctuary arrangements are rare, although numerous churches have Georgian
COMMUNION RAILS, some of them probably cut down from stair
rails. We are fortunate then that at Babington (1748–50), the
entire Georgian ensemble survives: communion table, rails,
pulpit, font, box pews and royal arms. Eight Bristol churches
could boast fine wooden REREDOSES, but the only survivor is at
St Thomas the Martyr. These were uncommon outside Bristol.
That *James Paty the Elder* of Bristol re-fitted the sanctuary at
Hereford Cathedral *c.* 1720 hints at the regional character of such
workshops; doubtless good work in Somerset by the Patys has
been lost. Brass CHANDELIERS, more tellingly called branches
in the C18, were made at Bristol and Bridgwater in imitation of
Dutch C17 pieces. Dated examples are at Croscombe (1707),
Keynsham (1717 and 1721), Mells (1721), and Easton-in-
Gordano (1731). A similar one at Backwell, dated 1786, is attributed to *William Wasbrough* of Bristol. Later Georgian furnishings
are not frequent. There are the elegant communion table, rails
and reredos-cum-screen at Christ Church, Bristol (*c.* 1789); otherwise a few simple but handsome oak pulpits, early C19 galleries
at Emborough and Great Elm, and the occasional survival of box
pews are all that can be mustered.

CHURCH MONUMENTS of the early C18 are plentiful. *Michael
Sidnell* of Bristol did standard pilastered tablets with pediments
(Yatton †1714, Tickenham †1715, Farrington Gurney, †1728),
and more florid ones at Stanton Drew (†1738). He also carved
the architectural frame of the Colston monument, †1721, at All
Saints, Bristol, designed by *James Gibbs*. At Wells Cathedral is an
ambitious monument by *Benjamin Bastard* of Sherborne, *c.* 1750.
The national scope of monumental sculpture at this time is
underscored by the numbers of London stonemasons signed or
attributed, e.g., at Axbridge 1712 attributed to *Woodman the Elder*,
and †1720 attributed to the *Hartshorne* workshop; at Wells, two
by *Samuel Tuffnell*, *c.* 1728, and that to Bishop Kidder, signed
Robert Taylor (*c.* 1690–1742). Other unsigned works probably
from London include that at Hardington, *c.* 1695, perhaps
by *William Stanton*. Few first-rank sculptors occur, and before
the late C18 only two. *Rysbrack*, apart from his equestrian
brass statue at Bristol, did the masterly effigy of Colston at All
Saints, Bristol, several wall tablets in the city, and the fine series

of busts at Redland Court chapel. *Grinling Gibbons* provided a rich though reserved tablet for Sir Robert Southwell at Henbury, Bristol, †1702. Named national figures are more noticeable after 1760. There is the Danish sculptor *Laurence Holm* (two monuments at Axbridge, †1760s); *Nollekens* once (†1793, Bath); *Flaxman* five times (one the delightful Dr Sibthorp, †1796, at Bath, another †1806 also at Bath, three at Bristol); *Sir Richard Westmacott* three times (Bathford †1810, Bristol †1816 and Frome †1827), and *Chantrey* eight times (three in Bristol, two in Bath, and Brockley †1828, Wells †1837, Weston-super-Mare †1841). Most monuments are tablets, usually with an urn, perhaps an allegorical figure or symbol such as an anchor (Hope) or a weeping willow (Mourning). The names of a few workshops occur all over N Somerset and beyond: the *Patys*, *Tyleys* and *Greenways* of Bristol, and *Ford*, *King*, *Reeves*, etc. of Bath. An oval garlanded tablet by *Coade* is at Keynsham, †1792. At the bottom of the scale in terms of status though not of interest must be the sweet timber tablet, †1803, at Shepton Mallet Methodist chapel, bravely painted up to look like marble.

For SCULPTURE other than monuments, Yatton church possesses two fine Baroque wooden statues from the organ at Bath Abbey, 1708. Of METALWORK, superb examples are provided by the wrought-iron screens and gates of *William* and *Simon Edney*, e.g. at St Mary Redcliffe, St Mark and St Stephen, Bristol. The best bear comparison with the work of Jean Tijou. Equal in delicacy and richness are the early C18 sword rests at St Stephen and St Mark. Newton St Loe has early cast-iron railings around a tomb of *c.* 1720. STAINED GLASS only features from the early C19: it is generally either heraldic or with bright geometric patterns, e.g. that by *Eginton*, at Wells Cathedral (1813) and Brockley and Kewstoke, *c.* 1825.

N Somerset has a number of early NONCONFORMIST CHAPELS, starting with the former Unitarian chapel at Shepton Mallet, of 1696, with hipped roof, pedimented doors and cross-windows. Then the surprisingly large and self-assertive former Rook Lane Congregational Church at Frome of 1707, its façade 61 like that of an up-to-date merchant's house. After that the best examples are again at Bristol, e.g. Wesley's New Room (1739–48) 64 and the unusually grand and architectural Friends' Meeting House at Quaker's Friars (*George Tully*, 1747). By contrast, the Meeting House of 1729 at Claverham looks like a plain village house from the street and has its recessed façade at right angles to it, a very modest piece of display. Its shuttered galleries are intact. Even more modest, yet still carefully proportioned, is the former Meeting House of 1718 at Lawrence Weston (now on the outskirts of Bristol).

With the success of Somerset Nonconformity in the C19, numerous early chapels and meeting houses were rebuilt. Developments after 1760 are characterized at Bath by the PROPRIETARY CHAPEL, i.e. privately owned but affiliated to the Church of England. *Timothy Lightoler*'s plan for the Octagon chapel p. 104 in Milsom Street probably derives from Nonconformist

architecture. Also octagonal was *John Palmer*'s Gothick proprietary chapel of All Saints, Lansdown (1794, bombed in 1942). At
Bath the only interesting Dissenting chapel before 1800 is that
formerly of the Countess of Huntingdon's Connexion, dated
1765. This is purely Gothick of the most playful kind; the pretty
street front with canted bay and Venetian motifs done with ogee
tops is in fact the Countess's villa; the chapel sits behind. C18
Nonconformists favoured a plain classical style, as at Beckington
Baptist chapel (1786). From the turn of the C19, Gothic details
were often applied to buildings of classical proportions, e.g. the
former Roman Catholic chapel at Shepton Mallet (1804), Oakhill
Methodist chapel (1825), and the pleasing Baptist chapel
at Paulton (1827), still with something of Batty-Langley Gothick
about the door. *Henry Rumley*'s handsome Grecian Baptist
chapel at Keynsham (brutally modernized inside) borrows its
details from his work at Queen Square, Bristol. Chapel INTERI-
ORS prior to 1850 have become, quite suddenly, a rarity. Among
those, Clutton Methodist Chapel (1810) has simple and near-
original joinery (only the ground-floor pews perhaps lightly
updated *c*. 1850) with an all-round gallery. It closed for the last
time on the day of the visit for this volume.

Civic and philanthropic buildings

Apart from Bristol and Bath (covered in their respective introductions), there are few early C18 examples of PUBLIC BUILD-
INGS. There is a gabled and mullioned charity school at
Kilmersdon (1707). That of *c*. 1713 at The Liberty, Wells, is in a
more up-to-date Georgian mode, and the Bluecoat School,
Frome (1720–4), has round-arched Wrennish windows and a
cupola. The poorhouse at Kilmersdon deserves mention too: like
three-storey cottages, but with an overscaled Baroque doorcase.
There are no town halls until the stately Georgian one at Wells
(1778–80), possibly by *Edmund Lush* of Salisbury. Stretching a
point chronologically we might mention the Roman Doric
market hall next door, by *Richard Carver*, 1835. Otherwise,
Axbridge has a small Late Classical town hall, 1830–3; Frome
can muster a small but elegant Assembly Rooms, *c*. 1819. Dr
Fox's asylum at Brislington, Bristol (*c*. 1801–3), was originally a
series of detached blocks with fireproof fittings, designed for the
segregation of patients by sex, degree of illness, and social class.

Transport and industry

TRANSPORT developments began to open up the northern part
of Somerset from the mid C18. Turnpike Trusts improved the
roads, and left the familiar TOLL HOUSES, often lodge-like and
with polygonal ends to give views along the roads – among the
best, a lovely thatched one at Stanton Drew, 1793; White Cross,
Hallatrow, 1818–19; and a Grecian example at Saltford, *c*. 1832.
Staging posts from Bristol and Bath included the inns at Old
Down near Emborough, and Cross, near Compton Bishop. Some

C18 inns gained large assembly rooms, as at Kilmersdon, and the Waggon and Horses near Doulting, c. 1790, with original iron windows and exterior staircase to its Long Room. BRIDGES include New Bridge (see p. 210), an improvement to the Bath–Bristol road, originally 1735–6, a fine six-arched bridge at Rode (1777), and the Monkton Combe viaduct (G. P. Manners, 1834).

Somerset is not a county of many CANALS, yet three ventures have left evidence. The Bath section of the Kennet and Avon Canal was opened in 1810 (engineer John Rennie), including the tunnel and elegant iron footbridges at Sydney Gardens, one with spandrels filled with diminishing circles. The Dorset and Somerset Canal (built 1796–1803, engineer William Bennett) left aqueducts at Coleford and Great Elm, and five great pits from a chain of balance locks near Mells; the link to Dorset was never made. The Somerset Coal Canal (Act 1794, completed 1805) took coal via the Kennet and Avon Canal to London. Parts of a chain of twenty-two locks survive at Combe Hay, and a tunnel portal at Wellow. The surveyor was William Smith, known as the Father of English Geology, who realized the principle of stratification of rock while surveying Somerset coal pits from Rugbourne Farm, High Littleton, and used his surveyorship of the coal canal to validate his ideas (see also p. 6).

MINING on the Mendip plateau had been carried on in a small way since medieval times, e.g. at Coleford. The discovery of coal measures at Radstock in 1763 led to development of the town, and new mines around Camerton, Wellow and Paulton: early structures there were long ago overbuilt. C18 INDUSTRIAL REMAINS are largely related to textile manufacture, e.g. the remains of wool and silk mills and of prosperous clothiers' houses at Shepton Mallet, Rode, Beckington, Frome etc. A whole industrial suburb survives at Trinity in Frome (begun c. 1660–1725, with later C18 additions), and small groups in semi-formal layouts at Sheppards' Barton and at Innox Hill, Frome. A regular terrace of brassworkers' cottages is at Kelston. Freshford has Dunkirk cloth mill, c. 1795, and an early C19 brewery.

ARCHITECTURE c. 1830–1914

Religious architecture

In CHURCH BUILDING the classical styles finally lost favour c. 1830, at least with Anglicans. However, the spate of Roman Catholic church building after the Emancipation of 1829 followed another course. H. E. Goodridge's Pro-Cathedral at Bristol (begun 1834), a vast Greco-Roman temple on the side of a hill, would have been a spectacular crown for Catholicism in the West of England, but the project foundered. At Prior Park, Bath, J. J. Scoles's client had equally monumental ambitions for the Roman basilican church of St Paul (1844), but again money delayed completion for decades.

The emerging archaeological spirit in GOTHIC REVIVAL church building was slow to mature; see e.g. *Goodridge*'s Holy Trinity, Frome (1837–8), with heavy paired spirelets at the w end, and the perfunctory Gothic alterations at Saltford, as late as 1851. At Bath, St Saviour, Larkhall (1829–32, probably by *Pinch the Elder*) follows St Mary, Bathwick, in its advanced handling of Perp details. St Michael (*Manners*, 1834–7), and St Stephen, Lansdown Road (*Wilson*, 1840), both also in Bath, are early moves towards E.E. of the earnest variety, as is Christ Church, Clifton (*Charles Dyer*, 1841–4), Bristol's first nod to archaeology. *George Gilbert Scott*'s first Somerset church was Nailsea (1843), around the time when archaeological accuracy began to inform his work; his church at Chantry (1846) is notably more correct. By *Rickman & Hussey* is the quite authentic-looking Dec of Christ Church, Clevedon (1839), although barn-like within. *Sir Charles Barry* designed the reredos at Wrington, 1832. *Benjamin Ferrey* did much as architect to the diocese of Bath and Wells, 1841–80; at Wells Cathedral he restored the Lady Chapel, 1844, and the w front 1870–4. His new churches tended to be small, e.g. Vobster, 1846. The brief fashion of *c.* 1840 for Neo-Norman is seen at Cleeve (*Manners*, 1838–40), Easton (*Carver*, 1841–3), Farrington Gurney (*Pinch the Younger*, 1843–4), and at Bishopsworth (*Fripp*, 1841–3) and Easton (*Dyer*, 1848) in Bristol.

Of HIGH VICTORIAN work we deal first with new churches. *Scott* in his mature years built St Andrew, Bath (1870–3), 'happily ruined' by bombing (Pevsner) and long demolished, as is *Street*'s masterpiece in this area, All Saints, Clifton (1863–8). The latter was a fine example of structural polychromy in brick, its sturdy banded nave arcades with passage aisles especially well handled. Such work is, as we might expect, absent beyond the cities. *Butterfield* is not seen to advantage. His first design was Highbury Chapel, Bristol (originally Congregational, now Cotham Parish church), of 1842–3, a work he later regretted. St John, Clevedon (1876) is big and has a porch-tower almost detached from the nave. It is not among his best. *Pearson*'s Oakhill of 1861 is small and quite plain. *Teulon*'s St Thomas, Wells (1856–7), has one of his best spires, slim and elegantly detailed, and elsewhere only a few of his characteristic oddities. The translation of his usual polychrome brick into bands of soft pink and cream stone under diapered roofs of blue and green slate is notably successful, but was not echoed by others in N Somerset. St Raphael, Bristol, by *Henry Woodyer*, 1859, another quite original work, was sadly demolished after minor bomb damage. By *Sir Arthur Blomfield* is the remarkably large and restrained vaulted chapel of Tyntesfield (1875; *see* p. 728), of French inspiration in its height, and densely buttressed and pinnacled.

The conservative inertia of clients, and perhaps Somerset's relative remoteness before and during the early days of the railways, encouraged continued reliance on local architects. This applied to a remarkable degree even in Bristol (notably the firm of *R. S. Pope* in its various guises) and Bath (dominated by the firm of *Manners & Gill*). Perhaps the best locally bred practitioner in the mid-Victorian period was *John Norton*; he also practised in London. He designed several good local churches (e.g. St John, Bedminster, 1855), most of which have been bombed or demolished. His church at Stapleton, Bristol (1854–7), is in a spiky, Midlands-inspired Dec, while Hewish (1864) is more French in character, with a semicircular apse. *C. E. Giles* of Taunton practised in Frome and London, and worked throughout N Somerset; the earnest C13 style of St Mary, Innox Hill, Frome (1863–4), is typical. The seaside towns have plenty of new churches but tend to fare better for fittings than for structure (e.g. two by *Manners & Gill c.* 1850 at Weston-super-Mare, dull Perp, and one by *C. E. Giles* at Clevedon).

High Victorian RESTORATIONS begin with *Scott*'s work at Bath Abbey (1860–73), the start of a half-century of restoration there, and completing the fan-vaulting of the nave. *Ferrey*'s restoration of the W front of Wells Cathedral (1870–4) achieved the stabilization of existing figures, and unfortunately replaced eroded Blue Lias shafting with Kilkenny marble. By comparison with restorations at other cathedrals, it might even be deemed sensitive. His work on parish churches as Diocesan Architect for Bath and Wells tends to be heavy-handed (e.g. Kelston, Publow, Keynsham and Corston, all 1859–63). His work of the 1870s was more respectful of local traditions, perhaps under the influence of his son. *Street* reinstated the nave of Bristol Cathedral, 1867–77, with the W towers completed by *Pearson* in 1888 (though this might legitimately be seen as a new structure not a restoration). Pevsner judged it 'rather dull, though admittedly very earnest'. More recent assessments have been kinder; Andor Gomme explained how Street's nave, in more conventional C14 forms than the choir, was designed to prepare one for the magnificence of the E end. The same deference informed his restorations of, e.g., Whitchurch (1861) and Yatton (1870–2). *Henry Woodyer* overrestored Doulting church in 1869–71, and almost completely rebuilt Barrow Gurney church for the Gibbs family, 1887–9; if one forgets what might have been lost, his work there is sumptuous. His restoration at Mells (1880) was less intrusive. *John Norton* too could often be overbearing, as at Westbury-on-Trym (1851–60), Chelwood (1861), Chew Stoke (1862–3), Winscombe (1863) and Clutton (1864).

New churches of the LATE VICTORIAN and EDWARDIAN period are uncommon in Somerset, except of course in the growing suburbs of Bristol and Bath. National names can be accounted briefly. *Bodley* appears with late works at Weston-super-Mare (All Saints, 1898–1902) and in Bristol at the House of Charity, Knowle, 1901–2, and St Aidan, 1903–4; also *Bodley & Garner*'s minor work of Peasedown St John (1892–4), and *Garner* alone in the restoration at Camerton (1891) and in the stupendous E part of Downside Abbey (1901–5). The abbey church, begun with the crossing (*Dunn & Hansom*, 1872–82), is the most splendid demonstration of the renaissance of Roman Catholicism in England. Otherwise churches at this period are mainly at Bristol; *George Oatley*'s All Hallows, Easton, 1899–1902, is perhaps the best of its date there, rather French Gothic. *Rodway & Dening*'s St Alban, Westbury Park, Bristol (1907–15), demonstrates their ability at spatial manipulation; later works did not live up to that promise. Greater freedom of handling is a hallmark of the Arts and Crafts, and an early example here is *W. D. Caröe*'s beguiling little church at Charterhouse on Mendip, converted from a miners' welfare hall *c.* 1908, with a nave fireplace. Roughcast walls, slate roofs, sloped buttresses and mullioned windows put one in mind of Voysey, while the pale oak screen is C17 in inspiration. St Nicholas, Portishead (by *Edward Gabriel*, 1911–12), appears more conventionally Gothic at a distance, but has segmental rather than pointed arches, and a slightly Baroque entrance with angels standing guard.

C19 CHURCH FURNISHINGS are of course prolific. Early work of interest includes the Jacobean Revival pews and gallery at Great Elm (1837), a response to the genuine C17 work there. The High Gothic taste is seen in *James Forsyth*'s carving and *Skidmore*'s ironwork at St Thomas, Wells (1857), and in the rich carving and inlaid floors at St John, Frome, *c.* 1865. More sumptuous is the private chapel at Tyntesfield, with glass by *Wooldridge*, coloured marble floors, and jewelled metalwork by *Barkentin & Krall*. For the numerous re-seatings and fittings in Perp parish churches, the fine poppyhead benches of 1859 at Wrington can stand as representative, while the Arts and Crafts taste is represented in *Sedding*'s superb screens and stalls at Axbridge (1880s) with birds, animals and swirling organic forms in the tracery. The *opus sectile* reredos at Rode (*Wooldridge* for *Powell & Sons*, 1873) is worth seeing too.

This volume covers much worthwhile STAINED GLASS. *Willement* is shown to advantage in his early and successful C13-style glass at Weston-super-Mare (1837), and at Wells Cathedral
95 (1843). *O'Connor* occurs frequently (see the vivid glass at St John, Frome, 1844–6), as does *Wailes*, e.g. at St Thomas, Wells (1857), and in a splendid Crimean War memorial window enlivening Chelwood, 1861. Also in the hot palette of this date, *O'Connor*'s glass at Whitchurch, and that at Lullington (probably *Lavers &
96 Barraud*). The glowing figures amid apple boughs of *c.* 1864 at Winscombe church were designed by *William Burges*, who also left the fine roundels at Winscombe Hall (as well as medievalizing painted interiors at Vicars' Close, Wells). A splendid set of
97 twelve *Morris* windows (1880–1921) is at Holy Trinity, Frome, to designs by *Burne-Jones*. *Kempe* left a rich series at Wraxall (1896–9), and another at Barrow Gurney (*c.* 1890), both for the Gibbses of Tyntesfield, unfortunately darkening the churches. Downside has a good collection from the 1880s onwards, by *Hardman*, *Lavers & Westlake*, etc.; their siting in small chapels means they cannot be enjoyed as a whole. The exception is *Comper*'s Lady Chapel glass (1899–1916 and later). 'Art glass' is occasionally found; the best, unfortunately rarely accessible, is
98 the brooding little panel of the Good Shepherd in a thorn thicket, at Knowle, Bristol, by *Christopher Whall*, a leading exponent. Kilmersdon has a good window by *Louis Davis*, 1914; St Mary,

Henbury, Bristol has a fine example of 1906 perhaps by *Margaret Chilton*; and Claverton has Edwardian glass by *Paul Woodroffe* and *H. W. Bryans.*

MONUMENTS that are anything out of the ordinary are less easy to find. At Arno's Vale cemetery (Bristol) is the best, and rarest for style: the big Indian chattri for Raja Rammohun Roy, by *William Prinsep*, 1842–3; also a cluster of chest tombs and obelisks by *Tyley* and others. *Burges*'s design for a small but rich military tablet at Banwell is worth noting. Of the end of this era is a plaster relief with peacock, †1886, by *Burne-Jones* at Mells.

NONCONFORMIST CHAPELS of the period are abundant but mostly unremarkable, with the adoption of Gothic in a modest way (Westbury-on-Trym, Bristol, etc.) from *c.* 1840. Most unusual is the archaeologically minded French Gothic exterior of Buckingham Baptist Chapel, Clifton (*R. S. Pope*, 1842–7). Classicism continues alongside for decades, e.g. Coleford, 1865, and Bourne Chapel, Two Mile Hill, Bristol, 1873. *T. L. Banks* produced the ambitious Gothic Congregational Chapel at Oakhill, 1872–3, and Ecclesiological planning makes a bizarre appearance in a tin mission hall at Batheaston, as late as 1892. Chapels everywhere are closing or being stripped. Intact C19 interiors that are in use are becoming the exception: among those, see Zion Congregational chapel, Frome, that at Stapleton Road, St Philip's, Bristol, and Shepton Mallet Baptist Chapel. Nonconformist architects tended to be favoured: *Foster & Wood* of Bristol (Wood was Methodist) cornered the market among Wesleyans in Bristol and beyond (e.g. the group built by Sidney Hill around Churchill and Winscombe, *c.* 1880–1900). In Bristol, *Frank Wills* deluged the Congregationalists with plate tracery. *W. Hugill Dinsley* designed the Wesley Memorial Chapel at St George, Bristol (1907); together with Churchill Methodist Chapel (above), it preserves more than anywhere else in this volume not just the fabric but the fragile atmosphere of gaslight, *Messiah* and Mr Lloyd George.

Victorian and Edwardian houses

In DOMESTIC ARCHITECTURE, *G. S. Repton*'s Camerton Court of *c.* 1838–40 continues the broadly Grecian style of the Regency, if a little heavier; the asymmetrical garden front with a columned loggia colliding with a canted bay is distinctly Victorian. Likewise, the terraces of Clifton kept up an extremely creditable Grecian into the 1850s. Then other forms break in. The castellar style noted during the Regency makes an ambitious and very visible return at Banwell Castle, 1845–7. The Tuscan Italianate which took hold in the hilly suburbs of Bath spread quickly, being popular with merchants and professional men who could retire to a distance from their places of business. Wadbury House, Mells (by *James Wilson c.* 1841), was for an ironmaster and *Edward Davis*'s Albury House, Wrington, *c.* 1846 for a solicitor. Wilson did much else around Bath in this style, e.g. the Red Post Inn, Peasedown St John, with *Fuller*, 1851. Jacobethan was also

86

favoured by Wilson, e.g. at Cholwell House, Clutton, 1855.
Less common was the rather French-looking Elizabethan of
Orchardleigh House, by *T. H. Wyatt*, *c.* 1856–8. The coastal resorts
mentioned under Late Georgian developments of course
expanded with the arrival of railways and the increase in middle-
class leisure. Terraces at Weston-super-Mare carry on the styles
of mid-C19 Clifton; Manilla Crescent was by *Henry Lloyd* of
Bristol, 1851. *Wilson* of Bath did much too. The big post-1860
villas below Hill Road, Clevedon, were mostly Gothic – perhaps
a preference of the Eltons – unlike their counterparts at Clifton.
Hans Price dominated Weston-super-Mare *c.* 1860–1910, with his
trademark grey-stone Gothic.

The most ambitious HIGH VICTORIAN HOUSE is *John
Norton*'s Tyntesfield, Wraxall, of 1862–4, one of the few C19
country houses in this area. His too, smaller but also lavishly
Gothic, is Chew Manor at Chew Magna, 1864, with C16 Flemish
and German imports and reused pieces from the underlying C17
house. Recently recognized is the Puginian work by *J. G. Crace*
at Uphill Manor, Uphill, *c.* 1856. It is, after Abney Hall and
Eastnor Castle, Crace's most complete extant scheme, although
his furniture was mostly sold off in the 1990s. Gothic was of
course popular for vicarages: *Pope & Bindon*'s lively High Gothic
one at Nempnett Thrubwell, 1860, employs red brick banding
and sharply pointed gables to enliven the grey limestone. *S. S.
Teulon*'s vicarage at St Thomas, Wells, 1866–7, is also excellent of
its type. Lullington vicarage (*George Devey*, 1866–7) is, by contrast, an unusually early borrowing from the C17 vernacular, and
pleasingly robust. The Victorians could be more sensitive to past
styles than is commonly perceived: *Manners & Gill*'s enlargement
of Ammerdown House (1856–7) was done almost imperceptibly
in the Wyatt style; *Hopper*'s Vanbrughian kitchen wing at
Kingsweston (*c.* 1847–9, demolished) fooled many observers too.

Diversity was the hallmark of the years 1880–1914, with Old
English, Queen Anne, Neo-Baroque and Neo-everything else. In
the prosperous suburbs of Bristol, some good work in the
Bedford Park style appears *c.* 1900 by *Henry Dare Bryan*, *Rodway
& Dening* etc. Also by *Dare Bryan*, a Voyseyesque pair at Leigh
Woods (1901–2), a contrast to its neighbours in the Alpine,
Jacobean or Gothic styles preferred by most of Bristol's mercan-
tile élite. Webbington House, Compton Bishop (*E. J. May*,
1907–8) may have been the best of the Old English style in this
volume before being ruined *c.* 1960. Lastly the rather Arts-and-
Craftsy house built for the archaeologist Dr Arthur Bulleid at
Midsomer Norton (*Rupert Austin*, 1908) is worthy of note.

Public, commercial and industrial buildings

There are relatively few CIVIC AND PUBLIC BUILDINGS to note.
At Bristol is the earliest Perp Gothic town hall in England, the
Guildhall, Broad Street, by *R. S. Pope*, *c.* 1843–6, and the ugly
Assize Courts by *Popes & Bindon*, 1867–70. *Brydon* produced
skilful work at Bath in the 1890s (Victoria Art Gallery, Guildhall

extensions etc.), but undoubtedly the most forward-looking and
original is *Charles Holden*'s Central Library at Bristol (1902–6);   108
see Bristol Introduction, p. 237. The rest is covered in the respective city introductions. Elsewhere, public buildings are modest.
At Weston-super-Mare, the odd rock-faced Italianate Town Hall
was by *James Wilson* of Bath (1856–9), much altered since. *Hans
Price* produced almost all other public buildings there until the
First World War. MARKET HALLS include Midsomer Norton by
Foster & Wood, 1859, Italianate; Clevedon, by *Hans Price*, 1869,
styleless but of unusual pyramidal form; and the railway-station-
like steel-framed structure at Radstock, by *T. Martin*, 1897–8.
Italianate was chosen for Frome's Literary and Scientific Insti-   p. 512
tute (now Museum), by *James Hine*, c. 1865–8, and for numer-
ous BANKS, e.g. *W. B. Gingell*'s at Weston-super-Mare, 1864.
Unexpected at Wells is a Venetian Gothic bank by *C. E. Giles*,
c. 1855. HOSPITALS of architectural interest include the former
County Lunatic Asylum at South Horrington near Wells (*Scott*   104
& Moffatt, 1845–8), like an enlarged Jacobean country house.
Theirs too is the Late Classical workhouse at Flax Bourton
(1837–8), the best survivor of quite a number in this volume
(Axbridge, Wells, Clutton, Shepton Mallet, Frome etc.).

EDUCATIONAL BUILDINGS begin with the Tudor Gothic of
the University College at Bristol, by *Charles Hansom*, from 1879.
The preference for that style was to endure well into the C20 at
Bristol (*see* p. 237). In the Bristol suburbs is the Gothic teacher-
training college of St Matthias, Fishponds (*Norton* and *Clarke*,   p. 366
1852–3). PRIVATE SCHOOLS frequently adopted collegiate
Tudor, as at Kingswood School, Bath (*James Wilson*, 1850–2) and
Clifton College, Bristol (*C. Hansom*, 1862 and later). RURAL
SCHOOLS were usually Neo-Tudor, e.g. Coleford, 1831, enlarged
as a National School, 1847. Gothic of course became the norm
from the 1850s, with Bristol architects usually employed in the
centre and w of our area (*S. B. Gabriel* at Dundry and Keynsham, 1857; *Lysaght* at Backwell, 1861; *Foster & Wood* at Wrington, 1857). The next type is the late C19 BOARD SCHOOL, always
lower and more spreading here than London schools, and slow
to take up the Queen Anne style. Apart from the group in Bedminster, Bristol, the Flemish Renaissance-style Walliscote Road
school, Weston-super-Mare (*Price & Wooler*, 1895–7), is among
the best. Of smaller schools there are *Walter Cave*'s timbered Arts
and Crafts school at Flax Bourton, 1895, and *Henry Dare Bryan*'s
Free Style design at Wells, 1898–1900. Lastly, the excellent design
by *Leonard Stokes* for Downside Abbey School, c. 1912, in an
abstracted mullioned style.

Advances in TECHNOLOGY and TRANSPORT are embodied in
Brunel's Clifton Suspension Bridge (1829–64), which is dealt   100
with under Bristol. Railway stations likewise come under the city
Introductions, except for *J. R. Hannaford*'s simple timber-and-
iron station building at Frome, 1850. Only the Great Western
Railway route through Bath to Bristol produced much in the way
of tunnels and bridges, e.g. *Brunel*'s series on the w outskirts of
Bath, and his fine (though obscured) bridge over the River Avon

at Brislington, *c.* 1840. PIER building began with a failed attempt at a chain pier at Weston-super-Mare, 1848. *Eugenius Birch's* screw-piling technique succeeded at Birnbeck Pier (1864–7).

100   Clevedon can claim to be the most elegant surviving pier in Britain (1868–9), its partial collapse and rebuilding (1970–98) making that claim the sweeter. The engineers used second-hand railway lines in the original structure. The iron-and-glass-roofed MODEL FARM at East Harptree (*Robert Smith*, 1858–9), with internal brick-and-iron arches supporting galleries, is related to railway station design. Otherwise the DOCK at Avonmouth is the only Victorian engineering project requiring mention, begun 1868–77, expanded 1902–8, with a monolithic reinforced-concrete flour mill (*F. E. L. Harris*, 1907–8) as a corollary. At the

102   turn of the C20, Bristol and Bath saw limited use of new materials and techniques; e.g. early *Hennebique* reinforced concrete at the Malthouse, Lower Bristol Road, Bath (*c.* 1900), and at Canon's Marsh railway sheds, Bristol (1904). The *Coignet* system was preferred for the second and third Cumberland Basin Tobacco Bonds from 1906.

ARCHITECTURE AFTER 1914

Architecture 1914–45

INDUSTRY and COMMERCE increased between 1914 and 1945, even in such a rural county as Somerset. Bookended by two world wars, the N Somerset area followed the wider rural pattern of fragmentation and uncertainty as increasingly mechanized farming required fewer people. Coal production peaked *c.* 1900–20, but the number of operational pits declined from thirty in 1920 to twelve by 1947. Long terraces of miners' housing built from *c.* 1914 around Radstock are one of the few reminders left, roughly following the standards established for COUNCIL HOUSING. The latter began in a small way even in rural districts, but nowhere followed Bristol's experiment on garden-suburb principles at Sea Mills from 1919. The development of interwar council estates at Bristol is explained in the city Introduction. Light industry, commerce, and to an extent, tourism, fuelled the urban spread around Bristol, Bath, Weston-super-Mare and some smaller towns. In conventional private housing development, the rural time-lag in fashions (which had been as much as forty years or so in the C18, and a decade or more even in the late C19) finally became vanishingly small, so that developments might be picked up by house builders at Frome or Weston-super-Mare via the architectural press within months of their appearance in Ruislip or Edgware. This also meant the demise of local materials and character in favour of what Osbert Lancaster called 'By-Pass Variegated'.

The ambivalence towards commercial applications of MODERNISM is shown by two examples. One of only two C20 buildings in this area by a world-class firm was *Breuer & Yorke*'s temporary pavilion for Crofton Gane's furniture company at the Royal Agricultural Show near Bristol (1936). *Page* and *Jellicoe*'s reinforced concrete restaurant (1934–5) at Cheddar Gorge suffered a worse fate, its form eroded by piecemeal changes and swamped in tawdry signage. The best Modern Movement HOUSES are Concrete House, Bristol (*Connell, Ward & Lucas*, 1934) and Kilowatt House, Bath (*Mollie Taylor*, 1935–8), both commissioned for prosperous intellectuals with individualistic tastes. The derivative streamlined *Moderne* style is seen e.g. at Knoll House, Frome (*Ronald Vallis*, 1935). By *Oliver Hill* is an unusual neo-colonial house at Tickenham, 1939–40. In stark contrast, *Lutyens*'s disciplined classical rebuilding of Mells Park, 1922–5, is the last major COUNTRY HOUSE in the volume. 112

PUBLIC BUILDINGS begin with the monumental Wills Memorial Building at Bristol University (*Oatley & Lawrence*, 1912–25), one of the last significant monuments of Gothic Revival architecture in England. Their fine physics building (1921–7) is in a C17 mode. Otherwise Neo-Georgian was the commonest style, e.g. Bristol Council House (*E. Vincent Harris*, 1938–52), its details barely sufficient to carry something on that scale. More characteristic are the enlargement of Weston-super-Mare Town Hall (*Fry, Paterson & Jones*, 1927) and the Post Office at Clevedon, 1938. *A. J. Toomer*'s former Police Station at Weston (1934) is arid Neoclassical, while *W. H. Martin*'s huge convalescent hospital at Kewstoke (1931–3) embraces the *moderne*, though still with Tuscan loggias. 109

Buildings for LEISURE are more numerous. Surviving 1930s CINEMAS include *T. Cecil Howitt*'s faience-clad Odeon at Weston-super-Mare, and its less pristine sister at Broadmead, Bristol; the sumptuous Forum at Bath (*Watkins & Willmott*); and the Regal, Wells (*E. S. Roberts*, in near-original condition until 2004). Earlier than all these is the Curzon, Clevedon (rebuilt 1920–2), with seemingly unique interior facings of pressed tinplate. *T. H. Mawson & Son*'s Winter Gardens, Weston-super-Mare (1924–7), has long Tuscan wings overlooking Italianate gardens and the sea, and a domed elliptical ballroom in the centre. Few interwar SWIMMING POOLS survive; Weston-super-Mare's Tropicana (1937) has lost its distinctive diving stages and may be redeveloped.

CHURCHES of 1914–45 must begin with *Sir Giles Gilbert Scott*'s completion of Downside Abbey. If ever there was excuse for building in period forms in the C20, it was here. Both the nave (1918–25) and tower (completed only in 1938) are nobly conceived, complementing Hansom's and Garner's Late Victorian Gothic work without slavish imitation. Scott's curving tracery is overtly un-medieval and un-Victorian. However, he considered the Early Christian-style church of St Alphege at Oldfield Park, Bath (1927–9) among his best work. Even in the cities, few ventured beyond the safe familiarity of the tail-end of the Gothic Revival. *F. C. Eden*'s s aisle at All Saints, Weston-super-Mare, is extremely refined traditional. *W. D. Caroe*'s church at Temple 92

Cloud, 1924–6, reinterprets Romanesque forms; the chapels at
Ashwick and Loxton are of high quality too.

FITTINGS generally are numerous. *Comper* re-fitted the sumptuous Lady Chapel (1898–1927) amongst much else at Downside, as already noted, and designed glass, reredos and rood
screen at All Saints, Clevedon (1917–24). Somerset's abundant
churches offer much STAINED GLASS. *Kempe & Co.* furnished
new glass at St John, Frome, 1923–30. The firm of *Bell & Son*,
the largest local producer, had followed Kempe's silvery style
until *Arnold Robinson*, its chief designer after the First World War,
steered a new course. The result can be seen in the splendid collection of smoky and mottled glass at St Alban, Westbury Park,
Bristol (1919 onward), and in smaller quantities elsewhere. The
same church has glass by *Margaret Chilton* and *Florence Camm*,
while *Karl Parsons* designed a fine war memorial window at East
Harptree, 1919. MONUMENTS can be covered briefly, as ambitious stonemasonry became too expensive for most. The Horners
of Mells commissioned from *Sir Alfred Munnings* a large bronze
equestrian statue of their son †1917. It stands on a plinth by
Lutyens, whose intended chapel to house it was never built. Also
by Lutyens is the abstracted block-like monument in Mells
churchyard to the McKenna family (†1932). *Sir Giles Gilbert Scott*
designed at Downside Abbey the crisp monument to Cardinal
Gasquet, †1929, a paraphrase of a late medieval chest tomb with
effigy under a canopy. *Eric Gill* carved a powerful Crucifixion
(†1931) at Canford cemetery, Bristol, and his pupil *Don Potter*
may have been responsible for a noble little tablet at Stowey
(†1940).

North Somerset did not escape wartime bombing. At Bristol
about one quarter of the medieval core was destroyed, and the
suburbs also suffered badly. Bath was blitzed in 1942, and
Weston-super-Mare received some heavy raids. The long period
of rationing and economic restriction which followed the peace
curtailed architectural innovation until *c.* 1955.

Building after 1945

The period *c.* 1960–80 saw perhaps the most radical changes to
Somerset since the Industrial Revolution, especially in towns and
villages near Bristol or Bath. A survey of Yatton, for example,
showed in 1974 that 72 per cent of its housing had been built
since 1945. Little of architectural merit resulted anywhere.

Post-war RELIGIOUS BUILDINGS include a few overtly
modern churches in the cities. The most important and remarkable is Clifton Cathedral (R.C.), by the *Percy Thomas Partnership*
(1965–73). While the exterior pink aggregate-faced concrete
panels have perhaps few admirers, the pyramidal profile rising to
three asymmetrical fins is nicely distinctive. It is inside that
the building delights, with its almost mystical manipulation of
light and space and crisply shuttered concrete. Christ the King,
Bristol, is by *Nealon & Partner* (1952–61), the favoured firm
for Bristol's Roman Catholic parish churches. More striking
is *Nealon & Tanner*'s double hyperbolic paraboloid roof at

St Bernadette, Bristol (1968). *Burrough & Hannam* were often [114] innovative, especially with the 'jelly-mould' church at Lawrence Weston (1950), of sprayed concrete over hessian, which survived for just a decade. St Peter, Weston-super-Mare (*Alban Caröe*, 1952), exemplifies the reinterpretations of traditional forms. Good FITTINGS include the fine organ case at Wells Cathedral (*Alan Rome*, 1974), and the jazzy inlaid chestnut chancel furniture at St John, Weston-super-Mare (*Stephen Dykes Bower*, 1962). There is abstract stained glass by *Keith New* at Bristol Cathedral and (surprisingly) Coleford; by *Harry Stammers* at St Mary Redcliffe, St Mary, Shirehampton, and St Cuthbert, Brislington; and by *Roger Fyfield* at Congresbury.

The coming of MOSQUES and GURDWARAS, mostly in Bristol, seems to mirror precisely the first architectural expressions of C18 Nonconformity. First in Bristol was a Sikh gurdwara established in 1958 in a small house in Easton; Muslims followed the same pattern. By the late 1960s some took over halls or mission chapels, e.g. Jamia Mosque, Totterdown, which by 1980 had the confidence to reface its Victorian chapel with a minaret and dome. Bristol's first purpose-built mosque in distinctively Muslim forms opened in 2001.

The biggest group of EDUCATIONAL BUILDINGS is the UNIVERSITY OF BATH, established in 1966 on a new campus in an [117] exposed landscape at Claverton Down. It is remarkably non-Bath in character. *Robert Matthew, Johnson-Marshall & Partners'* Development Plan (1965) provided for a technological university. The core megastructure, completed 1967–80, has a raised central spine, separating pedestrians from vehicles. *Alison & Peter Smithson's* additions, their major works after the early 1970s, were *p. 199* conceived as tassels to the fringe of the campus. Bristol has yet nothing like them, its 'campus' being discrete Victorian houses on public streets, and several dull post-war works at Tyndall Avenue, Clifton, by *Ralph Brentnall*. A new masterplan by *Feilden Clegg Bradley* (2006) aims to rationalize that central area, with an 'iconic', i.e. extrovert and very tall, new building on one of the highest hilltops in the city centre.

SCHOOLS began bravely after the war, with *Richard Sheppard & Geoffrey Robson's* experiment in aluminium construction (taking up the slack in aircraft factories) at Lockleaze, Bristol, from 1949, part-demolished. Secondary schools using the same technique were designed by the *City Architects' Department c.* 1951–5, e.g. Bedminster Down. As 1950s schools reached the end of their life, a replacement programme beginning *c.* 2000 produced good new schools in Bristol, e.g. by *Wilkinson Eyre* at Brislington, *NVB Architects* at Bedminster Down and Shirehampton, and *Alec French Partnership* at Henbury and Monk's Park. A City Academy at Redfield, Bristol by *Feilden Clegg Bradley*, 2005, is planned as a line zigzagging across a spine corridor, forming alternating triangles. *NVB Architects* also designed two distinctive primary schools at Rad- *p. 589* stock, making happy use of curved forms and timber cladding.

PUBLIC BUILDINGS include Bristol Crown Courts, of smartly striped stone (*Stride Treglown*, 1994), the contextual Magistrates Courts at Bath (1987–9), distinctive libraries at Wells, 1968, and

Nailsea, 1970–1 (both by the *County Architects' Department*), and
an exhilaratingly spiky theatre at Bath Spa University, by *Feilden
Clegg Bradley*, 2006. A small private hospital at Peasedown St
John, by *Foster & Partners*, is cleanly rectilinear and clad in aluminium alloy. The most significant post-war ENGINEERING projects are Royal Portbury Dock (engineers *Rendel, Palmer &
Tritton*, 1972–7) and the construction of the M5 motorway, especially the Avonmouth Bridge (1969–74) and the raised section
through the Gordano valley (1973). Good recent FACTORIES are
few: in Bath, *Yorke, Rosenberg & Mardall*'s Bath Cabinet Makers'
Factory (1966–7), and the Herman Miller Factory, Locksbrook
(1975), by the *Farrell Grimshaw Partnership*. The monumental
Imperial Tobacco factory at Hartcliffe, Bristol (*Skidmore, Owings
& Merrill* with *Yorke, Rosenberg & Mardall*, 1970–4) was perhaps
the major representative in N Somerset of International Modernism by world-class architects. It was stripped back to its rusted
steel frame then converted to flats in 2006–8. COMMERCIAL
ARCHITECTURE and PUBLIC HOUSING in Bath and Bristol are
discussed in the respective introductions. Elsewhere, really good
examples of either type are sparse.

A few late C20 HOUSES can be mentioned, e.g. the small developments by *Artist Constructor* at Ubley and Flax Bourton of the
early 1970s; *Potter & Hare*'s flat-roofed canons' houses at Wells;
and Modernist houses at Ubley (*Rebecca & Jim Dyer*, 2005–7),
Portbury (*Michael Axford Architects*, 1990–1) and Abbot's Leigh
(*Peter Meacock Central Workshop*, 2001–2). Most of these faced significant local planning objections, indicative of the continuing
distrust in some quarters of anything frankly new – while the
majority, the ersatz vernacular or the plain dull, go unremarked.

In the cities and towns, creative REUSE of old buildings and
brownfield sites is at last widespread; Bristol examples include
the Arnolfini (Bush House) and the Watershed, both converted
in 1975, which together set the pace for the regeneration of the
harbour. Rural areas have seen scattered conversion of industrial
buildings, and numerous chapel conversions for housing. Buckland Dinham Methodist chapel retains the gallery and auditorium intact, and *Richard Pedlar*'s sensitive conversion at Christ
Church, Rode Hill (1997–9) for a sympathetic musician owner
allowed the retention of the astonishingly tall nave and chancel
as a performance space.

We end as Pevsner did, with a glance at the current state. The
economics of home buying since 1970 has meant a huge influx
of second homers, a generation of country dwellers disconnected
from the land, and the craze for 'renovation' rather than conservation. Unmodernized cottages, even of the C18 and C19, have
become rare. The more prosperous villages in the Bristol com-
muter belt show a rash of repointed stone stripped of its traditional lime render and colourwash, and lurid red-stained
hardwood windows, or worse, uPVC, even in listed buildings.
This new age of domestic destruction may prove with hindsight
comparable to the age of Victorian church restorers. The careful
restoration and sensitive new elements in the Trinity area of

Frome, carried out in the 1980s, are even now being unpicked, with crass off-the-shelf plastic windows and doors inserted to make C17 weavers' cottages mimic estate houses. But there are positives too: among worthy CONSERVATION projects may be cited Rugbourne Farm, High Littleton, just one example of a building which, in Pevsner's day, might still have been demolished. At Tellisford, a ruined woollen mill has been brought back to use to provide electricity for the village. Proof that such projects can work even in sensitive locations must inspire hope for the rest of the county.

FURTHER READING

Somerset as a whole is uncommonly well served by standard county-wide works of reference, the N of the county rather less so. Recent *Victoria County History* publications relate only to S and W Somerset, so apart from vol. II (1911) on church history, there is little of use to us. COUNTY HISTORIES begin with John Collinson's *History and Antiquities of the County of Somerset* (3 vols), 1791, while John Rutter's *Delineations of the North Western Division of the County of Somerset*, 1829, usefully covers the area between Bristol, Chew Magna and Weston-super-Mare. The *Proceedings of the Somerset Archaeological and Natural History Society* (*PSANHS*; from 1851) are amongst the best of the archaeological journals in the country, and still address the historic county rather than the present one. The equivalent *Transactions of the Bristol & Gloucestershire Archaeological Society* run from 1876.

For GEOLOGY there is the new generation of maps and guides published by the British Geological Survey. Notable are the two packs (map and guidebook as one) for W and E Mendip by Andy Farrant, 2008. A similar pack is available for Bristol by C. Barton, P. Strange, K. Royse and A. Farrant, 2002. For the non-specialist, Alec Clifton-Taylor's enjoyable *The Pattern of English Building*, 1965, remains respected.

Introductory works and general surveys of the ARCHAEOLOGY include M. Aston and I. Burrow (eds), *The Archaeology of Somerset*, 1982; M. Aston and R. Iles (eds), *The Archaeology of Avon*, 1987; D. Dobson, *The Archaeology of Somerset*, 1931; and P. Ellis, *Mendip Hills, an Archaeological Survey of the Area of Outstanding Natural Beauty*, 1992. The Roman period is covered by K. Branigan and P. Fowler, *The Roman West Country*, 1976, and K. Branigan, *The Roman Villa in South West England*, 1977, and P. Leach, *Roman Somerset*, 2001. For Roman Bath there are Barry Cunliffe's accounts of 1969 (Society of Antiquaries) and 1995 (English Heritage), and his *Roman Bath Discovered* (4th edn, 2000). More detailed accounts are P. Davenport's articles 'Roman Bath and its Hinterland', and 'Aquae Sulis, the Origins and Development of a Roman Town', respectively in *Bath History* 5, 1994, and 8, 2000. Other sites are surveyed by J. Bennett, *Sea*

Mills, the Roman Town of Abonae (Bristol City Museum), 1985; W. Wedlake, *Excavations at Camerton, Somerset* (Camerton Excavation Club), 1958; M. Fradley, 'The field Archaeology of the Romano-British Settlement at Charterhouse-on-Mendip', *Britannia* 40, 2009; P. Rahtz and E. Greenfield, *Excavations at Chew Valley Lake*, Somerset (HMSO), 1977, and P. Linford, *Stanton Drew Stone Circles* (English Heritage), 1997. Journals of specialist interest besides the *PSANHS* are *Bristol & Avon Archaeology* (an unexpected bonus from the creation of the former County of Avon in 1974) and the *Proceedings of the University of Bristol Spelaeological Society*. The urban archaeological databases and/or historic environment records at the county and unitary authorities are accessible on line, and Somerset County Council's 'History of Somerset' pages are particularly helpful.

BRISTOL has a vast published history. The medieval city was recorded in the unique records of William Worcester (see the Bristol Record Society's scholarly edition by F. Neale, 2000). John Latimer's *Annals of Bristol*, 1887 and later (reprinted 1970) remains a fine source for post-medieval Bristol. Coverage has been extended to 1939 in five booklets by John Lyes (2002 onwards). B. S. Smith and F. Ralph's *History of Bristol and Gloucestershire*, 1972, gives a general survey. More recent volumes focus on specific themes or eras, e.g. D. H. Sacks, *The Widening Gate, Bristol and the Atlantic Economy 1450–1700*, 1993. Besides the *City Guide* by Andrew Foyle (2004), architectural descriptions include A. Gomme, M. Jenner and B. Little, *Bristol, an Architectural History*, 1979; W. Ison, *The Georgian Buildings of Bristol*, 1952; C. Crick, *Victorian Buildings in Bristol*, 1975; and T. Aldous, *C20, Bristol's Twentieth-century Buildings*, 2000. D. Merritt and F. Greenacre's *Public Sculpture of Bristol* is to be published by the Public Monuments and Sculpture Association (2011).

BATH'S post-Roman coverage starts with R. S. Neale, *Bath 1680–1850, a Social History*, 1981, and P. Borsay, *The Image of Georgian Bath, 1700–2000*, 2000. There are, surprisingly, fewer strictly architectural accounts than for Bristol. The *City Guide* by Michael Forsyth dates from 2003. Of earlier books, Mowbray A. Green's *The Eighteenth Century Architecture of Bath*, 1904, was followed by W. Ison's *The Georgian Buildings of Bath*, 1948. This and his Bristol book (above) are scholarly and entertaining. Neil Jackson, *Nineteenth Century Bath, Architects & Architecture*, 1991, is the best survey of the Victorian city. J. Tunstall's *Rambles About Bath and its Neighbourhood* (1847, 2nd edn 1876) includes much on the village churches. On WELLS, Marion Meek's *The Book of Wells*, 1980, is a good introduction, while Tony Scrase's *Wells, a Pictorial History*, 1992, has useful early illustrations.

Among the TOWNS, Frome is well covered, with R. Goodall, *The Buildings of Frome*, 2005, M. McGarvie, *The Book of Frome*, 1980, and R. Leech, *Early Industrial Housing, the Trinity Area of Frome* (RCHME), 1981. P. Beisly, *Weston-super-Mare Past*, 2001, furnishes an excellent introduction to the architecture and growth of the town. A few small towns are served by specific histories, such as Eve Wigan's *Portishead Parish History*, 1932. For the COUNTRYSIDE, R. D. Reid's *Some Buildings of Mendip*, 1979, provides a good though brief starting point, with a short but incisive text and good photographs. The late Robin Bush's *Somerset, the Complete Guide*, 1994, now hard to find, is a good introduction to present-day towns and villages. An idea of medieval growth around Bristol may be gained from R. L. Leech, *Small Medieval Towns in Avon*, 1975.

The CATHEDRALS of Bristol and Wells are covered in N. Pevsner and P. Metcalf, *The Cathedrals of England*, 1985 (2 vols, with bibliographies), while G. Cobb's *English Cathedrals, the Forgotten Centuries*, 1980, deals with Bristol and Bath. For Bristol, the context of religious life was examined in the British Archaeological Association's conference transactions, *Bristol in the Middle Ages, Almost the Richest City* (ed. L. Keen), 1997. J. Rogan, *Bristol Cathedral*, 2000, is the most accessible overall source for both history and architecture. For Wells there is a wealth of recent material. Dr Warwick Rodwell's *Excavations and Structural Studies, 1978–1993* (English Heritage, 2 vols), 2001, includes axonometric drawings of the building phases, and much else. Its essential counterpart is Jerry Sampson's *Wells Cathedral West Front, Construction, Sculpture and Conservation*, 1998. Tim Ayres, *The Medieval Stained Glass of Wells Cathedral*, 2004, contains many new discoveries and places the glass in the context of location and patronage. Bath Abbey has no recent studies of equivalent scale and depth. Works on other MAJOR CHURCHES include M. Q. Smith, *St Mary Redcliffe, an Architectural History*, 1995, while Aidan Bellenger's *Downside Abbey, an Architectural History*, 2011, is the first comprehensive coverage of the church, monastic and school buildings.

For the medieval PARISH CHURCHES, Kenneth Wickham's careful and beautifully written book *Churches of Somerset*, 1953, remains unsurpassed. John Harvey's *The Perpendicular Style 1330–1485*, 1978, has some Somerset references, while his pamphlet *Somerset Perpendicular, the Church Towers and the Dating Evidence* (1984, reprinted from two articles in the *Transactions of the Ancient Monuments Society*) is a mine of detailed analysis and dating. The first part, on towers, rebuts Peter Poyntz-Wright's flawed *Parish Church Towers of Somerset*, 1981 (*see* footnote, p. 27). D. T. Donovan and R. D. Reid's article 'The Stone Insets of Somerset Churches', *PSANHS* 107, 1963, helps to distinguish the occurrences of Blue Lias insets, which Pevsner often mistakenly identified as Purbeck marble. *Sir Stephen Glynne's Church Notes for Somerset* (Somerset Record Society), 1994, couples Glynne's C19 notes with John Buckler's illustrations of churches *c.* 1830. Comparison with today's structures is revealing for the effects of Victorian restorations.

The only coverage of ROMAN CATHOLIC CHURCHES is J. A. Harding, *The Diocese of Clifton, 1850–2000*, 1999, rich in social history but often frustratingly evasive on the buildings. For CHAPELS, Christopher Stell, *An Inventory of Nonconformist Chapels and Meeting-houses in South-West England* (RCHME),

1991, is the best survey, though by no means complete. Ignatius Jones, *Bristol Congregationalism, City and Country*, 1947, provides good dating and architectural information.

On CHURCH FITTINGS there is little consistent treatment. Early STAINED GLASS is surveyed by Christopher Woodforde, *Stained Glass in Somerset 1250–1830*, 1946 (reprinted 1970), with A. C. Sewter's *The Stained Glass of William Morris and his Circle* (2 vols), 1974–5, covering e.g. the Morris glass at Frome. Saxon SCULPTURE is well described in Rosemary Cramp, *Corpus of Anglo-Saxon Stone Sculpture*, vol. VII (SW England), 2006. For post-medieval MONUMENTS, there is Ingrid Roscoe's *A Biographical Dictionary of Sculptors in Britain 1660–1851* (2009).

Coverage of SECULAR BUILDING TYPES is patchy, and mainly through national surveys, such as A. Brodie, J. Croom and J. O. Davies, *English Prisons, an Architectural History* (English Heritage), 2002, or through specialist studies such as Jonathan Holt's *Somerset Follies*, 2007. Otherwise one has the DCMS listed building descriptions, now available at *www.heritagegateway.org.uk*; useful where revised as in Wells, but often thin on the villages.

Anthony Emery, *Greater Medieval Houses of England and Wales, 1300–1500*, vol. III (2006) covers such GREAT HOUSES as Clevedon Court, while many lesser or newer houses feature in Robert Cooke, *West Country Houses*, 1957. Nicholas Kingsley, *The Country Houses of Gloucestershire, vol. II, 1660–1830*, 1992, includes the northern outskirts of Bristol formerly in Gloucestershire, therefore surveying houses such as Kingsweston. W. J. Robinson's *West Country Manors*, 1930, is still valuable. Few country houses in N Somerset can claim national significance; the exception is Tyntesfield, on which the chief example of the flurry of writing since it was bought for the nation in 2002 is James Miller, *Fertile Fortune*, 2006. PARKS AND GARDENS are covered by the English Heritage Register of Historic Parks and Gardens, and by Tim Mowl's *Historic Gardens of Somerset*, 2010.

Sir Howard Colvin's admirable *Biographical Dictionary of English Architects, 1660–1840*, 1995, was used here; the 4th edition (2008) arrived when the gazetteer was all but finished. Sources for INDIVIDUAL ARCHITECTS include T. Mowl and B. Earnshaw, *John Wood, Architect of Obsession*, 1988, and D. Bernhardt's Ph.D. thesis on G. P. Manners's Bath practice (University of Bath, 2003). Articles on Thomas Baldwin, Edward Davis and C. E. Davis appear in the series *Bath History* (from 1986). Sarah Whittingham's monograph on *Sir George Oatley* was published in 2011.

Coverage of VERNACULAR ARCHITECTURE is partial. The Somerset Vernacular Buildings Research Group has concentrated mainly on the S and W of the county. Many building reports on individual houses further N are lodged at the Somerset Record Office; wider access requires printed or digital publication. Exceptions include Chew Magna, and an excellent booklet on Newton St Loe (2001). Linda Hall, *The Rural Houses of North Avon and South Gloucestershire*, 1983, touches the northern fringe of our area, though it provides useful comparisons with houses further s. John and Jane Penoyre, *Decorative Plasterwork in the Houses of Somerset 1500–1700*, 1994, includes some examples from the N of the county.

INDUSTRY and TRANSPORT start with the *Journal* of the Bristol Industrial Archaeological Society (1968 onward), covering a huge range of Bristol and Somerset topics. R. A. Buchanan and N. Cossons's *Industrial Archaeology of the Bristol Region*, 1969, remains the best survey of the subject. Specialist books include J. Binding, *Brunel's Bristol Temple Meads*, 2001; C. Down and A. Warrington, *The History of the Somerset Coalfield*, 1971 (reissued 2005); J. Cornwell, *The Bristol Coalfield*, 2003; and A. Smith, *The Nailsea Glassworks*, 2004.

Fuller BIBLIOGRAPHIES for Bath and for Bristol, including some works of wider relevance, will be found in the *City Guides* of 2003 and 2004 respectively. A more detailed bibliography on all aspects of English architecture is available at the Pevsner Architectural Guides' educational website, *www.lookingatbuildings.org.uk.*

GAZETTEER

ABBOT'S LEIGH

The manor was in 1140 given to the Abbey of St Augustine (now Bristol Cathedral), while the church remained with Bedminster. The manor house became the abbots' favoured retreat. It passed to the Norton family, and was replaced by Leigh Court, 1814–17.

HOLY TRINITY. Perp, nave rebuilt after a fire by *Pope, Bindon & Clark*, 1848–9. Original the s doorway with fleurons and the s arcade of three broad low bays with piers of standard section (four hollows). Post-dating the s aisle, and perhaps C15, a short three-stage w tower of Old Red Sandstone, with diagonal buttresses, embattled parapet, Bristol spirelet over the stair-turret. N arcade and aisle in imitation of the s, probably 1848–9. Pretty chancel ceiling, early C19, blue with white ribs and tracery. – FITTINGS. Simple oak stalls etc., 1932, style of *P. Hartland Thomas.* – STAINED GLASS. e window, *c.* 1869, signed *Henry Hughes* (*Ward & Hughes*). Chancel N, attributed to *Joseph Bell*, 1848. Chancel s, a single light by *Powells*, 1932. – MONUMENTS. Sir George Norton †1584. Elizabethan attached six-poster. Frieze and Corinthian columns fluted and reeded, no figures or inscription. – Sir George Norton †1715 and wife. Grey marble, large tablet flanked by Composite columns. Instead of a pediment, a truncated concave-sided gable (cf. a monument by James Paty the Elder at St Mary Redcliffe, Bristol). Volutes outside the columns, on plinths with portrait medallions. – P. J. Miles †1845, one of *E. H. Baily*'s best monuments (under the tower), the composition still in the C18 tradition. Tall pedestal with vase, flanked by big allegorical female figures, one seated, one standing. – Sir P. J. W. Miles †1888. Brass with rare photographic death portrait. – Many minor tablets.

WAR MEMORIAL. Cross by *A. C. Fare*, 1921. Medieval stepped base.

LEIGH COURT. Now a conference centre. Built 1814–17 for P. J. Miles, to replace the gabled Jacobean mansion of the Nortons. William Evans's researches show that the contractual architect, *Thomas Hopper*, took a reduced fee because the design is almost identical to Pythouse, Newtown, Wilts., by John Bennett (*c.* 1805). Even more curiously, Bennett

witnessed the contract for Leigh Court. The nature of the rela-
tionships is obscure, but *Bennett* must be considered at least
joint architect. It is the best house of its date in Somerset, especially excellent inside. Noble Grecian block of Bath stone, with
service wing and stables to the NW. Free-standing pedimented
SW portico of four giant unfluted Ionic columns, and a matching one to the garden front, NE. The SE side has a recessed
centre with four columns *in antis*, flanked by ground-floor
windows in segmental-headed recesses.*

The centre inside is a STAIRCASE HALL worthy of a palace,
rounded at both ends: a grandiose development of Hopper's
Ionic stair-hall with coffered vault at Melford Hall, Suffolk,
1813. Two wide flights rise parallel and meet at the first floor
in a U-shape. Rich brass-inlaid mahogany handrail, cast bronze
balusters. The upper floor has an Ionic gallery all round, and
a coved ceiling with glazed infillings of the coffers. It is reached
via a square ENTRANCE HALL with eight white marble
columns carrying a shallow dome, like a circular room within
a square. Six further principal rooms on the SW, SE and NE
fronts, with exquisitely executed Grecian plasterwork in pro-
fusion. The ceiling of the DINING ROOM (NW corner) shows
the early C19 turn to more naturalistic decoration, with vine
leaves and grapes. Most dramatic is the long LIBRARY in the
centre of the SE side, with a coffered ceiling; the adjacent
TAPESTRY ROOM has the richest ceiling, encrusted with
gilded anthemia etc. The MORNING ROOM (S angle) has a late
C19 Neo-Adam ceiling, frieze and window surrounds. In the
stair-hall, an ORGAN by *Flight & Robson*, perhaps c. 1820. In
two parts, flanking a door; plain mahogany cases with brass
scrolled frieze and trim.

On Abbot's Leigh Road, c. ½ m. SE, a former GATE LODGE to
Leigh Court. Severely Grecian. Between one-storey lodges, a
monumental arch framed by paired unfluted giant Ionic
columns with straight entablature, of the same order as the
house. *Humphry Repton* was engaged to redesign the grounds,
but little was done.

Some good Georgian VILLAS in Church Road, e.g. Abbot's Leigh
House, c. 1780–1800. To its SW, the folksy red sandstone
VILLAGE HALL (1896) must have been charming before the
introduction of ersatz windows. Opposite, on the main road,
the GEORGE INN, outwardly C18, with the medieval church
house at its core. THE PRIORY, Manor Road, is big unruly
Neo-Tudor by *Foster & Okely*, 1831–2. (Interior doors and
shutter panels with unusual cast-iron tracery.) In front, a grand
conservatory of 1836 with pierced parapets bristling with pinnacles. Away to the NW, another surprise in Harris Lane; two
admirably controlled Modernist villas by *Peter Meacock Central
Workshop*, 2001–2. That at the E square, the other a long rectangle abutting the boundary wall between. Flat roofs, white

---

*Here Pythouse differs, with two columns *in antis* and a smaller central staircase.
Both differences were dictated by the layout of the embedded preceding house.

render, and in parts, overhanging first floors on columns. The
rectangular house has a glazed ground floor to the garden, with
a swimming pool that begins indoors.

AMMERDOWN   7050

AMMERDOWN HOUSE. The nucleus was designed in 1788 by
James Wyatt for Thomas Samuel Jolliffe, who acquired the land
as bare sheep walks. It replaced Charlton House, the Jolliffes'
house w of Kilmersdon. Began 1789, fitted out by 1795, with
plasterwork by *Williams* of London. Of Bath stone, three
storeys with a tall rusticated ground floor, three bays wide E
and w, and originally two bays N and s. Only the E front is in
its original state. On the ground floor Venetian windows in
arched recesses; above, coupled giant Tuscan pilasters. Central
window on the first floor tripartite with an Ionic order and a
pediment over the wide middle opening. The house was
extended w in 1856–7 in the same style, by *Manners & Gill* of
Bath, with two rooms flanking a hall, and a recessed centre on
the upper floors. The s side thus arrived at its present state,
with three Venetian motifs on the ground floor, five windows
above between slightly projecting ends. At the NW corner an
ornamented entrance porch with paired columns, a smoking
room and additions to Wyatt's service wing running N, almost
certainly by *Gill & Browne*, all of 1877. The recessed upper
centre of the w front was filled in to mirror the E façade by
Lutyens, c. 1910–12.

The principal staircase has a rectangular well with a domed
lantern on a colonnade which has rounded ends and was originally solid, not glazed. The transition from the rectangular
lower parts to the rounded ends is by means of pendentives
decorated with, as it were, a classical version of Gothic fans
(cf. Wyatt's hall at Heveningham, Suffolk). It appears the stairs
have been rearranged, probably in 1856–7. The DINING
ROOM is as Wyatt left it: a wide curved recess in the N wall   79
flanked by niches, delicate plasterwork, marble chimneypiece
with vine carving. The DRAWING ROOM on the s front was
formed in 1857 from two rooms. Two fine marble chimneypieces here, and that in the Dining Room, are believed to be
by *Benjamin* or *Thomas Carter Jun.*; brought here c. 1877 from
Egremont House, London (interiors designed by Matthew
Brettingham, c. 1758–64). The hall and upper landing have
excellent Chinese late C18 wallpapers brought in in 1925.
Music Room on the first floor with a shallow Neoclassical
frieze of fans and figures.

The formal GARDENS with tall trimmed yew hedges and patterned parterres were redesigned by *Lutyens*, 1901–2, cleverly
turning an angle to link the house with Wyatt's ORANGERY of
1793 to the NE. – FOUNTAIN, late C17 Italian Baroque from

Merstham, Surrey, on the w forecourt. – STATUARY of *Coade* stone, late C18, from the foot of the column (*see* below), now in the formal gardens. N of the house, *Wyatt*'s STABLE BLOCK (*c.* 1788–95) is now a retreat and conference centre; additional floor, *c.* 1972. *Wyatt*'s Kilmersdon Gate, w of the house, originally the principal entrance, was disused by 1939, its fine Neoclassical LODGES now derelict. On a ridge in the park is AMMERDOWN COLUMN, 150 ft (46 metres) high, a memorial to T. S. Jolliffe (†1824), commissioned in 1849 from the engineer and architect *Joseph Jopling*, and completed 1855. Square plinth with oddly Soane-like segments above, and the column rising by smooth curves like a lighthouse. Formerly surmounted by a lantern of moulded glass in an iron frame.

ASHWICK

ST JAMES. Mid-C15 w tower with diagonal buttresses, panelled battlements and crocketed pinnacles. The nave and chancel, rebuilt by *G. A. Underwood* in 1825, were lost in a further rebuilding of 1876–81 by *Gill & Browne*. Four-bay nave with two-light windows in the low clerestory, narrow lean-to aisles, s porch and chancel, all with Geometric tracery. Nave piers of polished Dolomitic Conglomerate. Small s chapel by *W. D. Caröe*, 1915, with a tiny rib-vaulted apse; at the same time he extended the chancel. Plain moulded arches, tooled blocks, and floors of geometric black-and-white mosaic show his work. – STAINED GLASS. e window 1877, almost certainly by *Hardman*. – MONUMENTS. Richard Hardwick †1738 and Joseph Hardwick †1756. Two brass plaques in a stone frame; verse on time, and an image of a clock. – Richard Hardwick †1770, father of the above, and a clockmaker. Tall tablet with urn and cherub. – Good draped tablets by *King* of Bath, topped by urns, to the agriculturalist John Billingsley †1811, and Mary Billingsley †1828. – C15 churchyard CROSS, resited s of the tower in 1763 to obstruct the fives court and 'prevent the young people from spending so much idle time in that sort of exercise'.

ASHWICK COURT, NW of the church. s front at first glance quite Regency: stucco, symmetrical, with one-bay single-storey wings (added in 1927, l., and *c.* 2000). The three-bay centre is probably of 1698 (date on the stable behind). Hipped roof, tall chimneys and pedimented upper windows, originally crosswindows; one survives in the w return. Ground floor updated *c.* 1820–30 with ashlar porch, for the Strachey family whose eagle emblem appears above. Visible from the N are steep gables, mullioned windows and service ranges with sloped buttresses.

s of the church, a plain Gothic VICARAGE of 1881. s again at the five-way junction towards Oakhill, a former POUND

documented in 1638; now a walled garden. Adjacent is GAT-
COMBE HOUSE (formerly Lancet House), a Presbyterian
chapel of 1758, reworked as a house *c.* 1892; only the long-and-
short quoins and the proportions remind one of the C18.
Facing the junction, two thatched cottages with mullioned
windows; perhaps *c.* 1750.

AXBRIDGE

4050

Despite its smallness, Axbridge has all the requisites of a town.
The Anglo-Saxon *burh* had a mint by 997. The right to hold
markets was confirmed in 1204. C14 Axbridge clothiers navigated
the River Axe, which flows *c.* 1 m. SE.

ST JOHN BAPTIST. Built of Dolomitic Conglomerate and Doulting stone, in a fine dominant position above The Square and
just sufficiently retired from it. It stands at an angle revealing
the foreshortened W front, S aisle and porch, and the tall,
stately crossing tower. Repaired 1876–9 by *J. D. Sedding*, who
rebuilt the N aisle wall and added fittings throughout the 1880s;
this important scheme for his career was incomplete at his
death in 1891.*
    An early foundation is hinted at in the plan, with crossing
tower and big transepts; but what is visible now is nearly all
Perp. The chancel is more modest than the rest, typical of the
county. Attached to its N side was originally a vestry. Traces
remain outside, with a blocked door and stoup (Dec?). The
chancel and S transept were updated probably before 1400, the
rest following. The tower's lower stage is banded, with insignificant set-back buttresses and two-light windows (to E and W,
statue niches instead). Belfry stage perhaps later, with two-light
bell-openings flanked by two-light blank windows without
intermediate pinnacles, cf. Bleadon, Brent Knoll. Pierced
parapet with quatrefoils in lozenges, perhaps added in the C15
to agree with the aisles and porches. Small pinnacles and
higher stair-turret. The transept gables have the largest
windows – six lights to the S, five to the N (which is better
handled, probably later and unrestored). Here the reticulation
units are not subdivided, often in Somerset a sign of a pre-
1400 date, as is the continuous hoodmould. The W gable of the
nave is overlaid by the aisle walls. Broad low W porch. To its S,
a two-storey addition post-dating the S aisle, perhaps a treasury or muniment room and vestry. A will of 1429 specified
burial in the recently built porch, but this may refer to the W
porch or to the S; the latter also seems early C15, and probably of one build with the S aisle. All have the same parapet as
the tower, that of the S porch a C19 invention. Four-light aisle

* Paul Snell, Ph.D. thesis, University of Manchester, 2007.

windows. Main entrance through the s porch, very plain outside, perhaps in conscious contrast to the enrichments within. Perp panelled stone vault with single-chamfered ribs. Doorway flanked by triangular shafts; leaves in the spandrels.

The broad light INTERIOR impinges only after the arresting fact of the nave roof, a romantic piece of Jacobean Gothicism by a local plasterer, *George Drayton*. Prominently dated 1636 in two places. At the wall-plates, a narrow strapwork frieze. Thin straight and curved ribs form a dense lacy pattern of squares, lozenges and interlocked quatrefoils, with bosses or large pendants at strategic junctions, all heightened by colour and gilding. The design thus far is straightforward Jacobean, but the panels are cusped, and that can only be understood as a self-conscious or romantic allusion to the past. Corbels survive from the Perp roof as well. Nave arcades of four bays with slim piers of four shafts with wave mouldings between, the same as the crossing arches. The s aisle has small capitals to the shafts only, decorated with foliage. The N aisle has plainer capitals with three-ring mouldings, repeated in the two-bay s chancel chapel. Late Perp aisle and chapel roofs, canted and panelled, carefully restored by *Sedding*, preserving their 'power of design'. Medieval paint in one bay (N), a starred chequerboard in red and white. Wagon roofs in the transepts. Two-bay N chancel chapel with inscription in the ceiling cornice to John and Agnes Ruynon, probably late C15 (a son made a will in 1512). This agrees with the long-fingered angels in the capitals of this chapel only; they appear elsewhere *c.* 1470. The crossing also Perp in the details of its piers and arches, although its structure is probably older. The capitals have foliage like the s aisle, but smaller, tighter and perhaps earlier. An angel capital on the w crossing arch is C19. The tower has a remarkably early example of a large fan-vault, with big central bell-hole; from the probable neighbouring dates, before 1420. In the s chapel, E wall, remains of four Perp image niches.

FITTINGS. FONT. Perp, octagonal, the underside a close rank of busts of angels; two small quatrefoils on each panel above. Panelled stem. The fat roll mouldings seem very late. – Fine WOODWORK by *Sedding*: stalls, pulpit, bench-ends and fronts all with imaginative Perp tracery. Best of all the parclose screens, completed 1888, with remarkable Art Nouveau-like tracery details, door panels and lettering, and delicate Arts and Crafts hedgerow fruits and animals. – WALL PAINTING, s aisle. Christ showing his wounds. Red background with ornamental letters. Not too late in the C15. Repainted by the *Rev. H. R. Denison*, late C19. – FRONTAL, N chapel. Needlepoint by *Abigail Prowse*, daughter of the Bishop of Bath and Wells, worked *c.* 1710–20. It shows schematically how a communion table was arranged. – STAINED GLASS. E window, 1887, and s chapel E, 1897, both *J. Bell & Son*. – MONUMENTS. Brass to Roger Harper †1493, and wife. Kneeling figures, N transept. – Anna Prowse †1668. Big, stiff kneeling figure under an arch. Free-standing Composite columns, broken segmental pediment with a standing angel, plump cherubs, and curious angel-mermaids in coy poses like an Edwardian peep-show. On big volute brackets. Soft C17 colours revealed by conservation. – Probably by the same sculptor, William Prowse †1670. Life-size frontal three-quarter figure in an oval niche encircled by a wreath. Swagged Ionic columns, and outside thick garlands and volutes. The upper cornice bulges forward; above, an aedicule with coat of arms and allegorical figures. – Thomas Welsh †1675. Small wall monument without effigy. Corinthian columns and broken segmental pediment with a thick garland hanging across it. Perched on top, two allegories of Time. – John Prowse †1708, erected 1712. Attributed to *William Woodman the Elder* (GF). Grand Doric tablet, gadrooned urns and base. – J. Andrews †1720. Attributed to the *Hartshorne* workshop (GF). Baroque tablet, the ornament swirling so dramatically it almost prefigures the Rococo. Upper addition †1690, with arched cornice, arms and two cherubs. – Thomas Prowse †1767. Conspicuous monument signed by *Laurence Holm*.* High slate obelisk backdrop. Big tablet base with supporting volutes, waisted upper plinth on which a life-sized putto leans on a Neoclassical urn. – Also by *Holm*, Abigail Prowse, 1763; open pediment, urn. – Peter Fry †1787, by *T. Paty & Sons*. Usual draped urn. – Similar, to R. Chapman †1790. By *William Paty*.

TOWN HALL, The Square. Modest three-bay classical front with open pediment in the centre, and porch-balcony on cast-iron columns: c. 1830–3.

Former WORKHOUSE, St John's Court, Houlgate Way. By *S. T. Welch*, 1836–7. Now flats. Baleful Neo-Tudor. T-plan of two and three storeys, canted centre rising to a gable. Rubble rear wing (w) with octagonal tower to guard the (demolished) yards.

ST MICHAEL'S CHESHIRE HOME, Cheddar Road. *William Butterfield*, 1878. Built as a tuberculosis hospital. Gothic, high and gaunt. w façade with chapel beneath central gable. Projecting ward blocks at either end. High extension (s), 1882, lodge and chaplain's house, all Butterfield. The courtyard was covered by a four-gabled day room by *Beech & Tyldesley*, 1977.

PERAMBULATION. From the E, the winding approach along St Mary's Street reveals all the way many doubtless medieval or C17 houses (e.g. Maricourt, N side). Others smartened up with pedimented doors, fanlights and stepped voussoirs, e.g. Morecambe House, c. 1800. The lovely little SQUARE is a revelation. On the N side, the LAMB INN, refronted early C19, and THE OLD ANGEL, retaining its C17 façade. The l. return shows this to be pasted over a jettied three-storey medieval house. Bristol-fashion pent roofs over canted bays, blind central panel with pediment in the first floor. Just off the SW corner in Moorland Street, the OLD ALMSHOUSE, front renewed 1983 in C16 forms. On the best site, the corner of The Square and High

---

*Prowse was a gentleman-architect of Berkley, from an Axbridge family.

Street, a timber-framed merchant's house, probably *c.* 1500, called without reason KING JOHN'S HUNTING LODGE. Now the museum. Repaired by *Burrough & Hannam* for the National Trust, 1969, revealing square-framed panelling with regular curved braces. Shops occupied the ground floor. Moulded curved brackets at each post supporting the jettied upper storeys, and a replica of a C16 or C17 corbel head on the angle post where three braces support a dragon beam. Three gables facing N, one with ornamented bargeboard. Small cinque-cusped attic lights, first- and second-floor windows of 1968, with flattish ogee heads with encircled quatrefoils in the spandrels.

In the HIGH STREET, to the W, several timber-framed houses and many humble Georgian ones. Nos. 2–4 (N), C16, three-storeyed, jettied and close-studded. No. 9 has a C16 door with carved winged dragons in the head; No. 15, jettied but much renewed, good C16 plaster friezes in two rooms. No. 19 (S), the OLD MANOR HOUSE, refronted *c.* 1804 but with a C17 door and doorcase. (Also open-well C17 staircase, fine plaster ceiling, etc.) On the roof, a slate-hung belvedere room with ogee-capped roof, possibly 1752, the date on a weathervane. No. 27, a typically good C18 front. And so out along WEST STREET, which equals the entrance for picturesqueness. At the far end, COMPTON HOUSE. Long N front updated in the C18, leaving two half-blocked C17 windows. Tuscan porch. The S side with projecting wings was remodelled in the early or mid C18 as a new front. C17 four-seater PRIVY in the garden.

BABINGTON

ST MARGARET. Small and very lovably placed on the lawn in front of the house. Built 1748–50 by an unknown architect. Square projecting W tower, forming an open porch. Octagonal domed cupola on top, with an urn at the base of each diago-
nal face. Charming and simple interior: a three-bay nave with round-arched windows; coved ceiling; shallow apsidal chancel with a semi-dome: chancel arch with rosettes in the panelled soffit. Stucco cartouche in place of a reredos, with rays of glory, Rococo cherubs, etc.; lurid recent colour. – FITTINGS. All of a piece with the building. Crisply carved twisted ALTAR RAILS; panelled PULPIT with urn on the backboard; box PEWS, with a little hatch from the family pew giving a view of the altar. – FONT. Stone, baluster type, gadrooned rim. In the style of the *Paty*s. – ARMS. George II. Stucco. – Prominent hanging MON-UMENT to the Pacy and Mompesson families †1687–1726, erected perhaps *c.* 1760. Standing putto with inscription car-touche in front of a pink marble obelisk, possibly by *Thomas Paty* (cf. Hilliard monument, St Mark, Bristol; p. 258).

BABINGTON HOUSE. Now a hotel. Built *c.* 1705 for Henry Mompesson, perhaps lightly updated in the mid C18 (e.g. the window architraves, a little refined for 1705), and more radically in 1790 for the Knatchbulls. Deep rectangular plan with central light well. Two-storey seven-bay E front with heavy cornice (dentils in groups of five), hipped roof and dormers. Long-and-short quoins. Doorway with a shell-hood on fine carved brackets with exaggerated volutes and masks. Little decoration otherwise. N front with a deeply bowed centre added in 1790. Large square entrance hall with early C18 plasterwork (floral cornice; rectangular centrepiece with oval rose garland, and palm branches in the corners). Oak staircase with twisted balusters, ramped panelled dado. The fireplace is *c.* 1740–50. (The library, S of the hall, has oak panelling and a C17 chimneypiece, installed *c.* 1930.) The bowed addition has a dining room with drawing room above, an unusual arrangement in the country, with graceful Neoclassical plasterwork and doorcases. The staircase window contains C15 STAINED GLASS, four saints of Somerset provenance; other internal windows have C16 and C17 Continental glass.

A narrow cobbled yard leads to a pedimented late C18 STABLE BLOCK. Plain mullioned lights. In the S return, two oval windows or pitching eyes keyed into ornamented frames, perhaps earlier C18. In the grounds, SW, a stone-built domed C18 ICE HOUSE, *c.* 35 ft (10 metres) deep.

BACKWELL   *4060*

Three hamlets connected by suburban spread, with the church on rising ground to the S.

ST ANDREW, Church Lane. Outwardly mostly C15 Perp. Restored by *G. E. Street*, who rebuilt the N wall in 1872–3, without confusing further the architectural puzzles left by earlier builders. Hall (N side) by *Richard Westmacott*, 1980s. In 1980 a large stone was uncovered beneath the nave, from the W wall of a Saxon church which probably covered the chancel and first nave bay. Of Norman work, a fragment of chip-carving framing a squint (two cusped lights, perhaps *c.* 1536) in the chancel. Transitional S doorway (no doubt reworked); pointed hoodmould on trumpet label stops. By the C13 the nave, aisles and chancel were extant: see the blocked narrow S aisle windows, the inner frame of an E.E. window at the E end of the N aisle, single-chamfered depressed two-centred arch of the N doorway, the priest's door (chancel S) with continuous roll moulding, the sedilia with their completely renewed arches on shafts, and piscina (roll moulding with fillet). Next follows the S porch entrance which must be *c.* 1300; five orders of mouldings, alternately round and square, hoodmould with little scalloped labels. Of the same time or a little later the N chancel chapel in its first form – see the triple-chamfered arch towards the chancel. Then the Dec renewal of the N and S arcades; slender octagonal piers, double-chamfered arches. The E responds have two re-cut heads, once carrying the rood loft. The chancel arch and S chapel were renewed at the same time and in the same forms. The earlier N chapel arch is cut into by the chancel arch, as the W tower cuts into the W arches of the arcade. Perp also the S window to light the rood, and the vestry. Its ground floor has a quatrefoil opening into the chancel, and, above, an upper room with a slit window, probably the treasury.

The surprising and capricious TOWER is ashlar-faced, 103 ft 6 in. (31.5 metres) high, of four stages. Set-back buttresses with pairs of thin pinnacles at the third stage, then short diagonally set pinnacles reaching into the bell-stage. W doorway with two-centred head, five-light W window with panel tracery. Stages two and three have a narrow two-light window on each face. The upper has – an unheard-of perversity – a circle with a quatrefoil at the foot of the mullion, otherwise standard mid-C15 Somerset forms. The belfry stage is anything but standard. Broad two-light bell-openings with four-centred heads, Somerset tracery. The belfry lights are paired beneath a broad, low, ogee gable projecting through and above the parapet of pierced cusped triangles. Broad pinnacles set diagonally with four sub-pinnacles; higher stair-turret carrying a spirelet. All this is so curious that it has often been assigned to the C16 or the C17.* But the window reveals and parapet mouldings seem to match the C15 lower parts, and the clumsy SW pinnacle is clearly C17 and so different from the others that there is no reason to assume the rest of the top stage is not original. One is in a similar quandary over the CHANTRY CHAPEL N of the chancel. It is oddly vaulted with transverse ribs in a kind of mansard shape. The northernmost is probably early C14, with little ogee cusps at the outer angles of the mansard. The W side has a rough arch opening into the N chancel chapel. The structural evidence and that of the monuments are inextricably linked: *see* the Rodney monument, below.

FITTINGS. REREDOS with finely carved Crucifixion, by *Earp*, 1873. – SCREEN, early C16, with one-light divisions and broad four-centred doorways. Pretty tracery panels. Two friezes of foliage in the cornice. – LECTERN. By *Alan Rome*, 1966, in the style of Randoll Blacking. – FONT. Norman; circular with cable moulding. Later thick foliage band on the foot. – Tower SCREEN, *W. H. Randoll Blacking*, 1934. His also the pews and other fittings. – Splendid two-tier brass CHANDELIER, 1786, attributed to *William Wasbrough* of Bristol. – STAINED GLASS. E window *c.* 1881, *Clayton & Bell*, who probably also did the SW, †1899. Chancel S, by *Bell & Son*(?), †1879. N chapel E,

---

*Pevsner's comment about damage to the tower in 1603 is not substantiated.

George Cooper-Abbs (*Wippell*), 1945. N aisle N, *Camm Bros*, c. 1875–8. N aisle w, *Bell & Son*, †1884. – MONUMENTS. Sir Walter Rodney, †1466. Armoured effigy on tomb-chest with ogee niches under crocketed gables and containing long-fingered angels with shields. Behind this a Perp screen, probably early C16, of three four-centred openings; to the l. the doorway to the chapel behind, the other two filled with three-light tracery. Above the screen, a band with truncated inscription to Elizabeth Rodney †1536. Above this sits the oddest arrangement. First an outer crocketed gable between pinnacles, finials probably by *Street*. Within, another gable of mansard profile, rising to a little ogee point with big foliate finial. This gable is ogee-cusped. All like the early C14 tombs at Bristol Cathedral. Beneath this, later insertion of five panels with shields, again rising gable-like in the centre; early C17? What should we make of these puzzles? One viable theory is this. A tomb recess was made c. 1323 for Sir Richard de Rodney and his wife, framed by pinnacles and mansard gable, vaulted with one rib. In 1337 it was vacated when they were reburied at Keynsham Abbey, but reoccupied in 1466 for Sir Walter's tomb-chest. Elizabeth Rodney created the chapel in the early C16, cutting through the wall at the back of the recess, roofing it with mansard ribs roughly copying the *ex situ* C14 rib, and adding the screen. Her inscription was cut down to fit its present place over the screen, perhaps in the C17, when Rice Davis 're-edified' the chapel, possibly opening the w arch. – Rice Davis †1638. Brass with kneeling figures in a stone surround, tapered pilasters with bare-breasted female heads. – Good minor C18 and early C19 tablets, e.g. a woman standing by an urn (†1813) by *Tyley*.

CHURCHYARD. Fine C15 CROSS base and shaft, restored by *Alan Rome*, 1966. – GARNETT MEMORIAL. Big bronze crucifix, 1919–20, by the *Bromsgrove Guild* to designs by *George Oatley*, father-in-law of the man commemorated.

PRIMARY SCHOOL, Church Lane. By *T. R. Lysaght*, 1861–2. Asymmetrical Gothic schoolrooms and master's house. Prominent bellcote. Enlarged 1873 and 1892.

Backwell has good minor houses and farms. THE GRANGE, Church Town, has a C15 rear wing (altered), and a higher C17 addition with C19 Neo-Tudor porch and bays. Probably also late medieval is PARK FARM, Chapel Hill, Farleigh; see the three deep buttresses on the front, and rear newel stair. The mullioned windows etc. tally with the inscribed date 1637. Of the C17 and both with good original interior features, SORES COURT, Hillside Road, altered 1710; and COURT FARM, Church Lane, c. 1620–60, bulky and gabled, with continuous string courses. Opposite, its rather grand former stable, c. 1660–85, with oval lights keyed in to the frames. BACKWELL HOUSE, Backwell Hill Road, c. 1820, a superior Neoclassical composition in Bath stone. Five-bay front; serpentine Ionic porch, sunken panels and pedimented windows to the end bays, round-headed niches flanking the upper central window.

Shortly to its sw, BACKWELL DOWN, the perfect small estate for an Edwardian gentleman: C17 revival, by *E. A. Hellicar*, *c.* 1906–8. Nos. 121–123 Farleigh Road, *c.* 1900, have Ipswich windows, bulbous columned porches etc. Reputedly for the Tyntesfield estate, so possibly by *Walter Cave*.

3050

BANWELL

p. 30

ST ANDREW. A minster church existed by 885, later given to the Bishops of Wells. The present Perp structure, of Dolomitic conglomerate with limestone dressings, evolved from a probably Norman rebuilding. 'Improved' 1812–13, restored 1864–5, and repaired again, by *W. D. Caröe*, 1931–7.

Imposing w tower, *c.* late C14 to early C15, in composition and detail very like Winscombe and Cheddar. 101 ft (31 metres) high, with set-back buttresses connected diagonally across the angles. From their upper stages rise close-paired diagonal pinnacles. Top parapet with corner pinnacles and a pierced parapet with cusped triangles. Higher stair-turret with spirelet.* Big w doorway with hoodmould on two heads and an angel bust at the apex. Four-light uncusped w window. Above this, a two-light window partly blocked and flanked by niches with figures of the Annunciation. The lily in its vase in the blank part of one light; diamond stop-bar below. Above this stage another two-light window, and then two-light bell-openings flanked by identical two-light blanks. Shafts with pinnacles rise between them but do not reach the parapet. The trefoiled triangles of this parapet also on the aisles, clerestory and s porch (cf. Yatton). Tall rood turrets with pyramid caps. The clerestory is later than the tower, perhaps *c.* 1430–50: inside, the E face of the tower has a niche with a statue of St Andrew, evidently once external. The chancel is, as so often, treated more simply. No chapels. Two-storey s porch, good C15 or early C16 s doorway with fleurons in jambs and arch. Square hoodmould with traceried spandrels. Oval label stops with Masonic symbols of 1812–13, also the date of the three-light window above the outer door. Beneath the r. door jamb, part of a reused C10 grave-slab with knotwork. Above, a Perp image niche and the doorway to a porch gallery survive, with unconvincing timber gallery of 1938.

The INTERIOR is remarkably tall, with a fine wagon roof; wrought-iron ties of 1812–13 to the clerestory. The principals stand on shafts which rest on angels, and from the angels a very handsome pointed trefoil moulding runs round the clerestory windows; timber tracery in the spandrels (cf. Yatton aisles). Continuous tower arch of two wave mouldings with a deep hollow between. A lierne-vault inside the tower. Arcade

---

*An intended spire was taken only as far as the internal squinches.

of five bays, tall slim piers of the usual four-hollows profile. Small leafy capitals to the shafts only. Panelled aisle roofs; wagon roof in the chancel, with larger panels than those in the nave, the principals also on angels. The stalls have been destroyed, but a fine stone frieze and cresting remain, originally above them, and the ogee gable of the chancel doorway. The chancel arch finally has no capitals, but small angels at the springers.

FITTINGS. REREDOS. C19, high and broad, Perp panels and cresting. Is this the one 'lately erected' in 1829, by *R. H. Trickey* of Bristol, plasterer? – ROOD SCREEN. The best of the district. Datable 1519–21, and costing *c.* £40. Four-light sections, the main arch divided into two two-light sub-arches and the central mullion running up into the apex. Between the arches, sections of fan-vaulting form the coving, with gilded ribs. Two major and four minor friezes and cresting. Lavishly gilded, originally by *Robert Hoptyn* in 1524; renewed 1865. Altered by *Caröe*, 1935. – BENCHES. Plain C15, with simple poppyheads. – FONT. Circular, Norman, crudely carved with quatrefoils and plants in the C15 or C16. – COVER, Jacobean, spire-form with broad carved band. – PULPIT. Perp, of stone, with two-light blank tracery, a panelled foot and cresting. Probably from the same workshop as that at Bleadon. Staircase of 1884. – Octagonal SOUNDING-BOARD dated 1620, with rosettes beneath. – TOWER GALLERY. Screen below, of 1860. On its top, a band of foliate pattern from a pew-front set up *c.* 1584–90 by Bishop Godwin. – ROYAL ARMS. Overpainted 1805. – STAINED GLASS. N and S aisle E, small C15 panels. In a light-box, N aisle W, Netherlandish glass of the C15 and C16. Much mid-C19 glass. One in each aisle (1861 and 1863) is signed by *Warrington*. Did he also do the E window of *c.* 1850 with figures in three tiers? – BRASSES. Civilian and wife (W of the screen), *c.* 1480, 18-in. (46-cm.) figures. – Nearby, John Blandon †1554, without wife or head. – John Martock †1503, 28-in. (71-cm.) figure (S aisle wall). – MONUMENTS. Among several tablets by *Tyley*, Henry Emery †1826, lively Grecian. – Lieut. Charles Turner †1860. Long horizontal tablet, painted stone with regimental flag, designed by *William Burges*, 1861.

p. 90

BANWELL COURT (or BANWELL ABBEY). Now three dwellings. The house was rebuilt by Bishop Bekynton of Wells (1443–65) and later remodelled. Main block three-storeyed and T-shaped, possibly with C15 elements. In 1827 the S front was plain Georgian and without turrets. This was Gothicized *c.* 1870 by *Hans Price*, with a polygonal SW turret and projecting porch. The underlying C18 symmetry still evident. Some Perp blind tracery in the E gable, presumably *ex situ*. Making the transition to a low former chapel at the E, another 1870 turret, capped by a tall spirelet (later truncated) from an 1850s church in Weston-super-Mare. The chapel has a stepped, cusped three-light lancet window in its E wall (i.e. early C14 Dec), the most authentic medieval remnant, spoiled by a late C20 triple window below.

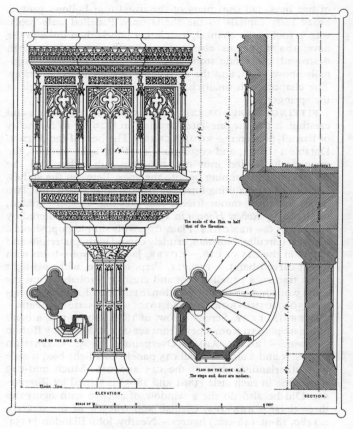

The scale of the Plan is half
that of the Elevation.

PLAN ON THE LINE C.D.

PLAN ON THE LINE A.B.
The steps and door are modern.

ELEVATION.

SECTION.

SCALE OF

Banwell, St Andrew, pulpit.
Engraving, 1849

BANWELL CAVES, *c.* 1 m. wsw of the village, on Banwell Hill.
An important early C19 garden layout. A stalactite cave was
discovered *c.* 1757. In 1824 attempts to make a new entrance
to it revealed the BONE CAVE, containing numerous animal
bones of *c.* 80,000 B.C. Held as proof of Noah's Flood, it
opened to the public in 1825 and became a great attraction.
On the slope above, Bishop Law built a three-room thatched
summerhouse with rustic veranda, 'after a plan given by
Buckler', 1827.* Its main room is now the hall, subsumed by
expansion in 1833 to a two-storey Picturesque *cottage orné*. It
was briefly, at the end of his life, the bishop's residence.

---

*The summerhouse of 1827 was seemingly preceded by another, perhaps on a
different site, which was noted as being 'tastefully fitted out for the reception of
visitors' in the *Bristol Times and Mirror*, 5 August 1826.

Extended further, perhaps *c.* 1870, and much repaired since.
A little Continental C15 and C16 glass installed as window
borders (more awaiting reinstatement), and some good marble
fireplaces, *c.* 1833. In the grounds, 1830s features intended to
evoke Druidic prehistory: a rubble ARCHWAY to the Bone
Cave (which has a fraction of its bones now stacked in neat
blocks); the LOWER GROTTO, of natural boulders with arches
and alcoves. Ruined in various degrees, a pebble-encrusted
SUMMERHOUSE, a GAZEBO, and the OSTEOICON, a Picturesque bone museum. Hidden in trees on the ridge
⅓ m. E, a MONUMENT erected by Bishop Law in 1840. Three-
stage octagonal viewing tower with four-centred arches and
hoodmoulds. Top stage and spirelet reinstated *c.* 1998.

BANWELL CASTLE, ⅓ m. SSE. A heavily castellated hilltop folly
built *c.* 1845–7 for Joseph Dyer Sympson, reportedly with work
by *R. Trickey* (*see* above). Unexpectedly convincing from the
road. Embattled gatehouse with circular turrets, higher tower
and long embattled wall to the SE. Within the gates, an oblong
coachhouse with square angle turrets, converted from a mullioned farmhouse, perhaps C16–C17. The main house three-
storeyed, oblong and keep-like, with turrets. S front more
domestic-looking and unenclosed. (Accomplished Gothic
interiors, restored by *Sir George Oatley*.)

In the village, some good cottages and C18 and early C19 houses
picturesquely disposed above retaining walls. In West Street, a
three-storey former MALTHOUSE, *c.* 1850; brick gable, stone-
built sides. Further W, THE GRANGE, a good Regency house
with fluted Ionic porch, the columns reputedly from a W
gallery in the church. Opposite, No. 39 dated 1761, with Bishop
Godwin's motto 'Win God, Win All'. It appears again at
TOWERHEAD, *c.* 1 m. E: built in the late 1580s, rebuilt *c.* 1840.
Modest Late Classical, including some *ex situ* arches and doorways from the Elizabethan house.

IRON AGE HILL-FORT, ½ m. NE of Banwell Castle. Roughly oval
and *c.* 500 by 200 yds (460 by 185 metres) in size, with the
rampart and part of the ditch still visible.

BARROW GURNEY

5060

The church and Court stand alone some distance NW of the
small village centre.

ST MARY AND ST EDWARD. The church of a Benedictine
nunnery with a parochial nave to its N. Much rebuilt 1821–3
and again, comprehensively, by *Henry Woodyer*; the chancel and
two-storey vestry in 1887, tower, nave and three-bay S aisle
(originally the nuns' choir) 1888–9. The body is low and sturdy
with big buttresses, diagonal at the corners, and Dec tracery.
Wagon-vaulted roofs. The low W tower was moved a few yards

w and entirely remodelled, with triple belfry lights and a bulky stair-turret. The w window (two lights, C15 Perp), and two openings at the w end of the s chapel are the only complete medieval features left. A corridor leads from Barrow Court to a lay vestry adjoining the w end of the s chapel. Unarchaeological tower arch with detail of *c.* 1300, and tierceron-vault of C15 Somerset type but with C13 fillets on the ribs.

FITTINGS. A splendidly rich and complete Victorian ensemble. Additions continued into the early 1890s. REREDOS continued up to frame the E window, with statuary in niches. – S aisle REREDOS and painted panelled surround, by *Kempe*, makers *Zwink* of Oberammergau. Carved and gilded, of miniature delicacy. – Brass ALTAR RAIL by *Singer*. – ROOD SCREEN. Perhaps by *Woodyer*, rather Dec in the tracery, with rood above. – Perp s aisle screen, by *Kempe*. – PULPIT with semicircular stair cut into the wall, under its own little vault. – FONT with tall, elaborately Gothic COVER. – IRONWORK. Fine filigree wrought-iron CHANCEL GATES, *Filmore & Mason*. – Entrance DOOR with dense ironwork depicting lions and a leafy tree, 1890. A copy of a C15 door at St Saviour, Dartmouth, Devon. – WALL PAINTING (s chapel E), all-over pattern by *Kempe*. Restored 1991 by *Alan Rome* and *Nimbus Conservation*. The scheme extends up into the vault. – STAINED GLASS. By *Kempe*, notably the E window, 1889 (a dense Tree of Life), and a suite of three, s chapel. – MONUMENTS. Joanne d'Acton, *c.* 1370s. *Ex situ* floor slab of encaustic tiles in rich greens and earth colours (lay vestry). – Francis James †1616. Eleven kneeling figures under paired arches, in the Elizabethan tradition. Well designed and carved tablet in a classical taste. – Catherine Bampfylde †1657. Small tablet finely done, Mannerist double broken pediment. – William Gore †1662. Attributed to *William Stanton* (GF). Big marble monument without figures. Inscription in oval laurel wreath. Black Ionic columns, broken segmental pediment. – Gore family, *c.* 1780–9, *T. Paty & Sons*; rectangular tablet, curvy base, flaming urn against an obelisk above.

CHURCHYARD. Fragments of the old church in the E wall. Medieval cross, *ex situ* and remodelled. To the N, a semi-private graveyard to the Gibbs family, with Crucifixion against the w wall.

BARROW COURT. The rooms aligned roughly N–S of the screens passage may be the only survivals of the house converted or rebuilt from remains of the Benedictine nunnery *c.* 1538–45. This was extended in the early C17 to form an E-plan, probably either for Francis James 1602–16, or for Sir Francis Dodington, *c.* 1626–40. Numerous original fittings of either C17 date, or both. The Court was added to and restored by *Henry Woodyer*, 1883–4, for H. M. Gibbs, son of William Gibbs of Tyntesfield. In contrast to his work in the church, Woodyer was faithful to the existing fabric. Altered by *Sir George Oatley*, 1946–8, as a diocesan training college. *David Brain* repaired the structure when it became a house again, 1989–93.

The porch of the E front is of the same depth as the wings. Four-light mullioned-and-transomed windows on ground floor and first floor, three-light mullioned windows in the gables. Doorway perhaps c. 1630–40, with cambered head, Ionic pilasters with strapwork waist-bands (or below-the-waist bands) with lions' heads, broken segmental pediment, reclining figures of Peace and Plenty. N front originally of two gables, extended W 1883–4 to give three, and unified by refacing. A T-shaped S wing presumably originated as a C16 or C17 service range, much altered as separate house and flats.

Inside, the screen between passage and hall has C17 elements, though much reconstructed. The hall (N) and dining room (S) both have *Woodyer* chimneypieces, the latter with Moghul elements. The hall has good stained glass by *Kempe*, c. 1887. At the back, a curving passage (c. 1883), once an aviary, with full-height glazing and cast-iron shutters. This leads to *Woodyer*'s book room added at the NW. To its E a parlour with unusual ceiling of all-over arabesques, and hunting frieze, c. 1630s. The staircase ceiling has gorgeous, if coarse, plasterwork with a frieze with big beasts. Thin-ribbed ceiling with, remarkably, some cusped tracery and a big bulbous pendant. Probably c. 1620–40, which tallies with the details of the staircase, much renewed in the 1880s. In the Great Chamber over the hall, a ceiling with ribs in squares and curves. Square panels with animals, stag, eagle, two-headed eagle, and also unicorn and pegasus. The same pattern in a tiny attached room, with possibly early C19 colour recently revealed. Panelling, friezes etc. in both rooms reworked in the 1880s, but the arched overmantel is authentic. Over one bedroom chimneypiece, heavy plaster figures of Justice and Mercy c. 1660, again painted perhaps 1800–50. A tiny oratory over the porch has a delightful timber vault and fittings by *Woodyer*, and *Kempe* stained-glass figures, 1899. On the second floor, a simple long gallery.

GARDENS. To the N and NW, formal gardens laid out by *F. Inigo Thomas*, 1893–7, embellished by obelisks, balustrades, Venetian gazebo, etc. Framing the view NW across to Tyntesfield is an exedra with massive Neo-Baroque gatepiers with urns. Twelve further piers carry busts of the Daughters of the Year, from girlhood to old age, by *Alfred Drury*, 1898. Also his, a lead statue of Nike, the Winged Victory. W of the house a plain stone BARN of the C14, now a house.

The VILLAGE nicely echoes the Court in its blend of C17 and C19 work. Many houses and farms were built by the Gores c. 1660–90: the grandest is HOME FARM, opposite the Court, built 1674 as the dower house. SPRINGHEAD FARM, an imposing E-shape with gables and polite doorcase, dated WG 1687, restored 1924–8; and the VICARAGE of 1679, remodelled in 1832. H. M. Gibbs desired a model estate village. C17 and C18 houses were restored and, one suspects, embellished, reportedly by *Walter Tower*, c. 1900 and later, the link no doubt being Kempe. *See also* the C17 FOX AND GOOSE INN, Bridgwater Road, 'restored 1916'. SW of the Court, WATERCATCH FARM, late C19, a model estate farm.

BATH

INTRODUCTION

That Bath was one of the centres of Roman life in Britain, with its hot springs, warm climate and appealing situation, is easily seen. But it is often forgotten how flourishing Bath was in the Middle Ages and that its prosperity, rooted in the cloth trade, continued to the very moment when the third Bath leapt to fame in the C18, the Bath of Ralph Allen and Beau Nash, of Bath stone and polite manners, of Smollett and Jane Austen, the spa *par excellence* of Britain.

The city lies in a loop of the River Avon, comfortably sheltered by land that rises steeply at once, a first step s towards the Mendips, the open plateau of Lansdown to the N, and the slopes of Combe Down to the SE. This last hilly margin yields some of the pale cream oolitic limestone – a warm honey-colour when weathered – of which Bath is almost entirely built. It is this that makes it the most coherent of English cities, for in other respects it is by no means a unified, planned whole, like, say, Edinburgh's New Town. The expansion that took place in a relatively short C18–C19 time span by speculating builders-cum-architects created a collage of unconnected, individual and often incomplete developments, shaped by accidents of land purchase, topography, and often financial over-ambition. Much of Georgian Bath remains, despite post-war demolition. Medieval and Stuart Bath, almost entirely overlaid by the Georgian, yet persists like a palimpsest in ancient streets and boundaries.

ROMAN BATH is described in the Introduction, pp. 13–15. For a detailed account of its major monuments, the celebrated Baths and Temple, *see* pp. 122–6, below.

From the Middle Ages to c. 1700

The SAXON RECONSTRUCTION under King Alfred in the late C9 was probably based on the Roman walls, but almost completely replaced the street pattern. As with Saxon town plans elsewhere, the chief features would have been a road running just inside the walls, thoroughfares linking the gates, and a grid of lanes or 'twichens' in between. The market place, now the High Street, was a wide wedge-shape just inside the N gate. The main E–W axis is now Westgate Street and Cheap Street. In the s sector, the Abbey, hot springs and Roman remains modified the Saxon grid pattern.

Little of the MEDIEVAL period survives other than the Abbey. Early maps show how the walls and the arc of the river contained the old city, with flood-plain meadows s and E.

At 24 acres Bath is one of the smallest walled medieval cities. The WALLS, over 20 ft (6 metres) high, were mostly demolished in the C18, along with the main city gates. A short crenellated length (restored) survives in Upper Borough Walls, another section on the corner of Old Orchard Street and Henry Street, further lengths in basements (e.g. beneath the Empire Hotel and markets, and at No. 1 North Parade). Of the gates, names remain as Northgate, Westgate and Southgate streets; also the narrow E gate, rebuilt in the C14, in a basement next to the Empire Hotel.

In 1091 the king granted John of Tours, Bishop of Wells, the whole city along with the Abbey, and until the C16 the Abbey was

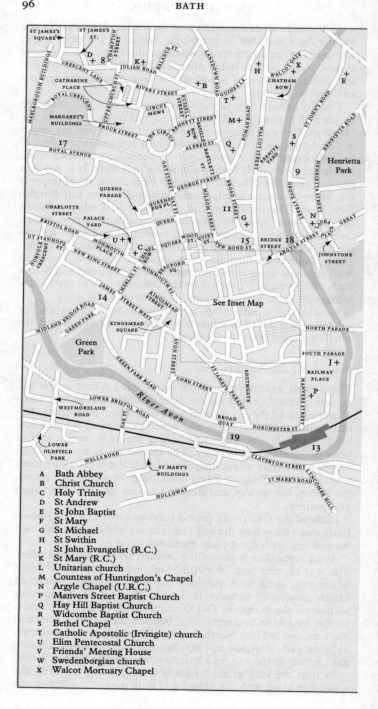

A	Bath Abbey
B	Christ Church
C	Holy Trinity
D	St Andrew
E	St John Baptist
F	St Mary
G	St Michael
H	St Swithin
J	St John Evangelist (R.C.)
K	St Mary (R.C.)
L	Unitarian church
M	Countess of Huntingdon's Chapel
N	Argyle Chapel (U.R.C.)
P	Manvers Street Baptist Church
Q	Hay Hill Baptist Church
R	Widcombe Baptist Church
S	Bethel Chapel
T	Catholic Apostolic (Irvingite) church
U	Elim Pentecostal Church
V	Friends' Meeting House
W	Swedenborgian church
X	Walcot Mortuary Chapel

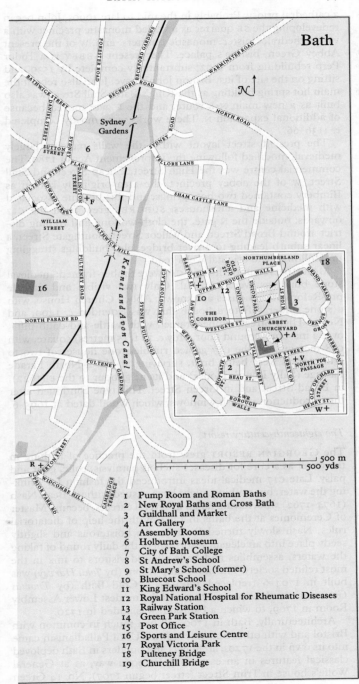

Bath

N

Sydney Gardens

FORSTER ROAD
WARMINSTER ROAD
BECKFORD GARDENS
BECKFORD ROAD
NORTH ROAD
BATHWICK STREET
DANIEL STREET
SUTTON STREET
SYDNEY PLACE
DARLINGTON STREET
PULTENEY STREET
EDWARD STREET
WILLIAM STREET
VELLORE LANE
SYDNEY ROAD
SHAM CASTLE LANE
BATHWICK HILL
PULTENEY ROAD
NORTH PARADE RD
Kennet and Avon Canal
SYDNEY BUILDINGS
DARLINGTON PLACE
PULTENEY GARDENS
R
CLAVERTON STREET
WIDCOMBE HILL
PRIOR PARK RD
CAMBRIDGE TERRACE

6

F

16

NORTHUMBERLAND PLACE
OLD BOND ST
TRIM ST.
BARTON ST.
SAW CLOSE
UPPER BOROUGH WALLS
UNION PASS.
UNION ST.
HIGH ST.
GRAND PARADE
THE CORRIDOR
CHEAP ST.
WESTGATE ST.
ABBEY CHURCHYARD
ORANGE GROVE
PIERREPONT ST.
HOT BATH ST.
BATH ST.
STALL ST.
YORK STREET
ABBEY GN.
NORTH PDE PASSAGE
BEAU ST.
LWR BOROUGH WALLS
OLD ORCHARD STREET
HENRY ST.
WESTGATE BLDGS
18
4
3
12
10
L
A
I
V
W
2
7

500 m
500 yds

1 Pump Room and Roman Baths
2 New Royal Baths and Cross Bath
3 Guildhall and Market
4 Art Gallery
5 Assembly Rooms
6 Holburne Museum
7 City of Bath College
8 St Andrew's School
9 St Mary's School (former)
10 Bluecoat School
11 King Edward's School
12 Royal National Hospital for Rheumatic Diseases
13 Railway Station
14 Green Park Station
15 Post Office
16 Sports and Leisure Centre
17 Royal Victoria Park
18 Pulteney Bridge
19 Churchill Bridge

37, 38,
p. 110

p. 126

a cathedral priory. Probably in the mid to late 1090s, John began redeveloping the SE quarter as a walled monastic precinct with a vast cathedral, cloister, monastic quarters, and, w of the present Abbey Green, bishop's palace. The present ABBEY is a Tudor Perp rebuilding from 1502, substantially complete by 1539, and sitting on the site of just Bishop John's nave. John also rebuilt the main hot spring building as the King's Bath. Stall Street was also built as a new main N–S route, and the E gate moved because of additional expansion N. These works were mostly completed c. 1136–66.

The present street layout within the walls remains largely medieval, modified following the Improvement Act of 1789. The commercial centre was the High Street, Cheap Street and Stall Street. W of the abbey precinct, the area originally known as Bimbery contained two hot springs, and this became associated with medicine and almshouses. SUBURBS grew from the C12 onwards: outside the N gate, the cloth-working and trading district around Broad Street, and Walcot Street; Southgate Street, a linear suburb leading to a river bridge; also buildings straggling up Holloway, the original Wells road.

Most HOUSES until the mid C17 were timber-framed; medieval stone buildings were unusual. Only two visible and datable pre-Reformation houses are known: Abbey Church House, with a stone undercroft to a house that was extended c. 1400, and No. 21 High Street, timber-framed with wattle-and-daub infill, over a masonry ground floor, only c. 16 ft (5 metres) square, with C18 recasing. By the C17 gabled rubble-stone houses of two to four storeys were being built, surviving at No. 4 North Parade Passage (Sally Lunn's House) and its neighbour to the E (1622), in Broad Street and in Green Street. This type continued after the introduction of sash windows, which Wood dated at 1695–6.

The eighteenth-century resort

The GEORGIAN RESORT grew from the practice of bathing in the water as a cure for diseases such as paralysis, colic, gout and palsy. Late C17 medical ideas introduced the fashion for drinking the water, but nothing might have ensued without Beau Nash (1674–1762) who, having failed in several careers, became Master of Ceremonies at the baths in 1704. With the help of dictatorial rules, Nash slowly turned Bath from a boisterous and slightly seedy place into an elegant resort where the daily round of taking the waters, assemblies and balls allowed visitors to mix in the most refined society. The first Pump Room (by *John Harvey*) was built in 1704–6 (replaced 1790–5), a Cold Bath (by *Thomas Greenway*) on the river in 1704, and the modest Lower Assembly Room in 1709, to which a ballroom was added in 1720.

Architecturally, Bath in 1700 still had much in common with Bristol and with other Somerset towns. Until Palladianism came into its own in the 1720s, architects and builders in Bath deployed classical features in an essentially Baroque way, as at General Wolfe's house in Trim Street (street begun 1707), No. 14 Green

Bath, Prior Park.
Engraving by Anthony Walker, 1752

Street (street built up in 1716), Beau Nash's house, Saw Close (by *Thomas Greenway*, 1720), and General Wade's House in Abbey Church Yard.* 55

The spectacular architecture that followed from *c.* 1725 was due in the first instance to Ralph Allen (1693–1764). An entrepreneur, he made a fortune transforming England's postal service, and in 1727 he bought stone quarries at Combe Down. In the same year he backed a scheme to make the Avon navigable from Bath to Bristol, so that he could ship his stone from wharfs at Widcombe down the river to Bristol and beyond. Allen's mansion of Prior Park, begun *c.* 1734, became an advertisement for his stone. Its architect was *John Wood the Elder* (1704–54), the last figure in the triumvirate that transformed Bath. Wood was born in Bath in 1704, the son of a small builder, and trained as a carpenter. In London in the early 1720s, he knew Edward Shepherd, developer of Grosvenor Square. In Yorkshire in 1725, his thoughts turned to planned developments at Bath, to which he returned in 1727, the year his son, the younger John Wood, was born.

The mid 1720s is the crucial moment for the change in Bath's architectural importance; the point at which its fashionability, established by Beau Nash, coincided with the presence of Allen, the wealthy promoter of Bath stone, and of Wood, a youthful and ambitious architect and speculative builder. Wood's Palladian formula of podium, *piano nobile* and attic storey, expressed in palace-front terraces, unified Bath's housing developments for the next hundred years. Georgian Bath began to set the pace for the whole of England. As a piece of town planning, it was unique in England and indeed in Europe; a city very rare as cities go,

*Rosewell House, Kingsmead Square, in a wild provincial Baroque probably by *Nathaniel Ireson*, is as late as 1735.

devoted almost entirely to leisure. Its fashionability increased as journey times from London decreased; before 1680 it took sixty hours, by 1790, just ten hours. Most of Bath's Georgian houses were intended not for permanent residents but as superior lodgings for the winter influx of visitors, leased entire or as suites of rooms. Bath's population rose from only *c.* 2,000–3,000 in 1700 to *c.* 6,000–8,000 by 1750, doubling to 15,000 by 1770, and again to 33,000 by 1800.

WOOD'S SCHEME as dreamed up in Yorkshire in 1725 makes clear the novelty and daring, the scale and style of his ideas. He suggested building in two areas: NW of the walls, i.e. the site of Queen Square, and SE of the Abbey. 'In each design', Wood writes in his *Essay Towards a Description of Bath*, 'I proposed to make a grand Place of Assembly, to be called the Royal Forum of Bath; another place, no less magnificent, for the Exhibition of Sports, to be called the Grand Circus; and a third Place, of equal state with either of the former, for the Practice of Medicinal Exercises, to be called the Imperial Gymnasium.' The desire to revive the splendour of a Roman city is accompanied in the *Essay* by a mythical glorification of British antiquity based on the legend of pre-Roman Bath as a great Druidic city ruled by its mythical founder, King Bladud. The Druidic stone circles were supposedly built to a Divine proportional system revealed in Solomon's temple, and disseminated by the Jews to the Druids before the Greeks and Romans. Wood thus invented a British – and specifically Bathonian – antiquity that surpassed classical antiquity.

That theory found architectural expression only at the end of Wood's life, in the Circus, his most successful achievement. With its correct and elegant superimposed orders, uniting the themes of Druid circle and classical theatre, it bears witness to his romanticism and infatuation with Roman grandeur. But Wood's firm faith in Rome – as seen through the eyes of Palladio – appears early, especially in the noble Queen Square, 1728–36. The square was by then already the focus of London's planned improvements, e.g. Inigo Jones's Covent Garden piazza (1630s); Bristol had joined in with Queen Square (1699). What distinguishes Wood's design from all examples except Covent Garden is that each frontage was planned to one consistent scheme, the N side being the grandest. Wood's is the first palatial treatment of the square in the English C18. All the larger terraces at Bath subsequently follow; London did not catch up until after 1750. Concurrently, Kingsmead and Beauford Square were developed by *John Strahan* of Bristol. Wood's ideals of order and discipline were evident next in North and South Parades, 1738–48. The scheme was part of the enormous Royal Forum idea projected in his *Essay* but which never took shape.

When the elder Wood died in 1754, Queen Square and the Circus were isolated and inward-looking showpieces. His son completed the great sequence, with Gay Street, finished after 1755, Brock Street (1760s), and at its end, the supreme Royal Crescent (1767–75). Unlike the other set pieces, Royal Crescent was left open at the S to unlandscaped fields. For the first time

70, 71

70

we see *rus in urbe*, with rural prospects as if from a country house, but with the advantages of town; an idea followed in the later crescents, and in the C19 development of the villa.

Royal Crescent set a precedent for crescents elsewhere, though their prevalence outside Bath has been exaggerated, and few appear until the 1790s; Bath's lasting legacy is the palace-front terrace rather than the contour-related crescent. Meanwhile, the streets around the *younger Wood*'s Upper Assembly Rooms of 1769–71 were laid out to that architect's design, but with elevations by speculative BUILDER-ARCHITECTS whose work is hard to differentiate, such as *Thomas Jelly*, *John Palmer* and *Thomas Warr Atwood*. The Woods' pattern for a simple, dignified and elegant terraced house front proved so adaptable and easy to copy that it became the standard – and this, as much as their designs, explains Bath's Georgian homogeneity.

NEOCLASSICISM provided a light, elegant and lively alternative to Palladianism, easily applied to the standard terrace. Robert Adam championed it nationally from the 1760s; his equivalent at Bath is *Thomas Baldwin*, architect to the city estates from 1775, taking over from Atwood at the Guildhall (1775–8). The slightly tired Palladian exterior was given a fine Adamish interior. Following the Bath Improvement Act of 1789 Baldwin introduced the style to the rest of the medieval town, notably at the delightful colonnaded Bath Street.

The next big expansion was *Baldwin*'s Neoclassical Bathwick estate from 1788, owned by the Pulteney family. The key to its development was to bridge the river, achieved with *Adam*'s fine Pulteney Bridge, 1769–74. The rigidly geometrical planning was on a vast scale, as can be seen by the length and width of the central spine, Great Pulteney Street.

Had the whole scheme not been curtailed by the financial collapse of 1793, when building almost stopped for a decade or so, it would have rivalled Edinburgh's New Town and dwarfed Wood's Bath. By c. 1800 Bath had also grown a mile E along the London Road to Grosvenor Place (by *John Eveleigh*, started 1791), and up the steep hillside to the N, with Camden Crescent (*Eveleigh*, c. 1787–8), Lansdown Crescent (*Palmer*, 1789–93), Somerset Place (*Eveleigh*, started 1790) and finally Sion Hill Place (*Pinch*, c. 1817–20). Lower down, Pinch designed Cavendish Place (1808–16) and Cavendish Crescent (1815–30), the end of Georgian development N of the city; also fine terraces such as Sydney Place (1804–8) and Raby Place (1818–25), in Bathwick. Pinch's late Regency works mark the culmination of a stylistic development away from the purity of Wood, and his death in 1827 marks the end of elegant terrace building in Bath.

Architects had various ways of dealing with hilly sites: by building crescents that snaked along the contours, as at Lansdown; or overcoming changes of level by raising roads or pavements over vaults (e.g. Walcot Parade), also seen at Clifton. Bath's terraces often step regularly uphill (e.g. Gay Street), whereas at Bristol irregular steps (e.g. Albemarle Row, Hotwells) seemed acceptable. The most elegant and unifying method is the ramped

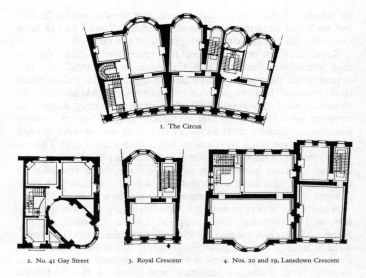

1. The Circus

2. No. 41 Gay Street   3. Royal Crescent   4. Nos. 20 and 19, Lansdown Crescent

Bath, comparative ground- and first-floor house plans (not to scale).

cornice and string course, first used at Barton Buildings (*Wood the Younger*, 1760s) and refined by *Pinch* at Sydney Place, etc. This device was rarely or never taken up at Bristol, for reasons unclear.

Much ARTISAN HOUSING was also built, now lost except for fragments such as *Pinch*'s Northampton Street of the 1790s. Never had such a large proportion of the populace, including the lowly, been housed with such dignity.

Some words must be said here about Georgian PLANNING and CONSTRUCTION, including points unique to Bath. The basement contained the kitchen; the attics, servants' or children's bedrooms. In a standard three-bay house, the ground floor usually had one main room front and rear (eating room and parlour). On the first floor, the *piano nobile*, a drawing room overlooked the street, sometimes with double doors to the rear room. Occasionally, as at No. 15 Queen Square and Nos. 7–8 Circus, the hall occupies the whole ground-floor front. Where view and orientation demanded, as at the Paragon and Grosvenor Place, the principal rooms might be at the rear and the staircase at the front.

Houses were usually of rubble, with ashlar facing the street only. The backs were often rendered to resemble ashlar. Normally of three storeys, the better houses also had basement and attics under double-mansard roofs. The basement was commonly built from ground level, with the street raised up on vaults (such built-up streets are only found at Bristol on very steep ground). The middle of the street vaults carried a drain for rainwater and, in some cases, sewage.*

---

* Bath's abundant supply of spring water from the hills was crucial to its expansion; the basis of the Corporation's agreement for Pulteney Bridge was that water would be piped across it into the city.

Early C18 WINDOWS at Bath have two sashes, each three panes
wide and high ('nine over nine'), with almost square panes and
ovolo glazing bars. By the 1730s the standard was three panes by
two – the more vertical 'six over six'. The tendency throughout
the C18 was for ever larger windows and thinner glazing bars. By
the mid C19, first-floor window sills were often lowered and small
panes replaced by plate glass. By 1870, what started as a fashion
became a condition of renewing leases.

Other PUBLIC BUILDINGS associated with the spa were
the *younger Wood*'s Hot Bath (1775–7), *Baldwin*'s Cross Bath   *p. 127*
(1783–4), altered by *Palmer* in 1798, and the Grand Pump Room,   72
by *Baldwin*, completed by *Palmer* (1790–5). The city's earliest
classical chapel is *William Killigrew*'s St Michael at St John's Hospital, rebuilt 1723. Of proprietary chapels, the first and most
important, St Mary, Chapel Row (by the *elder Wood*, 1732–4) was
demolished; *Timothy Lightoler*'s splendid Octagon, 1766–7, sur-   *p. 104*
vives. St Swithin, by *Jelly & Palmer* (1777–80) is Bath's only
remaining classical parish church, although C18 Gothicism never
took hold here as it did at Bristol, and such buildings as the
Countess of Huntingdon's Chapel of 1765 remained exceptional.

PLEASURE GARDENS modelled on the famous London
gardens offered dancing, walks, musical entertainments, and
refreshments. Harrison's Gardens (1708) were followed by at
least five others of varying duration and success. Sydney Gardens
(1795), the only survivor, had supper boxes next to the orchestra, as at London's Vauxhall.

Regency, Victorian and Edwardian Bath

As the fashionable early C19 resorts of Brighton and Cheltenham
eclipsed Bath, so visiting declined. There was a shift away from
urban housing and public amusements towards more sedate,
domestic priorities; a Romantic conception of Bath took hold, as
an English Florence with rural retreats in the hills. Speculators
turned to VILLAS on the fringes, which could be developed one
by one. The best are on Bathwick Hill, *c.* 1829–48 – *Edward
Davis*'s Oakwood, and *Goodridge*'s Bathwick Grange, Casa
Bianca, La Casetta and Fiesole. These are early examples of the
Italianate, with projecting eaves, asymmetrical planning, and
belvedere towers.

The cult of the PICTURESQUE found more extreme expression in William Beckford's intimate landscaped ride (of 1825–38)
from his house at Lansdown Crescent up to the severely Grecian
Beckford's Tower, by *Goodridge*. *Davis*, a pupil of Soane, designed   85
an even severer triumphal entrance, derived from Soane's
abstracted Grecian, for Royal Victoria Park (1829–30), among the
first great C19 public parks.

These belong to a handful of CLASSICAL REVIVAL buildings
in Bath designed or influenced by advanced London architects.
George Dance the Younger designed the spare Theatre Royal   84
(1802–5), *J. M. Gandy* the Doric House, Cavendish Road
(*c.* 1805), and *Wilkins* added (1809–10) to the Lower Assembly
Rooms a conspicuous Greek Doric temple portico (dem.), and

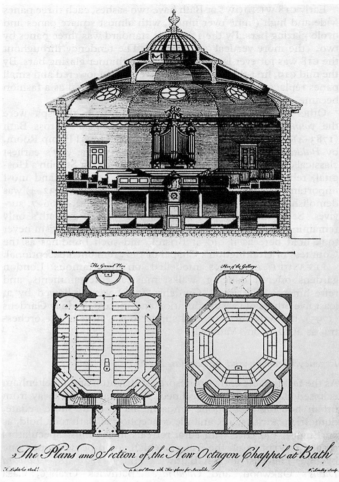

Bath, Octagon Chapel.
Section and plans

designed the Friends' Meeting House, York Street (1817–19).
Goodridge's Greek Revival work includes Argyle Chapel (1821),
probably the Bazaar (1824–5), the Corridor (1825), and much at
Cleveland Place.

In the C19 Bath follows the national tendency towards an
archaeologically correct GOTHIC REVIVAL, first at the *elder
Pinch*'s St Mary the Virgin, Bathwick (1817–20), unusually early
Neo-Perp. Three Commissioners' churches (*see* p. 234) were built
at Bath: Holy Trinity, James Street (1819–22, dem.); St Mark,
Lyncombe, 1830–2, by *G. P. Manners*; and St Saviour, Larkhall
(1829–32), built by *Pinch the Younger* probably to his father's

design. It derives from St Mary, Bathwick. Less scholarly is *Goodridge*'s Holy Trinity, Combe Down (1832–5) with its absurd polygonal spires. *Manners*'s fine St Michael with St Paul (1834–7) and *James Wilson*'s St Stephen, Lansdown Road (1840–5) are further steps towards medieval accuracy, and with St John (R.C.; 1861–3) by *C. F. Hansom* we find a confident Puginian Gothic. Bath's numerous CHAPELS include Widcombe Baptist (1820–2), Georgian Gothic; *James Wilson*'s grand Roman-revival Moravian chapel (1844–5); and the Manvers Street Baptist church (*Wilson & Willcox*, 1871–2), French Gothic.

The 'Battle of the Styles' is much in evidence: *Davis*'s Neo-Tudor villas at Entry Hill Drive (1829–36) competed with *Goodridge*'s Graeco-Italianate essays on Bathwick Hill, of the same years. *Manners* and his firm were equally capable of Tudor, Jacobethan, domestic Georgian, Neo-Norman (the Irvingite Church, Guinea Lane, 1841), or secular Gothic. The palazzo style makes a rare appearance at *George Alexander*'s Bath Savings Bank, Charlotte Street (1841). Typical of parochial SCHOOLS is the *younger Pinch*'s Tudoresque building for St Mary, Bathwick, 1841. The Jacobethan Blue Coat School (1859–60) by *Manners & Gill* may also be noted. Private schools tended to Collegiate Tudor, as at *James Wilson*'s Wesleyan Kingswood School (1850–2), or Gothic, e.g. the Royal High School (also *Wilson*, 1856).

Today's visitor may be surprised at the extent of COMMERCE AND INDUSTRY, which came to include gas, electricity, brewing, cloth, flour, building materials, printing and engineering by the latest C19. With them grew extensive middle- and working-class suburbs – Oldfield Park, Twerton, Weston, Larkhall. Transport developments are marked by the Kennet and Avon Canal (by *Rennie*, completed 1810), and of course the Great Western Railway (1840–1). *Brunel*'s Jacobethan GWR station is substantially intact apart from the roof over the lines. Green Park Station (1868–9, *J. H. Saunders*) for the Midland Railway hides its finely engineered roof behind a confident classical stone frontage. Industry lined Lower Bristol Road (between river and railway), including Stothert & Pitt, crane builders, at *Fuller*'s Newark Works (1857), and big cloth mills at Twerton from the 1830s. Particular to Bath is the extensive survival of fine SHOPFRONTS, a few Late Georgian, but most Late Victorian or Edwardian.

The only notable later C19 PUBLIC AND CIVIC BUILDINGS are *Brydon*'s successful additions to the Guildhall, the Victoria Art Gallery, and the Concert Room; all 1890s, and Neo-Baroque rather than Neo-Georgian. The SPA declined in the mid C19, despite some additions to the baths in the 1860s, the building of the bombastic French Renaissance-style Grand Pump Room Hotel, 1866–9 by *Wilson & Willcox* (dem.), and the arrival of the Midland Railway. In 1878–81, Major C.E. Davis discovered and excavated the Roman spring with its reservoir and the Great Bath. This signalled a brief Renaissance for the spa, resulting in *Davis*'s new Douche and Massage Baths for the latest 'Continental' treatments (1889, dem. 1971). The commission for the Neo-Roman colonnade around the Great Bath went to *Brydon* (1895–7). The

89

89

83

90

final surge of confidence in Bath's spa, and the last monument to the Victorian city, was *Davis*'s Empire Hotel (1899–1901), an enormous and eccentric Queen Anne Revival building.

The EDWARDIAN postscript saw a few Arts and Crafts buildings of the refined rather than the hair-shirt variety; Bayntun's Bookshop and Bindery, Manvers Street (*F. W. Gardiner*, 1901), and No. 108 Walcot Street (*Silcock & Reay*) are examples. *Voysey* contributed a charming, if uncharacteristic, house called Lodge Style (1909), *Silcock & Reay*, the Voyseyesque Gospel Hall at Claverton Down and a handsome Wren-style Baptist chapel at Oldfield Park. Of late Gothic churches, *Edmund Buckle*'s church of the Ascension, Oldfield Park (1906–7), is characteristic.

Bath after c. 1920

Big secular buildings of the post-Edwardian period in Bath are contextually classical: e.g. *Blomfield*'s remodelling of the Holburne Museum (opened 1916), and the Post Office, New Bond Street (1923–7). Of the C20 historicist churches, by far the most delightful – and least-known – is St Alphege, Oldfield Park (1927–9), an Early Christian basilica, which *Sir Giles Gilbert Scott* considered one of his own best works. New styles hid behind deferential façades, as at the Forum cinema (1933–4) – Corinthian without, wild Art Deco within. Alongside were glimmers of the conservation ideal, with the establishment of the Bath Preservation Trust (1934), and the restoration of the Assembly Rooms for the National Trust, by *Mowbray Green* with *Oliver Messel* (1936–8), a symbol of rediscovered Georgian Bath. The Bath Corporation Act of 1937 required a list of protected buildings to be drawn up, and 1,251 were identified (only façades were eligible).

The so-called Baedeker bombing raids of 1942 destroyed c. 1,050 buildings and damaged a further 19,147. Among the losses were the S side of Queen Square and the interiors of the Assembly Rooms. *Patrick Abercrombie*'s radical redevelopment framework was published as *A Plan for Bath* (1945). Never executed, its principles were free-flowing traffic, ring roads and roundabouts, zoning of the centre, and preserving the most important architectural set pieces in isolation (at the expense of lesser Georgian building). These ideas coloured Bath's planning policy until the 1970s.

POST-WAR BUILDINGS include intrusive council estates around the Georgian core, such as Snow Hill (1954–61), and the Ballance Street Flats by *Dr Howard Stutchbury* (1969–73). The S end of the centre was redeveloped from the early 1960s, with insipid Neo-Georgian blocks. Philip Street and the E side of Southgate Street were cleared for *Owen Luder*'s Southgate shopping centre (1969–72, since demolished). Kingsmead, much of its pre-Wood housing destroyed by bombing, suffered a similar concrete fate. The last major demolition was the Holloway area, for controversial housing by *Marshman Warren Taylor* (1969–70). In 1965 *Colin Buchanan & Partners* proposed a road tunnel under the centre from Walcot Street to New King Street. The scheme was abandoned after nearly fifteen years of debate, having blighted Walcot and spawned the reviled Hilton (formerly Beaufort) Hotel, by *Snailum, Le Fevre & Quick* (1972), which so intrudes upon views of Pulteney Bridge. New developments in Bath entailed the demolition of *c.* 1,000 Georgian buildings (*c.* 350 of them listed) between 1950 and 1973.

From the late 1960s, public awareness grew of the desperate need for CONSERVATION. Adam Fergusson's *The Sack of Bath, a Record and an Indictment* (1973) made Bath's destruction a national *cause célèbre*. Stronger Conservation Area legislation, and the birth of a national conservation movement, encouraged planners in the 1970s to refuse demolition proposals in favour of restoration (e.g. the s side of Kingsmead Square, and General Wade's House). Cleaning and restoration of soot-blackened and corroded Bath stone began with the Circus in the late 1950s: by *c.* 1990, little remained of the shabby, weed-strewn post-war Bath. Streetscape improvements included the restoration of overthrows and lamps, replacement of railings in squares, and some notable urban repair schemes, e.g. the Plummer Roddis Block, Northgate Street, by the *Alec French Partnership* (1980–3). Other schemes demonstrated the viability of lesser Georgian housing, such as St Ann's Place, New King Street, by *Aaron Evans Associates* (1987), and the possibilities of adaptive reuse, as at Green Park Station (*Stride Treglown Partnership*, 1982–4).

There is little honestly new architecture in the city centre.* Recent INFILL tends towards contextual classicism. Among the most persuasive is *Gerrard, Taylor & Partners'* Baldwin-style extension to the Roman Baths entrance, Stall Street (1971–2). By contrast, the most recent major contribution is the cardboard-thin and historically illiterate Neo-Georgian of the rebuilt Southgate precinct, by *Chapman Taylor*, 2006–10. Unmistakably of the C21, yet sensitive to its site, is the new Bath Spa building, by *Nicholas Grimshaw & Partners* with *Donald Insall Associates* (1999–2003). Bringing together themes of conservation, contemporary design, and adaptive reuse, the complex once more celebrates the hot springs that were Bath's making.

BATH ABBEY

An ex-monastic Benedictine church that has lost its associated buildings, much like Selby or Southwark. It is a very consistently designed C16 monastery church, one of the last to be built on such a scale. Traces of the (larger) Norman church remain within. The Bishopric is still called Bath and Wells: the two churches retain a joint title as equal seats following a papal decree of 1176.

* For the University of Bath, *see* p. 196, for significant post-war industrial buildings *see* Introduction, p. 70.

A 'convent of holy virgins' received land at Bath from King Osric in 675. The convent could have been built from Roman salvage, for which ample archaeological evidence exists. Perhaps, as at Gloucester, the community was originally a double house, i.e. for monks and nuns together, for in 757 a charter granted land to the 'brethren of the monastery of St Peter at Bath'. In 959 Edgar reunited the kingdoms of Wessex and Mercia, and in 973 he was crowned here by Archbishop Dunstan of Canterbury as the first king of all England. The Saxon church is entirely unknown to us. In 957 its 'marvellous workmanship' is mentioned. It was probably located under the present church: excavation has made clear that it was not s of the medieval abbey, and Cheap Street was an early route running E–W just to the N.

In 1088 John de Villula of Tours became Bishop of Wells, and following a decree of 1075 that bishops' sees ought to be in populous towns, obtained licence to remove to Bath. In 1091 the king granted him the whole city along with the abbey, both royal possessions. Here he resided, nominally as abbot; the former abbot became a prior, and the bishop's throne was in the priory church. Sustained resentment by the canons of Wells at their loss led to the joint bishopric title as a means of resolving the conflict.

The NORMAN CHURCH was begun by John of Tours, together with a cloister on the s side, monastic quarters, and a palace for himself in the SE corner of the close. Begun in the mid to late 1090s, the church was up to the lower vaulting at John's death in 1122. It was damaged by a fire that destroyed much of the city in 1137, and was consecrated c. 1148–61.

The Norman church was immense. The entire present church is built on the foundations of just the nave, and the E front incorporates part of the W wall of the Norman crossing and transepts. These had both E and W aisles (cf. Old Sarum, Wiltshire), and at the E end there was an ambulatory. The nave floor was c. 6 ft 6 in. (2 metres) below present level. The nave piers were apparently of the Tewkesbury type, as was the W end, with a giant niche flanked by turrets. Norman C12 chevrons, other decoration and sculpture are preserved in the Heritage Vaults Museum (see p. 113) and in the Choir Vestry s of the s aisle.

When Bishop Oliver King (formerly secretary to Henry VII) came in 1499 he found the Norman church 'ruined to the foundations', probably after a major structural collapse. King had a dream in which angels were ascending and descending a ladder from Heaven and a voice said: 'Let an olive establish the crown and a king restore the church.' Following demolition of the old nave, work began on the PRESENT CHURCH in 1502, and the new E end was ready for roofing in 1503. William Birde, in 1499 elected Prior, effectively the bishop's deputy, carried on the project, outliving King by twenty-two years. The church was substantially completed under Birde's successor, Prior Holloway (1525–33). Bishop King's master masons were *Robert* and *William Vertue*, who were also the king's masons. (Robert Vertue appointed *Thomas Lynne*, mason, to carry out the work.) William may have built the vaults at Henry VII's Chapel at Westminster

Abbey, and also the vault of St George's Chapel at Windsor. They promised Bishop King the finest vault in England though when this promise was made, neither the vault of Henry VII's Chapel nor that of King's College Chapel at Cambridge had yet been begun.*

After Dissolution in 1539 the monastery was sold to Humphry Colles of Taunton. He passed it on in 1543, by now stripped of its lead and other materials and the nave roof demolished, to Matthew Colthurst of Wardour Castle, Wiltshire, the M.P. for Bath. His son Edmund Colthurst gave the building to the city in 1572 as the parish church. Subsequent work included the crossing vault (late C16, paid for by the city) and S transept vault (early C17). Finally, Bishop Montague (1612–16) covered the nave with a plaster ceiling with timber Tudor-Perp ribs, like a flattened vault.

There were major RESTORATIONS by *G. P. Manners* (from 1833), and *George Gilbert Scott*, 1860–73. Manners cleared the congested Wade's Passage to the N side, 1825–35, and in 1833–4 he added pinnacles along the nave and choir, and to the turrets of the tower and the W and E end. He also added flying buttresses to the nave to match the originals of the choir, and replaced triangular pattern parapets to the aisles with battlemented ones of upright design to match the W front. Scott's more scholarly and comprehensive work included the reversal or replacement of Manners's alterations. His three-phase scheme, prepared 1860–4, was executed 1864–72. Scott made two substantial internal alterations. He replaced Bishop Montague's nave ceiling with the originally intended fan-vaulting to match the choir; and he opened the interior from end to end for use by very large congregations. Scott's pupil *T. G. Jackson* again restored the W front (more tactfully) in 1899–1901, and continued the replacement of Manners's work. Work in the 1990s included conservation of the W front and exterior, and making a museum in the C18 storage vaults on the S side.

The MEASUREMENTS of the church are: length 201 ft (61.3 metres), width 123 ft (37.5 metres), height of vaults 78 ft (23.7 metres), height of tower 162 ft (49.4 metres).

EXTERIOR

The church is quite exceptionally uniform. The outer walls sit on the Norman foundations, and much stone was reused in foundations and structure. The detail – and the uniformity – owe much to *Scott* and to some extent *Jackson*. Scott restored the E, W and large transept windows, and returned the pinnacles and parapets to their original appearance, changing solid pinnacles to lower, pierced ones. He also replaced Manners's flying buttresses to the nave (which were hollow) with structural ones, because he was also vaulting the nave. By 1906 Jackson had repaired and

---

*Above the choir vaulting the E wall has slots for horizontal timbers, perhaps for an intended flat ceiling before the decision to build vaulting.

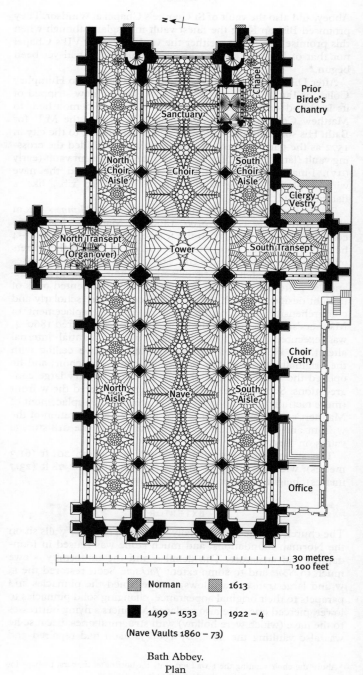

Bath Abbey.
Plan

North Choir Aisle

Sanctuary

Choir

South Choir Aisle

Chapel

Prior Birde's Chantry

Clergy Vestry

North Transept (Organ over)

Tower

South Transept

Choir Vestry

North Aisle

Nave

South Aisle

Office

30 metres
100 feet

Norman   1613

1499 – 1533   1922 – 4

(Nave Vaults 1860 – 73)

rebuilt flying buttresses on the SE aisle, built two new flying buttresses at the nave W end to correspond with those at the E end
of the choir, and replaced Manners's remaining pinnacles.
Jackson used Clipsham stone from Rutland, because Scott's
stone had deteriorated badly.

The CHOIR is three bays long. The aisles have broad five-light
windows, buttresses, battlements, and a parapet with pierced
arcading. Clerestory windows, also of five lights, higher and
with steeper arches. Flying buttresses between them, also
pinnacles, battlements, and a similar pierced parapet. The E
window is very tall, and square-framed at the top with traceried spandrels. It has seven lights and three transoms with
tracery below them, three-light sub-arches and elaborate panel
tracery. Plain three-light aisle windows, rising pierced parapets.
Low-pitched parapet over the main E window and turrets
flanking the choir. Polygonal turrets, rectangular before alteration in 1833. Exposed on the exterior of the E front, the bases
of two piers with strong coupled shafts to the cardinal faces
and thinner shafts in the angles, from which rose the Norman
crossing arches.
  The aisleless TRANSEPTS seem narrow in comparison with
the spaciousness of nave and choir. Battlements, parapet, pinnacles, and N and S windows (five lights, three transoms) all
much as the E end. The CLOCK in the N transept is to *Garbett*'s
design, 1834. Of the five-bay nave, nothing new need be said.
On its S side, a choir vestry in the form of a covered CLOIS-
TER, a war memorial by *Jackson*, built 1922–4.
  However, the WEST FRONT deserves attention as an original   37
and poetical version of the E end theme. Basically it is the same,
except that the big W window has only two transoms. Clearly
visible in the springing of the arch is stonework set to form a
lower head than was finally built. The tracery was renewed
c. 1865 by *Scott*. The aisle windows do not appear to be original either, but it is unclear when they were restored. Of the
carved figures, those noted below as original date from
1500–40, others from restorations of *c.* 1900 by *Jackson* (sculpture by *Sir George Frampton*); 1959–60 by *Lord Mottistone* and
Paul Paget; and 1991–2 as part of conservation of the W front
by *Nimbus Conservation Ltd*. The W doorway has a four-centred
head, richly moulded jambs and arch, and in the spandrels
good carvings of the Emblems of the Passion, with considerable evidence of polychrome. The side entrances are insignificant, and altogether the appearance of the relatively low aisles
in section, as it were, is not an advantage. The WEST DOOR was
given by Bishop Montague's kinsman Sir Henry Montague in
1617, and conserved in 2001–2. It is splendidly carved with
arms, drapery and cartouches, with some 1830s re-carving.
Flanking it are figures of St Peter and St Paul, of cruder,
provincial quality and almost certainly later than the original
carving, not too badly preserved as external C16 sculpture in
England goes. The buttresses between nave and aisle fronts are

decorated by the unique motif of ladders with little angels
ascending and descending. This commemorates Bishop King's
dream. The lower angels are original, retained to illustrate their
poor condition, the next pair up of 1959–60, the remainder of
1900. The descending angels are iconographically incorrect. In
its upper part the buttresses are polygonal, and here they are
flanked by three tiers of figures, some of which have been identified. The sequence is l. to r. On the lower tier St John the
Evangelist, the Virgin Mary, St Andrew and St John the
Baptist. The middle tier right-hand figures are St James and,
by *Peter Watts*, 1959–60, St Matthew. The top tier outer figures
are St Philip by *Laurence Tindall*, 1991–2 and St Bartholomew
(and canopy), *c.* 1900 by *Frampton*. Above the main doorway
are battlements, and in the middle is the statue of Henry VII
by *Frampton*. Above the main window is the Heavenly Host
(original and heavily decayed) gathered round a statue of
Christ in Majesty, and a cardinal's hat, showing that the work
was completed either under de Castello (*see* below) or his successor Wolsey. This in its present form is also by *Frampton*. In
the aisle windows are small figures in niches, perhaps C18. The
rebus on each angle buttress, the olive tree and the crown with
a mitre, is a pun on the name 'Oliver King'; renewed 1959–60.

Now the CROSSING TOWER. It is much broader than it is
long, being built on existing foundations of a bay of the
Norman nave; surprisingly this has no seriously upsetting
effect visually.* It has polygonal angle buttresses – not a Somerset, rather a Berkshire to Wiltshire motif – ending in polygonal turret pinnacles, and the same pierced arcaded parapet
as the rest of the church. Two-stage tower; the upper stage with
two bell-openings in square framing on each side (two lights
with two-centred arches N and S, four lights with four-centred
arches E and W). Below, the same composition and motifs are
repeated blank and much larger.

INTERIOR

38   The INTERIOR is impressive for its even lightness, with no break
at all from W to E. The High Altar is placed against the E wall.
The arcade is not high, the piers not specially slender. They
have four shafts and in each diagonal two broad waves. The
arches are four-centred and depressed. Tall clerestory, that is,
a tendency to even proportion between lower and upper stage.
The finest piece of architecture is the FAN-VAULT extending
throughout aisles, choir and nave. The square inner framing of
the E window indicates that the choir vaults were not planned
at once. Bishop King died in 1503, and on the vaults in both
choir and aisles are the arms of his successor Cardinal Adriano
de Castello (1504–18) (who never came to England) and of
Prior Birde. The fans are constructed in ribs and panels. The

---

* Oblong crossing towers were also intended for St George's Chapel, Windsor, and
St Mary Redcliffe, Bristol.

smaller aisle vaults have pendants. The tower vault dates from the time of Elizabeth I, and the s transept vault from that of James I. The nave received its fan-vaults only in the C19 as part of *Scott's* restoration. The Priory cloisters were demolished in the C16 but two entrance doorways remain. One leads from the nave to Jackson's choir vestry, now the bookshop entrance. The other is in the s choir aisle, now leading to the CLERGY VESTRY of 1613; the ceiling here shows what Bishop Montague's nave roof was like. W of this, the former entrance to the prior's lodging. Blocked NORMAN ARCHES survive in the E wall of the choir aisles, revealed by excavation (1863–71); they led from the Norman nave aisles to the transepts. Only the voussoirs of the N arch are visible, but the s arch has roll mouldings and, l., a column with block capital and chamfered abacus. *Tempus* with *Ivor Heal Design Group* created a Heritage Vaults Museum (opened 1994) in the s vaults. It contains Romanesque architectural remains and an archaeological *in situ* dig.*

FURNISHINGS

A splendid Georgian choir screen surmounted by an organ were replaced in Manners's 1830s restoration with a new screen further E, designed by *Edward Blore*. This and 1750s galleries in the choir were removed by *Scott*, who resited the organ in the N transept and renewed many fittings.

REREDOS. By *Scott*, 1875. – STATUES flanking the E window, 1929–39, by *F. Brook Hitch* from designs by *A. G. Walker*, architect *Sir Harold Brakspear* (St Alphege, St Dunstan, John de Villula, Bishop King). – SWORD REST (crossing pier). 1916. – STATUE (N transept). King David, one of three wood figures from *Abraham Jordan's* organ of 1708. (The organ was transferred to Wells in 1838 and sold to Yatton church (q.v.) in 1872.) – Five-light GASOLIERS by *Scott*, made by *Skidmore* of Coventry, 1870s. – TRIPTYCH SCREEN. E end of the N choir aisle, 1997; St Alphege surrounded by symbols of his martyrdom. Designer *Jane Lemon*, embroidered by the *Sarum Group*. – Wrought-iron RAIL (St Alphege Chapel). Originally the altar rail, probably by the Bristol smith *William Edney*. Given by General Wade 1725, sold in 1833, restored to the abbey 1959. – FONTS. E end of the N choir aisle, 1710. Moulded polygonal bowl with inscription band, and deep Baroque fluting beneath.† In Prior Birde's Chantry (E end of s choir aisle), a portable oak font of *c.* 1770. On a slender quatrefoil cluster column. Acorn finial. – W end of s nave aisle, carved stone font, by *Scott*, 1874. – PULPIT, by *Farmer & Brindley*, *c.* 1870. – ORGAN. Carved case and console by *Jackson*, 1912–14. The

---

* Outside the entrance a SCULPTURE of the Risen Christ carved by *Laurence Tindall*, 2000.

† COVER. Polygonal, like a spire. Given in 1604; now in the Heritage Vaults Museum.

'positive' organ case of 1972, cantilevered from the organ gallery, is the design of *Alan Rome*.

STAINED GLASS. A very large Victorian display. Some windows were replaced after war damage. Clockwise from the W end. N aisle, nave N wall. Windows 1–3 and 5 by *Clayton & Bell*, 1866–72 etc. Window 2 incorporates much glass from the original window of 1614, depicting the Lamb of God, symbols of the Evangelists, and seven shields of the St Barbe family. Window 4, *Bell* of Bristol, 1951, depicts the arms of C17 benefactors, salvaged from clerestory windows of *c.* 1604–20. One heraldic panel remains there. N transept, N and E walls, *Powells*, 1922 and 1924. N aisle, choir, window 2, *Powells*, 1947–56. NE window, *Bell* of Bristol, 1949, designed by *Edward Woore*. E window by *Clayton & Bell*, 1873, severely damaged 1942, restored by *Michael Farrar Bell*, 1955.* SE window by *Bell* of Bristol, 1952. Progressing E–W, S choir aisle, windows 1–2 by *Burlison & Grylls*, 1914 and 1870; 3, *Ward & Hughes*, after 1872, formerly in the N aisle. S transept E, by *Burlison & Grylls*, installed 1953. S transept S, *Clayton & Bell*, 1873, restored. S transept W, *Burlison & Grylls*, 1914. Nave S aisle, E–W, windows 1–4, *Clayton & Bell* (1868–73), and *Ward & Hughes*, 1869. S aisle W, by *Bell* of Bristol, 1869. W window, *Clayton & Bell*, completed in stages, 1865–94. N aisle W, by *Chance Bros*, 1862.

MONUMENTS. CHANTRY CHAPEL OF PRIOR BIRDE, begun in 1515: choir, S side, E end. Two bays with four-light four-centred openings on the long sides. Crested transoms, thickly foliated spandrels and frieze. Inside, an exceedingly pretty fan-vault; over the altar, closely panelled coving. Birde's rebus, a bird, is over the doorway and in the frieze, very characteristic of the early C16 (cf. e.g. Alcock's Chantry Chapel at Ely Cathedral, depicting cockerels). *Edward Davis* restored it in 1833 and finished Birde's carving. – WALL CROSS of bronze, wall ALTAR and wrought-iron GATE by *Sir Harold Brakspear*, 1930.

OTHER MONUMENTS. Many minor late C18 and early C19 tablets. Urns are ubiquitous. Signatures abound. The most widely patronized sculptors were *Thomas King* and *Reeves & Son*. They provide rich social documentary on those who retired to Bath, or who came to take the waters and failed to find a cure. The chief monuments are described from E to W on the S side, returning E on the N side.

CHOIR. Sir George Ivy †1639, and wife, r. of the altar; brass with kneeling figures. – Bartholomew Barnes †1605, and wife. Large hanging monument of alabaster and touchstone with the usual two kneeling figures facing across a prayer-desk. Unusually good sculpture, especially the kneeling children in the 'predella'. – Lady Miller †1781, by *John Bacon Sen.*, l. of the altar. A usual Bacon composition. Two female figures lean over a pedestal with an urn. On the pedestal portrait medallion in profile. Obelisk background.

---

*Thomas Bellot gave £60 to reglaze the E window in the early 1600s; fragments are preserved in the clerestory.

SOUTH CHAPEL. S wall. Granville Pyper †1717. Good, of reredos type, with well-carved cherubs. Attributed to *Edward Stanton* (GF). – Mary Frampton †1698. Bust on the top. – Dorothy Hobart †1722, also with bust on top. Signed *John Harvey* of Bath. – Elizabeth Winckley †1756; small oval tablet with profile portrait. – N wall. The painter William Hoare †1792. Very classical. A kneeling angel holds a portrait medallion. By *Chantrey*, 1828.

CHOIR SOUTH AISLE. Sir Philip Frowde †1674; excellent, a little swaggering bust in front of a trophy, with a small grotesque. Attributed to *Jasper Latham* (GF). – Admiral Bickerton †1832, by *Chantrey*, 1834. Grecian; a kneeling woman by an urn. – Dr Sibthorp. By *Flaxman*, 1796. A small monument. Sibthorp is shown landing in Greece: he began the first Flora of Greece.

SOUTH TRANSEPT. Several cheaper versions of compositions familiar from village churches, e.g. Elizabeth Moffat †1791, by *Reeves*, Mary Boyd †1763. – Joseph Sill †1824. Still the standing woman by an urn, but in a Gothic surround. – Jacob Bosanquet †1767, by *W. Carter*; a very fine relief of the Good Samaritan. – Archdeacon Thomas †1820, by *Gahagan*. Faith stands by a column with a Greek inscription. – Lady Waller †1633. One of the few earlier monuments. Alabaster and touchstone. She reclines behind her husband, Sir William, Parliamentarian commander at the Battle of Lansdown (1643). His effigy is defaced. Two children seated frontally at head and foot, behind big black Corinthian columns with a pediment. – Lady Wentworth †1706. Attributed to *Francis Bird* (GF). Two putti hold a medallion with a portrait bust.

SOUTH AISLE. Beau Nash †1761. Plain tablet with inscription in a Siena marble surround, 'Bathonie Elegantiae Arbiter'. – William Baker †1770, a merchant. By *J. F. Moore*. Allegorical relief with Justice, an anchor, a figure of Plenty and a Turk with a camel. – Anne Finch †1713, pretty cartouche with cherubs. By *Joseph Catterns*. – Caleb Hillier Parry †1822, eminent physician. Sarcophagus surmounted by books and a serpent. – Mrs Reeve †1664, and sons. Brass plate. Probably engraved by *George Reeve*. – William Bingham, by *Flaxman*, 1806. Flanking female genii holding wreaths. – John Hay Balfour †1791. By *Reeves*, with an awkward flying cherub. – Leonard Coward †1764. Weeping cherub at the foot between an urn and a skull. Against the S wall of SW porch. – Venanzio Rauzzini †1810. Swagged theatrical curtain engraved with a musical score. – SW porch. Lt-Col. John Mervyn Nooth †1821, with Fame blowing a trumpet.

NAVE W WALL. Herman Katencamp, by *John Bacon Jun.*, 1808. Large female figure, by an urn nicely wreathed with flowers. – Col. Alexander Champion †1793, by *Nollekens*. Obelisk and standing angel with portrait in an oval medallion.

NORTH AISLE (from W). Jonathan Henshaw †1764. Amply draped woman by an urn. – Lt-Col. Robert Walsh †1788. A broken column in an oval surround. – James Tamesz Grieve †1787. Simple sarcophagus. – Below, his wife †1757, with

charming relief of a reading man, an allegorical female figure
flying to ward off Death (a skeleton), and Father Time (by
Harris). – Brigadier-General William Steuart †1736. Telling
portrait relief in profile in a circular medallion against an
obelisk. – Bishop Montague †1618. By *William Cure*, mason
(who also provided the design) and *Nicholas Johnson*, carver.
Perhaps not entirely in its original state. Recumbent effigy on
tall tomb-chest. At both the head and the foot, two black
Corinthian columns carrying a piece of entablature; that is, not
a four-poster.

CHOIR NORTH AISLE. Henry Harington, M.D., †1816.
Relief with organ and music. – Fletcher Partis †1820. Relief of
the Good Samaritan. – Andrew Barkley †1790. Two standing
women with urn and portrait medallion. – Richard Chapman
†1572, and William Chapman †1627. Flanked by skulls. –
James Quin †1766, by *Thomas King*. Eloquent portrait relief in
an oval medallion.

CHURCHES

Church of England

CHRIST CHURCH, Julian Road. 1798 by *John Palmer*. The first
free church in England erected primarily for working-class
people unable to afford pew rents; also the first big Neo-Gothic
church in Bath, though Gothic only in a vague way, with wide
nave and aisles like a classical church. The simple design and
details reflect its charitable status. Plain w tower, with porches
of two bays' width spreading to either side. Battlemented
parapet, octagonal turrets and pinnacles by *Wallace Gill*, 1908.
Inside, galleries on tall quatrefoil piers. The ground floor had
800 free seats, subsidized by rented pews in the galleries. Small
quatrefoil windows lit the lower level, now segment-headed
rectangular. Apsidal chancel with nine lancet windows, 1865–6
by *J. Elkington Gill*. Numerous other alterations to *c.* 1945. –
WAR MEMORIAL by *Mowbray Green*, 1920. – STAINED GLASS.
Two in the s gallery by *A. O. Hemming*, 1890; two in the w
gallery by *Powell & Sons*.

HOLY TRINITY (formerly St Paul), St Paul's Place. 1872–4 by
Wilson, Willcox & Wilson. It replaced *Wood*'s St Mary's Chapel
to the E, 1732–4. E.E. gabled w front with heavy arcaded
narthex and lancets above, and boldly buttressed to the s. The
same architects added a N aisle, 1880–1, with a lower gable,
uncomfortably asymmetrical. (Aisle converted to a hall,
1953–4.) Otherwise derived from C13 French Gothic, fashionable in the 1860s. More advanced for the 1870s is the long,
continuous roof-line and semicircular E end, enclosing a barn-
like interior with no distinction between nave and chancel
except for the windows.

ST ANDREW, Julian Road. By *Hugh Roberts*, 1961–4. Simple,
dignified with a square tower open at the top. The chancel

has abstract stained-glass panels. It reuses rubble from old St Andrew, which occupied the adjacent green.[*]

ST JOHN BAPTIST, St John's Road. Originally of 1861–2 by *C. E. Giles*, E.E., with a low N porch-tower, barely attached like an Italian campanile. In 1869–71 *A. W. Blomfield* enlarged it to the S with an octagonal upper storey and spire to the tower, and a new Gothic nave and chancel with bands of alternating stone. The vigorous and bold additions overwhelm Giles's building. S windows with simple tracery and rose windows above. *Blomfield* punched through the S wall of Giles's nave, which became the N aisle. *Comper* decorated the ornate ROOD SCREEN in 1923. Small baptistery at the W end, 1879; mosaic floor and painted panelled ceiling perhaps also added by *Comper*. – STAINED GLASS. Sanctuary, W window and decoration of the sanctuary arch by *Bell & Almond*. – Nave and baptistery, *Clayton & Bell*. – Elizabethan-style CHOIR ROOM and SUNDAY SCHOOL (S), by *Browne & Gill*, 1881. Behind is the former rectory, BROMPTON HOUSE. Pre-1755, altered in the late C18. Poor extension by *Browne & Gill*, 1885.

ST MARY THE VIRGIN, Raby Place, Bathwick. Designed by *John Pinch* from 1810, built 1817–20. A fine Perp Gothic church, bristling with pinnacles. It replaced the decayed medieval church, and cost over £14,000. A large-scale, archaeologically leaning Gothic church is rare before 1818; the closest parallel – Edinburgh apart – is William Brooks's St Thomas, Dudley, Staffordshire, 1815–18. Pinch's W tower borrows partly from Somerset churches (*see* Batheaston for the pinnacles and battlements) and perhaps from the tower of Bath Abbey (the octagonal buttresses, not a Somerset feature). Three-stage tower divided by quatrefoil friezes, with twin belfry lights. Choir vestry, S side (now CHURCH HALL), 1906 by *Charles Deacon*, extended 1966.

High, spacious preaching-house INTERIOR, with Perp tracery in the tall aisle windows. Raked galleries on three sides, running between the nave 'arcades' – tall, thin columns of standard Somerset section (four hollows) carrying a flat timber lintel rather than arches. Over this lintel a clerestory, then a coved ceiling with plaster ribs. Pinch designed a chancel, but only built an angled apse. The pews initially faced W towards a three-deck pulpit; orientation reversed in 1866. Chancel of 1873–5 by *G. E. Street*. Early C14 Dec style, somewhat at odds with Pinch's Perp. *Clayton & Bell*'s decoration to *Street*'s design was overpainted 1906–10 when *Deacon* panelled the chancel and BAPTISTERY. A FRESCO of the Annunciation survives in the chancel arch. Deacon's work is a rich blend of Gothic, Art Nouveau and Arts and Crafts; his FONT is pink alabaster. *Sidney Gambier Parry* converted the sanctuary into a Lady Chapel in 1896, with marble and alabaster walls.

OTHER FURNISHINGS. Medieval FONT from the old St Mary, S porch. – ALTAR, an early design, 1886, by *Sidney*

88

---

[*] By *G. G. Scott*, 1869–73, with spire of 1878. Bombed 1942, demolished *c.* 1960.

Gambier Parry, carved by *Earp* of London. – The REREDOS (heightened and regilded, 1956) incorporates a four-section CI5–CI6 Netherlandish PANEL PAINTING from the studio of *Colijn de Coter*. – Brass eagle LECTERN, by *Street*, 1875. – METALWORK all by *Singer* of Frome. – Lady Chapel SCREEN with rolled brass scrollwork, copper lilies, and an arcade of brass palm branches. – Baptistery GATES of iron and German silver, a fine and individual design by *Deacon*. – PAINTING, the Adoration of the Child, by *Benjamin Barker*. – FRESCO outside the baptistery, 1906, by *Hemming*. – STAINED GLASS. *Clayton & Bell* executed the E and Lady Chapel windows. Baptistery, by *Powell & Powell*.

ST MICHAEL WITH ST PAUL, Broad Street. 1834–7; the most notable work of *G. P. Manners*. The medieval church was rebuilt in 1734–42 by the stonemason *John Harvey*, probably son of the mason of the same name; handsome, if outdated, classical. Manners increased the accommodation from 500 to 1,200. The splendid tower is tall and narrow, taking advantage of a slim V-shaped site with streets either side. The w face has a huge triple-stepped lancet window. Buttresses and corbel tables based on the E end of Salisbury Cathedral. Tall octagonal open lantern with elegant spire, rather Germanic (cf. Freiburg Cathedral). Polygonal porches flank the tower. The sides have the same buttresses and groups of stepped lancets. Inside, aisles as high as the nave, to accommodate galleries – removed, with Manners's pulpit and pews, in a reordering by *Browne & Gill*, 1899. Circular piers, tall and thin with four attached shafts. Quadripartite plaster rib-vaulting. Polygonal apse with blank arcading. Reordered 2006–7, with a glass-and-oak GALLERY forming a bridge across the tower arch. – ORGAN, 1847, by *Sweetland*, in good Gothic case. – SWORD REST next to the pulpit. – MONUMENTS. A good collection, Neoclassical and Gothic, under the tower.

ST SWITHIN, The Paragon. By *Jelly & Palmer*. Bath's only remaining classical-style parish church, built 1777–80, extended E with two further bays, 1788. The central square w tower, circular drum with arched openings, and octagonal spire (rebuilt in the early 1990s) were finished by 1790. All round the exterior are giant Roman Ionic pilasters, unusual for an CI8 church (cf. All Saints, Oxford; but that has a prominent attic above). Each bay has two tiers of windows, segment-headed and round-headed. w doorway in the base of the tower, flanked rather feebly by shapeless staircase lobbies that cut across the giant pilasters. Inside, three widely spaced giant Ionic columns on each side of the nave. The galleries were cut back behind them in 1881. Shallow sanctuary corbelled out over the Walcot Street elevation by *W. J. Willcox* in 1891, when the pulpit was brought forward to its present position. Pews removed and the crypt remodelled in reordering, 2006–7. – FONT. Arts and Crafts, 1901. – STAINED GLASS. E window, a post-Second-World-War Ascension, with Walcot church at the feet of Christ. – Innumerable MONUMENTS, lots with urns.

Paul Bertrand †1755, portrait medallion. – Jerry Peirce †1768, with an excellent, lively profile portrait. – John Palmer, the architect, †1817. – The novelist Fanny Burney (Countess d'Arblay) †1840, not of artistic interest.

Roman Catholic

ST JOHN THE EVANGELIST (R.C.), South Parade. 1861–3, by *C. F. Hansom*, who considered it one of his best works. Proof of how intensely the Gothicists hated the Georgian of Bath, and also a signal of mid-C19 Roman Catholic confidence. Late C13–early C14 Dec style, rock-faced, with dressed stone openings, a further defiance of the local ashlar tradition. Hansom added in 1867 the lofty W tower and 222-ft (68-metre) spire. The building reflects principles of honesty and severity laid down in Pugin's *True Principles of Pointed or Christian Architecture* (1841): small stones to enhance scale, steep roofs, structurally useful pinnacles. However, it lacks the sinuous intensity that Pugin might have achieved. The N side, with lean-to aisle, gabled transept, baptistery and porch appears 'one mass of gables' (*The Builder*). The N aisle and presbytery to the S were bombed in 1942 and rebuilt, the latter to a new design, by the *Alec French Partnership*, 1950s. The interior is architecturally somewhat thin; the original polychrome paint scheme does not survive intact. Very elaborate architectural and figure carving by *Earp* of London. W narthex, with baptistery and altar. Ambitious aisled nave with clerestory continued as a screen across the transepts. Broad polygonal apse with side apses, and polished Devonshire marble piers. Complete set of High Victorian FURNISHINGS. HIGH ALTAR, marble and alabaster, by *Earp* of London, flanked r. by a Blessed Sacrament altar, l. by Lady Altar and pulpit. The Lady Chapel altar came from a previous R.C. church in Corn Street. – Ornate iron CHANCEL SCREEN by *J. H. Powell* of *Hardman & Co.* – BAPTISTERY SHRINE, *Edward Hansom*, 1871. – STAINED GLASS. By *Hardman & Co.* Damaged in 1942. Apse windows of 1863, the earliest. Quite good and glowing in the aisle rose windows.

ST MARY (R.C.), Julian Road. An ambitious, unfinished church of 1879–81, by *Dunn & Hansom*. Much restored *c.* 1950 after bomb damage. Gothic Revival style, externally lower and more spreading than Puginian models. Nave and S aisle of five bays, chancel and S chapel of three narrower bays. The interior has marvellously delicate sculpture with birds, flowers and angels. Superb Italian marble REREDOS by *Signor Leonardo*, with figure paintings by *John Armstrong*, 1985. – On the N wall, five mural PAINTINGS by *Fleur Kelly*, 1997. – STAINED GLASS by *Hardman*.

Nonconformist

UNITARIAN CHURCH (former), Barton Street. 1795, attributed to *Palmer*. Also known as Trim Street Chapel. Rusticated

ground floor, tall arched windows above. Apse added and
interior altered in *Rundbogenstil*, 1859–60 by *W. J. Green*. Now
a pub.

COUNTESS OF HUNTINGDON'S CHAPEL (former), Roman
Road. *See* Public Buildings, p. 133.

KENSINGTON PROPRIETARY CHAPEL (former), London
Road. *See* p. 186.

ARGYLE CHAPEL (United Reformed), Argyle Street. By *H. E.
Goodridge*, 1821, a forward extension and rebuilding of
Baldwin's chapel, 1788–9. Greek Ionic portico *in antis* and pediment, influenced by Wilkins's Freemasons Hall (*see* Friends'
Meeting House, p. 140). The tall central door was originally a
window, with doors either side. Upper parts insensitively
altered in 1862 by *Hickes & Isaac*. Galleried interior, free-
standing central PULPIT with paired Ionic columns, and
directly behind, an impressive ORGAN CASE on a canted
plan, of 1888 but attempting to be in keeping with the
architecture.

MANVERS STREET BAPTIST CHURCH. 1871–2, by *Wilson &
Willcox*, with Institute and Sunday School extension, *Silcock &
Reay*, 1907. A simple gabled W front of squared rock-faced
Bath stone. Small, open NW corner tower with a continuous
arcade of horseshoe arches and a conical roof, based on early
French models (cf. the Cistercian church at Pontigny near
Auxerre and Notre-Dame-la-Grande, Poitiers). Galleried nave
with aisles, boarded roof. Apsidal E end spanned by a lofty
stone arch.

HAY HILL BAPTIST CHURCH, Roman Road. Craggy, rock-
faced Gothic, 1869–70 by *Wilson & Willcox*, with buttresses and
gable (cf. Manvers Street Baptist Church, above). Interior converted 1985–6 by *Carter Hughes Partnership*, with an inserted
floor.

WALCOT METHODIST CHURCH, Nelson Place East. 1815–16,
by the *Rev. William Jenkins* of London, a minister-turned-
architect who had built Methodist chapels in Sheffield, Canterbury, and elsewhere. It is more Methodist-looking than a
Bath architect would have made it. Two-storey five-bay front
with round-headed windows, and a Greek Doric porch on
paired columns. Three-bay pediment raised above the entablature on an attic, a solecism found elsewhere in Bath (*see*
pp. 153 and 172). Inside, a U-shaped gallery. – ORGAN. Built
in 1771 for the Assembly Rooms. – MANSE, W side, a handsome three-bay Grecian house with a Tuscan doorway and
banded rustication.

BETHEL CHAPEL, Grove Street. By *Alan Crozier Cole*, 1972.
Diminutive, with a correctly detailed pediment.

CATHOLIC APOSTOLIC (IRVINGITE) CHURCH (former),
Guinea Lane. 1841, by *G. P. Manners*, Neo-Norman, skilfully
designed on a cramped site. A segmental apse to the chancel,
lower than the nave, has scallop-capital engaged columns in
round-arched window reveals. Used by the Kingdom Hall of
Jehovah's Witness since 1976.

ELIM PENTECOSTAL CHURCH, Charlotte Street. Formerly Percy Chapel and Congregational Church. By *Goodridge & Son*, 1854. A spreading Lombardic Romanesque façade, with rich repetitive decoration and a blind ground-floor arcade. Two short corner towers with Italianate roofs, and a central rose window. A large decagonal lantern *à la* Parma or Cremona, on thin Purbeck columns. The space beneath is polygonal and galleried (now spoilt by a false ceiling). It had an early air-handling system by *Haden* of Trowbridge.

FRIENDS' MEETING HOUSE, York Street. *See* p. 140.

MORAVIAN CHAPEL (former; now offices), Charlotte Street. By *James Wilson*, 1844–5, in Roman Revival style. Without any of the humility of the C18 Moravians. A big assertive façade with giant Corinthian columns *in antis*. A heavy portico and rounded windows, with a touch of Vanbrugh's Baroque. It also contained the minister's house, schoolrooms, etc. 89

SWEDENBORGIAN CHURCH (former), Henry Street. By *Henry Underwood*, 1844, still remarkably pure Grecian. Pedimented portico of four three-quarter Ionic columns, plain angle pilasters and a splayed doorway set in a rusticated base. Now offices. Attached, E side, BLENHEIM HOUSE, the minister's house – same date, style and architect.

THOMAS STREET CHAPEL, Thomas Street. *See* p. 185.

Cemeteries

BATH ABBEY CEMETERY, Ralph Allen Drive, 1843–4. The best, most intact and last of three cemeteries laid out by the celebrated gardener and horticulturist *John Claudius Loudon* according to his scientific and hygienic principles. Free Gothic entrance gateway, probably by *Manners*, to a long rising main drive. Dominant MORTUARY CHAPEL by *Manners*, 1844 (originally projected to have cloister wings). Boldly Neo-Norman, with vigorous decoration, a square W tower and pyramidal spire. Numerous fine Greek Revival tombs. At the top of the Carriage Road, the Crimean monument, by *Samuel Rogers*, 1856, a Greek Revival obelisk. On the S border, Samuel Maxwell Hinds, by *Reeves*, 1847, based on the Choragic Monument of Lysicrates. Adjacent, Williams memorial, by *White*, c. 1848. A miniature Greek temple with paired fluted columns; draped urn, angel and mourner. At the N end is John Lambe, c. 1865; cable-banded column and phoenix.

ST JOHN'S CEMETERY, Church Walk, Bathwick. To the S is a Gothic former MORTUARY CHAPEL, now a picturesque ruin, which *Pinch* built of reused stone from the old church of St Mary Bathwick, after 1818. Three-stage tower with angle buttresses and pierced quatrefoil tracery.

WALCOT CEMETERY, Walcot Gate. MORTUARY CHAPEL, by *James Wilson*, 1842. Rather crude Neo-Norman, cruciform in plan. S of St Swithin's church, the ENTRANCE, with a vaulted mausoleum under. Also by *Wilson*, 1840, in a gloomy style

with two short towers and extinguished torches as the chief
ornament.

PUBLIC BUILDINGS

The Pump Room and Spa complexes

GRAND PUMP ROOM AND ROMAN BATHS, Abbey Church Yard
and Stall Street. The Grand Pump Room and baths played a
pivotal role in the life of Georgian Bath, as a combined social
and medicinal centre. The principal surviving baths are the
mostly post-Roman King's Bath and Roman Great Bath; a third,
the Queen's Bath, was removed in the late C19.

The GRAND PUMP ROOM, 1790–5, by *Thomas Baldwin*, completed by *John Palmer* after Baldwin's dismissal in 1793,
replaced John Harvey's Pump Room of 1704–6 (enlarged
1751). Baldwin's side elevation to Stall Street, w, designed as
a screen wall just three bays wide flanked by colonnades, is
particularly successful. It also forms part of his masterpiece of
urban planning that includes Bath Street to the w, a result of
the Bath Improvement Act of 1789 (*see* p. 142). The COLON-
NADES (the N open, the S blank) each have nine bays of
unfluted Ionic columns and a three-bay pediment containing
sphinxes facing a wreathed oval with a relief of Hygeia. The S
colonnade formed the frontage to the first phase, the New
Private Baths. These had dressing rooms with *en suite* baths;
the building is now the exit from the Roman Baths. *C. E. Davis*
added a corner block to the S in 1889, the Douche and Massage
Baths, which was replaced by a convincing shop and office
in Baldwin's style, 1971–2, by *Gerrard, Taylor & Partners*.
Baldwin's open colonnade to the N screens Stall Street from
the Abbey Church Yard. Between the colonnades the w front
is completely windowless, but made interesting by vermiculated rustication and four strongly modelled roundels on the
ground floor. Above are four pairs of coupled unfluted
Corinthian columns. In the three bays are slender arched
niches with balustraded aprons and pediments on consoles
with swagged friezes.

The seven-bay N FRONT facing the Abbey Church Yard is
less satisfactory, with a portico that relates uncomfortably to
the colonnade. Baldwin intended a detached portico (excavations in the 1980s revealed the footings for one). Palmer's main
alteration was to attach the portico to the N façade, giving it a
stuck-on afterthought appearance. The façade is wide with the
three-bay portico of giant Corinthian columns rising from the
ground. Its pediment remains below the main, intermittently
balustraded parapet. It contains an oak-and-acorn-wreathed
concave panel. In the entablature, a raised and gilded inscription, 'Water is Best' in Greek. Only the main architrave and

first-floor sill band carry across to tie the façade together. In between are five oval windows (more appropriate to an attic than a first floor) in rectangular panels. The angle bays break forward with large arched upper windows in the bays, the l. side with an elegant Ionic doorcase, balancing the entrance with the colonnade on the r. To the E is a successful continuation by *John McKean Brydon*, 1895–7, built following the discovery of the Roman Baths in the 1880s. It contains a concert room with a domed centre, with a Palladian pedimented front. A one-storey wall links this with the Grand Pump Room, r., and continues to the l. with a curved corner screening the Great Bath on the S side (*see* below).

The INTERIOR of the Grand Pump Room is no disappointment. It is one large saloon, 60 ft (18 metres) by 46 ft (14 metres) by 34 ft (10 metres) high, with attached giant fluted Corinthian columns, a coved ceiling and broad apses under elliptical arches at the E and W ends. The columns divide the long walls into five bays, each of those on the N wall with a window and a clerestory. Opposite, each second bay contains a fireplace and panel above, and the centre, a small glazed apse holding the fountain by *C. E. Davis*, 1888 (altered). The W apse has a serpentine-fronted musicians' gallery with a wrought-iron balustrade and, below, an orchestra platform, the E apse a STATUE of Beau Nash, the Master of Ceremonies, probably by *Joseph Plura*, 1752, from the old Pump Room. *Ian Bristow* redecorated the interior in the 1980s. The room is remarkably festive, especially when the musicians play. From the windows to the S can be seen the open-air King's Bath (*see* below), where men and women splashed about before Ralph Allen and Nash made the city a spa of polite manners. This explains why Nash in his Rules of 1742 had to preach to the patrons the elementary rules of good behaviour and to embroider on his theme with such forced jocularity.

The CONCERT ROOM by *Brydon* is of course thicker and richer in its decoration. Coffered dome with a lantern, apses with half-domes either end. Attached marbled Composite columns support the main entablature. A Venetian window at the N end and a Diocletian window at the S end light the apses. The planning and decoration derive from Wren's St Stephen Walbrook, London. Vaulted corridors on the N and E sides with porphyry Tuscan columns and paired pilasters. The Concert Room now serves as a splendid reception hall to the Baths complex beneath, laid out as a museum in 1897 around *in situ* Roman remains immediately N of the Great Bath, and extended in 1983 into the excavations under the Pump Room (*see* below).

To the S, Brydon's Doric colonnade encloses the Great Bath (*see* below), with a balustraded terrace above. Statues by *G. A. Lawson* on the parapet depict Roman emperors and generals with British connections. The N side has a loggia (glazed in the 1920s) of five Diocletian windows with triple keystones. Doorways at each end of this terrace are reflected by corner pavilions opposite. On the W side are further remains of *Davis*'s Douche and Massage Bath of 1889.

THE ROMAN LEVELS. The complex history of the Baths and Temple around the principal hot spring of Aquae Sulis is described on pp. 13–15. The Roman levels are described in the order in which they are encountered.

Directly beneath the Pump Room lies the TEMPLE PRECINCT. Excavations here in 1981–3 revealed part of the inner Temple forecourt, N of the Sacred Spring. In Roman times, this was a paved courtyard which continued under the Pump Room foundations to the N and around the Temple podium to the W. Areas are re-paved in Pennant stone. To the W several worn steps of the Temple podium can be seen through a gap in the Pump Room foundations. To the N, these foundations stand on the Roman precinct and the plinth where the sacrificial altar stood. Sufficient of this plinth has survived to enable its southern half to be reconstructed. Only the S side of the Temple Precinct bears any relation to its Roman form. A wall that formed the long outer N face of the SACRED SPRING survives, *c.* 3 ft (1 metre) high, and penetrated at mid-point by the entrance, its worn steps clearly visible. E and W of this wall are foundations of massive oolite buttresses added to take the thrust of the vault covering the Sacred Spring, and, centrally positioned, the four pier bases of the *quadrifrons* framing its entrance. To the E the main precinct entrance can be seen with difficulty beneath an electrical substation. The Roman Sacred Spring can be viewed from the N through windows at basement level. An open polygonal lead-lined reservoir was built in the C1, incorporated in the C2 within the SE corner of the colonnaded precinct around the Temple of Sulis Minerva. By the C3 it had been enclosed within an E–W rectangular stone building with a vaulted tile roof. The water level is now at the Roman level. Two square pillars, possibly statue bases, can be seen below the surface on the S side.

The OUTFALL DRAIN can be seen in two places here. The first is an iron-stained arch that served as an overflow from the reservoir in the outer E wall of the Sacred Spring. On the N side a flight of steps descends into the water. The drain passes beneath the Museum but can be seen again 80 ft (25 metres) further E where the outflow from the Great Bath joins it. On either side of the drain substantial Roman masonry is visible. To the S the outer wall of the Great Bath stands up to 6 ft 6 ins (2 metres) high. To the N, massive blocks prevented another great structure, either the precinct containing the *tholos* or possibly a basilican building, from collapsing the drain.

5   The GREAT BATH is the centrepiece of the bathing establishment. Despite the misleading C19 superstructure it remains one of the most dramatic monuments of Roman Britain. The chamber, aligned E–W, is 110 ft by 70 ft (34 by 21 metres) and contains a pool 60 ft by 30 ft (19 by 9 metres) and 5 ft (1.5 metres) deep. Steps on all four sides descend to a flat base still lined with sheets of Mendip lead. In the NW corner a shallow

channel feeds the bath from the King's Spring. The outfall sluice is in the N side near the E end. The pavements around the bath mostly consist of oolite slabs, worn to a smooth but uneven surface. Three *exedrae*, or alcoves, are set back in the N and S walls, the central ones rectangular, the outer ones apsidal. The chamber is enclosed by a wall surviving *c.* 3 ft– 10 ft (1–3 metres) high, which bears traces of impermeable lime mortar. On the N and S sides of the bath stand six piers, originally to support the roof but which now support the C19 galleries. In the C2 the piers were strengthened by adding blocks encroaching into the ambulatory on one side and over the top step of the pool of the other. The enlarged piers supported a heavy tile vault over the bath; this basilican superstructure would have included a clerestory for light and ventilation.

The principal component of the EASTERN RANGE was another rectangular bath, the 'Lucas Bath', 80 ft by 35 ft (26 by 10.5 metres), aligned N–S with steps at its N end. (Steps at the S end are presumed but missing.) It too was surrounded by a walkway. Its floor was later raised, and traces of this are visible. The C1 establishment was completed by a third pool further E again. Its base slabs are still visible, although in the C2 it was replaced by a suite of steam rooms with hypocausts, which underwent several stages of development, C2 to C4. These rooms were heated from furnaces on the N and E sides. The only surviving mosaic fragment in the Baths is visible in the far NE corner. In the C4 the steps at the N end of the Lucas Bath were blocked off and an apsidal immersion pool with a bench seat was installed immediately inside the doorway from the Great Bath.

Of Bath's three hot springs, the largest rises in the KING'S BATH to the W. It is the most rewarding of the baths, where one can look back through two thousand years of history and architecture from the C20 to the C1 A.D. The shape of the C1 Roman reservoir is preserved on the E, S and W sides. The floor of the later King's Bath was cut back to this line in 1979. The N side of the reservoir lies under the Pump Room. The vaulted chamber that enclosed the Sacred Spring in the C2 still gives the King's Bath its form today. The S wall below the C17 balustrade is mostly Roman and contains two apertures, both partly infilled. A third Roman aperture, used to connect to the Queen's Bath in the C16, was blocked up when that bath was removed in the late C19. *p. 126*

The four arched seated recesses on the E wall are all that remain of many built on the inner faces of the Roman chamber, probably in the late C11 or early C12, by the monks of Bath Abbey. Remains of Jacobean strapwork around the top, donated in 1624. The STATUE of Prince Bladud, the legendary founder of Bath, is possibly a composite from different medieval statues; added in the early C17. The bronze rings in the walls for bathers to clasp are further C17 donations. The orange staining indicates a higher water level in which bathers

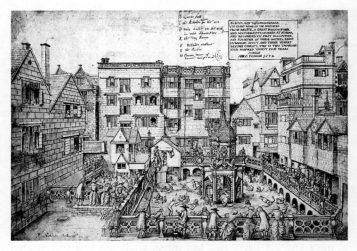

Bath, the King's Bath.
Drawing by Thomas Johnson, 1675

sat neck-deep. The water was lowered to its present level in the
1970s for archaeological assessment. The buildings above are
the remains of *Davis*'s Douche and Massage Baths of 1889,
built over Roman remains on the site of the demolished
Queen's Bath of 1576.

To the s lies the FRIGIDARIUM. In the CI it took the form
of a large unheated hall, whose original grandeur and simplicity are now difficult to appreciate. Screen arcades aligned with
the piers beside the Great Bath were matched at the N end by
three large apertures overlooking the Sacred Spring. From the
hall bathers would either turn E to the warm water of the Great
Bath, or w to the West Baths. Later, the *frigidarium* was divided
up. The area between the arcades was walled off and the 30-ft
(9-metre) wide cold Circular Bath, fed by a fountain on its
N side, was inserted in the floor. Outside the arcades, E–W
passages connected the Great Bath with the West Baths. The s
passage is well preserved, with pillars standing over 6 ft 6 in.
(2 metres) high.

The WEST BATHS started as a simple suite of warm (*tepidarium*) and hot (*caldarium*) steam rooms, typical of any town
bath house. Later, a circular *laconicum* (dry-heat sauna) was
added, and the *caldarium* replaced by a round-ended cold-
water bath. Central to the West Baths is the *tepidarium* whose
entire form is visible. It includes the best-preserved hypocaust
on the site, flues from the furnaces, and doorways to adjoining areas. To the w, a rectangular cold bath, also complete in
layout and with two sets of steps into it, can be seen beneath
Stall Street.

Bath, the Cross Bath.
Engraving after T. H. Shepherd, 1829

CROSS BATH, HOT BATH AND NEW ROYAL BATH. A coherent group in the SW sector of the medieval city, an area, with its therapeutic hot springs, associated since the Middle Ages with hospitals, baths and healing. The waters, for drinking and bathing, were enjoyed up to the 1970s, but fell into disuse. Restored and revived in the early C21 they continue Bath's function as a spa.

The CROSS BATH's history is complicated. Originally an irregular pool of Roman origin, it is mentioned in late C13 deeds and described by Leland in 1540. A medieval marble cross was set in the middle. Owned by the Church until the Dissolution, under City control from 1555. *Thomas Baldwin* as City Architect rebuilt it in 1783–4. On an almost triangular site with a narrow apex to the S, and a remarkably Baroque N façade with central bow and Adamish detail. Behind was an oval pump room. The bath was to the S. When Bath Street was cut through in 1791 (*see* p. 142), Baldwin's building became a misfit with a blank façade skewed to the splendid new E–W axis. In 1798, *Palmer*, the new City Architect, took down Baldwin's building, except for the W wall and bath, and rebuilt the dressing rooms and pump room. Baldwin's serpentine N façade was re-erected facing E towards Bath Street, and a new N elevation built to Palmer's design, with straight flanks canted back towards a segmental projection with Corinthian portico. The bath was converted in 1829–30 by *G. P. Manners* to provide vestibule and dressing rooms with reclining baths; the portico colonnade was infilled. *Manners & Gill*'s more drastic conversion in 1854 removed Manners's work and Baldwin's remaining internal structure. Further vandalized by *C. E. Davis*, 1885–8, enlarging and roofing over the bath (roof removed in 1952). All that remains of Baldwin's interior is an elegant relief carving of a vase and one patera.

In 1999–2003 *Nicholas Grimshaw & Partners* with the conservation architects *Donald Insall Associates* brought the Cross Bath back to life. A new elliptical lead roof, expressing Baldwin's original pump room, forms an entrance vestibule and cantilevered canopy with a glass apron. A new bath of similar size and shape intersects on plan with the canopy. At the point of intersection the hot spring rises through a brass and steel water sculpture by *William Pye*.

Diagonally opposite to the SE is the HOT BATH, built in 1775–7 by *John Wood the Younger*, replacing a medieval bath to the W. Wood's only civic commission in Bath is one-storeyed with a portico of paired Tuscan columns and a pediment. The symmetrical interior layout was radically altered by *A. J. Taylor* in 1925–7. The plan was square with an entrance at each splayed corner, facing a wall niche across the diagonal. To l. and r. were pairs of changing rooms. 'Slips' or steps descended between into a central octagonal bath, originally open. Externally this rises above the outer accommodation, with a balustrade on the enclosing walls, and is linked to the dwarf parapet of the outer façade by a shallow-pitched lead roof.

Now forming part of, and accessible from, the New Royal Bath (*see* below), the Hot Bath was converted into a treatment centre by *Grimshaw & Partners* and *D. Insall Associates* in 1999–2003. They restored the basic square-within-a-square plan together with the inner pool, now with a structural glass roof. Twelve surrounding rooms provide various treatments. Opaque glass shutters in the portico retract at night to provide glimpses of the pool.

To the E, *G. P. Manners* added the Tepid Bath in 1829–30 (dem. 1922). The entrance remains, as an extension to the N side of the Hot Bath. This has a serpentine façade enclosing a ramp for invalids. The doorway survives as a window. The Tepid Bath was replaced by swimming baths, replaced in turn by the NEW ROYAL BATH, by *Nicholas Grimshaw & Partners*, 1999–2003, opened 2006. This incorporates, besides the Hot Bath, No. 7 Bath Street as the entrance (*see* p. 142), now with a glazed ground floor by *Grimshaw* at the SW.

The New Royal Bath is a very high-quality building of its time, discreetly holding its own, tucked behind historic neighbours, knitting together the elements of the site. An unexpected commission for a firm associated so much with steel and glass and with non-contextual buildings. The plan forms a three-storey Bath-stone-clad cube raised one storey above the ground on pillars. In the SE corner are a cylindrical service riser and staircase, similarly clad. Staircase, lift and service tower to the N. The cube and cylinder are set within a glass enclosure hanging from steel-section columns. There are bathing pools on both ground and roof levels.

The ground-floor pool occupies the full area of the glass enclosure, spreading in free-form curves beyond the footprint of the cube. From it rise four powerful reinforced-concrete mushroom columns that support the cube, each capital spreading out to occupy a full quadrant of the soffit (cf. Frank Lloyd Wright's Johnson Wax Building, Wisconsin). The lowest level of the cube contains changing rooms, the middle level massage rooms in four segmental enclosures of curved etched glass that carry up the memory of the mushroom capitals. The inner space echoes the square-within-a-square plan of the Hot Bath. The top level has four free-standing circular glass-walled steam rooms, again informed by the columns, and a central shower. The glass enclosure finishes at this level, forming a glass-balustraded roof terrace. Finally, the cylindrical staircase leads up to a raised open-air pool with views across the city. Square with curved corners, it occupies all but a narrow perimeter of the cube. Circular corner enclosures – the leit-motif again – contain whirlpool baths. Between these are pro-filed stone surfaces like just-submerged Corbusian *chaises longues*.

Although rubbing shoulders with its neighbours, the archi-tecture is entirely articulated from the historic buildings which it incorporates, detached by glazed links and slots that intro-duce light and provide orientating views of rooftops and the Abbey, as do the porthole windows peppering the façades. The stone has grooved joints to express its character as panels. The water glows softly with coloured and fibre-optic lighting, and the natural heat of the water provides energy.

Civic and cultural buildings

GUILDHALL, High Street. By *Thomas Baldwin*, 1775–8. The High Street elevation is the best in Bath, and the Banqueting Hall is the best interior. An immensely extravagant riposte to the Upper Assembly Rooms (*see* p. 131), from which many, including civic dignitaries, were socially excluded. *John McKean Brydon* added large wings in 1893–7 and the Victoria Art Gallery in 1897–1900, forming a significant civic complex.

Complex circumstances surround the C18 commission, including an abortive start to another design. *Timothy Lightoler* produced a design in 1763, then in 1766 he won a limited com-petition (against Wood the Younger and Richard Jones). The following year the design was revised again. In 1768 the foun-dation stone was laid, but still there was no action. In 1775 the wealthy *Thomas Warr Atwood*, architect to the city estates and waterworks, produced a scheme, probably to the design of his clerk *Thomas Baldwin*. Work started amid accusations of jobbery, and acrimony over a rival scheme by *Jelly* and *Palmer*, when Atwood died in an accident on a building site. Baldwin quickly produced new designs. His EXTERIOR is in the Palla-dian country-house tradition with some fashionable Adamish detail. Rusticated ground floor with a vermiculated projecting centre. Above, a three-bay giant portico of three-quarter Ionic columns on pedestals. In the pediment the city arms flanked by festoons. The entablature frieze is carried across the broad wings, each of which has a pedimented first-floor window in an arched recess. Rectangular panels interrupt the entablature. The parapet has pedestal balustrading with stone vases. On the pediment a lead statue of Justice. *Brydon* added the dome (*see* below), and demolished Baldwin's low screen walls to the market with end pavilions on each side.

Rear additions were removed in the 1980s to reveal the splendid E elevation, very different from the front. Here the emphasis is on the end pavilions, each two windows wide with a pediment. The centre slightly recessed, three windows wide. This refusal of a central emphasis was presumably to show that there was no entrance in this front. Rusticated ground-floor façade; the tall first-floor windows on blind balustrading. *Œil-de-bœuf* attic windows in rectangular panels form a clerestory to the Banqueting Hall. The centre first-floor window is blind, to accommodate a fireplace inside, and the chimney is disguised as a classical Roman altar.

INTERIOR. The Banqueting Hall and staircase are masterpieces of up-to-the-minute late C18 decoration. Grand STAIRCASE in the SW corner, of Dutch oak, square in plan, with fine Neoclassical wrought-iron balustrading and stuccowork with oval paterae and festoons of husks. It leads to the sumptuous BANQUETING HALL, a double square in plan, 40 ft (12.5 metres) by 80 ft (25 metres), by 30 ft (9 metres) high. E and W walls of seven bays divided by engaged Corinthian columns. The second, fourth and sixth bays have arched recesses with mahogany double doors on the W wall. Plain intervening bays with large portraits by *William Hoare* and others, and, in the attic, *œil-de-bœuf* windows on the E wall and oval panels opposite. The main frieze is enriched with festoons of husks, bucrania, vases and anthemia and, in the recesses, fluting and paterae. In the centre of the W wall an orchestra gallery, and opposite, a fine chimneypiece with the city arms above and an ornamented lunette. The end walls similarly divide into three bays with an arched central recess with a fireplace, and paterae instead of ovals high up. A cove springs from a second frieze with Vitruvian scrolling. The flat ceiling has three large circular panels with elaborate radiating decoration, and three magnificent crystal chandeliers. The centre front room, W side, was the Common Council room. On the N side is a service stair and, originally, 'water-closets for the ladies'. On the ground floor, beyond a public hall, is the BRUNSWICK ROOM (centre E side), formerly a Sessions Court. To the S were the jury room and prison cells, and to the N, the Town Clerk's office and a weighing house.

In 1891 *Brydon* won a competition for extensive ADDITIONS, a S wing for municipal offices and a technical school (now offices) to the N. As executed in 1893–6, the scheme extends to twenty-six bays, of which the central five of the W façade are Baldwin. The rest, set slightly back, are by Brydon, following Baldwin's style but with exuberant Baroque touches. The curved corners repeat Baldwin's giant columns, but in Corinthian with friezes of figures by *G. A. Lawson*, derived from Belcher and Pite's Institute of Chartered Accountants, London (1888). Either side of the curved corners a single bay is set forward to mirror Baldwin's wings. To the corners, Brydon added two-stage domed belvederes in the style of Wren or Vanbrugh (cf. his later designs for Government offices in Whitehall): a fine addition to the skyline. The s wing is attached to the old Police Station (*see* p. 146) by an arched screen.

The s wing has some fine interiors. On the first floor a stone-vaulted corridor connects the committee room, Mayor's Parlour, and the COUNCIL CHAMBER. A square room with apsidal ends, and red scagliola Ionic columns and pilasters on all sides. Groin-vaulted ceiling with Neoclassical figures by *Schenck*. Rich mahogany woodwork, quite Baroque. City arms, woodcarving by *William Aumonier*. Circular window with the City arms, by *Kempe & Co.*, 1895.

VICTORIA ART GALLERY, Bridge Street. By *J. M. Brydon*, 1897–1900. A Baroque Revival continuation E of Brydon's N wing to the Guildhall. Two storeys, Doric rather than Corinthian. Blind first-floor façade, nine coved niches with alternating pediments. In the central niche, flanked by Ionic columns and pilasters, a marble statue of Queen Victoria, 1897, by *Andrea Lucchesi*. In the NE corner a semicircular entrance with canted ground floor. Doorway with an open pediment on blocked half-columns, in an arched recess. Paired Ionic columns in the first floor. Above, a meticulously restored leaded dome with oculi in the base. A single bay returns s into Grand Parade.

Off the circular entrance vestibule is a fine C17-revival stone staircase with mahogany newels, bulbous balusters and handrail, under a barrel-vault. Over the vestibule, a rotunda with six Bassae-order Ionic columns of Devonshire marble supporting a coffered dome with Signs of the Zodiac. Beyond is a top-lit picture gallery with a cast of the Parthenon frieze paid for by the architect.

ASSEMBLY ROOMS, Bennet Street. A large and noble block by the *younger Wood*, 1769–71.* Tucked away behind the Circus in an unimaginative setting. Originally called the New or Upper Rooms to rival the earlier ('Lower') Assembly Rooms, they were built by subscription to serve the fast-expanding upper town, and quickly became the centre of Bath society. In the early C20 the Assembly Rooms declined; the Ballroom became a cinema, the Tea Room a saleroom and market. Through the generosity of Ernest Cook, the Society for the Protection of Ancient Buildings (SPAB) rescued the building and gave it to the National Trust in 1931, who let it to Bath City Council. Restored by *Mowbray Green* with *Oliver Messel* as interior designer; reopened in 1938. Bombed in 1942, it was again restored in 1956–63, by *Sir Albert Richardson* with *E. A. S. Houfe*, and interiors once more by *Messel*. David Mlinaric

pp. 132, 133

---

* *Robert Adam* submitted a design, rejected as too expensive.

Bath, Assembly Rooms.
Watercolour by T. Malton, 1779

redecorated the principal rooms in the 1970s and, after collapse of plaster in the ballroom, the *David Brain Partnership*
carried out major restoration, 1987–91, with redecoration
based largely on Mlinaric's scheme.

The building consists of a U-shape of tall blocks, with a
single-storey centre to the w, the N side in Bennet Street with
seven upper windows with pediments, the s with nine more
closely spaced windows. The s side has square attic windows,
but the other façades gain strength from much plain walling
between windows and entablature. The Ballroom occupies the
entire N block; like the shorter Tea or Concert Room to the s,
it rises through two storeys. On the s side there were also
smaller public rooms. On the E side is a large Octagon (originally Card Room) with a full-height canted bay, the Ballroom
and Tea Room forming three-bay flanks. In the centre of the E
elevation is the Card Room, a lower addition of 1777 with pedimented N and s ends; architect unknown. Along the N front
runs a one-storey Doric colonnade for sedan chairs. This
returns along the w side as a plain corridor (rebuilt 1963) and
forms in the centre between the arms of the U the projecting
entrance portico. Inside, a corridor leads into a small octagonal hall in the centre of the building, top-lit with four chimneypieces. This opens into the three main spaces, which
interconnect elsewhere for ease of circulation.

The 105-ft (32-metre) BALLROOM has the proportions
1:1:2.5, i.e. a double cube and half-cube. The lower walls terminate in a Greek-key frieze. Above, a colonnade of forty
attached Corinthian columns and pilasters – garlands between
the capitals – frames clerestory windows and niches. Above the

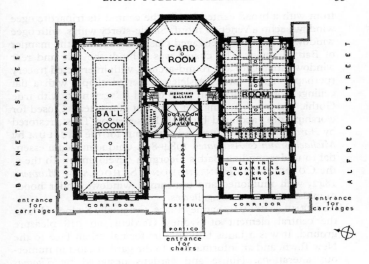

Bath, Assembly Rooms.
Plan

entablature, a coved ceiling springs from a Vitruvian scroll frieze. Five ceiling panels contain elaborate plaster roses. In the middle of its S side is a wide apsidal orchestra gallery, the iron balustrade with lyre decoration. The TEA ROOM, 60 ft by 40 ft (18 by 12 metres), has a splendid two-storey six-column screen in stone at its W end, Ionic below, Corinthian above, creating a magnificent Antique effect. The wall is set back, forming an entrance vestibule with a musicians' gallery. The other walls are treated like the Ballroom, the upper columns continuing around the room. Here however the bays of windows and niches create a double rhythm. Above the entablature is a continuous pedestal with trellis decoration, from which spring foliated bands in line with the columns. These rise up the cove and cross over one another on the ceiling, creating square and rectangular panels, originally with further embellishment. The gorgeous CHANDELIERS in both rooms are among the most important to have survived from the C18. The OCTAGON, 48 ft (15 metres) in diameter, is more simply treated, and relies on its shape for impact. The round-headed windows have Gothick glazing bars. The basement MUSEUM OF COSTUME opened in 1963.

BUILDING OF BATH MUSEUM, The Vineyards, Roman Road. Built in 1765 as the COUNTESS OF HUNTINGDON'S CHAPEL, for Selina Hastings, Countess of Huntingdon, a prominent figure in the Evangelical movement, 'to protect the residents from the evils of Bath society'. Among the first efforts in the Gothick style at Bath, and the first with ecclesiastical associations. The architect is uncertain. An exceedingly pretty little villa façade, the Countess's house, 1765–91; embattled front with a broad canted bay in the centre. Its tripartite ogee windows echo a Venetian motif. Single-storey wings, with ogee windows separated by engaged cluster columns in the manner of Batty Langley. The chapel was behind: the side and rear windows are bigger and round-arched, with intersected tracery (perhaps slightly later). Aisleless galleried chapel with a flat ceiling; Horace Walpole in 1766 called it 'very neat, with true Gothic windows', adding 'yet I am not converted'. Closed for worship 1981; acquired by Bath Preservation Trust, restored by *Aaron Evans Associates* and fitted out for the MUSEUM by *Michael Braun & Associates*, 1984–8. A unique museum essential to understanding Bath's Georgian development. To the S, the COUNTESS OF HUNTINGDON'S SCHOOLS, by *Manners*, 1842, with mullioned-and-transomed windows under hood-moulds. Now museum galleries.

HOLBURNE MUSEUM, Sydney Place. Originally Sydney House, the central element of Sydney Gardens, an C18 pleasure ground. It was a Janus building; its formal urban face to the New Town, and an informal face to the gardens, lost in numerous alterations. House and gardens designed by *Thomas Baldwin*, 1794, but modified in execution by his pupil, *Charles Harcourt Masters*, 1796–7. The house contained coffee, tea and card rooms, a ballroom on the first floor, and a pub in the basement for servants barred from the gardens. Originally three storeys, with the portico and rusticated ground storey as now, but with wings. In 1836 *John Pinch the Younger* added an attic storey when it became a hotel. Altered 1911–16 as a museum for the William Holburne art collection by *Sir Reginald Blomfield*, who reduced the four storeys to three, forming lofty galleries. An impressive five-bay façade, static and square, with rusticated ground floor and a bold pedimented Corinthian portico over a round-arched entrance loggia. Pedimented first-floor windows on thin pilasters and consoles. Five square second-floor windows were replaced by Blomfield with swagged medallions, a touch of *dixhuitième*. Over Pinch's plain attic cornice is Blomfield's parapet, with blind balustrading over the centre, flanked by brackets and vase finials. In place of the wings, Blomfield added single-storey Doric colonnades with rusticated end piers. Railings restored in 2000. Facing Great Pulteney Street, a charming pair of WATCH BOXES, 1830s, among the best surviving parish lookout posts anywhere. Each face has Tuscan pilasters and coved recesses, and an entablature with a triglyph frieze.

The building's rear formed one end of the gardens' central axis, a focus for entertainments. There was a first-floor conservatory over a loggia with Doric columns. From the middle bay of the conservatory projected a canopied orchestra stand on Corinthian columns, with a panel at ground level for transparencies. The building further embraced the garden with curved wings of private supper boxes, from where the concerts could be viewed. Blomfield swept it all away for an uninteresting staircase extension. An enormously contentious

glass-and-concrete rear EXTENSION by *Eric Parry Architects* [123]
was built 2009–10. Overtly new, with glazing below and vertical fins of blue-green ceramic above.

Educational buildings

CITY OF BATH COLLEGE, James Street West. 1957–63, by *Sir
Frederick Gibberd*. Dominated by a large general-purpose
block, with a raised projecting lecture theatre and pentagonal
assembly hall expressed as free-standing sculptural forms. The
scale and form are utterly alien to its context.

ST ANDREW'S SCHOOL, Julian Road. A delightful single-storey
building by *Nealon Tanner Partnership*, 1991. To the road, protective rubble base pierced by porthole windows. A colourful
steel-frame structure supports the roof, pierced by playful
metal vents.

WALCOT SCHOOLS (former). *See* p. 164.

BATHWICK ST MARY SCHOOL, St John's Road. 1841, by *Pinch
the Younger*. Tudor style. Additions probably of 1868. Sensitively
converted to housing by *Esmond Murray Architects, c.* 2002–5,
with two crisp new houses behind.

BLUE COAT SCHOOL (former), Upper Borough Walls. By
Manners & Gill, 1859–60, for 120 pupils. Jacobean with an
eclectic Flemish flavour. Extravagant five-stage corner bell-
tower, with clock, engaged columns and steeple, a reference to
the former building (1728, *William Killigrew*). Within, a Roman
tessellated PAVEMENT discovered during construction.

KING EDWARD'S SCHOOL (former), Broad Street. A distinguished Palladian building of 1752–4 by *Thomas Jelly*, erected
by the City Council. Two storeys, the bays 1:3:1, centre slightly
forward. Eared window architraves, on the ground floor with
segmental pediments and pulvinated friezes. Pedimented Ionic
doorcase. The main cornice modillioned. Each wing has a
balustraded parapet running into a large pediment with the
city arms. (Finials in the form of busts, carved by *Plura*, disappeared in the late C20.) The piers to the forecourt are contemporary, the connecting stone balustrading is early C20.
More than a hundred boys were taught in one large classroom.
Boarders slept upstairs. Vacant at the time of writing.

KINGSWOOD DAY PREPARATORY SCHOOL, off Sion Hill
Place. By *Feilden Clegg Design*, 1991–5. It cuts into the hillside
with a stepped section. Service accommodation forms the N
wall. Classrooms along the front, opening onto terraces for
summer. Between, a top-lit 'street'; at the E end is a top-lit
assembly space. The walls are load-bearing brickwork; zinc-
clad roof, with laminated bowstring trusses. For the senior
school, *see* p. 182.

Hospitals

ROYAL NATIONAL HOSPITAL FOR RHEUMATIC DISEASES,
Upper Borough Walls. Originally the General Hospital, then

Mineral Water Hospital. Primarily set up for the visiting poor to receive mineral-water treatment, it was built in 1738–42 by the *elder Wood* who gave his services free. His initial design was for a circular building. Ralph Allen and Beau Nash both contributed. Originally two storeys with basement for staff accommodation, reflecting the C18 'country house' approach to hospital design. Eleven-bay block with three-bay attached giant portico of Ionic columns. Attic storey added *c.* 1793 by *John Palmer*. Severely damaged in 1942. Eleven-bay W EXTENSION by *Manners & Gill*, 1859–60, and remarkably for that time, in similar style. Tympanum carving by *H. Ezard Jun.* of the Good Samaritan. Apsidal chapel (E side) with stained glass by *Wailes*. Central hall with big wooden staircase in Palladian Revival style. The extension has a fragment of Roman MOSAIC of blue and white swastika-meander design, *c.* 9 ft by 7 ft (3 metres by 2 metres), below street level. Probably part of a much larger pavement in a C4 dwelling.

For the Hospital of St John the Baptist, *see* p. 143. For the former United Hospital, Gainsborough Street, Bellots and St Catherine's hospitals *see* p. 144.

Railway stations

BATH SPA STATION, Dorchester Street. Part of *Isambard Kingdom Brunel*'s Great Western Railway. The Bristol to Bath section opened in 1840, Bath to London in 1841. The station buildings straddle a twenty-arch viaduct between two river bridges. A glazed roof over platforms and lines, similar to that at Temple Meads, Bristol (pp. 282–3), was replaced in 1897 by part-glazed platform canopies. The two-storey front faces N along Manvers Street, with an asymmetrical shallow-curved wing to the E, to resolve the street alignment. Front with arched ground-floor openings, Jacobethan ovolo-moulded mullions above, then three curved Flemish gables. *Porte cochère* on cast-iron columns, 1880s.

GREEN PARK STATION, Green Park Road. Architect *J. H. Sanders*, 1868–9, for the Midland Railway. An effort to impose polite Georgian conformity on a station façade. Rusticated ground floor, six first-floor Ionic columns flanked by pilastered pavilions, glazed cast-iron *porte cochère*. Forthright TRAIN SHED with much delicate detailing, by *J. S. Crossley*, Midland Railway chief engineer. A 65-ft (20-metre) cast- and wrought-iron vaulted glazed roof with small trusses over the platforms to either side. Little effort was made to reconcile the two structures where they meet. Closed 1966. Restored by *Stride Treglown Partnership*, 1982–4. The booking hall is a brasserie, the station houses shops, market and car parking.

Other public buildings

POST OFFICE, New Bond Street, 1923–7 by *Archibald Bulloch* of the *Office of Works*, distinguished and competent

Neo-Georgian, blending with its period neighbours without copying. Entrance at the narrow end, a Doric rotunda vestibule with a Venetian window above (cf. Gibbs's Mary-le-Strand, Westminster).

LEISURE CENTRE, North Road. On the S side of the Recreation Ground; visually intrusive. By the *City Architect's Department*, consultant *Sir Hugh Casson*, 1972. Concrete-framed, reconstituted stone infill, curtain walling to the entrance on the S side.

Park

ROYAL VICTORIA PARK, 1829–30 by *Edward Davis*, a pupil of Soane. A remarkably early British public park, pre-dating J. C. Loudon's Derby Arboretum (1839), and Paxton's park (1843–7) at Birkenhead. Instigated by local businessmen to improve the fields S of Royal Crescent, it includes ornamental plantations, walks and drives.

By the park gates in Royal Avenue, a WAR MEMORIAL, 1923; the standard design by *Sir R. Blomfield*. Raised on a plinth in a curved and rusticated recess with bronze lions, references to *E. Davis*'s adjacent RIVERS GATE. This has Soanian piers and arches, and classical *Coade* stone lions on top, 1833, from the Masonic Hall in York Street. Here and at the Marlborough Lane entrances, splendid new cast- and wrought-iron GATES were fitted in 2008, closely following those scrapped in 1942.

Just beyond in ROYAL AVENUE (W side), ROYAL VICTORIA PARK PAVILION, 1997, by *C. G. Davies*, timber-clad around a steel structure, with projecting eaves and a deck to the S. Further W, N of Royal Avenue, the outrageously large KEMBLE VASE, mid-C19, sculptor *S. S. V. Pieroni*. W again, centred on Royal Crescent, a BANDSTAND, *c.* 1887 by *C. E. Davis*; parabolic roof continuous with the walls, for sound reflection. Flanking it, a pair of Carrara marble VASES, a gift of Napoleon to the Empress Josephine, 1805. Possibly designed by *Percier & Fontaine*. Set in French AEDICULES of Portland stone, bequeathed 1874. N of Royal Avenue, a HA-HA of *c.* 1774–7 runs E–W.

Beyond Marlborough Lane, W, VICTORIA GATE, 1830, by *Davis*: a pair of severely trabeated, primitive Greek Revival triumphal arches. Centrepiece of the entrance is the VICTORIA COLUMN, 1837, by *G. P. Manners*. A crisp triangular obelisk on a base guarded by lions, within a circular balustrade. Adjacent (N), PARK FARM HOUSE, 1831. A charming *cottage orné* with splendid bargeboards, tall octagonal chimneys, oriels and hoodmoulds.

Davis's park layout followed the principles of Humphry Repton and J. C. Loudon. The drives were improved by *William McAdam*, 1835–43. The park W of Marlborough Buildings is quieter and more densely planted. In the NW quadrant, the BOTANICAL GARDENS. 1887, extended 1926. Within, N side, the TEMPLE OF MINERVA, a pavilion built by the Corporation for the 1924 Wembley Exhibition; re-erected here

1926. It has a three-bay colonnade with double columns. The
Jacobean strapwork parapet (s) has 'Aqua Sulis' in pierced
letters, the E parapet, 'City of Bath'. On the N side of the carriage drive, in the Great Dell, the SHAKESPEARE MONU-
MENT; a Roman altar, by *C. E. Davis*, 1864. Just NE, a colossal
Bath stone BUST of Jupiter, 1835–8 by *John Osborne*, on a
19-ft (6-metre) stepped plinth by *James Wilson*, 1861.

Bridges

In order, going downstream:

CLEVELAND BRIDGE, Cleveland Place, by *H. E. Goodridge*,
1827, for the Duke of Cleveland. Among the finest Greek
Revival bridges, combining the Antique with expressive use of
new materials. A single 100-ft (30-metre) span of parallel segmental cast-iron arches springing from stone piers. Heavy cast-
iron railings. Four handsome Greek Doric porticoed lodges,
from Stuart and Revett's *Antiquities of Athens*. Reconstructed
1928, strengthened 1992.

73   PULTENEY BRIDGE. 1769–74, built by William Johnstone Pulteney to *Robert Adam*'s quite original design. The idea of lining
a bridge with shops to a coherent plan has few precedents. It
connects Bathwick to the city, and was key to the development
of Pulteney's Bathwick estate (p. 173). Three segmental arches.
The upper structure is now much altered, but the s, downstream elevation retains a strong flavour of the original. Central
pavilion with an open pediment and a great Venetian window,
and wings with pavilion features over each pier. Square end
pavilions on the abutments, with domes and pediments and,

Bath, Cleveland Bridge.
Engraving after T. H. Shepherd, 1829

originally, porticoes facing outward. On the street elevations the flanks each have three arched shopfront openings with doorways between. All this sounds monumental. In fact, it is surprisingly small and friendly in its dimensions. In 1792 *Thomas Baldwin* added a storey, removed the porticoes and altered the shopfronts. After the NW pier collapsed, *John Pinch the Elder*, surveyor to the Bathwick estate, appears to have reconstructed the N side in 1802–4 to a plainer design and a deeper plan. The voussoirs to Adam's tripartite centre, evident on the street elevation, are all that remain of the original. In 1902–3 *Gill & Morris* demolished the SW pavilion for street widening, and rebuilt it to an Adam-style design in place of the three end shops. Adam's S river façade was well restored, except for these asymmetrical alterations, by *J. F. Bevan Jones* (drawings 1937, completed 1951). The timber shopfronts mostly date from a restoration of 1975 by *Vivian & Mathieson*, based on the 1880s model of Nos. 1–2, NW side.

NORTH PARADE BRIDGE, 1835–6, by *W. Tierney Clark*, engineer. The original structure was cast iron with rusticated ashlar piers. *F. R. Sisson*, City Engineer, rebuilt the span in ashlar in 1936–7. The bridge continues as a viaduct to the E, with two Jacobethan LODGES, 1835–6.

SKEW RAILWAY BRIDGE, Claverton Street. Built by *Brunel* in 1840, in timber. Two spans on a central pier in the river. Rebuilt in 1878 with wrought-iron lattice girders (strengthened with steel, 1960s). The line continues W above the roads on a Tudoresque VIADUCT by *Brunel*. Castellated parapet, four-centred arches, two-stage buttresses. Facing the city, a centre-piece flanked by semi-octagonal turrets with arrow slits.

CHURCHILL BRIDGE, Broad Quay, with a separate FOOT-BRIDGE, E. Single spans in concrete, opened 1964–6, replacing the Old Bridge (rebuilt 1304; enlarged 1754, 1847).

VICTORIA BRIDGE, Victoria Bridge Road. A suspension bridge by *James Dredge*, a local engineer, completed in 1836. Like all suspension bridges of the period, it uses chains of wrought-iron strips. They diminish in cross-section towards the middle. Its design principle differs in that the suspension rods are mounted at increasing angles towards the centre, spreading the load of the deck. Impressive ashlar pylons with tapered piers flanking a plain arch beneath a pedimented entablature. It was the prototype for more than a dozen in Great Britain and overseas; this is the only intact survivor.

For New Bridge *see* p. 210.

PERAMBULATIONS

1. *Central Bath, the south and south-west*

First (1a), the old city, including the former Abbey precinct, Bimbery – an area associated since the Middle Ages with healing and the mineral waters – and the Saw Close. (1b) explores how Wood the Elder and others made fashionable the E fringe between city and river, with the construction of streets, promenades and, later, the railway.

1a. The old city, to the south and west

We start in ABBEY CHURCH YARD, N of the Pump Room (p. 122). Opposite, Nos. 6–9, a late 1790s terrace by *Palmer*. E of these, a pleasant row of individual houses. Nos. 11 to 13 are early C18, No. 13 refronted and heightened, early C19. No. 14 was GENERAL WADE'S HOUSE. Wade – a founder of the city's fortune – probably lodged there. The house is of *c.* 1720, that is pre-Wood; the architect not recorded; possibly *Thomas Greenway*, or *Wade*'s own design. Above the ground floor the façade is a glorious showpiece, divided into equal bays by five giant fluted Ionic pilasters; probably the first use in Bath of the Palladian giant order over a basement storey. Provincial details – an even number of bays, window sills below the base of the Order, undersized Ionic volutes. The first- and second-floor windows are similar in size, with handsome garlands in between. An attic storey has panelled pilasters and a clumsy 'added-on' feel, both typical of *Nathaniel Ireson*, another possibility as architect. Restored for the Landmark Trust by *Brain & Stollar* in 1976. No. 15, attributed to *Greenway*, is also of *c.* 1720. Above the ground floor, superimposed pilasters at the angles and flanking the arched central windows. The first floor is Ionic with a straight pediment, the second floor Corinthian with a segmental pediment (cf. No. 14 Westgate Street and General Wolfe's House, Trim Street).

SHOPFRONTS. No. 15, *c.* 1850, with pilasters and four-centred arches. General Wade's House exceptionally fine, *c.* 1830, with double quadrant-ended bays and a continuous fanlight over. No. 13, *c.* 1830–5, attributed to *Edward Davis*. Soanish pilasters with incised decoration. Nos. 11–12, High Victorian with thickly carved cartouches. No. 10, by *Price & Titley*, 1875, smaller, with elaborate brackets. No. 8, *c.* 1830–40, with earlier arched openings behind, is designed for large square panes.

KINGSTON PARADE, the open space S of the Abbey, was the site of the cloister. Turning l. into YORK STREET, an oblique view S to Ralph Allen's town house (*see* below). Immediately E, the FRIENDS' MEETING HOUSE, 1817–19, built as a Masonic Hall, proves *William Wilkins* to be more severely Grecian than any of the Bath architects. Pedimented portico with four fluted Ionic giant columns based on the Erechtheum; the wings have single windows, originally blind. Within the portico is a symbolically blind doorway. The Great Room has two circular glazed lanterns. Opposite, Nos. 11–15, a terrace of equally severe design (lease 1819), perhaps also *Wilkins*. Eleven bays with giant pilasters rising from the ground. The capitals, entablature and three-bay pediment reflect the Masonic Hall.

Turning s into Terrace Walk (*see* p. 146), at once w is North Parade Passage. Off North Parade Passage to the s, NORTH PARADE BUILDINGS (formerly Gallaway's Buildings) completed 1750, a blind alley angled against the medieval wall. Probably by *Thomas Jelly*. First-floor windows alternately pedimented and corniced. Most have pedimented doorcases with Corinthian columns or pilasters, unusual for speculative lodging houses.

No. 4 North Parade Passage, SALLY LUNN'S HOUSE, is a rare example in Bath of an early Stuart house (as is the almost identical house next E, now part of the Huntsman pub). Four-storeyed with gables and inserted sash windows. Built by *George Parker* (lease 1622). Bowed mid-C18 shopfront. No. 3, also 1622, has an C18 façade. No. 2, RALPH ALLEN'S HOUSE, is of the same C17 type, refronted in the C18. Full-height C17 and early C18 panelling inside. Allen, a sub-tenant from 1718, acquired the lease in 1727 and built a detached E-facing wing at right angles behind, visible from a private alley off Terrace Walk. Allen later built Sham Castle (*see* p. 195) to improve his view. The design is traditionally attributed to *Wood the Elder*. However, Wood's *Description of Bath* (1765) is ambiguous: 'the Designs, as well as a Model for this Addition, were made while I was in London.' Like a miniature Roman temple, but oddly tall and narrow; three bays, a rusticated ground floor with a wide arched centre, and giant engaged Corinthian columns above. The large arched central window and the flanking lights suggest a Venetian motif here. In the side bays fleshy garlands. Steep ornamented pediment with torches on ball finials. The façade to the older house (l.) has matching garlands and cornice.

67

w of North Parade Passage is ABBEY GREEN, a delightfully irregular little square of late C17 or early C18 houses. On the corner of North Parade Passage, No. 2 (building agreement 1698) has mullioned windows in the s façade and gables to the rear. There are probably areas of timber framing behind render. Mid- to late C18 front. No. 3 to the s, late C17, has the remains of a double gable, a bolection-moulded doorcase, and voussoirs of the original narrow window openings. Mullioned windows to the sides. Rear wall timber-framed, probably contemporary. The s entrance to Abbey Green is ST MICHAEL'S ARCH, by the *City Architect*, 1973, an elliptical rusticated archway. On the w side, the CRYSTAL PALACE TAVERN, *c.* 1780, probably by *Thomas Baldwin*, with pavilion ends emphasized by arches below, pediments above. Doorcase pediment on delicately carved brackets.

At No. 1, N side, and to r. and l. in Church Street and Abbey Street, several houses with uniform elevations, built *c.* 1762 by *Jelly* and *Henry Fisher*, mason. No. 1 Abbey Green and No. 2 Church Street have nice staircases: carved tread-ends, two twisted balusters per tread, broad ramped handrails. No. 2 Abbey Street, ELTON HOUSE (*c.* 1699), has an irregular ground plan following earlier boundaries. In the basement a fine Baroque stone buffet with shell-hood, and an elaborate external doorcase, implying a ground-level rise in the C18.

Gabled rear wings N and S, the former with bolection-moulded stone fire surrounds. Soon after 1749 an ashlar façade was added and the rear recess infilled with a broad staircase, rounded at the half-landing for a sedan chair. A double-bowed shopfront was added to the NE frontage c. 1800. No. 4 is a fine Palladian house of 1756, probably also by *Jelly* (cf. his North Parade Buildings). The first-floor windows have two straight cornices and one pediment in the middle. Fine Corinthian pedimented doorcase, with the earliest wooden fanlight in Bath.

W along YORK STREET, on the l. is BATH CITY LAUNDRY, 1887–8, by *C. E. Davis*, adapted from a Dissenting chapel. Ionic pilastered ground floor, fanciful Baroque attic storey with pilasters on animal-head consoles. This returns to form an elliptical-arched 'bridge' over York Street, to bring water from the Queen's Bath (*see* p. 122).

W into Stall Street and a little to the N, BATH STREET is the finest piece of formal planning at Bath, by *Thomas Baldwin*, begun 1791. Part of the Bath Improvement Act of 1789 which replaced the medieval street pattern, it runs E–W from the King's Bath to the Cross Bath. Especially attractive for its modest size. Ionic colonnades of twenty-one bays on each side, varying in height to accommodate a gentle slope. These gave shelter for sedan chairs carrying patients between baths. They open into a semicircle to embrace the King's Bath (the NE segment truncated 1869) and into another at the W end. The upper façades have platbands with Vitruvian scrolls, the principal windows pediments and friezes with swags and paterae, on long, thin consoles typical of Baldwin. On the S side, Nos. 6–7 have *Baldwin*'s original shopfronts. Elegant console brackets and fanlights. N side rebuilt behind the façade for offices 1963, and again in 1988–9 by *Rolfe Judd Partnership* for shops. The replaced shopfronts have no doorways and do not step down the fall of the street. The development extends beyond the semicircular NW segment with a weak and incorrect classical façade, an unwelcome intrusion. The SW segment now forms part of the New Royal Bath complex (*see* p. 128). At the end, No. 8 Bath Street, the HOUSE OF ANTIQUITIES by *Palmer*, 1797, a small, early purpose-built museum for the Corporation. Niches in the façade contain statues from the C17 Guildhall of King Edgar and the mythical King Coel.

Closing the W end of Bath Street is the CROSS BATH with the nearby HOT BATH (*see* pp. 127–8). This area, known as Bimbery, had baths made fashionable from the late C16. Facing the Hot Bath are Hetling Court and Chapel Court. At the entrance from HETLING COURT on the l., S side, the four-column Tuscan portico of the HETLING PUMP ROOM, 1805, perhaps by *Harcourt Masters*. Now a visitor centre for the New Royal Bath.

Attached, to the W, is ABBEY CHURCH HOUSE (formerly Hetling House), big and gabled with a medieval core in the basement, perhaps once the ground level. At the E end two blocked openings, one pointed-arched; probably an original window and door. These remains are possibly part of the medieval St John's Hospital. The rest of the house, facing W onto Westgate Buildings, was built *c.* 1550 by John Clerke M.P., and extended E after 1591. It has a few original windows, a good staircase, and a big C16 chimneypiece in the Great Chamber with fluted Ionic columns, an overmantel with tapering termini-pilasters, and some strapwork. Most other internal features from a refurbishment of 1888. Bombed 1942, restored 1949–51. The W front and most of the block S of the Great Chamber were completely rebuilt.

On the N side of Hetling Court is the HOSPITAL OF ST JOHN THE BAPTIST, arranged around Chapel Court and entered from Westgate Buildings. Founded *c.* 1180 by Bishop Reginald Fitzjocelyn, providing homes for poor men and a priest under the Prior of Bath. The complex structures are dealt with chronologically. Earliest, in the SE corner behind the Cross Bath, is the chapel of ST MICHAEL, rebuilt in 1723 by *William Killigrew.* The first classical chapel in Bath. The apsidal interior is single-height but has two-storey windows, segment-headed below, circular above. Altered by *Browne & Gill,* 1879, with deplorable Venetian tracery; stained glass by *Ward & Hughes.* James Brydges, Duke of Chandos, built or rebuilt most of the rest as speculative lodging houses. His architect was *John Wood the Elder,* who had recent experience of London developments. First, in 1726–7, the lodging house on the N side of the courtyard. Varied window surrounds: on the ground storey, keystones that merge with a band course; above, architraves, a continuous sill and pulvinated friezes; on the second floor, eared architraves; modillion cornice. Rebuilt behind the façade in 1953–6 as FITZJOCELYN HOUSE. Inside is a fine stone Baroque buffet with shell-hood, from No. 15 Westgate Street. Then followed in 1727 the principal building on the E side, now JOHN WOOD HOUSE. This incorporated parts of the two-storey hospital of 1580, with colonnaded almshouses below and lodgings off a gallery above. The sober and dignified front has a heavy ground-floor arcade on pillars; above, the architecture matches Fitzjocelyn House. The back, facing the Cross Bath, was restored in 1991. Next, in 1728, was a range of lodging houses to the N, now demolished. In 1729–30 CHANDOS HOUSE was built to the W, a plain five-bay three-storey front facing N, renovated 1982–4. Good balustraded staircase. Nos. 4 and 5 adjacent (E), 1760s, were built by a carpenter, *William Sainsbury;* old-fashioned and provincial. No. 5 has a curious serpentine stair-rail, a showpiece of carpentry. The S side of Chapel Court was rebuilt in 1965–9 by *Alan Crozier Cole* as almshouse flats with a Master's Lodge. Echoing the Georgian buildings they replaced, but with aluminium windows and replica pre-Georgian gables. A lift shaft behind has a big Doric entablature.

An archway leads from Chapel Court through the colonnade of John Wood House to Hot Bath Street. Then S and E into BEAU

Street. At the w end, the GAINSBOROUGH BUILDING, originally the UNITED HOSPITAL, 1824–6, is by *John Pinch the Elder*. Bold and severe, unlike his delicate domestic work. The original building is like Wood's General Hospital (*see* p. 135), of eleven bays with a four-column attached Ionic portico and pediment, except that here the columns start on the first floor. *Manners & Gill* added a heavy attic storey and the Albert Wing in 1861–4. Their chapel of 1849 was rebuilt by *Wallace Gill* in 1864; *Browne & Gill* added another chapel in 1897–8.

Next to the e is BELLOTS, a C17 spa hospital poorly rebuilt by *Cotterell & Spackman* in 1859. Small façade with a slightly projecting centre, in ashlar with odd, splay-cut surrounds. Contrasting sandstone relieving arches, rather eyebrow-like. Lord Burghley's coat of arms of 1609, from the original building. In Bilbury Lane (N), ST CATHERINE'S HOSPITAL, of early C15 foundation, rebuilt 1829 by *G. P. Manners* in Tudor style around a courtyard. Converted to flats, 1986.

e along Beau Street, Stall Street is rejoined. Little of interest remains s of here. On the e side, MARKS & SPENCER, 1961 (additional storey, 1970) by *Monro & Partners*, among the better post-war commercial buildings in the s of the city. Also Neoclassical and of 1961, the former WOOLWORTH'S by *W. B. Brown*. Returning n across Bath Street, on the l. stood the Grand Pump Room Hotel by *Wilson & Willcox*. Demolished for the bland colonnaded ARLINGTON HOUSE, 1959–61, by *Wakeford, Jerram & Harris*.

To the n and at once w is WESTGATE STREET, the principal medieval e–w thoroughfare. No. 14, THE GRAPES HOTEL, the façade of *c*. 1720. Seven bays, four storeys; the centre bay framed by Doric three-quarter columns below, Ionic above and Corinthian at the top, under a broken pediment. In the first-floor drawing room a fine early C17 ceiling with thick ribs and heraldic escutcheons, the oldest remaining plasterwork of Bath. The e side has a C17 mullioned window and two blocked early windows. Opposite, Nos. 27–29 are a single composition, late C18. Further w (Nos. 22–23), the Egyptian-style former cinema of 1911–12. Extended 1920; interiors re-fitted 1926, both by *A. J. Taylor*. Façade with rusticated pilasters with stepped Art Deco drops. Classical auditorium; shallow-vaulted ribbed ceiling. No. 21, formerly the County Wine Vaults, confident 1870s Italian palazzo style, near the site of the medieval West Gate.

To the n, SAW CLOSE, originally an open space bounded n and w by the city wall; used from the C16 as a timber yard and for other industrial uses. By the 1850s there were pubs and wine merchants. On the sw side, the SEVEN DIALS development by *Aaron Evans Associates*, 1991. A successful essay in contextual classicism enclosing a courtyard, on a triangular site. Curved s end with a Doric colonnade and canopied balcony under a lead dome. Facing Monmouth Street (w), good ramped elevations to accommodate the slope. Stepped colonnade on the e, a little heavy-handed.

In the NW corner of Saw Close, the Theatre Royal foyer (*see* p. 172) is the principal house of a group of four by *Thomas Greenway*, 1720, extending W into St John's Place. Beau Nash lived there from 1743. Three storeys; E façade six windows wide; the S, five. Late Baroque, the mouldings characteristically overdone, as are the volutes to the door hood. (Wood the Elder: 'none but a Mason, to shew his Art, would have gone to the expense of those Enrichments.'). The Garrick's Head pub occupies part of the ground floor; over the entrance a bust of Garrick by *Lucius Gahagan*, 1831. *C. J. Phipps* added the brash *Rundbogenstil* ticket office and vestibule in 1862–3. Its northern neighbour was BEAU NASH'S SECOND HOUSE until his death in 1761. A later and more refined example of *Greenway*'s building. Three-bay entrance façade, five-bay return. Fine Corinthian doorcase – arched opening, rusticated surround, and a lion's head keystone. Two eagles on pedestals stand on the door hood. Sash windows with heavy ovolo glazing bars. The plan is simple but effective. Entrance hall with a small room to the r. and a fine staircase beyond an arch to the l. Ahead, the main room has three windows on the long E side, originally almost abutting the city wall.

Opposite, E side, is the PAVILION MUSIC HALL, built into an older structure in 1886. Remodelled as a theatre by *Wylson & Long*, 1894–6; new frontage with a two-storey loggia with giant flanking pilasters. Altered in 1956–7 as the Regency Ballrooms, now a bingo hall. To the N, on the corner of Upper Borough Walls, the former Bluecoat School (p. 135).

On Barton Street, N, the former Unitarian church (p. 119). Off to the E is TRIM STREET, begun 1707, the first C18 development to breach the medieval N wall. Now spoilt by TRIMBRIDGE HOUSE (the City Planning Office) on the NW corner, by *John Bull & Associates*, 1970. It at least conforms to the scale of the street. Incised moulding links the windows and an abstracted reference to giant-order pilasters marks the entrance. Opposite, a group of three houses dated 1724, with characteristically framed windows and keystones. One fine stone shell-hood. E of these, on the corner of Trim Bridge Street, an early house showing twin gable-ends. To the N, an arch known as TRIM BRIDGE, formed after 1728 as a carriageway to Queen Square (p. 152). No. 5, GENERAL WOLFE'S HOUSE, is florid provincial Baroque of *c.* 1720. Wolfe lived there briefly. Two storeys and five narrow bays, rusticated angle pilasters, doorway with fluted Ionic pilasters and segmental pediment. The window above has fluted Corinthian pilasters and another segmental pediment. The sashes later, as are the military trophies over the door. Gabled rear elevation. Unusual stone-panelled hall. The staircase has twisted balusters, the ground-floor front room an arched sideboard recess with plaster decoration.

Trim Street leads S to UPPER BOROUGH WALLS, where part of the medieval battlemented WALL survives, much repaired. Opposite, Parsonage Lane, and the parallel Bridewell Lane (W), part of the city's grid-pattern streets, probably of Saxon origin. In PARSONAGE LANE, on the w side, is a rare early, large-scale BREWERY (a lease of 1810 describes a 'newly built' brewhouse). Converted to the *Bath Chronicle* printing works in the 1920s, then to flats and retail in 1996–9 by *Aaron Evans Associates*, part of a scheme stretching w to Bridewell Lane.

1b. *South-east of the old city*

Here we deal with the SE sector, around the axis of Grand Parade, Pierrepont Street and Manvers Street. N of the Abbey is the REBECCA FOUNTAIN (1859–61), with marble statue and basin. It faces ORANGE GROVE, originally the churchyard of Bath Priory. From the early C18 a fashionable shopping area, landscaped in the 1730s with gravel walks. Beau Nash erected the OBELISK in 1734. During Bath's brief late C19 resurgence as a spa, *C. E. Davis*, City Architect, improved the area and remodelled the TERRACE on the s side in 1895–7. This plain row built 1705–8 was given gables, an angle turret, and shell-hoods to the first-floor windows. Opposite, N, the former POLICE STATION AND LOCK-UP of 1865 by *C. E. Davis*. A small but suitably bold palazzo, with three deeply recessed round-headed windows on the *piano nobile*.

Dominating all is the former EMPIRE HOTEL, by *Davis*, 1899–1901. Confident to the point of bombast. Five storeys with, for good measure, two attic storeys and a higher angle tower, once higher still. A large Loire-style gable and two smaller ones, Norman-Shavian tile-hung, sit side by side. Their scalloped architraves, along with numerous balconies, were removed when the Admiralty requisitioned the building in 1939. The river front is in the same frolicsome spirit. What can have gone on in the architect's mind? Elegant entrance canopies by *A. J. Taylor*, 1907. Little-altered ground-floor public rooms with heavy classical decoration. The first floor had suites with private sitting rooms. Demolition was averted in 1995–6, when *PRP Architects* converted the upper part into retirement flats and added a conservatory, s side. As part of the hotel scheme, *Davis* created GRAND PARADE on the E side, connecting Pulteney Bridge and Orange Grove.

The latter continues s into TERRACE WALK, its angle dictated by the medieval wall. The Lower Assembly Rooms (1709, rebuilt 1824) stood on the triangular space here. On their site a resited FOUNTAIN, 1859, by *Pieroni*. The houses at the N end are of *c.* 1728, behind late C18 fronts. No. 1, The HUNTSMAN pub, probably by *Wood the Elder*, was built as a house and shop, 1748–50. C18 stone shopfront: four Ionic half-columns, three arches, the middle one depressed and wider. Heads on the keystones, leafy spandrels.

To the E, PARADE GARDENS, never built up from its riverside level. From the 1730s it became a garden associated with the Parades (*see* below), designed by *Wood*. *Davis*'s COLONNADE supporting Grand Parade, with Italianate balustrading, now forms the NW boundary. Laid out by *Mowbray Green & Hollier*, 1930s, recalling Wood's formal plan, with a domed Doric KIOSK. To the S is *Wood the Elder*'s next major enterprise after Queen Square. NORTH AND SOUTH PARADES, with Pierrepont Street (W) and Duke Street (E), are one composition, a great square block laid out in 1738, built 1740–8; a fragment of the vast Royal Forum projected to extend S and E from here (*see* Introduction, p. 100). None of the houses faces the river. The long ranges have projecting ends and centres and central pediments, North Parade, Duke and Pierrepont Streets with twenty-five bays (3:7:5:7:3), South Parade twenty-nine bays (3:7:3:3:3:7:3). Costly foundations up to 18 ft (5.5 metres) high were required. Wood planned for the N and S ranges a palace treatment like that of Queen Square, with giant Corinthian orders; reduced at the insistence of developers to implied orders. Platbands, continuous first-floor sills, straight window cornices at the first floor, and modillion cornices. The windows altered, most balustrades removed. Some rear staircase bows for sedan chairs.

NORTH PARADE (originally Grand Parade) was intended as a shady summer promenade. Centre five-bay house with a full-width saloon on the *piano nobile*. In the garden of No. 14 (on the riverside) is DELIA'S GROTTO, a small pedimented folly with arched alcove. Duke Street runs S to SOUTH PARADE, intended for autumn and winter promenading. Started 1743; plots were still being assigned in 1749. Malton's view of 1775 shows front-area balustrades, urns at the parapet corners, and an obelisk finial on the pediment. Only No. 1 retains its balustraded parapet. Prominent (S) is St John the Evangelist (p. 119).

Now W to Pierrepont Street, a little N, then on the W side through ST JAMES'S PORTICO, by *Wood the Elder*, c. 1745: an opening through the ground floor of Pierrepont Street, with four Tuscan columns. Behind is PIERREPONT PLACE, a pleasant backwater. At No. 1, c. 1730, an Ionic pilastered doorcase with pulvinated frieze, and later pineapple finials. Inside, the best plasterwork of that moment at Bath: acanthus foliage, busts of the Four Seasons, a Baroque shell niche with a head. The continuation S, OLD ORCHARD STREET, has on the E side the MASONIC HALL, originally the Theatre Royal, by *Thomas Jelly*, 1750, enlarged by *John Palmer*, 1775. In its day the most important theatre outside London. It became a Roman Catholic chapel in 1809, then a Freemasons' hall in 1866. The exterior is undistinguished, the interior gutted. MANVERS HALL, W side, dated 1853, was a Roman Catholic school until 1868, now a chapel. The adjacent car park, S, has fragmentary remains of the C4 TOWN WALL, rebuilt in medieval times.

Old Orchard Street meets New Orchard Street, running W with NORTHWICK HOUSE, S side, 1962, by *E. Norman Bailey & Partners*, the first of Bath's stone-clad nonentities of this period. At the NE corner of HENRY STREET, the continuation E, PIERREPONT HOUSE and adjacent, N in Pierrepont Street,

KINGSTON HOUSE, *c.* 1808, form part of the projected, but never completed, Kingston Square. Pierrepont Street continues S as MANVERS STREET. Nos. 1–2 here, *c.* 1845, possibly by *Underwood,* are severe Greek Revival, commoner in Bristol and Cheltenham than here. *A. J. Taylor* linked them to Underwood's Blenheim House (*see* Swedenborgian church, p. 121) with a single-storey extension, 1924–5. Converted to a bank, 1975. On the E side, a little S, the nondescript reconstituted stone POLICE HEADQUARTERS by *J. G. Wilkinson,* Bath's Chief Planning Officer, 1962. S again, BAYNTUN'S BOOK-SHOP AND BINDERY by *F. W. Gardiner,* 1901, originally the Post Office sorting office, bold and convinced, conceding nothing to the Georgian tradition. Big arched ground-floor openings, mullioned-and-transomed windows, four gables and nice rainwater hoppers; converted by *Mowbray Green & Hollier,* 1938. The formal approach to the railway station (p. 136) is made by a pair of quadrant façades, late 1840s, originally the Royal (E) and Argyle (W) hotels. Laid out in accordance with the Great Western Railway Act, 1835. At least the ARGYLE HOTEL is probably by *H. E. Goodridge,* the railway's surveyor for this area. Giant Ionic columns and pilasters turn the corner, giving each façade equal importance. Tripartite first-floor windows with blind fanlights. Ground-floor frieze with good Grecian motifs. Closing Railway Place to the E, RALPH ALLEN HOUSE, possibly by *Underwood, c.* 1840; of three bays with banded rusticated pilasters.

W of the station, DORCHESTER STREET skirts the redeveloped Southgate shopping precinct (*see* below). On its S side, the BUS STATION, by *Wilkinson Eyre, c.* 2006–9, replacing the Neo-classical Churchill House (*W. A. Williams,* 1931–2). A steel-and-glass design with low wings and a tall drum, already nicknamed the Busometer, at the corner towards Churchill Bridge. To the N at the junction of St James's Parade and Somerset Street, the contextually classical FORUM cinema, by *W. H. Watkins & E. Morgan Willmott,* 1933–4, with an exceptionally complete Art Deco interior. Curved corner entrance with four giant Corinthian columns. 2,000-seat fan-shaped auditorium with cantilevered balcony and figured classical friezes. Now a church.

SOUTHGATE PRECINCT. By *Chapman Taylor,* scheme design 1996, built 2006–10. A mixed development of shops, restaurants and some flats, replacing a much-reviled shopping centre (*Owen Luder Partnership,* 1969–72). An improvement, but only because of its open streets rather than subterranean passage-ways, and because the plan provides at last for a clear diagonal avenue from the bottom of Stall Street to the station. For the architecture Bath's planners retreated yet again to the supposed safety of Neo-Georgian – here of the skimpiest sort. Like wearing paste jewellery to a coronation, Neo-Georgian is hardest to get away with when cheek-by-jowl with the real thing. The Bath stone cladding is only 2 in. (50 mm.) thick. The over-long façades, for that is all there is to consider, have

various Palladian and Neoclassical motifs side by side, untram-
melled by subtleties of scale or detail. And those details are
quite inadequate to the scale of the rest. Bath should be
ashamed.

2. The north-east city and its suburb

Showing the impact of the Bath Improvement Scheme of 1789.
From Abbey Church Yard, w through Baldwin's Pump Room
colonnade into STALL STREET and heading N, we meet the
main E–W thoroughfare: Cheap Street running E (see below),
and Westgate Street (see p. 144) running w. Curving round the
SE corner, No. 21 Cheap Street, the ROUNDHOUSE pub (formerly Abbey Wine Vaults), 1897 by C. E. Davis, with three
splayed bar windows. Diagonally opposite, No. 1 Union Street
was refronted and heightened by Willcox & Ames, 1885. In
French character, with profuse ornament and giant Corinthian
pilasters.

UNION STREET to the N was laid out by Baldwin as part of the
Bath Improvement Act, and built 1805–10. Nos. 6–8 (w side)
formed the centrepiece, a typical Baldwin composition with
paired Corinthian pilasters, garlands and rosettes. Nos. 9–11
refaced to match as a department store by Browne & Gill in
1891–2, sacrificing symmetry for unity. Nos. 23–25 (E) are
modern facsimiles. No. 20 has a C19 façade with engaged Ionic
colonnade at first floor. To the N, the w entrance to The Corridor (see below), and Upper Borough Walls, running E–W,
indicating the N boundary of medieval Bath.

Turning E into Northumberland Place and straightaway S,
UNION PASSAGE, parallel to Union Street, is an intimate thor-
oughfare of shops, rebuilt by Baldwin under the Improvement
Act with plain three-storey fronts. NORTHUMBERLAND
PLACE continues E as a charming narrow paved street with C18
buildings. At No. 7, a shopfront of c. 1820 with reeded pilasters
and lions' head capitals. Ahead, above the archway to High
Street, a pediment with the Coade stone arms of Frederick,
Duke of York and Albany. Turning S, Union Passage meets
CHEAP STREET, widened and refronted c. 1790, under the
1789 Act. Nos. 15–19, S side, are by Baldwin, with Doric
columns framing good shopfronts. On the N side, A. J. Taylor
rebuilt Nos. 5–6 (1925–9), along with other Georgian façades
in this part.

Continuing E into Orange Grove (see p. 146), to the l. through
Brydon's Baroque screen to a courtyard dominated by the
beautiful E façade of Baldwin's Guildhall (p. 129). To the E, the
slipway to the C14 EAST GATE. A narrow postern, with a
shallow pointed arch externally and a segmental arch internally. The city wall to the N survives in undercrofts. To the l.,
Newmarket Row includes the river frontage to the MARKET,
part of Baldwin's Guildhall complex of 1775. A modest two-
storey façade, with pediment and arched entrance. The market
within was rebuilt by Hickes & Isaac, 1861–3. Concentric

arcades around a twelve-sided dome on a drum with lunettes. Stone columns, of an indeterminate order, support the cast- and wrought-iron roof structure. Further arcades give access from E and W.

Returning E, onto GRAND PARADE, by *C. E. Davis*, 1890–5 (*see also* p. 146), raised on a long Doric colonnade. It overlooks PULTENEY WEIR, rebuilt 1968–72, architect *Neville Conder* of *Casson & Conder*, as part of flood-control measures. For Pulteney Bridge, *see* p. 138.

Clockwise past the Empire Hotel (p. 146), the N face of the Abbey makes a splendid ensemble with the Guildhall, which fills the E side of HIGH STREET. The street is probably of Saxon origin, and historically Bath's market place and its civic heart. At the S corner of Cheap Street, No. 13, early C18, has equal-sized upper windows, a pre-Palladian practice. Nos. 9–10 on the N corner, by *C. E. Davis*, 1895, are curved with large arcaded first-floor windows. Nos. 11–12, the CHRISTOPHER HOTEL, were C17 tenements. Rebuilt in bland Neo-Georgian in 1955; gutted and a rear C17 part demolished, 1997–8. Nos. 15–17, THE OLD BANK (now NatWest), were rebuilt above the base-ment by *Dunn, Watson & Curtis Green*, 1913–14. Standard Neo-Georgian; coffered domed banking hall.

Nos. 18–19 are the fashionably Grecian façade of THE CORRI-DOR, a speculation of 1825 by *H. E. Goodridge*, among the ear-liest outside London of this new building type. Originally of twenty-six units, now much altered, it is some 200 ft (65 metres) long, connecting with Union Street. Both entrances have Doric columns and pilasters renewed in red granite in 1870. At High Street, the three-bay centre is recessed between narrow pavilions, and has a first-floor pediment on consoles. In the attic, three lunettes and a wreathed pedestal. Tunnel-vaulted glazed iron roof of 1870 (originally wood-framed), but a double-height centre with an iron-balustraded gallery for a band. Frieze with wreath decoration (cf. the Choragic Monu-ment of Thrasyllus, Athens). Several shopfronts of 1870, tall of plate glass with quadrant heads. In 1833 Goodridge built the Corridor Rooms, miniature assembly rooms, behind the S side and entered between Nos. 7 and 8.

Next N on High Street, the dreary HARVEY BUILDING, 1964–6 by *North & Partners* under *Sir Hugh Casson*. Considered con-textual at the time; stepped plan, false mansard roof (then quite new and influential). To the r. is BRIDGE STREET, built in 1769 as the approach to Pulteney Bridge. On the S side, the Victoria Art Gallery (p. 131). At No. 7, an excellent Corinthian shopfront, *c.* 1830. *W. J. Willcox* rebuilt No. 9 in 1903 with giant Corinthian pilasters and urns on the parapet.

NORTHGATE STREET, directly N from High Street, lies almost entirely outside the medieval North Gate (dem. 1754), the principal entrance to the city. No. 17 has a curved shopfront by *Browne & Gill*, 1880–1. Opposite (W side), the PLUMMER RODDIS BLOCK, rebuilt by *Alec French Partnership*, 1980–3. It replicates its late C18 predecessor, except for the Tuscan colonnade. The front to Upper Borough Walls has double-height openings with cast-iron window frames and spandrels; a well-mannered intervention without pastiche. Nos. 2–3, C18, have Neo-Victorian shopfronts as part of the scheme.

On the N corner of New Bond Street is the 1920s Post Office (p. 136). Opposite, E side, the PODIUM, 1987–9 by *Atkins Sheppard Fidler & Associates;* shopping mall, supermarket and library. A crudely designed atrium leads to the river. Unconvincing and half-hearted classicism, using an architectural language foreign to its Georgian context. It has the merit of turning the reviled Hilton Hotel (p. 178) from a free-standing block, visually unconnected with its setting, into part of a quasi-terrace.

Ahead is St Michael with St Paul (p. 118) at a sharp corner in the *point-de-vue* up Northgate Street. Off W is GREEN STREET, laid out in 1717, and markedly old-fashioned, having escaped later planned interventions. No. 14 is a good four-storey gabled house with close-set sash windows. Broken segmental pediments over the outer windows. Shopfront *c.* 1850–60; cf. that at No. 19. No. 15 too is gabled. No. 3, set back on the N side, shows the transition from C17 vernacular; three gables, hood-moulds and a good shell-hood. First-floor sashes with bolection-moulded surrounds. Returning E, Nos. 4–6 are of 1769. Nos. 7, 8 and 8a, single-storey shops, 1908.

BROAD STREET runs N from St Michael: a medieval suburb with substantial early C18 survivals. Many older buildings survive behind Georgian façades. On the W side, No. 3 has a C17 roof structure suspended inside the present one, and (visible at the rear) a complete and rare section of C17 timber framing with brick-nogging. No. 7a has a rear outshut of *c.* 1680. In the N wall is a long four-light ovolo-mullioned window and a former doorway all under one dripmould (seen from Shires Yard – *see* below). Stone mullioned windows to the S side, behind a Late Georgian front block. On the E side, from S to N, No. 42, the small-scale SARACEN'S HEAD, *c.* 1700, dated 1713, has two gables, quoins and openings with chunky bolection surrounds. No. 41 of *c.* 1720, an early attempt at classical design, perhaps by *William Killigrew.* Quaintly asymmetrical, four windows wide with stone architraves and keystones. Superimposed orders with a pedimented entrance bay. Victorian shopfront. No. 38 had a datestone of 1709 (removed). An excellent example of the period, four-storeyed and twin-gabled, with quoins, heavy bolection surrounds and string courses at each floor. Shopfront, 1883. Through a gap on the W side, SHIRES YARD is a shopping arcade by *Bristol Team Practice,* 1988, in a folksy Cotswold vernacular. A pleasant courtyard then two awkward levels of shop inserted between old gutted buildings, linking with Milsom Street.

Further up on the W side is the former King Edward's School (p. 135). Finally, on the E side further N, the former YMCA, of 1887–8 by *T. B. Silcock,* with heavy but good classical detail, e.g. giant Ionic pilasters.

3. Queen Square, the Circus and Royal Crescent

QUEEN SQUARE begins the most important architectural sequence in Bath, enabling us to study the style and mind of *John Wood the Elder* at their best. After gaining experience in the building trades on big London developments, Wood settled at Bath in 1727. Queen Square, 1728–36, his first venture, marked the start of the upper town in earnest, setting fresh standards in scale, boldness and social consequence. Its great innovation is the treatment of a whole side of a square as one palace-like façade. This Wood did on the N side, a composition with a central emphasis. The E and W sides were conceived like wings enclosing a forecourt, though practicalities caused Wood to modify his plans here. The concept of individual dwellings as a single, unified composition was partly inspired by Inigo Jones's Covent Garden Piazza (1631–7), while the square plan perhaps echoed Wood's reconstruction in his *Description of Bath* of the Roman camp which he believed formed the basis of the city. A more direct influence was his familiarity with the design of the builder-architect Edward Shepherd for the N side of Grosvenor Square, London (*c.* 1720–5). This was intended as one palatial composition, influenced by Colen Campbell's first design for Wanstead House, Essex, published in *Vitruvius Britannicus* in 1715. Wood's N side of Queen Square fulfils Shepherd's thwarted design and is architecturally more assured and robust. Dean Aldrich's design for Peckwater Quadrangle, Christ Church, Oxford (1706–10), may also have influenced Wood.

The palace façade provided a sense of domestic grandeur that none of its tenants could afford individually. Wood financed the venture by leasing a site and sub-letting plots to builders (*see* pp. 49–50), stipulating the overall design while minimizing his own financial exposure. Additional land was leased as work progressed. The first of a series of ninety-nine-year leases was obtained from the ground landlord, Robert Gay, in 1728; building began in 1729. Wood had already sent Gay his plans for Bath in 1725. The square was to have been levelled, but the extra cost was risky for a speculative development.

The N SIDE, a terrace of seven (Nos. 21–27), is the grandest side of the square, and indeed one of England's grandest Palladian compositions before 1730. Twenty-three bays arranged 3:6:5:6:3, with rusticated ground floor, and a giant attached portico. Big pediment with three floriated vase finials. The columns are Corinthian, as at Wanstead. Richly decorated entablature with modillion cornice below a plain parapet. The pavilion ends have matching columns, and attic storeys in place of pediments. Distinctive impost mouldings to the ground-floor openings, and a plain band course above. Tall first-floor windows with plain pilaster strips and alternating pediments. Their original balustraded aprons were lost when the sills were lowered in the C19; the glazing bars mostly restored. Originally the basement areas had stone balustrading. Most houses retain dog-leg oak staircases with turned balusters, three per tread; some twisted balusters (e.g. No. 27).

Circumstances prevented Wood from building the W SIDE of Queen Square to match the E. Instead, he chose an equally monumental treatment: two broad villa-like corner blocks, identical in elevation, of seven bays and two-and-a-half storeys with a slightly projecting pedimented centre and a rusticated ground floor. Centre ground-floor openings in blind arches; flanking windows with Gibbsian frames, alternating pediments and massive keystones. The three centre first-floor openings have pilasters and alternating pediments. The returns are pedimented and the N corner block, Nos. 18A–20, has a pedimented rear façade. At No. 20 a side doorway with attached Ionic columns and pediment, a favoured Bath motif throughout the C18. Nos. 14–15, the S pair, retain three vases on the pediment. Originally the central house sat well back. In 1830 this was demolished and the forecourt infilled by the *younger Pinch* with three Neo-Grecian houses. *Mowbray Green & Hollier* converted them in 1931–2 for the BATH ROYAL LITERARY AND SCIENTIFIC INSTITUTION. Requisitioned 1940, reoccupied 1993. Projecting centre with raised attics, and fluted engaged Ionic columns (Wood's giant columns are always unfluted). Above the first-floor windows, a crisp anthemia and honeysuckle frieze. The ground-floor front rooms retain segmental niches with paired Ionic columns, the staircases of the outer houses, cast-iron balusters with Greek motifs. In the ceiling of the main first-floor room, four oval painted panels by *Andrea Casali*, 1750s, of Pan, Ceres, Pomona and Mercury. Bought at the Fonthill sale, 1823, reinstalled here 2003.

No. 15 has the grandest stair-hall in Bath, occupying the whole width of the front (as at Nos. 7–8 Circus below). It connects just the ground and first floors; a lesser staircase serves every floor. The staircase, removed in the 1920s, was re-created by *Donal Channer*, 1984–6. It ascends around three walls to a gallery landing. Fluted Corinthian newels, pilastered ramped dado. Lively stucco decoration to the upper floor, attributed to the *Lafrancini* brothers. The S wall has St Cecilia at the organ, framed by a moulded *trompe l'œil* archway. Niches at each side contain statues of female musicians and on the E wall stands a mythical figure with cymbals. Framed panels W and N depict musical subjects. The cove has acanthus scrolls and putti.

CHAPEL ROW, W, has a more modest stepped terrace by *Wood*, mid-1730s; all now have shopfronts. No. 1, at the E end, has an elegant late C18 doorcase at the side, with waterleaf capitals. The proprietary Chapel of St Mary, the first in Bath, was built on the N side in 1732–4 by a consortium including *Wood*. It was a fine temple after Inigo Jones's St Paul Covent Garden, though Doric not Tuscan. Demolished 1875. The aedicular MONUMENT, placed here 1976, is said to be constructed from its relics.

The s SIDE of Queen Square (Nos. 6–13) is less palatial. Middle pediment just three bays wide. The only other accent the blank arches around the ground-floor windows in the outer three and middle nine bays. The E section, by then part of the FRANCIS HOTEL, was bombed in 1942. *J. Hopwood* rebuilt it in 1952–3. Uncompromisingly C20 E extension facing Barton Street, 1977–80, by *Oxford Architects' Partnership* with much input by *Roy Worskett*, City Architect. Vertically articulated ashlar façade with bronze-anodized oriel windows.

The central GARDEN has a tall OBELISK of 1738 in honour of Frederick, Prince of Wales. Originally it rose from a circular pool and was 70 ft (20 metres) high. The trees are, of course, a Picturesque addition; the square was originally planted with low parterres. Stone balustrading was replaced in the 1770s by boundary railings (present railings 1978).

The s side extends E into WOOD STREET. The N side, Nos. 1–6, formed with No. 1 Queen Square the first phase of *Wood*'s development from 1729. Three storeys with a band course and cornice, otherwise plain. Nos. 1–6 have Corinthian shopfronts, 1871–4 by *J. Elkington Gill*. For the difference between *c.* 1730 and *c.* 1780 in Bath, see NORTHUMBERLAND BUILDINGS on the s side, a very fine Adamish composition of seven houses, the first speculative venture of *Thomas Baldwin*, 1778. Projecting pavilion centre and ends with pediments. Above the first-floor centre is a festooned frieze, continued to the sides as a band of scrolls, with large paterae over. For the first time in Bath in a consistent terrace the attic is brought forward as an extra storey. The result is top-heavy.

The simple E SIDE of Queen Square (Nos. 1–5), six substantial five-bay houses stepping uphill, matches the initial houses of Wood Street. The doorways are treated individually with especially elaborate Baroque designs at Nos. 2–3, probably commissioned by Richard, Earl Tylney of Castlemain and Wanstead House.

No. 41 GAY STREET, 1734–6, by the *elder Wood*, forms the NE angle of Queen Square. Here Wood's severity is replaced by heavy but cheerful Gibbsian-Palladian details. The diagonal corner has an applied semicircular bow. Ground-floor windows with heavy Gibbs surrounds, even heavier blocked Ionic columns above. Ionic doorcase with an arch and a grotesque mask keystone. Ingeniously planned, with a diagonally placed centre room of surprisingly modest dimensions. A semicircular bow flanked by fluted Corinthian columns is answered by a bow at the back. The room above, similarly planned and more spectacular, has a Venetian window in the bow with fluted Ionic pilasters, a curved pedimented Ionic doorway, and a matching chimneypiece. S of the entrance hall, tucked into a small triangular space created by the main room, is a charming powder cabinet containing a shell niche with a basin. Other rooms with corner fireplaces. Centred against the N wall is a good staircase. Despite the plaque, there is no evidence that either of the Woods lived here.

p. 102

Now a short detour along OLD KING STREET, E from the NE corner of Queen Square. At the SE corner is BONHAMS Auction Rooms, by *R. S. Redwood*, 1962, Neo-Greek Revival. At the E end, the irregular gabled back of Jolly & Sons' department store (*see* p. 161), by *J. Elkington Gill*, 1869, and *Browne & Gill*, 1885 (the two N gables). Half-timbered oriel by *C. E. Davis*, 1888. BARTON BUILDINGS off to the N is by *Wood the Younger*, 1760s. The first use in Bath of the ramped string course and cornice to link houses that step uphill. At the N end (rear of No. 34 Gay Street), a simple weatherboarded photographic studio by *H. J. Garland*, 1882, for W. Friese-Green.

Now to the N, up GAY STREET. The lower end as far as George Street is by the *elder Wood*, 1735–40, related to the E side of Queen Square, with string course and cornice broken at each step up. Continued to the same design by the *younger Wood* after 1755 to form the principal approach to the Circus. On the W side, the S-facing return of No. 2 Gay Street has blind windows and a pediment: a contextual design by *Davis*, 1870, when No. 1 was demolished for a road to Royal Victoria Park (*see* p. 137). In QUEEN'S PARADE PLACE behind No. 24 Queen Square, a pair of sedan chair attendants' LODGES, with Gibbs surrounds. Further up Gay Street, W side, No. 8 is an individual job for Prince Hoare, the sculptor. Corinthian pilasters on the ground and first floors frame the centre. Garlands over the ground-floor windows; the pediment over the upper middle window runs on into the architrave of the side windows. Here and in a few other places, one is led to believe that some had tired of the Woods' chastity.

CIRCUS. Gay Street runs straight into the Circus, the most monumental of the *elder Wood's* works. It would be even more so when seen as intended with the centre paved, and without the big central plane trees. Wood lived to see the foundation stone laid in 1754, but *Wood the Younger* carried out the work, granting leases for the SW segment, 1755–67, the SE, 1762–6, and the N, 1764–6.

Wood's architectural conception is original and powerful, yet the plan is very simple: three streets enter the Circus at even distances, none opposite another, giving the composition a static, enclosed, absolute character. A Circus so closed to the outside is very different from France, where aligned streets provide vistas, e.g. at Louis XIV's Place des Victoires. Moreover, the uninterrupted architraves close the circle tightly, like the hoops of a barrel. The Circus has one architectural motif only, carried through relentlessly without accents of height or relief. Coupled columns in three orders, Doric, Ionic, Corinthian, framing rectangular windows without architraves. The parapet, with later oval piercings, is crowned with acorn finials (a Druidic reference: *see* below). The metopes of the Doric entablature have 525 carved emblems including serpents, nautical devices and the Arts and Sciences. Most derive from a folio of no particular iconographic significance, *Emblemes* by George Wither (1635); others show fables,

Masonic devices and occupations; and some, of military trophies, are from the designs for Jones's palace at Whitehall (*see
also* below). Many were replaced in the 1950s. Linking the
second-floor Corinthian capitals are garlands and female
masks. This sustained depth of relief was something new for
Bath. In the C19 the first-floor windows were cut lower. The
glazing bars, reinstated in the 1950s, are too thin for the
1750s–60s. But the Circus retains most of its splendour.

The Circus represents a fusion of Wood's preoccupation
with Roman grandeur and his wild fantasies of Druidic civi-
lization, described in the *Essay* of 1749 (*see* p. 100). Tobias
Smollett, in *The Expedition of Humphrey Clinker* (1771), perceived the Circus as the Colosseum turned inside out; Soane
illustrated the comparison – disparagingly – in 1809. However,
Wood's building is circular, not elliptical like the Colosseum.
Wood possessed William Kent's *Designs of Inigo Jones* (1727)
which illustrated a proposal for Whitehall Palace, with an elaborately treated circular courtyard. He was familiar too with
Jones's theatrical reconstruction of Stonehenge, together with
William Stukeley's *Stonehenge* (1740) which asserts that the
megalithic circle had given Jones the idea for Whitehall. To
Wood the circle was perfect: 'the works of the Divine Architect . . . tend to a circular form' (*Origin of Building*, 1741).
In his *Essay* Wood imagined that this concept passed by revelation first to the Jews, then to the Druids. Wood deduced that
the first arch-Druid was none other than the legendary King
Bladud who, having established Bath, constructed the stone
circles at nearby Stanton Drew (q.v.), the precedent, according to Wood, of Stonehenge. Built into one of Stanton Drew's
circles, he supposed, was a Druid 'college', enclosing an area
'as spacious as the squares generally made in our modern
cities'. Significantly too, in *Choir Gaure, Vulgarly called Stonehenge on Salisbury Plain* (1747), Wood measures the diameter
of Stonehenge as 312 ft (95 metres), while the Circus encloses
318 ft (97 metres).

There are thirty-three houses set back behind wide areas:
ten in the N segment, eleven in the SW, twelve in the SE. Most
houses are three bays wide, some of four, and some have
entrances on the returns. These variations in width and
the irregular spacing of entrances usually passes unnoticed, since
the door openings, like the windows, are completely unadorned.
Much ingenuity was displayed in varying the plans. Nos. 7–8
p. 102
have front stair-halls, No. 9 has a groin-vaulted entrance hall,
and a stair-hall beyond, lit by a large Venetian window. Behind
the staircase a delightful little octagonal room with a coved
ceiling and a canted bay window. Above, the drawing room has
a good stucco ceiling. No. 10 has a Siena marble fireplace from
Beckford's Tower (*see* p. 184). Behind No. 11, a large colonnaded
garden building with round-arched openings.

Of the other streets leading into the Circus, Bennett Street to the
E (*see* p. 162) was built later, and does not form an overture to
the Circus. But BROCK STREET, leading W from the Circus,

is an understated prelude to the younger Wood's masterpiece. Eleven houses were built at the E end under leases granted by the *younger Wood* in 1763–70. In 1766 he acquired a further 19 acres in order to build Royal Crescent at the W end. Brock Street was lengthened to link with it. Flanking the start of Brock Street is a splendid pair of Doric porches to two Circus houses. Immediately beyond, more modest unornamented houses, generally with plain first-floor Venetian windows. On the S side, ground-floor Venetian motifs too, and many pedimented Ionic porches. Nos. 6–7 have interesting dovetailed plans giving No. 6 (where the younger Wood was a tenant in 1765) a wide back overlooking the Gravel Walk. MARGARET'S BUILDINGS, off Brock Street to the N, is an intimate paved street of shops that served these houses. Further W between Nos. 20–21, a semicircular archway that led to a chapel by the *younger Wood, c.* 1773, destroyed in the Second World War. Above the arch, a pedimented tripartite window with coupled Ionic columns. The composition is based on Hadrian's Arch in Athens, illustrated in Stuart and Revett's *Antiquities of Athens* (1762). No. 16, S side, has a fanciful Georgian Gothick porch with cluster columns, rare for Bath.

Brock Street gives no hint of the splendour to come until the very last moment. All one sees is the far end of Royal Crescent at an angle. The shock of arrival at the corner is one of the strangest and most pleasurable that town planning has to offer anywhere. It is tempting to say that this understatement was intentional, and to do so would place the scheme firmly within the English landscape garden tradition. But this is doubtful: like most Bath development, it is more likely the accident of site, topography and circumstance. Whether under different conditions the architect would have connected the Circus with Royal Crescent axially is uncertain, though the *Gentleman's Magazine* in 1754 stated that the connecting streets would be 'each terminated with a fine building'.

ROYAL CRESCENT was built in 1767–75 by *John Wood the Younger*. 70 Its large half-ellipse faces down a grassy slope towards Royal Victoria Park, originally fields. The elder Wood's developments were essentially urban and inward-looking. At Royal Crescent, his son continued the idea established at Queen Square of uniting a terrace with a classical palace frontage, but for the first time every resident overlooked a rural prospect, as if in a country house. Such an open composition was something quite new in town planning. With the advent of plate glass towards the mid C19, the Victorians intensified this contact by lowering the first-floor window sills.

Although construction began thirteen years after the elder Wood's death, something of the idea may be his. There are Druidic allusions in the name, the shape of the new moon, associated with pagan worship which according to Wood's *Essay* took place up the hill on Lansdown. Yet the plan-form is not a crescent; it is a half-ellipse, that is a half-Colosseum. As with Prior Park, compared in his *Essay* with an amphitheatre (*see* p. 201), Royal Crescent theatrically embraces its elevated site, overlooking, like a vast stage set, the landscape beyond. The extended arrangement of giant columns is an even more explicit reminder of theatre. A possible source is the colonnaded auditorium of Palladio's crescent-shaped Teatro Olimpico at Vicenza, based on his reconstruction of a Roman theatre, both of which Wood knew. He also owned a copy of Alberti's *Ten Books on Architecture*, in which theatres are said to take 'the shape of a moon in its decrease'. Royal Crescent thus fuses the palace tradition of Queen Square with theatrical and Druidic references. The symbolic crescent shape is so particular that it was to have few English successors. However, the palace façade was to be hugely influential, and recurs in big urban developments, e.g. by Baldwin at Bathwick (*see* p. 173) and the Adams in Edinburgh.

If the elder Wood's involvement is debatable, Royal Crescent's execution and details are undoubtedly by the *younger Wood*. Devoid of Druidic iconography, it has a completely plain ground floor, and engaged giant Ionic columns above. The entablature has a moulded architrave, plain frieze and modillioned cornice, and a balustrade. It is right that no emphasis on window or door pediments is allowed; 114 columns so closely set and so uniformly carried through are majestic, they are splendid. The only accents are subtle: coupled columns at the ends and around the central bay, where the first-floor window is arched.

The monumental semi-ellipse comprises thirty houses, three bays wide, except Nos. 14–17 in the centre and No. 30 on the end, which are four. The end houses, 540 ft (165 metres) apart, have five-bay returns that face forward, at 90 degrees to the ends of the curve. They were given a full architectural treatment as end pavilions, with coupled columns at the angles and central doorcases. No. 1, E end, was built first as a model to follow. Behind the uniform fronts is a diversity of plan, evident in the utilitarian, frequently angular rear façades.

p. 102

Several INDIVIDUAL HOUSES deserve mention. Going E–W, No. 1 (completed 1769, for Thomas Brock, Wood's co-lessee) was scrupulously restored by *Philip Jebb* and opened as a museum in 1970 by the Bath Preservation Trust. The window sills were raised to the original level, uniquely in Royal Crescent (conservation policy is now to retain C19 alterations). Entrance on the return, with a hall leading W to the dining room, E to the library, both plastered with sunk panels. Inner hall painted to resemble ashlar, with a wooden staircase. The first-floor layout similar. The reduced friezes are typically late C18. No. 2, bombed, was restored in 1948. The first-floor front room to No. 5 has an exquisite ceiling influenced by Adam, the corresponding ceiling to No. 12 a great circle of radiating strings connected by festoons with ribbon bows. Nos. 15–16 are the ROYAL CRESCENT HOTEL, restored in 1979 by *William Bertram & Fell*. No. 15 has an apsidal transverse hall and elegant curving cantilevered staircase with C19 cast-iron balusters. The first-floor front room has a deep foliated frieze and fine ceiling of earlier Palladian manner with birds with free-standing necks and wings. No. 16 is the hotel entrance. A large hall leads to a rectangular stair-hall with Venetian windows and a cantilevered open-well staircase. No. 17 was rebuilt in 1949 after war damage. The end house, No. 30, has fine Rococo ceilings.

Some interesting MEWS elevations face the gardens (for their street fronts, *see* p. 163). Late C18 coachhouse to No. 12, with a pedimented centre. Nos. 13–18 were all converted or rebuilt for the hotel between 1983 and 1998. No. 13 has an C18 Ionic temple front *in antis*. At No. 14, another temple front, a contextual design by *Hayward & Wooster*, 1877. To the rear of Nos. 15–16, the Neoclassical Dower House, 1985–6. The garden buildings to Nos. 17–18 are now the hotel's spa. No. 17 is by *James Wilson*, 1843, two storeys, five bays, with pavilion ends and monumental round-headed openings. No. 18, late C18 or early C19 Gothick. No. 19 has an excellent elevation by *Thomas Baldwin*, *c.* 1790. Projecting pavilion ends, each with a recessed round-headed window below a rectangular first-floor window flanked by half-pilasters with Prince of Wales's feathers as capitals. The pavilions flank an Ionic loggia. Above the cornice three garlanded panels with rams' heads, and a balustrade.

4. *Milsom Street to the upper town*

Commercial Georgian Bath, with its rich ensemble of later shopfronts, is the start of a gentle climb N to the residential upper town E of the Circus.

At the S end of Milsom Street is the attractive, pedestrian OLD BOND STREET. All one composition: on the w side, bland elevations typical of 1760s Bath (straight cornice, pediment, straight cornice); and on the E, of *c.* 1780, Venetian windows. Shopfronts: Nos. 7–8, magnificent double-bow fronts of *c.* 1800 with serpentine entablatures and typical reeded pilasters with lions' heads; w side, No. 14, 1955, Neo-Georgian, by *E. F. Tew*; Nos. 16–17, 1982, a pair of heavy pediments on Tuscan columns, by *Kenneth Boyd*; On the N end, E side, royal arms of *Coade* stone. The marble putto in the niche was part of the cross in the Cross Bath, dismantled in 1783 (*see* p. 127).

To the E is NEW BOND STREET, rebuilt for smart shopping, by *John Palmer*, 1805–24. The N terrace (1805) has paired houses separated by pilasters and ramped cornices. Elegant shopfronts, e.g. No. 12, and No. 19 by *A. J. Taylor*, 1906 and 1922; No. 21, typical mid-C19.

Returning to Milsom Street and a few yards N, QUIET STREET runs w. Nos. 7–11 (s side) are the former AUCTION MARKET AND BAZAAR, 1824–5, attributed to *Goodridge*. Nine bays, the three-bay centre marked by rusticated piers, below a segmental tripartite window with fanlight. Flanking round-headed niches containing statues of Commerce and Genius by

Gahagan. The centre of the parapet is stepped back, with a statue, a quotation from the Choragic Monument of Thrasyllus, illustrated in Stuart and Revett's *Antiquities of Athens*. Impressively large first-floor central room for exhibitions and meetings. Grecian and somewhat Soane-like, it is triple-square on plan with three shallow-domed ceilings, each with a glazed lantern, separated by segmental arches with Greek-key decoration. A large rear window corresponds to that at the front.

In 1871 the street's N side was cut back and refronted by *C. E. Davis*; debased classical. No. 1 JOHN STREET, facing W into Wood Street, has a façade of *c.* 1840. Three upper floors with triple round-headed windows flanked by panelled pilasters. Arcaded shopfront, 1858. In QUEEN STREET, off the S side, Nos. 2–3 and Nos. 11–11a (the latter originally a house); modest C18 double shopfronts with separate doorways, among the earliest in Bath, and flat-fronted oriel windows.

MILSOM STREET was laid out from 1761 to connect old Bath with the growing upper town. Developed jointly by the owning Corporation and their lessee, Charles Milsom; the street and first buildings were complete in 1768. Stepped houses linked by cornice, with bland elevations, the designer not recorded. *Thomas Jelly* was involved, and his partner then was *Palmer*; but Milsom's 1753 lease plans were drawn by *Robert Smith*, probably the churchwarden who made a design for a new church of St Swithin (Walcot). It remains the city's pre-eminent shopping street, with accordingly sumptuous shopfronts.

N of Green Street, No. 47 (E side) is 1780s by *Thomas Baldwin*; giant Ionic order and a rusticated ground floor. Restored by *Herbert W. Matthews* for a bank, 1908. It incorporates No. 2 Green Street on the return, rebuilt in a conforming style, 1930 and 1959. To the N, No. 46 has a façade of 1900 with Baroque touches, by *T. B. Silcock & S. S. Reay*, who had offices here.

p. 104
Behind, entered through a covered passage, is the most fashionable and elegant of Bath's proprietary chapels, the OCTAGON by *Timothy Lightoler*, 1766–7. The octagon plan was occasionally adopted for later C18 English churches, and favoured especially by the Methodists for preaching. The hidden exterior is a plain, windowless rectangle. Spacious interior 39 ft (12 metres) in diameter, with a gallery on eight unfluted Ionic stone columns. The gallery fronts have C20 plaster decoration. Entablature with a festoon frieze, then a shallow octagonal dome with delicate plasterwork, strings of husks, and a circular window in each facet. The saucer-shaped lantern sits on a drum decorated with swags. The ground floor has partly surviving recesses for invalids, two with fireplaces. Excellent wrought-iron chancel SCREEN with foliate decoration. Converted for the Royal Photographic Society by the City Architect *Roy Worskett*, 1978–9, which it remained until 2000.

p. 161
Further up, E side, SOMERSETSHIRE BUILDINGS, Nos. 37–42, five speculative houses by *Baldwin*, 1781–3. As city architect Baldwin could depart from the uniform street elevation in favour of a different scale and splendour. His composition is

Bath, Somersetshire Buildings.
Aquatint by T. Malton, 1788

on the palace-front principle, though the distance is lacking to appreciate the seventeen-bay façade. Rusticated ground floor with arched openings; a wide bowed centre and pedimented end pavilions with giant attached Corinthian columns. Balustraded first-floor windows, and above the centre windows panels with rams' heads and festoons. Lion-mask frieze. No. 42 has a red granite ground-floor bank front, 1892. At No. 41, the original ground-floor design was reinstated as the entrance to Shires Yard, 1988 (see p. 151). At No. 39 (centre), a bank since c. 1783, the ground-floor front room has one of the finest ceilings of its date in Bath; a large circular panel with delicate husk and drapery festoons, rams' heads, paterae, foliage and ribbons.

On the w side, Nos. 7–14 are JOLLY'S department store, opened in 1831, initially at No. 12. Partially C19 shopfronts, unified during refurbishment in 1994–5. Nos. 11–13 has the most extravagant in Bath, by *C. E. Davis*, 1879, colonnaded, with stone, polished granite, bronze and mahogany, deeply cut lettering, Art Nouveau fascias and bronze cartouches. Peacock friezes, leaded clerestory windows and strapwork within. The first-floor front rooms retain domestic vestiges. Continuing N, E side, No. 32 has an elegant front by *Silcock & Reay*, 1902, with mirrored soffit. No. 17, w side, had a Corinthian-columned shopfront, c. 1840, rebuilt and extended across No. 18 in the C20.

A pair of Italian palazzo BANKS form the N corners. No. 24, E, dated 1865, is by *Wilson & Willcox*, extended and altered 1884. Baroque in feel: a red granite corner entrance; ground floor rusticated, giant Corinthian columns above. On the w corner, No. 23, 1873–5, by *G. M. Silley*, with Ionic giant pilasters and lions' heads in the cornice. Extended by three bays to Milsom Street, 1890.

GEORGE STREET runs E–W at the top of Milsom Street; it was lengthened to the E when Milsom Street was laid out. Turning W, on the S side, Nos. 2–3 are *c.* 1760. Shopfront by *Wilson, Willcox & Wilson*, 1874, reusing Corinthian columns. Nos. 4–7 are a modest terrace, *c.* 1800. Nos. 8–12, mid-C18, are part of *Wood the Elder*'s Gay Street development (*see* p. 155). No. 11 has an exceptional Art Nouveau-influenced front of 1909 by *Spackman & Son*, with curvilinear glazing bars, bevelled glass clerestory and fanlight, and mirrored soffit.

A special feature of the N side of George Street at this W end (and many other streets of Bath) is a wide pavement raised high above the street, here with sturdy late C19 cast-iron railings. Off to the N is MILES'S BUILDINGS, a paved enclave by *Wood the Younger*, *c.* 1766–8. Nos. 3–4 have first-floor Venetian windows. Further E on the N side of George Street are EDGAR BUILDINGS, nine houses developed with Milsom Street from 1761. Projecting ends, and a pedimented centre terminating the view up Milsom Street. The centre first-floor window of each house pedimented. To the E, PRINCES BUILDINGS, *c.* 1764–5, of the standard *Jelly* type. Opposite (S side) is the ROYAL YORK HOTEL. By *Wood the Younger*, 1755–9; a long plain façade (6:7:6) with slightly projecting centre. The first-floor windows have cornices and a continuous sill. Remnants of a rear stableyard survive.

BARTLETT STREET climbs N from George Street. A little way up, on both sides, a former department store (Evans & Owens); tall Corinthian-pilastered shopfronts by *Browne & Gill*, 1882. The W side has a terracotta entrance arch, and paired first-floor windows with pilasters. E façade rebuilt 1892, by *Browne & Gill*. Bartlett Street leads N to *Wood the Younger*'s Assembly Rooms of 1769–71 (p. 131) and its surrounds: Alfred Street, Bennett Street and Russel Street, built simultaneously. Here one feels an absence of planning. Standard elevations with only slight variations; the upper windows have architraves, the first-floor windows, cornices too. ALFRED STREET, 1768–76, flanks the Assembly Rooms' S side. The SE range (Nos. 1–7) is symmetrical, with middle and ends projecting slightly, and a central pediment. No. 14 has an elaborate doorway with a bust of King Alfred over. Unusual C19 iron-work: an overthrow lampholder, conical torch-snuffers, and a windlass for lowering objects into the area. To the N, BENNETT STREET was built in 1770–6, along with RUSSELL STREET off its N side. Its lower W side has unmoulded first-floor Venetian windows.

5. *Marlborough Buildings to Roman Road*

A broad arc N and E from Royal Crescent, following several intact Georgian developments.

MARLBOROUGH BUILDINGS, W of Royal Crescent, brings Georgian Bath to an abrupt end. The long terrace, on the W side only, was developed from 1787. Ground floors rusticated with plain arched openings, a characteristic motif of the ending C18. Entirely plain above, except at Nos. 13–15, terminating the vista across from Brock Street. Here, pedimented first-floor centre lights in shallow arches, and floral festoons above the flanking windows. Larger rooms at the back, staircases to the front. Many houses at the N end have C19 and early C20 porch towers with bathrooms above.

Turning E at the top, in CRESCENT LANE are several good COACHHOUSES for Royal Crescent (see p. 159 for their garden elevations). No. 17, 1843 by *James Wilson*, has a yard flanked by wings with open pediments. No. 15, part of the Royal Crescent Hotel's Dower House, 1985–6, is by *William Bertram & Fell*; C18 gatepiers. For St James's Square to the N, see p. 165. Bounding the N side of the green here is JULIAN ROAD, approximately on the line of a Roman road; heavily bombed in 1942. At the W end, St Andrew's church (p. 116), and the adjoining school (p. 135). NORTHAMPTON STREET runs N from here, developed from 1791. *Baldwin* prepared designs but *Pinch* took over. Nos. 7–8 rebuilt in replica, 1998. The steep upper section, NORTHAMPTON BUILDINGS, was built cheaply. By *G. P. Manners*, 1820–6; his only speculative housing scheme.

To the N, a development of some architectural merit. BURLING-TON STREET, c. 1786 by *Palmer*, steps up from Julian Road. PORTLAND PLACE (*John Eveleigh*, 1786) forms a T-shape at the top; ten uniform houses on a raised terrace. Well-proportioned and quite severe, with a platband, continuous sills, strong cornice, and projecting three-bay pedimented centre. At Nos. 6–8 a disruptive attic storey by *C. E. Davis*, 1875. A high pavement with steps extends the whole length; central double ramp for sedan chairs, flanked by stone obelisks. Further E on Julian Road is LAMPARD'S BUILDINGS, ziggurat flats, 1960; *City of Bath Architects and Planning*.

Returning W to the triangular space behind Royal Crescent, and S via Rivers Street is CATHARINE PLACE by *Wood the Younger*, c. 1777–84. An intimate little square with central garden. At its S end off to the E, CIRCUS MEWS, late C18, now with dense small-scale developments grouped around courtyards, largely reconstructed using modern materials, 1986–95. On the S side houses by *Edward Nash Partnership*, 1995. Facing the street three-storey terraced houses, split-level front and back, entered from the staircase half-landing. Houses in the courtyard have spiral stairs around a structural column. To the N in RIVERS STREET MEWS are the best surviving Georgian mews in the city.

RIVERS STREET meanders E parallel to and S of Julian Road. By *Wood the Younger*, 1770s. Nos. 1–15 are later and lower than the rest on the N side. W end much rebuilt after bombing; Nos. 5–7 have first-floor Venetian windows. The earlier houses are standard Palladian, mostly with Tuscan doorways. No. 35 has a first-floor ceiling in the style of *Daniel Fowles*, one of the principal builders in this area.

At the end of Rivers Street is Christ Church (p. 116). Behind, the former CHRISTCHURCH INFANTS' SCHOOL by *Browne & Gill*, 1894, above an arcaded covered playground. The adjacent Tudor-style CHRISTCHURCH COTTAGES are by *Fuller & Gingell*, 1856. Set further set back, the MUSEUM OF BATH AT WORK occupies a rare former Royal Tennis court, built by *Richard Scrase*, 1777. Plain rubble, with nine bays of clerestory windows, originally extending lower. It became a museum in 1969. E of Christ Church, N side, Nos. 1–4 MONTPELIER, 1770–6, have first-floor Venetian windows.

Across Lansdown Road, GUINEA LANE descends steeply NE. On the S side, the former Catholic Apostolic church (p. 120). Below, the former WALCOT SCHOOLS, 1840, by *James Wilson*, now flats. Boldly detailed, with a commanding presence given its awkward triangular site. Basement plinth increasing with the slope, then two tall storeys treated as a giant, deeply recessed arcade. Within the bays narrow flat-arched windows with cornices, and round-arched windows above. The ends break forward. From the bottom of Guinea Lane, a big three-part terrace extends S along the E side of ROMAN ROAD: Axford Buildings, The Paragon, and Bladud Buildings. AXFORD BUILDINGS is by *Joseph Axford*, stonemason, 1767–73 (Nos. 28–32 rebuilt after destruction in 1942). It continues into THE PARAGON, 1768–75, by *Thomas Warr Atwood*. Twenty-one houses, slightly concave to follow the road, i.e. not a deliberate crescent. Standard elevations for buildings on Corporation property, three storeys with pediments to the middle first-floor windows. Massive foundations and a steep drop at the back; the largest rooms are here, for the views. Finally BLADUD BUILDINGS, 1755–62, probably by *Thomas Jelly* or *Thomas Warr Atwood*. Again the design is prescribed but, very unusually, the elevation is repeated on the rear. The centre house is pedimented and projects. Doorways mostly Tuscan. Nos. 1–8 have C19 shopfronts, No. 6 an early C19 full-height segmental bow above.

On a raised pavement, W side of Roman Road, the VINEYARDS. An unusual miscellany of styles and scales for Bath. From the N end, the STAR INN, a pub since 1760, with complete mid-C19 fitted interiors at the N end by *Gaskell & Chambers*. S part reconstructed 1928, by *W. A. Williams*, with interiors matching the older parts. No. 20 is a five-bay detached Palladian villa, c. 1765. Nos. 13–18 are attractively varied: Baroque keystones, Gibbs surrounds, pedimented sashes, Venetian windows, and at No. 14, a bow front. For the Building of Bath Museum, *see* p. 133. On the S corner of the pedestrian Hay Hill off to the W, HAY HILL HOUSE, quirky classicism by *C. E. Davis*, 1870.

Finally the S end of LANSDOWN ROAD. At the junction with Roman Road are FOUNTAIN BUILDINGS, c. 1775, two five-bay houses incorporating a fine five-bay mansion of c. 1730–40, restored by *Carter Hughes Partnership*, 1985–7. The pedimented centre bay has a wide rusticated arched doorway under a Venetian window. To its N on the E side is BELMONT, 1768–73, twenty houses on a raised pavement; Tuscan doorcases. No. 1 has a late C18 single-storey entrance vestibule, a gem by *Thomas Baldwin*. It has a serpentine façade, a round-headed entrance with niches either side and festoon panels above, flanked by thin double pilasters with long console brackets. On the W side is OXFORD ROW, *c.* 1775, a standard Palladian terrace possibly designed and certainly developed by *Thomas Warr Atwood*.

6. *St James's Square to the upper crescents*

Lansdown has splendid post-Wood terraces and crescents, stacked up the hill and with soaring views. They build on the precedent of Royal Crescent and point towards values of landscape and the Picturesque.

ST JAMES'S SQUARE, just N of Royal Crescent, is the most complete Georgian square in Bath. In 1790 Sir Peter Rivers Gay leased the land to four craftsmen, who commissioned the architect *John Palmer*. Work was complete by 1793. The precedent was Queen Square, here elongated into a N–S rectangle with four diagonal approach streets. The principal ranges are N and S, level along the contour. Central three-bay pediments with giant Corinthian pilasters, bow-fronted end pavilions. Each accent also has a first-floor arched window with a moulded band course above. The E and W sides step up the slope; plain, again with elaborated central and terminal accents; unfluted first-floor Composite pilasters here.*

PARK STREET, the NW diagonal exit, runs steeply uphill, part of an incomplete extension. The lower end by *Palmer c.* 1790–3. Nos. 19–24, W side, and Nos. 25–27, E, by *Pinch the Elder*, from 1808; quite grand, with full-height first-floor sashes. Nos. 19 and 27 break slightly forwards and have finely carved friezes over the first-floor centre windows. The street, formerly terminated by a proprietary chapel (*Palmer*, 1794, dem.), was intended to continue NW.

CAVENDISH PLACE, Cavendish Road, sits W of Park Place, facing W across High Common. By *Pinch the Elder*, 1808–16. It is one of the most distinguished early C19 terraces. Nos. 4–13 step evenly N uphill. This is not a palace façade: the architecture is astylar and lacks central or end accents. The Palladian tradition of rusticated ground floors and *piano nobile* continues, but the details follow Adam and Baldwin. Tall first-floor windows, the middle one accented with an entablature on reeded pilasters with console-capitals. Strong horizontal emphasis from the full attic with parapet, the cornice below it,

---

* Off to the SE is St James's Street; an opening on its E side leads to ST JAMES'S PLACE, a court of houses developed with St James's Square from 1790. The splendidly elaborate pedimented entrance and glazed shopping arcade behind are *c.* 1880.

a Pompeian-scroll platband under the second-floor windows, and a plain platband over the ground floor. These all ramp up successively, to give a cohesion that the Woods' climbing terraces never achieved. Especially notable iron- and leadwork, with overthrows, balconies, verandas, delicate fanlights etc. Nos. 6–9 rebuilt 1949. The curving front of the lower corner house, No. 3, required four windows rather than three; the device of two accented centre windows side by side on the first floor seems an unfortunate blemish.

Next, N, on CAVENDISH ROAD, is CAVENDISH VILLA, *c.* 1779, refronted. Then a pair by *Pinch, c.* 1810, WINIFRED'S DALE, early semi-detached villas on these NW slopes, with segmental bows, sharing a curved Doric porch. N again is CAVENDISH LODGE, Neo-Georgian apartments by *William Bertram & Fell*, 1996. Well-detailed and acceptable in scale, but the ostentation, formal axial approach and Cotswold dry-walling-effect stone are unsympathetic to this Regency neighbourhood.

CAVENDISH CRESCENT is a short, late crescent of 1815–30, by *Pinch.* Following the contour, eleven four-storey houses, with no central feature and somewhat austere except for cornices on long consoles over the middle first-floor windows, and extravagant radial rustication to the door openings. Opposite its W end, still on Cavendish Road, is the temple-like DORIC HOUSE, an uncompromisingly severe Grecian building by Soane's protégé *J. M. Gandy* for Thomas Barker, the painter, probably completed by 1805 (a one-storey design was shown at the Royal Academy in 1803). Remarkable elevation to Cavendish Road; a substantial plinth, then two storeys recessed behind column-screens. The ground floor is windowless, with four detached primitive Doric columns and engaged *antae*; unconventional concave capitals and large abaci. Entablature with modillion cornice. Attic storey with a superimposed colonnade of very short columns, sashes to the central bays, and a parapet with stylized acroteria. Pedimented S elevation, with a tripartite ground-floor window and a single window above. Despite the absence of triglyphs and metopes in the frieze, the effect is intended to be Greek Doric, and the blind wall behind a colonnade recalls temples in southern Italy and Sicily, such as the Olympeion at Agrigento. The double tier of columns, proportioned as they are, refer to the two-storey interior of a Greek temple, interpreted here on an exterior – something of an archaeological joke. N of the main temple block, a doorway flanked by Doric columns leads to a top-lit entrance hall; pretty curving staircase with iron railing, remarkably dainty after the forbidding exterior. Behind the closed wall lies the very unusual principal room, a double cube 32 ft (10 metres) long, a showcase for *Barker*'s giant fresco of 1826 of the massacre at Scio in 1822, perhaps inspired by Delacroix's painting of that subject (1824). To the W, a pear-shaped dining room. The N wing, extended with a second storey in 1822, was bomb-damaged and badly rebuilt *c.* 1952.

SION HILL climbs steeply W; shortly in the S side wall, a severe
Greek Revival doorcase to a demolished house. Then several
Late Georgian houses. SION HOUSE, three storeys; c. 1805,
probably *John Pinch*. At Nos. 11–14 a plain terrace,
c. 1795–1800, the grander No. 15 added in 1810–15. Some full-
height rear bows indicate the rise in emphasis on the garden
aspect during the Regency.*

Opposite (N), an outstanding cast-iron ENTRANCE SCREEN and
RAILINGS to Ernest Cook's embellishment of Summerhill,
Sion Hill Place (*see* below), by *Axford & Smith*, builders, 1932:
Regency pastiche of the highest order. Behind, SOUTH
LODGE, competent Neoclassicism, also by *Axford & Smith*,
and of 1932. E of the railings, rusticated gatepiers mark an
avenue running N to the remote and distinguished SION HILL
PLACE. By *John Pinch*, c. 1817–20, one of the last palace-
fronted terraces in Bath and the northernmost of its urban set
pieces. Nine elegant four-storey houses with big segmental-
bowed ends. Three-bay pedimented centre. Banded ground
floors.

SUMMERHILL, Nos. 1–2 Sion Hill Place, was substantially
altered in 1934–6 for Ernest Cook, benefactor of the Assembly Rooms (*see* p. 131). *Axford & Smith* remodelled and
extended the interiors, forming picture galleries on two floors.
Onto this addition was grafted a façade of c. 1738 by *Wood the
Elder*, a gratifying curiosity salvaged from Chippenham, Wilts.†
Since 1956 part of Kingswood School (*see* p. 182), now only
accessible through private grounds S of Sion Hill Place. Stylistically it resembles Wood's Bristol Exchange (p. 275). The
ground floor has chamfered rustication. Seven bays, the centre
framed on the upper floor by paired Corinthian columns with
a wider arched opening implying a Venetian window. To the
sides, Corinthian pilasters and pedimented windows. Frieze of
masks and festoons between the capitals. Modillion cornice,
pediment with pineapple finials, and a balustraded parapet.
Just to the W, the terrace of a late C18 house by *John Eveleigh*,
burnt in 1912. Inside its kitchen garden walls to the N,
Kingswood Day Preparatory School (*see* p. 135).

We return E to the crossroads at Doric House, where steps ascend
NE to the *pièce de résistance*, an almost unbroken line of mag-
nificently sited, sinuous crescents that follow the contour. First
and most unusual is SOMERSET PLACE, of sixteen houses.
Started by *John Eveleigh* in 1790, it was abandoned for financial reasons and only resumed c. 1820; the W wing has only five
houses though cellars were built for two more. Dominant

---

*To the W, where SION HILL turns S, is a finely detailed early C19 Greek
Revival villa, the central windows with segmental-arched recesses. Turning S downhill, SION COTTAGE (No. 23), c. 1760, Gothic with a castellated parapet; GOTHIC
COTTAGE (No. 27), a pretty *cottage orné* of 1797, unusually mixing Gothick and
classical.

†The façade was probably designed for Bowden Hill, Wilts., in 1738, but on the
owner's death the unfinished house was re-erected c. 1749–77 at Nos. 24–25 High
Street, Chippenham.

Bath, Somerset Place.
Elevation of the central feature

symmetrical centrepiece built first as a semi-detached pair, and
not curved in plan. United under a very big broken segmental
pediment, the break having reverse curves to a vase finial. In
the tympanum, paterae and swags. On the first floor a central
niche with an open pediment. Paired doors with Gibbs surrounds and icicle keystone masks. Simpler flanks: the E wing
descends, managing the slope with a tilted platband and
cornice. Nos. 5–7 and 10–13 were bombed in 1942 and rebuilt
as student hostels.

Somerset Place leads immediately up to LANSDOWN CRES-
CENT, by *John Palmer*, 1789–93. Twenty houses forming almost
one-third of a circle, with convex flanking ranges, LANSDOWN
PLACE WEST and EAST (*Palmer*, 1792–5). The convex-
concave-convex plan is remarkable. Wings are separated from
the centre by carriageways to the mews, but the effect is of one
continuous form snaking along the hillside. The weaknesses are
the ends (two bows set one bay in from the angles) and the
pedimented centrepiece: four Ionic pilasters spaced wider
in the middle to take a Venetian window. But its elevated
position, superb views, fine overthrows and lamps, and its
patinated stonework give unrivalled presence. The details are
simple: ground-floor rustication, continuous first-floor sills,
Vitruvian-scroll string course, plain frieze, modillioned
cornice, balustraded parapet.

William Beckford lived at No. 20, 1822–44, after leaving
Fonthill. The main entrance is at the side. The original Palmer
staircase rises only to the first floor. Beckford later acquired
No. 1 Lansdown Place West across the lane, and in 1824 linked
them with a semi-elliptical bridge by *H. E. Goodridge*, who had
already made designs for his projected tower at Lansdown
(p. 184). When Beckford sold No. 1 he retained the bridge,
which housed part of his library. It has three windows with
eared architraves. Above the balustrade, four urns with palms
or aloes of aluminium, seemingly original to the design. In the
garden behind is a small domed Islamic pavilion. He also
bought a strip of land to create an idyllic landscaped ride from
his house to Lansdown Tower, a mile away on the hilltop. In
1836 he purchased No. 19 and had *Goodridge* amalgamate it
with No. 20. Palmer's staircase was enclosed in a curious
inclined tunnel. It is lined with bands at intervals, giving the
effect of arches in perspective. On the ground floor is another
library, by *Goodridge*; arched recesses with mahogany bookcases, yellow scagliola pilasters.

Continuing E, Nos. 5–9 LANSDOWN PLACE EAST, bombed and
rebuilt in facsimile, 1946. Visible lower down, the handsome
plain HOPE HOUSE, 1790 by *Palmer*; segmental bows on the
garden fronts. Altered and extended in the C20 as part of Bath
High (now Royal High) School. The unusual porch with
reeded edges, segmental roof and thin columns matches those
of No. 1 Lansdown Place East, and No. 16 Brock Street.

Now S down LANSDOWN ROAD. At the junction with Lansdown
Grove (NE corner), the LANSDOWN GROVE HOTEL, 1770,
enlarged as a hotel *c.* 1860 and later. The original part has a
three-bay pedimented centre and canted bays. A few yards E
in LANSDOWN GROVE is a mid- or late C18 loggia in Batty
Langley Gothick; incorporated into Barcote House (*William
Bertram & Fell*, 1987). Further down on the E side, LANS-
DOWN LODGE, a detached mid-C18 mansion, enlarged 1835:
two storeys, five bays, pediment. On a conspicuous site on the
W side are the BALLANCE STREET FLATS, council housing
designed by the City Architect and Planning Officer, *Dr
Howard Stutchbury*, 1969–73. A prominent corridor-access
block of reconstituted Bath stone fronts the road, jutting out
against the slope so that the S end rears over its neighbours.
Upper walls slate-hung, a fashion influenced by Darborne &
Darke's 1960s London housing, forming sham mansards. 137
houses of 1773–83 that could have been refurbished were
demolished here, the apogee of the 'Sack of Bath' (*see* p. 107).
This disaster helped stem the tide of urban destruction by
planners, in Bath and nationally.

At YE OLDE FARM HOUSE pub (Jacobethan, by *F. W. Gardiner*,
1892), a short detour to the E completes the tour of the upper
crescents. First, in Camden Row, an early C19 Greek Revival
watchman's LODGE. Then CAMDEN PLACE steps uphill to
CAMDEN CRESCENT, a large fragmentary composition of
c. 1787–8, by *John Eveleigh*, with a magnificent prospect. The

plan was for thirty-two houses, twenty-two forming the crescent; of the wings, only Camden Place was built. A landslide at the NE end destroyed several crescent houses during construction, leaving eighteen standing, four to the r. of the centre. Even truncated, it is splendid; the vaulted substructure at the s end emphasizes the scale of the undertaking. The Palladian detail must already have been outdated when built. The centre and sw end have a rusticated base and an engaged Corinthian giant order, the centre committing the solecism of having five columns. In the pediment, the coat of arms of the 1st Earl of Camden, Recorder of Bath. The doorway keystones bear his crest, an elephant's head. Corinthian pilasters to the wings. The ground rises towards the centre, and the windows step up in groups of three, while the platband and entablature tilt with the slope.

Returning to Lansdown Road, at an angle below Camden Place is AINSLIE'S BELVEDERE. Laid out c. 1760; the datestone of 1806 to Nos. 2–3 may indicate a later phase. Nos. 3–5 are reconstructions. The descent to the city continues via BELVEDERE, late C18, the E side untidy. The w side steps downhill on a raised pavement; several Venetian windows. BELVEDERE VILLAS (E side) is a terrace of four in Baldwin's manner, late C18; pedimented ends with fluted pilasters and waterleaf capitals. Attic storey 1868. The houses beyond are dealt with in Perambulation 5 (p. 164).

7. South-west of the city centre

An excursion w of the medieval city, to the extremity of the considerable Georgian extension. Despite heavy bomb damage in 1942, several principal features remain.

KINGSMEAD SQUARE was begun in 1727 on land belonging to St John's Hospital, just w of the West Gate. One of the first planned developments in Bath, contemporary with Queen Square (see p. 152), and the first outside the city walls. The war-damaged s SIDE, by *John Strahan* of Bristol, was finally restored in 1974–6 by *David Brain & Stollar*. Heavy glazing bars replaced plate glass and new stone ground floors replaced C19 shopfronts. On the w side, ROSEWELL HOUSE, ornate provincial Baroque with German-Flemish influence, built 1735 for Thomas Rosewell. The style suggests *Nathaniel Ireson*, who was involved here in the 1730s. Five bays, three storeys, hipped roof. Angle pilasters, and a pilastered centre, with the heavy cornice rising over it to a segmental pediment. The flanking windows have heavy and very complex frames and keystones with busts. Even more elaborate centre window framed by bearded termini caryatids, their chests bulging forward. Second-floor centrepiece with fantastical gristly curves, gambols and garlands. Simple Ionic doorcase, perhaps later, flanked by inserted shopfronts. Wood's judgement was, 'nothing save ornaments without taste'. A heavy side elevation faces KINGSMEAD STREET, r. The entrance hall has full-height raised panelling; beyond, an excellent wooden staircase with three balusters per tread, the centre ones barley-sugar twisted, and ramped panelling.

To the E, WESTGATE BUILDINGS, originally c. 1760–71, following the curve of the city wall. Running S, the Neoclassical (former) COOPERATIVE WHOLESALE SOCIETY BUILDING, 1932–4 (W side) by L. G. Ekins. Adjoining to the S, Nos. 13–14, C18 survivors; Nos. 11–12 rebuilt after war damage.

Continuing S, ST JAMES' PARADE, c. 1768, probably designed by Jelly & Palmer. It required demolition of part of the medieval walls. Venetian first-floor windows, some Gothick glazing bars. Pedimented doorcases, Tuscan, Doric, Corinthian, and, at No. 19, SW side, Ionic. Shared pedimented doorcase at Nos. 39–40 (NE side), possibly by John Eveleigh: three columns with Tower-of-the-Winds capitals, elegant festoon frieze. Over the doorway of No. 33 a bust of Athena.

We return NW past the end of Westgate Buildings into JAMES STREET WEST. Most of Strahan's streets near here were obliterated in the Second World War. On the N side, ROSEWELL COURT (1961), insensitive five- to nine-storey council flats by Hugh Roberts. Beyond (W), the hostile eight-storey social security office, KINGSMEAD HOUSE, 1964–5, by W. S. Frost of the Ministry of Public Building and Works.

W of the road junction here is the former Green Park Station (p. 136). Beyond, S, is GREEN PARK, a terrace by John Palmer, 1790s and later; the green in front originally enclosed by a converging E range, lost to bombing. Here and at Norfolk Crescent further W (see below) can be seen the new Late Georgian style – taller, slimmer windows, iron balconies, verandas and overthrows.

To the N up Charles Street, NEW KING STREET runs W. Built 1764–70 by tradesmen including John Ford, mason, with Jelly, S side, and James Coleman, carpenter, N side. Plain but generous houses, most one or two bays wide with variations of detail. The N side has pedimented Tuscan doorcases. No. 55, NE end, was a symmetrical composition with its demolished neighbour. Nos. 7–9 rebuilt in replica. At No. 19 lived the astronomer and musician William Herschel; now a museum. Typical of the more modest C18 Bath interior – basement kitchen, ground-floor dining room, first-floor drawing room. Near the W end of New King Street is ST ANN'S PLACE, c. 1765, restored 1987. A paved court of two-storey artisan houses with continuous timber ground-floor lintels. Simple door hoods. The two-bay houses of GREAT STANHOPE STREET follow, W, again with Tuscan doorcases. Most of the N side rebuilt in facsimile, 1983. No. 24, S side, was altered by Edward Davis, c. 1830, in the manner of Soane; porch with Greek-key frieze and incised pilasters; pediment reduced to a slight angling of the parapet. Swept ironwork to the balcony, after Soane's house at Lincoln's Inn Fields, London.

Further W, terminating Georgian Bath in that direction, NORFOLK CRESCENT, a grand conception of eighteen houses with a radius of 420 ft (128 metres). Developed from 1792 by

Richard Bowsher, attorney. A planned axial street running W was halted by the financial crisis of 1793. Nine houses were completed by 1810. Four storeys, with arched ground-floor openings. Centre and ends with giant Ionic pilasters and pediments above the attic. Finely proportioned elevations, perhaps by *Palmer*; but the joinery, wrought-iron lamp standards (Nos. 7 and 14), and iron veranda-balconies with Greek-key decoration suggest the finishing hand of the *elder Pinch*, by this time a bankrupt whose affairs were in Bowsher's hands. Nos. 1–7 rebuilt, 1958. At the NE corner, a circular stone WATCH BOX, *c.* 1810. N of the green space, NELSON PLACE WEST, *c.* 1815, to a similar but smaller-scale design. Unfinished until 1973, when *Marshman Warren Taylor* added a matching W pavilion, and the big, nominally Georgian block of flats beyond.

We return to the city centre up Nile Street, N, then r. into Upper Bristol Road, thence to Queen Square via CHARLOTTE STREET. Laid out in 1839–40 by *G. P. Manners*, who also designed the terrace, N side, still ramped in the manner of Pinch. Next, N side, the former Moravian chapel (p. 121). Then

89 the REGISTER OFFICE, built as the Bath Savings Bank by the London architect *George Alexander*, 1841, in the Italian palazzo style of Barry's Reform Club; an early example of this style in a bank. Symmetrical, three bays on both principal elevations. Big rusticated quoins, heavy overhanging cornice. The windows of the *piano nobile* have Ionic aedicules, alternating pediments and balustraded plinths. Opposite, S side, Elim Pentecostal Church (p. 121). To its E, Palace Yard Mews leads S back to CHARLES STREET, with the former TELEPHONE EXCHANGE (E side), a slab of 1966–7 by *W. S. Frost* for the *Ministry of Public Building and Works*, a design of unbelievable perversity in this setting. Taller extension to Charles Street, 1971–2, with a slate-hung top.

Beyond, in MONMOUTH STREET, most remaining interest is on the N side. A turn N via Princes Street leads shortly W into BEAUFORD SQUARE, developed by *John Hobbs*, a Bristol sailmaker and timber merchant, in the early 1730s. The architect was *Strahan*. Two-storey cottages, Doric entablatures with triglyphs. Parapets ramped at the party walls and in the centre of each house; segmental pedimented doorways. Originally, all were three windows wide, those on the ground floor with a pulvinated frieze and cornice. To avoid window tax, several later had their windows paired with a slender central mullion. On the E side Nos. 2–4 and 21 are replicas of 1963–6. Bold Regency spearhead railings, overthrows and gates.

The intimate character of the S side is disturbed by the higher

84 THEATRE ROYAL, a design of *George Dance the Younger* carried out by *John Palmer* in 1802–5. A five-bay frontispiece of three storeys, set against a windowless block containing auditorium and stage. Ground-floor windows in blank segmental arches. Giant pilasters above, with sunk panels that are almost abstract, far removed from Palladian or Hellenic traditions. The deep frieze has Greek masks over each pilaster with

garlands between; above, restored lyre finials and a magnificent Hanoverian royal crest. Burnt out in 1862; interior rebuilt by *C. J. Phipps*, who also moved the main entrance to Saw Close (*see* p. 145). The auditorium has an intimate, horseshoe-shaped plan with three tiers of balconies on a cast-iron structure, and a shallow domed ceiling. The dress-circle balcony fronts have *trompe l'œil* panels and medallions. Refurbished 1982 by *Dowton & Hurst*, with a fly tower in an obtrusive lead-clad box, a necessary evil.

Back in Monmouth Street and continuing E, next, a vigorous bronze winged figure by *Igor Ustinov*, 1997, on the façade of the USTINOV STUDIO THEATRE. An otherwise uninteresting interwar building re-fitted by *Tektus* in 1995 as an adjunct to the Theatre Royal. Then on the corner of St John's Place is ST PAUL'S PARISH HALL, 1888–9, an amateurish design by the *Rev. Angus Clark*. It houses the EGG THEATRE (*Haworth Tompkins*, completed 2005), a small-scale elliptical auditorium for children. Opposite, Nos. 3–5 are humble remnants of *Strahan*'s Kingsmead development, No. 4 (dated 1731) unusually of brick.

8. *Pulteney Bridge to Bathwick*

Pulteney Bridge (p. 138) is the gateway E over the Avon to the Bathwick estate, one of the most impressive Neoclassical set pieces in Britain. Only a fragment was completed, the axis of an immense planned development of streets and circuses, instigated in the late C18 by Sir William Johnstone Pulteney. The scheme, designed by *Thomas Baldwin*, departs from the standard Palladian style of John Wood's successors, towards the fashionable Neoclassicism of Robert Adam. It was built between 1788 and *c.* 1820, the later parts by *John Pinch the Elder*, who succeeded Baldwin as estate surveyor *c.* 1793. Unlike earlier Bath developments, the streets were raised on extensive vaults, to form a level surface above the meadows. The houses therefore have basements and, near the river, sub-basements. The layout is simple: the short Argyle Street connects Pulteney Bridge with a diagonally placed square, Laura Place. Its NE continuation, Great Pulteney Street, forms the backbone of the New Town. It has short stub streets off, fragments of intended development now leading nowhere. At its NE end is Sydney Gardens, a very large elongated hexagon, with the Holburne Museum (originally Sydney House) as a *point-de-vue*. Of the terraces meant to surround the gardens, only the two western diagonals, Sydney Place, were built.

Now for the details. ARGYLE STREET, a unified composition, and a shopping street from the start, sets the scene. The s side has pedimented end pavilions and the N side divides into two blocks by Grove Street, the end houses projecting. Remarkable SHOPFRONTS: No. 16 (s side), late C18, has a deep bow front with radiating fanlights; No. 9, the Boater pub, similar; No. 8, Hale's Chemist, has a perfect Greek Revival shopfront with fluted Ionic columns. Many early fittings. Opposite, No. 6 (N side), another good C19 double shopfront with Corinthian columns.*

Opposite is Argyle Chapel (*see* p. 120). To the E, LAURA PLACE, like a small square set on the diagonal, with streets joining at each angle: characteristic of later C18 Bath (cf. St James's Square, p. 165). Central fountain basin, 1877, by *A. S. Goodridge*. To the N is Henrietta Street (*see* p. 177) and to the S, the unfinished stub of JOHNSTONE STREET (1794–*c*. 1805). Plainer houses with arched ground-floor windows, except the returns to Laura Place. The drop at the S end illustrates dramatically the artificial height of the street level.

GREAT PULTENEY STREET is among Britain's finest formal streets; cf. Adam's Portland Place, London, 1773–94, and Craig's George Street, Edinburgh, begun 1767. A monumental layout 1,100 ft long and 100 ft wide (335 by 30 metres) with palace-front terraces, the whole greater than the sum of the parts. Architectural details are spread thinly to provide maximum incident with economy of means, with vistas terminating with pediments, pavilions and giant Corinthian pilasters. At the E end the Holburne Museum remains always in view.

The standard houses have three storeys and three bays, attics in mansard roofs and rusticated ground floors. Windows are typically double-square, six-over-six panes, with thin late C18-type glazing bars (restored). Several wrought-iron scrolled overthrows remain; there are plans to restore the rest. The INTERIORS are fairly plain, with off-the-shelf components – cast-metal fanlights, plaster cornices, plain square balusters with cast-metal details to half-landings, chimneypieces with composition mouldings – but are nonetheless large and well proportioned, suitable for the London grandees who rented for the season. Cantilevered stone staircases, except at the E end, completed in wood after the onset of economic difficulties in the 1790s.

Construction proceeded E from Laura Place. On the N SIDE, two ranges divided by the stub of Sunderland Street, creating symmetry, or rather duality. Each has a centre of eleven bays of giant pilasters, with half-pilasters at the ends – a motif beloved by Baldwin – and a Vitruvian-scrolled platband. Three-bay pedimented pavilions flank the centre, each with an arched first-floor middle window with swags and paterae in the entablature. The flanks continue outward on each side thus: a plain fifteen-bay terrace; then five bays with paired giant pilasters at each end, and pedimented central window; then, at the

---

*To the N, in GROVE STREET, the former NEW PRISON, 1772–3. Pulteney commissioned *Robert Adam*, but *Thomas Atwood* took over. Externally it resembles a Palladian mansion. Five bays, the middle three recessed. Rusticated ground floor, where petty offenders were held; above, debtors' quarters, with pediments to alternate windows only. The building is raised above the old flood level on a basement, originally hidden by a forecourt; its exposure spoils the proportions. Converted to housing 1971 by *John Bull & Associates*.

extremities, projecting pavilions, three bays with pediment. No. 20 has a Greek Revival doorcase on Sunderland Street, *c.* 1830. No. 21, opposite, has a rather grand porch by *Baldwin*, with half-round columns and waterleaf capitals. Sunderland Street, merely the length of one house, was to have led to a vast square on the site of Henrietta Park. From here the terrace backs can be seen, with C19 extensions, and a few early cantilevered bathrooms on cast-iron brackets (once ubiquitous in Bath).

The S SIDE has three ranges separated by William Street and Edward Street. The centre range is the most impressive, being taller, with arched ground-floor openings, and balustrading. Three-bay pilastered end pavilions. Nine-bay centre, with five-bay pediment bearing the Duke of Cleveland's arms, intended to close the view from the unbuilt street opposite. At No. 53, a good double-bowed return to Edward Street, S, with an elegant Adamesque fanlight between. Simpler ranges W and E.

EDWARD STREET, a plainer side street branching S, begins a short walk through early C19 developments to the SE. The first-floor windows above each doorway have pediments. The big, later style continues in VANE STREET, off its S end, by *Pinch the Elder*. At the W end here is St Mary the Virgin (*see* p. 117) also by Pinch, as is RABY PLACE (1818–25) to its r., an elegant terrace climbing the lower slope of Bathwick Hill. Eighteen two-bay houses, with the attic storey brought forward. Characteristic ramped cornice; first-floor windows with cornices on consoles; plain pilasters separating the houses. C19 balconies with canopies. No. 18, stepped back, is later, built *c.* 1841 over the railway tunnel. Communal GARDEN with Grecian gatepiers. Next uphill, THE MOORINGS (*K. & L. Berney*, 1996–8), poor Neo-Georgian. Opposite, S side, BATHWICK TERRACE, attributed to *Pinch the Elder*, *c.* 1825. An incomplete terrace of three, at an angle to Bathwick Hill. Three bays with flanking pavilions and angle pilasters, and an end elevation splayed to the street with giant angle pilasters and a pediment on Ionic columns. Next E, GEORGE'S PLACE, a rank of shops, 1822–3. Buildings beyond the canal are described on p. 188.

SYDNEY GARDENS, by *C. Harcourt Masters*. Opened as a pleasure ground in 1795; a municipal park since 1909. The central C18 axis (the line of Great Pulteney Street) remains. Joining the main sloping axis, on the N side, MINERVA'S TEMPLE by *A. J. Taylor*, 1911, built for the Empire Exhibition, Crystal Palace, Sydenham; re-erected here 1913–14. Four Corinthian columns, big pediment with female figures and a wreathed head of Sulis. Further NE, the Great Western Railway, cut through in 1836–41, is crossed by a stone BRIDGE by *Brunel*, with a flat elliptical arch and pierced balustrading. Also the high retaining wall, with bold cornice and frieze. NE up the slope again is the KENNET AND AVON CANAL by *John Rennie*, excavated 1799–1810. It is crossed by two delicate cast- and wrought-iron FOOTBRIDGES made at Coalbrookdale, dated 1800, one with Chinoiserie balustrade, and also by stone ROAD BRIDGES flanking Sydney Gardens, also *c.* 1800, by *Rennie*.

83

These are drilled to resemble tufa and have swagged masks of river gods. Cleveland House (*see* below) closes the picturesque view s from the gardens across a succession of bridges. Terminating the gardens' central axis is a semicircular Ionic EXEDRA, by *Baldwin*, 1795. Rebuilt as part of SYDNEY HOUSE, beyond to the E, 1835–6, probably by *Pinch the Younger*; rebuilt again minus its curved wings in 1938.

Leaving the gardens at the top, 100 yds s along SYDNEY ROAD is the drive to the BATH SPA HOTEL. A very big Greek Revival mansion consisting of two two-storey blocks connected by a sturdy Greek Doric colonnade. s block of 1835, possibly by *John Pinch the Younger*. Projecting centre, ground floor with banded pilasters and tripartite windows, flanking a porch with paired Doric columns. In the first floor, angle pilasters and cast-iron balconies. Entrance hall with Soanian shallow-domed ceiling. Similar N block and colonnade by *Wilson, Willcox & Wilson*, 1878. In 1912 it became a hydropathic hotel, later a nurses' home. Converted back to a hotel, 1989, by *Alain Bouvier Associates*, adding a big wing in skimpy Palladian style. In the grounds, a Greek Doric TEMPLE and a tufa stone GROTTO, both c. 1835.

Straddling the canal, 50 yds W down Sydney Road is a remarkable Georgian office building, CLEVELAND HOUSE, by the *Elder Pinch*, 1817–20. Built as the headquarters of the Kennet and Avon Canal Co., and among the most refined canal buildings. Two storeys, five windows wide; ground floor with banded rustication and round-headed openings; first-floor windows with architraves and cornices, the middle one pedimented. Opposite, N side, RAVENSWELL and LONSDALE (now Sydney Gardens Hotel), 1853, possibly by *Goodridge*; Picturesque Italianate paired villas. KENNET HOUSE, s side, c. 1840, has a Gothic porch, hoodmoulds and steeply pitched bargeboards.

Finally in Sydney Road, 100 yds s, SYDNEY PLACE, part of the uncompleted architectural frame to Sydney Gardens; by *Pinch the Elder*, 1804–8. A speculative eleven-house terrace, the most beautiful of Bath's C19 buildings, the workmanship and uniformity of colour flawless. Four storeys, the attic brought forward; big and rather severe elevations. The slope is handled with great refinement and elegance by ramping all the horizontals, providing a unifying horizontal flow heightened by the lack of vertical accents. Each angle has a semicircular bay with the bands of decoration wrapping around like belts, achieving a remarkable unity. Less successful given the sloping site is the palace-front treatment with pedimented pavilions at centre and ends. Round-headed ground-floor openings. Adamish doors with delicate metal fanlights and trellised sidelights, and at the ends, corner Doric porches (the top house also has a charming Chinoiserie conservatory over the porch). Mostly original iron overthrows, railings and balconies. Well-planned if conventional interiors, fine stone staircases. For the first time in Bath, the first-floor windows extend down to the skirting boards. Sydney Place continues N of the Holburne Museum, forming the other completed wing of the Sydney Gardens hexagon. The terrace on its w side is by *Baldwin*, 1792–6; the usual palace front. Four-bay centre, two houses (each stealing a bay from the flanks) with paired doorways and Neoclassical window surrounds.

HAMPTON ROW, ⅓ m. NE of Sydney Place, is a slightly uneven terrace of artisan houses, 1817–19, by *Pinch the Elder*. Hidden behind, CLEVELAND POOLS, the oldest surviving Georgian public swimming pool in Britain. Constructed 1815–17. Here too the architect was *Pinch*, who was also a subscriber. The main pool has a semicircular centre with later rectangular extensions. On its axis, a small symmetrical house, originally the attendant's, flanked by curved single-storey wings with changing cubicles. Now derelict.

BATHWICK STREET runs NW from Sydney Place and forms the axis of the NW part of the Bathwick estate. First, N side, the CROWN INN by *Browne & Gill*, 1898, Tudorbethan. Off Bathwick Street to the s is DANIEL STREET. Begun with Nos. 35–37 (s end) to leases of 1792, by *Baldwin*, who was shortly bankrupted. The rest were designed by *Pinch the Elder* in 1810 as modest, nicely scaled two-bay houses. Arched recesses frame the ground-floor windows, with wide sashes that cleverly echo the narrower ones above in their glazing bars. Back in Bathwick Street, the houses on the N side are by *Baldwin*, 1788–92. Nos. 9–10 are replica infill. Nos. 1–8 have tripartite first-floor windows with pilaster strips, swagged friezes and pediments. They step slightly uphill with ramped string courses.

The w end of Bathwick Street is the centre of what was Bathwick village. Adjoining No. 1, BATHWICK HOUSE incorporates an earlier building, probably Bathwick Manor House. C17 mullioned window in the basement. Remodelled *c.* 1800, presumably by *Pinch*; three storeys, five windows (three only at second floor) and a Greek Doric doorcase. Attached to the NW, ROCHFORT PLACE is a late terrace of four by *Pinch the Elder*, *c.* 1827, comparable with his Bathwick estate designs elsewhere. Alongside is PINCH'S FOLLY, a surprising C19 Baroque Revival archway, on the site of *Pinch the Younger*'s builder's yard, but possibly erected by his son, *William Pinch*.

Opposite, Church Walk leads to the cemetery and church of St John the Baptist (*see* pp. 117, 121). On St John's Road, BRIDGEMEAD nursing home and day centre, *Feilden Clegg Design*, 1989–92. Double-height hall and conservatory set between angled blocks with semi-private spaces and residents' rooms. Clad in blockwork, steel loggias and brises-soleil. Raised on columns towards the river.

The SW turning from Bathwick Street is HENRIETTA ROAD. On the NW side, PULTENEY VILLA, admirably sympathetic Regency villa-style apartments by *Tektus Architects*, 2000–1. Beyond, HENRIETTA VILLAS, comfortable detached and semi-detached, *c.* 1840. The road curves s as HENRIETTA STREET, with simple terraces by *Pinch the Elder*, from 1797. At Nos. 25–26 and Nos. 22–23, E side, semi-elliptical archways mark the site (behind the terrace) of Laura Chapel, an elegant elliptical building by *Baldwin*, 1790–5, dem. *c.* 1920. The s end of Henrietta Street rejoins Laura Place.

9. *Walcot Street to Cleveland Bridge*

Walcot, N of the North Gate, was a suburb in Roman times; still a bustling district of trades and crafts, and, until the c19, a main route into the city. Uncertainty cast by Colin Buchanan's hated post-war road-tunnel scheme (*see* pp. 106–7) sustained the area's Bohemian character.

At the s end of WALCOT STREET, the reviled HILTON HOTEL by *Snailum, Le Fevre & Quick*, 1972; an overbearing slab, marring the view of Pulteney Bridge from the s. With the adjacent multi-storey car park, it formed part of the Buchanan traffic plan. The fenestration was obviously designed with some idea of keeping-in-keeping. Further N on Walcot Street, w side, Nos. 27–33, *c.* 1840, with good shopfronts. Steps at the side lead up into BROAD STREET PLACE. On the N, the YMCA BUILDING (*F. W. Beresford-Smith & Partners*, 1972) sitting high above Walcot Street on segmental arches. Upper walls slate-hung like a mansard roof, a fashionable device at that time.

Opposite, E side, is the CORN MARKET by *Manners & Gill*, 1855. Entered through a narrow classical building, a simple long hall raised on arches. Next E, in BEEHIVE YARD is the brick-clad BATH ELECTRIC TRAMWAYS DEPOT, by *Harper & Harper* and *G. Hopkins & Sons*, engineers, 1903. *BBA Architects* inserted mixed-use accommodation, incorporating a foundry beyond, in 2000–2.

Continuing N on Walcot Street. Nos. 68–70 are early c18, probably originally gabled. On the w side, late c18 STEPS ascend steeply to the Paragon (p. 164), its cliff-like back dominating Walcot Street. Next to the steps is LADYMEAD FOUNTAIN by *C. E. Davis*, 1860, Romanesque. On the E side, No. 88 and ST MICHAEL'S CHURCH HOUSE, one building by *Wallace Gill*, 1904; two gables and Jacobean-style windows, with attractive Arts and Crafts detail. Large recessed entrance arch with delicate lettered frieze. A carving of St George slaying the dragon in the swan-neck pediment. No. 108, c18, was extended by *Silcock & Reay*, 1905, with a pretty single-storey Arts and Crafts shop for the builders Hayward & Wooster; big mullioned-and-transomed windows, pediment, elegant lettering.

Next, the PENITENTIARY CHAPEL, by *Manners*, 1845. A bold design with heavy platband, continuous sill course, and five tall first-floor windows. Small circular lights between the bays and ground-floor windows are later additions. It served LADYMEAD HOUSE, No. 112, a female penitentiary from 1805, externally c19, but incorporating c17 remnants. Nos. 114–116, CORNWELL BUILDINGS is a delightful pair of shops, *c.* 1800;

a concave front like a miniature crescent, with concave reeded pilasters. Off E down towards the river, CHATHAM ROW, *c.* 1767, standard Palladian with a Venetian window on each end; dragged back from 1960s dereliction. Further N on Walcot Street, Nos. 109–119 (W side), mid-C18 with naïve Venetian windows and Gothick glazing. In ST SWITHIN'S YARD opposite, E side, are the Tudor-style ST SWITHIN'S SCHOOLS, by *Browne & Gill*, 1899–1901. Converted to housing, 2000–1. In WALCOT GATE off to the E is part of Walcot Cemetery (p. 121). Walcot Street concludes with No. 146, a rebuilding of 1900 with a Dutch gable by *F. W. Gardiner*.

Walcot Street merges into LONDON STREET. N of the junction with Roman Road running SW (*see* Perambulation 5) is HEDGEMEAD PARK, created after a landslip in 1881. At the junction, St Swithin (*see* p. 118). Continuing E on London Street, in NELSON PLACE off to the SE are C19 weavers' workshops with extensive first-floor glazing. WALCOT PARADE (N side) is a piecemeal Palladian terrace, *c.* 1770, on a high pavement.

In London Street, S side, CLEVELAND TERRACE (Nos. 4 and 6 with shopfronts of 1832) curves into CLEVELAND PLACE, the wedge-shaped junction with London Road. Developed by *H. E. Goodridge, c.* 1827–30, as a worthy approach to Cleveland Bridge (*see* p. 138), and Bathwick beyond. A fine Greek Revival design, with banded ground floors, tripartite windows, giant pilasters, wreaths and incised decoration after Soane. No. 9, CLEVELAND PLACE WEST, intended as the centrepiece, has incised Greek keys, and flanking wall panels with incised work. No. 7, and its opposite counterpart in CLEVELAND PLACE EAST, have giant pilasters, and pedimented first-floor windows. Particularly delicate and refined return elevation of Cleveland Place East into London Road. Goodridge's partiality for ironwork is evident from the balconettes. Terminating Cleveland Place East is the DISPENSARY of 1845. Good Late Classical front; five bays, rusticated plinth, central pediment on giant Ionic columns *in antis*. It had an ingenious circulation plan. Waiting rooms either side of the central entrance. Physician's and surgeon's rooms in the far corners with in- and out-doors, and a common top-lit dispensing room in the centre.

For London Road, Larkhall and Lambridge, *see* Outer Areas, p. 185.

OUTER AREAS

Bath's outer suburbs are dealt with clockwise in nine areas, beginning at the N with Lansdown. Many good things in these suburbs have tended to be eclipsed by the glories of the Georgian city.

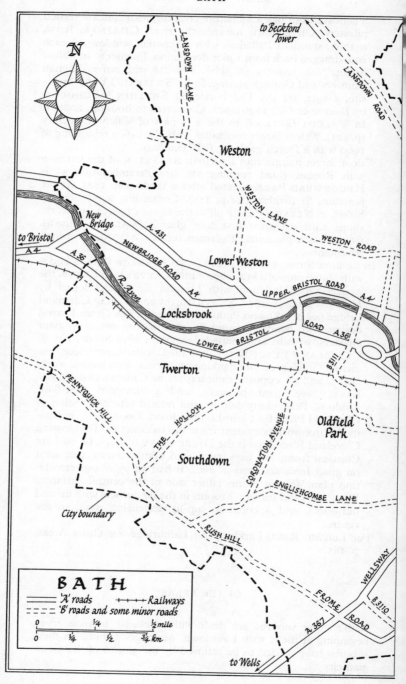

to Beckford
Tower

N

LANSDOWN LANE

LANSDOWN ROAD

Weston

WESTON LANE

New
Bridge

to Bristol
A 4

A 431

A 36

NEWBRIDGE ROAD
A 4

Lower Weston

WESTON ROAD

R. Avon

UPPER BRISTOL ROAD

A 4

A 36

Locksbrook

LOWER BRISTOL ROAD

ROAD

A 36

B 3111

Twerton

PENNYQUICK HILL

THE HOLLOW

CORONATION AVENUE

Oldfield
Park

Southdown

ENGLISHCOMBE LANE

City boundary

RUSH HILL

FROME ROAD

WELLSWAY

B 3110

A 367

to Wells

BATH
——— 'A' roads   +++++ Railways
- - - 'B' roads and some minor roads

0   ¼   ½ mile
0   ¼   ½   ¾ km

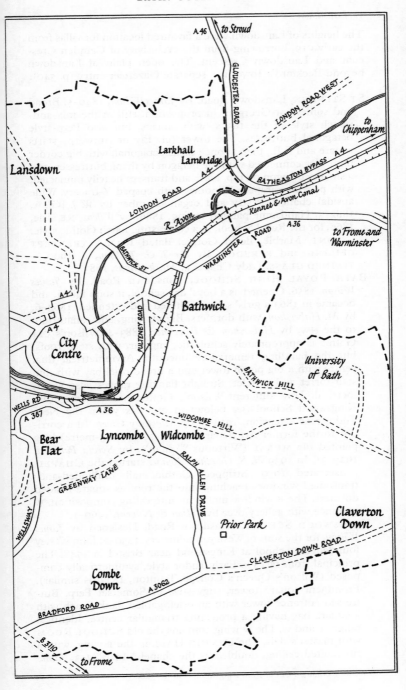

1. *Lansdown*

The heights of Lansdown were a favoured location for villas from
the early C19, borrowing from the exclusivity of Camden Crescent and Lansdown Crescent. The open plain of Lansdown
beyond Beckford's Tower is a separate Gazetteer entry (p. 540).

St Stephen, Lansdown Road. By *James Wilson*, 1840–5. Broad
and somewhat Georgian in proportion, still in the mix-and-
match style of the 1830s, with lancets, but also Perp-style
octagonal buttresses. The tower (cf. Ely or Antwerp) starts
square and E.E., then at once turns octagonal, with big corner
pinnacles connected with the octagon by flying buttresses, and
a smaller octagon on top. Nave and transept heavily pinnacled,
with pierced parapets. Windows with cusped Y-tracery. Wide
apsidal chancel, vestry and organ chamber by *W. J. Wilcox*,
1882–3. Handsome painted ceiling, 1886, by *Wilcox*. NE aisle,
1866, for the Royal School, in a contrasting harsh Gothic style.
– FONT. Marble, florid Gothic, dated 1843. – TRANSEPT
CEILING and REREDOS. By *Sir T. G. Jackson*, c. 1900. –
STAINED GLASS. Lady Chapel E, *Mark Angus*, 1983.

Bath Royal High School, Lansdown Road. By *James
Wilson*, 1856. Opened as a boys' day school, it soon failed, and
became in 1863 a girls' school. Altered and extended, 1864–6,
by *M. Habershon*, with dormers. Big SE wing, and sanatorium
to the NW, by *Habershon & Fawckner*, 1883–4. Wilson's C14
Gothic is appropriately scholastic, angular, with steep roofs,
but the handling remarkably uncouth. Asymmetrical dual
centre with a big porch tower and a broad oriel bay with thin
stair-turret and spirelet. Straight flanking ranges, also asymmetrical. How different Wilson's Gothic had become from
Kingswood School (*see* below) in only six years. Big Neo-
Tudor rear extension, 1924–5, by *Mowbray Green*. In a corridor to the former Art department, a 70-ft (21.5-metre)-long
painted tile MURAL ('Virtuous Woman'), by *Sylvia Packard*,
1929–31. In 1939 *H. S. Goodhart-Rendel* started the CHAPEL,
consecrated 1950. Stripped Gothic, tall mullioned-and-
transomed windows reaching into the roof as square-headed
dormers. The E window makes an interesting composition. W
entrance with gallery over by *Tolson & Nugent*, 1960–1.

Kingswood School, Lansdown Road. Designed by *James
Wilson*, for the sons of Wesleyan ministers, 1850–2. John Wesley
founded the school at Kingswood near Bristol in 1748. The
principal front faces S. Early Tudor style, symmetrically composed (Wilson's Queen's College, Taunton, 1843, is similar).
Prominent square tower, suggestive of Somerset Perp. Buttressed entrance tower with an oriel; gabled flanks, each with
a square bay having a projecting triangular centre. Identical
ranges E and W. The W wing contains the old SCHOOL ROOM
with master's dais. The DINING HALL in the E wing, with a
rib-vaulted ceiling, doubled as the chapel.* In 1882–3, *James*

---

*Wesley's original PULPIT from Kingswood is in the gallery.

Wilson & Elijah Hoole extended the hall by two bays; STAINED GLASS by *H. J. Salisbury*. Theirs too the barrack-like four-storey dormitory block projecting at the back, and to the E of this, the SANATORIUM, Swiss-chalet style. This was subsumed by additions of 1908, E, and 1929–30, a large W wing by *Hayward & Wooster*. Adjacent W, *Hoole*'s gymnasium, now ARTS CENTRE, 1891, Neo-Tudor.

Behind the main school, W side, the KINGSWOOD THEATRE by *Nugent Vallis Brierley*, 1993–4, closing the fourth side of a small quadrangle. The auditorium has an exposed tubular steel structure. Further W, the big FERENS TEACHING BLOCK, 1924–6, extended 1949, by *W. A. Forsyth*, with mullioned-and-transomed windows. W of Wilson's main building, the POSNETT LIBRARY, by *Forsyth*, 1935, Domestic Revival with a hipped roof. SW of this, the Y-shaped DIXON SIXTH FORM CENTRE by *Goldsmith & Tolson*, 1969–70. Free-standing at the SE, WAR MEMORIAL CHAPEL, by *Gunton & Gunton*, 1920–2, Neo-Perp. – STAINED GLASS by *Hugh Easton*, 1936.

ST STEPHEN'S PRIMARY SCHOOL, Richmond Road. 1839, by *G. P. Manners*, in the Jacobethan style he used where classical or Gothic was inappropriate. Extension by *Gill & Morris*, 1900.

CAMDEN ROAD shows the considerable distinction given even to small houses in Bath until the early C19. E of Camden Crescent (*see* p. 169), BERKELEY PLACE, S side, a mid-C19 terrace with banded ground-floor rustication and two-storey porches. UPPER CAMDEN PLACE, set back above the N side, is a picturesque late C18 and early C19 assortment, some by *Eveleigh*. Nos. 1–2 and 6–7, 1815, take advantage of the SE prospect, with segmental bays. LOWER CAMDEN PLACE, S side, early C19, possibly by *John Pinch*, are small, separated by plain pilasters. Set back high above, CAMDEN TERRACE, N side, six early C19 houses, possibly by *Pinch the Elder*, single-window width with reeded porches. The two projecting centre houses have a pediment with the Camden arms. PROSPECT PLACE, N side, a long terrace of cottages. Nos. 12 and 14, formerly one house, are 1736; No. 20, 1740, refronted 1811; the remainder mostly *c*. 1810. Further E is CLAREMONT PLACE, four pairs of small elegant semi-detached villas of 1817, with corner pilasters, acroteria and Soanian incised decoration. Probably *Pinch the Elder*.

In St Stephen's Place, S of the church, is ST STEPHEN'S VILLAS (originally almshouses). By *James Wilson*, 1843, institutional Tudor-Gothic. Projecting ends with buttresses. The original plan was quite grand; sixteen houses, chapel and hall, emulating Vicars' Close, Wells (*see* p. 686). A little way SE in Mount Road, HEATHFIELD, MULBERRY HOUSE and BELLA VISTA, Italianate villas, also *Wilson*, *c*. 1845.

The most isolated developments of Regency Bath lie NE of St Stephen. RICHMOND TERRACE, Richmond Hill, is possibly by *John Pinch*, 1790s. On RICHMOND ROAD (S end), RICHMOND LODGE, 1814, stylishly enlarged by *Browne & Gill*, 1885, for St Stephen's vicarage. NORTHFIELD HOUSE, W side, *c.* 1820, is a large Late Georgian villa (altered 1894–1903). Greek Doric portico with fluted columns and balustraded parapet, facing the garden. Proceeding N, YORK PLACE, E side, has a Roman Doric porch. Off Richmond Road to the E, RICHMOND PLACE, a long row of pretty artisan cottages, many rendered and colourful.

SPRINGFIELD PLACE, Lansdown Road, W of St Stephen's church. Semi-detached classical villas of *c.* 1820.

GLEN AVON, Sion Road, ⅓ m. NW of St Stephen's church. An eclectic, Goodridge-inspired Italianate villa, 1858–60, by *James Wilson* for himself. Gabled projecting block, three-storey belvedere, four-storey octagonal turret in between. Gabled and machicolated chimneystacks.

CHELSCOMBE FARM, ⅓ m. NW from the end of Fonthill Road. A five-bay house dated 1651, showing the new fashion for symmetry. Ovolo-mullioned windows, hoodmoulds, deep relieving arches.

BECKFORD'S TOWER AND LANSDOWN CEMETERY, Lansdown Road. 1¼ m. NW of St Stephen's church. Built in 1826–8 for William Beckford when, in old age, he lived in Lansdown Crescent below. It was both retreat and the terminating feature of Beckford's idyllic landscape garden (*see* p. 169). Following his death, Tower and grounds were donated to the rector of Walcot and consecrated as a cemetery in 1848, with the principal ground-floor room as a mortuary chapel.

Beckford's architect was *H. E. Goodridge*, appointed perhaps because he was young and compliant. Goodridge made several designs, including a 'Saxon' tower, as early as 1823. The final choice was Graeco-Roman: a picturesque fusion of a Neo-Greek tower rising 154 ft (47 metres) from an asymmetrical Italianate one- and two-storey house. This has round-arched windows with iron lattice grills, a triple-arched entrance loggia on the E side, a small single-storey apse to the N, and a triumphal-arch campanile above the S parapet. The surrounding graves, and the Tower's former function as a cemetery chapel, seem singularly appropriate. There is something bleak and sinister which penetrates into all its details. The windows for instance, have block-like sills and hoods and refrain from all mouldings. Equally elementary balustrades. The tall square shaft of the first stage is two-thirds plain with small windows, terminating in a great Doric entablature with a boldly profiled cornice. The belvedere stage has plain rectangular openings framing deeply recessed arches, and a reduced entablature with dentils. Plinth-like parapet decorated with panels of key fret and square corner blocks with roundels. The third stage is octagonal, after the Tower of the Winds. It acts as a plinth for the crowning octagonal lantern with cast-iron columns, adapted from the Choragic Monument of Lysicrates. The forms are ponderously, funereally, but very freely, treated: a design ahead of its time, with much that characterizes the change from Grecian to Victorian. The lantern was dazzlingly regilded *c.* 2000. The rich INTERIORS, originally filled with treasures, included an apsidal Scarlet Drawing Room (ground floor), a first-floor Crimson Drawing Room, and an Etruscan Library. A stone spiral cantilevered stair continues to the Belvedere.

Fire gutted the interior in 1931 and it was eventually converted to a house by *J. Owen Williams*, 1972. *Caröe & Partners* and *Mann Williams Structural Engineers* restored the tower in 1997–2000 as a Beckford museum, when something of the richness of the interior was re-created.

The elaborate gabled cemetery GATEWAY is by *Goodridge*, 1848. An eclectic layering of Neoclassical and Romanesque forms and decorations. The flanking walls (the railings replaced 2000) incorporate piers that had previously enclosed Beckford's TOMB at the Abbey Cemetery (it was moved here 1848). The tomb is a pink Aberdeen granite sarcophagus surrounded by a dry moat.

2. *London Road, Larkhall and Lambridge*

The long Late Georgian terraces and ribbon development of London Road can be followed for ¾ m. NE from Cleveland Place to Lambridge. To the NE, the late C18 and early C19 village of Larkhall survives largely intact.

ST SAVIOUR, St Saviour's Road, Larkhall. A Commissioners' church of 1829–32, probably by *Pinch the Younger* to the *elder Pinch*'s design. It cost £10,600. A plan approved in 1824 was Doric, the result is Neo-Perp, after St Mary, Bathwick (p. 117). W tower with octagonal buttresses, pinnacles and parapet. Tall windows. *C. E. Davis* added the chancel in 1882. Broad galleried interior, now subdivided, with tall, thin piers, and plaster tierceron-vaults. Fan-vaulted chancel. – Dec REREDOS by *J. D. Sedding*, 1886, marble and stone, richly carved by *Harry Hems*. – Original gallery PEWS. – ORGAN. By *Sweetland*, c. 1882, richly painted. – MONUMENTS. Many tablets. Frances Pottinger, †1842, by *Reeves*. The usual allegorical females, but flanking a Gothic tomb-chest.

LONDON ROAD.* Working SW to NE from Cleveland Place, first, N side, the KING WILLIAM IV pub, c. 1830, with bowed windows to THOMAS STREET. This rises steeply N with late C18 terraces at the lower end and, W side, the simple Grecian three-bay front of THOMAS STREET CHAPEL, 1830, now flats. The S side of London Road continues with WALCOT TERRACE, late C18; No. 9 was the BATH EAR AND EYE INFIRMARY, dated 1837, with a curious narrow prostyle Ionic porch with a bust of Aesculapius. One of many medical concerns around Cleveland Place. Opposite, N side, LONG ACRE was an early C19 terrace; *Mowbray Green* rebuilt the centre section as Bath Technical Institute in 1910. Four storeys, symmetrical front, with metal-framed windows. Next, SNOW HILL, a

*For London Road w of Cleveland Place, *see* p. 179.

housing estate for Bath City Council by *Terence Snailum* of *Snailum, Huggins & Le Fevre*, 1954–61; at the time, a model of slum redevelopment. A Scandinavian interpretation of classicism. Long parallel blocks with intrusive green copper roofs follow the contours, with one block stepping uphill. For 'focus', a twelve-storey point block, 1955–7. The upper terrace has prominent external staircases.

Then follows a somewhat scattered and sparse stretch. Set back on the S side, WALCOT POORHOUSE, rebuilt 1828: Tudor style, with a large blind quatrefoil dated 1848, when it became Sutcliffe Industrial Schools. Two C18 wings remain at the rear. Now commercial premises. Next E is Fortt, Hatt and Billings' furniture DEPOSITORY, with a Greek Revival front of 1926, by *A. J. Taylor*. The PORTER BUTT pub next door, 1800, has a stone barrel finial on the parapet. At right angles to the road, YORK VILLA, a large late C18 house once owned by the Duke of York, second son of George III. The Corinthian doorway has unusual garlanded quarter-columns. Large rear ballroom with coved ceiling. Opposite, off to the N, BRUNSWICK STREET; a remarkably intact early C19 artisan terrace stepping steeply uphill, W side: two-storey houses one window wide. Returning to London Road, set back (s), a SUPERMARKET by *Atkins, Walters & Webster*, 1999–2000: of stone, zinc roofing and aluminium cladding. A curved full-length canopy like an aircraft wing, on canted columns and struts, broken by a glazed entrance. A little E again, to the N, HANOVER STREET; E side, late C18, W side slightly later. Nos. 7–8 have doorcases with blocks and roundels to the corners.

Then London Road gathers strength once again, with KENSINGTON PLACE, a long frontage of *c.* 1795 by *Palmer*. Nos. 5 and 6 have recessed porches with flat segmental arches which gave access to the former KENSINGTON CHAPEL between. One of *Palmer*'s best designs, of 1795. Rusticated ground floor with three windows. Corresponding in the wall above, three tall, arched windows on a deep sill with consoles. The windows are framed by widely spaced pairs of pilasters, with a cornice that returns at the windows to form a springing for the archivolts. This pleasingly ambiguous arrangement also reads as three linked Venetian windows with blank outer compartments. Now a warehouse with an inserted floor, the chapel retains a panelled reredos. The only other accent is at No. 16: three-bay pediment, chamfered ground-floor rustication, Regency canopied balcony. The houses here still have pedimented doorcases with Tuscan demi-columns or pilasters. One feels that by 1800 architects at Bath devoted much less thought to such long terraces than the Woods had done.

A little E (s side), WORCESTER TERRACE, *c.* 1813–16, quite distinguished and crisply executed. Then BEAUFORT HOUSE (N), *c.* 1800 and later, hidden from the street behind tall gatepiers with Soanian caps. Symmetrical, seven windows wide with large segmental bays. The rear range is BEAUFORT LODGE, seen from St Saviour's Road, which joins London Road at

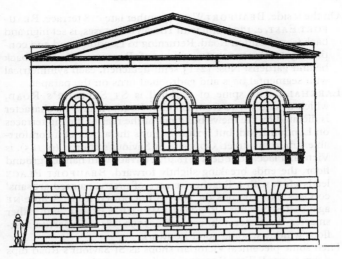

Bath, Kensington Chapel.
Elevation

a fork. In the angle of the roads is a former TOLL HOUSE,
c. 1820–30, the start of the Grosvenor turnpike to London.
On the S side is the bowed W end of GROSVENOR PLACE, by
John Eveleigh, begun 1791. Of the immense plan, only a hotel
and forty-one out of 143 houses were completed. A long terrace
with a gently convex centre, originally screening pleasure
gardens. Eveleigh went bankrupt, the gardens were abandoned
c. 1810, and much remained unfinished in 1819. At the middle
of the terrace is the hotel (No. 23), gaily ornate and somewhat
vulgar, almost Baroque. The ground floor has vermiculated
rustication, and arched windows with bearded icicle-mask keystones. Above, seven giant attached Ionic columns forming
an even number of bays, as at Eveleigh's Camden Crescent
(p. 169). One column stands wilfully over the doorway. The
shafts are decorated with bands of garlands, the lower band
left uncarved when money ran out, as were three of the six oval
plaques with animal reliefs over the first-floor windows. Only
the columns have a full entablature, but the modillioned
cornice breaks back across the bays. Balustraded parapet. The
central doorway with its later Doric porch was designed as an
entrance to the pleasure gardens. The flanks swell forward to
meet the hotel, punctuated by three-house pavilions that break
forward, one to the l. and two to the r. The houses are oriented
towards the garden view, with staircases at the front. No. 13 is
exceptional: five bays, Ionic doorcase, good ironwork, stair-hall
across two bays. Early C19 Greek Revival porches to several
houses. In No. 39, landscape MURALS ascribed to *Thomas
Shew*, c. 1828.

On the N side, BEAUFORT WEST, another late C18 terrace. BEAU-
FORT EAST, c. 1790, still with Tuscan doorcases, is set high and
back from London Road. Returning to London Road and continuing E, LAMBRIDGE, a row of Regency villas set back
behind gardens; Nos. 12–13 semi-detached, each symmetrical
with segmental bays and gadrooned urns on the parapet.

LARKHALL. The spine of Larkhall is ST SAVIOUR'S ROAD,
which diverges NNE from London Road. At first its character
is dictated by the mews buildings at the rear of the big terraces
on London Road; but it shortly gains the aspect of a comfortable suburban street. Opposite St Saviour's church (p. 185), is
Victoria Place, doubtless c. 1840; a terrace with banded ground
floor, the ends breaking slightly forward. BEAUFORT PLACE
leads off S, with a Regency terrace of pretty, painted artisans'
cottages; No. 10 ends the row with a bowed front. A little NE
again off St Saviour's Road is LAMBRIDGE PLACE, with rather
smarter three-storey houses of c. 1790–1810. Tripartite first-
floor windows, some good ironwork.

Then some piecemeal Victorian shops as St Saviour's Road dips
down towards THE SQUARE, really an irregular triangle dominated by the LARKHALL INN, a house of mid-C18 origins.
Symmetrical front with big sashes. Mansard roof, balustraded
parapet perhaps c. 1820–50. Apsidal rear wing of c. 1800, probably for a function room. To the N, BROOKLEAZE BUILDINGS,
a long stepped cottage terrace, c. 1800–20. Opposite, NEW
ORIEL HALL, a Neo-Tudor school by *James Wilson*, 1845, converted to community halls 2001–4. Behind it, NE, LARKHALL
PLACE, a terrace very like Lambridge Place (above), with
detached gardens opposite.

St Saviour's Road climbs NE from The Square. At Brougham
Place, two Late Georgian houses with first-floor balconies of
Caribbean extraction, i.e. the ends enclosed by walls. Another
¼ m. NE, beyond the bridge over the Lam Brook is DEAD
MILL, reputedly once a gunpowder mill, later a flour mill,
much rebuilt in 1900 (see the blue brick window arches).
Much of the stonework is clearly older. Adjacent is THE
FERNS, no doubt the owner's house, with C17 ovolo-moulded
mullions and an C18 roof.

3. *Bathwick Hill beyond the Kennet and Avon Canal*

The mile-long ascent of Bathwick Hill follows the early C19 shift
to a semi-rural idyll of Picturesque Regency and Early Victorian
villas. The descent, with rewarding views, concludes with industrial survivals along the canal.

We start where the Kennet and Avon Canal passes under Bathwick Hill. The CANAL BRIDGE, c. 1800, is by *Rennie*; uphill, w
side, is GEORGE STREET, a terrace of small two-bay houses.
Nos. 9–12, c. 1815, are cottagey with wide sashes; better proportioned, Nos. 1–8, c. 1820, by *Pinch*. Dividing George Street,
SYDNEY BUILDINGS runs S. Informal two- and three-storey

terraces, the E side with a raised pavement, *c.* 1820, a late and very high example. Above, the imposing rear face of Darling-ton Place. No. 1, *c.* 1830, perhaps by *Goodridge*, an unusually small and finely executed Greek Revival front, recessed in the centre. An industrial survival, a mid-C19 MALTHOUSE, con-verted to offices, 1972, by *Marshman Warren Taylor*. A timber structure with cast-iron columns; adjacent square kiln with pyramidal roof. No. 23, early C19 with C20 alterations, was a ticket office for the Kennet and Avon Canal. (For S of here, *see* below.)

Returning to Bathwick Hill, N side, stepping uphill, DUNSFORD PLACE, by *Pinch the Elder*, fifteen two-bay houses with Greek-key iron balconies. They accommodate the road with a slight concavity. Opposite, DARLINGTON PLACE leads off S. ADE-LAIDE PLACE, NW end, is a semi-detached villa pair with Neo-Grecian incised decoration. Unassuming houses on the W side, 1812–39, with porches. Nos. 1–8, by *Pinch the Elder*, 1824, are bigger, with good W elevations overlooking the view. No. 9, with a canopied porch, is 1812. Next on Bathwick Hill, ST PATRICK'S COURT, 1966, by *Hugh Roberts & Partners*, ugly flats that step uneasily uphill, having learned nothing from Pinch. Opposite, Nos. 39–40 and 36–37, 1827, by *Pinch* himself. Symmetrical, bow-fronted, pilasters at first floor, and Ionic doorcases. These alternate with villas, BAYSFIELD HOUSE, and LOMOND HOUSE, the latter 1839, probably by *Pinch the Younger*. Grecian Doric doorcases with iron balconies. Lomond House has immense brackets on the parapet. SION PLACE, S side, is an incomplete stepped terrace by *Pinch the Elder*, 1826, the houses separated by panelled pilasters.

Uphill from Sion Place is a sequence of neat, regularly spaced VILLAS designed or approved by the *Elder Pinch* as surveyor to the Bathwick estate, some with exuberant garden fronts. Dates given refer to leases; most have later alterations (e.g. No. 20, Jacobean-style; *Silcock & Reay*, 1897).

Nos. 1–5, all 1824–5, have pleasing Greek Revival details and varied compositions, e.g. at No. 2 small wings with symmetri-cal doors giving the appearance of two houses; at No. 3, out-dated Batty Langley-style Gothick detail over the door. No. 9 (SPA VILLA, 1820) was octagonal in plan, with a shallow-pedimented Greek Revival front; extended and squared off on one side by *Gill & Browne*, 1877, retaining the garden front as a centrepiece. An original Neo-Greek garden elevation at No. 10, with giant Ionic half-pilasters flanking the centre, and a bowed porch. Further interesting Grecian variations: e.g. the porch and double-bowed garden front at No. 15; mid-C19 wings and the decoration over the door to No. 18; fine detail-ing to No. 23, 1817. Finally, the pretty Tudoresque PRIORY LODGE, *c.* 1840.

On the steep upper slopes, a remarkable sequence of Picturesque Italianate villas, 1830s–40s, by *H. E. Goodridge* and others. First (N side) an asymmetrical semi-detached pair, CASA BIANCA and LA CASETTA, a speculation by Goodridge, *c.* 1846. The most Italianate of the group, with warm ochre stucco, rugged pantiles, chimneys as campaniles, and the obligatory tower. Terraces, loggias, and balustrades dissolve the boundary between house and garden. To the N is FIESOLE, 1846–8, built by *Goodridge* for himself, now a Youth Hostel. All the ingredients of the Italianate villa are here, but it seems clumsy, formulaic, and lacking charm. Entrance-hall staircase with Greek Revival balustrades from L. N. Cottingham's *Ornamental Metalworkers' Directory* of 1823. At the top of the stairs, a stucco panel depicting the architect and his wife. Opposite, s side, the big CLAVERTON LODGE. An austere street front, with origins *c.* 1820 evident on the garden side. Porch, top floor and dormered roofs added by *J. M. Brydon*, 1896.

Next on the N side is *Goodridge*'s earlier home, Montebello, now BATHWICK GRANGE, 1829. Large, not pretty and not explicitly Italianate like Goodridge's later villas, but an important contribution to the genre. In secluded grounds. The house is asymmetrical with a round-arched colonnade and a very tall campanile. Octagonal corner tower, now reduced in height, after the Tower of the Winds, Athens. A big conservatory was replaced with an extension by *Bennett Diugiewicz & Date*, 1998. Delightful lodge, 1848. Above, N side, is BATHWICK HILL HOUSE, probably *Goodridge*. Severest Greek Revival, presumably designed before 1829 when Goodridge took up the Picturesque. A strictly regular plan and crisp ashlar make the house appear monolithic. s (garden) façade with recessed centre with columns derived from the Tower of the Winds, Athens.

Opposite, s side, is OAKWOOD. A simple square villa of *c.* 1814 (i.e. the recessed and lower s wing) built by the landscape painter *Benjamin Barker*. Extended to the N after 1833 by *Edward Davis*, a pupil of Soane; an early example of Picturesque Italianate asymmetry, with shallow roofs, broad eaves, campanile, loggia and French windows. Davis's wing is of two phases; the w section has a projecting bay with a tripartite loggia above (now glazed). The E housed an art gallery with Venetian window. Coachhouse with a Tuscan watch tower behind. Further altered by *Gill & Browne*, 1879. Entrance vestibule and garden wing by *Brydon*, 1896. Davis's interiors owe much to Soane. Ashlar-faced rusticated staircase hall with segmental arches and incised ornament; dining room with Soanian starfish ceiling. Reconverted to a house in 1992–3 by *Forsyth Chartered Architects*. Regency garden laid out by *Barker*, with four small lakes linked by cascades, and a bridge of *c.* 1835.

Adjacent, E, WOODLAND PLACE, 1826, by *Goodridge*. A six-house terrace composed as pairs, with porches. On the gateposts, Grecian sarcophagi with acroteria. At No. 1 an elegant elliptical staircase; No. 6 has a stone plunge pool. WOODHILL PLACE opposite, also by *Goodridge*, is a semi-detached pair with a recessed centre and first-floor Doric loggia. A combination of Greek Revival and Italianate. Above the E ground-floor window a sunburst relief with a head of Apollo. Uphill again, s side, COMBE ROYAL CRESCENT by *David Brain Partnership*, 2001–2, three terraced houses crisply detailed in Pinch's manner with a touch of Soane. To the NE is the University (*see* p. 196).

Returning down Bathwick Hill to Casa Bianca, a gap opposite leads to a footpath across fields s of the road, following the backs of the Pinch villas. Behind Nos. 2–4 Bathwick Hill, HAWKSHEAD and WINGFIELD HOUSE, 1989–90, by *Hadfield Oatley*, single-storey, with corner glazing and chain rainwater drips. Further down, No. 22 DARLINGTON PLACE is by *Keith Bradley* of *Feilden Clegg Design*, 1996–7. A linear design with monopitch roof. Plain ashlar front with a clerestory and 'hole-in-the-wall' entrance. Inside, a raised threshold platform overlooks the living spaces.

Further down is the s end of Sydney Buildings. Nos. 30–38, SYDNEY PARADE, a small but dignified 1820s terrace by *Pinch*. Between Nos. 29–30, the path joins the KENNET AND AVON CANAL via an iron FOOTBRIDGE by *Stothert* adjacent to Widcombe Locks. Here are a Gothic LOCK KEEPER'S COTTAGE and an ornamental CHIMNEY, thought to be of a former pumping station. Shortly on the E side is the SOMERSET COAL COMPANY WHARF, with a warehouse completed 1814. Converted to offices.

4. *South and south-east of the Avon: Widcombe, Lyncombe and Holloway*

An area of great diversity. The expanses around Claverton Street, and Holloway to the w, were until the 1960s rich in early C18 artisan housing. To the SE, Widcombe village retains its character fully.

ST MARK (former), St Mark's Road. By *G. P. Manners*, 1830–2, a Commissioners' church. Perp Revival, battlemented and pinnacled, w tower rather in the Somerset manner. Polygonal chancel by *Thomas Ames* of *Wilson & Willcox*, 1883. It became Widcombe Community Centre in 1975, with partitioned aisles.

ST MARY MAGDALEN, Holloway. The chapel of a leper hospital built for Prior Cantlow of Bath, *c.* 1495. Restored in 1761. *H. E. Goodridge* added the chancel and small three-stage w tower in 1823–4. The tower arch was not cut through until 1889. E end rebuilt after bomb damage. Perp s porch with a canopied image niche, and hoodmoulds to the nave windows. Plain narrow nave with restored plaster barrel-vault, and more image niches, three to the N, two, s. – Ball-like FONT from Huish parish church (S. Somerset), 1980. – STAINED GLASS above the altar, *c.* 1950, by *Michael Farrar Bell*, containing C15 salvaged glass. – MONUMENT. Handsome tablet to Anne Biggs †1662; odd mannered top with a broken reversed scroll pediment, and high-relief reclining figures.

St Matthew, Cambridge Place. 1846–7, by *Manners & Gill*. Dull, Dec style. Prominently sited with a s tower and 150-ft (45-metre) broach spire. It had 1,250 seats. Now subdivided.

St Thomas à Becket, Church Street, Widcombe. Built by Prior Cantlow, 1490–8, on the site of a Norman chapel. The w tower plain, of two stages, with battlements and pinnacles. Arms of the Priory of Bath, high up on the e wall. Embattled Perp nave. Pierced chancel parapet from *C. E. Davis*'s restoration of 1860–1; he also unblocked the e window. s chapel screened from the chancel by complex c19 tracery. – REREDOS by *F. Bligh Bond*, 1914. – SCREEN. Finely carved oak, 1913. – FONT. Fine early c18 bowl on three cherubs, gadrooned base. – SCULPTURE. Part of a cross-head; circular centre with wedge-shaped arms and V-shaped angles, perhaps mid- to late c11. – Painted ROYAL ARMS, 1660. – STAINED GLASS, by *Lavers & Barraud*, 1861. Plants and flowers, but curiously no human figures.

Widcombe Baptist Church, Claverton Street. Formerly Ebenezer Chapel, dated 1820–2. Six bays of pointed windows with intersecting glazing, battlements, slated pyramidal roof painted with religious texts. Originally entered from the N; layout reversed and s entrance added *c.* 1980. Large square hall, galleried with Batty-Langley-style cluster columns. Big Jacobean-style Sunday School etc., by *Silcock & Reay*, 1910.

First Church of Christ Scientist, St Mark's Road. Built as a Temperance Hall in 1847. A handsome little building, pedimented, with Doric pilasters and full entablature.

Magistrates' Courts, North Parade Road. By *Chris Bocci* of Avon County Council, 1987–9. Steep slate roofs respond to the former La Sainte Union Convent, adjacent in Pulteney Road. By *J. Elkington Gill*, 1866–7, his largest sole work. Tudoresque, but unusually tall, gaunt and forbidding. Extension by *Browne & Gill*, 1880.

Widcombe School, Pulteney Road. By *Nealon Tanner Partnership*, 1995–6. The low single-storey building presents to the street protective rubble walls with a clerestory, and a shallow-pitch stepped roof, pierced with amusing metal vents.

Other Buildings. First, around Pulteney Road and Widcombe Hill. Claverton Street is a rather desolate dual carriageway since 1960s clearances. Near the e end, Widcombe Parade (s side), late c18. Originally twelve houses; four, w, replicated 1990–1. Further w, above the high abutment onto St Mark's Road, the former Temperance Hall (*see* above). On the N side here, Widcombe Footbridge crosses the Avon, a single-span wrought-iron lattice girder construction by *T. E. M. Marsh*, 1877.

Widcombe Hill, climbing from Claverton Street, w to e. First, s side, the Church Room and Institute, an amateur but not amateurish design by the *Rev. W. T. H. Wilson*, 1882, converted to a theatre by *Aaron Evans Associates*, 1997. Opposite St Matthew's church (*see* above) is Cambridge Place, by the *Elder Pinch*, *c.* 1825, detached and semi-detached villas, raised above street level. The central windows blind, except at Nos. 3 and 6. Uphill, S side, *Harcourt Masters*'s Widcombe Crescent with Widcombe Terrace, *c.* 1805, an attractive minor ensemble. WIDCOMBE CRESCENT has fourteen houses, quite plain. No central feature. Staircases at the front, allowing the rear principal rooms views of Beechen Cliff. The central houses have pretty paired entrances in shallow arches decorated with a floral boss and ribboned festoons. To the E, WIDCOMBE TERRACE, six tucked-away houses, the elegant W return elevation facing along the crescent; two full-height bows with parapet urns. Arranged back-to-front, the rear elevation achieving some grandeur, finely articulated after Adam, with a scroll frieze.

Further up on the S side of Widcombe Hill, behind a wall, AQUILA, a house by *David Hadfield*, 1997, single-storeyed with a Japanese flavour and pyramidal top lighting. On the N side, behind rusticated gateposts with pineapples, WIDCOMBE HILL HOUSE, late C18, one of the first villas here. CROWE HALL, S side, is a very grand mansion behind tall, banded gatepiers with pineapple vases. Originally of 1742 and 1780, rebuilt *c.* 1805, much altered since. After a fire in 1926 *Axford & Smith* rebuilt the W front sympathetically. Entrance front with giant Ionic tetrastyle portico; detailing to the blind flanks may be post-fire. Lavish classical interiors, mostly *c.* 1871; domed hall with screens of Doric columns on the long sides. Grand staircase, 1926. Extensive terraced gardens. The grotto below the S terrace is possibly of 1742. Late C18 coachhouse, pedimented with *œil-de-bœuf* window.

MACAULAY BUILDINGS, Widcombe Hill. Oddly isolated ⅓ m. E of Crowe Hall. Three villa pairs with bow fronts, 1819–30. Off the hill, more attached villa pairs.

PRIOR PARK ROAD. From Claverton Street, NW to SE. First, on the SW, RALPH ALLEN'S COTTAGES, by *Wood the Elder*, *c.* 1737, for Allen's stonemasons (his stone was shipped from the nearby wharf). A rare early example of small Palladian workers' dwellings; plain, three storeys (stone spiral staircases). Restored by *Hugh Roberts, Graham & Stollar*, 1983. At right angles beyond, PRIOR PARK COTTAGES, of *c.* 1820, rise steeply uphill. No. 2 has a fine Gothick front. The lane beside leads to the former MILLBROOK SCHOOL, by *C. B. Oliver*, 1902. Tudoresque, but with individual Arts and Crafts bell-hood and cupola. Back on Prior Park Road, separated from the road by a stream (SW side) are PRIOR PARK BUILDINGS, by *Pinch the Elder*, begun 1820. A monumental palace-fronted terrace with pedimented centre and ends. Opposite, pretty pairs of modest Late Regency villas, then Nos. 63–69, two Picturesque Tudor pairs dated 1843. ASHLEY LODGE, SW side, is a pretty mid-C19 villa. On the NE side, a former MILL, C18 or earlier (now a car dealership), with a good Venetian window. Here begins the more rural RALPH ALLEN DRIVE, the former drive to Prior Park (p. 200). The C18 LOWER LODGE, with a Venetian window and quoins, is by *Wood the Elder* (as is the UPPER LODGE at the top). Opposite, BATH ABBEY CEMETERY (p. 121).

OLD WIDCOMBE is an exquisite enclave in the combe below Prior Park. At the W end of CHURCH STREET, the rear of No. 5 Widcombe Hill is a village house of *c.* 1700, extended *c.* 1800 in the Palladian taste. No. 1, S side, SOMERSET HOUSE, early C19, one of an unequal pair with No. 2, has a powerful Greek Revival porch. A little further, N side, Nos. 11–12 are *c.* 1700, also mullioned. At the head of Church Street is St Thomas à Becket (p. 192).

WIDCOMBE MANOR lies NW of the church. Late C17, built for Scarborough Chapman, a Bristol businessman, and given a new principal S façade in 1726–7 by his grandson, Philip Bennet II. An elegant if provincial design, not in the local tradition, and by an unknown architect, perhaps *Nathaniel Ireson* of Wincanton. The honey-coloured main front is decidedly Baroque. Seven bays and two storeys. Giant fluted Ionic pilasters, coupled at the angles and as framing to a pedimented three-bay centre; garlands and an oval window in the pediment. Doric doorcase – flanked by arched windows – with triglyph frieze and segmental pediment. Three individual first-floor windows form something like a low Venetian window. The side windows have architraves with grotesque mask keystones and, at first floor, sills on consoles. The entablature has a pulvinated frieze, modillioned cornice and a high parapet; hipped stone roof. In 1840 *James Wilson* built the remarkably sensitive W elevation, with a canted bay, and pilasters to match the S front. Inside, a low, panelled hall with bolection mouldings, a good staircase with twisted balusters, and a first-floor landing with groin-vaulted side bays.

The forecourt has a two-stage bronze FOUNTAIN, said to be Venetian. Base with turtles and the Medici arms; above, satyrs and a cherub on a seahorse. In the extensive GARDEN is a small SUMMERHOUSE by *Didier Bertrand* with an C18 façade, moved from Fairford, Gloucs., *c.* 1961. Arched centre on rusticated Doric columns and flanking oculi with four keystones. Primitive blocks instead of triglyphs in the frieze. *Rolfe & Peto* added two lower TERRACES divided by a double staircase, and a sunken garden, *c.* 1930. The W extremity has a LAKE with an C18 cascade, and an early C18 MOUNT with a spiral path to its summit.

A two-storey GARDEN HOUSE S of the church is attributed to *Richard Jones*, Ralph Allen's clerk of works. Square in plan, with a three-arched loggia with engaged Doric columns; Ionic columns flank the upper windows. S again, E side, the former stables and service block, mid-C18 and C19 (now WIDCOMBE HOUSE). In front is a handsome C18 octagonal DOVECOTE with cupola, also an C18 garden grotto. Garden, and possibly the house conversion, by *Rolfe & Peto*, 1929.

HOLLOWAY. The name for both a district and the old main road to Wells, which climbs SW then S from the river bridge. At its foot, the controversial CALTON GARDENS, private low-rise housing by *Marshman Warren Taylor*, 1969–70. Despite attempting the linearity of Georgian terraces, it does great visual damage to Bath. To accommodate it, 381 houses were demolished in 1968, including many fine vernacular houses, under plans by the City Architect and Planning Officer, *Dr Howard Stutchbury* (architectural adviser *Sir Hugh Casson*). Above, N side, No. 88, PARADISE HOUSE, *c.* 1760, now a hotel. A wide symmetrical frontage with fine Palladian details; two Venetian windows with Tuscan columns, pedimented doorway. At the rear, a three-storey canted bay and a big single-storey Victorian extension. No. 90, dated 1761 and with Gothic windows. For St Mary Magdalen, adjacent, *see* p. 191. Below on WELLS ROAD (S side), ST MARY'S BUILDINGS by *Pinch the Elder*, *c.* 1820, a plain terrace stepped up steeply, with his characteristic ramped cornices.

5. Claverton Down and the University

Claverton Down consists of scattered buildings along the hilltops E of the city, without churches or public buildings. Only the campus of the University of Bath forms a coherent group. For the village of Claverton and Claverton Manor, *see* p. 460.

KING EDWARD'S JUNIOR SCHOOL, North Road, by *Alec French Partnership*, 1989–90. A steep site. The hall and dining area on the E side and two tiers of classrooms, staggered in plan to the W. Wedge-shaped open library between, to which all other spaces relate. It is lit by lights developed from the pitched roofs over the classrooms. STAINED GLASS window in the S wall by *Ros Grimshaw*.

SHAM CASTLE, off North Road. *Richard Jones* built it as an eyecatcher for Ralph Allen's townhouse in 1762, probably to a design by *Sanderson Miller* who had been approached seven years earlier (though Jones claimed the design was his). No more than a façade, with tall semicircular half-towers each side of an archway and square corner towers. Blind lancets and arrow loops.

KILOWATT HOUSE (now Woodside House), North Road. By *Mollie Taylor* of *Alfred J. Taylor & Partners*, 1935–8. Bath's only pre-war Modern Movement house, for the electrical engineer Anthony Greenhill. Of reinforced concrete with metal windows, it has a projecting semicircular stair-tower and transformer chamber to the garden front and flat roofs capable of being flooded for summer cooling. Greenhill was interested in acoustics, and his home was also his laboratory. W of the stairhall, a single-storey wing housing a recording studio lined with acoustic board. He produced 'colour music' which lit up an indoor 'cascade of glass', each musical note corresponding to a hue.

WESSEX WATER BUILDING, North Road. Office headquarters by *Bennetts Associates*, 1999–2000, based on environmental sustainability and a sensitive, low-key response to the steep site.

A wide central 'street' on five levels connects office wings (E) and ancillary accommodation (W). The cladding is glass and Bath stone, with large metal sunshades to the s.

Former GOSPEL HALL, Claverton Down Road. By *Silcock & Reay*, 1896–7. Charming, small and Voyseyesque, with much presence. Mullioned lights, and gable-ends that run out into buttresses. Their angled profiles continue above the roof-line as big kneeling angels whose wings lie back against the slope of the gable. Sturdy asymmetrical porch. Now a house.

UNIVERSITY OF BATH, Claverton Down. In origin a 1960s complex by *Robert Matthew, Johnson-Marshall & Partners (RMJM)*, with a spine vertically separating pedestrians and traffic. The campus has additions by *Alison & Peter Smithson*. Recent building is to a masterplan of 2001 by *Feilden Clegg Bradley*.

117   Occupying a 150-acre greenfield site, the campus is comparable to the seven new British 1960s universities (Sussex, Lancaster, Warwick, Essex, York, East Anglia, Kent/Canterbury), sharing with them a landscaped edge-of-town site, conceived as an antidote to the formlessness of the 'redbrick' universities. It belongs, however, to a slightly later trend for Colleges of Advanced Technology upgraded to university status. The new foundations attempted to integrate or at least juxtapose residence with teaching and research, with the aim of nurturing intellectual life by directing movement and interaction; part of a general idealism about reshaping the university.

RMJM published its Development Plan in 1965 and phase one was completed 1966–7, the rest by 1980.* Here, as at some other new universities, the plan was substantially decided by the architect and the Vice-Chancellor. The concept of a compact megastructure capable of expansion, with blocks latched onto a central axis, is similar to Lancaster (by Gabriel Epstein of Bridgwater, Shepheard & Epstein). Bath's pedestrian deck over road access is closest to Essex (Kenneth Capon, Architects' Co-Partnership). The use of the *CLASP* (Consortium of Local Authority Special Projects) building system aligns it with York, also by RMJM, but Bath's *CLASP* is a special version, with coloured concrete intended to resemble Bath stone.

Buildings and parts are classifiable under three heads: original megastructure, extensions, and detached pavilions-in-the-park. The sequence follows a clockwise circuit: the central campus; s to additions and teaching outliers; then W additions, N extremities, and the E side including the sports complex.

The basic framework of *RMJM*'s 1960s CAMPUS is an extendable pedestrian spine running E–W (cf. Cumbernauld New Town), above a ground-level service road (traffic consultant *Colin Buchanan*, for whom *see also* p. 106). The spine is flanked by the library, lecture theatres, department entrances, refectories and

---

*A proposed tower block breaking the wooded skyline was not built.

shops. Behind are teaching spaces, then workshops and laboratories: a front-to-rear hierarchy. Two tall, transverse slab blocks,
residences E and administration W, enclose the spine at its centre,
broadened here to form the 'Parade', the main social space. The
non-collegiate character comes across very strongly here. On the
s side, the hall and refectories define a grand flight of steps, originally intended as the principal approach. This relates the Parade
to the sunken grass amphitheatre and lake. On the ground, the
campus reads as one large complex sitting in a landscape. Subsequent additions have responded to the landscape and turned
the backyard spaces into fronts, rather as Cambridge colleges did
on a grander scale in the c18.

The BUILDINGS themselves have some individual presence
within the restrictions of system-building. On the SE side of
the Parade, building TWO EAST, ELECTRICAL AND ELEC-
TRONIC ENGINEERING, 1969, uses extensive glazing. Dominating the Parade on the N side is the LIBRARY, extended
forward by *Alec French Partnership*, 1994–6. This transformed
the 1960s architecture into a fashionably lightweight tension
structure, a transparent 'shop window'. Six cruciform steel
masts behind the glazing penetrate the roof, cantilevered
diagonal arms with tension rods support the structure. An
overhang shades the ground floor, a first-floor outer circulation route distances library users from the façade. Fixed
brises-soleil.

Detached a little w of the grass amphitheatre is UBSA (University of Bath Staff Association), built 1978–80 and 1984–5, by
Alison & Peter Smithson. The first phase, a single storey in
blockwork and concrete, became a plinth for the steel-framed,
glazed superstructure with a deep roof fascia. Adjacent, N,
SIX WEST, MANAGEMENT TRAINING CENTRE, by *Nugent
Vallis Brierley*, 1990–1. Supported independently on exposed
columns over an existing building. Access is by a ramped
bridge and a glazed spine. s of here is an isolated group. The
SOUTH BUILDING to the E, square with a courtyard, origi-
nally the Preliminary Building, 1965, was re-clad in the 1990s
by *Nick Hawkins* of Northcroft. Adjacent, w, the CHEMISTRY
TEACHING BUILDING, 2002–3, by *Quentin Fleming, Estates
Department Property Services, University of Bath*, wedge-shaped,
masonry- and metal-clad, with a segmental sheet roof. At the
SW of the group is the COMPUTER CENTRE, *Robert Matthew,
Johnson-Marshall & Partners*, 1975, plain, single-storey. N of
this, ONE SOUTH, CHEMISTRY RESEARCH BUILDING, by
Wilson Mason & Partners, 1999, has inward-sloping butterfly
roofs and two parallel top-lit galleried circulation spaces.

Returning NW to the main spine, EIGHT WEST, the SCHOOL OF
MANAGEMENT, s side, by *Nugent Vallis Brierley*, 1992–4,
together with Seven and Nine West (*see* below), form the w end
of the campus as defined in the Development Plan. Imposing
four-storey w front, with tall vertical glazing. Opposite, N side

and orientated N–S, SEVEN and NINE WEST, research and teaching laboratories by *de Brandt, Joyce & Partners*, 1994–7, N, and 1999–2001, S. They read as one building but are planned as two. Three and four storeys with a basement. Gleaming, heroic flue towers and stair-towers clad with glass blocks at both ends. Pre-cast panels express the columns and floors, with storey-high windows and stone infill. Metal-clad top floor, and a split-level, curved roof for mechanical plant. At the back, E side, the GLAXO LABORATORIES by *de Brandt, Joyce & Partners*, 1993–4. Designed as a two-storey pavilion, with a glazed link to the main building. The space between infilled, 1999. Aluminium-clad pyramidal roof in a witch's-hat finial.

The N side of the site was intended in the Development Plan for student housing. The first phase was WESTWOOD, by *RMJM*, completed 1976, straight blocks running E–W along the N boundary. *De Brandt, Joyce & Partners* broke away from this traditional hostel design at POLDEN COURT, 1993–4, to the W. It wraps around a courtyard on two levels to suit the contours. Mirrored to the E, BRENDON COURT (1987–90, *De Brandt, Joyce & Partners*) is a croissant-shaped building with solid, angular massing and small-pane windows derived from Lutyens's Castle Drogo.

Adjacent, SW, ONE WEST NORTH, completed 1978–81, the first of several campus extensions by *Alison & Peter Smithson*, their chief works after the early 1970s. At least superficially, they lack the fierceness and authority of their earlier works. However, the Smithsons' architecture has always meant to respond to place; here, RMJM's existing masterplan rather than the uneventful terrain. The architects described it as 'the first of a series of tassels' that would form a fringe to the mat of the campus. One West North (with the Department of Architecture and Civil Engineering, below) is significant for striving to break out of a grid pattern, towards a more humane architecture. It is three-storeyed, delta-shaped, with a zigzag back containing teaching rooms. Staircase walls act as wind-braces to a column-grid structure, a development of the grid-plan of the Smithsons' unbuilt Lucas Headquarters (1973). The exterior structure is exposed *in situ* concrete, with a thin reinforced-concrete 'cornice'.

EASTWOOD, further E, by *McDonagh Round*, was built in phases: 1972–3, 1983–4, 1984–5 and 1989–90. The last, ESTHER PARKIN RESIDENCES by *James McDonagh*, is a formal little building with classical touches. It has a central range with wings, and a ground-floor loggia with arches and rusticated voussoirs, like a semi-cloister. To the S, robust four-storey STUDENT HOUSING by *Feilden Clegg Bradley*, 2002–3, links geometrically to Eastwood and mirrors its courtyards. Rendered, with vertical windows, colonnades at ground level, and a curved stainless-steel roof.

p. 199 SE of here is SIX EAST, the DEPARTMENT OF ARCHITECTURE AND CIVIL ENGINEERING, an idiosyncratic late work by *Alison & Peter Smithson*, 1982–8, the E extremity of the campus.

Bath, University, Department of Architecture and Civil Engineering.
Axonometric drawing

It follows the Corbusian plan-as-generator tradition – the Smithsons called it 'developed from the inside outwards' – even if the results are strictly non-monumental. The materials suggest a rejection of the machine aesthetic of *CLASP*. Planned on two overlapping grids, one orthogonal, the other angled, with walls that bend and crank. The resulting spaces differ in shape, size and character, producing an oddly pedagogic building. Bearing walls and columns diminish in thickness according to need. Heavy uses like engineering laboratories occupy the ground floor, and at the top are tall N-lit studios. Bands of concrete emphasize the floor levels, inspired by the fortress of Sassocorvaro in the Duchy of Urbino (the Smithsons were influenced by Giancarlo de Carlo's C20 work at Urbino). The façade has infill of Bath stone, and vertical sliding aluminium windows that refer to sashes; the roof is stainless steel. Inside, the detailing is rather crude, intended to withstand modification.

EIGHT EAST, the CENTRE FOR POWER TRANSMISSION AND MOTION CONTROL, by *Feilden Clegg Bradley*, 2000–2, on the S side of the Smithsons' building, adds a final limb to the original RMJM plan. A linear building. The cladding is partly stainless steel; the remainder, crisply detailed Bath stone. Window openings are enlarged into horizontal bands, or two-storey-high with mullions and transoms. Bands of woven stainless steel shade the glazed entrance. To the E is the ARTS BARN, a converted agricultural building, intended as the centre of an arts complex. The ARTS THEATRE, SW, was *Alison & Peter Smithson*'s final 'tassel' to the campus fringe, built 1989–90, fitted out late 1990s; a windowless blockwork box with stainless-steel roof and fascia. The walls have ledges and pads, as if ready for other structures. Rectangular auditorium with side galleries, asymmetrical entrance lobby underneath.

To the s is the ENGLISH INSTITUTE OF SPORT (SOUTH WEST). Phase one, the SPORTS TRAINING VILLAGE, by *Denning Male Polisano*, 1994–5, is two large steel-clad sheds with segmental roofs linked by a flat-roofed entrance and café. Phase two, by *David Morley Architects*, 2002–3, w, linked by a covered colonnade.

6. Combe Down and the southern slopes, with Prior Park

A plateau separated from Bath by a steep escarpment with folded lower slopes. Combe Down grew from the C18 on the strength of its Bath stone quarries (*see* Prior Park, below).*

HOLY TRINITY, Church Road, Combe Down. By *Goodridge*, 1832–5. As fanciful and crazy as the best, shunning the early C19 tendency towards scholarly Gothic. The front has four buttresses; the inner ones become polygonal pinnacles of a tightly fitted octagonal tower with spire. Lancet windows. *W. J. Willcox* added the aisles and extended the chancel, 1883–4, in a serious C14 Dec style. Broad nave, very flat coved plaster vault with lozenge-patterned ribs. To the e, a Neo-Jacobean VICARAGE, *c.* 1840.

SMALLCOMBE CEMETERY, Horseshoe Road, Smallcombe Vale. Close to the city but remarkably isolated. E.E. MORTUARY CHAPEL by *Thomas Fuller*, 1855–6. Bellcote, stepped buttresses, triple-lancet e window. Good glass by *Powells*, 1895. – Octagonal NONCONFORMIST CHAPEL by *A. S. Goodridge*, *c.* 1860–1, E.E. with a porch and bellcote. – MEMORIALS. Hancock Mausoleum *c.* 1863, a Neoclassical adaptation of a Roman altar. – Ethel Pocock, *c.* 1924, headstone with bronze crucifixion and kissing figures.

PERRYMEAD ROMAN CATHOLIC CEMETERY, Blind Lane, Perrymead. 1858–62. Less formally planned than the adjacent Abbey cemetery. CHAPEL by *William Hill* (probably Hill of Leeds), 1859, plain Gothic with central belfry. EYRE CHANTRY, N of the gates, by *C. F. Hansom*, *c.* 1860. Small, elaborate Frenchified Geometric; polygonal e end, polygonal tower and spire. Rich interior: *Minton* TILES; alabaster ALTAR by *Charles Hansom*; IRONWORK by *Hardman*; STAINED GLASS by *J. H. Powell*.

PRIOR PARK, Combe Down. By *John Wood the Elder*, built *c.* 1733–*c.* 1750 for Ralph Allen, intended to demonstrate the high quality of stone from his nearby quarry. The house was to consist of a block flanked on each side by a square pavilion and a long wing beyond, all connected by galleries. Building started with the w wing, to house cattle, poultry and the

---

*The stone mines were in places less than 6 ft (2 metres) below ground. By the 1980s the surface around Church Road was unstable, threatening *c.* 700 houses. The mines were filled with *c.* 456,000 cubic metres of aerated concrete, 1999–2009; consulting engineers *Hydrock*.

stables. Wood was dismissed after a quarrel with Allen over alterations to his design by Allen's clerk of works *Richard Jones*. Jones completed the mansion in 1741 and designed the E wing, built by 1750.

p. 99

Prior Park is composed in the Grand Manner, the most ambitious and complete re-creation in England of Palladio's villas. It is situated at the head of a landscaped combe with breathtaking views over Bath. Now a Roman Catholic school; the garden belongs to the National Trust.

EXTERIOR. Wood's mansion is based on the unbuilt first design by Colen Campbell for Wanstead House, Essex, published in *Vitruvius Britannicus* in 1715. Wood's version is bolder, shorter by two bays, with taller proportions and a deeper portico. It belongs more firmly in the Palladian tradition of the villa on the outskirts of a town than other country house derivations from Wanstead: Wentworth Woodhouse, Nostell Priory, and Harewood House, Yorkshire. Like the Circus and Royal Crescent, however, Prior Park may represent several ideas. Unlike any of Palladio's villas, the wings are canted inwards, apparently to follow the contour; yet in his *Essay Towards a Description of Bath* Wood illustrates the plan as forming three sides of a duodecagon, a quarter of a mile in diameter. This may derive from Palladio's illustration of a Roman theatre based on a circle inscribed within a twelve-sided figure. Sitting on one of the hillside terraces, 'rising above one another, like the Stages between the Seats of a Roman Theatre' as Wood's *Essay* puts it, the house may be read as a theatrical analogy, with the city as spectacular stage set.*

The mansion appears large for a villa – fifteen bays wide with, on the N side, a giant Corinthian portico six columns wide and two deep – although the accommodation is relatively modest. Rusticated ground floor, treated as a vaulted basement, with alternating pedimented windows. The rather Baroque outer staircase leading to the entrance is an alteration of 1834. Best-preserved is the five-bay E elevation, with ground-floor windows in Ionic aedicules, and just one central Venetian window above. Very plain S front with an attached portico of six giant Ionic demi-columns; it appears one storey lower than the N, due to the falling ground. A splendid sweep of curved arcades connects the house with its pavilions.

That is where the original work ends. For the E WING, *Jones* threw Wood's intended pair of pavilions into one. It was again completely altered (together with the w wing – *see* below) after Bishop Baines, Roman Catholic Vicar Apostolic of the Western District, bought Prior Park in 1829. He converted the E wing into a school (St Peter's), and the w wing into a seminary (St Paul's). The E wing now consists, w side, of the square C18 pavilion with a Venetian window to each elevation, and continuing it a range of sixteen bays. The ground floor projects

*Inigo Jones used the same geometric figure in his reconstruction of Stonehenge, published in 1653, perhaps relating Prior Park also to Wood's interest in imagining Bath as 'a Druid metropolis' (*see also* pp. 100, 156).

(extended *c.* 1834). The half-storey above was raised to a full storey *c.* 1830. It has a central Venetian window. Above the central three bays, *John Peniston & Son* of Salisbury added a pedimented second floor in 1831, with sculpture in the tympanum transferred from Hunstrete House (*see* below). Set back on the roof is a small clock tower from the w pavilion of the E wing.

In the w WING yet more drastic changes were made. *Wood* had intended this range as an allusion to a Palladian agricultural building, using the Tuscan order, with projecting eaves and a pigeon loft. The executed version was gentrified with the roof concealed behind a parapet, and a raised banqueting room in the centre. In 1834 *H. E. Goodridge* remodelled it, raising the one-and-a-half storeys to match the remodelled E range, though without its raised centre.

Then in 1844 *Scoles* built the very large CHURCH OF ST PAUL to the E, completed by his son, *A. J. Scoles*. It has a severe closed ground floor with a heavily vermiculated and rusticated doorway. Above are giant attached Corinthian columns and pilasters, the capitals mostly uncarved. Pedimented clerestory windows with blind attic panels. An apse towards the house. Architecturally these changes are regrettable, as the total weight of the w wing is now greater than that of the centre.

INTERIORS. In 1836 fire destroyed most of the mansion's interior. It was rebuilt largely with fittings salvaged from the late C18 Hunstrete House, near Marksbury. These include garden sculpture, chimneypieces, plasterwork, joinery, doors, pilasters, the main staircase, and the windows with timber sills (not a Bath feature). To accommodate the windows, the sills were cut back, giving an odd reverse-slope. The E elevation retains original windows with thick glazing bars. In 1991 Prior Park was again ravaged by fire – the roof and third floor were lost, most of the second floor, half of the first and a third of the ground floor. *Ferguson Mann* reconstructed the building to the post-1836 scheme, including elaborate plasterwork by the firm of *St Blaise*; work completed 1995.

The ENTRANCE HALL, three bays wide with tall Corinthian columns, connects N and S fronts. A passage leads to the CHAPEL at the E end, the best-preserved from both fires (save for the ceiling, lost 1991). The most impressive of *Wood the Elder*'s interiors, a double-height space articulated by unfluted Ionic pilasters below Corinthian columns. Full-height coffered apse with a large reredos. The opposite end has a two-storey gallery of coupled columns, with small groin-vaults.

Before the 1830s the Chapel gallery was connected with a great Gallery that occupied the middle nine bays of the first floor, an unusual remnant of the long-gallery tradition. It was subdivided and extended after 1836 to form the ACADEMY HALL, spanning the width of the building, like the Entrance Hall below. Paired Corinthian pilasters, coved and panelled ceiling containing delicate plasterwork trophies. Fluted Corinthian doorcases. w of the entrance hall, the Hunstrete

STAIRCASE, by *John Stephenson* and *William Toms*, has fluted balusters with cable moulds. Three stone reliefs from a monument erected in the grounds by Allen commemorate General Wade's public works in Scotland. Other main rooms have coved ceilings, including the Drawing Room, now the LIBRARY (NW corner), with fluted Corinthian pilasters, Siena marble Ionic chimneypiece and plasterwork with garlands and cornucopia.

Scoles's CHURCH INTERIOR, one of the most impressive of its date, was completed only in 1882. On each side, the aisles run behind fluted Corinthian giant columns (some capitals uncarved). A straight entablature carries a coffered tunnel-vault with penetrations for clerestory windows. Tall apse with attached columns. The type comes from C18 France (e.g. Chalgrin's Saint-Philippe-du-Roule in Paris, begun 1774). *Charles Hansom & Son* completed the vaulted corridor, S, in 1867.

GROUNDS. The GARDENS (now National Trust) form a steep valley N of the mansion, with spectacular views over Bath. They were landscaped in three phases. The first, *c.* 1734–44, was a Rococo scheme executed with advice from Alexander Pope. At the top are the remains of MRS ALLEN'S GROTTO (SW corner), lined with Cornish minerals, and, a little E, a SERPENTINE LAKE and a small pedimented SHAM BRIDGE. Next, the garden was extended downhill, a cascade was formed halfway down, and the lakes and PALLADIAN BRIDGE were constructed. The bridge was built by *Richard Jones* in 1755, following Palladio's famous design, now at the RIBA. The drawing had been copied before at Wilton, Wilts. (1736–7) and Stowe, Bucks. (1738). The bridge is roofed and has pedimented end pavilions with arched openings linked by an Ionic colonnade. Finally, shortly before Allen died in 1764, '*Capability*' *Brown* removed the cascade to unite the garden in one great sweep, and further naturalized the planting. 66

SCHOOL GROUNDS, to the S. Re-erected N of the E wing, a heavily vermiculated pedimented ARCHWAY; formerly a pedestrian entrance from the road, a showy advertisement for Allen's product. Beyond is the PRIORY, originally the gardener's lodge, a very early Gothic Revival COTTAGE by *Richard Jones*, built *c.* 1740. The S front has a battlemented projecting bay, originally with a doorway, now with tripartite windows with hoodmoulds, and a bay of similar windows either side. C19 extensions, E and N. Entrance on the short, now gabled W front. To the N, in 1988 *Ferguson Mann* built a GIRLS' DORMITORY extension. Adjacent to the W, the PRIORY DAY HOUSE by *Ferguson Mann*, 1996–7, a grass-roofed, rubble-stone lean-to with a timber loggia.

E of the mansion uphill, the ruined OLD GYMNASIUM, extant by 1839, by the *Rev. James Baines*. This curious building reuses salvage from Goodridge's alterations to the W wing. It is long and narrow, enclosing on one side a sunken arena with an impressive gladiatorial entrance. Plain N elevation with a Venetian window and a widely spaced window either side.

The arena elevation has a primitive colonnade of baseless Tuscan columns and corresponding round-arched windows above. W of this, i.e. s of the mansion, a relocated rectangular GARDEN BUILDING of c. 1734–44, now a cricket pavilion. Plain, with a cornice, shouldered openings, and a vaulted interior with niches. This is probably the bath house of the earlier garden. Further W (s of Scoles's Chapel) is the JULIAN SLADE THEATRE and Sixth-Form Study Centre by *Ferguson Mann*, 1995. Ashlar and render. Its simple rectangular enclosure makes reference to classical details. Distinctive higher stairtower.

ST MARTIN'S HOSPITAL, Midford Road. 1836–8, built as Bath Union Workhouse. A model plan by *Sampson Kempthorne*, architect to the Poor Law Commissioners, of a hexagon framing Y-shaped wings, a plan also used at Abingdon, Berks. (now Oxon), 1835. Three storeys, classical. Executed by the City Architect *Manners*. Lunatic block of 1857. Simple E.E. CHAPEL by *Manners*, 1846. An aged inmate, *John Plass*, 'working with much zeal and industry laid all the stone'.

CHURCH ROAD is the centre of the former village of Combe Down. For Holy Trinity, *see* p. 200. Opposite, DE MONTALT PLACE, dated 1729, eleven cottages designed by *John Wood* and built by *Richard Jones* for quarrymen (cf. Ralph Allen's Cottages, Prior Park Road, p. 193), a very early instance of 'model' housing. The pedimented centre house was for Jones, Allen's foreman, later clerk of works. In Horsecombe Vale, ⅜ m. W, is VALLEY SPRING, a house by *Peter Womersley* for his brother John, 1972. Of reddish-brown brick, with no concession to regional style or materials. A linear composition of flat-roofed elements joined by fully glazed links. Vertical pairs of piers support floors and roofs, defined by horizontal timber fascias, leaving glazed corners unobstructed.

There are some good individual HOUSES on the southern slopes. The APPRENTICE STORE, Summer Lane, began as ancillary buildings to De Montalt mill: long two-storey stone ranges (c. 1852–86) with continuous upper windows. Repaired and converted with panache by *Threefold Architects*, 2006–8. Along the SE wall, a new lean-to living space with glazed front and a steel walkway weaving along the wall of the old structure. ½ m. NE, LODGE STYLE, Shaft Road, by *C. F. A. Voysey*, 1909, the most important C20 house in Bath and one of his most significant late works. Single-storeyed round a small courtyard, a typical Voysey grouping. The collegiate Gothic details are more revivalist than his early work. Inside, large open hearths, oak fittings, vaulted ceilings, and leaded casements.

LYNCOMBE HOUSE (now the Paragon School), Lyncombe Vale Road. Big, plain five-bay house, c. 1740 with a later C18 porch. In the same road is LYNCOMBE HALL. 1730s, on the old manorial site. Tall s-facing front with six Venetian windows.

ENTRY HILL DRIVE, Entry Hill. Five romantic Neo-Tudor villas by *Edward Davis*, built 1829–36, his first recorded commission after leaving Soane's office. Designs for seventeen houses were exhibited in 1828. GRANVILLE HOUSE was

Davis's home, 1835–41. Symmetrical, with entrance between projecting wings, tall Tudor chimneys and pinnacles. Last to be built were THE BRIARS and the principal house, ENTRY HILL HOUSE, *c.* 1836; asymmetrical with an oriel and battlemented parapets.

BLOOMFIELD CRESCENT, Bloomfield Road. By *Charles Harcourt Masters*, *c.* 1801. The poor man's Royal Crescent; fronted by pasture, with panoramic views to the N. Seven shallow houses with pedimented centre and shallow Greek detail implying some ambition, yet quite unpretentious. Convex entrance elevation of rubble stone.

7. Oldfield Park and Lower Bristol Road

Mainly uneventful late C19 artisan housing, with good industrial survivors along Lower Bristol Road.

CHURCH OF THE ASCENSION, Claude Avenue. Nave and aisles by *Edmund Buckle*, 1906–7. Big W window with Flamboyant tracery, plain untraceried aisles and clerestory. Contrasting again is the Perp E end by *F. Bligh Bond*, 1911. – FITTINGS. REREDOS, painted by *Christopher Webb c.* 1921. – ROOD SCREEN, oak, wiry Perp tracery, 1921; probably by *Bligh Bond*. – STAINED GLASS. Big E window of the Ascension; an early work by *Martin Travers*, 1913.

ST BARTHOLOMEW, King Edward's Road. Austere Neo-Perp, by *A. J. Taylor & A. C. Fare*, 1936–8. Half-demolished by a bomb in 1942; rebuilt on the old lines by 1951. Four-bay nave with clerestory and narrow passage aisles, intended for an eastern extension (crossing, S transept and two-bay chancel; unbuilt). Permanent E wall of 1980–1. Render and stone within, arcade mouldings that die into the piers. Glazed link to halls at the ritual NW, 1998–2000. – STAINED GLASS. By *Mark Angus*, late 1980s. Bold and welcome splashes of abstract colour in an otherwise monochrome interior. High rectangular seven-light E window, and a cross window below. Also three small W lights, *c.* 2000.

ST LUKE, Wellsway. E end by *Hickes & Isaac*, 1866–7. Plate-traceried C13 style. Small tower and a puny broach spire W of the N transept, seemingly a little later. Nave replaced by one of five bays, with S aisle and porch, and W baptistery (*Mowbray Green*, 1912–13); mechanical Perp. Striking truncated pyramidal timbering over the crossing. – STAINED GLASS. Deeply coloured E window. S chapel E, *Hardman*, 1966. S aisle first from E, *C. E. Moore*, 1934. N aisle, two by *Shrigley & Hunt*, 1925 and 1935.

ST PETER, Lower Bristol Road. By *C. E. Davis*, 1876–80. Now offices. C13 French revival. Strongly buttressed nave with narrow lancets, polygonal E end making some show. HALL (W) built as a temporary church by *Davis*, 1866–70.

OUR LADY AND ST ALPHEGE (R.C.), Oldfield Lane. By *Sir Giles Gilbert Scott*, 1927–9. Among the least-known of Bath's post-Georgian buildings, and one of Scott's favourite works.

Modelled on the Early Christian basilica of S. Maria in
Cosmedin, Rome, it is impressively simple, even severe. Three-
arched loggia with sturdy Byzantine columns, lean-to tiled
roof. Attached campanile, l., only half the planned height
because of fears over foundations. Exposed stone walls and
roof structure inside, arcaded aisles and blind apsidal sanctuary, flanked by a Lady Chapel and sacristy. Capitals exquisitely carved by *W. D. Gough*, with scenes from the life of Our
Lady, N, and St Alphege, S. – FLOOR, 'an interesting experiment in using small pieces of linoleum in the same manner as
marble'. – BALDACCHINO. Gilded oak carved by *Stüflesser* of
Ortisei and decorated by *Watts* of London. – Pendant LIGHT
FITTINGS by *Scott*, delightful gilded sunbursts. – ORGAN by
Rushworth & Draper of Liverpool, 1915, installed 1960, when
the w gallery was completed. – Attached domestic-scale PRES-
BYTERY, E of the church, completed 1958.

CHAPELS. OLDFIELD PARK BAPTIST CHAPEL, The Triangle, is
by *Silcock & Reay*, 1902–3. Two cuts above the average: 'Wre-
naissance' front with a giant Serlian motif on Ionic pilasters
with coved and rusticated central arch breaking into the pediment. Mullioned side windows. Pretty galleried interior with
pedimented organ case. – METHODIST CHAPEL, Shakespeare
Avenue. By *W. Hugill Dinsley*, 1906–7. Free Late Gothic. Four-
centred w window with flanking porches. Short tower and
spirelet.

ST JAMES'S CEMETERY, Lower Bristol Road. By *C. E. Davis*,
opened 1861. Asymmetrical Gothic lodge with oriel windows.
Attached triple-arched gateway. Small Anglican and Nonconformist CHAPELS, Dec, with transepts and five-sided apses.
Symmetrically arranged around a linking double arch with
spirelet truncated after bombing (1942).

TWERTON GAOL (former), Caledonian Road. By *G. P. Manners*,
1840–2. The first prison completed under the 1835 Prisons Act.
Closed in 1878; only the forbidding Palladian-style GOVER-
NOR'S HOUSE remains, now flats. With blocky detailing,
banded rustication over all three floors and unfluted giant
pilasters, the centre breaking forward. It also housed the
chapel, surgeon, magistrates, and service rooms.

Around BEAR FLAT. In a garden in Greenway Court, *c.* 350 yds
E of Wellsway, is an elliptical stone building, *c.* 1790–1810.
Originally a SUMMERHOUSE to No. 2 Devonshire Place, used
c. 1870–1900 as a synagogue. Conical roof of swept profile,
flying staircase to the main chamber. The sunken lower floor
has (blocked) oculi, and an oven for unleavened bread.
BLOOMFIELD HOUSE, Bloomfield Road, is perhaps by
Thomas Baldwin, *c.* 1791–1800. Two storeys with giant pilasters,
full attic and urns on the parapets. Ground-floor windows in
arched recesses. The N and S fronts have bowed centres.
Narrow arched entrance (N) with husk-and-patera decoration;
elliptical hall. One-bay w wing, perhaps *c.* 1900, with canted
bay in the return. From here, ENGLISHCOMBE LANE runs w,
with handsome houses of *c.* 1910–14; unusually good Art

Nouveau ironwork. To their N lies the MOORLANDS ESTATE, by *J. Owens*, City Engineer, and *P. Kennerell Pope*, Chief Assistant Architect. Bath's first completely new post-war council estate, completed 1950. Its frankly modern Bath-stone houses were seen as a model of respect for Georgian tradition.

LOWER BRISTOL ROAD. From the W end of Brunel's Claverton Street viaduct (*see* p. 139), a range of INDUSTRIAL BUILDINGS, among the few survivors of Bath's riverside industry. From the E, first CAMDEN MALTHOUSE AND SILO. Early C19 malthouse with gabled hoist on brackets. *J. G. Stone* raised the E part in 1913–14. Adjoining reinforced concrete silo to the E by *Hayward & Wooster*, 1913. Converted to offices and houses, with cantilevered glazed additions, by *K20 Design Company*, 1986. CAMDEN MILL. By *Henry Williams* of Bristol, 1879–80, extended by *F. W. Gardiner*, 1892. A large rectangular former steam flour mill. Now flats and offices (*Morrison & Partners*, 1974–5). Adjoining, W, *Gardiner*'s BAYER CORSET FACTORY of 1890, extended 1895. Red brick with stone-framed segmental windows. Rock-faced quoins. Further W, the NEWARK WORKS, 1857, by *Thomas Fuller*. Part of Stothert & Pitt's engineering works. Classical façade with battered rock-faced plinth. Large iron-framed windows below, thirteen bays of paired windows above, each framed by Tuscan pilasters, and a modillion cornice. A three-bay storey above for offices. To the l. a further thirteen, later, bays. W again, the former PITMAN PRESS. Early C20 Neoclassical façade, of Bath stone. In four phases (E to W) comprising eight, nine, eleven and four bays: respectively by *A. S. R. Ley & Sons*, 1929–34; *G. C. Lawrence* (*Oatley & Lawrence*) 1925–6; *Lawrence*, 1919; and *C. B. Oliver*, 1913. The entrance was souped-up in 1929 with fluted Doric half-columns and Art Deco-ish stepped parapet. Proposed redevelopment, 2010, retaining the façade.

For the Herman Miller factory, Lower Bristol Road, *see* p. 209.

8. *Twerton and Southdown*

Twerton stayed distinct from Bath until the C19, when remains of a woollen cloth industry survived. It is enclosed by the long GWR viaduct to the N.

ST MICHAEL AND ALL ANGELS, How Hill, Twerton. Low Perp W tower, C15, of three stages with diagonal buttresses. The first church was enlarged by *John Pinch*, 1824–5, rebuilt by *G. P. Manners* in 1839. *Edmund Buckle*'s Perp rebuilding, 1885–6, left only the medieval tower, and a C12 doorway inside the N porch: the l. column is deeply spiral-fluted, almost twisted, the r. column has horizontal zigzag decoration. Capitals with grimacing beast masks. Arch with lozenge frieze, one zigzag in the soffit, and a hoodmould with pellets. Low four-bay aisled nave. Broad arcades with standard Perp piers. – Elaborate marble REREDOS; a Last Supper under gabled

arches with cusps. – PULPIT. Oak, perhaps *c.* 1900, with
sinuous arches of indefinable provenance. Big angels at each
angle. – FONT. Norman, octagonal with deeply scalloped bowl.
Over-restored.

ST BARNABAS, Mount View, Southdown. 1957–8, by *F. W.
Beresford-Smith.* A triple cube, 90 by 30 by 30 ft (28 by 9 by 9
metres), on reinforced-concrete portal frames. Walls partly of
Bath stone-rubble from the blitzed St James, Stall Street. Tall
square-headed windows with mullions. Low S aisle and chapel.
– STAINED GLASS. Very big E window and four S chapel
windows by *M. Farrar Bell, c.* 1958, forceful and bright.

CHAPELS. TWERTON BAPTIST CHURCH, Mill Lane. *c.* 1830s,
round-arched windows. Entrance lobby and schoolroom,
1928. – Former ZION FREE METHODIST CHAPEL, High
Street, Twerton. Dated 1853. Gabled front. Round-arched
upper windows, porch with heavy blocking course, incised
panels. – SOUTHDOWN METHODIST CHURCH, The Hollow.
By *F. W. Beresford-Smith,* 1950–1. Churchy cruciform plan with
vestigial crossing tower.

HAYCOMBE CEMETERY, Whiteway Road. Opened 1937. Cruciform Neo-Perp chapel by *Mowbray Green & Hollier,* with glum-
looking masks at the bases of the mullions. CREMATORIUM by
J. G. Wilkinson, City Architect, 1961. A flat-roofed concrete
box, cantilevered at the E end. Detached octagonal Remem-
brance Chapel like a tiny summerhouse.

TWERTON GAOL (former), *see* p. 206.

I. K. Brunel's GREAT WESTERN RAILWAY (GWR) was constructed here *c.* 1839–40. It passes N of Twerton on a low stone
VIADUCT ⅓ m. long, with Lower Bristol Road directly to its
N. Solid walls with blind arcades, with occasional four-centre
arches for roadways, acting oddly like a medieval town wall
that preserves Twerton's sense of separateness from the rest of
Bath. At its E end, a former STATION, Neo-Tudor like most of
Brunel's GWR buildings, its three narrow storeys butted up
against the N side of the viaduct. The top floor is at platform
level, reached by external steps. Further W, twelve mill-
workers' houses were built into the viaduct. TWERTON
TUNNEL, ⅝ m. W of the church, has Tudor-arched portals
with octagonal turrets and battlements.

High Street curves roughly westward from the GWR viaduct to
the church, with vernacular C18 and early C19 terraces and
individual houses amidst unalluring 1960s shops. W of the
former Methodist chapel (*see* above), a row of vernacular Early
Georgian houses. Nos. 16–17, a pair perhaps *c.* 1700, with mullioned upper windows and continuous dripmould over the
ground floor (*see also* Nos. 20–21). Further W, No. 42, ROSE
COTTAGE, *c.* 1830s Neo-Tudor. CLYDE HOUSE is a polite
three-storey villa, perhaps *c.* 1800. W again, by the churchyard
wall in HOW HILL is the plain single-storey SUNDAY
SCHOOL, dated 1816. No. 9 How Hill is T-shaped, the rear
range C17 with ovolo mullions, the front mid-C19. NW of the
church, in Watery Lane, the former VICARAGE, by *G. P.*

Manners, 1845; his usual Neo-Tudor, with grouped octagonal chimneystacks.

N of the viaduct on Lower Bristol Road is a pre-1830s MALT-HOUSE, largely rebuilt *c*. 1900, with a reinforced concrete pyramidal roof to the drying kiln (N), an early British example of the *Hennebique* system. Converted to offices by *Edward Nash Partnership*, 2000–2. To the w *c*. 300 yds is the big single-storey BATH CABINET MAKERS' FACTORY (now part of Herman Miller), by *Yorke, Rosenberg & Mardall*, 1966–7. Notable for the first use in Britain of a Mero space-frame roof, developed in the 1940s by the German engineer *Max Mengeringhausen*.

9. *Weston, Lower Weston and Locksbrook*

Weston was a village NW of Bath until C19 suburban expansion.

ALL SAINTS, Church Road, Weston. First recorded 1156. Rebuilt in the C15 and again in 1830–2 by *John Pinch the Younger*, except for the low Perp w tower of three stages. *E. Harbottle* of Exeter added chancel and transepts in 1893, *Mowbray Green* a memorial chapel (SE) in 1921. Tall three-light windows with four-centred arches and Perp tracery. Battlements and pinnacles. Broad aisled nave with tall four-centred arcades on piers of Perp section, and a w gallery. – FITTINGS. ROYAL ARMS of William IV; by '*J. Jones* carver, of this parish'. – STAINED GLASS. Post-1893, except for the E window, *c*. 1860. Chancel N and s and the soft blue s chapel E are *c*. 1902 of Morris & Co. type. – MONUMENTS. A rich collection. Geoffrey, 'priest here while yet he lived', a C13 coffin-lid with a foliated cross. – Arthur Sherston †1641, Mayor of Bath. All that remains is a frontal demi-figure, the hand on a skull. – David Macie †1737, Baroque, Corinthian pilasters with inturned volutes after Borromini. – Jacob Barclay †1750, a lavish marble tablet with scrolls and open pediment, by *Prince Hoare*. – Similar tablet nearby to William Hall †1753. – General Joseph Smith †1790. Good large hanging monument: standing female figures l. and r. of a pedestal with trophy and urn.

E of the church is *Thomas Baldwin*'s TOMB to the architect Thomas Atwood †1775. A splendid Neoclassical vase on pedestal, with flutes, bucrania and garlands in the frieze. – N of the church a SARCOPHAGUS of 1795 with sharply angled sides and acroteria, on lion's feet.

ST JOHN, Upper Bristol Road. Begun in 1838 by *G. P. Manners*; plain E.E. revival. Probably of this phase, big plain lancets w and s, and the eaves billets. Enlarged by *C. E. Davis*, 1869; semicircular chancel (cf. St Peter, Lower Bristol Road), s transept, s porch. N transept, 1887. Plain interior with double transept arches and timber-clad roofs, unusually folded as if for transverse gables. Deep w gallery. – Circular PULPIT with all-over carving of foliage in trefoils.

CHAPELS. METHODIST CHAPEL, Newbridge Hill, 1890–1. Perp, with big ogee-capped pinnacles. – Yet more basic, the

COUNTESS OF HUNTINGDON CHAPEL, Trafalgar Road. After 1852, with flattened segmental arches, crude Y-tracery and stumpy pinnacles. – To the w on Weston High Street, the MORAVIAN CHURCH, by *F. W. Beresford-Smith*, 1955–6. Squat crossing tower.

LOCKSBROOK CEMETERY, Upper Bristol Road. By *Hickes & Isaac*, 1862. Landscaping by *Edward Milner*. Gothic LODGE, big plate-traceried upper windows, some mastic inlay. Iron GATES with splendidly flamboyant finials on the piers. Symmetrical E.E. CHAPELS linked by arches to a central needle spire. – Lady Mary Clarke †1895. Magnificent bronze sarcophagus by *E. Onslow Ford*, with seated angel.

NEW BRIDGE, Newbridge Road West. Rebuilt in the late C18 as a segmental arch spanning 90 ft (28 metres), with rusticated voussoirs. Widened in 1831–4 by *William Armstrong* of Bristol for the Bath Turnpike Trust. Battered upstream abutments, panelled pilasters; the spandrels have circular tunnels to reduce the weight. Ramped approaches on eight round-headed arches, blocked on the downstream side (i.e. not flood arches). The first bridge was of 1735–6, by *John Strahan*.

PARTIS COLLEGE, Newbridge Hill. Almshouses of 1825–7, by *Samuel & Philip Flood Page* of London. Bath's finest Greek Revival building. Established under the will of the Rev. Fletcher Partis to house thirty 'decayed gentlewomen'. An austere design, with a spacious quadrangle (open to the s) reminiscent of William Wilkins's Haileybury College, Herts., or Downing College, Cambridge, rather than an almshouse. Central chapel with a tall blind attic and unfluted Ionic portico. Two-storey flanks of thirteen bays, the last three accentuated. Sixteen-bay E and W ranges, also with three-bay ends accented by giant Doric pilasters, paired at the corners. In 1863 *G. G. Scott* made sumptuous Gothic alterations to the chapel.

ROYAL UNITED HOSPITAL (RUH), Combe Park. The hospital moved here from Beau Street (*see* p. 144) in 1932. *H. Percy Adams* and *A. J. Taylor* designed the Neo-Georgian ranges on three sides of a quadrangle. Two earlier buildings remain; the Bath and Wessex Orthopaedic Hospital (1922) and the Forbes Fraser Hospital (1924). RUH Central was redeveloped with a new main entrance and ward block, by *HLM Architects*, c. 1997–2002. Four symmetrical storeys, of coloured render, with the usual curved central roof over a full-height foyer.

ST JOHN'S HOSPITAL, COMBE PARK ALMSHOUSE, 2002–3 by *G2 Architects*. Arranged round a courtyard; landscaping by *New Leaf Studio*. An energy-efficient building of fifty-four units and chapel, the parts expressive of function. Highly articulated – even overworked – in Bath stone and brick, with roof terraces and bay windows. An unusual C21 example of an earlier building type.

Weston sits in a small, steep-sided valley through which the road from Lansdown runs SE to Bath, dominated by its church high up to the NE. W of the church is the VICARAGE, a pretty villa of 1802, attributed to *Baldwin*, with his favoured half-pilasters.

The doorway has thin double consoles and plain pilasters, the
window above a pediment with roundels and husks. The flanks
step slightly forward at first floor. Half-pilasters to either side
and angle pilasters. A path leads down to the pedestrian
CHURCH STREET. No. 30 is of three storeys with string
courses and a tall arched window through the upper floors; a
rainwater head is dated 1739. Beyond, a Late Classical terrace,
c. 1850. Fine mid-C19 GAS LAMPS opposite, flanking steps
down to High Street.

HIGH STREET at this point is a disconcerting mix of 1960s shops
and vernacular Georgian. Opposite the late C18 KING'S HEAD
pub, TRAFALGAR ROAD climbs NE, with minor Regency
houses and, further up, WELLINGTON BUILDINGS, a terrace
of early C19 workers' houses. High Street continues W with
noteworthy C17 houses, all with ovolo-mullioned window; e.g.,
No. 120, and No. 58, PENHILL FARM (apparently extant
1502), with a long mid-C17 front and broad relieving windows
arches. Many houses with C18 updatings, from the humble
(No. 61) to the quite grand (No. 109).

CROWN HILL climbs E from High Street to the sylvan setting of
WESTON PARK, with substantial Victorian villas. A long
wooded drive leads to CRANWELLS (now SUMMERFIELD
SCHOOL), Weston Park East, by *Wilson & Fuller*, 1850–2. A
near facsimile of Widcombe Manor, which Wilson extended
(*see* p. 194); giant Ionic pilasters and keystone masks. Doric
porch with emblems in the frieze derived from the Circus.
Exhibited at the Royal Academy in 1850, it marked mid-
Victorian Bath's rediscovery of Georgian architecture. A
Gothic-Tudor-Jacobean group of *c.* 1840 is attributable to
Manners, cf. his Romantic additions to The Moor, Clifford,
Herefs. (1827–9): gables, castellation, tall chimneys, oriels and
windows with hoodmoulds. They are: GLENFIELD, Weston
Park; THE RETREAT (now King Edward's Pre-Prep School),
Weston Lane; the present BATH PRIORY HOTEL; and two
asymmetrical semi-detached pairs, GRANVILLE and LITTLE
WOODCOTE, SOUTH LYNN and the simpler HERNE HOUSE
of 1833, Manners's own home.

HERMAN MILLER FACTORY, ¾ m. S at Locksbrook Road. By
Farrell Grimshaw Partnership, 1975. A cool and elegant furniture factory and store. A large-span steel structure of simple
primary and secondary beams with a hollow steel frame, clad
with demountable cream-coloured glass-reinforced panels.
Solid and glazed units, louvres and doors are all moveable.

BATHAMPTON

ST NICHOLAS, Mill Lane. C15 Perp W tower, with diagonal
buttresses and thin pinnacles. W doorway under square label,
three-light Perp window directly above. The rest much

restored. Nave and s aisle rebuilt 1754 by *Richard Jones* for
Ralph Allen, the work obliterated by C19 alterations. N aisle
added by *A. S. Goodridge*, 1858; organ chamber (*c.* 1878) and
vestries (1897) by *Wilson, Willcox & Wilson*; s aisle extended w
and the chancel restored in 1882. Here some C13 work seemingly remains, even if retooled, e.g. the steep chancel arch, with
multiple keeled shafts and moulded capitals. E window, three
stepped lancets. Running E from the N chapel, CHURCH
ROOMS by *David McDonagh*, 1992–3; a two-storey square
turned at forty-five degrees, each face gabled.

FITTINGS. Mostly C19. Australia Chapel (s aisle) fitted
1973–9; floor of Wombeyan marble, rails of blackbean wood. –
SCULPTURE. Outside at the E end, the figure of an ecclesias-
tic, its date disputed. Draperies in long close parallel vertical
folds, very long sleeves and a small defaced head. Possibly
c. 1100; given the subject, Pevsner's suggestion of rustic Elizabethan work seems less likely. – MONUMENTS. Two effigies,
a cross-legged knight (head and feet missing) and a lady
wearing a wimple, *c.* 1325. – Admiral Arthur Phillip, first Gov-
ernor of New South Wales and founder of Sydney, †1814. Rectangular tablet topped by a shaped black ground with urn,
cannon and anchor. By *King* of Bath. – Good tablets of similar
date, the best John Hume †1815, by *Reeves*, with a woman
leaning over an urn.

HAMPTON MANOR, Mill Lane, *c.* ¼ m. NNW of the church. The
front range is C17; see the blocked doorway in the s façade.
Refaced and enlarged at the back perhaps *c.* 1730–50, the interesting spacing of the front conditioned by the existing plan.
Seven bays, the windows in the flanks corniced and widely
spaced, the central three tightly grouped. The main doorway
has attached Doric columns, the window above Ionic columns.
This central motif breaks forward again. (Good C18 staircase.)
N again, a long stone TOLL BRIDGE, *c.* 1850s. Three slightly
pointed arches in the centre. Gothic trefoil parapets. Altered,
1870–2.

s of the church is the KENNET AND AVON CANAL (engineer *John
Rennie*, this section *c.* 1800–10). The C17 GEORGE INN sits
beneath the embankment, its upper windows level with the
water. Stone-slated roof, a reminder that Bathampton is at the
s tip of the Cotswolds. Just to the E, Mill Lane crosses by a
good stone BRIDGE with horseshoe arch. From here the HIGH
STREET runs w. Shortly (N side), THE GRANGE: the renewed
date 1661 agrees with the horizontal mullioned windows in
broad frame and cornice r. of the door. Vertical two-light
windows above. Sashes l. of the door from an C18 updating,
which formed a double-pile plan. In BATHAMPTON LANE,
c. ⅓ m. w, a good group of Regency villas in the Bath mode,
e.g. Avonstone, with raised two-bay centre.

IRON AGE ENCLOSURE, Bathampton Down, ¾ m. SW. With a
single low ditch and bank enclosing 78 acres. The earthwork
circuit overlies an earlier network of rectilinear fields

extending to the N and S. A sunken track associated with the fields cuts across the enclosure. For interpretation, *see* p. 12.

BATHEASTON

7060

The village forms a Y-shape, each arm spreading *c.* ½ m. from the junction of High Street with Brow Hill, which leads N to the church. Many late C16 or early C17 properties around this junction, masked by later fronts. High Street must have felt quite towny until most of its shops closed.

ST JOHN BAPTIST, Northend. Handsome four-stage W tower, 94 ft (30 metres) high, Perp with set-back buttresses and two-light windows and bell-openings. Higher SE stair-turret. N aisle by *John Pinch Jun.*, 1834, with Perp-looking arcade. The rest rebuilt or restored by *Frederick Preedy*: the chancel rebuilt in altered form (Geometric Dec), 1860; nave restored and a new aisle created by moving the medieval S wall and porch, 1866–8. – REREDOS, 1878, reportedly by *Sedding*. – FONT. Octagonal, on baluster stem, *c.* 1700–15. – FONT of 1869 with figures in quatrefoils; on marble pillars. – Chancel; encaustic tiles by *Godwin* of Lugwardine, 1860. – STAINED GLASS. Chancel S, *Clayton & Bell*, 1860. – MONUMENTS. Two small coffin-lids with foliated crosses, in the porch.

GOOD SHEPHERD (R.C.), No. 2, Northend. 1967. Rectangular, with monopitch roof rising to the SE angle, the upper E and S walls glazed in vertical blocks of vivid colour. The altar is on this diagonal axis, with seating in the round: an early example for this diocese of a parish church on Second Vatican Council principles.

CHAPELS. Former Congregational chapel, No. 193 High Street. By *Wilson & Willcox*, 1870–1. Prominent. Early Gothic, entrance beneath a short capped spire. Rose windows E and W. At Chapel Row, Northend, a simple Gothic Methodist chapel, 1876. Finally, a dilapidated 'tin tabernacle', Bailbrook Lane. 1892, rare because so Ecclesiologically correct, with chancel, transepts, porch and bell-tower. From the 1889 catalogue of *William Cooper*, London.

PRIMARY SCHOOL, School Lane. *Davies & Tew* of Chesterfield, 1858. Gothic. Surprisingly big bell-tower, two gables with spherical triangle lights.

NORTHEND has the most interesting houses. Starting opposite the church, working N, PINE HOUSE, dated 1672, and MIDDLESEX HOUSE, 1670, have steep gables with upright oval windows keyed into oblong frames, a leitmotif of this time. Pine House retains two-light mullioned windows. Both to the standard plan, i.e. single pile, two or three rooms in a row with the entrance and cross-passage roughly central. This is also

seen (N) at LOWER NORTHEND FARMHOUSE (three gables)
and at EAGLE COTTAGES, No. 110 North End. Again three
steep gables with upright ovals, and symmetrical ranks of five
two-light windows.

56   So to EAGLE HOUSE, *c.* 1724. Improbably attributed to John
Wood the Elder since Collinson noted that 'John Wood'
lived here.* Its charming provincial Baroque was surely not
designed by the ambitious Neo-Palladian responsible for
Queen Square. Showiest is the three-bay E front. Projecting
centre with an urn in a shell niche on the first floor, and an
eagle flapping on the pediment above, which frames the date
of these embellishments, 1729. The S front is of five bays and
two storeys, originally with a parapet, plain except for a Venetian motif squeezed in awkwardly, with blind flanking lights,
and the remarkably Baroque doorcase with pediment on Gibbsian Ionic columns. Pulvinated frieze, keystone with a crowned
head. To the W, a C19 addition, one-storey until raised and
Georgianized by *Mowbray Green*, 1906–8, obscuring another
datestone of 1724. (Fine chimneypiece with fluted Ionic
pilasters.)

In the HIGH STREET, BATHEASTON HOUSE, a five-bay clothier's house characteristic of its date, 1712. Long-and-short
quoins, bolection-moulded window frames. The cornices
project over the middle ground and upper floors. Many other
noteworthy houses: C17, with the familiar gables and mullions
(e.g. Nos. 163 and 264); and C18, e.g. No. 191, with typical
mansard roof and paired sashes. But what prettier than
No. 177? Symmetrical, full-height bows, *c.* 1780–1800.

BATHEASTON VILLA, Bailbrook Lane, London Road West. A
large early C18 house, famous for Lady Miller's poetry contests
in the 1770s. Even quoins, four-column Ionic porch. On the S
front a large embattled bow with Regency balcony. Jarring mullioned windows to the r., *c.* 1900. In the garden, a small domed
Doric ROTUNDA. Further W, BAILBROOK HOUSE, by *John
Eveleigh*. Now a conference centre. Designed in 1789, begun
1791, but completion delayed by Eveleigh's bankruptcy in
1793. An ambiguous composition: two blocks connected by a
one-storey entrance. Main house to the S, service wing to the
N, their fronts identically treated with giant Ionic pilasters,
defying C18 precepts of propriety. The link has a rich pedimented doorcase, flanked by arched windows with garlands
over. The S front of the S block has an arched rusticated projecting ground floor, forming a terrace above, with pedestals
and urns. The two storeys above have a projecting centre with
giant Ionic angle pilasters. Fine entrance hall with oval lantern,
Doric E and W galleries, and semi-elliptical fanlights across N
and S inner doors. Directly S, a central hall, and an elegant
staircase concealed behind doors. Upper landing with another
oval lantern. BAILBROOK LODGE, Nos. 35 and 37 London
Road West. Of seven houses planned, only this symmetrical

* The younger Wood did so, in 1781.

pair was built (for sale in 1831), by *John Pinch & Son.* Two-storey bows with trellised ironwork. Banded ground floor, plain pilasters above.

LITTLE SOLSBURY HILL-FORT, ⅔ m. W of Batheaston church. A single circuit of Iron Age earthworks, with some evidence for middle and later Bronze Age occupation.

BATHFORD

ST SWITHUN. Like the church of a Victorian metropolitan suburb, and with little atmosphere, as are unfortunately so many around Bath.* The reconstruction, paid for by the Skrines of Warleigh Manor, was by *Frederick Preedy*, with carving by *Boulton*. N aisle and porch 1855–6, S aisle and three-bay nave, 1871–2, big W tower, 1879–80. Deep chancel with two chapels, that on the N added 1911. Geometrical Dec tracery. Tower with tall pinnacles and paired belfry lights. Preedy followed the Somerset tradition of a taller stair-turret with pinnacle, yet the tower is E.E. not Perp. Double-chamfered arcades on octagonal piers, open timber roofs. Chancel wagon roof by *Alan Rome*, 1970, after a fire. Re-set Norman carving in the N aisle E wall; three animated heads, a small capital, and part of a small coffin slab with cross. The inner N doorway has columns with scrolly capitals, and an arch with an outer order of beading, all C19; the inner row of triple-banded chevrons may be re-tooled C12 work. Some old fabric may remain above the nave arcades, ashlar-lined in 1872, and in the exterior chancel walls. – FITTINGS. REREDOS. Deposition, carved by *Boulton*, 1872. Mutilated. – Oak STALLS, c. 1970. – FONT. Plain, probably C12. Octagonal bowl cut down from a square, with heavily scalloped underside. On a kind of 'waterholding' base, probably C13. – PULPIT. Oak, perhaps c. 1615–30. Finely carved relief panels, arched with foliage below, square with arabesques above. On the frieze, a biblical inscription, 'Blessed are they that hear the word of God and keepe it'.† – STAINED GLASS. E window by *Powell & Sons*, 1947, much white and gold. S aisle S, from E: *Frederick Preedy*, 1872; 1919; c. 1970, commemorating the fire, with C19 fragments. S aisle W by *Preedy*, 1872. N aisle N, from E: 1935 by *Powells*, with rich greens and blues; *Preedy*, 1877. N aisle W, *Preedy*, 1872. – MONUMENTS. Several crude C17 tablets. – Thomas Langton †1712, small square tablet with four cherubs (vestry passage). – Elizabeth Phillips †1759 by *John Ford.* Relief of a weeping putto and urn. – Betty Williams †1793, a big tablet

---

* The preceding church had a Norman chancel arch altered in the C15; a S transept (*Thomas Baldwin*, 1803, extended 1817–18) and a low saddleback tower, replaced in 1842.

† Cf. Monkton Farleigh (Wilts.), Croscombe (1616) and Dinder (1621).

with urn and Greek key at the sides. – John Symons, with an urn in a wreath, by *(Sir) Richard Westmacott, c.* 1810.

The CHURCHYARD has numerous chest tombs of *c.* 1780–1830. SE of the chancel one to Ann Nelson †1783, sister of Admiral Lord Nelson. Elaborate LYCHGATE, 1919.

BAPTIST CHAPEL, High Street. 1839. Small and simple; two round-arched windows and a pediment.

A stroll along Church Street, Pump Lane and High Street reveals many good cottages of the late C17, and smarter Georgian houses, evidence of a polite retreat from Bath. SE of the church in PUMP LANE, two cottages dated 1662, with mullioned hoodmoulded windows. From the S end of Church Street, first the OLD SCHOOL (*G. P. Manners*, 1837–9), the usual Neo-Tudor. EAGLE HOUSE must be *c.* 1750, attributed to *J. Wood the Elder*. On the entrance side, breaking into the pediment, a large arched staircase window with delicate late C18-style cobweb glazing bars. The ground-floor windows are on this side segment-headed. Handsome N front with broad canted-out centre containing a fine Venetian window with Ionic pilasters, a plainer Venetian window above, and a pediment. Behind high garden walls; the entrance gate has a good Gibbs surround.

To the N, more good houses on BATHFORD HILL. First TITAN BARROW (now Whitehaven) by *Wood the Elder*, 1748. The mason was *John Ford*. The garden front (NW) is only of five bays, yet most festive, with balustraded parapet, a rich and finely detailed frieze with garlands, and a three-bay attached portico of giant Corinthian columns. Pineapple finials on the pediment. The first, third and fifth ground-floor windows have pilasters and pediments. Very restrained entrance front with an advancing centre, pediment, and C19 porch. Big Neo-Georgian kitchen wing (l.), 1936–7. Original plasterwork in the former dining room. Nearby, ROCK HOUSE, No. 37 High Street. Deeds suggest a date *c.* 1723. Baroque, only three bays wide. Finely decorated door frame, steep swan-neck pediment with big scrolls. Above, a blind Venetian window with a shell in the arch, and a little C20 window in the central frame. The other windows have masks in the keystones. (Ground-floor room with decorative ceiling and shell-headed niches flanking the chimneypiece.)

BROWN'S FOLLY, ½ m. SE. Square tapering hilltop tower, erected in 1848 by Wade Browne, a quarry owner.

BECKINGTON

ST GEORGE. The most ambitious Norman tower of any Somerset parish church, big, broad, prominent, and vigorously decorated at the bell-stage. Chancel essentially Norman, updated in the C14, and the body of the church rebuilt in the C15, broader than it is long. Destructive alterations took place *c.* 1800 under *James Scaping* of Norton St Philip, and repairs under a 'pretended architect' of Beckington, *Henry Malpas*, in 1843–4. Much more thorough was *J. P. St Aubyn*'s restoration of 1872–3. Among much else he replaced the W and E window tracery, and lowered the sills in the S chapel to their original height. Decoration was by the *Horwood Bros.*

The tower was restored *c.* 1905–6. Originally it had clasping buttresses, but massive diagonal buttresses were added later. Low polygonal stair-turret. One small Norman N window, renewed Perp five-light W window. Two-light bell-openings, the main arches with chevrons, sub-arches on a colonnette. Flanking pairs of smaller blank arches – a strange anticipation of a convention of some Perp Somerset towers (Axbridge group). The arches have the continuous roll moulding of Bristol, Malmesbury, Glastonbury, etc. Inside the tower two blocked Norman windows, a panelled arch towards the nave and a Perp fan-vault.* The chancel is Norman (herringbone masonry behind the organ) with a Dec window by the S chapel. Ogee-headed PISCINA, simple SEDILIA, just two seats below a S window. Chancel arch of the same profile as the four-bay nave arcades, the piers not high, of standard section (four hollows). Unusual cresting on the arch springers (cf. Rode). Clerestory of straight-headed two-light windows, *c.* 1425, and an interesting roof with tie-beams. In each truss, five queenposts which have cusped four-way struts. Perp N aisle, with windows of 1873, but otherwise genuine Perp remains, e.g. stone panelling, image niche and piscina beside the altar. Among its roof supports, two surprisingly big animals in profile. S chapel of *c.* 1490, from a chantry bequest of 1484 by John Compton, clothier. S window of six lights and straight-headed.

FITTINGS. FONT. Of Purbeck marble. Plain, octagonal; circular stem surrounded by eight circular shafts. Perhaps C13 (cf. Wellow). – SCREEN, S chapel. Jacobean, with a half-wheel of turned balusters in the door. – Very early ROYAL ARMS, of 1574. In stone, Doric pilasters and pediment. – STAINED GLASS. E window, attributed to *Clayton & Bell, c.* 1873. W window and chancel N, *Horwood Bros,* 1873. S aisle SE, *Heaton, Butler & Bayne, c.* 1900. – MONUMENTS. Knight and lady *c.* 1380 (chancel), possibly Sir John de Erlegh II. Straight band over the recess, decorated with plain blank arcading and little hanging arches with small heads. – Lady *c.* 1370, W of the former. – Brass to John Seyntmaur †1485 and wife, 26-in. (66-cm.) figures (chancel). His figure stolen, both replaced with replicas.† – John Compton †1510 (S chapel; son of the founder) and wife, brass, 22-in. (56-cm.) figures. Samuel Danyel †1619, attributed to *Thomas Stanton,* perhaps *c.* 1655 (GF). Hanging monument with volutes, garlands, broken

51

---

*The restoration included a new fan-vault in the tower (*Building News,* 27 June 1873).

† Similar figures at Harpswell, Lincs., and Strelley, Notts., 1487.

segmental pediment, and a bust in a draped cloak or toga and wearing a laurel wreath. Erected after 1650 by Danyel's pupil, the celebrated Lady Anne Clifford. Nevertheless an early Somerset example of fully developed classical taste. – Harry Edgell, by *King* of Bath (1802), and Rear Admiral Henry Edgell †1846 by *T. Gaffin*, both with mourning widows. – Churchyard, unusual iron monuments: Charles Moody †1847, coffin-shaped, maker *Moody* of Frome; Caroline Davis †1858, Jane Davis †1874.

BAPTIST CHAPEL, 1786. A pleasing three-bay front with segment-headed windows, Doric pilasters and a one-bay pediment. Galleries with bellied cast-iron front on cast-iron columns, probably mid-C19. Panelled pulpit and Jacobean communion table.

Beckington is uncommonly rich in worthwhile stone houses. At Castle Corner (s end) is BECKINGTON CASTLE, a high compact Elizabethan mansion. Three steep gables to the street, two on the returns. Three-and-a-half storeys. Long-and-short quoins, continuous string courses above the windows. The street front has two six-light windows on ground and first floors, three four-light windows on the second. Most of the lights depressed-arched. Three-storey castellated porch, NE, with a polygonal projection. A similar turret and a service wing on the SW front added *c.* 1870. The house was seemingly built or rebuilt to an L-plan *c.* 1540–70 by the Long family, Beckington clothiers, and by the early C17 extended NE to form a near-square. Restored *c.* 1899 with a canted bay on the E side, and strapwork ceiling in the entrance hall. A seemingly genuine C17 ribbed ceiling on the first floor. Directly NE, the WOOL HALL, a high plain rubble-stone hall with external staircase, much altered, but essentially C16.

Nearby on Frome Road, BECKINGTON HOUSE, broad and comfortable, two-and-a-half storeys with three gables, dated 1628. Altered and enlarged in keeping *c.* 1850–1900. Further down (E side), BECKINGTON ABBEY (now three houses), the most important house at Beckington, reputedly built as the Hospital of the Augustinian Canons founded here in 1502. An irregular U-plan with long rear wings; the centre and rear r. wing probably the oldest parts. To the front the early C17 dominates with cross-windows. At the r. side a lower battlemented addition (dated rainwater heads, 1705?). To its l., i.e. the r. side of the C17 part, on the first floor an excessively large six-light window with a very high transom. This room has one of the most sumptuous plaster ceilings in Somerset, *c.* 1640, with a barrel-vaulted centre (cf. Herringston in Dorset, Barnstaple and Rashleigh Barton in Devon) springing from coved sides, perhaps reflecting the shape of an earlier timber roof. Strapwork with fleur-de-lys, pomegranates etc., and five pendants; the strapwork etc. derive from Jan Vredeman de Vries. Grotesque friezes to the sides, more strapwork on the coves and on the end wall. Restored *c.* 1979–84. The ceiling is

attributed by Anthony Wells-Cole to *William Arnold*, probable
architect of Montacute House. A big C16 fireplace was
removed *c.* 1950. In the corridor behind, remains of a late
medieval newel stair-turret, replaced by a dog-leg stair in the
C16. The r. wing adjoins here, with mullioned windows with
depressed-arched lights, and a wind-braced roof. It may represent the original *hospitium*. Opposite the r. wing an equally
long regular l. wing (perhaps also medieval), with some C16 or
C17 three-light windows. Very big ground-floor fireplace.

At the bottom of the Frome Road is the centre of the village. In
CHURCH HILL, branching off W of the late C18 Woolpack Inn,
the OLD RECTORY, C17, enlarged *c.* 1795 with a front range
of three bays. Tripartite windows, wide six-column Tuscan
portico. Returning to the centre and N up BATH ROAD, on the
E side, the OLD MANSE with three gables and mullioned-and-
transomed windows, mid-C17. (Fine splat-baluster staircase,
first-floor chamber ceiling with lions in panels. Also a plaster
overmantel dated 1670.) Almost opposite, THE CEDARS, C17,
tall and gabled, updated *c.* 1720 with sashes and a segmental
pedimented doorcase on Tuscan demi-columns. Early Georgian brick summerhouse with curly open pediment over the
doorway. Opposite The Cedars, GOOSE STREET leads E. Again
good cottages, showing both the continuation of C17 tradition
and efforts to keep up to date, e.g. No. 62, mid-C18, tiny yet
with a Venetian window. Opposite, Nos. 47 and 49, the rubble
walls much rebuilt. Formerly an open-hall house; arch-braced
jointed cruck roof with wind-braces, timbers felled in 1391.
Further E, Abbey House, No. 59 (C16, updated in the C17) with
two big gables; the same story at The Old House, Nos. 61–63
(first-floor fireplace dated 1663).

SEYMOUR'S COURT, *c.* ¾ m. NE along Goose Street. Built
c. 1460–80, probably for John Seyntmaur.* Symmetrical five-
bay front (S), two-storey porch with two-light upper window
with cinquecusped lights. The rest largely refaced perhaps
c. 1620–60; four-light windows, the service end (W) re-roofed.
The hall end is clearer; originally one or two rooms below,
probably a single chamber above, open to the roof. Arch-
braced collar-trusses with curved V-struts above the collars, as
crisp as when they were made. The rear wall has a big chimney-
breast to the hall, and three C15 windows like that over the
porch. The ground-floor E room has a C17 plaster ceiling with
profuse quatrefoils, fruit etc. Frieze identical to that at Laverton Manor Farm. Big Ionic chimneypiece of the same date.
Evidence of a private stair up to the chamber. Early C18 rear
wing with a cheese loft. Early C19 staircase at the rear of the
screens passage.

DEVIL'S BED AND BOLSTER. LONG BARROW 1 m. NE of Beckington, originally *c.* 85 ft (26 metres) long, with around twenty
scattered sarsens, of which less than half remain *in situ*.

---

*Not the home of Jane or Thomas Seymour, as tradition has it.

BERKLEY

ST MARY THE VIRGIN. The most ambitious Georgian church in any Somerset village. Rebuilt 1750–1, probably by *Thomas Prowse*, a gentleman-amateur architect who owned Berkley manor. Painted rubble walls; big Venetian motifs in the sides, embarrassingly bare, unmoulded inside or out. Small arched w windows, blocked later, and a low w tower, the only part ashlar-faced. Its base serves as a porch and has a pediment broader than the tower, accommodated by pushing the walls out like lateral buttresses; here and in the decorative details Prowse's inexperience tells. The tower top has an over-wide cornice. Balustrade with tall vases. The church plan derives from Wren churches such as St Mary-at-Hill, 41 ft (12.5 metres) square and 21 ft (6.5 metres) high, with four Ionic columns supporting a centre square with an octagonal dome, i.e. not a true dome but a domical vault. It has a lantern, as at St Stephen Walbrook. The stucco decoration is sumptuous and curiously worldly, full of Rococo C-curves and rocaille. The sections outside the central square have flat ceilings. Projecting low tunnel-vaulted chancel, the soffit marked by a band of scrolls. The church was much altered *c.* 1870, including removal of a w gallery and chancel screen. The inner doorcase is C19, probably including parts of the screen, e.g. the fruity festoons. Triple-arched E window of 1870, no doubt adapted from a Venetian motif. – FITTINGS. Victorian, not good. – MONUMENT of 1751 to the Newborough family, perhaps by *Thomas Prowse*. Pedimented on foliate brackets.

BERKLEY HOUSE, The main range is of 1730–2, designed by *Nathaniel Ireson* for Abigail Prowse, daughter of George Hooper, Bishop of Bath and Wells. A fine seven-bay front, the centre distinguished by a Doric-columned and pedimented doorcase with flanking arched windows, giant Ionic angle pilasters, and pediment with small Venetian window. Even quoins. Fine square hall; picture frames with excellent carved rocaille decoration, *c.* 1750. Amongst the portraits one of Thomas Prowse drawing a rotunda or tempietto.* Behind the hall, the staircase with Venetian window. Large square open well, three slim balusters to each tread: two elongated colonnettes, the middle one finely twisted. Unspecified alterations, 1767. Very plain rear wing, reputedly C17, but the roof pitch and brick window arches look early C19.

Next to the church, a small plain SCHOOL of 1861. At Home Farm, directly s, early C19 GRANARY on eight staddle-stones. Weatherboarded walls, unexpected in this county of stone. (To the SE at Lodge Hill, THE PHEASANTRY, a one-room plan, the ground and first floor dated 1581; original use unclear. Second storey dated 1783, with Y-traceried windows, perhaps for a hunting lodge or belvedere.)

---

* A near-identical portrait is in Axbridge Town Hall.

BINEGAR

and GURNEY SLADE

HOLY TRINITY, Binegar. Small w tower, probably c. 1400, but the continuous battlement mouldings perhaps later C15. Diagonal buttresses, battlemented parapet with blank arcading below the merlons. No pinnacles, but square plinths for them set on the diagonal. A niche on the parapet has an exceptionally fine and well-preserved C15 group of the Trinity; God the Father holding a crucified Christ, the Holy Spirit as a dove on his shoulder. The rest was rebuilt in 1858–9 by C. E. Giles in Geometrical C13 style. Small nave, N transept and chapel, two-bay chancel. Triple-chamfered tower arch. Medieval STOUP (vestry). – Jacobean ALTAR TABLE. – FONT. C15, with rounded arches on an octagonal bowl. – C19 OIL LAMPS on cast-iron brackets in the chancel. – STAINED GLASS. E window, 1913. – MONUMENTS. George Hellier †1736. Big tablet with scrolled cartouche and cherubs' heads. – S of the porch, CHEST TOMBS, that to Richard James †16?45 with a thick top slab (cf. Doulting).

Binegar is scattered on the Mendip plateau. TURNER'S COURT FARM lies ¼ m. N of the church. Nicely un-spruced up. Low L-shaped range, C16 or C17, with irregular fenestration. Attached l., a two-storey barn. At the r., a higher block with hipped roof, perhaps early C17.

GURNEY SLADE, strung out along a shallow valley to the E, grew up around quarries. One or two polite Georgian houses at the N end. Vernacular houses round the central junction, e.g. SUNNYVIEW COTTAGE, with mullioned windows and continuous hoodmould. At the S end ROCK HOUSE, dated 1844, with mullioned windows – surely survival rather than revival.

BISHOP SUTTON

HOLY TRINITY. Bald E.E. by S. C. Fripp, 1845–8, altered or repaired by E. B. Ferrey, 1877. Originally a chapel of ease to Chew Magna, but close to Stowey.

BLAGDON

ST ANDREW. Early to mid-C15 four-stage w tower, among the tallest of Somerset parish churches at 116 ft 6 in. (35.5 metres). Set-back buttresses ending in pinnacles at the bell-stage. The main tower pinnacles are separate. Parapet of pierced cusped lozenges. Higher NE stair-turret with spirelet. On each side two two-light bell-openings with transom, flanked by thin diagonally set shafts. Big niche above the w window. On the s side a very defaced relief, three figures with fleuron border, perhaps *c.* 1500. The rest entirely rebuilt in 1907–9 by *Frank Wills*, cousin of the Bristol tobacco barons who paid for it (*see* Coombe Lodge, below). He produced the Edwardian image of the ideal C15 parish church, slightly frigid in its perfection. Of rock-faced Dolomitic Conglomerate, very wide, high and symmetrical; four-bay nave, clerestory, aisles, NE organ chamber, high chancel. SE vestry remodelled as a war memorial chapel, 1918–19. Piers with the refinement of additional slim shafts in the hollows. The main shafts continue as wall-shafts up to demi-angel corbels.

FITTINGS of best craftsmanship, tweaked unobtrusively by *G. C. Beech*, *c.* 1957–65. – ALTAR PAINTING. *Chiaroscuro* Last Supper, by *Oswald Moser*, *c.* 1908. – SCREEN and ROOD. The only major addition, 1933–5, by *Sir George Oatley*. – COMMUNION TABLE (N chapel) *c.* 1650, altered. – SCULPTURE. Basin of a piscina, the lower sill fronted with four big-headed figures under arches. Possibly pre-Conquest. – ROYAL ARMS on canvas, Gothic painted frame. By *W. Burge*, Bristol, 1826. – Complete STAINED GLASS by *Powells*, *c.* 1909–16, some very good. – MONUMENTS. Good tablets in the tower.

CHAPELS. Small Baptist chapel in Mead Lane, 1875; builder's Gothic. Methodist chapel, Street End, rebuilt by *Frank Wills*, 1906, Perp.

COOMBE LODGE, ½ m. NW. 1930–2 by *Sir George Oatley*, for the Wills family.[*] His largest private house, a domestic version of the Cotswold manor style of *c.* 1600 used for his Bristol University commissions from the Willses. The structure is steel and reinforced concrete. The N-facing hillside site constrained the plan. The main drive from the SE is raised; a secondary drive to the service wing passes beneath. The best views of Blagdon Lake are from an impressive two-storey E window, which lights only the servants' stair. To the W, a U-shaped family wing with paired canted bays, and S-facing arcaded loggia. Interior planned around a stony octagonal vestibule. Elsewhere, oak panelling prevails, with 1930s decorative touches. Bathrooms and nurseries with charming painted tiles by *Carter & Co.* of Poole (*Truda Carter* and *Reginald Hill*).

Blagdon is splendidly sited on the N slope of Mendip, with Blagdon Lake below. East End, around the church, looks across to West End, which has most of the facilities; Street End sits higher up the hill. The SCHOOL (N end of Church Street) of 1842 was enlarged in 1894 and again by *Wills* in 1904; grey stone, small-paned windows, timber bell-cupola. A few polite houses, e.g. ALDWICK COURT, Aldwick Lane, *c.* 1791, seven-bay ashlar façade with unadorned openings. Anachronistic doorcase added 1921, along with two bays to its r. BLAGDON COURT, Station Road, is perhaps *c.* 1830s; E front with Diocletian window in a pediment. In its garden, a bungalow by the *Hubbard Ford Partnership*, *c.* 1985, with dramatic curving roof.

[*] Sarah Whittingham, Ph.D. thesis, University of Bristol, 2005.

Many early vernacular houses, e.g. GILCOMBE HOUSE, Church Street, C16, enlarged in the C17 and refronted in the C18; COURT FARMHOUSE, Station Road, early C16 at the S end, doubled in size in the C17.

BLAGDON LAKE. A reservoir supplying Bristol, built 1891–1902. Engineers *T. & C. Hawksley.* W of the dam (Blagdon Lane), two red-brick pumping houses with transomed-and-mullioned windows, flanking a chimney truncated in 1954.

BLEADON

3050

ST PETER AND ST PAUL. Chancel, nave and W tower only. Inside (N wall), two blocked arches with C15 piers of four-shaft-four-wave section indicating an intended aisle. Chancel said to have been dedicated in 1317, with motifs typical of this period: two-light windows with one tracery unit, varied and distinctive in detail. One lowside window, traceried below the transom. Cinquefoiled rere-arches. Priest's door (chancel S) cusped and sub-cusped within and without; inside, a big leafy finial. In the sanctuary, a tomb recess with cusped and sub-cusped ogee arch. Perp W tower of *c.* 1380–1440; three stages, diagonal but-tresses, simple tower arch, tierceron star-vault. Four-light W window, then a two-light window and above this, a triplet of identical two-light windows, the centre one only open. Pierced parapet with quatrefoils, pinnacles, higher stair-turret with spirelet. The chancel has the same outward form as in Buckler's drawing of 1828: the nave seating was extended 12 ft (3.7 metres) eastward in a restoration of 1858–9, by *John Palmer* (probably the Weston-super-Mare builder active in the 1840s). Further reordering by *Wilde & Fry,* 1900. Tower restored, 1924–5. N organ chamber, possibly by *Alban Caröe,* 1953–4. p. 28

FITTINGS. STALLS etc., simple oak, *c.* 1950s. – PULPIT. Perp, of stone, with two-light blank arches, frieze and cresting. Probably from the same workshop as the pulpit at Banwell. – FONT. Simple, circular with plain mouldings. Perhaps C12–C13. – Copper WEATHERCOCK, handsome folk-art by *Samuel Taylor,* 1833. – SCULPTURE. Excellent though defaced early C14 panel of Virgin and Child before a cross, with two kneeling figures (porch). Ogee arch above the group. Small demi-figure of an angel bearing a shield (nave N); said to be Saxon, but probably C15. – Encaustic TILES, *c.* 1280–1317, from the chancel floor. – STAINED GLASS. E window by *Marion Grant,* 1964. – MONUMENTS. Two civilians, very defaced, probably mid-C14. – Mary Tutton †1769, by *S. Haynes* of Bristol. Tall obelisk with pedimented relief of a seated woman by an altar with urn. – W of the church, C15 CROSS, with fluted tapering shaft and part of the head.

SHIPLATE HOUSE, *c.* 2 m. ESE. Good house of perhaps 1760–80, brick with stone dressings, long-and-short quoins. Centre pediment in a flat parapet.

BRISTOL

INTRODUCTION

The late Sir John Summerson wrote, 'If I had to show a foreigner
one English city and one only, to give him a balanced idea of
English architecture, I should take him . . . to Bristol, which has
developed in all directions, and where nearly everything has
happened.' Bristol has been a major centre of population, manufacture and commerce for almost one thousand years. It was
England's second city in the C14 and the C18, and became a
county in 1373. It remained in the diocese of Worcester until the
see of Bristol was created in 1542. Trade declined relative to the

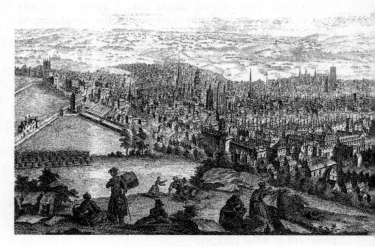

Bristol, from the north-west.
Engraving by S. and N. Buck, 1734

N of England after *c.* 1800, partly accounting for Bristol's piece-meal growth and the survival of so much pre-C19 architecture. Bristol reveals its charms slowly. Its uniqueness lies in the range and extraordinary juxtapositions of buildings, which, with the dislocation caused by Second World War bombing, produce a mystifying disjointedness. Today it is the seventh largest city in Britain and the regional centre of SW England.

The region's geography is the determining factor in Bristol's existence. It sits some five miles inside the mouth of the River Avon, which runs W to the Bristol Channel. The Channel has a tidal range of up to *c.* 50 ft (*c.* 15 metres), the second highest in the world; the force of these waters makes the Avon tidal well to the E of Bristol. The narrow, winding Avon channel proved a handicap to Bristol's C18 Atlantic trade. Otherwise Bristol possessed all the prerequisites for great wealth: a port and bridge-head, well placed to trade with the W coasts of Britain, Ireland, the Atlantic coasts of Europe, and the New World; river access to inland England; a focal point for trade in West Country wool and foodstuffs; access to coal, building materials, timber, and trade routes providing the raw materials for manufacturing.

The local GEOLOGY is complex. Central alluvial deposits are bounded by low hills of red Triassic sandstone at Redcliffe, College Green and beneath the Saxon town (*see* below). Higher slopes to the N (Brandon Hill and St Michael's Hill) are formed of Brandon Hill Grit, a red Carboniferous sandstone. Clifton sits on Hotwells limestone. From E of Bristol comes soft, flaky Pennant sandstone, widely used for rubble walling and flag-stones. Its dour battleship grey, often cast with soft blues, greens, ochre, or plum, is one of the underpinnings of Bristol's character. For fine work, medieval masons favoured Dundry stone from a few miles S. This creamy-white oolitic limestone weathers to a honey colour like Bath stone, but contains ribbon-like layers of

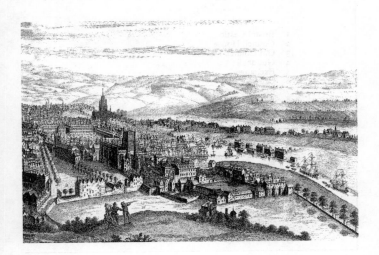

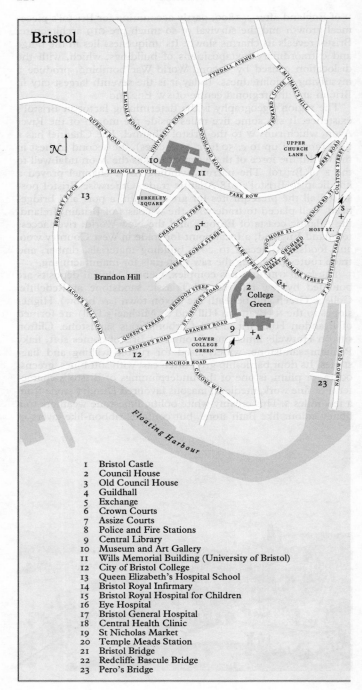

Bristol

1   Bristol Castle
2   Council House
3   Old Council House
4   Guildhall
5   Exchange
6   Crown Courts
7   Assize Courts
8   Police and Fire Stations
9   Central Library
10   Museum and Art Gallery
11   Wills Memorial Building (University of Bristol)
12   City of Bristol College
13   Queen Elizabeth's Hospital School
14   Bristol Royal Infirmary
15   Bristol Royal Hospital for Children
16   Eye Hospital
17   Bristol General Hospital
18   Central Health Clinic
19   St Nicholas Market
20   Temple Meads Station
21   Bristol Bridge
22   Redcliffe Bascule Bridge
23   Pero's Bridge

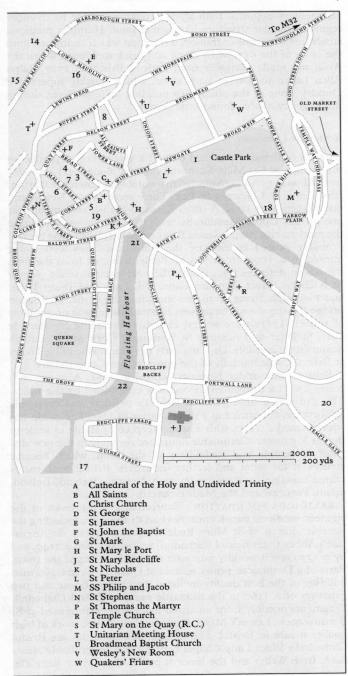

A	Cathedral of the Holy and Undivided Trinity
B	All Saints
C	Christ Church
D	St George
E	St James
F	St John the Baptist
G	St Mark
H	St Mary le Port
J	St Mary Redcliffe
K	St Nicholas
L	St Peter
M	SS Philip and Jacob
N	St Stephen
P	St Thomas the Martyr
R	Temple Church
S	St Mary on the Quay (R.C.)
T	Unitarian Meeting House
U	Broadmead Baptist Church
V	Wesley's New Room
W	Quakers' Friars

sedimentary deposits. Bath stone is distinguishable by its more regular, granular structure like coarse sand. Humbler medieval structures were timber-framed, a tradition which continued until the close of the C17, when stone and brick took over. When the Avon was made navigable from Bath to Bristol in 1727, Ralph Allen began to market Bath stone, which quickly superseded Dundry stone as the ubiquitous building material. Even during the Regency, stucco found little favour.

Roman and medieval

ROMAN settlement consisted only of a small port at Abonae on the Avon, now Sea Mills. Scattered villas lay along the Avon valley from Abonae to Aquae Sulis (Bath), notably at Lawrence Weston, Brislington and Newton St Loe. There were two at Keynsham, one of them very large. A small Romano-British settlement near present-day Upper Maudlin Street is the only known site within the modern city. Anglo-Saxon BRYCGSTOW (place of the bridge) probably existed at least by the late 900s; coins were being minted by *c.* 1009–16. It was probably defended from the first, the Saxon defences traceable in the near-circular street plan of St Nicholas Street, Leonard Lane, Bell Lane and Tower Lane, and E of High Street up to and including the castle. The Saxon bridge (on the site of the present Bristol Bridge) was presumably of timber. There were several churches, including St Mary le Port, St Peter and possibly St Werburgh, Corn Street, but no Saxon fabric is visible. Only the early C11 Harrowing of Hell relief at Bristol Cathedral tells of the power of pre-Conquest art.

Bristol came under Norman control in 1068. A motte-and-bailey CASTLE probably of wood was established by the 1080s. The C12 was a high point in Bristol's political and economic importance, confirmed in a royal charter of 1155. The castle was strengthened *c.* 1120, with a stone keep comparable in scale to that at Rochester. Commerce flourished, notably in the new districts of Temple and Redcliffe S of the Avon, which became centres of the wool and leather industries. Bristol soon maintained valuable overseas trades with Norway, Iceland, Ireland, Spain, Portugal and the Mediterranean.

RELIGIOUS FOUNDATIONS flourished: at least seven of the eighteen medieval parish churches had C12 origins, including the sizeable church of St Mary Redcliffe (before 1160). St Augustine's Abbey (later Bristol Cathedral) was established *c.* 1140, and by *c.* 1250 seven wealthy monastic foundations ringed the town. Parts of a Dominican priory remain at Quakers' Friars. Norman building of the best quality includes the chapter house and two gateways of *c.* 1160 in the monastic parts of Bristol Cathedral. Fragments possibly from an aisled hall house were reused at St Bartholomew, Lewin's Mead. Early English Gothic work of high quality is rare in Bristol. The outstanding examples are Bristol Cathedral's Elder Lady Chapel (using a mason, probably *Adam Lock*, from Wells) and the inner N porch of St Mary Redcliffe, both of c. 1220. The Wells workshop also influenced surviving sculptures at St James and St Bartholomew.

In 1240–7 Bristol Bridge was rebuilt in stone, and by c. 1300 was lined with houses. In the same years the River Frome was diverted through a new man-made channel, St Augustine's Reach, doubling the size of the harbour. Also in the mid C13 extensions of the Saxon WALLS followed the Frome N along today's Nelson Street. On the S, new walls protected Baldwin Street and Redcliffe. Similar projects, e.g. at Oxford, 1224–40, York, c. 1250, and Newcastle, c. 1265, were intended to regulate trade as much as for defence. These new walls, bridge, harbour and monastic foundations must have given mid-C13 Bristol a dramatic air of forwardness and change.

Bristol's wealth and prestige came, by the mid C14, no longer from wool but from fine woollen cloth, in high demand in Flanders and Italy. It was traded for wine and other goods in Gascony, Anjou and Poitou. Bristol was by c. 1330 the wealthiest town after London, and among the most populous at perhaps c. 10,000 residents. The Berkeley family were patrons of the innovative and capricious early C14 reworking of the eastern arm at St Augustine's Abbey, partly as a vehicle for their family tombs. The work has stylistic echoes at St Mary Redcliffe, also being remodelled on a grand scale.

Many of the PARISH CHURCHES were rebuilt or enlarged in Perpendicular style from the later C14. Among these are St Stephen, St Werburgh, All Saints, St John, St Peter, St Mary le Port, Temple and St Michael, Clifton (some later demolished or rebuilt). The best place to see the significance and wealth of early Perp work is in the later parts of the C14 rebuilding at St Mary Redcliffe, i.e. the upper parts of the choir, transepts and nave, perhaps completed c. 1390. The mercantile Canynge family were probably one of several donor families rather than sole patrons, as Victorian myth suggested. St John has two great rarities: a one-bay clerestory W of the chancel arch to light the rood, and a full crypt, built in two sections. The W part here has a vault matching that at St Nicholas; both are probably of c. 1350–80, and very fine. The best late Perp work is the Poyntz chapel at St Mark, decorated in honour of the patron's friendship with Henry VIII and Catherine of Aragon.

Medieval CHURCH FURNISHINGS include fragments of C14–C16 glass at Bristol Cathedral and St Mary Redcliffe, a fine C15 brass lectern now at St Stephen, and a rare candelabrum in the Berkeley Chapel of the cathedral. The cathedral misericords are of c. 1520. Bishop Miles Salley embellished the chancel at St Mark c. 1500–20, with a fine reredos and his own tomb in a matching style. The neighbouring Berkeley tomb and the similar late C15 Mede tombs at St Mary Redcliffe have richly ornamented canopies with lacy stonework. Sculpture includes the fine alabaster effigies of William Canynges the Younger †1474, at St Mary Redcliffe, and of Walter Frampton †1388, at St John. The Poyntz Chapel at St Mark was floored with richly decorated C16

23, 24, 25, 26

p. 269

39, p. 261

Spanish tiles, evidence of the strong trading links with the Iberian peninsula.

Surviving PUBLIC AND SECULAR BUILDINGS of the period are few. Illustrations of the C15 Guildhall show an asymmetrical façade with little sense of civic grandeur. Wealthy mercantile families such as the Canynges and Spicers had extravagant houses, often very tall and intended to impress.* High-status houses retained the medieval great hall open to the roof; by the C15 they were often not used for everyday living, but were decorated with symbols of military and civic status – a phenomenon that continued in Bristol as late as c. 1690. The best secular works are Guardhouse Arch, of c. 1520, now at Bristol Museum, and the remarkable surviving stair-tower at Inns Court, Knowle.

The sixteenth and seventeenth centuries

Bristol's population in the mid C16 was c. 9,500–10,000, increasing to c. 25,000 by 1700. The pattern of trade was also transformed. At c. 1630 just a few ships ventured to the Americas; by the end of the century, voyages to Virginia, the Caribbean and Newfoundland accounted for about half the ships leaving port. The effects of the Reformation included the demolition of Abbot Newland's untimely half-built nave at St Augustine's Abbey, though the abbey at least became a cathedral in 1542, giving Bristol city status. Monastic buildings were converted for use as guildhalls, schools (e.g. St Mark and St Bartholomew) or private houses. There was notable EXPANSION beyond the city walls during the C17. Scattered medieval outer suburbs (e.g. St Michael's Hill, Broadmead and Old Market) became more densely populated and suburban in character. King Street was laid out in the 1650s along the outer side of the S wall on Town Marsh, and housing straggled W towards Hotwells and S towards Bedminster too. The city was 'in every respect another London that one can hardly know it to stand in the country' (Samuel Pepys, 1668).

By the C16 Bristol's military importance was much reduced, and the castle was ruinous. Briefly refortified for the Civil War, it was demolished in 1655. No new churches were built in Bristol from 1530 until the C18. The rich legacy of CHURCH FURNISHINGS is best seen in the woodwork at St John. MONUMENTS are well represented, e.g. at St Mark, St Stephen and St James. Ionic columns support the canopy of Bishop Bush's monument of c. 1558 at Bristol Cathedral, the earliest surviving use of classical motifs in Bristol. Classical columns, perhaps crudely rendered, were considered appropriate for public buildings by the mid C16 (see below). However, classicism as an architectural style, rather than a source for applied details, was fashionable with the Court and aristocracy through the designs of Inigo Jones. Apart from the refacing at Ashton Court, Long Ashton, of 1633–4 (see

---

*An outstanding C14 fragment is the traceried oak door of c. 1330–50 from John Spicer's house, now at the Museum and Art Gallery.

Introduction, p. 47), it was another half-century before the gap between the taste of the Court and that of Bristol merchants began to close. Until then Bristol remained essentially Jacobean.

DOMESTIC BUILDINGS survive in good numbers, owing partly to the absence of a Bristol Great Fire. The best Elizabethan example is the Red Lodge, Park Row, of 1579–80. It originally had an Italian-influenced loggia. The interiors – especially the Great Oak Room – rival the best of their size and date in England. The richly decorated St Peter's Hospital (rebuilt 1612) and the Dutch House, High Street (1676; both bombed, 1940) were timber-framed, the latter of five storeys. Their height and ostentation are paralleled by examples in Newcastle. Others survive, e.g. at St Michael's Hill, King Street, Old Market, Victoria Street and St Thomas Street. Compared with Tudor work, the jetties are shallower or non-existent, with a pent roof or a moulded wooden beam at each floor. In King Street, five 1660s houses were treated as a unified symmetrical composition. Classical motifs include 'Ipswich' bay windows with arched centres, perhaps referring to the Venetian motif, and quasi-Ionic pilasters incised into structural timbers. Timber framing was replaced by brick with remarkable suddenness in the 1690s. 48

Surviving INTERIORS of the C17 are rare. A panelled room of the 1620s from Langton's Mansion, Welsh Back, was reconstructed c. 1906 at New Place, Shedfield, Hampshire, and highly decorated friezes or ceilings are at No. 33 King Street, and at the Llandoger Trow inn nearby. Stone chimneypieces of c. 1580–c. 1680 form a special group with a distinctive Bristol style (see Introduction, p. 46). There are fine examples at the Red Lodge, and at Red Maids School, Westbury-on-Trym (ex situ).

Bristol from c. 1700 to c. 1830

Bristol began to outstrip York and Norwich as second city after London from c. 1700, entering a golden age that lasted until c. 1750, by which time its population had doubled to nearly 50,000. It reached c. 67,000 by the 1801 census. The major commerce of these years was the slave trade. Early C18 Bristol saw new BUILDING MATERIALS. Brick quickly became the standard for housing. Bath stone, introduced from 1727, supplanted all rivals in the best public and domestic works. MANUFACTURING was carried on in small or mid-sized workshops, in the dense heart of the city. New industries included pottery and glass, which developed from the late C17 in St Philip's, Temple and Redcliffe. Nine glass kilns existed by 1696 – the largest concentration outside London. The only survivor is the truncated cone at Redcliffe, of c. 1780. The refining of Caribbean sugar has left only parts of one factory at Lewins Mead. Brass, an important export commodity for slave traders, was produced in Bristol by c. 1696, and Abraham Darby's brassworks was established c. 1702. At Arno's Court, Brislington, the nationally significant castellated stable block was built c. 1764, of iridescent purplish-black blocks of slag from 76

pp. 224–5

copper furnaces. For other examples of Bristol's craze for Rococo Gothick *see* Introduction, p. 53.

Commentators agree upon Georgian Bristol's social character: it had a large merchant class with money, but little concerned with taste or sophisticated society. Horace Walpole called it 'the dirtiest great shop I ever saw'. Its people were constantly 'in a hurry, running up and down with cloudy looks and busy faces' (Thomas Cox, *Magna Britannia*, 1727).

Bristol's new status resulted in PUBLIC BUILDINGS of some flamboyance but less refinement, such as the Baroque refacing of the Merchants' Hall for the Society of Merchant Venturers in 1719, perhaps by *George Townesend* of the Oxford family of masons. Civic pride was also expressed in almshouses, e.g. Colston's, St Michael's Hill, 1691–6, and the Merchant Tailors', 1701. Several medieval guilds rebuilt their halls, in their dying decades. Two façades at least survive; Merchant Tailors' Hall off Broad Street, and Coopers' Hall, King Street, both of the early 1740s and attributed to *William Halfpenny*. The best sculpture is *Rysbrack*'s great brass equestrian statue of William III in Queen Square. For its new Exchange (1741–3), the Corporation chose *John Wood the Elder* of Bath, an architect of national standing compatible with Bristol's sense of self-importance. He produced Bristol's most significant C18 building, a design of great sophistication and richness, interpreting Palladian models with academic rigour.

House building was transformed by the rise of planned TERRACES and SQUARES. The driving forces were two-fold: the desire for grander, more formal housing for the mercantile class, and the need for lodgings, as at Bath, to accommodate the growing number of visitors to the Hotwell spa. Of the latter type, Dowry Square, Hotwells is notable (1721 onwards), with villas and lodging houses up the hill in Clifton following in the 1740s. Of the former type, Queen Square (1699–*c.* 1727) is the first Bristol square, the grandest in scale, and the first piece of urban planning dictated by the Corporation. Houses were constructed piecemeal, the only coherence being dictated by building leases that stipulated regular brick fronts, cornices etc., in emulation of the City of London's post-Fire regulations. EARLY C18 HOUSES were generally of three, five or occasionally seven bays, and double-pile in plan. Special decorative devices include lesenes between adjoining houses, cherub rainwater heads, shell-hoods and foliate window keystones modelled as grotesque masks: see No. 28 Orchard Street and No. 29 Queen Square. The Late Baroque phase of urban housing is also seen at its liveliest at Nos. 66–70 Prince Street, *c.* 1725–8, probably by *John Strahan*, and in the 1730s façade of No. 59 Queen Charlotte Street, attributed to *Nathaniel Ireson*. The 1740s building boom saw the completion of Dowry Square, and the layout of King Square, Unity Street and Park Street, the beginnings of greater expansions northward from the later C18.

Baroque CHURCH ARCHITECTURE is limited to a fine rebuilding of the tower at All Saints (1712–17), and some minor

doorcases. Redland Chapel, by *John Strahan* and *William Half-* [60]
penny, c. 1739–43, was a merchant's private chapel, with refined
decoration and sculpture. Bristol was a centre of NONCONFOR-
MITY, though most early chapels have been lost. The best survivors are Wesley's New Room, Broadmead (1739 and c. 1748), [64]
the first purpose-built Methodist chapel, and the nearby Friends'
Meeting House (*George Tully*, 1747), perhaps the most architecturally ambitious of its type and date in England. In the later C18,
St Nicholas and St Michael were both rebuilt, in the 1760s and
1770s respectively, the former, by *James Bridges*, in a remarkably
early and accurate Neo-Perpendicular. A burst of church building in the 1780s produced Christ Church, Broad Street, St Paul,
Portland Square, and St Thomas in Redcliffe. The only national [75]
figure involved was *William Blackburn*, for the Unitarian Meeting
House at Lewins Mead.

Big VILLAS began to cluster at Clifton, already by the early C18 [69]
the most desirable location beyond the smoke and smells of the
city. Representative of the type is Royal Fort House (*J. Bridges*,
1758–61) with dazzling Rococo decoration. Also popular were [81]
several villages further out, notably Redland, Stapleton and Brislington; villas here were often updatings of C16 and C17 farms
or manor houses. Blaise Castle House (1790s, *William Paty*) is
typical of the modest but elegant Neoclassical villas built for the
wealthiest merchants. But for the nub of Bristol's character after
c. 1770, we must look one step down the social scale, to the
better-off middle-class stock of businessmen, shopkeepers and
investors in foreign voyages. For them was built the characteristic TERRACED HOUSING which spread rapidly from Park Street
across Clifton and Hotwells, Kingsdown, Montpelier and St [2]
Paul's: a northern fringe of leafy and spacious Georgian
SUBURBS unparalleled in England. The economics of their speculative development is detailed in the Introduction (p. 49). The
main proponents were the *Paty* family, and the typical Bath-
stone-fronted terrace of, say, Berkeley Square, is now referred to
as the 'late Paty style'. The most fashionable were of course in
Clifton, e.g. Royal York Crescent. They are only rivalled at Portland Square, St Paul's, designed c. 1787–8 by *Daniel Hague*,
where the planning approaches the scale and consistency of C18
London squares. Prince's Buildings, Clifton (1789), and Kingsdown Parade (1791) have pairs of houses linked by lower wings:
one step towards the semi-detached or individual villa which
displaced the terrace in Victoria's reign.

STREET IMPROVEMENTS in the medieval centre cluster
around the rebuilt Bristol Bridge (1760–9), e.g. in the 1770s, the
creation of Bath Street and Clare Street, which smoothed out
medieval alleys with new traffic routes, created smart shops, and
linked the commercial district with the quaysides more effectively. PORT FACILITIES begin with Sea Mills, the third wet dock
in Britain, c. 1712, an early and failed attempt to circumvent the
problems of Bristol's tidal harbour. In 1765 Champion's (later
Merchants') Dock was dug at Hotwells. After 1800 Bristol's population growth was much less spectacular than that of Liverpool,

Manchester or Birmingham, and her industrial capacity was fast overtaken. The creation of the Floating Harbour (engineer *William Jessop*, 1804–9) enclosed the formerly tidal harbour with lock gates, removing the limitation on loading and unloading caused when the tide went out and ships in harbour were lowered to the mud. But the cost increased harbour dues, and it came too late: Liverpool had overtaken Bristol in the Atlantic trade. Bristol became an early centre of the Abolition movement, which finally succeeded in 1833.

CHURCH BUILDING was given new impetus by the 'Million Pound' Act of 1818, intended for poorer and unchurched districts, and a further Act of 1824, under which three Commissioners' churches were built locally. Bristol's largest allocation funded the Grecian temple of St George, Brandon Hill (*Robert Smirke*), an affluent chapel of ease. The others, both thin Perp Gothic, were St Paul, Bedminster, by *Charles Dyer*, 1829–31, and *Rickman & Hutchinson*'s Holy Trinity, St Philip's, 1829–30. The Zion Congregational Chapel in Bedminster may stand for the numerous CHAPELS built or rebuilt in the early C19, most of them lost. PUBLIC BUILDINGS are more numerous, and outside architects were more frequently employed for these. After the economic collapse of 1793 the first building of note was the Clifton Assembly Rooms (1806, by *Francis Greenway*). *Charles Busby*'s Commercial Rooms, Corn Street (1809–11), looked to Liverpool and Manchester for inspiration. *C. R. Cockerell*'s Philosophical and Literary Institution, Park Street (1821–3), and *Smirke*'s Old Council House, Corn Street (1823–7), are both Greek Revival from scholarly sources.

Victorian and Edwardian Bristol

p. 415

Bristol's C19 economic strength lay in a diversified economy of up to a dozen key industries, e.g. sugar, shipping, iron-founding, soap-making, potteries, tobacco, chocolate-making and printing. They left no great monuments such as Lancashire's cotton mills. From *c.* 1840–60 there was economic stagnation as Bristol lost out to the industrializing North. Substantial growth from *c.* 1860 was driven by new industries and changes in the port's finances, slackening off after *c.* 1880. The population grew from *c.* 121,000 in 1831 to *c.* 352,000 in 1911. Victorian Bristol was prosperous yet commercially mediocre, without the monumental confidence and civic pride of, say, Manchester or Leeds.

105

PUBLIC AND COMMERCIAL BUILDINGS begin with the Victoria Rooms (*C. Dyer*, 1838–42), a Roman Corinthian expression of civic pride, and also of Clifton's growing status. Arno's Vale Cemetery is by *Charles Underwood*, 1837–9, part of a national trend for private cemeteries as city graveyards became over-full. Also notable are *Cockerell*'s Graeco-Roman Bank of England office (1846), *R. S. Pope*'s Guildhall of 1843–6, and the Assize Courts, Small Street, 1867–70 by *Popes & Bindon*. The Colston Hall (1864–73) by *Foster & Wood*, was Bristol's first major concert and meeting hall. The former Museum and Library, Queen's

Road, by *Foster* and *Ponton*, 1867, underscores Bristol's growing need for cultural facilities. None of these can compare with the scale seen in the Northern cities. However, Mid-Victorian banks and offices began to exhibit a brash self-confidence, often alluding to the commercial power of North Italian city states. Notable are the densely emblematic carved façade of the present Lloyds TSB bank by *Gingell & Lysaght*, 1854–7, and other showy examples in Corn Street. Shops are represented by a row in St Nicholas Street, by *Archibald Ponton*, c. 1866, and his excellent design for Pointing's Chemist, High Street, of about the same date (bombed 1940), in a more strongly Gothic idiom. No. 51 Broad Street (*Ponton & Gough*, 1868) is related to both. The Marriott Royal Hotel, College Green, and the Grand Hotel, Broad Street, are both of c. 1865 and Italianate. p. 292

A fine cast-iron Doric signpost of 1833 at Totterdown reminds us of the improvements by the Bristol Turnpike Trust, under its surveyor *John MacAdam*. Road gave way to RAIL with the opening in 1841 of the Great Western Railway from London to Bristol, under its engineer, *Isambard Kingdom Brunel*. Fortunately his original train shed, with its mock-hammerbeam roof and Tudoresque frontage, survives. With *Fripp*'s offices (1852–4) and *M. Digby Wyatt*'s GWR joint station (1871–8) it forms a fine complex. *Brunel*'s Clifton Suspension Bridge (1829–64), a road bridge, is perhaps the most recognizable symbol of Bristol to outsiders. In 1848 the city DOCK COMPANY was taken over by the Corporation, as were Avonmouth and Portishead docks in 1884. The harbour and rivers, already open sewers, stagnated after the harbour was docked in 1804–9: a Parliamentary Report in 1845 found Bristol among the dirtiest cities in Britain, with the third highest mortality rate (thirty-one per thousand). Cholera epidemics in part prompted improvements in hygiene and water supply, reducing the mortality rate to eighteen per thousand by 1883. p. 283 100

Industrial and warehouse buildings engendered a style known now as BRISTOL BYZANTINE, although deriving largely from North Italian models. Key examples are *R. S. Pope*'s warehouse at Narrow Quay, 1830 (now the Arnolfini), and *W. B. Gingell*'s basement warehousing at Bristol General Hospital (1852–7) with rock-faced walling and giant arches. *E. W. Godwin*'s Carriage Works in Stokes Croft (1862) and *Ponton & Gough*'s splendid Granary, Welsh Back (1869), display Sienese, Florentine, Gothic and Venetian motifs, and the influence of Ruskin. 99

The first CHURCH design of note in this period is *Henry Goodridge*'s megalomaniac hilltop temple, the Roman Catholic Pro-Cathedral, Clifton, begun c. 1834, never completed and long derelict. *Pope*'s St Mary on the Quay, 1839, is an austere, academic rendering of a Greek Corinthian temple for the Irvingite sect. Bristol was a bastion of Liberal Nonconformity and of Tory Evangelicalism; both fuelled a distrust of High Anglicanism and Ecclesiology, which appeared late, often attended by vehement protest. Local architects of course supplied most of the suburban churches (e.g. *S. B. Gabriel*'s St Jude, Braggs Lane, then a desperately poor district). *John Norton*'s Stapleton church (1854–7) and his spire for Christ Church, Clifton (1859) epitomize the taste for C13 earnestness. *Butterfield* explored Puginian ideas of honest construction at Cotham (1842–3), though unexpectedly for a Congregational chapel. His pupil *Woodyer* was responsible for St Raphael (1859). Then came *Street*'s All Saints, Clifton (1863), and *Ponton & Gough*'s Holy Nativity, Knowle (1870–83), a fine polychrome work of Byzantine-Gothic character. All three churches were High Anglican, and all were bombed. St Agnes (1885–7) is an original design, begun as a mission church to a poor suburb from Clifton College. The best later churches are *Oatley*'s All Hallows, Easton (from 1899), and *Rodway & Dening*'s St Alban, Westbury Park (1907–15). Restorations demanding note are the completion of Bristol Cathedral nave (*G. E. Street*, 1867–88), and the almost complete refacing of St Mary Redcliffe under *George Godwin* (c. 1842–72). The stained glass in the Cathedral Lady Chapel was restored by *Joseph Bell*, whose company operated in Bristol from c. 1840 until 1996; Bell glass can be seen of course in many local churches. As for Nonconformity, the former Grenville Methodist Chapel, Hotwells (1837–9), is among the earliest known uses of Gothic for a Nonconformist chapel in Britain. But classicism thrived, e.g. in the chapels of *Henry Crisp* and others, with Kensington Baptist Chapel, Easton, still Grecian as late as 1885–8. Others espoused Gothic in its churchiest garb, as at *Hansom*'s Clifton Down Congregational chapel, 1868.

HOUSING can be dealt with briefly. Clifton is a special case; its most splendid Grecian terraces and villas belong to the phase which began in the 1820s, but really took off c. 1833, perhaps prompted by a desire to vacate the city after the Riots of 1831.
103 Clifton's golden age was concentrated in the years c. 1833–48. From c. 1850 the terrace was superseded by the villa as the fashionable mode for housing. The grandest villas are around Durdham Down and in Sneyd Park. The suburban heartland of Clifton, Cotham, Redland, St Andrew's etc. was the province of local architects such as *W. H. Hawtin*, *George Gay* and *J. A. Clark*, whose works are nearly indistinguishable. Designs are characteristically debased Italianate, less frequently Tudor, Jacobean or Gothic, in grey or purple Pennant stone. *Foster & Wood* topped the bill throughout the C19, particularly for updatings, e.g. at Stoke House, Stoke Bishop. Edwardian housing includes the Voyseyish designs of *Henry Dare Bryan*, e.g. at Leigh Woods, just outside Bristol, and the Bedford Park-inspired Downs Park, near Henleaze.

EDUCATIONAL ARCHITECTURE starts with the University College (later University of Bristol), and the small group of buildings by *Charles Hansom* from 1879. These are conventional Neo-Tudor, evoking the great collegiate foundations of the late C15 and early C16. Both Queen Elizabeth's Hospital School (*Foster & Son*, 1844–7) and Bristol Grammar School (*Foster & Wood*, 1877–9) were founded in the C16, and chose styles to suit. A more expensive version appears at Clifton College (from 1862, by *Hansom*) in a richer collegiate Tudor. Board Schools after 1870 never adopted a 'trademark' style in the London manner, but clung to a dour Gothic or Tudor. *W. L. Bernard* was appointed as their architect only in 1888, and then not to the exclusion of others. Unlike in London, these schools frequently had just a high central hall with spreading single-storey blocks around. A group of five or six good schools survives in Bedminster and Southville, but the best and most metropolitan-looking design is *F. Bligh Bond*'s Higher Grade and Technical School at St George, 1894–5.

From *c.* 1880 mild forms of QUEEN ANNE and RENAISSANCE REVIVAL appear, e.g. at *Foster & Wood*'s Bristol Municipal Charities Offices, Colston Avenue. *Alfred Waterhouse*'s Prudential Building, Clare Street (1899), is in Loire Renaissance mode. *Frank Wills*'s distinctive free Gothic in red brick with giant pointed arches is seen at his Bedminster tobacco factories. The p. 415 Hippodrome, St Augustine's Parade (1911–12), is the last major theatre design by *Frank Matcham*. For the Art Gallery, Queen's Road (1900–5), *Wills* resorted inevitably to a weighty Edwardian civic Baroque. The ARTS AND CRAFTS MOVEMENT enjoyed some popularity in Bristol, notably in the pubs and offices of *Edward Gabriel*, *F. Bligh Bond*'s work at Shirehampton (e.g. the public hall, 1904) and *Dare Bryan*'s Congregational College (1905–6), Cotham. INDUSTRIAL BUILDINGS include the castellar Neo-Norman offices of Lysaght's Works in St Philip's, by *R. M. Drake*, 1891, with glorious tiled interiors. The young *W. Curtis Green* did the Counterslip Generating Station and the Brislington depot for the Bristol Tramways and Carriage Co. around 1900. Good commercial buildings survive by *Edward Gabriel* too. Bristol's outstanding Art Nouveau building is the scintillating tiled façade of Everard's Printing Works, Broad Street (1900). REINFORCED CONCRETE was employed fairly early in Bristol, for the GWR goods shed, Canon's Marsh (1904), which used the *Hennebique* system (now 'Explore'); the *Coignet* patent system was used for bonded tobacco warehouses at Cumberland Basin from 1906.

Bristol generally steered a middle course, ignoring the *avant-garde* in architecture. The exceptions are *Charles Holden*'s Central 108 Library, 1902–6, showing his awareness of the work of Mackintosh in Glasgow, and his Bristol Royal Infirmary work of p. 280 1909–12. After the library Holden produced nothing so uncompromising until his London Underground stations in 1932. *George Oatley*'s University buildings are latest Edwardian, the most prominent being the Wills Memorial Building (1912–25). 109 Of reinforced concrete beneath its stone face, in intention it is one of the last great monuments of the Gothic Revival.

From *c. 1914* to the twenty-first century

Bristol's population in 1921 was *c.* 368,000, growing to 442,000 by the mid century, but by 2001 this had decreased to *c.* 380,000 (excluding the S Gloucestershire growths of Bradley Stoke, etc.). Established industries such as printing, paper and packaging, tobacco, sherry importing, and chocolate-making flourished, alongside new ones such as aircraft manufacture. Central depopulation accelerated as working-class suburbs expanded s and e of the city, with smaller pockets of private middle-class housing; the converse situation applied in the leafier northern and north-western suburbs. Wartime bombing and the advent of a post-industrial economy meant the decline of traditional manufacturing. With the growth of Avonmouth Docks, Bristol ceased to be a commercial port in 1974. Within a few years motorways linked Bristol with London and the Midlands. Service industries took off from the 1970s, with media, technology and finance dominating.

Significant CHURCHES from before 1939 are confined to the Neo-Gothic of *Oatley & Lawrence*, and those of *P. Hartland Thomas*, stripped bare and showing glimpses of Modernism at Shirehampton and Brislington. Of PUBLIC BUILDINGS, only the bland Neo-Georgian of *E. Vincent Harris*'s Council House (1938–52) stands out, chiefly for its size and centrality. *Oatley & Lawrence* produced competent University buildings in pared-down Tudor or other revival styles. COMMERCIAL interwar buildings include *Sir Giles Gilbert Scott*'s former Friends Provident office, Corn Street (1931–3), and Electricity House, Colston Avenue (1935–48). *Cecil Howitt*'s Odeon, Broadmead, is the best cinema of its date to preserve much of its original appearance. *W. H. Watkins*'s super-cinemas have all gone. The Concrete House, Westbury-on-Trym (1934, by *Connell, Ward & Lucas*) is the finest MODERNIST house in Bristol, for a well-off intellectual. *Breuer & Yorke*'s two works for a furniture manufacturer (1935–6) were sadly demolished. During the 1930s slum dwellers were moved into COUNCIL ESTATES, e.g. at Shirehampton, Sea Mills, Knowle West and Fishponds, inspired by Garden City ideals.

The impact of Second World War bombing was enormous. About a quarter of the medieval city was destroyed, and much in Temple, Redcliffe, Park Street, Broadmead and Bedminster. After the war, the city was surrounded by a 'ring of blight' – a pattern common across the USA and Great Britain.

The City Architect *J. N. Meredith*'s megalomaniac Reconstruction Plan (1946) covered 771 acres, reduced by 1948 to just 4.5 acres of new shops at Broadmead. These were built *c*. 1950–60, against the wishes of traders and the public. The bombed shopping area around Castle Street became a wasteland. Traffic planning had already begun with the inner circuit road at Temple Way and Redcliffe Way, from 1936. Reports of 1952 and 1966 proposed a destructive outer circuit road, partly implemented at Easton, and resulting in much needless demolition at Totterdown in the 1970s. Plans for the centre featured destructive bridges across the harbour, and 'vertical segregation' by means of pedestrian decks above dual carriageways, an idea finally abandoned *c*. 1973.

There are two exceptional POST-WAR CHURCHES: Clifton Cathedral (R.C.), by the *Percy Thomas Partnership*, 1965–73, and

nearby, the angular All Saints (*Robert Potter*, 1962–7), with spec-   115
tacular fibreglass windows by *John Piper*. Unexpectedly, the most
striking fitting is at Southmead: *John Hoskin*'s huge steel sculp-   113
ture of the Exalted Christ, 1959. The advent of HIGH-RISE
HOUSING is represented best at Barton Hill, where cotton-
workers' terraces were replaced with fifteen-storey blocks of
1956–65, then the highest in the West of England. By contrast,
High Kingsdown, 1971–5, is a rare example of good low-rise,   120
high-density private housing. OFFICE BUILDINGS after 1945
were often abysmally dull, and big; the largest *c.* 1960–75 were
around 16,000–18,000 sq. ft (1,480–1,670 sq. metres). Among
the few of note is the Robinson Building, Victoria Street (*Group
Architects DRG*, 1960–3), admirably pure in line and colour.

Against such schemes, listed building controls offered little
protection for historic buildings, and demolition losses before
1975 probably equalled those from bombing. The Planning
Department negotiated privately with developers, resenting
the interference of the public and specialist bodies. Embryonic
amenity groups were formed from the late 1960s, and by 1975
the CONSERVATION MOVEMENT came of age. It was the turning
point in Bristol's post-war development. Public pressure began
to stave off destructive schemes, e.g. in the historic districts of St
Michael's Hill, Kingsdown, Clifton, and Old Market. The return
of *Brunel*'s S.S. *Great Britain* in 1970 heralded the regeneration
of the harbour, notably the Arnolfini Gallery (1975) and the   99
Watershed (1980–1), reusing derelict warehouses. The Planning
Department encouraged a contextual 'dockside warehouse' aesthetic for new builds, e.g. the Scottish Life building, Welsh Back
(*Burnet Tait Powell & Partners*, 1975). Big waterside HOUSING
SCHEMES began, and among the best COMMERCIAL PROJECTS
were Lloyds Bank, Canon's Marsh (*Arup Associates*, 1988–90),
and the River Station restaurant (*Inscape Architects*, 1998).

PUBLIC SPACES have been improved since *c.* 1980, especially
Castle Park (1978 and 1993) and the reinstatement of the C18
layout at Queen Square. The remodelled Centre has many faults,
but the concept is right: Bristol needs at this crucial hub a public
space, not a hole in the ground with water at the bottom of it.
Since the 1990s fashionable and expensive blocks of flats have
become ubiquitous, either new builds or created from reused
industrial buildings. Other trends include gentrification of the
inner suburbs, infill schemes and community-led developments.
Boding less well for the future is the Canon's Marsh redevelopment, *c.* 2004–10. The result is aesthetically impoverished, in
places poorly finished, and with exteriors brightly coloured in the
manner of the superficial makeovers given to 1950s and 1960s
estates. The other major inner-city scheme is Cabot Circus (masterplan by *Chapman Taylor*, 2003; built 2005–8), the extension of
Broadmead shopping district. It has dragged the centre of gravity
eastward, leaving the w end of Broadmead with many empty
shops and the hangers-on struggling to survive, swapping one
broken area for another.

CENTRAL BRISTOL

CATHEDRAL OF THE HOLY AND UNDIVIDED TRINITY*
College Green

Bristol Cathedral originated as an Augustinian abbey founded
c. 1140 by Robert Fitzharding, who became the first Lord Berkeley and died a canon of his foundation. His family continued as
the major patrons. The first buildings were probably just to the
E, later the parish church of St Augustine the Less, demolished
1962. From the C12 there remains the notable chapter house and
from the early C13 a Lady Chapel to the E of the N transept. But
Bristol's unique importance lies in the innovative and original
work begun in 1298 by Abbot Knowle (Treasurer from 1298,
Abbot from 1306): a new aisled choir and eastern Lady Chapel,
and S of the choir aisle the Berkeley Chapel, and its antechapel.
Knowle (†1332) and his successor Abbot Snow (†1341) were
buried before the rood altar in the nave. In 1339 the church was
still 'in ruins' according to a Bishop's Visitation, but by 1353

* Revised account by Bridget Cherry.

Abbot Asshe could be buried in the new choir. The S transept was rebuilt from the C14; N transept and crossing tower from the later C15, under abbots Hunt (1473–81) and Newland (1481–1515). By the Reformation a new nave had reached the sills of the windows. After Bristol became one of the six new dioceses in 1542, the E end was reordered for cathedral use and the incomplete nave replaced with houses. In 1859, a campaign to enlarge the inadequate accommodation was begun by Dean Gilbert Elliott; a destructive reordering of 1860–1 by T. S. Pope (advised by G. G. Scott) was much criticized. In 1866 Canon J. P. Norris began fundraising for an ambitious new nave, prompted by the rediscovery in 1865 of the C15 nave foundations. It was executed by G. E. Street in 1867–77, but the W towers completed only in 1887–8, after Street's death, by J. L. Pearson, who did further restoration work in 1890–1900. The C19 work is of Doulting stone, the C14 and later parts of the E end largely faced with Dundry limestone ashlar. Earlier walls are of red Brandon Hill Grit.

Exterior

Seen from College Green, the evenly balanced E end and nave are separated by the transepts and the Perp CROSSING TOWER, rising vigorously to two storeys, each face crowded with five two-light windows. Paired buttresses at each corner join halfway up to become broad diagonal ones; parapet with blank arcading and corner pinnacles. Street's W TOWERS with sturdy corner pinnacles provide a dominant accent from the W. His N PORCH is adorned with much sculpture. The prominent figures of Evangelists in the buttress niches date from 1878, replacing Church Fathers by *James Redfern*, torn down in 1876 by Dean Elliot following protests at their allegedly popish character. Funding diminished after this row, and Street's grand W end in the French manner remained without its intended sculpture. Street followed the choir in making the aisles as high as his NAVE, and in the window transoms, aiming for 'similarity at a distance'. But the details are in the more calmly ordered manner of the later C13, to distinguish his W end from the medieval parts. The nave parapet is similar to that of the E end, and to the E end parapets at Wells, with triangles filled by cusped lozenges; perceptively, Street designed Bristol's nave parapet long before fragments of the eastern arm's medieval one came to light. Pevsner called Street's western arm 'the respectable performance of a sensible architect'; Priscilla Metcalf, more sympathetic to Street's dilemma, saw it as 'a vestibule to a work of genius which he did not see it as his business to upstage'.

The four-bay ELDER LADY CHAPEL sits E of the N transept, an unusual position (cf. Ely); its early C13 date recognizable by the use of red sandstone, with stepped triple lancets divided by buttresses. The more elaborate E window is later C13, of five

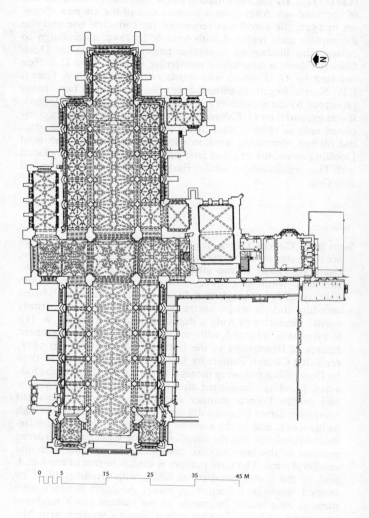

0 5   15   25   35   45 M

Bristol Cathedral.
Plan

lights with seven small circles containing quatrefoils, trefoils and a cinquefoil. Parapet and pinnacles are Perp. The C14 CHOIR AISLES are the introduction to the insistent ingenuity of Bristol work of this period. The heads of its tall windows alternate between a group of four quatrefoils, and an elongated quatrefoil between two trefoils. The transoms here had already appeared in the grander domestic halls, e.g. the late C13 Bishop's Palace at Wells. There is tracery also below the transoms: it can be read either as pairs of two-light arches with Y-tracery, or as intersecting ogee arches. The three-light aisle E windows show further variety in their tracery. The LADY CHAPEL's broad E window has nine lights, the three-light flanks under steep arches with reticulated tracery. The centre has first a mid-height transom band of three diagonal quatrefoils, then three bold stepped lights. Above them, a nastily spreading trefoil subdivided by minor tracery; Pevsner remarked on its 'perversity of design'. The N and S windows are like those of the choir aisle, but the western ones have only three lights and have transom bands of reticulation units. The S side is only accessible from the cloister; *see* p. 250. For monastic survivals beyond the cloister, *see* p. 251.

Interior

This account describes the medieval, eastern parts first. From the Norman church little evidence remains apart from the masonry of the TRANSEPTS. A small C12 window is visible high up in the E wall of the S transept, and there is a C12 block capital in the SW corner now helping to support the vault.* The ELDER LADY CHAPEL was added E of the N transept by Abbot David (1216–34), following the new fashion for elaborately decorated chapels dedicated to the Virgin (cf. the earlier ones at Glastonbury and Tewkesbury). Stylistically, the closest link is with Wells. Indeed two letters survive of *c.* 1220–30 to the Dean of Wells, asking for the loan of a mason called 'L', assumed to be *Adam Lock*, to 'hew out the seven pillars of Wisdom' for the Lady Chapel, and for contributions to building costs. The chapel is in the mature E.E. style, four bays long, vaulted and slender in its proportions, and using materials of contrasting colour. Shafts of Blue Lias (rather than the usual Purbeck marble) around the windows, between the bays and in the blank arcaded dado which has trefoiled arches. Much lively stiff-leaf carving, also genre scenes (e.g. St Michael and the dragon, a monkey playing a pipe, a goat carrying a rabbit) in the spandrels and in the piscina and sedilia, similar to the W parts of Wells nave. The roll-moulded string course below the windows even terminates in small heads swallowing the roll, as in Wells's N porch. The N windows are triplets of closely spaced stepped lancets, with fully detached shafts on the

---

* A Norman staircase in the thickness of the wall in the SE corner leads to a chamber over the Newton Chapel; another stair is hidden in the choir N aisle.

inside; the s wall has the same composition except that the windows are blank. The more advanced E window with different mouldings may be of *c.* 1270–80 (cf. Wells chapter-house staircase). The vault with its naturalistic foliage bosses is perhaps of the same date, quadripartite with ridge rib and transverse arches of equal width. In the s wall, two inserted Perp arches open into the choir N aisle, one housing a tomb. They have boldly quatrefoiled tunnel-vaults on ribbed coving, with disconcertingly large bosses, and belong with the C14 work to which we now turn.

The CHOIR is the great surprise. Bristol is a hall church, i.e. the aisles are the same height as the central vessel. Whatever the source of inspiration – suggestions include English retro-choirs such as Winchester and Salisbury, earlier French hall churches such as St-Serge at Angers, or, perhaps most convincingly, secular timber-framed buildings – the idea is adapted here with unprecedented originality. Pevsner, following the German art-historical interest in the handling of space, was in 1958 the first to alert English readers to Bristol's C14 work: he found the hall church with its diagonal vistas 'from the point of view of spatial imagination – which is after all the architectural point of view par excellence – superior to anything else built in England or indeed in Europe at that time'. Pevsner saw this work as the creation of a man 'of supreme inventiveness . . . who experimented with certain subtly applied discordances, with sudden straight lines and right angles in the middle of Gothic curves', and who achieved 'a superb synthesis of structural ingeniousness with spatial thrills'. Debate continues over whether Bristol choir is a 'European prodigy or regional eccentric', the title of an essay by Richard Morris.[*] Morris argues that building continued over a longer span, into the mid C14, and that the range of mouldings suggests several designers, rather than a single burst of creative energy from one master. But as to its wayward originality there is no dispute. The central vessel is broad rather than high (only 50 ft, 15.2 metres, to the apex of the vault), of four bays (or five, including the ambulatory). It has broad arches with two wave mouldings carried down the piers, interrupted only by capitals to thin triple shafts facing the nave. Continuous mouldings, a challenge to the consistent distinction of parts usual in E.E. work, became a characteristic of the Dec style, though precedents can be found in minor West Country detail such as the Wells nave triforium. *Thomas of Witney*, who worked at Wells, has been suggested as the designer; perhaps in the second decade of the C14.

The lierne-vault of the choir, that is a vault with additional ribs linking the ribs springing from the wall-shafts, is, with that of Wells Lady Chapel, among the first in the West Country. Richard Morris attributes it to *William Joy*, who also worked

---

[*] In Laurence Keen (ed.), *'Almost the richest city': Bristol in the Middle Ages*, BAA Conference Transactions, 1997.

at Wells. The principle appears earlier (Lower Chapel of St Stephen, Palace of Westminster, completed by 1297). The vault is best explained by saying that the designer first set out a normal vault with transverse arches, diagonal ribs, ridge ribs and one pair of tiercerons each way. Then, however, he studiously avoided the meeting of the tiercerons with the ridge rib, by splitting the ridge rib to form a chain of kite-like lozenges down the apex of the vault. Except in the eastern bays, this novelty is further emphasized by cusping the liernes forming the kites, as if it were window tracery; a trick taken up also at Wells choir, Tewkesbury choir and St Mary Redcliffe. Finally, the cusping stands proud of the vault cells.

The most striking feature of the AISLES is the unforgettable device by which the weight of the main vault is conveyed to the outer walls. Bridges that act as flying buttresses are thrown across the aisles from arcade pier to outer wall at the level of the main vault springers, like timber tie-beams on arch braces. (And, hall-church though it be, there is the further ambiguity that the arched braces imply lower aisle-height.) In the spandrels are mouchettes, big enough to look through them into the neighbouring aisle vaults. The aisles are vaulted transversely, each with two bays of rib-vaulting with ridge ribs. In each little vault the cell resting on the bridge is omitted, so that one can see through from vault to vault. Pevsner called this a 'flash of genius' which made 'the transverse arch and ribs on the middle of the bridge stand as it were on tip-toes, a tight-rope feat right up there', extending the diagonal vistas into the vaulting zone. The w bay of the s choir aisle has a vault of a different design, a more solid transverse tunnel-vault with eight ribs; possibly this and the simpler and adjacent Newton Chapel E of the s transept were the first parts to be built. The aisles have passages at the level of the window sills, which pass through the wall between the windows with arches of two convex (not concave) curves – a typical Bristol conceit. Within the gables so formed are excellent small heads, typical of the delightful minor sculpture throughout the E end. The passage's parapet is probably by *Pearson*. Stellate tomb recesses in the aisle walls are of the same type as those in the Lady Chapel (*see* below). A lower ogee-gabled niche with a half-octagon inner frame was extant in 1830, i.e. not a C19 remodelling as sometimes stated.

LADY CHAPEL, at the E end. Two bays, the same height and width as the choir. Restored in the C19. In the early C20 the original fittings were brightly coloured by *E. W. Tristram* based on surviving paint fragments. The resulting painted stonework and complete glazed scheme (albeit only partially C14) give some impression of a colourful medieval interior. Elaborately decorated C14 REREDOS, with three ogee arches and narrow steeply gabled niches between. The arches are cusped, the centre cusp on each side having straight sides. The centre, defaced at the Reformation, was restored after 1839, following the removal of a C17 altarpiece. In the mouldings is ballflower ornament. Frieze of big heads and fleurons. The elaborately transparent crested parapet above has the initials WB (for Abbot Burton, 1526–39). The sedilia and tomb recesses form part of the architectural design of the chapel. SEDILIA, much restored; four pointed arches, and above them, inverted arches like those beneath the crossing at Wells, with big finials. In the N and S walls three elegantly eccentric TOMB RECESSES, of the stellate design used in the aisles and Berkeley Chapel, now with effigies of later abbots (*see* Monuments, p. 249). They are Pevsner's '*nec plus ultra* of the ... cavalier treatment of Gothic precedent ... [a] sharply spiced meeting of straight and curved'. The inner half-octagon of straight lines has an outer frame of four concave semicircles on two quarter-circles. Their large scale is powerfully exotic, leading to comparisons with Chinese or Islamic forms, but the details echo native C14 art. There are familiar crockets and finials, and splendid heads and busts as stops, reminiscent of the miniature ornament on C14 metalwork and manuscripts.

The BERKELEY CHAPEL and its antechapel or sacristy lie S of the S choir aisle. The date is unclear. The tomb between chapel and S choir aisle is that of Lady Joan Berkeley (†1309), but the chapel may be a C14 reworking of something older (see the different ground level). The adjoining ANTE-CHAPEL is entered by a doorway with cusped and sub-cusped arches and ogee gable, flanked by steep gabled arches like those in the Lady Chapel reredos, though restored beyond redemption. The inner arch towards the ante-chapel is genuine and full of interest, with big roll mouldings dying into the jambs. The ante-chapel is full of puzzling curiosities. Below a flat stone ceiling is a miniature skeletal rib-vault of three bays: corbels with naturalistic foliage, transverse arches, cross-ribs, ridge rib and very big stylized bosses, are all here, but there are no cells to the vault. The first such flying ribs seem to be those of Lincoln's Easter Sepulchre, *c.* 1290; others, similar in type and scale to Bristol's, appeared in the pulpitum passages at Lincoln and Southwell, the former perhaps contemporary with Bristol's, the latter *c.* 1320–40. In the S wall are three deep recesses within ogee arches carved with huge knobbly leaves, the over-scaled detail similar to that in the arches off the Elder Lady Chapel. One recess has a flue leading to an outlet in a pinnacle; suggested as an oven for communion wafers. In the NE corner an odd diagonal niche below an open-mouthed head. The doorway into the chapel has an eccentric order of ammonites or snails, and an inner order of diminishing ballflower. Was this a mason's experiment, or is there some hidden meaning, related to the preparation of the Eucharist? The Berkeley Chapel is visually quieter, of two bays with a simple cross-ribbed vault with ridge ribs. Three-light windows, the middle light lower to make room for a dagger and two elongated trefoils in the spandrels. In the S wall three trefoil-headed niches with the perverse feature of straight gables over little carved heads. In the N wall, the tomb-chest of Lady Joan

Berkeley (mentioned above) is framed by another spiky stellate recess, as in the Lady Chapel. The chest has a capricious motif of three-quarter-circles left open at the bottom and connected by diagonal bars.

TRANSEPTS and CROSSING, although with Norman fabric, appear principally late C15–early C16. Perp S window, high up, because the monastic buildings adjoined here; a worn stair with vault over led to the former dormitory. The S transept vault, perhaps from the time of Abbot Hunt (1473–81), carries on the idea of the choir's lierne-vault; the N transept and crossing vaults confuse the design with additional ribs. Interestingly, here the idea of splitting the ridge rib to obtain liernes is no longer fully understood; there are pairs of additional liernes without that meaning, although the cusping is maintained. The N transept N window is by *Street*.

The interior details of *Street*'s NAVE are illuminatingly different from the choir, although he follows its proportions and main features. The eccentricities are toned down. A normal tierceron-vault; no cusped liernes. The piers have big naturalistic capitals to nave and arch, with Purbeck shafts. The aisles have bridges, but the vaults above are different, so that the gaps are vertical planes, not vault cells. The aisles have standard arched tomb recesses with big cusps.

Furnishings and stained glass

The most interesting C19 work is by *Hardman*, employed by Street for the stained glass in the new W end.* The dominant fittings were installed 1899–1905 to *J. L. Pearson*'s intentions, carried through after his death by his son *F. L. Pearson*.

LADY CHAPEL. STAINED GLASS. The coherence of the C14 windows is largely the result of *Joseph Bell*'s sympathetic mid-C19 restoration and repair. E window with Tree of Jesse across nine lights incorporating C14 pieces, notably the figure of the Virgin. Crucifixion in the upper central three lights, emphasized by the tracery pattern. N and S windows, standing figures against red or green backgrounds. The most complete of the old glass was placed in the SW window, which includes the Martyrdom of St Edmund.

CHANCEL. It is unclear which of the *Pearson*s designed the large High Altar REREDOS, 1899, with Cosmati-type inlaid pavement in front, and the PULPIT, 1903, with Flamboyant panels said to come from Abbot Elyot's pulpit of 1525. Wide ogee-arched SCREEN, 1904–5, by *F. L. Pearson*. – CHOIR STALLS from a rich early C16 refurnishing by Abbot Elyot (1515–25). Back panels and ends with Flamboyant tracery. – Twenty-eight fine MISERICORDS combining traditional subjects with narrative inspired by new Continental sources: scenes from the Romance of Reynard the Fox, others based on popular prints, with frequent use of nude figures and bawdy

* For a full account *see* M.Q. Smith, *The Stained Glass of Bristol Cathedral*, 1983.

detail. – The STALLS survived the Reformation removal of the medieval pulpitum and rood screen. Until the new nave was built, the crossing and two bays of the choir became the congregational space. The stalls were moved E beyond an elaborate stone rood screen acquired from the Whitefriars, given by Thomas White in 1542. It was removed in 1860, and parts incorporated in the SCREENS N and S of the choir, including, S side, fragments of the frieze, a shield with White's initials, merchant's mark and the arms of Edward, Prince of Wales. – Richly carved ORGAN CASES, 1682–5.

CHOIR AISLES. STAINED GLASS. At the N aisle E end, two windows of brightly coloured enamelled glass given c. 1665, an unusual date, with lively Old and New Testament scenes. Of a matching window, fragments now in the S choir aisle. In total contrast is *Keith New*'s dynamic and vividly coloured abstract Holy Spirit window (S choir aisle E, replacing the damaged C17 window), 1965.

BERKELEY CHAPEL. METALWORK. A rare late C15 candelabrum from Temple Church. Square leaves decorate the arms. In the middle, St George, with the Virgin above. – GLASS. medieval fragments in the ante-chapel, re-set. Lighter C20 tones are first seen in the delicately drawn Childhood of Christ series in the chapel proper, designed by the painter *Ernest Board* and *Arnold Robinson* (*Bell & Son*), 1925.

SOUTH TRANSEPT. SCULPTURE. A remarkable big slab with relief carving of the Harrowing of Hell; the disorderly and excited drapery suggests a late Saxon date, c. 1000–50. Found in the 1830s beneath the Chapter House floor. It stands on two colonnettes with decorated scalloped capitals, probably from the Norman cloister.

NORTH TRANSEPT AND ELDER LADY CHAPEL. STAINED GLASS. Medieval fragments in the transept E window, mostly early C16. By *Hardman*, the Elder Lady Chapel E, a dense Magnificat of 1894.

NAVE AND AISLES. STAINED GLASS. By *Hardman*, at the W end, an excellent rose window of 1877, N tower 1877 and 1887, S tower S 1883, all with standing figures below white canopies. The nave windows were to have two bands of small scenes, as in S aisle first from W, designed by *Street* himself, but these were not completed as planned. The present nave glazing followed wartime damage; the results do not complement the architecture. The N side has *Robinson*'s meticulously detailed figures of the local wartime Civilian Services, 1947, awkwardly set against clear glass to admit more light, as were the 1920s S nave windows, with dull figures of Bristol notables by G. J. Hunt.

Monuments

The earliest tombs are simple C13 coffin-lids, but the C14 rebuilding provided ostentatious spaces for monuments in the S choir aisle and off the N side for the Berkeleys, chief patrons of the

church. Three c15–early c16 abbots in traditional recumbent
position now occupy the Lady Chapel niches. The new Renaissance taste appears with the tomb of Bishop Bush †1558, the
first to occupy the see, with its cadaver below a flat canopy on
Ionic columns. But Bristol was a poor see; most bishops moved
on and were buried elsewhere. The chief post-Reformation
memorials are therefore secular. The local firm of *Tyley & Sons*
produced numerous minor memorials in the earlier c19. Later
c19 memorials to senior clerics revert to formal recumbent
figures or portrait reliefs.

LADY CHAPEL. Later abbots recumbent in the early c14
recesses: abbots Newbery †1473, Hunt †1481, and Newland
†1515. At Newland's feet two angels, such as are usual at the
head, holding a shield. In one of the niches of the Newbery
tomb-chest a headless statuette still stands.

CHOIR N AISLE. E, Bishop Bush †1558, Bristol's first bishop.
Cadaver under a low six-poster with tent top, short fluted Ionic
columns and chaste Roman lettering round the cornice, but
Gothic inscription on tomb below. – John Campbell †1817. By
Tyley. Urn on a square base, a seated woman in front. – Robert
Codrington †1618. Two of the usual kneelers facing each other;
but to the l. and r. standing angels pull up curtains hanging
from a big semicircular canopy. Broken segmental pediment
with achievement. – N wall. Robert Southey †1843, Poet Lau-
reate 1813–43. Bust by *Baily.* – Coffin-lid with a foliated cross
and inscription to 'Villam le [?]ometer'. c13, not *in situ.* –
William Powell. By *J. Paine Jun.*, 1771. Obelisk with inscription, above a big, remarkably classical base. In front of it a
seated genius with portrait medallion, equally classical. – Mary
Mason †1767, wife of William Mason the poet. By *J. F. Moore*
to a design of *James Stuart.* On the sarcophagus a medallion
showing husband and wife.

CHOIR S AISLE. E, Mary Spencer Crosett †1820. Big Gothic
tomb-chest, unusually of cast-iron, with marble Bible on
marble slab. – N, Harriet Middleton †1826. Big kneeling female
figure. By *Baily.* – S, Georgiana Worrall †1832. By *Tyley.* Relief
of a child in bed. – Lady Joan Berkeley †1309. Tomb-chest
without effigy, in arch between choir aisle and Berkeley
Chapel. – Maurice, 7th Lord Berkeley(?) †1326. In wall recess.
Military effigy. – Thomas, Lord Berkeley(?) †1243. In wall
recess. Military effigy with crossed legs. – Mary Brame Elwyn
†1818. By *Chantrey*, 1822. Woman seated on a Grecian chair in
front of an altar. – William Brame Elwyn †1841. By *Baily.*
Deathbed relief with mourning relatives.

NEWTON CHAPEL. E, early c16 Purbeck marble short
tomb-chest with lozenges. Late Perp canopy with panelled projecting sides against which stand spiral-fluted columns. Instead
of an arch a horizontal top with cresting. Quatrefoil-panelled
coving inside. S, Sir Henry Newton †1599. Big tomb-chest with
recumbent effigies. The kneeling children small against the
tomb-chest. The back architecture uninteresting. – Sir John
Newton †1661. Still with recumbent effigy. But the upper parts

very Baroque; two detached twisted columns, scrolly broken pediment and an achievement. w, Elizabeth Stanhope †1816. By *Westmacott*. A Flaxman conception. The young woman standing up and being received by an angel behind her. – Bishop Trelawny †1721, by *Alfred Drury*, c. 1900. Bronze Art Nouveau plaque with angels.

S TRANSEPT. S, Emma Crawfuird †1823. By *Chantrey*. Grecian altar with double portrait. w, Bishop Gray †1834. By *Baily*. Urn with portrait on pedestal; standing angels l. and r.

ELDER LADY CHAPEL. S, Maurice, 9th Lord Berkeley †1368 and mother. Recumbent effigies, slender figures, originally finely carved, on tomb-chest with ogee niches. Good C19 ironwork.

N TRANSEPT. N, Abbot David, resigned 1234, †1253. Coffin-lid, head in relief, very worn. – Major W. Gore †1814. By *Tyley*. Portrait medallion on base of an urn; two theatrical standing figures of soldiers l. and r. – Mary Carpenter †1877. By *J. Havard Thomas*, 1878. Bronze portrait medallion.

CROSSING. NW, Canon J. P. Norris †1891. By *Frampton*. Bronze relief portrait. SW, Jordan Palmer-Palmer †1885. Splendid Gothic brass with figure, by *Singer* of Frome.

NAVE. W end, Joan (†1603) and Sir John Young. By *Samuel Baldwin* of Stroud. Lively and robust. Only her effigy, recumbent. Tomb-chest with kneeling children. The lid is carried by two small winged genii at the corners. Crested canopy on black columns. – Sir Charles Vaughan †1630. Reclining figure. Two columns, and outside two remarkably quiet, classical allegorical figures. The top architecture also remarkably classical. Broken segmental pediment with two reclining figures and thick garlands below the open ends of the pediment. – N AISLE. Dean Elliot. By *Forsyth*, 1895. Marble recumbent effigy. – S AISLE. Dean Pigou †1916. By *N. A. Trent*. Recumbent effigy in wall recess.

For cloister fittings, *see* below.

The Precinct

The remains of the Augustinian abbey lie S of the church, interlarded with C19 work, and partly incorporated within the Cathedral School. The CLOISTER, with Perp traceried windows, is reduced to the E walk and a narrow N corridor, all C19 rebuilding. Of the Norman cloister, all that exists are the two colonnettes in the S transept. At the S end of the E walk is an early C14 doorway with depressed ogee gable. Crockets up both jambs and gable, partly cut into by the late C15 W wall of the E walk. Easily visible in the cloister, medieval STAINED GLASS fragments arranged as part of a post-war scheme by *Arnold Robinson*. – MONUMENTS. Eleanor Daniel †1774. Coloured marbles, big standing putto. – Elizabeth Draper, Sterne's Eliza, †1778. By *J. Bacon Sen.* A typical and very good work, with two amply draped standing allegorical figures. – Elizabeth Cookson †1852. By *Tyley*. With surround like a Rococo fireplace. The inscription is in the place of the hearth opening. – A. A. Henderson †1807. Figure of a kneeling young Roman.

CHAPTER HOUSE. E of the cloister is the VESTIBULE, of *c.* 1150–70. It is low, three bays wide by two deep, and originally carried a dormitory above, allowing the chapter house extra height behind. From the cloister walk three arched openings on columns with many-scalloped capitals. As the bays are not square, the arches between the aisles of the vestibule are pointed, an early occurrence (but cf. Malmesbury, and St John, Devizes, both Wilts.). The vault ribs have beaded fillets and big roll mouldings. The remarkably complete CHAPTER HOUSE is entered through a doorway at the back of the vestibule, flanked by twin-arched windows with a central column (probably of Blue Lias). The chapter house is rectangular, of two bays, and rises through the dormitory level to allow for an impressive high vault. The broad cross-ribs are thick with zigzag, while the wide, square-sectioned transverse arch has two rows of zigzag forming a frieze of lozenges. The side walls are lined with seats, above which are shallow niches with continuous mouldings. Above is a tier of enriched intersecting arches, the shafts alternately plain and spiral-fluted with beading, the arches all spiral-fluted with beading and a little nailhead. Higher again the entire wall is covered with a variety of interwoven lattice and zigzag. The W wall has intersecting arches up to the apex. In the E wall, much rebuilt after 1831, are three plain large windows. The whole ensemble is a striking example of what animated effects the late Norman style could achieve with abstract motifs.

The slype passage (an early C20 rebuilding) leads to the secluded CHURCHYARD to the E, from where one can study the irregular exteriors of C14 choir and C12 S transept with their projecting chapels.

BRISTOL CATHEDRAL SCHOOL, Lower College Green. Possibly of C12 origin. Re-founded in 1542 by Henry VIII. The buildings are a puzzle of medieval monastic remains, altered and extended in every century since the Reformation. Facing W towards College Square, the former DEANERY appears to be an early C17 house of seven bays and three storeys, altered in the C18. However, the cellars are probably medieval, and the inaccessible S wall has four Norman windows and later medieval stonework. C17 cross-gables at the back; before 1734 those at the front were removed, and hipped dormers and sash windows added. Ground-floor crenellated Tudor Gothic addition dated 1893, probably by *T. S. Pope & W. S. Paul*, with big mullioned-and-transomed windows, and a two-storey bay window, l. Open-well staircase, perhaps late C17, with newel posts continuous through three floors.

Adjoining the Deanery to the S, ABBEY HOUSE has a late Norman doorway, *c.* 1150–60, below ground level on the W front. Scalloped capitals and three orders of mouldings (two chevron bands, outer interlace pattern), perhaps by the mason

of the nearby Abbey Gatehouse. It was a porter's lodge to the
C12 abbey ranges eastward; the upper storeys were remodelled
in the C17, damaged by fire in 1940 and rebuilt in the 1950s.
Inside, a good chimneypiece with elaborate chamferstops,
c. 1590–1640, and a small room with plaster frieze of a similar
date. Behind the Deanery and S of the cathedral cloister, the
abbey FRATER, confused by C19 alterations, now forms the
heart of the school buildings. Large C16 windows in the second
floor and, at the W end, a fine if much-restored E.E. doorway
of c. 1240, which has triple columns with stiff-leaf capitals,
around a deeply moulded cusped and sub-cusped arch.*
Against the frater's S wall, a CORRIDOR is the only survival of
the former lesser cloister. In the cellars beneath the frater, evidence of a medieval staircase between the main and lesser
cloisters. The collegiate Tudor wings facing Anchor Road are
by *Roland Paul*, c. 1920–35. Excavations suggest the monastic
buildings extended S of the present Anchor Road.

The mid-C12 ABBEY GATEHOUSE lies W of the C19 nave, with
a postern gate and carriage arch. The larger arch has two orders
of mouldings on the N, four on the S, densely decorated with
nailhead, zigzags with angle rolls, and beaded interlace work.
Some column shafts have zigzag or spiral enrichment. Inside
the main arch, arcaded side walls and a vault, with decoration
as in the Chapter House. The upper parts were rebuilt c. 1500
(arms of Abbot Newland), modernized in the C18, and the late
Perp design reinstated in 1888 by *J. L. Pearson*, fairly carefully
for that date. It has double-height oriels, statuary niches, and
panelled parapets. Four figures of abbots on the S side by
Charles Pibworth, 1914.

CHURCHES

Church of England

ALL SAINTS, Corn Street. Now a Diocesan Education Centre.
A largely Perp parish church, so cramped by surrounding
buildings that little is visible externally apart from the C18
tower. This was rebuilt from 1712 initially by *Thomas Sumsion*,
a Colerne mason, but completed 1716–17 by *George Townesend*
with *William Paul*. Three stages, the lower two with oddly
assorted arches and windows. Belfry stage of simple recessed
panels with an oculus on each face, and an open-arcaded
domed octagonal cupola, cf. Wren's St Magnus Martyr,
London. Townesend's bell-shaped dome was replaced in 1807
by *Luke Henwood*, District Surveyor, with one of more conventional profile, restored 1930 by *Sir George Oatley*. *Thomas
Paty* rebuilt the three-bay N aisle wall 1782 in a reasonable imitation of Perp, at the same time as he reconstructed the NW

---

* There is uncertain evidence that it may have been moved here from the NW angle
of the cloister, the site now marked by a blocked arch.

corner as a coffee house to *John Wood*'s design (*see* p. 275). The
W wall, six-light W window and entrance are largely C19.
Adjoining at the SW, a rubble-walled GLEBE HOUSE (or parsonage) built in 1422, substantially rebuilt *c.* 1585 and heavily
restored 1905–6 by *Oatley*.

Inside, a high five-bay nave without clerestory, aisles and
long chancel. Two Norman bays survive at the W end, with circular piers, scalloped capitals and square-sectioned arches of
c. 1140. They supported structures built over both aisles, and
thus could not be removed in the rebuilding of *c.* 1430–50.
Awkwardly stilted piers at the junction with the Perp work.
Slim, elegant later piers, with four attached shafts, intervening
wave mouldings, and foliate capitals. In the S aisle, an oversailing bulkhead of the glebe house, with two tiny windows
from which priests could see the altars, and fragments of
painted C16 TEXT with foliate border. The chancel largely
rebuilt in 1850 and shortened by 6 ft 6 in. (2 metres). SEDILIA
and PISCINA beneath ogee arches, with coarsely scraped
stonework.

FITTINGS. REREDOS. Dec, of three bays, apparently from
Bristol Cathedral. – STAINED GLASS. E window by *Arnold
Robinson*, 1949; S aisle E, 1907–8 by *H. Holiday*. – MONU-
MENTS. Many good C18 tablets with urns, etc., principally by
the *Patys* and *Tyleys*. – William Colston, with Sarah Colston
†1701 (mother of Edward, below). Corinthian frame,
swan-neck pediment, putti opening a draped canopy to reveal
the inscription. Attributed to *William Woodman the Elder*
(GF). – Edward Colston †1721, wealthy merchant and Bristol
philanthropist. Colston's executors were governors of St
Bartholomew's Hospital, London, as was *James Gibbs*, from
whom they commissioned the architectural frame in 1728–9,
splendidly carved by the Bristol mason *Michael Sidnell* in black
and white marbles, with Ionic columns, putti and Colston's
arms. Gibbs recommended *J. M. Rysbrack* for the effigy, an
urbane and dignified reclining figure. – Troth Blisset †1805, by
Flaxman. Grecian figure in Gothic surround.

CHRIST CHURCH, Broad Street. A medieval foundation at the
site of the High Cross; rebuilt 1786–90 by *William Paty*. The
entrance front consists only of the base of the tower, according to Pevsner 'not a specially refined member of the large
progeny of St Martin-in-the-Fields' (Westminster). The upper
stage sits awkwardly over the pediment of the stage below.
Diminishing upper stages and an elegant octagonal spire
increase its apparent height. On the clock, two quarterjacks by
James Paty the Elder, 1728. Fussy Neo-Renaissance doorway
from *Henry Williams*'s disruptive reordering (1883). Bombing
exposed the featureless S side in 1940.

The aisled interior is the most accomplished of Bristol's surviving C18 churches. High windows, now with round-arched
tracery and poor coloured glass of 1883. Six tall Corinthian
columns form the arcades, originally painted to resemble Siena
marble. From their entablature blocks springs a 'vaulted'

75

ceiling – actually a series of pendentive domes held taut on elliptical vault-ribs enriched with guilloche. Suggested models include St Martin-in-the-Fields; Badminton church, Gloucestershire (1783–5); Sir Robert Taylor's Transfer and Stock Offices at the Bank of England (1765–8); and George Dance the Younger's Guildhall Common Council Chamber, London, 1777–8. Only the last had the essential element of Christ Church: the pendentive dome. *Paty*'s innovation was to employ twelve such domes together. Ceiling decoration of gilded Adamish grotesques and big rosettes. At the NW a tiny circular baptistery (1898), domed, top-lit and with Baroque plasterwork.

FITTINGS. Clumsy stone REREDOS of 1883. *Paty*'s original, with fluted columns twined with rose garlands, was reinstated in the 1920s as a ROOD SCREEN, with a big crucifix above. – Delicate demi-lune COMMUNION TABLE by *Charles & William Court*, 1791–2, to *Paty*'s design. Semicircular wrought-iron and mahogany RAIL. – PULPIT, with gilded cherubs on the panels. TESTER, 1816. – C17 octagonal FONT, reputedly from the long-demolished St Ewen's church. *Paty*'s mahogany baluster font is in the vestry ante-room. – WEST GALLERY with heavy carved front (1883) with an C18 cherub frieze below. Above, the ORGAN from the old church by *Renatus Harris*, *c.* 1708. – C18 wrought-iron SWORD REST. – Late C18 and early C19 MONUMENTS, mostly by the usual firms of *Paty*, *Wood* and *Tyley*.

ST GEORGE, Great George Street. By *Sir Robert Smirke*, 1821–3. The first of eight Commissioners' churches in Bristol, built as a chapel of ease for Brandon Hill. This design, with 1,416 sittings, cost over £10,000. It was reused at St James, Hackney. Austere Doric portico set imposingly above a broad flight of steps. The order is from the Theseum (Temple of Hephaestus, Athens). Above the pediment a narrow and bloodless domed lantern. This functionless portico is at the ritual E end. Congregational entrance towards Charlotte Street. Seven-bay sides with tall round-headed windows. Plain galleried interior. Reordered for High Church worship, 1871–6, with marble sanctuary fittings by *G. E. Street* and *Foster & Wood* (now in storage). Admirably converted to a concert hall by *Ferguson Mann* in 1985. *A. W. Blomfield*'s painted REREDOS of 1876 remains. Brick-vaulted crypt, now performers' and audience facilities.

ST JAMES, Whitson Street. Now THE LITTLE BROTHERS OF NAZARETH (R.C.). St James's Priory was founded in 1129 by Robert, Earl of Gloucester as a cell of Tewkesbury Abbey. The Benedictine nave became a parish church in 1374; the E end was converted to a large house at the Reformation, later demolished. W front of red rubble below, ashlar limestone above. Across the centre is a clever device: an interlaced arcade with every third column omitted, and three round-arched windows in the wider intersections thus formed. The ends are resolved with lancet arches. Above, an unusual and early wheel window, perhaps *c.* 1160, now badly weathered. Eight circular

Bristol, St James, wheel window.
C19 engraving

openings frame a central octagon, with rope interlacing and a
chevron band. The s aisle and tower may be late C14 or C15,
with later alterations. The building of a new tower was a condition of the grant of parochial use in 1374. It has two ashlar
faces and two (N and E) of rubble, and a Bristol Perp spirelet.
s porch and upper vestry room by *James Foster*, 1802–3,
in a well-observed Perp for its date, though, of course, not
archaeological.

Inside, a wide nave with five-bay Norman arcades of sturdy
circular piers with attached shafts at the cardinal points, and
multi-scalloped capitals. Round arches of stepped square
profile, with a roll in one angle, and outer mouldings of
lozenges and billets. Simple clerestory openings. The E wall,
with high triple window and Romanesque blind arcades (the
two tiers handled quite differently and very awkward-looking),
dates entirely from *S. C. Fripp*'s restoration, 1846. N aisle added
1864 by *Popes & Bindon*, to support the leaning nave arcade.
Now subdivided. Aberdeen granite piers with shaft-rings and
broad foliate capitals. The nave and s aisle have open timber
roofs, both with corbel heads perhaps of the late C15. In the s
aisle, a bizarre corbel – half woman, half pig.

FITTINGS. ALTAR of Portland stone slabs, 1990s. – Neo-
Norman FONT, probably 1864. – Stuart ROYAL ARMS. –
STAINED GLASS. E windows with geometric patterning, 1846.
s aisle, two by *Joseph Bell & Son*, 1900, 1909. – MONUMENTS.

In the s wall a stone effigy reputedly of Robert, Earl of
Gloucester (†1142), but with elegant linear drapery derived
from the w front sculpture at Wells Cathedral, thus probably
early C13. – Brass to Henry Gibbes (†1636) and family, in stone
frame with strapwork. – Sir James Russell †1674, first Gover-
nor of Nevis, with martial motifs. – Henry Dighton †1673,
probably by the same mason. – Thomas Edwards †1727, by
Michael Sidnell, a Corinthian design closely related to Rysbrack's Innys monument at St John. – Mary Edwards †1736,
possibly also by *Sidnell*, influenced by James Gibbs. – Thomas
Biddulph by *E. H. Baily*, 1842.

St John the Baptist, Broad Street (Churches Conservation
Trust). The last survivor of four churches over the city gates,
founded by 1174, rebuilt c. 1300–1400. Embattled late C14
tower and elegant spire with roll-moulded angles, over the
arched city gate, with portcullis slot and unusually elaborate
vaulting. On the s face are statues, possibly C17, of Brennus
and Bellinus, legendary founders of Bristol. Heraldry between
them. Embattled nave and chancel atop the wall. On the N side
is St John's Conduit (1866), which has flowed since 1376;
moved here in 1827–8, when its former site became a new s
entrance to the church, with pedestrian arches added to the
gate, by *Foster & Okely*. Late C14 six-bay nave, aisleless and
unclerestoried. Perp recessed windows with continuous arch
mouldings, divided by wall-shafts. Unusually, the e nave bay
has its own clerestory that lit the rood screen; cf. St Thomas
the Martyr (q.v.). Graceful moulded chancel arch and two-bay
chancel; vestry beyond, with an oriel possibly made or restored
by *Foster & Okely*, c. 1828–33.

CRYPT. A rare rib-vaulted crypt, entered independently from
the N side. The chapel of the medieval Guild of the Holy Cross,
partly independent of the church above. Early C14 e part of
three bays. Wall-shafts with moulded capitals supporting
tierceron star-vaults. Wider two-bay w part, perhaps c. 1380,
with more fanciful vaults, the same as at the crypt at St
Nicholas (*see* p. 265). Defaced PISCINA.

FURNISHINGS. COMMUNION TABLE (1635), with five
columnar legs and the sixth (centre front) a caryatid with
chalice. – C17 COMMUNION RAIL, uprights with foliage and
fruit, and spiral turned columns. – Unusual cruciform FONT,
1624, on scrolled legs with claw feet, cherubs' heads and
rosettes on the square body; open cover with a dove finial. –
READING DESKS made or remade in the C19, incorporating
C17 double-arched panels formerly part of a crypt screen. –
Late C17 brass LECTERN on baluster stem with acanthus decoration. – PEWS, c. 1621, altered in the C19. Not yet of box
type. – ROYAL ARMS of George I. – Early C18 wrought-iron
SWORD REST. Late C17 WEST GALLERY with arched panels
containing C18 paintings of saints in Dutch style. Below, fine
late C16 carved DOORS, set in a later screen. – STAINED GLASS.
N chancel, by *Bell & Son*, 1957. – Some medieval fragments
high in the nave. – MONUMENTS. Tomb-chest to the church's

patron Walter Frampton †1388, a very fine alabaster effigy with angels, and a dog at his feet. – Brass to Thomas Rowley and wife, †1478, 1 ft 10 in. (56 cm.) long. – Tablet to Andrew Innys †1723, by *Rysbrack*. – Crypt. Late medieval alabaster tomb-chest to unknown merchant and ten children. – Thomas and Chrystina White, †1542, slab with incised cross, Dec ogee canopy.

ST MARK (the Lord Mayor's Chapel), College Green. The church of a monastic foundation instituted by Maurice de Gaunt in 1220 (the church completed *c.* 1230) and transformed by his nephew Robert de Gournay into The Gaunt's Hospital. In 1541 it was granted to the Corporation for £1,000. Used as a Huguenot chapel from 1687 until 1722, when it became the official Corporation church.

The first church was unaisled and cruciform. Alterations of *c.* 1830 were largely undone in 1889 by *J. L. Pearson*, who rebuilt the N transept and made a new W entrance with flanking blind arcades in the E.E. style. Of the exterior only the W front, parts of the S side and tower are visible. In the gabled W end a big eight-light window, grouped 3:2:3, with a twelve-petalled rose window above. It is seemingly a C15 modernization of a C13 idea. The fabric is a replica of *c.* 1822 (cf. p. 395). Lower S aisle gable with an early C14 three-light W window overladen with ballflower ornament. At the SE, a tower of coral-pink sandstone with diagonal buttresses and Bristol spirelet. A mason's inscription dates its finishing to 1487. The narrow nave has E.E. three-stepped lancet windows (two being replicas by *Pearson*). Cambered timber roof, *c.* 1500, panelled, with moulded beams and gilded foliate bosses. Impressive Perp chancel rebuilt *c.* 1500 by Bishop Salley, all the lacy detail subordinated to a strictly rectilinear composition. Unusually three-dimensional four-seat SEDILIA and PISCINA. At the SW, two arches with wave mouldings dying against an octagonal central pier. They open into the S aisle of *c.* 1280, with three blocked Geometric windows. At the E, a panelled Perp arch leads to a lower S aisle chapel, of *c.* 1510. Panelled roof with Tudor rose and portcullis bosses, and four-light Tudor-arched S windows separated by elaborate canopied niches. The tower base forms the entrance to the Poyntz Chapel, added in 1523 as a chantry to Sir Robert Poyntz, †1520. Fan-vaulted in two bays with arms in the bosses. Eight elaborate canopied niches around the walls, and two deep recesses in the N wall, possibly confessionals.

FURNISHINGS. REREDOS, *c.* 1500. Delicate pinnacled frieze, three big niches beneath pierced octagonal domes. Statues *c.* 1917. – Altar TRIPTYCH painted by *Malcolm Ferguson*, 1990–1. – Fine large SWORD REST by *William Edney*, 1702, from Temple Church, as are the wrought-iron GATES (S aisle chapel), also by *Edney*, 1726. – ROYAL ARMS. Charles II. – WALL PAINTINGS. S aisle, three fragmentary early C16 paintings, representing the Nativity, Resurrection and Appearance of Christ to Mary Magdalen. – In the Poyntz Chapel, highly coloured C16 Spanish floor TILES, probably imported by Poyntz's son, with some medieval English armorial tiles.

STAINED GLASS. Continental glass of remarkable quantity and quality, mostly purchased at the sales of Sir Paul Baghott (Stroud, 1820) and William Beckford (Fonthill, 1823), installed without order and later disordered further. E window, main lights including SS Catherine and Barbara, French C16. Poyntz Chapel, E, three C15 bird roundels, and C16 saints from Steinfeld Abbey in the Rhineland, dated 1527. Nave N, second from E, orange-red heraldic glass, 1829; third, C16 French Mannerist glass from Ecouen, with much grisaille. Nave S, C16 French biblical scenes. S aisle E, St Thomas Becket, designed by *Benjamin West* for Fonthill, dated 1799. S aisle chapel, twenty-four Flemish C16–C17 roundels, and a squint with C14 roundel of a knight's head.

MONUMENTS, anticlockwise from NE corner. Chancel, N wall. Bishop Miles Salley †1516. Tomb-chest with thin blank arcading. Tudor arch with openwork spandrels. Frieze of the same design as the reredos. – Sir Maurice †1464 and Lady Berkeley. Big tomb-chest with eight blank arches with ogee gables. Big ogee or 'Berkeley arched' canopy with cusps and sub-cusps; extremely high finial rising above the superstructure. – Nave, N wall. Thomas Harris †1797. By *W. Paty*. Flowery garlands and angel bearing portrait medallion. – William Birde †1590. Unashamedly brash tomb-chest with superstructure on fluted Ionic columns, and frieze of biblical scenes. Caryatids and a shell pediment above. No effigy. – Sir Richard Berkeley †1604. Recumbent alabaster effigy in court armour.

S aisle. NW corner, Thomas James †1619, Corinthian frame with broken segmental pediment. – W wall, Henry Bengough, by *Chantrey*, 1823, a dignified if rather aloof seated profile figure. – S wall, William Hilliard †1735. By *T. Paty*. Big standing monument on rusticated base with arched recess. Black sarcophagus flanked by putti, with a good portrait bust. Open pediment and crowning obelisk. – Rare civilian effigy, *c.* 1360, placed on a C15 tomb-chest with quatrefoils and shields, under an ogee-arched recess. – John Cookin †1627. Poignant alabaster of a kneeling schoolboy with his books and pens, in Corinthian frame. – NE corner, Henry Walter †1737. Architectural tablet with cherubs' heads in the predella. Swan-neck pediment on fluted pilasters. – Late Perp tomb-chest with pointed quatrefoils and shields. – S aisle chapel, centre. Two effigies of knights, slim and with crossed legs, traditionally (but doubtfully) the founders Maurice de Gaunt †1230 and Robert de Gournay †1269. – E wall, Dame Mary Baynton †1667. Triptych composition with steeply pedimented flanks, domed baldacchino and four obelisks. Two kneeling sons hold back draperies to reveal their mother kneeling awkwardly in a niche. A late, provincial version of a London type developed by Maximilian Colt from *c.* 1615. – N wall, John Aldworth †1615 and his son Francis †1623, kneeling alabaster effigies, remarkably late Perp canopy. – Lady Margaret and Sir Baynham

Throkmorton, †1635 and 1664 respectively. Her reclining effigy, cradling an infant, clearly rearranged to make room for his and to effect the addition of their clasped hands. Coloured marble canopy with mutilated angels holding an inscription. – George Upton †1608. Stiff reclining figure. Splendid arched canopy with strapwork (cf. monuments to Snygge, St Stephen, Bristol, and Vaughan, Bristol Cathedral).

ST MARY LE PORT, Castle Park. Hidden behind post-war buildings E of High Street. Blitzed in 1940. The visible remains are Perp, but excavation (1962–3) revealed late Saxon or early Norman origins. The name Mary le Port indicates proximity to the market. Intact late C15 three-stage tower with simple Perp windows, arcaded battlements with central niche in each face, taller panelled stair-turret with crocketed spirelet. Low rubble walls describe a five-bay nave with rood-stair-turret, N porch, N aisle with E chapel, two-bay chancel.

ST MARY REDCLIFFE, Redcliffe Way.* St Mary lies in the suburb of Redcliffe, on a sandstone bluff, outside the medieval town walls. It is first mentioned c. 1160. Although eulogized as 'the fairest, goodliest, most famous parish church in England', its building history is obscure, and confused by C19 restorers who laid undue emphasis on the role of the wealthy Canynges family in the C14 and C15. Recent studies show that it was conceived as a coherent whole in the C14, but the order of work remains unclear. The unusually substantial and ambitious C13 predecessor must have conditioned and complicated the rebuilding, which probably began with the S transept, c. 1320–30. Burials and bequests of the 1380s–90s suggest the new E end was complete by then, and possibly the nave as well. St Mary has aisled transepts, an ambulatory and projecting Lady Chapel, a stone vault throughout and a clerestory so tall that it requires flying buttresses, and elaborate S and N porches. The church is 240 ft (73 metres) long inside and the spire rises to 292 ft (89 metres). Many English parish churches were totally rebuilt and given a dominant tower in the later Middle Ages but, as Pevsner remarked, aesthetically there is no other example 'so frankly endeavouring to be a cathedral'. It shares with Bristol Cathedral a taste for the eccentric, but the later details changed from fanciful Dec to more rigorous Perp.

EXTERIOR. The proud NW tower is C13, an addition to the previous building. Battered plinth with filleted roll, broad angle buttresses with trefoiled niches and crocketed gables. N and W windows with typical late C13 tracery. N, three stepped lancets with an encircled quatrefoil in the largest. W, four lights subdivided two and two with Y-tracery and a cinquefoiled circle in the middle. Above the N window, a row of trefoil-headed niches with C19 figures (two are copies of C13 originals). Bell-stage with two-light openings under ogee gables and much crocketing; the main buttresses end here with two-tiered ogee gables and pinnacles. Parapet with openwork frieze of cusped

---

*Revised entry by Bridget Cherry.

triangles, polygonal corner pinnacles. C14 ballflower motifs appear on the parapet and spire, which is very tall in relation to the tower. The early C14 spire of Salisbury is likely to have been the inspiration. The bands of decoration and the two tiers of transomed lucarnes with ogee gables are C19. Truncated by lightning in 1446, the spire was rebuilt only in 1870–2 by *George Godwin*, the culmination of an appeal launched in 1842 by the antiquary John Britton and the engineer William Hosking. As for the rest of the building, much of the exterior stonework which one sees now is refacing. Repairs were carried out by *A. W. Blomfield* (1890s) and *Sir George Oatley*, 1930–3. Godwin used grey Caen stone, Oatley used Clipsham stone to replace the original Dundry limestone.

The w wall of NAVE and S AISLE is C13, continuing the plinth of the tower. Renewed early C14 cusped and sub-cusped w doorway. Above, a tall Perp five-light transomed window below a low-pitched gable, with a parapet as on the tower. On the s side the TRANSEPT has an immensely tall four-light s window with two transoms and pretty flowing tracery above and below. Broad flanking buttresses with thickly crocketed gables. Remarkable upper w and e windows, of five lights treated as three normal lights framed by glazed quatrefoils, so that the centres appear to float (cf. Wells, doorways from transepts to choir aisles). Pevsner called this 'the questionable charm of the Bristol style of the early C14'. The Dec rebuilding probably began here. The other windows of the nave, choir and s transept have Perp tracery. The clerestory is very tall, the windows of six lights filling the whole space between the flying buttresses, with blind tracery in the spandrels and on the wall above the windows. Panelled and sub-panelled tracery. The parapet, continued round the transept, has pierced cusped triangles, again as on the tower, and delicate pinnacles. Aisle and Lady Chapel have pierced quatrefoil parapets and simpler Perp windows; in the choir aisles the arches are more angular. The lower masonry of the nave s aisle wall may be earlier than the Perp windows above. But apart from the s transept, the general effect is of Perp uniformity despite the minor variations. The only exception is the seven-light e window over the opening to the Lady Chapel, which does not rise to full height. It has reticulated tracery. The LADY CHAPEL was at first of one bay ending in two polygonal turrets now with ogee caps; the eastern bay is an addition, the passage beneath possibly C15.

Back now to the C14 S PORCH, richly decorated with pinnacles, pierced quatrefoil parapet and crocketed gables to the buttresses. Outer and inner entrances are cusped and sub-cusped with niches l. and r. Above the outer entrance is a tall niche flanked by two very odd windows, lancet-shaped, shouldered, and topped with very sharp, steep straight-sided triangles – a sign of the capriciousness more strongly expressed in the N porch. Side walls inside with five-light blind windows under four-centred arches, with central canopied niches. These

Bristol, St Mary Redcliffe, parapet, windows and doorway.
Engravings, 1813

are truncated by an inserted lierne-vault with cusped panels, the square centre subdivided into four – a bold design similar to the retrochoir vault at Wells.

In general, the N SIDE resembles the S side. N of the choir, a two-storey vestry and library above an undercroft. A second undercroft outside the N porch was added by *Sir George Oatley* in 1939–41, during clearances for the construction of Redcliffe Way. The exceptional N PORCH is the church's greatest curiosity. This was added *c.* 1320 in front of an older N porch. It is hexagonal, like the Eleanor Cross at Waltham of 1291, deliberately contradicting the clarity of the C13, avoiding 'the repose of rectangularity' (Pevsner). The outer doorway is framed by three bands of the most intricate foliage of that bossy, knobbly, flickering kind which replaced naturalistic foliage *c.* 1300. Tiny figures are almost hidden in the jungle of leaves. The doorway is ogee-cusped and sub-cusped. But the outer framing consists of concave arches, on the pattern of the tomb recesses in the cathedral, swinging up to points, the opposite of the pointed arch. The sources of the design have been much debated; the details can be paralleled in small-scale C14 English ornament but, as at the cathedral, the total effect is strangely exotic; Islamic or Indian influences have been suggested. The sides of the porch are covered in niches and crocketed gables, almost obscuring the upper windows. The newly fashionable nodding or three-dimensional arch (not found in the cathedral) is the prevalent arch form. The niches have lost their original figures, but their plinths are carried by many small figures, crouching men and the like. Virtually all the exterior was re-carved in the C19; some of the original plinth figures are displayed in the N aisle.

The porch interior is equally ingenious. Six piers against the six angles, between niches with seats, and hardly an indication of the ogee apart from the doorway, which surfs up above the line of the wall passage that runs around the walls and through the piers. Above the passage the wall panels are hollowed out in foliated niches. On the W side a tiny room recessed in the thickness of the wall, a later alteration possibly for the display of relics. Does the use of the porch as a cult centre explain its lavish treatment? Upper windows of three lights, a foiled shape in the middle. Vault with a hexagon of liernes in the centre, twisted so that its points face the outer walls rather than their corners. Big knobbly vault bosses and more figure sculpture hidden in the foliage throughout the porch interior. The INNER NORTH PORCH is excellent work of *c.* 1215–20. Blue Lias shafts, tall blank arcading l. and r., stiff-leaf capitals, elaborate arch mouldings. Quadripartite rib-vault. The arched top of the inner doorway is C19.

INTERIOR. 'The interior is of a splendour of which the Perp style does not often seem capable' (Pevsner). The whole church is vaulted, and the vaults richly decorated with bosses, so that the first impression is one of unity. Closer examination reveals a variety of detail, perhaps explained by a long building period, though the exact sequence is uncertain. A tour can start with the lower parts. The tower was given a C14 lierne-vault, cusped, like the choir vault of the cathedral. The C13 W wall of the nave also has C14 enrichment, with the inserted W window framed by panels with three-dimensional ogee heads. The S aisle wall has (much-restored) C14 tomb recesses similar to those in the cathedral, an ogee arch within an outer frame of concave curves. The S aisle also has a lierne-vault with cusps, but with the centre panel of each bay given concave sides. Curved ribs of this kind are very unusual in England; the closest comparison is Ottery St Mary, Devon. The vault must have been built with the S arcade of the nave (evidence in the roof space shows

East

North

South

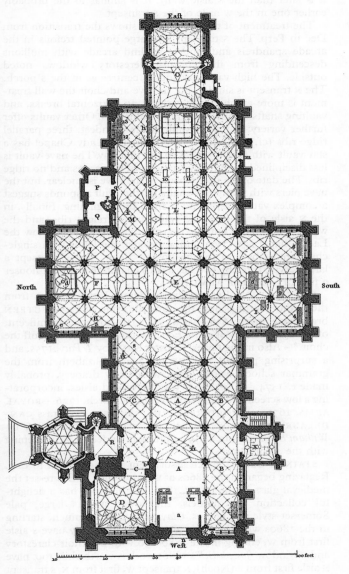

West

Bristol, St Mary Redcliffe.
Plan, 1813

it is later than the S aisle wall). It is similar to the probably
earlier one in the W aisle of the S transept.

The treatment of the upper parts shows the transition from
Dec to Perp. The S transept has large pointed trefoils in the
arcade spandrels and, above, a blind arcade with mullions
descending from the curious clerestory windows noted
outside. The high vault has square centres as in the S porch.
The N transept is similar, but in nave and choir the wall treatment is more emphatically vertical: no horizontal breaks, and
vaulting shafts thinner and more numerous. Other vaults offer
further variety; the choir vault is the grandest: three parallel
ridge ribs (cf. Gloucester, pre-1360). The Lady Chapel has a
star-vault with four lozenges in the first bay. The nave vault is
less disciplined, with many triangles of tiercerons and no ridge
ribs. The date of the upper parts of the nave is unclear, but the
nave piers with numerous shafts for the vault responds suggest
a complex vault was intended from the beginning. Finally, in
the N aisle of the nave the vaults have straight ribs, and the
window mullions continue down as wall panelling. Below the
Lady Chapel is a crypt and a passage, the latter with single-
chamfered ribs and foliage bosses. Below the N transept a
larger crypt, three by two bays, with chamfered ribs. (It houses
a fine C15 vestment ARMOIRE.)

FURNISHINGS. Repeatedly reordered. Little remains from
the medieval fittings or of the numerous side altars. – LECTERN
brass eagle, given 1638. – SCREEN, 1710 (tower). Magnificent,
of wrought iron; by *William Edney*. Originally it divided off the
choir.* – Also in the tower, baluster FONT by *T. Paty*, 1755, and
a surprising painted STATUE of Queen Elizabeth from the
grammar school, wood, large, with lively drapery, probably
made *c.* 1574. – C18 IRONWORK, nave and aisles, incorporating a low screen and gates from Temple Church, 1726. – ROYAL
ARMS, 1670. – SWORD REST, C18. – Elegant C17 brass CAN-
DELABRUM. – Lady Chapel. PULPIT, Dec style, 1856 by
William Bennett, from a C19 re-fitting intended to be in keeping
with the architecture.

STAINED GLASS. A rich assortment from medieval to C20.
Reglazing began in the 1860s at E and W ends. *J. Bell* re-set the
medieval glass in the tower, 1872. The tower N has a delightful collection of roundels, the tower W has large, pale
Somerset-style C15 figures. *Clayton & Bell* did much, starting
in the 1860s with the choir aisles E and the lively nave S aisle
first from W, ending in the 1880s–90 with the choir clerestory
and E window. *Joseph Bell*'s 1880s work is worthwhile too: nave
N aisle first from E (Noah); N transept W, first from N; S transept
W, first from N. Main W window by *Hardman*, 1868, with much
blue. Most spectacular, with arresting greens and purples, the
rich nave S aisle W, by *Heaton, Butler & Bayne*, 1867 (Life of
Moses). S transept S by *Comper*, 1914, pale figures in clear glass.

* *Hogarth*'s huge three-part altarpiece, 1755, is now at St Nicholas, *see* p. 266.

Lady Chapel, a complete set by *Harry J. Stammers*, 1965, a boldly drawn and coloured Life of Christ.

MONUMENTS. The C15 monuments testify to the importance of the citizens of Redcliffe. s aisle, in a wall recess: John Lavington †1411, worn stone effigy; foliated cross. – s transept. Civilian, a lively figure with purse and dog with a bone, late C15. – William Canynges the Younger, M.P. and five times mayor, and wife. Two stiff effigies beneath a routine late C15 canopy. – The same William Canynges †1474, shown as Dean of Westbury, where he retired after the death of his wife. Fine alabaster effigy with sensitive face, a bedesman at his feet. Brought from Westbury. – Choir N aisle. Pair of canopied tomb-chests for the Mede family; straight canopies with pinnacles springing from angel corbels, ogee arches between, chest and back panels with Perp panelling. On the w tomb effigies of Thomas Mede, three times mayor, †1475 and wife; the E one, for his brother Philip Mede, has a rectangular brass at the back, with kneeling figures, scrolls with prayers, and demi-figure of Christ, a type sometimes associated with Easter Sepulchres. – N transept. Large, slender military effigy with crossed legs, late C13. Assigned to Robert, 3rd Lord Berkeley (but later than him). – Nave N, high up, Admiral Sir William Penn †1670. Architectural, with cannons above curved inscription. His armour above. Attributed to *William Stanton* (GF). – In the tower several early tombstones with floriated crosses, and some good C17–C18 memorials, among them Richard Sandford †1721, by *James Paty the Elder*.

BRASSES. Lady Chapel (under carpet), John Juyn †1439. – Choir (under carpet), John Jay †1480 and wife, 3-ft (90-cm.) figures under canopies, kneeling children. – John Brooke †1522 and wife, also with 3-ft figures. – N choir aisle, brasses from Temple Church: merchant, 1396, half-figure; priest *c.* 1460.

ST NICHOLAS, St Nicholas Street. Prominently sited N of Bristol Bridge. A church was recorded here by 1154. Its chancel was built out over the s gate to the city. In 1760 plans for a new Bristol Bridge entailed demolishing gate, nave and chancel. *James Bridges*'s new design was begun 1762 on top of the old crypt, the s wall of which incorporates part of the medieval town wall. Following his departure in 1763, it was completed by *Thomas Paty*, 1763–9. Horace Walpole called it 'neat and truly Gothic'. Bridges intended to retain the decayed steeple but *Paty* replaced it with his own design. The lavish Rococo interior was destroyed by bombing in 1940 and a new interior created by the *City Architect's Department*, 1974–5, for a church museum (closed, now City Council premises).

Box-like nave with arcaded parapet and seven bays of five-light windows, probably the result of observing local Perp examples, and remarkably accurate for their date. The ogee intersecting tracery betrays its C18 origins. Windowless E wall with five spindly buttresses. Paty's w tower and slim elegant spire are every inch C18 Gothic. Clasping pilaster-buttresses with Gothic panels, parapet with pinnacles at the angles, and spire rising from within the parapet. Paired ogee belfry lights with cusped Y-tracery. Octofoil window over an ogee doorway on the N tower flank. Inside, a long, high nave with no remaining C18 features. Deep W balcony, 1974–5.

Some FITTINGS remain from its time as a museum.* Altar TRIPTYCH by *William Hogarth*, 1755–6, painted for St Mary Redcliffe. Depicting the Resurrection and Ascension, in total *c.* 53 ft (16 metres) wide by 28 ft (8.5 metres) high. Large religious work was an unfamiliar genre for Hogarth, who seems to have looked back to Continental models, and especially Sebastiano Ricci. Frames carved by *T. Paty*. – SCULPTURE. Four C14 statues of debated identity from Lawford's Gate and Newgate. – Very fine PULPIT, *c.* 1758, from Cowl Street Unitarian Chapel, Shepton Mallet. Hexagonal, on wineglass stem with large tester and flaming urn finials.

The CRYPT is one of Bristol's most precious survivals of medieval church architecture. It housed a chapel of the Holy Cross. Perhaps dating from *c.* 1350–80, of four bays divided by broad piers into a nave and a narrower S aisle. Generously carved vault bosses, mostly foliate but some with heads and C14 costume details. The present NE bay has a central boss depicting Christ crucified, and in the next bay W the Virgin and Child flanked by two praying donors. The whole vault is consistent, each bay a four-pointed star diagonally set around a lozenge, an identical pattern to the W bays of St John's crypt (*see* p. 256). The ribs have long concave sides to a narrow ridge, like the secondary ribs at St John. Half-hidden at the nave E wall, one arch rib, *c.* 1250, to a wider vault. A further bay existed to the E, presumably the chapel sanctuary. – FONT. Early C18 baluster shape with octagonal gadrooned bowl. – MONUMENTS. John Whitson †1629. Shallow standing monument with arched canopy on pilasters topped by pinnacles. Stiff reclining effigy. – Nearby on a C20 plinth, a second effigy of Whitson, by *Thomas Clark*, 1822–3, a close paraphrase.

ST PETER, Castle Park. A pre-Conquest foundation. The area was heavily bombed in 1940; the ruin remains as a memorial to Bristol's civilian war dead. Unbuttressed NW tower, with two-light Perp windows in the upper stages; at its base, possibly C11 stonework around the W door. Generous Perp nave and S aisle both *c.* 1400, the aisle with five-light windows. High N arcade with slender Perp quatrefoil piers. Narrow N aisle on Norman plan, with a large bullseye window. The tower and N arcade were consolidated with concrete 1975.

SS PHILIP AND JACOB, Narrow Plain. Established before 1174, then on the E outskirts of Bristol. Three-gabled nave and aisles. Ramped W gable, pinnacles and battlements, probably of 1764. The two N porches, tall square-headed aisle windows, and big projections N and S for gallery stairs are from a partial rebuilding by *William Armstrong*, 1837–41. Four-stage S tower with

---

*Lectern, sword rest and gates are at St Stephen's church (*see* below).

broad clasping buttresses and E.E. lancets low down, paired shafted lancets above, and Perp top stage with Bristol spirelet. Perp E window. Aisled nave, long chancel and N chapel. Perp wagon roof to the nave, with good C15 corbel heads and bosses. Broad arcades, remodelled 1764, when every second pier was removed and segmental arches added. The original cruciform plan is discernible in some fine work of *c.* 1200 around the former transepts. The once-vaulted tower room in the S transept has springers on short Purbeck shafts with excellent stiff-leaf capitals. From this transept to the chancel is an arch, now blocked, with moulded capitals and keeled roll mouldings. Of the corresponding N transept arch, part of the l. jamb remains. The aisles were probably built shortly after the transepts. The outer face of a good lancet window to the former N transept remains high on the E wall of the N aisle. Offset to the r., an arch with moulded capitals was inserted below to connect with the N aisle. Between the tower room and S aisle a fine, smaller E.E. arch: shafted inner order with capitals of shallow upright foliage, and continuous outer mouldings with deep hollows. This composite design probably derives from Wells-school work of *c.* 1200. Its E face respects the tower-room vault springers, so must post-date the vault. The E end is confused by recent unsympathetic partitions. Long chancel, probably essentially C13 but with Perp alterations including the simple wagon roof, and (to the N) blocked four-centred arches to the C15 Kemys Chapel, which took in the former N transept and extended E.

FITTINGS. Much-restored Norman FONT, square with scalloped underside. Oak COVER, 1636 (the later inscription plate is inaccurate): a cage of open arches, then eight big S-scrolls carrying a finial. – PULPIT, *c.* 1630. Octagonal, with two tiers of arched panels, and scrolled cartouches in the upper tier. Broad cornice on figure brackets, and later TESTER. – SWORD REST (in storage). Of 1610, the earliest in Bristol. A simple iron rod with flat metal ornaments at three points. – STAINED GLASS. E window (Day Memorial), restored by *Godwin & Crisp*, 1865. Glass by *Heaton, Butler & Bayne*, perhaps to designs by *E. W. Godwin*. Remarkably clear figures in purples, pinks and blue. N chapel, three N windows 1869–*c.* 1875, *Heaton, Butler & Bayne*. N chapel E, one big figure, *Bell & Son*, 1937. S aisle, Dunkirk Veterans window, 1995, by *Sampson & Son* of Bristol. – MONUMENTS. Many good tablets of *c.* 1750–1850. All below are in the N chapel. SW corner, head of a knight, early C14. – N wall, Henry Merrett †1692. Big architectural frame of barley-sugar columns, segmental pediment inside swan neck, and half-figure in an oval wreath surrounded by cherubs and skulls. – SE corner, John Foy †1771, by *James Paty Jun.* Obelisk with a portrait medallion. In the predella, good relief of a woman with children. –

ST STEPHEN, St Stephen's Avenue. A fine Perp church richly rebuilt in the late C15 on the site of a C13 cell of Glastonbury Abbey. At the SW, a majestic Somerset-type tower, paid for by the merchant John Shipward; the traditional date of 1453 is on unknown evidence. The base is perhaps C13 (see the arches within) and at a slight angle to the nave. Of four stages increasing in elaboration. Showy openwork crown with angled corner panels, derived from that at Gloucester Cathedral (1450s). William Worcestre recorded that the foundations were 31 ft (9.5 metres) deep, perhaps referring to piling undertaken when the Perp stages were added. Tower and crown have been repaired several times, most recently the angled panels to the crown replaced in reinforced fibreglass, 1970s. Good Baroque w doorway with blocked pilasters and segmental pediment, 1732–4, probably by *James Paty*. s porch with two rows of leaf carvings over deep concave mouldings around the entrance arch, and C20 parapet. Fan-vaulted interior with unusual flat panelled centre. In 1480 William Worcestre included a drawing of the porch's jamb mouldings, noting the ingenious work of the mason, *Benet Crosse*. He may have masterminded the whole rebuilding. The exterior was refaced gradually, 1777–1864. E of the s aisle, a MEETING ROOM by *Sir Giles Gilbert Scott*, 1936, altered 1950s.

Inside, the lower N wall pre-dates the C15 rebuilding, see the three ogee-arched tomb recesses; that at the w with C19 head (big bosses, cusps and sub-cusps). A high clerestoried nave with aisles and no structurally separate chancel, typically Perp. Elegant piers with concave sides and a thin shaft set in each curve, and angel capitals. Blocked rood door one bay w of the current chancel. w window possibly *c.* 1540. The arcade mouldings collide with the w wall; was it realigned in the C16? Baptistery beneath the tower; corner springers indicate lost vaulting, and the tower arches are essentially C13, the outer mouldings re-cut in the Perp rebuilding. Phased restorations replaced the roofs, floor, furnishings, glazing, and all the tracery except in the w window, without destroying the spatial unity: tower and aisles by *S. C. Fripp*, 1862; chancel by *Charles Hansom*, 1875; fittings by *Pope & Paul* 1886 and 1890. N aisle chapel created by *J. Ralph Edwards*, 1958.*

FITTINGS. Simple stone ALTARS in chancel and N aisle by *Edwards*, 1964. – REREDOS. *Hansom*, 1875; carver *Boulton* of Cheltenham. Very big, with cusped arches with central roundel depicting the Agnus Dei. Outer arches filled with painted relief panels by *Graeme Mortimer Evelyn*, 2010–11, on Slavery and Reconciliation. – Splendid late C15 brass eagle LECTERN, from St Nicholas, on a tall turned stem. – Elaborate PULPIT, 1890, maker *Harry Hems*. – BENCH-ENDS also *Hems*, 1886. – FONT. Possibly by *J. C. Moncrieff*, 1881, on marble pillars. – Magnificent wrought-iron SWORD REST and N chapel GATES, both by *William Edney*, *c.* 1710, from the blitzed St Nicholas. – STATUES of St Nicholas by *Gerald Scott*, St Leonard by *Ernest Pascoe*, 1958. – STAINED GLASS. E window by *Hardman & Co.*,

---

*James Russiello kindly suggested clarifications and provided names for the C19 restorations.

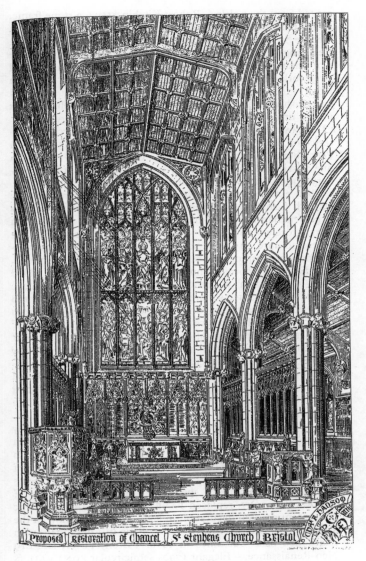

Bristol, St Stephen, interior.
Engraving, 1875

1882. *Clayton & Bell* glazed the N aisle (1898), tower (1901),
and probably the clerestory (1902–4). W window by *Arnold
Robinson, c.* 1945–50. Clearly drawn figures set in clear glass.
– MONUMENTS. (Reputedly) Edmund Blanket †1371 and his
wife, on a panelled chest, *ex situ*. – Sir Walter Tyddesley †1385,

resited from the s aisle. – Robert Kitchin †1594, a stone frame, tablet painted to imitate brass, with kneeling figures. – Sir George Snygge †1617, attributed to *Samuel Baldwin* of Stroud. Reclining figure in judge's robes, under an impressive Corinthian canopy framing an arch, a crest with arms, and strapwork (cf. the Still monument, Wells Cathedral). – Martin Pring †1626, an oval plaque with naïve figured surround embellished in 1733. – David Peloquin †1766. Obelisk with a plump urn, in fine coloured marbles. Style of *T. Paty*.

St Thomas the Martyr, St Thomas Street (Churches Conservation Trust). Founded before 1200. By the c15 it was a Perp church of some magnificence. Only the tower survived a fine classical rebuilding of 1789–93 by *James Allen*, a local statuary mason little-known as an architect.

Plain exterior with handsome e end. Neoclassical garlands beneath a shallow pediment, the wall below articulated by a large Venetian motif. A lunette in the arch was replaced with a crass rose window by *W. V. Gough*. Ramped parapets link the aisles and nave. c15 three-stage w tower with an unusual combination of clasping and set-back buttresses. Bristol spirelet, and diminutive corner pinnacles inside the parapet, all added 1896–7 by Gough. w entrance s of the tower; Five-bay nave arcade on substantial square piers with tunnel-vault penetrated by segmental clerestory windows. Transverse ribs spring from projections to the cornice, supported by Baroque cherubs' heads, the latter perhaps after Redland Chapel (p. 384). Lower flat-ceilinged aisles, with arched windows. The nave e bay was reordered as a chancel in 1878 by *Gough*, with contemporary CHOIR STALLS and ALTAR. Coffered sanctuary flanked by paired Ionic pilasters with one-winged cherubs squashed into the corners – a most unhappy design that shows Allen's inexperience.

FITTINGS. The woodwork is the glory of St Thomas, largely c18 and from the previous church. Fine REREDOS of Flemish oak, 1716 by *William Killigrew*, worthy of a Wren church in the City of London. The only survivor, and the best, of eight c18 reredoses in Bristol. The two-tier arrangement seems to have been a Bristol speciality. Garish paintings by *F. von Kamptz*, 1907, replaced PANELS with late c19 Aesthetic Movement painted decoration in leafy c18 frames (now in the s aisle). – Balustraded ALTAR RAIL. – Plain PULPIT (1740) with gadrooned base; cut down in 1878. – Stone FONT, late c19 Neo-Renaissance. – Elegant 1790s semicircular FONT RAIL (s aisle), mahogany with tapered supports and lozenge inlays. – Roman Doric WEST GALLERY, 1728–32, with inlaid clock. – ORGAN CASE, 1728 by *John Harris*, with foliage panels and cherubs' heads. – At the inner entrance, two small defaced c15 STATUES from the demolished Burton's Almshouses nearby. – Early c17 SWORD REST. – ROYAL ARMS, 1637, an unusually early survival, in a square frame still with strapwork and terms. Carved by *William Hill*.

TEMPLE (or HOLY CROSS) CHURCH, Temple Street. Gutted 1940. The Knights Templar built an oval church here *c.* 1150 (revealed by excavation), a variation on the circular model in London and elsewhere. Either just before or just after the suppression of the Templars in 1312, the church was rebuilt on a rectangular plan: the lost nave arcade and parts of the E end were probably from this campaign. Dramatically leaning tower (now c. 5 ft, 1.5 metres, out of true), begun c. 1390. Despite the subsidence, a third stage was added c. 1460; the corrected angle is obvious from the S. Frieze of cusped triangles below two fretted 'Somerset' belfry lights, separated by a shaft rising from the belfry-stage string course. Offset buttresses die into insignificant pinnacles below the parapet, giving a monumental flat-topped tower. No parapet and pinnacles; the masons must have lost their nerve. At the tower base three delicate Perp statue niches. Baroque NW doorway with big segmental pediment. Embattled N and S aisles with large early Perp windows. Rood-stair turret on the S, and further E a finely framed late C17 memorial, now much weathered; another is hidden high within the tower. Dec traceried E windows. Five-bay nave, the arcades now dismantled. Very long chancel with shorter flanking chapels, that on the N for the Weavers' Guild. Early C14 Dec windows in the E end, including, in the N chapel, square-headed windows of four cusped lights beneath convex-sided triangles. In the S chapel and throughout the nave, good Perp windows.*

Roman Catholic

ST MARY ON THE QUAY, Colston Avenue. Designed by *R. S. Pope* in 1839 for the Irvingites, but purchased in 1843 by the Roman Catholics, who added the legend in the entablature. An aloof Greek temple on a high base with a richly carved portico of six deeply fluted Corinthian columns. The order is from the Lysicratic Monument at Athens, which Pope also used at Brunel House (p. 314). Pilasters within the portico employ only the upper half of the full capital. Screen walls with channelled rustication. Returns pushing forward to the pavement, framing symmetrical entrance staircases rising through the plinth. Above the steps, tall blind windows in pilastered frames. The flanks look slightly unconvincing, like theatrical flats. The interior is a little disappointing; a plain box with tall side windows. The only enrichment is the narrower top-lit chancel: two fluted and gilded columns *in antis* at the front, and more around the walls, repeating the external order. Galleried N transept and another gallery on cast-iron Doric columns at the ritual W. – ALTAR with domed tabernacle, c. 1900 by *J. F. Bentley*. – FONT by *G. E. Street*, 1860, from St George, Brandon Hill (p. 254).

Other denominations

UNITARIAN MEETING HOUSE, Lewins Mead. 1787–91; now offices. Bristol's wealthiest Nonconformist congregation

---

* Some furnishings survive at St Mark, in the Berkeley Chapel at Bristol Cathedral, and at Holy Cross church (Inns Court, Knowle, S Bristol).

commissioned a new meeting house from *William Blackburn* of London, who was then designing a Bristol prison. A wide T-plan with the entrance at its foot and slightly recessed staircase wings filling the returns. The footprint is a rectangle 70 ft by 40 ft (21 by 12 metres). Ashlar façade with pedimented centre and a high rusticated basement. High centre window, a dignified tripartite arch with an order of acanthus and fern leaves. Elegant semicircular Ionic porch. Five arched tripartite windows (identical with that on the front) line the side and back walls. Boldly coffered ceiling, suspended on chains from the roof trusses. Galleries on thin cast-iron supports, the rear one now an organ loft. BOX PEWS frame a semicircular lobby beneath the organ gallery. Graceful mahogany PULPIT on an elegant stem. The pulpit stairs, box seats and a tiny railed COMMUNION TABLE are all of a piece with the pulpit. Converted to offices 1987 by *Feilden Clegg*, sensitively managed by glazing beneath the galleries, although the central pews were necessarily sacrificed. Outside are carriage yards (formerly with stables), and SCHOOLROOMS perched on the cliff to the N.

BROADMEAD BAPTIST CHURCH, Union Street. By *Ronald Sims*, 1969, replacing a C17 to C19 chapel. It sits over ground-floor shops, marked externally only by its canted and broken roofline since removal of a timber spire. Both spatially and in plan the chapel lacks coherence. Timber-clad ceiling of varied and canted profiles with four full-width lights running E–W. Full-immersion baptistery, a curving continuation of the pulpit. Raked W gallery backed by a glass wall. – STAINED GLASS. Some panels from the old chapel, by *Moon & Son*, perhaps 1920s.

WESLEY'S NEW ROOM, Broadmead. Effectively the world cradle of Methodism and its first purpose-built place of worship. John Wesley arrived in Bristol in March 1739. Finding inadequate accommodation for the worshippers, he organized the purchase of land for a 'new room' on 9 May. By June the first meeting was held in the unfinished shell. Rebuilding and enlargement were needed by 1748; the present structure is probably almost entirely of that date. In 1808 it became Welsh Calvinist, but was bought back and restored by *Sir George Oatley*, 1930.

External display was neither possible nor desired. A reticent roughcast S façade with one round-arched window above a Gibbsian blocked porch (by *Oatley*, to the C18 plan but of conjectural design). The interior exudes a magnetic calm: a plain, functional room with six Tuscan columns supporting the ceiling. Panelled E and W galleries lit by segment-headed windows. Stylistic similarities with the Friends' meeting house (p. 273) suggest *George Tully*'s hand. The constricted site necessitated additional top lighting, yet living space had to be provided above too. These requirements were reconciled by pushing an octagonal lantern through the upper room, with windows cut in the shaft. On the N wall, a two-tier pulpit (reinstated in 1930), sitting over the entrance lobby and reached by stairs down from the gallery ends. Central block of BOX PEWS reconstructed, 1930, but BENCHES in and under the galleries. The original colours were reinstated in 2005. *Snetzler* CHAMBER ORGAN, 1761, installed 1930. The upper rooms for visiting preachers are reached from the E gallery or by an external N staircase. Study-bedrooms off a large main room, John Wesley's bedroom with a fitted writing slope under the window. – SCULPTURE. S court, equestrian bronze of John Wesley, *A. G. Walker*, 1932. – N court, bronze of Charles Wesley by *F. Brook Hitch*, 1938.

REDCLIFFE METHODIST CHURCH, Prewett Street. By *Alec French & Partners*, 1962. A concrete box on a brick base, with a fully glazed wall facing St Mary Redcliffe.

QUAKERS' FRIARS, Broadmead. A most ambitious C18 Friends' meeting house, attached to fragments of the medieval Dominican friary. Simple, four-square MEETING HOUSE of 1747–9, by the Quaker *George Tully* and his son *William*. Widely spaced segmental-arched sashes, pedimented E entrance door dated 1747. This and the other masonry details by *T. Paty*. Ramped corners to the parapet. Panelled interior with Doric-columned galleries on three sides. Converted to a restaurant 2006–8 by *Alec French Partnership*, the space disastrously interrupted by a steel-and-glass gallery staircase. Pleasing caretaker's COTTAGE attached at the l., perhaps by *George Dymond*, c. 1833–5.

To the W are fragments of the monastic ranges of the BLACK-FRIARS. Their church to the N was established here in 1227–8. N of the courtyard, CUTLERS' HALL was possibly the friars' dormitory over the S cloister range. Used by the Cutlers' Company from 1499 until c. 1770 and purchased in 1845 for use as a Quaker school. A long two-storey range of rubble stone, with big E window of three E.E. cusped lancets, moved here from the Bakers' Hall range (*see* below). Small single lights on the long N side, possibly for the friars' cells. The S wall was rebuilt in 1850 with two-light plate-traceried windows, under *William Armstrong*, perhaps with his pupil *E. W. Godwin*. At the rear of the courtyard, on the site of the E range of the C13 lesser cloister, NEW HALL, a schoolroom of 1869, links Cutlers' Hall with the S range, BAKERS' HALL, probably the friars' infirmary of c. 1230–60. A patchwork of masonry with arches of the lesser cloister in the N wall. Part of a Perp window from the friary nave was re-set in the S wall in 1961. The upper hall has a crown-post roof with arch-braced collar-beams and wind-braces, conjecturally C14; repaired 1971–4 under *Alan Rome*.

PUBLIC BUILDINGS

Civic buildings

BRISTOL CASTLE. *See* p. 304.

COUNCIL HOUSE, College Green. *E. Vincent Harris* was appointed architect in 1933, after a mismanaged competition.

Harris specialized in civic buildings in a Neo-Georgian manner (e.g. Sheffield, Leeds). Building took place 1938–52, delayed by war and austerity. The official opening was in 1956.

The crescent plan closes the w end of College Green. Over a Portland stone basement, a high concrete-framed structure faced with brown Blockley Gloucester bricks, chosen here to avoid competing with Bristol Cathedral. The rigidly symmetrical four-storey façade has thirty-six repetitive bays of sashes emphasized further by a steep leaded roof; intermittent ground-floor window architraves provide inadequate variation. The composition is relieved only by full-height arched end pavilions leading via ramps to a lower domed *porte cochère*. The latter is spiced with Lutyens's influence – New Delhi in the dome and the Thiepval Memorial in the stepped profile and monumental arches. On the pavilion roofs are sculptures of majestic gilded unicorns (supporters of Bristol arms) by *David McFall*. Beneath the *porte cochère* is *Charles Wheeler*'s STATUE of John Cabot. Tall sculptures planned to stand before the pavilions were substituted by a shallow curving pool. The crescent plan, the unicorns and the central domed porch save the day – but only just. Harris's aloof and chilly achievement is difficult to admire.

The setting is not easy, with the cathedral, Norman gateway and Central Library close by. Harris swept away the raised and tree-lined College Green in 1950 for the billiard-table expanse that he hoped would 'make his building'. It does not. Harris turned to advantage a steep decline at the back, with a vast basement Rates Hall. Above, on the rear roofs, two children riding river horses, also by *McFall*.

The major INTERIORS are sited centrally. Curved ENTRANCE HALL with Doulting stone walls, and geometric floors of Belgian black marble and Bianco del Mara. Vast stony CONFERENCE HALL, with full-height w windows. The walls list the names of Bristol's mayors, 1216–1956, incised and gilded by *Angello del Cauchferta* and *Beryl Hardman*. Ceiling painted *in situ* by *W. T. Monnington*, in a semi-abstract design of atomic structures orbiting the earth. The COUNCIL CHAMBER adjoins to the N. Ceiling painted on canvas by *John Armstrong*; a remarkable fantasy on Bristol, with Bristol buildings along the sides, allegorical figures of Wisdom, Enterprise, Navigation and Industry in the corners, and a blue sea with innumerable close-packed sails occupying the whole centre. The two curving wings are served by spine corridors. In the s corridor, the Neo-Georgian LORD MAYOR'S RECEPTION SUITE evokes Bristol's C18 golden age, with panelling and pilasters in rich English walnut, and gilded details. Committee rooms in similar style.

OLD COUNCIL HOUSE, Corn Street. By *Sir Robert Smirke*, 1823–7. Smirke's larger scheme including a Guildhall (of 1823) was abandoned because the site was insufficient. Bath stone exterior articulated by *antae* and central recessed entrance between Ionic columns *in antis*. The frontage is a near-copy of

Smirke's design for the Royal College of Physicians, London. Despite its Grecian elements, the parapets include Italianate balustrades. Central figure of Justice by *E. H. Baily*. The three-bay w extension by *R. S. Pope* and *George Dymond*, 1827–9, housing the Magistrates' Court, replaced one by *Smirke* that proved to be inadequately lit. An accomplished design of deceptive simplicity. Inside, the hall has a coffered segment-vault. Staircase with brass Doric balusters and inlaid brass treads. The Council Chamber has a beamed and panelled ceiling with a lantern, and a remarkable decorative scheme (perhaps Late Victorian) of Grecian motifs with much gilding. A larger council chamber in thin Jacobethan style was added in 1899.

GUILDHALL, Broad Street. By *R. S. Pope*, 1843–6; Perpendicular Revival. A long three-storey façade with higher central tower and oriel, three symmetrically placed entrances under four-centred arches. The style was perhaps chosen to echo the previous C15 Guildhall, and with Barry's Houses of Parliament and New College, Oxford (1842), in mind. However, the oriel projects on very un-Perp curved brackets, and the odd extension of the hoodmoulds to the side gates, the round-arched parapet openings, and the wilful lines of the string course around the tower all suggest a classicist's attempt at Perp. Good sculptures of Bristol figures by *John Thomas* on the façade. Pope's building was harshly criticized at the time for being too small, badly planned, ill-lit and poorly ventilated. Most of the interiors except the main staircase have been modernized.

EXCHANGE, Corn Street. By *John Wood the Elder* of Bath, 1741–3, with the attached C18 and C19 market buildings, occupying a roughly rectangular plot between Corn Street and St Nicholas Street. Wood's outstanding public building is in the highest canon of C18 civic structures. It balances refined Palladian proportion and detail with more solid qualities likely to appeal to Bristol's mercantile oligarchy. Previously merchants had transacted business in the open-arcaded Tolzey nearby. In 1717 the Corporation started planning a replacement, and an Act was obtained in 1722.* In 1740 *George Dance the Elder* (the recent architect of London's Mansion House) was asked to submit designs. Almost immediately *John Wood* was also invited to participate. His local connections clearly prevailed, and building took place to his design. Among the craftsmen were *Thomas Paty*, 'ornament carver', *John Griffin*, 'ornament plaisterer', and *Benjamin & Daniel Greenway*, 'marble and freestone masons, carvers and vase-makers'. In 1745 Wood published a self-aggrandizing account of the design and construction.

The main entrance is from Corn Street. The flanks of this N range were originally occupied by a tavern and a coffee house, with a square vestibule in the centre leading to a

---

* In 1738–41 *William Halfpenny*, *John Jacob de Wilstar* and *George Tully* all submitted plans without success.

courtyard where the merchants transacted their business. In the E and W ranges were insurance offices, etc. The S range and the area beyond house St Nicholas Market. The eleven-bay N façade is a more tautly expressed development of *Wood*'s N range of Queen Square, Bath. Rusticated ground floor, plain arched entrance with iron-studded and bossed oak doors bearing massive lion masks. One-and-a-half-storey *piano nobile* with giant pilasters to the flanks, and deeply projecting attached columns in the three-bay pedimented centre. A Venetian window occupies the wider centre bay. The first-floor windows have alternating pediments on Corinthian pilasters. Beneath the entablature is a richly embellished frieze of garlands, after Inigo Jones's Banqueting House at Whitehall, with attributes of Bristol's trade. All the mouldings and breaks are richly embellished with egg-and-dart, waterleaf, etc. Fine C18 spear-headed iron railings front the area, with early C20 lamp standards beside the door. The plain but carefully composed side elevations have splendid doors framed with oak-leaf bands.

On the pavement in front are four brass 'NAILS', flat-topped balusters on which merchants transacted business – hence 'to pay on the nail'. Two are late C16, one with embossed foliage and scroll pattern, the others of 1625 and 1631.

The vestibule emulates Palladio's tetrastyle hall, with four Corinthian columns defining an inner square. Steps lead up to side doors surmounted by gods: Bacchus for the former tavern; and for the coffee house, where newspapers were sold, Mercury, messenger of the gods. In the S arch leading to the Exchange court, C20 glazed doors replace Wood's rich wrought-iron gates (now at Bristol Museum).

The Exchange proper is home to a teeming market. Wood argued for an Egyptian Hall after Vitruvius, i.e. a rectangular colonnaded room, the centre with a tall lantern-like second storey. It had recently been the model for Lord Burlington's York Assembly Rooms. The Corporation preferred an open court with arcaded walks, the traditional model for exchanges since Antwerp and London in the mid C16. But the executed design retains elements of Palladio's version of an Egyptian Hall, with its flat entablature over colonnades rather than arcades. The S and N colonnades are deeper than the sides, to make the most of the shade in summer and the sun in winter when the courtyard was open. Outer walls punctuated by niches below a fine frieze of shells, fruit and flowers, with a female head central to each bay. The E, S and W doorways have playful Rococo plasterwork in the tympana, with personifications of Asia, Africa and America, by the stuccoists *Charles Boni & Co.* Garish paint colours reduce the plasterwork to vulgarity. The architecture has been scandalously abused, parts of the capitals having even been sawn off to accommodate cables. In 1870–2 *E. M. Barry* added ranges of arched lights and terms (sculptor *E. W. Wynn*) above the colonnade to carry a high iron and glass roof. Barry's supporting stonework survives above a disfiguring replacement roof of 1949.

CROWN COURTS, Small Street. Originally the Post Office. The earliest part (l. of the arch) is by *James Williams* of the Office of Works, 1867–8. *E. G. Rivers* extended to the r. of the arch in 1887–9, mirroring the earlier work. Doric columns screen the recessed entrances. Extended s in 1908–9 by *John Rutherford*, heavy and unimaginative Edwardian classicism. Façaded in 1994 for new Crown Courts by *Stride Treglown*, with good polychrome striped masonry towards The Centre.

ASSIZE COURTS, Small Street. By *Popes & Bindon*, 1867–70. An unbalanced asymmetrical front, collegiate Perp at the r., with a tall central tower and a tight Gothic l. flank. The details are ugly. The building interconnects with the Guildhall in Broad Street, intended to give more space in the Guildhall courts. In an earlier design competition all three prizes were taken by *E. W. Godwin*, but *R. S. Pope* persuaded or bullied the Corporation to show favour, and Godwin's design was abandoned for one of precious little merit. It incorporated at least one room of *c.* 1530 with fine chimneypiece and fenestration, and a precious fragment of an arcade from a C12 hall house. After wartime bomb damage, the Tudor and Norman work were destroyed in 1961.

POLICE AND FIRE STATION, Nelson Street. By *Ivor Jones* and *Sir Percy Thomas*, 1928. A neglected building of considerable quality. The dramatic police-station entrance has massive blocked piers and exaggerated voussoirs beneath an open pediment. Higher former fire station to the N. Immediately W of Bridewell Street, the POLICE HEADQUARTERS EXTENSION by *A. H. Clarke*, City Architect, 1967, a dull eight-storey tower.

CENTRAL LIBRARY, Deanery Road. In 1899 Vincent Stuckey Lean bequeathed £50,000 for a new building for what was the second-earliest public municipal library in England (founded 1613). The competition in 1902 was won by the firm of *H. Percy Adams*, with designs by his assistant *Charles Holden*. As completed in 1906, it differs relatively little from the competition designs. It shows Holden's precocious maturity aged just twenty-seven; his education in the C19 tradition of historicism is evident (Neo-Tudor without, classical within). Why, then, is the library regarded as so significant in the development of the Modern Movement in Britain? Firstly, as Pevsner says, the styles are used with a 'freedom instigated by Mackintosh's Glasgow Art School' – juxtaposed, stripped down and stylized. Secondly, for the innovative exterior composition and handling of volume and mass, especially the s and E fronts. The plan is simple: entrance and staircase at the E end, with (originally) three floors of public space to the N; offices and storage to the s, on five floors, taking advantage of the sloping site. Holden used brick on steel framing, with facings of Bath stone. Internal ornament is kept to a minimum, and much is executed in plaster; but quality is never skimped. All the joinery and furniture was designed by *Holden* and executed in teak. *William Aumonier* did most of the stone carving.

108   Although the s approach was relatively unimportant, Holden held to the Arts and Crafts principle of equal attention to back and front. Bold chimneystacks and framing towers establish the dominant verticals here, and the central arched and buttressed bays echo the N front. There is a complex play of projection and recession reminiscent of the library wing of Mackintosh's Glasgow School of Art (1906–9) and Hill House, Helensburgh (also designed in 1902). Holden draws on the same set of ideas as Mackintosh – mathematical logic, spatial manipulation and Arts and Crafts respect for locale – while synthesizing a new and infinitely pleasing design. The design of the N front had to respect the adjoining Norman Abbey Gatehouse. Holden kept his parapet slightly lower, and the upper parts recessed. The gatehouse is echoed in the tower-like ends and round-arched entrance below a Neo-Tudor oriel window. Symmetrical centre of three segmental bays with pointedly small oriels against chequer panels of Westmorland stone. Between these are broad flat buttresses, and under the arches figure groups by *Charles Pibworth*, representing English literature. Beautifully detailed rainwater heads and downpipes. Westward extension of 1966–8 by the City Architect *A. H. Clarke*, associate architects *Burrough & Hannam*. Its N façade has square oriels and chequerwork, echoing Holden. Wide stone wall panels rise above roof level, the incomplete stubs of a planned third floor. Glass-canopied access ramp and entrance lobby added at the W end (2000, by *Architecton*). It all works surprisingly well with Holden's building.

INTERIORS. The VESTIBULE has narrow flanking aisles, and a low vault of pendentive domes tiled in turquoise vitreous mosaic. Walls and floor are faced in marbles, a setting that would do justice to the painted fantasies of Alma-Tadema. The secondary ground-floor rooms (originally Newspaper, Magazine and Lending libraries) are of lesser significance architecturally. At the end of this vestibule, a stone screen offers a glimpse of the high, light space of the main STAIRCASE, which rises in a single semicircular flight. A low vaulted corridor provides a dramatic spatial contrast to the READING ROOM, a cool, noble space similar in general form to Cockerell's Old University Library, Cambridge. Tunnel-vaulted with glass-block panels for top lighting and transeptal ends lit by floor-length mullioned windows. Two tiers of galleries. Three small oriels in the N wall light the area beneath the lower gallery, which continues around the room by means of narrow bridges across the transepts. The upper gallery has mildly Art Nouveau railings and, on the N side, a mullioned clerestory. The details are unexpectedly classical, given the faintly Tudor windows, etc.

The BRISTOL ROOM was designed for the fittings from the reference room of the former library in King Street. Panelling, bookcases and some furniture of *c.* 1740. At the s end a spectacular *Grinling Gibbons* overmantel, purchased in 1721 from Gibbons's studio sale by a Bristolian and donated to the old library. Beneath an open segmental pediment, drops of fruit, game birds and miraculously delicate sprays of corn, etc., carved with Gibbons's usual artistry.

MUSEUM AND ART GALLERY, Queen's Road. *See* p. 327.

Educational buildings

UNIVERSITY BUILDINGS. *See* p. 323.

CITY OF BRISTOL COLLEGE, St George's Road. 1998–2000 by *Unite*. Long and symmetrical; slightly canted flanks, bowed centre. Central triangular courtyard with glazed corner turrets, and an open spiral stair to the basement, with ceramics by *Linda Clark*. Other artworks by *Stephen Joyce* (bronze globe, etc.), and *Bill Guilding* (stair-drum mural).

QUEEN ELIZABETH'S HOSPITAL SCHOOL, Berkeley Place. Bare Tudor Gothic, by *Thomas Foster & Son*, 1844–7. Founded in 1590. Picturesquely asymmetrical gatehouse at street level, then vertiginous steps up to the symmetrical entrance tower, with double-height oriel above. Long, three-storey flanks of red rubble. The structural members are cast iron. At the roadside, N end, QEH THEATRE, by *Moxley Jenner*, 1990. A restricted site beneath high walls: striped brick and a glazed drum foyer. Polygonal auditorium in the round, reached by a bridge from the school grounds.

Hospitals

BRISTOL ROYAL INFIRMARY, Marlborough Street and Upper Maudlin Street. Opened in 1737, funded by subscription, as part of a national trend for founding charitable hospitals in the early and mid C18.

On Marlborough Street, the first infirmary building was replaced by the present OLD BUILDING, designed in 1784 by *Thomas Paty*, with *Daniel Hague* (probably as builder rather than architect). The unequal H-plan was constructed in stages, E wing 1784–6, centre block 1788–92, W wing, 1806–9. Three-storey centre of eleven bays arranged 3:5:3, with recessed bays beyond linking to the wings with the centre; the dignified design spoiled *c.* 1866, perhaps by *Henry Crisp,* who designed a ward wing at the SW in that year. On the SE side, a lancet Gothic CHAPEL with museum beneath, by *S. C. Fripp*, 1858.

Opposite on the N side of Marlborough Street is the Portland stone KING EDWARD VII MEMORIAL BUILDING of 1911–12. By *H. Percy Adams & Charles Holden*, also responsible for the Central Library (p. 277), it is an important step in the movement towards a plainer, more abstracted architecture, speaking through its massing and smooth surfaces. Hints are discernible of the geometries of Holden's London Transport Headquarters and University of London Senate House. Now only the SE front is easily visible, the least interesting part.

p. 280

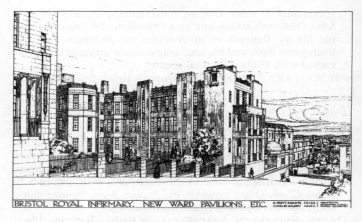

BRISTOL ROYAL INFIRMARY. NEW WARD PAVILIONS, ETC.

Bristol Royal Infirmary, King Edward VII Memorial Building.
Photolithograph, 1910

Ranged across the steeply sloping site are two tall blocks with
towers at the ends, and between them a deep courtyard formerly open at the sw, with two-storey loggias. The plan was
intended to provide maximum air and daylight to the wards.
A low wing with Lutyensesque dome fronts the street, with a
recessed entrance court at the NE end. A 1960s addition hid
the important sw elevations and destroyed the framing flight
of steps, diminishing the design immeasurably. This long
Maudlin Street extension (QUEEN'S BUILDING) is by *Watkins
Gray Group I*, designed *c.* 1965–6, opened 1973. Insistent repetition of grey concrete horizontals and slab-like mullions, with
projecting beam-ends. The building masks two big blocks on
the hill behind.

To the sw again, the yellow brick towers of BRISTOL ROYAL
HOSPITAL FOR CHILDREN by *Whicheloe Macfarlane*, 2001.
The front is varied with shallow projections, oriel bays, and
over the entrance a glazed quadrant with sun visors at each
storey. Window frames are jade-green; small areas of brilliant
pink, yellow and green. At the entrance, highly visible from the
street, is a SCULPTURE, Lollipop Bebop, by *Andrew Smith*,
2001.

Lower Maudlin Street has interesting subsidiary buildings.
On the sw side, a large brick HOUSE with a rainwater head
dated 1753, late for segment-headed windows and string
courses, and with a fine doorcase in the style of *c.* 1720. The
next house continues the string courses and parapet cornice of
its neighbour. Attics added 1886. Then the big red brick EYE
HOSPITAL by *Kendall Kingscott Partnership*, opened 1986. The
brief for elevational enrichment was more than fulfilled by
Walter Ritchie's THE CREATION, believed to be the world's
largest hand-carved brick sculpture. The five panels gain from
being set against darkened glass and black-painted panels.

BRISTOL GENERAL HOSPITAL, Guinea Street. By *W. B. Gingell*, one of his earliest Bristol works. Its core of 1852–7 is visible from the s and w, in an Italianate round-arched manner with a polygonal turret, originally with ogee dome. It sits over basement warehousing of massive rock-faced masonry. Much extended, forming by the early C20 a courtyard plan entered from Guinea Street. Additions: Gingell's Outpatients Department, designed 1871; N wing by *Crisp & Oatley*, c. 1895; a ward block next to the gates, 1905; a lodge, and SE wing with sun balconies, 1912. All work after 1900 by *Oatley & Lawrence*. The building is spoiled by unfortunate alterations.

CENTRAL HEALTH CLINIC, Passage Street. 1935, by *C. F. W. Dening*, the only pre-existing building incorporated in the 1940s plans for a Civic Centre. A relatively new building type in the 1930s. Brown brick and Portland stone. Deep U-shaped courtyard; stepped central tower, gently canted ends to the rear wing.

Markets

ST NICHOLAS MARKET, St Nicholas Street. A planned subsidiary to *John Wood*'s Exchange, executed 1744–5 by *Samuel Glascodine*, a carpenter-builder. There were three covered halls around an open square, originally with butchers' stalls. The s range of Wood's Exchange building, now a café, was originally the Gloucestershire Market Hall, and had no direct access from the Exchange proper. Its open arcaded front was blocked and glazed *c.* 1813 when it became a Corn Exchange. It opens onto the GLASS ARCADE, an avenue running E–W, lined with C19 wooden stalls. Glazed roof by *R. S. Pope*, 1854–5, repaired 2002–3. Pope added a pierced screen wall on the s to carry the roof. At its E end, *Samuel Glascodine*'s simple and pleasing Market Gate leads to the High Street via a vaulted arch, with narrow pedestrian entrances, now blocked. On the High Street front is a small pediment above a Serlian window. The untutored Glascodine may have been guided by Wood or another experienced architect. Inside the gate and s of the Glass Arcade, is *Glascodine*'s East Arcade Market Hall, now the ground floor of a pub. The arcaded first floor was added by *Pope* to carry the new roof in 1854. The richer niched screen wall N of East Arcade may be by *Wood*, or *Pope*'s attempt to emulate Wood.

Directly s of the Exchange building, on the site of the C18 shambles, is the arcaded MARKET HALL by *R. S. Pope*, 1848–9, with a very plain façade to St Nicholas Street. At the SW extremity is MARKET CHAMBERS (also *Pope*, 1848–9), replacing Glascodine's Somersetshire Market Hall.

Railway stations

TEMPLE MEADS STATION, Temple Gate. Temple Meads is actually parts of three stations, of which *Brunel*'s Great Western

Railway (GWR) station, 1839–41, is probably the world's first example of the mature form of railway terminus with integrated train shed, passenger and office facilities. The GWR was a Bristol initiative to provide a railway to London. Brunel became Chief Engineer in 1833, aged twenty-seven. The Bristol–Bath section was opened in 1840 and the whole line in 1841, controversially using 7-ft ¼-in. (2.1-metre) broad-gauge tracks.

First some orientation: in Temple Gate are Brunel's offices, Tudor Revival, with the train shed N of the approach ramp, no longer in railway use. To its s is the Jacobethan Bristol & Exeter Railway office, 1852–4, with ogee-capped towers. Facing down the approach, a big Gothic tower marks *M. D. Wyatt*'s Joint Station of 1871–8, with 1930s extension behind.

The GWR OFFICES, 1839–41, have a symmetrical Tudor façade, apparently of Dundry limestone. R. S. Pope has been proposed as joint architect, but the archive material suggests that *Brunel* was probably solely responsible. A tall oriel in a five-bay centre, and one-bay flanks outside octagonal angle turrets. Across the centre is a black-letter inscription on a long scroll: 'Great Western Railway Company Incorporated by Act of Parliament MDCCCXXXV'. The l. entrance arch was once matched by an exit arch at the r. The medieval revivalist Pugin thundered against the 'architectural display', the 'mock castellated work and . . . all sorts of unaccountable breaks' of the GWR stations; but Brunel saw nothing incongruous in using C15 collegiate Tudor to dress up a C19 building type. Having bridged the harbour to the E, the tracks came in above ground level on brick vaults, through which a road for passengers' carriages passes beneath the train shed. To the N was a goods depot (demolished), with dock and wharfs to take harbour traffic.

This new building type created complex problems that challenged even the most resourceful engineers. The train shed's impressive mock hammerbeam roof of yellow pine spans 72 ft (22 metres), with 20-ft (6-metre) aisles behind Tudor arcades. But the hammerbeams and arches are set-dressing to add architectural presence; the thin side walls over high vaults would not bear the outward thrust of true arched construction. Instead, in Brunel's first design, each bay was treated as two independent crane-like structures, not quite meeting at the ridge. Most of the weight was transferred to the slim iron columns of the arcades, which were bolted to the substructure on cast-iron rockers to allow fine adjustment during construction. Each column thus acted as the fulcrum for a cantilevered rafter, the downward thrust at the centre being resisted by a vertical iron tie-rod anchoring the triangulated frame over the aisle to the platform. This design was executed in amended form, with a crown-piece plugging the central gap and iron straps binding the two crane-like structures into a rigid portal frame. These compromises reintroduced some characteristics of arch construction and the consequent outward thrust

Bristol, Temple Meads Station.
Lithograph by J. C. Bourne, *c.* 1846

caused significant bowing in the columns and side walls. Brunel was still attempting to stabilize the roof in 1849.

The Bristol & Exeter line was constructed 1841–4, and joined the GWR lines from the first. There was originally a timber train shed across the present approach ramp at right angles to the GWR shed. S of the ramp, opposite the train shed, are the symmetrical Jacobean OFFICES, 1852–4, with shaped gables, towered roof-line and a pleasing Doric columned doorway. The architect was *S. C. Fripp*, Brunel's 'assistant' (probably meaning clerk of works) at the GWR station.

Matthew Digby Wyatt designed a Joint Station serving the GWR, Bristol & Exeter and the Midland railways, 1871–8, on a curving Y-plan. The Midland shed extended Brunel's train shed E, in similar if plainer style, but abandoning the mock hammerbeam roof. External walls of chunky pink Dolomitic Conglomerate from Draycott near Cheddar, with Bath stone dressings. The coarsely detailed tower had a French pavilion roof, destroyed by bombing. Austere red brick Gothic interiors. The new platforms were roofed by an elegant 125-ft (38-metre) arch formed of two segments, designed by *Francis Fox*, using the Cheltenham ironfounders *Vernon & Evans*. M. D. Wyatt had collaborated with Brunel at Paddington in 1851–5, and Sir Charles Fox, Francis's father, engineered the Paddington roof. It may have something to do with Wyatt's progressive views that the Bristol roof construction has interesting reminiscences of Viollet-le-Duc's *Entretiens* (particularly vol. II, 1872), with its programme for an iron-based architecture free from dependence on historical styles. A further extension by *P. E. Culverhouse*, 1930–5, added five platforms on the E side. Pared-down Tudor platform buildings in GWR chocolate-and-cream faience.

Bridges

BRISTOL BRIDGE. The reason for the modern settlement of Bristol, and once the only crossing over the Avon from Bristol to Redcliffe and the road to Bath. *James Bridges* designed the present structure in 1757–60, but the Corporation's indecision and disputes over alternative designs caused his departure in 1763. The bridge was built by *Thomas Paty*, 1764–7, on the pier foundations of the C13 bridge. Elliptical central arch, flanked by two semicircular ones. The long-and-short voussoirs and domed toll houses were based on Westminster Bridge of 1750. The toll houses were demolished for a widened deck standing on paired Doric columns, by *T. S. Pope*, 1861 and later, obscuring the arches beneath. A 1960s steel parapet completes the desecration.

REDCLIFFE BASCULE BRIDGE. *Sir George Oatley*, 1939–42. Designed to take the inner circuit road across the harbour to Queen Square. Chunky concrete piers, D-shaped control cabins.

PERO'S BRIDGE, St Augustine's Reach. Designed 1993–4, opened 1999, by the artist *Eilis O'Connell* with *Ove Arup & Partners*, engineers. Bristol's first example of the extrovert footbridges common to harbour-regeneration projects. A hydraulic ram raises the centre, with sculptural horns for counterweights. The staggered plan with refined opposing curves raises it above the run of footbridges. Named after Pero, one of few well-documented slaves, brought to Bristol in 1783: a symbolic acknowledgement of Bristol's role in the slave trade.

STREETS: CENTRAL AREA

The central area is bounded by St James Barton roundabout (N); Bristol Bridge (E); the Council House (SW); and Bristol Royal Infirmary (NW). Intact areas of historic buildings survive around College Green and Corn Street, and a few in the hospital quarter. Streets are dealt with alphabetically.

ALL SAINTS LANE. A narrow alley running SE off Corn Street. S of All Saints' church (p. 252) is ALL SAINTS' COURT, with modest early C18 town houses of brick. Then *Oatley & Lawrence*'s ALL SAINTS' HOUSE of 1903, pleasing though mild Arts and Crafts. Red granite plinth contrasting with ochre-coloured Ham stone. At the S end, E side, the MARKET TAVERN by *John Wood the Elder*, 1744–5, a rebuilding of the medieval Rummer Inn. A simple well-proportioned entrance front, to a 1:3:1 bay design, the flanks slightly set back. Internally the Market Tavern connects with a C16–C17 building eastward (upper room reported to have linenfold panelling).

ALL SAINTS STREET. On steep slopes just outside the E line of the medieval walls, entirely redeveloped with office blocks in the 1960s. The monolithic curve of PITHAY HOUSE (*R. S. Redwood & Associates*, 1966) demonstrates the architectural manner that mesmerized Bristol's post-war planners and builders. Excavation in 2000 W of Union Street revealed early medieval riverside houses.

BALDWIN STREET runs W from Bristol Bridge to The Centre. The central section was blandly redeveloped after bomb damage, e.g. the sweeping curve of BRIDGE HOUSE, 1961, and Nos. 27–29, NEW MINSTER HOUSE (1965), both *Alec French & Partners*. Nearer The Centre, EDINBURGH CHAMBERS (1896–8), where *Edward Gabriel* substitutes his usual vernacular detail for Baroque projections and recessions, with surprisingly tough blocked and rusticated ground floor and a domed corner. Then O'Neill's Bar, originally for Refuge Assurance by their house architect *Stanley Birkett*, 1926. The last gasp of classicism, in metropolitan-looking Portland stone. In Telephone Avenue, S, ARMADA HOUSE (*Henry Williams*, 1902) contains two Renaissance chimneypieces. In the hall, one of the late C16, with Ionic herms and strapwork overmantel. On the first floor, another of *c.* 1620 with rich strapwork and Ionic and Corinthian columns. The overmantel bears a later cartouche, 1700. On the N side between Marsh Street and St Stephen's Street is the former PEOPLE'S PALACE, a variety theatre of 1892 by *James Hutton* for the Livermore Brothers (hence LB in the fanciful aedicule).

The N side E of St Stephen's Street is typical Late Victorian commercial. First, the big façade of the former FISH MARKET, added in 1897 to the earlier market building on St Nicholas Street. Usually given to *W. B. Gingell*, but looking more like *W. V. Gough*'s Loire Renaissance style. Then Nos. 59–63, formerly a fish merchant's, now a pub. Of 1894, by *Gingell*, in his typical red-and-yellow brick style.

BRIDEWELL STREET. Named from old Bridewell prison, demolished *c.* 1878 for the POLICE COURTS by *Josiah Thomas*, 1879, E of the street, disused. Porch of flattened Renaissance design, with Aesthetic Movement railings and gates. Surrounded on three sides by the Police and Fire Station (*see* p. 277). No. 1 Bridewell Street is by *Alec French Partnership*, 1987, for Ernst & Young. L-shaped, with a glazed foyer in the return. White and scarlet cladding.

BROAD QUAY. The SE side of The Centre, and something of a hotchpotch. At the N end, Nos. 1–6 of *c.* 1830, possibly a refronting of C18 buildings. Towards the harbour, the seventeen-storey former BRISTOL & WEST BUILDING, by *Alec French & Partners* (1967–8). Remodelled by *AWW*, 2005–8, as a hotel, flanked by lower residential blocks over shops. For the latter, a polygonal dark brick extension, 1980, was demolished. To decrease its apparent bulk, the tower's concrete facing was replaced by curtain walling of blue reflective glass, and the top two storeys were replaced to a narrower profile.

BROAD STREET. One of the main streets of the late Saxon town, still giving a sense of narrow enclosure. It slopes picturesquely

NW from Christ Church to St John (p. 256), with the crashing post-war intrusions of Lewins Mead and the University buildings behind. At the s end, w side, Nos. 5–8 are of uncertain origin. The details match *Sir Robert Smirke*'s adjoining Old Council House (p. 274), and Smirke designed a smaller shop here. The present building may be a late C19 enlargement of Smirke's structure. Then HOLBECK HOUSE by *Sir Frank Wills*, 1911, a showy Baroque and Neoclassical blend. Next door, the narrow entrance of 1843 to ALBION CHAMBERS, built by 1833 and previously entered only from Small Street. Only as wide as its doorway, framed by Corinthian columns. Above, two storeys of tripartite windows topped by a pediment, with refined decoration throughout.

At Nos. 13–14, the former Branch BANK OF ENGLAND by *C. R. Cockerell*, 1846–7, a design of exceptional panache and subtlety, which yet maintains the necessary gravitas. In 1844 the Bank commissioned branches for Manchester, Bristol and Liverpool from its official architect, all in the same general mould: two storeys with superimposed Doric columns, and a pedimented attic. Bristol's branch had to be slotted into a continuous building line; it is set back a few feet to give visual separation, and enclosed by channelled return walls and projecting porches. Scholarly and correct Doric columns frame windows divided by firm grids of stone and a band of Greek-key ornament. By the 1840s Cockerell had moved away from his pure Grecian training to a Graeco-Roman idiom, evident in the break-back of the pediment cornice and the arcaded and railed attic. Now largely unused; little remains of Cockerell's interiors.

On the NE side of the street, the THISTLE HOTEL (formerly The Grand) by *Foster & Wood*, 1864–9, one of Bristol's most persuasive Victorian buildings, 'a cool but competent essay in the Venetian Quattrocento' (Pevsner). Designed as a five-storey block with lower flanks; only one flank was built, effecting the transition to Christ Church next door (p. 253). The high, bulky centre has an upper columned loggia below a massive bracketed cornice. It stands back behind a ground floor originally housing shops.

At No. 51, NE side, the former AVON INSURANCE BUILDING by *Ponton & Gough*, 1868; polychromatic Gothic, typical of Ponton. Middle Pointed arches on the first floor with much carving, paired shouldered arches on the second floor, and an arcaded attic. Ribbed masonry, giving a Ruskinian emphasis to the wall surfaces. No. 50, Hort's pub, is C18 with sturdy segmental-arched stone shopfront of *c.* 1870.

On the sw side is the Guildhall (p. 275). Further down are mainly C18 façades. No. 27, with a tall arched entrance, existed in this form by *c.* 1865–70, seemingly as a music hall. At No. 43, a rare survival of a C15 dwelling, refronted in the late C18. The jettied rear elevation in TAILOR'S COURT has probably original fenestration patterns; truncated timbers suggest the position of an oriel window. Also a C15 doorway, and two small mutilated C15 stone figures set in the wall. Adjacent is the former MERCHANT TAILORS' HALL, 1740–1, now apartments. Attributed to *William Halfpenny*. The façade has five big sash windows with alternating pediments, and a door at the E end. A fine shell-hood with the Tailors' arms and head of St John the Baptist may be re-set earlier work. Further up, SE side, is COURT HOUSE (1692), for James Freeman whose initials are on the shell-hood. A typically backward-looking provincial design. Three storeys of cross-windows with C20 casements. Staircase with twisted balusters, two C18 panelled rooms. Its Norman rear wall survives from an adjoining C12 hall (demolished 1859). At the end of Tailor's Court, ST JOHN'S CHURCHYARD, consecrated 1409. Tomb to Hugh Browne †1653, with crude effigies beneath a Late Georgian shelter.

Back to Broad Street, and the extraordinary EVERARD'S PRINTING WORKS, 1900–1. An architectural shell by *Henry Williams* faced with coloured Carrara-ware faience by *Doulton & Co.*'s chief designer *W. J. Neatby*. It depicts Gutenberg (spelt 'Gutenburg') and William Morris, each with his typeface, presided over by the Spirit of Literature. Above them a figure bearing a lamp and mirror represents Light and Truth. Edward Everard's name appears in his own typeface, with 'EE' in repoussé copper on the wrought-iron gates. The radial voussoirs, coved entrance and octagonal turrets perhaps derive from C. Harrison Townsend's early plans for Whitechapel Art Gallery (1896). Interiors demolished for NATIONAL WESTMINSTER COURT by *Alec French Partnership*, 1972, which includes the drab concrete intrusion to the r. Finally No. 35, a handsome three-storey house dated 1711, with jettied ground floor suggesting a C17 timber-framed house beneath. Good early C19 shopfront.

THE CENTRE. On conventional street maps this does not exist, being composed of St Augustine's Parade, Colston Avenue and Broad Quay. The Centre, focus of Bristol's nightlife and entertainment, sits between the commercial core, the harbour and College Green, yet is part of none of them. The buildings are described under their respective street names; the statues etc., down the middle are described below.

At the N end is the CENOTAPH (unveiled remarkably late, 1932), a competition win by *Heathman & Blacker*. It follows Lutyens's Whitehall model. To its S, a DRINKING FOUNTAIN, commemorating an exhibition of 1893. Further S is the STATUE of Edward Colston (1636–1721) by *John Cassidy*, 1895. Bronze plaques on the plinth, an early manifestation of Art Nouveau in Bristol. S again, the bronze STATUE of Edmund Burke by *J. H. Thomas*, 1894.

On the W end of The Centre, opposite Baldwin Street is *Ferguson Mann*'s octagonal mast-and-sail structure (*c.* 1997). Then a vigorous lead STATUE of Neptune, cast by *John Randall* in 1722 (the date and spelling on the plaque are wrong). Painted battleship-grey at his fifth re-siting in 2000, when this area was remodelled by the *Concept Planning Group*. The landscaping has too many changes of texture and surface. Three shallow pools with fountains, and to their w ten illuminated Millennium Beacons by *Martin Richman*. At the harbour, the pools finish in a stepped cascade. Few admit to liking it, yet it is a much-used public space, where open water would have impeded movement.

CHRISTMAS STEPS. A picturesque alley running uphill from Lewins Mead to Colston Street, largely of C17–C19 vernacular buildings, some timber-framed behind. At the top an arrangement of seats in niches, rebuilt 1881. Above the S side, we are told that Christmas Steps was 'steppered, done & finished September 1669' at the expense of Jonathan Blackwell, sometime Sheriff of Bristol. On the S side, the basement of Foster's Almshouses (*see* Colston Street) has arcaded shops with stumpy chamfered columns. By *Foster & Wood*, 1883. At No. 5, two small C17 figures in the first floor, from the Merchant Venturers' Hall. At the bottom, the THREE SUGAR LOAVES pub, built as a bakery *c.* 1747–8; old-fashioned hipped tiled roofs, deep cornice and flush-framed sashes. Heavily restored *c.* 1980.

CLARE STREET. Created 1771–5 by *Thomas Paty* to link Corn Street with Broad Quay. Some original houses (e.g. No. 10) survive with alterations. On the corner of St Stephen's Street, the former SCOTTISH PROVIDENT OFFICE, by *Oatley & Lawrence*, 1903. Small and immaculately detailed, yet the dome and subtly overscaled Baroque façades with giant Ionic columns lend unexpected grandeur. At the corner with St Stephen's Street, S side, No. 28 by *Henry Crisp*, 1883, was the company offices of the Bristol entrepreneur George White; a flashy design with Renaissance trim and ranks of dormers. No. 24, Ruskinian Gothic as late as 1890, by *Gingell*.

Further down, the PRUDENTIAL BUILDING (1899), by the company's architect *Alfred Waterhouse*. Of orange terracotta in the Loire-château style, high and compact with turreted corners. Massive chimneystacks and contrasting green slate roof. Opposite to the w is No. 15, the former COUNTY FIRE OFFICE, by *E. Henry Edwards*, 1889. It draws freely on Norman Shaw and much else, with an unusual arcaded attic. On the S side, the former CAPITAL & COUNTIES BANK. *Frederick Mew*'s narrow building of 1883 was widened in Neoclassical revival style by *R. M. Drake*, 1895, and again in 1924. At No. 2, *Charles Hansom*'s richly embellished shop and offices of 1881, in a hybrid Loire-Renaissance style.

COLLEGE GREEN. Framed on two sides by public buildings: the Cathedral (p. 240), Central Library and Council House (pp. 277, 273). Its roughly triangular shape describes the medieval precinct of St Augustine's Abbey. Levelled for the Council House in 1950. At the E apex, a marble STATUE of Queen Victoria, 1888, by *Boehm*, for her Golden Jubilee. To the S, the MARRIOTT ROYAL HOTEL, 1864–8, by *W. H. Hawtin*, richly detailed Italianate. Reopened *c.* 1990, with a weighty and less successful extension by *Denny & Bryan*. On this site was St Augustine the Less (rebuilt *c.* 1480, dem. 1962). w of the hotel are four terraced brick houses (now façades only). That at the l., of *c.* 1750, has moulded architraves and segmental windows (cf. George Tully at Dowry Square). On Deanery Road, a STATUE of the Indian reformer Raja Rammohun Roy by *Niranjan Pradhan*, 1997.

The NE side begins at Mark Lane facing The Centre, and curves w to the Green proper. Some fine C18 houses were bombed, 1940–1. First Nos. 44–47, shops of *c.* 1850, then two big offices filling bomb gaps, both by *Alec French & Partners*, 1962. At No. 38, the former CABOT CAFÉ by *La Trobe & Weston*, 1904, with its original crisp granite shopfront. Edwardian Baroque above; Art Nouveau copper window hoods and fine pomegranate mosaic by the client's daughter, *Catherine Hughes*, from a Charles Ricketts bookbinding of 1891. Inside, an Arts and Crafts staircase, and remnants of two tearooms with marquetry panelling, after the Glasgow fashion for artistic tearooms. No. 37, plain Georgian, has a big top-lit rear hall, originally the Royal Albert Rooms, *c.* 1846–9, with giant Ionic pilasters. No. 30 is mid-C18, of five pilastered bays (poorly refaced). Fine arcaded shopfront by *Foster & Wood*, 1865–6, of contrasting stones and mastic inlay.

COLSTON AVENUE. The N end of The Centre, now an elongated traffic roundabout. A broad space created by culverting the River Frome in 1892; for sculpture here, *see* The Centre.

Clockwise from Colston Street, first the COLSTON CENTRE by *Moxley Jenner & Partners*, 1961–73, a fourteen-storey rectangular tower over a long podium intended as a hub for pedestrian walkways over The Centre. Glazed walls behind balconies and vertical struts give it a visual lightness, anchored by a solid capping band. Perhaps too tall for the site, but with an elegance of its own. Beyond St Mary on the Quay (*see* p. 271) is NORTHCLIFFE HOUSE, newspaper offices completed 1929 by *Ellis & Clarke*. A stepped Art Deco clock tower with sculptural decoration, set slightly off-centre. Redeveloped 2002. At the head of The Centre is ELECTRICITY HOUSE, designed 1935–7 by *Sir Giles Gilbert Scott*. Completed 1948 after delays for war use. Of Portland stone with a prow-like composition. The top two storeys step back, with a loggia emphasizing the curve. To its SE, QUAY HEAD HOUSE, 1884 by *Foster & Wood* for Bristol Municipal Charities, a handsome Queen Anne composition that just misses the relaxed feel of Norman Shaw's work. To the s, a Portland stone office block by *C. F. W. Dening*, 1935; then ST STEPHEN'S HOUSE (*Alec French*, 1938) for Bristol & West Building Society, more severely disposed.

COLSTON STREET. Laid out *c.* 1870, replacing steep medieval lanes. At the bottom is COLSTON HALL by *Foster & Wood*, Bristol's major concert hall, in the Bristol Byzantine style, with polychrome brick and richly detailed cornices. Hall with warehousing beneath, 1864–7, the entrance front and lesser hall 1869–73 (the latter brought back into use, 2010). The seven-bay façade derives from Renaissance palazzo models, with an open arcaded ground floor and another above, originally glazed, now blocked by discordant concrete render with stone reliefs of c. 1960. Below, the outer arches were blocked and given small windows, by *Jones & Cummings*, 1899–1900. These changes mute the scale and rhythm. Fires in 1898 and 1945 destroyed the original staircase and main hall. Replaced in sub-Festival of Britain style by *J. N. Meredith*, 1951. The steep balcony is brought forward with staggered and angled boxes. Attached to the S, FOYER and rehearsal rooms, etc., by *Levitt Bernstein*, 2007–9. Plan of concave and convex curves, clad in brassy-coloured copper. Atrium marked externally by a sail-like roof and by full-height glazing over the entrances. Irregular glazing slots, corner roof terrace. The atrium is bridged by walkways to the bars, etc.

FRIARY HOUSE by *J. Ralph Edwards*, 1938, is immediately N. One of Bristol's first commercial Modernist buildings; recessed flanking bays, continuous horizontal glazing with slim mullions. Beyond, the dour and weighty former YMCA building (*Oatley & Lawrence*, 1930). Further up, FOSTER'S ALM-HOUSES founded in 1483, rebuilt in three stages by *Foster & Wood* 1861–83. Converted to flats from 2006. Fanciful Burgundian Gothic, after the Hôtel Dieu at Beaune, with diaper brickwork and tiling. Courtyard plan with corner towers and timber porches linked by balconies, and a charming open stair-tower with conical roof. Rich details, e.g. dragon hoppers, foliate eaves cornice, lead roof finials and an ogee-capped oriel at one corner. Terminating the N range, the CHAPEL of the Three Kings of Cologne, established in 1484. Refaced to a new design by *Foster & Wood*, 1883. Sculpture niches renewed and *Ernest Pascoe*'s statues of the Three Kings installed in 1960. Inside, a simple rectangular plan with collegiate stalls (woodwork mostly C19). E window by *Patrick Pollen*, c. 1960.

Above Christmas Steps is a good row of houses, c. 1710 to early C19, refurbished c. 1990 by *Peter Ware* and *Richard Pedlar*. Nos. 68 and 70 are mid-C17, with jetties, canted bays and gables.

CORN STREET. The commercial heart of Bristol, once the route from the High Cross towards The Quay. Now largely C18 and C19 banks and offices, many converted to bars and restaurants.

At the E end, S side, All Saints, *Wood the Elder*'s Exchange, and opposite, the surprisingly small Old Council House (*see* pp. 252, 275 and 274). Directly W is the astonishingly sumptuous LLOYDS BANK (originally West of England and South Wales District Bank) 1854–7, by *W. B. Gingell & T. R. Lysaght*. How they must have enjoyed knocking out their Grecian neighbour! Modelled on Sansovino's St Mark's Library, Venice, with repeated Venetian motifs, Doric below and Ionic above. Of Bath stone, with contrasting Portland stone sculpture. Originally five bays with a central door; the current entrance bay added at the l. probably c. 1925, all in Portland stone, upsetting the balance. All is overwhelmed with sculpture by *John Thomas* representing the towns where the bank operated, their rivers and products, and above, allegorical figures such as Peace and Plenty, Justice and Integrity. The weighty entablature has putti engaged in the pursuits of banking. In the banking hall, paired Composite columns and deep panelled coving around a 1920s glazed skylight. Next door, HSBC BANK by *T. B. Whinney*, 1921–3. Portland stone bankers' classicism, with a domed corner lantern.

Opposite is a row of commercial buildings that gives the street much character and unity. Flanking the Exchange are two narrow buildings probably by *Wood*, set forward to imply a shallow courtyard for his building. To the r. is No. 48 Corn Street built by *Samuel Glascodine*, 1746, originally the Old Post Office. The matching l. flank (then and now a coffee house) was built by *Thomas Paty*, 1782. Their heavy ground-floor arcades are repeated along this w side of the street. Adjoining No. 48 is LONDON & LANCASHIRE ASSURANCE by *Edward Gabriel*, 1904. A riot of classical motifs, with sculpture by *Gilbert Seale* and a high domed lantern. No. 40, of *c.* 1810–20, was in the C19 Miles and Harford's bank. *John Nash* designed something for them in Corn Street, seemingly not their later premises at No. 35 (below). Could No. 40 be his? Originally four bays, extended E *c.* 1925.

Further w, the Neo-Baroque NATWEST BANK (formerly the Liverpool, London and Globe Insurance) by *Gingell*, 1864–7, all rippling movement. A high ground floor with outer entrance bays, the next two storeys with a giant order stacked two high and four wide. An attic storey with caryatids and doubled pediment completes the visual indigestion. Excellent sculpture by *Thomas Colley*. The interiors rebuilt *c.* 1977, with a large marble relief by *Walter Ritchie, c.* 1977. It is joined internally with Nos. 32–34, formerly STUCKEY'S BANK, by *R. S. Pope*, 1852–4. Conservatively classical, with bold rustication and bracketed cornice. Doric banking hall by *Oatley & Lawrence*, 1914. p. 292

On the N side, w of Small Street first No. 47, formerly London and South Western Bank, four storeys by *James Weir*, 1878–80, with none of Gingell's swagger. Then the small but engaging former COMMERCIAL ROOMS, 1809–11. A merchants' club by the youthful *Charles Busby*, who later built much in Brighton. He adapted many features from Thomas Harrison's Liverpool Lyceum and his Portico Library in Manchester. Ionic portico flanked by narrow wings, and a high blocking course behind the pediment. Figure sculptures (Commerce, Bristol and Navigation) and the frieze inside the portico all by *J. G. Bubb*. Sober Great Room with black marble chimneypieces of Egyptian form, and pendentive dome with lantern supported on graceful caryatids after Soane's Consols Transfer Office (1798–9) at the Bank of England. At the rear, a mahogany buffet with caryatids, and above, a wind dial. Top-lit rear reading room.

At Nos. 37–39, the former FRIENDS' PROVIDENT BUILDING, 1931–3 by *A. W. Roques*; Portland stone elevation by *Sir Giles Gilbert Scott*. A lean Art Deco interpretation of Neoclassicism, enlivened with white 'anodium metal' windows, grilles and jaunty dancers above the door. Relief figures by *Hermon*

Bristol, Liverpool and London Insurance Company offices.
Engraving, 1870

Cawthra. No. 35 (now PIZZA EXPRESS) is of *c.* 1790, the façade
remodelled probably by *Gingell*, 1879. Previously ascribed to
John Nash *c.* 1811 (*see* No. 40, above), but signed and dated
plasterwork in the lantern proves that the interior existed in its
present form in 1791. C14 or C15 rib-vaulted cellar. Behind
a courtyard (now glazed in) is the banker's house, with a

Neoclassical plaster ceiling in the principal first-floor room. *William Paty* is the likely author. Nos. 31–33, originally a bank by *Gingell* 1862–4, refaced in Neo-Palladian style by *F. C. Palmer* for the National Provincial Bank, 1930. Brown brick, with four-column portico over a ground floor of Portland stone: all the polish but none of the charm of the C18. Gingell's luscious banking hall has a coved ceiling and central dome defined by beams.

DENMARK STREET. From The Centre, Nos. 1–11, s side, late C18–early C19 terraced artisan houses. The rear of The Hippodrome (*see* p. 295) dominates the N side. Opposite, THE GAUNT'S HOUSE, 1953 by *Alec French & Partners*, with relief sculptures on the upper storeys. Beneath are partly medieval cellars once associated with The Gaunt's Hospital. Beyond, a four-square C19 warehouse of Pennant rubble, converted to apartments *c.* 1998.

FROGMORE STREET. In the valley between College Green and the slopes to the NW, at the limit of the medieval city. The only building of obvious antiquity is THE HATCHET pub, timber-framed of 1606, largely rebuilt in 1967. Two-storey oriels and on the second floor even a little West Country timber ornament, an oval and a lozenge keyed in bars. Opposite, the NEW BRISTOL CENTRE *c.* 1963–6, by *Gillinson, Barnett & Partners*, brutal in scale and texture. It combined cinema, dance hall, ice rink, nightclub and bingo hall. SW end rebuilt as student accommodation by *Unite*, 2000. Towards Park Street viaduct is a neglected Greek Revival façade, *c.* 1830, with Doric attached columns.

HIGH STREET. Before the blitz of 1940–1, High Street was narrow and bustling, with tall C19 and earlier buildings. The E side suffered the worst, and is now lax and dissipated, with expanses of shabby paving (under which are C15 cellars). The derelict NORWICH UNION BUILDING by *Wakeford, Jerram & Harris*, 1962, deflates a prime site facing Bristol Bridge. Adjacent is the BANK OF ENGLAND (1964, extended 1976), both parts by *Easton, Robertson & Partners*. Bleak fenestration and a puny corner entrance.* On the w side, No. 41 is mildly Greek Revival (reportedly with part of a timber roof, perhaps C15). Nos. 44–45 have a veneer of half-timbering (*H. C. M. Hirst*, 1908) over a C17 core at No. 45.

LEWINS MEAD. Laid out *c.* 1250 between the bank of the River Frome and the steep escarpment to the NW; several religious houses were founded here. From Christmas Steps, NARROW LEWINS MEAD is a short alley leading NE to Lewins Mead. CENTRE GATE, offices by *Moxley Jenner & Partners*, 1984, re-creates the enclosure of the old street pattern. Opposite, a timber-framed house with mid-C17 upper storeys, the deep jetty suggesting a C15 or earlier core. On its r. is ST

---

*The corner at the top of High Street was the site of the C14 HIGH CROSS, removed in 1733, re-erected at Stourhead, Wiltshire, in 1764; and of the timber-framed DUTCH HOUSE (1676), bombed in 1940.

BARTHOLOMEW'S HOSPITAL, founded *c.* 1230–40, converted *c.* 1538 for Bristol Grammar School and later Queen Elizabeth's Hospital School. Adapted *c.* 1847 as housing and a print works. The moulded E.E. entrance arch was re-set lower in the C17. Inside, an arcade of *c.* 1250, and a precious C13 statue of the Virgin, perhaps from the Wells school. The historic buildings were refurbished (with Centre Gate, above) by *Moxley Jenner & Partners*, 1984, the new woven happily through the old. In the first courtyard are piers of two C13 arcades, one embedded in a later wall, with Norman capitals – perhaps reused C12 domestic work. This was the hospital chapel, double-aisled, with a s porch (now the street entrance). The rest is confused; four Tudor doorways, some C17 windows, and a Gothic school range, *c.* 1758–62, leading to an inner court. Here, a range of 'model dwellings for the industrial classes', 1856, three storeys with balcony access.

Lewins Mead begins to the NE, with a STATUE of a gaunt horseman, by *David Backhouse*, 1984. Next the SUGAR HOUSE, the last relic of the Bristol sugar industry; a refinery was established here in 1728. Simple rendered front with glass entrance canopy added in conversion to a hotel, 1999. In the hotel reception, a C19 engine-house chimney. A little NE, two bulky Brutalist offices: GREYFRIARS, 1974, *Wakeford, Jerram & Harris*, on the site of a Franciscan friary (*c.* 1250); and WHITEFRIARS, 1976, *D. A. Goldfinch Associates*.

LODGE STREET. A steep hill between Trenchard Street and Park Row. To the SW, Trenchard Street CAR PARK, a multi-storey monster of *c.* 1967. On the NE side are houses of *c.* 1800–10, including a double-fronted villa, with elegant tapering pilasters at the door. A *cause célèbre* in Bristol's conservation battles, saved from dereliction *c.* 1980–2 by *Ferguson Mann* for the Bristol Churches Housing Association. It included new houses behind in Lodge Place, around a garden court entered from Trenchard Street, through the façade of the former R.C. CHAPEL OF ST JOSEPH, built 1790. Roughcast-rendered wall with cornice, and four high Gothic windows. From 1861 it served as a school to St Mary on the Quay (p. 271).

LOWER PARK ROW. A steep medieval lane from Colston Street up to Park Row. At the top of Lodge Street, a terrace of *c.* 1790. No. 1 has a fine iron porch with leaded tent canopy, batwing spandrels and Chinoiserie details. Downhill, No. 10, an exceptional house of *c.* 1600–60 discovered under Georgian refacing in 1978, restored *c.* 1980 including much new work in the ovolo-moulded cross-windows, gables and roof. At the NE corner, small round-headed windows lighting cupboard-like recesses. Continuous string courses. The main front faces SW, now tight against the Ship Inn; a five-window range with two early C19 arched doorcases. At the bottom, ZERO DEGREES, a bar by *Acanthus Ferguson Mann*, 2003, on a steep triangular site. Render, steel and glass slotted neatly behind Pennant rubble walls, with a sweeping balcony facing Colston Street.

NELSON STREET. Largely disastrous 1960s redevelopment, including NELSON HOUSE (1967, *Angus McDonald & Partners*), disjointed slabs and a web of first-floor decks.

ORCHARD STREET. Built 1718–22 on the orchard of The Gaunt's Hospital, NE of College Green. As at Queen Square the Corporation leases specified uniform-height sash windows and brick fronts. Parapets replace modillion cornices, imitating the fire precautions of London building regulations. The fronts have unfortunately been painted white. No. 28 has unusually rich grotesque keystones, and a fine cantilevered mahogany staircase. At the NE, the street widens into a near-square; Nos. 15–18 have uniform pedimented doorcases on provincial brackets. The staircase hall at No. 15 has excellent Rococo plasterwork with lighthearted Chinoiserie motifs of *c.* 1740–50, possibly by *Joseph Thomas* who worked at Clifton Hill House. Opposite, No. 24A, by *W. G. Price*, 1938. Neo-Georgian offices in Bath stone for Bristol Municipal Charities. (In the former boardroom, a fine marble chimneypiece of *c.* 1770 from Kingsweston House, with a plaque depicting the Judgment of Paris.)

UNITY STREET, the SW continuation of Orchard Street, was opened up in 1742, perhaps in anticipation of Park Street (*see* p. 311). On the NW side, Nos. 2–4, built as a single centralized composition, perhaps by *James Paty the Elder*. No. 3 is of five bays with pedimented centre and Gibbsian blocked Ionic doorcase. Rusticated ashlar ground floors, Nos. 2 and 3 mutilated by shopfronts. The remaining houses similar if less grand. On the SE side, the former MERCHANT VENTURERS' TECHNICAL COLLEGE, an unfortunate Gothic concoction of red brick by *E. C. Robins*, 1880, partly rebuilt in 1906 by *Alfred Cross*. Converted to flats, 2004–6.

RUPERT STREET. Created by culverting over the River Frome in 1857 and 1879. Drastically remodelled in the 1960s. At the S end is FROOMSGATE HOUSE of 1971 by *Alec French & Partners*. A seventeen-storey monolith in drab concrete and orange brick. Directly NE, Bristol's first multi-storey car park, 1960, by *R. Jelinek-Karl* with structural engineers *Mander & Partners* and *E. N. Underwood*. Oval in plan with a continuous spiral ramp.

ST AUGUSTINE'S PARADE. The W side of The Centre. An irregular row, largely C18 and C19, and much altered, epitomizing Bristol's haphazard character. From Mark Lane, Nos. 1–2 (formerly Halifax Building Society), by *Alec French*, 1937. Five storeys, in Portland stone with bronzed doors and a balcony with Jazz Age motifs. Further N, the building line steps back for the HIPPODROME, a theatre and music hall of 1911–12, the last major design of *Frank Matcham*: for Sir Oswald Stoll, for whom Matcham had designed the London Coliseum (1904). The narrow access from St Augustine's Parade limited the opportunity for an appropriately grand façade, so Matcham built upward. Attic storey and tall roof, topped by an illuminated revolving globe, all removed 1964. To the l., an extension of 1964, continuing Matcham's channelled rustication. Domed auditorium, mostly original, with two galleries and gilded plaster decorations. The large stage had a tank beneath for water spectacles.

The next three houses have been amalgamated as the HORN & TRUMPET pub. The two on the l. are C18, then one perhaps of *c.* 1700, with moulded wooden cornices showing the transition from medieval jetties to string courses. DOMINIONS HOUSE is by *Arthur Blomfield Jackson*, 1898, for Star Life. Writhing Art Nouveau ornament, doorways with swan-necked pediments, and gabled bays. A further two storeys with steep turreted roof were not executed. Through the left-hand entrance is ST AUGUSTINE'S COURT, C18 houses and C19 warehouses, rebuilt as offices by *Moxley Jenner & Partners* and *Stride Treglown*, 1988–90. At the same time Nos. 26–30 St Augustine's Parade and St Augustine's Place, curving NW into Pipe Lane, were rebuilt according to their appearance *c.* 1860 (demolished behind). No. 26, three-and-a-half storeys with gables and jetties, is of C17 origin.

ST JAMES PARADE. A pedestrian way running E–W beside St James (p. 254), its former churchyard a park since 1882. On the N side, ST JAMES COURT, by *Holder Mathias Alcock*, 1996. Offices in Bath stone, with nicely detailed windows and brisessoleil. The E part incorporates the tower and triple-arched entrance to a former Presbyterian church (*J. C. Neale*, 1858). Spire removed *c.* 1970.

ST NICHOLAS STREET. The SW segment of the circle of streets inside the Saxon ringworks, later the line of the medieval walls, the curve most evident at the W end. On the N side, the former STOCK EXCHANGE, by *Henry Williams* (1903) for Sir George White. A stylistically backward-looking single-storey pavilion with a richly ornamented temple front of black marble columns. The doorcase derives from St Mary the Virgin, Oxford (1637). Good Art Nouveau tiling in the staircase, palatial lavatories with Edwardian fittings. On the S side, the FISH MARKET of 1873 by *Pope & Son*, now a bar. A single-storey hall with an iron-framed roof; badly weathered classical stone façade. Opposite, THE ELEPHANT pub by *Henry Masters*, 1867, with a carved elephant's head on the first floor. Then No. 18, GRESHAM CHAMBERS, one of several Gothic shops by *Ponton & Gough*, 1868, with good carved details. ST NICHOLAS CHAMBERS, handsome stone-fronted shops by *Archibald Ponton, c.* 1866. Round-arched windows with dragons in the spandrels. On the ground floor, cast-iron shafted columns; instead of capitals, moulded blocks masquerading as the ends of transverse beams running back into the building; the shopfronts set behind.

ST STEPHEN'S STREET. From Colston Avenue, Nos. 9–11 is a big overblown office by *J. H. Hirst*, 1873–5. Beneath a hubbub of decoration is a double-height arcade, the keystones not linked to the entablature. Each arch has a subsidiary segmental arch. High and busy attics. Adjacent offices of 1878, brick walls inset with terracotta heads. s again, the former BRISTOL TIMES AND MIRROR offices, 1902–4 by *Foster, Wood & Awdry* (now a hostel). Domestic Arts and Crafts applied with some success to offices, the ground floor perhaps influenced by Lethaby's Eagle Insurance, Birmingham. The upper parts borrow from late c17 Bristol merchants' houses.

SMALL STREET. Of late Saxon origin, and a favoured address for medieval merchants, now mostly occupied by the Crown Courts and Assize Courts (p. 277). Below the latter, NE side, is FOSTER'S CHAMBERS, once the house of the c15 merchant John Foster, with a gabled c17 front refenestrated in the c18. Interiors much altered.

WINE STREET. The E arm of the four late Saxon streets that converged at the High Cross, a major shopping street until the blitz of 1940–1. For the Bank of England, s side, *see* p. 293. Opposite, the high PRUDENTIAL BUILDING (1957), dull stripped classicism.

INNER CITY PERAMBULATIONS

1. *Around Queen Square*

The rectangular tongue of land s of the medieval city, then called Town Marsh, bounded by Baldwin Street on the N (*see* p. 285), the Avon to the E and s, and the diverted River Frome (St Augustine's Reach) on the w. The Marsh Wall ran N of present King Street, with gates at both ends, and quays to the N. The undefended s end of the Marsh was an archery training ground for the militia. Planned development started in 1650 with King Street, then Queen Square and Prince Street from 1699. Queen Square was the most fashionable Bristol address until the late c18, becoming commercialized in the c19.

From Bristol Bridge (p. 284), WELSH BACK leads s. After 1240 this was the secondary quay, serving the trade with Ireland and Wales. No. 3, WEST INDIA HOUSE by *Oatley & Lawrence*, 1903–4, has a narrow centrepiece with pilasters framing a double-height window. Directly s, the BRIGSTOW HOTEL, by *Helical Bar Development*, 2001, remodelled from offices of 1974; a clean grid composition. s of King Street is THE GRANARY, 1869 by *Ponton & Gough*, with exotic hints of Venetian, Moorish and Byzantine: 'the most striking and piquant monument of the High Victorian age in Bristol' (Andor Gomme). Powerful massing, soaring angles, and arcades of razor-sharp Cattybrook brick with black and buff polychromy (the black bricks, though, are painted). Stylistic comparisons suggest *Archibald Ponton* was the principal designer. The ground-floor arcade perhaps derives from Street's lost nave arcades at All Saints, Clifton. Seven grain floors, with intricately patterned

ventilation openings in arcades, each storey with a different
arch form. Machicolated battlements, swallow-tail merlons
and steep roofs. Ground-floor roundels were exit points for
grain chutes. Flues within the walls delivered warm air from
basement furnaces to dry the grain. Brick vaults insulated the
structure above the ground floor, but the upper construction
was not fireproof. Inside, massive brick piers carry ingenious
wooden Y-beams transferring thrust onto the E and W walls.
The joists are forcibly curved by cross-pieces to counteract the
tendency of the floors to bow under the weight of grain.
Converted to apartments, 2002, by *Barton Willmore*. Further S,
the SCOTTISH LIFE building of 1975, by *Burnet Tait Powell &
Partners*, perhaps the earliest Bristol emulation of the C19
warehouse style.

KING STREET, laid out in 1650, is rewarding for its gently
curving composition and harmonious juxtapositions. Here are
Bristol's best surviving Restoration merchants' houses. The
first six houses backed on to the Marsh Wall (i.e. the N side of
King Street); by *Thomas Wickham*, carpenter, completed by
1660; the leases prohibited 'noysome trades'. The S side leases,
of 1663, specified houses of regular design. Of these, the
famous LLANDOGER TROW inn is of *c.* 1664. Three showy
timber-framed houses (five until bombed in 1940), the best
Bristol survivors of their period. Three storeys and gabled
attics, with full-height canted bays, some with C17 'Ipswich'
windows. Shallow jetties and a broad unified composition give
the houses a Renaissance feel. Glazing appears once to have
been continuous between the bays. Renaissance details, e.g.
tapered pilasters with lozenges and coarse Ionic capitals. The
basements were used as warehouses (still with shuttered openings), the ground floors were probably always intended for
business. At No. 4, parts of the open-well stair, a C17 German
overmantel, and an C18 shell-hooded corner buffet survive.
The first-floor great chambers have two Tudor-arched chimneypieces, and good patterned ceilings.

On the N SIDE, w of Queen Charlotte Street, are the architecturally conservative ST NICHOLAS'S ALMSHOUSES, 1652–6,
largely rebuilt 1959–61 under *John K. Maggs*, for *Donald Insall*.
Eight regular gables to King Street (the three facing Queen
Charlotte Street are C19). Mullioned hoodmoulded windows.
Over the entrance hall was a tiny chapel, its floor removed
c. 1959 to form a double-height hall. The plaster barrel-vault,
dated 1656, has late strapwork and symbols of the Evangelists.
In the courtyard behind, a D-shaped mid-C13 BASTION from
the Marsh Wall.

To the w is the beautiful Georgian THEATRE ROYAL, including
Britain's oldest surviving theatre auditorium, in almost continuous use since 1766. Funded by forty-nine merchants who
subscribed £50 each, it received its royal patent in 1778. In
1946 the renowned Bristol Old Vic was established here, and
in 1972 improved back-stage facilities and a studio theatre were
created, with a new entrance through the adjacent Coopers'
Hall, by then redundant, at last providing a public face.

The COOPERS' HALL by *William Halfpenny*, 1743–4, has a five-bay façade with a rusticated ground floor and a big *piano nobile*, the central three bays with engaged columns and a pedimented attic flanked by massive volutes. The Corinthian order is close to that in Book I of Isaac Ware's 1743 edition of Palladio. However, the proportions are quite un-Palladian: squat basement, very tall sashes (a Halfpenny hallmark) in the *piano nobile*, and an over-steep pediment. To the w *Peter Moro*'s 1972 EXTENSION for a STUDIO THEATRE and offices. Brown brick, with four gables echoing the neighbouring forms, and carefully modulated recessions and projections. Moro removed the interior of the guild hall for a compact and practical new entrance, using render, glass and chrome, but replicating the ceiling plasterwork. The changes of level are integrated by a processional stair with gallery landing wrapped around the walls.

The upper foyer leads to the splendid AUDITORIUM of 1764–6. The proprietors paid £38 16s. 8d. for a plan of Drury Lane Theatre, London, from its carpenter, Mr *Saunderson*, and engaged *Thomas Paty* to build a theatre conforming with it as far as possible. Paty was probably responsible for the design beyond the basic principles. The auditorium is semicircular rather than the usual ellipse. Two circles were originally arranged as boxes; the Doric columns mark their partitions. Additional gallery tier added in 1800. A little of the original decoration survives, e.g. above the altered proscenium arch, acanthus plasterwork, and the paired Corinthian pilasters flanking the boxes. The rest achieved its current form with the installation of the starred ceiling by *T. S. Pope* and *C. J. Phipps*, 1881. The pea-green colouring is based on descriptions of the late C18 scheme. Moro's remodelling retained the 'thunder run' (a wooden trough down which balls were rolled to simulate thunder) above the ceiling.

Continuing on the N side, at No. 36 a crisp red brick flour warehouse, by *A. P. I. Cotterell*, 1905–6. No. 35, *c.* 1870, was a cork warehouse, in Bristol Byzantine style. Arched window recesses, attic arcades, and heraldic beasts. Refurbished *c.* 1975. Nos. 33–34, *c.* 1650–8, are by *Thomas Wickham*, a merchant's house and, attached, the earliest purpose-built warehouse to survive in Bristol. The house (No. 33) has stone party walls (the rear wall probably part of the C13 Marsh Wall) with a timber-framed gabled front; late C18 fenestration. Two-room plan, one behind the other, with stairs and lobby between. First-floor great chamber with plasterwork frieze of beasts' heads and shields, and a ceiling with a central quatrefoil with cherubs' heads, floral border and stylized branches of flowers and pomegranates.

Now for the S SIDE, working w from Queen Charlotte Street. No. 6 has an early C18 six-bay brick front with fine shell-hood, and grotesque keystones. The rear stair-tower, off-centre door and double-hipped roof suggest that two C17 gabled houses were amalgamated and refronted. Nos. 7 and 8 (*c.* 1665) were built as a pair with stone outer party walls but a central timber partition. Half-basements with shuttered doors, as at the

Llandoger Trow. Jettied upper floors. The jerry-built framing includes reused ships' timbers and barrel staves. Nos. 14 and 15, C19 stone and brick warehouses. Then more C17 survivors, with instructive later changes: Nos. 16–18 by *Francis Bayley*, shipwright, 1663–6; and Nos. 19–20 (*c.* 1665), perhaps also his. No. 16 was refronted and the gable cut back in the C18. (Reportedly with C17 ceilings and a Samson post.) No. 17, likewise altered *c.* 1700, has cross-windows and moulded platbands. No. 18 is the least altered. At No. 20 a shopfront of *c.* 1800, incorporating the C17 door. Opposite and a little w is the OLD LIBRARY, now a restaurant. The site was given in 1613 by Robert Redwood, and the library was rebuilt 1738–40, probably by *James Paty the Elder* who carved the masonry (much lost in brutal repairs *c.* 1970). Five-bay front with three-bay pedimented centrepiece and Composite doorcase. Projecting w wing, 1780s. The E gateway has an ogee gable of a type fashionable *c.* 1720–50. Fine oak staircase; the panelled reading room above removed to the new Central Library in 1906 (p. 277). Directly w, the MERCHANT VENTURERS' ALMSHOUSES of 1696–9. A cheerful vernacular interpretation of Colston's Almshouses, St Michael's Hill. Cross-windows, and bracketed door canopies; the carpenter was clearly taxed by the corner canopies. The missing w range of the quadrangle was bombed in 1941.

A turning s leads into QUEEN SQUARE, among the largest C18 squares in Britain. Bristol's first piece of formal planning, laid out in 1699 by the Corporation for merchants' houses, following the lead of St James's Square and Red Lion Square, London. The leases specified storey heights, regular brick façades and modillion cornices, with London's post-Great Fire building regulations in mind. They did not impose a single terrace design; various carpenters built single houses or small groups. Building peaked *c.* 1710–15 and was completed in 1727, after which Queen Square was overshadowed by the unified square of palace-front terraces, e.g. Queen Square, Bath, 1729. The square was bisected diagonally SE–NW by Redcliffe Way in 1936–7, removed in a visionary restoration by the Council's *City Centre Projects and Urban Design Team*, 2000–1.

At the centre is *Rysbrack*'s brass equestrian STATUE of William III, acclaimed by George Vertue as 'the best statue ever made in England'. Cast in 1733 and erected 1736. Designs were also invited from Peter Scheemakers (whose statue went to Hull). The asthmatic king is depicted as a lean and powerful Roman athlete, exuding nobility and purpose. The subject demonstrated the loyalty of Bristol's Whig oligarchy to the 1689 settlement.

The N side and most of the w side were burnt in the Bristol Riots of 1831, in which discontent over Parliamentary Reform and other local issues escalated into violent protests. At the centre of the rebuilt N SIDE is the CUSTOM HOUSE, 1835–7 by *Sydney Smirke*, Surveyor to the Customs Office. A bland design of five

Bristol, No. 29 Queen Square.
Elevation

tall arched windows over a banded ground floor. Paired
pilasters about the door, bracketed cornice. To its w are Nos.
69–72 (c. 1835), a truncated and altered terrace, a rather weak
design. Much better is the terrace E of the Custom House, Nos.
1–9, by *Henry Rumley*, c. 1833; of Bath stone, with giant
pilasters, fanciful Grecian capitals and fluted pilastered doorcase. Veranda balconies.

From the NE corner a detour into QUEEN CHARLOTTE STREET,
the s end of which was laid out with Queen Square. No. 59
(1709–11) has a showy Baroque refacing probably of the mid
1730s, perhaps unparalleled in England of its size and type.
Each storey has different flanking pilasters and window surrounds, those on the ground floor with lugs and 'ears' after
Borromini's Palazzo Pamphili, Rome, and inside the frames,
little scribed voussoirs. The façade is so similar to Rosewell
House, Bath (1735), now tentatively attributed to *Nathaniel*

Ireson of Wincanton, that it must be by the same. Ireson picked up elements of Roman Baroque through his work as builder to Thomas Archer, who in turn was influenced by Bernini and Borromini.* To the s, No. 61, *c.* 1705, shows the inexperience of Bristol builders in the use of brick.

The E SIDE of Queen Square illustrates later interlopers (e.g., at No. 13, a high brick warehouse by *A. P. I. Cotterell*, 1904–5; and mock-Georgian offices at Nos. 14–16 by *Alec French & Partners*, 1967). Then the big PORT AUTHORITY OFFICES by *W. V. Gough*, 1885, insensitive to context as one might expect for its date. Built when Bristol Docks Committee took over Avonmouth Dock in 1884, to a lavish Flemish Renaissance design in red brick and buff terracotta, with statues of the Continents on the first floor. Extended s in the same style, by *Gough*, 1902.

p. 301 The best surviving C18 houses are on the s SIDE. No. 29 (1709–11, by *John Price*, carpenter) has a showy five-bay brick façade with superimposed Doric, Ionic and Composite columns, and naïvely handled classical details such as window pediments balanced on the keystones, and columns that stop short of the eaves. Good mid-C18 iron gates, and ornamented gatepiers, all reinstated *c.* 1994. Central hall and staircase, with two rooms on each side, and rear closet towers. The narrow rear service court led to a warehouse and offices behind, a common arrangement for the houses that backed onto the quays. No. 30 is the best Neo-C18 replacement, by *Edmund Cullis*, 1919–21. Nos. 33–35 by *Alec French Partnership*, *c.* 1990; the Postmodern details do not succeed in such close proximity. W of Grove Avenue, Nos. 36–38 are of *c.* 1703; plainer than No. 29. The W end of this row, all of 1981–2, replaced C19 warehouses with pastiche of the weakest sort. At the SW angle behind No. 46 is the derelict SEAMEN'S MISSION CHAPEL by *Voisey & Wills*, *c.* 1880, appallingly refronted in concrete after wartime bombing.

The W SIDE of Queen Square was largely rebuilt *c.* 1832–40 after the riots, and is rather unsatisfactory for its irregular distribution of Greek Revival decorative features. *Henry Rumley* designed No. 57, formerly St Stephen's Parsonage; the rest, with the same features as Nos. 1–9 (N side), must be his too. The exception is Nos. 49–50, by *R. S. Pope*, 1832–3 in tuck-pointed red brick, with stepped voussoirs. PHOENIX HOUSE, 1834, Rumley's own residence, has a showy semicircular Greek Doric porch, and a large stone phoenix on the parapet. Nos. 54 and 55 (*c.* 1710) survived the riots, the former superficially updated with a wreathed window pediment.

We leave Queen Square where we came in, into the N end of PRINCE STREET, here dominated by the bulk of BROAD QUAY HOUSE; *Alec French & Partners*, 1981. The design evolved from a futuristic concept of 1973 into the existing

---

*Ireson's Ven House, Milborne Port, Somerset, and his White Horse Inn, Wincanton, have similarities to Queen Charlotte Street.

red brick polygon, in the then-favoured warehouse style. Segmental arches, slate mansards with buttress-like ties giving the roofs rather the appearance of a bell-tent. Towards Prince Street, ceramic panels by *Philippa Threlfall*. N of this lies NARROW QUAY. A little S along the waterfront is JURY'S HOTEL, by *Wakeford, Jerram & Harris*, 1964–6. Its multi-storey car park has structural screen walls of strident lozenge-patterned concrete. S of Farr's Lane is an early C18 three-storey sail loft, remodelled as the ARCHITECTURE CENTRE by *Niall Phillips Architects*, 1996. S again on the cobbled quayside is a bronze STATUE of John Cabot (*Stephen Joyce*, 1986), Bristol's adopted maritime explorer. Here at the meeting of the rivers Avon and Frome is BUSH HOUSE, now the ARNOLFINI ARTS   99 CENTRE. Its four-square bulk has an unexpected nobility, and its rejuvenation in 1975 symbolized a new Bristol. Built 1830–1 as warehousing and offices for Acramans, ironfounders, by *R. S. Pope*; a development of his Wool Hall (*see* p. 307). Extended with six bays to the N in 1835–6 to provide tea warehousing, making the E and W fronts asymmetrical. The symmetrical S façade combines round arches, classical proportions and a sense of impending Victorian solidity. Giant arches and rock-faced Pennant stone foreshadow the 1850s Bristol warehouse style. Remodelled as an arts centre in 1975 by *JT Group Ltd* with a new interior of reinforced concrete, and an additional floor in the glazed mansard. Interiors completely remodelled again by *Snell Associates*, 2003–5, with the creation of a basement, and a central stairwell.

Turning N, PRINCE STREET is a bleak stretch of mediocre postwar buildings linking Marsh Street with the harbour. It was laid out *c.* 1700 with Queen Square. Nos. 66–70 are the only C18 survivors, an impressive group N of Bush House. Nos. 68 and 70, *c.* 1725–8, built for the deal merchant John Hobbs, have his badge in the pediments. Architect probably *John Strahan*, who laid out Kingsmead Square, Bath, for Hobbs. No. 68, the Shakespeare Inn, has an open-well staircase between front and rear rooms and a full-width upper chamber at the front. No. 66 is of three bays, the centrepiece framed by giant pilasters under a segmental pediment; perhaps by *William Halfpenny* or *John Strahan*.

Opposite, THE GROVE leads E, retaining its unpolished dockside character. At its W end, a plain warehouse (now a pub), with small openings in Pennant walls, outmoded for *c.* 1878. The N side is now mainly offices. E of Grove Avenue the Postmodern rear of Nos. 33–35 Queen Square by *Alec French Partnership*, *c.* 1990. Further on, the former SAILORS' HOME (converted in 1874 from a warehouse). E again, the HOLE IN THE WALL pub, C17 or C18 and much modernized, with a porch-like projection, supposedly a look-out. Opposite, RIVER STATION restaurant, by *Inscape Architects*, 1998. Entrance and staircase in an angled glass projection. Steel balconies, curved roofs and tented canopies evoke a maritime quality. To its E is Bristol's earliest surviving TRANSIT SHED, *c.* 1865; iron-framed and originally open-sided, later timber-clad. Converted to another restaurant *c.* 1998.

2. Castle Park and Broadmead

Castle Park, NE of Bristol Bridge, was the site of Bristol Castle (C11–C17), then an area of late C17 houses and industry, and, by the late C19, Bristol's primary shopping district. It was heavily bombed 1940–1. To its N lies Broadmead, which developed around a C13 Dominican friary outside the town walls. From the C17 it was a centre of religious dissent. Despite the lighter bombing here, it was redeveloped in the 1950s to replace the lost shopping centre, a half-hearted and unpopular piece of planning.

CASTLE PARK. Here are the surviving elements of BRISTOL CASTLE, E of St Peter's church and N of a deep curve in the River Avon (dem. *c.* 1655). To the N, the KEEP foundations (*c.* 1120), originally probably *c.* 80 ft (24 metres) high and 80 ft square. Parts of the N and W walls, a well-shaft and a garderobe pit. Wall bases up to 16 ft (*c.* 5 metres) thick. To the s, C20 sunken walls mark the SALLYPORT, a defensive tunnel down to the moat. The C12 or C13 door jambs and tunnel are visible. To the E is a length of the castle WALL *c.* 6 ft 6 in. (2 metres) high, with two chamfered arrow loops, and fireplace openings from its incorporation in post-C17 structures. At the E end of the park, the CASTLE CHAMBERS, with glazed arches and brickwork fronting two rooms of uncertain function, related to the King's Hall (rebuilt 1239–42, dem.) which stood to the N. The s room, of *c.* 1225–50, possibly a porch, has fine moulded ribs on shafted columns, and stiff-leaf capitals (replicas). Perhaps part of the mid-C13 works at the castle overseen by the king's 'viewer', *William Mountsorrel*. The early C14 N room is simpler, with chamfered ribs. It may have been a separate entrance, later used as a chapel or antechapel.*

CASTLE PARK, site of the bombed Castle Street shopping district, retains the ruins of two churches, St Peter and St Mary le Port (pp. 266, 259). The park was fashioned in 1978 as a watered-down version of a scheme by *Sir Hugh Casson*, and enriched in 1992–3 with new landscape features and PUBLIC ART. NW of the church, Lines from Within, a tall abstract bronze by *Ann Christopher*. E of St Peter a hedged water garden by *Peter Randall-Page* and *Bristol City Council Landscape Architects*. To the N, *Rachel Fenner*'s Throne, of French limestone. SE towards the harbour wall a lively bronze drinking fountain by *Kate Malone*, with bas-reliefs. At the park's NE corner, a sculpture installation, Only Dead Fish Go with the Flow, by *Victor Moreton*, of white-glazed ceramic.

SE of Castle Park, QUEEN STREET runs s across the Castle Moat. w of the street is KING'S ORCHARD by *Leach Rhodes Walker*, 1982, refaced 2006; offices in orange brick, with housing to the

---

*Information from M.Litt. thesis by Michael Ponsford, 1979.

s. Opposite, its narrow end facing Queen Street, is the former SS PHILIP AND JACOB SCHOOL, of 1861, by *E. W. Godwin*, executant architect *J. A. Clark*. A long three-storey block of Pennant stone mainly with square-headed windows, and a plate-traceried arched window in the E gable. Built in drastically simplified form to bring it within budget; Godwin's elaborate Ruskinian design of 1860 had a tall Venetian Gothic tower. To the s in Passage Street, the former WESSEX WATER offices, by *BGP Group Architects*, 1978, a clean horizontal redbrick block raised on stilts. Behind, to its E, the 141-ft (43-metre) high former SHOT TOWER, by *E. N. Underwood & Partners*, engineers, 1968–9, a functional concrete structure treated as an aesthetic object, to great effect. Built for dropping molten lead into water to form perfectly spherical lead shot, a process invented at the predecessor shot tower on Redcliff Hill, of 1782. Distinctive angled top chamber over a Y-section shaft, the three arms originally carrying a staircase, a hoist and the dropping shaft. Remodelled 2005–6 by *WCW*; the top chamber intended as a boardroom or meeting space. On the N side is the Central Health Clinic (*see* Public Buildings, p. 281). Nearby to the E, SS PHILIP AND JACOB (p. 266), overshadowed to the N by the former ROGERS' BREWERY, Jacob Street, by *W. B. Gingell*, c. 1865, now offices. A tall rubble block with rock-faced rusticated basement, a much-altered fragment of the original design. Extended westwards as offices by *M. P. Kent Design Group*, 1980–2.

BROADMEAD, Bristol's post-war shopping centre, lies directly N of Castle Park. The plan finalized in 1946–7 by the City Architect *J. N. Meredith* provided for 145 shop units. It was built piecemeal, with many changes, 1950–60, with two streets (Broadmead and Merchant Street) crossing at a circular hub.

First, to the E, CABOT CIRCUS, the Broadmead extension built 2005–8 to a masterplan of 2003 by *Chapman Taylor*. Some 29 acres s and E of Newfoundland Street were cleared, and Bond Street was re-routed to enclose a new shopping area contiguous with the E end of Broadmead. Car park to the E by *Wilkinson Eyre*, linked by a bridge. Three covered streets converge on an internal hub or circus, surrounded by two levels of galleries, at some points not linked. Each shop façade is treated individually, with much cheap veneer of brick-like panels. The hub is covered by a shallow canopy of steel and glass (artist *Nayan Kulkarni*, structural engineers *Sinclair Knight Merz*). The key store, for HOUSE OF FRASER by *Stanton Williams*, is more tugboat than flagship: its E elevation, conceived as a dynamic cliff-like series of staggered verticals fractured by narrow glazing strips, was squared off and reduced to a disappointingly standard design in detailed planning. The Portland Roach stone-slab facing unfortunately reads from the roads like blank concrete. At plinth level is a textured bronze frieze by *Susanna Heron*, who also made the huge acid-etched windows. Further s, panels of sandblasted floral-patterned stone by *Timorous Beasties*, a design studio. The outer N face of

Cabot Circus has no shops: its long featureless wall was treated as a giant smorgasbord of builder's materials. Who said form follows function?

In the SE quadrant of the old Broadmead is Quakers' Friars, with the historic monastic buildings and Quaker meeting house at its centre, *see* p. 273. The formerly unlovely setting was revived as part of Cabot Circus in 2006–8 (*Alec French Partnership*). The backs of the 1950s ranges were rebuilt with shops facing into a square. Simple rectilinear façades and much stone facing, on the S side with an eighteen-storey tower of flats above, oval in plan and with a tilted roof slab. To the W in Merchant Street are the symmetrical, U-shaped MERCHANT TAILORS' ALMSHOUSES, dated 1701. Central shell-hooded entrance and, above, arms with richly modelled Baroque mantling. Interiors removed for the shopping centre to which it is now attached: THE GALLERIES, 1987–90, *Leslie Jones Architects*. This covers the SW quarter of Broadmead. Buff and orange brick with predictably thin Postmodern motifs, standard full-height glazed atrium. To the N is the central hub of Broadmead, with bland Bath stone quadrants by *J. N. Meredith*, built 1955–60. Then W into BROADMEAD (the street). On the N side is Wesley's New Room (p. 272). Then LOWER ARCADE by the brothers *James & Thomas Foster*, 1824–5, restored 1948. Its twin, Upper Arcade, was blitzed in 1940. The handsome façade is a scaled-down and adjusted version of Smirke's Old Council House (p. 274), with anthemion decoration on the entablature. Thirty-six two-storey shops arranged in nine bays marked by Ionic columns with a cast-iron frieze above, and narrow upper bows after the Burlington Arcade, London (1818). Glazed cast-iron roof with lion masks in the spandrels of the cross-arches.

On the S side is the former GREYHOUND INN. The C18 façade, with canted bays flanking a carriage arch, was 'preserved' as an entrance to The Galleries, *c.* 1987. To the W, No. 78, MARKS & SPENCER, by *James Monro & Son*, *c.* 1950, suggesting classical columns and entablature, represents the run-of-the-mill Broadmead designs. W again, at the junction with Union Street, the mildly Art Deco ODEON cinema, 1938, by *T. Cecil Howitt*, in cream and green faience. Full-height turret over a corner entrance, much altered, 1983–5. A little N, Broadmead Baptist Church (p. 272). N again, where Union Street meets The Horsefair, is Broadmead's original flagship store, built for Lewis's, by *Sir Percy Thomas & Son*, 1955–7. Six storeys of Portland stone on a triangular site. At the apex, a curved prow emphasized by a rectilinear grid with horizontal glazing strips divided by panels of stone. Roof terrace.

3. *Temple and Redcliffe*

Temple and Redcliffe lie in the deep curve S of the River Avon, and SE of the centre. Settlement was prompted by the presence of Bristol Bridge and the roads to Bath and Bedminster. In 1145 the E part was granted to the Knights Templar, who founded Temple Church and made the district their administrative centre in the West of England. The area was protected by a wall to the s from the C13, and the charter of 1373 brought it into the county of Bristol. The area is treated here in three walks which form a circuit, starting respectively at Bristol Bridge, St Mary Redcliffe and Redcliffe Bridge.

3a. Bristol Bridge to Temple Meads

The route SE of Bristol Bridge is now VICTORIA STREET, proposed in 1845 to Temple Meads railway terminus and completed c. 1872; the layout (not the building design) was by S. C. Fripp. BATH STREET is a short cul de sac running E from Victoria Street, across the former Courage Brewery site (previously George's), closed in the 1990s. Remodelled as mixed offices and apartments, by Atkins Walters Webster, in 2001–2. The 1930s KEG STORE in dark brick is on the l.; beyond, THE TOWER, c. 1925, tall and heavily classical. On the s side, a three-storey brick terrace by William Paty, 1789, later brewery offices.

Victoria Street was badly bombed and is now less than heartening. (For its SW side nearest Bristol Bridge, see Redcliff Street, p. 310.) The NE side after Bath Street, pleasingly varied Victorian Gothic, gives some idea of the original appearance; mostly façaded for offices or apartments in the 1990s. No. 2, the former TALBOT HOTEL (c. 1873), sub-Ruskinian commercial Gothic, with an arched entrance on the curve beneath a conical roof. Polychrome brick. The attic is almost an undetectable reinstatement, c. 1994. No. 8 may be by Henry Masters, who did much work here. No. 10, Platnauer Brothers' clockmakers' shop, a pilastered grid of load-bearing masonry and plate glass. No. 16, by J. Michelen Rogers, 1871, is brick and patterned terracotta, with big arched first-floor window, and a florid dormer.

Opposite on the SW side, Nos. 25–31, four gabled houses of 1673–5.* Three storeys with gabled attics, jettied ground floors and bay windows. Running s here, ST THOMAS STREET, an important medieval thoroughfare. On the r. is the former WOOL HALL (1828, R. S. Pope). Built as a market hall and warehouse, on spare classical lines. Tall façade with vermiculated plinth, narrow pedimented centre, windows grouped vertically in arched recesses. A forerunner of Pope's Bush House (see p. 303). The robust Pennant masonry feels very Victorian. Returning to Victoria Street, shortly another detour NE via Counterslip to the TRAMWAYS ELECTRICITY GENERATING STATION, 1899, an early work by W. Curtis Green. A hybrid of Neoclassical and Baroque elements, in red brick and Bath stone. Monumental SE façade, tall and narrow with a lunette

---

*The painted date comes from a deed of 1456 referring to shops here.

behind an Ionic columned screen. Venetian motifs below and in the returns. The NE side rises almost sheer from the water. Back on VICTORIA STREET, next to the C19 Gothic gateway to Temple Church (p. 270) is No. 58, by *W. V. Gough*, *c.* 1890s, for Temple vestry. Red brick with arcaded windows and a small Flemish pediment. Then the KING'S HEAD, C17 with a Late Georgian refronting and rare pub interior of *c.* 1865. To the SE is the SHAKESPEARE INN, with big oversailing gable, ground-floor jetty, and pent roofs at each floor. The date 1636, painted, unverified but quite plausible. Opposite, mediocre post-war offices. At the SE end, facing Temple Way roundabout is the former LONDON LIFE BUILDING, by *John Wells-Thorpe*, 1982. Its staggered masses achieve a pleasing three-dimensional quality. Five well-composed red brick storeys, screened by slim paired supports of contrasting aggregate. S of the roundabout between Redcliffe Way and Temple Meads Station, two Victorian hotels: the GROSVENOR HOTEL (1875, *S. C. Fripp*), high and four-square with coarse Flemish-looking attics; and to the SE the GEORGE RAILWAY HOTEL (*c.* 1866) with a statue of Queen Victoria presiding over the entrance.

3b. *Around St Mary Redcliffe*

Redcliffe sits upon a red sandstone bluff that gives the district its name. Sited outside the medieval town is Bristol's most famous church, St Mary Redcliffe (p. 259), with the busy circuit road nearby. S and W of the church is much good C18–C20 domestic architecture.

COLSTON PARADE, S of the churchyard, is a pleasant C18–C19 row. From the W, No. 12 (*c.* 1772), with a W front of brick, and on the N symmetrical stucco. FRY'S HOUSE OF MERCY, a small Gothic Revival almshouse of 1784, has Y-traceried windows symmetrical about the entrance. Interiors rebuilt. Nos. 1–5, *c.* 1760, possibly by *T. Paty*, have banded rusticated ground floors and Gibbsian blocked door surrounds, without the usual stepped voussoirs. At the E end, the SHIP INN, C17 or C18, refronted *c.* 1870. Behind is Redcliffe Methodist Church (p. 273). To the S, REDCLIFF HILL FLATS (*City Architect's Department*, 1955–64). Conceived by *J. N. Meredith*, later phases detailed under *A. H. Clarke*. Mainly of three- to five-storey blocks, with some up to thirteen storeys. In the centre of Somerset Square is a strange confection, a CONDUIT HEAD erected in 1849, from the destroyed Georgian square of the same name.

To the E along Prewett Street (N side) the stump of a brick-built GLASS CONE, probably *c.* 1780, truncated 1936. Now a restaurant. Glass and pottery were major C18 and C19 industries here. Return W to REDCLIFF HILL, cleared for 1960s road plans. On the W side is PHOENIX ASSURANCE by *Whicheloe Macfarlane Partnership*, 1974, long, bulky and relentlessly horizontal. S of Guinea Street is WARING HOUSE, 1958–60, the biggest and best of the Redcliff Hill flats (*see* above). The scalloped roof-line and barrel-vaulted canopy on the s side neatly echo the revetments to the river below.

To the NW, Nos. 10–12 GUINEA STREET of 1718 for Edmund Saunders, a slave trader, merchant and churchwarden at St Mary Redcliffe. Now divided into three. No. 10 has the original entrance, with a mid-C18 Gothick door, and an ogee gable, perhaps slightly later. Wavy arrises to the upper windows, and twelve grotesque window keystones, the best such group in the city. At No. 12, a good original staircase, and a fine stucco ceiling, with a fruity frame and delightful hunting scenes. A few yards N in ALFRED PLACE, two infill houses, designed by architect-artist partnerships for themselves. No. 2, by *Jonathan Mosley & Sophie Warren*, 2002. A severe white-rendered box over black timber boarding. No. 4 is by *Mike & Sandie Macrae*, 2001; an energy-efficient design, with lime-rendered upper parts and wave-like roofs.

Returning to Guinea Street, Nos. 18–19 may be part of Saunders's development, *c.* 1718. Everything beyond occupied by Bristol General Hospital, *see* p. 281. Where Guinea Street meets Bathurst Basin, to the N is the OSTRICH INN, perhaps mid-C18, updated *c.* 1830 with window pediments and margin glazing. It backs onto a rocky outcrop with tunnels known as Redcliffe Caves, probably the result of excavating sand for glass-making, and certainly not the slave dungeons of myth. Steps bring us up on to REDCLIFFE PARADE, two terraces with wide views N across the Floating Harbour and city. The w terrace and the first two houses E of Jubilee Place are of *c.* 1768–71; continued E *c.* 1800. Return E to Redcliff Hill and the end of this walk.

3c. *Redcliffe Bridge to Bristol Bridge*

N of St Mary Redcliffe, REDCLIFFE WAY was driven w through to Queen Square in 1939. From the Bascule Bridge (p. 284) the mills and warehouses on Redcliff Backs rise sheer from the harbour. The present line of Redcliff Backs was under water until the C14. On the bridge's NE flank, CUSTOM HOUSE, apartments by *Architecture & Planning Group*, 2001, trumpet the reinvention of Bristol harbour as another London docklands. Seven storeys with a stack of near-circular balconies cantilevered from the corner. Next door to the N is the Western Counties Agricultural Association (WCA) WAREHOUSE, by *W. H. Brown* of Leeds, 1909. A blend of gruff industrial and Edwardian classicism, and an early Bristol use of a reinforced concrete frame with brick cladding, with cantilevered oriels originally housing hoists. Converted to housing in 1997 by *Architecton*. E of the Custom House is the former WCA offices by *W. V. Gough*, red and yellow brick, old-fashioned for 1896–7.

From Redcliff Street, PORTWALL LANE runs E, formerly directly inside the C13 Port Wall. On the N side, some good late C19 WAREHOUSES of orange Cattybrook brick. No. 3, probably by *W. B. Gingell c.* 1880, with ground-floor segment-headed windows between square piers, and an arched corbel table. No. 4 (*Alec French Partnership, c.* 1990), the OPEN UNIVERSITY office, is a well-mannered addition. Nearby on Phippen Street (N) is CHATTERTON'S HOUSE of 1749, the only remainder of the small vernacular buildings here. Built by St Thomas parish for its schoolmaster, it was the birthplace in 1752 of the poet Thomas Chatterton. Against its S side is the pedimented façade of the SCHOOL HOUSE, relocated from nearby in 1939. Ashlar walls with simple classical motifs, somewhat old-fashioned for the apparent date of 1779.

Return E to REDCLIFF STREET, where on the E side is No. 60, THE ATRIUM, a tobacco factory by *Henry Crisp* and *H.C.M. Hirst*, 1883. An eclectic jumble of round arcades, classical cornices and pediments. Inside, a central top-glazed iron atrium. Converted to apartments. A few yards on (W side) is a medieval WALL with two blind arches inserted in earlier fabric, and a C15 ogee-arched stoup or wash-basin; a fragment of the house of William Canynges the Younger (1402–74), ship-owner, mayor of Bristol and benefactor of St Mary Redcliffe. The house was demolished 1937.*

N along Redcliff Street, where most of the W side is offices and flats, 1980s or later. The design concepts were negotiated 1970–7. At Ferry Street (W side), two brick towers of BUCHANAN'S WHARF, 1884, a granary and flour mill, converted to apartments 1988. REDCLIFF QUAY to the N is by *Alec French Partnership*, 1980–91. Buff brick over a limestone plinth with brown marble banding. On the long harbour façade, a confusion of metal balconies and brises-soleil. The PIAZZA to the N is dominated by a sculptural ceramic OBELISK, Exploration, 1991, by *Philippa Threlfall & Kennedy Collings*. To its N, Discovery House, part of the Redcliff Quay development, then BULL WHARF and BRISTOL BRIDGE HOUSE, both by *Angus Meek/R. Diplock Associates*, 1985. The harbour face of Bristol Bridge House is of carefully modelled buff brick alternating with curtain walling. Adjoining Bristol Bridge, NUMBER ONE VICTORIA STREET, by *Prudential Architects*, 1979–82. In harsh orange brick with angular projections, and giving the uncomfortable illusion that the lead mansards are dripping down like molten wax.

Opposite is the ROBINSON BUILDING, Bristol's first true tower block, of 1960–3, by *Group Architects DRG*. A custom-built post-war office block of such quality is a rarity outside London, although it has been criticized for its impact on distant views and on its neighbours. A square fifteen-storey tower of extreme elegance and simplicity on columns, with glazed foyer behind, and stilted podium-like conference and training facilities to the S. Crisp structural mullions and pre-cast wall panels finished with white marble aggregate. Glazing set behind the openings creates shadow and depth. The segment-headed windows are

---

*Behind on Redcliff Backs is a C15 rubble wall with two blocked windows, now grafted onto GUILD COURT, C20 flats; part of the boundary of Canynges's House.

the first deliberate echo of the Victorian warehouse style in post-war Bristol.*

4. Park Street and Brandon Hill

An anti-clockwise circuit, from College Green. Brandon Hill, topped by the landmark of Cabot Tower, is the highest point in central Bristol.

PARK STREET, climbing NW towards Clifton, was proposed in 1740 and laid out in 1758 by *George Tully*; building commenced in 1761, by *Thomas* and *James Paty Jun.* among others. At its bottom end, a cast-iron VIADUCT by *R. S. Pope*, 1870–1, crosses Frogmore Street. On the NE side, Nos. 8–18, Italianate stuccoed shops by *W. H. Hawtin*, 1867 and 1872. Opposite, Nos. 7–11 by *Henry Masters*, 1871, with a repetitive froth of carving around the windows. Extended and the interiors remodelled in 1936–8 by *W. H. Watkins*, for Avery's wine merchants, using fittings designed by the architect *Harold Peto*, c. 1906, from the Cunard liner RMS *Mauretania*. The ground-floor lounge bar was the *Mauretania*'s library, with mahogany panelling and a stained-glass dome; above Frogmore Street the gilded first-class Grand Salon, in a luscious C18 French style. Mauretania logo (1938) on the SE façade, Bristol's first 'moving' neon sign.

At the junction with St George's Road is the former BRISTOL PHILOSOPHICAL AND LITERARY INSTITUTION (1821–3), an early work by *C. R. Cockerell*. The Institution was founded in 1817, and was absorbed into the Bristol Museum and Library (*see* p. 327) in 1871, when this building became the Freemasons' Hall. At the corner is a circular portico, with a Corinthian order from the Temple of Apollo at Bassae in Greece, which Cockerell excavated in 1811. The portico relates poorly to the weaker returns, where insistent horizontal mouldings accentuate the sloping site (Cockerell noted this fault). Beneath the portico, a fine bas-relief by *E. H. Baily*: Bristol introduced to the Arts, Sciences and Literature. Bombed in 1940 and restored 1957–8, with rather bland interiors.

Beyond, the C18 HOUSES begin. Park Street was perhaps Bristol's first uniformly stepped terrace, with pilasters clasped by the cornices each side, rather than ramped parapets as at Bath. They have plain Bath stone fronts, three windows wide. About one third are post-war replicas, and most have unattractive C20 shopfronts. Either side of Great George Street, matching houses of c. 1762, of brick and with pedimented returns, attributed to *Thomas Paty*. No. 47 (s side) has an ornate arched shopfront of c. 1865–70.

GREAT GEORGE STREET, off Park Street to the l., climbs SW onto Brandon Hill. On the SE side are several ashlar-fronted three- and five-bay detached houses (Nos. 3, 7, 23–27) by *William Paty*, 1788–91, in his spare and elegant Neoclassical

* Information from Colin Beales and Elain Harwood.

manner, with rusticated ground floors and pilastered door-cases. Plans and details varied according to the clients' wishes. No. 7, now the GEORGIAN HOUSE MUSEUM, was built for John Pinney, a sugar planter on Nevis, and given to the city in 1938. Remarkably complete interiors, with study and powder room at the front, and rear reception rooms with restrained plasterwork and marble chimneypieces. Lateral stone staircase with geometric wrought-iron balustrade, and an unusual stone-lined plunge bath in the basement. On the NW side is ROYAL COLONNADE, described as recently completed in 1828. Probably by *R. S. Pope*, cf. e.g. his Brunel House (p. 314). Projecting ends frame a recessed ground-floor colonnade of an ill-advised 1:2:2:1:1:2:2:1 rhythm. At the top of the hill, No. 31 Great George Street, by *Alec French Partnership*, 1987–90; good Postmodern offices of red brick and Bath stone, in overlapping terraced blocks. Regency references in the eaves and a bowed oriel on the SW.

The SW end of Great George Street opens onto BRANDON HILL, a public park. The most visible remains of Bristol's CIVIL WAR DEFENCES are here, constructed in 1642–3 by the Cromwellian forces as part of a northern defensive line which ran to the Royal Fort and on to Kingsdown; they are among the most extensive and best-preserved of the period in England. First, on the lower S slopes, the overgrown WATER FORT, earthworks that defended the harbour approaches. From here, a linear EARTHWORK runs almost due N up the hill, with a spur and outwork halfway up. At the summit, a long angular BASTION of 1643–5, with well-preserved stone walls inside a bank and ditch. A circular fort here was demolished for CABOT TOWER, by *W. V. Gough*, 1896–8, commemorating John Cabot's voyage in 1497 from Bristol to Newfoundland. A tall pink sandstone tower with limestone dressings. Diagonal buttresses rise sheer without set-offs (giving rather the impression of a chamfered recessed panel to each wall); bulging balconies under Gothic gables, then a firm parapet balcony with corner pinnacles and flying buttresses supporting a strange octagonal cap, with a winged figure of Commerce surmounting a globe. Despite its Gothic enrichments, it defies stylistic labels; the distant profile is distinctive and successful.

Leaving the park, first CHARLOTTE STREET, laid out in the late 1780s by *Thomas & William Paty*, along with parts of Park Street and Berkeley Square. It has the characteristics already seen in their Great George Street work, but here terraced rather than as detached villas. This type of elevation became standard for Bristol, even where other architects were involved. Doric doorcases of a pattern-book design first used a few years earlier (*see* Rodney Place, Clifton, p. 339), some good cast-iron tented balconies of c. 1830, and raised pavements. On the SE side, Nos. 19 and 20, two villas of the 1820s. Over the ground-floor windows, semicircular panels with Adamesque radial fluting. Charlotte Street joins the upper part of Park Street.

BERKELEY SQUARE is tucked away to the SW at the top of Park Street. Planned in 1787, completed *c*. 1800, probably by *William Paty* (Thomas, his father, died in 1789). The SE side, originally left open, now has a soulless post-war University building in pastiche Georgian. Even without this, the square would be vexing. A trapezoid plan (no two sides equal or parallel) with sloping terraces on all sides, making any attempted symmetry hopeless. Nos. 9–10 has an Edwardian Baroque refacing by *John Bevan the Younger*, 1912. No. 15, BERKELEY SQUARE HOTEL, largely rebuilt in replica after war damage, makes a weak centrepiece to the NW side. In the central gardens, the re-erected upper parts of *John Norton's* near-replica of the medieval HIGH CROSS (1851) on College Green. At the square's N angle, on the l. is BERKELEY CRESCENT, built 1791–*c*. 1800 and planned with Berkeley Square. A tight curve of six houses on a high terrace pavement. Like the backs of Berkeley Square, it is of unfashionable brick. We emerge from here on to QUEEN'S ROAD. To the r., the Museum and Art Gallery, and, in front, Brown's Restaurant (p. 327). To the l. of Brown's, Queen's Road runs into the NE side of THE TRIANGLE, laid out in the early 1850s with grandiose metropolitan shops, resolving an awkward no-man's-land at the approach to Clifton. On the r. side, the Italianate ROYAL PROMENADE (1859, *Foster & Wood*), palatial in scale if repetitious; designed after John Marmont's Royal Promenade, Clifton (*see* p. 340). Much altered.

In Triangle West is CLIFTON HEIGHTS, Bristol's second tower block, 1962–5, by *Raymond Moxley*. Three-storey colonnaded podium; cleanly articulated twelve-storey tower above. A mixed scheme of shopping, restaurant, offices and flats, unusual for the early 1960s, and controversial for its proximity to C18 Clifton. Descending SW towards Jacob's Wells Road, a high revetment marks Upper Berkeley Place, with more *Paty* stepped terracing, *c*. 1790. Below in Berkeley Place is HILL'S ALMSHOUSE, 1866–7, by *Charles Hansom*. A high E-plan façade, Tudor Gothic, oriels, buttressing, gables and chimneys. Unusual rear elevation, with nine-bay cast-iron verandas on two storeys (now glazed in), with Gothic tracery. Low chapel, S.

Here begins JACOB'S WELLS ROAD, running S down a gully to the harbour. N of the junction of Constitution Hill is JACOB'S WELL, rediscovered in 1987. Inside an C18 or C19 stone structure, a warm spring flows from an opening in the wall. On a lintel above, a fragment of Hebrew script, interpreted as evidence of use for ritual washing of bodies prior to burial in a Jewish cemetery nearby on Brandon Hill. The lintel probably pre-dates 1142, when the spring became the property of St Augustine's Abbey. Almost opposite, high on the side of Brandon Hill, a plain, domestic-looking former POLICE STATION of 1836. Lower down, replacing *Elijah Hoole's* Artisan Dwellings of 1875, BRANDON HOUSE (1959) by *A. H. Clarke*,

City Architect; ten-storey slab-block housing. Beyond is the former HOTWELLS BATHS (designed 1881, opened 1887) by the City Surveyor *Josiah Thomas*; now a dance studio. Jolly red brick and yellow terracotta, with Flemish, Loire and Queen Anne elements.

From the roundabout with Hotwell Road, ST GEORGE'S ROAD leads E, then branches NE down into the hollow behind the Council House. Behind, c. 100 yds up the short hill called Brandon Steep, BRANDON COTTAGE of c. 1760–80, with ogee Gothick trim to the openings, perhaps by *Thomas Paty*. Back on St George's Road is BRUNEL HOUSE, by *R. S. Pope*, perhaps with *Isambard Kingdom Brunel*, 1837–9; façaded for offices by *Alec French Partnership*, 1984. Built as the Royal Western Hotel, part of Brunel's vision for an integrated route from London to New York: via the Great Western Railway to Bristol, crossing the Atlantic on the S.S. *Great Western* after staying overnight here. The scheme never materialized and the hotel became a Turkish bath in 1855. The impressive four-storey Greek Revival façade follows Jearrad's Queen's Hotel, Cheltenham, as one of England's earliest hotels to enjoy full architectural treatment. Inset from the ends, single-bay projections with high round arches, embracing a giant Ionic colonnade of eleven bays. Of the two-storey upper parts, the centre and projecting ends are treated as giant attached porticos, of a Corinthian order favoured by Pope, from the Lysicratic Monument at Athens. The two arched carriage entrances with radiating rustication were seemingly Brunel's idea. The r. carriage arch now leads to an open space behind, framed by gaunt ruined walls of a C19 building. In the centre, a bronze resin SCULPTURE, Horse and Man (*Stephen Joyce*, 1984).

5. Canon's Marsh

CANON'S MARSH, also called HARBOURSIDE, is an elongated D-shaped area N of the Floating Harbour and S of Brandon Hill. Originally water meadows; by the C18 shipyards and rope-walks had encroached. In the C19 it housed gas-works, timber and stone yards and railway sidings. With the closure of the city docks in 1973, it became derelict. In the 1990s, huge concrete tobacco warehouses at the E end gave way to prominent offices and the At-Bristol Millennium project. After decades of controversy, the W end was redeveloped c. 2004–10.

We begin at the S end of The Centre, where the cascade falls to the harbour (*see* p. 288). W of St Augustine's Reach are utilitarian transit sheds, converted to bars and restaurants. The first to be treated was the WATERSHED MEDIA CENTRE at the N end, iron-framed and originally with sliding doors to the quayside; 1894, by *Edward Gabriel*, converted by *JT Group Ltd*, 1980–1. Loire Renaissance N gable-end. S to Pero's Bridge (p. 284) and then W into ANCHOR SQUARE, of c. 1998–2000, part of a redevelopment scheme carried out to a masterplan by *Concept Planning Group*. It successfully interleaves buildings with high-quality public spaces. In the square, an alarming bronze rhinoceros beetle on a low plinth, by *Nicola Hicks*, 2000. On the N is ROWE'S LEADWORKS (*c.* 1886), straightforward industrial, of stone with a tall brick chimney. Converted to a restaurant. Flanking the square is the AT-BRISTOL complex, consisting originally of a nature exploratory, planetarium, cinema etc. Adjoining the leadworks, the BLUE REEF AQUARIUM and IMAX cinema of the complex, by *Michael Hopkins & Partners* (engineers *Buro Happold*). The wedge-shaped site is well exploited: at the apex, a blank brick drum of the Imax, from which the structure radiates in descending layers. A sweeping tent-like canopy on steel masts covers the botanic garden. Hopkins's interior spaces are excellent: a dark curving tunnel of sprayed concrete emerging into the high light-filled and brick-lined curve of the cinema foyer.

The EXPLORE building by *Wilkinson Eyre* (*Ove Arup & Partners*, structural engineers) was created from a goods shed of 1904 by *W. Armstrong*, engineer to the GWR, and *P. E. Culverhouse*. An early example of *Hennebique* reinforced-concrete construction. Railway sidings ran through an arcaded ground floor of surprisingly modern-looking elliptical arches, with a single-storey warehouse above. To the S, the mirror-finished metal globe of the PLANETARIUM. The glass N wall is pleasingly ambiguous at the NE corner, becoming a free-standing external screen with an opening to walk through. Inside, an elliptical beech-clad pod houses toilets and staircase. Outside the N front is Small Worlds, a cone SCULPTURE in fibre and coloured cement blocks by *Simon Thomas*.

S of Explore is MILLENNIUM SQUARE, by *Concept Planning Group*, framed E and W by striking metal-capped ventilation shafts to an underground car park by *Alec French Partnership*. At the NE corner, *William Pye*'s WATER SCULPTURE Aquarena, with arcs of mirror-polished steel, and fountains on stepped terraces. To the W, STATUES: Cary Grant by *Graham Ibbeson*, 2001; William Tyndale and Thomas Chatterton, both by *Lawrence Holofcener*, 2000.

To the S are offices for LLOYDS BANK (now Lloyds TSB), by *Arup Associates*, 1988–90; a broad crescent in pale limestone, enclosing an amphitheatre towards the water, but sitting uncomfortably with the later buildings behind. The design shuns the carefully cultured 1980s dockside aesthetic in favour of Beaux-Arts planning and civic gestures (cf. Arups' unexecuted scheme for Paternoster Square, London). Despite their Modernist principles here Arups deployed Postmodern classical references. From a distance, the giant paired columns appear like a free-standing screen that supports nothing. A curving top-lit 'street' enables a very deep plan. To the W is a rotunda-form staff restaurant completed 1994, linked by a low entrance pavilion.

The most controversial phase of the REDEVELOPMENT begins to the W. Beset since 1981 by abortive schemes, contention and planning inquiries, a masterplan by *Edward Cullinan Architects* was built after public consultation, *c.* 2004–10. The open spaces here are more generous than those of many equivalent schemes. Close to the harbour wall, the most successful element, glass-walled offices for CLERICAL MEDICAL, 2004–6 by *Aukett Fitzroy Robinson*, with brises-soleil through three storeys. Then the site is cut through by Cathedral Walk, allowing a tightly framed view of the Cathedral from the harbour. To the W is THE CRESCENT, a large curving block of flats (*c.* 2007–8), littered with balconies and canted rooftop excrescences. The visual incoherence of the whole scheme prompted the widely reported comment that 'Some bloke has dropped some Lego down by the harbour.'

At the E end of Canon's Marsh is the derelict remains of GAS WORKS established in 1823. It includes two rock-faced Pennant Stone retort houses with round-arched openings and gable oculi, and an engine house with chimney, all probably *c.* 1840. Important survivors of the Bristol Byzantine style, they are to be incorporated in the final phase of redevelopment. Also preserved is the powerful Victorian streetscape of Gasferry Road, cobbled and narrow between unrelenting high walls, with distinctively Bristolian cast-iron kerbs.

At the W apex of Canon's Marsh is CAPRICORN QUAY, successful flats by *Alec French Partnership*, 1998–2002, between the water and the line of Hotwell Road. Two sweeping curved blocks, divided by a sunken garden on the footprint of Limekiln Dock (extant 1626–1903). Returning E along Anchor Road are speculative offices (S side), built as part of the Canon's Marsh scheme, e.g. Nos. 1 and 2, College Square, with fully glazed façades, by *Stride Treglown*, 2006 onwards.

INNER SUBURBS

The inner suburbs form a ring around the city centre, with growth weighted towards the N and E, where Hotwells, Clifton and Kingsdown were established by the C18. To the S and W, the River Avon and the man-made channel known as the New Cut form the boundary with the outer suburbs. Three sub-sections: N and NW of the centre; E of centre, and S of centre (*see* map pp. 360–1).

NORTH AND NORTH-WEST:
HOTWELLS, CLIFTON AND KINGSDOWN

Places of worship

Cathedral (R.C.)

CLIFTON CATHEDRAL OF ST PETER AND ST PAUL (R.C.), Pembroke Road. Commissioned in 1965 from *R. Weeks, F. S. Jennett* and *A. Poremba* of the *Percy Thomas Partnership*; structural engineer *Frank Newby* (*Felix Samuely & Partners*), replacing the Pro-Cathedral in Park Place (*see* p. 321). It was the world's first cathedral designed in response to the Second Vatican Council's emphasis on liturgical essentials. The primary requirement was for a congregation of nine hundred, grouped as closely as possible around the altar during mass. The major elements were established in three months and were executed essentially unchanged, in 1970–3. Building was constrained by a four-acre suburban site and a small budget (*c.* £600,000), despite which the architects and craftsmen produced a church of superlative quality. It is three-dimensionally complex, yet the spatial arrangement is immediately clear, attaining a mystic simplicity through careful use of humble materials and masterly manipulation of light.

Set amidst Victorian villas, the cathedral has a surprising piquancy, yet it does no violence to its neighbours. The entrances from Clifton Park and Pembroke Road are reached via stepped bridges, with an additional processional entrance at the liturgical w. Exterior cladding is pre-cast concrete panels of pink Aberdeen granite aggregate, with contrasting white concrete piers. Concentric stages of walling rise to a steep double-pyramid roof. A crowning cross sits within the slim tripartite spire of bevelled fins, 167 ft (51 metres) high, with two bells from the former Pro-Cathedral. Presbytery to the N. *p. 318*
    The plan is an irregular hexagon subdivided into varied polygons, on a controlling module for all dimensions of an 18-in. (46-cm.) equilateral triangle. Exposed concrete walls inside, cast *in situ* with Russian redwood formwork, the crisp textures 116 dramatized by concealed natural lighting. The narthex leads to the BLESSED SACRAMENT CHAPEL, and a BAPTISTERY

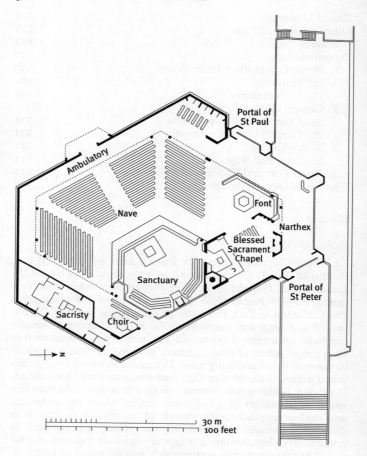

Bristol, Clifton Cathedral.
Plan

beneath deep galleries. LADY CHAPEL at the NW angle. There
is a palpable sense of emergence as one enters the nave – a
broad and simple space beneath a complex roof, with timber
acoustic cones. Seats in fan form, so that no one is over 50 ft
(15 metres) from the sanctuary steps: a more succinct plan
than at Liverpool, where seating 'in the round' places some of
the congregation behind the celebrant. The structure is based
on three concentric hexagons tied together with radiating
beams: the outer walls; the nave walls, supported on piers that
define a low ambulatory; and an inner ring suspended over the
sanctuary. This supports a funnel-like lantern which floods the
sanctuary with concealed light and gives an impression of ever-
increasing height.

FITTINGS. Portland stone ALTAR by *Ronald Weeks*, who also designed the LECTERN. – FONT by *Simon Verity*: of Portland stone with sculpted doves and fish, and a big Purbeck stone bowl, standing in a shallow pool lined with black stone. – ORGAN by *Rieger* of Austria. STATIONS OF THE CROSS in low-relief cast concrete by *William Mitchell*, each worked in an hour and a half. Their raw brutality jars with the setting.* – SCREEN to the Blessed Sacrament Chapel by *Brother Patrick* of Prinknash Abbey. – TABERNACLE of stainless steel, by *John Alder* (Blessed Sacrament Chapel). – Bronze MADONNA in the Lady Chapel by *Terry Jones*. – STAINED GLASS. Pentecost and Jubilation, by *Henry Haig*. Two colourful full-height panels of *dalle-de-verre* lighting the narthex.

Church of England

ALL SAINTS, Pembroke Road, Clifton. 1962–7 by *Robert Potter*. Designed on Liturgical Movement principles, emphasizing congregational participation, within a strong High Anglican tradition. It replaced *Street*'s church (designed 1863, consecrated 1868, completed 1872), blitzed in 1940; a mature work of a serious and self-confident architect rarely satisfied with the copying of old motifs and elements. After *W. H. Randoll Blacking*'s restoration plan of 1947 foundered, his partner Robert Potter (of *Potter & Hare*) demolished most of the ruins, incorporating in his new design the surviving tower, sacristy and narthex. The stump of Street's tower is topped by a slim timber spire clad in aluminium. To its N is the nave, with canted E and W ends and vertical glazing strips under folded roofs. Rubblestone ancillary buildings to the S with slit windows. The entrance through the tower leads to a light-filled glazed cloister, then into the subdued light of the nave with its richly coloured windows. Coffered concrete roofs based on a massive X-beam. S gallery against a fully glazed wall of blue. Angled sanctuary. N chapel, designed by *G. F. Bodley* as a narthex, 1907, recast by *Potter*. At the SE of the complex is a vaulted sacristy by *F. C. Eden*, 1922–3, with fine panelling. 115

FITTINGS. Incongruous Byzantine CIBORIUM by *Blacking*, 1952, over the altar slab. – Engraved slate PISCINA by *John Skelton*. – Drum-shaped FONT. – STAINED GLASS. W windows by *John Piper*, powerful and primitive, representing the River of Life and the Tree of Life, of translucent fibreglass panels built up *in situ*. N chapel, three N windows (1909), and a weak E window by *Christopher Webb*, 1967, with donor portrait.

CHRIST CHURCH, Christchurch Green, Clifton. By *Charles Dyer*, 1841–4; an early Bristol manifestation of movement towards archaeological Gothic. A large and prosperous, unified E.E. design, with a very tall spire, the broaches masked by pinnacles. Further work by *Ewan Christian* in 1857, the steeple added 1859 by *John Norton*, subtly suggesting a transition to 91

---

* *Mitchell*'s DOORS were replaced in glass, 1995.

C13 Geometric Dec. Aisles by *W. Bassett-Smith*, 1884–5. In places the details are coarse. Disappointingly mundane interiors, where the various building phases are more obvious. W gallery on timber-clad cast-iron columns, and a broad polygonal apse behind odd triple chancel arches like a screen. Its chilly Anglicanism was crystallized in John Betjeman's scathing poem 'Bristol and Clifton': 'Our only ritual here is with the plate'.

HOLY TRINITY, Hotwell Road. By *C. R. Cockerell*, 1829–30. The last classical Anglican church built in Bristol. Projecting central entrance on the S side, in a big arched recess with half-domed coffered head, a reference to Alberti's S. Andrea, Mantua. Framing this are broad Doric pilasters, with a sculpture of the Holy Spirit as a dove in the open pediment above. The central belfry over the pediment is barely related to the composition below. The flanks have two big round-arched windows on each side. Cockerell's nave was at right angles to the entrance axis, forming a cross plan around a shallow dome (cf. Hawksmoor's London churches); all destroyed by bombing. *Tom Burrough*'s plain refurbishment, 1955–8, made no attempt at restoration, but echoed the old design with a big elliptical dome.

ST JOHN THE EVANGELIST, Whiteladies Road, Clifton. By *S. J. Hicks*, 1841. Unarchaeological Perp. Aisleless nave, long three-light windows with transoms and four-centred heads. Enlarged cruciform E end by *S. B. Gabriel*, 1864. The ritual W (N) front has open traceried turrets after Rickman & Hutchinson's Holy Trinity, St Philip's, sitting awkwardly on short towers which have pairs of thin lancets. Subdivided as auction rooms, 1990.

ST MATTHEW, Cotham Side, Kingsdown. 1833–5 by *Thomas Rickman*. Mildly Perp. Aisles with tall regular windows with three lights and four-centred heads. Four-stage W tower; Rickman was archaeologically minded enough to add a Bristol spirelet. At the nave E end, chimneys disguised as turrets with big quatrefoiled caps. Four-centred arcades on square-sectioned piers with moulded angles, with galleries set behind. High clerestory with an ogee-headed niche on a big corbel between each bay. Interior divided at gallery level in 1989; hall beneath, church above. – ORGAN at the W end, with a Gothic case by *John Smith Sen.*, 1840. – STAINED GLASS. E window, 1927, by *Powell & Sons*. In the hall, four by *Arnold Robinson*, 1931–45.

ST MICHAEL ON THE MOUNT WITHOUT (former), St Michael's Hill. A C15 church for a growing mercantile suburb N of the city. Perp W tower of four stages, described by William Worcestre as 'new built' in 1480, with diagonal buttresses and SE stair-turret with spirelet. The body was rebuilt in 1775–7 by *Thomas Paty* in Georgian Gothic. Five-bay Pennant rubble nave with poverty-stricken mouldings. Aisles with Y-traceried windows, short chancel. E window of three lights with intersecting tracery. Oddly, the interiors are classical: arcades of vaguely Doric columns with fluted necks, supporting flat beams and a plaster tunnel-vault (post-war, after bomb damage). The aisles have flat ceilings. – FITTINGS. Late Victorian. – SWORD REST probably dating partly from 1683. – MONUMENTS. Joseph Percivall †1764, three graceful Neoclassical female figures against an obelisk, the central figure holding an oval portrait medallion. Signed *J. Walsh*, London. – Mary Stretton †1794, by *W. Paty*; the usual female leaning on an urn.

ST PAUL, St Paul's Road, Clifton. Tower and broach spire by *Manners & Gill* of Bath, 1853, the rest rebuilt after a fire by *Charles Hansom*, 1868; porch, 1905. Unexciting Pennant stone exterior. Nave with low pink sandstone arcade and sexfoil clerestory, wide aisles and tall narrow chancel, all under tie-beam roofs. – Impressive Perp timber REREDOS, 1903, with three *opus sectile* panels by *Powell & Sons*. In the aisles, ten more panels, all by *Powells*, of 1905–27. – Exceptionally complete STAINED GLASS sequence by *Hardman & Co.*, the E window probably of 1868, the rest 1871–87.

Other denominations

PRO-CATHEDRAL (R.C.), Park Place, Clifton. The saddest of Bristol's failed architectural visions. Begun in 1834 by Peter Baines, Vicar Apostolic of the Western District as a cathedral-in-waiting against the day when Catholic bishoprics were instituted. The architect, *Henry Goodridge* of Bath, envisaged a big Corinthian basilica, intended to have a giant portico projecting towards Park Place, attached giant columns along the windowless sides, shallow transepts and, over the crossing, a strange tempietto-like circular lantern. The steep quarried hillside subsided, funds ran out, and the project foundered. In 1846–8 *Charles Hansom* completed it as a functioning if aesthetically displeasing church. A light timber roof caps columns left without capitals, supported within by round wooden arches and complex bracing. W narthex, hall and N porch added by *Hansom* from 1876, in Lombardic Romanesque. It never became a cathedral. Unused since the R.C. Cathedral opened in 1973 (*see* p. 317). Proposed for conversion to flats, 2006; the latest of many such schemes.

UNITARIAN CHURCH (former), Oakfield Road, Clifton. By *Popes & Bindon*, 1864. Of orangey ragstone quarried on Durdham Down. Quite Anglican in appearance. Big saddleback tower, long paired lancet belfry lights, Geometrical Dec tracery. Closed *c.* 1985, now offices.

CLIFTON DOWN CONGREGATIONAL CHURCH (former), Christchurch Green, Clifton. 1868, by *Charles Hansom*. Spiky Dec with a high transeptal apse at the (ritual) NW. Triple-arched porch, finely vaulted. Only the W and N fronts survived conversion to housing *c.* 1987–8, by *Bob Trapnell* and *Domus Design and Build*.

HOPE CHAPEL (former Congregational), Hopechapel Hill, Hotwells. Possibly by *Daniel Hague*, 1786–8. Now a community centre. Founded by Lady Hope and Lady Glenorchy as a proprietary chapel serving Clifton and Hotwells. Rendered rubble with hipped roof, tall Y-traceried windows with four-centred heads, and panelled corner pilasters like those at Hague's St Paul, Portland Square (p. 350). Enlarged in the original style in 1838 by *William Harris*, to the ritual E and S; entrance front formerly with one tall central window, flanked by two shorter ones each with a door beneath, altered to four windows of equal height, and two doors beneath in the centre. The truncated pediment over the centre is also of 1838.

PEMBROKE CONGREGATIONAL CHAPEL (former), Oakfield Road, Clifton. By *W. H. Hawtin*, 1877. Cruciform. Big w window of five lights with Geometric Dec tracery and a double-arched entrance below. Now offices.

BUCKINGHAM BAPTIST CHAPEL, Queen's Road, Clifton. 1842–7, by *R. S. Pope*, who donated his fees towards the dec-oration. Rich French-influenced Gothic, rare for a Noncon-formist church of this date. An over-steep gable with a splendid but sham rose window that does not light the interior. Arcades of blind niches flanking the entrance, and five-bay return ele-vations, poorly related to the front. Inside, galleried hall, a flat-ceilinged with moulded beams, over-sized bosses, and big corbels with animated figures. Behind the dais-pulpit, a blind Gothic arch on classical pilasters. Scholarly Gothic and struc-tural truth had yet to impinge. Restored by *W. L. Bernard*, 1890.

GRENVILLE METHODIST CHURCH, Oldfield Place, Hotwells. Now flats. By *Thomas Foster*, 1837–9. A bequest of Thomas Whippie, an Anglican with Evangelical sympathies. Plain lancet style; gabled w front flanked by twin turrets, their big pinnacles lopped off. Among the earliest examples in Britain of a C19 Gothic Nonconformist chapel.

VICTORIA METHODIST CHURCH, Whiteladies Road, Clifton. By *Foster & Wood*, 1861–3. In banded pink and cream stones, and extravagantly pretty. A rather French-looking Gothic gabled front, the door flanked by low blind arcades in the plinth. Three tall windows with Geometric tracery. Deeply but-tressed sides, and a flèche. Within, the windows form contin-uous arcades down the sides, with cusped rere-arches echoing the cusped roof trusses.

EASTERN ORTHODOX CHURCH, University Road, Clifton. 1888, by *Henry Rising*, built for the Irvingites. Barn-like, E.E. style, some plate tracery. Short but lofty clerestoried nave with aisles.

SYNAGOGUE, Park Row. 1869–71, structural and exterior design by the Corporation surveyor *S. C. Fripp*; interiors by *Hyman H. Collins*. Bristol's C18 Jewish community settled largely in the Temple district; development of Victoria Street (*see* p. 307) forced the move here. Unprepossessing rubble exterior with Serlian entrance arch and rectangular triple windows above, with projecting Reader's House at the r. Inside, the ARK has curved mahogany doors (probably *c.* 1786), from the previous synagogue. Over it an arched canopy with gilded symbolic plants. WOMEN'S GALLERIES with latticed panels. Central

BIMAH (cantor's stage). C17 Dutch brass MENORAH (candelabrum), on an C18 base.

Bristol University

UNIVERSITY COLLEGE was founded in 1876 largely by the Rev. John Percival and Benjamin Jowett, Master of Balliol College, Oxford, with donations from local Liberals and Nonconformists. It gained university status in 1909 following a gift of £100,000 from Henry Overton Wills (1828–1911), quickly increased to £203,000 with donations from others. Wills was made the first Chancellor and is regarded as the University's founder.

The University does not have a campus in the sense of the out-of-town post-war universities. The first buildings (1879–1920s) are in the triangle between Queen's Road, S, University Road, W, and Woodland Road, E, including the Wills Memorial Building as the centrepiece. Later buildings stretch in a diffuse fashion from the 1960s Student Union building ½ m. W of the tower, to the borders of Cotham ½ m. N. Around Woodland Road, whole streets of big villas are occupied by the University. This is as close as Bristol gets to a campus, yet the area retains the character of a prosperous Victorian suburb.

A new MASTERPLAN by *Feilden Clegg Bradley* was adopted in 2006. It proposes a social heart for the campus at Tyndall Avenue, with the five-way junction at its W end becoming a 'gateway' to the University. The Arts and Social Sciences Library and other buildings on Tyndall Avenue will be redeveloped, as will the confused rear parts of the former Children's Hospital on St Michael's Hill. The Student Union building on Queen's Road will be abandoned for a more central site.

WILLS MEMORIAL BUILDING, Queen's Road. The University of Bristol's main building, by *George Oatley*, 1915–25. It houses an entrance hall, great hall, libraries, council chamber, and a majestic tower – a Bristol landmark. This monumentally scaled and exceptionally late example of the Perp Gothic Revival, wholly backward looking to the C19 and beyond to the C15, is nevertheless 'a *tour de force* . . . so convinced, so vast, and so competent that one cannot help feeling respect for it' (Pevsner). It was commissioned as a memorial to H.O.Wills by his sons. The structure throughout is of ferro-concrete, faced with Bath stone and carvings in Clipsham stone. Designed 1912–14; begun 1915–16, completed 1919–25, at a cost of c. £501,000.

The 215-ft (65.5-metre) TOWER is dramatically sited, angled and set forward on its plot at the top of Park Street, from which its whole height is framed by the stepped buildings. Oatley composed this consciously, pencilling his design onto a photograph. The main door in the plinth is the University's ceremonial entrance; above, the two-stage tower with one vast window on each face at each stage. The upper windows have three lights and blind tracery heads. Broad clasping buttresses, then thin pinnacles masking the transition to octagonal turrets with beautifully judged concave caps. The octagonal lantern with delicate tracery houses Great George, a bell of over nine tons. The fine carving was designed in collaboration with *Jean Hahn* of King's Heath Guild, Birmingham, whose big, lively gargoyle-like masks portray individuals on the University staff. Everything is subordinated to the bold composition necessary at this scale. What can be said against it? Compared with medieval towers, the proportions are too broad in relation to the height, but this gives majestic solidity to the distant silhouette and is hardly a fault. The traceried panels to the buttresses appear pasteboard-thin, and the tracery tends to be wiry and repetitive, and perhaps less inventive than at Giles Gilbert Scott's Liverpool Cathedral.

109   The ENTRANCE HALL continues beyond the floor area of the tower. It is vastly impressive, with panelled stone walls, and fan-vaulting higher at 75 ft (23 metres) than Wells Cathedral nave. Over the door is the prodigiously big Founders' Window, the glass replaced after war damage to a design by *D. Milner*, maker *Arnold Robinson*, 1953. Twin staircases run straight up 'as spectacular as their opposite number at Beckford's Fonthill and three times as solid' (Pevsner). They lead to a lateral fan-vaulted CORRIDOR; at its NW end the oak-panelled RECEPTION ROOM has a Neo-Jacobean plaster ceiling. The GREAT HALL is oak-panelled, with an apse behind the dais, and a hammerbeam roof with traceried panels. After bombing it was rebuilt in 1959–63 by *Ralph Brentnall*, Oatley's surviving partner, to a slightly simplified design. The COUNCIL CHAMBER to the SE is a truncated polygon, with a central light fitting in the vault, rendered as a rose window. The LIBRARY (SW wing) has fittings by *Oatley*, a Jacobean ribbed barrel-vault with pendants, and galleries joined by a bridge across the short end, reminiscent of Holden's at the Central Library Reading Room (p. 278). *Brentnall*'s library extension (completed 1962) continues the theme in a simplified fashion.

Other University of Bristol buildings are dealt with below, in two phases. Of its buildings adapted from other purposes, some are covered on pp. 344–5; the halls of residence under their appropriate perambulations.

The FIRST PHASE, 1880–1940. Building was initially sporadic. E of UNIVERSITY ROAD, a bald grey stone range N of a courtyard, built 1879–80. Intended as the first part of the QUADRANGLE for a sloping site with no axial approach; to be hidden later by a W entrance range facing University Road. Instead, tacked onto its W end is *F. B. Bond*'s pink sandstone ALBERT FRY MEMORIAL TOWER of 1904, really just a large turret. The rear range E of the courtyard was built in 1883. The extensions to the S, for ENGINEERING and the MEDICAL SCHOOL (now Geography), 1893–1904, are by *Edward Hansom* and *F. Bligh Bond*, in their Clifton College style: sandstone rubble walls, cusped mullioned-and-transomed lights, varied by incidental turrets and oriel windows with rib-vaulted bases. Facing

Woodland Road is the present Biology building, also by *Oatley & Lawrence*, 1910. Perp tower, turrets, oriels and bays. To its W, at the apex of University and Woodland roads, the ZOOLOGY AND BOTANY wing (1936–41), again *Oatley & Lawrence*. Collegiate Tudor pared down to the minimum.

To the NE, the former BRISTOL BAPTIST COLLEGE, Woodland Road. Built 1913–19 by *Oatley & Lawrence* for the world's oldest such establishment, founded 1679. Now also a University building. Jacobean style, in homely red brick, with varied projections. Composed along a narrow, sloping site, with a N entrance tower. Oatley's Arts and Crafts attention to quality and function is evident in the interiors and fittings. Neo-Jacobean staircase of oak with pierced finials. Staircase window, by *Arnold Robinson*, with much purple and brown. The former library (N wing) has some C15 and C16 glass.

Behind, on the hilltop of Royal Fort, is the H. H. WILLS PHYSICS LABORATORY, Tyndall Avenue. By *Oatley & Lawrence*, 1921–7, the University's best of this era. The main ranges of the L-shaped building are closely modelled on Kirby Hall, Northants, of *c.* 1570: very big mullioned-and-transomed windows between fluted Ionic piers, with scrolled brackets against a blank zone on top. Such emulation was old-fashioned by this date, but wholly in the spirit of the Willses' patronage. Between is a broad, high tower with suggestions of C17 motifs. On the S front a big Doric doorcase, with symbols representing discoveries in physics. Following H. H. Wills's wish to crown the Royal Fort with a ring of towers, the laboratory was just the NE corner of an intended great towered quadrangle around Royal Fort House (see p. 343), for which *Oatley* drew up plans in 1918.

THE UNIVERSITY AFTER 1945. In *c.* 1952 *Sir Percy Thomas & Partners* produced a masterplan for expansion, proposing a grandiose symmetrical composition on terraces descending SE from Royal Fort to Park Row, around an axial ceremonial stairway. Later buildings followed that plan only in general disposition, although much good early C18 housing was swept away before the plan for the lower tiers was abandoned.

At the E end of Tankard's Close is the MEDICAL SCHOOL, by *Ralph Brentnall*, started 1959. Dull brown brick, swamping St Michael's Hill when seen from the city.* Further W, the angular QUEEN'S BUILDING, or Engineering School, devised by *Oatley & Brentnall* in 1947, built in reduced form, 1951–8. Brick with green slate panels. Stylized classical references around the N entrance. Extended 2002–4 with two laboratory blocks by *Kendall Kingscott*; pale brick with broad horizontal bands of stone. The remains of the grand stairway of the masterplan lead S to the CHEMISTRY BUILDING, by *Courtauld Technical Services*, 1961–6. Two slab blocks with between them

---

*In protest at its ugliness, students staged the Funeral of British Architecture. Brentnall attended incognito as an undertaker, saying that, as the murderer, he felt obliged to see her decently buried.

a podium overlooking the city. On the S front, an angled cantilevered lecture theatre. Below the podium, a cloister-like sunken entrance court. To the SW in Cantocks Close, the SYNTHETIC CHEMISTRY BUILDING, by the *Percy Thomas Partnership*, opened 1999. The plinth is stone, with pale brick above. Curving triangular plan with a turret at the W apex. Full-height projections, swept roofs and four lead-clad chimneys.

Many of the significant purpose-built university facilities are in and around Tyndall Avenue, N of Royal Fort. At the W end is SENATE HOUSE, by *Ralph Brentnall*, opened 1965. A dispir-ited design, ashlar-faced, with bands of windows divided by narrow mullions. Next in line on this side, the CENTRE FOR SPORT, EXERCISE AND HEALTH, by *Nugent Vallis Brierley*, 2001–2. Brick towers at the ends, façade of conventional cladding and glazing, above which the long copper-clad upper parts bulge disconcertingly. *Brentnall*'s last major design for the University was the PHYSICS EXTENSION almost opposite, opened 1968. Notable only for bulk and desperate plainness. Adjacent, E, *Sheppard Robson*'s drum-shaped MATHEMATICS BUILDING, *c.* 2009–11. At the E end (N side) is the ARTS AND SOCIAL SCIENCES LIBRARY, by *Twist & Whitley*, opened 1975. It repeats their design for Belfast University. Fortress-like and austere, with minimal glazing to conserve heat. Indented corners and a second floor that reads like a big cornice, with long rows of small angled windows in box-like projections. To the NW in Woodland Road is a less intrusive addition, the ARTS FACULTY EXTENSIONS. Big Victorian villas by *George Gay*, *c.* 1862–72, are linked by simple and unobtrusive entrances and rear extensions, by *MacCormac & Jamieson*, 1979–84, planned around garden courts, with a high-level walkway behind.

Post-war additions away from the Royal Fort area must start with the STUDENTS' UNION BUILDING, Queen's Road. By *Alec French & Partners*, 1965. Perhaps Clifton's most bruising post-war intrusion. A large textured concrete slab at the W end, central recessed entrance and the E end raised over a basement swimming pool. A free-flowing curved staircase in the foyer. In Park Row, SW of the Wills Memorial Tower, is UNIVERSITY GATE, an Engineering faculty by *Atkins Walters Webster*, 1996. The Woodland Road front and the W end are the best parts, with juxtaposed roofs of swept curves. It incorporates part of the very long and pretentious Italianate façade of the Coli-seum, a skating rink then cinema, 1910.

For HAMPTON HOUSE (University Health Centre, formerly Homoeopathic Hospital), *see* p. 377.

Other public buildings

CLIFTON LIBRARY, Princess Victoria Street. Built as Christ Church Schools, 1852, by *Charles Underwood*, modestly Ital-ianate. Altered 1877, seemingly by *Charles Hansom*.

MUSEUM AND ART GALLERY, Queen's Road. By *Frank Wills* with *Houston & Houston* of London, 1900–5. It follows the national trend for civic art galleries (cf. Bradford, 1900–4, a very similar design). Originally the Art Gallery only; since 1940 it has housed the Museum too. Sir W. H. Wills of the tobacco firm donated the £40,000 cost and engaged his architect cousin. The result has been aptly described as 'fat Roman', less kindly as 'lunatic Baroque'. An over-scaled thrusting centre over a *porte cochère* (openings glazed in 2004). Above, an applied Ionic portico beneath an open pediment, with an inscription and arms. The portico frames a bowed oriel. Heavy parapets with seated figures by *W. J. Smith* representing Architecture, Painting and Sculpture. One big round-arched window in each flank: painted GLASS by *Joseph Bell & Son*, 1908. Inside, two full-height top-lit halls, the front hall with balustraded gallery, an imperial staircase, and the names of painters in swagged plaques. The lighter arcaded rear hall was added 1925–30 by *J. B. Wills*, Frank Wills's son. In the rear café, a spectacular mid-C17 stone CHIMNEYPIECE from Lewins Mead, some 12 ft (3.7 metres) high. A local mason's attempt to digest classical motifs, with naïve Mannerist figures perched on the pediment after Michelangelo's Medici tombs, but still with Jacobean strapwork.

MUSEUM AND LIBRARY (former), Queen's Road, Clifton. Now Brown's Restaurant. Built 1867–72, and described by Pevsner as 'the West Country's greatest compliment to John Ruskin'. *Archibald Ponton* designed the plan and *John Foster* the elevations, in a Venetian Gothic rendition of Colston Hall (*see* p. 289), with two tiers of arcading and lancet niches between the upper arches. Broad steps lead to a full-length entrance loggia, now part-glazed. Its arcade has rich foliate capitals with wild beasts. Shields above, 1894–5. Much was unexecuted, or was lost to bombing, e.g. a high pierced parapet with sculpture and corner canopies, ornamented cornices, etc. The interior was not reinstated in *Ralph Brentnall*'s rebuilding for the University refectory, 1949. Attached at the rear (and now part of the Museum and Art Gallery, above), the former museum LECTURE THEATRE of 1874, by *Stuart Colman*. The angled façade expresses a domed polygonal plan. Mannered lancets of excruciating thinness, and an ogee-traceried window after the Ca' d'Oro, Venice.

ROYAL WEST OF ENGLAND ACADEMY, Queen's Road. Founded 1845 as an Academy of Fine Art. The building of 1854–7 has Victorian Renaissance façades by *J. H. Hirst;* planning and interiors by *Charles Underwood*. The glazed first floor was originally an entrance loggia reached by an external double staircase, replaced by *S. S. Reay*'s entrance extension (1911–13), modified from a design by *H. Dare Bryan* with advice from *George Oatley*. It dampens the dynamism of the façade. Above, statues by *John Thomas, c.* 1857, of cast cement on slate armatures: Flaxman (l.), and Reynolds (r.). Inside, Reay's marble-lined staircase leads up to a rectangular domed vestibule with oil paintings in the lunettes by *Walter Crane*, 1913–14.

CLIFTON SWIMMING BATHS, Oakfield Place. Almost certainly by *Pope, Bindon & Clark*, 1849–50. This is a very rare survival of a C19 subscription baths. Symmetrical façade of two storeys plus attic, five bays with heavy cornice, faming pilasters and a Grecian battered door frame. Restored and reopened for swimming, 2006–8.

BRISTOL GRAMMAR SCHOOL, University Road. By *Foster & Wood*, 1877–9. The school was endowed by a bequest of 1532. It moved here from Unity Street. The Perp detail and composition of the Great Hall look back to Clifton College and beyond, yet the impression is bold, even handsome. Rubble walls of plum-coloured sandstone, with steep roofs, crow-stepped gables, a narrow N tower and openwork bell-turret. It contains classrooms below a hall measuring 140 ft by 50 ft (42.7 by 15.2 metres), and 50 ft high. This was planned as a single schoolroom, still with its built-in cupboards and canopied masters' chairs. Ranges towards University Road: to the N by *Frank Wills*, 1908, to the S by *W. V. & A. R. Gough*, 1912–14. To the S, a good SPORTS HALL by *Nugent Vallis Brierley*, 1990s.

CLIFTON COLLEGE, Guthrie Road, was one of the many new mid-C19 public schools. The first buildings, by *Charles Hansom*, opened in 1862. His later partner, *F. B. Bond*, continued after Hansom's death in 1888. The style is generally Perp, with a Dec chapel. From the l., the pink rubble-stone BIG SCHOOL projects S, a very high hall with large S window and strongly buttressed sides. Then in the centre PERCIVAL BUILDINGS (1869 and 1875) with cloister and oriel, and some fluid ogee tracery. To the r. a GATEHOUSE tower, 1889. CHAPEL and belfry 1866–7, with N aisle added 1881. *Nicholson & Corlette* ingeniously recast this chapel in 1909–10. The central parts of the side walls were removed, and two chapels set diagonally on each side, with rib-vaulting to a green copper-clad lantern inspired by the Ely Octagon. Near the chapel, a South African WAR MEMORIAL, a statue of St George by *Alfred Drury*, 1904. *A. Munby*'s SCIENCE SCHOOL of 1927 is plain and business-like; extended, 1960s. *Charles Holden*'s GATEWAY to College Road (1921) commemorates the school's war dead. Simplified Gothic, mundane after the glory of his Central Library (p. 277).

CLIFTON HIGH SCHOOL, Clifton Park Road. Built as a house by *Stuart Colman* (1875), sympathetically extended by *Sir George Oatley*, 1927. Colman's taste was experimental and often perverse; here, a rare and early Bristol example of Queen Anne. Confident red brick asymmetry, with quirky details such as the oriel on a miniature vault sprung from a column. At the rear, a gabled dormer bisected by a broad brick chimney.

ST MICHAEL ON THE MOUNT PRIMARY SCHOOL, Old Park Hill. A Board School by *W. V. Gough*, c. 1895, in his gruff version of Queen Anne. On the N gable an C18 sculpture of a putto.

CHILDREN'S HOSPITAL (former), St Michael's Hill. Tudor Gothic, by *Robert Curwen*, 1882–5. Symmetrical with cross-gabled ends, and the usual paraphernalia of bays, oriels and turret doorway.

MATERNITY HOSPITAL, St Michael's Hill. 1975. A big concrete slab that unforgivably disrupts the street's scale and line.

BRISTOL ZOO, Clifton Down. Founded in 1835. Of about that date are the pretty Neo-Greek LODGES, with a frieze of animal silhouettes (*c.* 1930s), and a glass entrance link by *LMP Architects*, 1996. The original landscape GARDENS by *Richard Forrest* of Acton largely survive. GIRAFFE HOUSE of *c.* 1860, like a Tudor Gothic villa with a heightened doorway, perhaps by *Charles Hansom*. CONSERVATION EDUCATION CENTRE by *Quattro Design*, 1999; a 'green' design, of rubble stone and timber cladding, with a glazed link to a circular tower. By the same architects, the TERRACE THEATRE, 2003; triangular, with a planted monopitch roof.

Bridges

CLIFTON SUSPENSION BRIDGE. The major Bristol work of *Isambard Kingdom Brunel*, designed in 1829 when he was just twenty-three, and built 1836–64. Brunel referred to it as 'my first child, my darling'. It has become for many the symbol of Bristol. Its visual impact is due to the great height of the gorge (245 ft, 74.7 metres, from high-water mark to the bridge deck) and the drama of the 702-ft (214-metre) span. It is also perhaps 'the most beautiful of early English suspension bridges ... largely due to the felicitous design of the stone pylons' (Pevsner). The suspension rods supporting the bridge deck appear wonderfully light and graceful.

100

William Vick, a merchant, bequeathed £1,000 in 1753 for a bridge across the Avon Gorge. By 1829 Vick's money had grown to £8,000, and designs were invited. Brunel submitted four, in various styles, based on the suspension principle, perhaps inspired by the competition judge Thomas Telford's recently completed Menai Straits Bridge. After a second competition a modified version of one of Brunel's designs was placed second. Brunel then persuaded the committee in 1831 to adopt his design anyway. It exceeded the 600 ft (183 metres) that Telford believed was the maximum possible, but Brunel calculated that suspension bridges could achieve much wider spans.

Brunel wanted his bridge to be 'simple and unobtrusive', and impressive 'rather by the grandeur of the ideas that it gave rise to than [. . .] by anything inconsistent with the surrounding objects'. However, the accepted 'unobtrusive' Egyptian design included sphinxes on the pylons, and cast-iron decoration of scarabs, etc. Work commenced in 1831. The massive Somerset-side abutment was built 1836–40, and the pylons raised by 1843. By then, the £45,000 available was spent, and work ceased. In 1853 the time allowed for construction by Act of Parliament expired. The project was abandoned and the ironwork reused at Brunel's Royal Albert Bridge, Saltash. Brunel died in 1859, and in 1861 members of the Institute of Civil Engineers resurrected the scheme in his memory, reusing chains from Brunel's Hungerford Bridge, London, then being demolished. Work resumed under *Hawkshaw & Barlow*, using three chains on each side instead of two and a wrought-iron deck frame instead of Brunel's timber and iron one. It was completed in 1864.

The piers on which the pylons stand are honeycombed with recently rediscovered vaults, to reduce the weight of masonry and increase strength. Brunel changed the original rectilinear design of the pylons before construction, for reasons unknown. Their apparently curving sides are in reality battered at two sensitively judged angles, the change of angle occurring at the level where the tall parabolic opening is bridged by a segmental arch over the carriageway; again a happy motif. They are of Pennant rubble below, with pale ashlar caps and cornices of harmonious proportions. The chains are fastened to iron saddles on top of the pylons and where they meet the ground, allowing the chains to flex. Tapering brick plugs anchor the outer ends into the rock. The planned cast-iron cladding of the pylons was happily omitted, revealing a magical fusion of engineering and architecture.

CUMBERLAND BASIN FLYOVER. By the *City Engineer's Department*; consulting engineers *Freeman, Fox & Partners*, 1962–5. Elegant gull-wing swing bridge on a central pivot.

LOCK BRIDGES, Cumberland Basin (beneath and just W of the flyover). By *Brunel*, 1844–8. Two bridges with decks suspended beneath wrought-iron tubular members. Brunel employed the principle again at Saltash Bridge, Devon.

Perambulations

1. *Hotwells and the Clifton slopes*

Clifton, with its big stone-built Georgian and Victorian houses in a spacious and leafy setting, has been described as 'preeminent . . . among English suburbs'. It is bounded by Durdham Down to the N, the Avon Gorge to the W, and a steep escarpment separating it from the city to the S and E. Hotwells nestles below, at the E end of the Avon Gorge. Together, Clifton and Hotwells cover just over one mile E–W, nearly two miles N–S.

A spa was established at Hotwells in 1630, and was purchased in 1676 by the Society of Merchant Venturers with the manor of Clifton. There followed a new pump room (1696), and Early Georgian lodging houses. The spa declined in the C19; the Hotwell House was finally demolished in 1867.

Before 1700 CLIFTON was a scattered hillside hamlet, with a few large houses (e.g. Goldney). Pope mentions 'very pretty lodging houses' in 1739, and, in a relation to Bristol like that of Hampstead to London, some wealthy merchants' houses on the

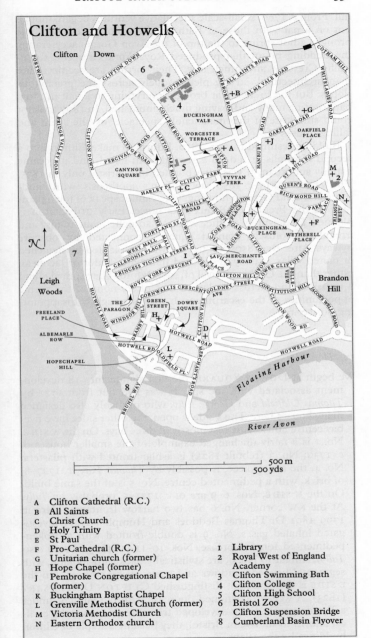

Clifton and Hotwells

Clifton Down

Leigh Woods

Brandon Hill

Floating Harbour

River Avon

500 m
500 yds

A Clifton Cathedral (R.C.)
B All Saints
C Christ Church
D Holy Trinity
E St Paul
F Pro-Cathedral (R.C.)
G Unitarian church (former)
H Hope Chapel (former)
J Pembroke Congregational Chapel (former)
K Buckingham Baptist Chapel
L Grenville Methodist Church (former)
M Victoria Methodist Church
N Eastern Orthodox church

I Library
2 Royal West of England Academy
3 Clifton Swimming Bath
4 Clifton College
5 Clifton High School
6 Bristol Zoo
7 Clifton Suspension Bridge
8 Cumberland Basin Flyover

hill. From *c.* 1760, small-scale speculative ventures began, though not on a par with those of Bath. In the 1780s a new borehole brought a hot spring to the top of the Avon Gorge, accelerating the building boom that produced Royal York Crescent, Cornwallis Crescent and much else. Their virtues are scenic rather than architectural, strung picturesquely across the precipitous slopes. But the French War brought everything to a halt in 1793, bankrupting many and leaving much unfinished. In 1807 a visitor could still write of the 'melancholy spectacle' of 'the silent and falling houses'.

Building resumed from *c.* 1810. Efforts to make Clifton into a second Hotwells or indeed a second Bath failed, and it became happily suburban. It was incorporated into Bristol only in 1835. The years *c.* 1815–*c.* 1850 saw Clifton's apotheosis, with handsome and solid Grecian housing. One cannot speak of town planning in the French or Beaux-Arts sense. Early C19 Clifton is planned for leisurely traffic, with no straight main roads, and irregular, profusely planted squares, connected by obscure byways. After the 1850s the terrace was supplanted by detached or paired villas, usually in debased Italianate, Tudor or Jacobean rather than the Gothic Revival of, say, Oxford. They sprawl N and E into Redland, across a plateau that offers none of the scenic opportunities of the escarpment. It makes a slightly disappointing postscript.

1a. *Hotwells*

We begin at DOWRY SQUARE, the first significant C18 development associated with the spa. It was laid out from 1721 by *Thomas Oldfield* and *George Tully*, who probably also designed many houses here. The s side is open; the other sides have five-bay centre houses, the rest mostly of three bays. On the W SIDE, No. 1 is a fairly unchanged example of the smaller houses of *c.* 1730; No. 3 (rebuilt 1822) is ashlar-fronted with pilasters; No. 4, the centrepiece, is possibly by *Thomas Paty, c.* 1747–8, of brick, with a pedimented centre. No. 5 is of the same build. On the N SIDE, Nos. 6–9 are of *c.* 1721–5, probably by *Tully.* At the NW corner, No. 6 has two narrow frontages. Here in 1799–1801 Dr Thomas Beddoes and Humphry Davy investigated inhaled gases. No. 9 is double-fronted with a broken-pedimented Ionic doorcase. Nos. 10–11 (1746, probably also *Tully*), similar to No. 9, are stylistically backward-looking, with segmental-headed windows and heavy string courses. On the E SIDE is the small but distinguished CLIFTON DISPENSARY (1823). A well-proportioned doorcase with big fanlight under a Tuscan porch. Fully developed tripartite windows, the earliest known to survive in Bristol; they became a staple of Clifton buildings by the 1830s.

Across Hotwell Road, DOWRY PARADE continues to the s; built 1763–4 by *Robert Comfort* and *Benjamin Probert* among others. Speculative five-bay lodging houses, a weaker imitation of

Albemarle Row (*see* below); but with cramped proportions and thin cornices without a parapet. They were subdivided, probably *c.* 1790–1800, resulting in crowded pairs of doors and blocked central windows. Single-bay houses of *c.* 1820 continue S. Opposite, CHAPEL ROW (Nos. 262–266 Hotwell Road) is the S continuation of the W side of Dowry Square, laid out *c.* 1725. Three houses with continuous string courses and cornices. No. 262 is particularly pleasing. S of Dowry Parade the Cumberland Basin road system (*see* p. 330) required the demolition of much C18 housing.

Continue W on HOTWELL ROAD, past HABERFIELD ALMS-HOUSES (*Pope & Paul*, 1889), a restrained design in brick and terracotta with two-storey porches. Nos. 288–290 Hotwell Road, a late C18 pair (one double-fronted), sport three full-height bows reminiscent of Cheltenham or Brighton. Past Granby Hill, the road curves N. From here, FREELAND PLACE climbs E, a steep backwater which even in the weakest sunshine, somehow evokes Tuscany. On the r., Nos. 22–23, a two-bay villa of perhaps *c.* 1830, later extended l., with central balconied porch. On the l., single-bay houses of *c.* 1820–5 step up from the Avon, pleasingly varied in details, most with small Gothic tented balconies. Where Granby Hill crosses, continue E into Cumberland Place, then N into ALBEMARLE ROW. A p. 334 brick terrace of 1762–3, built probably by *Thomas Paty* as lodging houses, the centre house pedimented. The house widths are irregular (from bottom to top, 5:5:5:5:3:3:5), and the steps up uneven, negating the attempted unity of front. Characteristic five-stepped voussoirs, even quoins at each party wall, and some Gibbsian doorcases. The double-fronted houses have a central hall with rear stair, and suites each side with closets at the rear.

HOPECHAPEL HILL leads steeply down to the E; for Hope Chapel, N side, *see* p. 321. Lower down, on the N side, North Green Street leads to THE POLYGON (1826–9), probably designed by *Richard Jones*. A twelve-house crescent (angled as the name suggests) with the fronts on the convex side. Simple three-storey houses with Regency Gothic balconies, facing uphill on to banked gardens, which lend them a verdant rusticity.

OUTLIERS. FOUNTAIN by *Tom Dove* of Birmingham, 1902, junction of Hotwell Road and Merchant Road. Cast-iron dome on slim pillars. It commemorates a missionary and Temperance pioneer. SE of Merchant's Road, ROWNHAM MEAD by the *Hubbard Ford Partnership*, completed 1980 on the site of Merchants' Dock (1765). The first big housing scheme of the harbourside regeneration, in a surprisingly harmonious vernacular style: red-brown brick, pantile roofs, stained timber-cladding. POOLE'S WHARF faces the harbour E of Rownham Mead. By *BBA Architects* (project architect *Patrick Bollen*), 1999. Pastiche Regency houses and flats. The small scale and planning are successful.

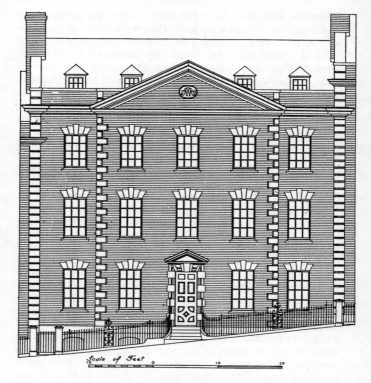

Bristol, Clifton, No. 5 Albemarle Row.
Elevation

CLIFTON VALE. At the upper end, a fifteen-house stepped
   terrace of *c.* 1836–41 by *Foster & Okely*. Severe but pleasing,
   with gently battered door frames and late Grecian balconies
   under the shallowest of pediments.
RUTLAND HOUSE, junction of Hopechapel Hill and Granby
   Hill. Large, mid-C18. Canted bays, icicle-work blocked
   columns to the doorcase.
Where HOTWELL ROAD runs NW into the Avon Gorge, some
   C18 survivors from the vicinity of the Hotwell spa. ST
   VINCENT'S PARADE, by *W. Paty*, was begun 1789 as a terrace
   of lodging houses. A little further NW, ROCK HOUSE, three
   storeys and five bays, depicted in an engraving of *c.* 1741. Deep
   Doric colonnade added *c.* 1800–10, tented balcony above.
   Then THE COLONNADE, 1786, built by Samuel Powell, lessee
   of the Hotwell, as shops for spa visitors. Gently curving brick
   front of thirteen bays with shopfronts beneath a deep Tuscan
   colonnade. A few yards N, almost beneath Brunel's Suspension
   Bridge (*see* p. 329), was the Pump Room.

1b. *Clifton slopes*

Covering the most important C18 developments on the s slopes of Clifton Hill, ending roughly at the limit reached at the slump of 1793.

On the N side of Clifton Hill is ST ANDREW'S CHURCHYARD. The Regency Gothic church, by *James Foster*, 1819–22, was bombed and demolished; the foundations remain. Good Gothic wrought-iron GATES and overthrow with lamp bracket. CLIFTON HILL runs E, with BISHOP'S HOUSE on the l.; in Bath stone ashlar, dated 1711, a fine and very early Bristol example of fully realized classicism. Perhaps by *John Strahan*, although there is no certainty of his being in Bristol before c. 1725. *George Townesend* is another possibility. Five bays (2:1:2), the projecting centre with banded rustication, seg-mental-pedimented Ionic doorcase, and a triangular pediment to the window above. The flanking windows have segmental heads and continuous architraves. The wings are later. On the corner with Clifton Road, E, is RICHMOND HOUSE (c. 1701–3), probably the earliest survival of Clifton's mercantile houses. Five bays also arranged 2:1:2. Later in the C18, the attic storey was raised and cross-windows replaced with sashes. Double-pile plan with central staircase. The small service quarters may indicate a true villa conceived for private retreat from the city.
Below at an angle is CLIFTON HILL HOUSE, 1746–50, a refined Palladian villa by *Isaac Ware*. Built for the Bristol linen draper and ship-owner Paul Fisher, it was the home in the mid C19 of the writer John Addington Symonds. Now a University hall of residence. An astylar Palladian entrance front of five bays and three storeys, with a heavy but sympathetic porch of 1853. Fisher's cypher and the date 1747 in the pediment, carved by *Thomas Paty*. He probably learned here the Palladianism that influenced his later work. The garden drops away to the E; the tall, astylar garden front is raised on a podium with low wings, like the Villa Ragona at Le Ghizzole by Palladio, whose *Quattro Libri* Ware had published in English in 1738. From the ground floor an external double staircase (after Lord Burlington's Chiswick House) leads down to the garden. The wings have been raised one storey. Smooth ashlar, with plain window openings, a Gibbsian door surround, heavily rusticated podium, V-jointed rustication on the ground floor, and orna-mented pediment. The DRAWING ROOM and DINING ROOM have fine chimneypieces, and ceilings by *Joseph Thomas* with fanciful Rococo plasterwork in strongly defined compart-ments. Stone staircase, with S-scrolled balustrade, and a Rococo ceiling. Flamboyant Regency Gothic study with plaster vault and ogee door surrounds. At the lower corners of the garden, two GAZEBOS (one now collapsed), probably c. 1690s.
To the N of Clifton Hill House, Lower Clifton Hill winds down to BELLEVUE, a speculative terrace begun c. 1792, probably

69

by *W. Paty*, but completed only *c.* 1810–15. Two-bay stucco backs facing uphill to a raised pavement, three-bay ashlar garden fronts with communal gardens. At its s end, Constitution Hill climbs steeply, back to Clifton Hill. Nearby to the sw is GOLDNEY HOUSE, also a University hall of residence. *George Tully* rebuilt a late C17 house here *c.* 1722–4, for Thomas Goldney II, merchant and fellow Quaker, possibly leaving parts of the old house as a service wing. Garden front of 3:1:3 bays, with a projecting centre. The Early Georgian part is the centre and the r. three bays only, extended by *Waterhouse* in 1864–5 to make it symmetrical, refacing the brick with Bath stone, and adding an ugly and prominent tower with a French pavilion roof. The fine 1720s parlour is heavily panelled in Cuban mahogany, with fluted pilasters and inlaid Doric frieze. Baroque chimneypiece of Hotwell marble, luscious overmantel in lime and pearwood in the style of Grinling Gibbons.

The ambitious GARDENS were created largely by Thomas Goldney III (1696–1768). The GROTTO of 1737–64 is one of the best in England, probably inspired by his father's account of a Utrecht merchant's grotto seen in 1725. Steps lead down to an arcaded chamber densely set with shells and minerals including tufa and 'Bristol diamonds', probably executed by Goldney himself. A cascade feeds a pool presided over by a river god. At one side, a 'lions' den' – a low cave with stone lions. *Thomas Paty* laid the marbled tile floor from Coalbrookdale in 1762–4; perhaps by him too the pretty Gothick façade of *c.* 1757. E of the house, an ORANGERY, probably *c.* 1750 (much restored *c.* 1933); of red brick, with segmental-headed sashes divided into groups of three by two entrances with rusticated surrounds. On its axis is a CANAL POND, 1758–9, very late for such a feature. Goldney extended the garden s, with a terrace (1753–4) and at its w end, a Gothick ROTUNDA (1757), perhaps reworking an earlier structure, and once colonnaded. On the terrace a sandstone WATER TOWER (1764), embattled and pinnacled, with lancets and portholes. Tower and rotunda may be by *T. Paty*. Nearby a lead STATUE of Hercules, on a Baroque stone plinth, in place before 1768. It may be one from Kingsweston by *John Nost the Elder*, 1715.

Adjacent to Goldney House gardens, GOLDNEY HALL, University accommodation by the *Architects' Co-Partnership* (*c.* 1966), successfully remodelled in 1992–4 by *Alec French Partnership*. The nine blocks were replanned as units each for eight students, and linked to create an irregular courtyard, with turret-like fire escapes. An L-shaped N block was added to close the courtyard. To the N up the slope, and w of our starting point, are BERESFORD HOUSE and PROSPECT HOUSE, a pair of lodging houses by *Thomas Paty c.* 1765, with his usual excess of Gibbsian blocks. w again is CLIFTON COURT (now the Chesterfield Hospital), *c.* 1742–3, probably by *William Halfpenny* for the brass-founders Nehemiah and Martha Champion. Side walls of black slag blocks, a by-product of brass making. Bath stone front, pedimented and with lower wings: over-large windows and quite un-Palladian proportions.

Clifton Hill continues NW towards SAVILLE PLACE, a small crescent started *c.* 1790 and completed in 1838 by *Charles Dyer* (Nos. 6–11), but a full half-storey lower. Here REGENT STREET begins, Clifton's main shopping street, developed from the 1860s, e.g. Nos. 10–14, NE side, shops by *Foster & Wood*, *c.* 1883. Soon on the SW is the most ambitious Clifton speculation, ROYAL YORK CRESCENT, *c.* 1791–1820, perhaps by *W. Paty*, a shallow curve of forty-six houses. Its developer was bankrupted in 1793, with ten houses finished and fifteen incomplete. After an abortive plan to convert it to barracks, completion was achieved slowly from 1809 to 1820. Its strengths are its contribution to distant views, contrasting an ordered sweeping composition with steep tree-clad outcrops of the gorge, and its impressive raised terrace, *c.* 20 ft (6 metres) high at the w end. The stucco houses are plain, with varied iron balconies; the only emphasis a trivial projection by the central pair. Interiors plain but elegant, with occasional surprises, e.g. a cantilevered staircase rising acrobatically through a five-storey U-shaped hall at No. 16.

PRINCE'S BUILDINGS runs N from the w end of Royal York Crescent. By *W. Paty*, 1789, an innovative design of quasi-semi-detached pairs with single-storey linking entrance wings. Much filling in above the links. To its s, spectacularly high on the escarpment is THE PARAGON, a short crescent by *John Drew*, 1809–14 (the w end completed by *Stephen Hunter* in modified form). Distinctive elliptical porches, standing almost free of the façades. The convex balconied backs face the view, as at The Paragon, Bath. Down to the SE is CORNWALLIS CRESCENT, *c.* 1791–*c.* 1835. Parallel to Royal York Crescent, almost as long, but bisected by a pre-existing right of way. The plain stucco backs have the entrances, the Bath stone s front has a terrace walk.

To the w, Windsor Place leads inauspiciously off Granby Hill to WINDSOR TERRACE, built 1790–*c.* 1810 to designs possibly by *John Eveleigh* of Bath. Its rampant disorder is as instructive as all the perfection of Bath. The speculator was William Watts, plumber, who invented a new process for lead shot. The site required a costly 70-ft (21-metre) high revetment. The two centre houses, completed by *c.* 1792, show the original conception, following Bath in its elaborate design. 1793 bankrupted all concerned, and work resumed in 1808 under *John Drew*, reusing the pilasters already cut on lower houses, hence the uncomfortable differences of scale. The pilasters stop short of the cornice, a visual disaster. Illiterate details, e.g. the cutting of grooved rustication over the windows.

CLIFTON WOOD is a backwater perched on a shelving plateau E of Hotwells, with cranky corners and wide harbour vistas. Few C18 houses, and mid-C19 terraces overlooking the harbour. w of Clifton Wood Road is CLIFTON WOOD HOUSE, of *c.* 1721, perhaps by *George Tully*. Eight bays, three storeys. Flanking the

original and handsome timber doorcase, two deeply curved
bows added *c.* 1800. No. 9 Clifton Wood Road is a tiny Gothick
cottage with shaped gable, perhaps *c.* 1790–1800.

2a. *Central Clifton, west side*

For Clifton's development, *see* p. 330. This perambulation
broadly covers Clifton from *c.* 1790 to *c.* 1850 when, with the
grandeur of Vyvyan Terrace, Worcester Terrace and Victoria
Square, Bristol's Belgravia arrives with a flourish.

Halfway up SION HILL, a platform affords excellent views of
Clifton Suspension Bridge (p. 329) and the gorge. Opposite,
the former ST VINCENT'S ROCKS HOTEL and PUMP ROOM.
Here in the mid 1780s Thomas Morgan drilled a borehole to
the Hotwell directly below, known as Sion Spring, beginning
Clifton's building boom of *c.* 1788–93. At the s end Sion Spring
House, a five-bay house (perhaps *c.* 1810–30) with tented
balcony, attached at the N to the four-storey building (1780s)
associated with the spring, with a seven-window range with
canted bays. Much altered and converted to flats *c.* 2001, with
first-floor curved glass front. Morgan's haphazard development of lodgings lies on Sion Hill to the N, *c.* 1780–90. Four-
and five-storey houses, with canted bays, curved bows, and
tented balconies added *c.* 1830. Every house has something
worth seeing, and they achieve delightful diversity (e.g. the
porch, No. 8) within an overall harmony.

Directly s of the viewing platform is the long-derelict GRAND
SPA PUMP ROOM, by *Philip Munro*, 1890–4, its parapet at
pavement level on Sion Hill and with a grandiose Neo-Renaissance entrance façade in Princes' Lane below. The owner
hoped to revive Clifton's fortunes as a spa, in conjunction with
the Clifton Rocks Railway, a funicular in an inclined tunnel
from the Pump Room to the bottom of the gorge. Attached to
its s, and also by *Munro*, the big Italianate AVON GORGE
HOTEL (1898). Opposite is ST VINCENT'S PRIORY, a tall,
narrow Regency Gothic house of *c.* 1828–31, with unusually
lively decoration. Big bow with narrow lancets, vaulted out at
the first floor from little colonnettes and with twisting figures,
reputedly copied from St Mary Redcliffe.

From here, the matching terraces of CALEDONIA PLACE and
WEST MALL run E, forming a long narrow square. To a single
design by *Foster & Okely*, 1833–40, an extension to an C18
development. Plain three-bay fronts with fine cast-iron
Grecian balconies with pedimented lattice panels, anthemion
etc. At No. 32 is the change to the C18 work, begun *c.* 1788,
probably to the design of *John Eveleigh* of Bath, with a thir-
teen-house terrace on each side – for Bristol at this date, a big
and unusually formal composition, but inadequately held
together by the pedimented ends and centre.

At the E end is THE MALL, a short street running N–S and the
closest thing to a centre in Clifton. The broad stone-fronted

CLIFTON CLUB (originally Clifton Hotel and Assembly Rooms) faces W to close the square. Of 1806–11 by *Francis Greenway*, who had trained with Nash.* Greenway and his two brothers ran a firm which undertook architectural design, building, statuary and landscaping, taking advantage of the vacuum that followed the collapse of 1793. They produced here one of the first big buildings in Bristol for over a decade, a somewhat incoherent nineteen-bay façade with bowed ends, recessed links, a big Ionic centrepiece with a full attic below the pediment. *Joseph Kay* completed the interiors. Much altered, with canted shopfronts, 1856 (r. flank) and two oriels squeezed into the central portico, 1894. N up The Mall and W into Portland Street for CARTER'S BUILDINGS, warehouses and workers' housing arranged in courts, almost unique in Bristol. Apparently of the 1790s, altered *c.* 1850. About half the residents of Clifton were working people serving the needs of the other half.

At the S end of The Mall is PRINCESS VICTORIA STREET, also originally for service premises. Nos. 29–31 are Edwardian Baroque buildings probably by *James Hart*, 1906, for Cowlin & Son, builders, both laden with swags, window aprons, etc. To the E is CLIFTON DOWN ROAD, with several good houses of the 1760s. Facing W down Princess Victoria Street is BOYCE'S BUILDINGS, 1763, speculative lodging houses undertaken for a wig-maker, and perhaps Bristol's first palace-front composition. Probably by *Thomas Paty*, cf. Albemarle Row, Hotwells, pp. 333–4. Originally three five-bay houses, the r. one demolished, the rest altered; the central pediment with Boyce's cypher hints at their former showiness. Directly N in Boyce's Avenue is CLIFTON ARCADE, a delightfully indulgent mishmash built as the Royal Bazaar and Winter Gardens by *J. W. King*, 1878; red brick shops with vaguely Moorish decoration. Behind is a little galleried arcade with an imperial staircase backed by a blind Gothic wheel window. Glazed roof on little cast-iron brackets with dragons.

Returning to Clifton Down Road (W side) is RODNEY PLACE, *c.* 1782–5, one of Clifton's earliest big planned terraces, in the late Paty style. Doric doorcases with triglyph frieze and an arched fanlight beneath open pediment; possibly the first Bristol use of a design that seems to originate with Sir Robert Taylor, *c.* 1744, and became very popular in Bristol perhaps via the pattern book of William Pain. Opposite are thee large late C18 houses: MORTIMER HOUSE, probably *c.* 1760–70; DUNCAN HOUSE and FREEMANTLE HOUSE, somewhat later, with a thick overlay of Victorian decoration by *Charles Hansom*, 1884, added when they were in use as a school. Shortly N is CHRISTCHURCH GREEN, a spur of the Downs which resisted development. At its SE corner are two resited MEMORIALS erected by General Draper of Manilla

---

* Greenway was bankrupt in 1809, later transported for forgery, and became known as the father of Australian architecture.

Hall nearby (dem.): a sarcophagus of 1766, to the 79th Regiment at the capture of Manila (1763); and an obelisk to William Pitt, whom Draper admired.

To the NE is CLIFTON PARK, with fine Greek and Gothic villas, 1830s–50s. On the N side, two free classical pairs, probably by *Charles Dyer*. Nos. 1–2 of 1836, Nos. 3–4 of 1845. The mutilated No. 5, by *Charles Underwood*, 1849, was the home of the developer Edward Clark, who with Charles Savery employed Underwood on many developments. To the N off College Road is WORCESTER TERRACE, c. 1848–53, also *Underwood*. The ends are treated as separate villas with bow windows on the returns, a clever device but seemingly never repeated. The pilastered terrace front is arranged 6:6:12:6:6, refined and meticulously detailed, if insufficiently varied. Curvaceous full-length balconies of cast iron. Back in Clifton Park are more villas in the Worcester Terrace style, also by *Underwood*. Nos. 8–9, of 1846, strike out in unapologetic Perpendicular Gothic. Similar in many details to *R. S. Pope*'s Guildhall, Broad Street (p. 275): these may be his too. Nos. 6–7 (1835), less convinced Regency Gothic, perhaps by *Pope* or *Dyer*.

To the S is the ambitious VYVYAN TERRACE, of fifty-seven bays arranged 3:3:3–12–3:9:3–12–3:3:3. Designed c. 1833, almost certainly by *Pope* (see the twelve-bay recesses, with loggias like Pope's Buckingham Place, p. 342). Planned as a nineteen-house terrace, and constructed piecemeal: Nos. 15–17 in 1833–4, the rest as late as 1841–7. Palatial centrepiece with eight giant Ionic columns *in antis*, reminiscent of Nash's Regent's Park terraces. The end pavilions have odd bowed balconies between attached columns. From the W end of Vyvyan Terrace, Lansdown Road runs S. Shortly on the l. are Nos. 1–4 KENSINGTON PLACE, an elegant and controlled terrace by *Underwood*, 1842, again for the developers Savery and Clark, with first-floor tripartite windows in segmental recesses.

Back again, and into the NE corner of VICTORIA SQUARE. The NE side, LANSDOWN PLACE, was built first, in 1842–5. Raised centre and ends, with slightly recessed links. Traditionally attributed to the firm of Foster, but the developers, Savery and Clark, frequently employed *Underwood*. The restrained classicism is like his Worcester Terrace (*see* above), and the SE return has a characteristic Underwood bow. For the development of the rest, The Society of Merchant Venturers' surveyor *John Marmont* planned a new square in 1847, incorporating Lansdown Place; it was not completed until 1874, and Marmont only designed two of the three remaining sides. ROYAL PROMENADE (NW) was complete by c. 1851; builder *William Bateman Reed*. An opulent palazzo design with round-arched windows in the centre and ends. Continuous stone balconies, attic arcades with cornice brackets. At the square's W angle, the related ALBERT LODGE, and PHARMACY ARCH, probably also by *Marmont*. The SE SIDE was developed c. 1865–72 with large villas. The best is No. 30, now a hotel, 1865, by *Archibald Ponton*. The rest, more Italianate, of 1869–70, probably by

103

J. A. Clark. The SW SIDE was designed in 1863, also by *Marmont.* The N end was built by *John Yalland*, 1863–7, the rest completed 1874. It is overburdened with powerful arcades of round and Lombardic arches: each bay is repeatedly subdivided vertically. As Late Georgian order finally lapses into indiscriminate mid-Victorian eclecticism, it is a good point to finish.

2b. *Central Clifton, east side*

We begin where Whiteladies Road meets Queen's Road, at the VICTORIA ROOMS, by *Charles Dyer*, 1838–42, assembly rooms intended 'as well for business as festivity'. It exemplifies a European trend *c.* 1840, away from Neoclassicism and towards Roman Corinthian grandeur. Magisterially scaled eight-columned portico, with pediment sculpture attributed to *Musgrave Watson*, 1841, depicting Wisdom in her chariot ushering in Morning and followed by the Three Graces; well-balanced and vivacious. Blind flanks with paired corner pilasters. The Beaux-Arts emphasis on high blocked parapets is especially marked on the return elevations. Main hall disappointingly remodelled (1935) for the University of Bristol. In the forecourt is the EDWARD VII MEMORIAL designed by *E. A. Rickards* (erected 1913) and executed by his favoured sculptor *Henry Poole.* The standing figure on a high plinth presides over fountains with writhing Art Nouveau bronze sculpture on aquatic themes. Roaring lions flanking the steps behind.

To the r., the former ROYAL COLONIAL INSTITUTE, designed in 1913 by *Bridgman & Bridgman*, opened 1921. The narrow S front has some presence, with a semicircle of giant Ionic columns. Unusual Mannerist details, e.g. deep scrolls breaking into the entablature. In the attic storey, half-Atlas figures carry globes. In front of the Victoria Rooms on a central island, the Gloucestershire Regiment's South African WAR MEMORIAL, by *Onslow Whiting*, 1904–5. A bronze soldier loading his rifle. To the SW is PARK PLACE, by *James Foster*, 1822–*c.* 1835. The round-headed porches are probably Edwardian.*

The W branch of QUEEN'S ROAD runs from the Victoria Rooms towards the centre of Clifton. On the r., big red brick flats by *Alec French*, 1935–7, faintly *moderne*, with what was probably Bristol's first underground parking.† Opposite, three large villa pairs, *c.* 1831–3, the model for Clifton Park and much else. At the E, the richest pair, EDGECUMBE HOUSE and THORNTON HOUSE, by *Charles Dyer*, with good Grecian and Italianate motifs freely mixed. Then the smaller BEDFORD and RICHMOND, richly varied. At No. 20 the W return has a rectangular bay with recessed quadrant corners, quite a Baroque

---

*NW of Park Place, No. 7 WETHERELL PLACE, a pleasing Gothic house of 1860 designed for himself by *J. A. Hansom*. In red brick with black diaper work, showing a Puginian concern for function in the asymmetrically disposed windows.

† Pevsner's fear that Clifton might be overwhelmed with such alien metropolitanism has thankfully proved groundless.

conception. From here, Queen's Road rises gently sw to Victoria Square. Opposite the University Students' Union (p. 326) is BUCKINGHAM PLACE, 1843–5, an irregular stepped terrace attributed to *Pope* on stylistic grounds. Next door is Pope's Buckingham Baptist Chapel (p. 322). On a high pavement (s side of Queen's Road) is RICHMOND TERRACE, *c.* 1790 and later, probably by *W. Paty*. Standard Late Georgian elevations. Unusually, it continues SE around two corners, forming three sides of an outward-facing square. The perambulation ends at the junction between Victoria Square (p. 340) and St Andrew's Walk, which leads sw to Clifton Hill (*see* Perambulation 1b).

3. North Clifton

For Clifton's historical development, *see* p. 330. Starting from Christ Church (p. 319), Nos. 1–9 HARLEY PLACE climb the slope to the w. A terrace begun *c.* 1788, but halted by the 1793 collapse and not fully occupied until *c.* 1819. Of Bath stone ashlar, the favoured material for almost everything to come. No. 9 has been refaced in a Soanian manner, perhaps by *Henry Goodridge* (cf. the Bazaar, Bath, 1824–5).

LITFIELD PLACE curves NW from Camp Road to Percival Road, developed *c.* 1827–35 by the Society of Merchant Venturers, who allowed owners to appoint their own architects, but strictly controlled the designs. At LITFIELD HOUSE (1829–30) the Society nominated *Charles Dyer*. A four-square design with paired pilasters, and a heavy Doric porch. Then three plain pairs of 1827–30, two of them altered. DORSET HOUSE, 1833–4, must be by *R. S. Pope* (cf. Royal Colonnade and Brunel House, pp. 312 and 314). Recessed colonnaded centre perversely arranged 1:2:3:2:1, 'a disorderly use indeed of what is not without reason called the orders' (Pevsner). ENGINEERS' HOUSE (formerly Camp House), by *Charles Dyer*, 1830–1, for the mayor Charles Pinney, broad and squat, has an American-looking two-tier portico and pedimented tripartite windows in the flanks. THE PROMENADE continues Litfield Place N, together forming a perfect continuum of domestic architecture of 1830–70, on the most substantial scale possible while maintaining an essentially suburban character. PROMENADE HOUSE, 1836–8, is perhaps by *G. A. Underwood* or *Charles Underwood*. Giant Corinthian pilasters around a deep bow with heavy attics. Then MAXWELL TAYLOR HOUSE, *c.* 1839 by *R. S. Pope*; windows framed by attached columns, and the same narrow wings as Dorset House. TRAFALGAR HOUSE (*c.* 1836) is probably by *Dyer* (cf. Engineers' House). The two-tier portico has non-structural arches between the piers, showing a new freedom from classical constraints.

From here on are several very large pairs, superficially classical, Jacobean or Italianate. At the N junction with Canynge Road, the MANSION HOUSE, by *George & Henry Godwin*, 1867, for Alderman Thomas Proctor. He always planned to donate it to the city, which accounts for its scale. Purple sandstone dug on

site, with big polygonal bays, and odd corbel-like eaves mouldings. On Clifton Down towards Bridge Valley Road are more
substantial villas, in various elaborations of Flemish Renaissance, Victorian palazzo and Jacobean. The Italianate AVON-
BANK (now the Blue House) and LLANFOIST are by *Henry
Goodridge* (1857). In front, a big canopied Gothic DRINKING
FOUNTAIN (*George & Henry Godwin*, 1872), given by Alderman Proctor.

PEMBROKE ROAD is a main route S–N through Clifton, built up
from the early C19. The rule here is Early Victorian terraces at
the S, mid-Victorian villas further N. Here we deal mainly with
exceptions. At the junction with Hanbury Road, CHANNINGS
HOTEL by *Thomas Nicholson*, 1879–82. Gloriously brash and
pompous, with two angular façades overwhelmed with bay
windows and rich carving. BUCKINGHAM VALE, E of Pembroke Road, was built *c.* 1847–50 probably by *Pope*. At Nos.
12–13 two houses are reconciled in an Ionic temple front: a
common device in London villas, but rare here. Nos. 60–64
Pembroke Road are two exceptionally pretty villa pairs of
c. 1852, with low belvederes flanking central verandas. At
No. 1 Alma Vale Road, directly S of All Saints (*see* p. 319),
EDWARDS' VAN GARAGE, 1899, by *Drake & Pizey*. Edwardian
Baroque, with Art Nouveau touches. Further N in Guthrie
Road (W side of Pembroke Road) is the tower of EMMANUEL
CHURCH (*John Norton*, 1865–9), E.E., flat-topped (intended
for a tall spire) with big louvred belfry lights. The rest demolished for old people's flats by *Futcher & Futcher*, *c.* 1978–80.
At the N end, E side, Nos. 1–3 Downside Road, big Italianate
houses, now the Bristol Old Vic Theatre School. Attached at
the rear, DANCE STUDIOS by *Ferguson Mann*, 1995, a light and
unhistoricist addition, fully glazed to allow views in. An early
example of a building type shortly followed by more prominent expressions.*

WHITELADIES ROAD forms the E boundary of Clifton. Now
mostly commercial in character, but with good Italianate villas
of *c.* 1855–65 at the S end, by *R. S. Pope* and *Henry Rumley*
among others. Between Belgrave Road and Tyndalls Park
Road, BROADCASTING HOUSE, by *BBC Architects*, 1987, a
good pastiche of its mid-Victorian neighbours. Further N (W
side), the disused ABC CINEMA, by *La Trobe & Weston*, 1921,
originally with a dance hall and restaurant. Superior and flashy
Hollywood motifs, e.g. pierced panels and carving on the
domed turret, spread-eagle wings down the flank, etc. At the
corner of Ashgrove Road (E side), the site of Trinity Methodist
Chapel (*Samuel Hancorn*, 1866), dem. *c.* 1978; its Gothic bell-
CUPOLA survives as a garden ornament. Near the N end of
Whiteladies Road, No. 106 (NATWEST BANK) by *Drake &
Pizey*, 1903–6, bulky free Baroque. Opposite, Nos. 155–157,
three quirky *Rundbogenstil* houses by *Gingell*, 1856. Three-and-

---

*For instance, the Laban Centre, Deptford, London (Herzog & de Meuron, 2002);
Dance City, Newcastle (Malcolm Fraser Architects, 2005).

a-half storeys, with belvedere towers, central arcade, bays, and more variety than any building can sensibly bear. (For the adjacent Redland Park United Reformed Church, *see* p. 385.)

Finally an enclave of convoluted lanes W of Blackboy Hill, the N end of Whiteladies Road; with C18 and later quarrymen's houses around the turnpike gate bordering Durdham Down. Signs of smartening-up: Late Classical terraces such as ANGLESEY PLACE, *c.* 1850; on RICHMOND DALE, a Gothic mission house and reading room (now school) in polychrome brick, *c.* 1860; and pompous brick shops on Whiteladies Road.

Outlying buildings

OBSERVATORY HILL. NE of the Suspension Bridge. At the highest point is the OBSERVATORY, a rubble-stone tower of an C18 windmill, recast in medievalizing dress in 1828–35, with a *camera obscura*. The hill is one of three IRON AGE PROMONTORIES fortified by earthworks overlooking the Avon Gorge. The other two, Stokeleigh and Burgh Walls, are on the W side of the gorge. They are all of similar size and shape and are probably contemporary.

OAKFIELD HOUSE, Oakfield Road, 1831, by *Dyer*, signed on the porch. A substantial villa to which *Charles Underwood* perhaps added the rear bow window.

CANYNGE SQUARE. Off Canynge Road. Latest-classical infill of 1840–9, on a trapezoidal layout. By *Charles Underwood*, completed by *Gingell*. Big linked pairs on the SW side. The other sides have terraces with windows in big relieving arches. One of two streets in Bristol still lit by Victorian gas lamps.

4. *Royal Fort and St Michael's Hill*

For the main cluster of University buildings around Tyndall Avenue, Woodland Road and University Road, *see* p. 323. SE of Tyndall Avenue, and now embedded in the University precinct, is ROYAL FORT, a five-sided fort of *c.* 1644 for the Royalist side. This was mostly demolished in 1655, and replaced by big houses of the C17 and C18. It became University property in 1917, and is now surrounded by University buildings of varying quality. ROYAL FORT HOUSE is Bristol's finest Georgian villa, built by Thomas Tyndall in 1758–61. *James Bridges*, who made the wooden model still in the house, was claimed in 1763 to be its architect, but a doggerel rhyme of 1767 appears to make claims for Thomas Paty and John Wallis: it was written probably by Wallis himself, perhaps to cast doubt on Bridges's authorship. The house is almost square in profile and plan, of three storeys, in Bath stone. The Vanbrughian N entrance front has arched first-floor windows, the W front is conventionally Palladian, of 1:3:1 bays and pedimented, and the S front has a canted bay, small first-floor Venetian windows, and two garden doorcases with pretty Rococo carving in the pediments. The relationship of the three façades is not entirely successful. Inside are incomparably the best C18 interiors in Bristol, at once playful and supremely elegant, with stucco by *Thomas Stocking*; masonry carving and fittings by *Thomas Paty*. From the N entrance, a central hall with a triple-arched screen leads via a lateral corridor to a staircase in the SE corner. Drawing room, parlour, dining room and study arranged around the hall. The HALL and corridor have a Doric entablature with elaborate metopes and, in the hall, four sculptural Rococo brackets. The STAIRCASE HALL has all-over plasterwork with sinuous Rococo designs reminiscent of C18 wallpaper. Its motif is vines alive with birds and squirrels, and with pastoral vignettes around the lower stems. Fine wrought-iron S-scrolled staircase balustrade. In the DINING ROOM are a Rococo ceiling, a lively rocaille mantel, and delicately undercut drops of hunting trophies. The doorcase has wreathed Corinthian columns and an extravagant Chinoiserie overdoor. Attached (E), a big contemporary service wing. [81]

The garden of Royal Fort House was sold for development in 1791, but the scheme foundered after quarrying had ruined it, and it was remodelled by *Humphry Repton* to hide both the scars and the new houses around Park Street. Small parts of Repton's scheme survive, as well as a section of the C17 FORT WALL, S side, and a mid-C18 brick GATEWAY, N side. Attached to the E of Royal Fort House is STUART HOUSE, simple but handsome, late C18 probably around a C17 core. Beyond is the C17 fort GATEHOUSE, with little original fabric; C18 outer arch, upper structure rebuilt *c.* 1950s. From here Royal Fort Road leads shortly down to ST MICHAEL'S HILL. Here at the brow of the hill are the former Children's Hospital (p. 329), and opposite, the bulky Maternity Hospital (p. 329). Below, a happy mix of C17–C19 houses, e.g. Nos. 65–67 (W) probably by *George Tully*, *c.* 1727, and No. 46, of 1711, a four-bay stone façade with panelled parapet, and open segmental pediment on Tuscan columns. Below, Winstone Court by *Derek Bruce & Partners*, 1977, a fine piece of infill incorporating, r., a late C18 house. The new work, with a glazed ground floor, is harmonious without slavish copying. On the W side, a long C18 row, the exteriors meticulously reconstructed from photographs by *Ralph Brentnall c.* 1960; interiors largely rebuilt. Nos. 49–51 and 39–41 are early C18.

COLSTON'S ALMSHOUSES (E side), founded by Edward Colston, are probably Bristol's earliest classical public building, of 1691–6. A homely courtyard of warm limestone with hipped roofs, arranged symmetrically around a steeply pedimented three-bay chapel with an inscription flanked by two oval windows. Cross-windows, the lower ones with alternating pediments. The doorways have gabled canopies, the chapel a higher segmental pediment. Adjoining, below, are three tall gabled houses of 1695, built to provide income for the almshouses. More of the C17 on the W side: Nos. 23–29, the upper pair *c.* 1637. Three storeys, gabled with two jetties, updated with C18 sashes. Immediately below is St Michael [54]

(p. 320). To the s in Old Church Lane, its former RECTORY has a pretty C18 Gothick façade, ogee-arched windows with intersecting glazing bars, presumably by *Thomas Paty* and of the date of the rebuilt church, i.e. 1775–7. The core is C16 or earlier: late C16 panelling was removed in 1910 (*see* Red Lodge, below). Lower Church Lane leads SW down to Park Row. At their junction, on a high platform, is SAVORY'S PRINTING WORKS, now a University building. By *Mowbray Green*, 1905, extended 1909. Arts and Crafts-influenced roughcast render and timber balconies.

Almost opposite on Park Row, RED LODGE, 1579–80, a remarkable late Elizabethan lodge, now a museum.* The site belonged to a C13 Carmelite foundation. In 1568 John Young acquired it and built a mansion (demolished for Colston Hall, 1863). Red Lodge was his garden lodge, of sandstone, originally rendered and painted deep red, gabled, and with an arched loggia to the garden – an Italian Renaissance idea. The distinctive window mouldings suggest that the architect may have been *Robert Smythson* or one of his team at Longleat. Red Lodge was extended in the C17 and comprehensively altered *c.* 1704, with hipped roofs, eaves cornice and long sashes. The N side was remodelled around a new staircase, the loggia incorporated into the rooms behind. The ground-floor PARLOUR has a C16 ribbed and moulded ceiling and chimneypiece with scrolled frieze. At the NW corner, the NEW OAK ROOM was re-fitted in 1965; fireplace of *c.* 1600, from the demolished Ashley Manor, Ashley Down, panelling from St Michael's rectory (*see* above). Coincidentally, its cornice is virtually identical to that in the Great Oak Room here, presumably by the same maker. Oak STAIRCASE probably *c.* 1704, nobly proportioned; three twisted balusters per tread, Ionic column-newels. The first-floor GREAT OAK ROOM is among the most elaborate English interiors of its date. The timber inner porch (cf. Montacute House, Somerset), probably contemporary, has shell-headed doors with paired Composite columns. Two richly embellished tiers of carving, each with its own order. The porch's upper cornice matches neither the lower one, nor that around the room. The walls have an arcaded dado with fluted pilasters, and above this, a regular grid of arched panels. Geometric ribbed ceiling, with pendants, decorative reliefs in the panels, and faintly Gothic ogee trefoils. Dominating all is the only major Bristol-school chimneypiece still *in situ*; attributed to the Bristol mason *Thomas Collins*, though a Longleat mason remains a possibility. It is very big and high, of carved limestone, with alabaster panels of Hope, Faith, Justice and Prudence. In the middle, Young's arms; the surrounding strapwork and paired terms derive from mid-C16 engravings by Vredeman de Vries.

In Red Lodge gardens is the WIGWAM, a barn-like structure by *C. F. W. Dening*, 1919–20, for the Savages, a society of

---

* This account incorporates new research by Nick Molyneux of English Heritage. Dendrochronology has established building and alteration dates.

artists. In the main room, two chimneypieces; one of 1682, with broken segmental pediment and seated figures, but still a cambered fire-opening, the other, of 1674, from the house of a wine merchant nearby; overmantel with arabesques, vine trails and tapering pilasters.* Park Row continues W, with minor incidents. LUNSFORD HOUSE, refronted *c.* 1738–9 around a C17 core, with a C19 rear wing. Brick, with a Venetian window in the projecting centre, and parapets ramped down to lower flanks. Then the faintly fortress-like VANDYCK PRESS, 1911, by *Mowbray Green*, now a University building, of rough-hewn rubble, with battered plinth. Plain and divested of historicism. Opposite, gabled brick shops by *Edward Gabriel*, 1905, and then Nos. 20–24, by *James Hart*, 1902. Originally a decorator's showroom (hence the samples of Baroque and Adam plasterwork) with houses either side. Eclectic references, e.g. Doric colonnades, C17 domestic in the wings. Here Woodland Road climbs back up to the University Precinct.

OUTLIERS. Two buildings marooned in the University precinct W of St Michael's Hill. TOWER VIEW, Cantock's Close, began as a summerhouse of *c.* 1750–80 (extended), for Lunsford House, Park Row (*see* above). It had probably two rooms above a single-arched loggia. In Park Lane, the MANOR HOUSE, rebuilt after a fire in 1691. Bristol's earliest surviving classical house, in provincial Restoration-Dutch mode. A handsome six-bay façade with shell-hood door placed off-centre, hipped roof and dormers. Single-storey wings, probably from an earlier C17 house. The cross-windows post-date a fire of 1978.

5. Kingsdown to Stokes Croft

A perambulation covering the residential NE fringe of the centre. John Betjeman described Kingsdown in the late 1950s as 'this airy suburb, this place of Georgian view-commanding terraces, trees, cobbled streets, garden walls and residential quiet'. That atmosphere is not lost.

We begin at ST MICHAEL'S HILL, the W boundary of Kingsdown. At No. 121, OLDBURY HOUSE (W side); now a University building. A gentry house of *c.* 1679–89, updated perhaps *c.* 1750, but retaining three C17 gables. Gibbsian doorcase with pediment in the Paty style. Opposite, alleys lead E into HIGH KINGSDOWN, housing by *Whicheloe Macfarlane* and the builders *JT Group Ltd*, after the demise of a destructive high- and medium-rise scheme in 1968. Low-rise houses of brick and tile, on a herringbone layout with walled gardens, inspired by Jørn Utzon's housing at Fredensborg, Denmark (1962–5). Built in phases, 1971–5. A green space and Victorian pub were left in the centre. On the N boundary, a long slab of flats intended to shelter the houses from an unexecuted road scheme (cf. Ralph Erskine's Byker Estate, Newcastle, planned

120

*A third timber chimneypiece is a mish-mash of C16 and later parts with coarse copies of the two Canynges effigies at St Mary Redcliffe, doubtless assembled in the C19.

1970). The zigzag ranges, walled alleys and courtyards give remarkable privacy. The only comparable English scheme is Bishopsfield, Harlow, by Neylan & Ungless, 1963–6.

To the E in Portland Street is KNIGHTSTONE HOUSE, by *Bruges Tozer*, 1974–9, also remarkably responsive to its site for the date. Angular flats around a rear courtyard, of red brick with blue soldier courses. It incorporates a Methodist chapel hall (*Foster & Wood*, 1883). In Alfred Place, S, a terrace of *c.* 1788, with canted bays with simple timber mouldings. To the S, a contextual addition of houses by *Moxley Jenner*, 1985.

Now E across Cotham Road South, to the heart of Kingsdown. KINGSDOWN PARADE runs NE along the escarpment. At the corner with Marlborough Hill, S, PRIOR'S CLOSE, by *Inscape Architects*, 2000–4, a community-led development. The tallest houses hold the C18 line and height, but the buff brick, render and aluminium-clad roofs avoid pastiche Georgian. Working NE, Nos. 20–28 typify the piecemeal mid-C18 houses, unified by bays, and with good railings etc. DEVON HOUSE, No. 34a, is unusually grand; ashlar-fronted, in the style of *William Paty*, *c.* 1790. At the NE end, long terraces for the respectable middle class, of *c.* 1791–1800; developer Charles Melsom, architect probably *W. Paty*. Nos. 48–86 (S side) form a near-uniform terrace, brick-fronted under later stucco. Doorcases with imposts carrying both curved brackets to an open pediment and a moulded inner arch around the fanlight (cf. Brunswick Square, 1784). On the N side, Nos. 65–101 are quasi-semi-detached pairs linked by originally single-storey entrance wings; a speciality of Paty. Long front gardens with pedimented gates (surviving at, e.g., No. 71), and no rear gardens at all.

At the NE end of Kingsdown Parade is FREMANTLE SQUARE. On the NW side, big villa pairs, perhaps by *R. S. Pope*, 1840s. The other three sides by *William Armstrong*, *c.* 1841–2; terraced, stuccoed houses with first-floor windows recessed in blind arches. Good teardrop fanlights. From the SW corner, SOMERSET STREET returns to the SW. A charming and relaxed backwater laid out probably *c.* 1737–8 by *George Tully*, at the northern limit of the grid-like blocks N of King Square; most houses of *c.* 1750–90. Haphazard extensions suggest a rise in the street's status in the late C18, e.g. No. 34, a mid-C18 cottage with three storeys at the l., of *c.* 1790. Further SW, Nos. 19, 18 and SPRING HILL HOUSE, *c.* 1770–80. Probably built by *Thomas* and *Isaac Manley* (cf. No. 26 Cumberland Street, St Paul's, p. 353); casually mixing canted bays, Venetian and tri-partite sashes.

SPRING HILL, a setted-and-stepped lane, descends steeply to Dove Street, where the harmonious C18 atmosphere is rudely shattered by DOVE STREET FLATS (*City Architect's Department*, 1965–8). Three big fourteen-storey slabs with lower links, which required the demolition of some 340 Georgian houses that could have been resored. Below is KING SQUARE, laid out by *George Tully* and built up slowly *c.* 1740–75. The SE and NE sides are dull post-war infill after bombing. On the SW side,

Nos. 2–7 (c. 1762), with familiar features suggesting *Thomas Paty*. Behind No. 7, a rare surviving coachhouse, c. 1760s, now derelict. On the NW side Nos. 12–15 are of c. 1760–70, with some ugly extensions.

JAMAICA STREET runs NE from King Square. On the r., Nos. 2–6 have simple and refined Greek Doric doorcases of c. 1810–20. Nos. 37–39 were built c. 1905 by *J. L. Priest & Co.*, ironfounders, as a carriage works; heightened in 1909. Bristol's belated first experiment in exposed iron-framed construction. Fully glazed lower façade between slim columns. Here we join STOKES CROFT, built up by the late C17. No. 104 is a fine example of the Bristol warehouse style, built as PERRY'S CARRIAGE WORKS by *E. W. Godwin*, 1862. Coursed Pennant rubble, ten bays and three storeys. On the ground floor, five broad segmental arches, originally open. Above, ten-light arcades to each floor, the outer arches narrower and pointed, lending a subtle tension. Disgracefully derelict, given its obvious significance. To the s, Nos. 74–76, a pair of shops also by *Godwin*, c. 1865, disfigured by later shopfronts, but with gutsy Gothic brick detailing. At the s end of the street, the former FULL MOON INN, c. 1695, has a three-storey gabled range at right angles to the street, with early C19 tripartite sashes and columned porch. Tucked away behind in Backfields, the crystalline Gothic former WESLEYAN DAY SCHOOLS by *Foster & Wood*, 1856.

OUTLIERS. HARFORD HOUSE, No. 2, Dighton Street. A mid-sized Palladian villa, after Clifton Hill House (*see* p. 335), and probably by *Thomas Paty*, c. 1760. Three-storey pedimented centre of 1:3:1 bays. The r. wing has been built up, giving a lopsided appearance.

CHARLES STREET. Nos. 4–5, modest brick of c. 1750. No. 4, occasionally open to the public, was from 1766 to 1771 the home of the Methodist leader Charles Wesley, and his son Samuel, the composer. Simple and evocative furnishings, and a re-created C18 rear garden.

EAST OF THE CENTRE:
ST PAUL'S AND ST PHILIP'S WITH ST JUDE'S

Places of worship

Church of England

HOLY TRINITY, Trinity Road, St Philip's. Now an arts centre. 1829–32, by *Rickman & Hutchinson*, characteristically Perp. It cost £8,231, of which the Church Commissioners contributed £6,031. Of Bath stone, with a showy gabled w front between polygonal pierced turrets. Lean-to aisles. Big Somerset-style w and E windows, tall three-light aisle windows with segmental heads. Shallow chancel, then a semi-hexagonal vestry, perhaps mid-C19. NE choir vestry, *W. V. Gough*, 1905. Harshly reordered *c.* 1980, with a floor inserted. Slender Perp piers without capitals. Flat panelled ceiling with bosses. Behind the piers, the gallery substructures survive. – FITTINGS. Mostly 1882. – MONUMENT. Ann Meloy and children; *opus sectile*, late C19. – Adjacent, N, a grim Gothic VICARAGE in red brick and stone, by *John Bevan Sen.*, 1889.

ST AGNES, Newfoundland Road. By *W. Wood Bethell*, 1885–7. An original design. Surprisingly costly at £9,520, a mission from Clifton College. High Perp tower at the NW, of pink sandstone with rich details, inventive flamboyant Dec tracery and a Somerset spirelet. Aisles, S chapel and a long chancel. The interior is 'unmistakably eclectic, and very good' (Gomme). Very high nave, plain red Pennant walls, tall circular piers with square capitals richly carved with figures. Bold arcades of square section with a small chamfer. Subdivided by *Philip Mann* of *Ferguson Mann*, 1993–7; the two w bays are now the halls, with offices above. The E end has been reversed, with an altar against the new w wall and new seating, but the old sanctuary FITTINGS largely kept. – Neo-Perp oak REREDOS by *W. W. Bethell*, 1900; also the SCREEN, now acting as a second reredos at the w end. – PULPIT, *c.* 1886–9, with mosaic figure panels. – Chancel FLOOR, also mosaic, with angels and saints. – STAINED GLASS. E window, 1892. Chancel S and S chapel E by *A. O. Hemming*, 1886. N aisle second from w, four figures by *Hemming*, 1889, resited and restored.

Adjacent, HALLS, 1882–93; the first part, also a schoolroom, with six gables facing the M32 motorway, by *C. F. Hansom*, 1882. Extended in seven phases. All in commercial use. In Thomas Street opposite the church, a small PARK established in 1883–4 by Clifton College. Pretty Gothic LODGE in polychrome brick, by *Hansom*, 1885.

ST JUDE, Braggs Lane, St Jude's. By *S. B. Gabriel*, 1848–9, converted to housing, 2004–5. Among the first Bristol churches to conform to Ecclesiological requirements. Aisleless buttressed nave and w tower, carefully observed C14 Dec windows, snaking tracery on the tower parapet. Attached to the NE, simple angular SCHOOL BUILDINGS.

ST PAUL, Portland Square, St Paul's (Churches Conservation Trust). 1789–94, by *Daniel Hague*, also the mason. Now a circus school. Externally Gothick of the Strawberry Hill variety, but hybrid-classical within (cf. St Michael, p. 320). The plan and general composition are entirely classical. A dispute over a rival design by *James Allen* caused bitter recriminations; it was rumoured that Hague's design had been influenced by the vicar. Bath stone ashlar. Ogee-headed windows with intersecting and Y-tracery, and pilaster strips with sunken panels, lozenges and quatrefoils, etc. The whole church is embattled and pinnacled. The tall three-stage tower projects from the w front, topped by two further stages with diagonal buttresses, diminishing in wedding-cake fashion to a stumpy pinnacle. Inspired, according to Hague, by the tower of the second Royal Exchange, London, 1667–71. The aisle windows have solid quatrefoil bands reflecting galleries that were removed in 1901. Nave arcades of tall columns with acanthus-leaf capitals, then a deep cove running into a flat ceiling. The ceiling has stucco arabesques in panels, and fine acanthus roses for the light fittings. More rich and very pretty arabesques frame the chancel arch. Throughout the interior are decorative bands of fluting with rounded ends or Gothic points, e.g. at the column bases and necks, in the coving, and in the pointed vault of *Hague*'s chancel. Here the N wall shows the original arrangement of two deeply sunk quatrefoil windows, placed high up. The chancel was extended by *John Bevan Sen.*, 1893–4, in an indeterminate and clashing Gothic style. Hybrid E window with vertical mullions through Dec tracery. The church was repaired 2002–4 by *Philip Hughes Associates* after long decay; a fine and sensitive reuse, maintaining most of the fittings, with a glazed vestibule beneath the w gallery.

FITTINGS. REREDOS with Agnus Dei, dumpy PULPIT, and coarse CHANCEL FURNISHINGS, all 1894. – WALL PAINT-INGS. Above the w gallery, uncovered *c.* 2003, two painted *trompe l'oeil* niches with pinnacles and saints, in poor condi-tion. These must be C19 overpaintings of the *trompe l'œil* cur-tained windows framing the organ recess, for which *Mr Freese* was paid £26 5s. in 1794. – STAINED GLASS. E window, *c.* 1894 by *Moon & Son*, remarkably old-fashioned. Three in the s aisle and one in the N, by *Joseph Bell & Son*. Tower N by *Arnold Robinson* (*Bell & Son*), 1949. – MONUMENTS. Col. Spencer Vassall †1807. By *Rossi*, 1810, to a design of *Flaxman*. Trun-cated black obelisk behind a winged figure of Victory mourn-ing over a shield inscribed Montevideo. – The usual tablets by *Tyley*, *Wood*, etc.

Other denominations

ST NICHOLAS OF TOLENTINO (R.C.), Lawford's Gate, St Philip's. Nave of 1848–50, by *Charles Hansom*. Routine Dec, of grey Pennant rubble, with starved s w spirelet. Later aisles with transverse gables. Low chancel, s chapel, sacristy and pres-bytery, all 1872–3. Reordered 2007–9, with a new s entrance and hall; by *O'Leary Goss*.

UNITARIAN MEETING HOUSE, Brunswick Square, St Paul's. Formerly Surrey Lodge, built *c.* 1830 as the entrance to the Unitarian Burial Ground behind. Low and domestic-looking, conventionally Grecian except for the recessed elliptical entrance arch flanked by Doric columns *in antis*. Extended by

Michael Lawrence, 1992, to replace Lewins Mead chapel (p. 271). – Glass DOORS etched with a circle of hands, designer *Richard Long*, 1991.

CONGREGATIONAL CHAPEL (former), Brunswick Square, St Paul's. By *William Armstrong*, 1834–5. Boxy, with heavy attached Ionic portico and channelled rustication. Greek Revival merging into Italianate.

CONGREGATIONAL CHAPEL, Stapleton Road, St Philip's. Italianate, by *Hans Price*, 1867–71, schoolrooms included. Open-arcaded lobby with gallery stairs at both sides. Triple window, bracketed cornice, open pediment. Inside, a high gallery on cast-iron columns that continue up to support big timber trusses.

CITY ROAD BAPTIST CHAPEL, St Paul's. By *Medland & Maberley* of Gloucester, 1860–1. A bold Romanesque design with aisles and clerestory, five stumpy pinnacles on the W front, and a big rose over the W door. Three-bay addition at the NE, dated 1885. Inside, unexpected arcades of big round arches on foliate capitals. Galleries on three sides. In 1905 a second row of circular windows was inserted beneath the N gallery.

PARKWAY METHODIST CHURCH, Conduit Place, St Paul's. By *Eustace Button*, 1971–2. Octagonal, with a central spike on the roof. – STAINED GLASS. E window of cast glass and resin, by *Geoffrey Robinson (Bell & Son)*, 1971.

UNITARIAN BURIAL GROUND, Brunswick Square, St Paul's. Established *c.* 1766–8. In the centre is a small C18 MORTUARY CHAPEL of brick.

JEWISH CEMETERY, Barton Road, St Philip's. Closed. A simple enclosure with high rubble walls. Probably established by 1753; the earliest surviving headstone is of 1762.

Public buildings

POLICE STATION, Trinity Road, St Philip's. By *Avon County Council Architect's Department (Chris Bocci)*, 1976–9. Of razor-sharp red brick with blue soldier courses. Forbiddingly windowless to Trinity Road.

ST PHILIP'S LIBRARY, Trinity Road. By *W. V. Gough*, 1896. Jacobethan, red and yellow brick, mullioned windows, prominent gables and a deep bay. Big elliptical arches on heavy columns across the reading room.

Perambulations

1. *St Paul's*

St Paul's expanded in the late C18 to accommodate growth on the fashionable N fringe. It became industrialized from *c.* 1870, with boot- and furniture-making prominent. Post-war dereliction exacerbated racial tensions here, but the area has been turned around since riots in 1981, with much commercial development.

We begin at BRUNSWICK SQUARE. A rather haphazard Georgian scheme, laid out with Cumberland Street to its w in 1766 by *George Tully*, although he did not design the houses. The N side remained open until a chapel was built in the 1830s. In CUMBERLAND STREET, the builders *Thomas* and *Isaac Manley* probably provided their own designs from pattern books. Bays, Venetian and sash windows freely mixed, e.g. at No. 26, s side. The N side has offices with replica façades, *c.* 1985–7. The w side of Brunswick Square is an incomplete terrace of three with Gibbsian blocked openings. Probably by *Thomas Paty*, as is the more orderly s side, also of *c.* 1766–71. Arranged 5:3:5:3:5 bays, with pedimented centre and stepped voussoirs. Sadly façaded for offices, 1981–3. The E side is probably by *William Paty*, *c.* 1784–6. The centre is de-emphasized in favour of higher end pavilions, a Neoclassical characteristic. Unusually, no lesenes between the houses. For the former Congregational chapel and Unitarian meeting house (N side), see p. 352.

Surrey Street leads w to PORTLAND SQUARE, laid out in 1787 and named for the 3rd Duke of Portland, then High Steward of Bristol. The houses partly financed the new church (*see* p. 350). Its architect *Daniel Hague* also designed the square, *c.* 1787–8; completed only *c.* 1823. Ambitiously planned, together with surrounding streets; the first design in brick was modified by bigger end pavilions and the substitution of Bath stone. Although spartan by London or Bath standards, the architecture is quite refined. *Thomas Pope*, father of R. S. Pope, was one of the builders. Continuous terraces on the N and s; four-bay centre and ends with full attics and, in the centre only, pilasters with acanthus capitals. Good Ionic doorcases, plain window openings. The w side is bisected by Surrey Street and the E side by St Paul's church. The side streets are simpler, and developed later, e.g. CAVE STREET, NW, built 1828.

In WILSON STREET, SE, a terrace of *c.* 1830 with reeded and round-arched doorways. Here too, the best survivor of C19 industry in St Paul's: a shoe factory, by *William Holbrow*, 1895. Red brick with stone banding and a Neo-Baroque doorcase. Now apartments. s of the square in St Paul Street and Pritchard Street, office buildings of the 1990s with atrocious pseudo-Georgian façades. A short way E along Newfoundland Street, N side, is the former MAGNET CINEMA by *Holbrow & Oaten*, 1913–14. Edwardian classical, with segmental arches and oculi. Top storey later. To the w is the SPECTRUM BUILDING by *BGP Group Architects*, completed 1984, offices with screen walls of blue glass, neon-lit at night.

2. *St Philip's with St Jude's*

The C12 church of SS Philip and Jacob (p. 266) was once the focus of a big parish extending some miles across present-day E Bristol. To its NE is Old Market, a broad early medieval route E from Bristol Castle. Heavy bomb damage to the w cut it off from the city, causing decline. Many C17–C19 buildings have been repaired since the 1970s.

We begin at the crossroads of Lawford Street and Old Market. On the NE corner is the PALACE HOTEL, an absurdly high and pretentious gin palace with French-looking details, 1869–70, attributed to *W. H. Hawtin*, to profit from a new railway station nearby. Good Victorian interior; partly surviving bar with brass barley-sugar columns etc. To the E is WEST STREET, now mostly late C19 commercial with some C18 houses. Further E, No. 20, a C17 gabled house with C19 half-timbering, on the verge of collapse before reconstruction, 2005–6. Back W into OLD MARKET, which widens at the site of the medieval Shambles. TRINITY HOSPITAL SOUTH (s side) was founded in 1402 by John Barstaple and rebuilt in stages by *Foster & Wood*, in Tudor Gothic with Burgundian details (cf. Foster's Almshouses, p. 290). Two Pennant-stone facing ranges, running N–S. The NE section, of 1857–8, has many breaks and projections, aiming at variety but verging on confusion. Perp chapel, 1867. SE addition of 1881–3, with timber stair-turret. Excellent W elevation hidden in Jacob Street; a shallow balconied courtyard with rich cusped and quatrefoiled timberwork, and inventive carving. N of Old Market is TRINITY HOSPITAL NORTH, 1913, by *F. Wills & Sons*, Tudor Gothic again but resolutely dull.
Most of the incident in Old Market is on the s side. No. 53, the mid-C17 MASON'S ARMS, gabled and jettied. No. 42 (N), a good early C18 house with alternating pediments. Double-bowed shopfront, c. 1800. Second floor replaced c. 1980. To its W, No. 41 of c. 1630–80, with a partial refronting, and Nos. 36–38, also mid-C17, bayed and jettied. This row was rebuilt behind c. 1980, destroying the C17 timber frames. Back on the s side, No. 59, KINGSLEY HALL, dated 1706, three storeys in chequered Flemish-bond brick, oversailing the pavement on stout columns. Then the big brick Gloster Regiment DRILL HALL, by *Paul & James*, 1914, converted to flats c. 2005. Nos. 70 and 71 are more gabled mid-C17 houses, with well-preserved jetty brackets. On the N side, the former METHODIST CENTRAL HALL, by *Kitchen & Gelder*, 1924, coarse Neo-Baroque with a domed lantern. Finally the STAG AND HOUNDS pub (s side), once home of the medieval Pie Poudre Court, which heard market disputes. Rebuilt c. 1690–1710 with oversailing upper floors on columns, a brick front with timber pilasters and string courses, and some cross-windows.

ST JUDE'S was a planned suburb N of Old Market, established c. 1700 with the laying out of Wade Street, Great Ann Street, etc., and Wade's Bridge over the River Frome (1711). Of this early C18 development almost all traces are now gone. From 2005 its NW end was redeveloped as Cabot Circus shopping centre; see p. 305. Nearby (s) is No. 7 REDCROSS STREET, a fine stone house of c. 1715–20, the birthplace of Sir Thomas Lawrence, portraitist to George III and IV. Three storeys by five bays, with elliptical shell-hood doorcase, the windows connected vertically by aprons and horizontally by string courses. Now horribly enveloped by pink aggregate-faced offices (*Elsom Pack & Roberts*, 1974). A little way E is GUILD HERITAGE HOUSE, Braggs Lane. By *Frank Wills & Sons*, 1912–13; a very early building designed for wheelchair users. Built for the 'Guild of The Brave Poor Things', a charity founded by Ada Vachell. Blunt red brick, with gabled centrepiece on Doric columns. It provided a hall, stage, classrooms, workshops, billiard room with wheelchair access, and a shop. Now local authority offices.

The part of St Philip's s of Old Market has fragmentary remains of C18 and C19 industry, amid run-of-the-mill new flats. In Jacob Street, one bold and original development, VERDIGRIS by *David Martyn* (*GCP Architects*), 2006–9. Behind a C19 brick façade, a green copper-clad tower, its top storey marked by orange-red panels and brises-soleil. At Old Market roundabout on Temple Way is the BRISTOL UNITED PRESS BUILDING. By *Group Architects DRG*, 1970–4, and always well regarded. Faced largely in purple tile and glazed brick with much blank walling, a conscious response to fears of terrorism. Staggered and set-back upper tiers, grouped towers with rounded angles. Printing hall (the N end of the building) demolished 2011. Directly s is BROAD PLAIN, a triangular space with trees in the centre. Of the C18 houses on the s side, the richest is No. 5, *c.* 1720, with shell-hood, serpentine window arches, foliate keystones and brick architraves. The E end of the row has bay windows of *c.* 1780, grafted onto earlier houses.

To the E of Broad Plain is the former THOMAS'S SOAP WORKS, a complex series of factory buildings between Unity Street, N, and Old Bread Street, s, now a shop. Soap boiling began here *c.* 1783; Thomas operated here from 1841, taken over by Lever Bros, 1912–53. N of Straight Street, a four-storey block facing Broad Plain dated 1884, remodelled possibly by *Gingell* from an 1850s building. Adjoining three-storey block on Straight Street of 1865, in Gingell's warehouse style (giant arcade and rock-faced masonry). s of Straight Street, a curtain-walled block by *A. E. Powell*, 1957–8, and adjoining to the E, a sharp red brick range of 1912 by Lever Bros' architect *James Simpson* (later Lomax-Simpson). To their s, the gaunt five-storey pan building where the soap was boiled. Recast in 1881 by *C. James*, from a lower 1840s building. The chimneys originally had flared tops on heavy corbel tables like that below the crenellated parapet; all after the Palazzo Vecchio, Florence. Much detail lost in a fire in 1902. On Old Bread Street, s, an arcuated stone block by *Foster & Wood*, 1865–7, with a taller brick block to the w, *c.* 1883, by *C. James*. Converted to dwellings, 2006.

From Avon Street, a snaking FOOTBRIDGE on an angled mast, by *W. S. Atkins & Partners Overseas*, 2000, leads s to TEMPLE QUAY, formerly a railway goods depot. Redevelopment was planned *c.* 1990 by the controversial Urban Development Corporation, and largely completed *c.* 1997–2002. The BRISTOL AND WEST BUILDING, by *Chapman Taylor* and *Stride Treglown*,

1997–2000, dominates the waterfront. Well planned, but with unimaginative elevations of contrasting yellow and red brick. TEMPLE QUAY HOUSE (*Stride Treglown*, 2001) is in a faintly 1930s idiom with horizontal windows flanking a recessed entrance.

OUTLIERS. Off Stapleton Road is ARMOURY SQUARE. An armoury was built here by the Board of Ordnance in 1805–7 against the risk of French invasion. In *c.* 1849–51 the central armoury building was demolished and one-bay artisan houses built in terraces against the boundary walls to form a street. Four plain double-fronted houses survive from 1805; No. 12, originally for the commanding officer; No. 19, the barracks, with the best-preserved façade; No. 39, for the armourer; and No. 46 for the storekeeper. At the top end, Colston Villas, a symmetrical pair of *c.* 1860 with a niche with a replica bust of Edward Colston. In 1978 the original was found to be *Rysbrack*'s terracotta maquette of *c.* 1728–9 for his monument at All Saints' church (p. 252); now at the City Art Gallery.

ST VINCENT'S WORKS, Silverthorne Lane. Formerly Lysaght's galvanized iron works. Neo-Romanesque OFFICES by *R. M. Drake*, 1891–3, with battered gateway and turreted corner entrance. Inside, an octagonal two-storey entrance hall beneath a glazed dome, with a painted frieze of shipping. The walls are wildly encrusted with *Doulton* tiles with Renaissance-inspired grotesquerie, extremely fine. Adjoining *Rundbogenstil* FACTORY of *c.* 1860, possibly by *Thomas Lysaght*, who briefly partnered W. B. Gingell and whose brother owned the iron works. Burned in 2005, awaiting rebuilding.

SOUTH OF THE CENTRE: SPIKE ISLAND

SPIKE ISLAND (a name only used from *c.* 1970) is a long spit of land s of the harbour, from Bathurst Basin in the E to Cumberland Basin in the W. It became nominally an island in 1809 with the digging of the New Cut to the s (*see* p. 234). Shipbuilding began here *c.* 1700. At the present-day Princes Wharf, William Patterson built Brunel's S.S. *Great Western* (1837), and his S.S. *Great Britain* further W from 1839. By the late C19 timber wharves dominated the W of Spike Island, replaced with expensive housing and leisure facilities in the recent harbour regeneration.

M SHED, Princes Wharf. Converted to museum use in 1978 from transit sheds by the Docks Engineer *N. A. Matheson*, 1948–51. Utilitarian brick on a steel frame, with sliding doors towards the harbour. Remodelled for the City Museums service by *LAB Architecture Studio*, 2007–10; glazed full-height entrance, rooftop gallery, and glass-planked W and S façades.

PERAMBULATION. Starting at Prince Street Bridge, to the SE is MERCHANTS LANDING, the second big harbourside development, by *Ronald Toone Partnership*, 1980–4. Big offices on Wapping Road, and to the E, varied brick and rendered houses of two to four storeys, with first-floor oriels. On the W side of Bathurst Basin, the WAREHOUSE and OFFICES of Robinson's

Oil Seed Manufactory by *Gingell*, 1874, the façades meticulously refurbished by *Roger Wilson* as part of Merchants Landing. Lively Bristol Byzantine buildings of yellow and red brick, similar but not identical, with Venetian ogee window heads, Moorish horseshoe arches, and plenty of cogging courses and panels of diagonal brickwork.

BATHURST BASIN was a small shipping basin formed with the Floating Harbour in 1804–9, from a medieval mill pond. Small Regency houses on the N side, probably *c.* 1820. On its N side, the LOUISIANA INN, formerly the Bathurst Hotel, also *c.* 1820, with elegantly fragile tented balconies on cast-iron columns. Wapping Road leads N to the harbour, where to the W is PRINCES WHARF, a general cargo wharf with most of its equipment and buildings intact, now a rarity. The Bristol Harbour Railway was laid here in 1872–6. On the quayside, four electric CRANES by *Stothert & Pitt*, 1951, two now working exhibits for the adjacent museum (p. 356). Beyond, on a semi-circular bastion, the elephantine *Fairbairn* STEAM CRANE (1875–8), with a curved box-girder jib. Further W on Wapping Wharf, THE POINT, by *Feilden Clegg Bradley*, 1999–2001, large rectilinear apartment blocks. Big render panels of red and blue, gunmetal-grey trim. The central block terminates in an astonishingly sharp front of five stacked balconies.

The preserved steamship S.S. GREAT BRITAIN by *I. K. Brunel*, built 1839–43, sits S of the elbow in the harbour, returned here in 1970 to the dry dock where it was built. A glass and steel lid with a shallow covering of water was inserted to protect the hull from further decay; structural engineers *Ove Arup & Partners*, architect *Alec French Partnership*, completed 2005. Nearby, the white-rendered OFFICE, *c.* 1839, with an exceptionally wide sash window lighting the draughtsmen's desks. S of the ship, the BRUNEL INSTITUTE (*Alec French Partnership*, *c.* 2006–10). Of stone, brick and timber-cladding, incorporating visitor, education and conservation centres. The structures echoing the ori-ginal engine factory and workshops of *c.* 1840. Sheltered by two blocks of flats in a dockside-warehouse aesthetic, by *Stride Treglown*, *c.* 2010.

GASFERRY ROAD leads S to the headquarters of AARDMAN ANIMATIONS. A bespoke design by *Alec French Partnership*, 2007–9. Some timber and copper cladding, and little canted oriel windows facing the road. A three-storey wedge-shaped building, with semi open-plan spaces. Curving timber and steel staircase in the atrium. Here is CUMBERLAND ROAD, the E–W spine of Spike Island. 100 yards W, the SPIKE ISLAND ARTS CENTRE, formerly a tea-packing warehouse, by *Beard Bennett Wilkins & Partners*, 1960. Of grey brick, with a long box-framed balcony, lower undulating roofs to the W. Long transverse packing hall with a glass-block barrel vault. Converted 1998, by *Niall Phillips Architects*.

Immediately W, MARDYKE FERRY ROAD returns N to the harbourside. Here is BALTIC WHARF (*Halliday Meecham Partnership*, *c.* 1983–6), private housing inexplicably mixing cottagey and stick-on Postmodern motifs. On the quayside, three SCULPTURES. First, *Vincent Woropay*'s bronze Hand of the River God, 1986; a hand holding a plinth, the crowning Hercules lifting an obelisk (after Bernini) now missing. To the w, Atyeo by *Stephen Cox*, 1986, fluid and abstract marble. w again is *Keir Smith*'s Topsail, 1987, with doughy clouds. Next w is UNDERFALL YARD, a working shipyard housing the harbour outlet sluices. Brick PUMP HOUSE with sharp, octagonal chimney (1888). Pedestrian gates E of the Harbourmaster's Office lead back to Cumberland Road, which soon curves NW past AVON CRESCENT, *c.* 1831–4. At its N end is the NOVA SCOTIA pub (probably *c.* 1821–8), plain Late Classical. Opposite on the island, two low terraces built by the Bristol Docks Co. (1831) for its workers, with gabled porches, wide eaves and half-dormers.

Further w along the quayside is CUMBERLAND BASIN (1804–9), where ships waited for the tide before leaving the lock-bound harbour. To the s, a conspicuous feature of Bristol's w approaches, three nine-storey bonded tobacco WAREHOUSES, designed 1903 by *W. W. Squire*, the Docks Engineer. Forbidding and bare, yet nobly proportioned, in three colours of brick. 'A' Bond (1903–6) at the E, has steel- and iron-framing with unreinforced concrete jack-arching. 'B' Bond (1906–8) to the w, looks identical, but its structure is the first major English use of the *Coignet* system of reinforced concrete. 'C' Bond (1919) is s of the river, and invisible from here. Adjacent to 'B' Bond (E) is ECOHOME by *Bruges Tozer Partnership*, 1996, built as a demonstration of environmental best practice, with a single-pitch roof canted s for solar gain.

At the E end of Cumberland Road, the ruinous GATEHOUSE of the New Gaol. By *H. H. Seward*, 1816–20. The gaol was burned in the Bristol Riots of 1831 and rebuilt by *R. S. Pope*. Closed 1883 and mostly demolished. A little w, Nos. 84–85, three-storey, *c.* 1835–40, with shallow pediment and over-scaled Greek Revival details, possibly by *Henry Rumley*. GOTHIC COTTAGE, No. 91, 1840. Three-storey symmetrical Tudor Gothic, converted to apartments 2002–3, with ludicrous half-timbered wings.

OUTER BRISTOL: EAST

For our purposes, E Bristol is a roughly wedge-shaped area NE of the city, bounded by the River Avon on the s, the M32 motorway on the N, and by s Gloucestershire on the E.

BARTON HILL AND REDFIELD

Barton Hill developed from *c.* 1840 around a cotton factory. Redfield straggles E along Church Road.

St LEONARD, Blacksworth Road. Modest but pleasing, an early work of *Robert Potter*, 1937–8. Render and Bath stone. Gabled W front with round-arched entrance; mullioned aisle windows. Copper-clad cupola. Nave and chancel in one, with low semicircular arches to a N aisle. W gallery with a handsome ORGAN CASE, from St Nicholas, city centre.

St LUKE, Avonvale Road. By *S. T. Welch*, 1842–3. Built for cotton workers. Pennant rubble, no aisles. W tower starting square, then an octagonal stage reducing to a squat Bath stone belfry. Nave with Y-traceried lancets. Wide barn-like interior with apsidal sanctuary; Dec tracery, *c.* 1893–1902. – Three mosaic and *opus sectile* PANELS installed 1960, from Christ Church, Ducie Road (dem. 1957/8).

St MATTHEW MOORFIELDS (former), Church Road. *J. C. Neale*, 1871–3. S aisle, 1887. Now flats and offices. Stub of a NW tower. W window with plate tracery. Off Cowper Street, the classical former HALL (1905) by *W. V. Gough.*

St PATRICK (R.C.), Dillon Court, Netham Road. 1994–5, by *JT Group Ltd.* Red and blue brick, gabled nave, lower aisles. Halls, etc. beneath. Overwhelming FITTINGS. Illuminated sea-green perspex ALTAR, LECTERN and FONT etc., by *Arthur Fleischmann*, 1972, installed 1995. – Six enormous photorealistic PAINTINGS by *Ramon Gaston*, 1989–92, cover the upper nave. – Barrel-vaulted NAVE CEILING, a riot of tempera by *Dumitru Pascari*, 2000; gilded Victorian-Renaissance motifs. – STATIONS OF THE CROSS of glass by *Stephen Bradley*, 1995. – STAINED GLASS from the former Pro-Cathedral, probably from *Hardman*'s series begun 1903.

Near Blacksworth Road, the plain former CHURCH, by *Sir Frank Wills*, 1922–3. Some plate tracery, later N aisle.

BRISTOL HINDU TEMPLE, Church Road. *Robert Curwen*, 1884. Formerly Methodist. Dec, with angled porches.

The FEEDER CANAL (engineer *William Jessop*, 1804–9) directs water from the Avon into the Floating Harbour. To the N was the GREAT WESTERN COTTON MILL, 1837–8, dem. in 1968.

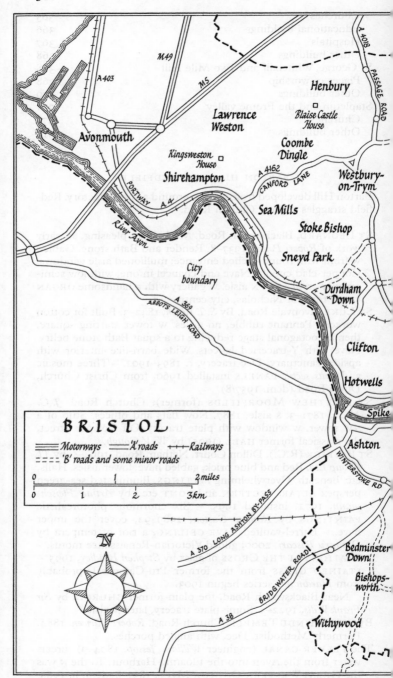

M49

A403

A4018

PASSAGE ROAD

Henbury

Blaise Castle House

Lawrence Weston

Avonmouth

Kingsweston House

Shirehampton

Coombe Dingle

A4162

CANFORD LANE

Westbury-on-Trym

PORTWAY A4

Sea Mills

River Avon

City boundary

Stoke Bishop

Sneyd Park

Durdham Down

A369 ABBOTS LEIGH ROAD

Clifton

Hotwells

Spike

B R I S T O L

═══ Motorways ═══ 'A' roads +++ Railways
- - - 'B' roads and some minor roads

0 .... 1 .... 2 miles
0 .... 1 .... 2 .... 3 km

Ashton

WINTERSTOKE RD

A370 LONG ASHTON BY-PASS

N

Bedminster Down

BRIDGWATER ROAD

Bishopsworth

A38

Withywood

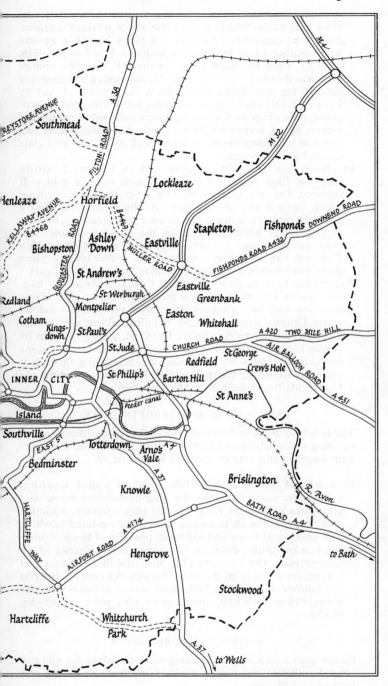

A three-storey former SMITHY and MECHANICS' SHOP survives near Maze Street, as do some 1840s workers' terraces. Most were demolished for BARTON HILL FLATS, a 22-acre neighbourhood unit by the City Architect *J. Nelson Meredith*, 1956–65. Then the highest flats in the UK outside London. First was BARTON HOUSE, Aiken Street, 1956, a fifteen-storey slab. To the N in Beam Street, the WELLSPRING HEALTHY LIVING CENTRE, by *Quattro Design*, 2004. Two storeys, rendered, on an H-plan. Curved forecourt wall with three Gothic arches. Metal GATES by *Julian Coode*. Staircase, a sweeping spiral of laminated birch, by *Walter Jack Studio*. Stained-glass screen by *Anne Smyth*.

In Queen Ann Road (W). BARTON HILL INFANT SCHOOL (1895, *F. Bligh Bond*), of red brick, with stepped gables. It replaced TILLY'S COURT HOUSE (1658, dem. 1894), from which came a C17 chimneypiece in the school hall, and a ceiling; a ribbed geometric design with pomegranates, flowers, and figures of Adam and Eve (cf. the Llandoger Trow's less elaborate versions, p. 298). Opposite in the RHUBARB TAVERN, C18 with late C19 extension, a fine chimneypiece dated 1672 with the initials of Thomas Day of Tilly's Court.

REDFIELD, ¼ m. N, grew up around CHURCH ROAD. To its S, set back on Victoria Avenue, a good brick villa *c.* 1810. Ionic doorcase with two windows either side; only three windows above. Unusual beaded cornices. In industrial use. N on Russell Town Avenue, CITY ACADEMY BRISTOL, glossy buildings by *Feilden Clegg Bradley*, completed 2005. Innovative plan; spine corridor running E–W, the classrooms zigzagging through it enclosing triangular courtyards. One block survives of the old Moorfields Board School (*J. Mackay*, 1900).

CREW'S HOLE AND TROOPERS HILL

The hilly and much-quarried N flank of the Avon valley. Copper-smelting was established by 1710, and in 1754 Reinhold Angerstein recorded fifty-one copper and lead furnaces.

In woodland above Crew's Hole Road, a walled GARDEN, *c.* 1752–77, associated with the long-demolished house and glassworks of William King. On the upper terrace, a Gothic GROTTO, *c.* 1750s. Of brick and stone once rendered in white, with chequered frieze and Gibbsian pilasters of black copper-slag blocks. Pointed doorway. Octagonal domed interior with a shallow pool. On Troopers Hill, N, a circular CHIMNEY of *c.* 1790, for a flue from the valley bottom. Another chimney at the bottom of Troopers Hill Road served a colliery engine house; C18 or early C19, square, two stages, some copper-slag blocks.

EASTON WITH GREENBANK

Easton grew into a sizeable working-class suburb in the mid C19 around collieries and wagon works. Greenbank to the NE was formed *c.* 1870–1910.

Places of worship

ALL HALLOWS, All Hallows Road. 1899–1901, by *George Oatley*. An outstanding though incomplete church in a piquant industrial setting. The style is Dec, *c.* 1300–30, French in its height and in some of the details. w front with three tall two-light windows. A tile-hung gable peeps over the angled parapet. Plain brick narthex by *Oatley & Lawrence*, 1939. Spacious interior with bare rubble walls. Nave with lean-to aisles, tall clerestory, polygonal sanctuary and a low ambulatory. A clever compact plan with shallow two-bay transeptal chapels beside the choir, opening out the E end. A High Church design with nine steps up to the altar, which is yet not too distant as there is no crossing. – FITTINGS. ALTAR designed by *Oatley*, oak with Perp niches, panels painted with Art Nouveau angels; maker *E. Aveling Green.* – Fine hanging ROOD by the *Birmingham Guild*, 1919–20. – Oak PULPIT by *Oatley & Lawrence*, 1913; saints carved by *Martyn & Co.* – Octagonal FONT on a short pillar with foliate capital. – STAINED GLASS. Apse lights by *Bell & Son*, 1948.

Former VICARAGE (N), by *Oatley*, 1897–8. Opposite, the CHURCH HALL, by *Oatley & Lawrence*, 1912–13, with broad Perp window.

ST ANNE, St Leonard's Road, Greenbank. An unprepossessing mission church with unexpectedly good fittings. By *Oatley*, 1899–1900. Plain paired lancets, arch-braced roof trusses.[*] *P. Hartland Thomas* reversed the orientation in 1925–6, adding a vestry and high shallow chancel. Porch, 1966. – FITTINGS. REREDOS by *Kempe*, from St Simon, Baptist Mills (now SS Peter and Paul, *see* p. 364); RIDDEL-POSTS with angel finials by *Comper*, from St Matthias College, Fishponds (p. 366). – TABERNACLE reportedly by *Martin Travers*, 1920s, from St Jude (p. 350).

ST MARK (former), St Mark's Road. 1848. By *Charles Dyer*, completed after his death by *S. B. Gabriel*. A serious Neo-Norman effort without the usual soullessness. Unarchaeological buttresses with fussy weatherings. Pennant rubble. Nave and chancel with small shafted windows. Big wheel window above the w door. NW tower with interlaced arcading at the bell-stage; two tiers of beasts squatting on the angles of its pyramidal roof derive from Thaon, Normandy, via Benjamin Ferrey's church at East Grafton, Wilts., 1844. Converted to housing *c.* 1989.

CASTLE GREEN CONGREGATIONAL CHURCH (now United Reformed), Greenbank Road. By *Frank Wills*, 1902. His brief was to avoid Gothic and 'ugly barnlike plainness'. Yellow brick with red bands, two short w towers with pyramid roofs. Round arches. Closed 2008.

KENSINGTON BAPTIST CHURCH, Stapleton Road. A competition win by a Glasgow architect, *Thomas L. Watson*, 1885–8. Remarkably late Greek Revival temple front of Bath stone. High basement. Above, Corinthian columns *in antis* and three

[*] *Oatley & Lawrence*'s ambitious plan for a replacement (1913), 70 ft (21.5 metres) to the vaults, was stalled by war.

tall windows. Pediment. U-shaped cast-iron gallery with elegant anthemion and lotus motifs.

ST MARK'S BAPTIST CHURCH, St Marks Road. *S. S. Reay*, 1911. Quite domestic-looking.

SS PETER AND PAUL GREEK ORTHODOX CHURCH (formerly St Simon), Lower Ashley Road. 1847 by *Hicks & Gabriel*, altered by *Pope & Bindon*, 1876. Plain neo-C13, with a NE tower with broach spire, awkwardly truncated in 1996. Nave arcade with moulded circular piers. – FITTINGS. Open timber screen, converted to an ICONOSTASIS. Over it a painted timber ROOD.

GREENBANK CEMETERY, Greenbank Road. Opened 1871, enlarged 1880. Gothic LODGE dated 1879, and elaborate wrought-iron GATES on a central pivot. Dec CHAPELS by *Henry Masters*, 1870–1, 'a High Victorian horror' (Pevsner). H-plan, the cross-stroke formed by a cloister topped by a polygonal turret with truncated spirelet. Chapels with apses at both ends. In poor repair.

EASTON MASJID (mosque), St Mark's Road. Occupying single-storey buildings formerly of St Mark's Sunday School, N of the church. Probably by *S. T. Welch*, 1858. Tudorish details.

SIKH TEMPLE, Nos. 81–83 Chelsea Road. A Gospel Hall, *c.* 1901, extended and refronted by *T. S. Bahra*, 1991–2.

Other buildings

On STAPLETON ROAD, immediately W of the railway bridge, a castellar TURRET, an early C19 garden building to Easton House, long demolished. To the N on Fox Road, the former OLD FOX INN, late C18, but with wide two-part sashes to the r., suggesting an early C19 extension. It was associated with bathing facilities in the River Frome by 1793.

Few INDUSTRIAL BUILDINGS with any presence survive.* On Co-operation Road, Greenbank, Bristol's only surviving CHOCOLATE FACTORY, formerly Packer's Ltd. Four utilitarian ranges of 1901–18, the first two at the W end designed by *Frederick Shove*. In between, glass-roofed yards bridged by iron walkways. To the E, offices by *Paul & James*, 1907. In Roman Road, Easton, a former CORSET FACTORY (*F. W. Gardiner*, 1898–9) for Bayer & Co. (cf. their Bath premises, p. 207). Three storeys, red brick, paired windows in Bath stone. A projecting attic, of cast iron with continuous glazing, was destroyed by fire in 1989.

EASTVILLE

Eastville continues the late C19 expansion from Easton along Stapleton Road.

NEW TESTAMENT CHURCH OF GOD (until 1976 ST THOMAS, C. of E.), Fishponds Road. 1888–9, by *H. C. M. Hirst*; nave

---

* Easton Way outer circuit road, opened 1973, erased the last of the district known as BAPTIST MILLS, the site of Abraham Darby's brass works, established *c.* 1702.

Mendip slopes near Westbury-sub-Mendip (p. 1)
Bristol, Hotwells and Clifton terraces, from the s (p. 332)

Bath, Roman Baths, the Great Bath, superstructure by J.M. Brydon, 1895–7 (pp. 124–5)

6	8
7	9

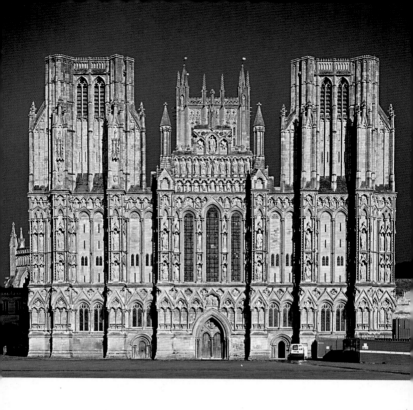

13 14 | 16
15 | 17

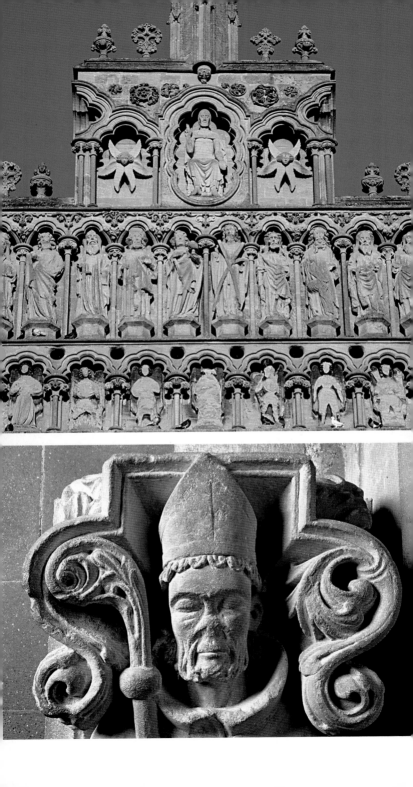

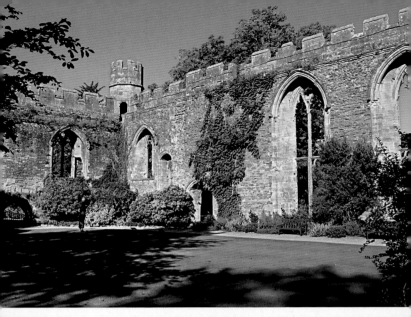

21. Wells
    Cathedral,
    Chapter
    House, vault,
    late C13 or
    early C14
    (p. 661)
22. Wells
    Cathedral,
    Lady Chapel,
    vault, *c.* 1320s
    (p. 662)
23. Bristol
    Cathedral, s
    aisle, vault,
    attributed to
    William Joy,
    early C14
    (p. 245)

21
22 | 23

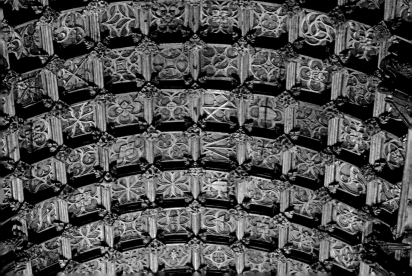

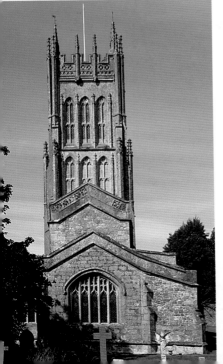

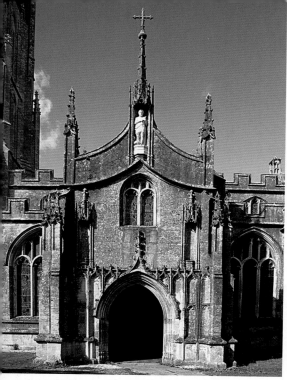

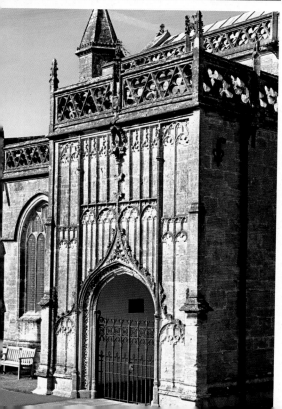

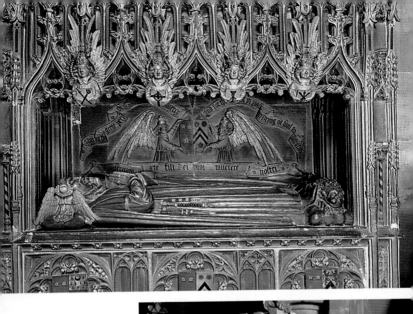

39 | 40
     41

54 | 56
55 | 57

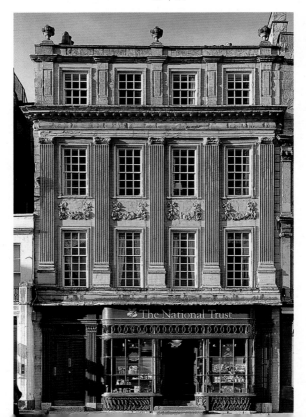

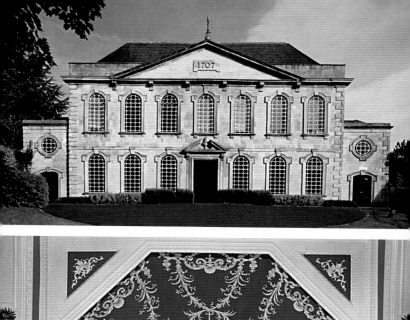

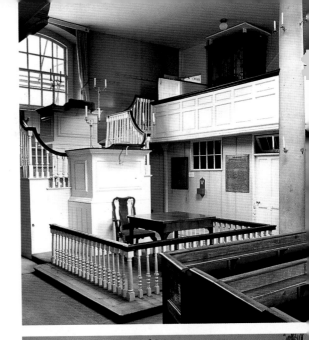

70. Bath, aerial view of
    Gay Street, the
    Circus and Royal
    Crescent
    (pp. 154–9)
71. Bath, The Circus,
    by John Wood the
    elder, built by Wood
    the younger,
    1755–67, detail of
    elevation
    (p. 155)
72. Bath, the Pump
    Room, by Thomas
    Baldwin, 1790–5,
    from Stall Street
    (p. 122)
73. Bath, Pulteney
    Bridge, by Robert
    Adam, 1769–74
    (p. 138)

| 70 | 72 |
| 71 | 73 |

74. Oakhill, Methodist chapel, 1825 (p. 573)
75. Bristol, Christ Church, by William Paty, 1786–90, interior (p. 253)

74	76
75	77

78	80 81
79	82

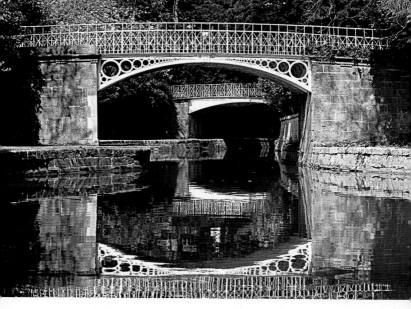

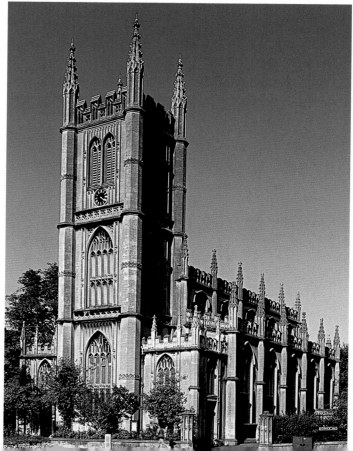

87	89
88	90

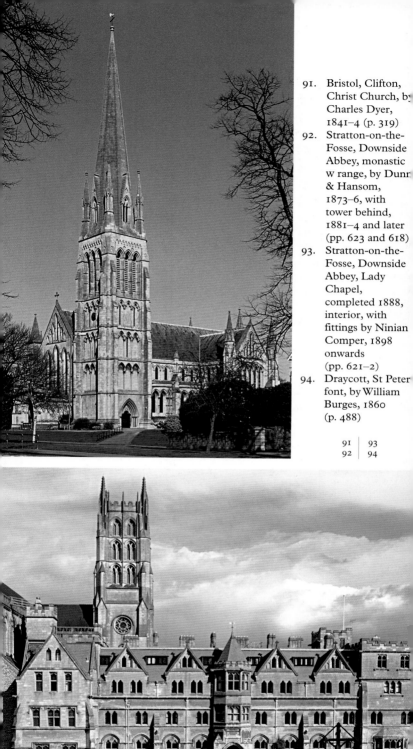

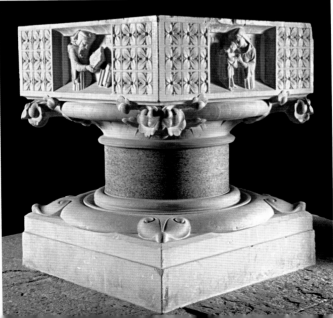

95. Frome, St John, s chapel E window, by Michael O'Connor, 1846, detail
(p. 509)
96. Winscombe, St James, E window, attributed to William Burges, 1863,
detail (p. 719)

the good shepherd

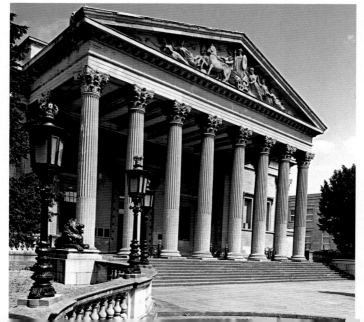

103. Bristol, Clifton, Royal Promenade, Victoria Square, by John Marmont, c. 1847–51 (p. 340)
104. Wells, former County Lunatic Asylum, by Scott & Moffatt, 1845–8 (p. 702)
105. Bristol, Clifton, Victoria Rooms, by Charles Dyer, 1838–42, portico (p. 341)
106. Wraxall, Tyntesfield, by John Norton, 1863–5, s front (pp. 728–9)

103
104 | 106
105

107
108   109

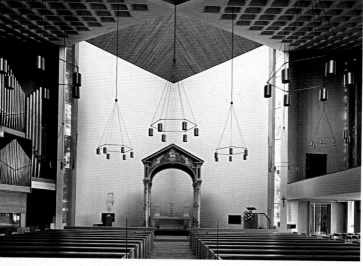

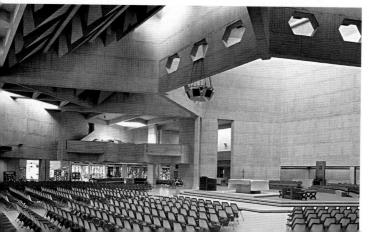

114. Bristol, Whitchurch Park, St Bernadette (R.C.), by Nealon Tanner Partnership, 1968 (p. 423)
115. Bristol, Clifton, All Saints, Pembroke Road, by Robert Potter (Potter & Hare), 1962–7, interior (p. 319)
116. Bristol, Clifton Cathedral (R.C.), by Percy Thomas Partnership, 1965–73, nave interior (pp. 317–18)
117. Bath University, by Robert Matthew Johnson-Marshall & Partners, 1966–80, campus, from the S (p. 196)
118. Weston-super-Mare, Weston College, by Bernard Adams, 1962–70 (p. 711)

114 | 117
115 | 118
116

119. Flax Bourton, houses by Artist Constructor and Bob & Tim Organ, *c.* 1971–3 (p. 503)
120. Bristol, High Kingsdown, housing by Whicheloe Macfarlane, 1971–5 (p. 347)

21. Peasedown St John, Circle Hospital, by Norman Foster & Partners, 2007–9 (p. 577)
22. Bath, New Royal Bath, by Nicholas Grimshaw & Partners, 1999–2003 (p. 128)

| 119 | 121 |
| 120 | 122 |

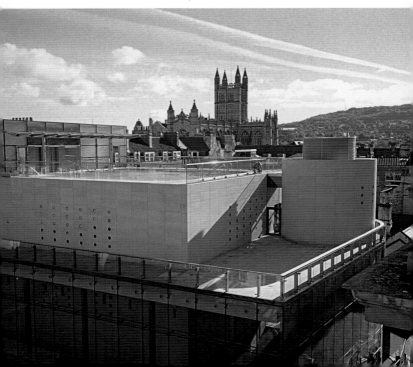

123. Bath,
Holburne
Museum,
extension by
Eric Parry
Architects,
2009–10
(pp. 134–5)

124. Bristol,
Gasferry
Road,
Aardman
Animations
headquarter
by Alec
French
Partnership,
2007–9,
interior
(p. 357)

completed 1903. Dec, austere Pennant stone with coarse mouldings, ambitiously big. Red and yellow terracotta banded windows (and nave arcades, now painted). An intended steeple not built. At the sides of the chancel are arches with crude Y-tracery, and the E window has a transom bizarrely placed a foot or two above the sill. Nave and aisles have an upper floor inserted. – Two *opus sectile* MONUMENTS by *Powells*, 1911 and 1919.

BAPTIST CHAPEL, Freeland Buildings. 1906 by *Benjamin Wakefield*. Small, brick, with a lunette and Arts and Crafts chequerwork in the gable.

PENTECOSTAL CHURCH, Fishponds Road (until 1997 Methodist). *H. M. Bennett*, 1901–2. Dec. Neo-Perp halls, *Charles White*, 1926–7.

BANGLADESHI MOSQUE, No. 468 Stapleton Road. By *Masood Akhtar Associates*, Birmingham, 2000–1. Small onion dome, four minarets. Coarsely detailed.

BRISTOL SIKH TEMPLE, Nos. 71–75 Fishponds Road. Three late C19 shops, refaced 1996–9, by *Lewis Foster Lewis*, with multi-cusped screen-like arcades to the windows.

FISHPONDS

The name appears to derive from two 'new pooles' formerly in the village centre, extant by 1610.

Churches

ST MARY, Manor Road. Built as a chapel of ease to Stapleton, by *James Foster*, 1820–1. Nave with short W tower and broach spire. The S wall has for decoration Tudorish arches framing the windows, like a blocked nave arcade. The N side was similar before a dull aisle was added, by *E. H. Lingen Barker & Sons*, 1901–2. Foster's chancel was replaced in 1871–3 by a deep apsidal trefoil-plan one with chapels, in a heavy E.E. style, architect *J. P. Seddon*. His planned recasting of the nave was never done. The plain, light nave now jars with the dim and elaborate chancel. Paired arches with foliate capitals and stumpy shafts to the side chapels. – Oak CHANCEL FURNITURE and PULPIT, 1913. – FONT by *Seddon*. Hexagonal with foliage panels. – MURALS, the Life of St Francis, by *Fleur Kelly*, 2003. – STAINED GLASS. Apse lights designed by *Seddon*, c. 1872. Two in the SE chapel by *Cuthbert Atchley*, c. 1930.

ALL SAINTS, Grove Road. By *E. H. Lingen Barker & Sons*, 1904–9. Chancel, S chapel, and clerestoried nave. Two further nave bays and a SW steeple were not built. Geometric tracery; six transverse gables to the S. – PULPIT by *H. T. Margetson*, sculptor, 1909. – STAINED GLASS. E window by *G. J. Hunt*, 1913.

ST JOHN, Lodge Causeway. *E. H. Lingen Barker & Sons*, 1910–11. Dec, with bellcote and W narthex. An eastward enlargement was planned. A near-replica of Barker's St Mark, Haydock, Lancs. (1910).

ST JOSEPH (R.C.), Forest Road. By *Sir Frank Wills*, 1923–5; E.E., with lancets and plate tracery, cf. St Patrick, Redfield. Apsidal chancel with ambulatory. – Unexpectedly sumptuous ALTAR AND REREDOS by *J. F. Bentley*, designed 1871, moved here from a Taunton convent in 1929. Of alabaster and serpentine; painted figures by *Nathaniel Westlake*. Canopied tabernacle niche. – STAINED GLASS. Three chancel windows, 1925, style of *Hardman*.

BAPTIST CHURCH, Downend Road. Built in 1851. It appears to have been altered externally, perhaps in 1902 when *La Trobe & Weston* added a gallery, schoolroom and parlour. Dec windows.

METHODIST CHURCH, Guinea Lane. Three congregations formerly in Victorian chapels commissioned this startlingly unchurchy design from *Roger Mortimer* of *Building Partnership (Bristol) Ltd*, 1966–7. Boxy grey brick walls, clerestory and flat roof. Timber latticed roof beams.

Educational buildings

ST MATTHIAS COLLEGE, Oldbury Court Road. Now the UNIVERSITY OF THE WEST OF ENGLAND, FACULTY OF HUMANITIES, LANGUAGES AND SOCIAL SCIENCES. 1852–3, by *John Norton* and *Joseph Clarke*, built as a women's teacher training college for the dioceses of Gloucester and Bristol and of Oxford, one of several opened after *c.* 1840.* Plain but attractive Gothic Revival, like Butterfield's St Augustine's College, Canterbury, begun 1844. The layout of Bishop Lonsdale College, Derby, was consulted. Much extended in the

Bristol, Fishponds, St Matthias College.
Engraving, 1852

* Research by William Evans and Sarah Whittingham.

original style, see the dated rainwater heads. Everything until
1904 is in Pennant rubble with brown stone-slated roofs. Most
upper windows are half-dormers with paired lancets. Elsewhere, mullioned-and-transomed lights, and for the main
rooms ashlar-roofed bays with Dec tracery. The oldest buildings form three sides of a lawned quadrangle. The central (w)
range has the main entrance in a tower in the NW angle. A
short central cross-wing was added by *W. L. Bernard*, 1893. s
of the w range, a wing with a first-floor examination hall by
F. S. Waller, 1859–60. The polygonal end projects picturesquely
into the quadrangle; attached at the r., a short square turret,
reached by a curving staircase with pierced parapet. In the sw
corner, the former CHAPEL, completed 1854. Very steep gables
with a bellcote, varied Dec tracery, and a quite noble five-light
E window. The s RANGE is by *W. V. Gough*, 1903–4, fitting in
with the 1850s work but more regular. The N side of the quadrangle has service ranges of 1852, ending with the former
PRINCIPAL'S HOUSE.

The rest of the campus is C20, except for the former PRAC-
TISING SCHOOL of 1852. Remodelled as a chapel, 1966; now
a lecture theatre. LIBRARY by *Kendall Kingscott*, 1992–3; buff
brick with contrasting bands. New practising school on Manor
Road by *W. L. Bernard*, 1894, now a doctors' practice. Red
Pennant Stone with C17 details in brick. Extended 2003 by
CMS (Bath), avoiding C19 echoes.

BRISTOL METROPOLITAN ACADEMY, Snowdon Road. By
Wilkinson Eyre, 2005–8. A two-storey spine running N–S, from
which three triangular modules of classrooms project eastward.
Spacious internal street – the usual layout now, to enable sur-
veillance and reduce bullying.

COUNCIL SCHOOLS (disused), Alexandra Park. By *Rodway &
Dening*, 1908–11. A good design with a homely, robust feel.

Former CHARITY SCHOOL, Manor Road. Built *c.* 1728. The educational reformer Hannah More was born here in 1745. H-
plan, the centre with tall windows flanking a pedimented
porch. The wings served as a master's house and an almshouse.
The l. wing had cross-windows later replaced by sashes.
Double-height schoolroom. Simple fittings, perhaps original:
wainscot, stone fire surround, built-in cupboards.

Hospitals

BLACKBERRY HILL PSYCHIATRIC HOSPITAL, Manor Road.
Formerly Manor Park. Built for naval prisoners of war in 1779:
adapted as Stapleton Workhouse, 1837–8, and again by
Medland & Maberley in 1860–4. Little C18 work remains. Many
signs of the early and mid C19, e.g. broad tripartite sashes. A
two-storey E range (Building No. 3, 1804) was adapted with a
three-storey cross-wing dated 1838. Some door surrounds have
heavy truncated pediments on massive brackets. The main
range faces the road; purple Pennant stone. Third storey
added, perhaps 1860–4. Central Tuscan porch.

Adjoining to the w, the former PAUPER LUNATIC ASYLUM, built 1858–61 and much extended. Closed (as Glenside Psychiatric Hospital) 1994; now the UNIVERSITY OF THE WEST OF ENGLAND, FACULTY OF HEALTH AND SOCIAL CARE. After long controversy and a competition, *T. R. Lysaght*'s expansive and self-satisfied Italianate design was selected in 1857. The style derives from Bristol General Hospital of 1852–7, by Lysaght's partner, Gingell (p. 281). Mostly two storeys, well-crafted of Pennant and Bath stone, with even quoins, paired round-arched windows, and a few canted bays. Occasional squat belvedere towers with pavilion roofs. The original build was only the central portion of the SE-facing spine. Irregular additions in conforming style: 1868–9 and 1875–6, then by *Crisp & Oatley*, 1880s–1908. Theirs too the three-storey entrance and administration block with tall clock tower behind, completed *c.* 1891. On the lawns (s), a former CHAPEL by *E. H. Edwards*, 1879–81. Robust E.E., with a tall coppered flèche. A pretty stair-turret in the NE angle. Complex roof struts over the crossing. Heavy REREDOS; sculptor *H. T. Margetson*. Good STAINED GLASS.

COSSHAM HOSPITAL, Lodge Road. *F. Bligh Bond*, 1903–7. A bequest of Handel Cossham for the local poor. Free Style, with Baroque touches. The main block is L-shaped. In the re-entrant angle, a dominant octagonal clock tower encircled by a wrought-iron balcony, with ogival dome and cupola. The wings are of Pennant stone, barely visible between windows linked vertically by Bath stone panels. Good LODGE with tall arched staircase window.

Other buildings

FISHPONDS ROAD, from SW to NE. At Station Avenue South, the LIBRARY, built 1911 as a cinema. Converted in 1927 by *W. S. Skinner & Sons*; single-storey, classical pedimented front. A little E, the PORTCULLIS INN, red brick, designed 1897–8 in the style of Edward Gabriel; canted bays, Tuscan porches. Further E, the former VANDYCK CINEMA, now a pub, by *W. H. Watkins*, 1926. Stylized classical. Tower-like ends, recessed centre with a thermal window above. To the E, a small PARK, 1887. First World War MEMORIAL of a bronze soldier, signed *Humphrys & Oakes*.

ST GEORGE, WHITEHALL AND TWO MILE HILL

St George developed in the C18 with mining and other industries. A centre of Methodism, with many C19 chapels.

Places of worship

ST AIDAN WITH ST GEORGE, Nags Head Hill. 1903–4 by *Bodley*. An interesting irregular design, mainly Perp with some flowing Dec tracery. Severe E wall with three gables. E window, placed high up. Incomplete two-bay nave with a blind W wall of brick. S chapel and very narrow S aisle with straight-headed windows, but no N aisle, and on that side five-light stepped lancets. One enters, oddly, into the S chapel; an unfortunate reordering has emptied the nave. Tall narrow chancel with two-arch arcade to the S chapel, the arches dying into the piers. The nave piers are square and without capitals; the chamfers of the arcades continue to floor level. The arches have inner orders of double-wave mouldings that finish oddly with sinuous curves, cut off flat without corbels. – Perp CHOIR STALLS, 1913. – PAINTING, Ecce Agnus Dei, by *F. G. Swaish*, 1921, from the reredos. – FONT, probably *Bodley*. – STAINED GLASS. E window by *Jack Compton* and *J. A. Crombie*, 1972. S chapel E in similar vein by *Crombie*, maker *James Clark & Eaton*, 1974. – HALL to the W, with dormers and flèche, by *C. A. Rowley*, 1915.

ST AMBROSE, Stretford Road. Impressive Perp revival, designed 1908–9 by *W. V. & A. R. Gough*, built 1912–13. Of red Pennant stone. Seven-bay nave, chancel with tall tower to its S. Big seven-light E window, the centre three buttressed for strength. Inside, much ashlar, arcades of four hollows, the shafts continued up to a wagon-vaulted roof with heavy tie-beams. Transverse arches between the aisle bays. – STAINED GLASS. E window in subdued colours, by *Percy Bacon*, 1913. N aisle W, 1922, style of *Arnold Robinson*. – HALL to the W, Perp with Art Nouveau flourishes, by *H. C. M. Hirst*, 1905. He added a second hall, 1907.

On Park Crescent, S, the BRISTOL AND ANCHOR ALMS-HOUSES, *Hirst*, 1906–7. L-shaped; two-storey centre with a quirky diagonal bay across the angle. Enlarged 1999, by *Kirkham, Williams & Lewis*, with cosy domestic references.

ST MICHAEL, Two Mile Hill. 1848, by *S. B. Gabriel*. Severe E.E. style with cusped lancets and a Geometric E window. Slightly later W tower with clasping buttresses and plain belfry stage. Flat parapet by *P. Hartland Thomas*, 1939. Arcade with circular piers, stiff-leaf capitals added 1898. N aisle only. – Oak REREDOS and COMMUNION RAILS, by *Herbert Read*, 1949. – ROOD, c. 1920. – PULPIT, stone with ogee arches, 1932. – STAINED GLASS. E window, 1950 by *Arnold Robinson* (*Bell & Son*), also one light of the N aisle W. Also by *Bell & Son* the silvery N aisle E (1913), and two N aisle windows (1921). Nave S, two by *Mayer*, c. 1901.

KINGSWOOD METHODIST CHURCH, Two Mile Hill Road. 1854, probably by *Henry Crisp*. Italianate, with pediment, quoined pilaster-strips, etc. (cf. Crisp's Hebron Methodist, Bedminster).

BOURNE CHAPEL, Two Mile Hill Road. Formerly Primitive Methodist, 1873. Imposing classical composition with long windows over three entrances.

WESLEY MEMORIAL METHODIST CHURCH, Bryant's Hill. A rare survival, entirely in its original state. 1906–7, by *W. Hugill*

Dinsley. Free Perp with an imposing W window, flanking porches, and r., a slim clock tower and spirelet. Wide interior with transepts and hammerbeam roof. Apsidal organ gallery. – FITTINGS all of 1907. – STAINED GLASS. Three by *Bell & Son*, depicting the Wesleys. The vestries and halls also completely preserved.

MINOR CHAPELS. The BAPTIST CHURCH, Summerhill Road, is Latest Perp, by *Charles White*, 1931–2. Dormers recessed into the roof slope, forming a sort of clerestory. ZION PRIMITIVE METHODIST CHAPEL (former), Whitehall Road (*T. & C. B. Howdill*, 1906–7), quite boldly composed, still debased Italianate. By the same architects, the BETHEL UNITED PENTECOSTAL CHURCH (formerly Salem Methodist), Church Road, 1903–4. Perp.

AVONVIEW CEMETERY, Beaufort Road, St George. 1882–3, by *Hans Price*. Gatehouse and small disused CHAPEL; Geometric Dec windows, tower and spire.

Other buildings

SPEEDWELL BATHS, Whitefield Road. 1937, by *C. F. W. Dening*, to a plan used at several suburban swimming pools (e.g. Knowle, Shirehampton). Brown brick, stylized pilasters. Closed 2006.

ST GEORGE HIGHER GRADE AND TECHNICAL SCHOOL (former), Church Road. By *F. Bligh Bond*, 1894–5. The first Technical School in the West of England and the most impressive C19 local authority school in Bristol, emulating the metropolitan fashions for height and bold Queen Anne details. One compact block, three-and-a-half storeys, of orange brick. On the second floor, big round-arched windows between pilasters, forming an arcade around the building. Ornamented gables with oculi and terracotta strapwork; continuous cornice of cut and rubbed brick.

AIR BALLOON HILL JUNIOR SCHOOLS, Hillside Road. Of 1905 by *La Trobe & Weston*, an Art Nouveau rendition of the School Board style. Grey Pennant with Bath stone, domed pylons at the entrances. Windows mostly segmental-headed casements beneath a pointed arch. Three square domed cupolas. The two-storey infants' block is oddly fortress-like.

SUMMERHILL JUNIOR SCHOOLS, Clouds Hill Road. At the top of the site, a single-storey building of *c.* 1880. On Plummers Hill behind, big Board Schools by *F. Bligh Bond*, 1899. Pennant stone, some Flemish elaboration. Incorporated (E) is a plain Baptist chapel of 1830.

At the junction of Clouds Hill Road and Summerhill Road, a Gothic DRINKING FOUNTAIN, 1896. Here stood DON JOHN'S CROSS, the medieval base and shaft-stump now outside the Library nearby. Off Hudd's Vale Road, a former POORHOUSE, 1800–1, reportedly the last design of *William Paty*. On a terrace over vaults; rubble with brick-arched openings, two storeys. A

nine-bay front arranged 2:5:2, the centre broken forward.
Now in commercial use.

STAPLETON AND THE FROME VALLEY

A hilltop village with views w to Bristol. For the former Glenside Hospital, *see* p. 368; for Heath House, *see* p. 381.

Churches

HOLY TRINITY, Bell Hill. The first church was medieval;
the second, *c.* 1690s, had a squat w tower. Bishop Monk
(whose new palace was nearby) paid for the present rich
design by *John Norton*, 1854–7. His best surviving church in
Bristol. Pennant walls, tall buttressed w tower, slim spire
of 170 ft (52 metres), densely crocketed with broaches
masked by pinnacles. Much carving by *Thomas Farmer*,
after that at Heckington Church, Lincs. Semi-octagonal
NE choir vestry, 1892. The nave has moulded capitals and
rich foliate label stops. Scissor-braced roofs with elaborate
cusping. In the chancel, a pointed wagon-vault with cusped
panels and demi-angels at the wall-plates. REREDOS of
1907, by *Powells*, designer *Charles Hardgrave*. Mosaic and
alabaster; central relief, *opus sectile* side panels. – Chancel
and sanctuary FLOORS of the same date. – PULPIT. 1857;
hexagonal, of Caen stone on serpentine pillars, with reliefs. –
FONT, alabaster, with ogee arches on angel corbels, 1857. –
Second FONT in the tower, Norman, perhaps C12, with a
modern base. – STAINED GLASS. Bright E window by
O'Connor, 1857. Chancel s, Annunciation, 1887, by *Kempe*, also
the s aisle first from E, 1888. Adjacent, a refined design by *Geoffrey Webb*, 1929. s aisle E, Adoration of the Magi, 1857, designed
by the *Misses Monk*, the Bishop's daughters, in the style of
O'Connor, who was no doubt the maker. w window by
Hardman, 1857. – MONUMENTS. Many from the old church.
Thomas Winstone †1757, sarcophagus with obelisk, putto, and
Rococo cartouche, probably by *T. Paty* (tower). Below, Mary
Harford †1798, Grecian with four female figures composed in
a sinuous S. By *Flaxman*, 1801. – Joseph Whitchurch †1772,
and family: festooned urn with a big swag and a pediment, over
a bombé curved base. Probably also *T. Paty*. – Isaac Elton
†1790, by *William Paty*; his usual Neoclassical frilled leaves and
husk garlands.

BAPTIST CHAPEL, Broom Hill. A simple classical box dated
1833, with pilasters. Enlarged 1905–6.

Other buildings

COLSTON'S SCHOOL, Bell Hill. The nucleus is the former
Stapleton House, red brick and mid-Georgian. Purchased in
1840 as a palace for the Bishop of Gloucester and Bristol.

Lavish alterations by *Decimus Burton*, 1841–6, costing another £12,408.* Rarely occupied, it was sold to Colston's School in 1858.

The GATES, with the Merchant Venturers' dolphins on the piers, are of 1859–61 by *Foster & Wood*, who also updated the quadrant-cornered LODGE. Inside the gates, red brick Edwardian SCIENCE BLOCK and former LIBRARY, by *Paul & James*, 1902–9. The Georgian STAPLETON HOUSE is to the S. Even quoins, segment-headed windows on the ground floor, flat above, with moulded architraves. Full attic storey above a deep cornice. C19 changes were deftly wrought and weathered down. The N front was the entrance in the C18, the bay pattern now 2:2:3:2:2. The narrow centre has a rich Doric doorcase with triglyph frieze. The two l. bays were added by *Burton* to make it symmetrical. He may have refaced everything in brick to disguise his addition. His new entrance front (E) has a solid porch with Doric pilasters, below a three-part centrepiece of narrow round-arched windows. The interior has been stripped of most fittings. A lofty hall leads to a top-lit staircase by *Burton*, with cast-iron balustrades, spoiled by a crude C20 flight above. In the Library, an Adamesque ceiling with cobweb centre and rinceaux, *c.* 1790. The room at the NE corner was the Bishop's chapel; double-height. On the S front, a long seven-bay room with a fancy panelled ceiling by *Foster & Wood*, 1859–61. Of the same date the oak-panelled school HALL off the SE corner. Behind it, jumbled remains of the C18 service wing.†

STAPLETON VILLAGE. Opposite the school gates, the BELL INN, 1900, by *P. W. Barrett*, with polygonal oriel-turret. Working E, Bell Hill becomes Park Road. First, STAPLETON COURT (now Colston's Lower School), N side. Perhaps *c.* 1730. Three storeys and five bays, the centre spaced more widely. String courses at each floor, breaking forward a little over the windows. Doorcase with segmental pediment on Corinthian pilasters. Staircase with turned and twisted balusters. Next door, the former RECTORY (also school property), with a Neo-Tudor front of *c.* 1841–5, and a brick rear range probably of the same date. The underlying structure is C17; in the maze of rear corridors, a charming late C17 dog-leg stair, with massive newels and turned balusters. Opposite, NE of the church, THE GRANGE, *c.* 1720–30. Pennant stone, three bays and three storeys; segmental-headed sashes. Angle pilaster strips formed of alternate deep and shallow blocks, like rustication. Later C18 wings. Good stable block with blind oculi in the first floor.

Park Road continues *c.* ½ m. NE, then SE into Broom Hill. On the NE side, the Baptist chapel (p. 371). ¼ m. SE, off River View, the remains of SNUFF MILLS. The present structure, probably C17 or C18, is a fragment, much reduced after 1926. C19 wrought-iron undershot wheel.

---

* Insisted upon by the Ecclesiastical Commissioners, despite the bishop's protests.
† R. J. E. Bayliff kindly made available his research on Colston's School.

WICKHAM COURT, Wickham Hill, is a farmhouse probably *c.* 1590, enlarged *c.* 1650–75. Two-and-a-half-storey centre with gables on all sides. Two upper windows ovolo-mullioned. This block was perhaps raised *c.* 1650–75 and a rear parlour and stair-tower added. Dog-leg staircase with pierced vase-shaped splat balusters. To the r. a two-storey wing, part of the early plan; three rooms in a row, the hall to the r. of the through passage. WICKHAM BRIDGE, SW, is early C17, with two arches.

BEECH HOUSE, Barkley's Hill. Formerly Stapleton Grove, apparently built *c.* 1764 for Joseph Harford. Bath stone ashlar, of two storeys. W front of five bays, with a fine Doric porch approached by little curved steps. Good cobweb fanlight. E front three windows wide, then a canted bay at the l. followed by a lower wing, probably early C19. Arched windows in broad arched recesses, and an Ionic porch with Doric triglyph frieze, a rare solecism.

LINDEN HOUSE, opposite (N), is an odd Neo-Gothic three-storey house (now flats) built for the Burden Institute, *c.* 1920s. At its W corner is a circular four-storey tower with two set-offs. This probably began as a windmill tower, castellated perhaps by *Thomas Wright*, *c.* 1760, as a *point-de-vue* for Stoke Park house (Gloucs.). A screen wall links it to another tower at the NW.

OUTER BRISTOL: NORTH

Bounded to the E by the M32, and to the W by the A4108 to Cribbs Causeway. Excepting the ancient settlements of Westbury-on-Trym and Horfield, the suburbs are mainly of 1850–1930.

ASHLEY DOWN, BISHOPSTON AND ST ANDREW'S

The Gloucester Road from Bristol via Horfield was rural until Bishopston was formed largely from the parish of Horfield in 1862. By 1900 middle-class villas stretched uninterrupted from Redland to Ashley Down.

Churches

St Bartholomew, Sommerville Road. By *W. Bassett-Smith*, 1893–4. Dec tracery, incomplete NW tower. Plain interior. – STAINED GLASS. E window and S aisle first and third from E by *Bell & Son*, 1901, 1913, 1915.

St Michael and All Angels, Gloucester Road. The church by *Welch & Clark* (1861–2) was demolished in 1997. Opposite, church halls of 1907–8, well adapted as the new church, by *Richard Pedlar Architects*, 2001–2. Pennant walls and mullioned windows. Slate roof raised above a new shallow clerestory.

Church of the Good Shepherd, Bishop Road. By *R. J. Beswick & Son*, Swindon, 1957–8. Fully glazed W gable and entrance. Low stone side walls with rows of small square windows. Shallow chancel behind a steep and elegant arch. Design reused at St Peter, Clevedon.

St Bonaventure (R.C.), Egerton Road. A presbytery, l. of the church, was built as a Franciscan friary in 1891. *Pugin & Pugin's* tall aisled church, 1900–1, was enlarged in 1907 with a W narthex and baptistery, confessionals, sacristy, belfry and side chapels. Austere interior with tall nave arcades; the arch mouldings stop short of the capitals. E and W windows of triple lancets, the central light stepped up at both top and bottom. – FITTINGS. An unfortunate reordering of 1974 was replaced in 2002–3 with SANCTUARY FITTINGS by *Rosemary Hatherly*; light oak with Gothic motifs. – Big hanging ROOD, 1927. – Stone SIDE ALTARS by *John Bevan Jun.*, 1922, going Art Deco, with stepped reredoses inset with marble patterns. – STAINED GLASS. E window of 1906; glowing colours, German in style; perhaps by *Mayer*.

Bishopston Methodist Church (former), Gloucester Road. By *Herbert Jones*, 1893. Two Dec W windows with a rose. Hall-like predecessor of 1890, to the S.

United Methodist Free Chapel (former), Berkeley Road. Now in commercial use. Perhaps by *Foster & Wood*, *c.* 1865; formerly with a Venetian motif and a later Italianate clock tower, both mutilated. It must have been an instructive contrast with the 1890s Gothic Methodist church to the N (above) and the opulent turn-of-the-century Perp at Horfield Baptist Church beyond (p. 382).

Zetland Evangelical Church, North Road. By *Oatley & Lawrence*, 1912. Its secular origin as an Institute and assembly hall shows. Twin segmental pediments (carved by *H. H. Martyn & Co.*), pedimented doorcase.

Other buildings

CITY OF BRISTOL COLLEGE, Ashley Down Road. Built as Müller's Orphan Houses, founded by the Prussian-born Rev. George Müller in 1836 in St Paul's. In 1845, seeking space and fresh air, a move to Ashley Down was decided. By 1886 Müller had received over £700,000 in donations, £115,000 of it for buildings. House No. 1 at the N end was built 1847–9, by *Thomas Foster & Son*. On a cross plan around a turret-like octagon, echoing workhouse planning – a feature avoided in *Foster & Wood*'s later blocks. These are plain Late Classical, two- and three-storeyed of Pennant stone with wide roofs and simple Bath stone Doric porches; fireproof staircases in stone or concrete, with cast-iron balustrades. House No. 2, s of No. 1, 1855–7; No. 3, s of Ashley Down Road, 1860–2; then, N of Sefton Park Road, Nos. 4 (1866–8) and 5 (1867–70). They housed 2,050 children. The effect is bleak, but conditions were humane for the time; all the houses were centrally heated from the first. In 1958 the orphanage became Bristol College of Science and Technology. Altered from 2003 to a masterplan by *PRP Architects*; House Nos. 1 and 3 now flats.

BISHOP ROAD PRIMARY SCHOOL. A Board School of 1895–6, probably by *W. V. Gough*, who designed extensions of 1902–5. Mullioned windows with round-arched upper lights, and a heavy central chimneystack.

BRISTOL NORTH BATHS, Gloucester Road. By *Lessel S. Mackenzie*, 1914–22. Edwardian frontage in red brick with much carved decoration, and somewhat Jacobean corner turrets with pepperpot domes. The pool was floored over and used as a cinema in winter. Closed 2005.

DAVID THOMAS HOUSE, Belmont Road, formerly David Thomas Memorial Church (Congregational), by *Stuart Colman*, 1877. The tall, emaciated spire exhibits his tendency to distorted proportions. Adapted as a lift shaft for five-storey flats by *Stride Treglown*, 1987, replacing Colman's nave.

In North Road nearby, a TERRACE perhaps also by *Colman*; unusually Gothic for Bristol, with brick cogging. To the E in Effingham Road, Nos. 25–27, by *W. H. Watkins*, 1905; Arts and Craftsy.

GLENFROME HOUSE, No. 280 Ashley Down Road, is *c.* 1827, one of a few isolated Regency villas built on the hilltop E of Montpelier. Nearby, ASHLEY HOUSE, by *S. B. Gabriel*, 1864–6. A good asymmetrical Italianate villa built for Charles Wathen, clothing merchant and later Mayor. Well-preserved interiors, despite institutional use.

COTHAM AND MONTPELIER

Montpelier began in the late C18 with scattered villas on the slopes E of Cheltenham Road, mirroring the slightly earlier development of Kingsdown. Cotham borders Clifton in the W at Cotham Hill; it was also established *c.* 1800, gradually spreading

E towards Montpelier. Both suburbs have numerous large C19 villas, single or semi-detached.

Churches

COTHAM PARISH CHURCH, Cotham Road. Originally Highbury Congregational Chapel, the first work of *William Butterfield*, 1842–3. Anglican since the 1970s. Remarkably faithful for its date to C15 Perp models, especially given its Nonconformist origins. Butterfield was the nephew of the benefactor, W. D. Wills of the tobacco family. Pennant rubble with limestone dressings, nicely composed on a shallow rise. Aisled nave with four-centred arcades on crisp octagonal piers. Shallow clerestory of triplet quatrefoils. W gallery. In 1863 *E. W. Godwin* added the apse and a S tower with, beneath it, a galleried bay beyond the aisle, like a sort of transept. The apse was extended E by one bay *c.* 1892–3, by *Frank Wills*. – STAINED GLASS. W window of 1950, commemorating the Rev. K. L. Parry, hymnologist. – MONUMENTS. Exterior N wall, a C19 memorial to five Marian martyrs burned at the stake here in 1555–7. – Rev. H. Arnold Thomas †1924, by *Eric Gill*, depicting the Good Shepherd.

OUR LADY OF OSTRABRAMA POLISH R.C. CHURCH, Cheltenham Road. By *Foster & Wood*, 1854–5. Built as Arley Congregational Chapel, paid for by John Holmes of Arley, Worcs. Italianate. Gabled W end with a handsome semicircular porch composed of three arches between engaged columns. Above is a short ogee-domed clock tower. Windows with Lombardic tracery, and a continuous shallow clerestory of little circles. – STAINED GLASS. One window from Poland, installed after 1968.

CHRIST CHURCH, Redland Road (formerly Wesleyan Methodist). By *Robert Curwen*, 1877–8. Rebuilt by *H. J. Jones* after a fire in 1897; his typical Dec tracery and thin detailing.

ELMGROVE COMMUNITY CENTRE, Redland Road (formerly ST NATHANIEL'S CHURCH). By *John Bevan Sen.*, 1872–3. Robust Geometric Gothic. Apsidal chancel, unfinished tower and spire, SE. Clerestory of paired circular lights. Inside, short piers with French Gothic capitals and square-profiled nave arcades. Chunky PULPIT with trefoil-headed arches.

IVY CHURCH, Ashley Hill. Built in 1791–2 as the chapel to a women's reformatory. Small and crude. Windows with mid-C19 Lombardic tracery. Painfully narrow W tower, its oculi converted to Romanesque windows. Thin spire replaced by a pyramidal cap.

WOODLANDS CHURCH, Woodland Road. Originally St Mary, Anglican. By *J. P. St Aubyn*, 1870–81. Tall and bulky, of pink sandstone. Geometrical style. Nave with aisles and clerestory. NW porch in the base of a planned steeple. The interior ruined by a concrete upper floor, *c.* 1990, now with housing above. Low circular piers with circular Perp foliage capitals. –

STAINED GLASS. E window probably by *Wailes*, *c.* 1874 (obscured). N aisle second from E, 1877, probably by *Lavers, Barraud & Westlake*, as is the N aisle W and S aisle first and second from E; third and fourth there, 1900 by *Bell & Son*. S aisle W, signed *Lavers & Westlake*, 1894. – MONUMENTS. Herbert Parker †1904, The Light of the World in *opus sectile*.

Other buildings: Cotham

COLSTON GIRLS' SCHOOL, Cheltenham Road. By *W. V. Gough*, 1891. Red Cattybrook brick striped with yellow, and overbearing buff terracotta Jacobean-Flemish ornament. Extended by *Gough* (1906); *Paul & James* (library, 1912), and *J. Ralph Edwards*, 1956. To the S, the blind façade of *J. K. Maggs*'s Britton Building, 1978, cleverly continues the striped brick while maintaining an up-to-date idiom. Inset sculpted bosses spelling out the school's name, by *Ernest Pascoe*.

FAIRFIELD HIGH SCHOOL, Fairfield Road. By *W. L. Bernard*, 1897–8. A Higher Grade school, costing £24,000. Mostly three storeys, of cyclopean red sandstone. Shaped gables. Considerable variety and panache.

COTHAM HILL. Clifton ends where COTHAM HILL leaves Whiteladies Road. Off to the W in Aberdeen Road, ABERDEEN TERRACE, 1849, probably by *R. S. Pope*. Late Classical, with idiosyncratic flat-topped pediment. On Cotham Hill (SW side), Nos. 39–45, by *George Gay*, 1843. Narrow entrance bays defined by pilaster-strips and little sections of raised parapet with arcading. On the NE side is the forbiddingly bleak CONVENT OF ST JOSEPH, 1868 by *C. F. Hansom*. Three storeys, no frills. At the top, S side, COTHAM HOUSE, its back to the road. Shown on Rocque's map, 1742. The Georgian part of the garden front is of seven bays and two storeys at the r., with a columned porch off-centre. At the l., a transverse wing (mid-C19?) with bow window and heavy balustrade. Altered *c.* 1900 by *George Oatley*, for Sir George White, transport entrepreneur: lavish Neo-Georgian fittings by *Bath Cabinet Makers* and *Smith & Co.*, Bristol. Towards the road, a two-storey Edwardian porch, and a quirky bow window decorated with 'Cotham marble'.

At the junction with St Michael's Hill by Cotham parish church (p. 376), the former HOMOEOPATHIC HOSPITAL, by *Oatley & Lawrence*, 1920–5, in a late Arts and Crafts Cotswold idiom, costing £123,000. Big Tuscan porch, high gabled wings, mullioned windows and diagonally set chimneystacks. All the wards had arcaded sun balconies. Adapted as a University student health facility, 2004–5, by *Narracott Oxford Mills*, with an inappropriate glazed entrance. Formal gardens of 1926–7 with rockeries of *Pulhamite*, an artificial stone. Opposite, the former WESTERN CONGREGATIONAL COLLEGE, by *H. Dare Bryan*, 1905–6. Now a medical practice. Loosely Jacobean. Y-plan, with a central entrance, behind which was an assembly hall. Angled wings containing, to the r., a library, and l., common room. These have big double-height bays. To the E, the Principal's House, lower and half-timbered. Scalloped boundary wall with ball- and obelisk-finials at the gates, exemplifing the Edwardian charm which Bryan did so well.

Nearby in Trelawney Road is TRELAWNEY PLACE, *c.* 1800. Three Neoclassical houses with single-storey entrance fronts and a lower floor at the back; an unusual type in Bristol (cf. York Road and Upper Cheltenham Place, Montpelier). Nos. 31–33 are by *Foster & La Trobe*, 1889; a confusion of chimneys, angles and gables.

COTHAM ROAD runs E from the top of Cotham Hill. Laid out in 1829; on the N side, W end, two 1830s villas survive, with pilastered and balconied fronts. Further E are villas of *c.* 1850–70. From Cotham Road South, COTHAM PARK runs NW. The turning is marked by two C18 OBELISKS with vermiculated rustication, the gatepiers to a house demolished 1846. Simple Italianate villa pairs of *c.* 1850 (e.g. Nos. 4–14, N side), and bigger houses, e.g. No. 16, late Greek Revival, in the manner of *Charles Underwood*.

CHELTENHAM ROAD. N of the junction with Ashley Road, the former ACADEMY CINEMA by *W. H. Watkins*, 1914. Red brick with Edwardian Baroque embellishments. The ceiling, plasterwork and balcony survive. A little N, at the angle with Bath Buildings, a tall pair of houses sharing a pediment, by *James Foster*, *c.* 1812. Further N, No. 174, a very handsome villa of *c.* 1830, with a wrought-iron veranda and Tuscan bracketed eaves.

Other buildings: Montpelier

The French city of Montpellier has long been associated with an elevated site, pure air and bathing facilities; the name seems to have attached to this district of Bristol by *c.* 1750. In 1764 Thomas Rennison improved a mill pond here as two baths, the largest 400 ft (123 metres) in diameter, with pleasure gardens etc. attached. No curative properties were ascribed to the waters; the purpose was recreational. Rennison's Baths survived until 1916. House-building began in earnest *c.* 1790, and from *c.* 1850 Montpelier became urbanized.*

The heart of the district is at the junction of Picton Street and Bath Buildings. Just to the N, off Bath Buildings, is MONTPE-LIER HEALTH CENTRE by *Vic Love Architects*, 1997. A nicely reticent red brick building with stained timber beams and a big gabled entrance. To the r., the OLD ENGLAND pub, three storeys, plain Georgian, built by Rennison as a coffee house 1764–72. To the SE is PICTON STREET, mostly built 1816–24 as a shopping street, and the most complete such survival in Bristol, though with largely Victorian shopfronts. The NW side is a near-continuous stepped terrace of one- and two-bay brick

* This account relies on Mary Wright's excellent *Montpelier, a Bristol Suburb*, 2004.

houses. Further N, PICTON LODGE, No. 43, *c.* 1827: full-height semicircular bows either side of the door, and big urns on the parapet. Adjacent to its gate, a parish LOCK-UP or charley box, *c.* 1828–32, for detaining drunks or criminals overnight. (Barrel-vaulted cells, one with manacles and an iron-studded door.) NE, on St Andrew's Road, the OLD VICARAGE of St Andrew's church (*John Hicks*, 1844–5, dem. 1969). By *S. B. Gabriel* and *J. A. Clark*, 1862. Sturdy Gothic, rather overpowered by a big 1990s addition.

The rest of the district is strung out. The contour dictates the near-parallel streets oriented SW to NE; St Andrew's Road uppermost, then Richmond Road, York Road, Cobourg Road and at the bottom, Upper and Lower Cheltenham Place. There are no crossing lanes, so one must zigzag back and forth to take it all in. We note only highlights and trends, for there is too much to cover house-by-house. Building began on leases of 1792, but the developer was bankrupted in the financial crisis of 1793. Intensive building *c.* 1810–30 established the present layout. The model was Kingsdown (developed *c.* 1760–1820 on similar terrain), but Montpelier was a step down the social scale, the houses more cottagey, though still classical. Their backs are often to the road, their best faces to the sloping gardens, many visible only from the next street down. Much survives amid later Victorian housing. First the larger villas, e.g., in Richmond Road, APSLEY VILLA (No. 128) and No. 109. Similar to Apsley Villa is YORK HOUSE, No. 68 York Road, dated 1823. Nearby, YORK COTTAGE, 1822, less regular and of three storeys, is an example of the humbler cottages. GADARA COTTAGE, No. 53 Cobourg Road, dated 1824, has a Gothic entrance arch in the garden wall, and a little brick coachhouse. Some simple terraces intervene: Nos. 73–93 Richmond Road, and Nos. 107–119 York Road, both *c.* 1820s. Nos. 96–104 Richmond Road are *c.* 1850, quite handsome, with rusticated ground floors and bracketed window hoods above. No. 36 York Road (with a Tuscan porch) and the neighbouring Nos. 2–6 Upper Cheltenham Place, *c.* 1830–5, look like a single-storey terrace, but the sloping ground allows two storeys at the back (cf. Trelawney Place, Cotham, p. 378). On the lower ground towards Ashley Road, Brook Road and Lower Cheltenham Place retain handsome artisan terraces of *c.* 1865, many by *J. A. Clark*, still with stepped voussoirs and classical door canopies.

A little way E, on Old Ashley Hill, ASHLEY HILL HOUSE. The earliest house here, extant by 1776, but surely rebuilt or refaced later, in brick with a round-arched Regency doorway, and a Victorian bay facing Old Ashley Hill. Opposite is ASHLEY GREEN, of 1831 by *William Okely*. Developed by J. E. Lunell, who also built e.g. SUSSEX PLACE, lower to the S, with plain but considered terraces of 1830–5.

THE MALTHOUSE, Fairlawn Road. An unusual industrial survival here. A four-storey stone maltings and kiln of 1876, adapted as thirteen houses by *Exedra Architects*, late 1990s.

EASTVILLE, LOCKLEAZE AND ST WERBURGH'S

Three disparate areas, sandwiched between Ashley Down, NW, and the M32 motorway, SE. Lockleaze was developed from the late 1940s to replace wartime losses. For the C19 parts of Eastville, *see* Bristol East, p. 364. St Werburgh's, to the W, is largely artisan housing *c.* 1870–1910.

ST MARY MAGDALENE, Gainsborough Square, Lockleaze. *Burrough & Hannam*'s church of 1960–1, an adventurous plan of interlocking octagons, was sadly demolished in 1997. The humdrum hall was adapted as a church by *Robert Narracott*, 1996–7.

ST WERBURGH (former), Mina Road. By *John Bevan Sen.*, 1877–9. Now a rock-climbing centre. Nave with W porch, aisles, SW tower, chancel. Beneath its refacing, much of the structure is medieval, from the C15 church of the same name in Corn Street, city centre. Its reuse in a poor or populous suburb was a condition of removal. The demolition and rebuilding cost £17,100, but £15,100 was recouped by selling the site. Four-stage tower probably of the 1460s–80s, with tall two-light windows and, above, two tiers of tall two-light bell-openings flanked by two-light blind windows. Higher stair-turret with a panelled top and openwork spirelet, repositioned from NW to SW for aesthetic and structural reasons. Pierced battlements in two tiers. There is no play at all with buttresses, corner shafts or pinnacles, giving the tower a spare silhouette. The nave was lengthened from four bays, but the uneven aisles were kept (the N is 3 ft wider than the S). The traceried heads of the aisle windows at least seem to be by *Bevan*, following Somerset models. The chancel entirely C19, as that at Corn Street had been removed in *James Bridges*'s remodelling of 1758. The interior stonework appears C19 (retooled or replaced?) Two-centred arches to the arcades, piers with four shafts between wave mouldings. Fan-vault below the tower. – FITTINGS. Most large fittings are now encased. – REREDOS. Ornate, Perp, with relief of the Last Supper. Perhaps *c.* 1890–1910. – The FONT (C15, octagonal, with scallop-shell panels) is not visible. – MONUMENTS. John Barker †1607. Behind a rock face, N aisle E. Stiff figure reclining on its side, flat canopy on Corinthian columns, and against the back a cartouche already with the gristly detail of the 1630s. – Robert Earle †1736, by *Michael Sidnell*. Rectangular tablet with Corinthian frame, swept top.

ST JAMES, Romney Avenue. By *Burrough & Hannam*, 1953, formerly Presbyterian, now Independent. Red brick on portal frames, with a big lozenge-shaped window fitted into the gable.

FAIRFIELD HIGH SCHOOL, Alfoxton Road. By the *Building Design Partnership*, 2003–6, accommodating 1,120 pupils. Right on the crest of the hill, and in appearance akin to contemporary office buildings. Irregular angled plan, a single-storey entrance in the centre, rising to six storeys behind. Assembly

hall in a central atrium with classrooms accessed from
balconies.

LOCKLEAZE SCHOOL, Hogarth Walk. By the *City Architect's
Department* (project architect *D. W. Salter*), 1951–4, extended
1958–9. The prototype of Bristol's early movement towards
system building, using long-span pre-stressed reinforced concrete beams. Closed 2004.

LOCKLEAZE JUNIOR AND INFANTS SCHOOLS, Romney
Avenue. By *Richard Sheppard & Geoffrey Robson*, 1948–50.
The prototype of *Bristol Aeroplane Company's* (BAC's) Mark I
prefabricated school-building system, using pressed aluminium throughout, intended to take up the slack in their factories once the need for prefabricated housing was filled by *c.*
1948. Junior school (demolished after 2006) completed in
1949. Brick-built halls and entrance, with two long classroom
blocks in parallel running N. Continuous glazing to the front
and canted fins expressing the classroom divisions. Lower corridors behind, above them clerestory strips to the classrooms.
Many fixtures and furnishings of pressed aluminium. The
infant school (N), completed 1950, now houses the junior
school too.

TESCO, Eastgate Road. By *David Daw*, consulting engineers
Buro Happold, *c.* 1985–6. Single-storey, with a wide-span roof
suspended from ten 46-ft (14-metre)-high steel masts.

A block of LABOURERS' DWELLINGS, Mina Road, St Werburgh's, by the M32 motorway. 1905–6, the only survivor of
five blocks erected by the Corporation in the E of the city from
1901. Brick, two storeys with open staircases to iron access
balconies.

HEATH HOUSE, Sir John's Lane, Purdown, on a hilltop N of the
M32. Of 1783–4; builder *John Hensley*; architect *Zachary Bailey*
of Bath. Elegant five-bay entrance front (w), relying entirely
on refined proportions; widely spaced central bays, outer bays
divided by even broader expanses of wall. Moulded window
frames with keystones; pedimented doorcase, Doric columns
with fluted necking, and fluted entablature. The S side has
semicircular bows flanking a three-bay centre. Restored as a
private hospital by *James Nisbet & Partners*, 1992–3, with new
blocks in the grounds.

HORFIELD

A hamlet of Saxon origin. Part of its common survives and one
farmhouse. Suburban development *c.* 1860–1930.

Churches

HOLY TRINITY, Wellington Hill. Of a small E.E. church nothing
remains; its once-circular churchyard may indicate a Saxon
foundation. The impression is of a low spreading country
church with a small W tower, big slate roofs over the C19 nave
and transepts, and a broad low crossing tower. The oldest part

is the W tower, with Perp belfry lights, and the date 1612 on the SW buttress. The rest was rebuilt by *John Hicks*, 1831; small, cruciform, aisleless and galleried. Of this, only a little masonry survives. Enlarged in 1846–7 by *Butterfield*, to accommodate soldiers from Horfield Barracks (*see* p. 383). Hicks's nave was given aisles, a SW porch and an enlarged chancel. The uneven quoins inside the nave windows, and the profile of their rere-arches, identify Butterfield's contribution. By *Henry Crisp* a pair of reticulated Dec nave dormers, 1876, one N, one S, just W of the crossing. NW vestry 1887, probably by *Crisp*. In 1891–3 Hicks's transepts and Butterfield's chancel were demolished for a bigger E end by *Crisp & Oatley*, at the instigation of the rector, who had the idea of a central lantern tower over the new crossing. Two-bay chancel with N and S chapels, originally symmetrical in plan; the style a slightly richer Dec than But-terfield's. *W. V. & A. R. Gough* made changes in 1911: the S chapel was extended E, and the S transept lengthened and given an E-facing porch. The transept was completed possibly in 1920. Finally, a blunt late Perp N transept extension, vestries and organ loft, by *P. Hartland Thomas*, 1929–30. He also cut a semicircular arch between chancel and S chapel, with an inven-tive cage-like piscina in its E pier. Overall, the interior is rather disjointed; the big E end and crossing lantern swamp Butter-field's more reticent nave.

FITTINGS. COMMUNION RAILS and CLERGY STALLS by *Hartland Thomas*, 1930. – CHOIR STALLS intended to match, 1933. – FONT (S transept), Perp, panelled, stone, octagonal. – Nearby, a WAR MEMORIAL by *A. R. Gough*, 1922. – STAINED GLASS. E window *c.* 1909, almost certainly by *James P. B. Young*. S chapel E, 1900, attributed to *Heaton, Butler & Bayne*. S transept E, 1950, *Joseph Bell & Son* (probably *Arnold Robinson*). – MONUMENTS. Standard C18 and early C19 tablets.

ST GREGORY THE GREAT, Filton Road. A big Romanesque-Byzantine affair in fiery red brick, 1933–4, by *A. R. Gough*. Cruciform, with a stubby octagonal central tower and a very short chancel. Sombre interior of purple and yellow brick; crossing with stepped squinches, then a shallow dome. – SANCTUARY FURNISHINGS by *John Crawford*, 1949, in the style of his former master Martin Travers (†1948), made as a war memorial and exhibited at the Festival of Britain, 1951. Tall oak REREDOS with a carved and painted crucifix; border painted with Instruments of the Passion, gilded TABERNACLE with Baroque sides, STATUES, etc. – STAINED GLASS. An oculus in the N chapel; a rather disdainful Christ in Judgment, by *A. J. Davies* of the *Bromsgrove Guild*, 1935.

HORFIELD BAPTIST CHURCH, Gloucester Road. 1900–1, by *R. Milverton Drake*, in Arts and Crafts Perp. Ambitious red Pennant Stone façade, with a very big W window under an ogee-pointed arch, flanked by squat towers originally with little cupolas. Repeated motif of a little cusp in the horizontals. Unspoiled interior seating 1,100: galleries to three sides, organ loft behind the dais. Three-and-a-half-storey HALLS at the r., by *C. H. White*, 1921–2; pared-down Neo-Tudor. Behind the chapel, GRIFFIN HALL, a school-chapel by *H. J. Jones*, 1895.

HORFIELD METHODIST CHURCH, Churchways Avenue. By *La Trobe & Weston*, 1897–8. Prettified Dec, typical of their style about this time. Little timber and tiled flèche. HALLS to the l., with stylized scissor tracery in narrow lancet lights.

WHITEFIELD MEMORIAL TABERNACLE (United Reformed), Muller Road. A former Congregational church by *Eustace Button*, 1933, is now the adjacent CHURCH HALL. In 1959 it merged with Whitefield's Tabernacle, displaced from Penn Street, Broadmead by redevelopment. *Button*'s new church (1959–60) is a plain brick box with his usual mullioned windows, and Jacobean-looking obelisks on the entrance canopy. Unexpected FITTINGS from Penn Street, of 1815. High panelled PULPIT, white and gilded: two curving staircases, concave base with Ionic columns. – Matching COMMUNION TABLE, a plinth with scrolled brackets. – Mahogany-cased ORGAN by *John Smith*, 1815, with big scrolls to a raised centre.

HORFIELD BARRACKS CHAPEL, off Wessex Road. Now offices. Of 1857, plain lancet style, with a w bellcote. Nine-bay sides, divided into threes by buttresses. Often wrongly attributed to Butterfield.*

Other buildings

HORFIELD SPORTS CENTRE, N of Dorian Road. 1980s, much extended with a swimming pool etc., by *Saunders Architects*, 2004–5. Wave-form roof.

HORFIELD PRISON, Cambridge Road. Begun by Bristol Corporation in 1874–5, but delayed in anticipation of the Prisons Act (1877). Cell blocks completed 1882–3 to a design by the Prisons Commission surveyor, *Alexander McHardy*. Building continued until 1889. Four-storey red brick blocks with heavy pilastered bay divisions, that for men with cells on both sides of an open well. Smaller block at right angles for women, with cells on one side only. Administration block and chapel, Italianate, with a short clock tower. Brutalist entrance block of ribbed concrete panels, 1970s.

On the N side of Holy Trinity church, the Perp Gothic former PARISH SCHOOLS, now Manor Farm Boys Club. w end by *Henry Crisp*, 1879–80; dull extension by *Oatley* 1900. Across the road, NW, a fine cast-iron LAMP STANDARD with drinking fountain, by *Macfarlane & Co.*, Glasgow, 1900. Horfield RECTORY stands s of the crossroads. Completed in 1825 for the Rev. Samuel Seyer, writer and historian. Simple Regency work. To the NW at Western Road on the edge of Horfield Common, a late C19 cast-iron URINAL, circular, with a filigree dome.

---

*The BARRACKS (1845–7, dem. 1966) were in the Late Classical style favoured by R. S. Pope.

DOWNEND PARK FARM, off Downend Park. Perhaps early-to-mid-C17, restored 1989. A wide three-bay façade with ovolo mullions containing (l. to r.) hall, unheated dairy, parlour, reportedly with *trompe l'œil* painting behind C18 panelling.

REDLAND

Redland bespeaks Bristol's Liberals at home after 1860, while Clifton to its w housed its Early Victorian Tories. Redland's w boundary is Whiteladies Road, and on the E the Cranbrook valley. The land was owned by the College of Westbury until 1539. In a deed of 1295 it was called Rubea Terra or Rouge Terre, probably from its red soil. It was dotted with wealthy houses by the C17, of which only the C18 rebuilding of Redland Court survives. With the sale of the Redland Court estate in 1864, suburban development began in earnest.

Churches

REDLAND CHAPEL, Redland Green Road. Now the parish church. Built by John Cossins, a London grocer, in 1740–3 as a private chapel to Redland Court (*see* p. 386). The architect's identity is much disputed: the most likely candidate is *John Strahan*, who certainly designed Redland Court, and whose other Bristol works have similarities with the chapel. However, two views of the chapel at the British Museum are signed by *William Halfpenny* as 'inventor and delineator'. Strahan died *c*. 1741–2, and in the latter year *Halfpenny* was contracted to oversee completion of the work (why, if the design was his?), visiting six days a week and forfeiting 3s. 6d. for every day missed.

The chapel stands in a high walled churchyard set on a broad green. Its style is a reserved Late Baroque, influenced by Gibbs. A handsome and ambitious w front, articulated by two pairs of Ionic pilasters, and a pediment with a lunette. The doorway has an eared segmental head, then garlands beneath a straight hood, against a rusticated ground. Standing on the door hood, a shell niche with volutes at the foot of the jambs. *Thomas Paty* contracted to carve the ornaments of the w front. Typical of Strahan is the shallow projecting panel around the niche. The front is crowned by an octagonal bell-cupola with leaded dome. 'Nothing could be simpler, or more decorative, than . . . the transition from the square to the octagon, and the ribbed, umbrella-like dome has just the festive quality the rest of the design demands' (Marcus Whiffen). The side walls have four plain arched aedicule-windows with pilasters. The chancel projects slightly and has only a blank Gibbsian-blocked arch high up, carried by two African heads. Small SE vestry by *John Norton*, from a restoration of 1859.

The interior seems to borrow from Gibbs, notably the w end of the nave (cf. St Martin-in-the-Fields, and the chapel at

Great Witley, Worcs.). First an octagonal vestibule, above which a w gallery opens into the church by three elliptical arches. Below the gallery and flanking the vestibule, two small spaces, opened to the nave via semicircular arches made by *Norton*, 1859. Three-bay nave with coved ceiling and cherubs' heads supporting the window jambs – *Paty*'s bill of 1741 refers to 'two cherubims heads in Stoca [stucco] over the panels at 10/6 each'. The E wall is arranged as a Venetian motif with the chancel arch forming its centre, and the sides panelled, with fluted Corinthian pilasters; all designed by *Halfpenny* and executed in 1742–3 by *William Brooks*, a London joiner, in Dutch oak. A deep entablature continues around the chancel apse. Its stuccoed vault has octagonal coffering, and winged cherubs' heads around the lunette. The altar painting is flanked by Commandment boards in the quadrant-curved corners, all framed by sumptuous drops of flowers and cherubs, etc. in limewood, by *Thomas Paty*. Cleaned and restored in 2006 by *Luard Conservation* under *Glyn Leaman Architects*.

OTHER FITTINGS. Altar PAINTING, a copy after Annibale Carracci by *John Vanderbank*. – COMMUNION TABLE, after a design for a side table by William Kent for Lord Burlington. A gilded eagle and winged half-figures supporting a marble top. – PULPIT by *Paty*, panelled, with prettily carved trophies in limewood. – FONT. Hexagonal baluster, 1755, by *Paty*. Replica cover, 2006. – SCULPTURE. Vivacious and informal marble BUSTS by *Rysbrack*, 1734: John and Martha Cossins (nave w wall), and in the vestibule, Martha's brothers William and John Innys, London booksellers who retired here.* – Walled CHURCHYARD with crude entrance piers (1753). – Good wrought-iron GATES with a fine overthrow, by *Nathaniel Arthur*, 1742.

ST SAVIOUR (former), Chandos Road. E.E., by *John Bevan Sen.*, 1882–9. Pennant and Bath stone, lancets and plate tracery. Double w bellcote. Altered *c.* 1976; converted to flats, 2002–3, by *Exedra Architects*.

REDLAND PARK UNITED REFORMED CHURCH, Redland Park. *Fripp & Ponton*'s Germanic-looking Gothic Congregational church of 1860–1 was bombed. Replaced on the old foundations, 1954–7, by *Ralph Brentnall*. Its pared-down Gothic shows his allegiance to his late partner Oatley's style.

TYNDALE BAPTIST CHURCH, Whiteladies Road. 1867–8, by *Samuel Hancorn*, a young Newport architect who died before it was opened. Conspicuous SW tower with pinnacles and big belfry lights, by *Crisp & Oatley*, 1893–4. Rebuilt by *Eustace Button*, 1957, after bomb damage, roughly on the old plan, retaining the tower, much of the w end and perhaps the chancel arch too. – STAINED GLASS. Nave S, 1960, and N, 1971, by *Geoffrey Robinson* (*Bell & Son*).

---

*John Strahan was portrayed in a fifth bust by *Rysbrack*, now lost, confirming his ties with the Cossins family and perhaps strengthening the case for his authorship of the chapel.

REDLAND GROVE METHODIST CHAPEL (former), Fernbank
Road. Of 1876; now offices. Perhaps by *Henry Crisp* (cf.
Hebron chapel, Bedminster, Bristol), who clung late to his
favoured Italianate. Imposing three-bay pedimented centre,
recessed flanks. Big triple-arched window above twinned
entrances between Doric columns.

TRINITY SCOTTISH PRESBYTERIAN CHURCH (former),
Cranbrook Road. 1907, by *Philip Munro & Son.* Red sandstone, a big nave with lean-to aisles and flying buttresses,
transepts and chancel. NW tower with castellated stair-turret,
and a slim Bath stone spire set inside the parapet – distinctly
Scottish details. A clean and reversible scheme by *Richard
Pedlar Architects* for conversion to flats was compromised in
execution by *Oxford Architects*, 2005–6.

SWEDENBORGIAN CHURCH, Cranbrook Road. By *Paul &
James*, 1899. Geometric Dec, with dormers.

Other buildings

REDLAND COURT, Redland Court Road. By *John Strahan*,
1732–5. John Cossins, a wealthy London grocer, bought the big
mid-C16 manor house in 1732, and replaced it immediately with
a grand house of Bath stone ashlar. In 1882 it became Redland
High School for Girls.

The compact central block is linked to square pavilions by
recessed one-and-a-half-storey wings. This Palladian conception is not thoroughly digested, and there are numerous
Baroque elements: the proportions and portico of the S front;
the tall and dominant urns on the parapet; and the compressed
composition of the N front. The central block faces S onto a
balustraded terrace with steps down to the lawns. It has a half-
basement and two storeys. The original five bays were widened
on the S to seven by *Thomas Paty*, 1747. The ground-floor
windows have intermittent rustication and big stepped voussoirs, borrowed from Colen Campbell's Houghton via *Vitruvius Britannicus.** The first-floor windows have plain
architraves and flat hoods. Projecting centre with rusticated
ground floor; above, a portico of engaged Ionic columns, reinforced at the angles by square piers, a Baroque doubling of the
outer order. Garlands above the windows and putti supporting a coat of arms in the pediment. The W pavilion is as built;
lower than the main block, with timber cupola. On the ground
floor both pavilions have fine original Venetian motifs with
Gibbsian surrounds, the centres treated as shell niches. The E
pavilion was raised in 1887 for the school, and further spoiled
by 1950s additions. The N elevation plainer, still of five bays.
Gibbsian doorway with segmental pediment, tightly flanked by
two windows – all with intermittent rustication and reading as

---

*See *Bristol: An Architectural History* for Michael Jenner's more detailed analysis of
the S front.

one motif. To the s on Redland Road, GATEPIERS with icicle rustication, magnificent urns, and fine wrought-iron GATES, c. 1735, attributed to *Nathaniel Arthur* (cf. his Redland Chapel gates).

The INTERIORS are much altered. On the N side, a central Doric ENTRANCE HALL, stone-floored. A fine doorcase with fluted half-columns and pediment leads to the panelled former DRAWING ROOM (centre s front). Marble chimneypiece with lion mask and draped pelt. Folding doors to the DINING ROOM (E). Here another good chimneypiece with a garlanded female head, probably by *Thomas Paty c.* 1747 (cf. his work at Clifton Hill House). Flanking the entrance hall, two oak STAIRCASES. The western one, with ramped rails and three twisted balusters per tread, curves tightly round a D-shaped space. The ceiling above the landing is vaulted and coffered, with a half-dome over the apse. The rectangular E staircase is simpler, and runs to the attics; turned balusters with some twisted fluting. The first floor of the W pavilion has *ex situ* painted panelling with bolection moulding, perhaps 1660–1715.

ADDITIONS for the school around the N courtyard. The LIBRARY (1903) was an art and science block. To its s, a HALL of 1911–12, by *Oatley & Lawrence*, Neo-Georgian with a prominent Venetian motif in the gable. To the W, a quite convincing imitation of the 1730s, built as a library by *Oatley & Lawrence*, 1910; carving by *Gilbert Seale*. SCIENCE BLOCK to the N, also *Oatley & Lawrence*, 1931–2.

REDLAND GREEN SCHOOL, Redland Court Road. By the *Building Design Partnership*, 2005–7. For c. 1,450 secondary pupils. Growing out of the sloping site, a long curving spine building rising to four storeys at the E, with a landscaped roof. On its s side, the now usual internal street, crossed by bridges to the Sixth-Form Centre, a big angled glass extrusion.

REDLAND HILL leads E from the roundabout at the top of Black Boy Hill. Almost immediately on the r., QUEEN VICTORIA HOUSE, now offices, built as a school by *W. L. Bernard*, 1885. Converted to a convalescent home in 1897–9, with a wing added. Of harsh red brick, four storeys with a big polygonal bay and Jacobethan doorcase. In the gardens to the s, a large OBELISK with wreaths, reportedly by *Turnbull & Rumley*, erected in memory of Princess Charlotte (†1817). Directly E again, ECOHOUSE, by *Exedra D. S. Drage*, 1997. A speculative design, of reused stone below and timber-clad living spaces above. Designed for optimal energy efficiency through siting, orientation, etc. Then REDLAND HILL HOUSE, now a school. Half of an early semi-detached pair, c. 1768–71, by *Philip West*, mason; r. house demolished in 1933. Three storeys, full-height canted bay at the l., front door in a Venetian motif, three bays of sashes to the r. From here, REDLAND ROAD runs SE, with big 1890s houses. At No. 157 the former VICARAGE to Redland Chapel, 1751. A plain box of three bays each side. The main doorcase (NW) has big keystones pushing into the pediment.

Off REDLAND COURT ROAD, the site of the Bishop's Palace (by *Caröe*, 1899, bombed 1940). It was replaced by a student hostel, itself demolished for ALDERMAN'S PARK, flats completed in 2004 by *Acanthus Ferguson Mann*, typifying the trend for high-density infill in affluent suburbs. Five storeys, red brick on a rubble-stone plinth. Serpentine plan with glass stair-towers at the back, and a circular tower adjacent.

GROVE ROAD leads NE from Black Boy Hill, with small Late Georgian houses. Nos. 8 and 9 began as one house, perhaps *c*. 1750–70. In the central bay, a first-floor oriel, and a Venetian window above. On the N side, Nos. 27–28, *c*. 1800–30, with recessed arches over the upper windows, and a wrought-iron porch. At the top of Grove Road, ELM LANE branches off S. On the W side, REDLAND VILLA, a small C18 core near the road, with a coachhouse to the r. now buried inside an angled entrance extension of *c*. 1840. Handsome Greek Revival garden front with recessed, balconied centre; also *c*. 1840. Elm Lane emerges on LOWER REDLAND ROAD. Off the S side, Elgin Park and Napier Road stand for the typical Italianate Redland housing of *c*. 1867–72. On the N side, more Regency and Early Victorian houses; Nos. 71–73, perhaps by *W. B. Gingell*.

On LUCCOMBE HILL a little E, THE OLD BARN of *c*. 1675 was embellished *c*. 1945–60 with crazy half-timbering, pieces from blitzed churches, etc. Next door, No. 20 is of *c*. 1820, with fine wrought-iron balconettes. At the E end of Lower Redland Road, THE SHAKESPEARE INN, an Edwardian classical remodelling by *Paul & James*, 1903. Red brick and Ham stone; near-original 'bottle and jug', stained glass and lavatories.

Off the E side of Whiteladies Road are numerous big villas of *c*. 1850–80, mostly Italianate. Nos. 11–31 Burlington Road are a Late Classical terrace of *c*. 1845, Bath-stone faced, and in the Clifton tradition. Perhaps by *R. S. Pope*. Three storeys, the end houses broken forward, iron balconies in the centre. Adjacent, a similar composition of *c*. 1855–60, but in ham-fisted Gothic.

SOUTHMEAD AND BRENTRY

Southmead's big 1930s and 1950s council estates merge northward into Brentry, laid out *c*. 1955–65.

ST STEPHEN, Ullswater Road. 1958–9, by *Gerald Wills* of *Miles & Wills*. Red brick, tower. The defining motif is a serpentine curve used in the porch roof, sanctuary steps and pulpit. Five concrete arches form the nave, with continuous clerestory on the S side only. S aisle, divided to form a hall in 1986. – FITTINGS. Behind the altar a forceful floor-to-ceiling SCULPTURE of the Exalted Christ, 1959, of sheet steel on a cradle of welded rods against a red ground. By *John Hoskin*, who then taught at Bath Academy of Art, Corsham, Wilts.

ST VINCENT DE PAUL (R.C.), Embleton Road. By *Kenneth Nealon*, 1953–5. Pale brick, tower with open bell-stage, U-shaped baptistery.

MONK'S PARK SCHOOL, Filton Road. By *Alec French Partnership*, 2006. With Henbury School the first phase of Bristol's school rebuilding programme. In the grounds, City Learning Centre by the same architects, 2001 (identical to that at Brislington, p. 418).

ROYAL VICTORIA PARK, Charlton Road. Formerly Brentry House, by *Humphry Repton & John Adey Repton*, 1802, with a landscaped park. It became a hospital in 1898. Converted to flats by *Stride Treglown c.* 2001–4, with new housing around, but leaving some parkland intact. The Reptons' house was modest, three bays on each side, of Bath stone ashlar, two storeys, with ground-floor openings framed by arched recesses with fluted tympana. Much enlarged *c.* 1830 in Greek Revival style, extending both the W and S fronts. On the W front the ends form tower-like projections linked by a six-column Greek Ionic colonnade; this and the date suggest that *R. S. Pope* may have been responsible (cf. Royal Colonnade, Great George Street, and Brunel House, St George's Road). The composition is slightly uncomfortable, although the overall impression is crisp and elegant.

WESTBURY-ON-TRYM, WESTBURY PARK AND HENLEAZE

Westbury-on-Trym is of Saxon origin, with a large medieval church. Westbury Park and Henleaze are suburban expansions of the late C19 and early C20 respectively, with the expected comfortable villas and some good churches and chapels.

Churches

HOLY TRINITY, Church Road. The early history of Westbury is more important from a national and regional point of view than that of Bristol. There was probably a Christian settlement here in 715, and by 803 a Benedictine monastery. In *c.* 961–3 Oswald, Bishop of Worcester, brought twelve monks from Fleury (St Bénoit-sur-Loire) in France and established at Westbury the earliest reformed monastic house in England. By 1194 the monks had been supplanted by a secular college of priests with a dean and five canons. This perhaps prompted an ambitious rebuilding as a collegiate church *c.* 1200, of which the present S aisle formed a parochial nave. Late in the C13 Godfrey Giffard, Bishop of Worcester, tried unsuccessfully to establish Westbury as a second capital of his diocese on the pattern of Wells and Bath. The church underwent a Perp remodelling under John Carpenter, the great benefactor of Westbury who was Bishop of Worcester from 1444, including a new tower and chancel. The work was largely completed between Carpenter's re-founding of the college in 1447, and his death in 1476. Westbury briefly attained cathedral status at this time. The church was heavily restored by *John Norton c.* 1851–60; ornamental carving by *Thomas Farmer*. Of the College more must be said, *see* p. 392.

The predominant impression of the exterior now is of Bishop Carpenter's C15 rebuilding, perhaps executed under the mason *William Roche*. The tower has a w doorway, a four-light w window with a figure of Carpenter above, and a higher sw stair-turret at the sw angle. The pierced and arcaded spirelet is *Norton*'s. N aisle extended at some point to end in line with the w wall of the tower. Most of the windows and battlements are Perp. There are two rood-loft turrets. Unusually for the C15, the chancel is polygonal. Below is a crypt chapel in which Bishop Carpenter was originally buried. The s porch has a turret giving access to a parvise, and inside the porch, evidence of a gallery.

The inner s doorway (over-restored in 1858) has continuous inner mouldings and a shafted outer order with stiff-leaf, a duality typical of E.E. work derived from Wells. The N arcade has circular piers with moulded capitals and nailhead decoration on one capital only. The s aisle, of *c.* 1200, has fatter piers, little carved leaf buds dotted around the capitals, and double-chamfered arches. Three stepped lancets at the w end, and a single lancet E of the porch. At its E end, outside the chapel, fine SEDILIA curiously high up, with filleted shafts. Arch mouldings of several rolls, continuous with the PISCINA. High up in three angles of the s aisle are short wall-shafts on stiff-leaf corbels, indicating an E.E. vault that was replaced by the present Perp panelled roof of timber.

The tower is connected with the nave arcades by angled pieces of uneven solid wall, tentative evidence of an earlier tower. The clerestory has five small two-light windows each side, and bigger windows above the rood. Over the chancel arch a square-headed window of five lights. N chapel two bays long; piers with the familiar four-wave section, two-centred arches. The s chapel, of three bays, has similar piers but slimmer and taller, with bulbous angular bases. Four-centred arches. William Canynges, the great Bristol merchant, was Dean of Westbury from 1469 to 1474; the s chapel was extended E for Canynges's Chantry, completed under Carpenter's successor, Bishop Alcock, i.e. 1476–86. Here is the most elaborate Perp decoration. In its s wall, three doorways to the former rood loft. The highest gave access from the rood loft to a sacristy for the parochial nave. The 3-ft-wide rood stair in its square turret allowed the priest to descend without marking his robes.

FITTINGS. Ogee-arched REREDOS of Painswick stone, angled around the apse. By *Norton*, who in 1862 raised money to have it painted and gilded (renewed 1958). Central panel carved by *Farmer* of the Last Supper, after a fresco at S. Onofrio, Florence. – PULPIT. Also by *Farmer* to *Norton*'s design. On marble pillars, reached through the pier of the chancel arch. FONT. Of the same genesis. – PEWS, 1850s, with a forest of tall poppyheads. – STAINED GLASS. Apse windows by *O'Connor*, 1860. Above the chancel arch, a good early example by *Joseph Bell*, 1852. S chapel: E, 1869 by *Heaton, Butler & Bayne*; S, first perhaps, second certainly, by *Percy Bacon Bros*; 1911, *c*. 1901; third, *Joseph Bell & Son*, 1910–11; at the head of the rood stairs, one by *Jones & Willis*, *c*. 1912. S aisle: first and second by *Bacon Bros*, 1903 and 1904; third by *J. Bell & Son*, 1903. S aisle W, 1925, probably by *Arnold Robinson*, for *Joseph Bell & Son*. N aisle N: first no doubt by *Hardman*, *c*. 1872; second by *Terence Randall*, 1952. – MONUMENTS. Bishop Carpenter †1476, between S chapel and chancel. A C15 cadaver under a Perp canopy of 1853. – Sir Richard Hill †1627, S chapel, E wall. A stiff reclining effigy in armour, under an arched canopy with strapwork. – To its l., Rose Large †1610; crude kneeling figure. – Miles Wilson †1567 and Elizabeth Revell †1581 (N aisle, E end). Purbeck tablet with arched top, on fluted pilasters. C16 paintings of a skull and tombs with effigies. –William Jefferis †1752, perhaps by *T. Paty*. Good Rococo monument, without figures.

ST ALBAN, Coldharbour Road, Westbury Park. A C20 church notable for its ambitious E end and Arts and Crafts glass. The first permanent church, now the hall to the N, is by *Crisp & Oatley* 1892–4. Picturesque flèche; Flamboyant Dec E and W windows. *Rodway & Dening* won the competition for a larger church. The first phase (1907–9) consisted of nave, aisles and transepts. Of silvery Brentry limestone, coursed and snecked. E end added 1913–15, including a NE tower of which only the base was completed. Bold massing, flying buttresses over the aisles, and varied Perp tracery. At the W end, a former baptistery, now glazed in, its top forming a gallery. Prosaic four-bay nave. Aisles as wide as the transepts, with moulded arcades that die into the piers. By contrast the chancel is bold and soaring, with solid side walls, pierced by two small arches into the S chapel. SEDILIA with deliciously sinuous embellishments. At the sides of the chancel are passage aisles formed by triple arcades on tall slender Perp columns. The passages emerge either side of the chancel arch through tall narrow openings, and have transverse segmental arches like bridges at each bay and against the E wall. The S aisle of the chancel can also be read as a N aisle to the big S chapel, given by Violet Wills in memory of her father. It too has a narrow passage aisle to its S, with a tiny second altar. The small N chapel became an organ loft in 1925.

FITTINGS. Oak REREDOS, 1937, by *Richard Nickson* of Liverpool, executed by *Herbert Read*; well related to the E window. Also by *Read* the finely wrought CHOIR STALLS, 1927. – S CHAPEL REREDOS, 1915, of Beer limestone with delicate lacy ornament, and relief panels. – STAINED GLASS. Much by *Joseph Bell & Son*'s chief designer, *Arnold Robinson*, was in memory of dead sons, a moving litany for the lost of the First World War: E window, S aisle, W windows, and N aisle second and third from E. The windows include some noteworthy pale glass with smoky striations of pink or blue. S chapel, all by

Powell & Sons, 1915, with pale Morris-like foliage. S transept S, by *Margaret Chilton*, 1915, depicting craftsmen and the completed church. N transept, *Clayton & Bell*, 1920. N aisle, first from E, 1929, designed by *Florence Camm* of Smethwick, with typical diaper leading. Four small lights (former baptistery), by *Margaret Chilton*, 1916.

ST PETER, The Drive, Henleaze. By *A. R. Gough*, begun 1927; competent Neo-Perp, as if of its lush Edwardian phase. *Gough* extended the church in 1937 with two nave bays, narthex and baptistery. The interior rendered but with much dressed and carved stone. Arcades with complex hollow chamfers. Aisles with stone diaphragm arches at each bay. Wagon roof with tie-beams. Lady Chapel created by extending the S aisle in 1960, by *T. H. B. Burrough*. – STAINED GLASS. E window and small baptistery light by *Andrew Younger*, 1966; in arresting red, gold and purple.

SACRED HEART (R.C.), Grange Court Road. By *Roberts & Willman*, begun 1939. Yellow brick, plain Neo-Romanesque. W entrance set in a tall arched recess with concentric steppings. Exposed concrete portal frames, but incongruous florid Neo-Georgian plasterwork around the altars and tabernacle.

TRINITY UNITED REFORMED CHURCH (Congregational), Waterford Road. By *Frank Wills*, 1906–7. Bulky and severe E.E. with plain lancets. Quite Anglican in layout. Porch at the (ritual) SW in the base of an incomplete tower, intended to have a spire.

BAPTIST CHURCH, Reedley Road. By *Nealon Tanner & Partners*, 1967–8. Brick, hexagonal, with a split roof with a clerestory between the two parts. A free-standing metal spire has been dismantled.

METHODIST CHURCH, Westbury Hill. By *H. J. Jones*, 1889–90. Geometric Dec traceried transept and W windows. Puny tower and spirelet at the ritual NW. Halls, 1953–90. Re-fitted and a glazed foyer added, by *Richard Pedlar Architects*, completed 2005. – Stardust, an ARTWORK by *Simon Thomas*, 2005, of raised stars sprinkled across the S transept wall.

WESTBURY PARK METHODIST CHURCH, Etloe Road. 1890, by *Henry Dare Bryan*, then just twenty-two. Geometric Dec, not innovative, but confident and well detailed, e.g. tracery bars raised for richness. A second NW porch is perhaps the base of an intended tower.

CANFORD CEMETERY, Canford Lane. Opened 1903. Small Gothic chapel, mildly Art and Crafts lodge; CREMATORIUM of 1956, brown brick with a big *porte cochère* under arches. – 50 yds r. of the main entrance, TOMBSTONE to Mrs A. Chute †1931 by *Eric Gill*, with a fine sculpted Crucifixion. – Next to the main drive, a monument to the Voke family, 1931; cinema-Art-Deco style.

Other buildings

WESTBURY COLLEGE, College Road (National Trust since 1907). For its early history *see* Holy Trinity church, p. 389. The college was re-founded in 1447 by Bishop Carpenter, who built the turreted quadrangle, with the River Trym to the N and buildings S, E and W: 'more like a citadel than a college' (Bishop Godwin of Llandaff, 1616). Converted to a house *c.* 1544. Used as Prince Rupert's CivilWar headquarters; when he left in 1643 he had it burned. Part of the S side survives – an embattled, four-storey gatehouse and a two-storey range to its W, terminating in a castellar circular turret with concave cap. The gateway has one large arch on the S side (now blocked), one for carriages and one for pedestrians on the N. It is vaulted in two bays with single-chamfered ribs of slender profile, ridge ribs on corbels, and shields and bosses in the vault. COLLEGE HOUSE, built *c.* 1709 on the W range, was burned and demolished in 1967. On the former quadrangle, WESTMINSTER COURT, old people's flats by *Power Clark Hiscocks Partnership*, *c.* 1971–4.

BADMINTON SCHOOL, Cote Lane. At its heart, NORTHCOTE HOUSE, a C19 Jacobethan mansion perhaps by *Foster & Wood* (cf. Frankfort Hall, Clevedon): Paul Pindar windows, shaped gables and a diagonally set turret. C20 additions include *Michael Axford*'s CREATIVE ARTS CENTRE, with much glazing, and the LIBRARY by *Casson, Conder & Partners*, 1969; a cool reworking of a Neoclassical pavilion, square with pyramidal roof, set against a bank so that from the garden terrace it appears to be of one storey. SANDERSON HOUSE by *Mitchell Taylor Workshop*, 2007–8, is a boarding house cantilevered over the boundary wall. Timber-clad, three storey, narrow windows with brises-soleil.

RED MAIDS SCHOOL, Westbury Road. Founded in 1634, on this site since 1911. Gothic gate LODGE with semi-octagonal end, possibly that designed by *Thomas Rickman* for E. B. Fripp, 1827–8. The core was Burfield House, its three-bay centre with segmental-headed windows probably *c.* 1725–50. To the l., an extension perhaps *c.* 1850, with fancy quoining and porch. To the r. a stark red-brick addition by *Sir Frank Wills*, 1910–11, and on the lawns in front, a long two-storey block with simplified giant-order piers, by *F. Wills & Son*, 1933–4. In the entrance hall of Burfield House, chimneypiece of *c.* 1620, with a flattened arch and frieze with lozenges and squares. It has been with the school since the C18. In the dining hall is a much grander one from the founder's house in St Nicholas Street. Of the usual Bristol pattern *c.* 1580–1600, with paired Ionic columns, and a scrolled frieze. Ceiling-height overmantel bearing the arms of Queen Elizabeth I between strapwork; paired Corinthian columns.

ST URSULA'S HIGH SCHOOL, Brecon Road. A Regency house with Doric porch. Bath stone garden front (SW), with sashes in arched recesses. Late Classical chapel (now library) by *John Peniston*, 1834–5. Severe three-storey additions for a convent, 1859–62, in the style of *Foster & Wood*, Italianate with a campanile.

ST MONICA HOME OF REST, Cote Lane. By *Oatley & Lawrence*, 1920–6. Given by Sir H. H. Wills and Dame Mary Monica

Wills, whose initials appear above the entrance. Lavish Neo-Tudor and Jacobean, costing *c.* £488,000. On plan, a long s-facing spine corridor serves big triangular wings which shelter paved parterres. Of pinkish local stone with heavy Bath stone dressings, steep roofs, and close-studded timbered gables, like a Norman-Shavian country house. Entrance porch set between two canted bays, forming an elongated hexagon, with fluted Ionic pilasters and strapwork in the spandrels, the most Jacobean element of the design. Converted to sheltered flats, 2004. – CHAPEL OF ST AUGUSTINE, 1920–6, N of the spine corridor. Bigger than many parish churches, overtly costly, and with no nod to contemporary and innovative reinterpretations of Gothic. Perp, ashlar-faced throughout. Fan-vaulted narthex beneath a gallery, then a three-bay nave. Wide E end with transepts leading into chapels open to the chancel. – SCULPTURE, Virgin and Child by *A. G. Walker.* – Big *Willis* ORGAN. Made for the patrons' house at Wrington, 1901.

In the grounds to the N, the former NURSES' HOME, now flats, *Oatley & Lawrence.* In a more austere ashlar-faced Jacobethan style, with a tower. To the W, THE GARDEN HOUSE nursing home, by *Williams Lester,* opened 2003. Low-pitched copper-clad roofs, rubble and timber cladding, with intervening deep buttresses.

WESTBURY VILLAGE. On the roundabout between High Street and Westbury Hill, a First World War MEMORIAL by *James & Steadman,* 1919–20, a garlanded obelisk. To the W, the MEN'S CLUB, 1897–8, by *W. L. Bernard,* red brick, timbered gables. Along High Street, N, some Georgian villas and cottages. No. 38 Church Road is of *c.* 1450–70, doubtless built for the church or college. Four-centred doorway, hall to the l. with a high two-light Perp window, and a smaller one l. again for the parlour. Service rooms to the r. of the cross-passage; here, Georgian sashes. In the C16 or C17 the hall was given a chimney and an upper floor was inserted. (C15 arch-braced collar-beam roof with wind-braces.)

In Trym Road, E, a well-preserved cottage terrace with margin-glazed sashes, perhaps 1830s. Rear court with C19 privies. Then a former BAPTIST CHAPEL, *c.* 1840; now Evangelical. Grey stone, with triple lancets in the W gable. E again, at the bottom of CHOCK LANE, some C17 cottages with the occasional surviving ovolo-moulded mullion.

VILLAGE HALL, Eastfield Road. Gothic, 1866–9, by *Foster & Wood* for Henry St Vincent Ames of Cote House.* Entrance wing for a library and a reading room, the hall sited laterally behind. It has a dramatic apsidal end with sharply folded roofs over five gables with rose windows.

POORHOUSE, Nos. 51–53 Eastfield Road. Built in 1802–4, converted in 1852 to two tall houses; Late Classical, in a high and visible position. In EASTFIELD, 100 yds E, some good early C19 houses; No. 40 a refined Grecian design perhaps by *Charles*

---

* *E. W. Godwin*'s design of 1866 bears no relation to what was built.

Underwood, c. 1840–5. Recessed centre with Ionic porch and Tower of the Winds columns *in antis* above.

N of Westbury-on-Trym. Off Passage Road is CONCRETE HOUSE, The Ridgeway, 1934, by *Amyas Connell* of *Connell, Ward & Lucas.** The most notable example of 1930s International Modernism in N Somerset and Bristol, and one of the least altered works of this important firm. A sleek rectangular slab, with much horizontal glazing on the S front; reinforced concrete frame with concrete infill walls. The white exterior was originally yellow. The recessed bedroom balcony at the r. is stopped short by the projecting main bedroom at the l., which, with the different elevational treatment here, lends the design a subtle dynamism. A signature of the firm's work is the prominence given to staircase blocks; here a fully glazed projection from the W return elevation rising above the roof parapet, with curving porch canopy running out to the drive. Integral garage at the N, and a rooftop sun terrace. Many original fittings, including built-in gramophone speakers. At Chapel Gardens off The Ridgeway, in the back garden of a late C20 house, the impressive RUIN of the W window of St Mark (or the Lord Mayor's Chapel), College Green (*see* p. 257). The splendid eight-light window was taken down in 1822 and re-erected here between turrets, as an eyecatcher in the park of a large house. Through it one now sees the sky: more intensely picturesque and romantic than any of the sham castles of Bristol or Bath.

S to Downs Park. On Westbury Hill to the S of the village, an early C19 LOCK-UP (E side), with wall-benches. Further up, the OLD POST OFFICE pub, extended in vibrant red brick and buff terracotta by *W. V. Gough*, 1888–9. At the junction of Falcondale Road and Westbury Hill, a former TRAM GARAGE of 1909 by *W. H. Watkins*, with twin gables, roughcast render, succulent moulded plasterwork. ½ m. E, in the fork of a road junction, No. 166 Henleaze Road, an early C19 Picturesque thatched LODGE, surely inspired by Nash's Blaise Hamlet (p. 400).

DOWNS PARK ESTATE was established *c.* 1903, the best of several Bristol emulations of the Bedford Park garden-suburb ideal. Many plots were developed using *Henry Dare Bryan* (who perhaps also designed the layout) and, from *c.* 1908, *Rodway & Dening*. Its impact is rather diluted by interwar and later infill. From the S end of DOWNS PARK WEST, first Nos. 1–3 by *James Hart*, 1905; handsome Early Georgian red brick. No. 7 was remodelled within by *Marcel Breuer & F. R. S. Yorke*, 1935–6, for Crofton Gane, furniture manufacturer, but these alterations are long gone.† To the N, No. 21 (1908–9, *Harold*

---

* Contributions from Elain Harwood; Society of Architectural Historians of Great Britain conference notes, 2002.

† In 1936 Gane commissioned *Breuer & Yorke* to design a temporary show pavilion of squared rubble and glass at Ashton Court. A milestone of early Modernist architecture in Britain, exemplifying the move towards more natural materials in the late 1930s; Breuer regarded it as one of his two best works.

S. Jacques) with vernacular and Voyseyish touches; and No. 27, bastardized Queen Anne (1908, by *A. P. I. Cotterell*). At the N end, W side, a very big pair by *Dare Bryan*, *c.* 1903–4, with overhanging tile-hung gables and smart Jacobean details. E along Henleaze Road, more pairs, and a group of three with Arts and Craftsy bays and gables (*Dare Bryan*, 1903–4); then into DOWNS PARK EAST. On the W, Nos. 65–79, four pairs with varied details by *Rodway & Dening*, 1911–12, already in the Neo-Georgian plummy brick that defined Dening's interwar work. Nos. 74–76, by *Dare Bryan*, designed 1903. Further on (E side), the best group, Nos. 42–60; the first three pairs by *Dare Bryan*, 1905–6; Nos. 42–44 and 46–48 by *Rodway & Dening*, 1908, the former perhaps the subtlest work at Downs Park: much tile-hanging, three jetties, and long catslides. The whole front above the ground floor reads as conjoined gables. Nos. 34–36, prominently dated 1910, again by *Rodway & Dening*. In NORTH VIEW, six three-storey shops at Nos. 23–33 probably by *H. Dare Bryan*, 1904.

In Durdham Park, bordering the Downs to the S, CARFAX COURT, a retirement complex. Two Victorian houses, the more imposing dated 1873, Jacobethan without too many frills. In 1989 *Ferguson Mann* added courtyard flats with C17 references in the mullioned bay. Further S off Redland Road, CAMBRIDGE PARK, a cul de sac entered through piers topped by lions. Big debased Italianate houses by *W. H. Hawtin*, 1865–7. Further S still in Coldharbour Road, the CAMBRIDGE ARMS, by *Edward Gabriel*, 1900–1. Jolly pargeted front; Venetian windows, Tuscan porches.

OUTER BRISTOL: NORTH-WEST

Including Avonmouth and other suburbs N of the Avon and W of the A4018. They are separated from the city by the enviable belt of Durdham Down.

AVONMOUTH

A Late Victorian industrial suburb, based around the docks which opened in 1877; the Miles family of Kingsweston were major investors, and their architects did much work here. Avonmouth is wedged uncomfortably between docks, railway line and motorway.

ST ANDREW, Avonmouth Road. E end, tower base and the E part of the nave by *W. Wood Bethell*, 1892–3. Pink conglomerate, with flamboyant Dec tracery. Austere additions by *P. Hartland Thomas*, 1935, of grey Pennant stone. He completed the tower, extended the nave (with quirky tracery in the W window) and the short S aisle. SW porch with typical stepped round arches. Gutted by bombing in 1941 and rebuilt by *F. L. Hannam*, 1955–7, with a new N aisle, emulating Hartland Thomas's simplified Gothic. N arcade a row of thin posts. – PULPIT, FONT and clergy STALLS from St Raphael, Cumberland Road, Bristol (by *Woodyer*, 1859), also bombed but not repaired.

CUSTOM HOUSE, Clayton Street. By the *Property Services Agency South West Region Design Office*; project architect *Derrick Long*, c. 1982. Suitably forthright in this setting. Of three storeys, faced with white marble aggregate. Chamfered window reveals. Low-pitched roof, incinerator pipe cutting through the roof.

LIBRARY (former National School), Avonmouth Road. Dated 1888. Elongated H-plan, Gothic, in red brick with black lozenges. Extended 1897.

AVONMOUTH DOCKS. The first dock was built 1868–77 and, with Portishead, taken over by Bristol Corporation in 1884. Enlarged to the N with ROYAL EDWARD DOCK, 1902–8; engineer *Sir John Aird & Co.* It added 30 acres of water, with a graving dock 850 ft (1metres) long. Between 1922 and 1928 the acreage of water was doubled. Since 1977 container ships berth instead at Royal Portbury Dock S of the Avon (*see* p. 580).

The working docks are inaccessible. Monolithic and largely featureless industrial buildings form an impressive backdrop to the suburb: e.g. the eight-storey Co-operative Wholesale Society FLOUR MILL, King Road Avenue, by *F. E. L. Harris*, 1907–8. White faience on reinforced concrete, one corner raised to a short tower. SPILLER'S MILL, eight windowless storeys of concrete (1930s); ADM MILLING (formerly Hosegood's), seven storeys with horizontal window bands, by *P. J. Clarke*, 1937–40.

AVONMOUTH BRIDGE. 1969–74, consulting engineers *Freeman, Fox & Partners*. It carries the M5 motorway 4,550 ft (1,400 metres) across the Avon. Twin box-girder construction, with a 570-ft (175-metre) central span, 100 ft (31 metres) above high water. The ten-span approach viaduct strides assertively over the rooftops.

On Avonmouth Road (S side), the MILES ARMS HOTEL by *F. Bligh Bond*, 1907. Neo-Georgian details, central columned balcony. Immediately w, a former METHODIST CHAPEL, by *La Trobe & Weston*, 1904, plate-traceried. On Avonmouth Road, w again, a three-storey terrace of shops, probably by *Bond, c.* 1900, a confusion of Neo-Georgian and Arts and Crafts motifs. Opposite, a former TRAM SHED by *W. H. Watkins*, dated 1915. Angled clock turret, oculi framed by palmy plaster foliage. In GLOUCESTER ROAD, outside the entrance to the first docks, the ROYAL HOTEL, part of a big brash terrace of shops *c.* 1880. Extended NE in 1892 by *Patrick J. Byrne*. Nearby on Portview Road, the FLYING ANGEL, a seamen's mission by *Oatley & Lawrence*, 1925–9. Now flats. Dark brick, mullioned-and-transomed windows.

HENBURY AND BLAISE CASTLE

Medieval Henbury was owned by the Bishops of Worcester. It had by the C17 several very large houses around the church, of which two survive.

Churches

ST MARY, Church Close. w tower, long aisled nave, aisled chancel. The earliest parts are late Norman – the nave arcades, and the N and S doorways. The w tower much altered, but its broad proportions and lack of buttresses, the chamfered tower arch on semi-octagonal responds, and the shouldered lintel of the stair-turret doorway point to C13 origins. Ogee belfry lights, with Y-tracery; coarse work of the C14, or C17–C18 and set in earlier openings? Simple N doorway, one capital with waterleaf decoration. This and the richer S doorway are latest Norman. The capitals trumpet-shaped, stilted segmental arch, keeled columns and arch moulding. The outer moulding continuous. Probably of *c.* 1200 are the fine six-bay nave arcades, work of the first order, and incidentally not at all of a Somerset character. They have tall, vigorous circular piers, plain moulded capitals and double-stepped pointed arches. Also of the C13, a curiously half-hearted clerestory: small cusped lancets with trefoiled rere-arches, in every second bay only, and above the spandrels, not the apexes of the arcade – a pinched and unhappy arrangement. C15 Perp aisle windows, and on the N side, brick battlements perhaps by *R. S. Pope* who raised the nave roof level in 1828. The chancel is steeply angled to the N. It was rebuilt by order of Bishop Giffard of Worcester in 1270–1, and probably at the same time given a spacious S chapel with triple-lancet windows. The PISCINA with a single cusp at the top of its inner arch looks earlier C13, perhaps from the previous chancel. *Rickman & Hutchinson*'s restoration of 1834–5 transformed the chancel in emulation of the S chapel, adding (e.g.) the E window of five stepped lancets, and a corresponding N chapel and vestry. In 1875–8, *G. E. Street* rather restored the *status quo ante*. How far the interior of these E parts is reliable, it is hard to say. The chancel arch has grouped shafts, the piers of the chapel a quatrefoil shape with keeled shafts or spurs in the diagonals.

FITTINGS. FONT. Octagonal, black marble, 1806. – Eight fine brass CANDELABRA, 1814. In the C18 tradition, but with Gothic quatrefoils in the branches. – STAINED GLASS. E window and chancel S, 1878 by *Daniel Bell*. Chancel N perhaps *Burlison & Grylls*, c. 1888. S aisle E and W, period pieces, by *Mayer & Co.*, Munich, 1877–8. Probably theirs too the N chapel N. S aisle, from the E: two by *Clayton & Bell*, c. 1878; third, possibly *Joseph Bell*; over the S door, *Clayton & Bell*, c. 1900; *Kempe*, 1890. N chapel E, behind the organ, a rarity by *W. R. Eginton*, 1805–6, the survivor of eight. N aisle, from the E: c. 1906 perhaps by *Margaret Chilton*, and very fine; *Bell & Son*, 1907; by *A. L. Moore*, 1907. *Arnold Robinson*'s N aisle W is a memorial to his brother, 1914–15. Vestry, some C16 Flemish glass, including the Virgin Mary. – MONUMENTS. In the tower, Sir Robert Southwell †1702, of Kingsweston. Designed by the military engineer *Sir Henry Sheeres*, executed by the workshop of *Grinling Gibbons*; very tall, with swept spire-like top and an urn. It cost £62.18s. – Sir Edward Southwell †1730; rebuilder of Kingsweston House. A noble hanging monument. Big black obelisk with ample white draperies hanging from a baldacchino and held up by two putti. Usually mistaken for the work of Gibbons. – Edward Southwell †1755. By *Thomas Paty*. Tablet with obelisk and palms. – In the church, Edward Sampson †1695, tablet with hanging garlands of finely carved flowers. – Edward Sampson †1848, the neighbour of the foregoing and a free copy of it. A comparison is entertaining. – John Sampson †1753, a fine piece of coloured marbles with palm branch and book against an obelisk. – Mary Teast †1766, by *Drewett*, 1790, with the hackneyed motif of a standing woman by an urn. – Mrs Harford Battersby †1823, executed by *J. C. F. Rossi*; with an addition for her husband †1852, both designed by *C. R. Cockerell*. An arch-topped tablet with base on Grecian volutes. – Isabella Cave †1827. By *Nicholas Bazzanti* of Florence. Fame holding out a wreath to a mourning woman.

The CHURCHYARD has a lancet Gothic VESTRY HALL, possibly by *Thomas Rickman*, c. 1830. – N of the church, Scipio Africanus †1720, a black servant of the Earl of Suffolk and Bruton. Both headstone and footstone have black cherubs' heads; the inscription begins: 'I who was born a pagan and a slave / Now sweetly sleep a Christian in my grave'. – Amelia Edwards †1892, egyptologist. Against the N chapel, an obelisk and slab bearing the ankh, Egyptian symbol of immortality.

Other buildings

BLAISE CASTLE HOUSE. Now a museum. In 1795–6 *William Paty* designed this small country house for the Quaker banker John Scandrett Harford. A restrained and graceful Neoclassical stone box. Pedimented NW front of five bays with a circular Ionic porch, half projecting and half carved, as it were, out of the building. Banded rustication to the ground floor. Five-bay SE façade, extended (r.) in 1832–3 by *C. R. Cockerell* with a six-column Ionic portico, into which the Picture Room projects, almost touching the four central columns. To the E a detached Doric conservatory by *John Nash*, c. 1805–6, on a concave quadrant plan, with Venetian openings at the ends. The balustrade, statues and urns around the house are *Cockerell*'s additions, reinstated 2006–7. In the hall, Neoclassical relief medallions by *Bertel Thorwaldsen*, c. 1833, and a plaster copy of part of the Parthenon frieze, c. 1820s. Cockerell's Picture Room has an oval domed lantern framed in an octagon. Bas-reliefs here also by *Thorwaldsen*. Scagliola Corinthian columns and a good marble chimneypiece. Well-proportioned library with free-standing Corinthian columns screening one end. Top-lit staircase with interlaced wrought-iron balustrade. LANDSCAPE by *Humphry Repton*, whose Red Book of 1795–6 was, unusually, implemented almost in full: a remarkably complete example of Picturesque ideals. The long driveway included hairpin turns, caves, rocks and hanging woods, to give arriving visitors shudders of terror.

The CASTLE is ¼ m. SW on Blaise Hill. A triangular sham-Gothic tower with corner turrets, designed by *Robert Mylne* in 1766 for Thomas Farr. David Lambert proposes a serious intent as a Whiggish emblem of peace and trade after the Seven Years War; three towers by Henry Flitcroft have similar icono-graphic meanings (Stoober's Stand, Wentworth Woodhouse (1748), Fort Belvedere, Windsor (1750), and Alfred's Tower, Stourhead). In a hollow just SE of Blaise Castle House, a pretty thatched DAIRY by *George Repton*, c. 1804, perhaps under Nash's direction. – ¼ m. S of the house, a woodman's COTTAGE, c. 1797, designed to give views from the house of homely smoke drifting from a woodland clearing. – On Henbury Road is a Tudor turreted LODGE by *Repton*, and shortly W, TIMBER LODGE, probably c. 1840s, in bark-covered logs like an C18 root-house. – STRATFORD MILL, an C18 watermill from near West Harptree, re-erected on the estate in 1954 when Chew Valley Lake was constructed (*see* p. 450).

[87] BLAISE HAMLET, Hallen Road. ¼ m. N of the house (National Trust). In 1810–11 *John Nash*, assisted by Humphry's son *George Repton*, designed ten dwellings as a place of retirement for Harford's estate workers. Pevsner called it 'the *nec plus ultra* of picturesque layout and design', which charms rather than irritates because of 'its smallness, its seclusion . . . and the nicely maintained degree of artificiality throughout'. Nine buildings are scattered around an undulating green with an emphatically off-centre pillar which is both pump and sundial. Avoiding the regimented almshouse model, each cottage differs from the others, or rather combines the same forms and materials differently. Limestone rubble, thatch, boarded gables, stone-tiled roofs, and brick are arranged to create Picturesque variety. Wide thatched eaves, dormers, gables or

half-hipped roofs cover the low compact cottages; each has at least one special feature, e.g. a dovecote gable or a sheltered seat. Over-sized chimneystacks of decorative cogged brick-work, some round, some square, set diagonally or in groups to break the roof-lines. CIRCULAR COTTAGE, with its dormer set symmetrically on a semicircular end, is perhaps first for Pic-turesque effect. DOUBLE COTTAGE combines two dwellings in one building. The hamlet is hidden behind a stone wall with a simple gate; Nash recommended modesty to maintain the pride of the recipients of Harford's generous charity. Nash's villa-retreat of Park Village, Regents Park, London (built from 1824), was a development of the Blaise concept of the Pic-turesque village.

WESLEY COLLEGE, College Park Drive. Big H-shaped main block, by *Sir Percy Thomas & Son*, 1951–3. Institutional Neo-Georgian.

HENBURY SCHOOL AND LEISURE CENTRE, Station Road. By the *Alec French Partnership*, 2005. Four wings radiate from a central entrance foyer. Blockwork below and coloured render above, with steel brises-soleil. Dual-pitched roofs with a clerestory strip at the break.

WOODSTOCK SCHOOL, Rectory Gardens. Formerly Henbury Awdelett or Henbury Manor House, built for the Sampson family in 1688. Steep gables, and unmistakable upright oval windows keyed into oblong panels. The entrance front has a full-width two-storey addition, probably mid-C19. It replaced a two-storey porch. On the N façade remains of one original cross-window. The original staircase has a square open well, thick twisted balusters, and pendants. In the grounds, a STATUE of Neptune from Henbury Court, demolished 1953.

BENGOUGH'S HOUSE, Crow Lane. By *Feilden Clegg*, completed 1996. Reserved and thoughtful. Much brown brick towards the road, the garden fronts timber-clad above steel balconies.

In CHURCH CLOSE, outside the churchyard gates, CLOSE HOUSE, C17 and symmetrical, two storeys with attic gables. Opposite, the Tudor Gothic SCHOOL of 1830, now a village hall, with an oriel window over the door. The school was for-merly housed in a long two-storey range with seven windows, perhaps C15. It may have started as a church house, cf. Chew Magna.

In HENBURY ROAD both S and N of the village centre are wealthy Georgian houses. Well up the hill to the S is CHESTERFIELD HOUSE of three bays, with all openings enriched by Gibbs sur-rounds and parapets curved up towards the corners, suggest-ing a date *c.* 1740–60. To the N is THE ELMS (E side), late C17, gabled, with C18 alterations. The continuity of character of Henbury is execrably broken by a large interwar pub at the main corner. At the junction with Station Road, HENBURY LODGE, *c.* 1760–80. Projecting pedimented centre with a Venetian window in the first floor.

In Station Road is NORTH LODGE, by *H. Dare Bryan*, 1902, a lodge to Henbury Court; Domestic Revival with fruity plasterwork and octagonal windows in one gable. To the E of Henbury around Crow Lane, large HOUSING ESTATES of terraces, three- and four-storey flats and a shopping arcade (*City Architect's Department*, 1954). It gives the area quite a New Town look.

LAWRENCE WESTON

Mainly post-1945 council housing, bounded by the M5 motorway and the levels of the Severn estuary.

ST PETER, Long Cross. By *J. Ralph Edwards*, 1961. A thoroughgoing Modernist design, nearly square, of pale brick with one gently curved side wall, and the opposite wall panelled with geometric-patterned concrete. Free-standing bell-tower. – STAINED GLASS. Panels set in concrete, by *Pierre Fourmaintraux*.

OUR LADY OF THE ROSARY (R.C.), Kingsweston Lane. Nave and aisles by *Kenneth Nealon*, 1952–3, completed by *Nealon & Partner*, 1957–8. Conventional brown brick.

QUAKER BURIAL GROUND, Kings Weston Lane. With arched gateway dated 1690. On Kings Weston Road, QUAKERS MEET, former Friends' Meeting House. Single-storeyed with a hipped roof and sash windows about an arched door, dated 1718. Closed 1893, now residential, and attached to a house. Nearby in ROCKWELL AVENUE, NE, a small housing development by *Architecton*, 1978. Dark brick, fragmented monopitch roofs, and bold and lively compositions.

ROMAN VILLA, Long Cross. Excavated 1948, a small villa after 268, the date of a coin in the foundations. Abandoned *c.* 370s. A wooden shelter covers a mosaic floor in the triclinium.

SEA MILLS WITH COOMBE DINGLE

Where the River Trym joins the Avon on its E bank was the Roman port of Abonae, the closest significant settlement to modern Bristol. Of the C17 or C18 mills on the Trym, nothing survived interwar suburban development.

ST EDYTH, Avonleaze, Sea Mills. By *Oatley & Lawrence*, 1926–8. A C20 variant of E.E., in florid red Pennant stone. Cruciform plan with a blunt, squat crossing tower. Lancet windows with Y-tracery. Nave with low aisles; temporary W wall replaced in Pennant stone by *Peter Ware*, 1993–4, with entrance and halls at the SW. Ashlar-faced interior, with tall nave arcades, the main arches filled at the top and framing a clerestory of triple lancets; elliptical subsidiary arches to the aisles. Octagonal piers also carry the transverse ribs of a pointed tunnel-vault. Transeptal crossing arches with unexpected central piers. Groin-vaulted crossing and chancel. – STAINED GLASS by *Arnold Robinson*, 1929–30.

METHODIST CHURCH, Sea Mills Square. By *Oatley & Lawrence*, 1930–1. Two storeys in dark brick with hipped roof. On the long side, a full-length lean-to narthex. Upper windows round-arched. Groined tunnel-vaulted interior, reminiscent of Oatley's chapel at Wills Hall, Stoke Bishop (1929). Converted to flats and worship area, *c.* 2007–8, by *Pentan Partnership*.

SEA MILLS DOCK. The third wet dock in Britain, built *c.* 1712; engineer *John Padmore*. Intended to mitigate the dangerous run up the Avon channel, it proved too distant from Bristol, and fell into disuse. A few walls survive, much decayed.

Sea Mills was developed by the City Council as a Garden Suburb, from 1919. Its radial streets, crescents, culs de sac, and generous greens were modelled on Raymond Unwin's *Town Planning in Practice* (1909) and the Tudor Walters Report (1918). Overall plan by *C. F. W. Dening* with *L. S. Mackenzie*, the City Engineer. Cottagey Neo-Georgian housing in red brick or render, many by *Benjamin Wakefield* or *Heathman & Blacker*. Radiating from the Pentagon are 250 'Dorlonco' steel-framed houses manufactured by *Dorman Long*, 1926. Outer skins of blockwork or of rendered corrugated metal; conventional pitched roofs.

CHERRY ORCHARDS (or Coombe Farm), off Canford Lane.[*] By *Godwin & Crisp*, *c.* 1870, for George Smith. The design is mostly by *Crisp*, though quite Godwinian in character. Rough-hewn but precisely cut stone. Gothic arches, square oriels, canted bays, half-timbering and brick-nogging. Good staircase with chamfering and pierced stringing. Now a residential care community. Careful single-storey extensions to the NW by *Feilden Clegg*, *c.* 1975–85.

SHIREHAMPTON WITH KINGSWESTON

The village became fashionable in the C18; it also has some unusually good Edwardian buildings by the Kingsweston estate architect, *F. Bligh Bond*, and briefly aspired to a garden suburb, *c.* 1910. *Vanbrugh*'s magnificent Kingsweston House broods hidden on its plateau above the village.

Churches and public buildings

ST MARY, High Street. Rebuilt by *P. Hartland Thomas*, 1929–30. Neo-Gothic, but handled with freedom, spirit, and an awareness of Modern Movement ideas. Pennant stone, five-bay nave, low windowless passage aisles, and wide straight-headed upper windows of five elliptical-headed lights and one transom, quite C16. Over the E end of the nave, a tripartite bellcote, big and square. No nave arcades, but reinforced concrete beams forming rectangular openings. – STAINED GLASS. E window by *Harry Stammers*, 1961. W window, a First World War memorial by *Arnold Robinson* (*Bell & Son*) 1930; resited and altered, 1962. Remnants of a complete scheme planned by *Robinson* in N aisle chapel, 1930, and organ chamber, 1946. Low down in

[*] Identified and researched by Dr Sarah Whittingham.

the w wall, a Nativity, *c.* 2004 (s side) and Deposition (N) of 2007, both by *John Yeo.*

ST BERNARD (R.C.), Station Road. Dec chancel 1902–3, by *E. Doran Webb* of Salisbury, hence the alien use of flint. Four-bay nave, 1928–9. – ALTAR. Portland stone, designed by *Robert Townsend,* 1973. – Hanging ROOD, designed and made by *Derek Wier,* 1973.

BAPTIST CHURCH, Pembroke Avenue. By *Benjamin Wakefield,* 1904–5. Scalloped cupolas flanking the gable, narthex with sinuous parapet.

METHODIST CHAPEL, High Street. Surely *c.* 1870. Pennant stone. Quite a dominant w front with pediment and Roman-esque windows.

PORTWAY COMMUNITY SCHOOL, Penpole Lane. 2004–5, by *NVB Architects.* Sports hall in the centre, with classrooms on a 'finger' plan to the E. Grey brick below, coloured render above.

NATIONAL SCHOOL (former), Station Road. By *Henry Rumley,* 1846–7. Tudor Gothic, red rubble. Extended 1892.

VILLAGE HALL, STATION ROAD, by *F. Bligh Bond,* 1903–4. Of local limestone, with Bath stone dressings, roughcast upper parts, and Cumberland slate roofs. Near-symmetrical entrance front with a succulently carved segmental pediment and oriel bows in the first floor. A similar bow on the SW side. In the angle between, a low clock tower with double-ogee cap. Vaughan Williams's *The Lark Ascending* was first publicly per-formed here, courtesy of the musical squire, P. Napier Miles.

Other buildings

In STATION ROAD, Nos. 24–30, a three-storey rank of shops by *F. Bligh Bond* in the same idiom as his Village Hall (above). His best surviving work for the Kingsweston estate is THE WYLANDS, High Street (1904), now a conference centre. Fas-tidiously detailed red brick and white woodwork. Dormers with alternating pediments, the segmental ones given serpen-tine bows. Tall bowed staircase window, small cupola. Oppo-site, s side, worthwhile Georgian houses. TWYFORD HOUSE, *c.* 1820, is symmetrical, with three-storey bows. PENLEA HOUSE, a little E, *c.* 1760, three storeys with canted bays. Then BRADLEY HOUSE, of about the same date. E again, THE PRIORY, Priory Gardens (now flats). Late C18 front. The rear chimneys and a Gothic arch in the hall suggest an earlier core. Nearby is a much altered C15 TITHE BARN. At the w, a C17 cottage created within the barn, and in the w gable wall, two four-centred arches. The E part has narrow C20 windows. (Ten-bay collar-beamed roof with wind-braces.)

Around THE GREEN are pleasant Georgian houses. In the centre, a domed DRINKING FOUNTAIN, 1897, of orientalizing filigree cast-iron.

Near the river, more Georgian mercantile reminders. On Station Road, THE LAMPLIGHTERS, an inn extant by 1768, catching

business from shipping. Three bays and three storeys, altered
c. 1800–20 with full-width balcony. MYRTLE HALL, Nibley
Road, is a late C18 brick villa with C19 bays. Further E, a former
GUNPOWDER MAGAZINE of 1749; storage of gunpowder was
banned in Bristol after the 1745 rebellion. Low rubble-stone
sheds with a jetty. Converted to a house.

Around PASSAGE LEAZE, ¼ m. SE of the centre, remains of an
ambitious scheme by the Shirehampton Garden Suburb Co.,
1910–13; supervising architect *George Oatley*. Forty-four houses
by *Frank Bromhead*, a pupil of Parker & Unwin, in the Letch-
worth vernacular.

Kingsweston House

KINGSWESTON HOUSE, Kings Weston Lane, on a wooded
escarpment overlooking the Severn estuary, is one of *Sir John Vanbrugh's* finest houses. Built for Sir Edward Southwell, Queen
Anne's Secretary of State for Ireland, *c.* 1710–22. It is rare in Vanbrugh's work for being essentially an entirely new build, and for
its small scale and compactness; nevertheless, maximum drama
is wrenched from just a few simple architectural elements judi-
ciously disposed. The usually quoted start date of 1710 may be
a year or two late: timbers on the second floor are dated 1711.
The house was covered in by 1713, the interiors substantially
completed probably in 1719, although work continued on subsidiary buildings. Built of ochre limestone quarried on site, which
has weathered to a glowing orange-pink; the master mason
referred to in a letter by Vanbrugh was 'Mr. Townesend', probably *George Townesend*, a younger son of the Oxford family of
masons, who settled in Bristol and designed a dairy at Kingsweston. *Thomas Sumsion* of Colerne also worked on the house.
His design of 1717 for an urn is in the Kingsweston Book of
Drawings. The house was much altered by *Robert Mylne*, 1763–8,
for Edward Southwell III. P. J. Miles of Leigh Court, Abbot's
Leigh (q.v.), bought it in 1833, and his son P. W. S. Miles commissioned changes from *Thomas Hopper*, 1846–7, executed by a
local architect, *Henry Rumley*. The house was sold in 1937 to
Bristol Municipal Charities for use as a school. Used as police
headquarters until the 1990s, it is now a conference centre;
grounds are generally accessible.

One arrives at the rear courtyard of a U-shaped plan (NE), based
on that of the preceding Tudor house known from Kip's
engraving of *c.* 1709. Vanbrugh recessed the three-bay centre
between angle turrets, but *Hopper* brought the centre forward,
destroying the carefully recessed planes. The severe NW
FAÇADE commands wide views across industrial Avonmouth.
A recessed centre between tower-like projections was replaced
by Mylne's canted bay, which smooths away the former tension
here.

The monumental ENTRANCE FRONT, SW, has a projecting
three-bay centre with round-arched windows between big 59,
p. 406

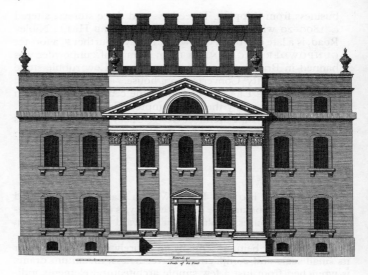

Bristol, Kingsweston House, south-west elevation.
Engraving by Colen Campbell, 1715

Corinthian pilasters, paired at the ends, and a lunette in the
pediment. The windows in the two-bay flanks have brutally big
flat surrounds. Parapet vases of *c.* 1717. One must stand well
back to see Vanbrugh's memorable square arcade of chimneys,
rising above the roofs to evoke the 'Castle air' he sought elsewhere, e.g. at the corner towers of Blenheim Palace. Regarding the chimneys, Vanbrugh proposed in 1713 'to make tryall
of the heights, etc. with boards ... for I would fain have that
part rightly hit off'. They were rebuilt in 1968, unfortunately
in Bath stone. The GARDEN FRONT, SE, is of nine bays, the
narrow three-bay centre broken forward, with an applied Doric
temple front of heavily rusticated pilasters and open pediment
to the ground floor framing the garden entrance. The first floor
has a square-hooded window tightly framed by narrow round-
arched windows. Then a big Palladian cornice in the centre
only, and a flat platband at the sides, with above them an attic
storey. Over the central attic is a raised blocking course or
further blind attic, with scrolled supports; Vanbrugh's alternative design with pediment was not executed.

Inside, a double-height SALOON, remodelled by *Mylne* with three
tiers of festooned picture frames, and a high dado with palmettes. Chimneypiece by *John Devall*, with a marble tablet of
fighting putti, replacing Vanbrugh's central door to the three-
storey STAIRCASE HALL. This has outer walls which retain
arched niches with *trompe-l'œil* painted statues and urns of
c. 1719. Here we must deal with *Hopper*'s work of 1846–7. His
Vanbrughian kitchen wing in the courtyard was demolished

c. 1938. He enlarged the staircase hall by moving its NE wall out, adding bathrooms and a corridor on the upper floors. Vanbrugh's open-well staircase rises to the first floor only, turning through three sides of a square. It formerly rose against the removed wall, but now appears to hang in mid-air, actually supported on wrought-iron stays. It is of oak (Vanbrugh's greatest houses all had wrought-iron staircase balustrades), with Doric newels, ramped rails, and two turned balusters per tread. *Hopper* destroyed Vanbrugh's complex spatial layering by removing the arcades between the balcony landings and the open central well. Cast-iron girders were inserted to support the landings, which were given balustrades like those of the C18 staircase. Hopper inserted a novel skylight with Greek Revival ornament; two layers of iron girders forming three-by-three grids, linked vertically by little arches sandwiched, as it were, between them. Two rooms on the NW side were remodelled as a LIBRARY.

The PARK was once heroic in scale. The Kingsweston Book of Drawings contains plans for a walled entrance court on the SW side, terminating the long vistas of the park, with gates with pyramidal obelisks on cannon balls as at Blenheim. If executed, it was lost when the formal features of the park were smoothed away later in the C18. – THE ECHO, a roofless summerhouse by *Vanbrugh*, terminates the garden's SE axis. Arcaded façade with heavy rustication. – N of the house is *Vanbrugh*'s Corinthian BANQUETING LOGGIA with a Venetian centrepiece, now forming the entrance to a Neo-Georgian brick house by *Niall Phillips*, slightly amended in execution by *Hardy Associates*, 2003–6. Nearby, *Vanbrugh*'s domestic-looking BREWHOUSE of *c.* 1718–20 has a theatrically over-scaled door keystone, reaching the sill of the lunette above, and machicolations attempting a romantic medievalism a generation ahead of its time. – GATE LODGE and nearby estate buildings by *F. Bligh Bond*, *c.* 1901–2.

NE on Napier Miles Road, *Mylne*'s STABLES of 1763, a robust three-sided court with lunettes over each door, and end walls modelled as blind triumphal arches. Opposite, and matching the end façades of the stables, twin LODGES flanking a large lily pond, which supplied ice to an C18 ICE HOUSE with domed roof, SW of the stables. By the pool, *ex situ* remains of BEWYS CROSS; probably C15.

Adjacent to Kingsweston House are two groups of buildings either influenced by Vanbrugh or designed with his involvement. 200 yds E of the house, Nos. 1–3 KINGSWESTON LANE are also early C18, very low, with enormous keystones to the ground-floor windows facing the road. Nos. 1–3 KINGSWESTON ROAD, on a rocky outcrop SE of the house, had been an inn since the early C18; *see* the plan for an ale house in the Kingsweston Book of Drawings. The present structure seems to be a version of that design, modified *c.* 1850 with two extra bays at the r. The segmental-headed door with broad flat surround, flanked by blind arches with little roundels above, appears to be C18.

SNEYD PARK AND STOKE BISHOP

Stoke Bishop was part of the property of the Bishops of Worcester. At the Dissolution it was granted, with Westbury-on-Trym, to Sir Ralph Sadleir. By the C17 and C18 there were a few houses for Bristol merchants, although the village developed mostly after 1860. To the SW is Sneyd Park (pronounced Sneed), a high limestone plateau above the Avon Gorge, enclosed as a deer park in 1274. The grounds of Old Sneed Park (built 1691, dem. 1972) were developed from 1853 with big houses, many since replaced. It has no pubs, few shops, indeed nothing but residential quiet.

Churches

ST MARY MAGDALENE, Mariner's Drive. A big E.E. church by *John Norton*, 1858–64; two nave bays, narthex, tower and spire, 1871–2; S transept and E apse, 1883. The tower has paired belfry lights. Narrow tiled spire with figure canopies rather than corner pinnacles. Grey Pennant relieved by bands of red stone. Inside, steep and sharply moulded nave arcades. Chancel arch on short free-standing shafts. Traceried rere-arches in the aisles. – FITTINGS. REREDOS by *Swayles*, flanked by mosaics of c. 1883. – PULPIT with much carving and FONT on marble pillars, both designed by *Norton* and carved by *White* of Bristol, who also did the rich foliate capitals and corbels. – S transept chapel re-fitted by *Comper*, 1923. – STAINED GLASS. Three apse windows by *Clayton & Bell*, 1897. W window, a Tree of Jesse by *O'Connor*, 1864. – MONUMENT. Churchyard, Caroline and Sir George White †1915 and 1916. By *Farmer & Brindley*. Panelled chest with Tudor roses.

University halls

In 1922 H. H. Wills purchased the 25-acre site of Downside to build a men's hall of residence for the University of Bristol. An inconvenient but time-honoured two-mile walk from the Wills Memorial Building, in part to safeguard the virtue of female students. Five halls were added after 1945.

WILLS HALL, Saville Road. By *Oatley & Lawrence*, 1925–9. First, at the N angle, DOWNSIDE, c. 1832–40, built for Alfred George. Neo-Tudor, with canted bays and fanciful twisted chimneys. The rear forms part of the quadrangle of Wills Hall, so was remodelled by Oatley to conform with its Cotswold manor house style at Wills's insistence. Three storeys with broad gables, around a quadrangle with staircases like an Oxford college. Some gables are pushed together, the second-floor windows running across in continuous bands. At the SE corner, a large oak-panelled dining hall with enormous queenpost roof. Oatley achieved a practical and high-quality building, fastidiously detailed, but at this scale without the charm of the Cotswold originals. Extended w with dull blocks by *Ralph Brentnall*, 1959–63, and a conference wing by *Hope & Bowden*, 1990. – CHAPEL of St Monica, NE of Wills Hall. *By Oatley & Lawrence*, 1928–30. In an austere somewhat Byzantine style, with semicircular apse. Plain interior with a groined tunnel-vault. At the direction of the patron, Dame Monica Wills, the model was P. Morley Horder's chapel at Westcott College, Cambridge. – SCULPTURE. Virgin and Child by *A.G. Walker*.

The best of the rest is HIATT BAKER HALL, Parry's Lane, N of Wills Hall. By *Sir Percy Thomas & Son*, 1966, still very crisp. Six three-storey blocks around a big dining hall. Brown brick with copper-clad panels over the upper windows, and copper-clad pyramids on the flat roofs. CHURCHILL HALL, Stoke Park Road, is by *Ralph Brentnall*, 1946–56, outdated, brick with octagonal motifs; BADOCK HALL, Stoke Park Road, by *Sir Percy Thomas & Son*, 1969, in soapy yellow brick with patterned tile-hanging. UNIVERSITY HALL, 1971, very dull, brown brick; DURDHAM HALL, 1993–4, with feeble Postmodern Cotswold allusions.

Other buildings

STOKE HOUSE, Stoke Hill (Trinity Theological College). Built by Sir Robert Cann. The doorway is dated 1669, in lettering not too trustworthy, yet the date fits the stylistic and documentary evidence. Excessively twisted columns, of three wound strands, naïve Corinthian capitals with masks, two big armed allegorical females in the spandrels, segmental pediment. The side walls of the porch have the leitmotif of *c.* 1670, upright oval windows keyed into oblong panels, here under steep open pediments. There are three ogee gables with

Bristol, Stoke House.
Engraving by J. Kip, 1712

truncated tops, still quite Jacobean in character. Otherwise the house is much altered; the original cross-windows were Gothicized probably *c.* 1765–70 (as painted by Turner in 1791). In 1872, *Foster & Wood* installed mullioned-and-transomed windows, and reinstated the pedimented ovals in the gables by reference to those on the porch. Double-height canted bays with projecting curved centres and strapwork cresting, after Salvin's Harlaxton, Lincs., 1830s. A pair of rooftop cupolas were removed in the C20. Attached at the back are two three-storey blocks, possibly earlier C17, one at an angle to the house. The oak staircase is characteristically mid-C17: still the Jacobean type with square open well, pendants, and flat balusters with alternating garlands and swags.

In the grounds to the E is a three-storey C17 LODGE, with four gables at each side. The CHAPEL, W of the house, is a remodelling *c.* 1960 of an C18 orangery, from which survives a Corinthian doorcase attached at the (ritual) SE.

STOKE BISHOP, AND S TO STOKE HILL. The centre of the village is where Stoke Hill meets Druid Hill. At the bottom of the hill, a picturesque Diamond Jubilee DRINKING FOUNTAIN, 1897 in an octagonal shelter. To the S is the VILLAGE HALL, 1885. An early work of *Edward Gabriel*, Bristol-born but by then practising in London and influenced by the Domestic Revival. At the l., a big multi-paned bay with 'Ipswich' centre, under a half-timbered gable on brackets.

STOKE HILL climbs SSE from the village. On the E side, some early C19 houses, notably No. 38, perhaps *c.* 1840. Gabled front with fretted bargeboards, upper windows under conical tented metal blinds. Next to the drive, an irregular five-sided Gothic FERNERY. No. 36 is sturdy and handsome Italianate, *c.* 1840–50. No. 30, *C. F. W. Dening*'s own house (1923–4, Neo-Georgian) was wrecked by modernization, *c.* 2006. Off W, No. 2 Church Road (*Ponton & Gough, c.* 1875–6), a big Gothic villa for Henry Fedden.

To the E, STOKE PARK ROAD forms a horseshoe around Stoke House (p. 409). E of Badock Hall (*see* University Halls, above) is CLAVERTON by *W. Wood Bethell*, slightly different from the published design (*Building News*, 24 January 1879). Eclectic Gothic, red brick with half-timbering. E again, THE HOLMES, same architect and date. Quite a different treatment, though still Gothic, in dramatic purple Pennant stone softened by Ham stone dressings. At the top of Stoke Hill begins Durdham Down. At the road junction, a WAR MEMORIAL by *W. H. Watkins*, 1920, an octagonal shaft with sword on a stepped base.

PARRY'S LANE AND COOMBE LANE. From Durdham Down, PARRY'S LANE runs NW. On the N side, COTE DRIVE has a few Neo-Georgian houses by *C. F. W. Dening*, 1923–4. At the end of the drive, COTE, a plain but substantial house of *c.* 1720. Two storeys and five bays; hipped roof, dormers, deep cornice, rusticated pilasters. Regency porch. ¼ m. NW, the ALL-ELECTRIC HOUSE, No. 26 Withey Close West. By *A. E.*

Powell, 1935, a demonstration house for the Electrical Association for Women, originally with every convenience down to a washing machine with attached meat grinder. Rendered brick, flat roof for the mandatory sun terrace, integral garage. On COOMBE LANE, NW, REDHOUSE FARM, dated by the owner to 1654. Politely refronted *c.* 1800, see the Doric porch. Opposite, CROSS ELMS, a pretty Regency villa with double-height arched window surrounds. On the NE side, the UNIVERSITY SPORTS PAVILION, *Oatley & Lawrence*, 1914, with long balcony and rooftop clock turret. ¼ m. NW, houses designed and built by *William Studley*, *c.* 1895–1905, with Neo-Perp embellishments from the Bishop's College, Queen's Road, Bristol (*Charles Dyer*, 1835–41, dem. 1902): e.g. SALISBURY HOUSE, 1902–3.

DRUID STOKE AVENUE, ⅝ m. S, was the drive to Druid Stoke House, *c.* 1800. The grounds were developed from *c.* 1905 with Domestic Revival houses, many by *R. Milverton Drake*, e.g. Druid's Garth, 1910; also No. 24, by *W. H. Watkins*, 1909–11, Free Style and rendered.

SNEYD PARK. Beginning NW of Durdham Down, No. 7 AVON GROVE, 1935, by *Mark Hartland Thomas*, secretary of MARS (the Modern Architecture Research Group). Built of rendered blocks. Strip windows, integral garage, and a rooftop sundeck, now with a glazed study by *Terence Haines*, *c.* 2001. Double-height galleried hall. Nearby, TOWER HIRST, Circular Road (*H. C. M. Hirst*, *c.* 1891–2). Stone with polychromatic lozenge patterning, three storeys and embattled, with a small half-timbered turret. More Modernist houses *c.* 1935 at No. 30 OLD SNEED PARK by *Mark Hartland Thomas*, and at ORCHARD HOUSE, Orchard Lane, off Mariner's Drive; by *A. E. Powell*, cuboid, with rooftop railings. COOK'S FOLLY HOUSE, Cook's Folly Road, is in a romanticizing castle-gothic style, *c.* 1855.*

ROCKLEAZE has big pairs of Italianate houses developed from *c.* 1860 by William Baker. The important exception is Nos. 10–11, a blunt design by *E. W. Godwin* (executant architect *J. A. Clark*), 1861–2. Rubble walls with asymmetrical windows and seemingly random blocks of whitish limestone and bands of red brick, all carefully organized. Canted brick heads to the window openings, foliate capitals. Overbearing dormers, probably *c.* 1932. No. 10 has some ghastly new glazing; No. 11, better preserved, has a double-height bay and evenly placed side windows.

DOWNLEAZE, developed for W. E. Walters by *H. Dare Bryan*, maps his stylistic development. Six pairs facing Durdham Down are eclectic Late Victorian, the first at the SW designed in 1888 when Bryan was about nineteen. By 1893–4, the first houses in the street behind (also called Downleaze) are entirely Domestic Revival, with jettied gables and pretty

---

*It incorporated COOK'S FOLLY, a prospect tower built 1693, but demolished in 1932 when the house was subdivided.

Neo-C17 porches. The best are Nos. 45–47 (1897–9), by Julian Road.

About ¼ m. NW in Pitch and Pay Lane is a nicely grouped small housing scheme by *R. Towning Hill* in conjunction with *SPAN*, 1963–5, extended *c.* 1969. Of traditional construction but with the first floors jettied out on reinforced concrete beams, the ends left exposed.

OUTER BRISTOL: SOUTH

For our purposes, South Bristol includes everything s of the River Avon and the 'New Cut', the man-made river bypassing the harbour. Historically this area was in the County of Somerset. Bedminster, Bishopsworth and Brislington were well-defined villages, the rest no more than hamlets or farmsteads.

For Whitchurch, outside Bristol's boundary, *see* p. 715.

BEDMINSTER, SOUTHVILLE AND ASHTON

Bedminster lay over the northernmost outcrop of the Somerset coal seams. The village grew from 3,000 people in 1800 to 78,000 in 1884, based on mining and manufacture. It remains proudly working-class; Wills's tobacco factories are the major industrial survival.

Places of worship

ST ALDHELM, Chessel Street. Big-boned, in boldly cast E.E., by *W. V. & A. R. Gough*, 1905–13. Its steep roofs sail nobly over the Victorian terraces. Meticulous purple Pennant masonry, and an unexpectedly French-looking apse. Apsidal s chapel. Romanesque chancel arch. Former VICARAGE of 1903, *W. V. Gough*.

ST FRANCIS, North Street, Ashton Gate. 1951–3, by *Potter & Hare*, on foundations of a C19 church blitzed in 1941. Simplified traditional style, yellow brick on concrete portal frames. N aisle, N porch door set in concave-curved aedicule, over which a tall tower was planned. E window by *Christopher Webb*.

ST PAUL, Coronation Road. Only the spindly Gothic tower survives of a Commissioners' church by *Charles Dyer*, 1829–31. The rest bombed in 1941, rebuilt 1956–8 by *Eustace Button*: anaemic Tudor Gothic. Timber FONT, *Sir George Oatley*, 1947–50, from the Seamen's Mission, Prince Street. Former VICARAGE to its s, by *S. B. Gabriel*, 1860.

HOLY CROSS (R.C.), Dean Lane. By *John Bevan Jun.*, 1921–6. A Byzantine-Romanesque concoction of hard orange brick. – STAINED GLASS. Imported E window by *Kempe*, 1890. Three by *Hardman*, 1920s.

CHAPELS. ZION CONGREGATIONAL, Coronation Road, 1829–30. Attributed to *R. S. Pope*. Funded by John Hare, oil-cloth manufacturer, in fulfilment of a youthful promise. Greek Doric entrance loggia but round-arched windows and simple mouldings. Now offices. Fine cast-iron Ionic balcony. – CONGREGATIONAL CHAPEL, Stanley Street South, *Frank Wills*, 1905–6. Small, brick-and-roughcast school-chapel, with battered piers. – BAPTIST CHURCH, Philip Street. By *J. C. Neale*, 1861. Big, stern and Romanesque. – BAPTIST CHURCH, East Street, 1893. By *W. H. Williams*. Dull. Pennant stone, round arches and rose window. – EBENEZER METHODIST CHAPEL, British Road. By *H. J. Jones*, 1885–6. Once Bedminster's wealthiest chapel. The grandly Corinthian pedimented front amputated for a deplorable façade of ribbed brick by *J. B. Ackland*, 1974–5. – Former HEBRON CHAPEL, Hebron Road. *Henry Crisp*, 1853. Big classical frontage with round-arched windows and rusticated plinth. Converted to housing *c.* 2001. Behind on Sion Road, HEBRON SUNDAY SCHOOL, 1885. Extravagantly Jacobean-Queen Anne, almost certainly by *Foster & Wood*. – SALVATION ARMY HALLS, Dean Lane. By *Oswald Archer*, 1908–9. Red brick and terracotta, with stepped gables.

Other buildings

POLICE AND FIRE STATION (former), East Street. By *George Oatley*, 1880–2. Oatley's master, *Henry Crisp*, may have contributed. A stern castellated design with a central tower. Now part of ST PETER'S COURT, an apartment conversion, 2005, by *Atkins Walters Webster*. A new five-storey block connects with the former LIBRARY, by *Frank Wills*, 1913, reopened as an art gallery. Red brick, Neo-Baroque detailing.

BRISTOL SOUTH BATHS, Dean Lane. By *C. F. W. Dening*, 1930–1. *Moderne* with some classical detailing.

SCHOOLS. The best surviving Victorian and Edwardian group in the city. – ASHTON GATE BOARD SCHOOLS, Greenway Bush Lane. By *Charles Hansom*, 1876–89, the later phases with *F. Bligh Bond*. Stridently Gothic, with a steep-roofed tower with dormers. In one gable, a twelve-light rose window. – BEDMINSTER BRIDGE BOARD SCHOOL, Stillhouse Lane. By *W. V. Gough*, c. 1895. In commercial use. Flemish gables and detailing, with massive brick chimneystacks. – MERRYWOOD BOARD SCHOOL, Beauley Road, by *Edward Gabriel*, 1894. Partly demolished, the rest a community centre and housing. Low red-brick blocks, linked at their angles. Handsome lantern topped by a bell-stage. – MERRYWOOD ELEMENTARY COUNCIL SCHOOL, Merrywood Road (now Southville Primary), 1907. *H. Dare Bryan*'s most charming Queen Anne idiom; red brick, curvaceous gables, white-painted arched windows, etc. Excellent wrought-iron gates. – ST MARY RED-CLIFFE PRIMARY, Windmill Close. *J. W. Trew & Sons*, 1885. On a steep hillside beneath Victoria Park. Rudimentary Gothic with plate tracery. Girls' block by *H. J. Jones*, 1902–3. – SOUTH STREET PRIMARY, by *W. V. Gough*, 1893–4. Imposing two-storey buildings with Flemish-Jacobean details, and soaring chimneys.

NATWEST BANK, No. 86, Bedminster Parade, c. 1919–20. Almost certainly by *C. H. Brodie*, National Provincial Bank house architect. An opulent, French-looking pavilion of Portland stone; arched bays between paired Corinthian columns. Good domed interior. Nearby in Stillhouse Lane, the VISION CARE CENTRE, for the R.N.I.B., 1993, by *Alec French Partnership*. Long and low. Hipped roofs, tall angle windows. Excellent use of materials, light and colour.

WILLS'S TOBACCO FACTORIES, East Street. The home of W. D. & H. O. Wills until the 1970s, when they moved to Hartcliffe (*see* p. 422). The red brick factories form an impressively ordered three-storey rank, designed by a cousin, *Frank Wills*. From the N: NO. 1 FACTORY, 1883–6, has a central entrance tower with steep pavilion roof over a big recessed Gothic arch. Wings with three giant Gothic arches and plate-traceried windows. Converted to shops and offices in the 1980s, when a walkway was made behind the façade. Extended S c. 1888, with taller arcades. Then the terracotta-faced and classical LOMBARD STREET BLOCK (1906–8). Subsidiary Tuscan columns to the windows. Rounded corner with bulging Venetian oriel and a domed turret. Converted to offices c. 1985.

Of the Southville cigarette factories, the main survivor is the TOBACCO FACTORY, Raleigh Road, by *R. Earle*, 1912, for Franklyn Davey, a partner in Imperial Tobacco. It continues Wills's style. Converted to an arts space, theatre and restaurant by *Ferguson Mann c.* 2000. Red Cattybrook brick, with unmoulded three-storey piers. No remnant of masonry framing between windows and piers.

Hidden in dense housing, some reminders of Bedminster's earlier history. Behind Diamond Street (W side), NORTHVIEW

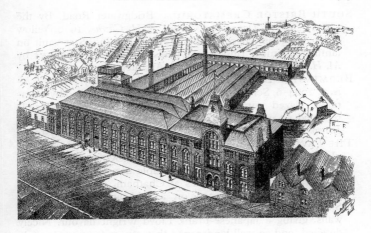

Bristol, Bedminster, Wills's tobacco factories.
Photolithograph, 1887

COTTAGE, a mid-C18 farmhouse of coursed Lias with hand-some bracketed door canopy. Surprising Rococo parlour ceiling with medallion heads. HAMPDEN HOUSE, No. 119 West Street, probably *c.* 1720–30; five bays, brick, with seg-mental door canopy. At the w end of North Street, a TOLL-HOUSE, perhaps *c.* 1820–30, bow-fronted with a veranda on iron columns, and Tudorish windows. s of St Paul's church, around ACRAMAN'S ROAD, small and pretty 1830s villas ellip-tical arches, Gothic arches, Grecian porches freely mixed. MOUNT PLEASANT (*Henry Rumley, c.* 1848–50) is a stone-fronted Late Classical terrace, before the descent to brick.

BEDMINSTER DOWN

A former mining community on a ridge, at the sw outskirts.

ST OSWALD, Cheddar Grove. 1927–8 by *P. Hartland Thomas.* Squat w tower with buttresses. Uncompromisingly straight parapets hiding the nave roof. Thomas was experimenting with the extreme paring-down of the Gothic system: mullions running straight up into the window heads; a band of idio-syncratic tracery across the middle of the w window, and uncommonly low sills, so that the interior appears all glass. The darker chancel was glazed off to form a hall, 1983, and the nave reoriented, 1998. Pointed tunnel-vault on flat beams, sup-ported on square piers, forming arcades of rectangular open-ings. Passage aisles, bridged at each pier by a transverse pointed arch and a segmental bridge higher up. Between each pair of arches is an iron grille. The effect is like buttresses taken inside the building.

SOUTH BRISTOL CREMATORIUM, Bridgwater Road. By the *City Architect's Department* under *A. H. Clarke*, 1970. Yellow brick octagonal chapel with clerestory lighting. Star-vault on laminated timber ribs. At the gates, elegant low OFFICES by *M. H. Kenchington*, Avon County Architect, 1975.

BEDMINSTER DOWN SCHOOL, Donald Road. By *NVB Architects*, 2004–6. School and community facilities, linked by a dramatic glazed entrance. Three storeys, coloured render. It replaced an early Comprehensive school (1954–5), using the *Bristol Aeroplane Company*'s prefabricated aluminium system.

THE PAVILIONS, Bridgwater Road. By *Arup Associates*, completed *c.* 1978 for the Central Electricity Generating Board at a cost of £16 million; now in multiple use. Like Arups' contemporary offices for Lloyd's at Chatham, Kent, it employs broad low forms planned on a grid around courtyards. Shallow-pitched roofs with deep overhanging eaves and glazed walls, giving a Japanese-Frank Lloyd Wright flavour. Nicely detailed, and so well landscaped that offices for 1,200 people facing open countryside all but disappear.

BISHOPSWORTH

On the SW fringe of the modern city.

ST PETER, Church Road. By *S. C. Fripp*, 1841–3. Neo-Norman, better externally than many examples of this date: authentically severe rubble walls and simple profiles. Short squat tower with pyramid roof over the chancel, and lower apse. A belfry stage reminiscent of that at Thaon, Normandy, was not built for lack of funds. Nave windows in wide bays divided by flat buttresses, and a corbel table. Triple windows high in the apse and in the W gable. Big N porch, 1964, reusing the Neo-Norman doorway. Five-bay arcades, awkwardly tall round arches with thick roll mouldings and half-shafts; embarrassingly spindly roof trusses. – Stone REREDOS, with encaustic tile insets. – FONT. Robust and square, on five columns, with Norman decoration. – PAINTING. A large, rather dull Visitation by *D. Alexander Guvenet*.

BISHOPSWORTH MANOR HOUSE, Church Road. A charming naïve house of *c.* 1720–30, a block of five by three bays. Mansard roof with a square of chimneystacks, four on each side, connected by segmental arches; a local mason's reaction to Vanbrugh's chimneys at Kingsweston. Central bay broken forward, with even quoins and steep pediment. The doorway has an elliptical arch rising out of the jambs without imposts or capitals, then a broken segmental pediment on brackets. Above, an elliptical-arched window with little pilasters. Good panelled hall and staircase with ramped rails. An apartment at the front comprises a large withdrawing chamber with double doors to a bedchamber. Nearby is CHESTNUT COURT, Vicarage Road, also early C18; five bays, door canopy on curly brackets.

BRISLINGTON AND ARNO'S VALE

Brislington in its pretty valley on the road to Bath was by *c.* 1760 dominated by large villas, and was described in 1830 as 'the favourite retreat of the Bristol merchants when got up in the world'. Land sales *c.* 1920 led to many losses and immediate industrialization.

Churches

ST LUKE, Church Hill. Largely rebuilt in the C15 with three-stage W tower, of red sandstone with diagonal buttresses and higher stair-turret. The buttresses end in pinnacles, the stair-tower in a bold spirelet with traceried panelling, as on the battlements. Image niche, S side, with small medieval figures. Good C15 S porch with ogee entrance arch, buttresses and pinnacles. C15 S arcade, the piers of Greek-cross section with shafts attached to the arms. Broad hollows between, also with thin shafts. A sixth bay towards the chancel is overlaid by a later arch, having broad panelled soffits with latticed transoms. N aisle, 1819, *James & Thomas Foster*; the arcade closely copied. E end extended 1873–4 by *Benjamin Ferrey*.

FURNISHINGS. Simple Jacobean PULPIT with two tiers of panelling, cut down from a two-decker by *Ferrey*. – Norman FONT, square bowl on cylindrical foot with scalloping. Restored. – STAINED GLASS. Much restoration 1948–9 after bomb damage. Very good E window, probably by *Arnold Robinson (Bell & Son)*, 1948. S chapel: E, 1900, attributed to *Powell & Sons*; S, 1908, attributed to *Burlison & Grylls*. – MONUMENTS. Maxse family †1798 and later, by *Foster & Co.*; draped urn. – Ireland family †1805–14, by *Lancaster*, three, near-identical. – The antiquary George Weare Braikenridge †1856, by *Tyley*, as Grecian as if done in 1820. – S porch, tablet to Stephen Stuart Bridges †1787, with a verse on the trials of illegitimacy: 'It now avails thee not, To whom related or by whom begot. An heap of Dust alone remains of Thee, It's all thou art and all the proud shall be.' – Churchyard. Five C19 railed monuments; the Clayfield-Irelands and Cooke-Hurles with Gothic plinths by *Tyley*. Near the porch, a big C13 PREACHING CROSS, hexagonal plinth, and a shaft with waterleaf brackets.

ST CHRISTOPHER, Hampstead Road. 1930–1, by *C. F. W. Dening*. Neo-Early Christian in brown brick. Gilt mosaic panel above the door. Plain barrel-vaulted interior with transepts, subdivided *c.* 1990.

ST CUTHBERT, Sandy Park Road. 1932–3, by *P. Hartland Thomas*. Red brick, aisled. W narthex. S porch, the base of an intended tower. Simplified Perp windows, five cusped lancets with mullions rising to the head of the arches. Round-arched doorways with concentric steppings. Basement hall. Unusually, a staircase up to the spacious white-painted nave, with mainly clear glazing. Pointed tunnel-vault with painted timber ribs. Generous three-bay arcades punched square through the walls without dressings of any kind. – FITTINGS. Mostly plain oak and built-in. – REREDOS with Art Deco-ish fluted panels. On top, gilded angels bearing candle holders. – S chapel REREDOS, The Dawn of Peace, painted by *F. G. Swaish*, 1917. – STAINED GLASS. N chapel E, by *Harry Stammers*, 1965. Vivid purple-blues, with primary colours in the figures.

CONGREGATIONAL CHURCH, Wick Road. By *Frank Wills*, 1901. His usual formula of Pennant stone and simple plate tracery.

CEMETERY, Arno's Vale. *See* p. 419.

Schools

BRISLINGTON ENTERPRISE COLLEGE, Hungerford Road. 2006–8, by *Wilkinson Eyre*, for 1,750 students, one of the second phase of Bristol's schools renewal programme. A crescent, or perhaps a necklace, of four two-storey blocks with entrances between; double-height street to the S. From this lead off five wedge-shaped 'pods' for *c*. 300 pupils each. Finishes mainly brick and render. In the grounds, the CITY LEARNING CENTRE by *Alec French Partnership*, 2001, an IT and communications centre. An award-winning scheme, taken from conception to opening in ten months. Flexible internal spaces, and an exposed steel frame clad with Kalwall, a semi-translucent material. Roofs in two planes, and a dramatic triangular projection, clear-glazed.

WEST TOWN LANE PRIMARY SCHOOL. *City Architect's Department*; *F. W. Fennell*, 1954. An excellent example of Bristol's post-war schools design. A long two-storey classroom block, the ends and base faced in rubble stone from medieval buildings demolished for the school.

Other buildings

BRISLINGTON HOUSE, Bath Road, was established 1804–6 by the Quaker Dr Edward Long Fox, who pioneered the humane treatment of mental illness. Almost the first purpose-built private asylum in England, and greatly influential on C19 asylum design. Closed 1951; converted to apartments and renamed Long Fox Manor, 2002.

The original plan was a seven-bay central block and three detached houses on each side; plain classical. Fireproof construction, stone with iron supports, window frames etc. A wall in the centre block divided male patients (and staff) from female. This segregation was carried through the flanking houses, with further division by social rank and severity of illness. By 1836 the centre had been joined to the flanks by one-bay wings with canopied bows on the garden (E) side, and the subsidiary houses also linked. In 1850–1 all was refaced by *S. C. Fripp*, forming a unified 500-ft (154-metre) façade in a grand Italian palazzo manner, and the internal divisions and iron fittings largely removed. *Fripp*'s CHAPEL, 1851, sits N of the main range. On a Greek-cross plan, pedimented arms and a high belfry. Exaggerated doorcase with segmental pediment. Gothic oak REREDOS, doubtfully from St Luke, Brislington, 1874. STAINED GLASS by *H. Hugh*, 1870s. In 1866, *Fripp* added a BALLROOM adjoining the chapel, with more Grecian motifs. On Bath Road, a LODGE of 1806 originally housing machinery to operate the gates; semicircular Tuscan porch. Much altered *c.* 1850.

The GROUNDS were important, exercise and fresh air, rural views, and the uplifting associations of Picturesque landscape features being integral to Fox's regime. Parts of the exercise-court walls survive on the garden front. Near Bath Road, an intriguing GROTTO, a primitive stone table and benches surrounded by standing stones, on a platform with a cave-like seat beneath. Wealthy patients had private VILLAS in the grounds. THE BEECHES (*c.* 1840, now a hotel) and SWISS COTTAGE (1819) survive; Picturesque Tudor Gothic. HEATH FARM, Ironmould Lane, to the NW, is a big gabled mid-C17 farmhouse, updated *c.* 1840 as the estate farm.

EASTWOOD FARM, off Wyndham Crescent, is a gentry house *c.* 1640–70, for a soap merchant. Four-square with hipped roofs. Ovolo-moulded stone window frames. Rear projection with fine open-well staircase; Ionic newels with scrolled finials and pendants, closed string carved like stone blocks, turned balusters. The first-floor chamber has a stone chimneypiece with strapwork overmantel, and ceiling figures of Adam and Eve and St Peter. WEST TOWN HOUSE, West Town Park. Perhaps C16 at the back, with an elegant Regency front block.

Much of the centre of old Brislington, including fine C17 farmhouses, was demolished in 1969–70 for shops and high-rise flats. In the former village centre, the WHITE HART INN, reportedly *c.* 1738, with big first-floor Venetian windows. CHURCH HILL HOUSE, Church Hill, is specially pretty; *c.* 1730, five bays and two storeys with a Venetian window, and an oval light in the pediment. LYNWOOD, No. 625 Bath Road, is inaccessible and semi-derelict. Of *c.* 1840 but parts possibly earlier, an enlarged *cottage orné* blending ogee Gothic and Tudor details. WICK HOUSE, Wick Road, was 'new built' in 1794. A marriage of classical and Gothic, awkwardly composed. Two canted bays, some Venetian windows. The most Gothic parts were matching single-storey flanks, demolished. Nearby in the garden of No. 209 (once part of the grounds), a Gothic brick SUMMERHOUSE in perilous disrepair. Details suggestive of *Daniel Hague* at St Paul, Portland Square (1789–94); might he have been responsible for the house?

ARNO'S VALE CEMETERY. Established by Act in 1837 and opened in 1839, this private cemetery soon became Bristol's most fashionable burial place. An example of the national trend for private cemeteries, e.g. Kensal Green, London, 1833–7. Space ran out *c.* 1987, but Bristol City Council gained ownership in 2003, and a charitable trust began restoration. The buildings are firmly attributed to *Charles Underwood*, *c.* 1838–40, the favoured architect of the developer and solicitor Charles Savery. Cast-iron GATES slide back through slots in the piers; inside, correct Greek Doric LODGES face each other. The idyllic and painterly Arcadian landscape has a circular drive backed by wooded slopes, against which are *Underwood*'s two mortuary CHAPELS: the Anglican chapel Roman Italianate, with projecting entrance, pilasters with shallow Corinthian capitals and an arched and pedimented belfry. The Nonconformist chapel has a Greek Ionic portico. It was converted to a crematorium by *H. G. Malcolm Laing*, 1927, with adjacent 'cloister' for interring ashes. The chapel became a visitor centre, with a steel-and-glass entrance pavilion to the w, by *Niall Phillips*.*

MONUMENTS. The most unusual is to Raja Rammohun Roy †1833, of Bengal, a cultural, religious and political reformer regarded as the father of the Indian Renaissance. He died in Bristol and was reburied here in 1843–4. His tomb, designed by *William Prinsep*, an artist to the East India Company, is a striking example of Victorian-Indian architecture, with a broad canopied dome on four columns, derived from authentic Hindu and Jain forms. Otherwise the best are on the slopes beyond the chapels. Thomas Gadd Matthews †1859, lavish marble sarcophagus on a curved chest, by *Tyley*. Nearby, a rare oak monument, to Heber Denty †1890, timber merchant. Tall obelisk to Mary Breillat †1839. Another nearby to Charles Melsom †1866, by *Tyley*. To the E, a Gothic chest tomb to Thomas Lucas †1856, again by *Tyley*. Two-stage octagonal Gothic pillar to the Tilly family, *c.* 1860.

ARNO'S COURT, Bath Road (now Arno's Manor Hotel). A C17 house was purchased by the brass manufacturer William Reeve *c.* 1740. In *c.* 1755–60 that house became the service wing to a plain mid-Georgian three-storey addition, in Bath stone ashlar. The new work is usually given to James Bridges, on the basis that the steeply canted bays are like his Royal Fort (1758–61).† The 1750s wing was given a superficial Gothic trim of battlements, intersecting glazing bars etc., probably *c.* 1764 when the estate buildings were gothicized (*see* below). The Gothic work is perhaps by *Thomas & James Paty*. At this date Reeve's choice of Gothic was quite progressive, as Horace Walpole had only a decade before begun the conversion of Strawberry Hill into a Gothic villa-retreat. Yet the symmetry and proportion remain firmly classical. SE entrance front with full-height canted bays framing a narrow centre. Thin ogee-arched tracery panels over the rectangular first-floor window openings, continued on the seven-bay NE side. Central porch, Gibbsian blocked pilasters with stalactite rustication, and a Rococo cartouche in the pediment. Within, one room and the

---

* Lindsay Keniston's research on the architects made available by kind permission of Arno's Vale Cemetery Trust.
† They are more like those at e.g. Rownham House, dem., or Nos. 22–24 Clifton Wood Road.

staircase have good Rococo ceilings probably by *Thomas Stocking*. Cheerless 1850s additions to the N for a girls' reformatory, by *Foster & Wood*; their chapel demolished.

Across Bath Road to the N, a decorative GATEWAY originally abutting the stables, relocated here *c.* 1992. Much Gothic panelling, termini and fancy ogee battlements. In ogee-headed niches are four statues of *c.* 1992, replicas of originals taken from medieval city gates demolished in the mid C18 – an example of Reeve's antiquarian interests. Ambitious STABLES 77 in the form of a mock-medieval castle, among the finest of their date in the country, now a pub. A square surrounding a courtyard, generously provided with battlements, towers and turrets. Built of blocks of compressed slag from Reeve's brass furnaces; their iridescent purplish-black against pale limestone dressings gives it a 'strange sinister gaiety' (Pevsner). In 1766 Horace Walpole mistook it for the Devil's Cathedral. Scratched on the entrance tower parapet is the date 1764, which must be about the year of building; stylistically the *Paty* brothers seem best to fit the bill. In the courtyard, some antiquarian fragments (e.g. a C16 tomb surround, head of Henry VIII, two C17 terms; much more now lost). The group effect is marred by the road between house and stables, and the removal of a Gothic bath house in 1957. Its façade is at Portmeirion, North Wales.

Former TRAM DEPOT, Bath Road, 1900–1, an early work by *W. Curtis Green*. Neo-Baroque, reflecting his training under John Belcher. Tram sheds behind, with big segmental roofs. On Whitby Road, NE, the GREAT WESTERN RAILWAY BRIDGE by *I. K. Brunel*, 1839, carrying the London line over the River Avon. Three elegant Tudor Gothic arches, obscured by additions.

HARTCLIFFE AND WITHYWOOD

Two suburbs of council housing developed on Bristol's S outskirts; planned by the *City Architect's Department* under *J. Nelson Meredith*, *c.* 1949. Occupation began in 1952. Intense social deprivation has only recently been addressed with any success.

ST ANDREW, Peterson Square, 1956, by *Burrough & Hannam*. Now looking rather shabby. Low-slung, with glazed gable and a concrete cross rising from a fin-like structure at the NW corner. – STAINED GLASS. Chancel S, cast glass and resin, by *Geoffrey Robinson* (*Bell & Son*), 1964.

ST PIUS X (R.C.), Gateacre Road. By *John Webster*, 1987. Quite secular; three triangular dormers on each side of the roof ridge, forming a sort of clerestory.

MERCHANTS' ACADEMY, Gatehouse Avenue. By *AWW Design*, 2006–8. A 1,000-pupil school arranged as six pavilions and a larger administration block, around an irregular polygonal cloister enclosing play space. Bold jungle motifs cover the entrance façade.

HARECLIVE PRIMARY SCHOOL, Moxham Drive. Mostly system-built, 1960s. In 2006–7, *Mitchell Taylor Workshop* designed for Hareclive the first Room 13 ART STUDIO in England; it cost only £157,000.* Intentionally raw-looking, the concrete block walls mostly blank. Two blue-clad angled lanterns.

COMMUNITY FACILITIES. Renewal has followed the riots of 1992; designs characterized by tough materials and community participation. The SYMES AVENUE regeneration by *Aedas*, 2005–7, includes shops and library, around an AREA CENTRE by *Hallett & Pollard*, 1993–4, with planted internal courtyard. Inventive use of colour and out-of-context vehicle components inside. The GATEHOUSE CENTRE, Hareclive Road, by *Quattro Design* (*Hugh Nettelfield*), opened 1995. Two wings flank a conical-roofed rotunda, the point of entry. By the same firm, WITHYWOOD COMMUNITY CENTRE, Queens Road, 2005–6, including a shared Anglican and Methodist church.

WILLS HEADQUARTERS (former), Hartcliffe Way. By *Skidmore, Owings & Merrill* with *Yorke, Rosenberg & Mardall*, 1970–4. How are the mighty fallen. Built for the relocation of 6,000 staff from Bedminster, and to produce a projected 600 million cigarettes a week. The five-storey office block rose above a two-storey reinforced concrete podium slung across a stream gully, the podium forming a dam so that the offices seemed to float on a lake. The cor-ten steel frame weathered as intended to a rusted patina. The two US practices, which had collaborated on the Boots D90 building at Nottingham (1967–8), regarded Hartcliffe as among their most prestigious European projects; when completed it was one of the most up-to-date factories in Europe. But plummeting cigarette sales meant that the factory was demolished *c.* 1999 for a retail park. The listed offices, stripped back to a skeleton like a vast abstract sculpture, have been controversially redeveloped as flats by *Acanthus Ferguson Mann*, 2006–8.

HENGROVE AND WHITCHURCH PARK

Hengrove is largely an interwar suburb between the Wells Road and Airport Road. To its s is Whitchurch Park, post-war private development.

CHRIST CHURCH, Petherton Road. 1934, by *Walter Rudman*. Low, red brick, with Arts and Craftsy-shaped w gable and tiled bell-hood. Transepts and chancel, 1939. The nave defined by semicircular concrete arches, of which there is no hint outside.
ST AUGUSTINE, Whitchurch Lane. Joint Anglican and Methodist. By *Moxley Jenner & Partners*, 1971–2. Future

---

*Room 13 is an innovative network of art studios run by the students, working with resident artists.

uncertain. Very high, of orange-pink brick with a single-slope roof. A belfry was dismantled, 1980s. Ranges of full-height slit windows, and a bulging s chapel. Above the altar, a resin-bronze SCULPTURE of Christ Triumphant, by *Ernest Pascoe*, 1972. – FONT. Early Norman tub font with Jacobean cover, from East Lydford, Somerset.

ST BERNADETTE (R.C.), Wells Road. By *Nealon Tanner Partner-ship*, project architect *James Leask*. Opened 1968. Overtly new and much admired. A square plan, set lozenge-wise with entrance and altar at the angles. The structure is based on con-crete beams arranged as two intersecting triangles, their bases linked in the foundations. The lower angles project like buttresses, channelling rainwater from the roofs. The tent-like aluminium-clad roofs, in the form of a double hyperbolic paraboloid, sweep up to a glazed chevron topped by a metal cross, and another peak sweeps forward over the entrance. Low red brick walls, also used for the narthex, which has a small Lady Chapel tucked in. White roughcast interiors. Square brick FONT with cover made of stacked metal tubes, echoing the roof shapes. – Suspended CRUCIFIX of alloy, by *Frank Roper*, 1982.

COUNTERSLIP BAPTIST CHURCH, Wells Road. By *Eustace Button*, 1957–8. Unadventurous, with mullioned segmental-headed windows.

CHURCH OF JESUS CHRIST OF LATTER-DAY SAINTS, Wells Road. 1965. Yellow brick. Stepped in plan, each step vertically glazed.

HENGROVE PARK, off Whitchurch Lane. On a 188-acre former airfield, community facilities and housing are being developed to a masterplan by *Clarke Bond* and *Broadway Malyan*, 2005. Phase I has three main elements. A SKILLS ACADEMY (concept design by *SMC Hickton Madeley*) was built 2007–10. For vocational training; curved pod form, influenced by air-craft hangars, with glazed ends, polymer roofs and chestnut-clad outer walls. The LEISURE CENTRE (*LA Architects*) and COMMUNITY HOSPITAL (*AWW Design*) were approved in 2008; building began in 2010. The latter will have a deep five-column portico over the NW entrance.

KNOWLE AND KNOWLE WEST

Knowle developed from *c.* 1880 and was briefly fashionable, with substantial Edwardian houses on Wells Road. The big council estates of Knowle West were built 1920–39.

Places of worship

HOLY CROSS, Marshall Walk, Inns Court. Completed 1999, by *Ferguson Mann*. The joint Anglican, Methodist and Pentecostal church is part of a community centre in a sorely run-down area. Rubble and rendered walls, and sparse fenestration: upswept roof with broad angled eaves, reminiscent of Le

Corbusier at Ronchamp. Slim, free-standing campanile faced with crisp Purbeck stone. – FONT, early C18, a fat gadrooned vase shape, from the blitzed Temple Church, city centre. – STAINED GLASS. Small richly coloured squares, chamfered into the thick rear wall, by *Louise Block*.

The MEDE COMMUNITY CENTRE, attached: coloured render panels, clerestory lighting with brises-soleil.

HOLY NATIVITY, Wells Road. *Ponton & Gough's* fine Byzantine church (1870–83) bombed in 1940; only the tower base survives; striped brick. Gothic upper stages and copper pyramidal spire by *A. R. Gough*, as late as 1931. The body of the church was rebuilt more simply by *Nicholson & Rushton*, 1954–8. Brown brick with inset strips of tile, round-arched windows, apsidal E end poised above precipitous slopes. Plain aisled nave with rendered apse and tunnel-vault; competent, but cold.

ST BARNABAS, Daventry Road. 1937–8 by *C. F. W. Dening*. Large, red brick, round-arched windows, without a tower. Nave demolished for sheltered housing built up against the church in the late 1980s. The S transept steps up to a big bellcote. Windowless semi-octagonal chancel. Tunnel-vaults. The long transepts and crossing, with an inserted floor, serve as a hall and the chancel as the church.

ST MARTIN, St Martin's Road. A daughter church to Holy Nativity (*see* above). 1900–1 by *W. V. Gough*; two further nave bays, 1907, a further two bays and W narthex with choir vestry below, 1939–40 by *A. R. Gough*. Plain Pennant stone exterior. Inside, crisp arcades of red Cattybrook brick against white-painted walls; aisles with transverse brick arches. Timber tunnel-vault on braced tie-beams, echoing Ponton & Gough's lost roof at Holy Nativity. – Octagonal FONT, 1909, and PULPIT, 1910, both by *W. V. Gough*. – ROOD by *F. Bligh Bond*, 1919. – STAINED GLASS. E window and Lady Chapel E by *Arnold Robinson*, 1947–8; traceries by *Geoffrey Robinson*, 1963. S aisle, small lights, 1930s, by *Arnold Robinson*. W window rose by *Geoffrey Robinson*, 2000.

CHRIST THE KING (R.C.), Filwood Broadway. *Kenneth Nealon's* modest church of 1952–3 (the area of the present nave), was heightened and enlarged in 1960–1 by *Kenneth Nealon & Partner*. Portland stone, copper roofs. Campanile, narthex, aisles. Curved NW baptistery with sculpture by *Ernest Pascoe*. Sparse interior: roughcast walls and exposed portal frames. – FITTINGS by *Christopher Marsden-Smedley*, the project architect. TABERNACLE and ALTARS of figured grey marble; FONT, on a stem growing out of the floor; baptistery SCREEN of big steel crosses.

ST GERARD MAJELLA (R.C.), Talbot Road. By *Pugin & Pugin*, 1908–9. Long aisled nave of Pennant and Bath stone. Lancet lights, square-headed aisle windows. Circular E window with bastardized Perp tracery. Elaborate REREDOS with gold mosaic.

CHAPELS. KNOWLE WEST BAPTIST CHURCH, Newry Walk, is by *Charles White*, 1933. Determinedly up-to-the-minute, like a little cinema. Art Deco motifs in stone panels at the corners and in a frieze. In Broad Walk, the CHURCH OF THE NAZARENE (formerly Knowle Park Congregational). By *G. C. Lawrence*, 1929–32.* Red brick, Perp w window, two-storey porches. KNOWLE METHODIST CHURCH, Wells Road, was intended as the Sunday School to a bigger chapel, never built. *La Trobe & Weston*, 1904. Flowing Dec tracery with Art Nouveau patterned glass. Hammerbeam roofs. Transepts. Exceptionally for a Free Church, a large MURAL on canvas of the Wise and Foolish Virgins, by *W. A. Chase*, 1909, in pinks, greens and blues.

Other buildings

BOARD SCHOOL (former), Greenmore Road, by *H. Dare Bryan*, 1897–8, converted to flats 2001. Red brick, single-storey blocks ranged around a hall, in a pretty Queen Anne style with swags and obelisk finials.

SOUTH BRISTOL HEALTH PARK, Leinster Road. An innovative attempt to integrate health and community facilities with public art. The WILLIAM BUDD HEALTH CENTRE, 2000, is by *Architecture & Planning Group*. Single-storey with opposing curved roofs and porthole windows. Metal GATES designed by *Hugh Nettelfield* with local young people. – LIFE PULSE by *Michael Pinsky*, 2006. On a hilltop, three masts with lights that respond to the heart beat when touched.

WATER TOWER, Talbot Road. 1905, perhaps by *Frank Wills*. Red Cattybrook brick, two giant arches on each face, heavy machicolated top.

ST SAVIOUR'S HOUSE, St Agnes Avenue.† Formerly the House of Charity, a girls' Industrial School run by the Anglican Sisters of Charity from St Raphael, Bristol; now occupied by a R.C. order. Designed in 1890 by *J. D. Sedding*, who died in 1891. His pupil *Henry Wilson* completed the first phase by 1892, plainer than the original plans, for lack of funds. Of limestone quarried on site, with Doulting stone dressings; tile-hanging, roughcast and non-structural half-timbering, especially to the E wing. A quadrangle plan, entered by a deep vaulted porch at the E; to its r. the girls' workroom, expressed by a very wide Ipswich window. Schoolroom in a big projecting square block at the NE corner; a compressed and less effective version of Sedding's design. It has two more Ipswich windows in curving bays side by side, the panels between the floors oddly rendered in concrete made to appear like rustication. Is this a later alteration? The part of the E wing l. of the porch is by *Bodley*, 1905. Service quarters in the N wing, and to the s the Sisters' accommodation, all of the first phase. The W side was closed *c.* 1894 by a low refectory with bow windows. SW corner rebuilt sympathetically after bomb damage, 1948. The QUADRANGLE forms a private garden, its walls varied by projecting bays, the

107

---

*Information from Dr Sarah Whittingham.
†This account draws on Paul Snell's doctoral thesis on J. D. Sedding.

alcoves between bridged by arches. Contrasting stone and roughcast render. The continuous CORRIDOR around the quadrangle has a wide inglenook fireplace on the S side, and nearby a fine window of the Good Shepherd in a thorny thicket, by *Christopher Whall*, 1894. On the N and E sides, high corridor windows for privacy.

The CHAPEL, intended for the SE corner, was finally added at the SW in 1901–2, to the design of *Bodley*, conventionally Gothic against Sedding's more personal Arts and Crafts style. A long space with college-style seats, and windows very high up. Timber wagon-vault with transverse ribs. Stone ALTAR installed *c.* 1998, from the Pro-Cathedral, perhaps by *Charles Hansom*, *c.* 1848. Three big sculpture panels, the original colours restored. – High timber REREDOS with a concave curved top. Three figures in niches. – STALLS. The fronts at the W end by *Sedding*, probably made by *Trask & Sons*. Coved top with a frill of carving. Narrow closing panels at the E end, by *Sedding*. – STAINED GLASS. E window by *M. C. Farrar Bell*, 1938, a highly coloured design that conflicts with the reredos. Side windows attributed to *Lavers & Westlake*, *c.* 1902.

To the ritual E (actually S), is a small MEMORIAL CHAPEL to A. H. Ward, founder of the mother church. A much cooler affair, by *Bodley & Hare*, 1908–9; chequered floor, panelled ceiling, ashlar walls. Five small windows, probably by *Kempe*, *c.* 1909–13. It is reached by a corridor outside the S wall of the main chapel, seemingly after 1909, with low flying buttresses as its roof-ribs. Two windows here, figures in glowing autumn colours, in the style of *Eleanor Fortescue-Brickdale*.

COUNCIL HOUSING at Knowle Park began in 1920 under the Housing Act of 1919; layout supervised by *C. F. W. Dening*, who designed several public buildings too. Tree-lined axial streets, with roads in concentric semi-circles or polygons. Cottagey red-brick houses by various architects (competition assessor Ernest Newton); the earliest (Broad Walk, Wellgarth Road etc.) amply spaced at twelve per acre. The denser westward extension known as Filwood Park or Knowle West was begun in 1931.

At Inns Court Green, E of Holy Cross church, a most surprising remnant: a STAIR-TURRET probably from the house of Sir John Innyn, lawyer; Bristol's 'most sophisticated piece of building from the early fifteenth century' (Andor Gomme). A buttressed half-hexagon, two storeys, with an arched doorway in a squared frame, and fine first-floor windows of two ogee lights with cinquefoil cusping and trefoils in the spandrels. Now attached to a mid-C20 building.

ST ANNE'S

Respectable early C20 artisan housing, and council housing of 1926–32.*

---

* St Anne's Well, shrine established in the C13, converted to a pottery *c.* 1650; ruins removed 1938.

ST ANNE, Langton Road. By *Henry M. Bennett*, 1904–*c*. 1907; Dec Gothic, no tower. A near-copy of his St Stephen, Soundwell, Gloucs. Simple chapel added s of the chancel by *Futcher & Futcher*, 1989–90, when the church was subdivided w of the crossing. Altar now at the crossing, with the wall behind mirrored to reflect the E window.

JUNIOR SCHOOL, Langton Court Road. By *William Paul*, 1899–1900. Low blocks in cyclopean masonry, and a charming miniature cookery classroom with polygonal roof. Extended in keeping by *Richard Biddulph Associates*, 2003.

LANGTON COURT, Highworth Road; a fragment of perhaps *c*. 1600, the earliest and least impressive part of a fine C17 manor house, the rest demolished 1902. In its grounds, SE, the LANGTON COURT HOTEL, by *Edward Gabriel*, 1903. His usual vernacular revival, with pargetted gables. No. 1 First Avenue, formerly St Anne's VICARAGE, by *P. Hartland Thomas*, 1924–5. A dramatic late Arts and Crafts evocation of C17 vernacular: Pennant stone, tall and severe, with gables and a big chimneystack. Ruined by replacement windows, *c*. 2005.

STOCKWOOD

CHRIST THE SERVANT, Stockwood Road. Chancel and N chapel of 1963–4 by *J. Ralph Edwards*, the rest of 1969 by *J. K. Maggs*. Grey brick. Slim tower with tall pinnacles faced with aggregate. Inside, a blind E wall of brick with alternate headers projecting, chequer-fashion. Deeply coffered timber roof. – STAINED GLASS by *Pierre Fourmaintraux*. N chapel, Christ in Glory; nave s wall, seven abstract slit windows in rainbow colours.

FREE BAPTIST CHURCH, Ladman Road. By *Kenneth Nealon & Partner*, 1963. Steep ridged roof and fully glazed w wall. Prestressed concrete portal frames, brought out at the eaves then angling in again, like elbows along the side walls.

TOTTERDOWN WITH WINDMILL HILL

Dense terraces for railway workers sprang up on the bare crest of Pylle Hill from *c*. 1860. Major clearances *c*. 1973, for an unbuilt road scheme. Windmill Hill to the w was developed *c*. 1880–1914.

ST MICHAEL AND ALL ANGELS, Fraser Street, Windmill Hill. *E. H. Edwards*'s church (1886) was burned and rebuilt to a new design 1926–7 by *P. Hartland Thomas* (some 1886 brickwork at the E end). Plain red-brick Gothic, with tranverse gables over the s aisle. Unmoulded nave arcades. – STAINED GLASS. E window probably by *Percy Bacon*, 1927. Lady Chapel E, *Arnold Robinson*, 1927. – Gaunt brick VICARAGE by *H. C. M. Hirst*, 1906.

CHAPELS. TOTTERDOWN BAPTIST CHURCH, Wells Road, is by *Alfred Harford*, 1880–1. Heavy and stilted Romanesque arches. w wall with six-light arcade, big triplet above. In Bushy Park, a METHODIST CHURCH by *Foster & Wood*, 1874–5. E.E. Geometric, long side parallel with the road, with projections at each end. The gables have stepped corbel tables. In Sylvia Avenue, VICTORIA PARK BAPTIST CHURCH, *Charles White*, 1929. Perp front only.

JAMIA MOSQUE, Green Street. Bristol's first mosque, 1968. Occupying St Katherine's mission chapel (bare brick Gothic, 1888–9). Remodelled with flat roof, dome and minaret by *Glyn Leaman*, 1979–80.

At Three Lamps junction, the Bath and Wells roads are marked by one of the finest SIGNPOSTS in England, a cast-iron column dated 1833, Roman Doric, surmounted by an entablature block then scrolly brackets carrying a lamp. The signs have openwork lettering in Egyptian type, pointing fingers, and terminate with more lamps. A little SE on Bath Road, the TURNPIKE pub, picturesque Tudor Gothic, probably built when the road was rerouted in 1832–3. An overgrown terrace above the Avon marks the old route.

CLANCY'S FARM, Berrow Walk. Nearest the road, a plain wing of *c.* 1850. To its W, a higher C16 or early C17 structure, cross-gabled, with a long C17 wing beyond. Some Tudor-arched openings. Adjacent was Lower Knowle Court (C16 and earlier, demolished).

4060

BROCKLEY

ST NICHOLAS (Churches Conservation Trust). Of Norman foundation, much rebuilt in the C15, with interesting additions begun by the Rev. Wadham Pigott of Brockley Court, *c.* 1820, and continued after his death in 1823. The architect may have been the same who rebuilt St John, Weston-super-Mare (the Pigotts also owned the manor there). Further restored 1842, repaired by *John Maggs* from 1989. Norman S doorway: attenuated shafts with scalloped capitals, one thin roll moulding around the arch with applied chevrons, doubtless Norman but altered in the early C19. The chancel has C13 lancets, illustrated in 1824. The usual Perp W tower with higher stair-turret, of three stages with diagonal buttresses and two-light windows, solid battlements. Tower arch with the familiar two-wave moulding. Short S aisle or manorial chapel, much altered in the 1820s – see the gable chimney, along the lines of a sanctus bell-turret, and inside, a Gothick pinnacled fireplace. To its W is attached a porch, perhaps C15, seemingly later than the aisle. Animated figures on the gable kneelers, *c.* 1820s. Corresponding N transept (organ chamber), again 1820s.

FITTINGS. REREDOS. *c.* 1820–30; ornate stone frame, painted panels. – PULPIT. One of a fine late C15 group (Bleadon, Banwell, Hutton, Wick St Lawrence). Corbelled out from the wall on several carved friezes, foliage as well as quatrefoils on the underside, and several more above the blank panels which are of two two-centred cinque-cusped lights. – BOX PEWS, probably 1820s. Oak benches (W) by *Sir George Oatley*, 1950. – FONT. C12, circular, with squat arcading, and big fluting on the underside. – COVER. Quite Baroque, with S-scrolls; perhaps mid-C17. – ORGAN CASE, 1820s. Twinned ogee tops. – ROYAL ARMS. 1842, painted by *W. Edkins & Son.* – STAINED GLASS, chancel and Pigott Pew. Collectors' pieces for the Regency fan. By *W. R. Eginton*, c. 1825. – MONUMENTS. Pigott family, probably c. 1794 (dates 1730, 1794 and later); in the style of *W. Paty.* Elegant, of coloured marbles, with urn on top. – Wadham Pigott †1823. By *Chantrey*, 1828. A big serious piece with a classically draped female mourner kneeling by an urn. On the pedestal good profile portrait.

BROCKLEY COURT, NE of the church. The principal house of the Piggotts from 1661 to c. 1825, when they moved to the Hall (below). Seven bays and three gables with characteristic upright oval windows in oblong frames. This front must date from shortly after 1661. Two cross-windows l. of the porch, the rest updated in the C18. T-plan with big rear wing, closed well staircase. Some C17 survivals within, notably a damaged stone fireplace with frieze, in the l. room. Hall and drawing room with bolection door frames, panelling, fluted Ionic pilasters etc., perhaps 1730s; cf. Brockley Hall. Attached at an angle beyond the rear wing, a lower wing, perhaps C16, doubtless the pre-Pigott farmhouse.

BROCKLEY HALL. Owned by the Pigotts since 1661, rebuilt perhaps c. 1730–50, enlarged c. 1825. Remains of an earlier house include two C17 basement windows with ovolo mullions. The quiet seven-bay SE front (one-five-one) is the core of the mid-C18 rebuilding. Its central five-bay saloon has panelling, and a good marble fireplace with Rococo pine frieze. Behind

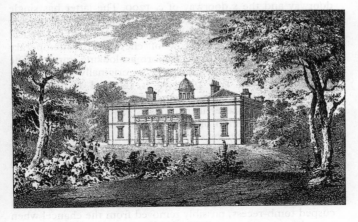

Brockley Hall.
Engraving, 1829

this an excellent open-well staircase with ramped rails, coiled curtail and twisted balusters; here, arches with pulvinated friezes and Ionic pilasters. Two flanking wings run back, forming a rear courtyard; the NE wing forms part of additions made for J. H. Smyth-Pigott *c.* 1825. The SE front received at that time a one-storey four-column Greek Doric portico, and within, a panel of Antique figures. There was an C18 cupola fitted up as an observatory. The walled garden (NE) is reached via a tunnel in the form of an early C19 Romantic GROTTO; flanking sphinxes and within the tunnel, a mutilated odalisque, the only survival of the Smyth-Pigotts' considerable sculpture collection. Good GATEPIERS, pilastered LODGE, also *c.* 1825.

BROCKLEY COTTAGE, Chelvey Batch. The thatched core probably C17. The charm is in the W front with its Early Victorian contribution for the Smyth-Pigott estate. It faces the main road to Bristol, a turnpike route *c.* 1837, which is perhaps the date of the alterations. Fancifully barge-boarded gables of different sizes and in happily accidental positions, with to the r. a stone-faced gable added at the same time; here, stone imitations of C17 jetty brackets, and Gothic windows. Someone had learnt the lesson of Blaise Hamlet (p. 400). Also some late medieval fragments on an outbuilding.

BUCKLAND DINHAM

A wool village on a high down, dropping steeply S to a secondary settlement by water.

ST MICHAEL AND ALL ANGELS. The earliest features in the nave, Norman S and N windows. With these go the plain N doorway and the S doorway of *c.* 1200. The latter has single colonnettes with a trumpet capital (r.), a foliate capital moving towards stiff-leaf (l.), and a depressed pointed arch on vertical springers, with an outer row of chevrons. Contemporary chancel arch, pointed on plain Norman-looking imposts. The outer entrance to the S porch was originally C13, plainly double-chamfered and pointed. It received a new lower entrance and a good fan-vault, *c.* 1490–1530. Abutting the porch and a little after it, perhaps *c.* 1250, the S chapel was added. In the position of an aisle, but with only one arch to the nave. Lancet windows and a group of three stepped lancets at the E end, cusped inside and with Blue Lias shafts. In the SE corner, a rare stone CANDLE SHELF, perhaps C15. Chancel also early C13, see the N lancet. Over-restored N transept endowed by Sir John Dinham in 1325, see the curious N window tracery (renewed). In the nave N side a half-broken cusped tomb-recess, possibly removed from the chancel when a small N chapel was added in the late C15. W tower, perhaps late C15, cf. Hemington. The middle stage with a pair of tall two-light transomed blank windows. Above them single three-light transomed bell-openings with Somerset tracery. Tower arch with continuous two-wave moulding. Restored by *G. G. Scott*, 1849–54.

REREDOS. Perp, *c.* 1900. – PULPIT. Oak with arched panels, early C17. – FONT. Circular, with a frieze beaded for half the circumference, the other half with angled crenellations, mid-C12. – MONUMENTS. N chapel. Demi-figures in relief, of Blue Lias, no doubt Sir John Dinham †1332, and wife †1361. The lower halves of the tombstones are flat. As a transition they have two shields each at waist height. Churchyard, Thomas Heale †1681. Big chest tomb with moulded arches. – Rev. Henry Clutterbuck †1883, shaft and cross on the stepped base of the medieval cross.

OLD PARSONAGE, s of the church. In origin a medieval prebendal house. The present structure largely pre-dates 1679, the date scratched on an attic window. Plain refronting, *c.* 1842. Opposite, a square BLIND HOUSE (lock-up) with pyramid roof, probably *c.* 1720–50. NW of the church, COURT FARM, the central two bays early C17, the ends early C19 refrontings. (An upper room has an early C17 plaster overmantel with fretted frieze and curly floral sprays. Also a cornice with bunches of fruit suspended on ribbons.) s of the church, a Gothic VILLAGE HALL of 1880; and behind, a former SCHOOL, *c.* 1847–8, enlarged 1853, 1876. Directly s, a farmhouse of *c.* 1650–80 or earlier, updated 1836–9 in Tudor Gothic style when it became the vicarage. C17 plan: three rooms in line, cross-passage to a rear kitchen wing. To the w, High Street has good minor C17 and C18 houses (many spoiled by replaced windows). Set back on the N side, the former EBENEZER METHODIST CHAPEL, 1811. Gabled, segmental-headed windows. Doorcase with keystones and a big segmental pediment on brackets, *ex situ* and *c.* 1730. Original gallery and stairs.

In the valley to the s, by the A362 road bridge, a PACKHORSE BRIDGE and a ruined DRYING TOWER for dyed cloth, both C18. A few yards N, a public BASIN for washing clothes, dated 1876.

OXLEY'S COLLIERY, *c.* ⅔ m. E, was established *c.* 1880. The tall brick CHIMNEY is the last such survival in the Somerset coalfields. 1 m. SE of the village, over the Mells Stream, MURTRY BRIDGE. Two big C14 arches with cutwaters, a third arch collapsed.

ORCHARDLEIGH STONES. Standing stones ½ m. SE of the village, all that remains of a once-imposing long barrow.

BURNETT

6060

ST MICHAEL. Much renewed. Nave and chancel. Oddly domestic-looking organ chamber and s vestry, perhaps C17 or C18. The nave s wall has one C13 lancet, the w window is original

Perp, perhaps *c.* 1380–1400. Otherwise round-headed mullioned nave lights, perhaps C18. Chancel arch without dressed stone, impossible to date. The chancel was lengthened *c.* 1886 and the s porch and bellcote renewed. – STAINED GLASS. E and w windows probably by *Bell & Son, c.* 1886. Nave N, *G. J. Hunt,* 1929. – BRASS. John Cutte †1575, Mayor of Bristol. The kneeling couple and their twelve children. Shield with the Bristol arms on the l., merchant's mark r.

MANOR HOUSE. At its N end part of one wing of a pre-C17 house, mostly demolished in the mid C18 when the remainder was extended and given a third storey. w front with heavy Georgian sashes and mid-C19 porch. On the E front, the canted bay with mullioned-and-transomed windows r. of the door is genuinely C16 or early C17, that at the l. mid-C18, reusing old stonework. In 1933–4 two C18 sashes over the door were replaced by mullioned windows, completing the misleading impression of a C17 façade. The dining room has a good stone chimneypiece of *c.* 1550 with scrolling frieze, and a timber overmantel with shell-headed niches, possibly C19.

On the main road, a steeply gabled former SCHOOL, 1858–9, with striking Dec tracery. Enlarged 1872.

BURRINGTON

HOLY TRINITY. The symmetrical E end faces the village square; projecting chancel, chapels with trefoiled parapets. Prominent rood-stair turret (N), with Perp panelling and a big spirelike pinnacle, outdoing Winscombe. Low C14 w tower, with Y-traceried belfry lights, diagonal buttresses and plain battlements. Below the w window, a diamond stop-bar, a Somerset feature (again, cf. Winscombe). Nave, aisles and chancel are of *c.* 1500. Splendid N DOOR; in the head, a little eight-arched arcade, and above, quatrefoils with shields. Big plain s porch. Low tower arch with two hollow mouldings; heavy moulded capitals run out at either side. Four-bay arcades with piers of standard section, also in the chancel arch and chapels. Thin capitals, decorated in the s arcade only. Three-light windows, more elaborate on the s side. In the aisles, wall-shafts ending in demi-figures of angels, with Instruments of the Passion. Handsome aisle roofs, flat with square panels. Wagon-roofed nave. Against the E respond of the s arcade a male figure placed horizontally, originally no doubt busy helping to carry the rood beam. Restored by *Foster & Wood c.* 1856–7 (new chancel and chapel roofs), and again under *J. D. Sedding,* 1883–4: new aisle roofs, chancel furnishings and floor, with marble insets and encaustic tiles by *Godwin* of Lugwardine.

FITTINGS. REREDOS by *Harry Hems,* 1908; Last Supper with fussy canopy. Its installation revealed a badly damaged relief SCULPTURE, now in the sedilia. Earlier medieval than anything else here. Christ flanked by two kneeling donors (the woman holding a distaff) and two censing angels. – PARCLOSE SCREENS. Oak, Perp, with spindly tracery, suns in the coving, and cresting. Early C20? – Intricate BENCH-ENDS by *F. Bligh Bond*, 1913. – STAINED GLASS. C15 fragments assembled over the N door, 1849; elsewhere medieval pieces in the tracery. E window, *Bell & Son*, *c.* 1880; also the vivid E windows of both chapels, *c.* 1857. s aisle, E to W: *Warrington*, 1865; *Kempe*, 1902; *Kempe & Co.*, 1920; *Bell & Son* (†1915). s aisle w, *Ward & Hughes*, *c.* 1881. w window, probably *Bell* and *c.* 1850. N aisle w, *Heaton, Butler & Bayne*, 1885. N aisle, first from w: *Kempe & Co.*, 1920; third, *c.* 1878, style of *Heaton, Butler & Bayne*; fourth, 1935, *Bell & Son* (probably *Arnold Robinson*). – MONUMENTS. Five big C18 ledger slabs rearranged in the porch: the earliest to Elizabeth Jones †1712, naïve pattern-book classicism. – Odd group linked to Thomas Whalley: his wife Elizabeth †1801, with urn; a similar tablet to her successor, August Utica †1807; Elizabeth's first husband John Sherwood †1770, obelisk with pediment.* – Albinia Jackson drowned †1810. By *Tyley*, epitaph by Hannah More. – In the churchyard, C15 CROSS. Square socket with two Perp arches on each face. Shaft and top *c.* 1910–14.

Burrington Combe has a number of CAVES. The most important is AVELINE'S HOLE, a rift cavern on the E side of the Combe with skeletal remains dating from the Late Upper Palaeolithic and Mesolithic periods (*see* p. 7). A panel of abstract geometric engravings, possibly of the early Mesolithic, was recently discovered.

On the edge of the Combe is BURRINGTON CAMP, an oval Iron Age earthwork measuring 120 yds by 80 yds (110 by 75 metres).

BUTCOMBE

ST MICHAEL AND ALL ANGELS. Small church sweetly placed on the side of a steep valley. Humble, but with an oddly ornate and quite originally detailed s tower, perhaps late C14. Three stages, plain embattled top. Set-back buttresses stop short at the second stage with pinnacles. Between these the angles of the tower itself develop into niches with nodding ogee canopies, from which rise short diagonal buttresses. Two-light windows, and two-light bell-openings. Nave with one-bay N aisle. s chapel added seemingly after the tower and to its E, with late C15 ogee lights, wave-moulded arch from the tower. The E wall has a mutilated niche with original colouring. Over-restored by *Clifton J. West*, 1868; new Perp-style arches to

---

*Whalley lavished £60,000 on MENDIP LODGE, s of Burrington. Of 1787–1804, dem. *c.* 1955. A remarkable big Gothick house with two-tier iron veranda.

chancel and N aisle. Later vestry, 1897, and organ chamber. –
PULPIT. 1922, with C15 blind tracery panels. – SCREEN of
c. 1500 from Blagdon, installed 1921, no doubt with new work.
Two-light divisions with extremely delicate tracery. Hand-
somely carved cornice, three bands of vines. – STAINED GLASS.
C15 fragments, S chapel E. Chancel, three by *Lavers, Barraud
& Westlake*, c. 1870. Tower S by *Westlake*, †1881.

PHIPPENS FARM. A simple late C18 house with early C19 alterations. (Two rooms with exceptionally rare all-round murals
in distemper and oils, c. 1832. Marbled dados; above, pastoral
subjects in blues on pink. Signed *Walters*, probably *Thomas
Walters* of Bristol.)

6050

CAMELEY

ST JAMES (Churches Conservation Trust). The outside gives
little hint of the uncommonly charming unrestored interior.
Handsome late C15 W tower (badge of John Benet, rector from
1483, S side). Of Dolomitic Conglomerate and local Triassic
sandstone with diagonal buttresses, two-light bell-openings
and a parapet with pierced cusped lozenge frieze. Fine W
window, three ogee lights, some inverted Y-tracery. The tower
arch is triple-chamfered. Also C15 the chancel, with simple
square-headed lights. Small low nave, partly Norman, with
exterior steps to the galleries. Porch rebuilt 1620, reusing
medieval wall-plates. The inner doorway, c. 1150–80, has keeled
nook-shafts, one with a scalloped capital, one with big
upstanding fronds; arch with unusual lattice mouldings.
Undecorated Norman chancel arch. Remnants of Perp arched
recesses for nave altars.

FITTINGS. REREDOS. Humble panelling, shaped top and
vases, perhaps c. 1710. – COMMUNION RAIL, early C18. –
PULPIT. Jacobean with tester, crudely carved but vigorous.
Adjoining READER'S DESK and FAMILY PEW of 1630. –
BENCHES, c. 1400, square-headed ends, quite plain. – BOX
PEWS, late C17 and C18. – FONT. C12, square, with three scal-
lops underneath on each side, cable moulding at the neck.
Waterholding base, possibly C13; COVER, 1634, crude S-scrolls.
– WEST GALLERY of 1711 with balusters still in the Jacobean
tradition. – Panelled SOUTH GALLERY of 1819 (*William
Penrold*, surveyor). – (SCULPTURE. Contentious wooden head,
assigned dates from the C10 to C17; due to be resited in the
tower.) Remarkable and varied WALL PAINTINGS, the best-
known feature. Nave N: C11 fragment of masonry pattern.
Adjacent, the foot of a big C14 St Christopher among crabs
and fish. Framing the chancel arch, red scroll patterns, c. 1200.
Royal Arms (three lions, c. C13), N pier of chancel arch. On
either side, at the altar sites, C15 gold, black and white damask
pattern. Near the pulpit, leafy damask perhaps of the same

period. Over the chancel arch, striking early C17 Command-ments, with coquettish cherubs. ROYAL ARMS of Charles I, framed. – MONUMENTS. Grave-slab reused in the porch floor, reputedly Saxon. – Cadwallader Jones †1692, astonishingly naïve classicism, beehive-shaped pediment. – Several by *Reeves* of Bath, that to John Rees-Mogg †1835 a vertical composition with draped altar.

A five-gabled Elizabethan mansion E of the church pictured in 1789 was demolished *c.* 1840. ¾ m. W is CAMELEY HOUSE. The W wing is late C17, with a big Gothick addition to the E, extant by 1766. This has ogee-headed windows. Porch with a re-set C16 doorcase. The prettiest motif is a two-storey embat-tled canted bay on the E return, with closely set ogee windows. It is repeated on the garden front.

CAMERTON

ST PETER. The development is not easy to grasp. The pre-Vic-torian church had a three-bay nave, N porch and two-bay chancel, with a N chancel chapel for the Carews, dated 1638. In 1842 *John Pinch Jun.* added a S chapel, and a long S transept immediately W of the chancel arch.* In 1891–2 *Thomas Garner* enlarged it further, making the chancel part of the nave, adding a new chancel, organ loft (S) and vestry, removing the transept, and elongating the S chapel as a four-bay S aisle. High-quality work in a slightly frigid Perp style. Embattled three-stage tower, perhaps early C16, with set-back buttresses, four-centred openings, and unusually big figure-stops to the hoodmoulds, including a woman with rosary, a lutist, and, on the N face, remarkably, a rhinoceros and an elephant. Embattled nave N wall and N porch Perp too. Then the N chapel, with end gables, battlements to the N, and straight-headed windows, renewed 1842.

FITTINGS. Mostly 1891–2, with REREDOS, ALTAR and other marble work, and perhaps carving too, by *Farmer & Brindley.* – Good oak STALLS and ROOD SCREEN. – PULPIT. Probably 1891. Modest Early Georgian style, with neat carved drops at the angles. – FONT. C15, octagonal on panelled stem. – COVER, *c.* 1620s; neat scrolled frieze. – STAINED GLASS. E window by *Bell & Son*, probably 1890s; six others by them, to *c.* 1906. N chapel E, *O'Connor*, *c.* 1865. – MONUMENTS. In the chapel, an impressive collection of Carew tombs. Sir John and Lady Carew, 1640. Recumbent effigies on a free-standing tomb-chest with kneeling children between coupled tapered pilasters. – John Carew †1683 and wife. The same composition but a standing angel by the heads of the figures, Doric columns, and in the middles of the long sides niches, each with

---

* *G. S. Repton* was involved, though seemingly not as architect.

a seated child. – Thomas Carew †1721. Big hanging monument with two busts and Composite columns. Curved top, urns and two reclining putti. – Lively reclining figure of a young woman in late C17 costume (s aisle).

CAMERTON COURT, in parkland NE of the church. A reserved and modest Bath stone villa by *G. S. Repton*, *c.* 1838–40. Two storeys, three bays by four, with intriguing asymmetrical s front – a one-storey Ionic colonnade, its l. end abutting a canted bay. Deep Tuscan *porte cochère* on the N. At the SW corner, a long Ionic conservatory, slightly later than the house. Well-preserved interiors. The top-lit cantilevered staircase has lotus-flower balusters of cast iron.

Of Camerton's mining past, a small POWDER HOUSE at Red Hill survives (*c.* 1870). At Camerton Heritage Local Nature Reserve, a fibreglass SCULPTURE of a coalminer originally displayed at the Festival of Britain, 1951.

Two Bronze Age ROUND BARROWS in Rowberrow Field, 1 m. SE on the s side of the Fosse Way. The only survivors of a once-larger barrow group. ROUNDHILL TUMP is large and well preserved while the second barrow, nearer the road, survives only as a low earthwork.

ROMAN ROADSIDE SETTLEMENT, astride the Fosse Way (now A367; *see* p. 577) between Peasedown St John and Clandown. It consisted of several lanes obliquely joining the Fosse Way and at least thirteen stone buildings, most of them fronting onto the Fosse Way. The extent of the undefended settlement is unclear but it occupied at least 10 acres. Traces of Iron Age ENCLOSURE DITCHES and a timber round house of the C2–C1 B.C. have been found.

CHANTRY

7040

Scattered hamlets centred on Little Elm. They gained parish status and a new name in 1846.*

HOLY TRINITY. 1843–6 by *G. G. Scott*, assisted in some details by *W. G. Brown* of Frome. Built for James Fussell of the local dynasty of edge-tool makers, who lived at The Chantry. A considerable advance over Scott's vaguely handled Gothic of Nailsea, just a couple of years earlier. Four-bay nave, lower chancel; tall Dec windows with varied tracery, highly Dec s porch and priest's door. w front with two diagonal buttresses, two lancet windows, and an extraordinary central buttress carrying a polygonal bell-turret with steep crocketed spirelet. Four angel corbels at the corners of the nave hold edge-tools etc. Large roof slates with half-rolls over the joins, intended to look like lead. – FITTINGS. All of a piece. – REREDOS. Stone, with

* Research by Dr Robin Thorne and Dr David Rawlins.

panels of saints painted on copper by *W. L. T. Collins* of Frome. – Oak CHANCEL SCREEN, slightly adapted by *Brown*, from *Scott*'s design. – STAINED GLASS by *Wailes*. E window, 1845, with scenes in medallions, consciously medieval, but not yet with the knowledge of details of *c.* 1300 which soon became the pride of the glass designers. – SW window depicting a rare Lily Crucifix. – MONUMENT. James Fussell †1845. Coffin-shaped slab with brass insets. Presumably by *Scott*.

THE CHANTRY. Probably by *John Pinch Sen.*, *c.* 1820–2. It sits directly SE of the church, overlooking it like a rectory. Built by his father for James Fussell, a mark of aspiration to gentility. The entrance front has two storeys and semicircular Doric porch, three bays with bowed centre over a high basement to the S, and an attic over the bow. Blind arches over some ground-floor windows. Fine PARK to the S, including two Romantic grottoes of the 1840s, and a 7-acre lake, also acting as headwater to maintain flow to the Fussells' iron works to the E (demolished).*

W of the church is YEW TREE FARM, *c.* 1650, with a mutilated medieval crucifix plaque reused as building stone in the entrance hall. N of the village near Pool House is BOS WELL, a stone-lined pool mentioned in a C10 charter.

CHARLCOMBE 7060

ST MARY. Nave and chancel, late Norman S porch. Much restored (1857–61), probably by *James Wilson*, under the supervision of *G. G. Scott*. Corbelled out from the W gable a surprising and picturesque square bell-turret, perhaps early C14, with two square openings and battlements. The yew tree SW of the church is much taller than the turret. Norman doorways. On the N side perfectly plain, tall, narrow and arched, on the S (renewed) with one order of columns carrying trumpet capitals. Organ chamber 1886. – FITTINGS. REREDOS, finely carved motifs in a coloured frieze, sculptor *H. Ezard*, 1862. – Norman FONT, plain circular bowl with upright leaves in two tiers decorating the underside. – PEWS. By *Robert Thompson*, 1967. – STAINED GLASS. Nave S, by *Ward & Hughes*, probably 1869. – PULPIT. Bath stone, curved, and perfectly plain. – MONUMENT. Lady Barbara Montagu †1765, by *Ford*. Female figure leaning on a pedestal.

CHARLCOMBE MANOR, Charlcombe Lane, *c.* ¼ m. SW. Late C17. A handsome five-bay S front with two steep gables containing oval lights keyed into square frames. Mullioned light with deep relieving arches above. Restored *c.* 1840, probably by *James Wilson*.

---

*At Railford, *c.* ½ m. NE, a ruinous mid-C19 CHIMNEY and water courses from the Fussells' second Chantry iron works.

CHARLCOMBE GROVE, NW of the village. A belvedered Italianate villa like so many on Lansdown; altered by *J. Wilson* *c.* 1860. To the E, mid-C19 garden terraces.

4050

CHARTERHOUSE

The loneliest and most expressive landscape on Mendip – that other Somerset of bleak undulating upland, its thin soil crisscrossed by dry-stone walls and pitted with industrial remains.

ST HUGH. A miners' welfare hall of *c.* 1890, converted by *W. D. Caröe*, 1908–13. Prosaic Voyseyesque exterior, roughcast with sloped buttresses dying into the walls. Simple rectangular mullioned windows under the eaves. Green slate roof with diagonally placed flèche added 1923. Reassuringly domestic interior with a fireplace, and at the W end, a low lean-to scullery, both from its time as a hall. Massive round-arched roof trusses. – Simple hand-crafted FITTINGS designed by *Caröe*, with sophisticated C17 touches. – Pale oak CHANCEL SCREEN, *c.* 1919. Hardly pointed enough to be called Gothic; delicately wrought fleur-de-lys etc., on twisted columns. – STAINED GLASS. W window by *Horace Wilkinson*. – Fine churchyard CROSS, 1909.

MANOR FARM, *c.* ¼ m. W. Believed to stand on the site of a Carthusian grange founded from Witham Abbey, extant by 1376. The present house is probably early C17. N front apparently fragmentary, and perhaps originally of E-shape. Two-storey porch. Garden front (S) completely flat, one gable at the W, two- to four-light windows, transomed mainly on the ground floor. The stone mullions and transoms have unusual restrained decoration of recessed panels on their narrow front faces.

ROMAN LEAD-MINING SETTLEMENT, evident in extensive landscape disturbance. Two enclosures can still be seen, one of them a possible fort. A small oval earthwork on Town Field has been interpreted as an AMPHITHEATRE.

There were medieval and later revivals of lead mining. A little S of the church, where the road curves across a shallow valley, can be seen on both sides of the road rows of circular depressions left by 'buddle houses' – tanks in which lead was washed. At Nether Wood, away to the NE, a series of 310-ft (95-metre)-long stone-lined condenser flues for lead smelting, late C19.

GORSEY BIGBURY HENGE MONUMENT, *c.* 1 m. W of Charterhouse. An important Bronze Age circular enclosure *c.* 200 ft (62 metres) in diameter, with its ditch inside the bank and a single entrance on the N side. Occupation extended from the Late Neolithic into the Early Bronze Age.

BLACK DOWN, 1½ m. NW of Charterhouse, is the highest point on Mendip (1,056 ft, 322 metres). Here are rare surviving

Second World War ANTI-AIRCRAFT LANDING DEFENCES; a grid of low mounds in long lines. An anti-aircraft ROCKET BATTERY survives in good condition, the only one known in England. Slightly later, a sophisticated system of lights was installed nearby to divert bombs from Bristol, with three extant CONTROL BUILDINGS.

CHEDDAR

Cheddar has a villagey air. Yet near the church lay a Roman villa and a Saxon royal palace; rare evidence in Somerset of such continuity. Lower North Street and The Hayes were a planned medieval extension to the medieval settlement. Mills E of Cliff Street were powered by fast-flowing streams. A brief industrial heyday, with shirt factories and paper mills at the foot of the Gorge, had waned by the early C20.

ST ANDREW, Church Street. Nothing remains of a Saxon monastery on or near this site. The size of the present church perhaps hints at its former importance. As usual, what is visible is mainly Perp. Expensively restored 1871–3 by *Butterfield*, who rebuilt the chancel arch, much of the chancel S wall and the S chapel. Most memorable is the 110-ft (34-metre)-high W tower – intended to carry a spire for which the squinches survive. It has set-back buttresses connected diagonally across the angles and crowned by tall diagonally placed shafts with pinnacles. The base perhaps built *c.* 1403–13, if indeed the headstops of the W doorway represent Henry IV and his queen. Above this an uncommonly tall four-light window, and two original statues of the Annunciation in niches. Stages two and three have two-light windows with split-Y reticulation units (used by *William Wynford* at Wells) and diamond stop-bars. The bell-stage has a triplet of two-light windows with intermediate pinnacles, the outer windows blank. To this point every detail is like Banwell tower. Pierced parapet with quatrefoils in lozenges, pinnacles and higher stair-turret with spirelet. N aisle, N porch and clerestory have the same pierced parapets with pinnacles. Three-light Perp aisle windows but two-light Dec clerestory windows. The chancel is C13; it projects only slightly between big chapels. One Norman head corbel survives between chancel and S chapel. Ambitious one-bay outer chapel E of the S porch, *c.* 1480s. Its S window straight-headed, divided into two arched three-light groups. Inside the tower, a lierne-vault and tower arch of two continuous wave mouldings separated by a deep hollow. As the clerestory windows make one expect, the nave arcades are C14. In point of fact they are rather mean. Octagonal piers with plain moulded capitals and arches with two wave mouldings, the piers not tall or substantial enough to cope with the height and width of the nave. The square sub-bases perhaps belonged to earlier piers. There are five-and-a-half bays. The S arcade has different mouldings at the W end – perhaps a rebuilding or extension; masonry joins show that the S aisle W wall post-dates the tower. Original nave and aisle roofs, that of the nave panelled, on thin arched braces (repainted 1873, following medieval traces). C14 arches with double quadrant mouldings from chancel to N and S chapels. The N chapel, which John Harvey suggested may be by *William Wynford*, is called *de novo fundata* in 1380: broad N window, two groups of three lights under a four-centred arch. Elaborately panelled and shafted arch from the aisle into the outer S chapel. On the E respond three richly detailed image niches, with C19 statues. E.E. PISCINA in the chancel, with moulded trefoil-arch and double basin on two attached shafts.

p. 37

FITTINGS. STALLS. By *Butterfield*, with good late C15 traceried panels in the fronts. Might these be from the chancel desks for which a Bristol carpenter was paid £2 in 1475–6? – SCREENS to N and S chapels. Late C15, three ogee lights per division, one thin cornice. – PULPIT. Stone, with small canopied niches, too small for statuettes, and busts of angels on the underside. Repainted 1873 following traces of medieval colour. – BENCH-ENDS. Many C15. Straight-headed, plain tracery. Allegorical heads etc. in the spandrels (N aisle). – FONT. Octagonal, trefoiled arches in shallow relief. Perhaps C13, but Sir Stephen Glynne thought it 'modern' in 1830. C17 COVER. – ALTAR TABLE. 1631. Bulbous legs, guilloche frieze. – PAINTINGS. Christ at Emmaus, large demi-figures. Late C17, by *Jan Erasmus Quellinus*. – Beneath the tower, big naïve panels, 1803, of Death and Time, in Gothick frames. – STAINED GLASS. Outer S chapel, two windows with mostly C15 fragments in the Somerset style, nicely assembled in 1873. Including Annunciation, St Barbara, etc. E window, colourful Ascension by *A. Gibbs*, 1873; four more, and part of the S clerestory, *c.* 1877. Nave N, *Beckham & Bell*, *c.* 1885–90. – MONUMENTS. Tomb-chest with four quatrefoils with shields. Tudor arch with big ferny leaves in the spandrels. On the lid brass to Sir Thomas Cheddar †1443, a 3-ft (0.9-metre) figure in armour. On the floor below, brass to his wife, *c.* 1475. The figure *c.* 33 in. (84 cm.) long.

CHAPEL OF ST COLUMBANUS, Station Road. In the grounds of Kings of Wessex School. The third on the site (*see* Saxon palace, below). A C13 rebuilding of the Saxon royal chapel. Re-dedicated 1321, for the Bishop of Wells. Plain oblong nave, with C15–C16 diagonal buttresses. Chancel demolished *c.* 1330 for a new E wall with trefoil-headed window (now blocked). Single-chamfered W doorway and lancet window above, round-arched inside. Ruined since *c.* 1910.

BAPTIST CHAPEL, Lower North Street. 1831. Simple but pretty. Round-arched windows, interlaced glazing. Italianate stepped gable with some mongrel strapwork. Spoiled by a recent porch.

METHODIST CHAPEL, Cliff Street. *Foster & Wood*, 1896–7. Gothic. Seven lancets in the W gable. Schoolrooms (r.), added by 1904.

Some minor PUBLIC BUILDINGS. The parish CHURCH ROOMS of 1894 have arched centres to the windows. A debased Italianate PARISH HALL, Church Street, began as a lecture hall and reading room. By *Cook & Hancorn*, 1859. Hannah More Court, Lower North Street, began as NATIONAL SCHOOLS in 1837; Neo-Tudor, with single-storey wings. To the W in The Hayes, CHEDDAR FIRST SCHOOL, by *John Bevan Sen.*, 1871–2. Gothic, sharp gables, plate tracery.

MARKET CROSS. At the junction in the centre, a C15 cross with stepped base. Late C19 cross-head. The shaft was surrounded probably in the C16 by a hexagonal roofed shelter with four-centred arches. The fabric was rebuilt in 1834, and much restored 1887.

Of Cheddar's MINOR HOUSES, only a few examples are offered. COURT HOUSE, Church Street, just S of the cross, is a red brick house of *c.* 1810–30, three bays with a wild display of rusticated stone framing. Next to the cross, ARUNDEL HOUSE, *c.* 1830, with Tuscan eaves and glazed veranda. To the W in Station Road, HANHAM MANOR, C14 or earlier. Hall (E), central solar in cross-wing, C17 additions to the W. (Solar roof with two-tier cruck-trusses felled 1341–2, with cusped arch braces and wind-braces. Very decorative, and comparable to the roof at St John's Priory, Wells.) FERN BANK, Lower North Street, is a pretty Gothick cottage, 1820s, for the Marquess of Bath. Finally THE HALL, St Andrew's Road. The asymmetrical projecting wings (two windows to the l. gable, one to the r.) support Pevsner's suggested C17 date. Recessed five-bay centre with gable over the central bays. Georgian sash windows.

CAVEMAN RESTAURANT, Cheddar Gorge. By *Russell Page* and *Geoffrey Jellicoe* in 1933–*c.* 1935. Little is left of this brave Modernist venture, originally with glazed front, roof terrace, and a restaurant with glass-block roof forming a pool. In the mid 1960s the café was partly rebuilt as shops, with a concrete cantilevered frame. Pool filled in, 1980s. Gaudy signage everywhere.

SAXON PALACE, S of Station Road. Excavated 1960–2, before building began on Kings of Wessex School; the school was resited to avoid the archaeology. Finds across the site and in the adjacent vicarage garden suggest that there was an extensive Roman villa complex or small town, with metalworking by the C2. The Saxon monastic site extended from the River Yeo (S) to a point opposite the Market Cross (NE), where there was an entrance. Three phases of Saxon royal palace building were uncovered, with a chapel and large timber hall rebuilt in phase two (after 930). This hall was *c.* 90 ft by 18 ft (28 by 5.5 metres), with inner rows of sloping posts, perhaps for an upper hall. It probably housed a meeting of the *Witan* in 941. King John rebuilt it as a hunting lodge, 1209–11. Also a smaller hall to its W, and ancillary buildings.

PREHISTORIC REMAINS. The caves of CHEDDAR GORGE have yielded evidence of Upper Palaeolithic hunters. The most famous cave is GOUGH'S (NEW) CAVE, the most productive Upper Palaeolithic site in Britain, yielding over 7,000 tools and weapons, as well as the skeleton of 'Cheddar Man', a very late glacial occupant dating from *c.* 7000 B.C. The less accessible SOLDIER'S HOLE, 200 yds beyond Gough's Cave, was also occupied by Upper Palaeolithic hunters. In LONG HOLE CAVE abstract engravings, probably Mesolithic, were discovered in 2005.

₄₀₆₀

CHELVEY

An isolated church and manor house grouped on a low rise. It supplied eels for the Norman royal larder, a reminder that salt marsh once extended this far inland.

ST BRIDGET. Norman S doorway of Dundry stone with one order of columns carrying scalloped capitals. Continuous inner roll moulding. Roll moulding in the arch. The blocked N doorway has inside an E.E. chamfered arch. Chancel of *c.* 1300, see the cusped lancets on the N side. The chancel E window looks late C15. The best date indicator for the S aisle is the two-and-a-half-bay arcade, with standard piers of four shafts with wave-moulded diagonals; perhaps *c.* 1380–1480. The reredos frame, image niches, ogee piscina, tomb recesses and aisle windows may be later C15; the claimed C17 date for the whole aisle is untenable. Uncusped windows, perhaps reworked in the C17 when the aisle became the Tyntes' manorial chapel. S porch with blind arcaded parapet, probably *c.* 1490–1530. In the porch, ogee-headed stoup, a reused C15 window light with glazing slot. Simple three-stage Perp W tower with arch to the nave with the frequent two-wave moulding. Only the parapet more elaborate: pierced frieze of cusped triangles and angle pinnacles.

FITTINGS. Much from an unrecorded late C19 restoration. – Straight REREDOS frame, *c.* 1500, with fleurons. Elaborate central canopy rising above the sill. Poor late C19 panels. To l. and r. tall image niches, the carving chiselled off. – A simple REREDOS frame also in the S chapel. – ROOD SCREEN. The stone dado and oak sill remain. – FONT. Originally square, mid-C12, see the big flutes beneath. The corners cut off to form an octagon in the C14. – COVER. C19, with small Jacobean panels. – MANORIAL PEW of the Tynte family. A good Jacobean piece with a high back, arcaded and with decorative frieze. A matching pew front in the nave has a shield dated 1621 WG, presumably for William Gregory, rector from 1619. – BENCHES. Some perhaps C15, plain with lozenge-shaped poppyheads. More of a different pattern at the rear of the nave. – STAINED GLASS. Small medieval fragments. – PAINTING (chancel N). A large rosette probably as decoration of a feigned ashlar block, possibly *c.* 1300. – MONUMENTS. Incised slab of unidentified limestone, to a knight, *c.* 1260–80 (cf. Bitton slab at Wells Cathedral). – In the S aisle S wall three matching Perp TOMB RECESSES. Broad crocketed ogee gables, blind arcaded bases. – Ledger slab to Robert Tynte †1636, a palimpsest with C15 floriated cross beneath the inscription. – Late medieval churchyard CROSS, shaft restored.

CHELVEY COURT. There seems little to clinch the phasing. The medieval house was rebuilt by Edward and John Tynte, *c.* 1618–60, on a single-pile plan with E-facing entrance front and a broad rear stair-tower (SW). The return N of the stairs filled in shortly after, forming a double-pile main range. From 1689, Chelvey was for 300 years a tenanted farm, explaining the spectacular survival of C17 decoration. A great hall to the S was demolished in 1805; see the S wall, blank but for a typically late C17 oval window keyed into an oblong panel, dated 1805 above. Externally the showpiece is the porch, probably *c.* 1663–9, at the S end of the E front. It has twisted columns (the r. one missing) and above them short tapering pilasters. Between these a steep open segmental pediment with coat of arms and garlands. Balcony above with pierced balustrade. The W front has broad mullioned-and-transomed stair windows, cross-windows to the later rooms, N. The room behind the porch has softwood panelling with C17 naïve woodgraining in bold symmetrical patterns. Directly N, a narrow panelled room with gilded bead-and-reel borders and blue-green graining. Fine C17 fireplace and overmantel with strapwork and coats of arms, probably *ex situ.* N again, a parlour with simple plaster wreath in the ceiling. Excellent three-storey oak staircase, *c.* 1650–80: massively proportioned, with a square well. Fat vase balusters, boldly turned. Above the stairwell, a dramatic pendant dropping some five feet, with fat garlands, surrounded by a thin ribbed rosette with flower motifs in the panels. The basement is on ground level at the W; here, a broad arched kitchen fire opening with six-row spit rack above, and in the room to its E, a chamfered fire opening, perhaps C15 or C16, with witch mark. Repaired and in parts remodelled since 1985 by *Keith Hallett.*

Big BARN S of the church, not a tithe barn but associated with the court. The E end is perhaps C15, carefully laid with showy bands of Pennant stone. Bigger W end added perhaps in the C16; long sides buttressed, projecting porch with diagonal buttresses. Two trusses of an arch-braced collar-beam roof. The first bay from the E has a full-height internal wall with pigeon loft.

CHELWOOD 6060

ST LEONARD. A small low church, on the track to a farmyard. Virtually rebuilt by *John Norton,* 1861. Small W tower with saddleback roof; the plinth from a rebuilding of 1772, the rest

Norton's. Two corbel heads in the E and W responds of the S aisle arcade said to be C13. – Big REREDOS, in Norton's E.E. style. – FONT. Norman, square cushion-capital shape with tiny corner volutes. Incised scalloped frieze at the top edge, incised rosette on the E face only. – STAINED GLASS. E window, fine Crucifixion by *William Wailes*, 1861. S aisle, various Flemish fragments, mostly C16. W window 1861, re-set here 1930–1. – MONUMENT. Martha Adams †1795. Crisp and refined tablet by *Reeves & Son*.

MALT HOUSE FARM, *c*. ¼ m. W. C16, altered in 1639 (dated panelling). Mullioned windows with hoodmoulds. In the room with the panelling a pretty plaster ceiling of thin ribs.

CHELWOOD HOUSE, I m. W. Seven-bay two-storey house of the late C17; three gables, the centre one projecting. Slim mid-C18 sash windows in flat frames.

CHEW MAGNA

The principal Chew valley village. Leland described 'a praty clothing towne, [with] a faire church'. Two rivers (the Chew, S, and Winford Brook, N) thread through it via numerous bridges. Vernacular cottages contrast with the smart villas of Georgian merchants, many doubtless by Bristol architects.

ST ANDREW. There are slight Norman remains in the arch of the S doorway, perhaps reused. The S arcade and the NE respond of the S chapel, are E.E., as are the pair of leafy label stops left when the westernmost window of the S aisle was replaced in the mid C15; see the initials above it, probably of Bishop Bekynton, 1443–65. What we see now is, externally at least, almost entirely Perp. A NE vestry was added in 1824, and the church re-seated and repaired by *John Norton*, 1859–60; otherwise the C19 left it relatively untouched.

p. 28

The memorably strong tall W tower of Dundry Ashlar, 99½ ft (31.5 metres) high, has four stages with set-back buttresses, pierced panelled parapet, finely moulded W doorway, elaborate five-light W window, then two-light windows on three stages (the bell-openings broader than the lower lights). From the topmost set-offs, little shafts continue up into the parapet to form diagonal corner panels from which rise thin pinnacles. All this is exactly as at Winford, although which came first is unclear. The tower base here must have been completed by *c*. 1440, before the N aisle, the W wall of which was built after, and abutting, the stair-turret of the tower.* For the N aisle money was left in 1443; it has four-light windows and battlements. The exquisite two-storey N porch is later (the r. return

p. 37

---

* A bequest of 1541 for the tower may relate to alterations, repairs or completion of the top.

overlaps a buttress), with a pierced parapet with cusped triangle frieze. Fine inner doorway, with four-centred arch under a square hood with ornamented spandrels. This porch may be explained by the former presence of a churchyard chapel, probably on the N side. The S porch is also Perp, bigger and plainer.

Inside, a very broad chancel arch on piers from which spring arches in four directions; the price of this bravado absence of walling is the leaning N arcade and the massive buttress added outside the N aisle. Of the S arcade, the octagonal piers and chamfered arches are C13, while the N has piers of standard Somerset Perp section (four hollows). These continue in the chancel arch. At the springing of the S chancel arch survives a little of the former narrower arch, matching the E.E. S arcade. Here one must ask why the S aisle is so broad? It contains the oldest work, and one might expect it to be smaller. Could it have been the Norman nave, with an E.E. arcade to a narrower N aisle on the site of the present nave? Or was it simply a large aisle with special status accorded by the Bishop's manor, from which a bridge entered the S chapel (extant in 1736, now marked by an upper S window)?

FITTINGS. ROOD SCREEN across aisles and nave. C15, a good piece, if not as spectacular as those of W Somerset. Two-light divisions with four-centred heads and panel tracery, three broad ogee-headed doorways, one leaf frieze and cresting (both added in 1860). Colours restored in 1750 and again in 1860, when the oldest bays were re-assembled under the chancel arch. – LECTERN. Originally a prayer-desk, probably from Chew Court, bearing the arms of Bishop Cornish who was vicar here 1505–13. – PULPIT. Oak, 1924, with apostles, and birds etc. among intricate undercut knotwork. – FONT. Norman. A circular lead-lined bowl with broad concave flutes like petals, and more at the base, fat and convex. – S DOOR, C15 with good wrought-iron hinges and seven scrolled straps. – MONUMENTS. Sir John St Loe †1447, perhaps with his second wife Agnes, on a tomb-chest with quatrefoils containing shields and small niches for statuettes between. The effigies of good quality. – Mysterious effigy called without reason Sir John de Hauteville. The knight in C14 armour reclines with one elbow on his shield. The pose resembles that of figures of Jesse in representations of the Jesse Tree, but is extremely rare in C14 effigies and exists in England nowhere in so pronounced a way before the late C16. The knight's legs are crossed, again more emphatically than the C14 did. Moreover, his foot rests on a lion, which means that owing to the distortion of the whole attitude the lion cannot lie on the tomb lid but must stand upright in a couchant attitude. These incongruities suggest that the monument must be a self-conscious imitation, probably of c. 1550–1650 (cf. those at Brading, Isle of Wight, believed to be mid-C17). In 1834 it was on a window ledge in the S chapel, but the flat back of the lion implies its original position was constrained. The present fanciful arched and cusped canopy is no doubt by *Norton*, c. 1860. – Edward Baber †1578, and Catharine †1601; the monument apparently later, but before 1643. Recumbent effigies on a tomb-chest with rather doughy three-dimensional cartouches. Upper a canopy without columns and with a shallow coffered arch, in which are cherubs' heads and more cartouche-work. Topped by an armorial crest in a pedimented frame, and figures of Justice and Fortitude; a third recently stolen. – Sarah Lyde †1662, oval frame still with strapwork. – Richard Jones †1692. Well-carved marble with pediment and flattened volutes with palms; up-to-the-minute and not by a local mason. – Samuel Collins †1713. Scrolly Baroque tablet with weeping putti and a trophy with pistols. – Elizabeth Jones †1714 (cf. the work of *J. Harvey* or *James Paty the Elder*). – Hodges Strachey †1746, pedimented tablet in coloured marbles, style of *T. Paty*. Sir Henry Strachey †1810. Woman at a sarcophagus, signed *J. Bacon Jun.*, 1816. – Lytton Strachey, writer, †1932; modest plaque. – STAINED GLASS. E window †1853, probably by *J. H. Powell*. S chapel E, *G. P. Hutchinson* (*Powell & Sons*), 1933. N chapel, 1934, *Eleanor Fortescue-Brickdale*, insipid.

In the churchyard, a splendid late medieval CROSS, on an octagonal plinth of seven steps with panelled risers.

BAPTIST CHAPEL, Tunbridge Street. By *Henry Lee* of Clifton, 1867. Plain and round-arched, except the incongruously fancy Gothic W doorway. Schoolrooms behind of 1887.

HOPE CHAPEL (former), Battle Lane. By *W. H. Clark*, 1874, for Free Methodists. Round-arched again.

OLD SCHOOLROOM, at the S entrance to the churchyard. An impressively large late medieval church house (99 ft by 23 ft, 30.5 by 7 metres), used for church ales, celebrations and the administration of charity. External stairs to two doors on the N side, the main entrance in the W gable-end. Original doorway with four-centred head and ogee gable, under a two-light window with cusped ogee heads. Flanked by simpler two-light windows, two on each floor. A panel above the door has the St Loe arms, and the date 1510 (now unreadable). In the gable a little figure, probably St Michael slaying the dragon. Roof eleven bays long, of arched-braced collar-beams and wind-braces, with a break in construction after the fifth bay from the E. The ground floor was later divided for use as a poorhouse and lock-up. Repaired 1972–3 for use as a village hall. To the N, MILLENNIUM HALL. By *John Casselden*, 2000. A courteous neighbour, of Dolomitic Conglomerate and glass with twin pyramid roofs.

CHEW COURT, immediately SE of the church. The manor house belonged to the Bishops of Bath and Wells in the C14, then from 1592 to the Baber family, local merchants made good, who probably made major alterations *c.* 1600. An L-shape; five-window N range, shorter E range. At its S end, a C14 gatehouse with four-centred archways. The room above has C17 mullioned windows and a late medieval arch-braced roof with wind-braces. To l. and r. of the outer entrance polygonal turrets, and immediately r. in the end wall of the E range, a small Perp window of two ogee lights, C14 or C15. Entry into the N range is by an arched doorway with Doric pilasters and strapwork frieze, c. 1600. Perhaps of the same date the five flanking ground-floor windows; the rest largely early C19 Neo-Tudor. Inside to the l. and r. rooms with fine bolection-moulded stone fireplaces, early C18. Of the w range only the entrance wall survives, with a small doorway.

CHEW MANOR, Battle Lane, NW. What meets the eye is all Victorian, mostly by *John Norton*, 1864, but according to dates inscribed also 1848. Norton was lavish in his display of Gothic fancies. Asymmetrical E and S fronts, with a square angle tower. Porch with two-storey oriel over, tall tourelle at the NE corner, and so on. The interiors are harder to date, because the C19 has brought in such a wealth of C16 and C17 woodwork, in large and small pieces and in most rooms. It is not recorded how much belonged to the house. The staircase seems original, however, of the early C17, with square well and flat open-work balusters. There is a fireplace with the right initials and the date 1615. Another fireplace is dated 1656, but the forms look earlier. The symmetrical outbuildings to the E look late C17 (circular keyed-in upper windows). Amongst the brought-in pieces, two South German reliefs from an altar of the early C16, martyrdoms of St Catherine and St Sebastian. Also a pretty series of panels in the Floris style (and in a ceiling!), probably Flemish, with a repeating date 1562.

VILLAGE. A little to the w of the church on High Street, Harford Square is a nicely undisciplined triangular space, dominated by HARFORD HOUSE of 1817. White-pointed sandstone, five very broad bays, the centre bay isolated by sections of blank wall. Rear addition with a bow, c. 1900. On HIGH STREET, w, the best of the C18 mercantile villas. ACACIA HOUSE (s side) is perhaps c. 1760–80, five bays with a pedimented centre broken forward. Slightly later and lower wings. Opposite, MYRTLE HOUSE, three tall storeys and three bays, another Late Georgian refronting. One fireplace possibly C15 or C16. Then THE BEECHES, built 1762 for Ephraim Chancellor; the most imposing of these villas, although not the biggest. Three bays with pedimented centre. Doorcase of a type that appears in Bristol c. 1790; open pediment on curved brackets, inner moulded arch around the fanlight. Low Venetian-windowed wings, possibly also c. 1790. It faces THE HOLLIES, with ground-floor bays and a Neoclassical grand porch. Further w, humbler cottages (N side), Nos. 35–43, early C19 with pretty trellis porches. On the s side, No. 24, THE RECTORY, a long range in two sections, dated 1672.

Battle Lane drops N to Spratts Bridge and Winford Brook. A little NE, THE ROOKERY, large early C19; its pretty bay-ended LODGE facing the bridge has Gothic cast-iron window frames and Tudorbethan chimneys. At the w end of the village is HIGHFIELD HOUSE, of c. 1830–40, with bracketed eaves, low-pitched roofs, and veranda.

E of Harford Square is Silver Street, following the Winford Brook. CHURCH HOUSE has a broad C18 or early C19 front, the short wings perhaps later; poor sham-Georgian alterations to the Ionic doorcase. Further E is the CHURCH HALL, dated 1923, vaguely Arts and Crafts, in rock-faced stone. Crossing Winford Brook, at the end of Butham Lane ELM FARM, perhaps C16 or C17. Smart C15 or early C16 ashlar doorcase with four-centred arch, cusped spandrels and hoodmould, apparently imported from Chew Court.

Tunbridge Road leads s from the centre. s w of the Baptist chapel, the OLD MILL, the survivor of at least four in Chew Magna. Three storeys, C19 breast-shot water wheel. Converted to an ecology centre, 2006–7. SE, TUN BRIDGE is a triple-arched late C15 bridge crossing the River Chew. Dumpers Lane leads w to DUMPERS HOUSE, a large farmhouse of medieval origin. Small two-arched bridge beyond, perhaps also medieval. Back on Tunbridge Road, s, TUNBRIDGE HOUSE, recast in the early C19, with a pretty wrought-iron porch, as good as anything in Bristol. Lastly FISHER LODGE, the rear wing perhaps C17, the front, with long-and-short quoins, c. 1730. Updated c. 1820–30 with two square ashlar bays and central porch-veranda (renewed late 1970s).

5060

CHEW STOKE

In a valley of a tributary of the River Chew, with steep hills N and s.

ST ANDREW, Church Lane. A small Perp church dominated by its three-stage w tower. It has diagonal buttresses, panelled parapet with statue niches in the centre of each side, panelled stair-turret with quatrefoil frieze and a big spirelet. Two-light windows and tall two-light bell-openings with Somerset tracery. The tower was restored in 1900. Aisles of orangey Butcombe sandstone, with chapels the full length of the chancel. Much detail added in *John Norton*'s restoration, 1862–3. He added a N aisle and chapel, and rebuilt the walls and nave arcades. Embattled s aisle and chapel. In the aisle, three-light arch-headed Perp windows, one with a transom. In the chapel a transomed four-light s window with four-centred head in square frame. The s porch has 1860s buttresses, outer arch, and parapet. The s chapel E window is C15, with little heads in the label stops; the chancel E window is Norton's, Dec and of three lights. N aisle with simple two-light Perp windows between buttresses. The interior swarms with Victorian demi-angels, 156 in all, giving the feeling that one is being constantly watched. They appear in bosses and corbels, in fours as the capitals to the moulded nave N piers, and wingtip-to-wingtip as a big frieze beneath the nave roof. The tower has a good Perp vault with a big circular bell-hole. Some of its details are Victorian additions. C15 tower arch with two broad wave mouldings. The extent of medieval fabric has been debated: C14 PISCINA, s chapel; the arch from s chapel to chancel seems

C15; and Norton would hardly have duplicated the simple chamfered arches in the S nave wall unless he was reusing old stone. To confuse matters, all is whitewashed. – FITTINGS. Mostly *Norton*'s. – Small REREDOS with green marble shafts. – Horrendous LECTERN, an orange marble column with a wooden eagle perched on a lump of quartz crystal. – S porch, STATUE of a female figure with an anchor, possibly C17. – STAINED GLASS. Similar E and W windows, the W dated 1863. Both perhaps by *O'Connor*. S aisle second from E, after 1945, perhaps by *Bell & Son*.

Churchyard. S of the tower, an early medieval square FONT, broken. Near the W gate a CROSS-SHAFT on a two-stepped square base, perhaps C14. Moved here 1953 from the flooded hamlet of Moreton (*see* below). – Built into the N churchyard wall, either side of a doorway, two fragments of an early C10 CROSS-SHAFT, one with intertwined ribbon animals, the other with plant ornament.

METHODIST CHAPEL, Chapel Lane. Begun 1815–16. This part has a hipped roof and two round-arched windows in the W wall. Oddly extended NE into an L-shape, 1899, by *J. Wood* (probably of Foster & Wood) half the old chapel becoming a classroom. Eaves brackets, half-timbering, Venetian window. Hall (W) by *Hicks Associates*, c. 2001–2.

PRIMARY SCHOOL, School Lane. By *S. B. Gabriel*, 1857. The usual grey stone Gothic. Extended 1926 and 1970.

Pilgrim's Way and Bristol Road form a loop in the village centre. School Lane branches SW, with a picturesque and very narrow two-arched BRIDGE alongside to the N, perhaps C17 or C18. Beyond the Primary School is YEW TREE FARM, with a cottagey C18 front. The roof has three cruck-trusses with unusually thin blades, cambered collars and evidence of smoke-blackening; felling date 1386. SW again is WALLIS FARM, nicely unmodernized, dated 1782. Do the steep roof pitch and through-passage plan indicate an earlier core?

Back to the bridge, and to the N along Pilgrim's Way (E side), the former RECTORY, 1870s; asymmetrical Gothic. Opposite, at the junction of Pilgrim's Way and Church Lane is the OLD RECTORY, built by Sir John Barry, rector 1524–46. The remarkably ornate front range is C16. A kitchen range was added at the NE in the C17, the L-shape filled in c. 1723, and parts were unified with Gothicizing additions c. 1829–39. On the S façade are four panels with arms in shields, including St Loe, Barry's patron, and an inscription with the date, 1529 (altered to 1629). Originally there were upper and lower halls at the W, and service rooms at the E end, possibly with a separate room above (cf. Congresbury vicarage, p. 479). This was lit by the large transomed two-light window in the E gable. The screens passage was removed in the 1830s. The ground-floor hall windows and that at the lower r. (two arched lights) appear original. C16 roof with two tiers of wind-braces.* W, beyond the church is CHURCH FARM, perhaps late C16 or early C17, an impressively long stone front with low irregular casements. Extended r. in the later C17.

OBELISK, Breach Hill Lane, c. ⅘ m. SW. Mid-C19, ashlar with rusticated base. A ventilation shaft for a water pipeline.

ROOKERY FARM, c. 350 yds further SW, 1720 (dated rainwater head). Impressive nine-bay front of two storeys. Projecting banded centre bay with pediment.

(PAGAN'S HILL ROMAN TEMPLE, 1 m. N of Chew Stoke. The complex included an octagonal building 50 ft (15 metres) across, and a well 30 ft (9 metres) deep. Built in the late C3/early C4 on a site periodically used from the Iron Age to the C7.)

CHEW VALLEY LAKE, c. ½ m. SE via Whalley Court Road. A reservoir for Bristol, mooted in 1933–4, built 1950–6 (A. E. Farr & Co., engineers). The outlet of the River Chew is marked by a faintly C17 style octagonal tower on the dam at the N.[*]

CHEWTON MENDIP

34, p. 28

ST MARY MAGDALENE, Church Lane. Chiefly known for its splendid tower, one of the highest parish towers in Somerset (126 ft, 38.5 metres). It is of Doulting Stone, whereas the church is of Lias. Its closest relative is Batcombe (Somerset South and West), also very late. It has three stages, the bell-openings repeated blank on the stage below, cf. Mells and Leigh-on-Mendip. The crown, however, is of the Glouces-ter–Dundry–St John's Glastonbury kind. The tower was unfinished, or at least the debt uncleared, as late as 1541, according to a will. Leland, a year or two later, calls it a 'goodly new high tourrid steeple'. The usual Mendip-pattern angle buttresses are here set forward from the corners of the tower, with diagonal bracing in the three angles. On them one set of pinnacles in relief. At the belfry stage, however, the buttresses become simply angle buttresses, coupled at each angle with a pair of diagonally set pinnacles ending just below the parapet. The crown has pierced arcading, a centre pinnacle on each side, and main pinnacles which are veritable square turrets, with slim detached pinnacles flying up the outer angles. Low W doorway with four-centred head, four-light W window (with two two-light sub-arches), statue of Christ above in a niche and six flying angels in relief to the l. and r. (cf. Batcombe, S. Som-

[*] Losses in the construction of the lake included CHEW TOWER, a small folly of c. 1770, and the hamlet of MORETON, near Moreton Point on the W side of the lake. Excavations before the reservoir's construction revealed evidence for continuous occupation from Early Bronze Age to medieval times. C1 Roman development of a native farm at Chew Park was succeeded by a small ROMAN VILLA. Slight evidence of a small group of medieval buildings, probably HOLY CROSS NUNNERY. Stratford Mill was moved in 1954 to Blaise Castle House Museum, Bristol (p. 399).

erset). The next stage has two tall blank transomed windows of three lights, with flanking diagonal shafts. Then the belfry stage, of the same arrangement but having open lights with Somerset tracery. The tower arch has ogee mouldings and one order of shafts, and there is a fan-vault under the tower, probably inserted after construction.

There are several Norman survivals. Especially interesting, to the l. of the chancel arch, a tall niche with slim shafts and beaded scallop capitals, and to the r. one identical column left when the chancel arch was widened unevenly in the C13. Pevsner suggested they housed side altars, but a tripartite chancel arch (cf. the daughter church of Ston Easton) is plausible too. Norman also the segmental N doorway of Bath stone with two orders of columns, decorated scallop capitals and a round outer arch with chevron decoration. Above the S doorway is a fragment of a Norman corbel table, perhaps *ex situ* as the doorway and aisle wall are in their present form post-Norman. The next building phase was the chancel and its S chapel, *c.* 1200–50. In the chancel a pair of trefoil-headed PISCINAS. The two-bay arcade to the chapel has quatrefoil piers with waterholding bases, stiff-leaf capitals and double-chamfered arches. Then follows the E portion of the nave arcade, perhaps late C13: quatrefoil piers on square bases; thin shafts in the four diagonals; fine moulded capitals; double-chamfered arches. The N chancel windows have spheric triangles in the tracery, *c.* 1280–1300. In the C14 the nave arcade was extended to the W, with octagonal piers. One Dec S aisle window, and one in the N wall of the nave. Other windows Perp. Late C15 or early C16, a third PISCINA and big three-seat SEDILIA sitting screen-like in the eastern arch between chancel and S chapel. The church suffered a heavy-handed C13-style restoration by *C. E. Giles & W. Robinson*, 1865. Theirs the big vestry and porch on the S side, pulpit and E window, with plate and bar tracery and trefoiled rere-arch. Tower restored by *Sedding*, 1889–90.

FITTINGS. ALTAR RAIL, S chapel. Mid-C17, fat turned balusters. – ORGAN raised over the S aisle and chapel on one column. Simple oak case, 1993. – E wall. Majolica tiles by *Maw & Co.*, 1865. – STAINED GLASS. Chancel N. Some good figures in yellow stain, *c.* 1450s (e.g. St Margaret, lower r.), arranged 1973. Much C19 glass, sadly darkening the church. E window *c.* 1865, nicely drawn, by *Robert Bayne* (*Heaton, Butler & Bayne*). The rest nearly all theirs, 1880 and later. Two nave S by *Bell & Son*, 1882. – MONUMENTS. Probably Sir Henry Fitzroger †*c.* 1350, and wife, †1388. Tomb-chest with bold quatrefoils in panels. Late C14, or erected in the mid C15 by their great-grandson, Sir William Bonville. – Frances, Lady Waldegrave, †1879, with profile portrait, by *Boehm*. – CROSS in the churchyard. Medieval head reinstated 1870, with four canopied figures; badly preserved.

MANOR FARM, Bathway. Reputedly for the Waldegraves' steward, *c.* 1700. Five bays, two storeys, hipped roof, cross-windows, finely coursed Lias stone. Further s on Bathway, PRIORY LODGE, late C18 Gothick, with a rustic tree-trunk veranda. It belonged to Chewton Priory, built shortly before 1791, demolished 1953. To the NW of its site, SAGE'S FARM, with astonishingly big interlaced Gothic windows rising chapel-like through two storeys; possibly removed from Chewton Priory *c*. 1858. E of Bathway, THE FOLLY, an irregular group of estate cottages, many dated 1785 (No. 35 with carvings of mason's tools).

CHILCOMPTON

ST JOHN, Church Lane. Isolated with only the manor house nearby, since the village migrated a little s. Two-stage w tower of the late C15. Three-light bell-openings, diagonal buttresses, battlements. Good w doorway under four-centred arch, square label stops. The rest rebuilt by *Jesse Gane*, 1839: four-bay nave and aisles, surprisingly big and high. Chancel and E chapels rebuilt again in 1897 by *F. Bligh Bond*. The E responds of the nave arcade have a second set of springers for new arches, presumably part of a design by Bond to rebuild the nave. – MONUMENT. Richard Seward †1581. Three stone shields with scallop shells etc., the remains of a canopied standing monument, destroyed 1839. – HALL to the s by *Richard Westmacott*, 1989–92, with a glazed link to the church.

ST ALDHELM (R.C.), Bowden Hill. A hall-like mission church of Downside Abbey, by *Francis Pollen*, 1976. – MURAL of St Christopher, by *Maurice Perceval*.

MANOR FARM. N of the church. L-plan, with mullioned windows under hoodmoulds. Rebuilt for the Stocker family, 1612 (dated N gable), altered *c*. 1790 and later. Attached DAIRY HOUSE, with a blocked attic light perhaps *c*. 1500. Former STABLES, C18, with cross-windows and two upright oval lights. BARN dated 1611. MILL COTTAGE is dated 1596, though the fabric appears late C17 (much renewal).

Plenty of nice houses on The Street, N to S. THE HOLLIES is C18 with a Venetian window in the centre, mullions elsewhere. Then SHELL HOUSE, plain mid-Georgian (dated 1752). Symmetrical, of three bays, broken pediment to the central upper window. The large shell-hood must be *c*. 1720, presumably from an earlier building. A little further s is EAGLE HOUSE, early C19, with an eagle over the pediment of a mid-C18 style doorcase. Opposite is GAINSBOROUGH, a long mid to late C17 range with mullions, extended l. in the C18. s again at the start of Bowden Hill is REED HOUSE, mid-Georgian, three windows each side of a pedimented door. DOWNSIDE HOUSE, Wells Road, is similar, but five bays wide. The building or rebuilding of so many big houses probably resulted from expansion of the local coal industry.

BLACKER'S HILL IRON AGE HILL-FORT, 1 m. SW. A promontory camp over 200 yds (185 metres) square and covering 15
acres. Originally with a substantial double rampart, one part
of which still stands 40 ft (12 metres) above its ditch.

CHRISTON

3050

ST MARY. The chancel has herringbone masonry and long-and-
short quoins suggesting an early Norman or pre-Conquest
date. The chancel, low central tower without transepts and the
nave are each on a different alignment, possibly indicating distinct phases. The tower has a corbelled parapet, mostly C19,
but good Norman double-headed corbels at the angles. Many
signs of a Normanizing restoration by *Charles Rawlinson Wainwright Jun.* (*Wainwright & Heard*, Shepton Mallet), 1875. His
father, also an architect, owned Christon Court. Norman
rubble s porch, the weight of the barrel-vault causing the
opening to bulge into a horseshoe. Norman doorway perhaps
c. 1170. Inner order continuous around jambs and arch; a trellis
of four chevrons, two forming lozenges parallel with the wall,
the other two at right angles to it. Nook-shafts with scallop
capitals, bearing an outer arch with two rows of chevrons, one
of them in the soffit, the points meeting at the angle; hoodmould of Greek key. The arches of the tower have again one
order of colonnettes, the shafts in the w arch twisted. Scallop
capitals, lozenges of facing chevrons in the arch, Greek-key
hoodmould. But all this is of 1875, seemingly a copy in plaster
of stone arches previously there. Rib-vault beneath the tower,
the most remarkable feature of the church: the ribs are crudely
done, of depressed form, and plainly roll-moulded. They
spring quite inorganically from dragons in profile at the
corners of the vault. Chancel lights with cinquefoiled rere-
arches *c.* 1300. Side lights Perp and square-headed, renewed
by *Godfrey Gray*, 1896; also Neo-Norman the E window of
1875. Nave windows, replacing Perp square-headed lights, with
mechanical detail. Barrel-vaulted nave roof with ridge rib and
small bosses, of 1536.

FITTINGS. Oak SCREEN of 1950 behind the altar, making a
little vestry. – Neo-Norman PULPIT, 1875 by *Wainwright*. –
FONT. Square bowl, early to mid-C12, with diagonal crosses
and scallop decoration. – STAINED GLASS. Tower S, small light
with fragments of C15 Somerset glass. E window, †1878, by *Bell
& Son*. Also by *Bell*, the w window, *c.* 1880. Nave S, small light
by *William Morris & Co.* of Westminster, †1926. Nave N, by *Bell
& Son c.* 1950, doubtless the work of *Arnold Robinson*. – MON-
UMENT. John Gore †1792 by *T. King*. Urn against an obelisk.

CHRISTON COURT.* Plain Late Georgian E front of five bays
with flat parapet. Underneath, partial survivals of a much

* With thanks to English Heritage, Research Department, Swindon.

larger house built for the Vaughan family in 1672 or 1674, of which much was pulled down in 1822 when the present E range was refronted. Doric porch, 1997. The C17 roof in this range takes account of something earlier at its N end. S wing with earlier C17 roof, and a bedroom with a stone fireplace. Oak overmantel dated 1672, possibly made up in 1822: still Jacobean despite the date, with caryatids and small standing figures of Justice and Peace in arches. C17 GAZEBO overlooking the road S of the house; bizarrely, it has a privy seat.

THE OLD GRANARY. Opposite the church. Mid-C19 barn, now a house. Rare surviving hypocaust system to heat the threshing floor, and embattled chimney.

CHURCHILL WITH LANGFORD

4050

ST JOHN, Church Lane. Founded c. 1170–90, largely rebuilt in the C14 and C15, restored 1879–80 by *Ewan Christian*. Lean three-stage W tower perhaps c. 1420–50, with tall tower arch of shafts and hollows (cf. Spaxton, S. Somerset, c. 1434).* Diagonal buttresses, higher panelled stair-turret. One two-light window on each face in the top stage, large W window rising into the second stage which also has a statuary niche. Parapets with the usual cusped lozenges (tower) or cusped triangle frieze (cf. Yatton, c. 1450). Tower vault star-shaped with tiercerons. The S aisle was preceded by a narrower one, from which a PISCINA survives: a cusped spheric triangle, c. 1290–1320. S arcade also probably C14: octagonal piers, double-chamfered arches. The aisle was rebuilt or widened (c. 1390 has been suggested), with ogee-light windows of c. 1450. Late C15 N aisle, evidently post-dating the tower. Arcade of standard four-hollows type. Large S-facing quatrefoil squint at the E end here.

FITTINGS. FONT. Norman, plain tub shape. Thick mouldings. – BENCHES. Perhaps C16 or C17, with ogee tops and foliage carving. – PAINTING. Last Supper by *John Simmons*, 1767, after a Flemish work. – STAINED GLASS. E window, *Clayton & Bell*, 1880. N aisle E, 1860 by *Joseph Bell*. N aisle, second and fourth from E with C15 fragments from Wakefield parish church (now Cathedral), installed 1948. N aisle W, *Mayer & Co.*, c. 1886. S aisle E, *Warrington*, c. 1861. S aisle S: first, probably *Heaton, Butler & Bayne*, c. 1880s; third, very traditional for 1968. S aisle W, c. 1857, and tower W, c. 1864, both attributed to *John Toms* of Wellington, naïvely drawn. – MONUMENTS. Early C14 knight (cross-legged) and lady, probably Sir Roger Fitzpayne †1322, S porch. – Small brass to Ralph Jennyns †1572 and wife, S aisle floor; said to be ancestors of Sarah Duchess of Marlborough. – Sarah Latch †1644. Perhaps by a Bristol

p. 455

---

* Poyntz-Wright's suggested Churchill group of towers, c. 1360–95, must be rejected.

Here lyeth Raphe Jenyns Esquyer which Dyed the xth day of Apryll in the
yere of our lorde God M CCCCC lxxii: and was burned the xviii day of the
same month, leavyng behynd hym Jhane his wyffe: and havyng by her
viii. chyldren that ys to wyte fyve Sonnes and three Daughters

Churchill, St John, brass, Ralph Jennyns (†1572) and wife.
Rubbing, 1970

sculptor, cf. Bridges monuments, Keynsham and Rodney Stoke (qq.v.). Big hanging monument of double arches flanked by columns; top achievement with strapwork. Naïve figure of her husband reclining behind, tenderly parting the shroud to reveal her face. In the base, eleven kneeling children.

ST MARY, Stock Lane, Langford. By *Samson & Cottam*, 1899–1900. Plain lancet-style nave and apse, in Dolomitic conglomerate. Tooled flat within and handsomely offset by golden timber roofs. – Tiled chancel FLOOR. – STAINED GLASS. Six by *M. Muraire* of Evreux, France, *c.* 1900–5; pious figures, painterly style. – s of the church, matching former acetylene GAS-MAKING HOUSE; electricity was still mistrusted in 1900.

METHODIST CHAPEL, Front Street. Given by Sidney Hill. By *Foster & Wood*, 1879–80. Surprisingly rich and churchy free Perp. Elaborately pinnacled apsidal narthex by *Silcock & Reay*, 1906. Low cloister to the schoolroom, with half-timbered gables, dated 1879. Attached to its E end, a timber-arched cloister to a covered carriageway and stables (1906). Walled and railed churchyard and precincts with original gas standards, gates etc. Almost unaltered galleried interior. – STAINED GLASS. Eight windows, *c.* 1880; a rarity for a chapel. Also in the cloister and schoolroom.

Opposite, also given by Sidney Hill, the VICTORIA CLOCK TOWER, *Foster & Wood*, 1897. Robust Gothic profile. Completing the group, further w on Front Street, SIDNEY HILL COTTAGE HOMES, by *Silcock & Reay*, 1906–7. Delightful low brick-and-tile almshouses forming a courtyard open to the s, inspired by Frederick Walker's painting Harbour of Refuge, 1872. Timber loggias, entrance arch with Wrennish cupola above.

CHURCHILL COURT, s of the church. L-shaped with a square tower at the angle. Of medieval origin, seemingly rebuilt in the mid C16 by Ralph Jennyns (*see* above). Of that date the rear wing, which has C17 mullioned-and-transomed windows, and a small shell porch, *c.* 1700. The tower has diagonal buttresses, probably C16, raised by a storey in the C17. In 1877 a new front was added for J. A. Giles by his brother, the architect *C. E. Giles*, and the tower given a brick storey for a water tank, removed 1904. Fine Neo-Baroque wrought-iron GATES (*Franken & Lefèvre*, Brussels, 1899), installed 1919.

LANGFORD, E of Churchill, is split by the A38. To the s is UPPER LANGFORD (parish of Burrington). OVER LANGFORD MANOR (formerly the Old Courthouse), Bath Road, lies ½ m. E of the A38. Of *c.* 1600, perhaps partly earlier, but much pulled about. The main interest the elaborate porch dated 1611, part of a once longer wing. Attached Corinthian columns, complicated friezes, steep gable with strapwork against rustication. Re-erected at Nailsea Court in 1911, later returned. In the adjacent corner, a C17 quadrant-shaped stair-turret. To the NE, LANGFORD COURT. C17 core (datestone 1651), see the gabled rear with ovolo-mullioned attic lights. The entrance front *c.* 1800. Round-arched lights frame the entrance. Smaller early

CI8 side projections. To the r., a Neo-Tudor dining room, *c.* 1840–50. Longer mullioned wing of 1875, l. Handsome late CI8 gatepiers with urns at the E entrance. In the gardens (NE) a late CI8 brick orangery with arched Gothic-glazed windows.

LOWER LANGFORD, N of the A38, bears evidence of wealthy Bristolian incomers. MILFORT, *c.* 1820 with semicircular Ionic porch. NASH HOUSE is early CI7, with ovolo mullions etc. Recessed centre, filled in *c.* 1820–40. MAYSMEAD, Maysmead Lane: mid-CI7 origins, transformed *c.* 1811 to a Gothick *cottage orné* with canted two-storey porch. E wing in similar style, *c.* 1900. SOMERLEA is of *c.* 1785, three storeys of sashes with stepped voussoirs: W wing of 1874, E wing *c.* 1906–13. NW of the village, LANGFORD HOUSE, Stock Lane (now a veterinary school). Modest villa of *c.* 1831, enlarged and ambitiously recast for Sidney Hill as an asymmetrical Italianate mansion, reportedly *c.* 1877. If so, it harks back to the mid-century: white stucco, bow windows, rooftop urns, and the indispensable belvedere. Langford did not escape Hill's abundant philanthropy: prominent in the centre, the VICTORIA JUBILEE LANGFORD HOMES, probably by *Foster & Wood*, 1887. Domestic Revival with repeating gables, big brick chimneys, and deep bows at the ends.

DOLEBURY IRON AGE HILL-FORT, I m. SE, and ¼ m. E of the *p. II* A38. Roughly rectangular with rounded corners and ramparts built of stone up to 20 ft (6 metres) high in places. The enclosure measures 500 yds by 250 yds (460 by 230 metres) disturbed in later times by lead mines. This hill-fort and DINGHURST CAMP, a short distance across the valley to the W, guarded one of the main northerly routes into the western Mendips.

CLANDOWN

HOLY TRINITY. 1847–9, by *Manners & Gill*. Simple Neo-Perp. Quite sizeable, with transepts. The tower in the angle between S transept and chancel clashes with the bellcote over the E side of the crossing. – Neo-Tudor former VICARAGE to the NW, also 1847.

CLANDOWN FARM, Pow's Hill. 250 yds W. Proof of the survival of CI7 vernacular forms, though lightly Victorianized. Simple two-storey W wing dated 1721; four two-light windows. Much grander extension of 1724 for the same family, still with mullions, five bays with two big gables. What prompted this ambitious enlargement?

CLAPTON-IN-GORDANO

ST MICHAEL, Clevedon Lane (Churches Conservation Trust). The dedication is explained by the siting, alone on a bluff. S doorway with a mutilated Norman tympanum without decoration. The blocked N doorway with a single chamfer is C13. So is the chancel S doorway with its continuous roll moulding and – though later – the W tower, with big short diagonal buttresses, a W window of two lights with Y-tracery under a hoodmould with dogtooth, and lancet bell-openings. The top has a corbel table of re-set late C12 corbels. C15 parapet of cusped triangles, not pierced. The tower arch is altered, but the thin keeled shafts are presumably original. C13 work in the church must originally have been more extensive and ambitious. Proof of that is the reused stiff-leaf in the reredos (*see* below). Next in order is the most interesting part of the church, the N aisle, perhaps *c.* 1280–1320; probably a manorial chapel for the Arthur family. Only one double-chamfered arch from the nave, N window with cusped Y-tracery, W window a lancet, E window a triplet of stepped cusped lancets. Cusped PISCINA. Of the Perp style there is a deep S porch, and a N chapel, its arch from the chancel with broad foliate capitals. Its E window of *c.* 1300 is reused. Evidence of late C15 remodelling of the chancel (E window, and square-headed N and S windows); also pretty crocket-like decoration on hoodmould in the nave S wall. Restored 1861–2, 1881–2 (by *E. W. Barnes*) and *c.* 1896–7. Plaster removed *c.* 1950.

FITTINGS. REREDOS. Perp fleuron frieze with embattled cornice and, flanking the altar, two polygonal projections formerly holding candlesticks. These are supported on *ex situ* Blue Lias shafts with excellent lush stiff-leaf capitals now used upside down. C19 ogee-panelled stonework above. Some authorities believe the lower part to be a C15 composition, others C17. It was described by Rutter (1829), so not a Victorian concoction as has been claimed. – BENCHES with ends with tripartite tops, the middle part rising finger-wise. Assigned to the early C14. – FONT. C13 quatrefoil bowl. Carved faces (probably C15) on the underside. – Remarkable oak TOWER SCREEN, *c.* 1280–1300, somewhat altered. A broad outer arch with two sub-arches, and above them a cusped circle, just like the tracery of a Geometric window. Slim attached shafts with plain trumpet capitals. Moved here from Clapton Court after 1860. – MONUMENT. Edmund Wynter †1672. Very big and vigorous, with kneeling figures in profile facing each other across a prayer-desk. This hackneyed Elizabethan pattern is given curious new life by the figure of their late son (a skull in his lap) sitting frontally under the prayer-desk as if in a little house. Behind the family group, a big arched recess with Victories in the spandrels, and a corbel-like trumpeting angel among clouds in the centre. Superstructure on Corinthian columns, their plinths having two ovals with emerging lions. Broken segmental pediment with central arms amid more broken curving forms and garlands. Two allegorical figures standing on the projecting entablature blocks. The panelled base has allegorical reliefs.

CLAPTON COURT. Of the medieval house of the Arthur family only the red sandstone rubble N wall and porch-tower remain. The tower is three-storeyed and embattled, with a broad moulded entrance arch. First- and second-floor front windows of two cusped arched lights. The porch bears the arms of Arthur impaling those of Berkeley, commemorating a mid-C15 marriage. To its r., a stair-turret rises in the corner from first floor to roof; next to it, high up a small C15 window. Then the broad chimney-breast of the former hall. The rest of the hall and its solar were demolished early, for the room built behind the chimney-breast had a mullioned window, blocked in the C17 by the addition of a rear kitchen. To the l. of the porch, a C15 straight-headed window with two cusped ogee lights; similar blind panels below a transom. Below that, another window with plain round-headed lights, perhaps late C16; the wing behind rebuilt *c.* 1840–60.

CLAVERHAM

4060

A spreading village without a medieval church.

ST BARNABAS, Jasmine Lane. 1877–9. A small lancet-style school-chapel.

FRIENDS' MEETING HOUSE, Meeting House Lane, ½ m. w of Brockley church. Dated 1729. Handsome three-bay centre at right angles to the road, with two arched windows and arched doorway. Square sundial with flaming finial rising above the eaves. Slightly projecting wings, originally with two almshouses in each. Inside, C18 gallery fronts at both sides, those on the w with hinged shutters above, added on conversion for the women's business meetings. The gallery spaces and staircases have been absorbed into the wings, now residential.

Three GENTRY HOUSES in the village. COURT DE WYCK, Bishop's Road, was a medieval manor house, ruinous and mostly cleared for a new house (now offices), *c.* 1819, for a Nailsea tanner. Plain, symmetrical Regency, with broad eaves; Ionic porch with twisted columns, perhaps reused. Behind, NW, a plain stone outbuilding, the remnant of a C14 private chapel which formed the NW corner of the old house. External steps, some blocked medieval openings. CLAVERHAM COURT, Lower Claverham, was the site of the other manor. S-facing main range of the C15, later developed to an H-plan with C17 w wing and late C18 E wing. Now inside, a two-light stone window with cinquefoil cusped lights, C15 or C16. w of the house, late medieval BARN and C17 STABLES. At Streamcross is CLAVERHAM HOUSE (rainwater head dated 1744). Five bays, two storeys, even quoins, parapet ramped at the angles with ball finials. C19 porch with Ionic pilasters and fancy capitals, flanked by ground-floor bays of *c.* 1860. At the l. a low wing of similar date.

Numerous good FARMS widely scattered in lanes to the N and NE. HOME FARM originated as a C15 open-hall house, as did ROSE FARM, Streamcross. GROVE FARM, Brockley Way, is perhaps *c.* 1580–1620, on an H-plan with hall to the r. of the cross-passage. Porch with flattened arch, early C17.

CLAVERTON

7060

For Claverton Down and the University of Bath, *see* pp. 195–200.

ST MARY. Squat plain w tower with saddleback roof behind a solid parapet, probably C13 – see the plain tower arch. The nave, N aisle and chancel were zealously reworked by *Manners & Gill*, 1858; earnest E.E. style. Vestry, 1891, by *J. S. Alder*. Medieval N chapel and N transept, the latter restored, 1904. – FITTINGS. Coloured marble FONT, 1866. Square bowl with reliefs. – STAINED GLASS. N transept N; assorted Continental pieces, e.g. Flemish panel with Tobias, St Peter, etc. The Taking of Christ, seemingly a fine early C14 German panel. Woodforde suggests it may be a good C19 copy. Nave s, armorials, two dated 1558. N transept w, 1891; copying a *Preedy* design of 1875. Arts and Crafts E window, *Paul Woodroffe*, 1904, also one in the N chapel. Chancel s, charming glass by *Alice Erskine*, †1921. Nave N, *Herbert Alexander*, 1907. w window, *Herbert Bryans*, †1916. Abstract single light by *Mark Angus*, 1983. – MONUMENT. William Bassett †1613 and wife. Two frontal three-quarter figures in niches chamfered at the top. Crowned by shields in odd eared panels topped by crests. – MAUSOLEUM of Ralph Allen †1764. In the churchyard. A square structure with three open arches on each side, crowned by a big pyramid. Within, a plain chest tomb. The architect was *Richard Jones*, the mason, *Robert Parsons*.

NE of the church stood the MANOR HOUSE, begun *c.* 1580, demolished 1823 in favour of a new house directly w (*see* below). MANOR COTTAGE (remodelled in the C19) may represent its service wing. Otherwise, all that survives is the spectacular TERRACES of 1628 leading down to the side road through the village. The lower two are walled with pierced balustrades; grand axial staircase fanning down to the lowest level. Gatepiers crowned by openwork obelisks. MANOR FARM adjoins on the N; late C17, windows mullioned to the s, early C19 Gothic to the N. To the N, a C15 BARN with hammerbeam roof, rare in Somerset; now a house.

CLAVERTON MANOR, The Avenue. By *Jeffry Wyatt* (later Wyatville), 1819–20, for John Vivian; now the AMERICAN MUSEUM IN BRITAIN. A fine and elegant Palladian villa, rather old-fashioned except that the *piano nobile* has been abandoned and the main rooms are on the ground floor. The E front has two segmental bows and between them two giant engaged Ionic columns above an elegant tripartite porch. A large screen wall was soon after added to its N, concealing an art gallery, and another to the S. The E front has two identical Ionic columns *in antis*. The S front is more conventional, five bays with a three-bay pediment on Ionic pilasters. Inside, a large stair-hall rising to a circular lantern and a frieze of bucrania and swags. Elegant cantilevered staircase with cast-iron balustrading of palmettes and anthemia, to the first floor only. S of the house is a pedimented COACHHOUSE; on the SE side a semicircular concave STABLE BLOCK.

BASSETT HOUSE, I m. S on the Warminster Road. 1836, probably by *H. E. Goodridge*. Italianate villa with symmetrical front. Originally a hotel for the Dundas Aqueduct nearby (*see* Wiltshire).

CLEEVE

HOLY TRINITY. 1838–40 by *G. P. Manners*. Neo-Norman, with nave, transepts, chancel, and crossing tower. The exterior is somewhat bald and the detail mechanical, but heavy plaster rib-vaulting throughout gives the interior more impact. The chancel is divided from the rest by three arches on two columns, a surprising idea in 1840, borne out as an Early Saxon habit by evidence found much later. Originally the narrow side arches had semicircular balustraded projections like balconies, for reading desks. Organ chamber, re-seating and general restoration by *C. H. Samson* of Taunton, 1888. – Standard Late Victorian STAINED GLASS.

WESTHANGER, S of the church. Handsome Neoclassical former vicarage, *c.* 1820. W front with recessed entrance behind a two-storey colonnade of paired Roman Doric columns with triglyph entablature – a nice somehow Italian effect. Big semicircular bow in the S return. The first owner went bankrupt and the bay to its E was completed only in 1851.

CLEEVE COURT, Old Bristol Road. Built for the Rev. T. S. Biddulph, *c.* 1820. A big Neo-Tudor house. Later C19 extensions. The chief interest is the main entrance, a late C15 doorcase from Court de Wyck (*see* Claverham): round-headed opening, fleurons in the jambs, elaborate ogee gable with crocketing, very big finial, flanking pinnacles. Door with ogee interlaced head. Adjacent, canopied Perp piscina, finely decorated. (Windows and other features within also from Court de Wyck.)

Former SCHOOL, Plunder Street. Plain Neo-Tudor, *c.* 1830s. Porches at each end. Adjacent C16 cottage, adapted as schoolmaster's house, 1836. Two small IRON AGE EARTHWORKS on Rodyate Hill, ½ m. SE, called Cleeve Toot and Cleeve Hill. They may have been associated with the hill-fort at Cadbury-Congresbury, I m. W (*see* Congresbury).

CLEVEDON

One of the most charming West Country seaside resorts, with much early C19 character. The medieval village lay inland at the foot of a ridge. In 1821 the Eltons of Clevedon Court initiated development of superior villas and lodging houses to the NW, on their land facing the Bristol Channel. Their estate manager *William Hollyman* developed many building plots, which were bought or rented for the summer by Bristol merchants, prompted by the mild climate and pure air. Hill Road, Wellington Terrace and The Beach show the speed of expansion after *c.* 1825. Railways arrived at Yatton in 1841 and Clevedon in 1847. Further growth took place from *c.* 1860 below Hill Road towards The Beach, with big Italianate or Gothic villas, comparable in concentration and effect with those of North Oxford. The philanthropic Eltons were the chief Victorian benefactors. Sir Edmund Elton's *Eltonware* ceramics (*c.* 1885–1920) can be seen throughout. The old village acquired the character of a small town, distinct in location and atmosphere. Despite C20 suburban expansion and some unwelcome redevelopment in the centre, Regency and Victorian Clevedon survives remarkably intact.

The suburb of Walton St Mary is included at the end of the entry.

RELIGIOUS BUILDINGS

ALL SAINTS, All Saints' Lane, East Clevedon. A low, countrified church built by Sir Arthur and Dame Rhoda Elton. *C. E. Giles's* cruciform plan of 1859–60 is obscured by early C20 enlargements. Rich furnishings, especially by *Ninian Comper*, compensate for a 'poor design' (Pevsner). Short crossing tower with stumpy, slate-hung broach spire. Lean-to aisles with simple plate tracery: elaborate Dec tracery in the S transept and chancel. On the E wall, a CRUCIFIXION designed by *Sir Edmund Elton*, cast by *Singer & Sons*, 1906. Hidden N of the chancel, three ceramic TONDOS after della Robbia, white figures on azure of the Virgin and Child and angels with fruity frames. W porch, extended 1924. Clerestoried nave of five bays with octagonal piers on clumsy bases. Crossing arranged as a choir, then a long chancel. Enlargements began with the small Lady Chapel E of the S transept, 1901, then two vestries,

1910–12, the chapel off the N transept, 1912, and the lengthening of the chancel, 1915. Over the S transept a music gallery of *c.* 1912. Baptistery (N aisle, W end) added 1913. S porch of 1922. Enlargements after 1910 are by *E. H. Heazell.*

FITTINGS. Oak and mahogany REREDOS by *Comper*, 1923, carved by *H. R. Gough* with alabaster figures of the Virgin and saints, in a gilded Perp frame. SEDILIA with carved diaper work, 1860. – W of the crossing, ROOD SCREEN by *Comper* designed 1917, of black oak with vaulted canopy. Open iron screen set in the lights. A gilded Calvary group above. – Lady Chapel. Big Perp niche with STATUE of the Virgin and Child, *Comper*, 1948. – BAPTISTERY mostly lined with marble, an *Eltonware* FRIEZE on its W wall (probably 1913), and FONT on five short columns, probably by *Giles*. Unusually the baptistery has its own altar, with stone FRONTAL adapted from *Giles*'s reredos of 1860. – STAINED GLASS. E window, *Kempe*, 1902. Three chancel windows by *Comper*, 1917. N transept N, *Comper*'s first Jesse window, 1924; E, a wheel window by *Hunt* of Clifton, 1913. S transept: N, *J. B. Capronnier* of Brussels, 1872; S, *Kempe*, 1903. S aisle, E to W: *F. C. Eden*, 1927; *Clayton & Bell, c.* 1861; *Wailes, c.* 1860; *Capronnier*, 1874; *Clayton & Bell, c.* 1860. S aisle W, *Comper*, 1923. Nave W, wheel window by *Comper*, 1920. N aisle W, *Comper*, 1923. Baptistery, two by *Comper*, 1918. N aisle, E to W: *Comper*, 1923; probably *Lavers, Barraud & Westlake, c.* 1870; *Clayton & Bell*, 1880 or later.

CHRIST CHURCH, Highdale Road. 1838–9, by *Rickman & Hussey.** Built for the expanding town as an alternative to the inconveniently distant St Andrew; subscriptions included over £1,800 from the antiquary G. W. Braikenridge. Early C14 Dec style, of local limestone ashlar, and unusually solid-looking for its date because of the deep buttresses to support the roof structure. Tall SW tower, remodelled by *Manners & Gill* in the late 1850s with new parapet and crocketed pinnacles, belfry lights with Somerset tracery, angel gargoyles and ballflower cornice. Other rich details typical of Hussey's influence on the firm by the 1830s, e.g. the varying Flamboyant tracery in the nave. W porch, the main entrance with the tower base as a vestibule. N porch, 1860s. The interior is plainer, as often with Rickman's churches. Big six-bay nave laid out like a chapel with no central approach to the short chancel. Deep W gallery on slim cast-iron columns. Unusual wind-braced roof on five broad stone diaphragm arches sprung from corbels. SE of the chancel is a CHURCH ROOM, 1920–1, enlarged by *Beech & Tyldesley*, 1969–70, in an L-shape extending E then N. – FITTINGS. Two ORGAN CASES of 1964 oddly placed flanking the chancel arch, hiding two rose windows which appear to have old stained glass. – PULPIT, Gothic, 1889. – Small ogee-panelled FONT by *Rickman*. – In the tower, a rare CHILDRENS' GALLERY by *Rickman*, with original benches. – STAINED GLASS. E window with much medieval and Renaissance

* Contributions from Megan Aldrich.

Continental glass given by Braikenridge. Especially finely painted French mid-C13 king from a Tree of Jesse, centre, and a Flemish C14 panel with the Coronation of the Virgin, l.

ST ANDREW, Old Church Road, well to the W of the town, on a hillside overlooking the sea. Late Norman with freestone of yellow Triassic limestone. The Augustinian Canons of Bristol controlled the church 1257–91. Restored by *W. D. Caröe* 1904–8. Low crossing tower with corbel table; upper stage with small arched lights, perhaps C17. Norman N transept and chancel, the latter with a sheila-na-gig, S side. The S aisle was added and the adjoining transept much enlarged in the C14, the transept's S window a Perp insertion in a visibly larger arch. Big plain C15 S porch with a newel stair, formerly to a Palm Sunday gallery. The E crossing arch, still round-arched but bluntly pointed, anticipates the transition to Gothic. Hood-mould with beast-head stops, and one capital with a rudimentary head, the other scalloped. Crude decoration perhaps no later than *c.* 1140–50; an outer order with incised lozenges, a heavier inner order with big lozenges around the columns and arch, the lozenges cut away to reveal a roll moulding beneath. Plain N arch of similar profile. Higher S and W arches, double-chamfered and elegantly pointed. These, the enlarged nave and S transept, and a new S aisle, are probably of one campaign shortly after the break with Augustinian rule, i.e. *c.* 1295–1320. Of the NAVE, the N wall is basically Norman. Dec and Perp windows, and a tie-beam roof by *Caröe*. Rood door above the pulpit. C14 S arcade with octagonal piers and arch mouldings curving into them like little corbels on the N and S faces. On the S aisle wall, six corbel heads and a green man, evidence of the C14 roof height.

FITTINGS. By *Caröe* and of *c.* 1904–8 the STALLS with faintly Art Nouveau pierced motifs, the Perp REREDOS, made by *N. & R. Hitch*, with much blue paint and gilding, and a big panel of the Supper at Emmaus, and oak ORGAN CASES, S transept, with Perp details but rather Baroque in the upper parts. – N transept arch, gilded timber SCREEN behind choir stalls, 1934. – Two iron SANCTUARY RINGS low down, N and S of the crossing. – PULPIT, cut down from a double-decker. Early C17 woodwork. Above the stairs, four C17 Dutch panels with scenes from the Life of Christ. Similar PANELS incorporated in the dado, nave W end. – PEWS, C19 with some older Perp-traceried pew-ends. – STAINED GLASS. E window by *Powell & Sons, c.* 1890. Chancel S, first from W, *Joseph Bell & Son,* 1958. Nave N, first from E, *Powell & Sons, c.* 1896, in pale bluish-greens. Nave W, highly coloured glass of 1862. – MONUMENTS. Chancel S, Derbyshire alabaster slab with incised armoured effigy possibly of Thomas Lovell, *c.* 1415. – Chancel N, in earlier arched recess, John Ken †1593, big plain chest. – S of the chancel arch and *ex situ*, Philippa Wake †1633, aged seven. Tiny recumbent figure. – S transept, chaste marble tablet by *Tyley* of Bristol, to Arthur Hallam †1833, the subject of Tennyson's *In Memoriam*. Greek Doric quarter-columns and pediment.

ST JOHN THE EVANGELIST, Queen's Road. Established by Sir Arthur Hallam Elton as a mission to the poor. By *William Butterfield*, 1876–8, altered 1909 by *C. G. Hare*. Not among Butterfield's best. Early Dec, of Pennant banded with Bath stone. It cost *c.* £4,000. Unbroken red-tiled roof, short transepts, and a saddleback tower-porch attached at its base to the SW corner. Narrow aisles, clerestory and, on the N side, extended vestries and N porch by *Butterfield*, 1883–4. Two-light clerestory windows with paired roundels in their heads. Nave with arcades dying into square chamfered piers without capitals. Original red and black Staffordshire tiled dado to repel 'disagreeable stains'. Butterfield's stencilling was painted out in 1904.

Very good FITTINGS. Gilded and painted timber ROOD BEAM, 1909, late Perp style, by *Hare*. It replaces Butterfield's chancel arch (his stone ROOD CROSS is now on the exterior E wall.) Calvary group erected 1918–20. – Wrought-iron CHANCEL SCREEN, and matching GATES E of the aisles, by *Hare*, made by *Singer & Sons*, 1909. – PULPIT. *Butterfield*. Walnut and oak, panelled with quatrefoil piercings. – REREDOS. Part of Butterfield's original scheme, red Devonshire marble and stencilling. Fine copper ALTAR FRONTAL, 1911, by *Barkentin & Krall*. – S transept LADY CHAPEL fitted up by *Hare*, with oak REREDOS, and ALTAR RAIL with lily panels. – STAINED GLASS. Much by *Heaton, Butler & Bayne*, 1878, well drawn and richly coloured. S transept S after Comper, *c.* 1930, with finely modelled figures against a pale ground. Clerestory by *Lavers & Westlake*, except N side, first from E (1912), and S side second and third from E (1916), by *Kempe & Co.*

N of the church, No. 1 St John's Road, the VICARAGE, of grey limestone, pleasing and simple.

ST PETER, Alexandra Road. (Now shared with the United Reformed Church.) By *R. J. Beswick & Son*, Swindon, 1959–60. Dominant steep roof, low stone walls with rows of square windows. Canted W wall of glass blocks between mullions, stepped up into a steep gable. Copper-clad flèche. Church rooms in the basement. Frame of concrete wishbone-arches, open to the roof. Narrower chancel beyond an elegantly steep arch. – FONT, *c.* 1966, a flared hexagon. – Painted COVER, a dramatic geometric abstraction of a Gothic spire. – STAINED GLASS. *Wippell & Co.*, 1966.

IMMACULATE CONCEPTION (R.C.), Marine Hill, 1886–7, by the *Rev. A. J. C. Scoles*. Bald E.E. lancet style. Big and barn-like.

METHODIST CHURCH (former), Lower Linden Road. By *Herbert Jones*, 1882–3. Geometric Dec, on a steep slope with basement Sunday Schools, etc. Long arcaded porch forming an unusual subsidiary entrance.

CONGREGATIONAL CHURCH (former), Hill Road. 1855–6, by *Foster & Wood*. Geometric Dec, with short S transept and a sharp spirelet above an open lantern-stage. Converted to flats *c.* 1990.

PUBLIC BUILDINGS

POST OFFICE, Albert Road. Neo-Georgian, 1938. Channelled Bath stone below, red brick above. Three central windows with scrolled brackets and heavy pediments.

MARKET HALL (former), Alexandra Road. 1869, by *Hans Price*. Rectangular, with two slated pyramidal roofs and small intervening clerestory giving a pagoda-like profile. On the upper roof a louvred lantern below a small square clock stage. The hall was open-sided with angle-braced timber posts. Converted to shops in the 1980s, when the sides were glazed and walled in; now a health club.

PUMPING STATION, Tickenham Road, by *Henry Dare Bryan*, 1901. An excellent Arts and Crafts design of coursed rubble and Bath stone, with mullioned windows, mildly Jacobean shaped gables, and a handsome square lantern. High chimney with a sculptural boxy projection near the top. Manager's house, dormered and with tile-hung gables.

HOLDLAND HOUSE, Old Street (formerly St Andrew's School). 1858, Gothic, of rubble stone with some brick in the dressings. The truncated tower had a spirelet with ugly lucarnes. Perhaps by *Pope & Bindon*, cf. their Bristol Assize Courts.

INFANT SCHOOL (former), Old Street. 1846, small and Tudor Gothic.

ST JOHN'S SCHOOL, Old Church Road. 1889, by *R. M. Drake* and *Henry Dare Bryan*, now the PUBLIC LIBRARY. Single storey, of red Cattybrook brick on Pennant rubble base, with big timber-framed windows. Half-timbered gables with bulls-eye windows in decorative square frames.

CLEVEDON COURT, Tickenham Road. Attached to a possibly C13 hall and tower house is an early C14 manor house reputedly built by Sir John de Clevedon. The usually quoted date of *c.* 1320 must be about right. The closest evidence is a document of 1337 referring to an old room, a new room (i.e. the present hall) and a chapel. Around 1430 the house was bought by the Wake family, who remodelled both cross-wings in the 1570s, with an ill-fated addition sitting w of the medieval w solar. In 1709 Clevedon Court was purchased by the Eltons, who remodelled parts around 1720. Alterations of *c.* 1763 in the Gothick fashion, perhaps by the *Paty*s of Bristol, were largely undone by 1860s changes and a fire in 1882, after which the Wakes' w wing was rebuilt by *C. E. Davis*. This was demolished in 1960 when the house was given to the National Trust. The original solar wing w of the hall survives, although little of its fabric is medieval.

At the r. of the s front the OLD HALL, conjecturally C13, sits at an angle between the tower house and the C14 work. Broad irregular chimney-breast, added later as shown by recent excavation. The C14 HOUSE is recognizable at once in the centre of the s front, with its buttressed porch. Between the new and old halls, the C14 service wing was rebuilt *c.* 1575, the ground-floor rooms having four-light transomed windows, the upper ones six lights and transom. Above, a little gable with star-like shoulders, a pedimented window, and up-to-date Renaissance ornament characteristic of the Wake alterations. Big transomed hall window of six depressed-arched lights, 1912, but approximating its appearance before the addition of a Gothic arched head in the 1760s. This is still visible as a relieving arch. Solidly buttressed CHAPEL projection mirroring the porch, but with diagonal rather than angle buttresses. The remarkable first-floor windows might be thought a wild Victorian invention, yet they are C14 Dec. A big, oblong S window completely filled by ogee reticulation; the similar E window is shorter because the altar stands beneath. At the NW angle is a spiral staircase corbelled out from the first floor. W of the chapel is the solar wing, 1570s windows and gable, much renewed after 1882. Quietly harmonious W FRONT by *David Nye*, 1960–1. It incorporates two windows arranged vertically in a Renaissance frame with coat of arms between, part of the 1570s work from the demolished W wing. The N FRONT has a staircase projection behind the hall over a vaulted cellar, *c.* 1720s, a depressed-arched window opening and C18 Gothick glazing. C14 N PORCH with portcullis slot, continuous chamfered moulding, 1720s door and glazed arched head.

INTERIOR. The S PORCH has an outer doorway with portcullis slot, and continuous double-chamfered inner doorway. In the SCREENS PASSAGE, chamfered-arched doorways to kitchen, buttery and pantry, their hoodmoulds connected. Higher central arch. To the l., the HALL, with early C18 doorway and plaster panelling replacing the medieval screen. Lower panels added *c.* 1960. Coved ceiling and Rococo rose of the 1760s, when the hall roof was renewed at a lower pitch. A plain Tudor-arched chimneypiece replaced a central hearth (there is a C14 smoke hole in the soffit of a Dec window in the E gable wall). The end windows, now partly blocked and hidden, sit two in each gable, one directly atop the other over lower cross-wings. The hall must have been wonderfully light. In the NW corner a big stone door frame, probably concocted *c.* 1830 by Mary Stewart, wife of the 5th baronet Elton, a friend of the antiquary Braikenridge. It consists of pieces of at least two chimneypieces of *c.* 1570–1600. Instead of a S bay window, there is below the chapel an ORIEL, a separate little room beyond a high chamfered arch. A further door leads to the room below the solar. Composite chimneypiece, the l. jamb with a deep hollow moulding, perhaps C15. Behind the Hall in the early C18 projection, a handsome STAIRCASE with turned balusters. It may have replaced a supposed medieval staircase which ran E–W up to the landing above. Here a Dec arch like those in the screens passage gives entrance to a lobby and thence to the solar, now the STATE ROOM, with C17 panelling installed *c.* 1920s. Rebuilding after the fire of 1882 revealed features of the adjacent CHAPEL, which had been panelled and used as a closet or boudoir since the C16. Ogee-headed piscina

r. of the altar, and a square-headed squint to the Hall, of two cusped lights. Stained glass in the reticulated windows by *Bell & Son*, 1883.

E of the screens passage is a triangular COURTYARD with a pump over the medieval well. The masonry puzzle here is hard to unravel. A doorway in the N wall with ogee-curved shoulders is identical to the outer vestry doorway at Wells Cathedral Lady Chapel, 1320s, so this range is, despite its Elizabethan windows, presumably coeval with the Dec manor house. Plain C13 doorway to the OLD HALL, which forms the E side of the courtyard. Converted to a kitchen perhaps when the new hall was built. A broad blocked arch, W side; why so big when facing such a small courtyard? Adjoining the hall's NE corner at a skew, a four-storey TOWER of uncertain provenance. It has just one room on each floor, internally *c.* 18 ft by 9 ft 6 in. (5.5 by 3 metres). Narrow slit windows suggest real defensive capability. Do the two represent the semi-attached hall and chamber tower of a courtyard house?* And which was built first, hall or tower? Masonry evidence is inconclusive.

Running N from the house up a steep slope is a battlemented WALL, probably medieval and connecting to a much rebuilt squat battlemented circular TOWER. Above this, a noble walled terrace with a small C18 SUMMERHOUSE, E end, facing a pretty octagonal GAZEBO of *c.* 1760. In the E gardens, a STABLE RANGE, *c.* 1720, and further E, a long BARN with some late medieval windows probably reused from a barn that sat S of the house.

PERAMBULATIONS

1. *The seafront and behind*

101 The starting point is CLEVEDON PIER, 1868–9, perhaps the most graceful of English piers, by the engineers *John Grover* and *Richard Ward*; contractor *Hamilton's Windsor Ironworks*, Liverpool. Happily unencumbered with the usual tat, it fulfils its original purpose, a landing point for Bristol Channel pleasure steamers. Eight elegantly wide arched spans, on trestles with legs of inverted V form. Constructed of wrought-iron Barlow rails of curved V-shaped section, purchased secondhand. Pier-head enlarged and realigned 1892–3 by *G. N. Abernethy*, carrying three cast-iron pavilions, the largest with a deep curving roof. In 1970 two spans of the pier collapsed during stress tests. The government consultant declared it beyond preservation, but it was saved by a determined campaign: the deck structure was restored by 1989, and the pier reopened fully in 1998. Architect *Peter Ware*; consulting engineers *Roughton & Fenton* then *Hyder Consulting*. Octagonal castellar TOLL HOUSE by *Hans Price*, 1869.

---

* On the model proposed by John Blair.

Directly N, the ROYAL PIER HOTEL, by *Hans Price*, 1869–70, partly burnt in 2003. A significant subsidiary to the pier. Rubble stone, Gothic windows with its name carved around a bay. The basement perhaps incorporates parts of the Rock House, an inn of 1822. Running S, the promenade, called THE BEACH, is virtually unchanged from the 1860s. Plots were sold in 1828. The villas are uniform and neat. The most handsome is Adelaide House, with Ionic pilasters at the angles, of 1842. Apsley House is of *c.* 1845, Brunswick House as late as 1853. Built into a wall (junction with Alexandra Road), a DRINKING FOUNTAIN by *Doulton & Co.*, 1895. Water-lily motif and green-blue glazes. At the S end, SPRAY POINT, low housing of the 1980s, blends successfully with the Regency work.

From the pier, Marine Parade leads N into Marine Hill. Along the cliff to the N WELLINGTON TERRACE, more 1820s villas and some horrible late C20 interlopers. Back to MARINE HILL, and near the Church of the Immaculate Conception (p. 465), the CONVENT, formerly the York Hotel, built 1834 by *George Fowler*, plain and lacking its stucco; a low bow-ended wing faces the sea, with big Ionic columns at the entrance. Then Nos. 2–3 semi-detached, of 1827. Niches with an anchor (l.) and mermaid (r.), added in the 1960s. Now for HILL ROAD; plot leases were taken up in 1825 by *William Hollyman* with *George Newton*, mason. No. 36 curves around the corner to Copse Road, with a fine shopfront of *c.* 1837. Pilastered and arched above, Ionic half-columns at the door. Inside, anthemion plasterwork and the mirrored fittings of an early C19 pharmacy. The N side of Hill Road was built first against a near-cliff (e.g. No. 85 Batson Cottage, *c.* 1825–30, by *Richard Gomer*). Shop extensions covered the front gardens from the mid C19, when brasher Italianate shops were built on the S side. Nos. 69–71, Eldon Villas, sit high above the road. Regency verandas, Gothic doors at the sides. At No. 45 triple-arched stone shopfront, 1865.

Terminating the shops, the former Congregational church (p. 465) with an incongruous five-storey addition. Hill Road continues SE with more comfortable villas. Opposite Christ Church, No. 1 Highdale Road, *c.* 1824–6, small, symmetrical and probably the first house on the hill. In Highdale Road, CLAREMONT (NE side), converted from two houses *c.* 1839 for the antiquary G. W. Braikenridge. Tall, Tudor Gothic, with a very big bay at the r. Now flats. Remarkable interiors, partly fitted up in the mid 1860s by the Rev. George Braikenridge using pieces from his late father's Bristol home, Broomwell House, Brislington. A panelled corridor ends at a fine door of *c.* 1823, based on a design by *A. C. Pugin* for St George's Chapel, Windsor, incorporating Flamboyant tracery, perhaps C15 Continental. Then a first-floor drawing room containing a ceiling from Broomwell House, an 1820s concoction with the arms of Bristol families. Tudor-arched trusses on figure corbels. A window to the coachhouse is framed by stone terms probably from a C17 chimneypiece. Further E, MOUNT ELTON, 1844, an early work of *S. W. Daukes* for Mary, Dowager Lady Elton. A large *cottage orné*. Three bay windows with deep ornamental frills at their eaves. The usual Tudoresque gables and chimneys.

2. East Clevedon

Scattered incidents begin at EAST CLEVEDON TRIANGLE. Trellis House and Ilex Cottage, small terraced houses by *William Hollyman*, 1827, each of three bays. Round-arched windows with interlaced glazing. A little way NW, Nos. 136–138 OLD STREET, originally an open-hall house, probably early C16, subdivided in the C17. No. 8 WALTON ROAD, The Grove, an elegant symmetrical villa of 1823–7; *Hollyman's* first development of a fashionable holiday residence, far from the sea but near Clevedon Court. To the N (W side) a war memorial in the form of a wayside CALVARY, *c.* 1920 by *Comper*. Further N, in All Saints Lane, the homely Gothic SAXBY COTTAGE, 1889, in memory of the first vicar of All Saints. N again on Walton Road, LITTLEMEAD, 1938, by *N. H. N. Darby*, a small *moderne* house for the painter, feminist and Communist Doris Hatt, and Margery Mack Smith. A reduced version of Sunway (*see* below) with D-shaped centre.

3. Town centre

THE TRIANGLE is the centre of old Clevedon, perhaps originally a village green. CLOCK TOWER, 1898, designed and paid for by *Sir Edmund Elton*, with much *Eltonware*; on the N side Father Time instead of a clock face. Sweeping concave roof. W of The Triangle in OLD CHURCH ROAD, S side, the CURZON CINEMA, 1920–2, built and probably designed by *Victor Cox*, monumental mason, incorporating a predecessor of 1912. Long symmetrical brick and stone front; shops below, big Ionic pilasters above. Broad gabled ends with arches and sunbursts. Auditorium entirely faced with decorative pressed tin panels, perhaps of a proprietary system known as Skelionite; the earliest and most complete example of its type in England. The boxes are missing. Further W, Nos. 88–90, 1892, the best survivors of Clevedon's penchant for extravagant bargeboards, dripping with icicles of turning and lacy festoons. SW towards St Andrew, TENNYSON HOUSE, Old Church Road, probably early C17, three rooms in line around a cross-passage, thatched and with two wooden ovolo-mullioned windows.

Good houses scattered throughout Clevedon. In DIAL HILL ROAD, No. 33, SUNWAY, *moderne* of 1934–5, by *N. H. N. Darby* of *Leete & Darby* for Victor Cox. Three rooms wide with a central D-projection, flat roofs. Sensitive additions by *Michael Axford Architects*, *c.* 1997. On the highest point in the town, ST EDITH'S, Dial Hill Road, 1874, originally a private school, now flats. Imposingly Gothic and ugly, with numerous projections and a high hexagonal entrance tower. In ELTON ROAD, villas of *c.* 1860–80, debased Italianate. Towards the seafront and a little earlier, the NORFOLK HOUSE, *c.* 1850, more Grecian though with a Victorian sense of mass and solidity. Further S, FRANKFORT HALL, Elton Road, *c.* 1850, by *Foster & Wood*, for Conrad Finzel, a Bristol sugar refiner. Lavish and overbearing Jacobethan, with semicircular bays. Now offices.

WALTON ST MARY

Formerly in the parish of Walton-in-Gordano (q.v.).

ST MARY, Castle Road. Of the medieval church by the late C18 only the tower base remained. But until 1838 it was the parish church of Walton-in-Gordano. Rebuilt 1869–70 by *John Norton* to serve the nearby rash of cliff-top villas. Nave on the old foundations, with wide N aisle, chancel and vestries, all Perp. To the tower base Norton added two upper stages, bell-openings with Somerset tracery and a Bristol spirelet. In the tower W window fragments survived of early C14 Dec tracery. Norton substituted Perp tracery, and seemingly too the doorway beneath. Tower arch with C14 wave mouldings. Timber roofs with small hammerbeams and angel terminals. S of the chancel arch, a small C15 trefoil-headed niche or piscina from the old church. Long chancel beyond a low screen wall. E window, E.E. style, with Purbeck shafts. Ribbed wagon roof painted with angels etc.

FITTINGS. Timber REREDOS, *c.* 1870, painted and gilded. – WALL PAINTINGS in the chancel, by the *Rev. R. Hautenville*, the first rector. – ROOD with Calvary group, by *P. Hartland Thomas*, executed by *Herbert Read*, 1948. – Fine wrought-iron CHANCEL GATES, 1870. – PULPIT, corbelled off the wall N of the chancel arch. – FONT, 1879, with trefoil-panelled sides of Purbeck marble. – STAINED GLASS. E window, incorporating a French medieval figure of a king, top centre. Nave S, from E: *Heaton & Butler*, *c.* 1873, with medieval fragments, top lights; *Gibbs*; *Ward & Hughes*, *c.* 1905. N aisle E, *Heaton & Butler*, *c.* 1873. N aisle, first from E, *Heaton & Butler*, *c.* 1877; second, *Jones & Willis*, *c.* 1916. In the N aisle W, two C16 Flemish figures.

Adjoining the tower a new entrance with CHURCH HALL to the W; *David Appleby*, 1969–70.

WALTON CASTLE, off Holly Lane. Begun *c.* 1615–20 as a hunting lodge or pageant fort by John (later first Baron) Poulett, but left incomplete, and completed as a private house *c.* 1980–2 by *Stuart Lennox*. Octagonal curtain wall with eight castellated casemates of varying sizes; some had been habitable and had fireplaces. At the centre, a three-storey octagonal tower with cross-windows and a projecting stair-turret. Top storey of 1980–2. New interiors; drawing-room plaster frieze copied from a C17 original at Barrow Court.

Possible IRON AGE HILL-FORT on Walton Castle Hill, 550 yds W of the church.

6050
CLUTTON

ST AUGUSTINE, Church Lane. Aisles, N and S chapels, long
chancel. Only the W tower, chancel arch and S doorway survived *John Norton*'s rebuilding of 1865, in a poor neo-1300
style. In the S porch, a late C12 doorway very like that at
Cameley, heavily restored. Early stiff-leaf capitals; finely
moulded arch, with a keeled roll moulding. The chancel arch
is also *c.* 1190, even more drastically restored. Keeled nook-
shafts, capitals without necking and with a kind of stiff-fruit,
as it were. The arch has two rows of chevrons at right angles
biting on an edge-roll. The tower is an interesting piece of C18
Perp survival; of weathered Dolomitic Conglomerate, the top
stage banded, diagonal buttresses ending in pinnacles. Pinnacles and battlements. Some of this may be C19 re-gothicizing,
but the windows, tall and mullioned with round-headed lights,
go convincingly with the semi-legible date on the tower: 1728.
– PULPIT. Painted figures of the Fathers of the Church, 1865.
– Small tower GALLERY by *Alan Rome*, *c.* 1970s. – STAINED
GLASS. E window probably *Clayton & Bell*, 1865. Likewise two
in the S aisle, 1870s.

METHODIST CHAPEL, Upper Bristol Road. 1810. Closed
c. 2005. Rendered front with round-headed openings and a
little decoration in the fanlight. Near-original interior, perhaps
the best survival of this date in N Somerset. Steeply raked
gallery on iron columns, continuous round all sides.

Alone on a rise S of the village, CHOLWELL HOUSE, by *James
Wilson*, 1855. Big square Jacobean Revival house for the Rees-
Mogg family. Adjacent to the church (E of the main road),
CHURCH FARM, typical early C17, with ovolo mullions, etc. In
Station Road, a small BOARD SCHOOL by *W. F. Bird* (1902).
Nearby, the RAILWAY INN, a mid-C18 mullioned farmhouse
with arched central upper window. Extended behind as a hotel
probably *c.* 1873.

6040
COLEFORD

A big, slightly bleak village. Coalmining was depleting woodland
here by 1619. The old centre is to the S, around Church Street.

HOLY TRINITY, Church Street. By *G. P. Manners* of Bath,
1830–1. Thin pre-archaeological Perp, typical of its date.*
Narrow W tower, aisleless nave, very shallow chancel. Tall
windows with poor tracery. – PULPIT and FONT, 1831. –
STAINED GLASS. E window by *Jones & Willis*, 1912; also one
nave S. Another by *Keith New*, 1958, semi-abstract, with much

---

* *John Sperring*'s sketchy seating plan (Incorporated Church Building Society) has
led to his misattribution as architect.

brown and violet. In the nave, fourteen figures of saints installed *c.* 1931; possibly Flemish and C17, believed to have come from Mells (Horner Chapel?).

METHODIST CHAPEL, Church Street. Dated 1865. Still classical; symmetrical front, Tuscan porch, rusticated ground floor. Quite big – Nonconformity was strong in the Mendip mining villages.

E of the church, a nice group composed of two single-storey former SCHOOLROOMS: of 1831, N, and opposite, a National School of 1847. Both Neo-Tudor. Also the gabled SCHOOL HOUSE between, 1847. The OLD RECTORY, S of the church, has broad Regency proportions but Neo-Tudor details. Of 1830–1, designed by *Thomas Thatcher*. From here Church Street descends S, at crazy steep angles, with picturesque C18 and C19 cottages terraced into the slopes above the King's Head Inn, of 1830. Coleford habitually dated its buildings. HIGH STREET turns off W; a little way along, in Mill Lane, a fine three-storey MILL with plain mullioned windows, rebuilt in 1794; internal iron-framed breast-shot wheel, with workings intact. Attached MILL HOUSE, possibly C17 in origin, with C18 alterations; the front updated *c.* 1850–70. N of High Street, a two-arched AQUEDUCT, *c.* 1800–1, intended to carry the ill-fated Dorset and Somerset Canal. Overgrown, and its ashlar facing robbed.

NEWBURY HOUSE, *c.* 1 m. NE, now a school. A big, handsome house of unexpected pink brick with stone dressings, windows with moulded architraves and keystones; all right for the date 1748 on a rainwater head. Five-bay centre facing N, with unequal wings set back. In the re-entrant angle, a mid-C19 stone porch, and a C19 bay window on the W front. To the W, a Late Georgian GAZEBO of grey brick with pyramidal roof. Good former COACHHOUSE, *c.* 1710–20, with segmental-headed cross-windows on the ground floor, bullseyes above.

To its SE *c.* 500 yds, in fields N of Page House Farm, rare archaeology of the Mendip COAL INDUSTRY; early post-medieval bell-pit mines. At the Works at Sharp Hill, a derelict WINDING ENGINE HOUSE from Newbury colliery, *c.* 1867. SW on Dark Lane, remains of MACKINTOSH COLLIERY (1867); the bed of a steam engine, remains of a steam-driven fan house and fan-drift, a tramway bed, and two stone-built late C19 miners' terraces. LUCKINGTON MANOR FARM, *c.* 600 yds N, is late C17. Two-and-a-half storeys, and a full-height stair-tower with oval lights in the return wall.

COMBE HAY

7060

CHURCH. From the road the church lies behind trees like many others. From the S however it stands immediately by the house, right on the front lawn, like a private chapel. Small Perp W tower with diagonal buttresses, battlements and pinnacles. Nave with short chancel and semicircular apse, altered in the late C18 with Y-traceried nave lights. N porch and narrow S aisle by *William A. Hill*, 1874. Reordered 2009. – MONUMENT. Robert Smith †1755, nice design with rocaille, two urns and an obelisk. By *Ford* of Bath.

COMBE HAY MANOR HOUSE. Built of Bath stone: the W front *c.* 1728–30, the S and E sides *c.* 1770–5. *John Strahan* has been suggested for the earlier work, *George Steuart* for the later. The W front nine bays wide and two storeys high, the middle three bays distinguished by giant pilasters, a pediment and a Venetian window on the ground floor, its centre formed by a concave niche. In the centre of the first floor, a big coat of arms in a Rococo cartouche. The S front, only three bays in width (but widely spaced bays), has a rather slim doorway with attenuated columns, and a recessed arch over, suggestive perhaps of James Wyatt or his influence. It is flanked by two broader tripartite windows with pediments. Plain upper floor. At each end, another concave niche with a concave oval in the first floor above. The plain E front is seven bays long, the central doorway of the same tripartite design as the S windows. (Excellent interiors, mainly of the 1730s to the W: Oak Room; morning room with fielded panelling, Doric pilastered fireplace with triglyph and metope frieze; three rooms with good fireplaces on the upper floor, one with relief bust and swags under a pediment, from Gibbs's *Book of Architecture*, 1728. To the E and S interiors of the 1770s: entrance hall with screen of two dark slender columns at the W end, dining room with lower exedra; staircase with oval glazed dome; drawing room with delicate Neoclassical oval ceiling. Design by *Wyatt* for a near-identical circular ceiling at the Victoria and Albert Museum.) – GROUNDS. Broad lawns on three sides, and to the E, an artificial lake, with a classical ROTUNDA on an island, *c.* early 1950s, in keeping with the style of house and grounds. N of the house STABLES, etc., with horizontal oval windows, i.e. *c.* 1700–20, with late C18 Diocletian windows below.

Numerous good houses. WATERCRESS COTTAGE is C17, low and humble, with small gables. A richly carved and figured stone chimneypiece in the hall, another dated 1624 in the chamber above, and decorative plasterwork. WEST HILL HOUSE, later and of higher status, reportedly with good C17 interiors too. At the NE end of the village, THE WHEATSHEAF pub, early to mid-C18. Broad and almost mechanically repetitive: four five-light windows below, ten of two lights above.

SOMERSET COAL CANAL. In 1794 a scheme was raised to transport coal from the Paulton and Radstock areas to the Kennet and Avon Canal at Limpley Stoke (Wilts.), and thence to Bath and London. Completed 1805, closed *c.* 1898. The engineer was *William Bennett*. The Paulton branch had to overcome a dramatic change of level at Combe Hay. The first design, for three stone caisson locks each 66 ft (20 metres) deep, was abandoned in 1799 after the walls failed. The solution was a chain of twenty-two locks over *c.* 1 m. At Rowley Bottom, E of the lane to South Stoke, five dry locks survive in good condition, with masonry up to 12 ft (3.7 metres) high.

COMPTON BISHOP
3050

with CROSS

Happily sheltered in a deep fold beneath the steep S escarpment of Mendip. The manor was settled on Wells Cathedral *c.* 1033–60.

ST ANDREW. The earliest fabric is C13, perhaps from the time of a consecration by Bishop Jocelyn in 1236. S porch outer arch trefoiled, on groups of three detached Blue Lias shafts; heavily moulded capitals. Inner doorway with Blue Lias shafts, upright stiff-leaf capitals (one renewed) and two outstandingly good headstops with curled fringes, no doubt by Wells masons. Contemporary the chancel. Chancel arch double-chamfered, the inner order on stiff-leaf corbels. Double PISCINA with trefoiled arches; small aumbry. The chancel E window with subreticulated tracery is Early Perp. N aisle added by *Manners & Gill*, 1851–2. Four-bay arcade. They also rebuilt the nave S wall and S porch in brownish sandstone. W tower base perhaps C13, heightened in the late C14. Angle buttresses and two-light Perp bell-openings. Pinnacles and parapet both 1883. – Finely carved C15 stone PULPIT. Tracery panels with leafy spandrels, carved friezes and cresting. Enlarged and moved, 1852. – FONT. Norman tub shape. – Big, noble Palladian MONUMENT to the Prowse family, almost certainly designed by *Thomas Prowse*, who erected it in 1751. Pediment on brackets with husk drops, scrolled frieze at the base. – STAINED GLASS. E window. Original glass *c.* 1375 in the tracery heads, the drawing and colour similar to contemporary glass in Wells Cathedral choir.

Unusually complete C15 churchyard CROSS, on four square steps. Head missing.

MANOR FARM HOUSE, Butts Batch. Early C17. Three regular gables, grouped two and one, flanking the porch and through passage. Ovolo-moulded mullioned windows under stopped labels. Attached barn (l.) now a house.

WEBBINGTON HOUSE, *c.* 1 m. W. By *E. J. May*, 1907–8, for H. A. Tiarks of Loxton. Set majestically against the side of Crook Peak. Big, with four asymmetrical half-timbered gables. Ruined by conversion to a country club and hotel *c.* 1960, and by the M5 motorway (opened 1973) which sweeps through below.

CROSS. ½ m. E of Compton Bishop, a staging post on the Bristol to Exeter road. Three coaching inns, all with canted bays to view the road: MANOR FARM, Cross Lane (the King's Arms by 1641); W on Old Coach Road, the NEW INN, and (250 yds W) the WHITE HART with Tuscan porch; these also C17, but more thoroughly rebuilt in the late C18.

COMPTON DANDO

St Mary. A puzzling church. The nave, s aisle and tower are medieval: the broad double-chamfered arcade, if original, suggests a c13 or early c14 date for the aisle. A plaque dated 1735 in the e wall indicates a remodelling, perhaps not only to the chancel; a rainwater head dated 1783 and a date 1793 on the s porch tie in with the classical parapets on this side. The ne vestry and organ chamber was added c. 1840–7, the chancel almost entirely rebuilt in 1905, with flamboyant Dec tracery. Big chilly interior, predominantly Victorian.*

w tower with diagonal buttresses, Perp in the w doorway (four-centred head, leaf spandrels). w window and tower arch with two broad wave mouldings, yet the odd cusped Y-tracery in the belfry lights seems Dec, and is not the result of restoration. Very large w window, of four lights with over-sized panel tracery. An unusual sexfoiled circle in the apex – is the tracery c19? The tower was repaired in 1674 (date on s face). In the bottom part of the e belfry light, a St Katharine wheel (after 1717). The nave s side has lower and upper windows, but oddly no clerestory windows on the n. The two-bay n arcade has a short pier and responds with the standard four-hollows moulding, and coarsely treated capitals with drunken ribbon-like moulding; all seemingly early c19 alterations. The vestry has a stone screen in E.E. forms, perhaps c. 1850s. Perp-style chancel arch, surely c19. The shafts have no bases. – STAINED GLASS. e window, 1963, perhaps by *J. A. Crombie*. Chancel s, possibly *Joseph Bell*, c. 1851. Four (nave and aisle) by *Powell & Sons*, 1867–71, each of three medallions on patterned ground; Presentation, Baptism and Temptation drawn by *Henry Holiday*, 1871.

Directly w of the church, a former RECTORY, by *S. C. Fripp*, c. 1849–51, conventional Neo-Tudor. The patchy red rubble walls suggest that he only remodelled the c17 rectory. Former SCHOOL and master's house, also c. 1850 and Tudorish, by the lane to the church. Prominent chimneys, iron diaper-framed casements. (COURT HILL HOUSE, Court Hill, is early c17, altered in the c19. Upper room with shield and gryphon frieze and c17 overmantel with pilasters.)

COMPTON MARTIN

St Michael. Perhaps the best Norman parish church in Somerset, with much mid-c12 work. Norman are the four-bay nave

---

* In the ne buttress of the chancel was a cornerstone from a c1 Roman altar from the temple of Sulis Minerva, Bath, depicting Apollo with his lyre, and an unidentified god. It was in the ne buttress of the n aisle in a drawing of 1717 (British Library). Removed 1997 for display at the Roman Baths Museum, Bath. There must have been a Roman settlement nearby – a find of moulds for brooches is now in Bristol Museum.

and its clerestory, both nave arcades, the chancel, and perhaps
the fabric of the low and narrow N aisle. In the space above
the chancel vault a small medieval columbarium to supply
pigeons for the priest's table. An entrance door high up in the
N wall, and near it, a smaller entrance for the pigeons, formerly
protected by a wooden louvre. The clerestory N side has four
small windows, a corbel table of monsters, heads, etc., and at
the eaves a fine chevron frieze delicately beaded. On the S the
clerestory is still visible inside the aisle, which in the mid C15
was heightened and extended with a S chancel chapel (Bickfield Chantry). Perp aisle windows, plain and uncusped on the
N, good-quality ogee tracery on the S, contemporary with the
heightening. The S aisle came after the W tower, for which a
legacy is recorded in 1443. The tower design is atypical of Somerset Perp. It is of four stages and rather busy. Diagonal buttresses. On the three set-offs truncated pinnacles. Each
buttress ends in a pair of thin pinnacles, independent of the
parapet. Unusually this is composed of concave-sided cusped
lozenges. Odd second stage which has only a small niche or a
small window and otherwise a system of diagonally set pinnacles disposed across the wall surface. Two-light bell-openings
flanked by niches. The tower arch has two ranges of cusped
panelling.* Restorations by *S. B. Gabriel*, 1858, including the
unfortunate replacement of the E window, and by *T. G. Jackson*
with *Harvey Pridham* of West Harptree, 1902–3.

Interior. The chancel is remarkably impressive, low and
austere, of two rib-vaulted bays. The transverse arch rests on
strong tripartite shafts with trefoil capitals. It is square in
section with chevron decoration to the W. Ribs of early profile,
a half-roll flanked by hollows. No bosses, but in the centre of
the W bay, four animal heads eating the ends of the ribs, in flat
relief. Norman PILLAR PISCINA, from Priddy. The nave
arcades have circular piers with regular scalloped capitals and
one-stepped arches. But the last pier on the S side has in
section eight rolls flanked by beading, with flutes between. All
this is twisted spirally, on the precedent of Durham Cathedral
and descendants, especially Pittington church, Co. Durham.
The chancel arch and the S arcade bay E of the spiral-fluted
pier have been re-cut with Perp mouldings, and latter arch also
heightened, the intention probably being to remodel the entire
S arcade. The resulting subsidence at the chancel arch forced
a halt, leaving a half-completed demonstration of the process
by which so many of Somerset's Perp naves must have originated. Norman arched altar recess, N aisle E. Perp N aisle roof
with big carved bosses.

FITTINGS. ALTAR RAIL. C17, heavy arcaded openings. –
FONT. Norman, circular, with a chip-carved zigzag frieze. –
SCREENS. S chapel. W side, *c.* 1500–20. Facing the chancel,
possibly a C17 imitation. – ORGAN. Pretty Gothic case by

p. 37

9

* A mason's mark (tower arch N side) may recur at Wells Cathedral and at North
Cadbury: their dates agree with the 1440s date proposed for Compton Martin. Jerry
Sampson, unpublished report, 2003.

Groves & Mitchell, c. 1850. – STAINED GLASS. E window by *Murray* of London, 1902. Two lancets with symbols of Evangelists by *Wailes*. Chancel N, *J. H. Powell*, 1871. By *Hardman Studios*, 1943–50: two porch lights; three N aisle windows; four clerestory lights. – MONUMENTS. Thomas de Moreton, *c.* 1290 (N aisle). Rare civilian effigy, of Blue Lias flatly carved (cf. Paulton). – Ann Abraham †1800, by *Henry Wood*. Seated woman with anchor.

SE of the church, PARSON'S HILL, the former rectory. Rear wing late C17 or early C18, front range by *E. J. Andrews* of London, 1841; overbearing Jacobethan, like a workhouse. A few good vernacular houses, e.g. Earl's Farm, The Street (N side), late C16 or early C17. (Later C17 rear stair-tower, splat baluster staircase.)

MOAT FARM, Bickfield Lane, 1 m. N. A late medieval manor house, its moat partly dry. Formerly larger. Alterations have left confusing evidence. To the SE, a two-storey gabled porch with double-chamfered doorway with four-centred head. Inner doorway with tracery spandrels. Projecting wing to the l. with blocked windows and doorway. On the W side three-light windows with arched cusped lights, and deep buttresses.

4060

CONGRESBURY

ST ANDREW. The site of a royal monastery by the late C9; the village name suggests a dedication to St Cyngar or Congar.* Externally a stately Perp church with tower and spire, aisled nave and clerestory; but the E.E. church consecrated in 1215 soon makes itself known. Restorations 1825, 1856, 1880 (re-seating, and S chapel by *E. B. Ferrey*). *Burrough & Hannam* reordered the chancel, 1958.

The two-stage Dundry stone tower is not of a Somerset type; diagonal buttresses, no special emphasis on bell-openings, and W doorway with two delicately moulded orders of niches in the jambs. Battlements and diagonal pinnacles. Elegant spire with ribbed angles and a decorated band. One-bay chapels, that on the S with piscina and tomb recess, also a prettily painted ceiling, probably 1880, on C15 head corbels. Embattled aisles, large windows with ogee lights *c.* 1450–90, and S porch with a sumptuous C15 inner doorway (fleurons in the jambs, ogee gable with very big finial, slim flanking pinnacles). Square-headed windows to the upper porch room, probably of 1825.

p. 19   *SCULPTURE from that building was found in 1995 under the floor of a barn in Brinsea Road; now at Taunton Museum. Fragments of exceptionally big, refined figures on a free-standing column, perhaps associated with an altar or shrine in the church. Probably early C11. The figures were depicted in architectural frames of which the arched tops survive, Christ's head has one hand raised in blessing, the other holding a cross. Two other pieces form a figure shown waist to knees, with crisply stylized drapery also seen in C10–C11 manuscripts.

There are indications of the C13 building in the N chapel E window which has reticulated tracery; the N door, with big roll moulding and chamfer; and the outer porch opening, with colonnettes of which the moulded capitals remain, a double-chamfered arch, and a hoodmould on stiff-leaf stops. This last must be *ex situ*, and was probably originally the inner doorway. The interior also is evidently E.E., remodelled. In the chancel a fine E.E. double PISCINA. The four-bay s arcade has double-chamfered arches and circular piers, surrounded by four detached Blue Lias shafts (replaced 1856). The waterholding bases are C13. A little later but still C13 the Bath stone N arcade; unusual piers of four attached shafts with chamfered angles between, the capitals and arches moulded. Similar the chancel arch and those to the chapels. Set into the chancel arch halfway up two apparently C14 heads. They may be connected with the rood beam (rood-loft doors in the N aisle). The tower arch has C13 double-chamfered jambs; the arch appears re-cut with C15 wave mouldings. Dec clerestory, perhaps 1320–50; two windows to each bay, reminiscent of East Anglia. Wagon roof in the nave, the ribs renewed 1951–2, reusing the C15 square bosses which include seven green men. Good head corbels throughout, those supporting the nave roof in attitudes of pain from toothache, neuralgia etc., perhaps referring to William of Bitton II (Bishop of Bath and Wells 1267–74) who generated a posthumous cult as a healer of such ailments. – FITTINGS. FONT. Norman tub with cable moulding, on C13 base with four Blue Lias shafts. – C17 spired COVER. – SCREENS. Stone bases to rood screen and parclose screen (s). The rood screen itself of oak, in one-light divisions and with a finely decorated three-band cornice, all much reconstructed. s aisle screen also C15 but seemingly more altered. – STAINED GLASS. E window with C15 fragments in the head, the rest of 1889 by *Bell & Son*, reordered 1958. s chapel, two of 1880. s aisle, war memorial (one window for each of the three services), style of *A.L. Wilkinson*, c. 1950. s aisle w by *Roger Fyfield*, 1971, pleasing ground. – MONUMENTS. Hester Richardson †1810. Graceful shield shape with urn. – Mary Merle †1851. By *T. Tyley*. Marble tablet with wreath, a butterfly and sweet sprays of naturalistic lilies of the valley etc. – CROSS (churchyard). C15, on stepped base. – SCULPTURE. *See* footnote opposite.

VICARAGE, NE of the church. A remarkable building of two parts, p. 40
C15 and early C19. Square three-bay w block of c. 1824, with a handsome if severe Doric-columned porch *in antis*. Probably by a Bristol architect; the living was owned by Bristol Corporation. Attached is the vicarage of rendered rubble, built c. 1465–70 by the executors of Bishop Bekynton. His arms appear in the fine, asymmetrically placed two-storey gabled porch. Outer doorway decorated with dogtooth, usually a C13 device. In the gable a panel with an angel. To the l. three windows with buttresses between (the hall), to the r., one light to the service rooms. The ground-floor windows and that over the porch have transoms. The first-floor lights not aligned with

those below. A semi-public lower hall, which was from the first ceiled, was used for church business. Directly above it, reached by stairs along the rear wall, the priest's private hall, with arch-braced collar-beam roof. Over the screens passage and service room, a solar; its chimneypiece has an inventive frieze of cusped daggers and quatrefoils in circles.* A small study over the porch. This compact plan with lower and upper halls was adopted elsewhere in the C15, e.g. Chew Stoke, Gothelney Manor (sw Somerset), and Dunchideock, Devon.

Large spreading village with, at its centre, a big C15 CROSS on five-stepped base. THE BIRCHES, Mill Lane, has an imposing front, c. 1760–80, three storeys with arched door hood. Further s, No. 26 Venus Street, thatched, externally C17. Rather thoroughly restored c. 1982, when it had smoke-blackened upper cruck roof trusses, i.e. originally an open-hall house, floored in the C16. URCHINWOOD MANOR, Urchinwood Lane, lies c. ½ m. E. Dated 1620 on the porch, sw wing added c. 1645, probably by John Taylor, a Bristol merchant. Good C17 panelling, some imported in the C19, and drawing room with plaster ceiling of 1620 and frieze with running vine borders.

CADBURY IRON AGE HILL-FORT. A single circuit of ditch and bank following the contours of a hill now covered by woodland. Built in the mid C5 B.C., abandoned before the end of the Iron Age, but reoccupied on the Roman abandonment of Britain.

CORSTON

6060

ALL SAINTS. Low w tower, diagonal buttresses with many set-offs, one-light lancet bell-openings, and single-chamfered arch towards the nave. Later battlements and a very short recessed octagonal stone spire. The w face of the tower was altered in 1622, in simplified Perp forms; lower window mullioned with round-headed lights under a square head; above, two lights under a round relieving arch. Chancel and nave C13, but very restored. E window of three stepped lancets. Restored by B. Ferrey, 1863–5, including a new N aisle and porch, chancel arch and vestry. – FONT. Early C14?; octagonal, on a tall octagonal stem. – ROYAL ARMS. 1660. On canvas. – STAINED GLASS. E window, *Powells*, †1902.

MANOR FARM. Nine bays, two storeys, hipped roof – an impressive, though simple front. Doorway with shell-hood, and cross-windows on the ground floor, i.e. c. 1690–1720. Almost opposite the church, OLD COURT HOUSE, late C17, three storeys with small ovolo-mullioned windows and off-centre porch. What lies inside?

* Cf. one at Kingston Seymour Manor, c. 1470–80.

CROSCOMBE

A linear settlement in a steep valley of the River Sheppey, which crosses and re-crosses the road via bridges and weirs. In its cloth-making heyday in the C15, it maintained seven guilds – Yonglens (young men), Maidens, Webbers (weavers), Fullers, Hogglers (labourers), Archers and Wives.

St Mary the Virgin commands the steep hillside N of the village. One of the most complete survivals of Jacobean church furnishings in Somerset, and among the richest in England. The building is of Dolomitic Conglomerate and Doulting stone, mainly of the C14–C16, and has uncommonly complete churchwardens' accounts from 1475. The church was by 1318 'in ruinous disorder', usually meaning under repair. Nave rebuilt c. 1420–40. In its roof a boss refers to Sir William Palton, †1449. He endowed in his will the s chancel chapel, complete by 1459. The oldest survival is the C13 s aisle; corbels over the door may represent Edward I and Queen Eleanor, i.e., c. 1270–90. C15 window tracery. Also of the C13, the outer doorway to the s porch (two orders of columns and a complexly moulded arch). Unusually there are two early C16 attachments, the treasury (sw) and the clergy vestry at the NE, built 1507–9 by *John Carter*, mason, of Exeter. The former has small barred lower windows; above was the guilds' meeting room. The two-storey vestry was built as a chapel of St George; it has a ribbed tunnel-vault. Carter was paid £37 11s. 8d. for it in 1512. The w tower, 108 ft (33 metres) high, is probably later C14. It has diagonal buttresses, battlements with blank arcading, pinnacles, and a fine spire with angle rolls and a single band of arcading, entirely rebuilt by *Caröe & Passmore* c. 1937–9. Aisles and s porch with parapets with blank arcading (cf. St Cuthbert, Wells). Straight-headed windows, four-centred arch over the s aisle e window only. Five-light chancel e window, and above it an inscribed name referring to the early C16. Clerestory and chancel have battlements instead of a parapet, and pinnacles. The tower arch low and triple-chamfered, i.e. C14 rather than C15. Later fan-vault. Arcades of five bays, the piers also clearly C14: four shafts with thinner shafts in the diagonals. Three-light clerestory windows. Unusual chancel arch, springing from corbels high in the spandrels of the nave arcade, and consisting only of a moulding run very close to the roof-line. Panelled wagon roof in the nave with big bosses of lozenge shape. On them two kneeling figures, coats of arms, etc. The chancel roof was remodelled in 1664, when sparse lozenge decoration was applied. In 1860 *Wainwright & Heard* altered the belfry, removed a w gallery and renewed the w window tracery. *Sedding*'s exterior restoration of 1889–90 was remarkably conservative.

The spectacular fittings commanded respect even in 1831, when *C. R. Wainwright Sen.* did repairs and added seating.

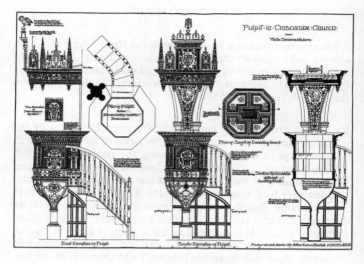

Croscombe, St Mary the Virgin, pulpit.
Drawings, 1889

First the Jacobean contribution, probably all *c.* 1616 (the date
on the pulpit), and mostly given by Hugh Fortescue, lord of
the manor. SCREEN. Probably by *John Bolton*, who made the
remarkably similar though smaller chapel screen at Wadham
College, Oxford (1612–13).* Now moved one bay w. Gloriously tall, with two tiers of two-light openings on delicate Ionic
columns, each pair of arches joining in a pendant instead of a
column. Many obelisks, on top as well as within the upper
arches. Instead of the medieval rood, a fine big achievement of
arms of James I surmounted by strapwork. – Matching PAR-
CLOSE SCREENS and STALLS. – PULPIT. Big and richly carved
with gilded Corinthian pilasters; large tester crowned by strapwork and obelisks. The carving flatter and more refined than
that on the screen. Dated 1616, given by the Bishop of Bath
and Wells. – Twin READERS' DESKS to match. Oblong, with
lively caryatid figures (N side) or herms (S) on the fronts. – The
front of the nave has fine C17 BOX PEWS. On the ends blank
arches and arabesque-work, and on many, similar elaboration
inside. – High up in the chancel, a PLAQUE with the Fortescue arms to commemorate all this. – FONT. Octagonal, Perp,
with heavy horizontal mouldings on stem and bowl (cf. Meare,
Weston Zoyland, both in S. Somerset). – BENCH-ENDS, at the
back of the church. Perp, with poppyheads and plain tracery;
C15. One with a finial figure of a priest, S aisle. Cross-facing
benches (S aisle) and box pews (rear of the N aisle) probably
of 1831. – CHANDELIERS. Brass. One dated 1707 with six del-

* Philip Bisse, a benefactor to Wadham at this time, was also an Archdeacon in this
diocese; a relative was rector at Croscombe.

icate branches, the other Rococo revival, *c.* 1850. – STAINED
GLASS. S aisle E by *Comper*, 1925, incorporating C15 pieces in
the tracery. – MONUMENTS. Chancel E wall, two medieval
tomb-slabs. – Two brass plates with whole families kneeling, to
James Bisse †1606, and William Bisse †1625, attributed by
Adam White to *Francis Grigs*. Long Latin inscriptions. –
Thomas George †1741, Doric, by *Curtis* of Bristol.

CHURCH ROOM (churchyard, N). Built 1480–1, perhaps as a
priest's house. Rubble stone. At the SE angle, a small jettied
section. Two tall Y-traceried windows inserted in the C19. Fireplace with big four-centred opening.

LONG STREET winds through the village. It was straightened and
re-routed in 1852. From it lanes climb steeply up. In Church
Street (N) the MANOR HOUSE, the true claimant of three so
named in the village. Probably built for the Palton family
in the late C14; divided up by 1448. Later occupied by the
Fortescues, it was a Baptist chapel from the early C18 (now
Landmark Trust). Large hall at the E end, with two two-light
N windows and one on the S, all with central transoms. At the
SE corner, a blocked arch to a demolished oriel. At the W end
of the hall are doors to a former screens passage, and internal
doors to the service end. Four-bay arch-braced collar-beam
roof with wind-braces. A C15 stone lamp bracket on the S wall
bears the Palton arms. The external E gable wall has two fireplaces from a former solar wing.

The OLD MANOR HOUSE, Long Street, stands hard by the road
at the E end of the village. Late C15. A broad front with the
doorway towards the W, then a hall oriel like a full-height
porch. Ground floor glazed on three sides, the angles with
detached panelled uprights, and a two-light window above.
Ogee heads flanked by quatrefoils in circles. Other windows
mullioned with hoodmoulds. Big sloped buttress at the E end.
The hall is low, with moulded beams and a fireplace with big
traceried spandrels. The oriel is reached through a panelled
arch, and has a most rare detail: a stone ceiling like a flattened-
out fan-vault, and in the middle angels holding initials vari-
ously interpreted as those of John Selwood, Abbot of
Glastonbury (improbable), of Hugh Sugar, Treasurer of Wells
1460–89, or the 'IHS'.

To its W, a plain Gothic PRIMARY SCHOOL, probably designed
by its builder *Henry Knight*, 1869–70. Opposite is GRIFFEN
MILL, three storeys, probably C18 with C19 fenestration. To its
W, PARSONAGE FARM, L-shaped, C16 with C17 alterations,
then PARSONAGE HOUSE, C17 at the back, refronted by one
of the *Wainwright* family of Shepton Mallet, *c.* 1800–15; good
doorcase with ornamented entablature. Adjacent is the OLD
RECTORY, *c.* 1828–37, a simple villa with columned porch.
Further W at the junction of Church Street, the late medieval
CROSS, on a three-stepped base. Throughout the village are
C16–C18 stone houses.

Further W, on the S side the MANOR HOUSE, Old Street Lane.
Also pre-Reformation. Doorway with hoodmoulds on

headstops, perhaps C15 or C16. Irregular fenestration; some mullioned lights; others mullioned-and-transomed, perhaps c. 1580. All now with crass plastic-framed glazing. Further W on Long Street is PARADISE HOUSE, C17, with a classical front of c. 1820. Adjacent (W) is ASHLEY HOUSE, tall, gabled and perhaps c. 1650–80, the upper windows mullioned. Ground floor updated in the C18 (rainwater head dated 1728).

MAESBURY CAMP IRON AGE HILL-FORT, 2¼ m. NW of Shepton Mallet. Roughly oval, enclosing an area of 6¾ acres within a single bank and ditch.

5040

DINDER

and DULCOTE

ST MICHAEL AND ALL ANGELS, Dinder. Mainly Perp, on the site of a probably Norman chapel. Until *Foster & Wood*'s restoration of 1871–2 entrance was from the S. Small three-bay nave with a W tower that seems taller because of its narrowness. It has diagonal buttresses, battlements, and a tall NE stair-turret. Two-light bell-openings with Somerset tracery. Lengthened chancel and NE organ chamber, 1871–2. Dec tracery in the E and S windows. Nave and N aisle with panelled battlements. Simple S porch. A small high window at the SE lit the rood loft. At the SW angle a medieval Mass dial. Foster & Wood lined the walls with Doulting stone, and installed a tie-beam roof. The chancel arch and E nave wall were rebuilt using old materials; the arch is chamfered and perhaps C14, as is the triple-chamfered tower arch. Three-bay C15 arcade; four shafts with hollows between, small moulded capitals. A small re-set PISCINA. Also a Norman arch moulding re-set over one S window, with beads and fine dragons' head terminations (with very doggy features). – PULPIT. Dated 1621. A very uncommon Early Renaissance design, of stone. Big scrolling foliage frieze, with egg-and-dart and acanthus leaf in the top mouldings. Four tall flat panels bearing isolated rosettes, fleur-de-lys, and two triangle-trefoils; an ingenious cipher for the Trinity. – FONT. Perp, the usual octagon with quatrefoil band. – STAINED GLASS. A jigsaw of late medieval fragments assembled in the rood-loft window. E window and chancel S windows by *Clayton & Bell*. N aisle w, c. 1872 by *Hardman*, much faded. – Good oak LYCHGATE, N, by *Cuthbert Atchley*, 1930.

Dinder is as pretty as any village in N Somerset, its main street bounded by a C19 leat tumbling over little weirs. On the N side, HIGHER FARM and Nos. 1–3 Riverside are typically C17. At the W end, the Neo-Tudor OLD RECTORY (now two houses), by *George Basevi*, 1827–9, as a *cottage orné* for Dr Richard Jenkyns, Master of Balliol College, Oxford, and later Dean of Wells. Extended E and W c. 1847, by *Jesse Gane*, with a new porch and lengthened windows. Shortly W again is DINDER HOUSE, c. 1801–3. The architect was possibly a *Mr*

Nicholls of Bath, surveyor. A long ashlar-faced two-storey box above a basement. In the middle of the s front, a broad three-window bow. Each flank has framing giant Ionic pilasters, and on the ground floor a tripartite window. One-bay additions at each end by *Vulliamy*, *c.* 1850. Single-storey addition to the N, 1929, in keeping. (Semicircular entrance hall (N) leading to a curving stone staircase, and curved double doors to the bowed breakfast room.) To the sw, a low Italianate LODGE by *H.E. Goodridge*, 1834. The drive crosses a most elegant C18 BRIDGE, a rusticated elliptical arch with serpentine balustrades. GARDENS remodelled with a spiral canal linked by earthworks to a box spiral in front of the house. By *Calonder Landscape Architects*, 2008.

In the lane opposite the church, WISTARIA HOUSE, *c.* 1730s. Five bays, two storeys, symmetrical mullioned windows with edge-rolls, and a shell-hood on acanthus brackets. Good staircase with ramped rails and tapered column-balusters. ½ m. N in wooded grounds is SHARCOMBE PARK, perhaps *c.* 1830 but largely rebuilt after a fire in 1922. Quite Regency-looking.

DULCOTE lies ⅝ m. W of Dinder, beneath the long quarried ridge of Dulcote Hill. At the T-junction a memorable rock FOUNTAIN of 1861. To its sw, a former SCHOOL-CHAPEL of 1860; simple Gothic, with a bellcote. N of the junction, the OLD MILL HOUSE. A steep-roofed brick gabled range to the N was part of a grist mill, remodelled probably *c.* 1748. Handsome W range, of *c.* 1760–80, built over the older gable; brick, with pedimented doorcase. Ruined mill buildings to the E.

On the escarpment N of Dinder and Dulcote are ANTI-INVASION DEFENCES of 1940–1; part of Stop Line Green, which ran E through Somerset and Wiltshire. It includes numerous pillboxes, and anti-tank cubes.

DOULTING

6040

Doulting is notable for its stone, a yellowish Inferior Oolitic limestone used for Wells Cathedral and much else in Somerset. Here also St Aldhelm died in 709; the spring became a pilgrimage site. Church and village owe much to the C19 interventions of the Pagets of East Cranmore (S. Somerset).

ST ALDHELM. A happy sight from the road, with its spire, stone-tiled roofs and highly ornate s porch. The plan is cruciform, with an aisleless nave with clasping W buttresses, probably late C12. The octagonal crossing tower, perhaps *c.* 1240, has two-light belfry windows under superordinate arches. Shortish spire, perhaps C15, with a pretty band of decoration. Also C15 the transepts. The E arm is C19, in the style of *c.* 1300; reticulated s window and ballflower cornice. Porches N and S. All drastically over-restored in 1869–71 by *Woodyer*, for the Rev.

R. H. Horner of Mells and Sir R. H. Paget,* when the church was almost entirely dismantled. The rebuilding used much original stone, certainly the nave and transepts, and probably much of the N porch. Also the tower and spire, rebuilt 'exactly as before' – excepting the six feet added to the tower. Woodyer's new chancel, organ chamber and vestry with their crisp, competent but lifeless details show little of his nervy inventiveness. He altered or added the chancel and s transept parapets, to accord with that of the N transept, quatrefoiled, C15; also the C12-style corbel table around the nave. Two-storey s porch of c. 1500, with a concave-sided gable (cf. Mells). Its s front was replaced by Woodyer. Reasonably faithful to the old stonework, which now embellishes a wall of the former vicarage garden, disembodied and laid out like an architect's drawing. Angle buttresses connected by a diagonal and rising to detached pinnacles, cf. the towers of Leigh, Mells, etc. Crocketed ogee-gabled door framed by two tiers of panelling. Above, canopied niches flanking a pretty window. Another niche in the gable. Delightful fan-vaulting in two bays with rose centres and big pendants.

Within the N porch, a reversed and re-set late C12 doorway with an order of colonnettes and segmental arch on vertical springers. The r. capital has waterleaf, and the l. little flutes. On the back of the arch, a band of quilted lozenges. Woodyer replaced Perp nave windows with lancets, single and grouped. Their rere-arches have Caernarvon-arched heads with foliate enrichments. Crossing arches double-chamfered. Above, a bold ribbed vault with big bell-hole. The transepts are the least changed: the old window openings have C19 tracery, e.g. uncusped panel tracery in the N and s windows. Good transept roofs of C15 Somerset type, with tie-beams resting on stone demi-angels, and more big angels with spread wings launching from the sides of each tie-beam.†

FITTINGS. Mostly of 1869–70. REREDOS with saints, central gable and a cross of malachite. – Oak CHANCEL SCREEN with wrought-iron filigree in the lights. – FONT, C15, octagonal. Panelled stem, bowl with lively demi-figures of angels, and a band of quatrefoils. – STAINED GLASS. E window, chancel s, and s nave w c. 1870, probably by *Hardman*. s and N transepts probably *Clayton & Bell*, c. 1860 and 1870–1. s transept E, †1904, probably *Morris & Co*. Nave N, †1894 by *O.C. Hawkes* of Birmingham. Nave s, first from E, c. 1915, good Arts and Crafts perhaps by *Arnold Robinson* (*Bell & Son*). w window no doubt *Burlison & Grylls*, †1877. – MONUMENT. Richard Paget †1794, by *Lancashire* of Bath, oval with urn.

CHURCHYARD. Big late C15 CROSS on four-stepped base. Blocky plinth with detached angle shafts, and shaft with attached angle shafts (cf. Dinder). The head missing. Many

---

* *See* Paget in *PSANHS*, 1884, and compare John Buckler's drawings of 1833.
† *PSANHS*, 1907, states that the transept roofs were 'carried out by *Halliday* of Wells about fifty or sixty years ago, but so well done that they appeared original'. Can this be trusted?

CHEST TOMBS with heavy top slabs, the earliest near the N gate dated 1640 and coffin-shaped.

DOULTING MANOR (formerly vicarage), Church Lane. L-plan, with long rear wing then low service ranges. The S garden front is C18; five bays and two storeys, even quoins, Gibbs surrounds below.

VILLAGE. In a valley W of the manor house is ST ALDHELM'S WELL. Behind an outer wall with a trough, the water rises from two openings in a second wall, possibly C18. The village centre, at a crossroads NE of the church, wears a curiously almshousey air from the ranges of estate cottages provided by Sir Richard Paget, 1881–1901. High chimneys, oriel bays, and a gatehouse with arms and initials liberally displayed. The architect was *G.J. Skipper* of Norwich. S of the crossroads is MANOR FARM, a handsome ashlar-faced house of two storeys with hipped roofs, seven bays with cross-windows. The high transoms suggest a late date, perhaps in this remote part as late as 1720. Robust C18 barns frame the farmyard, on the S side of which is the noble medieval TITHE BARN, one of four belonging to Glastonbury Abbey (the others all in SW Somerset). Dendrochronology has pushed back the dating to 1288–90 (felling dates). Of local stone with stone-tiled roof, and two gabled porches on each long side. The porches have segmental arches, the gable-ends deep central buttresses with three set-offs. Vent holes in the form of cusped spheric triangles, a Dec leitmotif. (Fine roof with raised base crucks with trusses against the end walls, two collar-beams on arched braces and penetrations from the porch roofs; one collar-beam on arched braces.)

Doulting parish rises N for *c.* 1½ m. to Beacon Hill, where the Old Frome Road crosses the Mendip heights. (The part of the parish S of Doulting is in the SW Somerset volume.) ⅝ m. NW of Doulting is BODDEN CROSS, a cluster of C17–C19 houses and farms around a now dismantled medieval CROSS. From here lanes lead E to CHELYNCH. A hamlet grouped around the POACHER S POCKET INN, licensed in 1702. C17 (small rear window); naïve late C18 pedimented doorcase. On the lanes E of Chelynch, some wealthy farms including Temple House Farm, with cross-windows; *c.* 1690–1710. NE again is LONG CROSS, where the TURNPIKE HOUSE of 1790 has been 'restored' to nothing. ½ m. NW at Beacon Hill, the WAGGON AND HORSES INN, also *c.* 1790, probably in response to enclo- sures and turnpikes. Still with mullions, rectangular in section with slightly chamfered angles. Original cast-iron diamond casements. At the r., the coachhouse and stables, with steps to a long room above.

DOWNHEAD

6040

ALL SAINTS, Park Lane. Small, with C14 W Perp tower, nave and chancel rebuilt 1751, dated on the porch. Tower with diagonal buttresses, battlements with continuous mouldings, big gargoyles, and pinnacles, probably C15. Triple-chamfered arch into the nave, without capitals. C18 segment-headed windows, with late C19 Perp-style tracery to E and W. – PULPIT doubtless of 1751. – Norman tub FONT.

CRANMORE TOWER (parish of Cranmore, SW Somerset). 1¼ m. SW of Downhead; via Slait Hill, then N on Furzeclose Lane. A prominent landmark on a wooded ridge. An Italianate belvedere or folly tower by *T. H. Wyatt*, 1862–4, for J. M. Paget of Cranmore Hall. 148 ft (45.5 metres) tall, and slim in proportion, with continuous balcony halfway up, balconies under the paired arched windows on each face, and a pyramidal roof with heavy cornice.

WATERLIP, 1 m. W again. A few cottages, a tiny former chapel (1874), and unusual rural ALMSHOUSES for quarrymen. Central plaque 'Domino et pauperibus ES 1699', continuous driphood over the ground floor. Badly modernized; ovolo mullions lost.

DOWNSIDE ABBEY see STRATTON-ON-THE-FOSSE

4050

DRAYCOTT

ST PETER, School Lane. By *C. E. Giles*, 1860–1. Modest. Plain lancet nave, apse, transepts, bellcote. Chancel arch on fat short circular piers with naturalistic foliage. Good decorative wrought-iron CHANCEL SCREEN and CROSS of 1894, by *George Fellowes Prynne*, noted for his screens. – FONT. 1860, by *William Burges*. Attributed on the strength of a sketch in his notebooks, a newspaper report naming 'R. Burgess', and on stylistic grounds. Commissioned by Burges's patron H.G. Yatman. Maker possibly *Nicholls* of London. In the Transitional style of the late C12. Circular foot with short granite shaft, broad foliate capital supporting a square bowl with an all-over squared flower pattern, cf. Burges's reredos at Waltham Abbey, Essex. The sides have reliefs of the Four Ages of Man; the earliest known example of designs reused in the font at Studley Royal, Yorks., and at Tower House, Holland Park, London. – STAINED GLASS in the apse by *Lavers & Barraud*, 1861.

94

DUNDRY

5060

Perched on an escarpment, Dundry has magnificent views over the distant centre of Bristol. The Romans first quarried its fine limestone, much favoured by Bristol's medieval masons.

St Michael. The 97-ft 6-in. (30-metre) tower is one of the most 31, p. 28 spectacular of Perp Somerset towers. A stone dated 1482 inside probably relates to the addition of the crown a few decades after the tower was finished.* Set-back buttresses, w doorway, five-light w window, two tiers of blank two-light windows above, and two-light bell-openings. Ogee-headed lights, i.e. after c. 1440. It is, in spite of all its proud display, not entirely satisfactory aesthetically: the heavy NE stair-turret mars the lean profile, and the crown is quite unrelated to everything below. It is wider than the tower, sitting like a crown on a head. With its cousin at St Stephen, Bristol, it derives ultimately from Gloucester Cathedral's central tower of the 1450s. The parapet is pierced with arcading, and the arcade has tiny pierced qua-trefoiled circles in the spandrels. The main pinnacles are big and square and wholly transparent, with four tiers of arcading, their own completely detached buttresses and flying buttresses and pinnacles, and crowned by pierced battlements and open-work spirelets. It is a showy rather than a beautiful finish. A refacing took place in 1828–30. The church is surprisingly small. It was much rebuilt in 1860–1 after a lightning strike, by S. B. Gabriel, who re-set the s wall and windows to form a s aisle. The nave piers with their E.E. capitals seem entirely Victorian, as is the chancel arch, though its N pier and the NE chancel respond are medieval, with C18 graffiti. The three stepped and chamfered arches of the N arcade seem also C13, with thick quarter-roll mouldings at the soffits. N wall with a deeply moulded blocked doorway, perhaps C15, and a Late Georgian window with interlaced tracery. – FITTINGS. PULPIT and FONT of 1860–1. – High Victorian ALTAR RAILS of wrought iron and brass. Matching CANDELABRUM now over the font. – STAINED GLASS. Probably by *Wailes*, 1860s.

NW of the church, the Gothic PRIMARY SCHOOL. 1857–8, by *Gabriel*, of grey limestone. Enlarged by *Maynard Froud* in 1896, again in 1912. Good minor C17 farmhouses, e.g. CASTLE FARM, Castle Farm Lane, and GROVE FARM, Dundry Lane, with mid-C17 panelled front door and big stair-tower.

BAPTIST CHAPEL, Maiden Head crossroads, ½ m. E. 1828, updated (presumably with the foiled rose above the door) in 1877.

DUNKERTON

7050

ALL SAINTS. W tower perhaps late C14, three stages with diagonal buttresses. The top stage appears later, of brownish ashlar, with Perp two-light belfry openings. C15 parapet with continuous moulding. Three-light W window with reticulated tracery,

---

*The involvement of Bristol's Society of Merchant Venturers is at least part myth; they were not established until the mid C16.

perhaps C19 renewal. Small nave and chancel, restored after a
fire by *C.E. Davis*, 1859. He added a S porch and rebuilt most
of the N wall. The quoins at the E end are perhaps C12 or C13.
Ashlar-faced within, giving an entirely Victorian feel. – ALTAR
RAIL, STALLS, LECTERN, PRAYER DESK, PULPIT etc. all of a
piece, wrought iron and brass by *Singer* of Frome. – Quite elaborate ORGAN, also *c.* 1860, the lamp brackets and angel finials
also by *Singer*. – STAINED GLASS. All by *Clayton & Bell*, including E window, †1879.

Across the valley N of the church, THE GRANGE, Tudor Gothic
of 1825 and 1860 on a mid-C18 core. Shortly W, CROOKED
COTTAGE, The Hollow, dated 1695. Typical of the date the
upright two-light windows and oval openings keyed into square
frames. In the valley bottom on the Bath Road, the OLD
SWAN: the date 1719 refers to an enlargement of an earlier
house, again with C17 mullioned windows.

WITHYDITCH. A hamlet ½ m. W. Plain BAPTIST CHAPEL of
1839, with two arched windows on each side. Unusually intact
interior, gently rearranged in the 1870s. Nearby schoolroom
also *c.* 1840, with a smart pedimented front topped by a figure
of a praying child (plastic windows). Down the lane (l. side),
OLD FARMHOUSE, *c.* 1670–90 with ovolo mullions and an
upright oval light in the gable-end. Extended *c.* 1730, with a
smart shell-hood and bolection doorcase.

EAST HARPTREE

5050

ST LAURENCE. Norman S doorway with segmental arch. Arch
and jambs framed by two roll mouldings, the outer one interrupted by widely spaced chevrons forming a kind of crenellation. In the chancel, a little billet moulding, perhaps re-set.
Otherwise the chancel seems C13, see the two trefoiled PISCI-
NAS, and internal evidence of a triple lancet E window
(replaced by a two-light window with C19 tracery). Big nave S
window with good late C15 tracery. N aisle perhaps 1440–90;
three-light windows, diamond label stops, six-bay arcade of the
usual four shafts and hollows. The eastern arch overlaps the
chancel wall in a curious way. Also Perp the ogee-moulded
chancel arch, perhaps a re-cutting of something earlier. W
tower with diagonal buttresses. Four-centred W doorway and
window with ogees and inverted cusping, signs of the late C15.
Upper stage perhaps completed in the early C16; see the
masonry changes, and two tiers of small Tudorish lights.
Higher stair-turret without spirelet. Parapet dated 1633,
pierced with pointed quatrefoils in square panels, small
pinnacles. Big plain S porch, probably C16: entrance arch of
narrow bricks visible within, an unusually early example of
brick in Somerset. Re-seated *c.* 1881–3. The first plans were by
Street, *Sedding* took over at his death, but completion was by

J. T. Micklethwaite & Somers Clarke. Of this date, big diagonal buttresses added to the chancel, and the w porch window.

FITTINGS. SCREEN, Perp style, probably of 1881–3. – ROOD figures, 1931. – PULPIT. Jacobean, the usual classicizing arches, lozenges and guilloche. – Several C15 BENCH-ENDS. – FONT. Norman, plain tub-shape. – WOODWORK. Reused C17 panels in tower screen, aumbry doors, dado panelling. – WALL PAINT-ING. Over the E window, figures probably by *Clayton & Bell*, c. 1883. – STAINED GLASS. Chancel. Four in the style of *Clayton & Bell*, c. 1884. N aisle; four almost certainly by *Burlison & Grylls*, c. 1917–18. Nave S; fine war memorial by *Karl Parsons*, 1919. – MONUMENT. Sir John Newton †1568. Splendid tomb-chest with recumbent effigy. Against the front of the chest twenty kneeling children. Six-poster with fluted columns, debased Ionic capitals and a broad entablature with arabesque frieze. Tudor roses beneath the canopy. Re-erected in the S porch.

HARPTREE COURT, Whitecross Road. Built 1795–7, probably by *Charles Harcourt Masters*, for Joshua Scrope. A long S-facing front of Bath stone, with Greek Doric four-column porch (two pairs) perhaps c. 1820. Five-bay centre with three-bay pediment, arched ground-floor windows, and a nice tripartite doorway. Then lower three-bay wings leading to one-bay pavilions with pediments and on the ground floor tripartite windows. Mid-Victorian service wing to the l., but done in keeping. The garden front is similarly arranged, but with two deep bows in the centre, a composition Masters used at Wid-combe Terrace, Bath. The narrow space between is bridged by a gently convex porch on two unfluted Ionic columns. In the wings, the ground-floor windows are set in triple blank arcades. Sash glazing largely reinstated c. 1985. Good Neo-classical interiors. Square entrance hall with fluted Greek Doric columns forming arcades on two sides. Simple wrought-iron staircase balustrade, delicately restrained plasterwork and good marble chimneypieces in the main rooms. *Masters*'s signed plan for the grounds was implemented in modified form: N of the house, unfussy lawns and a chain of ponds over which an elegant stone bridge carries the drive.

MIDDLE STREET runs N–S, with roughly rectangular enclosures defined by parallel streets each side, perhaps a planned medieval layout. At the S end off Coombe Lane, scant earth-works remain of the Norman RICHMONT CASTLE, probably ruinous by the time Sir John Newton robbed the stone for a new house shortly before 1540. Scant earthworks survive on a spur above a wooded combe.

EASTWOOD MANOR FARM, c. 1 m. E, is a plain large farmhouse of the C17 to C19, possibly the successor to Newton's house. Extraordinary MODEL FARM buildings of 1858–9, designed by *Robert Smith*, a Devon agriculturalist. Originally water-powered, with corrugated iron and glazed roofs covering 1¼ acres. Main front in five parts: in the centre a high gable rising to an eccentric Gothic bellcote, flanking this two big glazed lunettes as in a railway terminus, then further smaller gables. Inside, two courts surrounded by brick and iron arches behind which are cast-iron galleries for grain storage. EASTWOOD MANOR, *c.* 300 yds w, is a variegated Gothic mansion by *E. T. Boston*, *c.* 1885. Someone wisely omitted a proposed octagonal lantern over the porch.

EAST HORRINGTON

ST JOHN EVANGELIST (former, East Horrington). 1838, by *Richard Carver* of Taunton, in his customary lancet style. Nave with w porch and bellcote and lower chancel. Now a house.

CHILCOTE, ⅓ m. SE. At MANOR FARM is a barn which was a C15 manor house possibly connected with a prebend attached to Wells Cathedral. Three single-light windows with ogee arches, and two two-light windows, one blocked and with transom. A four-centred doorway with panelled soffit. (Wide fireplace with four-centred opening.) CHILCOTE MANOR, opposite, is Gothic with a short clock tower, *c.* 1870s.

EASTON

ST PAUL, Wells Road. 1841–3, by *Richard Carver*. Slightly mechanical Neo-Norman, but with solid proportions and details hinting at the new archaeological spirit. Cruciform plan without tower. Short chancel, w bellcote. Cusped open timber roof. – STAINED GLASS. E window probably by *T. W. Camm*, *c.* 1880.

EASTON-IN-GORDANO
with PILL

ST GEORGE. The medieval tower is architecturally interesting. Its bottom stage, of pink Dolomitic Conglomerate, may be *c.* 1250–1320: see the small chamfered w lancet, four relieving arches inside, and the most unusual design of the tower arch – quadruple-chamfered on semi-octagonal responds. These appear too short: the floor-level was raised in 1872. Caernarvon-arched w doorway, also 1872. The tower was remodelled and raised to three stages *c.* 1440–1500, this work having affinities with Chew Stoke and perhaps Portishead. Set-back buttresses, pinnacles, battlements with blank arcading and in the middle of each side a niche with statue. Good panelled spirelet over the NE stair-turret, which has its own battlement (cf. Chew Stoke). Two-light bell-openings, and below them more windows of two lights, These have transoms with pretty tracery beneath, of cinquefoiled ogees with a band of quatre-foiled circles in the spandrels. Tall three-bay nave with clerestory, lean-to aisles and square chancel, by *Ewan Christian*, 1871–2, replacing a much-derided nave (*Edward Brigden*, 1822–7). Handsome geometric mosaics lining the sanctuary, in subtle colours.

FITTINGS. Late C19 REREDOS. Red and white marbles, with reliefs of the Nativity and musical angels. – FONT. Late Norman square bowl with trumpet scallops; re-cut no doubt in 1872, when the lurid marble step, shafted foot, and COVER were added. – CHANDELIER. Two tiers; 1731. – STAINED GLASS. Complete set attributed to *Bell* of Bristol, mainly 1870s–90s. – MONUMENTS. Samuel Sturmy †1669; rare painted monument to a sea captain and scientific instrument maker, with his portrait in the gabled top. He gave to the church a manuscript of *The Mariner's Magazine*, his treatise on tides and navigation. It could be borrowed on security of £3. – Roger Soudon †1703. Composite columns flanking a painted inscription. Naïve bust in an oval medallion, one hand on heart, the other on a book. Cherubs' heads and a skull in the base. – Numerous tablets, the best to Cordelia Wilkins †1774, by *Allen* of Bristol.

To the S in St George's Hill, ST GEORGE'S HALL, *c.* 1830, the former rectory. Three-bay front, Ionic tetrastyle portico. Some good farmhouses, e.g. HAPPERTON FARM, Happerton Lane, three-room cross-passage plan with two-centred doorway, perhaps C15 or C16; UPPER HAPPERTON FARM, mid-C18, five bays with Gibbsian door surround. COURT HOUSE FARM, Marsh Lane, has a re-set datestone of 1630, a double-pile plan with two attic gables, blocked mullioned windows. BARN with arched-braced trusses, i.e. perhaps late medieval.

PILL adjoins Easton-in-Gordano to the NE. It is bleak but char-acterful. The small silted creek or pill just inside the mouth of the Avon has Victorian granite walls. From here pilots rowed ships up into Bristol, and the Pill hobblers transferred cargo from ships moored in the Severn. C18 and C19 cottages line twisting lanes and alleys impassable to the motor car. Facing the harbour mouth on the E, WATCH HOUSE, *c.* 1850, a single-storey former custom house.

HAM GREEN HOUSE, Chapel Pill Lane, SE. The C18 mansion became the centrepiece of an isolation hospital from 1899; now the headquarters of a cancer care charity, restored and extended by the *Alec French Partnership*, 2002–6. Bath stone ashlar. The S-facing wing is the earliest: perhaps *c.* 1730s, five bays, with segmental windows and door pediment. The E ele-vation fronts a three-storey addition with canted bays flanking a bowed Tuscan porch, *c.* 1790–1840. NE of the house, a fine hexagonal GAZEBO, *c.* 1760. Lead-covered ogee dome, rubble with brick angles, sash windows with ogee-Gothick blind-traceried heads; cf. Arno's Court and Goldney House, Bristol, attributed to the *Paty* family. On the bank of the Avon, a mid-C18 WATER GATE for visitors. Whitened rubble wall of crescent form, low circular towers at each end.

EMBOROUGH

ST MARY THE VIRGIN (Churches Conservation Trust). A sweet and unassuming country church looking as it might have done *c.* 1800: all clear glass and flaky limewash, and a little musty within. A faculty exists for restoration by *J.D. Sedding*, 1885; if carried out, it must have been the gentlest of repairs. The well-proportioned central tower was re-roofed in 1316, so must be C13 at least; it has diagonal buttresses and a parapet with pierced cusped lozenges. Small chancel; three-bay nave with C13 N aisle. Small S porch with pediment, probably late C18 or early C19. Of about the same date the intersecting tracery in several windows. Drunken nave arcade with double chamfers and no capitals, propped by round transverse arches in the N aisle. Here the Geometrical E window with trefoiled rere-arch is typically C13. In the chancel (S), a two-light Perp window unblocked in a 1920s restoration by *Robert Marchant*, who added the frieze and floral plasterwork to the barrel-vaulted nave ceiling. – PULPIT. Plain, panelled, C18. Later base with scrolly arches. – Unadorned tub FONT, perhaps C12. – Small panelled MUSICIANS' GALLERY on Doric columns, C18. – ARMS of George III, by *Joseph Emery* of Wells, 1817. Unsigned Decalogue boards etc., also 1817. – MONUMENTS. Mostly to the Hippisleys (*see* below). – Robert Bath †1822. Pedimented frame, portrait roundel.

MANOR FARM, SW of the church. Mainly C15, owned by the Hippisleys of Ston Easton from 1570 until the 1950s. Broad E front, probably remodelled *c.* 1570–1640, with central porch leading to a cross-passage. Two- to four-light mullioned windows, the largest, N of the porch, transomed. At the N end, a gabled solar wing with diagonal buttresses. On the N wall, a big four-light window with transom, probably inserted *c.* 1640s, when the solar was upgraded to create a great chamber.

OLD DOWN INN, at the crossroads of the A37 and B3139. A coaching inn by 1710, claiming a date *c.* 1640. Late C18 or early C19 front with three-bay centre, pedimented porch on columns, and higher two-bay flanks, perhaps later.

ENGLISHCOMBE

ST PETER. An exceptionally interesting building consisting of a tall nave with big S chapel, central tower, and chancel. The nave walls, tower and part of the chancel are Norman, see the chancel corbel table, the tower s wall and especially the inside. There are here, however, puzzling irregularities. Both E and W tower arches are C13, chamfered and pointed, where one would expect round arches, but they rest on Norman attached demi-columns with decorated scalloped capitals. The E arch has also part of the Norman moulding at the r., and a monster face to one of the capitals. In the chancel's NW angle, the capital from a Norman column, part of a system of blank arcading which can still be seen in the N wall under the tower, telling of a donor's high ambitions. Here the arches have three-dimensional chevron with bead decoration. Most surprisingly, the arcading continues behind the NW pier of the tower and reappears at the E end of the nave. How can this be explained? The Norman tower in fact began square, but its W wall was rebuilt E.E. to give a shallower rectangular plan, presumably after some damage. The evidence for this is in the thicker E parts of the nave walls, and outside (N), where both Norman clasping buttresses survive, showing the larger dimensions of the original tower base. See also the NE stair-turret, flat and oblong, in its original state, with a narrow Norman doorway inside. The s chapel has a single triple-chamfered arch from the nave. On its W side (now within a C19 porch) an extremely pretty little double squint of cusped spheric triangles – i.e. a motif of c. 1290, which gives a latest date for the chapel. (It was altered, perhaps c. 1500–40: square-headed s window with panelled reveals inside, embattled parapet.) Next the chancel was rebuilt Dec, see the fine tall early C14 windows to the E and s (inside, a second blocked s window). The pretty PISCINA with cusping and ogee points is perhaps also early C14, re-tooled. The E window has (renewed) reticulated tracery, and the E front outside is gabled, embattled, and has polygonal angle pinnacles. In 1885 *Willcox* of Bath restored the church, quite gently. – Fine FONT with square bowl, angled underside with chamfered corners, octagonal stem. Possibly Norman, re-cut in the C13. – Ogee-domed COVER, with big coarse crock-ets; perhaps C16. – SCULPTURE. *Ex situ* medieval figure of a child in swaddling clothes, above the chancel arch.

Former RECTORY, SE of the church. Late C16 or early C17, long and low; cross-passage plan. Mullioned windows. Panelled C18 gatepiers with urns. Attached, S, a sturdy TITHE BARN, origi-nally the property of Bath Abbey. Gabled porch entrance to the s, deep buttresses with offsets on the E gable. Raised cruck roof, felled 1314–58, with arch-braced collars and wind-braces. Repaired 1993–4.

FAILAND

5070

ST BARTHOLOMEW, 1 m. N at Lower Failand. A daughter church of Wraxall, by *E. W. Barnes*, c. 1885–7. Of Old Red

Sandstone quarried on site. Charmless and urban-looking
Dec. Big transepts, porch-tower with tall broach spire. Patron
saint over the door, by *John Roberts*, 1987.

FARLEIGH HUNGERFORD

St Leonard. Built by the first Lord Hungerford to replace the
church taken into the castle, and consecrated in 1443. Evidently a product more of duty than of ambition. Thin unbuttressed w tower with plain parapet and pyramid roof.
Straight-headed windows, mostly of two cusped ogee lights
under hoodmoulds. Low chancel arch. The chancel interior
entirely Neo-Gothic, probably of *c.* 1830–40. Pretty tripartite
E wall. Re-seated and the gallery removed in 1898. – PULPIT.
Of 1898, with eagles with huge beaks carved against the angles.
– COMMUNION RAIL. Good early C18 work with openwork
scrolls and figures, probably Continental. – PAINTINGS. By
Philipp de Loutherbourg (1740–1812): The Taking of Christ, and
Christ appearing to St Peter. – STAINED GLASS. Head of a
knight, late C14, in a N window (in the border the initials of
Sir Thomas Hungerford †1397). Many fragments in the E
window, Netherlandish. – MONUMENTS. Dorothea Torriano
Houlton †1799 and John Houlton †1839; Mrs Shirley †1828,
Lady Wilson †1864. All Gothic with canopies.

p. 498
Farleigh Hungerford Castle, *c.* 300 yds NE. On a hilly
outcrop with rising ground to its s, and to the N and E a stream
in a steep defile with hills equally high on the other side; not
a good defensible site. Here the Montfort family built a manor
house (perhaps C13); foundations of its latrine tower are at the
NE corner of the inner bailey. That house was purchased in
1369 by (Sir) Thomas Hungerford, who was pardoned in 1383
for fortifying it without licence. An outer bailey was added
c. 1430–45. The Hungerfords' estates were sold in 1686 and the
castle stripped of stone and decorative pieces *c.* 1705–35. In the
later C18, the inner bailey buildings collapsed piecemeal and
the outer bailey served as a farm. The ruins were consolidated
after 1915 when it came into public ownership.

In its heyday the castle must have been exceedingly impressive; it is of the regular type in which strength was coupled
with architectural order. The Inner Bailey was a rectangle
c. 200 ft E–W by *c.* 175 ft N–S (62 by 54 metres), with circular
angle towers and on the s side, the least protected, a big gatehouse with two semicircular bastions. In all this it followed the
Edwardian tradition of Harlech as continued or revived by
such South English castles as Bodiam, Sussex. But Farleigh is
earlier, larger and more diffuse than Bodiam, which was begun
in 1386 and is very compact. Farleigh's towers are slimmer, and
its walls longer. Fortification counted here in the end far more
than regularity; for the NE tower was stronger and thicker than

the others and projected further. The S and W sides are further protected by a formidably deep stone-lined ditch, filled in to the E of the gatehouse in the C16 or C17.

Of the INNER BAILEY, except for the ruinous SE and SW towers, much has to be read from the exposed foundations. There were buildings along the S, E, and W walls, but the main hall and kitchen range, principally *c.* 1370s, bisected the courtyard from E to W. From the stone forecourt a central porch led to a staircase, and this to the first-floor Hall – see the foundations of two C15 piers in its undercroft. To the E lay the Great Chamber, connecting with the range against the E wall, in which by the C16 and C17 were the best family rooms. The kitchen lay W of the hall, with a separate entrance from the S court. Behind the kitchen against the N wall, the bakehouse and brewhouse. Between the hall range and the N wall was a small private garden. More survives of the irregular polygonal OUTER BAILEY to the S, added *c.* 1430–45 by Sir Thomas's son Walter, a courtier and soldier of the first importance under Henry V. Entrance to the Outer Bailey is from the E via a big gatehouse, square in plan and without turrets or embellishment. At the W end, another gatehouse, this time ruined. Two round angle turrets on the S side, originally closed on the inside. Also *c.* 1430–45, a BARBICAN was added to the inner bailey gatehouse; visible as foundations only. E of the chapel (*see* below), a two-storey PRIEST'S HOUSE of *c.* 1430; two arched doorways, and another with a moulded frame in the N end, now leading into a C17 extension. Windows mostly C17 or C18. A curved recess for a newel stair in the SW corner.

CHAPEL OF ST LEONARD. Built in the mid C14 as a parish church (i.e. before the present castle). Enclosed by the outer bailey *c.* 1430–45, it became the castle chapel. Simple W porch, early C16. Large nave and chancel in one. E window of three lights with elementary panel tracery under a depressed arch, of *c.* 1440 and identical to the W window of the parish church. Five square-headed windows in the S wall, blocked in the C18. N chapel added *c.* 1400 to house the tomb of Sir Thomas Hungerford. Broad depressed entrance arch, with very odd mouldings. Chequered marble floor, *c.* 1660. Roof timbers felled 1600–21. Underneath the chapel is a tunnel-vaulted crypt, perhaps *c.* 1600.

FITTINGS. REREDOS and PULPIT made up *c.* 1832 of early C17 pieces. – FONT. Plain lead-lined octagon on a circular foot, perhaps C13 or early C14. – GATES to the N chapel, writhing curls of wrought iron, *c.* 1660. – In the crypt, six C17 LEAD COFFINS, in human form and four with moulded face masks; the best collection of its type in Britain. – WALL PAINTINGS. To the r. of the E window a gigantic figure of St George, and adjacent on the S wall, a fugitive donor (Sir Walter Hungerford?); both *c.* 1440. The N jamb of the E window has a fine C15 white-on-blue brocade pattern. – In the N chapel, remnants of an all-over scheme devised by Lady Margaret Hungerford *c.* 1658–65 to frame her husband's monument,

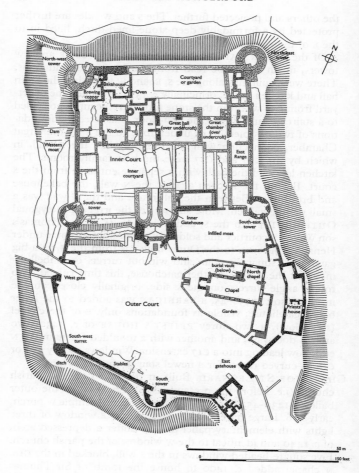

Farleigh Hungerford Castle.
Plan

announcing no less than their apotheosis at the Last Judgment. As depicted in 1842, the scheme had chequered floors in perspective, a figure rising from the tomb beneath the N window, then heraldic devices between the windows, largely still visible. Upper frieze of apostles framed by classical columns (extant in the NE corner). The ceiling beams have well-preserved clouds and cherubs with golden ribbons. The plaster ceiling, doubtless the climax of the scheme, was lost in the C18. – STAINED GLASS. In several windows Netherlandish and German glass of the C16 to C18, introduced in the C19.

MONUMENTS. In the chapel, except where stated. Sir Thomas Hungerford †1397 and wife. Big tomb-chest with five elongated quatrefoils with shields. Between them (N side), tiny figures of mourners, three knights and one lady. Recumbent effigies on top. Fine iron railings added *c.* 1440, with two ornamental bands, and cut plate finials (cf. Bekynton's Chantry, Wells Cathedral). – Sir Walter Hungerford †1596 (chancel s wall). Tomb-chest with fluted pilasters, triglyph frieze and geometrical panels, vividly picked out in green verditer and pinkish-red. – Sir Edward Hungerford †1607. A near-copy of the last. – Mrs Mary Shaa or Shaw †1613. Tomb-chest with kneeling family against its front. Strapwork-framed brass above. – Sir Edward Hungerford †1648 and wife, planned and erected by her *c.* 1658–65. Weighty white marble chest with baluster corners, festoons, cherubs, acanthus leaf, and arms on the end. A polished black marble top bears excellently carved recumbent effigies, his armoured and with the Hungerfords' wheat-ears and sickle. Attributed to *Thomas Burman.*

FARLEIGH HOUSE, *c.* ½ m. sw of the castle. Large, ostentatiously asymmetrical, castellated and turreted pile, with outbuildings, lodges, etc., all equally romantic. The first house, apparently gabled and simple, was built for the Houlton family in the early c18 when they abandoned the castle, from which much stone and fittings were robbed. This may be represented now by a detached w wing of two storeys with two-light mullioned windows and a castellated central feature, with big turrets and towers behind. The present main block began *c.* 1806–13 as a symmetrical two-storey house in fanciful Regency Gothic with big traceried church-like windows, elaborate pinnacles, and a low conservatory along the garden front (s). In the late c19 (or *c.* 1906?), the house was given a third storey and refronted (less symmetrically) in conventional Neo-Tudor style. To the E, chapel-like former STABLES, with traceried s window and a belfry or spirelet above. Nearby, a stage-set Gothic GATEWAY, *c.* 1806–13, buttressed and gabled with pierced parapet, and a lodge.

FARMBOROUGH

ALL SAINTS. Simple Perp w tower, diagonal buttresses, embattled parapet with thin pinnacles. At the NE, a polygonal stairturret. Chancel rebuilt *c.* 1793–4, Geometric N aisle and porch added during comprehensive restoration by *J. Elkington Gill,* 1869. The nave s wall has odd elongated two-light windows said to date from the c18, with arched lights and a straight hood. Of the same date the blocked s doorway. Some medieval fragments built into the nave s wall inside. – FONT. Perp, octagonal with quatrefoil panels. – PEWS, 1869. – STAINED GLASS. Tower; three life-size figures from Christ Church, Brighton, 1838, installed here *c.* 1931. The l. and r. ones are copies from Reynolds's famous windows at New College, Oxford. Nativity, by *Gilroy Stained Glass, c.* 1990s.

PRIMARY SCHOOL. 1857, by *S.B. Gabriel* of Bristol. Gothic, grey limestone, with Picturesque bellcote on the E gable, master's house with canted bay, etc. Enlarged 1895.

Further E, the MANOR HOUSE. Dated 1667 and an exceptionally interesting example of minor domestic architecture of that date. Front (originally symmetrical, extended E in the C19) with four-light mullioned windows. Broad middle projection with big gable, containing the porch, l., the staircase, r. The porch has a four-centred arch, a nicely lettered inscription, and a small oval side window keyed into an oblong panel. The staircase has straight flights, balustrade with openwork panels, plain, oblong and oval. Restored 2000–4 by *Chedburn Ltd*, including at the E end, rear, an apsidal stair-tower with stone newel stair.

FARRINGTON GURNEY

ST JOHN BAPTIST. The Norman church was demolished for this staid Neo-Norman essay by *John Pinch Jun.*, 1843–4, standing alone in fields E of the village. Big clerestoried four-bay nave, aisles, W tower. – FONT. Square, on short pillars, in the Italian mode. – SCULPTURE. Above the W door, a re-set medieval Trinity group, minus the dove. Framed by Renaissance tomb ornaments. – MONUMENTS. Mostly to the Moggs, the earliest (†1728) by *Michael Sidnell*. Arched top, leafy capitals, shaped base with palm fronds. – George Mogg †1818. Black slate, fluted pilasters but a big curvy top, most un-Grecian. Signed *I. Wood*, Bristol. – Several more conventionally Grecian, by *Reeves & Son*. – Early C14 churchyard CROSS; three-stepped square base, and part of an octagonal shaft.

MANOR HOUSE, Main Street. For the Mogg family, probably mainly of 1637 (dated porch). Four-gabled S front, asymmetrically placed gabled porch with semicircular opening. Two-light ovolo-mullioned windows. At the back, C18 mullions and a C19 Gothic porch. (W. J. Robinson mentions a date 1691, and a staircase with twisted balusters.)

OLD PARSONAGE, Main Street (junction with Bristol Road). Fine house of perhaps *c.* 1680–90, of red sandstone. The E façade, originally the front, has five widely spaced cross-windows, pedimented on the ground floor, with central pedimented doorway. The house was turned round *c.* 1710–20, by the addition of lateral corridors along the W side, with symmetrical wings projecting by one bay. The wings are roofed separately, hipped towards the courtyard and with gabled outer returns. Handsome W front, still with cross-windows, a backward-looking feature for *c.* 1720 (later sashes in the first floor of the wings). Pediments on the ground floor, as on the E side. Doorway with semicircular hood on carved brackets. Open-well staircase at the N end, *c.* 1710–20.

FAULKLAND   7050

A compact churchless village begun as a planned market town by John de Courtenay under a charter of 1263.

The triangular village green, remnant of the market square, retains STOCKS with a stone seat and flanking monoliths of uncertain origin. On the NW side THE GREEN FARMHOUSE; late C18, symmetrical and in the Bath tradition. Next door, THE GREEN FARM has mullions and continuous string courses; mid-C18 (cf. FAULKLAND HOUSE, NE side, nearly identical before C19 alteration). SW of the green is HORSE-POND FARM, of c. 1700, unpretentious and unspoiled; five bays, vertical mullioned openings.*

TUCKER'S GRAVE INN, c. ½ m. E. Vernacular mid-C18; mullioned windows. Rare early to mid-C19 pub interior over three rooms, with minimal bar counter, fitted benches, tongue-and-grooved dados and C19 lettering on the tap-room door.

HASSAGE MANOR, c. 1 m. NE. A mellow composition, owned in the C16 by the Bayntons. Of this period the W wing, originally the service end, with timber casements of two to four lights. The graceful E wing, dated on the porch 1677, for Henry Coles of Frome, has a hipped roof, transomed-and-mullioned windows, and upright oval lights keyed into panels, here unusually as dormers. The proportions and thick walls of the dining room (r. of the porch) suggest it may incorporate parts of a medieval Hall. Screens passage with timbered wall to the hall, done, with other sensitive repairs, by *Peter Bird* of *Caröe & Partners*, 1982–3. The rear (N) door squeezed tightly between projecting wings. Doorcase c. 1720s, with fluted pilasters flanked by blind arches, *ex situ*; canopy on scrolly brackets, not one with the frame. The E side has blocked C17 openings, and 1950s sash windows in C18 style. In the N façade more sashes, probably c. 1812. Behind the dining room, a fine splat-baluster staircase of 1677, with heart-shaped cut-outs and massive panelled newels. In the NE room, a broad chimneypiece probably of 1677 with fluted Ionic pilasters and scrolled frieze; inset, early C18 panelled surround to reduce the opening. Good Neo-Georgian wrought-iron GATES by *John Beauchamp* of *Caröe & Partners*, c. 1990s.

HIGHCHURCH FARM, Chickwell Lane, ½ m. S. A manorial house mentioned in 1395–6. Entrance front (N) with mullioned windows under square hoodmoulds; W end possibly altered or rebuilt in the C19. From the S, the high gabled E end appears to be a late C16 or C17 cross-gabled house of two-and-a-half storeys.

---

*TURNER'S TOWER, 1 m. WSW, c. 1885, was demolished in 1969.

FELTON

with LULSGATE

St Katherine and the Noble Army, Felton Common. Designed by the vicar, the *Rev. Joseph Hardman*, 1865–6. Plain nave and apse, cusped lancets. NW tower, *c.* 1892.

FELTON was just a hamlet until the C20. FELTON HOUSE FARM is L-shaped, the E front (dated 1742) late C17 with cross-windows and gabled porch in the angle. On the projecting N façade, a late C18 doorcase and strange mortar joins. The S front is a mid-C18 updating of a C17 wing.

BRISTOL INTERNATIONAL AIRPORT, Lulsgate, *c.* ¾ m. W. Bristol's airport was transferred in 1957 to this former RAF airfield. The terminal designed in 1990 by *Yorke, Rosenberg & Mardall* was built 1999–2000 after protracted planning inquiries. A rectangular block sheltered on all sides by the projecting roof structure which forms an angled canopy like a giant cornice. Glazed screen walls reveal the structural columns behind, from which spring triangulated struts in four directions. Extensions are planned at both E and W ends, almost doubling the size of the terminal. The original brick-built reception building and control tower (*J. Nelson Meredith*, 1955–7, much altered) cowers, like a biplane next to an airliner, a little SE.

FLAT HOLM

An island in the Bristol Channel, *c.* 6¼ m. WNW of Weston-super-Mare. As at Steep Holm (q.v.) there was prehistoric activity, and possibly a medieval chapel. LIGHTHOUSE of 1737, and a FOGHORN building of 1906. Ruined C19 gun batteries, barracks (1869), and cholera hospital (1896).

FLAX BOURTON

St Michael. Small nave, S porch. Perp windows, but the lower nave walls reportedly older. Early C16 features in the chancel. Sturdy W tower with diagonal buttresses, battlements, *c.* 1370–1430. Dull N aisle by *E.B. Ferrey*, 1880–1. Could the tall narrow S door opening be Saxon? Its Norman exterior stonework perhaps an addition: one order of spiral-fluted columns, one decorated scallop capital, the other with little upright volutes. Arch with zigzag decoration and an outer moulding with an ornamental scroll. Above, a Norman relief of St Michael and the Dragon. Also Norman the single-stepped chancel arch with edge-roll. Two orders of strong columns faintly patterned with chevrons. Scallop capitals on the l., leaves, small volutes and an animal's head on the r. Flat chevrons on the abaci, ending on the l. side with a winged dragon. Three further dragons' heads on the abaci. – REREDOS. Mosaic and tile with line painting of Leonardo's Last Supper, maker *W. B. Simpson & Sons*, *c.* 1882. – ALTAR RAIL. Quietly good, by *Alan Rome*, 1970. – FONT. Norman, square, underside with big trumpets. – STAINED GLASS. E window, *Lavers, Barraud & Westlake*, 1880. Chancel, *Ward & Hughes*, 1893, 1903. N aisle, *Kempe & Co.*, *c.* 1916, 1929.

Opposite the church, the former ANGEL INN, perhaps *c.* 1650–75, mullions, continuous string courses. Also C17, CHURCH FARMHOUSE, Post Office Lane, with asymmetrical gables. At the end of this lane, five highly individual houses by *Artist Constructor* and *Bob & Tim Organ*, *c.* 1971–3. Varied plans attempting to resolve Serge Chermayeff's observations on community and privacy. Polygonal and angled forms, one to three storeys with tower-like features.

BOURTON HOUSE, 200 yds E of the church. Front of five bays, two storeys, *c.* 1720s. Arched windows, Doric pilastered doorcase with semicircular hood on acanthus brackets, with the arms of Gore and Langton. The back has some ovolo-mullioned windows and gabled attics. In the C18 part, high-quality oak joinery in the staircase hall, with star parquetry, dog gate, carved tread-ends, Ramped rails, and beneath the landing, a later semi-dome. From the landing are semicircular steps up to the front range. Fine stucco ceiling over the stairs with big trumpeting angel in high relief, musical trophies, cornice like a corbel table. A little E, SCHOOL HOUSE, Main Road. By *Walter Cave*, *c.* 1895. Schoolmaster's and caretaker's dwellings each with broad half-timbered gable, lower centre housing a village reading room.

Former WORKHOUSE, Cambridge Batch, ¾ m. E. *Scott & Moffatt*, 1837–8. A design reused, e.g. at Williton (SW Somerset). Now flats and offices. Very large, Late Classical style. Octagonal centre with pediments in the diagonals, wards to a complex symmetrical plan. Arcaded link to the Gothic CHAPEL by *John Norton*, 1860. Adjacent, big former POLICE STATION, also *Norton*, 1858. Serviceable Gothic.

GATCOMBE COURT, Ashton Watering. The porch and everything to its l. (w) is C17; two gables with cross-windows. (Door dated 1664, staircase 1683.) To the E, a projecting wing. In its end gable a three-light mullioned window with cusped ogee heads (probably 1450–1500). A similar one in the re-entrant angle, cut into by the C17 wing. – ½ m. NW is KINGCOTT FARM, Gatcombe Lane. Medieval, altered early C17. L-plan, with C17 stair-tower in the re-entrant angle. C15 doorways front and back in the main range. Recently repaired and enlarged by *Chedburn Dudley*, *c.* 1998.

7050

FOXCOTE

ST JAMES THE LESS. Of medieval foundation. Rebuilt 1720–1 by Dorothy Smith, 'a very strict Presbyterian' (see Rook Lane Congregational Chapel, Frome). W tower projecting from the nave, but very narrow like a bellcote (cf. Hardington). The battlements and pinnacles probably C18, emulating Perp. Small nave and chancel with arched windows. The nave has dressed stone, long-and-short quoins and a flat parapet on the S side only. S doorway of a domestic type: attached Doric columns, segmental pediment. Interior unadorned, fittings mainly C19. – PULPIT. Oak-panelled, of 1721, with probably later fruity drops at the angles. – ALTAR RAILS. C18, much altered. Later balusters. – MONUMENTS. Robert Smith †1714, and Dorothy †1721. Standing marble monument of reredos type, not by a local mason. Baroque composition, reminiscent of works by John Nost. Composite columns flanking a bowed tablet without figures. Base with trophies and supporting volutes. Semicircular top, with cherub heads, clouds and gilded rays in the tympanum. Then a further triangular pediment. – Rev. Robert Smith †1769. Obelisk; below, seated weeping putto between an urn and a skull.

7060

FRESHFORD

A charming village in a bend of the River Avon. From the hilltop church, lanes descend to the wooded river valley which forms a fine backdrop N and S. Evidence of C17–C19 cloth working and brewing contrasts with the gentle influx of affluent merchants attracted to Bath, or retiring from it, after 1700.

ST PETER, Church Hill. The W tower is low, of three stages, with diagonal buttresses with stepped set-offs. Embattled parapet with continuous mouldings, ogee-headed belfry lights, all late C15 characteristics. The W doorway was converted to a four-centred window with Y-tracery, perhaps early C19. Short nave, with more early C19 windows. S porch also C19. Lower short chancel, rebuilt and enlarged 1858–9, probably by *C. E. Davis* (see the rectory, below). N aisle added 1736, extending level with the chancel E wall. Interesting aisle windows, very tall mullioned two-light windows with ogee tops: they can only be interpreted as a survival of C16–C17 tradition. Quatrefoil arcade piers with depressed segmental arches. – FONT. Plain, octagonal, probably early C14.

METHODIST CHAPEL, The Tyning, Sharpstone. Opened by John Wesley, *c.* 1783, doubtless refaced or rebuilt. Single-storey, simple lancet lights.

MANOR HOUSE. NE of the church. Built for a clothier *c.* 1719, attributed to *Thomas Greenway* of Bath. On an L-plan. Fine

sw-facing entrance front of five bays; sashes with bolection surrounds, panelled aprons, hipped roof. A rear service wing at
the l. incorporated a pre-c18 cottage. Shortly after 1796 *John
Pinch* gave Greenway's SE return a Neoclassical bow, and
added a taller plain block beyond in the angle of the L-shape.
Enlarged in keeping *c.* 1886–92, by *T. W. P. Isaac*; his NE range
included a balancing bow for the SE front.

Opposite the church is MANORTHORPE, a good house *c.* 1720;
cf. General Wolfe's House, Trim Street, Bath. Of five bays and
two storeys, the upper sashes with panelled aprons. The doorcase has Doric pilasters and broken pediment, continued
above with Ionic pilasters framing the central window. (Handsome staircase.) Down CHURCH HILL, NW, the OLD PAR-
SONAGE, with gables and some c17 mullions, sashed in the
c18. (Above, in Crowe Lane, the gaunt former RECTORY, 1859
by *C. E. Davis*, Tudorish, with sharp gables.) Behind the Old
Parsonage is a former BREWERY, early c19; a straight three-
storey rank over very high basements. Adjacent, a refined
three-storey house in the Bath mode, *c.* 1820–40.

In the High Street, 150 yds SW, the attractive Gothic PRIMARY
SCHOOL, 1849; bellcote, plate tracery etc. Cross-wing (SE),
after 1870. L-shaped rear wing by *Gareth Wright* of *Sogol Architects*, 2000–1, with timber balconies. High Street shortly turns
back towards the church; many attractive houses, e.g. VINE
COTTAGE, *c.* 1710, and THE CORNER HOUSE, with pretty
Gothick pointed windows, *c.* 1780–1800, at the junction with
The Hill. A little way down here is OLD HOUSE, a plain five-
window front, *c.* 1730–50, with four later bays at the r. At the
foot facing up the hill, HILL HOUSE, updated *c.* 1760s; pedimented doorcase on brackets, round-arched centre window
with heavy keystones. Round the corner, past the INN, with
c17-looking gables, mullions and hoodmoulds (dated 1713,
perhaps repairs) to FRESHFORD BRIDGE over the Frome.
Three semicircular arches with cutwaters. Late c15 or early
c16; Leland mentions (*c.* 1540) its 'faire new arches of stone'.

SHARPSTONE lies N of the Frome, 300 yds SW on The Tyning
and l. at the cemetery. First, SHARPSTONE COTTAGE, a graceful Regency marriage of Gothic windows with Italianate
(stucco, deep bracketed eaves). Past the Methodist chapel (*see*
above), THE HERMITAGE, high on a bank. Perhaps late c14,
much rebuilt in the c19. High, gabled with mullions and transoms. (Stone newel stair, three roof trusses with arch-braced
collars and cusped wind-braces.)

DUNKIRK MILL, in the valley ¼ m. w then s. A woollen mill of
1795, now houses. Bath stone, three regular storeys (once five),
segmental-headed windows with central mullion. Big arched
cart entrances.

HAYESWOOD CAMP. Battered remains of a quadrilateral earthwork with inner rock-cut ditch, enclosing 1¼ acres. Of uncertain date; finds from a trial excavation in 1932 ranged from
flint implements and flakes through Iron Age pottery to c3–c4
Roman pottery.

FROME

The largest town on Mendip, with a population c. 25,000. Its name derives from its river which flows N to the Avon. A monastery was founded c. 685, on or near the site of the parish church. By the C15 the town had expanded to S and E (Gentle Street and Vicarage Street), and N to Cheap Street and the Market Place. There were weavers by 1327. The high point for the woollen industry began c. 1650, leaving stately late C17 and C18 houses, and the rare surviving early industrial housing at Trinity. By the 1720s the population had 'prodigiously increased' (Defoe) and was reckoned to be higher than that of Bath and perhaps of Salisbury. In 1730 seven waggons of cloth were sent to London each week (*The Voyage of Don Manoel Gonzales . . . to Great Britain*). Dissenters outnumbered Anglicans by as many as four to one; Frome's chapels do not disappoint. Early C19 improvements were instigated by Thomas Bunn, who envisaged a Grecian Frome to rival Bath. In 1826 it had 'all the flash of a Manchester' (Cobbett), and by 1831 a population of c. 12,000. The cloth trade collapsed c. 1840 and, despite diversification, until c. 1980 the town declined too. With regeneration since the 1970s, Frome seemed at last to have turned a corner, but now faces the difficulties of inappropriate redevelopment.

PLACES OF WORSHIP

St John, Bath Street. A low, embattled, spreading church on a hillside just S of the centre. It has a cruciform plan with lean-to aisles, E chapels, and a tower and spire in the place of a S transept. Of the monastery church founded by St Aldhelm c. 685 nothing structural survives. Scattered indications of a sizeable rebuilding c. 1160–70. An E.E. tower was built S of the crossing c. 1300, and in the later C14 the N transept was rebuilt and the nave lengthened. In the C15 chapels clerestory, upper tower and spire were added. The C19 did much to alter and confuse: piecemeal changes were wrought by *Jeffry Wyatt*, 1814, and *Benjamin Ferrey*, 1844; from 1852, the Rev. W. J. E. Bennett added High Anglican fittings; finally he had the fabric almost entirely rebuilt under *C. E. Giles*, 1862–5.

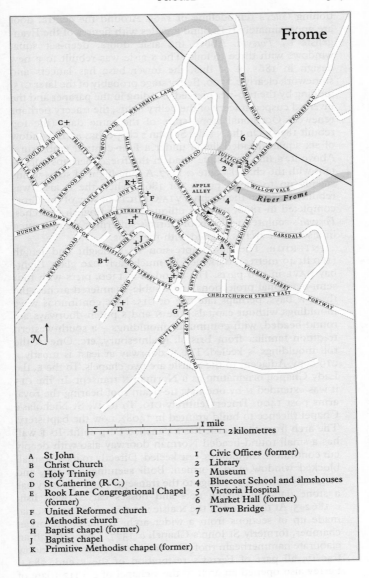

Frome

A	St John
B	Christ Church
C	Holy Trinity
D	St Catherine (R.C.)
E	Rook Lane Congregational Chapel (former)
F	United Reformed church
G	Methodist church
H	Baptist chapel (former)
J	Baptist chapel
K	Primitive Methodist chapel (former)

1	Civic Offices (former)
2	Library
3	Museum
4	Bluecoat School and almshouses
5	Victoria Hospital
6	Market Hall (former)
7	Town Bridge

EXTERIOR. The w approach is via an ample forecourt closed by a pretty five-arched Tudor Gothic SCREEN by *Jeffry Wyatt* (later *Wyatville*), 1814. Both resulted from clearances for the creation of Bath Street (*see* p. 514); Wyatt was working for Lord Bath at Longleat. The w front ('pitiable': Pevsner) is a recasting of the medieval gabled nave with low lean-to aisles. Wyatt faced it in ashlar and renewed the windows, perhaps conditioning *Giles*'s remodelling of 1865. Around the central door are approximately E.E. blind arcades with figures of the Evangelists by *Forsyth*. Above the aisle doors, deep-set squat windows with three trefoils. The S aisle was rebuilt to a new design in 1865. E of this, the tower base has lancets and stonework clearly *c.* 1300. Belfry stage probably of the later C15, judging by the two-tier pierced arcading in the parapet and the inverted cusped tracery of the belfry lights, the tracery perhaps renewed. Octagonal stone spire of the same date (the top rebuilt 1830). On the N side, St John's chapel has a C16 window of six square-headed lights under a four-centred embrasure. Above it, a fine grotesque head in the frieze, perhaps consistent with the chapel's date *c.* 1377. A long flight of steps winds steeply up to the N porch (of 1862, when the N aisle was rebuilt), lined on the E with a VIA CRUCIS or Way of the Cross completed in 1866, perhaps unique among English churches. *Forsyth*'s sculpted tableaux of Christ's sufferings are presented in a series of arches aligned with the steps.

INTERIOR. The first impression is of height and length (160 ft; 49 metres), darkened by much early C20 glass. Eight-bay NAVE in two parts. The E end of *c.* 1300, piers with four semi-octagonal projections and double-chamfered arches; the three W bays, perhaps late C14 or C15, have continuous wave mouldings without capitals. The N and S porch doorways are round-headed, with continuous mouldings – a south-western tradition familiar from Bristol, Malmesbury, etc. One of the roll mouldings is keeled. The N doorway at least is mostly a C19 copy. Adjacent to the N aisle are two chapels. To the E, the Lady Chapel, originating as a Norman N transept. In the C15 it was extended N by one bay; tie-beam roof bearing the royal arms post-1409. Tracery entirely C19. To its W, St Nicholas's Chapel (licence to build granted in 1408), now the baptistery. The arch from the N aisle has a panelled Perp soffit. Its E wall has a small round-headed Norman doorway also with deeply cut continuous mouldings, one keeled. Directly to its N, a small blocked window, also Norman. Both seemingly *in situ*, and originally external openings to the transept. The baptistery has a stone dado of fishing nets and bosses carved with fish, *c.* 1862–5. At the E end of the N aisle is a reworked C12 piscina, made up of sections from a wider arch. To its E, the organ chamber, formerly St John's Chapel, *c.* 1377. Chancel with an elaborate hammerbeam roof, Dec sedilia, Geometric E window tracery, all part of Ferrey's restoration of the E end, 1844. Ferrey also opened an arch to the S chapel of *c.* 1412 (date of endowment), and re-roofed it. Fine ogee-arched piscina, C15. Finally the tower, with a triple-chamfered E arch without capitals, and a S window with a trefoiled rere-arch, both perhaps *c.* 1300.

FURNISHINGS. REREDOS. Of red-veined marble, by *Forsyth*, *c.* 1865. – Another in the N chapel by *Kempe & Co.*, 1924. – PULPIT. By *Phillips* of London, 1859. Big and quite low, in the North Italian style. – FONT. C13 type, quatrefoil on four Purbeck shafts; if original, re-tooled. – ROOD SCREEN, highly coloured and gilded, with vaulted canopy, by *Kempe*, 1892; rood figures by *Zwink* of Oberammergau. – Wrought-iron SCREEN to the N chapel, by *Singer*, with integral gas fittings.* – SCULPTURE. In the tower, two *ex situ* fragments discovered in 1865. Part of a C9 cross-shaft depicting a reptilian animal with interlace, work of the West Saxon Lacertine group. Below, a small dog-like creature with raised tail, perhaps C11. – Eighteen big medallions depicting miracles and parables in the nave arcade spandrels, *c.* 1862–5. – TILES. *Minton* floor in the S chapel, 1844; originally in the chancel. – Inlaid FLOOR (baptistery), depicting the Virtues and Deadly Sins, by *Clayton & Bell*, *c.* 1860–5. – STAINED GLASS. E window by *Clayton & Bell*, *c.* 1865. Chancel N, 1844, and S chapel E, fine and richly coloured, 1846, by *O'Connor*. S chapel S, *Wailes*, 1840s. Tower S, *Mark Angus*, 1985. N transept, three by *Kempe & Co.*, 1923–4. NW window by *O'Connor Jun.*, *c.* 1865. Fragments of heraldic glass in the baptistery chapel; 1517. Aisle windows by *Kempe & Co.*, 1924–30.

MONUMENTS. In the N transept unknown gisant or cadaver. – George Methuen †1640, clothier, the family later to ascend to Corsham Court, Wilts.; a good standing monument with steep broken pediment, Corinthian columns, kneeling effigies (vestry). – George Locke †1735. Big tablet with swept gable, columns and Baroque ornaments, by *James Paty the Elder* of Bristol. – Richard Stevens †1796 (baptistery). By *Thomas Cooke* of London. Stevens's Asylum, a charity school for girls, with men's almshouses, was demolished in 1956. In the centre an urn. To its l. two charity children, to its r. an old man, and the distant prospect of the Asylum. – Lucy Georgina and Louisa Boyle, daughters of the Earl of Cork and Orrery, †1827 and 1826, by *Sir R. Westmacott*. Two standing young women holding each other. – Isabella Henrietta Countess of Cork, †1843, by the younger *Westmacott*. Seated female figure with an open book. – Many C19 brasses, doubtless by *Singer*. – Outside, against the chancel E wall, monument to Bishop Ken †1711. The tomb is coffin-shaped and covered by a cage of iron hoops with a gilt crozier and a mitre. Gothic canopy of 1844 by *Ferrey*.

CHRIST CHURCH, Christchurch Street West. By *G. A. Under-wood*, 1817–19. The first Anglican expansion in Frome. This odd-looking church began as a nominally Gothic (but not Perp) four-bay aisled nave with high clerestory, and a chancel within the short battlemented tower. This had three blind arches in anticipation of a cruciform E end, finally achieved in 1929. W gallery added by *Charles Long*, 1828. The church was Gothicized by *Manners & Gill*, 1851 (parapets, Perp tracery in the aisles – except the S aisle W, still with original Y-tracery). Re-seated, 1868. Chancel by *Harold Brakspear*, 1904–5; Perp E window, heavily buttressed angles. S porch heightened as a full transept in 1899. Brakspear added a shallow Lady Chapel E of

---

* Fine late C17 wrought ironwork from the N transept, believed to be tomb railings, is in the Victoria and Albert Museum.

the N transept in 1929. The slim iron columns of the nave were unfortunately encased in reinforced concrete to brace them when the galleries were removed in 1960, by *Ronald Vallis*. Reordering by *Lawrence King*, 1968. – ROOD SCREEN. By *Herbert Read*, 1910. In the style of Voysey. – STAINED GLASS. E window by *Kempe*, 1905.

HOLY TRINITY, Trinity Street. 1837–8, by *H. E. Goodridge*. His brief was to design an effective termination to Trinity Street, though he never saw the site. The resulting ritual W (actually E) front is in the Commissioners' style. Three doorways tightly grouped under starved gables, three stepped lancets above, heavy flanking spirelets over the gallery staircases. Small W gallery, shallow chancel. Big ritual S transept, 1851. – FITTINGS. Wrought-iron chancel SCREEN the full width of the nave, by *Singer & Sons*, 1903 (resited). – PAINTINGS. Two by *H. T. Ryall*, Entombment and Crucifixion; Early Victorian. – STAINED GLASS. E window, 1875 by *Horwood Bros* of Mells. In contrast, twelve sumptuously coloured lights by *Morris & Co.*, 1880–1921, to designs by *Burne-Jones* of 1869–96. – To the l., lancet-style SCHOOL of 1840, extended by *W. G. Brown*, 1887. Remodelled as halls etc. by *NVB Architects*, 2004; glazed link with upcurved timber canopy.

ST MARY, Innox Hill. 1863–4, by *C. E. Giles*. Small and aiseless, with sharply geometrical polygonal apse and a big ornate bell-cote. Lancet windows. – REREDOS, E.E. style. – FONT, 1844. Square, on green marble columns. – PULPIT. Solid sides with all-over pattern of inlaid slate. – Hanging ROOD in the form of an anchor, placed here 1952. – STAINED GLASS. Three apse lancets by *Clayton & Bell*, 1864. Nave S, third from E, *Hardman*, 1966.

A low former SCHOOLROOM is attached at the N, with a triangular dormer of four lancets. Connected to its N, a picturesque VICARAGE, originally houses for schoolmaster and curate. The whole complex by *Giles*, 1864,

ST CATHARINE (R.C.), Park Road. By *Martin Fisher*, 1967–8. Blockwork walls. Polygonal with conical roof.

ROOK LANE CONGREGATIONAL CHAPEL (former), Bath Street. Of 1707, and exceptionally handsome. Its size and pride remarkable at so early a date. Paid for by Robert Smith, clothier, of Rook Lane House; the builder, *James Pope*, perhaps also made the design. In 1717 the congregation numbered 1,000. Gatepiers with urns and railings, all probably of 1862, enclose a rising forecourt. Seven bays, with five-bay pedimented centre, the windows round-arched with Wrennish ears; cast-iron frames of 1862. Doorway with broken pediment. At the outer corners, set-back entrance additions of 1862 by *W. J. Stent*, in keeping. Closed in 1968, the chapel became derelict; repaired 1992–3, by *Plincke Leaman & Browning*. Inside, two big stone Doric columns with separate entablature blocks, and between them a shallow elliptical dome (reinstated from archaeological evidence, 1992–3). The ground floor is used for exhibitions and performances. U-shaped gallery used as offices by *NVB Architects*, who in 2002–3 added a steel and glass link to a rear wing with a monopitch roof; admirable and uncompromisingly new.

UNITED REFORMED CHURCH (former Zion Congregational), Whittox Lane. 1810, refaced by *Joseph Chapman Jun.* in 1888, in North Italian Romanesque. Gabled front red sandstone shafts to the windows. Schoolroom behind, 1837. Charmingly quirky octagonal former SUNDAY SCHOOL (s), perhaps also by *Chapman*, 1875.

METHODIST CHAPEL, Wesley Slope. 1810–12, by *James Lester*, a builder-architect. Tuscan porch. Plain five-bay front, round-arched first-floor windows. Gallery with external staircase extensions. Upper floor inserted.

MINOR CHAPELS. Most important the big former BAPTIST CHAPEL, Catherine Street. Now housing. 1813, on an older site. Five bays by seven, rising up behind the rooftops of the narrow street. Offset from the chapel is a fine screen wall to the courtyard, and a pure Greek Doric portico with paired columns, *c.* 1845. In South Parade, a former BAPTIST CHAPEL by *J. Davis*, 1850. Ashlar-fronted, one-three-one bays with flanks advancing. It replaced a grand chapel of 1708. Red brick Italianate schools behind, 1860. A small PRIMITIVE METHODIST CHAPEL, Sun Street, primitively altered *c.* 1880. Finally a good DISSENTERS' CEMETERY, Vallis Way; 1851, with a small Romanesque chapel.

PUBLIC BUILDINGS

CIVIC OFFICES (former), Christchurch Street West. By *Halliday & Anderson* of Cardiff, 1891, as offices for the Board of Guardians. Free Victorian Renaissance.

LIBRARY, Justice Lane. *Somerset County Council Architects' Department*, *c.* 1990. Two storeys, rubble-faced, with cupola, and entrance set back beneath an overhanging polygonal first floor with much glazing.

MUSEUM, North Parade. By *James Hine* of Plymouth, *c.* 1865–8. *p. 512* Built as a Literary and Scientific Institute. On a flatiron plan, the narrow end facing the Town Bridge and Market Place. Three storeys, Italianate with round-arched openings, of Bath stone sparingly inlaid with pink Mansfield stone. Cast-iron balconettes by *Singer*.

BLUECOAT SCHOOL and ALMSHOUSES, Town Bridge. A 57 rebuilding of *c.* 1720–4. The design is oddly disjointed. The deeply projecting two-storey centre is quite Baroque, with quoins, four big arched windows, and a doorway with a figure of a charity boy in the broken pediment. Above this, statue of a charity woman in a niche. The figures ('Nancy Guy' and 'Billy Ball') were carved by *William Langley* in 1724. Little cupola and clock on the roof. Three-storey wings with vernacular mullioned windows; each wing bisected by a broad chimneystack. Near the bridge, two statues of charity girls, from the demolished Stevens's Asylum (*see* p. 509).

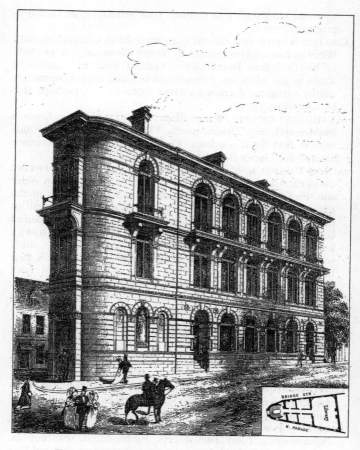

Frome, Museum (Literary and Scientific Institute).
Engraving, 1869

COMMUNITY HOSPITAL, Enos Way. By *DK Architects* of Bath,
2006–8; two ranges with opposing roof slopes, linked by a
recessed entrance.

VICTORIA HOSPITAL, Park Road. By *B. V. Johnson*, *c.* 1899–
1901, altered. Small and quietly Neo-Georgian.

MARKET HALL (former), Market Yard. By *W. J. Stent* of
Warminster, 1873–5. Gable-ended, two colours of brick; simple
Italianate. An arts centre since 1998.

RAILWAY STATION, Wallbridge. By *J. R. Hannaford* of the GWR,
opened 1850. A rare, largely unaltered survival of an early
covered station. Timber-clad through-shed with a low office
range to the w. Timber-framed corrugated-iron roof with iron
tie bars and clerestory ventilation.

Town Bridge. By *G. A. Underwood*, County Surveyor, 1821. Unusually it has houses on the w side, as at Pulteney Bridge, Bath. The early c18 bridge here had houses, so it was probably a case of fulfilling leases, rather than emulation.

PERAMBULATIONS

1. *From the Market Place to St John's church*

The Market Place lies s of the Frome bridge, widening to a wedge as it rises to Bath Street, which tips into it from the se. It was originally in two parts, but the making of Bath Street *c.* 1810–13 prompted the clearance of a dividing block. Few buildings now have visible pre-c18 fabric. At the nw corner is the Greek Revival NatWest Bank, built as assembly rooms *c.* 1819–21. The likeliest designer is *John Pinch Sen.*, who made an unexecuted design now in Frome Museum, but *Jeffry Wyatt* or *G. A. Underwood* are possible too. Ground floor with arches, originally open, forming a market hall (blocked *c.* 1874). First floor with Ionic columns paired with pilasters. Remodelled by *Oatley & Lawrence*, 1920–3; how much is theirs? Then (n), the George Hotel, much remodelled 1754–5 and refronted *c.* 1874. Three bays and three storeys. n again is the four-storey Crown Inn, refronted very plainly *c.* 1820, but the mullioned back with a bullseye in one gable accords with a date 1697 within. On the e side next to Town Bridge is the Blue Boar Inn of 1691, with later sash windows. A panelled pier at the l. is from the lock-up of 1724, demolished *c.* 1961–3. To the s of Cheap Street is Lloyd's Bank, *c.* 1840, with Renaissance refacing by *W. J. Stent*, 1874. Opposite, in the market square, a former drinking fountain, 1871, by the artist and author *E. V. Boyle*, an unusually early design by a woman. Octagonal basin, shaft with foliate cross.

Cheap Street climbs e from the Market Place. Picturesque, narrow, and already old when first recorded in 1500; numerous timber-framed houses behind later fronts. On the n side, No. 4, c16 or c17 with ovolo-mullioned oriels, double jetty at the rear, and c17 staircase. Nos. 5 and 6 also *c.* 1550–1650. Nos. 7 and 7a on a double plot, with c16 timber front, stone behind. No. 11 is the best timber-framed house in Frome, perhaps *c.* 1530–60 and elaborately carved, e.g. Tudor roses beneath the jetty. Pentice roof over arcaded shopfront of *c.* 1900. Opposite (s side) is No. 13, on the corner with Eagle Lane. One c17 upper window; early c20 half-timbering following previous forms. Behind the n side runs Apple Alley, a chance for the archaeologically-minded to inspect the backs.

n of Cheap Street again is King Street, equally old. The Angel Hotel has an early c19 front, but was extant by 1668. se, two good c18 houses owned by the Sheppards, prominent clothiers. Iron Gates was built a little before 1696, and altered *c.* 1725–50. Five-bay front, segment-headed windows,

pedimented doorcase. Good C18 staircase with turned balusters. Attached at right angles behind is COURT HOUSE,
c. 1700–10. Its centre also has segment-headed windows and a
shell door hood. To their E, the bare KINGSWAY shopping
precinct (*L. R. Ings*, 1976) disrupts the older character. King
Street climbs s past the THREE SWANS INN, low and gabled,
C16 proportions, and up to CHURCH STEPS. Here at their
foot, a SPRING in the N churchyard wall, with arched well-
head by *C. E. Giles*, *c.* 1865–6. On the W side of the steps is
OLD CHURCH HOUSE, *c.* 1600, with stone basement and
ground floor, and two timber-framed storeys (once gabled)
oversailing on a moulded bressumer. A five-light mullioned-
and-transomed C17 window r. of the door. Church Steps rise
to the forecourt of St John's church.

2. *South and east of St John's church*

Sunk into the SE corner of the churchyard, a relocated C17 lock-
up with a hole in the domed roof for food and air. NE of the
church in SAXONVALE was Merchant's Barton, dem. *c.* 1970.*
VICARAGE STREET runs E. The Gothic ST JOHN'S HALL (N)
is by *C. E. Giles*, 1854, originally a school with playground in
an arched undercroft (now blocked). Next, the VICARAGE of
c. 1744–9. Suggested designers *Henry Spencer* or *Nathaniel
Ireson*. Three-bay centre with set-back wings (returns filled in
and a boxy Ionic porch added, mid C19). The windows flanking the doorway have heavy Gibbs surrounds and stepped keystones. Opposite, Nos. 27–28 have C18 fronts, and a moulded
arch of the early C16 between. Adjacent, No. 26, handsome
mid-C17. E again at the junction with Garsdale, GARSTON
LODGE, Regency Gothic with battlemented parapets, shallow
ogee-arched windows and porch on clustered shafts. Rebuilt
c. 1800–13 around a possibly C16 core, and refaced *c.* 1830.

Back to St John, from where GENTLE STREET climbs s; a pedes-
trian lane with good houses of the C16 and later. No. 12,
ARGYLL HOUSE (W side), was built *c.* 1768–9 for Mary Jesser,
of a prominent family of clothiers. A handsome and fashionable façade with two Venetian windows on each storey. Fine
Chinese Chippendale staircase balustrade. NW wing *c.* 1820.
Further up, No. 9, KNOLL HOUSE, 1839; three storeys, heavy
Tuscan porch, banded ground floor with segment-headed
windows. Gentle Street narrows towards the bulky mid-C19
LAMB BREWERY. Four storeys, converted to flats 2004–5, with
the steep roof reinstated.

BATH STREET descends from the crossroads with Christchurch
Street N to the Market Place. Laid out 1810–13, replacing
narrow lanes on land owned by Lord Bath. At the top, No. 10,
altered *c.* 1760–74, with sash windows symmetrical about the
door. (Staircase, *c.* 1720, with a Chinese Chippendale dog gate,

---

* A first-floor ceiling with ribs, stars and flowers, dated 1650, is at Priory Barn,
Bradford-on-Avon, Wilts. A copy is at Mells Manor.

1760s.) Nos. 11–15 are all lower and gabled, mid-C17. The steeply curving N end of Bath Street was mostly complete by 1820. On the r., terraced shops with ramped parapets, Bath-fashion; at No. 4 an Ionic shopfront, *c.* 1835. At No. 19, a good faience butcher's shopfront *c.* 1920.

3. *South from the Market Place*

Mainly C17 and C18 expansions. NW of the Market Place is CORK STREET. Nos. 3 and 3b, mid-C17, with mullioned-and-tran-somed first-floor windows. Built as a piece. The gables raised to form a full second floor with cross-windows, *c.* 1690–1700; a third gable (l.) removed. (Fine first-floor ceiling *c.* 1650; vine scrolls, shield, griffin frieze.) Then at right angles, MONMOUTH HOUSE, perhaps *c.* 1730. Plain, five bays. The home of Thomas Bunn, Frome's arbiter of taste, who in 1819 installed plaster replicas of the Parthenon frieze in the entrance hall, by *John Henning.* To the NW, and originally belonging to Monmouth House, a later C17 cloth workshop with Tudor-arched doorway and cross-windows; now a house. An often-misinterpreted type. Back to the corner with Market Place, from where STONY STREET climbs steeply S. No. 16 is prob-ably of 1688 – see three steep pediments shaved off at the first floor, and the rear with cross-windows, and dated lead rain-water goods. From the top of Stony Street, CATHERINE HILL winds up again to the W and SW. Individual buildings are sec-ondary; the lasting impression is a jumble of hilly lanes and hidden courts of various styles and ages. Off Catherine Hill to the S by steps through a covered alley is SHEPPARDS' BARTON, a close of early to mid-C18 houses erected piecemeal for Sheppard's cloth workers, and reshaped *c.* 1820. It leads into SOUTH PARADE. On the NW side, next to the Baptist chapel, a quite humble former FRIENDS' MEETING HOUSE, a rebuilding of 1821. Opposite, a four-storey TEXTILE MILL, *c.* 1825. To the NW of South Parade, WINE STREET and HIGH STREET (both complete by 1755) have minor C18 houses. High Street, which in no way justifies its name, leads back to Cather-ine Street, the W end of which is largely C19. Off to the NW, THE PIGGERIES, perhaps the best recent infill in Frome. By the *Architecture & Planning Group*, 1994–8. Two- to four-storey houses between winding stepped paths.

The NE boundary of The Piggeries is WHITTOX LANE, running N off Catherine Street. Here is MELROSE HOUSE, Frome's best pre-C18 house, probably *c.* 1690–5, as witnessed by the tall blocked cross-windows facing the street. Grand though not large, one room deep and two wide. The main front is at right angles to the street, its cross-windows replaced *c.* 1720; also the pediment and urn to the doorcase, cornices over the windows, and the good staircase. Main rooms with bolection-moulded panelling, the blocked W windows converted to buffet cupboards. Conservative repairs *c.* 1998–2001 uncovered a series of seven C18 overdoor panels on the ground and first

floor, with painted landscapes, battle scenes etc. Shortly N,
Castle Street leads W to Trinity.

4. The Trinity area

An important survival of early urban workers' housing, *c.* ½ m.
NW of the centre. Some half-a-dozen streets of dense terraced
housing built *c.* 1660–1725 for the woollen industry. Its population in 1785 was 2,084. As the leases fell in *c.* 1760–1825,
many houses were altered or refaced. Semi-derelict by the mid
C20, it was then understood as an early C19 district with a few
older cottages. Two 1960s schemes cleared everything NE of
Trinity Street; a Clearance Order for the rest was mercifully
delayed by the local government reorganization of 1974, and
in the interim Trinity's true nature was rediscovered.* Successful rehabilitation by *Moxley Jenner & Partners*, 1980–4, sacrificed long rear plots for parking; some houses knocked
two-into-one, a few demolished. Most original features were
retained. Trinity is regarded as a nationally unique example of
an early industrial suburb. Despite this, the scholarly repairs
are being unpicked, with uPVC double-glazing appearing
everywhere.

p. 517 Development began just before 1660 with the NW side of Vallis
Way between Castle Street and Naish's Street. Lower-status
housing spread NE along Castle Street and the E end of Trinity
Street, complete by 1685; then Selwood Road, the centre of
Trinity Street and the S end of Naish's Street (by *c.* 1705);
finally the NW end of Trinity Street, and the demolished streets
to its NE, by *c.* 1725. The simplest houses consisted of one room
with a door straight off the street; others had two rooms side
by side or one behind the other. Some wide houses had a third
room to the rear. All might have a newel stair winding up next
to the chimneystack, or in the larger plans, a cross-passage to
a rear stair projection. Interiors include chamfered and
stopped beams (often plastered), scratch-moulded panelled
doors and stair risers, and ventilated cupboards.

At the S end of VALLIS WAY, No. 4, eight bays, pre-dates 1697
(refenestrated). Then No. 5 with stone cross-windows, a stairwell bullseye, and the legend 'Time trieth troth June ye 3 JS
1697'. Nos. 6–9 were similar before alterations. None had
gables. In CASTLE STREET, No. 23 is unusual for being
refronted in brick and ashlar, perhaps 1730–50; the grandest
house in Trinity, of five bays. Behind, the former SELWOOD
PRINTING WORKS of Messrs Butler & Tanner, built in three
dated stages, 1866, 1870 and 1876, by *Joseph Chapman Jun*.
Rubble stone with brick dressings, window openings in arcades
of three to five. Nos. 1–3 are *c.* 1680, gabled and mullioned.

---

*R. Leech, *Early Industrial Housing: The Trinity Area of Frome*, RCHME, 1981.

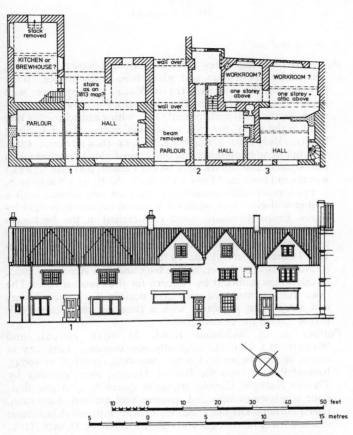

Frome, Nos. 1–3 Trinity Street.
Elevations and ground plans, 1981

No. 7 is of the same date, but of three storeys, with brick-vaulted cellars. On the N side here, shabby and dispiriting flats and shops (*Ronald Vallis*, 1962 and later), the intended fate for all of Trinity. Exemplifying the change in thinking is WILT-SHIRE'S BARTON, opposite; infill by *Moxley Jenner & Partners* completed 1984. Rendered three-storey flats, vernacular in spirit without copying. Behind (S), Naish's Street, where Nos. 29 and 30 (NE side) of 1705 are perhaps among the last to be built with attic gables. SW of Holy Trinity (*see* p. 510) in GOULD'S GROUND is FOUNTAIN HOUSE, built 1818, the former vicarage of Holy Trinity, with two-storey central bow to the garden (N).

OUTER AREAS

1. *North and east*

Across Town Bridge a few diversions around NORTH PARADE, laid out by Act of 1797, with plain three-storey houses. To the E, following the river is WILLOW VALE, a pretty street with good C17 and C18 houses. The FEATHER FACTORY is a three-storey textile mill, perhaps early C19, with gambrel roof, a rare form in the SW. Converted to housing with a new stair-turret by *Bruce Yoell*, 2001–3. Further E, Nos. 14–16, a terrace, *c.* 1720, with tall slender windows and bolection-framed doorways with thin semicircular hoods. W of North Parade, BRIDGE STREET was the old road out of town. On the l., the BLACK SWAN pub, *c.* 1750, plain and symmetrical. Now an arts centre, with a timber-and-glass rear addition achieved on a tiny budget by *Aaron Evans Architects*, 2000–1. Attached at the back is a former DRYING HOUSE for dyed cloth, of 1796, converted to a tourist information centre, 1994. A circular tower about 16 ft (5 metres) across and 19 ft 6 in. (6 metres) high. To the N, No. 13 Bridge Street, of five bays and two storeys, *c.* 1700. Nicely unencumbered by concern for the classical rules. The door frame is moulded with ears; outside this Ionic pilasters and steep open pediment with a Baroque cartouche. Pediments too on the ground floor.

Further N in Welshmill Road, MENDIP HOUSE and WELSHMILL HOUSE, originally one dwelling. Late C17 in origin (a C17 beam and some panelling reported in 1974). Remodelled *c.* 1790 for Robert Meares, dyer, possibly by *Thomas Baldwin*. Central tripartite doorway, alternate first-floor windows pedimented, paterae and garland decoration, raised corners. On the S façade, a niche with tall Adamesque urn and frieze of husk garlands. To the N, No. 35, INNOX HILL, a pretty *cottage orné*, *c.* 1820, recently extended. Tudor openings under square labels. E again, Nos. 4–11 are early C19 three-storey weavers' houses; behind, further terraces forming a secluded court. Returning to North Parade, NORTH HILL HOUSE was first rated 1779; an elegant plain house of the Le Gros family, silk manufacturers. Overbearing C19 attics. FROMEFIELD is the NE continuation of North Parade; where it joins Bath Road is FROMEFIELD HOUSE, *c.* 1797, for the clothier George Sheppard. Some Adamesque ornament, flat parapets, five-bay entrance front with pediments and blind arches over the windows in the first, third and fifth bays. Tripartite entrance. The heights of openings etc. on the two main façades are misaligned.

E of the centre, two mills survive at WALLBRIDGE, both now housing. N of the eponymous bridge, a three-storey stone tweed mill, a rebuilding of 1868, two bays by seven. The last woollen manufactory in Frome, closed 1965, adapted as flats, 2005–7. To its S, E of The Retreat, a three-storey mill, extant by 1727.

2. *South and west*

s of the centre, clusters of diverting buildings lead off in two directions. At Wesley Slope, opposite the roundabout at the top of Bath Street, are good Methodist SCHOOLS, adjacent to the chapel. Two houses sandwiching a low school range of 1858, plain Gothic, by *W. J. Willcox*, who added the low range and another house to the NW in 1863. Leading off NW is Christchurch Street West, an C18 development. On its N side, ROOK LANE HOUSE has three big gables. Probably the site purchased in 1607 by Robert Smith, clothier, whose descendants built Rook Lane Chapel nearby. Updated with sashes etc. in the C19. At the corner of Wesley Close, BUNN PILLAR, 1825, the survivor of four marking the entrance to a Grecian crescent planned by Thomas Bunn. Circular, with channelled rustication and anthemia etc., round the cap. Adjacent in Christchurch Street West, a Gothic former POLICE STATION by *C. E. Davis*, 1856–7. Irregular; triple-arched entrance under a big window. In Park Road, CHRIST CHURCH SCHOOLS (now flats) by *G. G. Scott*, Jacobethan, 1844, with additions of 1899–1900 by *W. G. Brown*. Christchurch Street West continues W; the PACKHORSE INN (N side) has coupled doorways with replicas of steep swan-necked pediments and vases. W of Christ Church is WEST LODGE, 1778–80, with a serpentine pediment to the doorway and Venetian windows l. and r. of the centre (cf. No. 12 Gentle Street).

To the s of Wesley Slope is KEYFORD, both district and road. Again, C18 and later fronts hide older structures. The CROWN INN is late C17, mullioned and gabled; then No. 27, a pretty mid-C18 shopfront, two bow windows, good fanlight. A little to the E in Lock's Hill, a MEDICAL CENTRE by *Jeremy & Caroline Gould Architects*, 1995–6. Low, with the upper floor in a big slate roof which projects at the s, with spiral escape staircase beneath. A little SW is STONEWALL MANOR, Lower Keyford, again mid-C17 with the usual gables and mullions, on an impressive scale. Much restored *c.* 1900 in C17 style (early C17 plaster ceiling in the hall).

FROME TOOL AND GAUGE, Manor Road. A striking single-storey factory, mid-1960s, blue engineering brick with reinforced-concrete shell roofs in three curving parts.

WORKHOUSE (former), Weymouth Road, by *Sampson Kempthorne*, 1837–8. Based on his Y-shaped radial plan of 1834. Three storeys, plain classical with gabled centre in each wing, within a hexagon of low service buildings, the latter half-demolished in conversion to housing, *c.* 1990s.

KNOLL HOUSE, Whitemill Lane, ¼ m. SW. A good *moderne* flat-roofed house by *Ronald Vallis*, 1935. Round-ended balcony.

GREAT ELM

7040

ST MARY MAGDALENE. An early church. The nave has the herringbone masonry typical of Saxo-Norman work. A blocked

Norman N doorway to the chancel, also a small window with a renewed head which may well be Norman. The squat w tower was added in the C13. Its proportions and absence of buttresses at first also look Norman, but the w doorway is E.E. One order of colonnettes, arch depressed-pointed, starting on vertical springers. Dogtooth in the hoodmould. Window with round arch and a pierced quatrefoil above. Tower arch (behind vestry doors) on responds with moulded capitals standing on corbels. The tower has a big saddleback roof. Big N transept added in 1837, with crude trefoil-headed lights. Probably at the same time the tracery of the nave s windows and of the e window was replaced; the cusped rere-arches in the nave are C13. Nave ceiling of the C17; thin ribs with leaves, stars or bosses at the intersections. In the transept an able imitation of 1837. – PULPIT. Plain, mid-Georgian. – BOX PEWS. Jacobean. The ends with semicircular heads, their centres hollowed out and carved with shells, as at Mells. In the transept, C19 pine copies. – GALLERY of 1837, bow-fronted, on Doric columns, Jacobean-style arched panels.

NW of the church stands GLEBE HOUSE, with a low L-shaped Tudor part and a three-storey early C19 addition at the w. In one room a plaster ceiling of c. 1630 with some of the same motifs as the church roofs. s of the church a small green, with a Neo-Tudor former SCHOOL, c. 1830. Some 350 yds SE is a river bridge; SE of the bridge was one of Fussell's six IRON WORKS in the area; built c. 1792. Pits for three water wheels.

HAPSFORD HOUSE, c. 1 m. E. Built for George George, a Frome cloth manufacturer, c. 1815–20, extended c. 1834. (Two-storey blocks flanking a single-storey centre, with Tudor Gothic details. Verandas and canted bays to the garden. Large grounds with lakes and an island GROTTO, pre-1839.) At Hapsford Bridge (E), an early C19 MILL, apparently iron works. Much renewed 2006–7. Nearby is MURTRY AQUEDUCT, c. 1796–1800, built to carry the intended Dorset and Somerset Canal over the Mells stream. Possibly by *William Bennett* of Beckington, surveyor to the canal company. Three low elliptical arches with jointed voussoirs, and pilasters between the arches. For Murtry Bridge, *see* p. 431.

TEDBURY IRON AGE HILL-FORT lies in woodland ½ m. SW of the village, its earth rampart still 12 ft (3.7 metres) high in places. Its defensive location is enhanced by the Wadbury and Fordbury valleys to the N and s. One of a group of hill-forts in the vicinity (cf. Mells).

GREEN ORE

Green Ore is a huddle of cottages and pub around a busy cross-roads. At BEECHBARROW FARM, c. ¾ m. SW, at the SE side of the Bristol road, is a SCULPTURE representing Romulus and

Remus with the she-wolf, reportedly copying the image on a banknote. Made *c.* 1945 by *Gaetano Celestra*, a prisoner-of-war, in recognition of the kindly treatment of Italian prisoners. Concrete on an iron frame, raised on a four-legged plinth.

Nearby stands PEN HILL MAST, a guyed steel television and radio transmitter, erected 1967. 1,001 ft (305 metres) high, on one of the highest points on Mendip.

HALLATROW   6050

THE GRANGE, Paulton Road, modest-sized, is dated 1669; one or two ovolo-moulded windows survive, without their mullions. About 1800 the ground-floor openings were given fanciful ogee heads (cf. Cameley House). Unusual star-patterned glazing. In Hart's Lane, ⅓ m. NW, HALLATROW COURT, dated 1674. Three bays at the l. of 1873.

WHITE CROSS, ⅔ m. WSW. At the road junction, a toll house built for the Bath Turnpike Trust, 1818–19. In the gable-end, a blind Gothic arch with quatrefoil light in the first floor. Much modernized.

HARDINGTON   7050

ST MARY (Churches Conservation Trust). Small and forlorn amongst big utilitarian C20 farm buildings. Nave and chancel, and a tiny oblong tower, its top at least of the late C15 with battlements and pinnacles. One w window and a niche above it. Late C14 nave with lingering Dec influence in the windows. Much was rebuilt in the early C17, see the small two-light windows, e.g. in the chancel. Uneven chancel arch, possibly Norman, of basket-arch shape. Restored 1858–9 by *Sir G. G. Scott*, including rebuilding the E and S chancel walls; repaired 1963–7 and 1973–5. The interior has a Georgian air, with silvery oak fittings: two-decker PULPIT and ALTAR RAILS, *c.* 1780, BOX PEWS, early C19. – ROYAL ARMS of Charles I, repainted 1817. – WALL PAINTINGS. N wall, fragments of crude foliate patterns in red, possibly C16 or C17. – MONUMENT. Col. Warwick Bampfylde †1694. Fine standing wall monument of   65 white marble some 12 ft (4 metres) high. A trophy on the base, inscription on a swagged cloth with garlanded volutes to the sides, swept top with two cherubs, more garlands and an urn. Attributed to *William Stanton* (GF).

Hardington is now just a church and a farm. The C15 house was ruinous by the C18, although an early C17 wing was repaired by 1802 as a farmhouse, demolished *c.* 1952. Earthworks of garden terraces s of the church were largely bulldozed in 1977.

The STABLES of the manor house of the Bampfyldes, *c.* 1690–1700, survive NW of the church. Once among the grandest of its type in Somerset, now at extreme risk. A long two-storey range with finely moulded cross-windows and upright oval pitching eyes in the S front, very big and high central doorway and broken pediment. Corresponding doorway in the N side, so perhaps the stables acted as a sort of gatehouse. Big holes punched in the walls for its use as a barn.

On the hillside to the NW, the tall narrow KEEPER'S LODGE, dated 1581, with a first-floor banqueting chamber.

7050

HEMINGTON

ST MARY. A church with interesting work of several periods, particularly the C13 and early C14. Restored in 1859 and 1862 by *G. G. Scott*, with a prim Transitional S porch with mechanical carving. Norman chancel arch with moulded imposts, two orders of columns with scallop capitals. Two-stepped arch. E.E. S doorway of *c.* 1230 with a stilted arch on columns with moulded capitals. Continuous inner roll moulding. The S aisle clearly of the same date, with windows shafted inside with Blue Lias shafts which carry trefoil rere-arches. The two-light tracery is Dec, perhaps a century later. The N side is aisleless, also with Dec windows and Perp square-headed clerestory lights above – an oddly domestic effect. The arcade piers (four bays) are circular with circular capitals and double-chamfered arches. Ambitious two-bay S chapel, early C13, the central pier towards the chancel circular, with four detached Blue Lias shafts; leaf sprays on the base. W and E responds on corbels, the E one with upright stiff-leaf. Double-chamfered arches. W tower of three stages with diagonal buttresses, yet with the second displaying two blank tall transomed two-light windows (cf. Buckland Dinham). Three-light bell-openings above with Somerset tracery. It must be late C15 or very early C16. Arch to the nave with two wave mouldings. Good roofs: nave on big demi-figures of angels, S aisle roof also on corbels. – BENCH-ENDS. Unusually, C17 with heavy fleur-de-lys finials. – FONT. Plain, circular, Norman, with two friezes of lobes. – S door perhaps C15, renewed tracery to the external face. – STAINED GLASS. E window designed by *G. E. R. Smith (A. K. Nicholson Studio)*, *c.* 1938. – MONUMENTS. Edward and Katherine Batcheler †1667. Heavy proto-classical tablet, still with strapwork. – Samuel Vigor †1711. Bolection frame, broken pediment and crude incised pattern. – In the churchyard, two good Neoclassical CHEST TOMBS to the Craddock family.

Former RECTORY, W of the church. Five-bay centre of the mid C18, flat door hood, segmental-arched window above, prominent keystones. Big S wing, early C19.

For Upper Row Farm, *see* Laverton.

HEWISH

4060

Thinly strung out along the A370 Weston-super-Mare road.

ST ANNE (former). 1864, by *John Norton*. Paid for by John Phippen, Mayor of Bristol. A spacious transeptal church in the E.E. style, with rather bleak plate tracery. Wide semicircular apse of thirteen lancets under trefoil-headed rere-arches with Blue Lias shafts. S transept with statue of Madonna and Child below a big rose window. A tower was raised to 70 ft (21.5 metres) on the boggy soil before it collapsed. In its place, a small circular turret with conical roof in the angle between nave and N transept. Made redundant, 1979, and converted to two houses, with an intermediate floor inserted.

Attractively grouped with the former VICARAGE (E), and Gothic PRIMARY SCHOOL (W), given by Phippen, 1868, perhaps also by *Norton*.

HIGH LITTLETON

6050

HOLY TRINITY. Small Perp W tower, perhaps late C14. Angle buttresses, two-light windows. Pinnacles of 1903. The rest rebuilt by *Wilson & Wilcox*, 1884–8. NE chapel added *c.* 1890–7. Arcade piers with attached shafts of polished Purbeck marble. – STAINED GLASS. All probably *Bell & Son*, *c.* 1885–97.

HIGH LITTLETON HOUSE. A very interesting house of *c.* 1710. Five bays, two-and-a-half storeys defined by moulded string courses, elaborately framed doorway flanked by Ionic pilasters. On the ground floor and first floor are tall cross-windows with the segmental heads of Wren and the Early Georgians, in the attic, normal rectangular cross-windows. A balustrade screens the basement area, which has two symmetrical staircases down to kitchen and offices. The rear updated *c.* 1800 with plain sashes and a columned porch.

RUGBOURNE FARM, Timsbury Road, *c.* ¼ m. E. An impressive manor house usually assigned to the late C17, although there is some evidence for a date *c.* 1630. This would be remarkably early for a double-pile plan in Somerset. Three storeys, symmetrical five-bay front with ovolo mullions, the transoms removed except in three windows in the centre of the first floor. Upright oval lights in the attic gables. Four early C18 sash openings replacing mullions. Decorative thistle-and-rose C17 ceiling in the parlour. The blocked second-floor lights are to be reopened, and missing transoms replaced.

The main street has late C19 miners' terraces, and some small C18 houses, e.g. PEMBROKE HOUSE, dated 1777, with symmetrically placed oblong mullioned windows. Some local mason must have had a penchant for the ogee-Gothick windows fashionable in late C18 Bristol: e.g. Cottage Farm,

Timsbury Road, dated 1724, enlarged in the Gothick style
c. 1780–1820. It appears too in even more humble cottages.

HINTON BLEWETT

Nice triangular green open to the countryside on the s. The
church tower appears behind a row of cottages to the N.

ST MARGARET. Perp, though with interesting C16 and C17 work
and restoration and fittings by good C20 names. Of Blue Lias
with a Doulting stone arcade. Perp w tower, low and square
with diagonal buttresses and a higher stair-turret. Parapet with
pierced quatrefoils in squares, in the style of the 1630s (cf. East
Harptree). Square w window with mullions, probably also C17.
Nave with square-headed windows, crude s porch, small rood-
stair turret. Over the priest's door (chancel s), the initials and
arms of Simon Seward, rector 1514–59. He added the N aisle
and its eastern chapel *c.* 1553, a most unusual date. More
square-headed windows, with quatrefoil tracery. Arcade with
short piers of standard type (four hollows), but unconventional
moulded capitals broken by flat projections. The same design
for the arches of the N chapel. The chancel arch oddly re-cut
with mouldings curving in deeply at the base. Sensitively
restored by *Robert Marchant*, 1927–8, with rough grey rendered
walls. – ALTAR RAILS. Simple C17 style, by *Vivian Young*, 1939.
– PULPIT and tester. Dated 1638, possibly much renewed. –
BENCH-ENDS. Square-headed with tracery, late C15 or even
C16. – FONT. Norman, square, in the shape of a cushion capital
with little angle volutes. A frieze of lunettes beneath the rim,
little sprays of foliage around the foot. – TOWER SCREEN.
Anthony Methuen, 1955. – STAINED GLASS. E window *c.* 1919,
Virgin with St Michael and St George.

HINTON CHARTERHOUSE

HINTON PRIORY. The charterhouse of *Locus Dei*, founded at
Hatherop in 1222, moved here by a grant of 1227. Initial building was complete in 1232. The founder was Ela, widow of
William Longespée (cf. Salisbury). In the same year she
founded an Augustinian nunnery at Lacock, Wiltshire. Hinton
is thus the second Carthusian house in England, after Witham
(*Somerset: South and West*). Much more is visible here than at
Witham, namely the chapter house, the refectory, and parts of
the guesthouse. Excavations in 1951 and *c.* 1958 revealed the
main cloister 226 ft (70 metres) square. Of this, shallow earthworks survive. Around its W, S and E sides were fifteen houses

rather than cells: Carthusians, it will be remembered, lived in solitary silence, each in a house with its own walled garden. Of the CHURCH to the N, almost nothing survives but much can be deduced. It was only 100 ft (31 metres) long, without aisles or transepts, and consisted of five cross-ribbed bays. Between the church and the main cloister was a small cloister, about 38 ft (12 metres) square. These were characteristic Carthusian features: unlike other orders, the communal buildings – church, chapter house, refectory etc. – were of lesser significance, individual provision greater.

The CHAPTER HOUSE, c. 1230 or a little later, stood at the SE corner of the small cloister. It remains in impressively good condition; a two-storey, rectangular tower-like building, with cross-gabled attic storey. Rubble walls with broad flat buttresses, chamfered at their bases. Single lancets on the upper floor. To the E, a lower wing with a later dovecote on the upper floor. Attached to the N face of the chapter house, a deeply projecting two-storey stair-tower with gabled roof. The stair gave access to the church roof, and to a tunnel-vaulted room in the tower (possibly a sacristy?). Remains of a trefoil-headed piscina, and above it (r.) a vault springer from the church. Single-chamfered ribs spring from a triple shaft with moulded capital, carried in turn on a small corbel. The W side of the stair-tower has a lean-to containing a narrow vaulted corridor with chamfered transverse arches, leading S from the church to the chapter house. The chapter house itself is rib-vaulted in three bays, one and two with single-chamfered ribs, but three, a little later, separated by a broad arch, with ribs of fine, partly filleted moulding. The vaults rest on moulded (and also freely carved stiff-leaf) capitals and stand on corbels or shafts with fillets. One corbel is reeded, another reeded and violently twisted. On the E side, stepped triple lancets. In the S wall, a trefoil-headed piscina with a little stiff-leaf in the small spandrels. The W entrance doorway has a fine moulding and stiff-leaf stops to the hoodmould. Otherwise most doorways are depressed two-centred arches with simple chamfers. Above the chapter house was a LIBRARY of two vaulted bays, also with chamfered ribs on shafts with perfectly preserved moulded capitals. The shafts again stand on corbels. The room has lancet windows.

The REFECTORY stands c. 30 yds W. Its date seems to be c. 1300, and like the chapter house, its S wall is aligned with the N walk of the large cloister – see the corbels on the outside S wall. Its undercroft is vaulted in two sections: to the E, three bays of single-chamfered ribs on two central octagonal piers, and on corbels with octagonal capitals; to the W, a smaller room with transverse vault, no central piers, and a big hooded fireplace. The featureless refectory above became a barn. It is accessed from the N by external stairs. Remains of some blocked lancets; C19 roof.

HINTON PRIORY, 80 yds N. Embedded in a later house, parts of a probable C15 GUESTHOUSE near or attached to the priory gatehouse. Best-preserved is the disorderly N front: r. of centre, a polygonal stair-turret, to its l., the broad chimney-breast of the hall, then the main entrance. Big end gables, random mullioned-and-transomed windows. In the late C16 the Hungerfords gave the house essentially its present form with two symmetrically projecting wings to the S. Theirs too, a second spiral staircase, and a handsome ribbed and restrainedly ornamented plaster ceiling on the first floor. The house was restored and enlarged (probably the low E wing) by *Snailum & Pictor*, 1933.

About 1 m. E is the hamlet of FRIARY by the River Frome, originally the lay brothers' quarters. One of two or three such sites in Britain, and the only one not built over. Some medieval work is doubtless embedded in the five cottages. At the river bank, some ruinous walls with a C15 window; possibly a mill.

ST JOHN BAPTIST, Green Lane, ⅓ m. E of the High Street. Much has been added or moved. The basic pattern is probably a late Norman church with a W tower, with a slightly later two-bay S aisle. The church was lightly updated in the early C13, the late C13 and the early C14. Unusually for Somerset, there is little Perp work; it was owned by, and frequently in conflict with, the Priory. C12 the S doorway with continuous roll moulding and hoodmould with big headstops. The broad unbuttressed tower has a triple-chamfered tower arch with simple capitals, and two early C13 lancets with deep inner splays (two more in the S aisle). The top of the tower was renewed in 1770, see the characteristic windows with Gothick Y-tracery. S porch probably added in the C13; its entrance has a moulded arch with a fillet and stiff-leaf corbels (cf. the Charterhouse, i.e. *c.* 1230). In the chancel, a late C13 two-light window with unfoiled circle above and cusped rere-arch, and another, smaller, with cusped lights and a sexfoil. C19 E window. In the S aisle a two-light window with cusped lights and a quatrefoiled circle. Renewed Dec S aisle E window; three lights, the centre opening into a trefoil top. Tudor Gothic N aisle, probably by *Zebedee Scaping* of Norton St Philip, 1825. Reseated 1849 by *G. G. Scott*, who reportedly did more restoration in 1866. – FONT. Norman, tub-shaped, with a chevron band at the top. – STAINED GLASS. E window by *Kempe*, 1889. Much of the early C20 too. – MONUMENTS. John and Margaret Shutt, 1668, still with strapwork and skulls. Two arms clasping a heart. – John Painter †1809, by *W. Brewer*; mourning figure with an urn.

HINTON HOUSE, Green Lane. Parts of Hinton Priory's grange are embedded: the jambs and hinges of an *in situ* tithe barn door were uncovered in 1887, 1949 and 1951 in the N (service) range. The present house began with a fine rebuilding in 1701 for a London barrister. S range of seven bays (2:3:2) and two storeys with a balustrade and hipped roof. Slender sash windows, even quoins, porch with pediment on Ionic columns. The ground-floor windows have triangular pediments. Top-lit

staircase of 1810–13. *Manners & Gill* reworked the E front in
1847–8; plain, of six bays without pediment. Higher parapet
with urns. They moved the porch to the S, making the handsome garden front into the entrance. (Some panelling from
Hunstrete House, Marksbury.)

Next to the church, a small Gothic former SCHOOL, by *William
White*, 1860; L-plan with altered porch in the angle, plate
tracery. The village has the usual Somerset quota of solid
stone-built cottages, C17 and later. No. 40 High Street must
be *c.* 1715 (elliptical doorcase, three upper windows in flat
frames), subdivided and refenestrated in the late C18.

ROMAN ROAD. Traces of 550 yds (500 metres) of the road from
Bath to Poole Harbour were visible within living memory as
an earthwork WSW of Pipehouse, 220 yds E of the B3110 road.
Ploughing has all but levelled the earthwork although its line
can still be discerned as a cropmark.

HOLCOMBE   6040

The C12 old church is delightfully isolated in fields, with Downside Abbey rising distantly behind. The centre of the village has
moved 1 m. S.

OLD ST ANDREW (Churches Conservation Trust). Small W
tower without buttresses, possibly C14 or C15, but the mouldings, pinnacles and small round-headed lights probably C16 or
early C17. Nave and chancel; here too, evidence of C16/C17
rebuilding or updating; see the little scrolled kneelers to the
gables. Re-set in the S porch, a Norman doorway with one
order of spiral-fluted columns with scallop capitals, the arch
with four rows of chevrons, and an outer billet moulding. A
C16 angel above. The r. capital is a re-cut block with part of a
C7–C9 Latin inscription, now upside down. It defies more than
the most conjectural reading. Charming whitewashed interior
with plaster wagon-vaulted nave. – FITTINGS. Mostly white-
painted, C18 fashion. – Two-decker PULPIT composed of
reused panels of *c.* 1630, with simple lozenges and scallop
patterning. – PEWS. Early to mid-C18 on the S; higher late C18
box pews with ramped top rails on the N. Hat pegs above. –
Small MUSICIANS' GALLERY with vase balusters, perhaps
c. 1740–60. – COMMANDMENT BOARDS. Signed *Joseph Emery*
of Wells, 1817. – ROYAL ARMS. 1726. – N of the tower, a late
C19 cross, a memorial to the Scott family, including Robert
Falcon Scott †1912, Antarctic explorer.

ST ANDREW, Holcombe Hill. 1884–5. Small and dull. Red
Pennant Stone, with lancets. Bellcote, S porch. – FONT.
Norman, from the old church, with plain round mouldings. –
STAINED GLASS. E window by *A. L. Moore*, late C19. Nave N,
Christopher Webb, 1946.

ST CUTHBERT (R.C.), Common Lane. An C18 coachhouse, converted in 1926. – Good STAINED GLASS window by *John Redvers*, 1987.

ESE of the old parish church is the Regency OLD RECTORY, and behind, its COACHHOUSE, C16 or C17, perhaps originally a priest's house; the only secular survival of the medieval village site.

HOLCOMBE MANOR, Brewery Lane. A simple late C18 house in the Bath fashion. Pilastered porch with pretty elliptical fanlight. Briefly the home of the family of Robert Scott, whose father managed the brewery adjacent. The three-storey BREWERY building is now residential.

GIANT'S GRAVE, 1 m. NE of Holcombe at Charmborough Farm. Badly damaged chambered long barrow, originally 115 ft by 60 ft (35 by 18.5 metres).

3050   HUTTON

ST MARY, Church Lane. Perp nave, C19 S aisle and chancel. Tall W tower started perhaps *c.* 1430. Diagonal buttresses and paired two-light bell-openings of which only the two inner lights have openings. The paired lights are framed by attached pinnacles as at Locking. W doorway with hoodmoulds, angel headstops, big W window with ogee tracery. The upper stages have almost round-arched heads to the lights, perhaps indicating a second phase for completion in the late C15. Top parapet pierced with trefoils in triangles (cf. Yatton, *c.* 1450). Pinnacles. Higher stair-turret with spirelet. Lierne-vault with many bosses inside the tower. Tower arch continuous (no capitals), two wave mouldings with a deep curved hollow between. Chancel arch similar. In 1849 *S. C. Fripp* rebuilt the chancel and added a four-bay S aisle, reusing the C15 windows; the moulded piers and arches reveal no understanding of Perp forms. Vestry extended to provide new meeting room etc., by *Arturus (Julian Hannam)*, 2003. – FITTINGS. REREDOS of 1858, Gothic panels with painted boards. – PULPIT. Perp, of stone, set high against the N wall on an attached pillar. Blank two-light tracery, leaves in the spandrels, top frieze of quatrefoils then a sort of undercut dogtooth; leaf cresting above (cf. Banwell, Bleadon, Brockley, Wick St Lawrence). – PEWS. 1785, with doors (nave N). – STAINED GLASS. S aisle, W end, 1909, signed *Clayton & Bell*. – MONUMENTS. Brass to John Payne of Hutton Court, †1496, wife and eleven children. 30-in. (76-cm.) figures. – Thomas Payne †1528, wife and children. Recess in the chancel N wall with four-centred panelled arch. Kneeling brass figures. – Nathaniel Still †1626. Sophisticated classicism for that date, perhaps by a Bristol mason. Small hanging monument of cream marble and slate; swan-neck pediment, scrolled sides, heavy mouldings. Kneeling family group. –

Joseph Smith †1825, by *Lancaster & Walker*, Bristol. Grecian sarcophagus, Gothick frame.

HUTTON COURT, Church Lane. The oldest parts are mid-C15, and much added to during the C17 and C18. It forms a square around a small courtyard. At the SW corner, a three-storey embattled tower. Attached S range housing the Hall, still with open arch-braced collar-beam roof; above the wall-plates, a row of tracery panels. N range appearing early to mid C17 with several mullioned windows, but with a wind-braced roof, and at its E end, one truss of a hammerbeam roof. W range probably C17, refaced in the early C18; five bays, two storeys, framed windows, parapet, quoins of even length. A bedroom here has good C17 panelling and arched overmantel with atlantes and caryatids. In the W and S fronts, Gothick interlace glazed sashes, probably late C18. A porch was added to the tower after 1859. (A little way to the S, a ruinous early C18 SUMMER-HOUSE.)

Hutton is otherwise uneventful. Opposite the church, the OLD RECTORY by *Hans Price*, c. 1870; large and Gothic with good timber porch. Also his, the nicely composed PRIMARY SCHOOL, Main Road, 1872. To the W, SUTHERLAND HOUSE originated as a farmhouse (the E wing), perhaps C17. Handsome addition of 1826 with a deeply bowed end facing the entrance to the village.

IFORD   8050

Despite its idyllic appearance, Iford's fast-flowing stream gave rise to mills from the first. The county boundary cuts through the manor house and its splendid garden, developed from 1899 by Harold Peto. For these, *see* Wiltshire.

SERVICE RANGES around the courtyard W of the house (i.e. in Somerset) are probably of medieval origin and served as wool workshops, then as coachhouse, barns etc.; now housing. Nearest the main house a range with Neo-Perp oriel window; adjoining, W, an C18 range with cross-windows.

In front of the manor house, a two-arched BRIDGE of c. 1400, much rebuilt. Above the cutwater a big figure of Britannia with a trident. Added by Peto, c. 1899, reputedly from Salisbury.

KELSTON   7060

ST NICHOLAS, Church Road. Small; chancel, nave, S aisle. Broad sturdy W tower with diagonal buttresses. Saddleback roof behind a solid parapet (cf. Swainswick). Perp belfry lights, but the slit windows below suggest the C13. So does the tower arch, low, pointed and with two broad chamfers. The rest mostly from *Benjamin Ferrey*'s ruthless restoration, 1859–60. – STAINED GLASS. Chancel S window, early C14 saint, assigned to France; much restored. Opposite C15 saint, probably from the Netherlands.*

MANOR FARM, W of the church. Large seven-bay BARN, probably for Shaftesbury Abbey's estate, *c.* 1500; moulded four-centred arch to the porch entrance, angle buttresses, kingpost roof. Directly S, a gabled DOVECOTE, perhaps *c.* 1600. Restored, 1982–3. N of the church, a big stone VILLAGE HALL, also *c.* 1600, with outside steps on the N gable.

Kelston has many mid-C19 ESTATE COTTAGES built for the Neeld and Inigo-Jones family; see Nos. 9–12 Bath Road, with inscription in a fancy pedimented surround. Opposite, a public PUMP shelter, 1858. The Neelds built TOWER HOUSE, NE of the church, by *James Thompson* of London, 1835. Eminently solid, though with little charm in the details. Round-arched eclecticism; is it meant to be Romanesque or Italianate? Severe ashlar walls, paired round-headed lights. At the NW, a shockingly designed tower, the upper cornice corbelled out, tiny lights between the corbels. On the l., a stair-turret on a corbel. Possibly influenced by H. E. Goodridge's unexecuted Norman designs for Beckford's Tower (p. 184).† Italianate terraced garden.

KELSTON PARK, ½ m. SSE. By *John Wood the Younger*, *c.* 1767–8. A plain house, five bays by five, of two storeys over a half-basement. Entrance front (N) with deep porch on paired Gibbsian-blocked columns. Over it, a tripartite window with broken swan-necked pediment over the centre. Above, a small one-bay pediment, barely breaking the parapet. The E and S sides have no such accents; just a frieze and cornice over each ground-floor window. It was enough, it seems, to perch the house and its terrace over a cliff-steep escarpment with views S across the Avon valley. (Drawing room (centre S) with Corinthian fireplace and good panelled ceiling with circular centre. The library ceiling has an octagonal centre and profuse guilloche moulding.) Joined to the W side by a recessed service wing, later C18 STABLES. The W front has a three-bay pediment. Low S front of nine bays with central Venetian window and one-bay pediment. Insensitive infill in the courtyard was replaced by a top-lit drum-shaped reception building when the complex was converted to offices; by *Aaron Evans*, mid-1990s. The wooded PARK was laid out by *Capability Brown*, 1767–8. Two early C19 LODGES by *H. E. Goodridge*.

KELSTON MILLS, *c.* ¾ m. NW. From William Champion's brass mills, *c.* 1760s, two annealing ovens (tall pylon-shaped stone chimneys). Two terraces of workers' cottages.

---

*SCULPTURE fragment stolen in 2004. A Crucifixion scene with a cable border, possibly C13 rather than Saxon.

†Amy Frost, Ph.D. thesis on Goodridge, University of Bath, 2009.

KENN

ST JOHN EVANGELIST. Small Norman w tower with later roof, a stepped stone pyramid with crockets up the angles. Slit windows, one with round arch and fish-scale on the lintel. Nave and chancel all in one. Tall two-light E window, c. 1300, with cusped Y-tracery. Restored by *Foster & Wood*, 1861, rebuilding most of the nave and chancel in its previous form, and raising the walls by several feet. Tower roof also altered and the stepping made regular. – FONT. Octagonal, stem surrounded by shafts. – SOUTH DOOR. Interlaced ogee tracery, Perp. – STAINED GLASS. All by *Joseph Bell*, 1862, except the E window, c. 1876. – MONUMENTS. Christopher Kenn †1593. Erected by his widow Florence, who reclines on the base cradling an infant. Above on a shelf, the familiar Elizabethan kneeling figures, her husband and two daughters. – CROSS. C14, stepped base, big square socket. Restored 1920.

SCHOOL HOUSE (former), NE of the church. Small, Neo-Tudor, dated 1841. VICARAGE to the NW, by *J. H. Spencer* of Taunton, 1879.

KENN COURT. SW of the church. C16 manor house of the Kenn and Stalling families. The former front, facing the road, has two storeys of four mullioned-and-transomed windows. SE return transformed into a new entrance front, c. 1814: semicircular Doric porch, round-arched window above.

LAKE HOUSE FARM, ¾ m. NW. E-plan house of c. 1600, with S-facing two-storey porch. In the longer E wing a large utilitarian fireplace with moulded Tudor-arched opening. Much developed and subdivided since c. 2000.

KEWSTOKE

ST PAUL. Fine inner s doorway, c. 1100–50. One order of colonnettes with spiral-fluted and decorated scallop capitals. Arch with lozenge frieze (two chevrons), beaded crenellation frieze, hoodmould with billet and small chevron. Late C13 nave and chancel; see the two-light E window with a cusped spheric triangle, two nave windows with cinquefoiled rere-arches (copies of 1849) and the cinquefoiled head of the N doorway. Perp w tower with moulded tower arch, pierced parapet with quatrefoils in lozenges, pinnacles, and a higher stair-turret with spirelet. Perp clerestory with plain parapets. Short s aisle, perhaps C13 (see the small trefoil-headed light now inside the porch), with double-chamfered moulded entrance arch, and three-light square-headed window, possibly C16. Attached to its w side, late Perp porch with pierced parapet like the tower. Nave N wall rebuilt in 1849, uncovering a medieval wooden reliquary containing a cup. Ogee-headed rood-stair door s of the chancel arch. Chancel partly rebuilt in 1854. Vestry and organ chamber, 1906–7. – FITTINGS. REREDOS by *Herbert Read*, 1923. Stone, delicate relief panels. – ROOD SCREEN and FIGURES also *Read*, 1938. Also a smaller screen. – FONT. Circular with an octagonal bowl like a moulded capital and a base like that of an arcade pier. Probably C14. – PULPIT. Perp, stone, with small blank arches carrying tall crocketed finials. Decorated frieze and cresting. – Simple BENCHES and STALLS, 1962 and later, *Burrough & Hannam*. – ROYAL ARMS. C18, repainted by *Thomas Penny* of Bristol, 1831. – STAINED GLASS. E window and rose 1921, *Kempe & Co*. Nave N. *Paul Jefferies*, 1963. Dark abstracted figures. S chapel. Heraldic glass *c*. 1825, *W. R. Eginton*, some replaced in replica *c*. 1949.

PRIMARY SCHOOL, 1909. Pretty Edwardian classical window frames with serpentine heads. Brick, rubble and Bath stone.

Prominent on the shoulder of Worlebury Hill, a women's CONVALESCENT HOME for the Birmingham Hospital Saturday Fund, *W. H. Martin*, 1931–3. It cost £60,000. A long white-rendered *moderne* block with flat roof, canted on plan as if embracing the Channel air. Tuscan loggias on the ends of the wings. Axial terraced gardens on an imperial scale. Reopened 2006 as a private psychiatric hospital, with loss of good Art Deco interiors.

The hamlet of NORTON lies to the E. HOME FARM, long, low and C17; upstairs, a plaster overmantel dated 1660. NORTON COURT FARM, C17, has a rear stair-turret.

NEWTONS, ½ m. E, off Queensway. Now buried in housing. A small gabled house new-built in 1627 now forms the rooms l. of the front door. Extended and refronted in 1710 by John and Frances Selwood. Coursed silvery Lias, of six bays and two storeys, gabled roof. Timber cross-windows with leaded lights. Porch with pediment on baluster-like columns. Dormers also with richly moulded pediments. Interior much altered. C17 kitchen with bressumered fireplace and spit jack, and a newel stair within its W wall. Open-well staircase with moulded vase balusters, with much reused material. Triple C18 dog-gates. Over the staircase, stucco ceiling of 1710; floral wreath centre. Rooms r. of the entrance with three good C18 landscape panels.

6060 ## KEYNSHAM

The medieval town developed S of the parish church along the High Street. From the C16 until 1776 the Bridges or Brydges family, cousins of the Dukes of Chandos, had a mansion on or near the Abbey site (*see* below). Brass mills established in 1706 created a minor boom, with an influx of Dutch and German workers. Much has been lost to depressing urbanization *c*. 1960–80, and to floods in 1968.

KEYNSHAM ABBEY. Keynsham had a Saxon minster; finds include a cross-shaft and fragments of grave markers. A

Victorine ABBEY (a reformed Augustinian order) was founded
c. 1167. It was rich and important, and the Norman stonework
particularly fine. The plan has been recovered: *c.* 100 yds E of
the parish church, and on roughly the same alignment, a cruciform aisleless church with S cloister, big rectangular chapter
house on its E side and abutting the S transept (cf. Bristol).
Running E from the SE corner of the cloister was a big dorter.
Secondary cloister to the S, service buildings etc. to the W.
Keynsham by-pass was driven SE to NE through the site of the
cloister and W end in 1964–6. *In situ* remains: a long stretch of
precinct wall forming the rear boundaries to the E side of High
Street; the stump of a late C15 pier from a N chapel in the
garden of No. 3 Abbey Park; in the park adjacent some low
walls of chapter house, S transept and cloister. Numerous
remains *ex situ*, including on the C17 gateway in Station Road,
and an Agnus Dei boss in the wall of the Crown Inn, Bristol
Road.*

ST JOHN BAPTIST, High Street. In a dominant position.
Founded *c.* 1270, appropriated to the Abbey in 1292, and much
rebuilt in the C15. A steeple E of the N aisle collapsed in 1632
in 'Tempestuous weather', destroying parts of the chancel,
vestry and nave, leaving the tower 'crazed from the top to the
foundation'.† Heavily restored by *Benjamin Ferrey*, 1861–3;
mason, *W. Sheppard*.

Chancel of the C13, with broad clasping buttresses, single
lancets and a C19 ballflower cornice. S aisle with Late Dec ballflower cornice. Perp N aisle with battlements and big gargoyles.
Both have W stair-turrets to the roof. C15 S porch with
tierceron-vault. Inside, four broken TOMB-SLABS from the
abbey, C15. The brief of 1634 gives a *terminus post quem* for the
start of the new W tower; a bell hung in 1654 and the weathercock dated 1655 indicate completion. A good example of
Gothic survival, based loosely on Somerset models. The
masons were *Baylie* and *Butler*. The bottom stage is of Blue
Lias with contrasting stone bands at regular intervals, now
cement-covered except on the N, and a Perp W window. Next,
each face has a tall blind mullioned-and-transomed window
arranged four-over-four, with cusped round-arched lights, not
a Somerset form (but cf. Colerne, Wilts., and Dursley,
Gloucs.).‡ The top stage has short bell-openings with incon-
gruous-looking Perp tracery. Stubby pinnacles, parapets with
blank arcading near the angles, and the centres pierced with
the familiar cusped triangles. SUNDIALS of 1741.

The INTERIOR is remarkably spacious, with a wide eight-
bay nave and wide aisles too. Much C19 restoration, with
some earlier elements such as a late C13 PISCINA with two
basins. Ferrey's incongruous chancel arch replaced a C17

---

* Stonework retrieved from gardens includes Norman arch mouldings, late C12
vault-ribs of distinctive heart-shaped section, E.E. bases, pieces of Dec and Perp
tracery, and a vaulted C15 niche, suggesting continual piecemeal development up
to Dissolution in 1539.

† Brief for rebuilding the church, 1634.

‡ David Martyn; he suggests the possibility of early C18 tower alterations too.

asymmetrical opening. He rebuilt the nave arcades using the old stonework. On the N, two-centred arches and Perp piers of four shafts with wave mouldings; on the S, octagonal piers, arches with two concave mouldings. From the former tower to the nave is a good C15 Perp arch, with tall narrow capitals of delicate foliage. Entirely *Ferrey*'s design are the Perp aisle windows and nave and chancel roofs. Late medieval aisle roofs much repaired after 1632, with relief patterns; some lively bosses in the S aisle.

FITTINGS. ALTAR, late C16 or C17, thick baluster legs. – SCREENS. To the S chapel, of three-light divisions with panel tracery and a vine frieze. Coved and panelled top with big suns in splendour, the badge of Edward IV, indicating construction after 1461. Between chancel and S chapel, a much altered screen, *c.* 1630s, perhaps originally at the chancel arch. Arcades with naïve Ionic columns and arabesques. High pedimented centre with the Stuart arms flanked by strapwork. Other arms probably post-Restoration. – PULPIT, 1634. With arched foliate panels below horizontal ovals. – FONTS. N aisle E, 1725. Bath stone, a fat decorated baluster on a twisted knop, with a small bowl. Another of 1863. – Good multi-tiered CHANDELIERS, no doubt of local brass, 1717 and 1721. – STAINED GLASS. E window, 1961, by *Arthur Walker*; makers *Maile & Son*. – MONUMENTS. The Bridges monuments so crowd the chancel as to distract one even from the altar. N side, E to W: Sir Henry Bridges †1587. Recumbent effigy on a big tomb-chest with caryatids and terms. Two-arched canopy on tapering Ionic pilasters, allegorical figures above. – Thomas †1706. Pilastered, with segmental pediment. – George †1677 with naïve bulging Corinthian columns. – Henry †1728. Baroque cartouche, curved hood. – S side, E to W: Philippa †1628. Arched tablet with reclining figures in the spandrels. – Most prominent of all, Sir Thomas †1661. It has elements in common with George Rodney's monument at Rodney Stoke; and Sir Thomas's mother, Lady Anna, was indeed a Rodney. Very big hanging triptych with four twisted columns, after Bernini's baldacchino in St Peter's, Rome. Thin central effigy kneeling in a niche carved with clouds and a trumpeting angel. The sides have weighty broken segmental pediments, and mutilated angels which once reached up to crown him. – Lady Anna †1705. Oval tablet with palm branches and a winged skull. – N aisle: Joane Flower †1659, under a broken arch. Clumsy scrolls topped by female heads. – Margaret Simpson †1792, a *Coade* stone oval plaque with garland border. – Minor tablets by *King, Lancaster, Tyley* etc. The best to Benjamin Milward †1833, by *Olive Greenway*.

ST FRANCIS, Warwick Road. 1957–8, by *F. W. Beresford-Smith*. On pre-cast concrete arches. Windowless canted W end with columns forming a loggia. Copper-clad cupola with a narrow spike.

ST DUNSTAN (R.C.), Bristol Road. By *Roberts & Willman*, 1935. Purple brick, mildly Romanesque with Art Deco-ish stepped windows. Interior remodelled 1979 by *Ivor Day & O'Brien.* – STAINED GLASS. w oculus by *Mark Angus*, 1980. Twelve panels by *John Yeo*, *c.* 1990s.

BAPTIST CHURCH, High Street. 1834–5, doubtless by *Henry Rumley*, who surveyed the previous chapel before demolition. Fluted Doric pilaster doorcase like those by Rumley in Queen Square, Bristol. A handsome stuccoed façade with arched windows and recessed centre. Schoolroom of 1858, r., with an intrusive addition by *Gordon Swift*, 1988, of reconstituted stone – could they not have continued the stucco? Inside, only the gallery survived a brutal modernization of 1975–6.

VICTORIA METHODIST CHURCH, High Street. By *Robert Curwen*, opened 1887. Small, Perp, with transept-like projections for the gallery staircases.

THE TOWN. At the NW end is BRIDGES ALMSHOUSES, Nos. 48–54 Bristol Road, of 1685–6. Originally six terraced houses, with two- and three-light ovolo-mullioned windows, and continuous dripmoulds. Two coats of arms in deeply curled cartouches. N of Station Road junction is OLD VICARAGE GREEN, by *Peter Smith & Partners*, 1971–6. Flats and terraces of town houses, around a long green. Yellow brick with tile-hung top storeys, raised over garages. Dominant pillar-like verticals. Opposite, on the side of No. 7 Bristol Road, a blind Perp window (reportedly from Stanton Drew) and two small niches, one with Norman fragments from the Abbey. These enhanced the outlook from the neighbouring OLD MANOR HOUSE, much altered in the C20 as a hotel. The present structure is *c.* 1620–50. Updated *c.* 1870 with a big dining room (r. side), and an odd little tower for asymmetry. Within a C19 Tudoresque porch, a C17 doorcase with pediment on short pilasters. Central cross-passage with hall to the r. It has a broad fireplace with moulded and cambered bressumer. At the back, a C17 closed-well staircase.

STATION ROAD runs E from St John's church. At the entrance to Park House is a re-erected late C17 GATEWAY from the Bridges' mansion stable: of one storey with hipped roof, central door and eight tall cross-windows with an oval light above each. 1670–90 would be about right for these features. The arched doorcase, now the gateway, has a steep pediment, pulvinated frieze, and rusticated piers in the form of large rounded blocks – an unusual conceit. On the reverse, fragments of Saxon and later carving from the Abbey, including a Norman variant on Greek key from a frieze in the chapter house.

On low-lying water meadows is Cadbury-Schweppes's SOMERDALE CHOCOLATE FACTORY, built when Fry's relocated from Bristol 1921–32. Steel-framed red brick blocks of four and five storeys, probably by *E. W. Hilton*, dated 1924, 1928 and 1933. Domed octagonal turrets face the river. Closed in 2010. From 1925 to *c.* 1930, Fry's erected some seventy workers' houses around CHANDOS ROAD, modelled no doubt after Bournville, Birmingham. ¼ m. E is BRASS MILLS, Avon Mill Lane. A fragmentary survival. A former outbuilding at the river's edge, probably early 1830s, now a pub, its s wall entirely of copper slag blocks. Nearby is the manager's house, 1852, with clock tower and bell-cupola.

The HIGH STREET has relatively little of interest. From the N, No. 12 has C16 or C17 mullioned-and-transomed windows. No. 23 has an C18 façade but a fine late C16 or early C17 ceiling on the ground floor; double-ovolo-moulded beams. Southward, the ugly w side is mainly 1960s. At the junction with Bath Hill, COUNCIL OFFICES and LIBRARY, by *John Hodges* of Somerset County Council, 1965. Four storeys with inverted-V canopy roof, in conjunction with shops and a prominent skeletal steel CLOCK TOWER. Opposite on Bath Hill, TEMPLE COUNTY PRIMARY SCHOOL. 1855–7, by *S. B. Gabriel.** Grey limestone, plain Gothic with cusped lancets and plate tracery. A few vernacular survivals in TEMPLE STREET (e.g. the Ship Inn, mid-C17). All overwhelmed by the horrible CHEW PARK CENTRE, 1974–6 by *Design & Planning Associates*, project architect *Peter Ashby*. Shops, flats, offices and leisure centre, up to five storeys, in brown brick and aggregate-faced concrete. To the s, DAPPS HILL drops down to the River Chew. Dappifer's House (Nos. 6–8) is an attractive pair, the external features probably mid-C17 but possibly on a Tudor core. Again with ovolo mullions. Further down, a two-arched stone BRIDGE, perhaps C17, with a cutwater. s again, Nos. 6–8 Chew Cottages, plain workers' houses dated 1824, and quite well preserved externally.

CEMETERY, Durley Hill. ¾ m. N. Two small chapels by *C. E. Davis*, 1877–8, joined by an arch with spirelet.

ROMAN VILLA, excavated 1922–4 and now covered by the cemetery and the main Keynsham–Bristol road. The villa, the largest in the region, took the form of three corridors around a courtyard and dated to the late C3–C4. Its sophisticated layout included two hexagonal *triclinia* fitted with figured mosaics that included representations of Europa and the bull, dancers and sea creatures. The mosaics are now kept in Keynsham Town Hall.[†]

CHANDOS LODGE, Durley Lane, 1 m. N of the centre. A hunting lodge for the surrounding deer park, built by Sir Thomas Bridges in the late C17. Modernized with flush sashes *c.* 1700–10, and much altered later. (In the first-floor great chamber, now partitioned, a plaster overmantel dated 1663 with the royal arms, and painted achievements on the walls.)

KILMERSDON

with CHARLTON

In a deep hollow with a dramatic approach from the w, the church tower rising nobly at the bottom of a long straight hill.

---

* Oddly, the competition winner was *Henry Masters*.
[†] Another ROMAN HOUSE, excavated in the 1920s within the gates of the Somerdale factory, measures 50 ft by 35 ft (15 by 11 metres). Foundations left exposed. An inscription of A.D. 155 was found in 1931 reused in a wall.

Mostly owned by the Jolliffe family (Lord Hylton of Ammer-down), giving it the air of an estate village, with some rows of C18 and early C19 cottages.

St Peter and St Paul. The Norman church consisted of nave and chancel, of which evidence survives in the nave s wall: a small window, a plain narrow doorway (now opening into the vestry of 1898–1900), and stretches of fish-scale frieze with big corbels, evidence of the roof level before the C15 clerestory. This has two square-headed windows only. The chancel was rebuilt *c.* 1878–81 by *E. B. Ferrey*, who re-set many Norman fragments in the walls (human and animal heads, angels, foliage and geometric motifs) and reused stonework where possible, e.g. the chancel parapet. Inside, the N chancel wall has remains of a Norman window, and inset Norman fragments including palmettes of classical inspiration. Four-stage w tower of Doulting stone, probably *c.* 1475–90, with set-back buttresses connected by diagonals hiding the angles. The buttresses develop into diagonal pinnacles, the diagonals quite uncommonly into groups of triple pinnacles which reach up above the battlements, the middle one being tallest. w doorway and window with hoodmoulds on good headstops. Then two stages with blank two-light windows with niches l. and r., then the three-light bell-openings with Somerset tracery. Ornate embattled N aisle and chapel, probably added *c.* 1445–65; deeply buttressed and with heraldic beasts probably representing the patron William Botreaux (†1462). It has a fine panelled ceiling, two panels with possibly later gilding and black-and-white chevrons. Four-bay N arcade of four-centred arches with piers of standard shape (four hollows). Tower arch with the same moulding and deep triple-panelling towards the nave. The chancel arch, N chapel arch and that connecting chapel and chancel have similar features, and panelled soffits too. Corbels of demi-figures of angels for a higher nave roof. More such angels, but bigger, for the chancel roof.

FITTINGS. PULPIT. 1898, made up of older panels. – FONT. Octagonal, Perp, with quatrefoils. – Wrought-iron chancel screen by *Singer*, 1879. – A good C15 stone screen (N chapel) with strong two-light divisions, ogee tracery.* Demi-figures of angels in the cornice. – benches. Plain and solid, C15 Perp (also C19 imitations). – Traceried C15 door (vestry). – sculpture. Two saints by *Peter Watts*, 1962, in elaborate C15 image niches flanking the N chapel E window. – stained glass. All made by *Powell & Sons*. E window by *Henry Holiday*, 1880, with single figures reminiscent of Burne-Jones. Also by *Holiday*, N aisle, first and second E (1886, 1890). N chapel E, by *Louis Davis*, 1914, a handsome late example of Pre-Raphaelite types, although the technique is rather that of the graphic artist. – monuments. Robert James †1528, and Richard James; four-arched hanging monument dated 1595

* Reputedly from the medieval St Andrew, Holborn, London, dem. 1675. The Rev. Henry Shute was incumbent both here and at Holborn.

(vestry). – Mary Goodman †1745, with obelisk, by *Prince Hoare*. – Twyford family †1765–76, one signed *Thomas Paty*; big pedimented tablets. – Jolliffe memorials in the tower; Thomas S. Jolliffe †1824 by *King* of Bath. – Churchyard. Thomas Jolliffe †1918, by *Lutyens*. With flanking Doric columns. Probably also by him, Mary Lepel Jolliffe †1912. – GATE, N of the church, by *Lutyens*, 1900; three triangular piers on circular paving, symbolic of the Trinity, stone-tiled pyramid roof. Surely the model for his shelter at Mells (1908).

SW of the church the JOLLIFFE ARMS and adjacent house with pedimented doorways, C18, forming a good setting with the small square in front of the church tower. At the S end of the pub, a late C18 wing with big Venetian windows, reportedly a courtroom. Opposite, the BLIND HOUSE or lock-up, C17 or C18, with Gothic opening and pyramid roof.

In CHURCH STREET, No. 24, the OLD VICARAGE, has some blocked late medieval openings facing the church, and a small C15 lantern chimney on the W gable. Otherwise mainly C18 and C19 externally. E of the church, a former Wesleyan CHAPEL of c. 1850; a reserved symmetrical front. Behind is a building with hipped roof, converted from a cider house earlier in the C19. Next door, Nos. 17–19, THE BARRACKS, an early C18 poor-house, now cottages. Three storeys, small two-light windows and much plain wall. The over-scaled Vanbrughian doorcase to No. 18, rusticated pilasters and massive stepped keystones beneath a pediment, is surely *ex situ*. In Ames Lane, NE, OLD SCHOOL HOUSE, five bays and two storeys, built as a Charity School in 1707 by the Rev. Henry Shute, also Treasurer of the Society for Promoting Christian Knowledge (SPCK). Upright mullioned windows, big central gable; nothing of the C18 in the exterior yet, nor in the balustered staircase inside. On the hilltop to the NW in School Lane, a former RECTORY of 1852, bare Neo-Tudor.

MANOR HOUSE, Silver Street. The r. part dated 1664, with two big symmetrical gables and mullioned windows (mullions square with an outer rebate, not ovolo; a local variation). At the l., a tall early to mid-C18 block; sashes in moulded frames with keystones.

CHARLTON lies c. 1 m. W. Just to the NE, an early C19 DORIC GATE to Charlton House (dem.). Four stone columns, timber entablature with triglyphs and metopes.

For Ammerdown House, *see* p. 79.

KINGSTON SEYMOUR

ALL SAINTS. In a churchyard surrounded on three sides by water, the ditch bridged to the W by a C19 lychgate. W tower with spire, perhaps C14, with later (C15) parapet sitting oddly on the splayed foot of the spire. The parapet has two tiers of arcading, broad and with ogee heads below, narrow vertical openings above. N wall of the nave raised and Perp windows and a pierced parapet with cusped triangles added, all *c.* 1450–75. Of about the same date the s aisle and two-storey porch, the outer arch possibly C14 and re-set. Tower arch of the standard four shafts and four hollows. The chancel arch may also be C14, the double chamfers re-cut in the C15 with ogees (see the awkward bases where the mouldings stop). Trefoil-headed C13 PISCINA in the chancel. Also (N side) a delicate late Perp niche with little figures around vaulted canopy, *ex situ*; the corbelled base and angel over seem C19. Four-bay s aisle arcade of the four-hollows type, C15, with small foliate capitals to the shafts only. C15 ogee-cusped PISCINA, s aisle E, and a late C15 squint through the jamb of a s chancel window. Wagon roof in the nave. In 1865–6 *Popes & Bindon* rebuilt the chancel and added vestry and organ chamber. Theirs too the flat s aisle ceiling on C15 demi-angels. Further restoration, 1905–6.

FITTINGS. FONT. C12 base, bowl of cushion capital form. The rim of the bowl looks to be an addition. – ROYAL ARMS. Charles I. On canvas. – STAINED GLASS. E window by *Warrington*, 1865. Heraldic w window by *Roland Paul*, 1917, replacing one by *W. R. Eginton*, *c.* 1825. – MONUMENTS. Plaque in the porch, perhaps C18, commemorating the flooding of the Somerset Levels and the Welsh coast in 1606, with great loss of life: now thought by some to have been a tsunami. – E of the church, Perp tomb-chest with quatrefoils. – C15 CROSS on stepped base; late C20 head.

Picturesque Gothic former SCHOOL, *c.* 1857–8, SW of the church. Opposite, the OLD MANOR, a dull Gothic rebuilding by *Thomas Bruford*, after the medieval manor house (*c.* 1475–85) burned down. The withdrawing room at the w end of the medieval house survives as the kitchen, with a very handsome C15 stone chimneypiece with shafted sides, fleurons in the jambs, big panelled frieze with cusped daggers and quatrefoils, cf. Congresbury Rectory. Around the village, good minor FARMHOUSES, e.g. Gout Farm (three-room cross-passage plan, *c.* 1500); and Hope Farm, restrained Late Georgian. Of the same period, a local tradition of pretty latticed timber porches, e.g. Middle Farm, Middle Lane.

LANGRIDGE

ST MARY MAGDALENE, Langridge Lane. Short Norman w tower with saddleback roof. Buttresses only at the foot. Coarse pointed tower arch inside. Finely carved Norman s doorway consisting of a continuous inner roll moulding, two columns with spiral roll moulding flanked by beading (cf. Compton Martin), scallop capitals (the r. one with an upright leaf), zigzag on the arches, and an outer arch moulding with chip-carved rosettes. Much restored or remodelled Norman chancel arch on groups of three stepped columns with spur bases and scallop capitals. Two orders of chevrons in the arch, pellets inside the hoodmould. Above the arch a small former window. The nave seems, from restored windows, to have been rebuilt in the C14. Chancel over-restored and extended with an apse by *C. E. Davis*, 1872.* – PULPIT. Jacobean with tester: finely carved panels with arabesques and arches, probably re-assembled. – BENCH-ENDS. Carved by the then rector and his friends *c.* 1880. – FONT, perhaps early C14; square bowl with chamfered corners. – STATUE. A very remarkable Anglo-Saxon figure of the Virgin and Child, *c.* 1000–50. The mother has a very long face, the child oddly stylized hair. – MONUMENTS. C14 effigy of a lady, under the tower.[†]

COURT FARMHOUSE. A T-shaped house. It is now thought the wing running N–S may be a C12 first-floor hall (cf. Saltford), and that the E wing perhaps began as a detached kitchen block, joined to the hall range and refaced as the main house perhaps *c.* 1709, when the farm was bought by the Blathwayts of Dyrham. Symmetrical three-bay S front with ovolo-mullioned lights. The W range has in its S gable a large transomed two-light window with cusped arched lights. (The first-floor Court Room has a fine C17 chimneypiece with fluted Ionic pilasters.) Partly overlaying the gable of the W range, a projecting square three-stage tower. Three-centred arches connect internally with the Court Room, i.e. it is a medieval addition, probably defensive.

TADWICK MANOR HOUSE, *c.* ¾ m. NE. Mid- to late C17, with three unevenly placed gables. Mullioned windows.

7060

LANSDOWN

A bleak limestone plateau N of Bath, at the SW tip of the Cotswolds. For Beckford's Tower and suburban Lansdown, *see* Bath (p. 182).

CHAPEL FARM HOUSE. L-shaped. Its S-facing rear service wing originated as the C15 chapel of St Lawrence. See the buttresses N and S, and three blocked two-light Perp windows. (Ogee-arched piscina within.) The W wing was formed by extending northwards from the W end, perhaps *c.* 1540–1600; see the old angle buttress still emerging from the W wall.

GRENVILLE MONUMENT, *c.* 1 m. E of the main road. Erected in 1720 to the Royalist leader Sir Bevil Grenville, killed 1643 at the Battle of Lansdown. *c.* 25 ft (8 metres) high. Square rusticated base, slightly diminishing to a square stage with two

---

* Faculty for rebuilding the chancel (1930) possibly not executed.
† Stolen, a brass to Elizabeth Walsche †1441, a 3-ft (90-cm.) figure in widow's weeds with a dog at her feet.

inscriptions, and trophies and arms in relief, carved by the second *John Harvey*. Griffin on top bearing Grenville's arms. Harvey perhaps acted as architect too. Restored by *Edward Davis*, who removed Grenville's coat of arms to his house (*see* pp. 204–5), *c.* 1835.

ROMAN INDUSTRIAL SETTLEMENT, Little Down Field, on an exposed promontory at the NE extremity of the Lansdown plateau. The discovery of stone moulds suggests that it was the site of pewter manufacture.

LAVERTON

7050

ST MARY. An exceedingly strange W end, like a Westwork in Germany, i.e. a broad erection with a saddleback roof, a little taller than the nave. Two small single lights, perhaps C12 or C13. Three-light Tudor window high up. Big (later) buttresses of strong batter, without set-offs. Within the N porch, a Norman doorway: one order of scallop capitals, and around the arch, two rows of chevrons. The biggest surprise within is that the tower and nave are one space. Double-chamfered chancel arch without capitals. The chancel was much renewed and a S vestry added in 1847. Nave restored 1859 by *W. G. Brown*. – FITTINGS. FONT, octagonal, Perp. – CHAMBER ORGAN in a mahogany case like a bureau, *c.* 1800. Installed 1942. – CLOCK MECHANISM, *c.* 1790 in a case by *William Bertram*, 2000. – STAINED GLASS. E window of 1868. – MONUMENT. John Yerbury †1691, Corinthian frame, broken pediment.

MANOR FARM. E of the church. L-shaped, the N part probably late C16 or C17 with mullioned windows, the higher S end remodelled in the mid C19. Inside, a fine plaster ceiling quartered with broad ribs containing four big quatrefoils, abundant scrolling roses, thistles etc. At the centre, a mermaid in her vanity. Dense frieze dated 1627. The same room has an early C17 oak overmantel with caryatids from No. 1 Manor Farm Cottages. A little N, LAVERTON HOUSE, formerly the vicarage, perhaps 1750–75, with round-arched central upper window. Opposite, MANOR FARM COTTAGES, formerly the manor house, again C17 with mullioned windows and one big blocked mullioned-and-transomed window.

UPPER ROW FARM, *c.* ½ m. NW, has a felling date for the roof of 1491. NW and SE of the farm, earthworks of the deserted village of Row, occupied *c.* 1100–1500.

LEIGH WOODS

5070

Finely sited on the wooded W side of the Avon Gorge. Leigh Woods began *c.* 1864 as a select residential development linked to Clifton by the Suspension Bridge (*see* p. 329).

St Mary, Church Road. By *John Medland*, 1891–3. Nave and polygonal apse; the intended aisles unbuilt. Poor C13 Gothic, of red Pennant Stone. The date is revealed in the pretty barge-boarded dormer windows and shingled sw saddleback tower with bell-turret, fulfilling the brief for a rustic appearance. – FITTINGS. Oak, Neo-Perp. – STAINED GLASS. Mostly *c.* 1893–1910. Three apse windows, the nave s, first from e, and the small light behind the font, by the rarely seen *W. G. Rich*, 1892. w window, *Burlison & Grylls*, 1905. Nave n, w end, by *Morris & Co.*, 1916, depicting Valour (designer *Dearle*) and St George, a reused *Burne-Jones* design. Nave n third from e by *Geoffrey Robinson*, 1961, with splendid sultry colours. – MONUMENT. Canon John Gamble †1929; tablet by *Sir George Oatley*, lettered by *Eric Gill*, 1930. – LYCHGATE. 1919–20, also *Oatley*.

GATE LODGE, Abbotsleigh Road. *Foster & Wood*, 1877. Ambitious upper lodge to Ashton Court (*see* p. 548). Neo-Tudor. Asymmetrical polygonal towers, that on the r. with a taller turret.

The winding avenues of Italianate, Gothic and Old English VILLAS are worth a stroll to see how Bristol's wealthiest Victorian merchants lived. From the w end of Clifton Suspension Bridge, immediately on the l. is BURWALLS, Bridge Road. By *Foster & Wood*, 1873, for Joseph Leech, newspaper proprietor, sold in 1894 to one of the Wills tobacco clan and extended by *Frank Wills*. Orange brick, Jacobean of varied profile and mannered details, with ogee-capped tower. Big bedroom block for the University of Bristol by *Powell & Moya*, 1981. High on a bluff nw of the bridge, ALPENFELS, North Road. For Francis Fox, chief engineer to the Bristol & Exeter Railway, *c.* 1872. A square stone house in Swiss chalet style. Further w on North Road, BELVEDERE, *c.* 1880, with an extraordinary veranda 'like a racecourse stand' (Andor Gomme) on top of the roof. w again, BRACKEN HILL HOUSE, 1894–6, for Melville Wills. A rambling essay in the Norman Shaw style; red brick, tile-hanging, fruity pargetting and a Jacobethan ogee-capped tower. Fine gardens with *Pulhamite* outcrops, 1917–27. Lastly, THE WHITE HOUSE and GRANGE FELL, Abbotsleigh Road, by *H. Dare Bryan*, 1901–2. The best example in n Somerset of the Voyseyesque. A semi-detached pair, completely asymmetrical. Roughcast with hipped tiled roof, double gables rising through the roof pitch. Mullioned and leaded casements with shutters, two square bays under a shared roof, l. Grange Fell (r.) has a barrel-vaulted entrance hall, and more original fittings (heart-shaped cut-outs, handmade window and door furniture, etc.).

LEIGH-ON-MENDIP

33   St Giles. The Doulting stone w tower has the most sophisticated decoration of all the Mendip churches; a date *c.* 1475–90

has been suggested. It derives from that at Mells, of which Leigh was a chapelry until 1860. It is 91 ft 6 in. (28 metres) high and of four stages, having angle buttresses with diagonals filling all three angles, the typical Mendip plan. The diagonals have two set-offs like a buttress, closely stepped as at Wells and Salisbury. In the top stage three tall openings, each of two lights, with a central transom and Somerset tracery. The composition repeated with blind lights in the stage below. Each corner has two pairs of pinnacles set on the diagonal, the lower pairs rising from the buttress set-offs at the second stage and finishing at the top of the third, the upper pairs starting between the lower ones at the third stage, and rising to flank the main corner pinnacles at parapet level. Here, battlements with big pierced quatrefoils, and little trefoils below. Two attached shafts on each face of the parapet form intermediate pinnacles: a total of twenty-eight pinnacles – eight on the buttresses, twenty at the top. A remarkable performance. W doorway with ogee gable reaching up in front of the foot of the four-light W window (two-light sub-arches). On the S side a small window flanked by niches. Tower arch with wave moulding. Under the tower springers of an uncompleted vault.

The clerestoried nave is equally decorated but short. Its high blank E wall drops abruptly to a low chancel, an unsatisfactory composition. The nave is probably later than the tower, let us say c. 1490–1520. Masonry joins date the aisles after the tower. The small N and S chapels were added, probably together, after the aisles. The S side has parapets with two rows of pierced quatrefoils on the clerestory, and a single row on the aisle, dated 1620 (possibly a repair or alteration). The chancel is below the nave floor level, and must pre-date it, although altered and re-roofed c. 1500. Uneven nave arcades of two-and-a-half bays, the W pair lower and narrower. Piers of standard type (four hollows), but the crude moulded capitals and bases differ on N and S (i.e. aisles of different dates). The chancel arch and chapel arches have octagonal capitals and bases. Three-light windows in aisles and clerestory, in the aisles straight-headed. The chapels have ogee-arched lights in square frames, and on the S side, a PISCINA of similar pattern to the lights. A bigger plain-arched PISCINA at the E end of the S aisle. Late Perp chancel E window of five lights, under a four-centred arch and with a transom in the tracery. Excellent tie-beam roofs of Somerset type in nave and chancel on big angel corbels, and decorated with demi-figures and whole figures of angels. Also decorated bosses, and fine decorated wall-plates of vines etc. in the chancel. Panelled aisle roofs, late medieval on the N. Over the sanctuary step, angel corbels for a Lenten veil. The church was partially restored or repaired in 1884, 1898–9, and (by *Whitaker & Hole* of Paulton) in 1909.

FITTINGS. PULPIT. Oak, Neo-Perp, late C19 or early C20. – FONT. Norman, plain, square bowl with two heavy scallops on each side, on a circular foot. Early C17 oak COVER of eight S-stays forming a crown. – BENCHES. An uncommonly complete set, late C15 and simple, straight-topped, with tracery decoration. – A possibly C13 STOUP in the S porch. – STAINED GLASS. Medieval fragments assembled in the W window, with roundels including the Instruments of the Passion (cf. Westwood, Wilts.); some possibly Continental. – MONUMENTS. Three similar Ionic tablets, probably by the same family of masons; John and Francis Johnson, *c.* 1720; Hannah Moore †1722; John Hartgill †1786.

At the E end of the village is GREAT HOUSE FARM, with a damaged datestone of 1596 in the gable wall, and a cipher below with knotwork. The other features appear mostly mid-C17. Facing W at the junction with Leigh Street is the OLD VICARAGE, *c.* 1700, six bays wide. Continuous driphoods, small windows with moulded mullions. The village is ranged along LEIGH STREET which rises wide and quite straight to the W. The houses largely C17–C19, an unusual number with dates (mostly 1680–1700). The changing form of the mullions can be traced: heavy C17 ovolos, getting somewhat thinner *c.* 1700, and until *c.* 1750 with narrow concave mouldings, single or doubled. Plain mullions with simple edge-rolls occur throughout the C18. PRESCOT HOUSE (S side) is a much altered open-hall house perhaps *c.* 1470–1530, floored across during the early C17.

LITTON

ST MARY. Sturdy Perp W tower with diagonal buttresses and oblong stair-turret. Embattled parapet on a corbel table of assorted heads and stiff-leaf, probably reused. Also demi-angels bearing the arms of Archdeacon Thomas Palton and Prebendary Richard Harewell (*see* below), who rebuilt the tower *c.* 1395–1416. Four-centred W doorway, good late C15 window above with inverted split-Y tracery. The nave must have been rebuilt wider, and aligned with the tower. Off-centre chancel arch, a blocked chancel N window with C13 trefoiled rere-arch, and a square pillar piscina, possibly Norman. Narrow S aisle, with piers of standard type (four hollows). The pier at the chancel arch is made to carry four arches, a task to which it is hardly equal, creating an unusual openness. The distorted masonry suggests the chancel arch came last. Crude N aisle of 1841, superficially matching the S. Big S porch with diagonal buttresses, that at the SW with a medieval mass dial, and notched footholds for C17 or C18 fives players to retrieve their ball from the roofs. Restored *c.* 1905–10, when the interior acquired unsightly ribbon pointing. Major repairs by *Anthony Methuen*, 1956. – FONT. Octagonal, Perp, with pretty foliage in quatrefoils. Panelled stem. – PULPIT. Mid-C17, with rectangular cartouches, arches, scrolly base panels. – Some C15 BENCH-ENDS. – STAINED GLASS. E window by *J. Bell & Son*,

1890. w window, *John Potter*, 2000. – MONUMENTS with good floral borders, one outside, †1731 and †1732.

OLD RECTORY, directly S of the church. The entrance range early C19, with sash windows under hoodmoulds. A long rear wing with patchwork masonry is perhaps C16 or C17. Rising behind it is the circular chimney and gable-end of the hall built *c.* 1400 by Prebendary Harewell, nephew of the Bishop of Bath and Wells. Little else of this early range survived a Gothic facelift *c.* 1870.

In the little village centre below the church, some good vernacular houses, e.g. the King's Arms, mid-C17 and Brookside House, 1754. A little SE, on the road to Ford, Spring Farm, late C16, probably truncated at the l. on the line of a former cross-passage. At the hamlet of SHERBORNE, ⅔ m. NW, a former FULLING MILL for woollen cloth, *c.* 1750s, oddly domestic and architectural. Round-arched upper window flanked by blocked mullioned lights, doorcase with triangular pediment.

LOCKING

3050

ST AUGUSTINE. Perp w tower perhaps *c.* 1380–1440; its stylistic features are long-lived ones. Diagonal buttresses. w doorway flanked by triangular shafts with pinnacles. The usual upper two-light windows, but the heads of the arches pushing up through the string course above, an unusual variation. Like Hutton, the bell-stage has paired two-light bell-openings of which the outer lights are blank – a variant of the more ambitious triple arrangement with the outer windows blind. Attached pinnacles between and around each pair, rising from the base of the stage, i.e. well below the window sills. Pierced lozenge parapets intended to have a central subsidiary pinnacle on each face. The rest is C19: N aisle added 1814 by *Charles Knowles*, builder, nave rebuilt 1816, chancel in 1833. The windows Perp, probably replicating old patterns, but the mullions of an un-medieval square section. The N arcade has two tall sturdy classical columns (of no particular order), quite a surprise after so many identical Perp piers all around. The tower arch has a continuous triple chamfer, the chancel arch (also continuous) a double wave moulding with a rebate between, probably reused C15 fabric. – FITTINGS. Chancel PANELLING, made by the village woodworking class, 1914–17. – FONT. Square, and more interesting than most Norman fonts in Somerset. Bath stone. At the angles four primitively carved standing figures stretching out their long arms to join hands. The sides are decorated with interlaced and beaded plaits which turn out to be snakes. – PULPIT. Late C15, gaudily painted stone, with blank tracery and deep cornice of quatrefoils and vines. – STAINED GLASS. Much of *c.* 1860–5: E window and N aisle N, first from E (1866), signed *J. Bell*. Probably also his the two chancel S lights and two in the S aisle. N aisle N, third, traditional, by *Maile Studios*, 1967.

N of the main road by-passing the village, the former RAF LOCKING, dominated by a square brick water tower, *c.* 1939. The RAF site is to be mixed commercial and housing, retaining the former chapel.

EARTHWORK. At Locking Head, ⁴/₅ m. N of the church. A small Norman motte-and-bailey castle which, with the similar site at Worle, may have commanded the surrounding Levels.

5070

LONG ASHTON

Densely built-up for *c.* 2 m. along a S-facing slope. Of its five manors, Ashton Court and Ashton Phillips survive.

ALL SAINTS. Early Perp. The W tower has the arms of the Lyon family and was probably largely rebuilt by Thomas de Lyon late in the C14. The chancel, chapels and N wall as far as the porch were rebuilt in a restoration of 1871–3, by *B. & E. B. Ferrey*. The tracery of the aisles and E end is consistent, of three ogee lights, i.e. later C15; C19 work seemingly faithful at least in outline. Tower of three stages, not tall but sturdy. Diagonal buttresses, doorway with two-centred arch and good headstops, four-light W window, two-light upper window, two-light bell-openings, battlements and pinnacles, and spirelet on the higher stair-turret. The body of the church also embattled; medieval sanctus bellcote on the nave E gable. Wide interior, four-bay arcades, the piers with wave mouldings between four attached shafts. The same moulding in the chancel arch and chapel arches. N aisle roof of medieval timbers assembled from other parts of the church in 1873. Small C18 FONT with gadrooned bowl built into the tower arch as a stoup. First-floor tower room with big oak-framed oriel facing E; *William Bertram (Bertram & Fell)*, 1991–4.

FITTINGS. REREDOS. 1871–3, three arches with marble shafts. – FONT. Perp, octagonal, with two blank ogee-headed panels to each side. COVER. Descending dove by *Ernst Blensdorf*, 1950. – Excellent ROOD SCREENS, *c.* 1480–1500, with three-light divisions under two-centred arches in the aisles, two lights in four-centred arches in the nave. This and minor differences in the cornices suggest the sections may be altered or of different dates. Doorways of the same height and richly cusped. Top with a foliage frieze, a cresting, another foliage frieze, and two more crestings. Repainted 1872. – Good TOWER SCREEN by *George Oatley*, 1919, originally a lobby to the W door. – STAINED GLASS. Chancel S, C15 fragments. By *Clayton & Bell*, E window, 1872, S aisle first from E, *c.* 1889, and W window, 1919. S aisle: second from E, probably *Arnold Robinson*, *c.* 1935; third, *Powell & Sons*, 1906. N aisle second

from E, signed *Joseph Bell*, 1910. N aisle, some Continental glass
from Ashton Court, C17 or C18.

MONUMENTS. Two defaced late C13 effigies in the N porch,
one inscribed to William de Snowden. – In a recess (S aisle),
ex situ C15 tomb-chest with quatrefoil decoration and a lion on
the E return. – Sir Richard Choke †1486, a Judge of Common   40
Pleas, and wife, a very fine Perp monument (cf. Mede tomb,
St Mary Redcliffe, Bristol). Recumbent effigies on a tomb-
chest with three big quatrefoils with shields. Angels against the
back wall hold a shield. Canopy with four hanging ogee gables
and five demi-angels. Straight top. – Under the tower, good
identical tablets of the Smyth family †1697 and *c*. 1715 (the
former signed *George Townesend*, Bristol). Fluted Corinthian
pilasters. – Excellent array of early C19 tablets, classical
(*Thomas Clark*, *c*. 1810) and Gothic (*Tyley*, *c*. 1849). – The
Smyth monuments continue Gothic as late as 1916 (Lady
Emily †1914, designed by *Oatley*, portrait by *E. F. Fabian*). –
CHURCHYARD. Base and shaft of a medieval CROSS, moved
here 1882. – Fine C17 CHEST TOMBS to the Whiting family, S
of the church.

CONGREGATIONAL CHAPEL (former), Long Ashton Road. By
Frank Wills, 1892. Gothic, with a pretty rose window in the
gable.

SCHOOLS. In Church Lane, the PAROCHIAL SCHOOL, dated
1818, small and square with hipped roof and Gothic Y-
traceried windows. On Long Ashton Road, the former
NATIONAL SCHOOLS, by *James Wilson*, 1860–1. E.E., irregular. Master's house (r.), schoolroom (l.) with elaborate bell-
turret and spirelet.

Until the C20 Long Ashton consisted of three distinct areas on
Long Ashton Road, the smartest at the W. Here, No. 3 Church
Lane, a chantry priest's house of *c*. 1495. Five two-light
windows under square hoodmoulds around a four-centred
doorway, now a window. Altered and restored in the C19. A
little W, a priest's house of *c*. 1540, similar. SW of the church,
PARSONAGE FARM, outwardly Late Georgian, conceals
medieval fabric. The roof of its C15 seven-bay BARN was burnt
in 1966. Back on Long Ashton Road, the ANGEL INN, extant
in 1495 when it became a priest's house. It was the church
house by the early C16 and an inn before 1597. Refenestrated.
(Roof with three arch-braced collar-beam trusses.) Minor late
C18 and early C19 villas and refronted cottages continue for
some distance W. Typical of the Domestic Revival infill, BARN
HEY, No. 73 Long Ashton Road, *Foster & Wood*, 1903. Also
theirs, the former VILLAGE CLUB, 1879. W again, the SMYTH
ALMSHOUSES, *Edward Gabriel*, 1900–2. Pleasing single-storey
range, of rubble. Red-brick chimneystacks in pairs joined at
the top by arches. Wide bays with dentil cornices, central clock
turret.

LOWER COURT FARM, N of the by-pass. The main range runs
N–S and, according to Collinson's *History of Somerset* (1791),
formed the E wing of the C13 manor house of Ashton Phillips.

Much altered, probably in 1663: two big transverse gables and mullioned staircase windows at the back (E), mullioned-and-transomed ground-floor windows at the W. On the W front, a stepped buttress, perhaps where another wing adjoined. To the S a complete little Perp CHAPEL. Three-light E window with panel tracery, two-light N window with cusped ogee heads (i.e. late C15). Plain bellcote.

ASHTON COURT
Bower Ashton

The house is oriented SW–NE; for simplicity, this will be referred to as W–E. All building dates before the C19 remain conjectural.

Set in a beautiful deer park, Ashton Court is at once exciting, puzzling, neglected and intensely sad. The core of the present house is *c.* C14–C15. It was owned by the mercantile Smyth family from 1545 to 1946. There were major remodellings in the late C16, C17, C18 and C19. Deliberate historicism and imported fittings make interpretation a minefield. Purchased by Bristol City Council in 1959; parts are now used for functions, but other parts are a shell and in dangerous condition, despite the building's Grade I listing.

45 EXTERIOR. The W entrance court has a C16 gabled E range, with shallow two-storey porch to the hall. Left of the hall is a C15 cross-wing, not visible from here. The fanciful Gothic outer porch and Perp windows all round the courtyard are *c.* 1803, inspired by one genuinely Perp hall window. These alterations attributed to *James Foster*, who designed a porch identical in detail and date at St James, Bristol (*see* p. 254). At the inner angles are matching buttressed projections: at the r., C16, and at the l., *c.* 1767, built for internal access to the NW wing of the same date. This wing, with ogee Gothick trim, is perhaps by *Thomas Paty*. It has an imitation Elizabethan stair-turret and gables with blind ovals and Doric chimneys, either of the 1760s or 1803, but echoing the C17 work of the S wing, which is masked by a two-storey corridor added to its N side *c.* 1803.

The W half of the S front is late C16, with a classical refronting of 1633–4, spuriously attributed to Inigo Jones. The builder was Thomas Smyth, M.P. (1609–42), who knew Jones's refurbishment of St Paul's Cathedral. Smyth married into the Poulett family, who did similar work in the mid C17 at Brympton D'Evercy and Hinton St George in Somerset (S and W). This connection perhaps produced Smyth's mason-architect, one familiar with Jones's innovations.* The S front has thirteen

---

*The Smyth letters reveal that *Christopher Watts*, freestone mason of Bristol, went with Thomas Smyth to Rodney Stoke quarries in 1633. He made Smyth's (lost) tomb in 1642, witnessed a bargain for the church of St Augustine the Less, Bristol, in 1648 and was probably buried there in 1653. Gervase Jackson-Stops suggested his name for the pink stone chimneypiece at Ashton Court, and linked it to Watts's work at Sherborne Castle and Stalbridge, Dorset. Was he master mason for the whole SW wing?

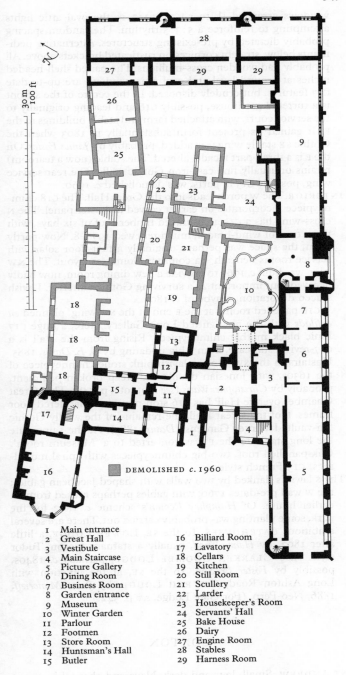

1 Main entrance
2 Great Hall
3 Vestibule
4 Main Staircase
5 Picture Gallery
6 Dining Room
7 Business Room
8 Garden entrance
9 Museum
10 Winter Garden
11 Parlour
12 Footmen
13 Store Room
14 Huntsman's Hall
15 Butler
16 Billiard Room
17 Lavatory
18 Cellars
19 Kitchen
20 Still Room
21 Scullery
22 Larder
23 Housekeeper's Room
24 Servants' Hall
25 Bake House
26 Dairy
27 Engine Room
28 Stables
29 Harness Room

DEMOLISHED c. 1960

30 m
100 ft

Long Ashton, Ashton Court.
After a plan of 1885

windows arranged (l. to r.) 3:2:3:3:2, the oval attic lights attempting to reinforce a 5:3:5 rhythm. The random spacing probably dictated by pre-existing structures. Alternating pediments below, straight cornices on rusticated brackets above. All probably had wooden cross-mullions. The paired shell-headed niches at ground level and oval attic windows are up-to-date C17 features, but crudely disposed. In the centre of the s front is a turreted gatehouse, possibly C16 and leading originally to the service court, with attached farm and stable buildings to the E. It gained its present form substantially in 1803 when the Gothic SE stable wing was added, probably by *James Foster*. On the E is a three-part façade, altered. The stable (now a tearoom) retains unusually fine cast-iron Gothic stalls. The rear service wing, possibly C15 in parts, was demolished *c.* 1960.

INTERIOR. The W porch leads into the Great Hall. The C18 chimneypiece incorporates an earlier carved alabaster panel. The N cross-wing has a C15 arch-braced timber roof of six bays, with three tiers of wind-braces, much renewed 1977–8. Now partly open, the space was perhaps originally a first-floor solar with service rooms beneath – a common Somerset layout. The NW wing was built *c.* 1767 to provide a new dining room, now badly decayed, but important as a surviving Gothick interior. Lavish stucco decoration, maybe of *c.* 1803.

C18 panelled rooms at the E end of the SW wing, planned *en enfilade* with the now gutted Long Gallery. Here, a huge C17 Ionic black marble chimneypiece. Rising from the Hall is a C17-revival staircase, from a big updating by *C. E. Davis*, 1885. Upstairs in the SW wing, a lavish pink stone chimneypiece of the 1630s, with Jonesian details and steep broken pediment, probably by *Christopher Watts* (*see* footnote, p. 548). The 'Great Chamber over ye Hall' has C16 stop-moulded chamfered door frames. E of the Great Hall, the remains of the wildly Gothic fan-vaulted Winter Gardens (*Davis*, 1885). At the same date the long stable to the E was converted to a 'Museum room'. Oak-panelled roof, two big chimneypieces with spiral mouldings, C15 French style.

The s lawn is flanked by two walls with shaped Jacobean gables; the w wall pre-dates 1760, with gables perhaps reused from an earlier house. Of *Humphry Repton*'s scheme *c.* 1802 for the park, some planting was probably carried out. There are several ambitious GATEHOUSES. To the SE, LOWER LODGE, a little after 1802, by *Henry Wood*, usually a statuary mason. Tudor style. Also CLARKEN COOMBE LODGE, perhaps *c.* 1840s, possibly by *Foster & Son*. To the SE, at the junction with Long Ashton Road, CHURCH LODGE, by *John Moncrieff*, 1886, Neo-Perp. (For Gate Lodge, *see* p. 542.)

3050

LOXTON

ST ANDREW. Small, low, and dark. Nave and chancel in one, s tower acting also as the porch, and N and s chancel chapels.

Late Norman s doorway with segmental arch and pellets in the hoodmould. The tower was built soon after, with a squint from porch to nave. No buttresses. In the nave w of the tower a tall lancet, cinquefoiled inside. The N chapel, with plate-traceried E window and a very pretty cusped trefoiled window in the w gable, is probably late C13. All 'thoroughly restored' by *Ponton & Gough*, 1873. Nave roof and w window tracery renewed by *Price & Jane*, 1900. Chancel re-fitted in memory of H. F. Tiarks by *G. E. S. Streatfeild*, 1913, with a polished Draycott stone floor. *W. D. Caröe* rebuilt the organ chamber and added a vestry (now chapel) in 1925–6, reached from the nave by two unequal segment-headed arches. – FITTINGS. ROOD SCREEN, *c.* 1500, with one-light sections and three densely carved friezes, crested top. Much restored with the rest of the chancel, 1913. Oak-panelled chancel and sanctuary sumptuously carved by *Harry Hems*, enclosed like a college chapel, with fittings all of a piece. – PULPIT. Late C15 Perp, carved from one block of Doulting Stone, on a trumpet foot resting on a human demi-figure. Small niches and buttresses with pinnacles. – FONT. C14, plain. – STAINED GLASS. E window by *Hardman*, typical of their designer *Dunstan J. Powell*, 1913. Nave N, *Kempe & Co.*, 1924. w window, *Hean & Maerchant*, 1904. (Vestry; Second World War memorial, by *Arnold Robinson* (*Bell & Son*), 1948.) – CROSS. Churchyard. C15 tapered shaft on steps. Restored 1910.

In the village, much late C19 work for the Tiarks family. Former RECTORY, 1884. Gothic, with bold asymmetrical roofs and a fine cast-iron porch-cloister. Of the same date, to the NW, THE LODGE, probably by the same architect; prominent tourelle. For Webbington House, *see* Compton Bishop.

LULLINGTON

ALL SAINTS. Perhaps the most enjoyable Norman village church in Somerset, consisting of nave, short central tower, chancel and s transept. Restored and the nave extended w by *T. H. Wyatt*, 1862. The Norman elements are mid-C12, and the showpiece is the N doorway. Two orders of columns, the inner on the l. with horizontal chevrons, on the r. with spiral twisting. Capitals with animals in profile, Samson and a huntsman. Lintel with grooved foliage. Tympanum with the Tree of Life and two beasts (a griffin and a lion?). Frame of rings round the tympanum. In the arch three-dimensional chevrons and then an outer order of beakheads – a rarity in the county. The hoodmould on two headstops rises to form a steep gable framing a seated figure of good quality. Paterae l. and r. Norman also the corbel table of the nave, two N windows, and the simpler s doorway with one order of columns with decorated scallop capitals. Also Norman the base of the tower; the w arch remarkably elaborate, with three orders of columns, the middle ones spiral-twisted. Capitals with animals, also in affronted pairs. Other capitals scalloped and decorated. Decorated abaci. Fragments of chevron decoration survive in the arch. The E crossing arch is simpler, though it also had originally three orders of columns. The W and E arches are pointed, a revision perhaps c. 1280 when the S transept was added (much restored arch from the nave, aumbry, square PISCINA with head of a king). Chancel rebuilt in the early C14, with straight-headed three-light side windows having inverted arches in the tracery. Good cusped ogee piscina. A S porch was added and the upper tower rebuilt (two-light bell-openings, battlements, SE stair-turret) in the late C15, completed 1508. In the tower base, two square-headed windows with quirky early C16 tracery.

8   FITTINGS. FONT, of Bath stone. The most richly decorated Norman font in Somerset. Tub-shaped with four bands: at the top, a row of faces linked by foliage emitting from their mouths, then an inscription (*Hoc fontis sacro pereunt delicta lavacro*), then rosettes, and at the bottom intersected arches on twisted coupled shafts. On the rim another (partly defaced) inscription. – STAINED GLASS. E window probably *Lavers & Barraud*, 1862, in the hot mauve and turquoise palette of the day. Surely theirs too the S transept S and E. Chancel S, c. 1912: good art glass. Painterly S window, central tower, by *J. L. Vanderpoorten* of Brussels, 1862. – MONUMENTS. Finely carved and well-preserved C12 Norman tomb-slab; the hand of God emerging from clouds and blessing a cross. – W churchyard wall, two parts of a Norman grave-slab with a cross and chevrons.

The ruinous VILLAGE was purchased from the Longleat estate by William Duckworth of Orchardleigh c. 1855. He brought in *T. H. Wyatt* in 1862 to design the former SCHOOL N of the village green; big S gable with fifteen-light iron-framed window (later bellcote). The C16 GLOUCESTER FARMHOUSE at the W end of the village was enlarged, plain Neo-Tudor (*W. Brown & Sons*, Frome, 1861), using materials from the old Orchardleigh House. *George Devey* transformed the centre around the green into an estate village with pairs of cottages, probably with the canopied pump. PUMP COTTAGES, dated 1861, and CORNER COTTAGES are Picturesque revivals of C17 and C18 forms: half-dormers, mullions, and round-arched canopies on curvy brackets – a remarkably early hint of the C18 revival that led shortly to the Queen Anne style. N of the church, COURT FARM, late C16 with the usual mullions under high relieving arches. To its N, EARTHWORKS indicate a larger early medieval village. To the E, LULLINGTON HOUSE, 1866–7, the former vicarage and *Devey*'s best work here. Harmoniously asymmetrical, with stone tiles, brick chimneys and mullioned windows, evoking the C17 but firmly Victorian. Intact plan and fittings, including hot-air central heating system by *Haden* of Trowbridge. (Also by *Devey*, Park Farm, 1863, c. ¼ m. NE.)

For GLOUCESTER LODGE, *see* Orchardleigh House, p. 575.

MARKSBURY

St Peter. Founded in the C12. Small aisleless nave with w tower, structure mainly C15. There is little Perp left after C17 and C18 rebuildings and restoration in 1875. Tower much remodelled in 1634 (date over the w door). A plain mullioned window above of the same character and date. The upper stages were reworked in a stark unbuttressed style after 1780, with round arches and monstrously big obelisk pinnacles. One Perp belfry light survives. More remodelling on the s side of the nave, with an inscription of 1627. – FONT. Norman, of block-capital shape. – MONUMENTS. William Counsell †1674, slate tablet. – Wadden †1682. Pilastered tablet in cartouche. – Boulter family †1782–1836, by *W. Brewer*.

From the main road, Marksbury is over almost as soon as it has begun. In a side lane, BECKET'S PLACE, dated 1668, with diagonally set chimneystacks and continuous string courses. Edge-moulded mullions were inserted as late as 1801 in the first floor of two cottages in a lane going NW towards Marksbury Vale.

Hunstrete House, 1½ m. w. Now a hotel. The site of a mansion of the Pophams of Littlecote, Wilts. The surviving house was built probably in the mid or late C18, and enlarged in the 1820s when the mansion was in decay. Plain seven-bay Regency front of Bath stone. The Early Georgian doorcase from the mansion has pilasters and a big segmental pediment with swags and a coat of arms. The mansion, c. 300 yds NW, was refronted c. 1770–97 by *Daniel Green*, a local mason, to form a very large block in a grand but outdated Palladian manner for Francis Popham and then for his widow Dorothy. Popham also developed the park with a chain of lakes to the N. Apparently never lived in, it was demolished c. 1832–6. The best fittings went to Prior Park, Bath (*see* p. 200). It had a fifteen-bay N front, of which the central five arches of the rustic basement survive as a sort of FOLLY. Excavation in 2007 partially revealed the plan of the E and N façades.

Stantonbury hill-fort, ⅔ m. NW of Stanton Prior. Single ditch and bank enclosing c. 10 acres and divided in two by a ditch. The WANSDYKE (q.v.) is incorporated into the N bank.

MELLS

Contrary to legend, the nursery-rhyme plum pulled out of a pie by Little Jack Horner has nothing to do with Mells or with the Horners, who purchased the manor in 1543. The village is nevertheless a plum, with its grouping of church and manor house among the happiest in Somerset, the church tower rising strong and trustworthy above the high trimmed hedges of the garden. From the 1880s the Horners created an artistic and political salon at Mells: thus the village boasts works by *Lutyens, Burne-Jones, Eric Gill* and *Gertrude Jekyll* for some of the great names of early C20 English society.

p. 28 ST ANDREW. The TOWER, 104 ft (32 metres) high, was in progress from *c.* 1446, when a bequest was made towards its building. It belongs to the group (cf. Leigh-on-Mendip) which has large blank windows below the bell-stage and repeating its design. The arrangement of buttresses and pinnacles is as ingenious as any in Somerset. Angle buttresses each with three diagonal infills. From the buttresses rise diagonally set tall pinnacles which end at the stage of the blank windows. From the belfry stage, a second set of diagonally placed pinnacles rises from the buttress set-offs to the parapet, forming a lively group with the main angle pinnacles. All the pinnacles are slightly detached from the mass of the tower. W doorway with crocketed ogee gable and (renewed) five-light window above. On the N and S the lowest stage is completely bare. Then follows the rich surface pattern of the three tall transomed two-light windows, all blank, and above, the same arrangement open, as belfry lights. The plain battlemented parapet is not altogether successful as a conclusion to the richness below.

The church exterior is of Doulting stone, fully embattled, with a fine Perp bellcote and Sanctus bell on the nave E gable. The fabric of nave and aisles appears all of a piece, probably built *c.* 1400–80. Leland (*c.* 1540) said the church was built 'yn tyme of mind', i.e. the late C15 or early C16, though this could refer to completion of the porch and vestry which distinguish the side towards the village. The semi-octagonal two-storey VESTRY was funded mainly by a London draper named Garland in 1485; on the S face, the arms of the Merchant Tailors' Guild. The windows small, of two lights with four-centred heads. The rich S PORCH, *c.* 1500, is two-storeyed with a concave-sided gable (cf. Wellow, Doulting) swept up to a pinnacle with a delicate niche rising in front of it. The angle buttresses carry detached pinnacles. The entrance is ogee-gabled and is flanked by panelling. Above, two niches. Unusual two-bay fan-vault almost identical to that at Doulting; eight fans frame a large central rose surrounded by four small traceried roses in the diagonals.

There is also a fan-vault inserted in the tower, its springers built out to square up the space. Its design derives from the high fan-vaults at Bath Abbey, designed *c.* 1503, with bands of quatrefoils around each fan. The execution is poor, indicating a local mason's copying.* The half-bay of solid wall terminating the nave was built with the tower – see the cracked masonry at the join, N side. The nave arcade is not high, of four bays, the piers with the standard wave mouldings between four shafts. The same repeated in chancel arch and tower arch, the

---

*Linda Monckton, Ph.D. thesis, 'Late Gothic Architecture in South-West England', University of Warwick, 1999.

latter with cumbersome shafts. Two arches into each chancel chapel; a narrow access arch with a much bigger one to its W, evidently later (see the altered jambs of the smaller arches), and probably to hold a monument. The exterior of the N or Horner Chapel with its pierced quatrefoil parapet shows it was an addition, perhaps c. 1500. In the chancel, a C13 cusped PISCINA. Another in the S chapel, C15 with cusped ogee arch. C19 restorations: S chapel roof by *W. G. Brown* of Frome, 1846; W window and W door, 1851; new chancel roof, and the plaster ceiling in the nave replaced by a tie-beam roof, c. 1859. A major restoration of 1880 by *Woodyer* included facing the chancel and porch with ashlar, new tiled floors, chancel fittings, pulpit and seating.

FITTINGS mostly of 1880. ALTAR of inlaid marble with two C19 Indian floral panels given by the Horners. – REREDOS with scenes of the Passion and Crucifixion, by *G. Vennell*. – SCREENS. C15 screens to the N and S chapels were replaced with near-replicas (but with wider tracery lights), c. 1855. *Woodyer* installed the elaborate chancel screen; carver *Stillman* of Bath. – LECTERN, 1855, its stand including pieces of C15 tracery from the screen lights. – PULPIT. Stone, with foliage panels. Carver *Vennell*. – Some Jacobean benches, the ends with a semicircular top and three finials; blank arches below. More reworked as dado panelling, c. 1880, when the *Clark* brothers of Mells made the panelled and traceried bench-ends. – Norman tub font. A cable moulding round the base. – Three good brass CHANDELIERS, one dated 1721. – EMBROIDERY. A big and impressive piece entitled *L'amor che muove il sole* from Dante's *Paradiso*, depicting the Guardian Angel of Humanity. Designed by *Burne-Jones*, worked by his friend *Lady Frances Horner*, c. 1880–3. – STAINED GLASS. C15 figures in the N aisle. E window by *Hardman*, 1881. Chancel N (1882), chapels and aisles (badly faded) by the *Horwood Bros*, local men trained at St Andrew's College established in Mells by the rector in 1843. N chapel E, a fine design by *William Nicholson*, 1930. W window by *Hudson*, 1851. – MONUMENTS. Chest tomb by *F. Nicholls* of Lambeth, 1872, replacing older monuments to Horners. Perp style. – Laura Lyttelton †1886. Relief with a peacock perched high up, displaying its long tail. Plaster on wood. Designed by *Burne-Jones*. – Mark Horner †1908, a small plinth designed by *Lutyens*, executed by *Eric Gill*, a very early work. – Raymond Asquith †1916, bronze wreath by *Lutyens*, with lettering cut by *Eric Gill*. – Edward Horner †1917, an equestrian monument of manageable size, moved from the N chapel to the W end of the N aisle, 2007. Tall plinth by *Lutyens* derived from the Whitehall Cenotaph; sculpture by *Sir Alfred Munnings*, 1920.* – Michael McKenna †1931 (NE corner of the churchyard). By *Lutyens*, 1932. A dramatically sculptural chest tomb: a solid block of Portland stone with a raised cross on top. Laurel banded sides,

110

* *Lutyens*'s unexecuted mausoleum for it had four full-height columns forming a Greek cross with barrel-vault.

below which the corners are cut away in big coves. – Siegfried
Sassoon †1967. Simple headstone.

MANOR HOUSE, W of the church. Initially the house appears
Elizabethan; a single-pile range aligned E–W, of two-and-a-half
storeys, and five gables on each long side. Mullioned-and-transomed windows of three to six lights, and a canted bay on the
W return. The earliest part, i.e. beneath the third gable, is of
the later C15 when the manor belonged to Glastonbury Abbey.
The Horners extended it to the W perhaps c. 1550–70; to this
phase belong two slim columnar buttresses, polygonal with
concave sides. Extended equally to the E, c. 1580–1600. Early
C17 additions to the N, which formed an H-plan, were dismantled slowly from 1763 as the family removed in stages to
Mells Park. In 1794 the *Gentleman's Magazine* said 'half the old
house is mouldering in ruins, the rest is occupied by a farmer'.
The Horners returned c. 1901, and the surviving S range was
much restored by *Lutyens*, with further changes to c. 1905. In
the W parlour a geometrical ceiling of c. 1905, based on a lost
ceiling of 1650 at Merchant's Barton, Frome. The drawing
room (E end) has an early C16 fireplace with a big frieze of five
quatrefoils containing shields and fleurons, brought from a
house in the village, c. 1920s. C17 ceiling with simple corner
sprays, perhaps also *ex situ*. To the E, a single-storey music room
and adjoining garden room by *Lutyens*, c. 1922, Neo-Tudor to
the entrance front, plain within, glazed round arches opening
S onto a Tuscan pergola. Lutyens's plans of 1904 in the family
archive projected a wing from the NW corner, then running W.
Instead a low kitchen range was built to the S, by *Owen Little*,
c. 1905–8.

MELLS PARK, 1 m. WSW. The deerpark was enclosed from 1604
for the Horner family. A lodge was replaced c. 1725 with a
house by *Nathaniel Ireson*, as the Horners vacated the manor
house (above).* The Horners returned to the manor house
c. 1901, and after a fire in 1917 Mells Park was rebuilt 1922–5
by *Sir Edwin Lutyens* for the McKenna family.† It is in the
restrained and sober classicism he preferred for country houses
after 1900 (e.g. The Salutation, Sandwich, Kent), by contrast
with his early Picturesque designs. Some details (e.g. the Gibbs
door surround) exhibit his characteristically playful treatment
of classical forms. Of fine ashlar stone and two storeys, seven
bays by four. Giant Doric pilasters, coved eaves and a hipped
roof, reminiscent of C17 Commonwealth houses. Tall windows
with shutters, and raised aprons below the first-floor sills.
Lutyens incorporated the surviving C18 service court with its
arcaded way leading N to the STABLE COURT of 1761, probably by *John Wood the Younger*. GARDENS on the E, S and W sides,
c. 1926, arranged around stone-walled terraces connected by

---

*Extended with bay-fronted wings in 1763 by *Daniel Hague*; altered by *Soane*
c. 1794 and 1804–24.
†Sir Reginald McKenna was a friend of Lutyens and chairman of the Midland
Bank. Their connection resulted in several buildings, including the Bank's headquarters at Poultry, London, 1924–39.

steps. Designed by *Lutyens* with *Gertrude Jekyll*, who was Pamela McKenna's aunt. To the w, paths and terraces, part of improvements by *W. S. Gilpin*, 1825–32. The Gothic LODGE W of Mells is early C19, probably by *Chapman* of Frome. Some of the Georgian park layout is discernible.

Mells was called by Leland 'a praty townelet of clothing'. Its main interest is NEW STREET, the approach to the church, though not aligned on the porch. It was built by Abbot Selwood of Glastonbury Abbey (which owned the village) *c.* 1470 as part of a plan to rebuild Mells with four straight streets meeting in the Roman fashion. The terraced houses had one room each side of the entrance and a stair-turret by the back door. Most have been updated, but Nos. 4, 6 and 9 have four-centred doorways and some C15 two-light windows.

SELWOOD ROAD, running E to W at the bottom of New Street, was realigned *c.* 1790 to accommodate a plain new RECTORY to the W, much rebuilt after a fire in 1929. GAY STREET, W of the Rectory, has good vernacular houses, e.g. GARSTON GATE, 1598. S again, BLIND HOUSE or lock-up, early C18, square with Gothic arched door. Back in Selwood Road is the TALBOT INN (C15, altered *c.* 1790), and E of New Street, low cottages with late C18 diamond-paned iron windows. Opposite, a TITHE BARN (now village hall), the roof having felling dates of 1395–1414. Much altered, and shortened at the N end. E again, a WAR MEMORIAL by *Lutyens*, *c.* 1920; low curving seats backed by high walls with clipped yew hedges above, central figure of St George on a Doric column. To the SE is HOLLYCROFT (lease of 1689): eight bays with cross-windows, porch, and small oval lights in rectangular frames. 100 yds E at Woodlands End, a triangular stone-roofed SHELTER and seat by *Lutyens*, 1908 (cf. his lychgate at Kilmersdon), one of three well-heads in the village commemorating Mark Horner; inscription by *Eric Gill*. Just S of the bridge over the Mells stream, a pair of ALMSHOUSES, late C17, each of five bays with two-light windows and hipped roof. The village SCHOOL at Mells Green is at its core a C17 farmhouse, quite high and gabled. ½ m. SW, CLAVEY'S FARM, *c.* 1650; some ovolo mullions and an early C18 doorway with semicircular hood.

FUSSELL'S IRON WORKS at Wadbury, E of Mells. Founded in 1744, it made edge-tools (i.e. scythes, spades, etc.). The Wadbury works, known as Lower Mill, were occupied 1841–*c.* 1891. Linear ranges almost 400 ft (123 metres) E–W, fed by weirs and leats from the S. In various states of decay; the offices stand to two storeys. To the NW, within Wadbury Camp (*see* below), is WADBURY HOUSE by *James Wilson*, *c.* 1841, for Thomas Fussell. A big Italianate villa, Bath-fashion.

A little E of Conduit Hill, the great pit survives of a BALANCE LOCK, constructed *c.* 1799 as part of the uncompleted Dorset and Somerset Canal (*see* p. 59); designed and patented by *James Fussell*. It could lift a barge of ten tons up to 20 ft (6 metres). ½ m. E below the summit of Barrow Hill, another four pits, partly masonry-lined, mark the easternmost limit of the failed venture.

IRON AGE HILL-FORTS. KINGSDOWN CAMP, on the E Mendip plateau 2¾ m. NNW of Mells, is a small heart-shaped single bank and ditch enclosing half an acre. These defences were built soon after the Roman conquest over a late Iron Age ditch. NEWBURY HILL, a small enclosure of 200 yds by 150 yds (190 by 140 metres), 1 m. NE of Mells, has been all but obliterated by ploughing. WADBURY is ½ m. E of Mells and a similar distance from Tedbury hill-fort further E (*see* Great Elm). Its enclosure is 500 by 300 yds (460 by 280 metres), bounded on its S side by the rocky gorge of Mells stream and on the other sides by ditches and stone walls.

7060

MIDFORD

76　MIDFORD CASTLE, Midford Road. The most eccentric of the substantial villas around Bath, beautifully sited overlooking a wooded valley. Built for Henry Disney Roebuck, *c.* 1775, probably after *John Carter*'s design for 'a Gothic Mansion' (*Builder's Magazine*, 1774). An early example of the taste for geometric-shaped villas, mainly triangular and sometimes castellated, e.g. Carr's Grimston Garth, Yorkshire (1781–6). It is tower-like, three-storeyed, on an ingenious trefoil plan. (It was said in 1899 that this 'ace of clubs' plan commemorates a gambling feat by Roebuck.) Raised on a plinth containing service quarters. The two principal floors have pointed windows with ogee hoods, the upper windows, straight hoods. To give the appearance of towers, the parapet is heightened over the turrets like a screen wall, and pierced with quatrefoil openings in blind arches. Each floor has a central lozenge-shaped hall leading to three main rooms, surprisingly varied in plan: D-shaped, horse-shoe, or rectangular with a bow. Charming Rococo ceilings attributed to *Thomas Stocking*, chiefly light foliage in circular or octagonal compositions, one with free-flying birds.

Castellated also, the early C19 GATEHOUSE (four-centred arch, quatrefoils in the spandrels) and the picturesque group of STABLES and former CHAPEL. This has a tower with pinnacles, and a cupola. To the NE is a ruined summerhouse known as THE PRIORY, extant in 1791. A two-storey circular tower with a higher circular stair-turret, embattled, with quatrefoil windows. Originally it had a nave and apse, with ogee-headed niches. On the brow of steep descent is a restored rustic HERMITAGE, also C18.

MIDFORD MILL, on the main road, is a three-storey C19 rebuilding. The attached miller's house has a gabled front, late C18 or early C19, on a probably C15 core: see the enormous chimney-breast, a depressed-arched chimneypiece, and massive collar-beamed roof with wind-braces.

MIDSOMER NORTON 6050

A small market town which expanded under the impetus of coal mining from the C18. Post-industrial decline and redevelopment have spoilt what must once have been an attractive setting.

ST JOHN BAPTIST, Church Square. The w tower was rebuilt in 1674 (dated on tower arch) with set-back buttresses ending in obelisk pinnacles. Round-arched tracery in the belfry lights, small upright ovals in the second stage. On the s side high up in a niche, a STATUE of Charles II. Parapet with corner and intermediate pinnacles. w window with curious tracery of lancets and a big circle connected by bars, probably of 1828–30, when the body of the church was rebuilt by *John Pinch Jun.* Tall lancet windows with three-light tracery; battlements and pinnacles. One of Pinch's better interiors. Tall arcades of the Perp Somerset standard (four hollows). Roof on arched braces with traceried spandrels. In 1875 *C. E. Giles & Richard Gane* produced plans for enlarging the E end, though what was carried out is unclear beyond the insertion of Perp tracery. In 1924–6 *W. D. Caröe* lengthened the chancel by one bay, reusing the Perp tracery and earlier parapet. In 1935–6 he removed the galleries and their E staircases, replacing that on the s with a low Lady Chapel. – FONT. Norman, circular, with a small scalloped top band. – STAINED GLASS. E window by *Kempe*, 1889. – MONUMENTS. Harbord family, 1678. Ionic pilasters, broken pediment with cartouche. – George Savage †1747. Still Baroque; Composite columns. – Sarah Smith †1829, by *Chapman* of Frome. With a fat little putto seated by an urn.

HOLY GHOST (R.C.), High Street. A C15 tithe barn, part of a grange of Merton Abbey. Converted by *Giles Gilbert Scott*, 1907–13, as a mission of Downside Abbey. Six bays divided by big buttresses. At the third bay from the r. a high transeptal entrance with depressed arch. Granger's loft above lit by a transomed window with ogee lights. It serves as the church's ritual s porch. In the ritual w gable, two big square-headed lights by Scott. The interior was courageously left barn-like, with whitewashed walls and the fine roof exposed. Arch-braced collar-beams and two tiers of wind-braces. – Sumptuous gilded and carved TABERNACLE, 1794. Probably Bavarian, from the R.C. church in Warwick Street, Westminster. – Chancel PANELLING perhaps late C17. – Timber STATUE of Virgin and Child, Dutch, *c.* 1630. – PAINTINGS. Late C18 Flemish Stations of the Cross.

METHODIST CHAPEL, High Street. 1859. Geometric Dec, in the manner of Foster & Wood. Quite imposing despite the truncated spirelet l. of the gable.

SOMERVALE SCHOOL, Redfield Road. 1963–5, probably *Somerset County Architects' Department.* Long two-storey block with occasional three-storey sections. Concrete frame, the corner posts exposed by breaks in the grey brick infill. Water tank on stilts at the w. These features refer to the Smithsons' influential school at Hunstanton, Norfolk, but lack its compositional clarity.

The River Somer flows through the HIGH STREET, though now harshly canalized. Here there is only one handsome house left, now the COUNCIL OFFICES, No. 19: a three-storey five-bay stone house with Gibbs surrounds to all the windows and the doorway. In the style of Thomas Paty of Bristol, c. 1750–70. In the square to the W, the TOWN HALL, formerly market hall, by *Foster & Wood*, 1859–60.* Of yellow Lias, Italianate. Round-arched openings with pointed voussoirs of Pennant banding. A little way W is No. 11 The Island, modest Georgian c. 1760. Red sandstone, with a Venetian window. In High Street, NW of the square, the GREYHOUND HOTEL and adjacent BANK of the same build: plain Italianate with brick banding, c. 1860. NE of the parish church, THE PRIORY; mullioned front perhaps of 1712 with arched door hood and heavy keystone. (Within, traces of a possibly medieval structure.)

DYMBORO HOUSE, North Road. By *Rupert Austin*, 1908, for Dr Arthur Bulleid, archaeologist. Now three houses. An unexpected and pleasing Arts and Crafts house on an L-plan facing S and E. Coursed stone, stone-tiled roof, big mullioned-and-transomed windows. The angles between entrance, staircase and main rooms are deftly managed by an octagonal lobby with Neo-Georgian panelling.

MANOR HOUSE, Millard's Hill, Welton, ½ m. N. Tower-like porch, embattled and with a round-arched entrance and a round-headed window above. Dated 1620. It is centrally placed in a three-bay front with mullioned windows. (On the first floor, an unusual Renaissance chimneypiece with figures supporting the mantel.)

MONKTON COMBE

ST MICHAEL. Rebuilt 1863–5, by *C. E. Giles*. 'Rather a terrible piece of architecture' (Pevsner). E.E. with plate tracery, short W tower with stepped lancet bell-openings and saddleback roof. Horseshoe chancel arch. N aisle in keeping, i.e. dull, by *E. H. Lingen Barker*, 1886.

Next to the church is CHURCH FARM, the symmetrical front C18. At right angles, facing the churchyard, a range which is probably C16 or earlier, with hollow-chamfered mullioned and four-centred lights. To the SW, a square C16 DOVECOTE with blocked mullioned gable lights. (Ashlar nesting holes.) In Mill Lane, the LOCK-UP, probably c. 1776, with domical stone roof. At the foot of the lane by Midford Brook, former FLOCK MILLS, with a four-storey early C19 office building. Iron-framed windows in segmental openings.

---

* *The Builder*, 6 October 1860. Thomas Harris Smith, previously credited, was a brewer.

MONKTON COMBE SCHOOL. Taken NE, from the N end of Mill Lane. First, slightly recessed, a Neo-C17 block of 1937 by *Skinner Bros*, incorporating the hall behind. To the E, a wide-fronted farmhouse, dated 1714 but still entirely C17 in style. Then a Neo-C17 block, *c.* 1960, by *Eustace Button*. Adjoining Maths and Science block by *Tektus*, opened 2008; nicely judged in scale and proportion. Just to its W, the school CHAPEL, by *A. Beresford Pite & J. S. Hodges*, 1924–7. Mild Neo-Gothic, inventive curvy tracery in the W window. At the W (ritual S) side a short porch-tower with louvred bell-openings and a quirky dome. Small aisle beside the porch by *George Pace*, 1964. – STAINED GLASS. E window by *Deirdre Ducker*, 2001.

Above the village on Shaft Road (N), COMBE GROVE MANOR, now a hotel. Long Late Georgian front with bowed centre, altered 1858 with segmental-headed windows. On Brass-knocker Hill, ½ m. E, massive rusticated gatepiers, late C18, with urn finials. Opposite, Nos. 1 and 2, early C18 mullioned cottages with three rather Baroque urns at the eaves. A little lower, COMBE HILL HOUSE, a Gothic villa of the 1790s. The most interesting elevation is the E, with a full-height bow (l.), then a concave front of six bays.

VIADUCT carrying the A36 road across the valley E of Monkton Combe. Eleven arches of Bath stone, reserved classical details. By *G. P. Manners*, 1834.

For the Dundas Aqueduct, *c.* ¾ m. NE, *see* Limpley Stoke, Wiltshire.

NAILSEA

A town with three centres connected by suburban infill. Coal mining and glassworks drove its growth until the C20. It now serves partly as a satellite to Bristol.

HOLY TRINITY, Church Lane. A chapel of ease to Wraxall until 1811. Perp throughout. Tall four-stage W tower with diagonal buttresses, two-light windows and bell-openings, a parapet with pierced cusped lozenges, and a higher stair-turret. W doorway, W window. Corner pinnacles and stair-turret cap, 1903. Crude S porch dated 1712. S wall buttresses added 1861 by *S. C. Fripp*. He replaced the roofs. Hall by *Nealon, Tanner & Partners*, 1983–5. It obscures the Perp manorial N chapel (now organ chamber). Tower arch with unusual moulding, double ogees and hollows. No chancel arch. Crocketed ogee PISCINA with pinnacles. Arcade of five bays of which four lead into the aisle, one into the chancel chapel. The unusual piers have four shafts, and four wide hollows with thin shafts set in them. Broad foliate bands around the capitals. Arcade in two sections of subtly different designs; the two eastern arches probably *c.* 1440–90 (for a chantry chapel?) extended W perhaps before 1540. Where the rood loft was, the capitals have the lion of St Mark (N) and the bull of St Luke (S) with a remarkable figure defecating towards the nave; a reminder of the earthly alongside the divine. Reordered by *Chedburn Ltd* in 2003–4, including full-immersion baptistery and moveable seats. Effective colour scheme by *Henry Haig*. – Mid-C19 REREDOS. From Wraxall. Installed 1893. Caen stone, ogee-gabled ends. – FONT. Perp, octagonal, cusped square panels, one marked out but not carved. – Interesting late C15 stone PULPIT on polygonal stem; access through the N wall. Each side with a two-light blank panel. – ROYAL ARMS. 1714–26; charming painted stone relief. – STAINED GLASS. E window doubtless by *Hardman*, 1878. – S aisle E, C15 fragments collected here 1861. – S aisle from E, *Heaton, Butler & Bayne*, 1887; and *John Hall & Sons*, 1926. – MONUMENTS. William Cole †1657; engaged Doric columns, swan-necked pediment, curvy base. – Late medieval CROSS-SHAFT.

W of the church, a humble TITHE BARN, *c.* 1480. Seven trusses of an arched-braced collar-beam roof with wind-braces, repaired 1972. Used as a school from the early C19, enlarged in the late C19. Adapted and restored for community use by *Architecton*, 2009–11.

CHRIST CHURCH, Christ Church Close. 1842–3 by *Scott & Moffatt*. Still in the Commissioners' tradition, but the W front, with three stepped lancets and bellcote above, hints at the robustness of Scott's later work. Nave with paired lancets, chancel with single lancets, S porch. Plain interior. Organ chamber and vestry by *R. Milverton Drake*, 1885–6. – FITTINGS mostly early C20, Perp. – HALL by *Jones, Biggs & Mann*, 1975–6, masking the S side. Uncomfortably irregular plan, avoiding graves. – Former VICARAGE. 1844, presumably by *Scott & Moffatt*.

ST FRANCIS (R.C.), Ash Hayes Road. By *John Webster*, 1985–6. Pale brick, square in plan with the internal axis on the diagonal. Pyramid roof. Linked hall and presbytery.

CHAPELS. METHODIST, Silver Street, completed 1999. Gable-end of blockwork verticals alternating with Pennant stone. Of the C19, only the UNITED REFORMED CHURCH, Stockway North, is still in use. Classical, the usual pedimented front, 1837.

SHOPPING PRECINCT, Somerset Square. Planned 1962, by *BGP Group* (*Roger Gallannaugh*), built 1970–2. Bland bush-hammered concrete arcades and brown brick, with staggered and jettied upper floors. Lively octagonal LIBRARY (*Somerset County Architects' Department*, 1970–1) sunk in a stepped well; ribbed concrete panels and vertical glazing, central lantern.

NAILSEA GLASSWORKS, E end of High Street. Established by J. R. Lucas in 1788 and closed in 1873. The 13½-acre site produced mainly window and bottle glass. Much of what survived was buried beneath a supermarket car park *c.* 2001–3. What remains is bounded to the W by the Royal Oak, an C18 inn. Attached to its E side, a long rubble-stone shed with later corrugated roof, which in 1870 housed two French kilns. Also the base of New House GLASS CONE, *c.* 1826–9. Nearby, swinging pits for the production of sheet glass. Off High Street (E end), some HOUSES survive, e.g. New Rank, *c.* 1820s, and Woodview Terrace, much modernized.

MIDDLE ENGINE PIT, Golden Valley (Nailsea Park). A remarkable survival of a colliery engine house and horse gins, *c.* 1840s. The pit operated 1846–50.

NAILSEA COURT, Chelvey Road, *c.* 2 m. SW. Historically highly instructive and interesting, despite conversion to three houses, *c.* 2001–2. The main (Hall) range runs E–W; its S front has a full-height gabled porch at the E end of the Hall. From its E end a range runs N, with three gables facing E and two S. The Z-plan is completed by a squarish block at the SW; two gables E and two S, the latter with a canted bay. There are four periods, the C15, the Elizabethan (perhaps two phases), an undefined period later in the C17 or *c.* 1700 (perhaps two phases), and restoration and new SW wing by *Arthur Stratton*, *c.* 1910–13. This replaced a ridiculous castellar turret-cum-water-tower erected *c.* 1906 by *R. Milverton Drake* to buttress the walls where a C16 range was removed. Of the late C15 one ornamental piece remains, a two-light window with cusped ogee-arched lights found during the C20 rebuilding (cf. hall windows at Tickenham Court and the upper porch window at Yatton Rectory). Structurally what survives of the C15 house is as follows: the Hall, with a separate, buttressed bay-room at its dais (W) end which had another small room over (as testified by one remaining slit window to watch arrivers); the narrow stair of the porch now hidden by panelling; an oriel window on the upper floor of the porch; the kitchen (now Library) E of the porch and the former screens passage, and part of its large fireplace. The Elizabethan enlargements are visually better documented. There are two *in situ* chimneypieces one above the another in the SW wing. In a room NW of the Hall and in the room above are two fireplaces, one with the initials of Richard Cole of Bristol and his wife, the other with the date 1593. A pre-existing porch was raised to full height with a new entrance arch and restrained classical entablature. In the E range a new, larger kitchen was provided N of the old one; the old kitchen and the rooms above both were made into additional living quarters. On the upper floor a fireplace with the initials of George and Elizabeth Perceval who lived at Nailsea Court 1551–82. There is in addition the date 1582, perhaps apocryphal. The windows have depressed-arched lights, a feature more at home *c.* 1550 than *c.* 1580. Smaller features worth noting are the buttery hatch and two doorways W of the Hall proving that an additional and more spacious staircase had been supplied there. Now for the late C17. The porch staircase was blocked by panelling which looks in style *c.* 1670. A further staircase was put in E of the Hall. Then, perhaps *c.* 1700, the Hall was given a new fireplace and tall cross-windows on two floors. Whether the horizontal subdivision of the Hall was carried out then or earlier cannot now be said. Also *c.* 1700 a new stone doorcase from the Hall to the E staircase and to the bay-room. Finally the C20 wing, with imported pieces, notably panelling from No. 18 Fore Street, Taunton, an overmantel from Over Langford Manor, Churchill, and a plaster ceiling from Ashley Manor, Bristol. – In the gardens, SE, a former BARN. Buckler's drawing of the 1820s shows typical C15 to C16 features. Remodelled before 1910; buttresses added, and large mullioned-and-transomed windows inserted.

NEMPNETT THRUBWELL

ST MARY. Norman S doorway. Only part of the plain arch remains. Under it is a smaller lower Perp doorway. Perp W tower with set-back buttresses and two-light bell-openings with Somerset tracery. Parapet with blank arcading, square pinnacles, higher stair-turret with a quatrefoil frieze, battlements. Spirelet renewed, C19. Good wagon roof with bosses in the nave, resting on head corbels. Re-seated by *Popes & Bindon*, 1865. Chancel rebuilt in a well-designed Neo-Dec, 1896–7, by *Edmund Buckle*. – FONT. Circular on circular stem. Blank arcading, re-cut in the early C16 with close tracery on the bowl and small naïvely carved demi-figures. – SCREEN. Four-light divisions with Flamboyant tracery, coving with ribs, angel-figures against the main posts. Given its character, perhaps by Buckle.* – MONUMENT. Beale family, c. 1710 and later. Big bolection frame. – CROSS. Square four-stepped base, late medieval.

OLD RECTORY, ¼ m. S. By *Pope & Bindon*, 1860. An exemplary High Victorian Gothic rectory, of grey stone enlivened by decorative red brick bands. Sharply pointed arches, timber porch.

(FAIRY'S TOOT NEOLITHIC CHAMBERED TOMB, SSW of Howgrove Farm, a little E of Butcombe. Destroyed before the mid C19. An antiquarian account describes three pairs of chambers either side of an axial passage and a porthole-type entrance slab.)

NEWTON ST LOE

HOLY TRINITY. Externally low, spreading, and much restored. Then the spacious and arresting early C14 Dec interior, particularly surprising in Somerset where the best work is so often Perp. The S porch and S aisle are most interesting. The porch has a double-chamfered arch dying into the jambs. Ornate ogee-headed S doorway with a continuous hollow moulding

---

*The source for Pevsner's attribution to E.W. Pugin is uncertain.

and ballflower. Immensely broad aisles. The four-and-a-half-bay s arcade has broad quatrefoil piers with thin shafts in the diagonals, moulded capitals with ballflower, and depressed two-centred double-chamfered arches. The W respond differs slightly, and seems to belong more to the C13 than the C14. The S aisle E window (renewed) has a shafted, cusped and sub-cusped rere-arch, and hoodmould on headstops. Three-light S windows, in reveals also with double-chamfered arches dying into the jambs. Restored in 1857 by *C. E. Davis*. He added the N aisle and rebuilt the chancel in lavish Dec, adhering closely to original forms. A squint and rood-loft door are preserved. Perp W tower, perhaps late C14, with diagonal buttresses, two-light bell-openings, and strange pinnacles, slim, panelled and tapering, perhaps C18. The tower arch is double-chamfered, on demi-shafts with polygonal capitals.*

FITTINGS. REREDOS. Marble relief in triptych frame, 1891. – PULPIT. Lavish Neo-Perp, early C20. – FONT. Small circular bowl on a fringe of stiff-leaf, 1857. – PEWS. All 1857; Perp carved panels. – STAINED GLASS. Chancel N, small light by *Geoffrey Robinson*, 1972. – MONUMENTS. Joseph Langton †1701, also his parents †1716 and 1719. Surprisingly stately, restrained and dignified standing monument, worthy of Westminster Abbey. Drapery and armorials in the base, seraphs' heads supporting free-standing Corinthian columns, big segmental pediment with two putti and an urn. The inscriptions are divided by a central fluted pilaster, the only solecism. The carving is of the best, the design in the taste of Gibbs. The area corresponding to the vault below is surrounded by a cast-iron RAILING with ball and spear-head finials, the earliest piece of cast iron in Somerset, and perhaps the south-west of England. That also points to Gibbs's influence. – A splendid array in the N aisle, including Dame Anne Cobb †1749, white urn against a sar-cophagus, by *Prince Hoare*; Susannah Warburton †1766, bombé tablet with palm branches; Abel Moysey †1780, of coloured marbles. Standing woman by an urn; obelisk background.

The VILLAGE is remarkably unspoiled, with C17–C19 cottages among twisting lanes and fertile orchards, preserved first by the Langtons, and since 1941 by the Duchy of Cornwall. Outside the churchyard, the FREE SCHOOL of 1698, a low two-storey five-bay front with upright two-light mullioned windows and a semicircular door hood on carved brackets. Restored and enlarged, 1911. Opposite, STONEWALLS, dated 1715, with three-light mullioned windows, suspended, as it were, from continuous string courses. One-bay pediment with a two-light mullioned window. Here the C17 and the C18 meet. Down the street, the OLD RECTORY, Bath stone ashlar. Perhaps C18, with an Italianate W front in the Bath style, *c.* 1840s. To the S, minor C17 houses, some thatched; that by the green at the village centre has a Baroque cartouche of *c.* 1700 over the door.

*The cellar doorway is puzzling. Can it be Transitional and re-set?

NEWTON PARK (Bath Spa University). Among the finest C18 country houses in Somerset, noble and reticent. It began as a fortified manor house of the St Loe family, c. 1290–1320, enlarged by the Botreaux family in the C15 and further altered for the Langtons, Bristol merchants, owners from 1666. Joseph Langton demolished all except the keep, gatehouse and service ranges (*see* below), for a new house to the N by *Stiff Leadbetter*, c. 1761–5.

This is a large villa rather than a mansion, cf. Leadbetter's Nuneham Park, Oxfordshire (1756–63). The two-storey main block has a comfortably spaced seven-bay entrance front (SE). Balustraded parapet and three-bay pediment with Diocletian window. The ground-floor openings have alternating pediments. No further decoration. One-storey quadrants with arched windows curve forward to identical service pavilions, of five bays and one-and-a-half storeys, with big pediments and recessed cupolas. The garden side (NW) is even plainer. Central canted bay with pedimented doorway. Another canted bay on the SW return. Refined Neoclassical INTERIORS, sensitively repaired by *Gerrard, Taylor & Partners*, 1946–7, after wartime occupation; interconnecting rooms of various geometries, around a rectangular staircase hall, architecturally the most attractive space. Fine wrought-iron balustrade of S-scrolls carried round three sides of the upper landing, and an Ionic columned gallery (SW). Above, graceful spandrels and a circular glazed dome. The main rooms have delicately detailed stucco ceilings, friezes over the doors of exceptionally crisp Rococo carving, and very good marble fireplaces. The central saloon on the garden front has a curved bay inside the canted exterior, and the best chimneypiece, of white marble with terms and a relief of the Sacrifice of Isaac. The ceiling of the room in the W corner has oval and circular Neoclassical plaster reliefs in the style of Wedgwood jasperware, amidst Rococo foliage. The canted bay in the SW front is resolved within by a most attractive octagonal room with Adamish motifs in the plasterwork; more appear in the rectangular Doric entrance hall; triglyph frieze with bucrania and paterae in the metopes. All this betrays Leadbetter's familiarity with e.g. James Stuart's *The Antiquities of Athens* (1762).

PARK remodelled by *Capability Brown* c. 1761–5, with lakes set steeply below the house to its N and W. *Repton*'s Red Book (1796–7) proposed new lakes with a Palladian bridge; little was done apart from re-routing the ¾-m.-long drive from the N across open hillsides and picturesque wooded glades.

To the SW, modified by Brown as a picturesque eyecatcher, is the KEEP of the St Loes. It is difficult to see now what is original C13 work. The keep was still in use in the C16; see the (restored) three tiers of four-light transomed windows with arched lights. Spiral staircase in the W wall (with two tiny medieval windows) with a C16 big rectangular staircase projection to its N. GATEHOUSE, NW of the keep, probably C15. Machicolated outer front with square angle towers, the carriageway splendidly vaulted in two bays, and with original gates. OUTBUILDINGS SW of the keep. Two long ranges originating as stables or service rooms, probably *c.* 1666. Stone-tiled roofs, ovolo mullions, depressed four-centred door openings. Partly regularized and modernized for the Training College. – LODGE, NE, in Newton St Loe; Tudor Gothic, *c.* 1845.

The house became a teacher training college in 1947, and is now the main campus of Bath Spa University. The earliest EDUCATIONAL BUILDINGS, N of the mansion, were designed under *Molly Gerrard* (*Gerrard, Taylor & Partners*). The Bath stone GYMNASIUM (now restaurant), 1950, revives the modified Neoclassicism of the 1930s. Noteworthy UNIVERSITY THEATRE, by *Feilden Clegg Bradley*, 2006: fronting the road, a low curving curtain wall of almost unbroken ashlar, contrasting with a glazed entrance and the bulky auditorium rising behind. Upper parts clad in white stone bristling everywhere with regular vertically set shards of black slate.

(ROMAN VILLA, ⅔ m. NE of the village. Uncovered and destroyed during construction of the Great Western Railway in 1837. An elaborate mosaic including geometric decoration and a representation of Orpheus and the animals is now at Bristol Museum.)

NORTH STOKE

ST MARTIN. At the NE end of the village. Short, broad, two-stage W tower. The proportions, the semicircular tower arch and clasping buttresses suggest C12 origins. The buttresses were regularized, perhaps in 1731 (date plaque). Parapet and short pinnacles perhaps also C18. Simple S porch. The angles of the nave are not square, and it aligns neither with the chancel nor the tower. Uneven pointed chancel arch without mouldings. Interesting late medieval roofs, in the nave just collar-beams to each pair of rafters, in the chancel in addition straight braces. Nave and chancel over-restored *c.* 1858 (chancel windows renewed and the roofs raised) and in 1888 by *C. E. Davis*. – FONT. Perhaps *c.* 1200. Square bowl with chamfered angles, flaring out to form the foot. – WOODWORK. Inner and outer S doors both perhaps C16 or early C17. – MONUMENTS. Ward Family, 1770, by *Ford*. In the base, a mourning woman against an urn, with weeping willow and obelisk. Inscribed obelisk top missing.

CHURCH FARM, W of the church, is *c.* 1700–10: hipped roof, three-bay front with bolection-framed openings and cross-windows. Restored 1885. THE MANOR HOUSE, *c.* 150 yds W, must be *c.* 1670 (cf. Becket's Place, Marksbury), mullioned but with straight eaves, with a good shell-hood added *c.* 1700. MANOR HOUSE FARMHOUSE, symmetrical and mullioned, has two big gables flanking the central entrance. (First-floor chimneypiece with overmantel dated 1664.)

LITTLE DOWN PROMONTORY HILL-FORT, 400 yds E of the church, at the E extremity of the Lansdown plateau. The triangular earthwork encloses 15 acres. Remains of two Bronze Age ROUND BARROWS, badly eroded by ploughing, lie E of the fort's single entrance. One of these produced fragments of a gilded bronze sun-disc, now in the British Museum.

6060 NORTON MALREWARD

HOLY TRINITY. Rebuilt excepting the short w tower and late Norman chancel arch by *James Wilson*, 1861. The nave has thirty-six eaves corbels with symbols, designed by the *Rev. R. A. Taylor*. Tower of White Lias with Dundry dressings, perhaps C15, with diagonal buttresses. Solid battlements; every merlon has its own pinnacle. The chancel arch, doubtless resurfaced, has authentic irregularities. To the w one order of twisted colonnettes with beading between the main spirals. Stronger inner columns with scallop capitals. The outer two orders of chevrons are arranged at 90 degrees point-to-point; the inner order, at 45 degrees to the wall, has little beads in the points. Outer pellet moulding. – STAINED GLASS. Three (s aisle) by *Bell & Son*, c. 1900. – MONUMENTS. Civilian and lady, c. 1325. Big, weathered coffin-lid, with two heads in relief (cf. Norton St Philip). – Coffin-lid with two foliated crosses; C15. – Shute Adams †1766. Attributed to *Thomas Paty*. Handsome oval tablet under open pediment with urn.

MANOR FARM, N of the church. A once impressive Early Georgian façade; two storeys, originally of 3:2:3 bays marked by superimposed pilasters, Tuscan and Ionic. The r. three bays were burnt c. 1900. In the two-bay part, the windows are arched. Pedimented doorcase in the third bay, the pilasters framing it on one side only. Attic storey and segmental pediment noted by Pevsner have been removed.

MAES KNOLL IRON AGE HILL-FORT, ½ m. NW of the village. A triangular enclosure of 30 acres at the E extremity of Dundry Hill, much eroded by ploughing. The N and NE ramparts are overlain by the bank and ditch of the Wansdyke, a linear boundary of the C7 (*see* Wansdyke).

7050 NORTON ST PHILIP

ST PHILIP. The w tower is a curious design, due to a rich citizen called Jeffrey Flower, †1644, who reputedly rebuilt the tower and much of the church to his own ideas, perhaps reusing material from Hinton Priory. The tower seems a modification of the Mells–Leigh type. Set-back buttresses, battlements, higher stair-turret, pinnacles, but none of that play with pinnacles which the local masons indulged in. Shallow C15 W porch, *ex situ*. The outer doorway has niches l. and r. The inner has bearded heads in the spandrels. Flat stone ceiling with a wheel centre, like a flattened fan-vault, and on the l. and r. big animals in profile. Three-light transomed W window with, above, a small panel arranged as three niches. The middle stage has a blank transomed window, its lower lights replaced by another row of three niches. The bell-openings have a transom pushed right up to the springing point of the arch.* More oddly, the S and N side of the tower have three-light ground-floor windows, and yet more rows of niches. The rest of the church seems externally all Perp – nave without clerestory, gabled aisles, N and S chapels – but over-restored by *Scott*, 1847–50. Chancel restored by *G. P. Manners* before 1847. Very simple S porch; outer door with square hood, perhaps C16, and a good wagon roof with big square bosses. The inner S doorway with its depressed, two-centred, single-chamfered arch may be C13. The three-bay nave arcades are confusing. On the S side, two arches with double wave mouldings, i.e. C15, on circular piers with four filleted demi-shafts, i.e. early C14. The easternmost arch is lower, pointed and double-chamfered. On the N side, the W bay has a depressed arch with double-panelled soffit, perhaps C16. The arch from N chapel to chancel is similar. The central nave bay has a two-centred arch with ovolo mouldings and the queerest responds, no doubt C17. Tower arch with wave mouldings and shafts, but two odd shaft-rings below the capitals, and a tower vault of a design unknown to the C15: probably all C17 too. The chancel and its arch seem more securely C15, four shafts and hollows. The S chapel arch has panelled soffits, *c.* 1500. At the W end of the N aisle, a daring free-standing oak pod (for vestry etc., under a glass meeting room). By *Chedburn Ltd*, 2000–5. – FONT. Perp, with quatrefoils and shields. – STAINED GLASS. Chancel N and S by *Wailes*, probably *c.* 1847–50. – MONUMENT. Effigy of a civilian, *c.* 1460, under a cusped arch. Tomb-chest with quatrefoils. – Two relief heads from a possibly late medieval monument to the 'Fair Maids of Foscott', conjoined twins. The story was noted by Pepys.

Opposite the church an ambitious Neo-Tudor SCHOOL dated 1827, reportedly by *J. Thomson* of London. Embattled, with four angle pinnacles. In CHURCH HILL, good C17 and later cottages. MANOR FARM was the home of the Flowers 1523–1666, but was rebuilt *c.* 1690. Imposing nine-bay two-storey front with cross-windows, two bolection-framed doorways, entirely regular and symmetrical but for a subsidiary entrance in the second bay from the r. Facing, a former C18 stable with upright oval windows. NW, a C15 DOVECOTE.

---

* Are all these threes a conceit on the Trinity? The Flowers had Catholic and Royalist sympathies, and gave money for the restoration of Bath Abbey.

HIGH STREET, to the N, has narrow burgage plots probably indicating the town planted in the C13 by Hinton Priory, who held the manor from 1232. The GEORGE INN is among the most remarkable medieval inns in England, begun in the later C14 by the priory, and used for storing wool and cloth before the annual fairs (Hinton's fair was transferred to Norton St Philip in 1345 and became one of the most important in Somerset). To the front only the ground floor is of stone. At the r., some mullioned windows, perhaps C16, and a short external staircase, later than the main structure. The porch has a four-centred archway, with worn stone seats within. To the l. two canted lightly buttressed bays with cusped arched two-light windows, probably late C14. The original stone upper storey was replaced *c.* 1430–1 with two timber-framed storeys on jetties. The first-floor overhang rests on the porch and ground-floor bays. On the first floor three pretty oriel windows on triplets of curved brackets, not symmetrical with the composition below. Square framing with some downward braces. The s end was shortened by two bays *c.* 1700. Both ends have octagonal pierced chimneys, probably C15. The rear of the main range is all of stone, closer to its original C14 state. More elaborate archway from the cross-passage, a polygonal stair-turret, and two-light cusped windows. The room l. of the cross-passage was originally open to the roof, with galleries at first and second floors. This well was infilled in 1510. The main roof has collar- and tie-beam trusses, with noble arch braces over the former well, and two tiers of wind-braces. The lower rear buildings face a nearly triangular courtyard, with rooms open to the roof on two sides. s range (perhaps a barn originally) roofed *c.* 1457–8, E range *c.* 1478. The w range with a low timber-framed gallery is probably C15.

Good C16–C18 cottages s of the inn, e.g. The White House, 1658; low, gabled and mullioned. Opposite, a simple BAPTIST CHAPEL of 1814. Gothic windows. Further s, a garden gate incorporating a Perp arch, *ex situ.*

WICK FARM, *c.* 1¼ m. NE. Low, stone-roofed. Prominent two-centred entrance arch with continuous roll mouldings, deeply undercut; i.e. C13. Altered in the C17 and C18. Truncated cross-wing at the l. (Smoke-blackened raised cruck roof with diagonal arched wind-braces; timbers felled 1371/2.)

NUNNEY

ALL SAINTS. Three-stage w tower with diagonal buttresses, bell-openings with Somerset tracery, and a pierced parapet *c.* 1500, with quatrefoils below, arcaded merlons, and continuous top moulding. In the second stage, a C15 or C16 panel with the badge of the Paulets. Of the same period, the s porch. The chancel is C13 but almost completely rebuilt in 1874 by *Gill & Browne*. Two N lancets, renewed, as are the N and S doorways with depressed pointed double-chamfered arches. Aisle tracery of *c.* 1300, reworked probably when the W bays were added, by *G. A. Underwood* and *John Crocker*, *c.* 1818–26. Transepts *c.* 1330–50, with reticulated tracery. The arch from the aisle into the N transept is also original. The arcades otherwise are later C14; no capitals, double-chamfered arches (cf. Frome). Two squints flanking the chancel arch, *c.* 1400. The nave wagon roof, *c.* 1500, was replaced in 1958 by *Anthony Methuen*; jarring tiled ceiling of 1966–7. – FONT. Norman, circular, with coarse spiral fluting. Square base with big leaves. Polygonal COVER, of Jacobean type, yet dated 1684. – CHANCEL SCREEN. C15, densely carved frieze and cresting. In the C17, some upper mullions replaced by ball finials, and lower panels by tracery and scallop borders. – WALL PAINTING. Above one of the nave piers, late C14 figure of St George, in a lively attitude against fleur-de-lys, Richard II's White Hart and the motif of a noose (or the circular cordon of the Paulets' badge?) – STAINED GLASS. N aisle second from E, †1906, by *A. L. Moore*; his too the W window. – MONUMENTS. N chapel. Five effigies cramped together in the early C19. C14 knight probably of the de la Mare family (on a window sill). – A knight, probably Sir John Paulet †1437, with his lady on a tomb-chest with shields in quatrefoils. – Effigies probably of Richard Prater †1580, and his wife (*see* below) on chest with Ionic pilasters and shields in cartouches.

NUNNEY CASTLE. Neither large nor in a commanding position, yet aesthetically the most impressive castle in Somerset, expressing monumentality by its strictly symmetrical plan. Surrounding it, a moat and a stream to the S. In 1373, John de la Mare, later Sheriff of Somerset, received licence 'to fortify and crenellate his manse at Nunney'. Regular and concentric plans first appeared in Britain in Edward I's late C13 castles of Harlech and Beaumaris, square or oblong in plan with mighty angle towers around a central courtyard, but these were an exception. A tendency across all architectural forms to regular and rationalized plans emerged with the Perp style from *c.* 1350. Nunney is a compact oblong range forming a double square 78 ft by 39 ft (24 by 12 metres), without courtyard but with round angle towers, the short sides so narrow that the towers almost meet. This type has a tradition in the North, back, it seems, to the C13 – cf. Tarset and later Langley, both Northumberland – and is akin to a fortified tower house rather than a true castle. The design is attributed to *Henry Yevele* or an associate, mainly on the strength of the window tracery and the geometrical plan. In 1542, Leland described 'the stayres narrow, the lodginge within somewhat darke'. These problems were alleviated, probably by Richard Prater of London who bought it in 1577. He also constructed an inner bank between the walls and the moat. Slighted in 1645 after a two-day siege.

28, p. 572

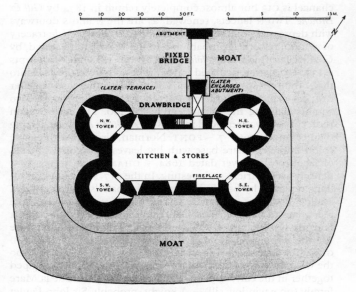

Nunney Castle.
Plan

The N wall collapsed in 1910; the moat was reinstated and the structure stabilized and repaired by the *Office of Works*, 1926–30.

Originally the walls had machicolations all round, battlemented parapets, and conical-roofed turrets over the towers. The centre had a high-pitched stone roof. Slits lit the lower floors; the big square windows are late C16, as is the full-height circular staircase in the NE tower. A bridge leads to an undefended N doorway, then into a tiny vaulted lobby from which a staircase rises as at Stokesay Castle, Shropshire, straight up in the thickness of the wall. The ground floor housed offices and kitchen, see the big fireplace with a brick oven. The s wall contained all the fireplaces on the three upper floors. The second-floor Great Hall has tall, deeply splayed two-light windows, s. The N side also had them before the collapse. They have four-centred heads, cusped lights and short vertical bars framing a quatrefoil with an ogee lower lobe (cf. Henry Yevele's work in London, *c.* 1370s). The hall fireplace was blocked later. The third floor contained the solar and perhaps a guardroom, and in the sw tower, a chapel, with the only traceried windows in any of the towers. An altar slab forms the sill. There were garderobes on the first floor in the NE and sw towers, and on the third floor in the NE and SE towers. In the SE garderobe and in three family chambers on the second and third floors are iron hooks for cloth hangings, and in the hall, wooden dowels to take hooks for heavier hangings: rare survivals of physical evidence for wall hangings.★

Originally there was a curtain wall outside the moat except on the s protecting the service ranges. Within its line, to the NE, a late C15 BARN; two buttressed porches with moulded jambs, their arches and gables removed.

MANOR HOUSE, NW of the castle and within its former bailey, was rebuilt c. 1700–10 by William Whitchurch. Handsome, five bays with hipped bell-cast roof. Lower windows with alternating triangular and segmental pediments and pulvinated friezes; steep broken door pediment. Pronounced Baroque touches, e.g. the frieze which runs into the window frames, and windows linked vertically by their frames. (Good C18 staircase. Rear cellar windows possibly earlier than the house.)

Opposite the church, a C12 CROSS on a four-stepped circular base. Late C19 head. SW of the castle in HORN STREET, a lesson in changing fashion. Nos. 18–20 of 1693, initialled for RAS, with mullioned lights, continuous string courses. No. 22 for IAS, 1724, is still in the C17 style, with ovolo mullions. The new taste for classical symmetry and sashes at No. 16 (also for IAS, 1738) develops to quite gentlemanly effect in St Peter's Cottage, 1744. Then ROCKFIELD HOUSE, a large villa of c. 1804–5, by *John Pinch*, with his favoured central bow.

(WHATLEY COMBE ROMAN VILLA, I m. NNE of Nunney. Excavated in 1837, 1848 and 1958; discoveries included a *triclinium* containing an Orpheus mosaic (now mostly destroyed). Probably late C3.)

OAKHILL

ALL SAINTS. By *J. L. Pearson*, 1860–3. Small and quite plain. Grey limestone rubble banded with ashlar. Uncusped lancets. Nave and chancel, big s porch with dogtooth to the door. Good w bellcote of battered profile. – STAINED GLASS. *Clayton & Bell*: E window, 1879; w window, 1881.

CONGREGATIONAL CHURCH (former), High Street. By *T. L. Banks* of London, 1872–3, for the brewery owner John Spencer. Strikingly churchy E.E., aisled nave, transepts and apse; big plate-traceried w window above a low five-light arcade. NW porch-tower with short two-part spire with intervening clock stage.

METHODIST CHURCH, Bath Road. Dated 1825. Simple, symmetrical, two storeys, Doulting stone façade. Gothic windows and a blind quatrefoil. Side windows with interlace glazing.

NW of All Saints', a SCHOOL by *Benjamin Ferrey*, Gothic, perhaps also 1860s. In HIGH STREET, COOMBE HOUSE, probably c. 1700. Hipped roof. Three-bay centre flanked by one-bay

★Information from Tony Harcourt.

wings. Segmental pedimented door with bolection architrave, cross-windows on the upper floor. Low down to the SE, two cottages dated 1723; narrow concave-moulded mullions, continuous driphoods in places. Further W, the site of the brewery (established 1767 but closed in the mid C20; now housing). W again, big stone MALTINGS of c. 1860, round-arched and with rock-faced dressings. OAKHILL HOUSE, Dean Lane, is hidden by high walls; extant by 1792, altered in the 1820s for the vicar of Ashwick (q.v.), perhaps by *G. A. Underwood*. Front of two storeys and six bays (1:4:1) with Doric porch in the l. return. (Good plasterwork in the main rooms.)

S of the High Street, PONDSMEAD of 1874, by *T. L. Banks* for Frederick Spencer, the brewery owner. Broad irregular S front, incoherent Gothic with half-timbering. Survivals of the C18 park of its predecessor; on a dam between two lakes, a series of GROTTOS with tunnels, a RUINED ARCH and a HERMIT'S CELL. E of Zion Hill is OAKHILL MANOR, originally Hillylands, of 1881 for John Maitland Spencer. Picturesque Tudor style; gabled wings, recessed centre with a big hall window of five lights and three transoms. In a lane to its N, the very low DOWER HOUSE, mid-C18, with a central Venetian motif breaking the eaves with a little eyebrow.

ORCHARDLEIGH

ST MARY. Secluded on a little island in the grounds of Orchardleigh House. Later C13 chancel and small nave with W bellcote. Regency Gothic N chapel for Sir Thomas Swymmer Champneys, c. 1800. In 1878 *Sir George Gilbert Scott* began a restoration, completed with much tact and respect in 1880 by *J. Oldrid Scott*. The S porch (replacing a W door) is of 1878. The chancel seems to have been decorated lavishly in the C13, exhibiting quite a personal taste for minute motifs and vivacious figures. Windows of two lights with a circle in bar tracery. Narrow priest's door (N); the head pointed-five-cusped, with an extremely odd glazed pointed trefoil above. PISCINA with Credence, under a trefoiled nodding gable on heads. More heads stopping the window hoodmoulds. AUMBRY (N), trefoiled opening beneath a steep arch, and in the tympanum a tiny seated figure of Christ triumphing over Death (a skull) and two censing angels. Original door with iron hinges. By the altar, pedestals carrying small figures, a king on the l. with two pages, a queen on the r. with a dog and a page. They act as corbels for lost statues. Also two small corbel-figures to hold a lenten veil. In the nave, two-light windows with circles. A large cusped tomb recess with engaged pinnacles, early C14, was converted into the arch to the N chapel for the Champneys (now vestry). – FONT. Oldford stone, c. 1300, tub-shaped with leaf friezes. Later sexfoil medallions containing small seated figure reliefs. – PULPIT. Oak, Jacobean; the top of a three-decker. – CHANCEL SCREEN. 1878–81, sharply cusped. – STAINED GLASS. Mostly mid-C15, perhaps from a Bristol workshop; re-set by *Clayton & Bell*, 1879. E window, large saint and angels. Chancel N and S, eight small apostles. W window, angels, and demi-figures of an abbot and a king. Nave S; pale glass by *Clayton & Bell*, 1879. – MONUMENTS. Two unsigned Champneys tablets (†1791 and 1793); obelisk grounds with mourning females. – Sir Henry Newbolt, poet, †1938. Nicely lettered slate tablet; he married a Duckworth (*see* below). – Neoclassical urn with swags and bucrania, to Sir Thomas Champneys's dog †1796 (see Newbolt's poem 'Fidele's Grassy Tomb'); resited in the churchyard 1989.

ORCHARDLEIGH HOUSE. The Champneys' inconvenient and decaying medieval house S of the church was bought in 1855 by William Duckworth, a Manchester solicitor, mainly for the 600-acre park of 'high down and far horizon, its deep woods and . . . shimmering lake'. He commissioned a new house from *Thomas Henry Wyatt*, 1856–8. It is picturesque, irregular, and very big (originally thirty-five bedrooms). Wyatt's luxurious Elizabethan-French-château design, notably in the roofscape, was contrary to the client's wish for an unpretentious Old English style. It included the latest technology: fireproof wrought-iron and concrete construction on *Fox & Barrett*'s system, and extant kitchen ranges etc. from *Jeakes* of Bloomsbury. The eventful entrance side (N) is L-shaped, with the service wing stepping forward at the l. Entrance like that at Burghley, a Doric triumphal arch motif. Over-steep French

Orchardleigh House, from the south-east.
Engraving, 1872

pavilion roof above. In the l. corner a tourelle, to the r. a big bowed oriel. The s front is symmetrical, with broad canted bays flanking a recessed centre with veranda (ornamental cast-iron by *Edward Cockey*). At the w end, the lusciously carved stone skeleton of a big conservatory, now framing a rose garden. Interiors comfortable but not overpowering: oak staircase with strapwork balustrades and arches on oak columns; fine joinery by *Holland & Hannen*; lacy Renaissance plasterwork in the drawing room. In the hall, a little heraldic glass by *Heaton & Butler*. Terraced GARDENS to the s, laid out by *W. B. Page* with advice from *Wyatt*.

Miraculously, the house and 300 acres of park have been clawed back from the brink of ruin since *c.* 2003. Of the C18 and early C19 heyday under the 'lesser Beckford' Sir Thomas Champneys, a Romantic BOATHOUSE remains at the E end of the lake; a dilapidated Doric temple with dock beneath. At Lullington, the equally Romantic GLOUCESTER LODGE, *c.* 1815 (conspicuously dated 1434), possibly by *Jeffry Wyatt*, who made designs for a new house. Castellated and turreted gatehouse, flanked by quadrant walls with more turrets and castellations. At Murtry (s), a pair of sober Tudor LODGES, *c.* 1825–30, and a little way N by the drive, WOOD LODGE, a *cottage orné*, *c.* 1790–1810. In its pretty bowed end, intricately leaded French doors.

PAULTON

HOLY TRINITY. The tower is dated 1757 on a quatrefoil. This refers to an updating, for the w doorway, the bell-hole and domical vault within appear C17. Clearly C18 are various quatrefoils (some ogee) and ogee-headed windows, the corbel table at the top, and the obelisk pinnacles on the buttresses, a medieval Somerset form. The bell-openings are just possibly C15: could the pierced parapet and top pinnacles be too? The rest was rebuilt in 1839 by *John Pinch Jun.*, nominally Perp. Aisled interior (slim shafted piers) in the local tradition, though in typical early C19 proportions, broad and high with big w gallery. In 1862–6, *John Norton* rebuilt the chancel, added an organ chamber (N), enlarged the vestry and re-seated the nave. – REREDOS. Norton's usual Neo-C13 style, stone with gabled ends. – STAINED GLASS. Very good E window by *Horwood Bros*, 1863. s aisle, probably *Joseph Bell*, 1865. – MONUMENTS. Blue Lias effigy of a praying knight in long surcoat, the head under a trefoiled arch on two headstops; *c.* 1290. – Knight, *c.* 1360, in two pieces and badly mutilated.
BAPTIST CHAPEL, Winterfield Road. Founded 1721, rebuilt 1827. Gabled front with high Gothic windows flanking a quirky Tuscan doorway. Engaged columns, open pediment. 'Batty Langley' inner doorcase with clustered shafts and ogee fanlight breaking into the pediment; perhaps C18? The sides have

pilasters and two tiers of ogee windows. Late C19 gallery on
scrolly brackets with ornate cast-iron panels.
(Two adjacent ROMAN HOUSES were discovered in 1818 1¼ m.
w of the village, in an unusual upland location. One house contained a hypocaust room and a number of other small rooms;
the other contained a series of large rooms.)

PEASEDOWN ST JOHN   6050

ST JOHN. 1892–3 by *Bodley & Garner,* 'a work of which they
cannot have been proud' (Pevsner). Built to serve a growing
working class. Nave, transepts, s porch. Polygonal bell-turret
with spirelet on the w gable, rising from a shallow projection
which also houses the w window. Loosely Dec windows, some
in four-centred openings. N aisle, *c.* 1905.
BATH ROAD runs die-straight through the village, mostly miners'
housing of dour grey stone. At the sw end, the surprisingly
Italianate RED POST INN, by *Wilson & Fuller,* 1851. CIRCLE   121,
HOSPITAL, Foxcote Avenue. By *Foster & Partners,* 2007–9.   p. 578
Low and compact rectangular form of Corbusian purity, integrated with the rural landscape. The sunken plinth of grey-
brown brick has on top the largely glazed level of the main
spaces, surrounded by a planted terrace. Jettied upper floor
clad in aluminium alloy and pierced by long horizontal glazing
slots. A double-height top-lit street articulates the interiors.
METHODIST CHAPEL, Carlingcott. Builder's Gothic, 1851. Fittings mainly of 1889.
FOSSE WAY. To the s, part of the ROMAN ROAD passing roughly
NE–SW through the E end of N Somerset now the A367 in this
section. Laid out by the army soon after the Roman invasion
of A.D. 43. Not all sections of the road may have been completed by the time the military frontier moved w into the Midlands and South Wales. It remained in use throughout the
Roman period. The line of the road can be seen in many places
in present roads and hedgerows, and stretches of the raised
agger can still be seen also on Bannerdown and Odd Down to
the N and s of Bath.

PENSFORD   6060

Pensford's cloth market was among the largest in late medieval
Somerset; copper was milled in the C18, and coal mining boomed
briefly in the early C20.

ST THOMAS BECKET. Surrounded on three sides by the River
Chew and a mill leat. Low C14 Perp w tower with pitched roof
inside the parapet. w doorway with a finely moulded two-
centred arch. Inside the tower, an odd tierceron-vault with very

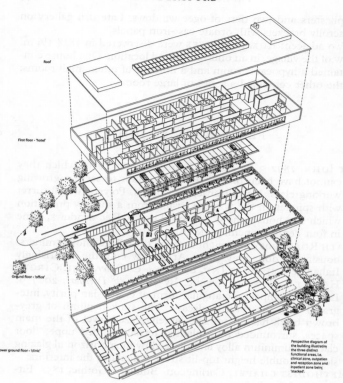

Roof

First floor - 'hotel'

Ground floor - 'office'

Lower ground floor - 'clinic'

Perspective diagram of
the building illustrative
the three distinct
functional areas, i.e.
clinical zone, outpatien
and reception zone and
inpatient zone being
'stacked'.

Peasedown St John, Circle Hospital.
Exploded perspective, 2008

large circular centre and four small circles on the four diagonal ribs – all for bell ropes. (– FITTINGS stored in the tower.
Perp font, C17 pulpit, benefaction boards, fine medieval bell-
frame.) The body of the church, rebuilt in 1869 by *C. E. Giles*,
converted to a house 2009–11.*

Close to the church the three-arched CHEW BRIDGE. Built over
the eastern arch on its S side, BRIDGE HOUSE, C18 to the river
but C16 behind, timber-framed, with an overhang and a gable.
Below the jetty a Georgian shop window. The A37, cut through
by the Bristol Turnpike Trust *c.* 1830, bisects the village expos-
ing the backs of the cottages in High Street and Church Street.
To the E, facing the triangular market place, an octagonal mid-
C18 LOCK-UP with hemispherical ashlar dome and ball finial.
To its S, the three-storey GEORGE AND DRAGON INN, probably 1752 (the date formerly in nails on a door). Broad window

---

*Fragments of a Crucifixion and an Adam and Eve from the CHURCHYARD CROSS
survive in a house wall in The Barton.

frames with keystones. Three bays, then a quoined projection
(r.) over a carriageway; this bay has both pediment and a triangular parapet over, indicating a local mason still unsure of
his classical language; cf. Stanton Court, Stanton Drew. Crossing the valley to the w is the Pennant stone RAILWAY
VIADUCT, 1873, of sixteen arches.

BELLUTON HOUSE, *c.* ¾ m. NW. *c.* 1800. Six bays, pedimented
doorcase l. of centre. Two Venetian motifs in the double-gabled
end.

PORTBURY   4070

ST MARY. The church appears Perp and low because of its aisle
windows and sturdy w tower, but within it is broad and spacious, and not Perp but Norman, E.E and Dec. Its scale and
quality are explained by the fact that Portbury was a subsidiary
residence of the lords of Berkeley. Chancel virtually rebuilt by
Ewan Christian, 1870–1, with new roofs to the nave also. He
probably restored the aisles and porch, *c.* 1875. Big Norman s
doorway with double columns. Scalloped capitals, and arches
heavily decorated with a chain of lozenges and a kind of Greek
key on the extrados as well as the intrados, meeting at the
angle. Norman chancel; see the broad flat clasping buttresses
at the E end, the priest's doorway (s), and above all the jambs
of the chancel arch. Groups of five shafts with scalloped capitals, the farthest projecting one keeled, perhaps as late as
c. 1190. The shafts are set high: either the chancel floor was
originally raised, or the jambs have been raised later; certainly
the pointed chancel arch is Dec. In the s chancel wall, a fine
triple SEDILIA and PISCINA, *c.* 1250. Trefoiled arches with filleted roll moulding on Blue Lias shafts. Hoodmoulds on re-
cut headstops. Much was done and redone *c.* 1300, primarily
the addition, or rebuilding, of aisles. There was already a s aisle,
with a chantry established *c.* 1189–1200 by Robert de Berkeley. Here, another good SEDILIA and PISCINA group with trefoiled heads and Blue Lias shafts, also *c.* 1250. The w and E
windows of the N aisle survive (of three and five stepped cusped
lancets, respectively). Five-bay arcades with continuous
double-chamfered arches and piers. Stone seats against the
aisle wall, and around the arcade piers too; unusually generous provisions at a time when wooden benches were rare. Also
about 1300 the chancel windows were enlarged. The E window
has cusped intersected tracery and a rere-arch, the s side one
of stepped cusped lancets and one with Y-tracery below a quatrefoiled circle. Squint from the N aisle into the chancel, indeed
almost a narrow chapel, with three stepped lancet windows,
again *c.* 1300. Next the remarkable early C14 Dec N chancel
chapel with pointed tunnel-vault of parallel chamfered ribs (cf.
Backwell); late C15 N window. Good corbel heads throughout
the nave and aisles, those in the s aisle bigger and perhaps later.

Embattled Perp w tower, angle buttresses, four stages, perhaps c. 1380–1450. Deep s porch, probably C15.

REREDOS. Seven-arched, marble, 1914. – BENCHES, s aisle. Plain, squared ends, ogee-scrolled stops, perhaps C17. – FONT. Norman, square, scalloped beneath, on squat circular foot. – SCULPTURE. Two odd head corbels, one with rather East Asian features (both chancel N); were they for the lenten veil? – STAINED GLASS. s chancel first from E, *Bell & Son*, 1876. Two adjacent attributed to them, including the E window, †1894, artfully composed in unusual pale glass, perhaps by *F. H. Bell*. – BRASS. Sarah Kemish †1621, a small engraved tablet with kneeling figures.

THE PRIORY. Conjecturally the prior's house to a cell of Augustinian canons attached to Breamore Priory, Hants, from at least the C13. In 1860 it was reportedly ruinous, with 'four bare walls'. It is L-shaped, facing s and E with a plain rubble tower in the angle. An ashlared front faces E, with a broad chimneybreast, embattled parapet, and at the NE corner, an angle buttress topped by an improbable pinnacle. Much of this is C19. (Internally, a first-floor hall over a barrel-vaulted undercroft.) Tower with one transomed two-light window, perhaps C15. The secondary wing is probably medieval (evidence was found of a lost arch-braced roof and of a garderobe at the w end) but has C17 ovolo-mullioned windows.

OLD VICARAGE, 200 yds s of the church. By *A. C. Pugin*, c. 1830. Tudor Gothic. Thomas Rickman's diary, 1832, reports it as 'miserable within'.

ROYAL PORTBURY DOCK. *Rendel, Palmer & Tritton*, engineers, 1972–7. The latest chapter in Bristol's attainment of a deep-water port, after Avonmouth (q.v.). Cellular diaphragm wall construction. One of the busiest UK container and vehicle ports, and with the largest entrance lock, taking vessels up to 41 metres (134 ft) wide and 300 metres (984 ft) long. The site covers 2,600 acres.

BANK HOUSE, Sheepway, w of the M5. By *Michael Axford*, 1990–1, for himself. Low block-and-render walls and mono-pitch roofs. Screened from view to the s, continuous glazed walls and roof on three sides of a narrow U-shaped swimming pool.

CONYGAR HILL. Small triangular Iron Age HILL-FORT whose earthwork follows the contours of a flat-topped hill s of and overlooking The Priory. In the centre is a round barrow. Another small encampment a short distance away to the s.

PORTISHEAD

Until the early C19 an agricultural village with fishing and trading from a creek ending at a tide mill at the NE end of High Street. Bristol Corporation instigated seaside development in 1828, but without a proper beach, Portishead never rivalled Clevedon or Weston-super-Mare. A pier for steamer passengers and railway arrived in 1849. The creek was re-cut as a dock for transatlantic shipping in the 1870s. Industry and power stations arose alongside, while the village became a modest town. Since industrial demise in the 1980s, the dock has been reinvented as a marina with dense housing alongside.

CHURCHES

St Peter, Church Road South. Largely Perp, much repaired 1816, with minor restoration in 1832. Restored again 1905, and reordered 1980. Dominant four-stage w tower, 99 ft (30 metres) high. w door with sub-reticulated five-light window above. Set-back buttresses with intermediate set-offs at each stage. The string courses wrap round the buttresses. From the buttress tops, little shafts continue up into the parapet to form diagonal corner panels from which rise square pinnacles with spirelets and four sub-pinnacles each; tower top restored 1832. One two-light window at each stage, blind until the third stage. In all respects above, it is like Chew Magna and Winford. It had probably reached the second stage *c.* 1450–90, with completion perhaps *c.* 1500; see the ogee lights in the upper stages, and the change from diamond to circular label stops. Pierced parapet with cusped triangles, with a central pinnacle on each side. The tower arch has two wave mouldings with a casement between.

Of the second third of the C14 the E window and the double-chamfered chancel arch, of the late C14 the two-bay nave arcade; square piers with four demi-shafts on them and right angles cut out of the corners, a move towards the four-hollow standard. Broad arches with chamfer and ovolo mouldings. Arcade proportions distorted when the floor was raised by several feet in 1816. The s porch probably C15, with finely marked s doorway. Handsome GALLERY above, 1816, open to the nave; also a tower gallery with the same arcaded front. The s windows are straight-headed. The E bay of the nave is of 1878–9, when the chancel was rebuilt 11 ft (3.4 metres) to the E: a very skilful job by *W. Bennett,* a builder-architect. Old materials and complete features were reused or copied. The N aisle is bridged by a four-centred stone arch, pierced quatrefoils and daggers in the spandrels, on a corbel head in C15 headdress, but with C19 features. Is any of this medieval? The N aisle has late C15 four-light windows; pinnacles replaced 1832. N chapel (now vestry), 1878–9. Nave roof of slatted panels, 1980, wagon roof in the porch, medieval lateral beams in the N aisle.

FITTINGS. FONT. Norman. Square on a circular stem, with impressive angle volutes. – PULPIT. A plainer relation of the fine local group of stone pulpits, perhaps early C16, re-tooled. Bath stone, on a fat moulded stem; two cusped blind arches on each face. Friezes, fleurons below, running vine above. – SCULPTURE. In the chancel s wall two small head brackets, one holding in his mouth the metal ring for the lenten veil. –

STAINED GLASS. Chancel s first from E, *Lavers & Barraud*, *c.* 1857; hot palette. Three in the chancel, probably *Clayton & Bell*, late 1860s. By *Bell & Son*, the N chapel E, 1879, nave S, first from E, 1885, and third, 1928. Nave S, second, good Arts and Crafts glass by *Mary Lowndes*, 1904.

ST NICHOLAS, Nore Road. 1911–12 by *Edward Gabriel* as the National Nautical School's chapel. Severely masculine late Perp. – Oak STALLS and ORGAN CASE with somewhat C17 gilded finials, shells and sprightly dolphins.

UNITED REFORMED CHURCH, Woodhill Road. By *Wills & Voisey*, 1875–7. The design was seemingly Voisey's. E.E. Rock-faced interior, with striking timber roofs. Closed 2010.

CONGREGATIONAL CHAPEL (former), West Hill. Unusually good Gothic for the date, 1840; pinnacles, buttresses, rose window over the door.

FRIENDS' MEETING HOUSE, St Mary's Road. Established 1669–70. Small and thatched, probably a converted cottage. One room with C18 panelling and benched dais.

PUBLIC BUILDINGS

AVON AND SOMERSET POLICE HEADQUARTERS, Valley Road. By *Bruges Tozer*, completed 1995. Buff brick, tiled roofs, aluminium brises-soleil. Main block around a quadrangle, curved glass-and-steel corner entrance. Three-storey operations centre with continuous glazed top storey beneath generous overhanging eaves.

NATIONAL NAUTICAL SCHOOL (former), Nore Road. 1904–6, by *Edward Gabriel*, whose father-in-law Henry Fedden was the sponsor. Two-and-a-half storeys over a vaulted terrace, 382 ft (116.5 metres) long and rigidly symmetrical. Eleven-bay flanks with giant pilasters and segmental pedimented ends, a borrowing perhaps from Aston Webb's Royal Naval College, Dartmouth. 90-ft (27.5-metre)-high clock tower with cupola, squashed tightly between the wings. N, the MASTER'S HOUSE; more relaxed, roughcast and gabled. Converted to flats, 1988–92. *See also* St Nicholas.

PRIMARY SCHOOL, Station Road. *Batterham Matthews Design*, *c.* 2001–3. A long two-storey block in buff brick, facing away from the road. Double-height entrance and hall, fronted by a downward-sweeping curved wall of blue render. Splendid stainless-steel turnstile GATES by *Matthew Fedden*.

PERAMBULATION

The medieval centre is around St Peter. SE is COURT FARM. The earliest part, a small C15 manor house, is low down to the E. Probably ceiled from the first, the hall on the upper floor with two-light transomed windows N and S. Arched-braced collar-beam roof. The E bay is lost. Big two-storey W addition, late C16 or early C17. Purchased in 1619 by the Corporation of Bristol, which either built or remodelled this part to accommodate its visitations. Three-light mullioned windows with segmental or four-centred heads on the S front. Close-set between them, two broad chimney-breasts, heating a large hall with dais W of the cross-passage. Tall SW angle turret added later in the C17 as a belvedere for the Corporation to view its lands and shipping; polygonal, stone with red brick angles. Its only access is external. The older portion remained as living quarters after 1619. Chimneypiece dated 1664 with initials of the tenants, the Chappell family.

THE GRANGE, at the S end of High Street, was the second manor house. Low end (r.), early C15 at latest, with smoke-blackened true cruck roof. Rare evidence for Somerset of gabled smoke louvres formerly on both sides of the roof ridge. The service end (l.) had a solar above. This was rebuilt in the C17, two-and-a-half storeys with gables and hoodmoulds. At the N end of High Street, the WHITE LION INN: early C19 front with shallow bows, the long four-storey back wing an C18 tide mill which closed c. 1810–15. High archway cut through the mill for a road, probably also in the early C19.

The Corporation's seaside development, laid out by *George Dymond*, starts at the S end of WOODHILL ROAD with a Neo-Tudor LODGE dated 1828. A little uphill, ADELAIDE TERRACE, c. 1830–5, at first devil-may-care Jacobean with shaped gables but turning classical higher. Further E in WOODLANDS ROAD, large Neo-Tudor villas, e.g. Woodside, 1836, probably for and by *J. R. Sturge*. On a headland, E, the Neo-Tudor ROYAL HOTEL, 1829–30 by *Dymond*. Private development followed, e.g. a three-bay villa in Beach Road West, dated 1832. Of later infill, most notable is DORMERS, Woodland Road, by *Sir Banister Fletcher*, perhaps c. 1910. Low, brick and tile, with six curiously regimented dormers. The W end of this northern promontory is BATTERY POINT, site of a Civil War FORT, 1643–4, refortified c. 1850 and c. 1939, finally abandoned 1946.

PORT MARINE. The site of two power stations (1926–9 and 1949–55), redeveloped from 1999 (masterplanners *Scott Brownrigg & Turner* and *Llewelyn Davies Yeang*) with housing by various architects. Inside the granite dock walls and lock of 1872–9, a smaller marina lock of 2000–1.

WOODHILL CAMP. Now indistinct remains of earthworks, probably Iron Age, on the headland overlooking Woodhill Bay.

PRIDDY

A scattered former lead-mining village high on Mendip.

ST LAWRENCE. The church has instructive differences and irregularities. The plan was cruciform, perhaps C12 or C13, with a

Perp N aisle (see the long-and-short quoins outside). Perp chancel chapels, to the N late C15, that to the S perhaps earlier. An E.E. S porch was attached W of the S transept, but a Perp rebuilding of the porch reused the earlier doorcase. C13 stoup within. Restored by *E. B. Ferrey, c.* 1880–3; first the exterior of nave (S wall partly rebuilt), chancel and aisle, then the tower. Short W tower, possibly late C14. The S belfry light is simple Perp; the stone head has spalled away. Diagonal buttresses with three set-offs. Parapet with pierced cusped triangles perhaps *c.* 1450, renewed in 1705. Triple-chamfered tower arch without capitals. In the chancel an early C14 lancet window; its rere-arch is a reused C13 grave-slab with foliated cross. The N arcade piers have four shafts between diagonals. At the second bay from the W a transverse quadrant arch to brace the arcade, with wall-shaft of standard section. Stone bench along the aisle wall. Panelled chancel arch.

Pre-Reformation REREDOS. A defaced canopied niche survives N of the E window. – SCREEN. Across nave and N aisle. Late C15, simple one-light divisions, with typical Somerset tracery. Cambered doorheads, probably C17. – PULPIT. Stone, Perp, tall, with two slender sides of a rectangle, converted from the remains of a rood stair. – PULPIT *c.* 1620–40. Oak, with usual Somerset decoration. Cut down in the C19. – Norman tub FONT, repaired 1883. – FRONTAL. 'Water-flowers' (irises?), embroidered on blue Italian brocade. Probably late C15.

ASHEN HILL BRONZE AGE BARROW CEMETERY, 1 m. NE. There are eight barrows in a row aligned roughly E–W, comprising seven bowl-barrows and one possible bell barrow. Investigation at various times has shown that all covered cremation burials.

PRIDDY NINE BARROWS. A Bronze Age barrow cemetery, 1 m. ENE. There are only seven bowl barrows evident, aligned roughly NW–SE ascending the summit of North Hill. They are all large barrows, up to almost 10 ft high and up to 80 ft across (3 and 25 metres). Most were investigated in the C19, revealing evidence of cremation burials.

PRIDDY CIRCLES, 1½ m. NE. Akin to henge monuments except that here, all have the ditch outside the bank. There are four circles each 165–185 yds (150–170 metres) across, aligned roughly N–S and extending for ¾ m.; the N circle separated from the rest by a gap of 500 yds (460 metres). They probably date from the Late Neolithic/Early Bronze Age and are almost certainly associated with the barrow cemeteries around them.

6060

PRISTON

ST LUKE. Norman nave and chancel of nearly equal length, with the tower between. Deep S porch, perhaps Perp, and Perp three-light W window. All is confused by an illiterate

Neo-Norman restoration by the *Rev. J. Hammond*, completed in 1860–1 after his death. The little remaining Norman work is re-tooled: the s doorway, with segmental arch and nook-shafts with cushion capitals; the corbel table outside, nave s, the heads re-set too wide apart (i.e. reusing only the best); and the lengthened nave windows. The most obtrusive and ignorant work is in the arches under the tower, which also has blocked Norman windows. Upper tower rebuilt in 1754. Round-headed windows with Y-tracery, pronounced set-offs, and pierced balustrade with shaped finials. The chancel was heavily restored to Dec forms, with elaborately cusped and sub-cusped rere-arches, reticulated tracery in the e window, cinquefoils in circles elsewhere, and a priest's door with ogee gable. – Good Dec ogee PILLAR PISCINA. – FONT. Octagonal, Perp, with arms and emblems. – DOOR. The s door *c.* 1350–1400, ironwork *c.* 1200; six straps with split curls, lower hinge with foliage scrolls. Upper hinge replaced. – WEATHER-VANE. 1813, very big at 5 ft (1.5 metres) high. – ROMAN COFFIN with broken cover. Found at Hill Farm, 1917. – STAINED GLASS. e window attributed to *Heaton, Butler & Bayne*, after 1869. – MONUMENTS. Over the porch entrance. Thomas Wats, parson, †1589; inscription starting 'Priston repent'. – Tablets by *Hoare* (Elizabeth Jenkins †1766), a handsome unsigned one (†1774), *King* (†1790), *Lancashire* (†1798).

PRISTON MANOR. A boxy stone villa, *c.* 1830, of three bays with broad eaves and a balustrade. Four-column Doric porch. Set-back wing to the l.

PRISTON MILL, *c.* ¾ m. NNE. Flour mill, *c.* 1780–1820, of rubble with segmental-headed lights. Four storeys, double-gabled roofs. Working mill gear with oak shafts etc., driven by a cast-iron pitchback wheel.

PUBLOW

ALL SAINTS. Founded from Keynsham Abbey. Blue Lias with Dundry dressings. Fine tall w tower of four stages (cf. Winford, Dundry and Chew Magna). Set-back buttresses ending at the bell-stage in diagonal pinnacles. Tall panelled parapet and main pinnacles, taller panelled stair-turret. The base perhaps early C15 (two-centred door decorated with fleurons, and four-light w window with lozenges in the tracery). Upper stages *c.* 1440–90, two tiers of blank two-light windows, and tall two-light bell-openings, all with the characteristic ogee tracery which Pevsner called 'Dec reminiscences'. Belfry lights infilled with Somerset tracery. The third-stage windows have the most attractive detail of a transom made up of lozenges. Tower arch with double wave moulding. The rest is hard to date, as *Benjamin Ferrey*'s restoration (1859–60) renewed the clerestory windows, probably the e window (Dec reticulation), and much else. Further restored *c.* 1911, reportedly to plans by *Sir Arthur Blomfield* (†1899). The clerestory is obscured by the aisle roofs, which continue unbroken over the chapels to give an even triple-gabled E end. In the E wall, an odd niche with a tracery screen made up of parts, with fragments of C16 or C17 mouldings. Parch marks suggest there may have been an apsidal chancel. Two-storey S porch with two niches above the door, the upper one with its medieval statuette. Most aisle windows square-headed; C19, following C15 forms? Low four-bay arcades with double-chamfered arches, often a Dec feature. Perp piers (the usual four hollows), possibly re-cut from Dec octagonal piers. The chapels open from the chancel with one wide and one narrow arch, the former originally probably to house monuments, the latter as passages. A finely moulded two-centred 'pedestrian' arch on the N pre-dates the panelled arch of *c.* 1500–40 opposite.

PULPIT. Jacobean, with blank arches over rosettes. – FONT. C13, square bowl with cutaway lower corners, octagonal stem. – STAINED GLASS. By *Hardman*, the E window, 1866, and well-composed W window, 1871. N aisle E, *Arnold Robinson* (*Bell & Son*), 1939. N aisle W, *John & Laura Gilroy*, 2000, with local figures and settings. – MONUMENT. James Jefferies †1757. Scrolly cartouche with cherubs.

Big former RECTORY by *Ewan Christian*, completed 1878; transomed and mullioned.

PUXTON

HOLY SAVIOUR (Churches Conservation Trust). A chapel of ease to Banwell, built probably in the C13, though not the first church here. Much repaired. The short C15 W tower leans heavily W, despite timber raft foundations. Diagonal buttresses, parapet with pierced quatrefoils. The nave was lowered and re-roofed in the C16. In its N wall a two-light E.E. window (w) and one Dec. On the S side, one Perp, square-headed (w), one perhaps C17 Perp survival, round-arched. N porch with the St Loe arms and the date 1557. Inside, a nicely unrestored air. Low ceiling at the height of the tie-beams. Chancel arch of two ogees with a rebate between, perhaps C16. Tower arch C15, two continuous wave mouldings. Organ chamber and chancel roof, *c.* 1880. – Base of a stone ROOD SCREEN, Perp. The ROOD BEAM is cut off flush with the N and S walls. – FONT. Norman, tub shape. C17 scrolled COVER. – Jacobean PULPIT and READER'S DESK, possibly once a two-decker although not made as such, see the non-matching decoration. Also Jacobean ALTAR RAILS, with turned finials and balusters, scallop decoration. – C17 or C18 wrought-iron HOUR-GLASS HOLDER beside the pulpit. – Plain C16 BENCHES. – BOX PEWS,

perhaps *c.* 1740s. – COMMANDMENT BOARDS etc., painted by
Job Nicholls, 1825. – ROYAL ARMS. Painted by *Mr Sess* of
Banwell, 1775. Directly s of the church, a large circular field
surrounded by a ditch or moat, perhaps for drainage rather
than defence.

QUEEN CHARLTON

Charlton, formerly owned by Keynsham Abbey, was acquired in
1544 by Henry VIII's sixth queen, Catherine Parr, hence its
prefix.

ST MARGARET. A Norman or Transitional structure, originally
cruciform; the s transept demolished. Nave and N porch were
rebuilt by *Benjamin Ferrey*, 1859–61, reusing the old tracery.
Sturdy central tower, its big Norman openings having two sub-
arches with roll mouldings. Inside, the tower rests on single-
stepped pointed arches. The w and E arches, with semicircular
responds, carry scallop capitals. The N and s arches without
demi-shafts. Plain abaci. Norman masonry in the w front,
perhaps the N doorway, and in an arch near the church; *see*
below. Two arches to a lost s chancel chapel are excellent E.E.
work. Octagonal pier with stiff-leaf. In the w respond plainer
tripartite stiff-leafs instead. The E respond enriched by figure-
work: beast, and a human head bitten by beasts (a motif also
seen at Wells). No neckings to the capitals. The tower was given
an extra stage perhaps as late as the 1530s: diagonal buttresses,
Perp bell-openings, parapet with pierced arcading, pinnacles.
– FONT. Bowl perhaps originally a C12 square cushion-shape;
later re-cut octagonal. C19 foot. – STAINED GLASS. E window
by *Powell & Sons*, 1950. Two two-light war memorial windows
by *Bell & Son*, 1921. Chigi memorial, 1949, *Bell & Son* (probably *Edward Woore*). Chancel N, *James Crombie* (*Roy Coomber*),
2000.

On a pretty green by the church, a medieval CROSS on a square
stepped base. Restored 1887. w of the church is the MANOR
HOUSE. Long varied front, early C18 in the centre and l., one
mullioned light giving away the C16 core (two big rear gables).
Three-bay centre *c.* 1730; probably original sashes, doorway
with a broken segmental pediment and urn. Two urns on the
parapet. Long wing to the r., 1857, much modernized. (Central
hall with a C16 chimneypiece, moulded ceiling beams with
pendants.) Opposite the house, a re-erected NORMAN ARCH.
Was it the s doorway of the church? One order of fluted
columns with leaf capitals, trefoil-decorated chevrons around
the arch, outer hoodmould with big billets. Shafts replaced in
Bath stone.

RADFORD *see* TIMSBURY

RADSTOCK

Pevsner called it 'really desperately ugly . . . without dignity in any building', yet Radstock is among the best survivors in England of a small Victorian colliery town. Commercial mining began *c.* 1763. The centre, of White Lias stone, was redeveloped *c.* 1860–1914 by the Waldegrave family.

ST NICHOLAS. Set apart on the S edge of the town. Of the medieval church the low late C14 W tower, S porch and W three bays of the nave and aisle remain. Three S windows square-headed, perhaps *c.* 1500–40. Over the S porch, a canopied niche. Also a C15 PISCINA. Tower arch with attached shafts and decorated capitals. N aisle added by *William Armstrong* of Bristol in 1832, then all thoroughly refaced and extended E in 1878–9 by *Wilson, Willcox & Wilson*, in dull Geometrical style. The little rood doorway (S) shows the former length of the nave. – REREDOS. By *Harry Hems*, 1904. – PULPIT, 1889, with some alabaster and mosaic. – FONT with cable moulding, *c.* 1150. – SCULPTURE. Fragment of a Roman infantry soldier's grave-slab. – Part of a C15 cross-shaft and its head; under a cusped gable, a small mutilated Crucifixion, and an eroded Virgin and Child on the reverse. In the E wall of the porch in 1910. – C15 incised panel of woman with harp (vestry). – STAINED GLASS. Chancel. Three by *Bell & Son*, *c.* 1910–20. Nave S, second from E, by *A. L. Wilkinson*, 1948. N aisle, third from E, one panel by *R. J. Newbery*, late C19. N aisle W by *A. L. Moore*, 1898. – MONUMENTS. From Writhlington church. Bridgett Salmon †1691; colloquial Baroque, an oval plaque framed by Doric columns, swan-neck pediment above. – Anna Maria James †1818, by *King*. Scroll and draped urn.

ST HUGH (R.C.), Wells Hill. Plain stone barn, perhaps C17–C18, opened 1929 as a Mission from Downside Abbey. Much repaired after a fire in 1991.

METHODIST CHAPEL, Fortescue Road. By *Robert Curwen*, 1901–2. Gothic, but with round-arched Lombardic windows. Halls behind on a difficult angled site; Curwen likened their planning to a Chinese puzzle.

VICTORIA HALL, Church Street. A Working Men's Institute of 1866, enlarged 1897 by *W. J. Willcox*, and again as Urban District Council offices 1902. Round-arched upper windows, bracketed eaves, scrolly gablets.

p. 589 PRIMARY SCHOOLS. Two uncommonly good schools opened in 2005, by *NVB Architects*: ST NICHOLAS, Kilmersdon Road, and TRINITY, Woodborough Lane. Timber construction with red cedar cladding. At St Nicholas, a roughly oval hall with slit windows, and a wedge-shaped class block (E) with curving projections at intervals. Trinity has a similar hall, leading to a wave-form façade with projecting canopy on steel columns.

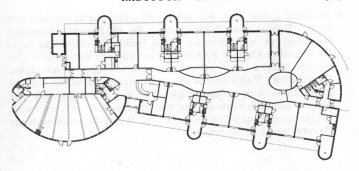

Radstock, St Nicholas Primary School.
Plan

MUSEUM, Waterloo Road. Market Hall of 1897–8, by a local sur-
veyor-architect, *T. Martin*. Enlarged 1925; converted 1998–9,
architect *Robert Taylor*. Steel-framed with clock turret,
and double slate roofs with continuous clerestory between.
Mezzanine floor inserted on conversion.

Opposite the Museum, a PIT-HEAD WHEEL from Kilmersdon,
erected *c.* 1995. Remounted in 2005 on a split brick pillar by
Sebastien Boyesen, carved with plant forms alluding to the
geology of coal. Next to the Museum, the former BELL
HOTEL, 1880, probably by *Wilson, Willcox & Ames*; mildly Italianate with canted bays. From Coomb End (w), a footpath
leads to Middle Pit POWDER HOUSE, *c.* 1870, with triple-skin
roof of stone slabs, bitumen and concrete; a rare survival.

REDHILL 4060

CHRIST CHURCH. 1843–4, by *James Wilson*. Spartan lancet style.
w tower, short chancel. Organ chamber and vestry, 1897. –
FONT. Bizarre: circular bowl, eight attached shafts on Perp
bosses. 1844? – STAINED GLASS. E window by *A. K. Nicholson*,
1932.

SCAR'S FARM, Lye Hole Lane. Surprisingly strong Gothic farmhouse *c.* 1860 with capped turret in the angle. Worthwhile C17
houses to the s, e.g. Lyehole Farm.

REGIL 5060

ST JAMES. Small school-chapel, 1864–6, by *G. T. Robinson* of
Leamington. Hints of his roguishness in the (ritual) s side.

A medieval house here was splendidly enlarged in the late C17 by the Babers (*see* Chew Magna). By 1832 only a fragment remained as a farmhouse. Two buildings claim the site: REGILBURY COURT FARM is plain C19 with some minor C17 features. Yet a map of 1782 seems to support its claim. REGILBURY PARK seems the more likely candidate: an C18 print shows it as a regular block of five gables by two. The present house is reduced, yet still impressively C17, with attic gables, numerous ovolo mullions, etc. If not the remains of the Babers' house, what was it?

RICKFORD

4050

A hamlet in a winding conifer-clad valley, suddenly revealing a large pond by the road; like a Victorian chocolate-box view of an alpine landscape. A landscape of mills and tanneries was prettified *c.* 1895 by Lord Winterstoke to improve the approach to Coombe Lodge, Blagdon (q.v.). He enlarged the mill pond and rebuilt the small BAPTIST CHAPEL to its w. Half-timbered, with a short capped tower. It became a Masonic Lodge in 1965, with the happy addition of an external staircase. Similarly Picturesque GAUGE HOUSE.

RODDEN

7040

ALL SAINTS. Beside a pond, with Rodden Farm directly N, and views over gentle green hills. Founded perhaps *c.* 1200, it became a chapel of ease to Boyton, Wilts., from 1289. The small early C16 nave was repaired in 1639–40 (see the straight-headed windows with hoodmoulds, and the date over the s door) by the Rector of Boyton, and a new chancel added. N vestry, *c.* 1820. In 1832 the nave was lengthened by one bay, with a shallow projecting w tower, by *Charles Long* of Frome. Embattled parapet, plain round-arched belfry light, w window with minimal Perp tracery. – FITTINGS. PULPIT. Plain oak, C18. – FONT. On a shaft with three columns surrounding, perhaps 1832. – PEWS. Some probably of 1640. – STAINED GLASS. Mostly mid- to late C19. Nave SE by *S. Walker* for *Maile & Son Studios*, 1947, good quality.

VILLAGE HALL, NE of the chancel. Built *c.* 1826 as a schoolroom for children from Sheppard's cloth mill, *c.* 1826. Three windows with paired depressed arches and hoodmoulds. Rodden expanded after Sheppard's CLOTH MILL was established in 1793; it had closed by 1883. Scant remains of the mill at Rodden Manor Farm *c.* ⅔ m. SW. Between this and the church, RODDEN MANOR. Five gabled bays, only the centre one late C16, timber-framed, jettied with a four-light oriel and a little diagonal bracing. Gabled stone wings dated 1663. Lower extension to the l., when it was used as almshouses in the C18 and C19. (Parlour with plaster overmantel, perhaps 1663; grotesque frieze, cf. Laverton Manor Farm, floral motifs below, and the A'Court arms.)

RODE

8050

A wool village with abundant stone houses.

ST LAWRENCE. Modest by Somerset standards. Sturdy w tower, clerestoried nave, aisles, chancel. Scant evidence of Norman fabric; two *ex situ* fragments of twisted column, and a moulded stone in the vestry wall, under a C19 arch. Renewed by *C. E. Davis* of Bath, 1873–4, including the N vestry, organ chamber, and a fan-vault in the tower. Some N aisle windows of *c.* 1770 were replaced with square-headed Perp lights. s aisle windows of three ogee lights with label stops, i.e. later C15. The tower is later (see the SE buttress, and part of a door frame within the aisle). Three stages with three-light windows and belfry openings, battlements. Big five-light w window (tracery of 1874). The N porch has a fanciful C19 E.E.-style outer arch. Inner doorway with wave-moulded arch and a small ogee cusp, mid-to late C15. Tall panelled tower arch. Perp arcades of four bays. Standard piers (four hollows). A little cresting above the capitals (cf. Beckington). Chancel arch of the same section. The aisles have C15 wagon roofs with bosses. – REREDOS. Fine *opus sectile* Last Supper, with patterned flanks. By *Wooldridge* for *Powell & Sons*, 1873. – Oak ALTAR RAIL with twisted balusters, *c.* 1720–50. – FONT. Octagonal, Perp, with rosettes in quatrefoils. Nicely panelled stem. — WALL PAINTING. Late medieval, possibly the Virgin (s aisle). – STAINED GLASS. E window, *Lavers, Barraud & Westlake*, 1873. – MONUMENTS. Part of a C13 grave-slab with trefoiled cross (vestry). More reused in the squint s of the chancel arch. – C15 recess with cusped canopy, brattishing and shields. – Anne Hawkins †1739. Swan-necked pediment, gadroons, columns.

CHRIST CHURCH, Rode Hill. By *H. E. Goodridge*, 1822–4, for the Rev. Charles Daubeny, Archdeacon of Salisbury. An amazing conception, E.E. and Tudor, the detail wilful and in places quite independent of Gothic precedent; spirited to the point of recklessness. The inspiration is King's College Chapel, Cambridge. w front flanked by gaunt polygonal panelled turrets, pierced for bell-chambers, then with a ring of gablets below big stepped spires. Converted to a house by *Richard Pedlar Architects*, 1997–9, retaining the spatial integrity of the nave. Exaggeratedly tall five-bay nave and chancel in one, with low passage aisles. Attenuated upper nave windows with wayward Geometrical tracery. Hoodmoulds drop down the sides of each arch to horizontal stops. Chancel arch reaching to the roof ridge, and a plaster rib-vault in the chancel bay. Altar surround with a gabled canopy on thin colonnettes. Small rooms behind new glazed doors in the aisles and beneath the w gallery. Here, a timber and plaster vault with heads of wildly indeterminate parentage. – MONUMENT. Rev. Charles Daubeny †1827. Gothic with two allegorical statues.

To the E is the former rectory, DAUBENY HOUSE. Late C18, remodelled by *Goodridge*, 1824. Sashes with interlaced glazing and square labels. Gothic porch.

BAPTIST CHAPEL, High Street. Dated 1786, sturdy, gabled and well proportioned. Rubble walls. Door canopy on brackets. Five round-arched windows, interlaced Gothic glazing. Three-sided gallery, other fittings removed *c.* 1990. Now multi-denominational. To the N, a former SCHOOLROOM of 1839. Flattened Gothic openings.

Evidence of medieval settlement in fields s and w of the church, and C15 houses in the present centre *c.* ½ m. NW, suggest that the village expanded towards the River Frome in late medieval times. On HIGH STREET, facing Church Lane, Nos. 23–25a have C18 façades; inside, a nine-bay smoke-blackened collar- and tie-beam roof, the timbers felled 1427–9. Opposite, the CROSS KEYS INN, early C18 but with a conspicuous red brick former BREWERY behind of *c.* 1884–1900, extended 1903. Four storeys, two chimneys. s again, No. 16, apparently C17, refronted for the Node family, clothiers. Urban-looking six-bay façade, *c.* 1800–30, semicircular porch on Greek Doric columns. At the SW end of the village MAYFIELD HOUSE, substantial late C18, for a clothier. Italianate porch of *c.* 1850, and a three-storey early C19 mill attached (converted, 2007). Lower Street has cottages crowded engagingly behind High Street.

At the bottom of Rode Hill, a six-arched BRIDGE over the Frome, *c.* 1777, and a late C18 former CLOTH MILL. Three storeys, segmental-headed windows with one mullion. On the E bank, RODE MILL HOUSE, early C18, hipped roof, five bays. Adjacent coachhouse, with good Venetian window to the room over, and a glazed door in the first floor with external steps. To its r. handsome Early Georgian STABLES. Three bays, with segment-headed cross-windows and circular pitching eyes. To the r. and perhaps a little later, another coachhouse with big arched doors and similarly placed openings.

LANGHAM HOUSE, NW of Christ Church, is of 1792, reputedly by *Thomas Baldwin*, enlarged 1810. Three storeys and five bays, ground-floor windows in blind arches, parapet urns. (Good interiors; Tuscan-columned hall, plasterwork, etc.) Park-like gardens.

MERFIELD HOUSE, Straight Lane. 1810, of Bath stone, two-storey flanks with three-storey bowed centre to the garden front (cf. Pinch the Elder at Chantry, q.v.).

RODNEY STOKE

St Leonard. The interest lies in the superb Laudian woodwork and the Rodney monuments. Plain w tower with diagonal buttresses and battlements. Above the w door, three angel busts, then an early Perp two-light window with figured hoodmould. Two-light bell-openings. Three-bay nave, built after the tower (see masonry joins, s). The details suggest a renewal *c.* 1470–1500: circular label stops, pierced arcaded parapet with pinnacles, ogee tracery, sub-reticulation with inverted cusping (renewed but trustworthy). Fine four-light w window, with similar details, perhaps inserted after the tower was built. N and s chapels with pierced parapet (quatrefoils in lozenges) and pinnacles. s chapel from *B. & E.B. Ferrey*'s restoration, 1878–9. N chapel added after the nave, with ogee-headed doorway. Plain N porch with an ogee-headed Dec stoup. Perhaps also Dec a cusped piscina with two-centred arch. High canted tower arch with one shaft between shallow concave mouldings. – FONT. Norman, cup-shaped bowl with broad twisted flutes. – Dominant chancel SCREEN (1625). Still built on the principles of Perp screens, i.e. with big one-light sections with strapwork arches, and extravagant five-tiered cornice worked with fans, foliage and winged beasts. In the position of the rood loft, a singers' gallery; turned balusters with little arches. – PULPIT with two tiers of blank arches. – Conical FONT COVER with similar motifs. – ALTAR RAIL, turned balusters. – ALTAR TABLE, 1634; bulbous legs, guilloche frieze. – BENCH-ENDS. Lively tracery and foliage motifs competently carved by villagers, *c.* 1900–14. – STAINED GLASS. Nave s, by *William Aikman*, 1920. Richly coloured and textured.

MONUMENTS. Five to the Rodney family. Sir Thomas Rodney †1471. Tomb-chest, in a chancel recess opened up to the N chapel perhaps in the early C16. The effigy in armour, recumbent. Four-centred arch with cusps and sub-cusps, long-fingered angels as the main bosses. On the chest, five weepers, three with rosaries. Above, tall attic with five spiky shields (cf. The Rib, Wells); embattled cresting, restored pinnacles. The chapel side has crude carving and a non-matching cusped arch. On the chest, three shields (later?) with reliefs of the Virgin, Christ, and St Anne (centre), St Erasmus disembowelled (l.), and St Leonard (r.). – Sir John Rodney †1527. Rearranged. In the former Easter Sepulchre recess, a cusped Tudor arch with embattled cresting, concave octagonal shafts at the sides. Under the arch not a tomb-chest but a low wall with three shields in panels. – Three entertaining C17 monuments in the N chapel. Anne Lakes †1630. Rearranged. Sarcophagus base. Recumbent alabaster effigy below a thin arch on naïve Ionic columns. Inside the arch, stars and clouds. – George Rodney †1651. Big plinth with strapwork. Shrouded demi-figure rising from the coffin between standing earthbound putti. An angel on clouds blows a trumpet in the open segmental pediment. – Sir Edward Rodney †1657 (donor of the woodwork) and wife. Two busts in oval recesses. Angels seated l. and r., a third in clouds above. Canopy with pulled-up curtains. The later two, in Pevsner's words, are 'homespun', perhaps in Bristol.

MANOR FARM. N of the church. The Rodneys' seat was rebuilt c. 1800 as a gentleman farmer's house; three storeys, tripartite sashes. In the farmyard, S, a tall late C16 SUMMERHOUSE or guest quarters, now a barn. Of three bays. First-floor chamfered cross-windows with hoodmoulds. High raised doorway with a broad arch, classical entablature and originally flanking columns on high plinths. Three-light mullioned-and-transomed window in the W gable. (Cross-passage plan; unheated rooms below, one large chamber above.)

ROWBERROW

4050

ST MICHAEL AND ALL ANGELS. Late C14 Perp despite restoration in 1851–3 by *J. E. Cox* and 1865 by *John Norton*, who rebuilt the E wall (the E window probably renewed by Cox), the vestry E and W walls, and the chancel arch. Also Norton's the nave tracery, N side. Nave SE tracery probably C15. Three-stage tower without buttresses, pierced parapet of cusped lozenges, semi-octagonal stair-turret, mid-C19 spirelet. – FONT. Perp, octagonal, with knobbly foliage panels, one with Agnus Dei. – SCULPTURE. Fragment of a C9 cross-shaft, discovered in the churchyard, 1865; a ribbon animal, its tail interlaced around the body. Probably of common origin with a piece at Colerne, Wilts. – ROYAL ARMS. 1637.

ROWBERROW ROUND BARROW. See Shipham. For Dolebury hill-fort, directly N of the church, *see* Churchill with Langford.

RUDGE

8050

METHODIST CHAPEL. Dated 1839. In use and untouched by the C20. Small gabled front with pedimented doorcase and three arched windows, quite old-fashioned. Late C19 fittings. Tiny gallery, dais-pulpit with wrought-iron panels. Twisted brass lamp standards.

OLD MANOR, N, has a broad and imposing façade inscribed and dated 1692 for SAP. Two storeys and three gables. Cross-windows, door with bolection surround, pulvinated frieze and pediment. The façade is an updating of an earlier C17 house, the plan three rooms in a row, formerly with a cross-passage. Updated c. 1825 with a new staircase (removed) and rear corridor. Rear staircase extension, 1994.

ST CATHERINE

ST CATHERINE. Low w tower; three-light bell-openings with Somerset tracery, battlements and pinnacles. The tower arch has a trumpet capital (r.), on a short shaft. If *in situ*, this may date the base of the tower as late C12. The chancel was embellished or rebuilt *c.* 1490 by Prior Cantlow of Bath. Four-light E window with expensive panel tracery, repeated in straight-headed frames in nave and chancel. – PULPIT. Late C15, panelled, with C19 colour. – FONT. Probably late C12 or early C13, an odd design with thin blank pointed arcading and interlace, on a fluted stem. – WALL PAINTING by *Powell & Sons*, 1880. – Most interesting STAINED GLASS. Four-light E window, with Virgin, Crucifixion, St John and St Peter. Kneeling below St John, Prior Cantlow with Latin inscription dated 1490. Figures much restored in 1846, the date of some heraldic glass. Chancel s, also *c.* 1490: St Catherine without her wheel as frequently found in Somerset. – MONUMENT. William Blanchard †1631, and wife. Big kneeling figures between black Corinthian columns; broken pediment and achievement.

ST CATHERINE'S COURT. Remains of a large grange farmhouse and retreat built for Prior Cantlow, *c.* 1490–1516, visible in the mullioned NW entrance front. Three symmetrical gables, central entrance; hall (r.), parlour (l.) and Great Chamber above. Enlarged and made more monumental, probably *c.* 1610, by William Blanchard; see the broad two-storey porch. Doric entrance with triglyphs, canted corners with classical niches on the ground floor, and arched side lights with baluster mullions. Above, a continuous three-sided window. The house was altered *c.* 1841–5 and a SE wing added 1914–15 by *W. H. Bidlake* for the Hon. Richard Strutt. Inside rearranged, with imported or copied panelling, chimneypieces etc., complementing the existing work. Fine Neo-Jacobean library ceiling. Drawing room ceiling of 1915 with late C17-style oval garland and panels. In the Great Chamber, a plaster frieze with beasts, shields and Blanchard's initials, cf. a frieze with Strutt's initials on a landing. Fine gardens with TERRACES descending at the NE (cf. Claverton), begun *c.* 1610. Italianate gardens by *M. H. Baillie Scott*, *c.* 1920. Doric orangery of about the same date.

TITHE BARN, NE of the church. Probably C15, with varied roof trusses (some raised crucks, one hammerbeam).

GREY HOUSE, St Catherine's End. Mullioned windows under hoodmoulds and three steep gables with upright oval windows keyed into oblong panels, typically late C17. (Equally typical a fireplace and heavy bolection-moulded door surround.) Big gatepiers.

CHARMY DOWN. Plateau ½ m. w of the church with prehistoric finds over a long period: mid-Neolithic pottery and flint scatters, a few Bronze Age round barrows, and an extensive Bronze

Age field system surveyed in 1941 in advance of the construction of an airfield.*

6060

SALTFORD

ST MARY, Queen Square. Low unbuttressed w tower, perhaps C13: in 1789 it had a saddleback roof, cf. Swainswick. Top stage rebuilt with obelisk pinnacles and battlements in 1832. The lower stage has small blocked slits. Neo-Norman w door with continuous roll moulding is probably from alterations *c.* 1851, when the s porch and a s vestry were removed, the nave and chancel much rebuilt, the small Perp windows replaced by plain lights with intersected and Y-tracery. The Perp lights (nave N) may be original. Pretty gallery, 1832. – FONT. A remarkable, seemingly C13 piece. Circular bowl on a flared octagonal base with eight well-carved heads. – PULPIT. Made of C17 pieces. – STAINED GLASS. w window by *Geoffrey Robinson*, 1975. Thick cast glass in resin.

MANOR HOUSE, w of the church. A rare survival of a Norman first-floor hall house, probably *c.* 1148, among the oldest continuously inhabited houses in England. Some remarkably good features survived alterations of the late C15 and mid C17. The Norman range is in silvery limestone, of three storeys, with lower ranges E and w, probably C16. A N wing at the E end of the main block collapsed in the 1940s. The front was rebuilt *c.* 1640s, roughly dated from two fireplaces (*see* below), with small mullioned lights under deep relieving arches. A lion crouches on the E gable apex. Within are huge ceiling beams, a segmental Norman arch on plain imposts, and some moulding of the same form. In this room, a plaster overmantel with cartouches, dated 1645. The fireplace is C15, installed when the storage room beneath was made habitable. Timber lintel with central quatrefoil flanked by arcading. The first-floor hall has two excellent mid-C12 windows of two lights. One (blocked) below the E gable has stone window seats. That in the N wall has inside paired colonnettes with scallop capitals and a lozenge frieze (i.e. two parallel chevron friezes meeting), outside a chevron frieze and a hoodmould with nutmeg decoration. The friezes are similar to one at Hereford Cathedral made before 1148. To its l., the *ex situ* head of a two-light window, C14 or C15. On the E gable a big carved beast. A second beast is now on the door hood. First-floor w room chimneypiece dated 1637. On the second floor, traces of WALL PAINTING, *c.* 1200, including a seated Virgin and a Wheel of Fortune.

*The Monkswood Hoard of Middle Bronze Age objects and fragments of personal adornment was found in the 1930s during the construction of the Monkswood Reservoir, 500 yds N of Charmy Down.

SALTFORD HOUSE, High Street. 1771, perhaps by *Thomas Bennett*, for himself. Five bays, three storeys, of Bath stone. Plain but for a pedimented doorcase. (Good mahogany staircase, three turned balusters per tread.)

TOLL HOUSE, Bath Road. Greek Revival for Bath Turnpike Trust, *c.* 1832, origin-ally with Doric colonnade *in antis* (infilled).

SHEPTON MALLET

6040

A small town on the s edge of Mendip, poised on a hill s of the River Sheppey which once drove Shepton's numerous mills. A Roman trading settlement has been excavated on the Fosse Way just E of the town, and the core of the church is Saxon. A market charter was issued in 1234/5, and the economy must by then have included wool. Manorial rights belonged to the Malet family in the C12, but passed after 1536 to the Duchy of Cornwall. In the C16 and C17 broadcloth and the vari-coloured fabrics known as Spanish medleys were major products, and Defoe mentions knitted stockings. There is ample evidence of all this in the fine clothiers' houses. By 1790 there were *c.* 4,000 workers in the wool trade, which suffered over the following two decades a collapse unmatched elsewhere in Somerset. A brief revival came after *c.* 1830 with finer hand-finished silks, crêpes-de-chine and velvets. Brewing boomed from the mid C19. The centre of Shepton, shabby and run-down since the 1930s, has seen a minor renaissance since *c.* 1975.

CHURCHES AND PUBLIC BUILDINGS

ST PETER AND ST PAUL. The Saxon nave was extended one bay W *c.* 1180–90, the aisles and new chancel added, and perhaps the first W tower too. The present TOWER is what attracts externally, as is the rule in Somerset. Of holey Chilcote stone, it seems to date from *c.* 1380 or shortly after. John Harvey proposed that *William Wynford* designed or at least influenced it. One must visualize it with a set-back octagonal spire like Croscombe; a spire was indeed begun, then discontinued and the stump roofed over. The tower has angle buttresses, each corner with three diagonal infills across the angles. These infills diminish, though not in unison with the buttress set-offs, and the buttresses terminate below the belfry stage. This stage is somewhat narrower than the tower below, allowing space for an unusual treatment at each corner, by which two free-standing diagonally set shafts rise from the tops of the but-tresses and are crowned by pinnacles. Shafts and pinnacles are connected with the tower by thin panels of stone like infilled flying buttresses, forming a narrow V-shape on plan. At belfry level these abut against diagonal angle shafts which finish with the expected pinnacles on the parapet. This play with diagonal and square-set buttresses and shafts reminds one of Wynford's sw tower at Wells Cathedral, also designed in the 1380s. From him also came the fashion for flat-topped towers, which may account for the decision to abandon the spire here. The parapet has pierced quatrefoils in lozenges. Higher stair-turret, NE. w window of six lights, 1859–60. Above this three niches for stat-uary (weathered medieval figure of the Virgin; two of 1930). At this level on the N and S sides are two-light windows instead. Two-light windows on all sides above this, and then two-light bell-openings flanked by blank two-light windows. The bell-stage does not dominate sufficiently, perhaps because of the original intention for a spire.

The clerestory was added c. 1500, and the splendid roof shortly after but the medieval aisles and transepts were replaced by the present AISLES in 1835–7 by *Richard Carver* of Taunton and *C. R. Wainwright Sen.*, surveyor. They have three-light Perp lancets, if that term can be permitted. The E end of the CHANCEL is a part-rebuilding of c. 1851. One enters beneath the W tower which has fan-vaulting within, c. 1500. Perp tower arch with two wave mouldings. The first impres-sion is of the narrow nave with its glorious roof high up, a ver-itable roof for the whole hill on which the town stands. Then the attention is drawn to the extraordinary double-width aisles of 1835–7. They are more pronounced without their galleries (the W removed in the mid C19, the others in 1966). The former entrances over the N and S porches now look like musicians' galleries.

Detailed examination must start in the nave. The late C12 ARCADES, of three bays with square chamfered piers, were pierced crudely through pre-existing walls. The arches are wider than the nave itself. Evidence of Saxon long-and-short work is visible from the aisles at all four angles of the Saxon nave, i.e. at the chancel arch, and two piers to its W. This nave must have been 37 ft by 14 ft 6 in. by 25 ft high (11, 4.5 and 8 metres). Uneven masonry joins (revealed c. 1905) show where the Norman chancel was added. The double-chamfered arches have an inner order standing on short shafts, and these shafts have in the second and third bays Norman trumpet capitals, fashionable c. 1180–90. They stand on corbels of early stiff-leaf foliage with stems tied and sharply twisted to one side. In the

E bay Perp angels are attached to the shafts. The CLERESTORY initially had a tie-beam roof; see the recesses for the beam-ends. It also had figures between each window, for which shallow niches survive. The six bays do not align with the arcades. Window tracery replaced in 1881.

And then the ROOF, the most glorious of all the wagon roofs of England, solid and trustworthy, the back of a strong and nimble animal and yet extremely richly wrought. It probably dates from c. 1510–20. There are 350 panels and over 300 bosses, without any repetition in the design. The motifs of the panels are not in themselves eminently imaginative – quatrefoils of all kinds, wheels of three or four mouchettes, and so on, but together they appear as close and dense as the foliage of an arbour. The principal beams, not otherwise recognizable in a wagon roof, are given angel figures at their springing points, with more in between, flat against the wall-plates.

The double-chamfered chancel arch belongs to the early C13, with triple shafts on stiff-leaf corbels, rather like at Wells. The N and S chapel arches are double-chamfered also. The chancel roof is presumably of c. 1851; of the wagon type too, but lower and simpler, on the usual busts of angels. Double PISCINA under a trefoil-headed arch, c. 1220s. N of the chancel a two-storey Perp vestry with odd E windows, now containing the organ. Somewhat reordered, 1990–5.

FURNISHINGS. Simple STALLS by *J. D. Sedding*, 1887–9, con-temporary with his minor restoration. Some horizontal linen-fold. He also re-pewed the church. – Perp stone PULPIT of c. 1530–50, like a wineglass on a tall stem. Canopied and gabled Gothic niches, but in them Renaissance cornucopia, vases with flowers, etc. The base has a band of blind quatrefoils contin-ued out and tying it to the pier. The pulpit at Cheddar is similar but lacks the Renaissance ornament. – FONT. C11, probably just pre-Conquest; a squat bowl on a short foot (cf. Little Billing, Northants). Nearby, a Perp-style octagonal font of 1835–7, presumably by *Carver*. – ORGAN CASE, C18, with nice scrolly foliage and an angel blowing a trumpet. Formerly on the W gallery, remodelled c. 1860 to fit the tight N chancel arch. – SCULPTURE. A fragment of a corner shaft with deeply carved interlace, probably late C11. – DECALOGUE. Big and intrusive triptych, painted saints in the flanks. Possibly C18. – STAINED GLASS. W window c. 1861, probably by *O'Connor*, very brightly coloured. S aisle E by *John Yeo*, 2000, in blues and golds. Oth-erwise much clear glass inserted by *S.E. Dykes Bower*, 1953–4. – MONUMENTS. Effigies of two Knights, cross-legged (N aisle W and E ends), mid- to late C13. That at the E end may be Hugh de Vivon †c. 1249. – Edward Barnard, 1641, bust in a surround of gristly scrolls (tower). Attributed to *Edward Marshall* (GF). – Joan Strode, big brass plate dated 1649, with the whole family kneeling in a perspective interior with Corinthian columns. In the centre a skeletal figure of Death aiming a spear at the wife. Also attributed to *Edward Marshall* (GF). – Surrounding them, more C17 and C18 tablets without effigies, e.g. Jane Barnard

†1658 and Joan Strode †1679, the latter attributed to *Edward Pearce* (GF), with swags, cherub's head and skull. – Elsewhere, C18 and C19 classical tablets by *Paty* and *Wood* of Bristol, and *King* and *Reeves* of Bath.

R.C. CHURCH (former), Townsend. Opened 1804. A curious design. Along the street four bays of large pointed windows with intersected tracery. Small central door with a quatrefoil over. The church belonged only to the r. bay of this façade and extended at right angles behind it, with plain lancets. The other front windows are inside divided into two storeys.

UNITARIAN CHAPEL (former), Cowl Street. Built 1696. Four-bay front with hipped roof. The middle windows tall and round-arched, inserted in 1758 when a rear wing was also added, and with intersecting tracery of 1837–8. Late C17 outer bays. Steeply pedimented doorways and cross-windows above, also with pediments. (Pulpit and tester of 1758, now in St Nicholas, Bristol.)

BAPTIST CHURCH, Commercial Road. Originally Congregational. The chapel and schoolroom of 1801, of which two round-arched windows with interlace glazing survive at the rear, was extended forward by four bays in 1814. Big shaped gable added to the front in 1887, the good and complete galleried interior of the same date. – MONUMENT. Bartlett Giblett †1802, by *Chapman* of Frome. Gothic tablet with a draped urn.

METHODIST CHURCH (former), Paul Street. Dated 1819, the design derived from Walcot Methodist Chapel, Bath (so perhaps by the *Rev. William Jenkins*). Big, of five bays and two storeys, and a heavy Tuscan porch with complex Gothick fan-light beneath. Round-arched windows with interlaced glazing, the centre three in arched recesses. Over the centre are blind panels below a raised pediment. Ramped curves run down to its l. and r. Interior floored across at gallery level. – MONUMENT. Eliza Byron †1803 (gallery). Against a black ground, a big tablet with a crown finial. Marbled timber.

CEMETERY, Waterloo Road. Opened 1856. Gothic lodge, gates and simple paired Dec chapels by *Wainwright & Heard*. Entered by a bridge over Cowl Street.

PRISON, Cornhill. Probably the oldest purpose-built prison in England still in use. The house of correction of *c.* 1625 was rebuilt in 1790. Further adapted in 1817–20 by the County Surveyor *G. A. Underwood*, under the direction largely of the magistrate Sir John Coxe Hippisley, to form a rectangular courtyard of severe three-storey blocks in silvery limestone, with pronounced receding and projecting articulation. Low hipped roofs. Massive entrance on Cornhill, with channelled rustication, over-sized cornice, and moulded round arch to the door. Underwood's core survives, with big late C19 additions. Closed in 1930 but reopened in 1966.

POLICE STATION, Commercial Road. Formerly also the Court House. By *Wainwright & Heard*, 1858, of the local grey stone with Jacobean Revival shaped gables. Nicely asymmetrical, with the entrance to the Police Station at the base of a slim tower tucked into a corner. It has lost its ogee dome.

WHITSTONE SCHOOL, Charlton Road. First parts completed 1960, officially opened 1965. Presumably by *Somerset County Council Architect's Department*. Two-storey flat-roofed blocks with horizontal strip windows and reconstituted stone facing, slightly *retardataire*. Nearby, former GRAMMAR SCHOOL buildings by *W. J. Willcox*, 1899, Free Jacobean-cum-Renaissance.

Former COTTAGE HOSPITAL, Princes Road. By *G. J. Skipper* of Norwich, 1879. Now flats. Timber verandas, and domestic-looking gables and bays.

WORKHOUSE (now housing), Old Wells Road. In 1836 an existing building was seemingly converted or extended by *Jesse Gane* for the Shepton Mallet Union. This is probably the three-storey cruciform building at the rear; the mill-like E arm has flat mullioned windows that could be C18. At the crossing point is an octagon, typical of 1830s workhouse planning. The E wing facing the road, dated 1848, is by *C. R. Wainwright Sen*. Three storeys, plain Late Classical, with pedimented centre.

PERAMBULATION

The natural starting point is the MARKET PLACE at the lower end of High Street. The church lies back to the E and does not enter into the picture although, seen from afar, its tower dominates the town unmistakably. Of the roofed timber SHAMBLES or market stalls of *c.* 1450, the N row survived until 1912. Three stalls remain, resited and largely reconstructed in the 1970s. The handsome MARKET CROSS consists of a tall pinnacle built in 1500 by the will of Walter and Agnes Buckland. Rebuilt in the C17 or C18 without its original buttresses. The hexagonal arcade surrounding it is perhaps of *c.* 1700–50 and the upper part of the pinnacle was enriched in 1841 by *G. P. Manners* of Bath. At the S side of Market Place, a Gothic DRINKING FOUNTAIN by *H. W. Hickes* of Bath, 1868. Doulting limestone, granite and Serpentine. Dominating Market Place's E end, but unfortunately drawing back from it, is THE ACADEMY, a fortress-like performing arts centre, designed by *Wyvern Design Group*, 1974–5 as a community centre and theatre. The materials are bush-hammered concrete beams, reconstituted Bath stone, and some Purbeck rubble. Towards the church, the Academy has darkened glass and angular lead-clad attics. The scheme included a library behind a replica C18 façade in the Market Place, and shops with flats above continuing round the corner to the N, maintaining the enclosure of Town Street.

GREAT OSTRY, W of Market Place, has an unusually uniform terrace of seven three-storey weavers' houses, perhaps of *c.* 1650–80. Each house gabled, with ovolo-mullioned windows. S up the HIGH STREET, Nos. 12–16, early C19, with Gothic details on classical window surrounds. No. 21 is conspicuous for its four high storeys, a Victorian shocker, 1879. A butcher's shop in debased Italian Gothic with bulls' head capitals. Above

the crossroads with Paul Street and Commercial Road, High
Street climbs gently, with C18 and early C19 houses. At the top,
the CENOTAPH by *C. F. W. Dening*, 1920, a classical plinth
stepped in at the top.

PAUL STREET runs E from High Street. On the N side, set back
in gardens, THE LAWN is a pretty, set-back pair of Georgian
houses with pedimented doorways. The l. house forms a projecting L-shape with the doorway in the corner. Adjacent is a
disused TELEPHONE EXCHANGE, a good design of 1953, by
C. J. Woodbridge (Ministry of Works). Red brick, with a five-part
concrete balcony boxed out on the first floor. Pevsner
remarked that it 'deserves passing notice in a county so devoid
of modern architecture'. Opposite, Nos. 6–22, a humble C18
row with varied doorcases of better than expected quality, up
to the former Methodist church (*see* above).

Now for the lower town, starting again at the Market Place,
where to the E is the CHURCHYARD with its C18 lime trees. SW
of it is No. 8 Market Place, a big T-shaped house built for
Edward Strode *c.* 1675–8 (felling dates of the roof timbers);
carefully repaired *c.* 2003–7 under *Caröe & Partners*. Two
storeys plus cellars and gabled attics. Ovolo-mullioned
windows, ogee-kneelered gables. The plan of the S range was
a W cross-passage gable, a large hall and parlour, with stairs at
each end. N range originally two tenements, the rental from
which funded Strode's bread charity; divided vertically and not
connected internally with the S range. N gable wall rebuilt and
refenestrated *c.* 1890s. Fireplaces in both ranges have painted
plaster in the openings, some to a design also found at Alhamp-
ton Manor, Ditcheat (SW Somerset); white, black and red
chequer patterns with diagonal divisions in each square, and a
running braid border. The S range attic fireplace has a rarer
design of freely painted circles, dots and fleur-de-lys. Directly
adjacent, with their blank backs to the church, are STRODE'S
ALMSHOUSES, founded in 1699 'to honour God and to doe
good'. The style is, as expected, still pre-classical, but with
straight eaves rather than gables. Continuous string course,
cambered doorheads and two-light ovolo-mullioned windows.
Much restored and perhaps altered in 1862, and again in the
1980s, when each two houses were thrown into one. To their
W, a four-house row, with gabled BREAD HOUSE for distribution of bread to the poor; dated 1862, by *Wainwright & Heard*.

CHURCH LANE, N of the church, has at its E end WICKHAM'S
ALMSHOUSES by *Benjamin Ferrey*, 1868; Gothic and gabled,
with a pent roof over the ground floor. W is the OLD
GRAMMAR SCHOOL founded in 1627 by George and William
Strode. The building is perhaps *c.* 1600. Two storeys and seven
bays, mullioned windows with arched lights. Plain late C18
annexe to l. On PETER STREET, the entrance with the blunt
instruction: *Disce aut discede* (Learn or Leave). This is reached
via an alley r. of the Rectory. Here are more Georgian houses,
the wealthiest No. 27, with a broad front of irregularly spaced
windows, and pedimented door.

This is the start of the clothiers' district in the valley N of the centre. The tangle of descending and ascending lanes are the town's most attractive feature. Pevsner's account of 'big and sombre houses' and 'deserted or half-abandoned villas' has been superseded by renewal of variable quality, but the serendipitous mixture of mills and clothiers' houses retains an air of melancholic decline. Peter Street pitches steeply E into LEG SQUARE, a seemingly accidental space framed by handsome C18 houses such as EDEN GROVE and THE HOLLIES, both with pedimented doorways between attached Tuscan columns. The latter has C17 windows at the rear of the E wing. From Leg Square, two exits lead E. On the S side of the Sheppey, CORNHILL rises towards the massive prison walls. First on the r. is the OLD MANOR HOUSE; late C18, three tall storeys with Venetian motifs on the ground floor, tripartite windows above. Beyond the prison Cornhill becomes TOWN LANE. Here on the S is WHITSTONE HOUSE, U-shaped with high projecting gabled wings, and a good Doric triglyph doorcase, all consistent with the date of 1762 on the lead rainwater hoppers. NE of Leg Square is the former TOWN MILL, an C18 woollen mill rebuilt as a corn mill after a fire in 1868: square, pyramidal roof, and a tall square chimney behind. GARSTON STREET leads E parallel with the River Sheppey. Its N side is a near-continuous row, over ¼ m. long, of varied C17–C19 cottages.

LONGBRIDGE, W of Waterloo Road, has further remains of the cloth industry. On its N side, Nos. 2–4, three gabled and uniform weavers' houses of c. 1690–1700, each two bays wide, with pedimented cross-windows (cf. Cowl Street Unitarian chapel). Moulded doorcases also with pediments. Attached to the r. an early C18 addition, attempting some architectural grandeur with much restless quoining and alternating blocks in the window surrounds. Three-storey wing at the back, perhaps earlier C17. W again is the CROWN HOTEL of c. 1800. To its r., the entrance to DRAYCOTT, once the most interesting street in the town. S of Draycott is the enchanted and gloomy group called SALES HOUSE, now flats, with its back to the street. It was the mill, dyehouses and mansion of a clothier, dated 1769 on a rainwater head. Three-storeyed with a full-height canted porch-bay. Lower, far-projecting wings of three storeys with two-light mullioned windows. The mill building itself has been demolished. Up the steep gardens a ruinous octagonal SUMMERHOUSE, mid-C18 with two storeys of round-arched openings, most blocked.

COWL STREET climbs N from the Crown Hotel. On the E side, LONGBRIDGE HOUSE, C16 and C17. L-shaped, the longer and probably earlier part parallel with the street, to a cross-passage plan with four-centred doorway and ovolo mullions. In the centre of the garden elevation, a long canted single-storey bay window with eight round-arched lights. Opposite stood Monmouth House, a fine C17 double-gabled house demolished in 1965, with other good buildings, for the unworthy grey-brick council flats of HILLMEAD. Closing the N end of Cowl Street, and always providing the backdrop for the lanes below, is the high RAILWAY VIADUCT with rock-faced piers, opened in 1874, widened in brick, 1892, and part rebuilt after a collapse in 1946.

Former ANGLO-BAVARIAN BREWERY, Commercial Road. Now Anglo Trading Estate. Begun in 1863–4 with the lower Italianate side ranges, and a two-storey centre block, enlarged and heightened to four storeys for Anglo-Bavarian after 1871. Complex plan of 2:1:3:1:2 bays, each division stepping forward to a pedimented centre. Heavy Italianate trim, with broad Bath stone frames to the openings. At the sides are tall towers, once with pavilion roofs. A big chimney rises behind. Good solid maltings etc. N and W, some as late as 1884.

OUTER TOWN

1. East: Charlton

In KILVER STREET, on both sides, big C20 BREWERY buildings clustered around a mid-C19 nucleus: on the E side, an archway marked Kilver Street Brewery, and a plaque 'FMS 1860', perhaps an early phase of developments by the Showering family. Tall C19 ranges behind, one formerly a crêpe-de-chine factory, another making textile machinery. In the C20 the brewery was famous for Babycham, and for the plastic Bambi that pranced on the factory roof. Just to the N is KILVER COURT, an L-shaped range of mid-C17 houses (see the gabled back), updated c. 1700 with pedimented cross-windows (now blocked), and again in the mid C18.

S of Kilver Street, on Charlton Road, the THATCHED COTTAGE RESTAURANT, c. 1650, with irregular thatched roof. Further E, CHARLTON HOUSE HOTEL, with a C17 rear wing and the façade updated in the early C19, of six bays. Debased Italianate porch, perhaps c. 1850. FIELD FARM, S, is a 42-acre estate of 360 houses, begun c. 1994, on Duchy of Cornwall land. Masterplan by *Robert Adam Architects*, architects *Oldfield King*. Neo-vernacular with classical accents, inspired by the Prince of Wales's Poundbury, Dorset.

2. West: Bowlish

A satellite of Shepton Mallet until a road was pushed through to Croscombe in 1850. Several fine clothiers' residences. The most impressive is OLD BOWLISH HOUSE, with a front of seven bays and two-and-a-half storeys. Doorway with pediment on attached Ionic columns. On the first floor the second, fourth and sixth windows with pediments. Balustraded parapet. Most sources date the façade c. 1720, but the proportions and details point surely to c. 1750–60. At the back mid-C17 windows, and inside a fine open-well oak staircase through both storeys, with an openwork scroll balustrade, probably c. 1650. There was still a woollen mill in the grounds in 1836. N up Forum Lane is BOWLISH GRANGE, a long high range once a mill, with mullioned windows at the r., and a regular three-bay C18 house front to the l. On the S side of the Wells road is BOWLISH HOUSE, almost the equal of Old Bowlish House for grandeur, dated 1732 on the rainwater hoppers. Seven bays and two storeys with alternating pediments to all the openings. Broad Doric triglyph doorcase with pediment, gatepiers with urns, and a mounting block to the r. (Good open-well staircase with twisted balusters.) Rear wing perhaps late C17. Adjacent is COOMBE HOUSE, a big three-storey villa of c. 1820. ½ m. W, DARSHILL HOUSE has an early C19 HANDLE HOUSE for drying teasels used in cloth manufacture. Of brick, with chequered vent holes in panels between solid piers.

3. North: Downside

TURNPIKE HOUSE. On the A37 a little N of the C17 Downside Inn. Neo-Tudor c. 1850, with a little oriel in the gable. In the narrow lanes ½ m. W, WINDSOR HILL FARM, c. 1700–50, with mullioned windows. MILL HOUSE FARM, a little N, is Late Georgian with three-storey mill attached.

SHIPHAM

4050

ST LEONARD. A restless design by *James Wilson*, 1841–3. Short chancel, nave and SW porch-tower, loosely echoing the medieval plan. Square tower base with E entrance, the upper part octagonal. Long transomed belfry lights, rather Perp, but cusped Y-tracery to the nave, and reticulated Dec E window. None are medieval. Reordered 1899 by *Edmund Buckle*, who perhaps added the C17-style plasterwork to the chancel vault. – WOODWORK. Fixed like a reredos, a long pierced panel with Perp-looking arcade, vesicas and inverted arches above, friezes of square fleurons, circles in rows and in fours. C16? – STAINED GLASS. One in the nave signed *Bell & Son*, 1914.

The village centre is The Square, a broad irregular space from which a network of lanes and alleys straggles untidily E, where C18 miners staked claims and built on the waste. MANOR HOUSE, S, is long and mullioned, a classic three-room plan with cross-passage, seemingly C17. Showy naïve classical gatepiers of the late C17 to COURT HOUSE (rebuilt c. 1890), opposite the church. Behind, a ruined C19 CALAMINE KILN. Calamine mining peaked c. 1790–1830, supplying the Bristol brass works. This period shows in polite but modest Regency houses such as LITTLE COURT, N of The Square, and BAY TREE HOUSE, on Turnpike Road, which was laid out in 1826–7. N, at Broadway, a well-preserved TOLL HOUSE.

ROWBERROW ROUND BARROW, ½ m. NNE of Shipham. Of Early Bronze Age bowl type, 65 ft across and 7 ft high (20 and 2.2 metres).

SHOCKERWICK

8060

SHOCKERWICK HOUSE. The traditional attribution to John Wood the Elder, *c.* 1750, is doubtful. Possibly of *c.* 1775–85 by *John Palmer*, whose signed elevation is in Bath Library. He seems to have enlarged and remodelled it in the late 1790s. S façade to the road above broad grassy slopes. Main block of five bays and two-and-a-half storeys, with giant angle pilasters. In the centre, a three-bay attached portico of giant Corinthian columns with a pediment. The ground-floor openings are heavily rusticated. Lower wings, originally single-storey with three arched openings and balustraded parapet. These may be part of the original design, or slightly later. Their extra storey, with just two windows, is by *George & Yeates*, 1896–7. They also added a four-columned portico to the simpler entrance front. This has a Venetian window with floating pediment on the first floor, and a simple tripartite window above. The composition of the upper floors is more in Palmer's style than that of the Woods. Also of 1896–7, the low service wing in vernacular Georgian style, and a rather Lutyensesque LODGE to the S. Low wing for a billiards room, 1907. Late C18 ORANGERY a little to the E.

LOWER SHOCKERWICK FARM, NW, is dated 1793, with mansard roof and flat parapet, but ovolo-mullioned windows under hoodmoulds. A C17 house remodelled. A similar story at the larger UPPER SHOCKERWICK FARM. Good C18 BARN and GRANARY.

SHOSCOMBE

7050

PRIMARY SCHOOL. Gothic school-cum-chapel of 1868, a cut above the average. E bellcote and reticulated gable window. Caernarvon-arched lights on the S side.

PAGLINCH FARMHOUSE, Shoscombe Bottom, ½ m. SW of the school. L-shaped with mullioned-and-transomed windows. Good doorcase with cambered head and fluted pilasters, dated 1632 in the spandrels. Above, a blocked trefoil-headed lancet window, i.e. a medieval feature.

SIDCOT

FRIENDS' MEETING HOUSE. Handsome, single-storey, originally of 1817, but completely remodelled by *Theodore Sturge*, 1925–6. Round-arched windows.

SIDCOT SCHOOL, opposite the Meeting House, was established by the Society of Friends in 1699 and re-founded 1808. Main building designed by *S. W. Daukes*, 1834, built 1838. Five bays and three storeys, with two-storey wings of three bays. Deep eaves on paired brackets. Edwardian additions. ROSE COTTAGE, s, may be by *Daukes*. The former Headmaster's House is by *Fred Rowntree*, 1905, Neo-Georgian.

Sidcot has some pleasing early C20 houses amid later suburbia: PENHAVEN, Hillyfields. By *C. R. Ashbee c.* 1910–12, for S. A. Maltby, a master at the school; small, brick and cottagey. Bigger and with consciously Arts and Crafts touches is MONKSHAVEN, Fountain Lane, for T. B. Clark, of the Quaker shoe manufacturers. By *W. H. Bidlake*, 1897–8. Extended (E gable) in 1908. On Bridgwater Road (A38), several comfortable houses by *Oatley*: HALE (1902–4), DOWNFIELD and GATCOMBE (both 1906–7).

SOUTH HORRINGTON see WELLS

SOUTH STOKE

ST JAMES. Low three-stage W tower, C15, with diagonal buttresses, two-light bell-openings and embattled parapet. Heavy stair-turret with swept cap. S porch with Norman doorway. One order of columns patterned with lozenges, in which are nailhead ornament, l., and fleur-de-lys and dots, r. Lintel with low-pitched top, chip-carved. Tympanum with a trellis pattern of roll mouldings. Arch with rosettes, three-dimensional chevrons and a kind of flat plait. S aisle and chancel rebuilt 1845 and *c.* 1850, by *G. P. Manners*. Restored 1885 by *J. C. Atwell* of Bath. – PULPIT. Stone, polygonal, probably Perp but re-cut.

MANOR FARMHOUSE, W of the church. E part *c.* 1670–5, with similarities to the Packhorse Inn (*see* below), but C15 arches within. Extended in the C19. Fine BARN, probably *c.* 1485–1500, with deeply projecting porch entrance and another projection for a DOVECOTE. Arch-braced collar-beam roof with wind-braces. At the NW corner, an early C19 ENGINE HOUSE with apsidal end. E of the church, THE PACKHORSE INN. The date 1674 probably indicates a remodelling. Two-and-a-half storeys, three straight gables, ovolo-mullioned windows. Doorcase with cambered head. The cross-passage plan survives. Chamfered beams, door frames etc., typical of the later C17.

Sloping green in the centre. BREWERY HOUSE, NE, is Picturesque Gothic of *c.* 1834, with wide embattled gable like a full-width pediment, flanked by thin square turrets. Embattled service wing at the l. THE PRIORY, SW, is 1850; Neo-Tudor, with tall chimneystacks. SOUTHSTOKE HALL. Reportedly of medieval origin. Six-bay Late Georgian S front with metal-roofed veranda, then a big wing with a canted bay at the E end. Its LODGE by the green is strange, *c.* 1840, with approximately E.E. ornaments, a bellcote in the apex of the steep gable and another on the porch roof.

8050   STANDERWICK

STANDERWICK COURT. In wooded parkland, a plain two-storey mansion perhaps *c.* 1720–40, for the Edgell family. Six-bay entrance front, seven bays to the garden. Some original sashes, with ogee-moulded rebates like mullions of a few years earlier. Garden windows and enclosed semicircular porch of *c.* 1790. Lower range at the back, perhaps late C17, the former house relegated to service quarters. Pretty Neoclassical ceiling of *c.* 1790 to a panelled room inside. Exceptionally fine mid-C18 staircase installed (with modifications) in the C19; turned and twisted balusters, ramped rails, fluted Ionic newels. Large arch-headed stair window of seventy panes. The early C18 staircase became the servants' stair. – ICE HOUSE, mid-C18, standing unusually tall with a stone beehive dome on a square base. – Former STABLES, W, a handsome early C18 block of seven bays; tall round-headed windows below, oculi above. There is possible evidence of a deserted medieval village in the park; a church was demolished before 1454, although its ruins appear still on a map of 1736.

REDBRIDGE COTTAGE, Rudge Lane. C14 with many alterations and much updated *c.* 2003–6. Some small two-light stone-framed C15 or C16 windows in the porch and on the S front, and a raised cruck-framed N gable with brick infill, rare for this district. (In the main range, a near-perfect C14 wind-braced roof with cranked collars.)

5060   STANTON DREW

ST MARY. An unusual plan: nave, N aisle, NE chapel as long as the chancel; tower in the middle of the N side, with two-storey porch of *c.* 1470–1520 to its N. Rubble masonry mainly of Blue Lias, Dundry stone dressings. Tower with angle buttresses at the base, diagonal where the tower is rebuilt. E of the tower, another chapel, probably C15. The chancel may date from the

C13, though the strange stepped four-lancet group in the NE chapel is C19. Dec N doorway, heavily moulded, with ogee gable and thin pinnacles. Much rebuilt in 1847–8 by *S. C. Fripp*; the odd vaguely Perp-looking mouldings of the arcade, the chancel arch, and the arch into the N chapel with its convex sides and convex capitals and abaci may belong to that date. The same mouldings also for the openings to tower and Lyde Chapel. – FONT. Circular tub-shaped bowl, possibly C12 or C13? Circular base like an upturned bucket with four thick demi-shafts and tripled moulding at the neck: perhaps a much later invention. – MONUMENTS. Cornelius Lyde †1717. Baroque tablet with cherubs' heads at the foot. Signed by *Michael Sidnell*. – Also his, Lyde family †1738, a good piece of reredos type, more classical, with Ionic pilasters and broken pediment. Influenced no doubt by Sidnell's work for Gibbs and Rysbrack. – Elizabeth Adams †1768 and Samuel Price, erected 1777, nearly identical and notably backward-looking, still with broken pediments and floral pilasters. – Minor Neoclassical tablets: John Adams †1788, by *William Paty*; John Kernan †1804, *Foster & Co.*; Coates family †1791–1813, *Jones & Co.*

CHURCH FARM, E of the church. Two ranges slightly offset, that to the W seemingly once a church house with, in the N gable, an early C15 tall two-light window, with transom and flowing reticulation. Inside this range's S end, on the upper floor, a big blocked arch with trefoil-cusping. It is supposed to be part of a former two-storey opening, perhaps the bay window of a hall. Mid-C18 E façade, with paired sashes and central porch.

RECTORY FARM HOUSE, Bromley Road. Mid-C15 rectory (later a schoolroom). Long N front with assorted windows including two four-centred lights with mullion and transom, at the l. end a four-light window over one of six lights, and between them, forming a single composition, two shields, one with the arms of Bishop Bekynton of Bath and Wells (i.e. *c.* 1450s). Which windows are *in situ*? (The plan is a large inner room divided from adjoining small rooms by a framed screen. Roof part-medieval.) Opposite, STANTON COURT, handsome five-bay three-storey Georgian front with quoins. Centre bay with a triangular parapet over the pediment, provincial and uncertain (cf. the George and Dragon, Pensford). The doorway has a segmental pediment on Doric pilasters. (Inside, in studs on a door, the date 1753. One attic light with C17 ovolo mullions.) N again, W side, is MILL PLACE, an ashlar-faced house of *c.* 1820 for a retired Bristol sugar planter. Three bays, two storeys, Doric portico, broad eaves. Yet lower, the BRIDGE with two ribbed pointed arches; C14 or C15. N again up the slope, on a triangular junction, a TOLL HOUSE, hexagonal and thatched, with Gothic arched windows. For West Harptree Turnpike Trust, *c.* 1793.

STANTON WICK FARM, *c.* 1 m. SE. Dated 1666 on a sundial. Symmetrical front with big central gabled projection. Ovolo-mullioned windows and traces of cross-windows too.

4   STONE CIRCLES. A group of three circles of different sizes on
     private land on the E side of the village. Also THE COVE, a
     structure of three massive stones adjacent to the village pub,
     and HAUTVILLE'S QUOIT, a single standing stone *c.* 750 yds
     to the NE beyond the River Chew. The remains of avenues
     approaching two of the circles from the E can still be seen.
     Most of the stones are local conglomerate. In 1776 William
     Stukeley estimated there to be around 160 stones in the group,
     although barely half that number are visible today and only a
     few of these remain upright. The largest circle, over 110 yds
     (100 metres) across, was one of the biggest in the country. For
     the discoveries of 1997 and their interpretation *see* p. 9.

6060   STANTON PRIOR

ST LAWRENCE. Three-stage Perp W tower with diagonal but-
    tresses. Late C15 two-light bell-openings with Somerset tracery
    (cf. Farmborough). Deep C13 N porch, see the unmoulded
    two-centred entrance arch on the plainest imposts. The S
    doorway apparently also C13. The rest essentially of 1860, by
    C. E. Davis. – FONT. Octagonal, perhaps C13. – MONUMENT.
    Thomas Cox †1650, an interesting hanging monument. The
    architectural elements still derived from the Jacobean style, but
    all the cartouche-work of the typical gristly character of the
    mid C17. Large broken semicircular pediment with standing
    angel. Below, the two main figures seated frontally and leaning
    with an elbow on a prayer-desk with a skull. The woman is
    holding a baby. Kneeling children in the 'predella'.
CHURCH FARMHOUSE, W of the church. Dated 1737, with mul-
    lioned two-light windows. The OLD RECTORY, E of the
    church, and POPLAR FARM, 400 yds NE, show the influence
    within a few decades of Georgian Bath. Taller, more regular,
    and ashlar-faced with mansard roofs and sashes.
STANTONBURY HILL-FORT. *See* Marksbury.

2060   STEEP HOLM

An island in the Bristol Channel *c.* 5½ m. W of Weston-super-
    Mare. Archaeology has revealed evidence of Neolithic activity
    and a probable Roman signal station. High up at the E end was
    an Augustinian PRIORY, extant only to *c.* 1260, served by a
    Prior, twelve canons and a few lay brothers. Rudimentary
    narrow church, partially excavated 1978–86. – FORTIFICA-
    TIONS. Built from 1860 as part of the line of 'Palmerston Forts'
    defending the approaches to Bristol and Cardiff; parts of the
    gun batteries and round-arched stone barracks (dated 1867)
    stand.

STOKE ST MICHAEL
or STOKE LANE

ST MICHAEL. 1838 by *Jesse Gane*, except for the w tower with diagonal buttresses. Late Dec belfry openings, *c.* 1320–50, with two ogee-headed lights and an ogee quatrefoil, but not yet with vertical bars. See also a doorway in the ringing chamber. C15 battlements, gargoyles and pinnacles. Below the belfry, square-headed two-light windows, perhaps C16. w door is a C19 cutting down of a lancet, just *c.* 16 in. (40 cm.) wide. Oak roof with ogee-braced trusses, perhaps of 1905 when the church was altered. – STAINED GLASS. With Art Nouveau lilies and angels, 1905. – MONUMENTS. Edward Morris †1672, one of several Blue Lias tablets with naïve incised ornament. – Katharine James †1780. Long brass plaque, rounded at the top and bottom, with leaf border.

w of the church, a low cottage with blocked door in the E gable opening into the churchyard; presumably a priest's house, and perhaps C15 or C16. Nearby in Tower Hill, the MANOR HOUSE, *c.* 1690. Square plan, hipped roofs. Symmetrical, of five bays with two-light mullioned windows, and oval light above the door. To its r., a carved C19 shop window. Four rooms around a central passage; at the rear a good splat-baluster dog-leg staircase. Immediately s, the KNATCHBULL ARMS. Late C17. Mullioned hood-moulded windows, gabled dormers. Porch with gable and on the side two characteristic oval windows. The ears of the doorway are characteristic too. w on Stoke Hill is TOOSES FARMHOUSE, *c.* 1650; cross-passage plan, chamfered doorcase with four-centred arch.

MANOR HOUSE FARM. ⅝ m. E. Dated 1696, five bays and two storeys with upright two-light windows. Projecting rear wings. The porch has two Roman Doric columns. They possibly came from the ruined MANOR HOUSE to the w, *c.* 200 yds N of Somers Farm, reputed without evidence to have been owned by the Dukes of Buckingham. It was quite small, and E-shaped. Only the ivy-clad w wall and the entrance façade (s) remain. This had an ovolo-mullioned and transomed window in the end of each projecting wing, and one in the recessed part between porch and wings; one frame survives, w of the porch. Round-headed porch opening with panelled jambs. In the w wall, parts of a fireplace with a finely moulded and stopped jamb, and parts of a herringbone brick fireback. All suggest a date *c.* 1590–1625.

STOKE BOTTOM, *c.* ¾ m. NNW, had stone and fulling mills in 1545. A short-lived paper mill was established by the Fussells (*see* Mells) in 1803. A little w of Stoke Bottom Farm is a complex of leats, sluices and mill ponds, with ruinous early C19 mills. Intermingled are ruined walls and outbuildings of Stoke House (C18, dem. 1928). FOSSE FARM, *c.* 1½ m. w. Big fancy datestone, 1759. Symmetrical, with four mullioned windows about the porch. 100 yds w of Blake's Farm, a PIT for bull baiting. Roughly oval amphitheatre: *c.* 100 yds (90 metres) wide and 15 ft (4.5 metres) deep, access ramp from the N.

STON EASTON

ST MARY. A little church of nave, narrow aisles, chancel and three-stage C15 W tower with diagonal buttresses, continuous moulded battlements and small belfry lights with Somerset tracery. S aisle cased in ashlar *c.* 1740s, with ramped parapet and Gothic door frame. Perp-style tracery of *Sir Arthur Blomfield*'s restoration of 1890–1 (organ chamber added, chancel largely rebuilt, roofs renewed with pretty dormers). Small N doorway, on the axis of Ston Easton Park, so probably C17. Perp arcades with four shafts and hollows, ring-moulded capitals. Norman chancel arch on single columns with cushion capitals. Arch with a heavy inner edge-roll, two rows of chevron, and outer chequered billet moulding. Ogee openings outside the arch, 1890–1. – FITTINGS. By *Blomfield*. Perp style. – FONTS. Elegant baluster with acanthus decoration, mid-C18. Second font and COVER, 1890–1. – STAINED GLASS. All 1891. E window probably by *Heaton, Butler & Bayne,* Blomfield's favoured firm. Two by *W. G. Taylor,* S, with unpleasant mauve flesh tones. – MONUMENTS. John Hippisley †1664. Ionic tablet with broken pediment. – John Hippisley Coxe †1769. Plain white marble obelisk. – Henry Hippisley Coxe †1795. Neoclassical tablet on Gothic arched ground, Greek-key borders. Probably by *Reeves*, who did several more in the church. – William Mills †1805 (churchyard); chest-tomb type on unusual oval plan, like a big pillbox.

MANOR FARM, E, is simple Late Classical, *c.* 1830–60. In the village, ¼ m. N, MIDWAY HOUSE, early C18, of five bays with mullioned lights and continuous string courses.

STON EASTON PARK. Now a hotel. In 1635 'lately erected' for John Hippisley V or his son. An estate map of *c.* 1700 reportedly shows a tall house with gabled projecting porch, of which C17 roofs and some mullioned windows remain. The N side was refronted *c.* 1700–10 and is of ten bays arranged 2:3:3:2, irregularly spaced, and without break or projection. Two storeys over a basement of generous segmental-headed windows with nearly square panes. Narrow ground-floor sashes with segmental pediments, flat cornices on the first floor. At the W end, the Painting Room and the adjacent room have bolection panelling and fireplaces of corresponding date. The two E bays of this front are an extension, or rebuilding, for the Drawing Room. Probably *c.* 1740–60, when the main interiors were refashioned.

The S front has three storeys and eleven bays (1:1:2:3:2: 1:1) stepping forward and back at each break. The seven-bay centre was probably dictated by the C17 house (see the

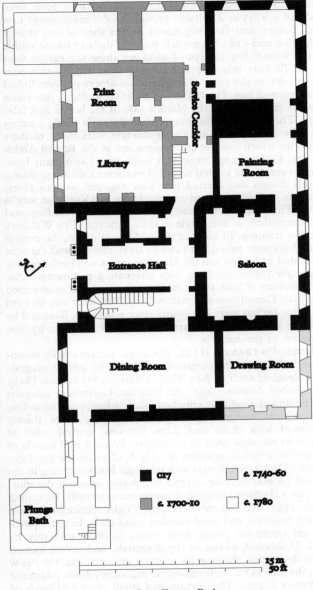

Print Room

Service Corridor

Library

Painting Room

Entrance Hall

Saloon

Dining Room

Drawing Room

Plunge Bath

■ c17
□ c. 1740–60
■ c. 1700–10
□ c. 1780

15 m
50 ft

Ston Easton Park.
Plan

mullioned windows to the basement) and may have been updated c. 1755 as a suitable prelude to the magnificent new Hall, Saloon and Drawing Room. It was then of two storeys only. The mid-c18 changes left parts of the c17 house visible at the w end; five storeys of windows show the earlier floor levels. To hide this, the s front was extended by two bays c. 1769–86, in the form of a square two-storey pavilion linked by a recessed bay. The balancing addition to the E, one room deep, is revealed from the blank E side of the house as a false front. The pavilions have low-pitched pyramid roofs, a rather outmoded Kentian motif. Other changes were made to the s front, for which five variant designs are at the British Architectural Library, none exactly as built. One has a giant Ionic portico across the central recess. A rusticated doorcase shown in this design was carried out: four engaged Roman Doric columns with triglyph-and-metope frieze and Vitruvian scrolls above. This work is attributed to *Thomas* and *William Paty*, and is characteristic of their style c. 1780, influenced by William's London training. To balance the additional width, the central seven bays were raised from two to three storeys, and the attic decorated with urns and the Hippisley arms amid oak-leaf festoons. First-floor windows with alternating pediments. Attic and pavilions of Bath stone; earlier parts rendered in imitation of ashlar. Demolition was narrowly averted after sale in 1956 but some fittings were lost (some since regained). Restored by *E. F. Tew* from 1964, and carefully altered c. 1978–82 by *Tom Foster* for its present role.

Simple ENTRANCE HALL, not large. Exceptionally sumptuous SALOON in the centre of the N side, its quality suggesting a designer such as *John Wood*. A date c. 1755 is most likely. The timber doorcase from the Hall has Corinthian columns and pediment, profusely enriched foliate frieze, etc. The ceiling is nearly as sumptuous: modillion cornice, frieze thickly encrusted with shells and floral festoons, central relief of Jupiter as an eagle with thunderbolts. Framed wall panels of *trompe l'œil* reliefs in grisaille, notably Apollo over the fireplace. Simpler DRAWING ROOM with fine light Rococo ceiling in the style of *Thomas Stocking*, c. 1750. Worth special notice the staircase, in a U-shaped space not expressed externally. Its ceiling also c. 1750s. Mahogany stairs with a tight semicircular turn, turned balusters and good scrolled tread-ends. In the E pavilion, an octagonal plunge-bath room c. 1820, probably by *G. A. Underwood*; niches in the diagonals, and severe incised linear decoration showing his training under Soane. On the w side, the LIBRARY, with reinstated mahogany Ionic pilastered bookcases c. 1770. The cornice had small vases and busts of *Wedgwood* Black Basalt ware, of which Shakespeare is original. Fine mid-c18 chimneypiece with enriched frieze; pedimented overmantel with the original painting, a Roman architectural *capriccio* including the Pantheon. Charming PRINT ROOM, where prints from Raphael, Domenichino, Roman vistas, etc., are pasted symmetrically and decoratively on the wall. Two built-in cupboards with Chippendale-style glazing bars, Rococo friezes and broken pediments. In the w corridor, *ex situ* secondary stairs *c.* 1740–50.

PARK. SE of the house, an unusual C19 OBSERVATORY; two Pennant sandstone slabs cramped together with iron in a standing triangle, with mounting holes for a telescope. The view to the church was obtained by clearing parts of the village *c.* 1740–50. Drive rerouted *c.* 1981. C18 iron GATES from Merstham, Surrey (via Ammerdown House, *see* p. 79). N of the house is a narrow terrace, then steep banks dropping to a valley, with no scope for formal gardens. *Humphry Repton*'s partly executed Red Book of 1791–2 created a Romantic stream with a series of weirs, and bridges E and W. The latter is backed by a small castellar gate. Adjacent early C18 COTTAGE romanticized with crowstepped gables and battlements. In trees to the N, an C18 ICE HOUSE. W of the house, semi-derelict mid-C18 STABLES.

WHITCHURCH FARM, ¾ m. E of the church. A prebendal property of Bath and Wells from *c.* 1140. The core a medieval hall house, exterior late C16 or early C17. Two-and-a-half storeys and four bays, front; mullioned windows with stopped labels, projecting gabled wing at the r., and datestone HGE 1633. Two-storey porch dated GCD 1613, with good four-centred doorway, foliate frieze and decorated spandrels.

Five small and much eroded Bronze Age ROUND BARROWS were excavated in 1941.

STOWEY

5050

ST NICHOLAS AND ST MARY. Small but not without interest. Of Butcombe Sandstone. Small three-stage w tower, perhaps late C14 or early C15; parapet with the usual pierced cusped lozenges. Exceptionally tall three-light Perp w window. Square-headed nave lights and some C17 alterations, C17 N porch. The nave's NE corner has the shears mark of the wool-staplers' guild. – SCULPTURE. N chancel wall. Small C15 statuette of Virgin and Child, possibly repaired and *ex situ*. – FONT. C14, octagonal, panelled in cusped squares; on one face a scallop shell. – PAINTINGS. By *Henry Strachey c.* 1907–8. On canvas, around the chancel arch a dominant Day of Judgment, other scenes covering the chancel. – ROYAL ARMS. 1660, with strapwork. – MONUMENTS. William Jones †1748. Handsome hanging monument by *T. Paty*. Pedimented base on which recline two putti. Obelisk above with rocaille cartouche. – Elizabeth and Mary Jones †1783 and 1791. By *Moore & Smith* of London. Charming, of coloured marbles, with an inset oval relief. – Henry Strachey †1940. A fine tablet with thickly carved tree forms, beautifully lettered. Signed *D.P.*, probably *Don Potter*, a pupil of Eric Gill.

STOWEY HOUSE, directly N. An L-shaped gabled C17 house to the w. Doubled in size by a Georgian addition, also L-shaped, its s wing back to back with the older part. The N front of the C18 part has a canted bay and plain sashes. Castellated E front, with most windows mullioned; two sashes. Good pattern-book ogee-Gothick doorcase of the type made by the Patys and others in Bristol c. 1760–70.

SUTTON COURT. Now flats. Of a fortified manor begun c. 1310 by William de Sutton, the embattled wall and a three-storey tower on the N front remain. This is square and has a taller circular stair-turret. A C15 or early C16 hall was added to its s. The panelled arches between it and the tower and in axis with the s porch may be original, as may also a small one-light window in the s porch. About 1558 (former date on a fireplace) Bess of Hardwick and her second husband Sir William St Loe added a NE wing with a parlour and a chapel above. It looks a little earlier than 1558, still with buttresses in the earlier Tudor tradition. (The C16 roof remains above C19 ceilings.) How much of the two-light cusped and the plain mullioned-and-transomed windows here and on the s side is original, cannot now be said. The house had more or less its present size by the early C18, by when it belonged to the Stracheys (painting with a family group in the hall). The entrance side appears largely as it is today in Buckler's drawing in the Pigott Collection but the house was radically remodelled and re-detailed by T. H. Wyatt, 1858–60. The s front is an incoherent composition of two storeys and eight bays, five random gables, shallow projections, various canted bays and mullioned-and-transomed windows in three styles. The central s porch has a pretty semicircular door hood on carved brackets, and above it a sundial dated 1734 with the Strachey arms.

KNIGHTON SUTTON FARM, ¼ m. NE of Sutton Court. Late C17 front of five bays and two storeys with tall and slender cross-windows, utterly spoiled by double glazing.

STRATTON-ON-THE-FOSSE

ST VIGOR. A dedication repeated only once in England. Unbuttressed w tower with early C17 details, e.g. solid parapet, uncusped two-light windows with round heads (cf. Corston, Holcombe Old Church). No signs within or without that these are later alterations. s porch perhaps c. 1500, with deeply moulded arch and an image niche above; Norman inner doorway with plain round arch. Nave, two-bay N aisle (or Knatchbull chapel) rebuilt on medieval foundations in 1782, its E and w windows Tudor-arched with interlaced tracery typical of their date. Chancel rebuilt 1765, but since re-gothicized. C18 no doubt also the plain plaster vault of the nave. Restored by B. & E.B. Ferrey, 1879, including the chancel roof, three s windows and probably the reticulated E window too. Two arches to the N aisle, that at the E CI5, with wave moulding and a hollow. Chancel arch also probably CI5, with deep hollows. Uneven tower arch, probably CI7. – PULPIT. Perp, stone, simple slender panels. – Plain Norman tub FONT. – DOOR. CI5, with tracery. – ROYAL ARMS. 1805. – STAINED GLASS. N aisle E and W: much CI5 glass, a patchwork of small fragments, with some good heads. Big angel (W) probably from an Annunciation. – MONUMENTS. Knatchbull Chapel: tablets to Knatchbulls and Longs, mostly draped urns by *T. King* of Bath, 1760s–1818. The best, unsigned, is to Norton Knatchbull †1782, with an oval relief with seated woman. – Nave: James Salmon †1784, by *King*; mourning widow leaning on a broken column. – George Long †1787. Unusually sculptural work by *William Paty*; urn, standing mourner with very full and rich drapery.

ST BENEDICT (R.C.). By *C. F. Hansom*, 1857. Dec. Single vessel with ritual S porch and short capped tower. Former schools attached to the l., of the same date.

CHRIST CHURCH, Downside, I m. SW of the abbey. Now a house. 1837–8 by *John Pinch Jun.* and *C. R. Wainwright* (perhaps executing Pinch's design). Lancet Gothic with a bell-cote. Later CI9 chancel. *Pinch* altered the adjoining house as the VICARAGE in 1838.

Adjacent to St Vigor, the MANOR HOUSE, late CI7 with mullions above, sashes below, and a pedimented doorcase (renewed). At the junction of Church Lane and Fosse Way, good WAR MEMORIAL, by *Dom Ephrem Seddon*, 1922–3. Column with corner shafts, and a big finial with a Crucifixion. A little S is the KING'S ARMS, South Street; late CI8, with Venetian motif over a pedimented door. NE of the village at Killing's Knap is MANOR FARM, mid-CI8. Seven-bay S front with narrowly placed windows and a semicircular door-hood; N front less regular, also mid-CI8, with a CI9 two-storey porch.

DOWNSIDE ABBEY

The Benedictine monastery of St Gregory was founded at Douai, France in 1606. It soon established a school for English Catholic boys. Following Revolutionary persecution, the house was re-established in England in 1795, and moved to the Mount Pleasant estate at Downside in 1814. Here stood Downside House, now part of the school. A chapel was added in 1823 and a school range in 1853–4. *A. W. N. Pugin* made plans in 1839 and 1841–2 but nothing was built. Then in 1872 a new beginning was made, with plans by *Dunn & Hansom* for a vast monastic abbey church, cruciform and aisled, with a high French spire after St Pierre, Caen. The monastic ranges were planned around a cloister to the S: the W range was completed in 1876, the first part of the church in 1882. Work continued until 1938 under *Sir Giles Gilbert Scott*. Concurrently large additions to both monastery and school buildings created the closely integrated if somewhat disorderly complex S of the church.

pp. 619, 620

CHURCH OF ST GREGORY THE GREAT. Among the largest post-Reformation Roman Catholic churches in England, 328 ft long and 74 ft high to the vault ridge (100 and 22.5 metres), giving an impression of cathedral splendour and at the same time of great earnestness and sobriety. It is Pugin's dream of the future of English Catholicism at last come true.

The public approach reveals first the EAST END, planned on the grandest French cathedral precedent, with an ambulatory and radiating chapels, and a further-projecting Lady Chapel. The E end was built 1887–90, all by *Dunn & Hansom*. *Frederick Walters*'s Perp SACRISTY at the NE (1913–15) is the most conventional part. Behind rises the seven-bay CHOIR, by *Thomas Garner* 1901–5, with flying buttresses added by *Sir Giles Gilbert Scott*, 1930s. Its free Perp tracery contrasts with the more earnest C13 style of the transept with its big rose window, and again with Scott's idiosyncratic forms, best seen in the flowing tracery and parapets of his eight-bay NAVE of 1923–5. At the NW, a domestic-scale public porch slightly mars the impression of grandeur. The temporary W front looks fine with its rough lias and plain tall lancet windows. The S side of both nave and choir has two tiers of windows at aisle level – actually gallery chapels over a cloister. Against the S transept is the commanding TOWER 166 ft (50.5 metres) high, higher than any in the county except the crossing tower of Wells. It would have been taller still with the intended spire. *Dunn & Hansom*'s part (1881–4) was completed to the second of the three tiers of bell-openings, narrowing by carefully judged stages. It is oddly fenestrated (slim lancets with high rose windows above, originally clock faces), sitting uncomfortably with the paired Y-traceried bell-openings of rather C13 character. *Scott* added the third tier of openings in 1937–8, the tracery and terminations of the pinnacles and sub-pinnacles around the parapet echoing Somerset Perp forms.

The church is rib-vaulted throughout in C13 French forms, although otherwise the architecture is not uniform, by no means a disadvantage. We begin inside at the CROSSING of 1880–2. Here and in the E arm there is an almost Spanish effusiveness, with thick naturalistic capitals and rich sculptural detail, mostly carved by *Wall* of Cheltenham, 1880–1914. The N transept began as a temporary sanctuary, accounting for the generous altar of what is now the chapel of St Oliver Plunkett. The S transept is filled at gallery level with the screened-off organ. This first phase included one bay of the choir and one of the nave, fixing to some extent the elevations of the CHOIR of 1901–5. Garner eliminated the triforium for taller clerestory windows, without harming the overall unity. It is fundamentally E.E. The choir is square at the E end, contradicting the plan form with its ambulatory and radiating chapels; an odd and very English expedient. Hidden behind the triple lancets in this E wall, an apsidal RETRO-CHAPEL defined by a screen wall; by *Scott*, 1934–5. At the same time he reordered the choir by bringing the High Altar W of the stalls, an idea suggested by Comper in 1925. The E arm is asymmetrical in plan, and

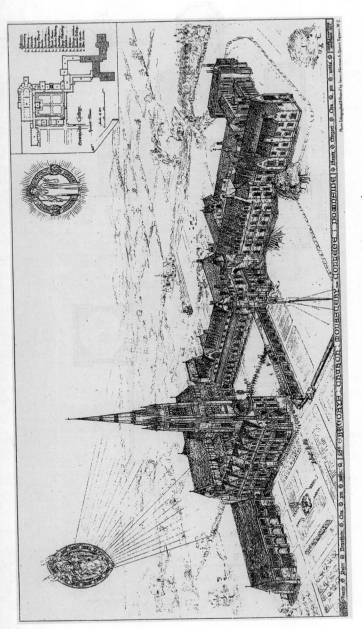

Stratton-on-the-Fosse, Downside Abbey, aerial perspective.
Engraving, 1879

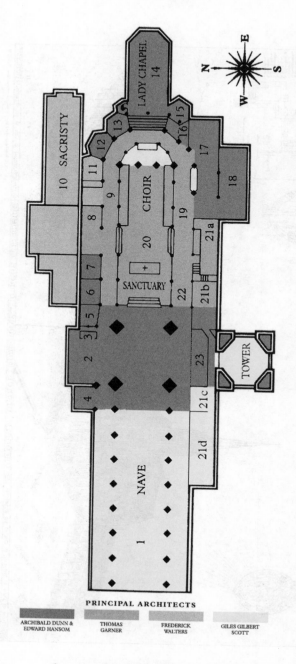

PRINCIPAL ARCHITECTS

| ARCHIBALD DUNN & EDWARD HANSOM | THOMAS GARNER | FREDERICK WALTERS | GILES GILBERT SCOTT |

Stratton-on-the-Fosse, Downside Abbey.
Plan

more complex than the standard French *chevet* with roughly equal chapels. The CHOIR N AISLE has conventional side chapels: at the W, Holy Angels of 1880–2, then St Placid and Seven Sorrows of 1891–2, all by *Dunn & Hansom*. The fourth (St Sebastian) is by *Garner*, built with the choir, and the fifth (St Sylvia) by *Walters*, with the sacristy. Then, on the NE side of the ambulatory, two polygonal chapels (St Joseph and St Vedast, by *Dunn & Hansom*, 1888–90); the axial Lady Chapel and, on the SE, the hexagonal Sacred Heart Chapel, both completed 1888. The E end of the S choir aisle has just two big rectangular chapels; St Benedict, and on its S side St Isidore, both *Dunn & Hansom*, 1887–9. *Garner*'s CHOIR S AISLE has on its outer side a blank wall dividing it from the monastic N cloister, on top of which is a series of GALLERY CHAPELS reached by stairs from the aisle. *Scott*'s NAVE reproduces Dunn & Hansom's forms only in the vault, elsewhere abstracting them in Scott's typically enjoyable manner. The arcade piers lose the roundness of the crossing's clustered shafts in favour of jutting polygons. Narrow passage aisles continue the lines of the ambulatory, and the triforium gallery has ogee arches and quatrefoils in place of lancets and trefoils. But there is continuity with Garner's choir and this is due to the monastic community, which rejected designs by Scott that contrasted more strongly.

FURNISHINGS, STAINED GLASS and MONUMENTS. From W to E. – NAVE N AISLE. MONUMENT to Abbot Ramsay †1929, by *Scott*. – N TRANSEPT. Elaborate ALTAR, REREDOS and TABERNACLE with central pinnacle 30 ft (9 metres) tall, by *Dunn & Hansom*, 1882; carver *Wall*. Gilded oak RELIQUARY of St Oliver Plunkett, on tall stone columns. By *Dom Ephrem Seddon*. STAINED GLASS. Two windows and a big rose above, by *Hardman*, 1882. – CHAPEL OF ST LAWRENCE, W of the N transept. Refitted by *Walters*, 1898. ALTAR with Perp SCREEN behind. RELIC CUPBOARD painted by *N. H. J. Westlake*, 1898. STAINED GLASS. Two by *Lavers & Westlake*, 1882. – S TRANSEPT. Stylized Gothic ORGAN SCREEN of repeated vertical openings, by *Scott*, 1931; carver *Ferdinand Stüflesser* of Ortisei, in the Italian Tyrol. – CHOIR. STALLS. 1931–3 by *Scott*, after the late C14 stalls at Chester Cathedral. Carved by *Stüflesser*'s workshop, with densely pinnacled canopies and statues above. Front two rows of seats 1951, also *Stüflesser*. STAINED GLASS. E window. *Comper*, 1936, in vivid indigo and gold. – SACRISTY. Splendidly architectural oak fittings by *Walters*, c. 1915. Altar, reredos, fitted cupboards and vesting benches, all with linenfold.

CHOIR N AISLE. MONUMENT. Thomas Garner †1906. Central crucifixion panel by *G. F. Bodley*, the rest executed after Bodley's death probably by *F. A. Walters*. – CHAPELS. CHAPEL OF THE HOLY ANGELS. Small Flemish TRIPTYCH of c. 1540, derived from an original by Pieter Coecke van Aelst, possibly painted by a disciple of his who painted an identical triptych at the church of the Beguinage, Leuven, Belgium. PARCLOSE SCREEN by *F. C. Eden*, c. 1930–3, Perp with flattened ornament. – CHAPEL OF ST PLACID. Far-from-placid fittings, c. 1915–16. ALTAR and REREDOS; panels with six saints painted by *Dame Catherine Weeks*, coloured and gilded by *Geoffrey Webb* who also designed the archangels above. PARCLOSE SCREEN by *F. C. Eden*. STAINED GLASS by Messrs *Hardman*, 1892. – CHAPEL OF THE SEVEN SORROWS. REREDOS by *Hansom*, carver *Wall*, 1892, recoloured and gilded by *John Tolhurst*, 1955. In its centre, a Crucifixion PANEL, probably from the region of Regensburg, Germany, c. 1480–90. PARCLOSE SCREEN by *F. C. Eden*, c. 1920. STAINED GLASS by Messrs *Hardman*, 1892. – CHAPEL OF ST SEBASTIAN. Refitted under *Comper*, 1929; by him, the REREDOS with alabaster figure of St Sebastian, and a Perp stone SCREEN (the w bay completed by *Gilbert Sumsion*, 1972). Later C15 PAINTING of five saints attributed to *Francesco Botticini*. MONUMENT. Van Cutsem family, by *Comper*, c. 1929; low tomb with Purbeck marble slab. – CHAPEL OF ST SYLVIA. Medieval ALTAR SLAB from Cannington, Somerset, installed early 1930s. Big stone RELIEF of the Crucifixion, by *Dom Hubert van Zeller*, c. 1960s. – CHAPEL OF ST JOSEPH. STATUE. St Joseph with the infant Christ, designed by *Dom Hubert van Zeller*, carved by *Dupré*. – STAINED GLASS possibly by Messrs *Hardman*, c. 1890–2, as is that in the Chapel of St Vedast.

92   LADY CHAPEL. Sumptuous fittings by *Comper*, begun in 1898: ENGLISH ALTAR with alabaster and gilt REREDOS; fine square TESTER hung from the vault, 1912, with a Coronation of the Virgin on the underside; on the screen wall behind, four gilded RELIC CHESTS and a ROOD, also c. 1912; SCREEN AND GATES, 1927–8, fine Spanish-inspired wrought-iron; STATUE of the Virgin, c. 1915, on the trumeau at the entrance, of painted and gilded limewood. STAINED GLASS. A set of nine by *Comper*, three in the apse fitted 1899–1911, the rest c. 1919–27. MONUMENT. Edmund Bishop †1917, inscription by *Eric Gill*, l. of the Lady Chapel entrance. – SACRED HEART CHAPEL, s of the Lady Chapel. Decorated with ceramic reliefs by *Adam Kossowski*, c. 1954–6. STAINED GLASS, three by *Comper*, 1915–c. 1916.

CHOIR S AISLE. An outstanding limewood SCULPTURE of the Virgin and Child, with freely handled swirling drapery. Attributed by Pevsner to *Nicolaus Gerhaert* of Leiden, 1465–6, or to a Strasbourg follower of Gerhaert, perhaps an altar statue for Konstanz Minster. Since ascribed a more likely date *c.* 1470. – MONUMENTS. Cardinal Gasquet †1929. By *Scott*, carver *E. Carter Preston*; a marble effigy with beautifully linear and stylized angels, beneath a stained and gilded pine canopy mixing Gothic and Renaissance forms. Bishop Peter Baines †1843. Alabaster effigy by *Wall*, 1913.*

CHAPELS, choir S aisle. CHAPEL OF ST BENEDICT. Furnishings by *F. A. Walters*, 1896. Fine triptych REREDOS, painted by *N. H. J. Westlake*. PARCLOSE SCREEN by *Walters*, 1897. STAINED GLASS, two by *Lavers & Westlake*, 1896–7, densely drawn. – CHAPEL OF ST ISIDORE. Fittings by *Garner*, 1901. Marble pavement made by *Farmer & Brindley*. STAINED GLASS by *Lavers & Westlake*, E window *c.* 1894, S 1896. – GALLERY CHAPEL OF THE BLESSED RICHARD WHITING. STAINED GLASS, one by *N. H. J. Westlake* (*c.* 1907?), the l. †1915, by *Geoffrey Webb*.

OTHER BUILDINGS. Of the MONASTIC RANGES, the W RANGE   93
is by *Dunn & Hansom*, 1873–6: 'dismal Victorian neo-Gothic, restless without being picturesque' (Pevsner). Originally of two storeys; two gabled attic storeys added *c.* 1899. There is more poetry in the austere rib-vaulted cloister on the ground floor of this range. Dogtooth on the ribs. Its N continuation runs alongside the abbey nave and passes through the base of the tower. This part served as a temporary church, 1876–82. The S side of the cloister garth appears open, with a raised terrace walk which sits above the PETRE CLOISTER, also 1870s; this is at the basement of the W range, owing to the falling ground. Also at basement level in the E range, the WELD CLOISTER, remodelled *c.* 1950, has simple, heavy chamfered vault ribs. This was overbuilt with a three-storey GUEST WING and refectory by *Francis Pollen* (of *Brett & Pollen*), 1970–5. Buff brick and concrete, with repeated angular projections in the attic storey. A glazed bridge links the first floor with *Pollen*'s fine polygonal LIBRARY to the E (1966–9), managing six floors without dominating either the abbey or the school. The blind two-storey base is square, with catalogue and reading rooms above, then a two-storey polygon of book stacks with obscure-glazed walls. The core is a spiral staircase.

The REFECTORY range, a high collegiate Perp hall by *Dunn & Hansom*, links the SE corner of the monastic cloister with the school. DOWNSIDE HOUSE, or Old School, built *c.* 1700, is somewhat buried among the later school buildings. Of three storeys with mullioned two-light windows and steep hipped roof. A T-shaped lancet-style addition against its W side was built in 1823 by *H. E. Goodridge*: transepts contain a chapel at first floor, what appears to be an aisled nave was school accommodation. In the chapel, a good white alabaster STATUE of the

---

*Not on display: small DIPTYCH of Christ and his sorrowing mother, after the style of *Simon Marmion*, *c.* 1475–1500; St John Baptist, large oil PAINTING attributed to *Lazzaro Bastiani*, a pupil of Mantegna, late C15; fine ivory CRUCIFIX attributed to *Andreas Faistenberger* (1646–1735).

Virgin and Child, by *Wall*, 1883. Adjacent to its w is an L-shaped school range of 1853–4 by *Charles Hansom*, rather Puginesque in style. For the early C20 expansion, the community was fortunate in selecting *Leonard Stokes* as its architect. He envisaged two quads s and se of the earlier buildings, separated by a range with a towering s entrance. Of this only one-eighth was built, in 1910–12; a big tower connecting with Hansom's range, and from it an L-shaped wing with big gable ends, running s and then e. It shows the happy combination of tradition and originality so typical of Stokes. Especially characteristic the square tower in the w range with its restrained Arts and Crafts detail, and the alternation of rough and smooth stone to unite all parts of the composition and to emphasize the vertical connection between the wide mullioned-and-transomed main windows. *Sir Giles Gilbert Scott* in 1932 and 1939 completed the s range at its e end and added the L-shaped Science Block to the w of Stokes's tower, in a consciously similar though plainer and squarer style. *Brett, Boyd & Bosanquet* added a theatre, gymnasium and two school houses to the e of Old School, *c.* 1956–8. A little way ne, a three-storey girls' school house by *NVB Architects*, opened 2006.

7060

SWAINSWICK

St Mary, Upper Swainswick. Small Norman nave and chancel, with a simple Dec w tower, Dec s porch, C15 N aisle and chapel. Many restorations and repairs. Chancel twice extended, the last time *c.* 1921–4. Late Norman s doorway. One order of columns with scalloped capitals. Arch with three-dimensional chevrons, hoodmoulds with dogtooth on two headstops. The w tower is squat, plain and unbuttressed, with saddleback roof behind a parapet. Two double-chamfered arches inside, opening e and s. Built perhaps in the C13, within the nw corner of the Norman nave. On the se tower pier is a demi-angel in a shaped niche. The Dec work on the nave s side is of quite a high order. Porch entrance with big ogee head, well modelled (without capitals). Stoup inside with ornate gabling. e of the porch, a three-light reticulated window of dramatic ogee profile. Standard Perp N arcade, big panelled arch between chapel and chancel. In the chapel's N wall a shallow four-centred arched recess with leafy spandrels, like a fireplace. – Altar with C17 frame. – Font, octagonal with moulded underside (re-cut?), on a cylindrical E.E. foot. – Royal Arms. 1647. – Monuments. The architect John Wood the Elder, †1754. Plain, self-effacing ledger slab. – Mary Morgan †1794, by *Reeves*. Tablet with draped urn.*

---

*Brass to Edmund Forde †1439, chancel floor, a 2-ft (61-cm.) figure. Stolen 2002, leaving inscription plate and three lettered scrolls.

Swainswick, St Mary.
Wash drawing, by Samuel Hieronymus Grimm, 1790

MANOR HOUSE, NW, is mid-C17. Tidied up a little too thoroughly in the C19, with flat parapet, boxy Gothic porch and regular four-light mullioned windows. To the w, a BARN dated 1629, of seven bays, still with buttresses and tie- and collar-beam roof. 150 yds NNE of the church, HILL HOUSE. Garden front (s) with plain C18 centre with sashes, but a steeply gabled section at the r., perhaps late C16 or C17, with some ovolo mullions. 175 yds E is BEECH HOUSE. A simple early C18 house of ashlar, pilastered, with pedimented centre. C19 square bay, r.

TELLISFORD

ALL SAINTS. s porch perhaps C15. Unbuttressed, three-stage w tower, *c.* 1490; parapet with shallow crenellations, square-headed belfry lights with Somerset tracery, and small quatre-foils only in the middle stage. Tall tower arch with continuous wave moulding. The nave windows with diamond stops must be of about the same date, but in the chancel two Dec s windows. The inner s doorway is the most interesting feature architecturally. Late Norman arch with a row of heavy moulded chevrons frontal to the face, and an outer row of flat-tened chevrons. The columns are E.E. with typical moulded capitals, the large headstops of the hoodmould believed to be *c.* 1320. Tall chancel arch of 1854, replacing a narrow opening with Norman fragments. – PULPIT. Small, oak, dated 1608 in the typically short blank arches, heavily incised with linked circles. Very similar to the pulpit at Westwood, Wiltshire, a few miles away. – FONT. Octagonal, quite plain, perhaps *c.* 1200 but much reworked. – Other fittings good Neo-Perp, 1931–6: CHANCEL SCREEN incorporating late C15 cornice. – STAINED GLASS. E window, *Clayton & Bell*, 1863. W window, late C19, by *Horwood Bros.* Also theirs, nave S, E of porch, 1884. Much better the window W of the porch (*Powell & Sons, c.* 1908). – MONUMENTS. Proficient Neoclassical tablets by *Chapman* of Frome, to Edward Crabb †1810 and Ann Crabb †1816.

CRABB HOUSE, polite early to mid-C18, of five bays, depressed-arched upper window over a doorcase with broken pediment. Early C19 roof. Rear wing with mullioned lights. To its l., cobbled steps twist steeply down to the river and TELLIS-FORD MILL, a cloth mill from at least 1574, run by the Crabb family *c.* 1710–*c.* 1900. Rebuilt as a hydro-electrical generator *c.* 2002–8, by *Klaentschi & Klaentschi.* E across the valley VAGGS HILL FARMHOUSE, dated 1615, for Peter Crooke, clothier, who took over the mill. Ovolo mullions, semicircular stair-turret with broad newel stairs, handsome hall fireplace with interlace in the frieze.

TEMPLE CLOUD

ST BARNABAS. By *W. D. Caröe*, 1924–6. An unusual date for a country church, and a good addition to Somerset's stock. Grey-brown rock-faced Pennant walls with Pennant dressings; long and low, to a simple rectangular plan. Short transeptal organ chamber, vestry to its E. Round-arched openings. Sturdy bellcote (SW) with its own little roof and chimney. Weighty round-arched roof trusses. – REREDOS. Ambitious relief trip-tych (Risen Christ with musical angels) carved by an aunt of the soldier commemorated. – Fine STALLS, PULPIT etc., of 1925. Neo-C17 motifs. – VICARAGE by *Herbert Passmore*, late 1920s; styleless.

POLICE STATION and COURTS (former). By *James Wilson*, 1857. Big grey-stone Jacobean Revival. *Wilson* also rebuilt CHOL-WELL HOUSE, S of the Clutton, in the same style in 1855 for the local magistrate, William Rees-Mogg.

CAMBROOK HOUSE, Eastcourt Road. The former Clutton Union workhouse, by *Jesse Gane*, 1836–7. Late Classical. Three-storey main block, with centre pediment, stepping down to long single-storey wings. Behind was a semi-hexagonal range (replaced by housing, 1980s), more usually associated with the Y-plan layout of workhouses.

BRIDGE HOUSE, S on the Wells Road. A characteristic Mendip farmhouse *c.* 1750; symmetrical, four mullioned windows, and an arched light above the door.

TICKENHAM

ST QUIRICUS AND ST JULIETTA. A rarity for Somerset – a parish church which is not predominantly Perp. The earliest survival is the narrow unmoulded chancel arch with simplest imposts, probably no later than 1100. The sizeable nave and chancel are also essentially early Norman. Early in the C13 aisles and a S chapel were added. The walls were simply cut through with chamfered and pointed arches. The S aisle was originally two bays only, that is the two W bays. The second pier of the S arcade, originally the easternmost, was singled out for additional decoration of the angles on its W face, two shafts with fine (though re-cut) stiff-leaf capitals. Several early Norman cathedral and abbey naves (e.g. Romsey, Norwich, Peterborough) have one pier similarly distinguished in plan or decoration, believed to indicate the position of nave altars or of a screen separating laity and clergy. Could this have applied in such a small church? The S doorway could belong to this original S aisle. Of c. 1230 the S porch and its outer door. This has slim Blue Lias colonnettes with moulded capitals and a little very small dogtooth, and a trefoiled pointed arch. About 1300 the S chapel was either given new windows or rebuilt, see the cusped lancet, two-light window with Y-tracery, and three-light window of three stepped cusped lancet lights. At the same time the chancel received a three-light E window with intersected tracery. Mid-C14 Dec, the S aisle W window and especially the N aisle windows which are straight-headed with reticulated tracery. The C13 S aisle was extended E in the late C15 to join the S chapel – see the ashlar walls and Perp window with ogee lights. Square-headed windows were inserted E and W of the porch, perhaps 1500–20. Also Perp, the blank-arcaded S aisle parapet. Three-stage W tower with diagonal buttresses, c. 1450–90. W doorway, four-light W window, two-light blank windows, two-light bell-openings with ogee-headed lights. Late C19 crown, in the right spirit: tall diagonally set pinnacles, crenellated parapet with blind arcading, an image niche on each side, higher stair-turret with blank arcading and a spirelet. Tower arch with two wave mouldings.

FURNISHINGS. ALTARS. Stone and alabaster slabs on fine glazed *Eltonware* columns, 1895. – PULPIT. Oak, Jacobean, decorative relief panels in two tiers. – FONT, c. 1300. Square bowl with blank trefoiled pointed arch-heads, on a strong central stem with four slim Blue Lias shafts. – Neo-Perp SCREEN, S chapel. 1911. – ROYAL ARMS. Charles II. Carved and painted. – STAINED GLASS. The only complete C14 figures in Somerset apart from Wells Cathedral. All restored (*Joseph Bell*, 1877), and again by *Alfred Fisher*, 1981. In the S chapel, excellent small figures of Christ Crucified (cf. Wells Crucifixion, c. 1320), and Christ in Majesty. Two N aisle windows with heraldic shields probably c. 1370–90, and

another figure in the typical C14 green. E window, *Wippell &
Co.*, 1969. – MONUMENTS. Three good effigies: two knights,
one of *c.* 1240–50, the other cross-legged later C13, and a lady
of *c.* 1300. – Samuel Bave †1715, by *Michael Sidnell*; fluted
pilasters, broken pediment.

TICKENHAM COURT. Immediately N of the church. A most gratifying survival, a late C15 hall and at its W end running S, small
and great solars. Planned as one but built in two phases: Hall
of 1471, solar wing *c.* 1476 or shortly after. The hall has large
two-light windows with ogee heads on the N and S sides, and
front and back doors for a screens passage along its E wall. Two
blocked doorways with four-centred heads in the E wall led to
a service wing, seemingly replaced as early as 1571–5 by a long
wing running N from the W end of the hall. High up between
the two windows two shallow corbels on each side, with blank
quatrefoil decoration. What purpose can they have served? Hall
roof with collar-beams and arched braces; evidence of decorative cusped wind-braces, removed. In the angle between hall
and solar, two blocked arches to a lost oriel chamber. The joint
in the wall of the solar wing shows its extent. This wing must
have looked very festive with its large windows. In its S gable
wall, a large arched upper window (originally at least four
lights) has been reopened with plain glazing. In the E wall one
straight-headed transomed four-light window survives. The
upper lights are ogee, the lower pointed; all are cusped. Private
newel stair in the W wall at the N end of the solar wing. The
first-floor great solar has a good roof with collar-beams, arched
braces, and three tiers of wind-braces.

THE ORCHARD, Orchard Avenue. Colonial Neo-Georgian, by
Oliver Hill, 1939–40. Timber-framed, of Canadian red cedar,
boarded below, shingled above. Slightly projecting centre with
pediment, round-arched garden entrance below, shuttered
casements. A little W, EAST END FARM (i.e. the E end of Clevedon), C17, two storeys with gabled wings projecting at the sides.

CADBURY CAMP IRON AGE HILL-FORT, 3¼ m. E of Clevedon.
Roughly oval in plan, with a double circuit of ditches and banks
enclosing 6 acres. Additional outworks added protection on the
W side and outside an entrance on the N side.

TIMSBURY

ST MARY. The embodiment of Pugin's *Contrasts*. E end by *Scott*,
1852. Long chancel with shorter chapels. Rich blend of Dec
and Perp: dense tracery, solid parapets with quatrefoil friezes,
prominent angle buttresses. Bald Commissioners'-style W end,
by *G. A. Underwood*, 1826. Short tower with tall pinnacles,
four-bay nave with typical Y-tracery under four-centred heads.
Inside, harmonious despite the mixed parentage. Four-centred
arcades to narrow aisles, thin imitation Perp piers. W gallery,
remodelled 1852. – STAINED GLASS. Splendidly coloured E

window, *Wailes*, 1863. Chancel N and S, each with two Evan-
gelists, probably also Wailes. S chapel E by *Joseph Bell*, *c.* 1886.
N aisle, one by *Hardman*, 1906. – MONUMENTS. Sir Barnaby
Samborne †1610. Armoured recumbent effigy. Chest-tomb
base remodelled perhaps in 1826, with bald fluted pilasters. –
Plenty of minor early C19 work, especially by *King* (†1815),
Lancashire (†1814, †1846), *Greenway* (†1808, †1826), *Reeves*
(†1823, a kneeling woman by an altar; also †1837, †1841),
H. Wood (†1842), *Tyley* (†1843). – Churchyard. Two good chest
tombs. Bartholomew Smith †1782. Angled scrolls at the
corners. – Rev. Bartholomew Deeke Smith †1815; flared
sarcophagus.

Four chapels are still in use. The best is the METHODIST
CHAPEL, 1805. Tall, with round arches, naïve pinnacles on the
gables. Galleried interior, complete pine fittings, perhaps 1880s.

CHURCH COTTAGE, Church Hill, has one upper-cruck roof
truss, felled 1444–5.* Many worthwhile polite Georgian
houses, unusual for a mining village. PARISH'S HOUSE, ¼ m.
E. Attributed to *Thomas Baldwin* of Bath, *c.* 1816. Three bays
by three, ashlar-faced. Entrance side (N) with segmentally projecting porch with Doric columns and triglyph frieze; flanking
windows set in arched recesses. On the S side, a shallow central
bow. The offices, E side, were the original C18 house. Behind
the porch lies a circular lobby. Elegant top-lit hall, square with
rounded corners and an open-well cantilevered staircase. At
the W end of the village, VALE HOUSE (Cheshire Home), 1802,
and ROSEWOOD MANOR (formerly Kenny's) *c.* 1800, both
three storeys and ashlar-faced with ground-floor Venetian
windows. Vale House has its back to the road. The Venetian
motif occurs too in the early C19 OLD RECTORY, a little E of
the church.

RADFORD FARM HOUSE, ⅝ m. SSE. Dated 1759. Three storeys
and three bays, even quoins at the angles, flat parapet. Paired
sashes with broad flush surrounds under cornices. The surrounds bond in one place on each side with the wall. Flat
doorway as well.

TYNTESFIELD *see* WRAXHALL

UBLEY

ST BARTHOLOMEW. Red sandstone. C13, with Perp aisles.
Restored 1875 by *John Prichard* of Llandaff. C13 W tower (see
the N lancet and the stair-turret doorway inside), chancel
(two lancets), and chancel arch, the latter re-cut with Perp

*TIMSBURY HOUSE of *c.* 1610, NW of the church, was demolished in 1961.

mouldings. Upper tower and tower arch (two wave mouldings) remodelled perhaps *c.* 1390–1410. A square stair-turret rises oddly high above the s parapet, competing with the small ribbed spire. s aisle probably C15; parapets with pierced cusped lozenge frieze, humble arcade with standard piers (shafts and hollows) and double-chamfered arches. Good late C15 tracery, E. N aisle widened in the late C14 (see the w wall and window), the four-centred N windows probably C16. N arcade perhaps altered later too, crudely mimicking the s.

ALTAR. Dated 1637, bulbous legs, robust patterning. – REREDOS. Made up in the late C19; a medley of C16 or C17 carving. – SCREENS. Probably 1875. – PULPIT. Early C17, arched panels. – FONT. Norman, square bowl of cushion-capital form with big lobed corners. – Gothic chamber ORGAN; good early C19 mahogany case. – STAINED GLASS. E window by *J. B. Capronnier,* 1877. By *Bell & Son,* the w window and two others (chancel and N aisle W), 1910s. s aisle, a spirited design by *John Hall & Sons* (*J. A. Crombie*), 1965.

METHODIST CHAPEL. Proudly elevated, with a little display of debased Lombardic tracery, *c.* 1870.

On the grassed triangle outside the church, a big MEMORIAL CROSS, 1901. To the s, tucked unobtrusively behind other houses, TREES, a sleek and subtle rectangle by *Rebecca & Jim Dyer* (*RD Architects Ltd*), 2005–7, for themselves. A remarkable feat in a conservation area, and preferable to the usual 'renovations'. Red cedar-clad first floor which seems to float at the level of the tree canopy over a ground floor fully glazed to the s and w. The first floor projects on these two façades, for shade and articulation. Open-plan interiors, and a shallow monopitch roof nicely judged to read from within. A little w of the church, a group of overtly modern houses of *c.* 1969–70 by *Artist Constructor,* with *Peter Smith*: polygonal plans, in a Spanish idiom.

UPHILL

At first glance a southern suburb of Weston-super-Mare. Protected from the sea by the outcrop on which stands the medieval church. s is the little creek or pill of the River Axe, the Roman port of Axium. It traded in the C17 as a duty-free port, and was still active in the 1860s.

ST NICHOLAS, Uphill Road South. 1841–4 by *James Wilson.* Hints of Commissioners' Gothic. Aisleless nave of Bath stone, thin open timber roof. The w tower is square at the base, changing to an octagon with big detached corner shafts hiding the diagonals, and attached at the top by little pieces of tracery. Angle pinnacles. Incongruously high rubble-stone chancel, 1891–2, by *G. F. Burr* of Hastings. Also his, N porch, baptistery etc. – FONT. From Old St Nicholas. Octagonal and apparently

Uphill, Old St Nicholas.
Engraving, 1829

of two dates, the underside with upright leaves and crockets
C13, the foliage of the bowl re-cut in the C15. – STAINED
GLASS. E window by *Bell & Son*, 1882. Another by them in the
nave, 1876.

OLD ST NICHOLAS (Churches Conservation Trust). Isolated
and perilously close to a high cliff edge, with views across Somerset and the Bristol Channel. The plan is essentially Norman:
nave, central tower without transepts, and chancel. No W or E
windows. Nave roof removed in 1864. Norman are two chancel
lights (N), one S tower window with Mass dial above, and the
two nave doorways, both very minor. In the tympanum of the
S door, a cross within a circle, and another Mass dial. Over
the N door an interlaced design of lobes within a circle. Tower
probably rebuilt in the C15; see the coursed stonework, Perp
tower arches, pinnacles, and stair-turret with spirelet. Pierced
parapet of quatrefoils in squares, generally in Somerset a Tudor
motif, reinstated 1930. Also a blocked nave window (SE), late
C15 ogee-headed lights. N porch rebuilt using the old materials after it collapsed in 1904.

UPHILL MANOR, Uphill Road South. Described in an Act of
Parliament of 1799 as 'lately built' for Simon Payne. A drawing
survives at the Society of Antiquaries, London. But the present
picturesque castellated Gothic mansion is as enlarged by *Henry
Rumley* of Bristol, *c.* 1835, for Thomas Tutton Knyfton Jun.,
and its extension E *c.* 1856 by *James Wilson*. The S front is probably largely by Rumley. Low, with simple battlements. Wilson's
work is Perp; E porch and corridor, octagonal hall rising to a
large turret, big gabled drawing room, and conservatory to its
S. Fine interior decoration of *c.* 1856 by *J. G. Crace*, inspired by
his collaboration with A. W. N. Pugin, 1844–52, and his most
complete extant scheme after Abney Hall, Cheshire, and
Eastnor Castle, Herefs. In the drawing room, *Pugin*-designed

wallpaper, stencilling derived from his *Floriated Ornament* (1849), and a splendid iron radiator cover, possibly by *Hardman*. Castellar GATE LODGE, by *Wilson*, 1859.

For the General Hospital, Grange Road, *see* Weston-super-Mare.

UPPER MILTON

5040

MANOR FARM HOUSE. The symmetry of the E front suggests a date *c.* 1675–95, supported by the upright oval windows in the gables of the two projecting wings. Between them lies a recessed three-bay front with mullioned windows of two to four lights under hoodmoulds. S side updated with sash windows. (Two fine splat-baluster staircases, three early C18 panelled rooms.)

VOBSTER

7040

ST EDMUND (former). By *Benjamin Ferrey*, 1846. No W tower, short two-and-a-half-bay nave with S porch, and a chancel. Dec details. Tall interior with thick leaf corbels for the hammer-beam roof. Redundant 1983, now a house.

A few C17 and later houses where the road winds across a valley. At the centre, a BRIDGE with four low arches, reportedly of 1764. About ½ m. W are the ruins of VOBSTER NEW PIT, a breach colliery extant 1861–84. Standing remains include two banks of twenty-eight brick coking ovens. About twelve are intact. SE of Vobster Cross, a well-preserved ½-m. section of the bed of the Dorset and Somerset Canal, *c.* 1798–1800.

WALTON-IN-GORDANO

4070

ST PAUL. Built 1838–9, possibly incorporating an earlier chapel. Plain nave with short transepts, small W tower with saddleback roof. C15 N porch from Walton St Mary (*see* Clevedon). Chancel perhaps by *John Norton* who restored Walton St Mary, *c.* 1869. – FITTINGS. Mostly Perp, early C20. – FONT. Perhaps C14, from Walton St Mary. Plain octagonal. – STAINED GLASS. Reputedly made by the *Rev. Rawden Hautenville*, rector 1866–80. Remarkably C20 in flavour. Nave N 1870, S, 1873. E window (three lancets) in same style. He may have also painted the pointed wagon-vault its startling emerald colour with patterned ribs.

MANOR HOUSE. Long S front, *c.* 1700. Two storeys, gabled ends, eight leaded casements on each floor. Hipped dormers. Squarish addition to the W, *c.* 1780. Little changed externally since it was painted by S. H. Grimm *c.* 1789 (British Library).

WALTON ST MARY *see* CLEVEDON

WANSDYKE

Late C6/early C7 linear earthwork with its bank on the N side, extending from Odd Down to the S of Bath to Maes Knoll via Stantonbury; the bank overlies the defences of both hill-forts. Other visible sections can be seen SE of Breach Wood, Englishcombe; in the S bank of the lane E of Englishcombe church; 330 yds W of the A39/B3116 road junction, Compton Dando; 550 yds E of Compton Dando; and 875 yds N of Norton Malreward. Called West Wansdyke to distinguish it from East Wansdyke, Wilts. For interpretations, *see* p. 18.

WARLEIGH MANOR
1 m. S of Bathford

7060

On the wooded E slope of the Avon valley. A surprisingly early Tudor Revival villa by *John Webb* of Staffordshire, *c.* 1814–15 for Henry Skrine, replacing a house *c.* ¼ m. S. Enlarged in keeping by *J. S. Alder* of London, 1907–8. Picturesque castellated towers and turrets. Originally rectangular with thin turrets, some big oriel windows and cusped tracery in the glazing bars. Made more asymmetrical in plan and elevation by plainer additions, especially on the entrance front, NW. To the E, lower castellated outbuildings and an orangery, also buttressed and embattled.

WELLOW

7050

A large village with abundant honey-coloured limestone and the money to build with it.

ST JULIAN. A proud, little altered, stylistically very uniform church, masculine rather than refined. If the date *c.* 1372 could be established, its historical importance would be high indeed; but the source of the tradition is unverified. On the basis of

John Harvey's careful analysis of Somerset Perp, some details of tracery, hoodmoulds etc., suggest a date after *c.* 1440. Wellow's uniformity is in fact only an impression; for the chancel is by *Bodley & Garner*, 1889–90 – proof of how self-effacingly they could work. General restoration by *B. Ferrey*, 1845. Externally the robust W tower is (of course) dominant. Set-back buttresses continued above into diagonally set pinnacles which appear as an unusual motif above the battlements – joining hands round the corner, as it were. Higher SE stair-turret. Three-light W window with transom, and three-light bell-openings. The tower, like the rest of the church, is ashlar-faced. Nave, aisles and chancel all have battlements. In addition there is a S rood-stair turret also embattled, and a S porch with the concave-sided steep gable that occurs elsewhere in NE Somerset (cf. Mells, Doulting). Three-light Perp windows in the aisles and clerestory, the former with C15 ogee heads and expensive tracery details. Light spacious interior. Four-bay arcade with standard piers (four hollows and shafts). The same standard moulding in the tower arch. Good C15 nave roof, shallow-pitched with tie-beams on wall-posts resting on big demi-figures. Also good roofs in the S aisle and N (Hungerford) chapel. In the chapel's N wall, a shallow recess, with a quatre-foiled front below and a four-centred arch above. On the ledge an inscription referring to the building of the chapel: 'For love of Jesu and Mary's sake, Pray for them that this lete make.' The N chapel was restored by *Browne* of Bath, 1878, and again in 1950–2. A simpler recess, also with a four-centred head, in the N aisle wall.

FURNISHINGS. Perp ROOD SCREEN of one-light divisions with a broad four-centred doorway above which the divisions carry on. It has well-carved leaf spandrels. Elaborate Neo-Perp rood loft and figures by *Alban Caröe*, 1950–2, painted and gilded. – A simpler Perp SCREEN, also of one-light divisions, between the N aisle and its chapel. – BENCHES. Many old bench-ends with poppyheads and simple Perp tracery. – DOOR. Fine S door with six divisions and reticulated tracery. – FONT. Eight-lobed bowl on fat circular foot with eight attached shafts. Perhaps late C13. Ogee-domed COVER, 1623. – SCULPTURE. A series of twelve excellent small carved heads, probably early C14, re-set in the chancel E and S walls, 1952. – WALL PAINT-INGS (N chapel, E wall). They represent Christ and the Twelve Apostles, a unique subject so far in English medieval wall painting. The date probably *c.* 1500. Uncovered and restored *c.* 1951. – MONUMENTS. Effigy of a priest, *c.* 1400, N aisle. Dorothy Popham †1614. Tomb-chest with reclining effigy, sculpturally very poor. Under a low canopy, with black columns framing four small arches of which the middle two rest on a shorter column.

Opposite the church is CHURCH FARM, perhaps 1690s; a good L-shaped house with regular three-light windows and stone roof. To the W, a TUNNEL ENTRANCE to the former Somerset Coal Canal, *c.* 1800 (engineer *William Bennett*). MANOR

HOUSE, *c.* 150 yds w along High Street, is in two sections, the earlier a tall cross-gabled wing with rear porch dated 1634. Set half a storey lower, a later C17 wing; mullioned windows with hoodmoulds. A wooden overmantel with the Hungerford arms and small caryatids standing on larger heads was returned to the house before 1955. C17 winder stair with C18 twisted balusters. In Farm Lane, a circular thatched DOVECOTE belonging to the Manor House. C17 or earlier.

(ROMAN VILLA, 1 m. w of the village. Site of a large villa with two corridors whose rooms included hypocausts, baths and mosaics. Two flanking outbuildings created a courtyard whose open end was closed off with a wall. Another villa is known at White Ox Mead.)

STONEY LITTLETON CHAMBERED TOMB, ½ m. SSW of Wellow on a low promontory on the E side of the Wellow Brook. It has a trapezoid mound 100 ft (30 metres) long, originally flanked by quarry ditches which provided stones for the mound. A recessed forecourt at its SE end, revetted with dry-stone walling, leads to the entrance of two large orthostats supporting a lintel. Beyond this, a gallery gives access to three pairs of side chambers and an end chamber from which human bones were recovered.

WELLS

INTRODUCTION

Wells invites clichés: jewel, venerable, unique. They wash blandly over the uninitiated reader, but to arrive here is to realize with shocking suddenness that they are unavoidable and true. The city (for city it is, despite a population barely over 10,000) is justly famed for the early and purely English Gothic of its Cathedral, and its virtually complete gated medieval precinct, with the exquisite moated Bishop's Palace. As if all this were not enough, one emerges from the precinct into a lively market place, from which a few shopping streets of pretty medieval and Georgian buildings lead W to a fine parish church. For the traveller, Wells's memorable distinction is that from most directions, it is obscured until one is almost upon it. This is most intensely felt on the old approach from Shepton Mallet, where at the last possible moment, one rounds a wooded hillside to be confronted close-up with the glorious Cathedral, only to have it disappear again as the road descends. Only from the W may one experience the gentler thrill of distant views and gradual revelation. Moreover, one may walk N–S across the city and be in fields again in only two-thirds of a mile. The reason is that Wells sits between the Mendip Hills which rise gently to the N, and Palace Fields, the Bishop's park, which since 1207 has impeded expansion to the S.

The situation on a spring line accounts for the eponymous WELLS SE of the cathedral which still 'bubbles up so quick a spring' (Celia Fiennes, 1698). Some excavated Neolithic tools hint at early settlement, of which little else is known, but the view that Wells was first a Saxon settlement has been revised by the excavation of a small late Roman sepulchre S of the Cathedral. Small but undeniable finds of C1–C4 pottery and building material imply significant settlement, perhaps to the S around the Bishop's Palace, and possibly a military presence nearby. The springs were probably venerated in Roman times. There was a Saxon MINSTER by 766. SW of the Cathedral, the market place lies on a NE–SW axis that, as we now know, continued the alignment of the Saxon cathedral oriented on the springs. That alignment was first suggested in 1909 by W. H. St John Hope and sceptically ignored. But excavation in 1978–80 showed that the C10 cathedral, as well as earlier buildings, lay obliquely across the site of the present cloisters, on an axis from St Andrew's Well to the market place. The High Street and its surrounding grid are thought to have been laid out from that, with the parish church c. 450 yds W. So it seems we have here a partly preserved Saxon town plan, a secular layout generated by a church layout, all oriented on a spring of possibly pre-Christian sanctity. The area around St Cuthbert may have developed as a discrete Saxon community.* Markets and fairs were probably held by the C10, possibly in the (W) entrance court or atrium of the Cathedral (the garden site W of the present cloisters), but there was no burghal status, mint or defences, so Wells could not have rivalled Bath, Taunton or Ilchester.

Wells's medieval significance was reinforced by a charter of 1160, granting the right to hold three markets in the 'broad places'. Its boundaries were outlined by charter of 1201. Wells prospered from the C13, coincidental with the regaining of cathedral status in 1244, and was by the C14 the largest town in Somerset, based on wealth from wool and from its ecclesiastical status. In 1341 the burgesses received the right to 'enclose and fortify' the town, but after prolonged litigation it was withdrawn. Of the C15, Bishop Bekynton's rebus liberally displayed upon his

---

*A Saxon chapel of St Etheldreda existed in present-day Southover, re-dedicated after 1170. Demolished by 1542 (Leland).

works ensures he is the best-remembered of Wells's ecclesiastical builders. Bekynton had Renaissance intellectual interests, had travelled to France, and his Archdeacon, Andrew Holes, knew Florence.

There was much rebuilding from the C16, including some canonical houses and a market and assize hall. Good timber-framed buildings survive. But more noticeable in the centre is the extent of C18 brick and stone town houses, especially in Chamberlain Street and New Street. Wealth in this period came still from the woollen trade and especially stocking knitting. In 1735 Wells was said to be very flourishing, and chiefly inhabited by gentlemen and able tradesmen. The Town Hall and Assize Courts of 1778–80 and the Doric market hall (1835) represent the only significant post-medieval public buildings in the centre. Renewal of façades in High Street continued in the early C19. The widening of Broad Street and laying out of Priory Road in the late 1830s were the first major changes to the street plan since Tor Street in 1207. After 1870 there was little new building in the centre, but there was gradual, and now unremarked, restoration of medieval detail around the Market Place and Precinct. C20 suburban spread E, W and a little to the N has not harmed Wells's essential unity and smallness of scale. Since *c.* 1980 there has been significant backfilling in the lanes around High Street, both residential and commercial, without great harm but without leaving any positive architectural imprint.

CATHEDRAL CHURCH OF ST ANDREW

INTRODUCTION

The Cathedral as we now see it, the second at Wells, is mainly the work of two building periods. The first, from *c.* 1175 to *c.* 1250, saw completion of the eastern arm, transepts, nave and west front, and achieved the creation of a completely English yet completely Gothic style: Wells was the earliest English Gothic building to use pointed arches exclusively. Its second phase, *c.* 1285–*c.* 1345, saw the E end remodelled, construction of the crossing tower and the upper chapter house, and the dramatic strainer arches inserted; at that time Wells – together with Bristol – represents the most original treatment of architectural space of which Europe was capable. The only major later works are the Perp upper W towers and the rebuilt cloister.

The earliest surviving written record of the church is a charter of 766 referring to 'the minster near the Great Spring at Wells for the better service of God in the Church of St Andrew'. Excavation E of the cloister has also established the existence of a Saxon cemetery (burials of the C7–C11) around a small late Roman mausoleum. The relatively small SAXON CHURCH almost certainly lay obliquely across the site of the present cloister, at the

centre of a linear family of structures. This linear pattern was well
established for middle and late Saxon churches, cf. Canterbury,
Winchester Old Minster. Its form will remain uncertain unless
the cloister garth is excavated, but it is surmised to have had a
modest nave, probably with *porticus* at each side for important
burials. The W entrance court has been alluded to (*see* p. 637).
An apsidal E end lies under the E cloister walk; the tip of its curve
was recovered in excavation. Its foundations, at least 6 ft (1.8
metres) deep, suggest a crypt below. Wells became a cathedral in
909. In the mid C10 the Roman mausoleum was replaced with a
Lady Chapel, later enlarged. About the time of the Conquest
Bishop Giso built a link between the chapel and the eastern apse
of the Anglo-Saxon cathedral a few metres W, and erected claustral buildings on both sides. These seem to have been demolished
c. 1090 by Bishop John de Villula who moved the bishopric to
Bath, leaving the canons to 'live in common among the people'.
This lower status may have inhibited the usual Norman rebuilding, leaving the way clear for the Gothic experiment. Some building work at Wells was dedicated in 1148, and documents hint at
new foundations on a new alignment. There is no proof yet that
the later C12 plan was influenced in position of piers and outer
walls by that work.

p. 642

An entirely NEW CHURCH, the present one, was begun
c. 1175–6 by Bishop Reginald (†1191). Paul Binski sees this ambitious rebuilding as a bid to regain cathedral status, supported by
the C12 *Historiola*, a posthumous memoir of Bishop Giso written
some time after 1174, which sets out the historic precedents for
Wells as a bishopric. Construction began at the eastern arm
which from the start was as long as it is now and surrounded
by a square-ended ambulatory. A period of unrest followed
Reginald's death, yet work was sufficiently advanced to allow for
demolition of the Saxon church *c.* 1195–6 (excepting the
Lady Chapel) and the projection of the E walk of the intended
cloisters. Around 1200 it seems that seven Anglo-Saxon bishops
were reinterred in the new church, with five being marked by
newly commissioned tomb effigies (*see* S choir aisle), evidence of
the centrality of Wells's episcopal lineage in this new venture.
Transepts and crossing (with one or two E bays of the nave
sufficient to bolster the crossing) were begun in the mid
1180s. The unusual use of Chilcote stone in this part of the building occurs just at a time when Glastonbury, after a fire of 1184,
may have been monopolizing the Doulting quarry. Construction
of the nave began from the E *c.* 1191–5 and was completed as
far as the N porch break *c.* 1209. Bishop Jocelyn (succeeded
1206, out of England 1209–13, †1242) completed the nave, N
porch and W front. The craftsman in charge is thought to have
been *Adam Lock* (†1229) followed by *Thomas Norreys*. The
church was consecrated in 1239 and, after *c.* 154 years, cathedral
status was restored in 1244, with the bishopric renamed Bath and
Wells.

17

10, 12

The work of the period c. 1286–c. 1345 began with the decision to complete a 'nova structura' long since begun, which must be the chapter house, followed by a new E end with Lady Chapel, E transepts and retrochoir, and a new presbytery with renewed choir. The impetus for the new E end was probably the desire to provide, with easy access to side chapels, for processions associated with the Use of Sarum, the Salisbury liturgy which had been adopted at Wells by 1298. The style strongly suggests that *Thomas of Witney* was the master mason from shortly after 1306; probably synonymous with 'Thomas le Masun' named in deeds. He was probably responsible for the early C14 changes to the cathedral's E arm before moving on to Exeter by 1329. For the beginning of the Lady Chapel we have no date, but it was called 'newly constructed' in 1326 (Bishop Bitton I was reburied there in 1319). The retrochoir, containing part of the Lady Chapel vaulting-structure, was necessarily built with it. In 1325 several documents mention a 'novum opus', probably the eastward extension of choir and presbytery to join the retrochoir. Bishop Drokensford's burial took place in 1329 in the E transept S of the Lady Chapel. The mason *William Joy*, who may have trained in Bristol, was in charge from 1329. The high vault of the choir was presumably complete by c. 1340.

A new campanile (central tower) was begun in 1315 and there was a grant for roofing it in 1322. In 1338 the church is called 'enormiter confracta' and 'enormiter deformata'. It is thought that that refers solely to the effects of the new crossing tower on the crossing piers and that the astonishing strainer arches were the remedy. They can therefore be dated c. 1338–40, though the last phase of the plan for stabilizing the tower may have been concluded as late as 1356, partly postponed by the Plague, of which Joy may have died.

It may be assumed that the whole eastern arm was complete by 1345 at the latest. Later work tends to be underplayed in its effect on the cathedral. Early signs come in the early C14 choir grilles with their mullions extended downward as panelling, and the great E window tracery. Much simpler C15 tracery replaced the E.E. throughout nave and transepts. But its grandest appearance was in the late C14/early C15 W towers, the SW tower probably designed by *William Wynford*, in the noble mid-C15 rephrasing of the central tower's exterior – a wonderful achievement of calm power – and in the insertion of its late C15 fan-vault. Among the parish churches of Somerset are progeny of the central tower (Ilminster) and the W towers (Wells St Cuthbert, Wrington, Evercreech). Finally, the cloisters, where rebuilding began at the E range c. 1420, together with Bishop Stillington's new Lady Chapel (1477–86) on the site of the old. Completion of the W range was not until c. 1508.

EXTERIOR

The Cathedral was built mainly of limestone quarried at Doulting near Shepton Mallet, with Blue Lias shafting for contrast on the west front. The W towers are 124 ft high (38 metres), the crossing tower 182 ft (55.5 metres). The whole cathedral is 415 ft long; the C13 cathedral was c. 325 ft long (127 and 99 metres).

Early work: choir, transepts, nave and north porch

It is comparatively simple to appreciate the work of the first period outside. The subtler points of development come out more clearly inside. Church building as a rule started in the Middle Ages from the E. This was so at Wells too, beginning with the late C12 CHOIR. The best viewpoint is in the Camery churchyard to the E of the cloister (for which *see* p. 673). The broad aisle buttresses remain and the corbel table, and of the clerestory the narrower buttresses, the string course which goes round the original windows like a hoodmould, and again the corbel table. The break between the late C12 work and the early C14 remodelling is obvious enough, and it takes place in the clerestory one bay further W than in the aisle. Here interpretation has been radically revised by the discovery in 2008 that the late C12 wall plinth of the N choir aisle continued uninterrupted around the eastern arm; in other words, the eastern arm was not (as appears from the S side) a three-bay E.E. building lengthened to six bays in the C14, but was from the start as long as it is now. The three Dec bays represent a remodelling only. The visual break is, with the upper west front, the most awkward transition in the building phases at Wells.

p. 663

The main TRANSEPTS come next. They have both E and W aisles. But they differ in other ways. That on the S side is more easily visible than in monastic cathedrals, where extensive buildings usually rise to the E of the cloister. It has broad buttresses, three ground-floor windows, then a row of blank pointed arches with continuous roll moulding – the hallmark of Wells, as we shall see – cut into by the lowered sills of three stepped lancets above. The gable again has three stepped lancets, the central one wider and blank. On the buttresses stand tall polygonal pinnacles like chimneys, their long shafts with blank arcading, again without any capitals. The E aisle windows were enlarged in conjunction with the new presbytery, i.e. are not of the simple early C15 forms that most other windows are.

At the S end of the S transept's W aisle is the Chilcote stone doorway from the E walk of the cloister, of c. 1184–9; this was the first processional entrance to the E arm, hence its elaboration. It is tall and rather narrow, suggesting the loftiness of the earlier cloisters, with an inner continuous chamfer, then two pairs of columns on each side separated by a step in the jamb. The columns have one shaft-ring and stiff-leaf capitals. The capitals are more developed than in the choir, less than in the nave. Broad arch with delicately undercut filigree of stiff-leaf and scrolls arranged in oblong sections. The hoodmould on headstops is damaged by the later cloister.

On the N transept the pinnacles on the buttresses are in three tiers, with blank panelling. The blank arcade below the main

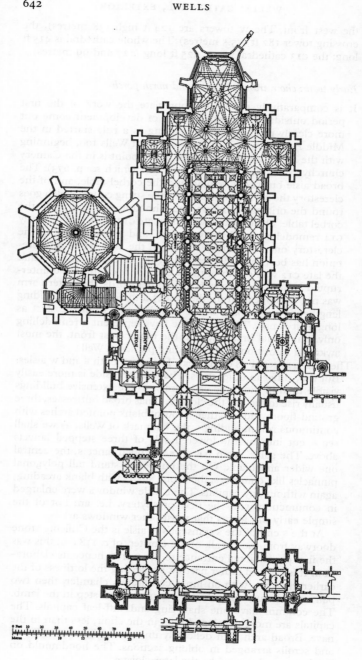

Wells Cathedral.
Plan

upper windows has six arches, of which the two outer ones are higher. The window zone consists of three tall arches of even height and two narrow blank bays l. and r. Under the tall arches are three stepped lancets, and above the lower of them paterae of stiff-leaf foliage, the first appearance of another Wells leit-motif. In the gable finally there are twelve stepped blank arches with continuous moulding. Above the middle pair stiff-leaf in the spandrel. The greater variety of motifs in the N transept than in the S is perhaps a sign of later completion.

The NAVE foundations were laid, on the best calculations, c. 1185–90, and the walls begun c. 1191–5. Its compositional system is again very simple. Broad buttresses below, narrow p. 658 buttresses above. The lower buttresses have on the N side stepped set-offs – four steps on the first, three on the second – which Salisbury made a speciality. Corbel tables on aisle and clerestory. The window tracery again Perp and the parapet raised. More ornate only the doorways, and especially that leading into the church from the N under the porch. It is placed five bays from the crossing and six bays from the west front. This N entrance is a twin doorway with a middle post or trumeau. The trumeau has three shafts with shaft-rings, and two hollows between. Each doorway has a continuous mould-ing, which is, however, stopped short by the trumeau. The whole entrance is enriched by one order of columns with shaft-rings, one outer continuous keeled moulding, and a keeled hoodmould on two small busts. In the capitals, the standing figures of a monk (with a scroll) and a bishop, with stiff-leaf behind them – the first figured capitals which we meet. The part of the arch which they carry has, surprisingly, a row of Norman chevrons, set at an angle of 45 degrees.

The NORTH PORCH is treated so sumptuously that we cannot doubt where the principal entrance was meant to be. The porch has externally completely plain sides (except for the Perp parapet of the same design as everywhere else; see below) but a highly enriched façade and interior. Two flat nook-shafted buttresses flank the entrance. They end in polygonal pinnacles, again with blank arcading without capitals. The doorway has eight orders of columns with shaft-rings plus two facing into the interior. They follow an odd rhythm. From outside, the wall first projects as a polygonal attached shaft, then recedes, allow-ing space for two columns. Then it projects again, and so on. The rhythm is shaft–column–column–shaft–column–shaft–column–column–shaft–column–shaft, and then the columns at the opening proper. The capitals are purely stiff-leaf on the r., but full of figures on the l. (five capitals represent the Martyr-dom of King Edmund). The arch mouldings repeat the same rhythm: keeled rolls over the coupled columns, a frieze of the most puzzling ornament over the single columns. It is unques-tionably again a paraphrase of the Norman chevron motif (cf. decoration at Glastonbury in the same period). Two crenella-tions with triangular merlons at 45 degrees to the surface meet in the middle a similar chevron set at 90 degrees, that is pointing straight at us. Stiff-leaf sprays inhabit this spiky frieze. The hoodmould is a filigree band of thin stiff-leaf scrolls. In the spandrels are two oblong panels with reliefs: one with a man and a beast, the other with a scaly mythical animal. The gable of the porch contains a group of six stepped blank lancets with continuous moulding. The highest pair in the middle has a short shaft on a corbel. Below it, inside this pair of blank arches, a group of three small stepped lancet windows (of the tracing house described below). Four bits of stiff-leaf and minor figure-work above. The conception of all this is developed from the N rather than the S transept.

The inside of the porch is a masterpiece of the E.E. style, of a richness which is at the same time orderly and measured. Two rib-vaulted bays; on detached double shafts in the corners, on triple shafts in the middles. The shafts have shaft-rings and stiff-leaf capitals. The walls are covered with tiers of arcading, first a tier of four blank pointed arches per bay with continuous moulding and spandrels filled with symmetrical stiff-leaf arrangements, then the sill moulding with hanging sprays of stiff-leaf. The moulding is cut off at the ends of each bay by tailed monsters biting into it (cf. Elder Lady Chapel, Bristol). The upper blank arcades are almost in two layers in so far as they have their own supporting shafts close to the wall but are separated from one another by two detached shafts standing behind one another. So there is much depth in this blank arcade, but depth in front of a clearly maintained back surface. That is E.E. at its best and most English, in the same spirit as contemporary work at Lincoln, the cathedral which was built by St Hugh of Avalon, Bishop of Lincoln. The shafts of this arcade again all have shaft-rings and stiff-leaf capitals. Arch mouldings with keels and fillets. The outer moulding of each arch intersects a little with that of the next immediately above the capitals. In the spandrels rings of stiff-leaf and also figure motifs. The lunettes above have blank windows with Y-tracery uncusped – and detached from the wall – once more the desire for a distinction between front layer and back layer. This must be one of the earliest appearances of the Y-motif anywhere. The vault makes no difference in girth or mouldings between transverse arch and diagonal rib. Fillet on the middle member of each rib and arch. The room over the N porch contains one of the two TRACING FLOORS known to survive in England (cf. York), with a maze of incised lines from generations of masons' working drawings set out on the smooth plaster.

The west front

10, 16   The WEST FRONT, with its great screen of sculpture, was called by John Harvey 'the most nearly perfect of any among English cathedrals', a view diametrically opposed to that of Pevsner, who found the unmitigated contrast between the C13 sculpture screen and the Perp upper towers unsatisfactory. The west front was perhaps planned and laid out with the nave *c.* 1185–90, and constructed *c.* 1215–48, first under *Adam Lock* (†1229) then under *Thomas Norreys*. The Wells style so far has been one of amplitude, of firmly rounded forms set against nobly sheer surfaces. Now we find something spare instead, harsh uprights and horizontals, angular gables, long marble poles detached from the wall, almost like steel scaffolding. This difference, which Pevsner attributed to a change of designer from the western nave and the N porch, may be due in part to a maturing of Lock's style, but is perhaps more due to changes of emphasis by Norreys. The west front must have been rising by *c.* 1215, being built in pyramidal fashion from the centre outwards. The central section was probably complete with its sculpture and de-scaffolded for the Cathedral's conse-cration in 1239. Here we describe first the architectural struc-ture then the sculpture, solely for clarity of organization and language: ultimately the reader must attempt to view them as an indivisible whole.

The west front below the Perp towers forms a broad rec-tangular screen, divided vertically into five parts by six mighty buttresses. The towers were set out as one with the nave, and it seems that the designer placed them outside the aisles to achieve a broad screen with a flat top and a central gable, as at Lincoln and later at Salisbury. Norman towers had been set outside aisles (Old St Paul's, St Botolph, Colchester). The same plan was envisaged in the rebuilding of St Albans (1195–1214), and was carried through at Ripon, *c.* 1220–30 (here W towers were built outside the width of the aisleless nave). The late C12 foundations were seemingly laid out for western transepts, but the clasping buttresses at the tower angles represent an early C13 change, with transepts converted to towers. These were carried only as high as the rest of the screen front, and their finishing *c.* 1248 with rubble masonry inside implies that higher towers were not envisaged.* Further, the walls between the massive buttresses are no thicker than those of the aisles. The geometry of the west front in both plan and elevation is based on rectangular and square modules, related to the width of the nave and to the distance between the pulpitum door and the High Altar. The height of the C13 towers to the top of the sculpture screen conforms exactly to these geometries, additional evidence that no higher structure was intended. The massive buttresses increased the space avail-able for sculpture, with subsidiary diagonal viewpoints for the figures on their sides, and provided major vertical and frontal divisions which underscore the iconography of the sculpture. They were possibly topped by pinnacles like those surviving on the two central buttresses. The extreme NW and SW but-tresses are deeper than the other tower buttresses, making the west front to the base of the central gable a perfect double

p. 649

---

*Pevsner argued that the breadth of the façade and depth of the buttresses implied an intention for upper towers of unprecedented height to achieve visual balance.

square; final proof that their designer was concerned with a conceptual geometrical system that reinforced the meaning of the sculpture, rather than with structural or aesthetic requirements.

Between the buttresses are the three tall nave w lancets, only slightly stepped, and pairs of blank lancets of equal height in the w faces of the aisles and between the tower buttresses. The blind lancets in the towers were not originally glazed like those in the centre, but had frames fixed in them presumably for louvres.* The openings were blocked in the late C14 or early C15 when the upper towers were added, and given slit windows. These Pevsner regarded as a blemish, 'as if pygmies had come to inhabit this mighty rock'.

At the outer corners the buttresses connect with the deep N and S buttresses by diagonal braces which hide the angles of the towers. As the towers project so far beyond the aisles the whole system of the façade is carried round them. The horizontal zones are, one, the plinth with its portals; zone two, the lowest tier of standing figures in paired gabled niches, with the angels and biblical quatrefoils above; zone three, two further tiers of standing and seated sculpture in gabled niches, with the Resurrection tier above them in low cusped niches; zone four, at the base of the centre gable, the nine orders of angels and Twelve Apostles above them; and zone five (upper gable) the seated Christ. This grid of insistent verticals and horizontals gives the odd feeling of steel scaffolding. The sunk quatrefoils in zone two break round the corners, resulting in dents in the outline. It occurs more noticeably at the sides of the triple niche in the central gable. This apparent solecism (which also occurs at Salisbury) seems to deny the stony solidity of the front; the designer treated it as a screen which, like embossed cardboard or leather, could be pressed round corners.

In the plinth are the three portals, the middle one reaching up into the next zone. Pevsner regarded them as ridiculously small, even 'niggly' by comparison with Reims and Paris. But as he pointed out, most English w doorways are equally small. There may have been a conscious symbolic contrast between the grand lay portal of the N porch and the narrow way of the canons' doors to the w. The portals have marble shafts, the nave doorway also has a trumeau (of C19 Purbeck, its only occurrence here). The stiff-leaf capitals are renewed. The arches are firmly moulded, and there are also inner continuous mouldings and hoodmoulds on headstops. Above the aisle entrances instead of the gabled circles, there are windows – Perp now. Between the portals, there are paired statuary niches with their own little nodding trefoil gables beneath each main gable.

*A document of 1343-4 makes ambiguous mention of a bell-tower towards the Deanery. Was this a lost free-standing tower, or a wooden superstructure on the C13 base of the NW tower? Jerry Sampson favours the latter, and suggests that the disparity between this and the upper SW tower may have encouraged the completion of a matching NW upper tower, which was almost certainly intended from the start.

All the motifs so far are familiar from the work further E. But the west front has two novelties, both used insistently: slim marble shafting, and gabled arcading. The shafting was originally of paler Blue Lias quarried locally, mostly replaced with machine-cut 'Kilkenny marble' by *Ferrey*. Its darker colour against the pale Doulting stone heightens the impact of the shafts, which in zone three are elongated to 'stove pipes', reinforcing the feeling of scaffolding. They have vertical rows of crockets behind – a motif first used at Lincoln (cf. Geoffrey's piers where E transepts and choir aisles meet).

In zone three the six weighty buttresses take over the chief display of sculpture, again in single and paired niches with gables. The marble shafts carry arches high above the upper image niches. Where the statuary is paired on the sides of the buttresses, the sub-arches form a Y-motif under a main arch with intersected mouldings (both seen also in the N porch). The stepped gable above the nave is in three tiers, the lowest of cinquefoiled arches, the rest of trefoiled arches, and the topmost with a cusped oval niche with Christ in Glory flanked by trefoiled niches with angels. More quatrefoils break round the angles. Big shafted pinnacles like spirelets flank the gable.

The UPPER WEST TOWERS were added in the C14 and early C15, standing bold and bare on the mid-C13 front. Some (including Pevsner) have found the contrast with the C13 work jarring; others have seen them as a brilliant and creative response to the constraints imposed by the earlier work. They are also the source for a group of Somerset towers. The SW tower was mainly paid for by Bishop Harewell in his lifetime, i.e. before 1386, and the master mason was *William Wynford*. Bishop Bubwith left money for the NW tower in 1424, specifying completion of the west front by replicating Wynford's SW tower. Each C13 buttress is continued by one with two thin diagonal buttresses. In the N tower the two facing W have richly canopied niches with images. These C14 or C15 main buttresses end with gables and pinnacles. At that point they throw back an inclined plane up to the bell-stage, like a huge final set-off. Out of those develop big diagonal buttresses divided into two and panelled, with thin diagonal angle shafts. The paired two-light bell-openings have diagonally set shafts between, and simple Perp tracery. Their distinguishing feature is the very long blank continuations below; they read as immensely long windows, left blank up to their transoms. Compared with the crossing tower, where the intention is balance, all uprights are stressed much more vigorously; the effect is unmitigated verticality. The W towers have no crowns whatever; their upward thrust is abruptly cut short by a blank arcaded parapet with the smallest of battlements. The single pinnacle on the apex of the nave gable may have been a trial for pinnacles on the twin buttresses of the W towers.

Before leaving the architectural aspects of the west front, two more things must be said. First, RESTORATIONS (prior to the work of 1974–86) added a hardness to what was somewhat wiry from the beginning. In fact, the restorations of 1903 and 1925–31, with their cement-sloping and metal clamps, were far more damaging than *Ferrey*'s work of 1870–4 more often blamed. The warping effect this must have had on the judgement of observers has been somewhat mitigated by the conservation in 1974–86, under *A. D. R. Caröe* then under his son *Martin Caröe*. The weathered medieval carving was repaired, cleaned and given a lime-based sheltercoat, a technique employed successfully here by *Professor Robert Baker*. Second, to visualize the façade as it was *c.* 1250 we must remember what part COLOUR played. Surviving paint fragments show that the backgrounds of the niches were often strong red or green, with blue shafting, and mouldings of pink, red or brown. Robes were predominantly white, with richly coloured linings and borders, and we can assume from evidence elsewhere that gold was extensively used too. The paint scheme was seemingly abandoned (perhaps at the same time as the sculpture, *see* below) and little colour can have been applied to the upper or outer areas of the front. Colour was concentrated around the central door, the most important point liturgically. It is almost impossible for us to imagine its effect upon the façade. It may have served much like a painted Gothic polyptych – even, it has been suggested, intended as a larger version of the high reredos inside.

Sculpture of the west front

The façade of Wells is the richest receptacle of C13 SCULPTURE in England, what Pevsner called 'a reredos as never reredos had been seen before'. It must be repeated now that the figures cannot be seen in isolation from their richly decorated gabled niches and firm framework of roll mouldings contrasting with lively stiff-leaf. In the past the west front has often been described purely aesthetically, as a sort of vertical art gallery; but recent studies have focused as well on iconographic and liturgical interpretations. Still, arriving at definitive meanings is difficult: there is no contemporary documentation for its construction, much sculpture was destroyed by iconoclasts, restorers or weather, and some was never installed (particularly on the SW tower). Most of the surviving sculpture is unidentifiable, having lost detail and colour. Of 297 surviving figures, apart from the central subjects of Christ, the Virgin and Child and the Coronation of the Virgin, only ten others can be identified with complete or near certainty. Given that the centre section of the front was complete probably by 1239, the first figures were probably carved somewhat before Pevsner's suggested date of 1235. The upper sculpture was completed before the front was ready to take it; inevitably, many pieces do not fit in their frames as nicely as the earlier ones. Perhaps because of financial problems, the sculptors' work was terminated *c.* 1242, with the figures on the S and E sides of the SW tower still uncarved, and leaving much completed statuary to be installed later: this led to errors in positioning (mostly cor-

Wells Cathedral, conjectural appearance of west front, *c.* 1250.
Drawing, 1998

rected at the time). The front was probably complete up to the
upper string course by *c.* 1248. It is now clear that the sculpture
was designed to a single iconographic programme.

The subject of the west front is the history of the universe from
the Creation to the Second Coming. It is divided into earthly
time (zones one to three, everything below the gable, laid out
on a rectangular grid) and eternity (zones four and five in the
gable, laid out as a triangle). The locations of key figures conforms with this geometry. The layout can be summarized thus.
In zones one to three, the s side deals with Old Testament subjects, the N side New Testament, although this division does
not apply in the central section, which deals with Mary, Christ
and the Incarnation. Subjects were intended to be read from
the centre outwards. Horizontally, the rectangle below the
gable (the temporal) is divided into the lowest tier, the history
of the old covenant with the Jews; the middle or window zone,
the present new covenant with Christ's Church; and the upper
tier, the future resurrection of the dead. So the iconographic
programme reflects the architectural tension between vertical
and horizontal axes which Pevsner remarked.

   In the tympanum of the middle doorway, in a deeply sunk
quatrefoil, is a seated Virgin with the Child, and in flanking
spandrels remains of censing angels. The figures are badly
damaged, being so accessible, but must have once been
amongst the best at Wells, as befitted this position. Heads and
hands carved by *Arthur Ayres,* 1970. Above is the Coronation
of the Virgin in a niche with a broad shouldered trefoiled gable
(Pevsner found it 'incomprehensible' and 'absurdly small').

These two badly mutilated figures must once have been fine; the sharp long parallel folds have a good deal of vigour. The proposed completion of this group in 1973 (maquettes also by *Ayres*) was abandoned after public outcry.

Zone two, up to the string course below the main windows, showed the Birth of the Church. The standing statuary (mostly lost) seems to have depicted deacons, subdeacons and holy women, etc. They were grouped in pairs. On the back of the NW tower, for some reason, plenty of low-level sculpture escaped the iconoclasm of the C16 and C17. They are, it has repeatedly been said, the best of the Wells statues. When they were cleaned in 1980, carving 'of staggering quality' was revealed – or, at least, remains that implied the original existence of quality. Here is the fine group often known as the Four Maries, certainly the Virgin and Mary Magdalen, possibly with Saints Anne and Elizabeth. In the spandrels between each pair are sunk quatrefoils, originally filled with demi-angels. What remains of them is good sculpture. The sharp-eyed will see an elating detail here: in the centre, inside each of the angel quatrefoils are three singing holes served by a gallery in the thickness of the W wall (for their liturgical use, *see* p. 651).

Above the gables, the biblical quatrefoils conform to a general scheme of the marriage of Christ and the Church, as found in C12 to C13 English Psalters. They are treated as detached stories, rather than single figures, and have a redemptive emphasis. On the S side, scenes of the Fall, from Genesis including the creation of Adam, Adam and Eve, Adam delving and Eve spinning, and Noah's Ark; and on the N side, scenes of Redemption from the Gospels, including the Transfiguration and Christ among the Doctors. Pevsner rightly quibbled with their small scale and cramped subjects; it was clearly difficult to balance the available architectural space with the requirements of such a big and ambitious sculpture programme.

Zone three, the zone of the W window, has two tiers of figures representing the Historical Church, one statue on each tier against the front of the buttress and two on the sides. At this height the destroyers could do less damage, so although the figures are defaced, the intended impression can still be obtained. On the S, churchmen and confessors, with only one king; on the N, largely royalty and saintly martyrs, including both Anglo-Saxon royal martyrs (Saints Ethelbert, Oswald, Edward and Kenelm firmly identified) and universal saints such as St Thomas Becket. Solomon and Sheba, the only biblical figures in zone three, flank the base of the main W window's central lancet. They stand above and either side of the Coronation of the Virgin, and echo it iconographically, representing the marriage of Christ and his Church, the passing of truth and wisdom from Jew to Gentile. Seated in tier three on the fronts of the buttresses flanking the W window are two kings holding charters, possibly representing grants of land and rights to Wells and its Cathedral, echoing the claims of the C12 *Historiola* for Wells as a bishopric (*see* p. 639).

Above tier three, directly below the upper string course, is the so-called Resurrection tier, showing the dead climbing naked from their graves, some joyful, others dumbstruck, in the last moments of earthly time. The Last Judgment, their division into redeemed and damned, has not yet occurred.

Finally zones four and five, the central gable, represent the Eternal realm. The figures, and probably the central pinnacle, were carved c. 1450–75, when the upper towers were completed, but their subjects broadly fulfill the original intention. First a row of angels, and above them a row of holes for sounding trumpets, served by a walkway for the musicians in the nave roof above the high vault. Above these, the Twelve Apostles, and finally a seated Christ in Glory. The two flanking niches have six-winged angels: these and the upper half of the Christ figure designed by *David Wynne*, 1985. It has long been clear that the design of the figures was adjusted according to their position. The upper figures are taller and thinner in proportion, with arms adjusted to allow for foreshortening; faces are tilted downwards and robes, chins and noses are flattened so as not to obscure the parts above. The bases on which they stand are more steeply sloped. Pevsner thought the upper figures 'weird and gaunt', perhaps due partly to erosion of the limbs. He also differed from most scholars in regarding the quality of the west front sculpture as distinctly second-rate, by comparison with the angels in the transepts at Westminster Abbey, with sculpture in the w portals of Reims, begun c. 1230, and with work at Chartres (Ste Modeste, St Theodore, Visitation, c. 1225–35). The supremacy of France as the artistic inspiration at Wells is now disputed; wider stimuli may have been shared by English and French artists. For instance, the siting of sculpture in gabled niches (rather than against columns as in France) occurs in the clerestory glass at Canterbury, and on metalwork shrines (e.g. Aachen) by c. 1200. Biblical figures in quatrefoils occur at St Albans, and, c. 1220, in the illuminations of the Lothian Bible. Cathedral seals, e.g. Canterbury, 1232, depict similar compositions of linear vertical buttresses and a w gable, with iterative canopied statuary niches. C13 church furnishings (e.g. the Naumburg screen, the Salisbury pulpitum) employ a similarly brittle, shallow decorative language.

The west front had an important LITURGICAL FUNCTION in the Palm Sunday procession. A version of the Salisbury liturgy known as the Sarum Use had been adopted at Wells c. 1273–98. It included an elaborate Palm Sunday ritual re-enacting the entry of Christ into Jerusalem. The procession left the church and re-entered via the w door, outside which the 'Gloria Laus' was met with responses from the singing holes, and perhaps with angels trumpeting from the upper holes too: so the walls functioned as the gateway to Christ's Jerusalem, symbolically also the entry of the saved into the New Jerusalem. In these terms, the west front may also be envisaged as an expressive and vividly coloured stage set, fitted for sound and peopled with representations of the Church past, present and future.

Chapter house

The substructure of the CHAPTER HOUSE was begun on an unconventional site NE of the N transept, and must have been done soon after Westminster chapter house was laid out; i.e., as we shall see inside, the work at Wells must have started by *c.* 1250–5. The undercroft, passage to the undercroft, and staircase to the chapter house were all laid out together and built to a level above the top of the plinth. Then work apparently stopped and was only resumed in 1286. Yet the window tracery on the staircase is still in a transitional style: two circles with sexfoils below one large circle with three small encircled sexfoils, the spandrels not yet pierced as in bar tracery, but a little sunk. Presumably these stair windows were at least designed, if not built, in the 1250s.

11 The chapter house proper, however, as proved by its window tracery, cannot have been completed until about forty years later. That is, work must have proceeded in the 1290s after work on the substructure resumed in 1286. (A document of 1307 refers to building expenses for the chapter house in the past tense.) Some tracery details are identical with those of side windows at St Etheldreda, Ely Place, London, of *c.* 1290. Ogee arches are frequent in the chapter house windows, but otherwise the tracery here is still a little closer to late C13 traditions than is that of the new E end. The chapter-house workmen were obviously not the same as those on the Lady Chapel (*see* below). The chapter-house windows are splendidly broad, of four lights, divided into two-plus-two. Each light has an ogee head and a pointed trefoil above. Each two lights have a circle with an ogee sexfoil, each four lights a large circle again with an ogee sexfoil. Buttresses with gables decorated with ballflower. Big gargoyles. Top frieze of two-light openings with Y-tracery in continuous mouldings, lighting the roof space. Then a later pierced parapet with diagonally set pointed quatrefoils and diagonally set pinnacles.

Lady Chapel

11 The LADY CHAPEL was begun at an unknown date in the early C14, outside the old E end. Toothings above the roof of the present retrochoir, apparently intended for flying buttresses, have been thought to prove that the Lady Chapel stood detached for a long time, but no such buttresses were apparently ever built there; moreover, the plinth of chapel continues in one build round part of the retrochoir. The involvement of the Lady Chapel with the retrochoir will become clear inside. There is reason to assume that the chapel was complete by 1319. The very original design of the window tracery looks earlier than that; for it contains no ogee forms. The motif of the window tracery is arches upon arches – a kind of pre-reticulation – and the arches are really spherical triangles, each pointing upwards. Jean Bony saw knowledge of Islamic forms behind this, and also compared this staggered piling-up to the

Bishop's Throne at Exeter. The parapet of the Lady Chapel has an openwork frieze of cusped triangles, and it may well be that this motif began here and was then extended to the presbytery and its clerestory, the crossing tower, and most of the cathedral. It was copied in the eastern arm of Bristol Cathedral, and in many Perp Somerset churches.

Retrochoir, east transepts and presbytery

The RETROCHOIR and EAST TRANSEPTS, for reasons which the interior will reveal, must have gone up a little after the Lady Chapel; the roof timbers of the SE transept (St Katherine's Chapel) were felled in 1325, indicating virtual completion of the work by the late 1320s. These E transepts are only as high as the aisles, not branching from an E crossing as at Lincoln and Salisbury. The window tracery is more varied and unquestionably later than that of the Lady Chapel. The E chapels of the retrochoir (e.g.) have reticulation, a mature ogee motif, and also a kind of straightened-out reticulation which, though in accordance with certain occasional and interspersed perversities of the early C14 at Bristol, seems to point, in this consistent presentation, to the proximity of the Perp style. The E transept E windows have a motif of intersected ogee arches, familiar from Bristol Cathedral, the end and W windows are again reticulated. The choir aisles carry on with intersected ogees or reticulation.

The PRESBYTERY has a clerestory of the same stage of tracery design as its aisles. But in the three W bays the design is curiously bleak, as if money or zest had given out. The most extraordinary piece of the design is in the high gable of the presbytery. The great seven-light window here, undoubtedly close to the Perp style, thus cannot be earlier than 1335 or so (and the heraldry in the glass, without French fleur-de-lys in Edward III's arms, belongs to the period 1327–39). The main division is into 2:3:2 lights, achieved by running the two chief mullions right up into the main arch – a hallmark of the Perp. The three-light centre has Perp panelled tracery, a new development in the 1330s. Each outer section has two ogee lights with one reticular unit above, but squeezed in above that, an off-centre foiled circle towards the centre of the window – a painfully lop-sided arrangement. This wilfulness is Dec, in the Bristol spirit, but the rest, to say it again, must be called Perp. The gable over the window is as curious. It has what normally would be two two-light windows (to the space between vault and roof) with Y-tracery and an almond-shape above, subdivided into four almond-shapes. But every curve is rigidly straightened out, and the whole made into a pattern of lozenges echoing the pitch of the gable.

Crossing tower

The CROSSING TOWER belongs to the years 1315–22. However, its exterior was altered c. 1440, after a fire in 1439. It is a noble design, calm, peaceful, and deeply satisfying. The C14 work stands on a short storey left of Jocelyn's time – with the slim blank arcades with continuous moulding that his master mason liked so much. This low lantern was raised in 1315–22 by a tall storey with, on each side, three pairs of very elongated lancets – a form derived, it is proposed, from the towers of Ketton, Rutland, and Witney, Oxon. This last reinforces the stylistic case that *Thomas of Witney* designed the crossing tower at Wells. The master of *c.* 1440 then filled in the lancets and decorated them in his own taste. The arrangement now appears of three two-light bell-openings with a transom, repeated below by blank two-light windows without transoms, a composition dependent on Gloucester's central tower. The proportions of the whole are wonderfully felicitous. Each light of the bell-openings is given a small foiled circle and on it a gable; the blank openings below have a short piece of quatre-foil frieze above each light. The buttressing is brilliant: the C14 clasping buttresses are continued and end in pinnacles with attached sub-pinnacles, and little statuary niches in each face of the buttress at parapet level. The three panels on each face of the tower are separated by slimmer buttresses. All but-tresses have at half-height little ogee gables. The intermediate ones then turn diagonal, ending in shorter pinnacles above the parapet, which has the same frieze of pierced cusped triangles as on the Lady Chapel.

INTERIOR

Early work: choir, transepts and crossing

Since we know that work started at the E end and proceeded to the W, it is to the CHOIR that we must look to see what was planned at Wells under Reginald, a few years before Bishop Hugh started work on his choir at Lincoln. But of Wells's late C12 choir only the piers and arches of the three W bays survive (for it was from the start as long as it is now, *see* p. 641). The three E bays were taken down to plinth level and rebuilt in the early C14, as part of scheme for a new Lady Chapel, E transepts and retrochoir. The three W bays were given a surface remodelling only; the reason may be that, with the central tower beginning to subside (and still without its strainer arches), the masons did not dare dismantle the choir further W. In any case, we have to look to the transepts to envisage the original choir design.

The master of Wells, while adopting certain Gothic features, was in almost complete disagreement with the recent French tendencies to height and verticality so notable at Chartres. The earliest evidences of his work are the piers and arches in the three W bays of his choir. The piers are broad and complex in section, spreading generously rather than pulled together, and his vaulting shafts do not stand on their capitals. Horizontals are not sacrificed to verticals. The piers in particular are without doubt a demonstration – an anti-Canterbury demonstration soon to be an anti-Lincoln demonstration as well. They consist of a solid core of Greek-cross shape and attached to it twenty-four shafts, in groups of three to each main direction, and three to each diagonal. The abaci are square over the diagonals, polygonal in the main directions. The arches have a variety of roll mouldings, three for each diagonal, four under each arch, two plus two for the outer mouldings, and a hood-mould in addition (chipped off in the choir, on headstops in the transepts). The capitals in the choir are the most telling feature of the earliest phase. They are of the stiff-leaf variety, but the leaves are small, in one or two rows, still rather like the crockets of French capitals. Only one at the NW end, by the crossing, is livelier and has a small head peering out. The aisle walls are divided by triple shafts as well.

Above the arcade in an English cathedral of the C12 or C13 one would expect a gallery. At Wells there is a triforium instead, i.e. a middle storey without outer windows. In the three W choir bays, hidden in the aisle roofs behind the curious stone grille the C14 placed in front of it, is a low triforium grouped in pairs and detailed with continuous mouldings, exactly like the E and W sides of the transepts. So we can safely look to the TRANSEPTS for an impression of the whole of the design of Wells in c. 1180–90. The only important difference between choir and transept is in the development of stiff-leaf foliage, here both bigger and freer. The leaves curl more boldly, the motifs are larger, the carving deeper. One other difference is obvious, and it probably indicates the building sequence within the transepts. The E aisle capitals are wholly foliage, the W aisle capitals introduce with some gusto many attractive figures: a bald head, a man pulling a thorn from his foot, fights, a grape harvest, a bridled woman etc.

The first pier of the N transept E aisle from the crossing has a peculiarity worth noting. The shaft to the E is cut off, and there is a long stiff-leaf corbel instead, with a lizard on it – forerunner of so many long foliage corbels in English cathedrals. And the first capital directly E of this, on the corner between N choir aisle and the N transept, has different foliage from the others, more like the capitals on the chapter-house staircase. Both features are perhaps evidence of renewal after damage in 1248 by a 'tholus', or lantern, falling from the crossing tower.

By contrast with the galleries at Canterbury or Lincoln, the Wells triforium forms primarily a horizontal band, in which respect it follows that of the C11 at the Trinité at Caen. In the transepts it is grouped into two openings per bay, and the vaulting shafts in between start, not on the capitals below, but on corbels above the triforium sill. So the sill is one uninterrupted horizontal, by contrast with Chartres where the triforium is always subordinated to the verticals. The openings have continuous mouldings (a roll, a chamfer and an inner roll), a favourite motif at Wells, and one which can be traced back to the late Norman of e.g. Bristol. The corbels of the vaulting shafts incidentally again have foliage and heads on the E side,

seated figures on the w. The profile of the transept aisle vault-
ribs is three rolls arranged trefoil fashion, of the high vaults
two rolls flanking a triangle or spur. The aisles have no bosses,
the high vaults have bosses with soberly treated stiff-leaf. Here
we must remember the stiff-leaf of the doorway from the s
transept to the cloister. There also capitals are reminiscent of
crockets, and of about the same date (*see* Exterior, p. 641).

It is worth emphasizing the oblong shape of the transept high
vaults. Durham already had oblong vaults, but the Wells vaults
are understood in the French Gothic way. They are the one
really French Gothic motif at Wells. For the memorable fact
remains that Wells, though in nothing else French, is yet wholly
Gothic. Not at Canterbury, Glastonbury or Chichester (where
the Gothic retrochoir is exactly contemporary with the start at
Wells) is the round arch eliminated. Wells is the first Gothic
building in England in which the pointed arch is used exclusively.

The gable walls of the two transepts are identical inside,
although they differ outside. There are windows below, separated by triple shafts, and windows above with depressed two-
centred rere-arches. But between these two zones the triforium
runs as a blank frieze of five arches, not subdivided. This horizontal continuity becomes the main innovation of the nave
and a memorable feature of the Wells interior.

12   The STRAINER ARCHES are grossly scaled, without doubt
the most obtrusive motif at Wells, and deserving of attention
for that reason alone. The crossing tower of 1315–22 had begun
to sink and its piers to buckle very soon after its completion.
The sensational way in which it was strengthened, probably
c. 1338–40, is incidentally further proof of Wells's dependence
on Bristol. In fact, *William Joy*, then master mason at Wells, is
thought to have trained at Bristol. The strainer arches on three
sides of the crossing are huge, and they are – according to how
one looks at them – two intersected ogee curves or an arch
standing on its head on a normal arch. The inverted arch is of
slightly flatter profile. This is exactly like the choir aisle tracery
and the sedilia of the E Lady Chapel at Bristol. Also the huge
gaping eyes in the spandrels are direct reflections of the
mouchettes in the spandrels of the aisle bridges at Bristol. The
arches rise straight from the ground, without responds to carry
them, and a thin triple-chamfer with quadrant moulding is
carried on all up the crossing piers. A tower can be shored up
in other ways. That this is the way chosen here shows once
again, with no punches pulled, what the Dec style is concerned
with in England in matters of space. No smooth vista along
the nave and up into crossing tower. Let it be filtered through
these gargantuan meshes. The obstacle to the eye is worth
more than the vista. Also added, to brace the inside of the
CROSSING TOWER, were stone grids with the same moulding,
as austere as works of the C20. These are concealed by the
splendid fan-vault dating from *c.* 1480, by *William Smyth*. It
has ogee-cusped panelling and reversed cusping forming a

thick band of concave lozenge form around the central bell-hole.

Having dealt with the strainer arches, one can absorb enough of the turn of the C13 to be able to decide what the master of Wells was after. The crossing ought to be visualized as it was without them, also without the fan-vault in the tower. The crossing has its details of *c.* 1200 (now only seen by ascending above both C15 fan-vault and C14 stone grid): two tiers of arcading, both now blank, but the upper perhaps intended to let light in. They have shafts with moulded capitals, and the lower tier yet smaller blank arches inserted oddly in their lower halves. That view is now doubly barred.

Nave and west end

The NAVE interior is, in its finishing, completely of Jocelyn's time, and is rightly taken as early C13 Wells par excellence. It is perhaps best to view it facing W, although the interior of the west front, while closer in design to the nave walls than are the strainer arches, is yet not in harmony with the nave either. Even so the purity of the nave will win; for here – this cannot be stressed enough – is a design of great intrinsic beauty and of supreme consistency preserved without any later interference, not even in the vaults. Its designer – perhaps the man who had designed choir and transepts, but at a more mature age – drew his conclusions from what has already been called Wellensian as against French: the stress on horizontals. The nave is ten bays long. Piers, aisle shafts, aisle vaults, high vaults are as in the transepts (except that the aisle vaults have small bosses of stiff-leaf). As in the choir, the piers have the subtle touch of keeling the shafts pointing to the diagonals. But the great innovation is this. The grouping of the triforium with the vault bays (here it would have to be in threes, not twos as in the transepts) is given up, and it runs through from E to W as one seemingly interminable band. To achieve that, the designer pushed up the corbels for the vaulting shafts to just below clerestory level, removing one more interference of the vertical with the horizontal.

12,
p. 658

These principal features have a second effect besides horizontal stress, and one which is equally important. One feels sheltered between walls at Wells in a way one does not in a French cathedral; perhaps the horizontality and solidity of the walls are presented almost too bluntly here. Lincoln also allows the horizontal its English place; but one does not feel horizontal strips, as one feels at Wells, even at ground level. For so massive are the piers and so finely subdivided that, in perspective, they also form an unbroken band.

Some more differences between the nave and its aisles and the transepts and their aisles must now be pointed out, although they are subordinate to the ones described so far. The triforium openings are shorter than the arches described by their mouldings, and in the spaces between are paterae of

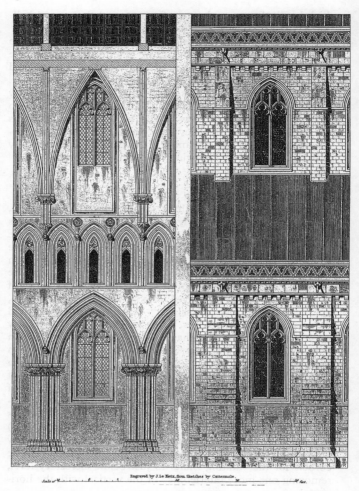

Scale of

Engraved by J. Le Keux, from Sketches by Cattermole.

Wells Cathedral, bay elevations, nave.
Engraving by J. Le Keux, 1824

stiff-leaf, and another in the spandrels between the arches. This
and the bosses of the aisle vaults point in the direction of
increased richness, and we shall see presently that within the
nave such a development also took place.

Meanwhile the inside of the west front must first be looked
at. It is clearly designed to a different scheme: John Bilson in
his paper on Wells of 1928 suggested this meant a different
designer, but Jerry Sampson concludes that similarities to the
Elder Lady Chapel at Bristol probably indicate this is a
maturing of *Adam Lock*'s style. The doorway has a depressed
two-centred arch and is flanked by trefoiled blank arcading. As

on the exterior there are numerous marble shafts (though here of Draycott marble as well as Blue Lias). The aisle doorways place their depressed arches on vertical springers. The zone of the big w windows was reshaped in the Perp period. The horizontal ribs are patent, also above, where the Perp capitals carry E.E. arches with dogtooth decoration. Stiff-leaf also reappears in the top spandrels.

As the towers stand out to the N and S, there are separate chapels under them, vaulted with eight ribs around an opening for hoisting bells. There is a certain restlessness in the design owing to the fact that the capitals of the window shafts and those of the blank arches sit higher than those of the vaulting shafts. In the S wall of the S tower, up in the lunette, is a prettily cusped stepped blank arcade such as are to be found also at the E end of Ely Cathedral.

John Bilson showed a break in style running through the nave along a joint clearly definable and, as building operations go, naturally lying further w on the ground floor than on the upper floors. It runs up six bays from the E below, five bays from the E above. Some of the differences are not easily visible: vertical instead of diagonal tooling, and larger ashlar blocks. But the abandonment of headstops at the ends of the hood-moulds e.g. will be noticed by everybody. This 'break' was probably due to the Interdict, during which Bishop Jocelyn was out of England, i.e. 1209-13, a proposition supported by the dendrochronolgical dating of the nave roof: the E part of the nave, although completed c. 1209, was only roofed after the interdict, with timbers felled in 1212-14.

The most telling change is that in the character of the stiff-leaf capitals. Wells is the best place in England to enjoy and study stiff-leaf. Stiff-leaf foliage was an English speciality anyway; C13 capitals of stylized foliage as beautiful as those of Wells and Lincoln do not exist anywhere outside England. They make the crocket capitals of France look dull. Wells presents us with the whole gamut of stiff-leaf, from the timid beginnings of the choir to the classicity, as it were, of the E bays of the nave and to the Baroque effusiveness of the w bays and the tower chapels. The capitals here assume indeed a lushness, a depth of carving, a fullness in their overhang which goes quite beyond what older men had attempted before. But what date does this end of the work represent? There is no certainty, whatever answers have been attempted. What can be said is that the choir was the work before Jocelyn, that the nave was probably begun c. 1191-5, work to the w of the break resumed c. 1215, and the west front was rising by about the same time. Work on the nave must have been complete well before the cathedral was consecrated in 1239.

Chapter house

Next, the interior of the CHAPTER HOUSE, beginning with the UNDERCROFT, and its access passage. The doorway from the N choir aisle into it has one order of Blue Lias shafts, two capitals rather like those near the W end of the nave (one with birds and grapes), a depressed two-centred arch the inner mouldings of which die into the jambs, and a gable on large and excellent headstops, and with bar tracery: a quatrefoil in a circle. This is the first bar tracery in the cathedral, and bar tracery was not introduced into England until 1245–50 (at Westminster Abbey). That provides a convenient *terminus post quem*. The passage to the undercroft is low, but impressively treated, with wall-shafts, stiff-leaf capitals which look earlier than those of the doorway, rere-arches of the windows dying into the jambs, and with transverse arches, ribs, and a ridge rib, again the earliest in the cathedral. Ridge ribs are a Lincoln innovation, but had by 1260 also been used at Westminster, at Worcester, at Ely etc. The rolls of ribs and arches have fillets. Bosses with figure-work. The undercroft itself has a massive central pier with eight attached shafts against an octagonal core. Surrounding it, a circle of eight sturdy circular piers to support the chapter-house floor above, with circular moulded capitals; two have dogtooth, a rarity at Wells. Single-chamfered vault ribs. Most of the wall-shafts have waterholding bases (a feature occurring at Hailes Abbey, Gloucs., 1246–51). The barred windows have rere-arches. The Perp stoup or lavabo with a carved pet dog inside gnawing a bone should not be overlooked. How enviably free from considerations of propriety the Middle Ages were! The entrance for visitors from the N choir aisle is by *Martin Stancliffe* (*Purcell Miller Tritton*), 2008.

The STAIRCASE to the chapter house is *c.* 1250s, like the substructure. Although its windows have plate tracery, the little spaces between are moulded and sunk, but not yet pierced as in bar tracery. Plain doorway from the transept E aisle with a depressed pointed head and continuous moulding.* The staircase (with its steps so delightfully uneven) is vaulted in two bays with ridge ribs. The two S vaulting shafts are placed on two charming figures. The capitals now turn noticeably more naturalistic (all upright leaves, somewhat like the one transept capital renewed after the earthquake) – again a sign of the second half of the C13. That goes with the tracery of the windows, as we have seen and can now see again; for the former N window is now above the doorway to the bridge which leads to the Vicars' Hall. It has four lights with two sexfoiled circles and one large eight-foiled one above, not as fully pierced as bar tracery.

With the entrance to the chapter house we are firmly in the C14. The walls are very thick, and so the wall-shafts and trumeau and tracery, all very light and transparent, are duplicated in two identical layers with a little vaulted space between. The outer as well as the inner entrance has above the paired doorway arches a large spheric triangle. Large open cusping, with no finesses; like great thorns. The reveals or side walls of

---

*The doorway is *c.* 1180: an intended grand entrance to the staircase was never made.

the little intermediate lobby have blank arcading with a curious top consisting of a large almond-shape filled with sexfoiled circles top and bottom, and two eight-foiled almond-shapes side by side in the centre, the whole like a paraphrase on the theme of the elongated quatrefoil. The vault again has ridge ribs, and a large boss. In the entrance, and indeed on the stair-case, occurs the Blue Lias shafting so fashionable throughout the C13.

The octagonal CHAPTER HOUSE is one of the most splendid examples in England of what might be called the tierceron style, developed at Exeter in the last quarter of the C13 and most fully in its presbytery of c. 1291–9. Tiercerons were first used at Lincoln, and next at Ely and Westminster Abbey. But it is only where they are multiplied and three pairs sprung from one springer that the palm-tree effect results, which makes Exeter so memorable an experience. Yet the Wells chapter house goes beyond Exeter. From the central pier of the West-minster chapter house sprang sixteen ribs. The number was twenty at Lincoln. At Exeter, if one continued the scheme of the vaulting shafts full circle one would arrive at twenty-four. At Wells, thirty-two ribs rise from the pier. (A further step was to be the centralized fan-vault, about half a century later, at Hereford.) The shafts, and the bench and plinth on which they stand, are of Purbeck marble, indicating the fall from favour of Blue Lias just after 1300.

At Wells clusters of five wall-shafts support the vault from the corners. The walls have the usual seats under blank arcad-ing below the windows, seven bays on each side. These have Blue Lias insets, probably built a little before the central column. The cusping of the arches undulates. The gables rest on head corbels and have crockets. Pointed trefoils in the span-drels and slim little buttresses and pinnacles between the gables. The whole panel of each of the seven bays is framed by a frieze of ballflower. The window surrounds are also decorated with two rows of ballflower. The vault has at its apex an octagon of ridge ribs. This does not stand in line with the sides of the outer octagon, but (inevitably) side against corner, and corner against side. The same had already been done at Lincoln (and was to happen on a more elaborate scale in the relation of Ely lantern to the Octagon vaults below). The bosses are still fairly near to nature in their foliage.

In comparing the chapter house with the Lady Chapel, L. S. Colchester suggested that the chapter-house design was by a different man working with knowledge of the Westminster court style (as exemplified e.g. in the tracery of St Etheldreda, Ely Place, London, of c. 1290), rather than someone working entirely in the West Country tradition. Yet this man clearly knew the Exeter vaulting system; and Exeter's window tracery has many details of the St Etheldreda type. (Peter Kidson, in fact, suggested that he came from Exeter.) In describing the Lady Chapel, on the other hand, we shall find ourselves refer-ring, not to London or to Exeter, but to Bristol.

Lady Chapel and retrochoir

The LADY CHAPEL in its interior is so much part of the whole
rebuilding of the E end that the one cannot be described
without the whole. It is indeed the great fascination of the parts
that they are so inseparable, and the way in which this great
master has interpenetrated Lady Chapel and retrochoir is a
feat of Dec spatial imagination as great as that at Bristol. The
Lady Chapel at first sight seems easy enough to understand.
It seems a room of one bay with an apse of three sides of an
octagon. Trefoiled wall-shafts with knobbly capitals, windows
of that ingenious tracery which has already been described (*see*
p. 652). Fleuron band below the windows. The S doorway and
the sedilia are of excellent quality, with nodding ogee arches,
crockets and finials: in fact, the sedilia were repaired by *Benjamin Ferrey* in 1843, and the S doorway re-carved at the same
time, revealing the maturing attitude to Gothic of Early Victorian architects; Ferrey had been a pupil of the elder Pugin. But
then as soon as one looks back or up into the vault, one real-
izes that one is in a room meant to be read as an elongated
octagon, and moreover an unequal one, the E end more sharply
pointed than the W. The W sides of the octagon stand on two
clustered shafts and merge into the retrochoir. The vault has
the first liernes of Wells, roughly contemporary with those of
Bristol choir.* They are made to appear a star within a star.
From each shaft rise diagonal ribs and three pairs of tiercerons.
The inner star is formed by the third tiercerons and not by
liernes, but the outer consists of liernes. Bosses and sprays of
knobbly foliage at the rib junctions. The central boss has Christ
Enthroned. The only aesthetically unresolved problem is that
of the difference in height between the Lady Chapel and the
retrochoir. Here the master of Bristol, having a hall-church to
play in, was in an easier position. At Wells the three W arches
are lower than the others and the space above them is disappointingly filled by blank arches.

The RETROCHOIR is all of a piece with the chapels flanking the
Lady Chapel and with the E transepts, and all are part of the
same ingenious spatial conceit, introducing further surprises.
From outside, one has seen how much lower all this is than the
Lady Chapel, and also how square and rectangular and normal
it seems (like Salisbury, except that there the E transepts are not
part of the E end composition). But inside, the sensitive visitor
is at once thrown into a pleasing confusion. There are six clusters of shafts in the retrochoir plus the two intermediate piers
at the E end of the choir itself. It takes time to realize why they
are all placed as they are. The two easternmost and largest piers
we have already located as part of the Lady Chapel octagon.
Then there are piers to mark the W ends of the two eastern side

*John Harvey has pointed out that the Lady Chapel's subtly irregular vault is like
a dome, its E–W section forming a perfect semicircle. Jean Bony called it a domical
net vault with Islamic overtones. Its cleaning and the C19 painting of the centre
with rich arabesques further emphasizes its mysterious ambiguities.

Wells Cathedral, bay elevations, choir.
Engraving by J. Le Keux, 1824

chapels, the chapels which flank the Lady Chapel. They naturally stand in axis with the chapel walls. Moreover they are in
axis with the arcade between choir and choir aisles, and they
form part of the initial rectangularity. But the next two clusters
a little to the w of these are again in axis with the Lady Chapel
w piers. That is unexpected, in fact unnecessary, but it is where
the designer reveals his genius. For by this means, floating in the
open space of the retrochoir, an elongated hexagon is formed –
at right angles to the elongated octagon of the Lady Chapel.
That the two intermediate piers of the E arcade of the choir are
not in line with the w piers of the hexagon is an additional
complication which, instead of heightening the aesthetic

significance of the whole, only involved the designer in unnecessary difficulties as soon as he had to invent and set out vaults. It will be realized that in several places odd triangular spaces would have to be vaulted, and the master makes his appreciation of this known by giving the w pier of both E chapels a triangular shape. The Dec style always liked the diagonal and so also the triangle. Yet however one sorts it out, some difficult spaces were bound to be left over.

It will no doubt by now be obvious to anyone who has tried to follow this description that English Dec space can be as intricate and as thrilling as German Rococo space. The vaults here are all of the new lierne kind except for the E chapels which are easily disposed of by diagonal ribs, ridge ribs and one set of tiercerons. The E transepts, being rectangular, could again receive a lierne star without much difficulty, though one should remember that liernes were still a very new toy. But the retrochoir's combination of various lierne stars with triangles was a problem. How it is done cannot be described and can only be drawn by the expert. But one should not shirk the effort of understanding it. It is like penetrating a piece of complicated polyphonic music. Nor was the master wholly successful. In one place indeed he has broken down, or someone took over who was incapable of understanding the original plan. From the massive NE and SE piers of the choir rise, amongst other arches and ribs, three to the E which must have turned out to be so useless that lions are called in to bite them off. This is a ruthless procedure and one which a less naïve age would not have allowed itself. A clue to the identity of the master mason here is the two-stage base of each retrochoir pier. This unusual formation is identical to that of the front piers of the Exeter pulpitum (completed 1324), built under *Thomas of Witney*, who was probably in charge in both places. The retrochoir windows are also now generally accepted as Witney's.

Later work in the choir

20,
p. 663

The CHOIR offered less scope for spatial play. In the aisles the difference in the shafts (e.g. the use of Purbeck marble) and in the capitals from the work of c. 1200 is at once seen. The vaults are lierne stars of yet a different pattern (without any diagonal ribs or ridge ribs), and they were substituted for the original, simple, quadripartite vaults in the w bays also. There are again no real bosses but rather sprays of foliage, where the ribs meet. The choir is, especially in its upper parts, the foremost piece of design in England of the few but interesting years between Bristol and Gloucester. If the Wells E end was complete by 1326, we have every reason to assume that the high walls and vaults belong to the 1330s. They are therefore not earlier in date than the Gloucester S transept, though they are earlier in style. For while Gloucester, in spite of certain motifs and attitudes which are inspired by Bristol and must be called still Dec, is in its essentials Perp, the choir at Wells, in spite of certain motifs which are in the Perp spirit, and of which some have already been commented on, is in its essentials Dec. This must be demonstrated.

The contrast with the late C12 choir arcades is of course evident everywhere: now more finely divided piers, the principal shafts of Purbeck marble with foliage capitals, the less stressed parts without any capitals – a Bristol device. Thus a continuous moulding runs up all the way to the vault and frames arcade bay and clerestory bay together (shades of the Glastonbury transept?). But the memorable feature of the Wells choir is the delicate stone grille between arcade and clerestory, an exaggeration of classic French mid-C13 ideas. The w front of Strasbourg above the parts of 1275 etc. is the best-known example. But no interior example is as intricate as this Wells stone filigree. Verticals are resolutely emphasized, and between them are three canopied niches in each bay with brackets for images, and two narrow spaces to the l. and r. The verticals are thin shafts set in pairs, again with narrow ogee niches between. The wall-passage in front of the clerestory windows breaks forward in a significant little triangle above every one of these shafts. Moreover, the wall-passage runs through the piers with diagonally set, ogee-headed entrances, and there are ogee-headed blank panels above them.

As far as possible the same grille was laid over the late C12 upper wall further w. That all is a little flatter could not be avoided. Yet an attempt is made even here to obtain a feeling of air between transparent front and solid back – by means of a canting forward of the narrow side pieces l. and r. of the outer buttresses. So far the Dec elements only have been mentioned. But the panelling of a wall-space as such is the favourite Perp idea, and the fact that the buttresses – glorified mullions – stand directly on the arcade arches below, is also Perp. In connection with that the tracery of some of the windows must again be remembered with their unmistakable Perp motifs: the great E window of c. 1335–9, with its main mullions to the top of the arch, has been described (Exterior, p. 653).

The vault is a *tour de force*. Though it keeps transverse arches, it has no intention any longer of stressing bays. There are e.g. no diagonal ribs except those tying together two bays at a time. There are also no ridge ribs, and instead a lierne pattern crystallized in cusped squares at the ends of a saltire cross – a rectangular, wholly arbitrary pattern. Lower down at the sides of the vault, kite-shapes lie over the diagonal ribs, with the quirk that their cusps seem to bite down on the rib as it runs through underneath. This cusping and the way it is raised off the surface of the vault is an innovation at Wells, imitating the Bristol choir (cf. also the Tewkesbury choir vault of c. 1340). Again no bosses, but leaf sprays at the junctions.

29

FURNISHINGS AND MONUMENTS

Described from E to W.

Lady Chapel and east end

LADY CHAPEL. SCULPTURE. Mary as a peasant, with Jesus, by
A. G. Walker (early C20?). – STAINED GLASS. E window drastically but conscientiously restored by *Willement*, 1845. In the
other windows a jumble of fragments, quite effective, including much original figure-work, especially in the tracery lights
and in the canopies of the main lights. This must date from
c. 1315–20. The SE window is the most complete. Most of the
glass in the N windows is contemporary but comes from other
parts of the church. Amongst details to be looked for is a panel
with two of the Three Magi, a trumpeting angel, and several
canopies. Also bases for figures; said to be the earliest such
occurrence in England. Another innovation is the use of yellow
obtained from silver nitrate. Here yellow is still absent in the
tracery lights, but plentiful in the main lights.

RETROCHOIR, EAST CHAPELS AND EAST TRANSEPT. Magnifi-
cent brass LECTERN, given 1661. Signed *William Burroughs* of
London (he made the lecterns at Lincoln and Canterbury).
Big bulbous stem on four lion feet, symmetrical scrolly foliage
in the gables; acanthus-crested ridge with candle sconces. –
SCREEN. NE transept; fragments of an Elizabethan or early C17
screen, with arches and unfluted columns, extended in the
early C20 to incorporate a tomb canopy E of the door. – COPE
CHEST. The oldest dated piece of furniture in the United
Kingdom; oak felled 1111–43. Stepped column bases round the
sides, fan decoration on the lid. – SCULPTURE. NE transept.
C15 stone relief above the altar: Ascension of Christ. Only his
feet are visible in the clouds. – TILES. NE transept; section of
early C14 encaustic floor tiles of Bristol–Lower Severn manufacture, in carpet-like patterned strips with foliate borders. –
STAINED GLASS. Of about the same date as in the Lady
Chapel. In the SE chapel S window heads of bishops. Above, a
Christ in Majesty. In the E window a Christ apparently from a
Coronation of the Virgin. In the NE chapel N window more
heads of bishops, and above, another Christ in Majesty. The
SE transept S window is from Rouen, early C16, and of the
school of *Arnold of Nijmegen*. NE transept N, by *Powells*,
designed by *G. P. Hutchinson*, 1902. – MONUMENTS. SE chapel.
Canon John Martell †*c.* 1342. Perp tomb-chest. Canopied
niche to the E. Three canopies with steep, concave-sided gables
with tracery. Panelled vault inside. – SE transept. Bishop Drokensford †1329. Tomb-chest, with low ogee-headed arches.
Dean Gunthorpe †1498. Big tomb-chest without effigy; five
shields in panels. – W wall: small brass to Humphrey Willis
†1618. Probably by *Richard Haydocke*, Fellow of New College,
Oxford. Kneeling figure with a remarkable display of inscriptions. On the r. his hat, sword, violin etc., on the l. the *Armatura
Dei*. He looks up and says: '*Da Mihi Domine*'. Two cherubs
answer: '*Petenti dabitur*' and '*Vicisti recipe*'. – NE transept. Dean
Godelee †1333. Tomb-chest like Drokensford's with low ogee-
headed arches. Of the effigy no details are recognizable. –

Bishop Creyghton †1672. Bulgy sarcophagus. Big recumbent alabaster effigy. – John Milton †1337. Recumbent effigy.

Choir

CHOIR ENCLOSURE. BISHOP'S THRONE. CI4 with magnificent stone canopy of ogee arches and pinnacles, almost as high as the choir arcades. Painted marbling was removed in 1848. The stone STALL CANOPIES and PULPIT with nodding ogee arches were designed by *Salvin* as part of his restoration of 1848–54. *James Forsyth* worked on this restoration and may have carved the stalls. For Salvin's attentions to the pulpitum *see* Crossing, below. The CI4 oak stall canopies which they replaced were different, and had been mutilated in 1633 by the introduction of gallery seating. The sub-stalls are medieval. There remain sixty-three MISERICORDS of *c.* 1330–40, the same decade as Chichester's and Ely's (plus one of the CI7): fifty originally belonged to the upper stalls, from which Salvin removed them; sixty are now attached to the lower rows. They are among the best in England, carved with a delicacy fit for a less menial purpose. Amongst the subjects here are mermaids, a pelican, a hawk and a rabbit, a lion and a griffin, a monkey and an owl, a puppy and a kitten, a cat playing the fiddle, a man slaying a dragon. Three are displayed in the s aisle at the corner of the retro-choir, including the finest, of Alexander borne aloft by griffins. The subject appears on misericords elsewhere (Lincoln, Chester, Manchester etc.), yet this must be the most beautiful example. – CI4 entrance SCREENS to the choir aisles; crocketed ogee arches flanked by buttresses. – ORGAN CASES by *Alan Rome*, 1974. CI8 style, incorporating two trumpeting angels by *J. Forsyth* from the 1857 case. On the Victorian base. – STAINED GLASS. E window. Tree of Jesse. One of the finest examples of mid-CI4 glass painting in England. The date is probably *c.* 1339 (no fleur-de-lys in the royal arms in the borders). Large standing figures, under canopies, which is unusual. Much yellow and green, hardly any blue: like 'a meadow full of buttercups and daisies with a patch of red poppies here and there'. Clerestory: the two NE and the two SE windows have large impressive figures of saints, also original, and a year or two later than the E window (fleur-de-lys now present in the borders). Tracery heads: on both sides, small figures belonging to the Resurrection. W of the old windows, stained glass on the s side by *Willement*, 1846, on the N side by *Joseph Bell* of Bristol, 1851. 29

CHOIR SOUTH AISLE. STAINED GLASS. In the tracery heads some of the best early CI4 glass, e.g. a Christ Crucified, a Virgin accompanied by angels, and a St Michael. These figures have all the sophistication and fragility of the architecture of the same moment and also its leaning towards the excessive. In one window heraldic and figure panels of the CI7. – MONUMENTS. The interesting monuments at Wells are the retrospective effigies of seven Saxon bishops in the choir aisles.

Five are thought to date from *c.* 1200 and were made as standing, not recumbent, figures. They may originally have formed part of a great reredos, each with his relics housed in a chest below his effigy, and with lead fillet inscriptions set in the stone. Of the four figures in the S aisle, three are of this type, firmly modelled with deep rounded regular drapery folds and a deep rounded treatment of the features as well. Yet by the canopies at their heads the original stone block is still felt, and much of the carving seems sunk rather than raised. Canopies vary from trefoiled pointed to a curious shape with lobed sides and straight head. The first from the W has wilder drapery than the others. But all three are work of one workshop (for two more, *see* choir N aisle below). The figure at the E end is quite different, and is one of the two made as recumbent effigies carved in the style of William Longespée (1227) at Salisbury and therefore of *c.* 1230 (for the other, *see* choir N aisle).* This effigy must be by one of the west front men, and is far more independent of the coffin-lid; he really seems to lie on it. The pillow instead of a canopy especially helps to create that verisimilitude. The figure wears a low Saxon-style mitre, and there is a frieze of small stiff-leaf along the edge of the lid. When the presbytery was extended *c.* 1325 all the effigies were laid down on the benches of the aisles and their lead fillets made into plaques and put inside the accompanying bone chests. (The present stone bases on pillars date from 1913.)

OTHER MONUMENTS in the choir S aisle, from the E: chantry of Bishop Bekynton (bishop 1443–65), dedicated 1452, but made some years earlier. Cadaver below in the opened winding sheet; six low oddly bulbous shafts with little ogee gables and, attached above them, demi-figures of angels with wings spread into fern-like leaves. Recumbent effigy of painted and once jewelled alabaster, on a slab carried by the six shafts. E of the effigy, a chantry chapel in the form of a high canopy, depressed arch with openwork tracery, demi-figures of angels as cusps, straight top. Intricate little three-bay vault with pendants. Round chantry and tomb, an iron railing, sturdy and unrefined, with coarse little heads as decoration, and excellent lock-plates (cf. iron gates, S transept; also Farleigh Hungerford chapel). – Bishop (Lord Arthur) Hervey †1894. Design by *J. L. Pearson*, effigy by *Thomas Brock*, 1897. – Bishop Bitton II †1274. Incised slab, coffin-shaped, the figure under a trefoiled gable. Among the earliest incised slabs in Somerset; cf. that at Chelvey, of *c.* 1260–80. – Bishop Harewell †1386. Alabaster effigy, pair of hares at feet.

CHOIR NORTH AISLE. STAINED GLASS. In the tracery again some original figures: St Michael, Christ Crucified, St John the Baptist. In the window E of the doorway to the chapter-house undercroft, glass by *Westlake*, 1885. In the UNDERCROFT several roundels with early C14 glass. – MONUMENTS. Three

---

*These probably represent Bishops Giso and Dudoc, who were buried in the apsidal transepts of the Saxon cathedral.

more of the C13 series, two of the earlier ones, the third again
of *c.* 1230 (*see* choir S aisle above). The earlier have a cinquefoiled canopy, and a trefoiled pointed canopy on stiff-leaf
corbels with two angels in the spandrels; the later again lies
free of any canopy and wears the low mitre. – E of the choir
door, Bishop Ralph of Shrewsbury †1363. Good alabaster
effigy. – W of the choir door, Bishop Berkeley †1581. Tomb-
chest with cusped circles and shields, primitive Roman lettering on lid, no effigy.

Crossing and transepts

CHOIR SCREEN or pulpitum. Of the time of the completion of
the choir, and indeed still Dec rather than Perp but made as
good as new in 1848 by *Salvin*, who moved the whole centre
forward. Stone, two-storeyed. Tall ogee-headed niches below
with brackets for images; low ogee-headed niches above; battlements. The doorway is ogee-cusped and sub-cusped, with
openwork cusping and encircled quatrefoils in the spandrels.
– On the W strainer arch, ROOD FIGURES, 1920, by *G. Tosi* to
the design of *Sir Charles Nicholson*.

NORTH TRANSEPT. SCREENS. To the E aisle: stone, late C15 Perp.
To the choir aisle: a remarkable piece, presumably early C14
when the choir was being finished. Ogee doorway with thin buttresses and pinnacles like that from the aisle into the choir, but
flanked by a vertical band of cusped and sub-cusped lozenges
(cf. St Mary Redcliffe, Bristol, S transept windows). – DOOR to
the chapter-house staircase. C14, with tracery. – The famous
Wells CLOCK is more visited than anything else in the cathedral.
Made *c.* 1390. There is no evidence for Peter Lightfoot as its
maker. On the dial the heavenly bodies are represented as they
seem to move round the earth in twenty-four hours and thirty
days. The small ball in the centre represents the earth ('Spher-
icus architypum globus hic monstrat microcosmum'), flanked
by larger circles indicating the moon (l.) and her age (r.). The
three outer circles of the dial show the day of the month, the
minute and the hour. Above the dial, a procession of four small
jousting knights on horseback. On the quarter hours, they
gallop round in opposing directions like a Victorian child's toy,
one knight unseated at each rotation. – To the r. of the clock a
seated figure known as Jack Blandiver. It may also date from *c.*
1390 and would then be the oldest CLOCK JACK in the country.[*]
– SCULPTURE. In the W aisle, N wall, over the entrance to the
stair-turret: Wise Virgin(?). Very good small figure by one of the
west front masters. Beneath the clock, Christ the Redeemer, by
E. J. Clack, 1956. – STAINED GLASS. Clerestory E side. Decap-
itation of St John. Probably by *Arnold of Nijmegen*; dated 1507.
The inscription is in French. Renaissance details in the ornament. N lancets by *Powells*, 1903; highly praised at the time.

[*] On the outside of the transept wall a simpler DIAL and two QUARTER-JACKS, in
late C15 armour.

Chapter-house staircase, some of the oldest glass surviving in the cathedral. It dates from *c.* 1290 and consists of patterns in ruby, green, blue and white with grisaille. In the chapter-house tracery lights some early C14 glass, also some C15 heraldic glass. – MONUMENTS. Bishop Cornish †1513. Tomb-chest with shields on cusped fields. Tudor-arched canopy, straight top with cresting and pinnacles. No effigy. Against the E wall mutilated figures of Christ and the kneeling bishop. – Bishop Still †1607. Attributed to *Maximilian Colt* (GF). Recumbent alabaster effigy flanked by two black columns. Shallow coffered back arch, spandrels with shields and ribbonwork. – Bishop Kidder †1703, by *Robert Taylor*; cf. his masterpiece, to Thomas Deacon (Peterborough Cathedral, 1721). Perhaps erected *c.* 1720 by the bishop's daughter, whose reclining figure is depicted, rather daringly dressed and looking up to the two urns of her parents. Broken segmental pediment on Composite columns. Below, swagged drapery with three cherubs' heads.

SOUTH TRANSEPT. FONT. Bath stone bowl of the C9 or early C10; circular with arcade of blank arches and vestigial leaf motifs in the spandrels. Carved figures in seven of the arches have been chiselled off and the round arches re-cut to blunt points. The composition is in the tradition of Mercian sculpture (cf. the Hedda Stone of *c.* 800 at Peterborough), and the carving more primitive than on the similarly tub-shaped fonts with carved figures under arcades at Hereford Cathedral and Rendcomb in Gloucs. Probably moved here *c.* 1196, when the S transept was newly completed and served as the main entrance. – FONT COVER. Naïve Jacobean, S-scrolls. – SCREENS. As in the N transept, but with C15 iron GATES probably from the Bekynton Chantry (S choir aisle). – STAINED GLASS. E side, clerestory, two saints by *W. R. Eginton*, 1813. Two E windows by *A. K. Nicholson*, 1921. – MONUMENTS. Some of the most important in the cathedral. Thomas Boleyn †1470, E aisle. Alabaster monument of *c.* 1400, from Nottingham, the tomb-chest with two panels of the most familiar themes: an Annunciation and a Trinity, but of an expressive power rarely achieved in English alabaster. Between the two panels three standing statuettes and shields. Effigy also of good quality though no match for the two panels. Heavy canopy of stone; big superstructure with blank arcading. – William Byconyll †1448 (E aisle). Tomb-chest with ogee arcading. Back wall and coved ceiling with plain panelling. Heavy straight top. – Bishop William de Marchia †1302 (S wall). The new retrochoir may have been envisaged as a site for his shrine but a petition for canonization in 1324 was unsuccessful. To the l. of the monument a separate chantry altar. The historical importance of the monument depends on whether one is entitled to assume that it was – as was usual – made shortly after his death. If so, it represents Wells at the beginning of the great work about the E end. The tomb is in a recess with a canopy. The effigy, of excellent workmanship, lies on a low base with a frieze of detached heads on it, a weird, as yet unexplored conceit. Three arches, ogee-cusped ogee gables with crockets and big finials. If this is indeed c. 1302–5, the ogees are the first in Wells. Vault with ridge ribs and bosses. On the back wall three figures in bad condition. Two of them are angels. Against the E and w walls just one head each, of a grossly exaggerated size: one man and one woman, possibly Christ and Mary (cf. frieze of the Lady Chapel reredos, Bristol Cathedral). The touch of the sensational that turns up so often in the style of the early C14 is certainly present. – The surround of the CHANTRY ALTAR is livelier. One arch only with pierced ogee cusping. Panelled spandrels, straight top. The panelling in the spandrels is so much a Perp motif that it makes one consider whether the altar was not set up a generation later. Back wall with three ogeeheaded niches, the middle one wider. Openings like small windows towards the big s window behind. Brass plate to commemorate the burial here of the Countess de Lisle †1463.

Nave

PULPIT. An extremely interesting stone pulpit is attached to the Sugar Chantry (which is earlier than the pulpit; see below) and can only be reached from inside the chantry. Its interest lies in the fact that it is of solid, monumental and very plain Italian Renaissance forms, handled without any hesitation and without any hankering after prettiness, and yet is as early as the time of Bishop Knight who gave it, and whose arms appear on it. His bishopric began in 1540 and he died in 1547. He was an able politician and a valued adviser of Henry VIII. In 1527 he had been to Rome in connection with the divorce case, and he had spent many years in the Netherlands. His pulpit is one of the earliest attempts in England at a serious understanding of the Renaissance, as early as Lacock Abbey and Old Somerset House. It is circular with broad projecting piers and an inscription (in a mongrel mix of classical lettering and black-letter) that reads in part: 'preache thov the worde be fervent in season and ovt of season reprove rebvke exhorte wail longe . . .' – Under the NW tower: oaken PYX CANOPY, a great rarity. Circular in plan, 4 ft (1.2 metres) high, with pierced tracery, and traces of red, blue and gilt paint. It seems to be of the C14. Formerly in the undercroft, where Britton's engraving shows it, but originally presumably in the C14 sanctuary. – STAINED GLASS. W window, 1670. An important document of the use of enamelled glass, rather than an enjoyable work of art; also much repaired after damage from westerly gales. Centre light by A. K. Nicholson, 1931. s aisle, four two-light windows by C. E. Kempe, inserted 1905–6. Some tracery lights with C15 glass: s aisle, westernmost and easternmost windows; N and s clerestory, easternmost windows. – MONUMENTS. A pair of chantry chapels (the only ones besides Bekynton's, s choir aisle): N, to Bishop Bubwith †1424 and s, to Treasurer Hugh Sugar, 1489, by William Smyth. Of identical form; a hexagon, the sides canted out simply to gain space between two piers of the nave arcade. In the architectural details much difference. The E wall in the earlier with quatrefoil-panelled coving, in the later a fan-vault instead of coving and demi-figures of angels in the frieze. The tracery of the earlier contains an odd reminiscence of the C13, rounded trefoiled lights though with Perp panels above. In the later the windows are arranged in four lights with two two-light sub-arches. The doorways of the earlier four-centred, of the later ogee-headed. There seems little stylistic significance in these changes. They are no more than variations within the same style. Whatever else the nave and aisles may have contained has been cleared out by restorers.

CLOISTERS

The original cloisters of the period *c.* 1200–25 were rebuilt in the C15. The new cloisters belong to a distinctive West Country tradition that emanates from Worcester (*c.* 1377), reaching Wells via the lost cloister at Exeter (*c.* 1390–1413).* The EAST WALK was begun by Bishop Bubwith *c.* 1420–4, represented by the eight N bays, including the library above, and completed by his executors in the 1450s. The gap may be explained by the construction of the NW tower. The E cloister is wider than its predecessor; see the fine S door of *c.* 1215–20 with cusped arch outside, which is not central to the walk. Six-light windows with transoms and two-centred heads, divided into three-light sub-arches. Here begin the ogee-headed lights found after *c.* 1440 in Somerset parish churches. Much pretty cusping. The vaults start on solid springers like fan-vaults, the pattern built up with liernes to an octagonal centre (as in the E walk at Worcester). Central square bosses with concave sides. On the upper floor the LIBRARY, a splendid room originally 160 ft (49 metres) long and intended as the cathedral library from the beginning. It must be the largest C15 library in England. Small windows of two lights. Book presses and fine panelling of 1686, three matching presses added 1728. The Perp wooden screen at the N end comes from Vicars' Close. Cambered beamed ceiling supported on fine head corbels; twelve are *c.* 1260, probably from the old cloister range.

The S and W walks follow the design of the E range except in some matters of detail. They too have C13 outer walls. New inner walls were raised on top of the C13 wall-bench. The SOUTH WALK was begun by the executors of Bishop Bekynton †1465 and completed, after an unexplained pause, in 1507–8. This is single-storey. The square bosses no longer have concave sides, the fan springers are replaced by conventional ones, and the capitals are decorated foliage bands. WEST WALK, done probably *c.* 1460–80 (references to paving stones in the accounts of 1480–1 may indicate completion). It overlaid the fine C13 porch which was the main lay entrance to the

---

* Linda Monckton, 'Late Gothic Architecture in South-west England,' Ph.D. thesis, University of Warwick, 1999.

cathedral. Later blocked, reopened 2007–8 (*see* below). Segmental inner arch on stilted springers, with single Blue Lias shafts and stiff-leaf capitals. The offices above have the same small two-light windows as the library. The roof has collar-beams on arched braces and one tier of wind-braces. Against the w wall, a late medieval porch with an *ex situ* stiff-leaf boss. Under the CLOISTER GARTH is a stream in an underground chamber set at an angle to the garth (another reminder of the Saxon cathedral). It was clearly associated with the supply of water direct from the holy wells. Until the late C18 it retained a C15 stone superstructure. Against the lower wall of the E walk, two small open structures with stone roofs, possibly for altars. – MONUMENTS, NE to NW. Many ejected from the Cathedral, often incomplete. Thomas Linley †1795, also his daughters Elizabeth Ann Sheridan and Mary Tickell, by *Thomas King*. Urn on a base with musical instruments. Peter Davis †1749, Recorder of Wells, 'a Man eminently learned in the Laws of his Country . . . Unambitious but Uniform'. By *Benjamin Bastard*. Obelisk, and standing in front of it the solitary and silly figure of a putto holding an inverted torch which looks like a cornu-copia. – George Hooper †1727. By *Samuel Tuffnell*. Grandiose standing wall monument. Two attached columns with open scrolly pediment and achievement. Two putti standing outside the columns. – Abigail Hooper †1726, rich tablet of coloured marbles with broken pediment, also *Tuffnell*, 1728. – John Berkeley Burland †1804, by *John Bacon Jun*. Relief medallion with the dying man held by a woman. – John Phelips †1834. By *Chantrey*, 1837. Big, grave seated figure in a gown. – Many tablets with urns, the best to Abraham Elton †1794, by *William Paty*.

The Camery

The CAMERY churchyard sits E of the cloisters and S of the choir. It served as a burial ground from the C7 to C11 and was walled to the E *c.* 1200. Beyond lies the holy well dedicated to St Andrew, from where water was carried to the town through a conduit constructed *c.* 1190–5 beneath the cloister. Here was the mid-C10 Lady Chapel, which alone had been saved when the old cathedral was swept away in 1196. It was then 'restored' and joined to the E range of the new cloister. Interest in the chapel grew: ordinations were held there, and it became packed with the burials of clergy and influential lay benefac-tors. It was tripled in size *c.* 1276 probably by the addition of aisles and an eastern extension. In the C14 a small building with side benches, possibly a consistory court, was erected N of the chapel in the angle between the E cloister and S transept. Entrance was from the S transept. This building and the whole of the chapel were demolished and replaced by a large cruci-form LADY CHAPEL of 1477–88, the foundations of which are marked in the grass. Designed by *William Smyth*, and funded by the absentee Bishop Stillington. He was buried here in 1491.

The archway from the cloister to the Camery was the entrance to the chapel; outside it may be seen the panelled W wall formerly within the chapel. Parts of two vault-rings built on to the bench of the E cloister are from the vaulting of Stillington's chapel, cf. Smyth's contemporary vault under the crossing tower; also at Sherborne Abbey. But here he made the innovative addition of large pendants (cf. the Divinity School, Oxford, and St George's Chapel, Windsor). In 1552 Stillington's Lady Chapel was demolished by Sir John Gate, the king's collector of lead.

In *c.* 1500, on the site of the former consistory court building, a chapel dedicated to the Holy Cross was built. A stone screen, of which the upper tracery survives *in situ*, divided this chapel from the cloister. Inside, the foundation for the altar has been discovered, together with a single tomb.

On the S side of the Camery, adjoining the cloister's SE corner, new CHOIR PRACTICE ROOMS etc., accessed through a reopened C13 doorway in the cloister. Oak-framed open passage, main space roofed with arch-braced oak trusses. Further E, WORKSHOPS. Both are by *Martin Stancliffe* (*Purcell Miller Tritton*), *c.* 2005–7, and have banded rubble and ashlar walls towards the Cathedral.

W of the cloisters, i.e. towards Cathedral Green, is the CLOISTER GARDEN, a walled enclosure roughly following the lines of the W atrium of the Anglo-Saxon Cathedral, although that space extended further S. Against the W cloister range are various appendages, one with the same blank-arcaded parapet as the W towers of the Cathedral. This structure remains from the previous cloister, for it contains a richly moulded E.E. arched porch which is now the entrance to the cloister from the VISITOR CENTRE. This is by *Martin Stancliffe* (*Purcell Miller Tritton*), 2007–8. Of two storeys, oak- and steel-framed, with slate roof and rendered walls. Echoing the atrium's Saxon function, a new public entrance marked by a leaded spirelet breaches the medieval garden wall towards Cathedral Green. Neatly incorporated is the N gable of the (ruined) CHORISTERS' HOUSE, built 1354 by Ralph of Shrewsbury, furnishing a date for the introduction of standard Perp forms to Wells. Restored transomed two-light Perp window. The house was built at an angle to the cloister, i.e. on the old Saxon alignment, implying that some Saxon structures survived here into the C14.

BISHOP'S PALACE

Without doubt the most memorable of all bishop's palaces in England, combining high architectural interest with exquisite beauty of setting. It remains a proud entity of its own, distinct from the Cathedral or close, isolated from the precinct by the high cloister wall and by its moat and crenellated wall – a fortified mansion, even if the moat is now an ornamental sheet of water, and the wall no more than the enclosure for lawns and spreading trees. The present character, the product of the gentle romanticism of the C18 and early C19, must be put aside if one wants to visualize the medieval palace. However, historical considerations cannot spoil the intense pleasure and the gentle melancholy with which the visitor wanders amongst the verdure and the ruins.

The site, s of the Cathedral and cloisters, was probably used for this purpose from the C10. King John granted Bishop Jocelyn licence to empark 500 acres (now Palace Fields, to the s) in 1207, usually taken to mark the start of the present palace. A hall and chapel were erected by Bishop Burnell at the end of the C13, but the irregular pentagonal MOAT and curtain WALL with semicircular angle turrets were not added until c. 1330–40. The moat, which was wider than now, is crossed by a small drawbridge (the chains are a C19 fiction, but the portcullis slot is functional) to the mid-C14 GATEHOUSE. This has two polygonal towers, that to the l. with a late C16 oriel. Most of the arrow loops enlarged in the early C19. Four-centred archway with big quite plain roll mouldings; to the vault inside simple, single-chamfered diagonal ribs. At their crossing four lions' heads. The w tower has a porter's lodge, otherwise the towers were arranged as lodgings. The angle turrets in the curtain wall are open to the inside, that at the NW incorporating a two-storey oratory or retreat, an early C19 adaptation.

And so to the COURTYARD. To the E is the MAIN RANGE built by Bishop Jocelyn. This building is surely proof, with the Cathedral's front, of his determination to re-establish Wells as the primary episcopal seat. The masonry evidence also suggests it was begun at this time. After a break, when Jocelyn left England at the Interdict, work was completed; perhaps in the 1220s. It is seven bays wide, originally of two storeys with a rectangular stair-turret at each end; that at the s survives, against the late C13 chapel (*see* below). On the ground floor, twinned lights with trefoil heads, not original and of uncertain date. There were far-reaching C19 interventions. The façade was evened out *c.* 1810 with the entrance moved to the centre (previously in the next bay l.), but the porch is by *Benjamin Ferrey*, who undertook a restoration for Bishop Bagot, 1846–7. He also reinstated four regular buttresses with characteristically close-stepped set-offs, replicated from the C13 originals on the E façade, where lancets also survive. The shape of the first-floor windows is original. They are of two lights, trefoil-pointed with a quatrefoil above in plate tracery and odd trefoiled hoodmoulds. These are also *Ferrey*, reportedly from evidence found. His is the attic storey with three gabled dormers ('silly', thought Pevsner). The s and N gables have big quatrefoils in the gables. Paired lights like the w front (the sills lowered by *Ferrey*). Projecting NE wing off the solar, a little later

Wells, Bishop's Palace, chamber window.
Engraving, 1866

than the main range, probably containing a private chamber
with a garderobe. Big Tudoresque first-floor oriel, *c.* 1825.
Inside, two rooms deep (a rarity in a medieval house). On the
first floor a narrow gallery runs the full length of the W front,
with three broader chambers behind. The three UNDER-
CROFTS are well preserved. Beneath the gallery, one of seven
bays, originally partitioned into two or three rooms. Once
excellent late C15 fireplace with kites and a frieze of cusped
squares, removed in the early C18 from Bishop Bekynton's N
range (*see* below). Centre of the frieze and mantel renewed,
with coarse leaf carving and uncusped kites. Behind this, the
largest undercroft, perhaps originally for servants or guests,

double-aisled and of five bays. Painted vault imitating masonry studded with little rosettes. The solar undercroft (N end, now subdivided) was square with a single central column. The columns are of Blue Lias, bases and capitals have simple and robust E.E. mouldings, and the ribs are single-chamfered. Transverse arches are not specially emphasized. Against the walls, arches and ribs rest on moulded corbels. At the SW angle of the range, a wide spiral staircase of Jocelyn's time which was superseded by a new main STAIRCASE, c. 1608–16. This was altered to a dog-leg c. 1810. Newel posts with rectilinear strap-work and C19 dragon finials; balustrade of square Ionic columns and within each arch a ball-headed tapering baluster connected with the capitals at impost level (cf. Laverton). The undersides of the upper flights have plaster decoration and open pendants finishing the newels. The windows of the first-floor GALLERY have trefoiled rere-arches on shafts painted to look like marble, replaced by *Ferrey* to the old pattern, but the details flashy and mechanical. That these interiors have 'neither the charm of the Early Gothic Revival nor the truthfulness of the best of the later C19 Gothicists' (Pevsner) is partly due to the C16-style ribbed ceilings, dado panelling and florid door surrounds of papier mâché by *George Jackson & Sons*, installed by 'an ignorant upholsterer from Bath' engaged directly by Bishop Bagot, to Ferrey's displeasure. The same continues through the bigger chambers behind. In the SE chamber, two mutilated and blocked C13 windows. These rooms were open to the roof: fragments of high-quality painted decoration survive above the ceilings.

p. 676

There must have been kitchens and service rooms to Jocelyn's range, perhaps on the site of the NORTH RANGE added by Bishop Bekynton (1443–65). Its battlemented KITCHENS overlook the courtyard, with two-light trefoil-headed windows seemingly of the C17 or C18. Where it adjoins the C13 range is a projecting porch-tower, c. 1608–16, with pan-elled outer arch. The inner porch doorway is mid-C15, with four-centred head, pinnacles and fleurons around the arch. The HALL, which runs N to the curtain wall, is best seen from the E gardens. It was built as a hall with chamber above, an early example. Three very tall straight-headed windows on the ground floor, two C15, that at the S a replica of 1956. Three cusped lights with transoms. A floor was inserted as part of remodelling, c. 1810; with incongruous C19 sashes in the upper rooms, and cutting across the C15 windows. The hall screen is fine early C17, *ex situ* or at least much cut about, with decorative frieze and central arch with the usual freely worked straps, curlicues, mythical beasts etc. NE of the hall, and opening off it, the sturdy three-storey ORIEL TOWER with attached stair-turret and diagonal buttresses. The ground floor probably served as a private audience chamber. A very fine mid-C15 WALL PAINTING has been discovered above its ceiling, of a lady in fashionable dress, a fragment of a sumptuous decorative scheme. Overlooking the moat, the N side of the hall and its SOLAR is intensely picturesque, with seemingly random close-set openings and breaks. Here, two Tudor oriel windows. The larger is five-sided, with glazed quatrefoil frieze at the foot (introduced c. 1810) and transomed lights with ogee heads below, segmental heads above; rib-vaulted ceiling. The other is canted, with a panelled ceiling and the arrangement of the lights reversed. In the ceilings of both, a demi-angel carries the arms of Bishop Knight, i.e. 1541–7.

The CHAPEL of Bishop Burnell (1275–92) just touches the SW angle of Jocelyn's palace. It is a building of great beauty, especially internally, lofty and spacious and of happy simplicity, with a rather French character suggested by the high proportion of glass to wall. It has been suggested that it is a reworking of Jocelyn's chapel, the lower walls and perhaps the W doorway c. 1210–30. High up on each face, small ventilation openings of cusped spheric triangle form, typical of the late C13. The exterior is of small red stone with white stone dressings. The W doorway is segmental-arched, nearly semicircular, has Purbeck marble colonnettes, and a hoodmould on headstops. Three cusps in the arch; originally five, the lowest ones pared off when the floor level was raised in the C19. Inside it is five-cusped on no capitals and again has hoodmould and headstops. The chapel is three bays long, with tall three-light side windows and a vault high up which has ridge ribs and tiercerons and bosses carved beautifully with naturalistic foliage. The wall bosses to the lateral ribs carry heads instead. Between the windows are slim Purbeck shafts of trefoil section, on head corbels (some lumpen C19 restorations). The windows have double shafts and mullions with small capitals; their tracery patterns one ought to learn by heart to remember what the late C13 is like in Somerset. W window of five cusped stepped lancet lights, E window of six lights, grouped in three plus three with intersected tracery and, in the middle, an eight-foiled circle. The other windows have tracery as follows: three spheric triangles with cusped trefoils inside, three almond-shapes arranged trefoil-wise, with cusping that includes ogee details, i.e. completed after 1300; three circles with sexfoils. Spheric-triangle tracery occurs in two-light form at the entrance to the Cathedral chapter house. SEDILIA and PISCINA with Purbeck marble shafts, simply cusped pointed arches, the cusps a little pierced, sunk pointed cusped trefoils in the spandrels, and again hoodmould and headstops. – ALTAR and CHAIR by *David John*, 2006, of maple inset with Ancaster stone, on an Ancaster floor slab lettered by *John Rowlands-Pritchard*. – Good STALLS designed and carved by *Miss A. Ardagh*, 1906, with faintly Morrisy panels of fruit. SCREEN of similar date. – STAINED GLASS. Isolated panels within borders, including jumbled medieval fragments from Rouen collected by Bishop Law. Installed by *Thomas Willement*, c. 1832–5.

The chapel was originally accessible from Bishop Burnell's new HALL. Its roofs were plundered for lead in 1552, and the E and most of the S walls dismantled by Bishop Law c. 1824,

18

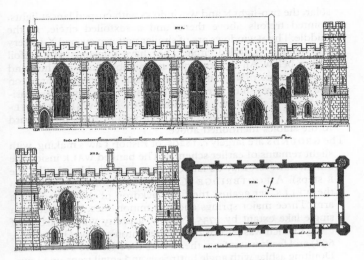

Wells, Bishop's Palace, Burnell's Hall.
North and west elevation and plan, 1836

leaving only a Picturesque screen across the gardens. When complete it must have been one of the most inspiring of the century in England, 115 ft long and nearly 60 ft wide (35 by 18 metres), almost as large as that of the archbishops of Canterbury. Burnell was Chancellor and friend of Edward I: a hall of this size was surely planned with an eye to entertaining kings (as he did at Acton Burnell, Shropshire, *c.* 1283). The hall is not square to the chapel or to Jocelyn's range, perhaps respecting the course of a stream that ran to the N. The embattled parapet is for show (the four immensely tall N windows tell us that) and it is remarkable that before 1300 the bishop could open his hall so wide to the outside. Four octagonal angle turrets, again with many-stepped set-offs, a notably early example of the fashion for such turrets. They must have made this block look very self-confident. The SW turret was the garderobe, with tiny vaulted roof inside. That at the SE corner stands as a solitary cliff, with the stub of the S wall and the jamb of its first window. The hall was aisled in five bays with columns of timber or stone. Encaustic tile fragments made in Glastonbury suggest the quality of the floor.

The hall possessed already – one of the earliest known examples – the English standard arrangement of porch, screens passage, and kitchens accessible from the passage. The porch (demolished *c.* late C18) was two storeys high and projected deeply; the position of the screens passage is shown by scars on the N wall. W of the screens passage were service rooms lit by small lancets, then a low central door through the W wall of the hall to kitchens on the site of the C19 stables to the W. S of this door, the solar chimney flue survives. Lighting the solar, the two-light N and W windows with cusped lancet lights, pointed trefoils above them, and a sexfoiled circle, in the middle. The N windows are of similar pattern: cusped Y-tracery and again a sexfoiled circle. They have transoms with trefoil arches below. All the tracery is remarkably fine and thin, and the stonework of the same dimensions as the windows at Acton Burnell, Shropshire; seemingly the same mason was responsible. Parts of the tracery reinstated, 1830. New VISITOR FACILITIES by *Caröe & Partners* were approved in 2010, for the yard to the stables mentioned above.

The GROUNDS are largely *c.* 1820s, of Bishop Law's making, with slight remains of earlier schemes. The banked WALK inside the S wall, however, may be late C17 (see a scrolled bracket by the E steps). A FOOTBRIDGE (*Caröe*, 1926) crosses the moat to the WELLS, set against the fine backdrop of the cathedral's E arm. Three major springs and two minor ones, now feeding a single lake extant by 1735. Nearby, a pretty WELL HOUSE of *c.* 1451 which was part of Bishop Bekynton's *Nova Opera* (*see* p. 698) and feeds water from the wells to the Market Place conduit. Doulting ashlar with angle buttresses and small transomed two-light windows. Pyramid roof, finial with crouching dog.

BISHOP'S BARN, SW, is early C15. For the bishop's home farm. Local squared rubble with Doulting stone dressings. Cruciform plan, thirteen bays marked by buttresses with two set-offs. Small transomed slit windows, and opposing central porches to the threshing floor. Entrance arches with chamfered segmental heads. The roof has two collars, one tier of curved wind-braces, and two tiers of tenoned and chamfered purlins.

THE PRECINCT

Cathedral Green

The entrance to CATHEDRAL GREEN from Market Place is through PENNILESS PORCH, built *c.* 1451 by Bishop Bekynton (his rebus in the angle to the W of the outer N wall). Some of the lower masonry is earlier, possibly indicating an Anglo-Norman gatehouse on this site. It would originally have sat on the axis of the Saxon cathedral and its atrium. The arch seems to lead E but then turns N. It is as monumental towards the town as Bekynton's Bishop's Eye to its S (*see* p. 699), but not in so monumental a position. Polygonal towers to the W. Archway with four-centred head decorated with fleurons. Foliage in the spandrels. Shields and windows above. On the second floor three niches and between them two-light windows with their lower parts blank. Towards Market Place, the first-floor window tracery, battlements and carved details were reinstated *c.* 1906–12. First-floor chamber with fine oak panelling, perhaps *c.* 1610–50; decorated frieze and Ionic pilasters framing the later chimneypiece.

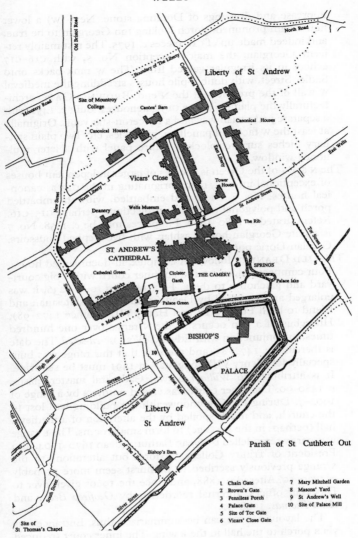

Wells, Cathedral Precinct.
Plan

1 Chain Gate	7 Mary Mitchell Garden
2 Brown's Gate	8 Masons' Yard
3 Penniless Porch	9 St Andrew's Well
4 Palace Gate	10 Site of Palace Mill
5 Site of Tor Gate	
6 Vicars' Close Gate	

Doulting ashlar with angle buttresses and small transomed two-
light windows. Pyramid roof, finial with crouching dog.

BISHOP'S BARN, sw, is early C15. For the bishop's home
farm. Local squared rubble with Doulting stone dressings.
Cruciform plan, thirteen bays marked by buttresses with two
set-offs. Small transomed slit windows, and opposing central
porches to the threshing floor. Entrance arches with chamfered

doorcase and dressings of Doulting stone. Next (w) a lower house with prominent porch looking too Georgian to be true, and indeed made up of C18 pieces *c.* 1975. The rest mainly reticent Georgian; the major exception No. 5, with C16–C17 echoes in its irregular gabled front. The w rank backs onto Sadler Street, with double-pile houses straddling the medieval w wall of the precinct. At the N end, BROWN'S GATE, architecturally the plainest of the C15 gatehouses. Built *c.* 1451 with a separate pedestrian way and a tierceron-star vault. Originally at least the w face had panelling, pinnacles, etc. Two plain statuary niches survive; blocked centre panel with a later mullioned window.

The N SIDE of the Green is a series of larger independent houses of exceptional interest, many originating in the C12 as canonical houses. No. 6 is low and embattled, with an embattled porch and polygonal turret-like projections, perhaps C15–C16. Refenestrated *c.* 1780–1800. Fireplaces may be *c.* 1558. No. 7 is a Late Georgian house, ashlar, with five-stepped voussoirs. Grecian Doric porch, *c.* 1820s.

The OLD DEANERY follows. A complex, ill-documented house. Four compact ranges around an inner court, with a big courtyard and gatehouse to the E. First referred to in 1236, it was enlarged and enriched by Dean Gunthorpe (a statesman and friend to both Edward IV and Henry VII, in office 1472–98). His rebus of a gun occurs in the N range over one hundred times, in conjunction with Edward IV's *rose-en-soleil*. The date is therefore *c.* 1472–83, and the idea that this range was built specially for Henry VII's long stay in 1491 must be set aside. It is attributed to *William Smyth*, Cathedral master mason *c.* 1480–90. The inner court was closed on the E by a range of 1602–7. During the Commonwealth the building was lost to the church, and much spoiled by the alteration of a medieval hall (perhaps in the w range) to form small rooms. The E range was partly remodelled by Dean Bathurst, dean 1670–1704, also President of Trinity College, Oxford; but alterations to the s range previously ascribed to Bathurst seem more probably *c.* 1730–50. Altered *c.* 1888, and since the 1960s given over to Diocesan offices. Internal reordering by *Geoffrey Beech* and *Alan Thomas*, 1988–91.

The layout *c.* 1500 can be summarized thus. Entrance was via a porch to the hall in the E wing. The inner court (reduced to a light well by encroachments since 1800) gave access to kitchens and offices on the ground floor of the N wing, with principal chambers unusually on its upper floors. Domestic quarters were in the s and w ranges, of which the lower walls are C13, remodelled by Gunthorpe in Chilcote stone. The s FRONT faces the Green and gives a brief impression of C18 Gothick. What establish the Gothic are seven regular buttresses with C13 bases, enveloped and heightened in the late C15; and at the angles, two prettily panelled polygonal turrets. The C15 battlements (possibly restored) have shields and Tudor roses in the merlons, perhaps marking Henry VII's stay in 1491. That

DEANERY, WELLS,

Wells, Old Deanery, bay window.
Elevation and section, 1836

it also looks C18 is due to a complete refenestration: the C15 buttresses frame six windows on two storeys, with their original sash-bars. This work is usually credited to Dean Bathurst, but appears later than 1704 (plain Palladian architraves, and rectangular rather than square panes). In the w range the same sashes continue. Here, a vernacular late C17 porch with steep pediment and little upright oval windows keyed into oblong panels, the fashion in N Somerset c. 1670–90 (see also the E front). This must be by Dean Bathurst, and he surely cannot have been responsible at the same time for the Palladian-looking windows. Gunthorpe added the sumptuous three-storey N RANGE of Chilcote stone and Doulting for some of the finer work. Irregular fenestration and a square tower at its SW corner, which in 1796 had tall shafted pinnacles. In front of it, the NW corner is slightly set back, with Y-traceried lights of *c*. 1800–20. Then follow from W to E a fine double-height square oriel rising from an arched base, with a big four-light Perp window at each floor, certainly late C15. Directly E, a canted first-floor bay with pinnacled parapet rising from a row of gun barrels, and bands of shields above and below the lights bearing Edward IV's *rose-en-soleil* with guns. Its tracery is like that at Eltham Palace, Kent, *c*. 1475. Pevsner thought the whole bay might be C18, but it is without doubt genuine. Then a broad chimney-breast, and two two-light windows with transoms. E of the house, a spacious COURTYARD reached by an embattled gateway, with a carriageway and a pedestrian entrance outside but only one very wide archway inside, and a chamber above. The S courtyard wall W of the gatehouse has a broad terraced top (cf. Berry Pomeroy Castle, Devon). N of the courtyard, another C15 house, originally free-standing, with transomed two-light windows. To its SE, an early C19 four-centred gateway leads to low L-shaped former STABLES.

The E range of 1602–7 has an off-centre porch, mullioned-and-transomed windows on the ground floor, and late C17 cross-windows in the porch. Flanking the Georgian upper windows and in the upper porch, more late C17 oval lights as in the W porch. The HALL, presumably secondary to that in the N range, lies in the expected position S of the porch; a big room but low, with early to mid-C17 panelling, naïve Ionic pilasters about the door, and a big stone chimneypiece of the late C15, better preserved and more decorative than the similar one in the Bishop's Palace.

Off the screens passage, in the ground floor of the N range, the present reception office, with Neo-Georgian oak staircase by *Alan Thomas*, 1988–91. The doorway from screens passage to inner court is C15. Immediately to its r. what was the N wall of the court, with two plain doorways into the former kitchen and offices on the ground floor of the N range. The first floor was reached by a broad staircase in the NW tower, a straight flight under ascending chamfered arches to the first floor, then continuing as a spiral. The first-floor HALL was ceiled from the beginning, as its original moulded beams show. Original rough screen with chamfered muntins, formerly one bay E of the W wall, resited at the E end. In the W wall, i.e. in the former screens passage, a good C15 lavabo. On the N wall, side by side are the square oriel and the canted bay window seen from without, both elaborately vaulted, the canted bay with pendants bearing white roses with gun motifs.* More again in the spandrels of the fireplace to their E. Opposite this in the S wall, another canted oriel looking into the inner court. It has the *rose-en-soleil* again on a shield outside, and a fan-vault with one pendant and two shields bearing Gunthorpe's arms. E of the hall, a former withdrawing chamber houses the recent

*Linda Monckton compares these vaults with one in the banqueting hall at Sudeley Castle, Gloucs. (*c*. 1469–78). They are responses to developments in chantry chapels.

staircase, and floating on the wall above, another Gunthorpe fireplace. Above the hall, a large room (now divided by another *ex situ* plank-and-muntin screen), perhaps the Dean's private CHAMBER, with the upper four-light oriel window, a Gunthorpe fireplace and more moulded beams. To its W, some small mezzanine rooms accessible from the spiral stair. One has three two-light windows peeping down into the hall.

Lastly, in the S range, the central ground-floor room has a ceiling with massive beams, perhaps medieval, covered by C17 or C18 plaster mouldings. Eared chimneypiece *c.* 1750 with swag and mask in the frieze. At the SE corner, a handsome and roomy dog-leg staircase, of mahogany rather than oak, *c.* 1730–50. Three finely tapering turned balusters to each tread, acanthus tread-ends. It leads up to a very handsome panelled room in the centre of the S range, much like a combination room in a Cambridge college. Fluted Ionic pilasters in pairs, rich dentil cornice, profuse leaf or egg-and-dart mouldings, and a fine fireplace with acanthus frieze. Can all this be as early as *c.* 1700 as is usually supposed, or might it be of the same date as the staircase?

Next, the MUSEUM (or Chancellor's House). Apparently C16 core. Recessed centre, with Venetian upper windows, paired sashes below. Wings, that at the r. with two mullioned windows (one blocked), perhaps C17. Updated in Regency Gothic *c.* 1828, with a very big canted bay on the gable-end of the W wing. Window in matching style in the E wing. Good early C19 staircase. The MUSIC SCHOOL was the Archdeaconry, rebuilt by Archdeacon Holes, i.e. 1450–70. It had a hall with battlements and angle turrets, cf. the Deanery S range. The S side was sashed in the C18, and the hall was horizontally subdivided. Completely altered by *Edmund Buckle*, *c.* 1888–9 for Wells Theological College. Of the C15 work, only the two angle turrets survive. Off-centre entrance via a low porch slung between a tall projecting stair-turret, l., and a very broad and deep polygonal bay window, r. Of the former screens passage there is a surviving door jamb and part arch at the front and on the outside of the E gable wall, three blocked doorways originally leading no doubt into kitchen, pantry and buttery. Inside at the E end of the N wall, i.e. where the passage's rear door would have been, is a most interesting cinque-cusped arch with C13 mouldings, now blocked as a recess. In the mid C19 the E gable had a circular window of late C13 forms, and a C13 cusped lancet survives low down in the N wall next to the rear door. C15 timber roof with collar-beams, long arched braces, and four tiers of wind-braces arranged in two ogee crosses above each other. Deeply undercut frieze at the wall-plate, with blank arcading above. *Buckle*'s limed oak fittings for the college library include arcaded galleries of C17 form, reached by spiral stairs.

CHAIN GATE, the most elegant of Bekynton's gates, was built *c.* 1459–60 to provide the Vicars Choral with a bridge from their Hall (*see* Vicars' Close, below) directly into the Cathedral. The bridge is in the form of an enclosed windowed passage

p. 688

approached via the top of the chapter-house staircase, and sitting over the gateway. The carriageway has a broad four-centred arch (formerly barred at night by a raised chain) over which is a tierceron-vault with a central square. Flanking pedestrian passages with pretty traceried panelling above the entrances. They are screened off from the carriageway by depressed-arched openings. One passage is longer than the other because placed below a square projection in which, above, the transition from the bridge to the Vicars' Hall is managed – a modification completed by 1465. Previously the entrance to the Hall was axial to the bridge. The covered upper passageway has three-light transomed windows with four-centred heads and prettily cusped tracery; the two windows over the central arch have a statuary niche in place of a central light, with original statuettes. Panelled battlements, with pinnacles reinstated in a restoration c. 1889–90, by *Ewan Christian*.

Vicars' Close

42   VICARS' CLOSE is, architecturally speaking, of the highest inter-est. The vicars of Wells were subordinate members of the cathe-dral in orders or minor orders acting as vice-prebendaries, i.e. instead of absent prebendaries. They had existed since the cathedral was reorganized in the C12. Bishop Ralph of Shrews-bury established them in 1348 as a College of Vicars Choral and gave them their quarters, New Hall or New Close (called Vicars' Close since the early C20). It is the most completely preserved of its type in Britain, with facing terraces on each side. 456 ft (139 metres) long, subtly decreasing in width from S to N, either a deliberate perspective effect or the result of pre-existing boundaries. The twenty-one HOUSES of identical plan were complete by 1353–4.★ They are of course not in their orig-inal state. The walled and gated front gardens were added c. 1410–20 by Bishop Bubwith. By c. 1450 the houses were in poor repair, but Bishop Bekynton's bequest c. 1466 rectified this, adding the tall chimneystacks (which bear *inter alia* his arms and those of the See), continuous roofs and eaves course which are responsible for the still happily unified impression.

    Entrances were originally to the S of the chimneystacks, leading into a hall. The high end (N of the chimney) was lit by two-light windows front and back. The S end was screened as a small room (surviving at No. 7), perhaps for a servant. At the rear was a stair-turret with timber stairs and incorporating a latrine, with a second conjecturally above. There was a door to the rear yard, and in the rear wall of the hall, a lavabo, of which the best survivor is at No. 9. The first floor was arranged as a large and a small chamber like the ground floor. The fenestration seems to have varied a little, but generally the hall

---

★ This account relies on Warwick Rodwell's summary in R. Hall and D. Stocker (eds), *Vicars Choral at English Cathedrals*, 2005.

windows were transomed, of two lights with cusped ogee heads, within squared frames; similar but smaller main chamber windows without transoms. The original roofs were possibly thatched, irregularly stepped, and the party walls did not continue up to the ridges.

The exterior of No. 22, restored by *J. H. Parker* and *William Burges* in 1863–4 and refurbished 1991, gives a good idea of the C15 appearance. Hall ceiling painted with vines and floral borders by *Burges*. The front garden retains its little battlemented gate (see also Nos. 5, 27 and two at No. 13, which also has a section of wall approaching the original height of *c.* 6 ft, 2 metres). Other houses show signs of change: at No. 18, three canted bay windows; No. 16, two houses amalgamated and refronted in brick, of five bays with pedimented doorcase, *c.* 1780–90 (cf. doorcases at Kingsdown Parade, Bristol). No. 14 has a s-facing wing of *c.* 1490, filling the space between house and chapel. It is distinguished by a big four-light window, with shields in the dado. The ground-floor part is Victorian. The house to the r. of the chapel is perhaps late C15 or early C16, refaced in the C19; it hides the front of the northernmost house of the E range. The Close was closed to the N by a chapel, to the S by the Vicars' Hall.

The CHAPEL, with LIBRARY above, was built *c.* 1424–30. S front of creamy Chilcote ashlar. Bellcote with Bekynton's arms, added *c.* 1443–65. E window of three lights under a depressed arch. The S front is bisected by a narrow buttress, with two storeys of two windows each side. The chapel windows Perp, of two lights under two-centred arches, with flowers and leaves around the jambs. The entrance bay (l.) has the door inserted beneath the arched window head. Original oak door with the arms of bishops Bubwith and Stafford. Smaller upper windows with straight heads. The battlements and the spandrels of the ground-floor windows have charming but inexplicable decoration, of reused early C13 spandrel carvings from the Cathedral: perhaps an early antiquarian impulse, they were present by 1790. C15 panelled chapel ceiling, with moulded beams. Medieval ALTAR SLAB, Perp image niches with crockets and big finials. – SCREEN (W). One-light divisions with foliage frieze and cresting, restored 1885–6 by *J. D. Sedding.* – REPOUSSÉ PANELS with standing figures in the Arts and Crafts taste. By *Heywood Sumner*, 1893, set in fine panelling by *Henry Wilson*; the figures accompanied his lost sgraffito decoration for *Sedding.* – STAINED GLASS. By *Clayton & Bell*, 1875–6, with some mid-C15 heads and canopies in the tracery. – The library roof, a C19 copy, has wind-braces in the form of inverted arches.

The VICARS' HALL in part pre-dates the College foundation, but now forms part of a composition which is essentially C15. Here the college administered its business and the vicars ate. It is amongst the greatest attractions of the Wells precincts. The lofty UNDERCROFT, originally perhaps a single-storey hall, is late C13; its vault marked by attached wall-shafts with moulded

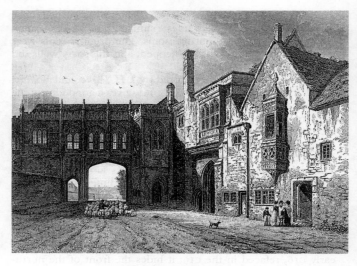

Wells, Chain Gate and Vicars' Hall.
Engraving, 1824

bases and capitals. The small cusped windows are C14. Vault painted by *Burges c.* 1863; similar decoration in a room to the w. The Hall was added above *c.* 1345–8, and there are appendages E and W. The s front which is obscured at the w end by Chain Gate is quite unmonumental. It changes in height and projects and recedes, and the fenestration differs in size and height. It was partially refaced in the early C15. The gateway was pushed through the E end at an uncertain date – *c.* 1365 and *c.* 1460 have been claimed. It is divided into a pedestrian and a carriage arch on the outer side, one broad arch on the inner. The arch mouldings are deeper than those of Chain Gate, but the tierceron-vault is very similar. Above on both sides, but not by any means in axis, are shallow canted oriels, *c.* 1500–23, from a remodelling by Richard Pomeroy, keeper of the fabric. His arms and inscription are in the glazing. On the N side, two transomed two-light windows side by side, with wave-moulded jambs typical of the master mason *William Joy*, i.e. *c.* 1329–48. The tracery is not yet divested of Dec ogee curves. In the gable-end E of the gateway there is also a delightful C15 s-facing oriel window, very daintily decorated with friezes and quatrefoil panels, Another, facing w in the Hall's w wing, is by *J. H. Parker*, 1863. Originally the approach to the Hall from the Close was by stairs against the N wall. Now it is reached by a wide straight staircase in the long three-storey STAIR-TOWER which projects deep into the Close. This forms a porch open on all sides; within it, a very close and intricate lierne-vault.

The entrance to the Hall from the stair is opposite that from Chain Gate. A panelled screen on the w was originally matched by one on the E forming a screens passage. Pointed wagon-roof below the collar-beams, possibly C16. In the W gable a four-light window of c. 1460, with reused C14 tracery (three quatrefoils). Late C15 or early C16 E window of three lights with cinque-cusped ogee heads. On the S wall a big fireplace, probably early C16, with very elongated beasts in the spandrels and unidentified initials. To the r., a stone pulpit probably of c. 1620, tucked in above and behind the fireplace, for the steward to read from the Bible during meals. A pair of WOODEN FIGURES, of c. 1330–40, are taken to represent the Annunciation, with the three Magi and the Child Christ playing with St John beneath.

To the W a small C14 kitchen with large fire opening, original timber roof and an open drain in the stone floor disgorging into the street. It retains a medieval stone sink. From the hall, a narrow newel stair leads up to the EXCHEQUER on the second floor of the stair-tower, with original fireplace and ornamented lavabo and again an original roof with wind-braces. At its N end is a small MUNIMENT ROOM with a remarkable survival, a C15 deed chest, looking just like a modern cupboard of card-index boxes. From here another newel stair leads down to a TREASURY over the porch, the most secure and hard-to-reach location.

St Andrew Street

ST ANDREW STREET runs E from Vicars' Hall, with two substantially medieval houses facing one another. On the N side, behind high walls is TOWER HOUSE (customary residence of the cathedral precentors, 1338–1734), so called from a square three-storey tower at its NE end. It has a polygonal stair-turret at the SE angle. A long main range running N–S, presumably early C14 from the blocked two-light Dec window with a transom in the S gable. Elsewhere, mostly C18 and C19 sashes. (It had originally a first-floor hall with undercroft at the S end. The hall has a S window with a trefoiled rere-arch behind a round-arched head, and Elizabethan panelling. Good four-bay roof with heavy cambered and arch-braced collars, two tiers of wind-bracing, brattished wall-plates with quatrefoil frieze. Two staircases, one of them a spiral up the tower. The other, next to the hall, much altered, but its stone roof exists with transverse arches. A short medieval range projects W, set one bay back from the S gable. Its ground-floor room has a four-compartment ceiling with moulded beams, a four-centred panelled inner arch of a broad window or oriel and a small recess with a flue. Two-bay roof, identical in detail to that over the main range.)

THE RIB, opposite, was a canonical house in the gift of the bishop. C14 or earlier, on a site occupied since c. 1130. The gabled E–W range is largely mid-C15. Handsome porch added a little later at the W end of the N side. Diagonal buttresses, four-centred door and a good three-light window above (cf. Chain Gate), with shields beneath the window bearing a W, probably for Walter Osborn, a canon *c.* 1464–84. W service wing demolished *c.* 1950, the E solar wing replaced by the early C16 cross-wing. Three-bay s front with two full-height buttresses; arched heads still to the upper lights, the lower windows inserted probably in 1802 when the double-height hall was floored and staircase inserted. In the N wall of the ground-floor E room, a broad panelled arch with moulded elliptical head, probably C14. It may have led into a bay window or a separate oriel. C15 six-bay roof to the main range: remains of a quatrefoil frieze above the wall-plates, arch-braced trusses, four tiers of wind-braces, wall-shafts in two corners carried on stone angel corbels. – STAINED GLASS. In the oratory over the porch, a seraph and Osborn's initials, perhaps *c.* 1470.

The Liberty

THE LIBERTY runs N from St Andrew Street in an L-shape (called East Liberty and North Liberty until the late C20). Developed from the C12 with canonical houses, there are now few pre-Georgian survivals but most had medieval predecessors. In the E arm (formerly East Liberty), No. 25, of C13 origin, was rebuilt *c.* 1606–10, reusing stonework from Bishop Stillington's Lady Chapel (*see* p. 673). Altered in the C18 and C19 but restored by *Robert Potter*, 1969. On an L-plan with a staircase in the rear angle. Two storeys with attic, symmetrical s front with two gables, gabled W porch. Mullioned windows under hoodmoulds, of four, three, and two lights, and sashes on the first floor. Two re-set C15 demi-figures of angels acting as label stops to a s doorway. (The porch gives onto a hall to the s, and kitchen to the N. In the kitchen, a broad cambered fireplace, and a C15 rear window of four lights, straight-headed with two-centred heads to the lights; no doubt from Stillington's chapel. At the NW end, remains of a stone newel stair to the kitchen chamber. A late C16 attic chimneypiece may be a C19 insertion.) The rest are occupied by Wells Cathedral School. No. 23, *c.* 1819–25, tall and block-like with spare Grecian details, in the manner of contemporary Clifton villas. Projecting porch. To the l. of the entrance a pretty staircase with thin iron railing and apsidal N end. Agreement to rebuild No. 21 was made in 1737. Pretty staircase, right for the date, with three slim balusters to each tread, one of them twisted, and carved tread-ends. Early C19 porch. In the basement N wall, a C17 ovolo-mullioned window.

No. 19, built for a wealthy physician, Dr Claver Morris, 1699–1702, is a telling example of domestic architecture in Somerset at that date. Five bays and two storeys with a projecting central porch, deep eaves cornice and a hipped roof. Raised above a half-basement, giving an imposing presence. Upright oval windows in the sides of the porch, with thickly moulded frames. The upper windows have original bolection-moulded surrounds with sashes. Sash windows appeared in Bath only *c.* 1695–6, so this is early for Somerset. The lower surrounds and door pediment appear to be *c.* 1780–1820. At the back, a much altered regular arrangement of openings with one early C18 sash frame surviving. The first-floor side windows have stone mullions and moulded frames of *c.* 1700 with pulvinated friezes but on the N side, C17 hood-moulded and cambered basement openings. Some good original panelling, bolection-moulded doorcases, robust open-well pine staircase with heavy newels and fat turned balusters. Over the porch, a tiny closet with fruity garlanded ceiling. To its N, set back behind a deep courtyard, DE SALIS HOUSE. Abutting parallel N–S ranges, the rear range C14 (rare late C14 barrel roof; curved rafters and some moulded ribs) and the E-plan front perhaps late C15 (four-bay roof with arched-braced trusses, wind-braces and ridge purlin). Much C17 and C18 updating. Central porch with thin diagonal buttresses, pinnacles and a four-centred head. Hoodmould on big headstops, moulded beamed ceiling within. The gabled projection to the l. (a solar?) has the hoodmould of a window with a two-centred arch. A third large window with a two-centred arch is blocked in the S gable-end of the house. Vaulted undercroft. Rear range externally Regency Gothic. Former outbuilding with two buttresses and four-centred openings.

At the elbow of the street is THE CEDARS. Built 1758–61 for Charles Tudway M.P., three times Mayor of Wells, and owner of a sugar plantation in Antigua. By *Thomas Prowse*, a gentleman-architect with property in Wells, and grandson of Bishop Hooper of Bath and Wells. The builder was *Thomas Paty*. Of two storeys and nine bays (1:2:3:2:1), the centre and ends recessed. Parapet with intermittent balustraded sections. Central doorway with attached unfluted Ionic columns and a pediment. Jarring conservatory, w, *c.* 1866. Mahogany staircase with two turned balusters per tread under an octagonal dome with Rococo garlands (cf. Berkley church, p. 220). Two rooms have magnificent Rococo ceilings by *Thomas Stocking*. The fine Neoclassical decoration in the central saloon – stucco figures in oval medallions, husk garlands, a circular relief with Aeneas and Anchises etc. – may be a decade or two later. NW of The Cedars, a 340-seat RECITAL HALL and teaching space was approved in 2009, by *Eric Parry Architects*. In College Road, NE, handsome STABLES of rosy brick around a paved yard (*c.* 1755–8).

w of The Cedars, No. 11, *c.* 1764–5. Central Venetian motif for the doorway, flanked by two-storey canted bays. Windows with moulded architraves and small plain keystones. Next, ST ANDREW'S LODGE, built for a Charity School founded 1713, apparently not occupied until 1726. Reticent five-bay two-storey front with stone cross-windows, pedimented on the ground floor. Semicircular moulding over the door, with a carved figure of St Andrew. Then RITCHIE HALL, built for the Cathedral School by *J. D. Sedding*, 1883–4; Perp, single-storey front with a low porch tower. Its E end incorporates fragments of the CANONS' BARN, a tithe barn for the parish. The Dean and Chapter were confirmed in possession of the site in 1176, and a charter of about the same date refers to the barn. The NW corner seems original, with large quoins, but the present E wall crudely inserted between the piers suggests truncation. There were narrow aisles inside: three pairs of square piers *c.* 18 ft (5.5 metres) tall, with slightly curved, not chamfered corners. No capitals; plainest abaci. Of Chilcote stone, like some contemporary parts of the Cathedral. POLYDOR HOUSE follows. Early C14 but updated *c.* 1719 for Archdeacon Hunt of Bath. Sash windows, pretty shell-hooded door decorated inside by two cherubs' heads, and a fine spacious open-well staircase to the r. of the entrance, with carved tread-ends and slender turned balusters. Earlier features include the irregular façade with varied eaves heights, one or two mullioned windows, a C17 attic gable at the w, and two buttresses flanking the doorway. C17 rear range. In the former outer back wall is part of an upper window of the C15. (Also a C16 newel stair, and a C17 panelled room with fielded ceiling. Arch-braced collar-roof. Main trusses carried on two carved demi-figures of angels with shields; three purlins, chamfered wind-braces.)

Across the street, four CANONS' HOUSES by *Potter & Hare, c.* 1967–9. Overtly modern, stone-faced below with rendered overhanging upper floors, originally flat-roofed. The flat roofs leaked and pitched roofs were substituted (*Beech Tyldesley,* 1983); a shame, visually at least.

THE TOWN

CHURCHES

32   ST CUTHBERT, St Cuthbert's Street. Though in such an inconspicuous position that it might easily be overlooked were it not for its tower, St Cuthbert is the largest parish church in Somerset, and one of the most interesting. In many Somerset churches the tower is so grand and elaborate that the church is a disappointment. That is here not so: the church can fully hold its own. The Anglo-Saxon dedication makes a pre-Conquest foundation virtually certain, but there is nothing now to tell of it. A re-dedication *c.* 1122–35 may imply some rebuilding* but the core is now C13. The church at that date was cruciform, with a crossing tower (cf. Congresbury, Yatton), five-bay nave with aisles, S porch, and a treasury in the mirror position on the N side. The Perp rebuilding began probably with the chancel and w tower, both perhaps *c.* 1390. So the church gave the unusual spectacle of a w and a crossing tower.

p. 28   The W TOWER is high – in fact the third highest of Somerset parish churches (122 ft, 37 metres) – but does not seem

---

*Of a Norman PILLAR PISCINA, the scalloped bowl was stolen and the pillar recently smashed.

excessive, because it is broad too. Heraldry on the w face indicates major gifts towards its construction *c.* 1385–1400 and *c.* 1435–50. It has been suggested that *William Wynford* was responsible, just after he designed the Cathedral's sw tower, which in any case is clearly the inspiration for the long panels. The Bishop gave worked stone in 1426, and stones in the tower with a Cathedral mason's mark bear this out. Completion was probably achieved *c.* 1430. It has set-back buttresses which near the top sprout out into two tiny attached pinnacles, then a short pinnacled shaft set on the diagonal and finishing below the parapet. Behind rise the very tall square main pinnacles accompanied by thin pinnacled shafts, a complex arrangement. But the principal parts are robust enough to prevail. Embattled parapet with blank arcading. w doorway, six-light sub-arcuated w window, three niches above it, and then, beginning just above the nave roof, the very tall belfry stage modelled on the pattern of the cathedral w towers, but handled more sensitively. On each side two three-light bell-openings with Perp tracery, only the tracery heads open. The lights are extended blank below for the whole height of the top stage, with a transom band of quatrefoils just as in the Cathedral. The unity of handling is emphasized by three wiry shafts framing the main lights, which soar from the base of the stage to the heads of the belfry lights. After the tower, the nave and aisles were remodelled in separate campaigns. In the late c15 or early c16, outer aisles or chapels were added in the two bays between transepts and the porch and treasury projections, giving the church its marked width at this point. The s side is ashlar-faced and has blind arcaded parapets like the tower, though here not embattled. On the N side, reddish sandstone rubble walls and plain parapets. The aisles, chapels and transepts mostly have large simple Perp five-light windows, *p. 37* with two-centred heads. The s transept acquired its s window *c.* 1402. The exceptions are the clerestory of after 1575 (where the cusping is more elegant too) and the vestry. The c13 church is only obvious externally in the Treasury windows, small cusped lancets and a two-light window with a cusped circle in plate tracery, the near-identical s transept E window, and the s doorway, with the deep mouldings and fillets of *c.* 1300.

The INTERIOR reveals a building process that was one of the most curious in Somerset. In the nave, the early c13 piers were heightened by the Perp masons, simply by adding another 9 ft (2.8 metres), to the same moulding as before. The arches also remain, with two pairs of chamfers, and the hoodmoulds with their headstops. The piers are square with four groups of triple shafts. The w bay of the nave arcade is entirely Perp as is clear from the different w responds, i.e. the E.E. nave was extended to join it to the newly built tower. One bay w of the heavy crossing piers, another difference occurs: the piers on both sides have filleted shafts in the diagonals rather than right angles (cf. Cathedral nave). The N capital also has stiff-leaf foliage, while that on the s has simple ring-mouldings like the other C13 capitals. But one bay further W on the S, the capital has trumpet-shaped scallops instead, which at first appears very conservative. Perhaps this was the shape the carver received from the hewer and into which he was to work his foliage. But this instructive feature at St Cuthbert's can be compared with one capital in the nave of the Cathedral, on the S side, in which also trumpet-shapes still appear surrounded by leaves. Was there some ritual reason for this differentiation at St Cuthbert? And why are the capitals thus distinguished not at the same bay?

The site of the crossing tower is clear from the pieces of flat wall E of the nave arcade. Then the arches into the transepts (the diagonal shafts here have no fillets and the arches are triple-chamfered, as was often done under towers); then a shorter wall before the chancel arch, with the same responds as the transept arches. These walls are the crossing piers pared off after 1561 when the tower was dismantled: the capitals here, of the same date, linked by their abacus mouldings. Perhaps the most impressive Perp feature is the immensely tall tower arch, broad enough to be panelled with three sets of arches side by side. Complicated lierne-vault with bosses under the tower. The windows have already been described. They admit ample light, and in addition there is the clerestory added *c.* 1475–1525. Between its windows wall-shafts rise on demi-figures of angels, carrying a low-pitched Somerset roof with tie-beams for every second principal and tracery over. There are demi-figures of angels against the middles of the tie-beams and also against the principals without tie-beams. They carry books with symbols which defy translation. The colouring devised by *Stephen Dykes Bower*, 1961–3, is a triumphant reminder of late medieval spectacle. Unusually for Somerset, a five-light window in the E gable of the clerestory. The chancel chapels of three bays have standard Perp piers with four-wave mouldings. The aisles have wall-shafts too, in the N chapel ending in heads.

The OUTER S CHAPEL interestingly attempts a Perp version of the nave piers. The triple shafts in the main direction are again found, but then two tiny wave mouldings side by side in the diagonals. Small capitals with discrete sections of foliage or animal carving. The E arch is panelled. Fine cambered roof uncovered in the 1950s and restored by *Alan Rome*, 1960; moulded main beams and big square bosses, blind traceried panels of extreme inventiveness and delicacy. Four demi-angels per bay above the wall-plate. It probably dates from 1500–20, cf. S Somerset roofs, e.g. South Brent, Somerton. The OUTER N CHAPEL is more ambitious, probably *c.* 1480–1500. Piers and responds shafted and with ogee-headed panels like the panels surviving in the Cathedral from Stillington's chapel. In its E wall, the preserved former W window of the N transept, unblocked *c.* 1848 as an unglazed traceried screen. It is of three lights, richer than all the rest, with cinque-cusped heads; cf. the S aisle windows at Chard, SW Somerset, *c.* 1453. This suggests an approximate date for the remodelling of the N transept and a *terminus post quem* for the outer N chapel. Low late C15 SACRISTY E of the N chancel chapel; heavily moulded ribbed vault resting on corbels and with ridge ribs. The tower base and W end of the nave and N aisle were reordered by *Caröe & Partners*, 2007–8.

Of the FURNISHINGS, the most remarkable though unfortunately very fragmentary survival is the REREDOSES of the transepts. Figures hacked off at the Reformation, uncovered *c.* 1849–50. The S reredos was a Tree of Jesse made *c.* 1470 by *John Stowell*.★ Jesse is clearly recognizable, propped up on one elbow like a reclining effigy from an Elizabethan tomb. The other figures stood in niches, two tiers of three on each side of the E window (on the r. the last wrapped round onto the S wall), and one tier of nine above. They are separated by vertical strips of vine foliage of the type, set horizontally, seen in rood screens. Over 400 high-quality sculpture fragments survive (no longer on display), with much original colour and gilding. Of three types of stone, probably indicating a High Altar reredos as well. The heads with protruding cheek-bones have much character and individuality. The N reredos has two tiers of five niches under two-centred heads; minute and refined vaults and pinnacles. – REREDOS (chancel) by *Forsyth*, 1867. Caen stone, five crocketed gables, relief of the Last Supper. – PULPIT. Dated 1636, and uncommonly rich in its carving. Base brackets modelled as eagles. Three-dimensional cartouches below larger shields with naïvely carved figures from the Old Testament (Jacob and the Angel, David and Goliath, Samson and the lion, Jonah in the mouth of the whale, Daniel in the lions' den); coupled colonnettes at the angles with arabesques. Stairs, 1861. – FONT. Perp, panelled and octagonal. COVER, possibly late medieval in parts, with C18 painted inscription. Restored by *W. H. Randoll Blacking*, 1950–1. – ROYAL ARMS. 1631, in Jacobean surround. Another, smaller, of 1660. Both coloured and gilded oak. – STAINED GLASS. E window by *Wailes*, 1851. Chancel N and S perhaps made up by *Joseph Bell*, *c.* 1850s, although the S at least was painted by *Mrs Tudway*, and dedicated to family members. S chancel chapel E, 1865, *Bell*. Also his the window over the chancel arch, *c.* 1867. S transept E, C15 fragments, re-set. W window, *Clayton & Bell*, 1872.

MONUMENTS. Henry Clark †1587. Mutilated recumbent stone effigy; in the N chancel chapel, armorials from his big standing monument, demolished *c.* 1848. – Henry Luellin †1614. Alabaster and stone standing monument with kneeling figure under Corinthian canopy. – Henry Keillinghusen of Hamburg 'who came to see this countrye and learne the language', †1615. Marble tablet with winged skull. – Francis Hayes †1623. Good gilded brass with kneeling figure, in

★ Cf. the mid-C14 Jesse reredos at Christchurch Priory, Hants (now Dorset), and a surviving C15 Jesse figure in oak at St Mary, Abergavenny, Gwent.

scrolled alabaster surround with *memento mori*. – Robert Kingston †1743, scrolled tablet with pediment, prominently signed *Nathaniel Ireson*. – Canon H. Barnard †1855. Enamelled brass by *Waller Bros*, 1857.

ST THOMAS, St Thomas Street. 1856–7, by *S. S. Teulon*. Among the liveliest Victorian churches in N Somerset, with one of Teulon's best spires, inventive without becoming wayward. Broad polygonal apse. The style adopted is the favoured Geometric, with some early C14 motifs borrowed from Wells Cathedral. Prettily banded limestone in buff, cream and coral, diapered slate roofs, wrought ironwork by *Skidmore*. Cross-gabled N aisle. Inside, Doulting ashlar with Ham stone around the arcades. Low Church layout (e.g. no chancel arch or screen). S aisle added 1866, also *Teulon*. N arcade piers originally polished like marble, with fine capitals carved by *Thomas Earp*. Wind-braced crown-post roof, ending with a half-wheel of trusses over the apse. Sensitively reordered since 1980, and restored 1996–7, by *Alan & Ann Thomas*. – Complete and largely original decoration and fittings. REREDOS. Mosaic panels by *Salviati*, painting and stencilling by *Fisher*. – ALTAR RAIL by *Skidmore*. – Angular crystalline FONT made by *James Forsyth*, and PULPIT, both designed by *Teulon*. – SCULPTURE. Bas-relief (S transept) by *Josefina de Vasconcellos*, 2002. – STAINED GLASS. Five apse windows by *William Wailes*, 1857, rich and colourful. N aisle, vine-patterned green glass, *Thomas Wilmshurst*. S aisle w, 1866, attributed to *Richard Clayton*.

SE is the former VICARAGE by *Teulon*, 1866–7. An original design, to an irregular plan with service wing at an angle (now a separate house). Inside, a splat-baluster staircase and screen with Moresco-Gothic piercings. To improve the view, Teulon removed slum cottages opposite the church and built ST THOMAS'S TERRACE, 1868–9, Gothic with tall almshousy chimneys. Further w on St Thomas Street and also by *Teulon* is the master's house of St Thomas' School (1859, dem.).

ST JOSEPH AND ST TERESA (R.C.), Chamberlain Street. Originally a convent chapel (*see* Carmelite House). By *C. F. Hansom*, 1877; chancel and nuns' choir by *Hansom & Bond*, 1888. Dec, w door under gabled canopy on curved brackets.

BAPTIST–UNITED REFORMED CHURCH, Union Street. For the Baptists, 1827. Three bays, two storeys. Arched windows, doorway with attached Doric columns and straight architrave.

METHODIST CHAPEL, Southover. Built 1838. Restrained façade, with round-arched windows, interlaced glazing bars, Doric doorcase. Enlarged 1865 (perhaps of this date the arched organ recess on floriated pilasters). Original panelled gallery. School-room to the r., 1881.

PUBLIC BUILDINGS

TOWN HALL, Market Place. 1778–80, probably by *Edmund & William Lush* of Salisbury. Replacing a mid-C16 market house and assize hall to the N. It holds its own in a modest Georgian way against the medieval gatehouses. Two storeys, nine bays arranged three-three-three, of Doulting ashlar. Rusticated, arcaded ground floor, originally open for markets. Arms framed by husk garlands and paterae in the pediment of the centre which was brought forward to form a deep *porte cochère* in 1861. The balcony, the rustication, quoins, and three oculi below the pediment are 1932–3, by *W. D. Caröe*. Brick rear wing, 1854, for court rooms and cells. The two-bay w addition some time after 1861. Secondary staircases inserted by *Charles Brown*, 1905–7. Only the the former Council Chamber has any presence; rich plaster cornice of 1861.

Former MARKET HOUSE, Market Place. By *Richard Carver*, 1835. Low but handsome Roman Doric façade, triglyph frieze and a central attic with little arcaded lights. The hall was originally open, on free-standing columns. Enclosed *c.* 1903 for a Post Office, by introducing incongruous arches on pilasters between the columns.

LIBRARY, Union Street. By *Somerset County Council Architects' Department*, 1968. Neighbourly infill in a narrow side street, with raked top lighting, and clever use of full-height slit windows. Two-storey addition of 1992.

CATHEDRAL SCHOOL. *See* The Liberty, pp. 690–2.

BLUE SCHOOL, Milton Lane. At the w end of the site, former Secondary Modern buildings *c.* 1959, of yellow brick. Additions by *Beech Tyldesley & Partners*, 2002–6. To the E, former Grammar School buildings of *c.* 1962–5 by the *County Architects' Department*; dark brick with concrete lintels, three-storey centre with an apron of single-storey classrooms.

ADULT EDUCATION CENTRE, Portway. By *H. Dare Bryan*, 1898–1900, for the Blue School girls. A pretty example of the freedom from imitation of the past then current amongst the brighter architects. Low L-shaped range with broad curved s gable, corner turret with panelled top, shallow dome and a tall spike. Extended 1913. (Largely original interiors.)

WORKHOUSE (former), Glastonbury Road. By *S. T. Welch*, 1836–7 (cf. Axbridge). Two-storeyed, symmetrical stone front with projecting centre and ends. Over the porch the façade rises in canted form to a third storey with gable and some mean pinnacles. The centre and ends fenestrated with Tudor arches and thin tracery – the recessed flanks with plain sashes. The rear range forms a T-shaped layout with an octagonal block halfway down to control the yards. Extensive N ranges, 1871. The usual afterlife as a hospital ceased *c.* 1990s; converted to council offices by *Caroe & Partners*, 2003–7.

COTTAGE HOSPITAL (former), St Thomas Street. By *John Belcher*, 1895. Attractive. Steep broken pediments and other mildly Restoration motifs. Converted to housing, 2011.

For the former Mendip Hospital, *see* South Horrington, p. 702.

PERAMBULATION

The MARKET PLACE is an ideal preparation for the spacious majesty of the cathedral and its precinct. An irregular L-shape, its traffic mostly pedestrian, nicely re-paved 1993. The s arm

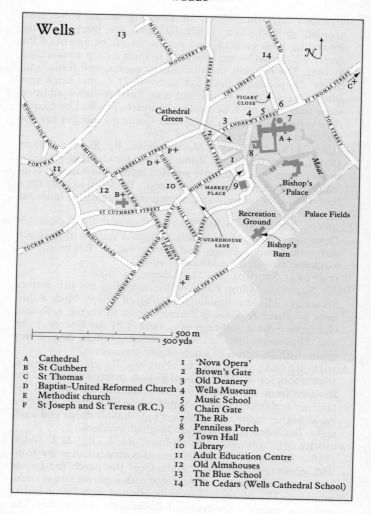

Wells

A	Cathedral
B	St Cuthbert
C	St Thomas
D	Baptist–United Reformed Church
E	Methodist church
F	St Joseph and St Teresa (R.C.)

1	'Nova Opera'
2	Brown's Gate
3	Old Deanery
4	Wells Museum
5	Music School
6	Chain Gate
7	The Rib
8	Penniless Porch
9	Town Hall
10	Library
11	Adult Education Centre
12	Old Almshouses
13	The Blue School
14	The Cedars (Wells Cathedral School)

is roughly square, the site of a C17 canonical house with walled garden, all demolished for the modestly dignified Town Hall. Of the main arm, the N side is one remarkably even row of shops, built all at one time, and much earlier than one would at first suppose. They are Bishop Bekynton's NOVA OPERA ('New Work'), *c.* 1451–3. The concept, not fully realized, was for a regular square with a central conduit and matching terraces, N and S, framing the contemporary gateways to the Cathedral and Bishop's Palace. If completed it would have made a display of Renaissance order unparalleled in English towns before the C17. The *Nova Opera* had originally twelve three-storey houses, of one bay separated by thin buttresses (three remain). The original appearance is unrecorded, but eight houses have Georgian canted bays, perhaps suggesting Perp predecessors. At the E end, half of one small upper cusped arched light, and part of the original upper cornice. The C15 parapet was embattled too. No. 21 has a big original four-centred archway at the back and roof timbers with two tiers of wind-braces. Good Victorian shopfronts, notably at Nos. 17–23, a matching iron-framed array, *c.* 1880–5.

The E side gives a more original impression, dominated by the BISHOP'S EYE. Like a college gatehouse, it has polygonal turrets at all four corners (the battlements of the E pair reinstated *c.* 2000), a wide archway with four-centred heads and a lierne-vault inside, a frieze of shields and then windows on two upper storeys. The W face has three original but badly preserved figures and between them two two-light windows on each floor set into a regular panelling arrangement (cf. St Cuthbert, Wells; Linda Monckton suggests *John Stowell* as designer). The Perp tracery and crossed arrow loops are *c.* 1900–4. To the E face, one tall middle niche on a long shaft and bracket. The battlemented three-bay houses N and S were part of the original composition; that to the N given battlements and mullions etc. *c.* 1932–3 by *Caröe*, sweeping away Georgian alterations. For Penniless Porch, *see* p. 680.

The S side of Market Place is less regular. There are gables here as well as parapets, and at the W end, four harmonic variations on the theme of the Georgian canted bay. No. 8 is late C16, with timber oriel. The best house is the CROWN HOTEL, timber-framed, three-storeyed, with three gables, three canted bays and upright oval windows between them. Full-width pent roofs at each storey. This is *c.* 1650–80, perhaps updating a late C16 building (see the set-back stone door jambs in the entrance-way). In the rear courtyard, more elaborate carved oriels on brackets with pretty arabesque-work. (In one room, a steep arch-braced roof with wind-braces; also several C16 stone fireplaces, C17 plasterwork and a splat-baluster staircase.) At the W end of Market Place, a triangular FOUNTAIN replacing Bekynton's conduit (*see* p. 680). By *Charles Harcourt Masters*, 1799; unusual Gothic Revival. Very rocky rusticated base, spire-like superstructure with ogee-headed openings, clustered shafts at the angles, icicle-work pinnacles, and an ogee cap.

SADLER STREET, N, is a nicely varied collection of Georgian and later shopfronts, and a scattering of C15 to C17 features. The E side was developed *c.* 1370, with housing straddling the wall of the Cathedral precinct. No. 7, W side, is C17, with two gables, two canted bays, wooden mullions, and some pargetting; good C19 shopfront. Further up, the SWAN INN, first mentioned in 1422, much rebuilt 1768–9. The façade, with very broad sash windows, perhaps early C19. Large C16 chimneypiece in the l. ground-floor room and fine linenfold panelling in the dining room, both imported in the late C20. (At No. 29 two good panelled rooms, one C17, the other early C18.) On the E side, Nos. 20–22 were built *c.* 1451 with Brown's Gate (*see* p. 682). Some C15 fabric within, especially a big stone overmantel with brattishing and florets.

HIGH STREET is not straight, which helps to increase interest in the humble but hardly anywhere unattractive houses. The E end is narrow and enclosed. NATWEST, unexpectedly convincing Venetian Gothic, was Stuckey's Bank by *C. E. Giles*, 1855, and had a balcony with Ca' d'Oro tracery, removed in the early C20 when ground-floor alterations were made, probably by *George Oatley*. Inside No. 8, almost opposite, an excellent mid-C17 dog-leg staircase with heavy pierced balustrade with bold roughly symmetrical scrolls, fleurs-de-lys, etc., pendants and finials. Broad arched fireplace with brick fireback dated 1673, and a C15 roof. Where High Street curves and broadens stood the Middle Row shambles, demolished *c.* 1754–64. Much was refronted *c.* 1760–1840 in brick or Doulting stone, e.g. the former STAR HOTEL, a C16 inn with central cobbled coach entrance, and further W, the KING'S HEAD INN, which conceals a timber-framed range of 1511, and hall roof *c.* 1318–19 (upper crucks, collar-beams, cinquefoil-cusped arched braces, cusped wind-braces). No. 46 has a faience façade, *c.* 1930, built as a butcher's shop, with C17 allusions and two bowed oriels. No. 56 still has its C16 gable and jetty, a type common before the refrontings. Set back at the W end of the High Street, AVENUE HOUSE, a five-bay house *c.* 1800–20, with delightful lacy two-storey wrought-iron veranda.

The street forks here, with BROAD STREET to the S. The first impression is indeed of a broad, Georgian Street. The widening was done *c.* 1835–49, with regular plain three-storey houses on the W side. At the same time, PRIORY ROAD was laid out. S is ST JOHN'S STREET, where No. 2 (W side) incorporates fragments of the HOSPITAL OF ST JOHN, founded *c.* 1220. The main building was replaced by the former Central School (*Edwin Hippisley*, 1858–9, Gothic, with a good capped tower). No. 2, facing the street, was probably an early C14 guesthouse: it has blocked medieval openings in the Georgianized façade and S gable. On an L-shaped plan with hall, passage, and service room in the main range. Later wing behind, with remains of a spiral stone stair at the junction. The hall has a well-preserved and decorative base-cruck truss roof of 1314–15; five two-tier crucks with cusped arch-braces, upper crucks and three tiers of wind-braces. Extremely early use of carpenters' marks in both Roman and Arabic numerals.

On ST CUTHBERT STREET, the CITY ARMS, a C16 inn with low two-storey ranges around a courtyard. It was the city gaol until *c.* 1800. Much altered, with misleading antiqued features. W is PRIEST ROW, facing St Cuthbert. At No. 10, reputedly the priest's house, a C15 four-centred doorway. Running off to the E, LLEWELLYN'S ALMSHOUSES, rebuilt *c.* 1887–8, by *Charles Brown*. To the N in CHAMBERLAIN STREET, the OLD ALMSHOUSES. The main range was probably erected *c.* 1436–40, certainly by 1446, with Bishop Bubwith's bequest (1424). Chapel (E), then a gabled porch bridging the former course of a stream; four-centred door under square label with image niche above. Then a long one-and-a-half-storey range with half-dormers (largely rebuilt *c.* 1850), high hall or Guild Room at the w. The CHAPEL roof has collar-beams, arched braces, and four tiers of ogee-shaped wind-braces arranged in two crosses one above the other. Five-light Perp E window with STAINED GLASS by *Joseph Bell*, *c.* 1850. A small straight-headed N window has *ex situ* glass of 1434–43, with the royal arms and those of three founders. (The GUILD ROOM was divided into two floors *c.* 1850 and restored 1995–6; the roof is still visible.) Later almshouses behind, visible from St Cuthbert's church-yard. BRICKE'S ALMSHOUSE is *c.* 1636–8, originally four houses with small mullioned lights symmetrically arranged. In its centre, a curious sedilia-like feature, half classical and half Gothic: four seats set within round cinquefoiled arches on Doric colonnettes. Above, four little round-headed niches under gables (or pediments?) with ball finials, again supported on miniature Doric columns. Within each gable, a cusped ogee arch. Its showiness was presumably intended to remind residents and town of the donor's beneficence. Two s-projecting ranges at the w end, one detached and replacing Still's Almshouses of 1614. Both 1884, probably by *Charles Brown*.

E along CHAMBERLAIN STREET, in appearance almost wholly Georgian, but probably laid out by the early C13. There is first on the l. ST CUTHBERT'S LODGE, early C18, of eight bays, with a spacious staircase to the r. of the entrance, of three windows' width. Each tread has one turned and one twisted baluster. The gatepiers of the stables are also original. More Georgian houses follow. MELBOURNE HOUSE lies back, with five bays and a doorway with attached Doric columns. No. 28, HARPER'S ALMSHOUSE, is an unusually plain vernacular building with a possibly earlier core, rendered with leaded casements. Established 1713, for 'old decayed woolcombers'. Almost opposite, No. 17 has a roof felled 1444–5. No. 22 has exceptional joinery of *c.* 1720–40, including a complete pan-elled parlour with chimneypiece and enriched mouldings (also a fine stucco ceiling with mermen over the stairwell). On the N side is a break where houses were cleared *c.* 1730 to create a vista for a new-built mansion opposite, where now stands CARMELITE HOUSE of *c.* 1810–30. A long two-storey façade with broad overhanging eaves, projecting pedimented centre with entrance recessed behind Greek Doric screen with solid segmental tympanum. A convent from 1875 (its chapel is now St Joseph and St Theresa, *see* above). Now flats.

At the street's E end (N side), a row of good plain Georgian fronts. No. 8 has a C15 rear range with smoke-blackened roof; perhaps others hide similar secrets. Opposite, Nos. 1–9, a modest classical terrace of *c.* 1840. Then N into NEW STREET, at first like Chamberlain Street in character. Decorated door-ways, e.g. No. 1 with Gibbs surround and pediment. No. 9, Ritchie House, begins a series of larger houses *c.* 1760–90, all ashlar-faced and most of five bays. No. 2 (opposite), then to the N, Beaumont House, and No. 19, the latter the Assize judges' lodging in the C19 and C20. On the w side, a more modest but varied row.

OTHER BUILDINGS

E OF THE CENTRE. TOR STREET was laid out *c.* 1207 when the road from Shepton Mallet was re-routed around Bishop Jocelyn's new park. On the w side, the high park wall; on the E, low cottages, many doubtless of medieval origin. ST THOMAS STREET, running E from the top, was established by the C12, and was called Byestewalles. It too is cottagey, with rear courts at right angles. On the N side, Nos. 3–5 may represent a service range and hall of *c.* 1400, with four-centred doorway marking the screens passage. No. 9 has a C16 arched doorway flanked by square ground-floor bays; C17 and C18 fittings. Nos. 26 and 28 (s side) have been dated by dendrochronology to 1511 (A-frame roof with cranked collars, ridge-piece and in-line butt purlins) and 1485 (beamed ground-floor ceiling). No. 25 is an exception, polite ashlar-fronted, late C18, with large bow window, pedimented doorcase. Another C15 four-centred doorway at No. 41, with headstop; the doorway at No. 53 may be *c.* 1400, window mullions C17. For St Thomas and its associated buildings, *see* p. 696. Further NE in Hawker's Lane, BERYL HOUSE by *Benjamin Ferrey, c.* 1838. A Neo-Tudor villa of grey limestone. Broad straight staircase with good Gothic detailing.

W OF THE CENTRE. In Princes Road, the former REGAL CINEMA, good Art-Deco-with-water, by *E.S. Roberts*, 1935. Original raked balcony, wavy combed stucco, big fountain grilles flanking the proscenium arch. Further out, in WEST STREET, a former MILL, C19, on the site of one of the bishop's two mills in the out-parish of St Cuthbert. N in PORTWAY, No. 71 is a *moderne* house of 1936, with the usual flat roof accessed by a tower.

OUTLYING BUILDINGS

KING'S CASTLE. Small Iron Age HILL-FORT I m. E of Wells, roughly triangular in shape within woodland, with banks still *c.* 6 ft (2 metres) high in places.

SOUTH HORRINGTON. The recently invented name for a former hospital and its redeveloped grounds, on Bath Road just beyond the city boundary. The MENDIP HOSPITAL (County Lunatic Asylum) was built in 1845–8 to a Neo-Jacobean design by *Scott & Moffatt*, of pink sandstone quarried on site, with Bath stone dressings. At the main gate (w), a strikingly pretty LODGE, shaped gables, ogee-domed turret. The main buildings face s onto spacious lawns with cedars, enjoyably like a country house, and without any sense of gloom. Numerous cross-wings and projections, shaped gables, occasional strapwork, big square lantern over the main entrance. Late C19 ward additions apparently by *G. T. Hine*, consultant to HM Commissioners in Lunacy. Large grounds with farm, orchards, laundry, gas works etc., made the community largely self-sufficient. In 1870–1 *Parr & Strong* added a big, coarsely detailed CHAPEL. Over its crossing a broached octagonal tower rising to a fat spire. The last patients left in 1991. Sensitive conversion to housing *c.* 1996–2001, by *BBA Architects*, with judicious pruning of the service buildings, and bland new houses behind.

WEST HARPTREE   5050

The church and many houses are of orange-pink Dolomitic Conglomerate.

ST MARY. Simple Norman w tower with clasping buttresses and two slit windows. Copper-clad splay-foot spire, a type rare in Somerset, perhaps C13 or C14. N doorway also Norman, although entirely rebuilt, with a single order of columns with scalloped capitals. The arch is segmental, as often in Norman parish churches in this part of Somerset. Some reused mid-C12 corbel heads. The long-and-short quoins at the NW angle of the nave are also C12. Three-bay s arcade with Dec octagonal piers and the first arch from the E double-chamfered, as are the openings into the s chapel. The two arches at the w indicate a Perp extension of the aisle. Much original Perp work in the s porch, with stairs to a former gallery. In 1865 *C. E. Giles* added a transeptal vestry (N), and rebuilt the chancel and much of the interior in a lifeless E.E. style. Pretty Dec PISCINA (s aisle); cusped ogee opening with trefoil spandrels. – SCULPTURE. W nave wall: part of a Perp vaulted niche canopy with medieval colour traces, and two (C13?) corbel heads.

The church stands partly screened by yews, at a broad junction full of interest in all directions. To the NE, the OLD VICARAGE, with a symmetrical façade of square-headed two- and three-light mullioned windows, *c.* 1670–90. A third storey and staircase tower were added in 1724, and no doubt the round-arched door canopy too. s of the church lies GOURNAY COURT, a sizeable house of red sandstone begun perhaps *c.* 1600 by Francis Buckland, updated or completed *c.* 1640–60 by his son. Restored *c.* 1910 by *J. D. Coleridge*, intended for the epileptic son of King George V, but never occupied. Further altered by *G. C. Lawrence* (*Oatley & Lawrence*), 1929 and later. The front is seven bays wide and two-and-a-half storeys, with four straight gables. Windows of cross-type, perhaps mid-C17. Distinctive two-storey porch with attached Doric columns below, Ionic above, and a glazed upper storey. Over the porch a strapwork balcony with a segmental-headed loggia behind, topped by a curved gable squeezed between two of the straight ones.

The porch bears the arms of Buckland and Phelips (a marriage *c.* 1642); does this apply to the porch or to the whole front? The rear E wing may be late medieval, see the buttresses. (In the ground-floor E room, panelling of *c.* 1600 from Beaudesert Hall, Staffs., installed *c.* 1935. In the room above, a fireplace with royal arms, strapwork and caryatids in the overmantel, oak-leaf-wreathed ceiling. Early C17 staircase with arched balustrade, vases and fruit on the newels.)

W of the church, TILLY MANOR. Built for the Roynon family in 1659, as dated on an overmantel with strapwork cartouches in a ground-floor room. The ground-floor windows are lustily embellished by steep swan-necked pediments with nicely carved heraldry cartouches, and above these, quite detached, puny segmental pediments. The first-floor windows are upright with a mullion, but the middle window is much larger and must once have been a balcony door. But the façade was altered early in the C18, and (perhaps at the same time, certainly before 1829) a third storey and two wings were removed. The shallow-pitched roof seems early C19. The main door has an elaborate frame with ears, then an independent surround of fat pilasters on bases which are Ionic capitals, probably injudiciously reused material from the C17 doorway. Also of 1659 the open-well staircase, with pierced strapwork panels.

₅₀₄₀

WEST HORRINGTON

A small village strung along the side of a hill, *c.* 2 m. ENE of Wells. About ½ m. N, in the deep valley of Biddle Combe, a packhorse BRIDGE (rebuilt late C20) leads to a ruined C18 BUDDLE HOUSE: a circular stone beehive-shaped structure for extracting lead ores by sedimentation. One door opening; *c.* 13 ft (4 metres) in diameter internally.

₅₀₄₀

WESTBURY-SUB-MENDIP

ST LAWRENCE. Low battlemented W tower, nave, Perp S aisle and chapel. Heavily restored in 1886–7 by *W. V. Gough*. Late Norman single-stepped tower arch on prominent trumpet capitals showing signs of turning to crockets; short wall-shafts on corbels, the l. with early stiff-leaf, the r. with fluting. Gough removed a buttress blocking the Norman N door and reconstructed the segmental arch. Single columns, plain cushion capitals with projecting corners (cf. Ubley font). Early C14 chancel: two-light E window with encircled quatrefoil, cusped rere-arch, N lancet window, unaltered piscina. S aisle and porch, *c.* 1450–1500: three-light ogee-headed windows. The porch is ashlar below, rubble above. Parapet with trefoiled tri-angles (cf. Yatton), continuing on the aisle. Pinnacles over the buttresses. In the porch, a cusped stoup with embattled cornice. Three-bay arcade of standard shafts-and-hollows section, also the S chapel arches. Chancel arch with continuous moulding. The aisle has wall-shafts carrying corbel heads for the roof. Similar heads in the nave. – REREDOS. 1887. Over-elaborate, niches with plants, gabled centre. – PULPIT. C15, stone, two tiers of narrow panels, on a good head corbel. – FONT. Dec but entirely undecorated. – MONUMENT. George Rodney †1586. Like a reredos in the S chapel. No effigy but an inscription beneath a flattened segmental arch. Fluted and reeded Doric columns with a surfeit of entasis and egg-and-dart capitals. Heavy entablature.

WESTON-IN-GORDANO

ST PETER AND ST PAUL. Unbuttressed late C12 S TOWER, rubble, of three stages. Small plain lancets, Y-traceried belfry lights. Corbel table, solid parapet. This makes for an unusual plan but cf. Loxton. The S porch may be early too, see the double-chamfered outer arch, perhaps re-set in four-centred profile in the C15 when the inner door arch was renewed. Over this, a rare PALM SUNDAY GALLERY, with ogee-arched door in the E wall to its staircase. C15 brattished beam, panelled underside C15 stoup with arcaded interior. Simple nave, the windows all Perp, two on the N of late C15 type with the mullions in the tracery divided at both top and bottom. The tower arch by contrast has a continuous double chamfer, c. 1300. S CHAPEL (now vestry) abutting the tower's E side. Probably constructed c. 1536 when it is mentioned in the will of Sir James Perceval. Its arch has responds of the standard four-hollows pattern. Square-headed windows with attenuated mouldings and flattened rere-arches. – ALTAR. Medieval slab on six *Eltonware* columns, c. 1890s. – STALLS. Reputedly from Portbury (q.v.). Probably early C14. Stall dividers finishing with trefoils. Five primitive MISERICORDS with wyvern, flowers, human heads. – ROOD SCREEN. Late Perp base and beam, wiry tracery added in the C19. – PULPIT, perhaps late C12, set into the nave wall. Its staircase is cut through the jamb of the tower arch. Another of c. 1620. Standard Somerset pattern of ornamented arches in panels. – BENCHES. Very plain, lozenge-shaped poppyheads. Some bench-ends with ogee-scrolled stops are perhaps C17. – FONT. Norman, square, like a big cushion capital. – STAINED GLASS. In the head of the E window C15 fragments, angels and musical instruments. More C15 fragments, chancel S. Main lights in both c. 1860, possibly by the *Rev. R. W. Hautenville* (cf. Walton-in-Gordano etc.). W window, 1908, a Perceval memorial designed by *Anne*

Perceval; maker perhaps *Bell & Son*, who signed the nave s, 1917. – MONUMENTS. Richard Perceval †1483 (nave N side). Canopy with big ogee arch, blind arcaded panel and with quatrefoils above. Low arcaded base with inscription in French on its top. Under the canopy, a panel with three crudely modelled angels; perhaps a C17 or C18 restoration of something mutilated by iconoclasts. Can the French inscription be trusted? – Sir Ascelin de Perceval †C12. Outside s door; reputedly the oldest chest tomb in England, very plain and massive. Later brass plate. The alterations to Richard's tomb make one question whether this has not got something to do with the ancestral pride of later Percevals. – Churchyard CROSS. By *Anne Perceval*, 1912.

WESTON LODGE, off Valley Road. Five-bay centre, perhaps *c.* 1720–50, three storeys, the attic lights blocked on the s front. Double-pile plan, rooms of very modest size. Enclosed porch with rusticated round arches. Two-bay wings, probably early C19, as high as the centre but two-storeyed.

WESTON-SUPER-MARE

A fishing village, possibly Saxon in origin, which was conscious of its seaside attractions by 1805, when summer visitors were already coming to bathe and take the air, encouraged by the social cachet of the rector, the Rev. Wadham Pigott (*see* Brockley). The first guidebook came out in 1822. Bristol's proximity helped, with villa retreats purpose-built for mercantile families. Only faint echoes of the pre-C19 village remain in the tangled layout and street names around the parish church of St John. The railway arrived in 1841, relatively early among seaside resorts, prompting development of terraced lodging houses. The contribution of *c.* 1840–65 has much character, at first still sub-Regency, later Italianate or Tudor at the developer's whim, with a penchant for bargeboarded gables too. Pevsner's appeal for 'some preserver's sympathy' has been only partially heeded. The town centre is cramped and unlovely and gives no hint of the broad w-facing seafront. It shelters beneath Worlebury Hill to its N, which supplied abundant grey, purple and blue Carboniferous

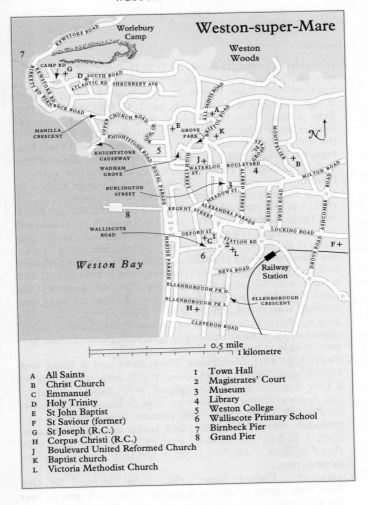

Weston-super-Mare

A All Saints
B Christ Church
C Emmanuel
D Holy Trinity
E St John Baptist
F St Saviour (former)
G St Joseph (R.C.)
H Corpus Christi (R.C.)
J Boulevard United Reformed Church
K Baptist church
L Victoria Methodist Church

1 Town Hall
2 Magistrates' Court
3 Museum
4 Library
5 Weston College
6 Walliscote Primary School
7 Birnbeck Pier
8 Grand Pier

0.5 mile
1 kilometre

Limestone for Weston's Victorian villas. It also occurs in pink and buff, often used decoratively. These villas, and the terraced suburbs stretching E, define Weston's character. Much is by *Hans Price*, Weston's resident architect (fl. 1861–1912). Surprisingly heavy bombing (1941–2) caused losses in the centre. There are some decent public buildings from Weston's C20 role as a centre of local government. The churches are emphatically second in order of interest, but not without surprises. The population in 1811 was 163; in 2001, 71,700.

For Worle and Uphill, and for the islands of Steep Holm and Flat Holm, *see* the separate gazetteer entries.

CHURCHES

Anglican

ALL SAINTS, All Saints Road. By *G. F. Bodley*, 1898–1902. Conspicuously good and beautifully furnished. S aisle and chapel,
1925, by *F. C. Eden*. Externally at least he followed Bodley's
design. Likewise the NW porch, by *C. G. Hare*, 1911–12. Free
Perp W front with three gables; aisle gables each with one
slender lancet (Early Dec tracery) breaking the sheerness of
the wall, under the nave gable two slender two-light windows
higher up, separated by a buttress. S porch by *Robert Potter*,
1955, still Gothic. He reordered the wide interior 1959–60.
Piers of eight attached shafts and boarded wagon roof. – By
Bodley the PULPIT, carved by *Zwink* of Oberammergau, the
FONT (its tall classical cupola COVER by *W. H. Randoll Blacking*, 1949), and the SCREEN and STALLS, made 1913. ROOD of
1919. – S chapel SCREEN by *Eden*, 1926. Ethereal, panels open
down to the floor. – SCULPTURE. Madonna and Child by *Laurence Broderick*, 1964 (S porch); statues in the S chapel E window
to *Eden*'s design by *Alfonso Noflaner*, c. 1925. – STAINED GLASS.
E window by *Kempe & Co.*, 1917. By *Eden*, the chancel N; the
fine S chapel E, c. 1925; S chapel S, from St Saviour, 1933, successfully rearranged here by *John & Laura Gilroy*, 2002; and S
aisle W, 1924. S aisle S, W end by *Leonard Pownall*, maker *Liddall
Armitage*, 1926; unfortunately bright, with photorealistic portrait. N aisle W by *Harry Stammers*, 1953.

CHRIST CHURCH, Montpelier. Nave, aisles and W tower with
broach spire, 1854–5, by *Manners & Gill*; earnest C13 style for
a Low Anglican parish. Completed with chancel, chapel (S)
and organ chamber (N), 1877 by *Price & Grosholz*. Clerestory
by *Price & Wooler*, 1889. Plain interior, octagonal piers with
moulded capitals. Entrance and HALL etc. by *Architecton*,
2004–5, tucked into the slope to the N. – STAINED GLASS. By
Powell & Sons: E window, 1932; W window, 1955, lighter and
more dynamic.

EMMANUEL, Oxford Street. 1846–7 by *Manners & Gill*.
Perp, little vigour or charm. Somerset tower with spirelet over
the stair-turret. Pinnacles removed 1947. The two W bays of
the nave subdivided for halls, by *Alan Rome*, 1979. Low
alabaster chancel wall. – PULPIT. Alabaster, serpentine and
marbles (†1908). – FONT, 1919. White marble angel with
bowl, after Thorwaldsen, originally en suite with the war
memorial (*opus sectile* tablet, *G. J. Hunt*). – STAINED GLASS. E
window, c. 1890, figures re-set in clear glass 1957 during
reordering. Two from *Wippell & Co.*: 1939 (*George Cooper-
Abbs*), and 1946.

HOLY TRINITY, Atlantic Road. Now Elim Pentecostal; savagely
subdivided. By *Henry Lloyd* of Bristol, 1859–61. Big E.E.
clerestoried nave, aisles, transepts. SW spire with pinnacles and
lucarnes. Inventive nave arcades with sharp narrow arches at
intervals. Organ chamber and vestry by *E. H. Edwards*, 1885. –

STAINED GLASS. E and W windows by *J. Bell*, 1861. Also his, S transept W; hot colour palette. – N aisle, a two-light window, mainly C15 fragments.

ST JOHN BAPTIST, Lower Church Road. The medieval parish church was largely replaced in 1823–4 with a new nave and tower. Chancel rebuilt 1837, N aisle added 1844 by *Thomas R. Hannaford*. Porch heightened *c.* 1888 by *Edmund Buckle*. S aisle 1890, by *Price & Wooler*. Four-stage tower (top stage added 1840) with pinnacles. Inside, an early C19 impression from the broad Tudor arcades (panelled on the S) and Gothic three-sided gallery, gilded on white. The W gallery is probably mid-1820s. Its continuation over the S aisle is unusual for 1890. Chancel reordered by *S. E. Dykes Bower*, 1961–2.* His beautifully spare STALLS have black-and-gold chequered inlay. – PULPIT. 1905, ornate, Caen stone and green marble, pierced Gothic panels of alabaster. – FONT. Norman, square. Three scallops on each side below the bowl. – Neo-Perp SCREENS and REREDOS (S chapel), 1926–8. – PAINTINGS by *A. O. Hemming*, 1901, flanking the chancel arch. – STAINED GLASS. C15 figure of a saint, N aisle. E window, presumably the glass provided by *Thomas Willement* in 1837, given by Bishop Law of Bath and Wells. Seventeen panels with the life of David and scenes from the Passion, in yellow and blue, successfully imitating the C13 style, except in the lettering. Bomb damage repaired in 1949 by *Bell & Son*, who believed it to be 'ancient' and may have antiqued it accordingly. – MONUMENTS. Elizabeth Smyth, by *Chantrey*, 1841. Portrait profile on an altar. Emily Pigott, by *Weekes*, 1844, large praying figure of a woman. Nearby, four Grecian tablets all by *Tyley*, 1843–55, two with regimental colours and draped flags. – Boer War Memorial, *c.* 1902; alabaster relief of a soldier, by *Harry Hems*.

ST PAUL, Walliscote Road. 1911–12 by *P. G. Fry*; Neo-Perp, impressively big clerestoried nave with aisles. A SE tower never rose above the aisle. Nave and chancel gutted by incendiary bombs 1941; the aisles were almost untouched. Portland stone piers with arches dying into them above the capitals. Restored on the old lines by *Harold Jones (Fry, Paterson & Jones)*, 1954–7. – FITTINGS. Unexpectedly rich, repaired after the fire with scorch-marks left as a reminder. – High stone REREDOS and alabaster PULPIT (1912); S chapel SCREEN and REREDOS, 1914; W screen, 1917; FONT, alabaster, 1921. All by *P. G. Fry*, maker *Boulton* of Cheltenham. – Art Nouveau PRAYER-DESK (S chapel), *c.* 1912. – STAINED GLASS. E window designed by *F. W. Cole* for *Morris & Co.*, 1957. Powerful colours and composition; Christ with trumpeting angels. Calmer W window, 1917, also restored by *Morris & Co.*, with much old glass. S chapel E, 1908 by *Jones & Willis*. S chapel S, two by *Daniells & Fricker*, *c.* 1912. Aisles, mainly post-war. Four from *Wippell & Co.*: two of them by *J. A. Crombie*, St Francis (*F. W. Cole*, 1960), and St Paul (*Roy Coomber*, 1964).

*The SCREEN of 1902, noted by Pevsner, was removed.

ST PETER, Baytree Road. 1964–5 by *Alban Caröe* (*Caröe & Partners*). Low brick walls, much roof, glazed W gable. SW tower (dem. 1989). – STAINED GLASS. E window by *Roy Coomber*, 2007.

ST SAVIOUR (former), Locking Road. Busy apsidal E end by *S. J. Wilde*, 1890–2, preyed upon by a squat and sinister three-bay nave, 1901–2 by *Wilde & Fry*. Converted to flats, 2005–6.

Roman Catholic

ST JOSEPH, Camp Road. 1858, by *C. F. Hansom*; nave and chancel, bald and primitive Gothic. Aisles and W porch by the *Rev. A. J. Scoles*, 1893.

CORPUS CHRISTI, Ellenborough Park South. By *John Bevan Jun.*, opened 1929. Neo-Byzantine with Portland stone W front. (Brick interior. Round-arched arcades, brick and stone piers, capitals with early Christian symbols by *G. Hillman*. Baldacchino.)

OUR LADY OF LOURDES, Baytree Road. Opened 1938. Pareddown Gothic, in buff brick and stone. Lady Chapel and sacristy, 1976.

Nonconformist

BOULEVARD UNITED REFORMED CHURCH, The Boulevard. By *Gordon W. Jackson & Partners*, 1959, reusing the foundations of a bombed Congregational chapel (*T. L. Banks*, 1876). Without resort to Gothicisms. Copper-clad spike. – PULPIT. Purbeck stone with prow-like reading rest. – STAINED GLASS. E and W windows, abstract *dalle-de-verre* by *A. E. Buss*.

BAPTIST CHURCH, Lower Bristol Road. By *Hans Price*, 1866. Big Geometric S transept window and a smaller pair in the W gable. Open belfry with spirelet.

ELIM PENTECOSTAL. *See* Holy Trinity.

VICTORIA METHODIST CHURCH, Station Road. By *Fry, Paterson & Jones*, 1935–6. Strikingly churchy free Perp, impressive 65-ft (20-metre) tower. Of Pennant with Ham stone dressings. – FITTINGS. A good period piece; boxy oak chancel stalls, pulpit, etc. with stylized Gothic details, raked pews. – STAINED GLASS. E window, 1935, possibly *G. Maile & Son*. W window with big figures; maker unknown, 1935. Vestibule, *Maile Studios*, †1970.

PUBLIC BUILDINGS

TOWN HALL, Oxford Street. A mixed bag, begun by *James Wilson* of Bath, 1856–9, with Italianate windows and a campanile. Much enlarged and reclothed in Free Renaissance dress by *Hans Price*, 1897. Extended N in Post Office Georgian,

1927, by *Fry, Paterson & Jones* with *Harold Brown*, Borough Surveyor. Red brick s wing, 1980.

MAGISTRATES' COURT, Station Road. The former Police Station of 1934, by *A. J. Toomer*, County Architect. Impersonal classical revival, with Fascist Roman details. Behind, a Brutalist POLICE STATION by *Bernard Adams*, County Architect, 1970.

LIBRARY, The Boulevard. By *Hans Price*, 1899–1900. Cattybrook brick and Bath stone. Self-important classical motifs jostling around the entrance, contrasting expanses of plain wall above, then glazed Ionic loggias. Two figure panels by *Harry Hems* below a central second-floor oriel.

WESTON COLLEGE UNIVERSITY CAMPUS, Bridgwater Road. By *Arturus*, 2005–7. Mainly two-storey blocks; wave-form roofs, now a cliché for such buildings. Three-storey cupola at the hub, with vertical glazing and blue-green render. Crescent-shaped sixth-form block to the s, linked by a glazed bridge over the main entrance.

WESTON COLLEGE, Knightstone Road. The Technical College by *Bernard Adams*, County Architect, 1962–70. Planned as 'a really vigorous piece of punctuation', amply fulfilled in eight storeys of bulky Brutalism. Three-storey blind projection at the SE, with serrated textured concrete panels. S extension by *Stride Treglown*, 1997. Immediately N, the former SCHOOL OF SCIENCE AND ART by *Hans Price*, 1892. Hyperactive Jacobethan-cum-Flemish Renaissance; attractive ceramic panels. [118]

PRIMARY SCHOOL, Walliscote Road. Board School of 1895–7 by *Price & Wooler*. A vigorous Flemish Renaissance composition, with shaped gables, lanterns and cupolas.

GENERAL HOSPITAL, Grange Road, Uphill. By *Percy Thomas Partnership*, designed 1981 for 252 beds, with expansion anticipated. Symmetrical composition, repeated pyramidal roofs, overhanging eaves, latticed metal balconies.

BIRNBECK PIER. Now derelict. The first seaside structure at Weston, oddly sited round a headland N of the town. It utilizes a rocky islet for the seaward end. By *Eugenius Birch*, 1864–7, using his screw-piling technique. The Pavilion and Reading Room were rebuilt by *Price* in 1897–8 after a fire; clock tower; lifeboat house (N side), 1889; and another to the s, 1902. A further pier branches N from the island, *c.* 1900 for pleasure steamers.

GRAND PIER. 1903–4, among the last big pleasure piers to be built in England. Designed by *P. Munroe*, contractors *Mayoh & Hayley*. Shortened by 500 yds in 1916. The lighthearted PAVILION with domed turrets was replaced in 1930–2, the successor destroyed by fire in 2008. Its replacement, by *Angus Meek Architects*, was opened 2010. A high glazed entrance, tall corner turrets referring to the 1903 design, wave-form roofs sweeping down towards the sea, and a 59-ft (18-metre) atrium crossed by two bridges. A 276-ft (85-metre) revolving observation turret was proposed at the seaward end.

PERAMBULATIONS

1. *The seafront*

From the high revetments at Anchor Head (N end) to the former
sand dunes s of the town runs almost 1½ m. of rock-faced SEA
WALL. Engineer *T. J. Scoones*, 1883–5. E of Anchor Head,
MANILLA CRESCENT by *H. Lloyd* of Bristol, *c.* 1851; debased
Italianate of the Clifton variety. Two seven-house terraces with
scrolly balconies and dormers. A little s is KNIGHTSTONE, like
Birnbeck an islet. Seawater and warm baths were established
here in 1820, and by the late 1820s a stone jetty replaced the
shingle causeway. In 1832, the existing BATH HOUSE was built
on the rock by Dr Edward Long Fox (*see* Brislington, Bristol)
to augment his treatments for mental illness; a two-storey Late
Classical structure with three-bay pediment and columned
porch. Adjacent SWIMMING BATHS and PAVILION THEATRE
by *J. S. Stewart*, both opened 1902. All three buildings redeveloped as flats by *Acanthus Ferguson Mann*, 2005–7; towering
additions with monopitch roofs confuse the lively pavilion
skyline.

Further s and set back from Knightstone Road, ROYAL CRES-
CENT. Under construction in 1847, the grandest conception at
Weston. Oddly gloomy, with castle-like giant segmental arches
embracing the two upper storeys. Small first-floor balconies
with fish-scale stonework; bracketed eaves. In front, PARK
PLACE, *c.* 1845, with pretty villas still in Regency mode, most
spoiled by hotel alterations. At the junction of Knightstone
Road and Victoria Place the OLD THATCHED COTTAGE,
probably Weston's oldest surviving house. Built *c.* 1791 as a
summer residence for the Rev. Leeves of Wrington. Self-
consciously Picturesque originally, but only a slice survives (as
a fish-and-chip shop), with bay windows and steep gables. s
again, the ROYAL HOTEL, or at least the s end of it, was built
1808–10, with an arcaded loggia. Extended and refaced in
mildly debased Italianate with a *porte cochère*, by *Gabriel &
Hirst*, completed 1849. Also by them the adjacent ROYAL
TERRACE, now part of the hotel.

The centrepiece of the esplanade is the WINTER GARDENS,
1923–7 by *T. H. Mawson & Son* with *H. Brown*, Borough Surveyor. Single-storey. Neo-Georgian, central oval ballroom with
a flattened dome. The long Doric-colonnaded wings were originally partly open, giving sea views from Mawson's formal
Italian GARDENS behind; those mostly lost to a dull shopping
centre, *c.* 1992–3. From Regent Street s runs the BEACH
LAWN, 1885, with a tiered cast-iron fountain by *Coalbrookdale*.
On the seafront, a pretty PAVILION of 1905, perhaps associated with Grand Pier. A little s, the TROPICANA open-air pool,
opened 1937, by *H. Brown*, using the *Coignet* reinforced-concrete system. A dramatic concrete-arched diving platform was
sadly demolished *c.* 1983. Aloof from the town, the GRAND
ATLANTIC HOTEL, Beach Road, begun 1854 as a private

school (two storeys, 3:5:3 bays) but converted to a hotel and much enlarged by *John S. Whittington* of Manchester, 1889, with polygonal corner turrets. Finally a little further S, ELLENBOROUGH PARK, *c.* 1855–61, by *W. B. Moffatt* (formerly of *Scott & Moffatt*), to attract retirees from the Indian service. Long gardens running back from the sea, flanked by belvedered villas and terraces formally laid out, with an elegant, mildly Italianate crescent at the E end. ⅜ m. S is CLARENCE PARK, laid out 1882. Intact pavilion, lodge, and fountain.

2. The town centre

Best explored from GROVE PARK, opened *c.* 1890, formerly the grounds of Grove House, owned by the Pigotts (*see* Brockley), lords of the manor in the early C19. Their Neo-Tudor house was bombed except for a small extension (1880s), now council offices. Adjacent to St John, GLEBE HOUSE, modest early C19 with shutters and curved metal window hoods. Good WAR MEMORIAL, a tall plinth with a winged Victory by *Alfred Drury*, 1922. Plinths added after 1945 by *Walter Cave*. On the park's W side, ORIEL TERRACE, Lower Church Road, facing the parish church. By *James Wilson* of Bath, 1847–8. Shaped Jacobean gables, strapwork nameplate in stone, cross-windows, and a single oriel. SOUTH TERRACE around the corner is of similar date and design, though humbler. Then in WADHAM STREET, BLAKEHAY ARTS CENTRE, a Baptist church of 1850 remodelled 1862 in Italianate forms by *Hans Price*. Nos. 3–6, a former coachhouse and warehouse by *H. Dare Bryan*, 1896; three storeys, red brick with broad arches and stripy stone voussoirs, elaborate S gable.

HIGH STREET runs S from Grove Park too. First (E), high gabled shops by *Price*, 1889. Then the PLAYHOUSE THEATRE, by *W. S. Hattrell & Partners*, 1969. Brutalist façade with seven boxed-out panels of textured glass fibre, sculpted by *William Mitchell*. Shortly (W side), LLOYDS BANK, 1864, by *W. B. Gingell* of Bristol. Italianate, shorn of its rich carving in the 1960s. Nearby in South Parade the former STUCKEY'S BANK, also 1860s; a convincing Florentine palazzo with bracketed eaves. Returning to the S part of High Street, No. 44, W. H. Smith, with former reading room above faced with reliefs in lead, symbolizing Bath, Somerset, Taunton and Bristol, and a quotation from Shakespeare. Typical work of their in-house shopfitting department under *Frank C. Bayliss*, *c.* late 1920s. Nos. 31–33, formerly BURTON'S, is a typically good façade with glitzy Jazz Age motifs (elephant capitals!) by their architect *Harry Wilson*, *c.* 1932. Where Regent Street meets High Street and Meadow Street is SILICA, by *Wolfgang Buttress* with *Conran Architects*, 2006: part news kiosk and bus shelter, part public sculpture. Egg-shaped base rising smoothly into a needle-like spire with steel rings.

w of High Street, in Richmond Street, a purpose-built transatlantic CABLE TERMINAL, by *S. J. Wilde*, 1889; rare and early of its type. Embellished with globes depicting the Americas and Europe, and logos of the New York Commercial Cable Co. N from the centre, the ODEON CINEMA (corner of Walliscote Road and Locking Road) is by *T. Cecil Howitt*. Modernistic of 1934–5, impressively blank tiled faience walls and low tower set in a re-entrant angle, with a flat cap raised on short round pillars. Largely intact but subdivided interior. *Compton* organ with splendidly jazzy illuminated Art Deco glass case, one of only two in the country *in situ*. On the same *moderne* note, in Station Road and Neva Road to the SE, housing by *N. Darby* (*Leete & Darby*), *c.* 1936; flat-roofed, few original metal-framed windows left.

In Burlington Street, *c.* 200 yds N, the MUSEUM, built 1912 for the Gas Light Co., the last known design of *Hans Price*. Long classical Bath stone front with big arched ends. N again, THE BOULEVARD, 1864, a consciously French plan, aligned on the spire of Christ Church to the E. On the S side, the WESTON & SOMERSET MERCURY OFFICES, 1885, by *Price*, with big quadrant-glazed corner and a high tower gabled in Flemish forms. A few doors away, No. 28 Waterloo Street (1874) was *Price*'s office. To his own design, wisely avoiding styles. To the E, hidden off Stafford Place, unexpected amid Victorian villadom, a house by *Clough Williams-Ellis & Lionel Brett*, 1950–2. SW bedroom added 1954, the kitchen (NE), *c.* 1964. A long simple bungalow raised over terraced gardens; backward-sloping monopitch roof overhanging at the front, with Mediterranean-style balconies and arched basement doorways.

3. *Worlebury Hill*

Some dispersed incidents on the hillside N of Weston. For Worlebury hill-fort, *see* p. 11. At the seaward end, ATLANTIC TERRACE, *c.* 1862, spec-built with Holy Trinity church as a nascent desirable suburb; three-and-a-half storeys, Italianate. More confidence than judgement. Probably by *Henry Lloyd*. Nearby, THE SHRUBBERY, smart houses of *c.* 1860. In Shrubbery Avenue, a Gothic tower (now a house) provided a water supply for the estate by 1859. THE CHALET, South Road, a villa of 1862, was altered by *Price & Wooler*, 1888. Fancy-dress Bavarian timber balconies, fretwork and overhanging gables; the home of W. H. Wooler, who was German. *Wooler* designed Nos. 83–85 Upper Church Road, 1892, a remarkable pair with Moorish horseshoe arches and tiles, seemingly after a visit to Spain and North Africa. To its N, the Grove Park estate typifies the firm's domestic work in the 1890s, with shaped gables, bays and Flemish motifs.

WHATLEY

ST GEORGE. Restored in 1859, and by *G. E. Street*, 1869–70. Of the C13 perhaps the inner S doorway (continuous double-

chamfer). Two-stage W tower with diagonal buttresses, plain
Perp belfry lights. Solid parapet with pinnacles, possibly from
repairs of 1820. Within the parapet, an elegant spire with roll-
moulded angles, perhaps later C14 (cf. Croscombe; St John the
Baptist, Bristol). Simple S porch, perhaps C17 or C18, with
rounded outer arch. A S transept was consecrated as a chantry
chapel for Sir Oliver de Cervington in 1350; the arch double-
chamfered, the inner chamfer on corbels with a little foliage.
– Plain C12 tub FONT. – Oak STALLS with tall poppyheads,
probably 1859. – ORGAN. By *T. C. Bates* of London, *c.* 1840. –
Brass CHANDELIERS, one dated 1838. – MONUMENTS. Sir
Oliver de Cervington †*c.* 1348, in his chantry. A cross-legged
knight, in armour of *c.* 1325–30. Tomb-chest with ogee-arched
panels with some ballflower. The detail must once have been
uncommonly fine. The arms on the shield, e.g. three stags, are
carved and not painted. Fine arrangement at the feet also of a
stag amongst leaves. – Elizabeth Welsteed †1679. Naïvely mannered hanging monument. Inscription between Ionic pilasters,
with cherub peering out between raised curtains above, as if
on stage. Broken segmental pediment with arms, above intervening brackets, inverted scrolls and fruity festoon.

MANOR HOUSE. C15 GATEHOUSE NW of the church. Double-
chamfered arch, the outer face (W) with a big hoodmould and
tracery spandrels. The E face plainer, with external steps to the
rooms above. The HOUSE lies directly N and parallel with the
church. Ostensibly C17, with three- and four-light mullioned
windows, and an off-centre porch listing westward, of two
storeys with flat door opening. A detached wing projecting at
the E end has a small window of two arched cusped lights,
perhaps C15 or early C16.

WHITCHURCH   6060

ST NICHOLAS. Granted to Keynsham Abbey in the late C12,
perhaps prompting the building or rebuilding of a Transitional
cruciform church here; much of *c.* 1190 survives in the chancel,
N transept and the low unbuttressed central tower. This was
heightened by a few feet in the C15, with unadorned bell-
openings, parapet and pyramid roof. In the chancel (N), one
Transitional lancet (another to its W C19), and one on the S
inside. The N doorway may just be earlier C12, still round-
arched, with one chamfer and a big roll moulding. S transept
absorbed in a late C14 or early C15 S aisle with S chancel chapel.
Perp N and S porches. Restored in 1861 by *G. E. Street.* The
pointed crossing arches are single-stepped, on filleted corbel
shafts with scalloped and trumpet capitals. In addition the
crossing piers have short thinner shafts cut into the angles on
the W side of the E and W arches, and on the inner sides in the
N and S arches. These also have fillets, and two have capitals
with two tiers of upstanding fronds, a forerunner of stiff-leaf.

All the shafts are set in deep slots in the piers. The chancel E
window is of *c.* 1300–20 with Perp additions, and possibly
minor re-setting by *Street*. Odd Geometrical bar tracery of
three cusped lancet lights, the middle lower and narrower to
allow space for a quatrefoiled spheric quadrangle. The N
transept N window identical. Both have mullions with very slim
shafts and leafy capitals inside. These were set in later; the Perp
W window has the same shafting. Four-centred nave arcade
with piers of the standard four-hollows section, S chapel the
same. C15 bossed wagon roofs to nave and aisle. – REREDOS.
Marble and encaustic tile, 1861. – FONT. Norman; square,
cushion-capital shape. – SCREEN, S aisle (perhaps *ex situ*). Of
c. 1500, cf. Wrington. Three three-light divisions, ogee lights
with segmental inner arches, attached pinnacles, dense vine
cornice and cresting. – PARCLOSE SCREEN. One-light divisions
with X-tracery, probably late C15. – STAINED GLASS. E window
by *O'Connor*, *c.* 1862. Nave N, first from E, probably also
O'Connor; hot mauve and turquoise. – MONUMENTS. Holbeach family, 1735, by *W. Lydyard* of Keynsham. Grey marble,
Doric pilasters, gadroons. Two the same by *T. Tyley*, *c.* 1842,
with Grecian scrolled tops.

By the church, the former PARISH SCHOOL by *Henry
Rumley*, 1837; Neo-Tudor, altered.

(LYONS COURT, ¼ m. W of the church. Probably a C13 steward's
house for Keynsham Abbey lands; owned by the Lyons and
Holbeach families until 1688. Altered in the C17, much repaired
in recent decades. On an irregular Z-plan; W entrance front with
service end to its N, hall in the centre now divided by a first
floor, and a long later wing offset to the S. Medieval survivals
include a W door to a screens passage with two four-centred
doors to the service end; r. of the main entrance, a two-light hall
window with cusped arched lights and hoodmould; a tall
blocked double-chamfered arch to the r. in line with the W wall
of the hall (perhaps the arch to an oriel bay), now inside a later
projection; some two-light windows at the back. In a service
room (N wing), a spice cupboard and a small stone niche. Over
the former hall, moulded wall-plates with two head corbels, and
a three-bay wind-braced collar-beam roof.)

For Whitchurch Park *c.* ½ m. N, see Bristol.

WICK ST LAWRENCE

Here 'the Fennes be almost at hand' (Leland).

ST LAWRENCE. W tower with SW stair-turret, nave and chancel,
two-storey S porch. All Perp, thoroughly restored and
extended by *Foster & Wood*, 1864–5. C16 or C17 wagon-vault
(earlier roof-line over the tower arch). – PRAYER-DESK. 1865?
Robust Gothic with latticed front. – PULPIT. Brought from

Woodspring Priory, reputedly in the late C16. One of the finest medieval stone pulpits in Somerset, very daintily detailed, with panelled stem, panelled body, and friezes of quatrefoils, fleurons, horizontal leaf-trails, etc.; cf. simpler pulpits at Banwell, Bleadon, Brockley and Hutton. – FONT. Norman, plain bowl on circular stem. – STAINED GLASS. E window by *Michael Lassen*, 1989. Chancel S and nave N by *Clayton & Bell*, c. 1865. – MONUMENTS. James Morss †1730. 'Far from dry ground, mistaken in my course, I stick in mire, brought hither by my horse. Thus vain I cry'd to God, who only saves; In death's cold pit I lay, ore'whelm'd by waves.' Grim confirmation of Leland's words.

Near the church a big C15 CROSS on high steps; square socket with cusped panels. Adjacent, BANKSEA COTTAGES, with irregular walls, seemingly the late medieval church house. Used as a poorhouse by 1762, much altered in the C19 and after. Many good C17 FARMHOUSES in the parish, perhaps enabled by drainage schemes, e.g. Icelton Farm, with broad moulded fire-opening.

WINFORD   5060

ST MARY AND ST PETER. Tall four-stage W tower of Dundry stone, with set-off buttresses. The top three stages have only one two-light window in each face, blind in the two middle tiers. Lozenge-shaped label stops with concave curving outlines. Parapet with openwork arcading, slim crocketed pinnacles. In all these respects the tower is especially like Chew Magna, and built perhaps c. 1450–1500. Tower arch with a moulding of two broad waves. The W doorway is Perp only in its lower parts. Above, it belongs to 1796–7, when the body of the church was rebuilt by *James Allen*. Three-light W window with typical intersected tracery. Aisled nave and chancel with large, slightly bleak, pointed windows with wrought-iron Y-tracery. E window with Perp-style tracery, a late C19 insertion. Arcade piers of the Somerset standard section (four hollows), probably reused Perp, startlingly high plinths (of 1796?). Ceiling panelled with acanthus rosettes; winged cherub corbels (cf. Allen's work at St Thomas, Bristol). – ALTAR RAIL. Georgian, turned balusters like the GALLERY. – PULPIT. Pierced arcading, Gothic, no doubt 1796. – BENCHES. 1868, by *Thomas Drew*, the Dublin architect. What brought him here? – ROYAL ARMS. Oil on canvas, George III. – BENEFACTION BOARDS, 1810 and 1813, liberally embellished with the churchwardens' names. Creed and Decalogue similar. – STAINED GLASS. E window, c. 1889, probably *Clayton & Bell*. In the aisles, armorials by *Arnold Robinson* (*Bell & Son*), 1945–7.

S of the church is THE COURT. The thickness of some external walls suggests that Norman fabric has partially survived at least two rebuildings, the last of 1593 (datestone over the door). The front faces s into a narrow forecourt between wings. Some sashes, but also chamfered mullioned windows. A cross-passage runs N to a big stair-tower on the N front, which may once have been the main entrance, facing the church. Here, a three-light window and signs of a porch over the rear door, now internal. This side is very irregular otherwise, with four small two-light windows – grim and impressive. E front with three-light windows below hoodmoulds. (The room W of the cross-passage, perhaps once the hall, has a very large inglenook, and remains of a newel staircase. E parlour with stone door surround and fireplace probably of 1593.)

A little W is the OLD RECTORY, the smallest type of C15 priest's house, one-up and one-down. A rear window with two arched trefoil-cusped lights was destroyed by fire in the 1960s. Door with a four-centred arch. Hall-kitchen to its l. and lean-to buttery to its r., later heightened.

RECTORY (former), Old Hill. 1 m. sw. Built in 1716 (dated rainwater head) for Peter Webb, rector 1714–24. Five bays and two storeys with a central break forward. Bolection-moulded window surrounds, handsome shell-hood on sturdy brackets. A double-pile plan. Cross-windows to the stair at the back of the main block. The lower service range has some possibly late C17 features (beam with stepped and run-out chamferstops; ogee mullion-and-transomed window). Tiny lobby between hall and staircase, with a little leafy groined vault in stucco. Good staircase of 1716 rising to the attic, with turned balusters, carved tread-ends, ramped rails, fluted newel posts, doggate. A single front attic room like the memory of a long gallery, with groined vault.

POWDERMILL FARM, Littleton, ¾ m. ESE. C16, enlarged in the mid C18 for the manager of a gunpowder mill, extant 1748–1830s, whose ruined late C18 CLOCK TOWER stands by the stream, N.

WINSCOMBE

ST JAMES. Serenely placed on the hillside with views N across a valley. Of the church consecrated in 1236, only the font and perhaps one lancet (chancel N) survive. Perp nave, aisles and tower. No clerestory. In 1863 *John Norton* rebuilt the chancel (and the s pier of its arch), uncovering extensive E.E. work during demolition, inspiring the details of his replacement. Proud four-staged W tower, 100 ft (31 metres) tall, perhaps *c.* 1380–1440, and similar to Banwell, Cheddar, Weare (S. Somerset), Mark (S. Somerset), Bleadon and South Brent (S. Somerset). Set-back buttresses connected diagonally across the angles, rising to pairs of tall diagonal shafts ending in pinnacles. W doorway and W window and then two stages with a single two-light window in each face, partly blank. They have diamond stop-bars below the sill, and the lower w window has flanking niches for Annunciation figures (cf. Banwell and Cheddar); in one of the blank lights remains a vase with a lily. Two light bell-openings flanked by identical blank windows. Shafts between, finishing just below the intermediate parapet pinnacles. Main pinnacles at the corners, pierced parapet with quatrefoils in lozenges. Higher NE stair-turret with crocketed spirelet. Both aisles later than the tower. N aisle and porch with the same ornate parapet as the tower; the s aisle has a pierced parapet instead with trefoils in triangles. Five-bay arcades, the piers with the four-shaft-four-wave profile. Small circular capitals to the shafts only. Capitals of the chancel arch and chapels enriched by Perp leaf crestings. Tower arch of two continuous wave mouldings, lierne-vault in the tower. The one-bay chapels and N aisle have essentially medieval roofs (the latter repaired 1928, *Oatley & Lawrence*). Nave roof, with two tiers of angels with outspread wings; by *Norton*.

FITTINGS. REREDOS, 1907. – STALLS by *George Oatley*, 1908. – FONT. C13, and very uncommon. Big, circular bowl like a broadly detailed moulded capital, on a base like that of a pier. – BENCHES. Plain, straight-headed, with tracery. – CANDELABRA. Splendid thirty-six-light coronet of 1884, and a more elegant one of 1903. – STAINED GLASS. A highly rewarding C15 and early C16 collection. N chapel E, exceptionally complete, with Crucifixus, Virgin, St John, and St Anthony, four pairs of kneeling donors at the foot, and angels in the tracery. Collected here from other windows by *W. Warrington*, 1850. N chapel N with Virgin, St Catherine and the Baptist. S aisle S, first from E, also latest Perp: St James, a bishop and archbishop. Simple and restrained colour. The swapped feet of the archbishop and St James restored to their rightful owners, 1984. Chancel N, given by Peter Carslyght (monogram PC), vicar here 1520–32. St Peter the Deacon, St Peter the Apostle, and St Peter the Exorcist. White ground with colour almost entirely orange-yellow, produced by silver-stain. In the upper arches Renaissance detail appears in a minor way. Much better aesthetically is the E window, given by J. A. Yatman of Winscombe Hall, who promoted the rebuilding. Design attributed to *Burges*, 1863. Three single figures on top of each other in the side lancets, four in the middle one, forming a stylized type of Jesse window. Splendid glowing colours on greeny-blue ground, pretty apple and apple-leaf ornament, understanding use of leading. Aisles. Yatman memorial by *Bell & Son*, 1896; also three by *Lavers, Barraud & Westlake*, 1879, 1882 and 1901. – MONUMENT. Sarah Knollis †1825, by *Harris* of Bath. Weeping woman kneeling over an urn. Weeping leaves frame the inscription. – WAR MEMORIAL. Celtic cross, by *George Oatley*, 1920 (churchyard).

96

OLD VICARAGE. E of the church. 1836. Recessed entrance with Greek Doric columns *in antis*.

ALL SAINTS, Sandford, *c.* 1½ m. N. By *Price & Wooler*, 1883–5, a compact design. Nave and chancel, w porch, robust double bellcote. On a little knoll with LYCHGATE to the E.

Several CHAPELS in the parish, notably the diminutive METHODIST CHAPEL, Hill Road, by *Foster & Wood*, 1898–9. Given by Sidney Hill (*see* Churchill with Langford). Richly ornamented free Perp.

WINSCOMBE HALL, Winscombe Hill. Now a care home. Begun in 1855 for John Augustus Yatman, by *William Railton*; desultory mid-Victorian classical. In 1858 *William Burges*, who had designed furniture for Yatman's brother, was engaged to design furniture and interiors. He did further work in 1862, 1871 and 1875, the principal structural changes being the rather French corner tower on heavy Romanesque arches in the rear court, and the similar loggias flanking the garden front. In the former dining room, stained-glass panels of the four elements represented by Sylph, Gnome, Undine and Salamander, with coloured borders (a better version of a design used at Cardiff Castle, 1877, and Tower House, London, *c.* 1877–8).

BARTON. A delightfully remote hamlet *c.* 1¾ m. W. BARTON FARM, C17, was extended W in 1703 (datestone on E gable), with taller and more regular fenestration (good fittings of 1703). HOME FARM also C17, with good contemporary fittings and rare detached kitchen. WEST END FARM has one bay of a true cruck roof felled 1278–9, the earliest known example in Somerset. Higher up, in a fold under Crook Peak, BARTON ROCKS, *George Oatley*'s weekend and summer home, 1900–2. As self-effacing as its designer, sturdy and well-crafted of local stone. Big pyramid roof with catslide to the S.

WOODSPRING PRIORY

3060

On a remote part of the Bristol Channel coast, at or near the site of a late Norman chapel of St Thomas the Martyr founded by Reginald FitzUrse, one of Becket's assassins. The manor passed to his grandson, William de Courtenay, who also founded a house of Augustinian Canons (of St Victor) at Doddlinch (probably near North Curry, S. Somerset) *c.* 1210. By 1226 that community had transferred to Woodspring. E end enlarged *c.* 1291–1317, but the church was never big: two-bay aisleless nave, central tower, chancel, S chapel. Excavation (1993) revealed the position of a possible C13 N transept, though there is no sign of transepts in what survives. Chancel shortened and the rest remodelled *c.* 1491–1530s after a fire, accounting for its outwardly late Perp appearance. The Tudor work is of greyish Dundry ashlar, contrasting with the golden Triassic limestone of the C13. In the early C16 a N aisle was added, with abbot's lodging at its W end, but much was unfinished at the suppression of the order in 1536. The chancel, chapels and most of the claustral buildings were demolished, and the nave, N aisle and prior's lodging remodelled as a farmhouse, which was extended in the C18.

Woodspring Priory.
Engraving, 1829

The CHURCH was partly restored and embellished in an antiquarian spirit *c.* 1829, for J. H. Smyth-Pigott, by *John Buckler*. Repaired since *c.* 1970 by *Caröe & Partners* for the Landmark Trust. The gabled W front has polygonal corner turrets with quatrefoil parapets, and a very large blocked window with a depressed four-centred head. This form continues throughout. Three storeys of plain mullioned lights were inserted. Scars of a pinnacled ogee frame of the former W doorway, and of two image niches above. The S side of the nave has two blocked C16 windows (one infilled between the tracery showing the original arrangement, of transomed lights in two pairs). A matching third window, lighting the tower base, reopened 1970. Below it, a small blocked doorway. Various smaller windows with mullions, C16 and later. At its W end is the roof-line of a former W cloister range. Nave parapet of pierced quatrefoils with central bosses. The TOWER has a parapet of 1829 copying that of the nave, diagonal buttresses, two-light windows to the N and S, and above these three-light bell-openings with Somerset tracery. The openings are continued blank below a transom (cf. e.g. Othery, S. Somerset). The E face has a blocked arch to the lost chancel, and traces of the jamb of the first S window. Two good medieval heads at roof level. In the tower base, a fan-vault with quatrefoil in a square at the centre, inserted *c.* 1829. It is set over lofty panelled arches, their piers mutilated by a demolished pulpitum, tombs, etc. Another lofty arch leads into a three-bay N AISLE, with large blocked windows with depressed four-centred heads: it must have seemed almost entirely glazed. Evidence of much post-Reformation rebuilding to the upper walls, and of inserted floors. Several finely moulded responds, rectangular in plan, indicate a lost stone vault. The early C16 PRIOR'S

LODGING abutted the W end of the N aisle, and was incorporated in a westward farmhouse extension dated 1701. Upstairs,
an early C16 chimneypiece has polygonal ends and unfinished
fleuron frieze. SW of this range, *ex situ* arches from a former
gatehouse; an entry for pedestrians and one (two-chamfered,
with segmental head) for carriages.

The CLOISTER lay S of the nave: its outer W wall survives to
full height, with four grotesque gargoyles. A plain porch at its
N end perhaps C16 or later, and part of a stair-turret to the cel-
larer's range over the refectory at its S end. In a wall directly S
of the tower, a two-centred ARCH made up of pieces, probably
in the early C19. Cusped and sub-cusped inner arch, as was
usual for tomb recesses *c.* 1300. A little S of the lost chancel is
the C15 INFIRMARY, now a barn. It has tall transomed two-
light windows with depressed ogee lights under two-centred
heads. Hoodmoulds with square label stops. Good arch-braced
collar-beam roof with three tiers of wind-braces, one bay at the
ridge with the braces inverted to allow for a smoke louvre. On
the S side was a projecting chapel with infirmarer's quarters
above.

The TITHE BARN lies NW, as no doubt did the other agricultural outbuildings. Probably late C15, of stone, seven bays
long. Central transeptal entrance with angle buttresses, their
bases protected by circular spurs. An opposing N entrance was
removed in the C19. Two subsidiary doorways with continuous double-quadrant mouldings, and a matching additional
doorway at the E end, after 1829. Restored and re-roofed (arch-
braced collar-beams, curved wind-braces) by *E. J. McKaig*,
1935.

WOOKEY HOLE

ST MARY MAGDALENE. By *B. & E. B. Ferrey*. Chapel-like. Nave
with the base of an intended SW tower serving as a porch,
1873–4. E end, 1876–7. – Excellent Neo-Perp WOODWORK by
F. E. Howard, 1923. – STAINED GLASS. E window, 1877, *Lavers,
Barraud & Westlake*.

SCHOOLS, by *Wilson & Willcox*, 1870; enriched gables, some plate
tracery, and a decorative capped tower. Immediately below in
the centre of the village, the PAPER MILL. Of 1855–8, the last
survivor of a significant Mendip industry. A mill existed before
1610, utilizing the waters of the River Axe which rise in the
caves behind. Splendidly forthright buildings, three-storey
front range of nineteen bays, with slate roofs and raised ridge
vents.

GLENCOT, *c.* ½ m. S, is by *George & Peto*, completed 1887,
for W. S. Hodgkinson, the mill-owner. Jacobean manner, of
rock-faced pink Draycott stone with Ham Hill dressings.
Asymmetrical and gabled, irregular mullioned-and-transomed

windows, some in square bays. Tall garden front rising from a balustraded terrace. Opulent Jacobean-style interiors. In Titlands Lane, staff COTTAGES, *c.* 1897, Neo-C17. Probably by *George & Yeates*. Perhaps also theirs, THE CROFT, a pleasing Voyseyesque terrace SW of the mill; *c.* 1900–10. Big chimneys and gables, broad mullioned lights.

CAVES. The GREAT CAVE open to public view is situated at the top of the ravine from which the River Axe emerges; occupied in the Late Iron Age. HYAENA DEN cave, 60 yds S of the Great Cave, consists of a large chamber and a narrow passage beyond, periodically occupied by hunters and animals during the Upper Palaeolithic. The large number of hyaena bones found gave the cave its name. Caves in EBBOR GORGE, ⅔ m. NW of Wookey Hole, contained material left by Palaeolithic hunters.

WOOLLARD

6060

The C16 three-arched bridge was swept away by floods in 1968. On the W approach to its successor, CHEW COTTAGE and NEW BRIDGE HOUSE have at their core a much-altered C15 chapel, which was a dependant of Keynsham Abbey. In the W gable, slight remains of a Perp window; tracery head of another inside. Also part of an unusual frieze of shields in trefoils. Opposite, the former BELL INN, putatively a priest's house, with a blocked late C15 window in the E gable. Arched and cusped lights, fine small-scale decoration in the spandrels. C17 or C18 front, reusing a C16(?) doorhead. (Two-room plan with cross-passage, semicircular rear stair-turret. Two fine C15 panelled ceilings with moulded beams.) W again, PARADISE ROW, dated 1782, estate cottages for the Pophams of Hunstrete.

WOOLLEY

7060

ALL SAINTS. 1761. John Wood the Younger is traditionally named as architect, but evidence is lacking. Small and unpretentious, combining Gothic and classical motifs and, in Pevsner's view, not much to Wood's credit. Nave and polygonal apse. Pedimented W front entirely blank but for a Gothic-arched doorway with foiled oculus above. Above the pediment, the parapet ramps up to a short bell-tower: square, with an oculus on each face and urns on the top corners, then an octagonal domed cupola. In the nave, plain side windows with Y-tracery. The chancel arch perhaps a remodelled remnant of the ruinous medieval church on the site – pointed, with the Somerset standard responds (half four-hollows). – FONT. C18; slim vase baluster, bowl with leaf decoration. – MONUMENTS. Two pretty tablets of coloured marbles, one with arms, one with an urn; †1763 and 1767.

MANOR FARMHOUSE, N of the church. C17, symmetrical three-bay front with windows under hoodmoulds. (Fine chimney-piece with fluted pilasters, foliage and fancy stops, in the ground-floor r. room.) Altered in the C19. At the l., a lower projecting range, also C17 and probably the earliest part. Contemporary BARN.

7050

WOOLVERTON

ST LAWRENCE. Now a house. So low it lies virtually hidden in its own churchyard. Attractive tower, probably C15, very small, narrow and unbuttressed, with tiny single lights, narrowing to a bell-stage and spirelet with two decorative bands (cf. Holy Trinity, Bradford-on-Avon, Wilts.). S porch with pointed tunnel-vault on leaf corbels. C15 chancel arch. All over-restored in 1888–9.

WOOLVERTON HOUSE HOTEL. Chunky late C19 rectory evoking the C17, with broad chimneys, mullions, angled bays etc. At MANOR FARM, a handsome broad-eaved farmhouse, c. 1840, nicely unscraped but needing repair.

3060

WORLE

Submerged in overspill from Weston-super-Mare. The old village is ranged high on the hillside along Church Road.

ST MARTIN. Founded c. 1125–50, from which time must date the S doorway. One order of colonnettes, decorated scallop capitals, one-stepped plain arch. Some lumpy stonework at the base of the tower may be Norman too; the rest rebuilt in the C15 – see the W doorway with fleurons up the jambs and along the arch. Two heads as hoodmould stops, the bust of an angel at the apex. Low angle buttresses at the foot of the tower, which is short and simple and needs none further up. Pierced parapet with quatrefoils in lozenges, higher stair-turret, and short spire of oddly broken outline, getting suddenly steeper near the summit. Nave and N aisle largely C15 too – see the nave SW window, with spear-shaped label stops, a variant of the diamond stops fashionable after 1440. Flat-headed window E of the porch – perhaps early C16. N aisle prominently buttressed, with the same parapet as the tower. Rood-stair turret with spirelet. N vestry and organ chamber, 1870, by *John Norton*, who drastically restored. He rebuilt the four-bay nave arcade which was nearing collapse. Piers of standard section. – ALTAR. Black Irish marble and encaustic tiles by *Godwin* of Lugwardine, 1870. – REREDOS. Last Supper in Perp alabaster frame, by *Jones & Willis*, 1905. – STALLS with early C16 misericords. Simple motifs, including a dragon, twice two heads under one cowl, and twice the initials of Prior Richard Sprynge, prior of Woodspring and vicar of Worle (1499–1516). – FONT. Norman, octagonal bowl on flared foot. – PULPIT. Perp, Caen stone, *c.* 1550, with blank tracery and leaves in the spandrels. – WEST GALLERY. 1988–9, by *Coffin, Jones & Roden*. Simple Gothic. – ORGAN. Exceptional Baroque case and pipework made in Frankfurt, 1662, installed here *c.* 1860s.

SCHOOL, w of St Martin. Converted by *John Norton* (*see* above) out of a medieval BARN. The buttresses remain. E along Church Road, No. 121 is a robust three-storey house of *c.* 1850, with iron-and-glass veranda and fine C19 porch-conservatory with Gothic filigree ironwork. At the top of The Scaurs, BELL HOUSE, the front C17 but the core medieval (remains of a true cruck roof in the rear l. wing). In Highlands Lane, s, THE CAMPUS, by *David Morley Architects*, 2003–6; two schools, library, sports and community facilities. Distinctive and pleasing two-storey composition with the library at one end; roof and wall in a single curve, glazed end wall.

NORTH SOMERSET COURTS, The Hedges, St Georges. By *Building Design Partnership*, opened 2006. Fully glazed crescent front with external steel posts and brises-soleil; broken in the centre by a rubble-stone turret entrance. Inverted V-shaped roofs with overhanging eaves, well-handled stone stair pods at the ends. Clean geometries, most marked in the linked block of probation service offices; but a jarring mix of steel, glass, purple panels, alien yellow rubble and hard red brick.

BRIMBLEWORTH FARM, St Georges. C15, with a jointed cruck roof above its inner room and lower end. The open hall was later ceiled and its roof replaced. The unusual length of the lower end (29 ft, 9 metres) suggests it may have been a longhouse.

CASTLE BATCH, NE of Worle. A Norman motte-and-bailey castle; a small, compact earthen ring, once moated.

WRAXALL

4070

ALL SAINTS, Wraxall Hill. Impressively Perp without, and what is not in the Perp style hardly tells. Yet it has a Norman s doorway with one order of columns carrying scallop capitals, and the much-renewed outer entrance to the two-storey s porch seems E.E. Two orders and capitals with stiff-leaf decoration. In the arch mouldings are keeled rolls. The small doorway to the upper floor also seems E.E. Restored in 1851, and again in 1893–4 (*Sir Arthur Blomfield*), when the s aisle

and chancel were lengthened by one bay, reusing old
material. The impressive effect is chiefly due to the w tower, a
design of some originality. Stripes of grey and buff stone, now
barely noticeable. Diagonal buttresses with many set-offs,
parapet with blank arcading, and in the middle of each side a
niche for a statue (only the w niche present in 1788). Big
square pinnacles each surrounded by pretty minor ones.
Higher stair-turret with spirelet. Two-light windows, one to
each stage. The string course rises around their heads to form
a hoodmould, quite an individual feature and, one feels, an
early one. Two-light bell-openings with Somerset tracery. The
interior is the gloomiest major church in Somerset – thanks to
the stained glass. The Perp details here indicate the C14. Four-
bay N arcade with piers of standard four-hollows section, but
broadly treated and with a band of moulded capitals and abaci,
impossible after 1400. The details of tower arch and chancel
arch (continuous mouldings) also are not of any of the conventional late Perp patterns. N aisle perhaps remodelled in the
early C16, with Tudor-arched E window. The S pier of the N
chapel has two green men with foliage, c. 1500.

  FITTINGS. REREDOS. 1893, stone and marble; Transfiguration. Flanks with bold mosaic panels. – Delicate S chapel
REREDOS, Annunciation, by *Kempe* (1891). – Perp SCREENS.
– Splendid ORGAN CASE atop the N chapel screen. By *Blomfield*, 1892. – FONT. Big, octagonal, C15 Perp, two blank ogee
arches on each side. – Next to it, attached to a nave pier a
charming little BOOK-REST on a demi-angel. – STAINED
GLASS. Chancel S, two by *T. C. Tute*, figures re-set in clear
grounds to lighten the sanctuary. Otherwise, all are by *Kempe*,
lavishly bestowed by the Gibbses of Tyntesfield (q.v.), 1896–9.
Much admired, though Pevsner was right that there is 'no thrill
of deep colour in the darkness'. – MONUMENTS. Sir Edmund
†1512 and Lady Anne Gorges. Two recumbent effigies on a
tomb-chest bearing the bold and grandly conceived motif of
one big coat of arms flanked by two angels. Of high quality,
c. 1500–15. – William Mathew †1781. Elegant tablet with urn
by *T. Paty & Sons*. Similar one of 1792. – J. Lucas †1817 by
Tyley. The 'afflicted parents' standing by an urn. – Louisa
Lucas †1807, perhaps also Tyley. Seated allegorical figure
against the curved pedestal of an urn. – James Vaughan †1857.
Oval. Crazy Neo-Norman borders. – In the churchyard, a C15
CROSS on octagonal stepped base, head reinstated 1893. –
SCHOOLROOM (N) of 1809. Perp windows, mid-C19. –
Master's house of 1827, Neo-Tudor, like a gate lodge.

Wraxall shows throughout the improving hand of the Gibbs of
Tyntesfield. S of the church, the SCHOOL, 1879–81 by *Butterfield*, Gothic, of red rubble with a small capped tower. E on
Bristol Road, the former BOYS' SCHOOL, 1856; grey stone,
steep gables, buttressed porch, bayed gable facing the road. E
again, the BATTLE AXES INN, also *Butterfield*, 1880–1, with
adjacent village CLUB HOUSE. Both Gothic with plentiful
half-timbering.

WRAXALL COURT. Immediately NW of the church. Core of *c.* 1720, with three-bay S front, hipped roofs behind parapet. The porch is from its predecessor, dated 1658 with the initials of Samuel Gorges. Arched entrance flanked by attached Ionic columns on high pedestals. Enlarged *c.* 1830 in a sub-Soanian style, suggesting perhaps H. E. Goodridge or Edward Davis, with bow-fronted symmetrical wings. To the rear, an imperial staircase, vaulted hall and lateral corridor; round and segmental arches with simple incised lines in the soffits. Restored 1911–12, including new C17-style study ceiling.

BELMONT HOUSE, Belmont Hill. Plain classical villa, rendered and lined like ashlar. The pilastered five-bay centre of the SW façade may represent the original house of *c.* 1760. Wings and entrance front (NW) of *c.* 1820. Arched windows between engaged Doric columns in the centre. Rear court infilled *c.* 1895 for a rackets court. Arched steel, iron and glass roof, partly replaced on conversion to a theatre by *Ivor Day Partnership*, *c.* 2004–8.

BIRDCOMBE COURT, ¾ m. w. An astonishing survival. A medieval manor house, the hall and cross-passage perhaps C13, with a solar wing added to the S in 1441–2. The earliest documentary evidence (licence for an altar) is 1331. The entrance front (E) has a five-storey porch tower, square and buttressed. Originally projecting, but the flanks were brought forward with a three-storey Neo-Gothic wing to the N, *c.* 1837. The tower has two-light windows, cusped on the first and second floors, i.e. C15. Heightened by two storeys and given an ogee-capped roof probably in the early C17. Weathervane dated 1633. The porch's outer arch is as wide as a carriageway, four-centred with broad mouldings. Another arch to the N now blocked by the N wing; the porch must have functioned something like a *porte cochère*. It has a tierceron-vault resting on head corbels. Arms in the bosses refer to the Courtenays, Percevals and possibly the Gorges. The two-centred inner doorway is earlier than the tower but still C15 – see the wave mouldings and square label stops. The back doorway is simply stepped; perhaps C13. Of the screens passage, the moulded head beam survives, and two doorways with triangular heads to the S, originally leading to kitchen and offices. The ground floor of the solar has C15 moulded beams. Staircase *c.* 1883, from Clevedon Court. N of the screens passage was the hall, with a huge C17 stepped chimney-breast. Later subdividing E–W wall. One truss survives, of arch-braced true crucks with sharply cranked collar, possibly late C13 or C14. The solar roof has four arch-braced collar-trusses with two tiers of wind-braces, the lower cusped. It encloses the C13 gable-end of the hall, with pigeon holes.

CHARLTON HOUSE, *c.* 1½ m. N. Now The Downs School. The N front is from a rebuilding probably *c.* 1585–1610; two projecting wings with curved gables and bay windows. To the l. of centre, a Victorian two-storey porch. The house was enlarged in the early C19; see the plain sashed S front. Remodelled and the W wing rebuilt *c.* 1883, for the Gibbs of Tyntesfield, by

Henry Woodyer. Windows are mullioned-and-transomed on the ground floor, mullioned only above. The E wing is the oldest part, with in the E wall (now inside) a two-light window with arched lights, perhaps early C16. Other windows Elizabethan or Jacobean, where they are not renewed. W of the cross-passage, the hall (mostly C19) retains a gorgeous Jacobean stone fireplace with clustered colonnettes reinforced by termini caryatids and other figures. In the overmantel abundantly draped figures of Charity and Justice.

TYNTESFIELD, ½ m. E. A High Victorian country house, exceptional architecturally and for the near-intact survival of most of its works of art, furnishings and ephemera. Built for William Gibbs (1790–1875), whose fortune came from fertilizer. Far from Gibbs's business interests, Tyntesfield was made possible by the railway age. In 1843 Gibbs bought a modest Tudor Gothic house built *c.* 1813. It was greatly enlarged by *John Norton* in 1863–5, creating a dramatic and strident Gothic mansion without any hint of gloom, beautifully sited on wooded slopes. The high-quality furnishings include much by *J. G. Crace* and *Collier & Plucknett* of Warwick. William Gibbs's great-grandson died in 2001, and a sale seemed inevitable – perhaps the last such complete Victorian ensemble to be threatened with dispersal. It was acquired instead by the National Trust in 2002.

The long rising approach from the SE gives glimpses of high turrets and pinnacles. The centre of the S front is all that is recognizable of the Regency house, although heightened and remodelled by Norton: three windows wide and three storeys, with a central canted bay. To its l., Norton's drawing room. Arcaded loggia probably by *Henry Woodyer*, part of a major remodelling for Gibbs's son Antony, 1887–90. E entrance courtyard with a single-storey library wing S of the porch. A high tower over the porch was demolished in 1935. Fine naturalistic stone carving by a *Mr Beates*, e.g. the porch bosses. The entrance corridor leads to a spectacular library lined with golden oak, with an arch-braced collar-beam roof, fitted bookcases and *Minton*-tiled window seats. The dining room was extended E and N by *Woodyer*, with three bay windows screened by columns. Oak-panelled ceiling integrated with the chimney-surround. Top-lit hall with impressive timbered roof by *Norton*. His original imperial staircase was rearranged by *Woodyer*. The lower flights rest on arcades of coloured marble and granite. Drawing room 51 ft (15.5 metres) long, with panelled ceiling. Uncomfortable Renaissance Revival chimneypiece from Venice, added 1910. Billiard room with timber clerestory roof; inglenook added by *Woodyer*, fixed central-heated billiard table by *James Plucknett*, *c.* 1889. The plinth wall survives from an immense domed conservatory demolished in 1917.

CHAPEL. Astonishingly big and magnificent, by *Arthur Blomfield*, 1873–5. Blomfield's inspirations were the Sainte Chapelle in Paris, George Gilbert Scott's Exeter College Chapel, Oxford, and perhaps Butterfield's Keble College Chapel, Oxford, which was paid for by the devoutly High Church Gibbs. The chapel is reached by a bridge from the N wing. Basement let into the hillside, intended but never used as a burial crypt. SW belfry turret with large crocketed pinnacle. Three-bay stone-vaulted nave, with W gallery and shallow transepts. Apsidal sanctuary. – FITTINGS. Arcaded REREDOS with mosaics designed by *Henry Wooldridge* and made by *Salviati*. – Tessellated FLOORS of faience, marbles, bluejohn and onyx by *Powell & Sons*. – STAINED GLASS. Nave more muted than the apse, all designed by *Wooldridge* for *Powell & Sons*, excepting a small 1930s light. – MONUMENTS. Jewelled memorial crosses by *Barkentin & Krall*.

GROUNDS. S and W of the house, formal terraced gardens. Stable Court by *Woodyer*, 1889. Jubilee Garden with Neo-Baroque gardener's offices and dilapidated orangery, both *c.* 1894–7, probably by *Walter Cave*. The supporting paraphernalia is remarkably intact, notably the red brick electricity-generating house of 1889, possibly *Woodyer*. Model farm of 1881 and later, saw mill, water supply and gas works, ensuring near self-sufficiency.

WRAXALL CAMP (or Failand Camp), near Longwood House. Small Iron Age enclosure with traces of associated fields. A decorated late Iron Age bronze collar was found at Wraxall.

WRINGTON

4060

ALL SAINTS. Wrington and its church were owned by Glastonbury Abbey from the C10 until 1539. Among the most majestic of North Somerset's Perp churches, crowned by a good tall W tower (113 ft 6 in., 35 metres), possibly *c.* 1430. The bell-openings are continued as blank panels below, as at Evercreech (S. Somerset); both derive from St Cuthbert, Wells, and ultimately from William Wynford's SW tower at Wells Cathedral. The masons' marks in the tower are reported also at St Cuthbert (Jerry Sampson). Twin bell-openings, each of two lights, divided by a diagonal shaft rising to a central parapet pinnacle on each face. Set-back buttresses ending in diagonal pinnacles. The chief pinnacles are independent of them, square turrets with their own angle pinnacles. Pierced parapet of cusped triangles. Big four-centred W doorway under a square moulding with traceried spandrels; panelled jambs and voussoirs. Sophisticated six-light W window; with sub-arcuation, something one expects at the very close of the C15; perhaps inserted after completion of the tower. Two-light N and S windows. Counting the blank lower extension, they have two transoms. Extremely pretty turret for the Sanctus bell on the nave E gable. The aisles and clerestory have the same pierced parapets as the tower. Only the tall S porch has pierced quatrefoil lozenges instead. Aisle windows of four lights, clerestory windows of three. The chancel E window, a correct replica of the original, a design of *c.* 1300; five lights with a large circle in the head which contains a sub-cusped quatrefoil. The buttresses at the E angles of the chancel have spirited Dec image niches; nodding double-ogee arches with sub-cusps and ballflower, and above them, by contrast, triangular gablets with crockets. Above the S doorway a statue of Christ seated; defaced. Inside, the church is tall and impressive. It has a lofty tower arch of three panels, canted in plan, with shafts between the panels. Tower fan-vault comparable to those at Bishop Alcock's Chapel, Ely, and St George's Chapel, Windsor. The clerestory is later than this tower, see the former roof-line above the tower arch. The arcades are of four bays with an uncommon section, four shafts and four wide concave diagonals with a thin shaft set in. Two-centred arches. The chancel arch is exceptionally wide. In detail it corresponds to the arcade as do the one-bay chancel chapels. The small capitals have leafy decoration, cf. Winscombe. On the arcade E responds demi-figures of angels, formerly supporting a rood beam. The church was restored in 1859 by *Foster & Wood*, including repair of the early C16 nave roof, and new chancel ceiling.

FITTINGS. REREDOS. Elegant Neo-Gothic, designed in 1832 by *Charles Barry*; carver *John White*. – Fine CHANCEL FURNISHINGS by *Alan Thomas*, 1998, oak and wrought iron. – SCREEN across chancel and chapels. Of *c.* 1500 (cf. Whitchurch), with C19 repairs. Two-light divisions, the usual enriched cornice with brattishing, running vine, etc. Less usual, a foliage band below the lights. – ROOD figures of 1940. – PULPIT. Caen stone, typically High Victorian, 1859. – PEWS. High-quality poppyheads and traceried bench-ends, 1859, by *William Ship*. – FONT. Of Dundry stone. Octagonal, Perp, and richly decorated with demi-figures of angels and elaborately detailed quatrefoils. – STAINED GLASS. A good Victorian array. E window by *Joseph Bell*, 1860. Chancel N and S, both *Clayton & Bell*, the S *c.* 1876, the N a memorial to Hannah More, 1884. S chapel E, *Joseph Bell*, 1860. S chapel S no doubt *Mayer & Co.*, *c.* 1890. S aisle, from E: first (1871) and third (*c.* 1875) by *Clayton & Bell*; second clearly *Powell & Sons*, 1906. N aisle, from E: first 1879, *Clayton & Bell* again; third, over N door, no doubt *Joseph Bell*, *c.* 1860. Also his and of the same date, the tower W window, with Old Testament prophets after the Sistine Chapel, an exceptionally early example of influence from Michelangelo. *Bell* probably glazed the clerestory. – MONUMENTS. Effigy of a priest, *c.* 1340, formerly in a garden wall of Wrington House. – Hannah More †1833, of Barley Wood near Wrington; plain tripartite Gothic tablet by *E. H. Baily*.

PRIMARY SCHOOL. Lively Gothic, by *Foster & Wood*, 1857. Big Perp windows with vertical tracery lights, a picturesque timbered porch and entrance running low along the front, master's house (l.) with capped tower in the angle.

BROAD STREET, shortly NE of the church, forms a wide curve, and was presumably the site of the market granted by charter of 1332. The former RECTORY, s side, has a late C17 wing at the sw, with a square block added *c.* 1710; this reduced from three to two storeys in the 1950s with a hipped roof, giving it an exemplary Queen Anne appearance. Five bays, broken segmental pediment. More good C18 houses, e.g. WEBBSBROOK HOUSE, Silver Street, symmetrical and with full array of early C18 sashes; typical thick glazing bars in squarish panes. To the N, where High Street meets Chapel Hill, ALBURY HOUSE, attributed to *Edward Davis*, *c.* 1846 for John James, solicitor. An excellent Italianate essay, cf. Fiesole and Oakwood, Bath (*see* p. 190), e.g. a first-floor loggia on the w front treated as a Serlian motif. The usual belvedere tower here substituted with a sturdy belfry over the N front. Many original interior fittings, bracketed cornices, anthemion motifs on doors and shutters.

BARLEY WOOD, Long Lane. A pretty cottage, originally thatched, built *c.* 1801–2 for Hannah More, writer, philanthropist and social reformer. Enlarged by *Ernest George* in 1900 for H. H. Wills of the Bristol tobacco family, altered again by *Chester Jones*, 1933. The canted bay l. of the entrance, and the long veranda on the s front are original in design, though renewed. Half-timbered porch of 1900. Now in institutional use. In the garden, Neoclassical URNS commemorating John Locke and Bishop Porteous, erected 1802 and 1805 respectively.

WRITHLINGTON

A bleak hilltop mining village, formerly with the last working colliery in N Somerset (closed 1973).

ST MARY MAGDALENE (former), Church Hill. Rebuilt 1874. Redundant 1981; now residential. Small three-bay nave with bellcote, N aisle, chancel, s porch.

WRITHLINGTON SCHOOL, Knobsbury Lane. By *Aedas*, 2007–10. Cool, partly metal-clad exteriors. Two curving wings form a vesica shape in plan, bridged by a central atrium. It replaced a good design by *R. Oliver Harris*, County Architect, 1954–5.

The old settlement on Church Hill has one or two C18 farmhouses, and the OLD RECTORY, the rear probably 1700–50, the front early C19; Bath stone, plain Late Georgian.

YATTON

ST MARY. Built of Dundry stone, and essentially Dec, though Perp work dominates at first sight. The nave was enlarged and

given aisles and a fine s porch in the mid C15. Thoroughly
restored 1870–2 by *G. E. Street*, who rebuilt the s chancel wall,
probably using the old materials. The C13 church was aisled
and cruciform, with a crossing tower, the hub of the design. It
rests on arches which were given a Perp shape (two-wave
moulding) when the spire was started. At the same time the
tierceron-vault with a large bell-hole was put in. The first and
second tower stages have lancet windows, single, or double
with Y-tracery, i.e. forms of the late C13. One is visible from
inside the nave, indicating the lower roof-line before the
clerestory. The top stage was altered in the C15 with simple
Perp belfry lights, then a parapet pierced with a frieze of
cusped triangles, diagonal pinnacles, higher panelled stair-
turret. Finally the truncated octagonal spire, under construction in 1456,* which must have reached a considerable height,
for the angle is steep. It was strengthened or repaired in 1582,
but in 1595, it was reduced to its present height. Late C13
too are the transepts: s transept s window, a design of some
individuality, five lights with intersected tracery, but, for
variety, with quatrefoiled circles in the outermost intersections
of the first tier. The arch from the n transept into the aisle is
double-chamfered without capitals – a Dec form. A little later,
c. 1325, the tomb recesses in the n transept (*see* below). The
five-light n window of the n transept is a Perp insertion in the
Dec opening. Another Perp remodelling is the chancel, with
finely moulded window reveals; the foundations may be C13 or
even earlier. But the chief work of the late Middle Ages at
Yatton was the remodelling of the nave and aisles and the addition of the s porch and the n chapel. Beginning probably
c. 1440, the nave was heightened with a clerestory and lengthened, and the aisles rebuilt, all to a consistent design. s aisle
roof timbers felled in 1445. The n doorway (rather obscured
within a glazed entrance; *see* below) has fleurons, an extravagant ogee gable with big finial, and then side pinnacles. The
tripartite w front has its only counterpart in Somerset at
Crewkerne: large transomed w window, three plus three lights
under sub-arches (renewed tracery), under a steep central
gable, seemingly a reminiscence of the early C14 structure. In
the gable a statuette of the Trinity. The centre flanked by robust
polygonal turrets with caps. Lower versions flank the lean-to
aisles, which have four-light windows (two plus two under sub-
arches). Clerestory and aisles have the same type of pierced
parapet as the tower (nave parapets renewed, 1870–2), probably all *c.* 1450 or within a few years. The later s porch was
made to agree. The parapet of the n chapel, however, is pierced
with a frieze of cusped lozenges and there is, to add more ani-
mation, a NE angle turret. The s porch is the most highly decorated in Somerset, its façade composed round a four-centred
entrance arch, and scrolling foliage running up the jambs and
around the arch. Ogee door hood with more foliage and

36

*The dates come from churchwardens' accounts.

remarkably naturalistic crockets. Flanking the entrance, blank panelling sending up ogee-curved crocketed feelers towards the central arch. Above the arch, the panelling is higher and finishes with a row of blind arcading beneath a flat parapet. Inside the porch a lively thin-ribbed lierne-vault. Inner doorway with four-centred head and fleuron frieze.

The s porch and N chapel have often been ascribed to the munificence of Sir John and Lady Isobel Newton of Court de Wyck, Claverham. He died in 1488, leaving 40s. to Yatton, regretting having given nothing to the church during his life. She died in 1498, but the churchwardens' accounts show that her first contribution was not until 1496. The N chapel seems to be later than the porch, and became the Newtons' chantry chapel (see below).

Light and spacious INTERIOR. Lofty five-bay nave arcades on slim, multi-shafted piers of uncommon section: a Greek cross with concave quadrants in the diagonals, demi-shafts to the ends of the cross-arms, and slim shafts set in the hollows. The E responds have heads. Otherwise the shafts have small capitals with varied foliage, except those facing the nave, which rise to the roof, their upward élan only checked by the sill course of the clerestory which curves round them. This course is decorated with fleurons. The clerestory has two-light windows. The wall-shafts end with little heads which carry the roof principals. Wagon roof with demi-figures of angels on the wall-plate and carved bosses. In the aisle also wall-shafts. They carry depressed pointed trefoiled arches of wood with closely panelled tracery, and on these rest the wall-plates. Wall-shafts in the aisles are a motif more at home in SE than in N Somerset. N chapel restored c. 1906 by F. Bligh Bond (his SCREEN of local Perp forms). It is of two bays with very prettily traceried windows. Those to the N have four-centred arches. The arches from the W and the chancel are panelled. Rich image niches flanking the altar. To the r., a PILLAR PISCINA.*

FITTINGS. Splendid brass and enamel LECTERN, presumably of 1872. – SCULPTURE. Life-size oak figures of St Peter and St Paul, in Baroque attitudes, for the organ of Bath Abbey in 1708, whence a third figure has been returned. Acanthus frieze from the same instrument incorporated in the C20 organ case. – STAINED GLASS. Chancel E and three S all Clayton & Bell, the SE recorded in 1877. Chancel N signed Henry Hughes, c. 1865. N chapel E by Powells, 1928–9. Medieval heraldic glass in the tracery, incorrectly restored 1872, corrected under Roland Paul, 1927. Also by Powells the two N windows, 1951. N aisle, two by Clayton & Bell: first from E c. 1900; second, 1926, no doubt by Reginald Bell.

MONUMENTS. Two recesses with broad cusped ogee gables in the N wall of the N transept. In them two civilian effigies of c. 1325, presumably man and wife, worn. – Sir Richard Newton †1449 and wife †1475. Fine alabaster monument of c. 1475 (cf.

---

* In the N aisle on a window sill, the base of a shaft, probably for another statuette.

William Canynges's monument at St Mary Redcliffe, Bristol). Tomb-chest with ogee niches filled by figures of angels carrying shields (a usual motif of the alabasterers, cf. Clifton, Beds.; Millom, Cumbria). Recumbent effigies with some original red colouring. – Sir John Newton †1488 and Isobel of Cheddar †1498. Tomb-chest with quatrefoils in a recess. Recumbent effigies. Broad buttresses and pinnacles l. and r. of the recess. Low Tudor arch with pretty openwork cusps, openwork tracery in the spandrels and much crocketing. Against the back wall relief of the Annunciation. Above the arch frieze of ten niches for figures. Only one half of a figure is left. Fleuron frieze on top and cornice. – Henry Grimsteed †1714. Signed *Michael Sidnell*. Broken pediment, simple tablet with volutes and palm leaves. – Hannah Markham †1768. Perhaps by the *Patys*. Tablet with inverted volutes, marble obelisk and draped urn. – WAR MEMORIAL. Cross-shaft and crown of 1921. The stepped base may be that recorded as new in 1524–5.

N of the church an octagonal MEETING ROOM by *Andrew Pittman*, 1974–5, the roof rising to a truncated cone echoing the C15 spire.

CHURCH HOUSE. N of the church. Largely rebuilt 1471–3, the date of all medieval survivals. Converted to almshouses *c.* 1621. Altered 1728–9 and later. Mainly of Dundry stone, with decorative quoins of Blue Lias in the E gable. Original window openings at the E end. Blocked late medieval door on the N front, originally to a cross-passage. Raised cruck-trusses forming a six-and-a-half-bay roof. The eastern two bays were originally a double-height kitchen and brewhouse with open hearth. The W end had a great chamber on the first floor. Dividing wall between the ends removed in the C18.*

OLD RECTORY, SE. A former prebendal house with an impressive C15 front. Buttressed two-storey porch to the W with screens passage behind, buttressed cross-wing with two unequal gables to the E. Four-centred heads to porch entrance and doorway. Above the porch a large transomed two-light window with tracery, cf. Tickenham Court. The hall was to the l. of the porch; here, a smaller straight-headed window with transom and mullion. Handsomely traceried, quatrefoiled circles in the spandrels. Other windows of the later cross-type. (Arch-braced roof with cambered collars, and wind-braces.) A probable service end W of the screens passage has been lost.

The village is large and the points of interest scattered. On the SE edge, HILL COURT by *George Oatley*, 1907–9, pleasing Neo-Georgian in the manner of Leonard Stokes or Ernest Newton. On High Street, a dignified WAR MEMORIAL in the form of an Ionic column, by the *Rev. F. Peert*, 1922. COURT FARM, Chescombe Road, is perhaps a C17 reworking of a C15 hall house. In the much modernized front two timber two-light windows with round-headed and trefoil-cusped lights. (Arched-braced roof with wind-bracing.)

*With thanks to John Thorp, Keystone Historic Buildings Consultants.

(HENLEY WOOD. Site of a ROMANO-CELTIC TEMPLE on a small wooded hill, just NE of Cadbury-Congresbury hill-fort (*see* p. 480).)

(WEMBERHAM ROMAN VILLA, 2 m. W of Yatton. Excavated in 1884. Of two storeys, on an unusual plan. The villa yielded a fine red, white and blue pavement.)

GLOSSARY

Numbers and letters refer to the illustrations (by John Sambrook)
on pp. 746–753.

ABACUS: flat slab forming the top of a capital (3a).

ACANTHUS: classical formalized leaf ornament (4b).

ACCUMULATOR TOWER: *see* Hydraulic power.

ACHIEVEMENT: a complete display of armorial bearings.

ACROTERION: plinth for a statue or ornament on the apex or ends of a pediment; more usually, both the plinth and what stands on it (4a).

AEDICULE (*lit.* little building): architectural surround, consisting usually of two columns or pilasters supporting a pediment.

AGGREGATE: *see* Concrete.

AISLE: subsidiary space alongside the body of a building, separated from it by columns, piers, or posts.

ALMONRY: a building from which alms are dispensed to the poor.

AMBULATORY (*lit.* walkway): aisle around the sanctuary (q.v.).

ANGLE ROLL: roll moulding in the angle between two planes (1a).

ANSE DE PANIER: *see* Arch.

ANTAE: simplified pilasters (4a), usually applied to the ends of the enclosing walls of a portico *in antis* (q.v.).

ANTEFIXAE: ornaments projecting at regular intervals above a Greek cornice, originally to conceal the ends of roof tiles (4a).

ANTHEMION: classical ornament like a honeysuckle flower (4b).

APRON: raised panel below a window or wall monument or tablet.

APSE: semicircular or polygonal end of an apartment, especially of a chancel or chapel. In classical architecture sometimes called an *exedra*.

ARABESQUE: non-figurative surface decoration consisting of flowing lines, foliage scrolls etc., based on geometrical patterns. Cf. Grotesque.

ARCADE: series of arches supported by piers or columns. *Blind arcade* or *arcading*: the same applied to the wall surface. *Wall arcade*: in medieval churches, a blind arcade forming a dado below windows. Also a covered shopping street.

ARCH: Shapes *see* 5c. *Basket arch* or *anse de panier* (basket handle): three-centred and depressed, or with a flat centre. *Nodding*: ogee arch curving forward from the wall face. *Parabolic*: shaped like a chain suspended from two level points, but inverted. Special purposes. *Chancel*: dividing chancel from nave or crossing. *Crossing*: spanning piers at a crossing (q.v.). *Relieving or discharging*: incorporated in a wall to relieve superimposed weight (5c). *Skew*: spanning responds not diametrically opposed. *Strainer*: inserted in an opening to resist inward pressure. *Transverse*: spanning a main axis (e.g. of a vaulted space). *See also* Jack arch, Triumphal arch.

ARCHITRAVE: formalized lintel, the lowest member of the classical entablature (3a). Also the moulded frame of a door or window (often borrowing the profile of a classical architrave). For *lugged* and *shouldered* architraves see 4b.

ARCUATED: dependent structurally on the arch principle. Cf. Trabeated.

ARK: chest or cupboard housing the

tables of Jewish law in a synagogue.

ARRIS: sharp edge where two surfaces meet at an angle (3a).

ASHLAR: masonry of large blocks wrought to even faces and square edges (6d).

ASTRAGAL: classical moulding of semicircular section (3f).

ASTYLAR: with no columns or similar vertical features.

ATLANTES: *see* Caryatids.

ATRIUM (plural: atria): inner court of a Roman or C20 house; in a multi-storey building, a toplit covered court rising through all storeys. Also an open court in front of a church.

ATTACHED COLUMN: *see* Engaged column.

ATTIC: small top storey within a roof. Also the storey above the main entablature of a classical façade.

AUMBRY: recess or cupboard to hold sacred vessels for the Mass.

BAILEY: *see* Motte-and-bailey.

BALANCE BEAM: *see* Canals.

BALDACCHINO: free-standing canopy, originally fabric, over an altar. Cf. Ciborium.

BALLFLOWER: globular flower of three petals enclosing a ball (1a). Typical of the Decorated style.

BALUSTER: pillar or pedestal of bellied form. *Balusters*: vertical supports of this or any other form, for a handrail or coping, the whole being called a *balustrade* (6c). *Blind balustrade*: the same applied to the wall surface.

BARBICAN: outwork defending the entrance to a castle.

BARGEBOARDS (corruption of 'vergeboards'): boards, often carved or fretted, fixed beneath the eaves of a gable to cover and protect the rafters.

BAROQUE: style originating in Rome *c.*1600 and current in England *c.*1680–1720, characterized by dramatic massing and silhouette and the use of the giant order.

BARROW: burial mound.

BARTIZAN: corbelled turret, square or round, frequently at an angle.

BASCULE: hinged part of a lifting (or bascule) bridge.

BASE: moulded foot of a column or pilaster. For *Attic* base *see* 3b.

BASEMENT: lowest, subordinate storey; hence the lowest part of a classical elevation, below the *piano nobile* (q.v.).

BASILICA: a Roman public hall; hence an aisled building with a clerestory.

BASTION: one of a series of defensive semicircular or polygonal projections from the main wall of a fortress or city.

BATTER: intentional inward inclination of a wall face.

BATTLEMENT: defensive parapet, composed of *merlons* (solid) and *crenels* (embrasures) through which archers could shoot; sometimes called *crenellation*. Also used decoratively.

BAY: division of an elevation or interior space as defined by regular vertical features such as arches, columns, windows etc.

BAY LEAF: classical ornament of overlapping bay leaves (3f).

BAY WINDOW: window of one or more storeys projecting from the face of a building. *Canted*: with a straight front and angled sides. *Bow window*: curved. *Oriel*: rests on corbels or brackets and starts above ground level; also the bay window at the dais end of a medieval great hall.

BEAD-AND-REEL: *see* Enrichments.

BEAKHEAD: Norman ornament with a row of beaked bird or beast heads usually biting into a roll moulding (1a).

BELFRY: chamber or stage in a tower where bells are hung.

BELL CAPITAL: *see* 1b.

BELLCOTE: small gabled or roofed housing for the bell(s).

BERM: level area separating a ditch from a bank on a hill-fort or barrow.

BILLET: Norman ornament of small half-cylindrical or rectangular blocks (1a).

BLIND: *see* Arcade, Baluster, Portico.

BLOCK CAPITAL: *see* 1a.

BLOCKED: columns, etc. interrupted by regular projecting

blocks (*blocking*), as on a Gibbs surround (4b).

BLOCKING COURSE: course of stones, or equivalent, on top of a cornice and crowning the wall.

BOLECTION MOULDING: covering the joint between two different planes (6b).

BOND: the pattern of long sides (*stretchers*) and short ends (*headers*) produced on the face of a wall by laying bricks in a particular way (6e).

BOSS: knob or projection, e.g. at the intersection of ribs in a vault (2c).

BOWTELL: a term in use by the C15 for a form of roll moulding, usually three-quarters of a circle in section (also called *edge roll*).

BOW WINDOW: *see* Bay window.

BOX FRAME: timber-framed construction in which vertical and horizontal wall members support the roof (7). Also concrete construction where the loads are taken on cross walls; also called *cross-wall construction*.

BRACE: subsidiary member of a structural frame, curved or straight. *Bracing* is often arranged decoratively e.g. quatrefoil, herringbone (7). *See also* Roofs.

BRATTISHING: ornamental crest, usually formed of leaves, Tudor flowers or miniature battlements.

BRESSUMER (*lit.* breast-beam): big horizontal beam supporting the wall above, especially in a jettied building (7).

BRICK: *see* Bond, Cogging, Engineering, Gauged, Tumbling.

BRIDGE: *Bowstring*: with arches rising above the roadway which is suspended from them. *Clapper*: one long stone forms the roadway. *Roving*: *see* Canal. *Suspension*: roadway suspended from cables or chains slung between towers or pylons. *Stay-suspension* or *stay-cantilever*: supported by diagonal stays from towers or pylons. *See also* Bascule.

BRISES-SOLEIL: projecting fins or canopies which deflect direct sunlight from windows.

BROACH: *see* Spire and 1c.

BUCRANIUM: ox skull used decoratively in classical friezes.

BULL-NOSED SILL: sill displaying a pronounced convex upper moulding.

BULLSEYE WINDOW: small oval window, set horizontally (cf. Oculus). Also called *œil de bœuf*.

BUTTRESS: vertical member projecting from a wall to stabilize it or to resist the lateral thrust of an arch, roof, or vault (1c, 2c). A *flying buttress* transmits the thrust to a heavy abutment by means of an arch or half-arch (1c).

CABLE OR ROPE MOULDING: originally Norman, like twisted strands of a rope.

CAMES: *see* Quarries.

CAMPANILE: free-standing bell-tower.

CANALS: *Flash lock*: removable weir or similar device through which boats pass on a flush of water. Predecessor of the *pound lock*: chamber with gates at each end allowing boats to float from one level to another. *Tidal gates*: single pair of lock gates allowing vessels to pass when the tide makes a level. *Balance beam*: beam projecting horizontally for opening and closing lock gates. *Roving bridge*: carrying a towing path from one bank to the other.

CANTILEVER: horizontal projection (e.g. step, canopy) supported by a downward force behind the fulcrum.

CAPITAL: head or crowning feature of a column or pilaster; for classical types *see* 3; for medieval types *see* 1b.

CARREL: compartment designed for individual work or study.

CARTOUCHE: classical tablet with ornate frame (4b).

CARYATIDS: female figures supporting an entablature; their male counterparts are *Atlantes* (*lit.* Atlas figures).

CASEMATE: vaulted chamber, with embrasures for defence, within a castle wall or projecting from it.

CASEMENT: side-hinged window.

CASTELLATED: with battlements (q.v.).

CAST IRON: hard and brittle, cast in a mould to the required shape.

Wrought iron is ductile, strong in tension, forged into decorative patterns or forged and rolled into e.g. bars, joists, boiler plates; *mild steel* is its modern equivalent, similar but stronger.

CATSLIDE: *See* 8a.

CAVETTO: concave classical moulding of quarter-round section (3f).

CELURE OR CEILURE: enriched area of roof above rood or altar.

CEMENT: *see* Concrete.

CENOTAPH (*lit.* empty tomb): funerary monument which is not a burying place.

CENTRING: wooden support for the building of an arch or vault, removed after completion.

CHAMFER (*lit.* corner-break): surface formed by cutting off a square edge or corner. For types of chamfers and *chamfer stops see* 6a. *See also* Double chamfer.

CHANCEL: part of the E end of a church set apart for the use of the officiating clergy.

CHANTRY CHAPEL: often attached to or within a church, endowed for the celebration of Masses principally for the soul of the founder.

CHEVET (*lit.* head): French term for chancel with ambulatory and radiating chapels.

CHEVRON: V-shape used in series or double series (later) on a Norman moulding (1a). Also (especially when on a single plane) called *zigzag*.

CHOIR: the part of a cathedral, monastic or collegiate church where services are sung.

CIBORIUM: a fixed canopy over an altar, usually vaulted and supported on four columns; cf. Baldacchino. Also a canopied shrine for the reserved sacrament.

CINQUEFOIL: *see* Foil.

CIST: stone-lined or slab-built grave.

CLADDING: external covering or skin applied to a structure, especially a framed one.

CLERESTORY: uppermost storey of the nave of a church, pierced by windows. Also high-level windows in secular buildings.

CLOSER: a brick cut to complete a bond (6e).

CLUSTER BLOCK: *see* Multi-storey.

COADE STONE: ceramic artificial stone made in Lambeth 1769–c.1840 by Eleanor Coade (†1821) and her associates.

COB: walling material of clay mixed with straw. Also called *pisé*.

COFFERING: arrangement of sunken panels (coffers), square or polygonal, decorating a ceiling, vault, or arch.

COGGING: a decorative course of bricks laid diagonally (6e). Cf. Dentilation.

COLLAR: *see* Roofs and 7.

COLLEGIATE CHURCH: endowed for the support of a college of priests.

COLONNADE: range of columns supporting an entablature. Cf. Arcade.

COLONNETTE: small medieval column or shaft.

COLOSSAL ORDER: *see* Giant order.

COLUMBARIUM: shelved, niched structure to house multiple burials.

COLUMN: a classical, upright structural member of round section with a shaft, a capital, and usually a base (3a, 4a).

COLUMN FIGURE: carved figure attached to a medieval column or shaft, usually flanking a doorway.

COMMUNION TABLE: unconsecrated table used in Protestant churches for the celebration of Holy Communion.

COMPOSITE: *see* Orders.

COMPOUND PIER: grouped shafts (q.v.), or a solid core surrounded by shafts.

CONCRETE: composition of *cement* (calcined lime and clay), *aggregate* (small stones or rock chippings), sand and water. It can be poured into *formwork* or *shuttering* (temporary frame of timber or metal) on site (*in-situ* concrete), or *pre-cast* as components before construction. *Reinforced*: incorporating steel rods to take the tensile force. *Pre-stressed*: with tensioned steel rods. Finishes include the impression of boards left by formwork (*board-marked* or *shuttered*), and texturing with steel brushes (*brushed*) or hammers (*hammer-dressed*). *See also* Shell.

CONSOLE: bracket of curved outline (4b).

COPING: protective course of masonry or brickwork capping a wall (6d).

CORBEL: projecting block supporting something above. *Corbel course*: continuous course of projecting stones or bricks fulfilling the same function. *Corbel table*: series of corbels to carry a parapet or a wall-plate or wall-post (7). *Corbelling*: brick or masonry courses built out beyond one another to support a chimney-stack, window, etc.

CORINTHIAN: *see* Orders and 3d.

CORNICE: flat-topped ledge with moulded underside, projecting along the top of a building or feature, especially as the highest member of the classical entablature (3a). Also the decorative moulding in the angle between wall and ceiling.

CORPS-DE-LOGIS: the main building(s) as distinct from the wings or pavilions.

COTTAGE ORNÉ: an artfully rustic small house associated with the Picturesque movement.

COUNTERCHANGING: of joists on a ceiling divided by beams into compartments, when placed in opposite directions in alternate squares.

COUR D'HONNEUR: formal entrance court before a house in the French manner, usually with flanking wings and a screen wall or gates.

COURSE: continuous layer of stones, etc. in a wall (6e).

COVE: a broad concave moulding, e.g. to mask the eaves of a roof. *Coved ceiling*: with a pronounced cove joining the walls to a flat central panel smaller than the whole area of the ceiling.

CRADLE ROOF: *see* Wagon roof.

CREDENCE: a shelf within or beside a piscina (q.v.), or a table for the sacramental elements and vessels.

CRENELLATION: parapet with crenels (*see* Battlement).

CRINKLE-CRANKLE WALL: garden wall undulating in a series of serpentine curves.

CROCKETS: leafy hooks. *Crocketing* decorates the edges of Gothic features, such as pinnacles, canopies, etc. *Crocket capital*: *see* 1b.

CROSSING: central space at the junction of the nave, chancel, and transepts. *Crossing tower*: above a crossing.

CROSS-WINDOW: with one mullion and one transom (qq.v.).

CROWN-POST: *see* Roofs and 7.

CROWSTEPS: squared stones set like steps, e.g. on a gable (8a).

CRUCKS (*lit.* crooked): pairs of inclined timbers (*blades*), usually curved, set at bay-lengths; they support the roof timbers and, in timber buildings, also support the walls (8b). *Base*: blades rise from ground level to a tie- or collar-beam which supports the roof timbers. *Full*: blades rise from ground level to the apex of the roof, serving as the main members of a roof truss. *Jointed*: blades formed from more than one timber; the lower member may act as a wall-post; it is usually elbowed at wall-plate level and jointed just above. *Middle*: blades rise from half-way up the walls to a tie- or collar-beam. *Raised*: blades rise from half-way up the walls to the apex. *Upper*: blades supported on a tie-beam and rising to the apex.

CRYPT: underground or half-underground area, usually below the E end of a church. *Ring crypt*: corridor crypt surrounding the apse of an early medieval church, often associated with chambers for relics. Cf. Undercroft.

CUPOLA (*lit.* dome): especially a small dome on a circular or polygonal base crowning a larger dome, roof, or turret.

CURSUS: a long avenue defined by two parallel earthen banks with ditches outside.

CURTAIN WALL: a connecting wall between the towers of a castle. Also a non-load-bearing external wall applied to a C20 framed structure.

CUSP: *see* Tracery and 2b.

CYCLOPEAN MASONRY: large irregular polygonal stones, smooth and finely jointed.

CYMA RECTA and CYMA REVERSA: classical mouldings with double curves (3f). Cf. Ogee.

DADO: the finishing (often with panelling) of the lower part of a wall in a classical interior; in origin a formalized continuous pedestal. *Dado rail*: the moulding along the top of the dado.

DAGGER: *see* Tracery and 2b.

DALLE-DE-VERRE (*lit.* glass-slab): a late C20 stained-glass technique, setting large, thick pieces of cast glass into a frame of reinforced concrete or epoxy resin.

DEC (DECORATED): English Gothic architecture *c.* 1290 to *c.* 1350. The name is derived from the type of window tracery (q.v.) used during the period.

DEMI- or HALF-COLUMNS: engaged columns (q.v.) half of whose circumference projects from the wall.

DENTIL: small square block used in series in classical cornices (3c). *Dentilation* is produced by the projection of alternating headers along cornices or stringcourses.

DIAPER: repetitive surface decoration of lozenges or squares flat or in relief. Achieved in brickwork with bricks of two colours.

DIOCLETIAN OR THERMAL WINDOW: semicircular with two mullions, as used in the Baths of Diocletian, Rome (4b).

DISTYLE: having two columns (4a).

DOGTOOTH: E.E. ornament, consisting of a series of small pyramids formed by four stylized canine teeth meeting at a point (1a).

DORIC: *see* Orders and 3a, 3b.

DORMER: window projecting from the slope of a roof (8a).

DOUBLE CHAMFER: a chamfer applied to each of two recessed arches (1a).

DOUBLE PILE: *see* Pile.

DRAGON BEAM: *see* Jetty.

DRESSINGS: the stone or brickwork worked to a finished face about an angle, opening, or other feature.

DRIPSTONE: moulded stone projecting from a wall to protect the lower parts from water. Cf. Hoodmould, Weathering.

DRUM: circular or polygonal stage supporting a dome or cupola. Also one of the stones forming the shaft of a column (3a).

DUTCH OR FLEMISH GABLE: *see* 8a.

EASTER SEPULCHRE: tomb-chest used for Easter ceremonial, within or against the N wall of a chancel.

EAVES: overhanging edge of a roof; hence *eaves cornice* in this position.

ECHINUS: ovolo moulding (q.v.) below the abacus of a Greek Doric capital (3a).

EDGE RAIL: *see* Railways.

E.E. (EARLY ENGLISH): English Gothic architecture *c.* 1190–1250.

EGG-AND-DART: *see* Enrichments and 3f.

ELEVATION: any face of a building or side of a room. In a drawing, the same or any part of it, represented in two dimensions.

EMBATTLED: with battlements.

EMBRASURE: small splayed opening in a wall or battlement (q.v.).

ENCAUSTIC TILES: earthenware tiles fired with a pattern and glaze.

EN DELIT: stone cut against the bed.

ENFILADE: reception rooms in a formal series, usually with all doorways on axis.

ENGAGED or ATTACHED COLUMN: one that partly merges into a wall or pier.

ENGINEERING BRICKS: dense bricks, originally used mostly for railway viaducts etc.

ENRICHMENTS: the carved decoration of certain classical mouldings, e.g. the ovolo (qq.v.) with *egg-and-dart*, the cyma reversa with *waterleaf*, the astragal with *bead-and-reel* (3f).

ENTABLATURE: in classical architecture, collective name for the three horizontal members (architrave, frieze, and cornice) carried by a wall or a column (3a).

ENTASIS: very slight convex deviation from a straight line, used to prevent an optical illusion of concavity.

EPITAPH: inscription on a tomb.

EXEDRA: *see* Apse.

EXTRADOS: outer curved face of an arch or vault.

EYECATCHER: decorative building terminating a vista.

FASCIA: plain horizontal band, e.g. in an architrave (3c, 3d) or on a shopfront.

FENESTRATION: the arrangement of windows in a façade.

FERETORY: site of the chief shrine of a church, behind the high altar.

FESTOON: ornamental garland, suspended from both ends. Cf. Swag.

FIBREGLASS, or glass-reinforced polyester (GRP): synthetic resin reinforced with glass fibre. GRC: glass-reinforced concrete.

FIELD: see Panelling and 6b.

FILLET: a narrow flat band running down a medieval shaft or along a roll moulding (1a). It separates larger curved mouldings in classical cornices, fluting or bases (3c).

FLAMBOYANT: the latest phase of French Gothic architecture, with flowing tracery.

FLASH LOCK: see Canals.

FLÈCHE or SPIRELET (lit. arrow): slender spire on the centre of a roof.

FLEURON: medieval carved flower or leaf, often rectilinear (1a).

FLUSHWORK: knapped flint used with dressed stone to form patterns.

FLUTING: series of concave grooves (flutes), their common edges sharp (arris) or blunt (fillet) (3).

FOIL (lit. leaf): lobe formed by the cusping of a circular or other shape in tracery (2b). Trefoil (three), quatrefoil (four), cinquefoil (five), and multifoil express the number of lobes in a shape.

FOLIATE: decorated with leaves.

FORMWORK: see Concrete.

FRAMED BUILDING: where the structure is carried by a framework – e.g. of steel, reinforced concrete, timber – instead of by load-bearing walls.

FREESTONE: stone that is cut, or can be cut, in all directions.

FRESCO: al fresco: painting on wet plaster. Fresco secco: painting on dry plaster.

FRIEZE: the middle member of the classical entablature, sometimes ornamented (3a). Pulvinated frieze (lit. cushioned): of bold convex profile (3c). Also a horizontal band of ornament.

FRONTISPIECE: in C16 and C17 buildings the central feature of doorway and windows above linked in one composition.

GABLE: For types see 8a. Gablet: small gable. Pedimental gable: treated like a pediment.

GADROONING: classical ribbed ornament like inverted fluting that flows into a lobed edge.

GALILEE: chapel or vestibule usually at the W end of a church enclosing the main portal(s).

GALLERY: a long room or passage; an upper storey above the aisle of a church, looking through arches to the nave; a balcony or mezzanine overlooking the main interior space of a building; or an external walkway.

GALLETING: small stones set in a mortar course.

GAMBREL ROOF: see 8a.

GARDEROBE: medieval privy.

GARGOYLE: projecting water spout often carved into human or animal shape.

GAUGED or RUBBED BRICKWORK: soft brick sawn roughly, then rubbed to a precise (gauged) surface. Mostly used for door or window openings (5c).

GAZEBO (jocular Latin, 'I shall gaze'): ornamental lookout tower or raised summer house.

GEOMETRIC: English Gothic architecture c. 1250–1310. See also Tracery. For another meaning, see Stairs.

GIANT or COLOSSAL ORDER: classical order (q.v.) whose height is that of two or more storeys of the building to which it is applied.

GIBBS SURROUND: C18 treatment of an opening (4b), seen particularly in the work of James Gibbs (1682–1754).

GIRDER: a large beam. Box: of hollow-box section. Bowed: with its top rising in a curve. Plate: of I-section, made from iron or steel plates. *Lattice*: with braced framework.

GLAZING BARS: wooden or sometimes metal bars separating and supporting window panes.

GRAFFITI: *see* Sgraffito.

GRANGE: farm owned and run by a religious order.

GRC: *see* Fibreglass.

GRISAILLE: monochrome painting on walls or glass.

GROIN: sharp edge at the meeting of two cells of a cross-vault; *see* Vault and 2c.

GROTESQUE (*lit.* grotto-esque): wall decoration adopted from Roman examples in the Renaissance. Its foliage scrolls incorporate figurative elements. Cf. Arabesque.

GROTTO: artificial cavern.

GRP: *see* Fibreglass.

GUILLOCHE: classical ornament of interlaced bands (4b).

GUNLOOP: opening for a firearm.

GUTTAE: stylized drops (3b).

HALF-TIMBERING: archaic term for timber-framing (q.v.). Sometimes used for non-structural decorative timberwork.

HALL CHURCH: medieval church with nave and aisles of approximately equal height.

HAMMERBEAM: *see* Roofs and 7.

HAMPER: in C20 architecture, a visually distinct topmost storey or storeys.

HEADER: *see* Bond and 6e.

HEADSTOP: stop (q.v.) carved with a head (5b).

HELM ROOF: *see* IC.

HENGE: ritual earthwork.

HERM (*lit.* the god Hermes): male head or bust on a pedestal.

HERRINGBONE WORK: *see* 7ii. Cf. Pitched masonry.

HEXASTYLE: *see* Portico.

HILL-FORT: Iron Age earthwork enclosed by a ditch and bank system.

HIPPED ROOF: *see* 8a.

HOODMOULD: projecting moulding above an arch or lintel to throw off water (2b, 5b). When horizontal often called a *label*. For label stop *see* Stop.

HUSK GARLAND: festoon of stylized nutshells (4b).

HYDRAULIC POWER: use of water under high pressure to work machinery. *Accumulator tower*: houses a hydraulic accumulator which accommodates fluctuations in the flow through hydraulic mains.

HYPOCAUST (*lit.* underburning): Roman underfloor heating system.

IMPOST: horizontal moulding at the springing of an arch (5c).

IMPOST BLOCK: block between abacus and capital (1b).

IN ANTIS: *see* Antae, Portico and 4a.

INDENT: shape chiselled out of a stone to receive a brass.

INDUSTRIALIZED or SYSTEM BUILDING: system of manufactured units assembled on site.

INGLENOOK (*lit.* fire-corner): recess for a hearth with provision for seating.

INTERCOLUMNATION: interval between columns.

INTERLACE: decoration in relief simulating woven or entwined stems or bands.

INTRADOS: *see* Soffit.

IONIC: *see* Orders and 3c.

JACK ARCH: shallow segmental vault springing from beams, used for fireproof floors, bridge decks, etc.

JAMB (*lit.* leg): one of the vertical sides of an opening.

JETTY: in a timber-framed building, the projection of an upper storey beyond the storey below, made by the beams and joists of the lower storey oversailing the wall; on their outer ends is placed the sill of the walling for the storey above (7). Buildings can be jettied on several sides, in which case a *dragon beam* is set diagonally at the corner to carry the joists to either side.

JOGGLE: the joining of two stones to prevent them slipping by a notch in one and a projection in the other.

KEEL MOULDING: moulding used from the late C12, in section like the keel of a ship (1a).

KEEP: principal tower of a castle.

KENTISH CUSP: *see* Tracery and 2b.

KEY PATTERN: *see* 4b.

KEYSTONE: central stone in an arch or vault (4b, 5c).

KINGPOST: *see* Roofs and 7.

KNEELER: horizontal projecting stone at the base of each side of a gable to support the inclined coping stones (8a).

LABEL: *see* Hoodmould and 5b.

LABEL STOP: *see* Stop and 5b.

LACED BRICKWORK: vertical strips of brickwork, often in a contrasting colour, linking openings on different floors.

LACING COURSE: horizontal reinforcement in timber or brick to walls of flint, cobble, etc.

LADY CHAPEL: dedicated to the Virgin Mary (Our Lady).

LANCET: slender single-light, pointed-arched window (2a).

LANTERN: circular or polygonal windowed turret crowning a roof or a dome. Also the windowed stage of a crossing tower lighting the church interior.

LANTERN CROSS: churchyard cross with lantern-shaped top.

LAVATORIUM: in a religious house, a washing place adjacent to the refectory.

LEAN-TO: *see* Roofs.

LESENE (*lit.* a mean thing): pilaster without base or capital. Also called *pilaster strip*.

LIERNE: *see* Vault and 2c.

LIGHT: compartment of a window defined by the mullions.

LINENFOLD: Tudor panelling carved with simulations of folded linen. *See also* Parchemin.

LINTEL: horizontal beam or stone bridging an opening.

LOGGIA: gallery, usually arcaded or colonnaded; sometimes free-standing.

LONG-AND-SHORT WORK: quoins consisting of stones placed with the long side alternately upright and horizontal, especially in Saxon building.

LONGHOUSE: house and byre in the same range with internal access between them.

LOUVRE: roof opening, often protected by a raised timber structure, to allow the smoke from a central hearth to escape.

LOWSIDE WINDOW: set lower than the others in a chancel side wall, usually towards its w end.

LUCAM: projecting housing for hoist pulley on upper storey of warehouses, mills, etc., for raising goods to loading doors.

LUCARNE (*lit.* dormer): small gabled opening in a roof or spire.

LUGGED ARCHITRAVE: *see* 4b.

LUNETTE: semicircular window or blind panel.

LYCHGATE (*lit.* corpse-gate): roofed gateway entrance to a churchyard for the reception of a coffin.

LYNCHET: long terraced strip of soil on the downward side of prehistoric and medieval fields, accumulated because of continual ploughing along the contours.

MACHICOLATIONS (*lit.* mashing devices): series of openings between the corbels that support a projecting parapet through which missiles can be dropped. Used decoratively in post-medieval buildings.

MANOMETER or STANDPIPE TOWER: containing a column of water to regulate pressure in water mains.

MANSARD: *see* 8a.

MATHEMATICAL TILES: facing tiles with the appearance of brick, most often applied to timber-framed walls.

MAUSOLEUM: monumental building or chamber usually intended for the burial of members of one family.

MEGALITHIC TOMB: massive stone-built Neolithic burial chamber covered by an earth or stone mound.

MERLON: *see* Battlement.

METOPES: spaces between the triglyphs in a Doric frieze (3b).

MEZZANINE: low storey between two higher ones.

MILD STEEL: *see* Cast iron.

MISERICORD (*lit.* mercy): shelf on a carved bracket placed on the underside of a hinged choir stall seat to support an occupant when standing.

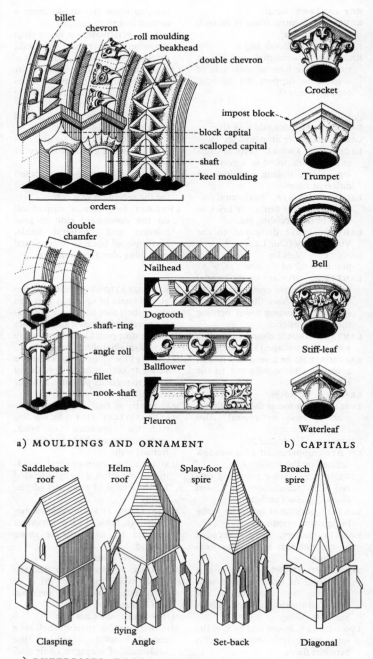

billet

chevron

roll moulding

beakhead

double chevron

Crocket

block capital

scalloped capital

shaft

keel moulding

impost block

Trumpet

orders

Bell

double chamfer

Nailhead

Dogtooth

shaft-ring

angle roll

fillet

nook-shaft

Ballflower

Stiff-leaf

Fleuron

Waterleaf

a) MOULDINGS AND ORNAMENT

b) CAPITALS

Saddleback roof

Helm roof

Splay-foot spire

Broach spire

Clasping

flying

Angle

Set-back

Diagonal

c) BUTTRESSES, ROOFS AND SPIRES

FIGURE 1: MEDIEVAL

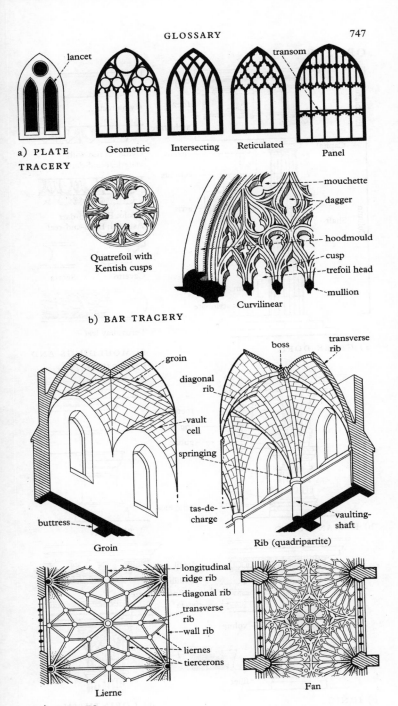

a) PLATE TRACERY

Geometric   Intersecting   Reticulated   Panel

lancet

transom

Quatrefoil with Kentish cusps

mouchette
dagger
hoodmould
cusp
trefoil head
mullion

Curvilinear

b) BAR TRACERY

groin

diagonal rib

vault cell

springing

buttress

Groin

boss

transverse rib

tas-de-charge

vaulting-shaft

Rib (quadripartite)

longitudinal ridge rib
diagonal rib
transverse rib
wall rib
liernes
tiercerons

Lierne   Fan

c) VAULTS

FIGURE 2: MEDIEVAL

ORDERS

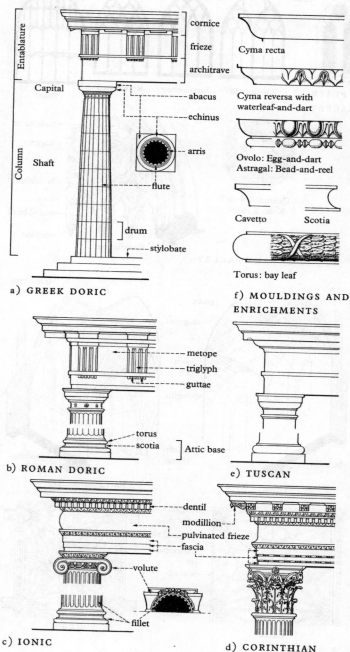

a) GREEK DORIC

f) MOULDINGS AND ENRICHMENTS

Cyma recta

Cyma reversa with waterleaf-and-dart

Ovolo: Egg-and-dart
Astragal: Bead-and-reel

Cavetto   Scotia

Torus: bay leaf

Greek Doric labels: cornice, frieze, architrave, abacus, echinus, arris, flute, drum, stylobate; Entablature, Capital, Column, Shaft

b) ROMAN DORIC

labels: metope, triglyph, guttae, torus, scotia, Attic base

e) TUSCAN

c) IONIC

labels: dentil, modillion, pulvinated frieze, fascia, volute, fillet

d) CORINTHIAN

FIGURE 3: CLASSICAL

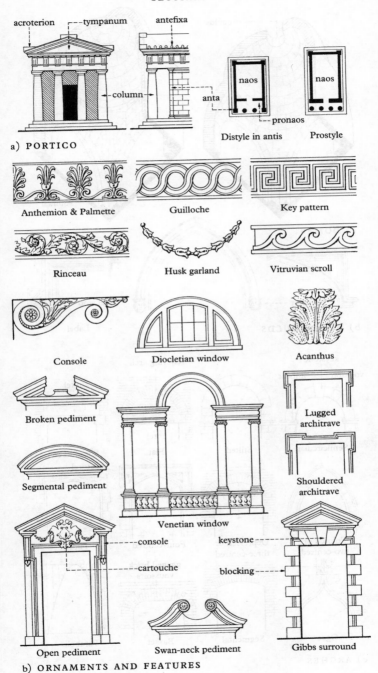

a) PORTICO

Anthemion & Palmette

Guilloche

Key pattern

Rinceau

Husk garland

Vitruvian scroll

Console

Diocletian window

Acanthus

Broken pediment

Lugged architrave

Segmental pediment

Shouldered architrave

Venetian window

Open pediment

Swan-neck pediment

Gibbs surround

b) ORNAMENTS AND FEATURES

FIGURE 4: CLASSICAL

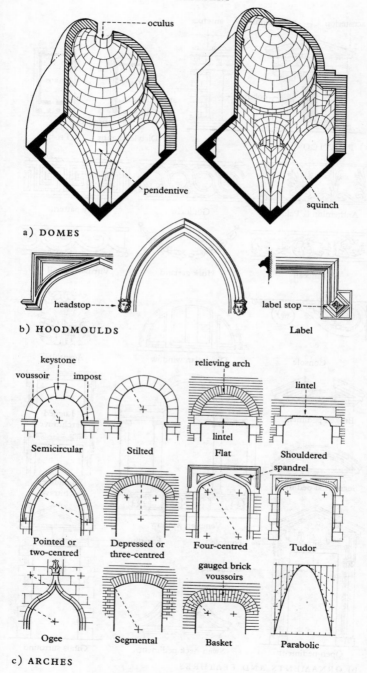

a) DOMES

b) HOODMOULDS   Label

c) ARCHES

FIGURE 5: CONSTRUCTION

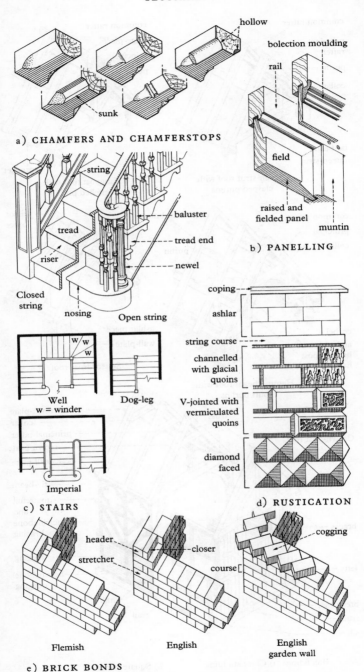

a) CHAMFERS AND CHAMFERSTOPS

hollow

bolection moulding

rail

field

raised and fielded panel

muntin

b) PANELLING

string

baluster

tread

tread end

riser

newel

Closed string

nosing   Open string

Well
w = winder

Dog-leg

Imperial

c) STAIRS

coping

ashlar

string course

channelled with glacial quoins

V-jointed with vermiculated quoins

diamond faced

d) RUSTICATION

header

closer

stretcher

course

cogging

Flemish   English   English garden wall

e) BRICK BONDS

FIGURE 6: CONSTRUCTION

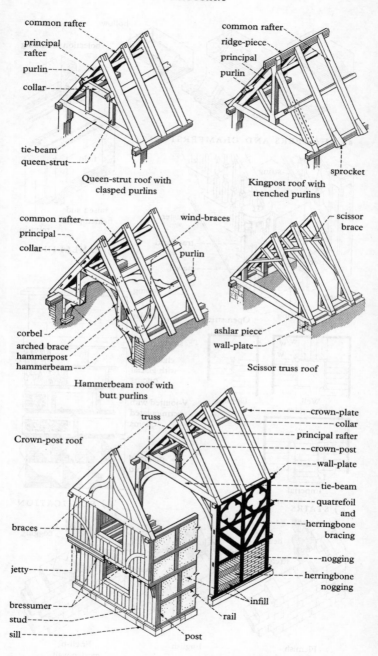

Queen-strut roof with
clasped purlins

- common rafter
- principal rafter
- purlin
- collar
- tie-beam
- queen-strut

Kingpost roof with
trenched purlins

- common rafter
- ridge-piece
- principal
- purlin
- sprocket

Hammerbeam roof with
butt purlins

- common rafter
- principal
- collar
- wind-braces
- purlin
- corbel
- arched brace
- hammerpost
- hammerbeam

Scissor truss roof

- scissor brace
- ashlar piece
- wall-plate

Crown-post roof

- truss
- crown-plate
- collar
- principal rafter
- crown-post
- wall-plate
- tie-beam
- quatrefoil and herringbone bracing
- nogging
- herringbone nogging
- braces
- jetty
- bressumer
- stud
- sill
- post
- infill
- rail

Box frame: i) Close studding   ii) Square panel

FIGURE 7: ROOFS AND TIMBER-FRAMING

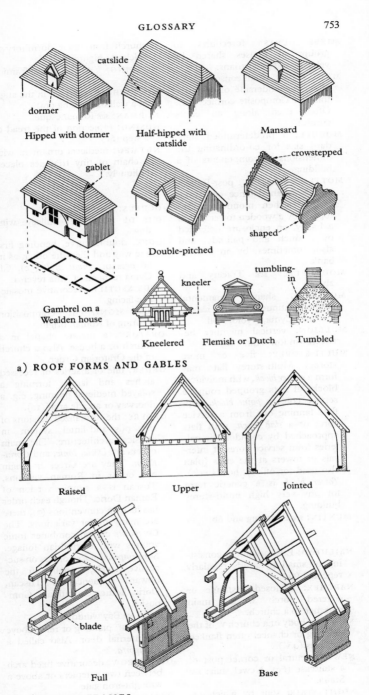

Hipped with dormer

catslide

dormer

Half-hipped with catslide

Mansard

gablet

crowstepped

shaped

Double-pitched

Gambrel on a Wealden house

kneeler

tumbling-in

Kneelered

Flemish or Dutch

Tumbled

a) ROOF FORMS AND GABLES

Raised

Upper

Jointed

blade

Full

Base

b) CRUCK FRAMES

FIGURE 8: ROOFS AND TIMBER-FRAMING

MIXER-COURTS: forecourts to groups of houses shared by vehicles and pedestrians.

MODILLIONS: small consoles (q.v.) along the underside of a Corinthian or Composite cornice (3d). Often used along an eaves cornice.

MODULE: a predetermined standard size for co-ordinating the dimensions of components of a building.

MOTTE-AND-BAILEY: post-Roman and Norman defence consisting of an earthen mound (motte) topped by a wooden tower within a bailey, an enclosure defended by a ditch and palisade, and also, sometimes, by an internal bank.

MOUCHETTE: see Tracery and 2b.

MOULDING: shaped ornamental strip of continuous section; see e.g. Cavetto, Cyma, Ovolo, Roll.

MULLION: vertical member between window lights (2b).

MULTI-STOREY: five or more storeys. Multi-storey flats may form a *cluster block*, with individual blocks of flats grouped round a service core; a *point block*, with flats fanning out from a service core; or a *slab block*, with flats approached by corridors or galleries from service cores at intervals or towers at the ends (plan also used for offices, hotels etc.). *Tower block* is a generic term for any very high multi-storey building.

MUNTIN: see Panelling and 6b.

NAILHEAD: E.E. ornament consisting of small pyramids regularly repeated (1a).

NARTHEX: enclosed vestibule or covered porch at the main entrance to a church.

NAVE: the body of a church w of the crossing or chancel often flanked by aisles (q.v.).

NEWEL: central or corner post of a staircase (6c). Newel stair: see Stairs.

NIGHT STAIR: stair by which religious entered the transept of their church from their dormitory to celebrate night services.

NOGGING: see Timber-framing (7).

NOOK-SHAFT: shaft set in the angle of a wall or opening (1a).

NORMAN: see Romanesque.

NOSING: projection of the tread of a step (6c).

NUTMEG: medieval ornament with a chain of tiny triangles placed obliquely.

OCULUS: circular opening.

ŒIL DE BŒUF: see Bullseye window.

OGEE: double curve, bending first one way and then the other, as in an *ogee* or *ogival arch* (5c). Cf. Cyma recta and Cyma reversa.

OPUS SECTILE: decorative mosaic-like facing.

OPUS SIGNINUM: composition flooring of Roman origin.

ORATORY: a private chapel in a church or a house. Also a church of the Oratorian Order.

ORDER: one of a series of recessed arches and jambs forming a splayed medieval opening, e.g. a doorway or arcade arch (1a).

ORDERS: the formalized versions of the post-and-lintel system in classical architecture. The main orders are *Doric*, *Ionic*, and *Corinthian*. They are Greek in origin but occur in Roman versions. Tuscan is a simple version of Roman Doric. Though each order has its own conventions (3), there are many minor variations. The *Composite* capital combines Ionic volutes with Corinthian foliage. *Superimposed orders*: orders on successive levels, usually in the upward sequence of Tuscan, Doric, Ionic, Corinthian, Composite.

ORIEL: see Bay window.

OVERDOOR: painting or relief above an internal door. Also called a *sopraporta*.

OVERTHROW: decorative fixed arch between two gatepiers or above a wrought-iron gate.

OVOLO: wide convex moulding (3f).

PALIMPSEST: of a brass: where a metal plate has been reused by turning over the engraving on the back; of a wall painting: where one overlaps and partly obscures an earlier one.

PALLADIAN: following the examples and principles of Andrea Palladio (1508–80).

PALMETTE: classical ornament like a palm shoot (4b).

PANELLING: wooden lining to interior walls, made up of vertical members (*muntins*) and horizontals (*rails*) framing panels: also called *wainscot. Raised and fielded*: with the central area of the panel (*field*) raised up (6b).

PANTILE: roof tile of S section.

PARAPET: wall for protection at any sudden drop, e.g. at the wall-head of a castle where it protects the *parapet walk* or wall-walk. Also used to conceal a roof.

PARCLOSE: *see* Screen.

PARGETTING (*lit.* plastering): exterior plaster decoration, either in relief or incised.

PARLOUR: in a religious house, a room where the religious could talk to visitors; in a medieval house, the semi-private living room below the solar (q.v.).

PARTERRE: level space in a garden laid out with low, formal beds.

PATERA (*lit.* plate): round or oval ornament in shallow relief.

PAVILION: ornamental building for occasional use; or projecting subdivision of a larger building, often at an angle or terminating a wing.

PEBBLEDASHING: *see* Rendering.

PEDESTAL: a tall block carrying a classical order, statue, vase, etc.

PEDIMENT: a formalized gable derived from that of a classical temple; also used over doors, windows, etc. For variations *see* 4b.

PENDENTIVE: spandrel between adjacent arches, supporting a drum, dome or vault and consequently formed as part of a hemisphere (5a).

PENTHOUSE: subsidiary structure with a lean-to roof. Also a separately roofed structure on top of a C20 multi-storey block.

PERIPTERAL: *see* Peristyle.

PERISTYLE: a colonnade all round the exterior of a classical building, as in a temple which is then said to be *peripteral*.

PERP (PERPENDICULAR): English Gothic architecture *c.* 1335–50 to *c.* 1530. The name is derived from the upright tracery panels then used (*see* Tracery and 2a).

PERRON: external stair to a doorway, usually of double-curved plan.

PEW: loosely, seating for the laity outside the chancel; strictly, an enclosed seat. *Box pew*: with equal high sides and a door.

PIANO NOBILE: principal floor of a classical building above a ground floor or basement and with a lesser storey overhead.

PIAZZA: formal urban open space surrounded by buildings.

PIER: large masonry or brick support, often for an arch. *See also* Compound pier.

PILASTER: flat representation of a classical column in shallow relief. *Pilaster strip*: see Lesene.

PILE: row of rooms. *Double pile*: two rows thick.

PILLAR: free-standing upright member of any section, not conforming to one of the orders (q.v.).

PILLAR PISCINA: *see* Piscina.

PILOTIS: C20 French term for pillars or stilts that support a building above an open ground floor.

PISCINA: basin for washing Mass vessels, provided with a drain; set in or against the wall to the S of an altar or free-standing (*pillar piscina*).

PISÉ: *see* Cob.

PITCHED MASONRY: laid on the diagonal, often alternately with opposing courses (*pitched and counterpitched* or *herringbone*).

PLATBAND: flat horizontal moulding between storeys. Cf. stringcourse.

PLATE RAIL: *see* Railways.

PLATEWAY: *see* Railways.

PLINTH: projecting courses at the

foot of a wall or column, generally chamfered or moulded at the top.

PODIUM: a continuous raised platform supporting a building; or a large block of two or three storeys beneath a multi-storey block of smaller area.

POINT BLOCK: *see* Multi-storey.

POINTING: exposed mortar jointing of masonry or brickwork. Types include *flush*, *recessed* and *tuck* (with a narrow channel filled with finer, whiter mortar).

POPPYHEAD: carved ornament of leaves and flowers as a finial for a bench end or stall.

PORTAL FRAME: C20 frame comprising two uprights rigidly connected to a beam or pair of rafters.

PORTCULLIS: gate constructed to rise and fall in vertical grooves at the entry to a castle.

PORTICO: a porch with the roof and frequently a pediment supported by a row of columns (4a). A portico *in antis* has columns on the same plane as the front of the building. A *prostyle* porch has columns standing free. Porticoes are described by the number of front columns, e.g. tetrastyle (four), hexastyle (six). The space within the temple is the *naos*, that within the portico the *pronaos*. *Blind portico*: the front features of a portico applied to a wall.

PORTICUS (plural: porticūs): subsidiary cell opening from the main body of a pre-Conquest church.

POST: upright support in a structure (7).

POSTERN: small gateway at the back of a building or to the side of a larger entrance door or gate.

POUND LOCK: *see* Canals.

PRESBYTERY: the part of a church lying E of the choir where the main altar is placed; or a priest's residence.

PRINCIPAL: *see* Roofs and 7.

PRONAOS: *see* Portico and 4a.

PROSTYLE: *see* Portico and 4a.

PULPIT: raised and enclosed platform for the preaching of sermons. *Three-decker*: with reading desk below and clerk's desk below that. *Two-decker*: as above, minus the clerk's desk.

PULPITUM: stone screen in a major church dividing choir from nave.

PULVINATED: *see* Frieze and 3c.

PURLIN: *see* Roofs and 7.

PUTHOLES or PUTLOG HOLES: in the wall to receive putlogs, the horizontal timbers which support scaffolding boards; sometimes not filled after construction is complete.

PUTTO (plural: putti): small naked boy.

QUARRIES: square (or diamond) panes of glass supported by lead strips (*cames*); square floor slabs or tiles.

QUATREFOIL: *see* Foil and 2b.

QUEEN-STRUT: *see* Roofs and 7.

QUIRK: sharp groove to one side of a convex medieval moulding.

QUOINS: dressed stones at the angles of a building (6d).

RADBURN SYSTEM: vehicle and pedestrian segregation in residential developments, based on that used at Radburn, New Jersey, USA, by Wright and Stein, 1928–30.

RADIATING CHAPELS: projecting radially from an ambulatory or an apse (*see* Chevet).

RAFTER: *see* Roofs and 7.

RAGGLE: groove cut in masonry, especially to receive the edge of a roof-covering.

RAGULY: ragged (in heraldry). Also applied to funerary sculpture, e.g. *cross raguly*: with a notched outline.

RAIL: *see* Panelling and 6b; also 7.

RAILWAYS: *Edge rail*: on which flanged wheels can run. *Plate rail*: L-section rail for plain unflanged wheels. *Plateway*: early railway using plate rails.

RAISED AND FIELDED: *see* Panelling and 6b.

RAKE: slope or pitch.

RAMPART: defensive outer wall of stone or earth. *Rampart walk*: path along the inner face.

REBATE: rectangular section cut out of a masonry edge to receive a shutter, door, window, etc.

REBUS: a heraldic pun, e.g. a fiery cock for Cockburn.

REEDING: series of convex mouldings, the reverse of fluting (q.v.). Cf. Gadrooning.

RENDERING: the covering of outside walls with a uniform surface or skin for protection from the weather. *Limewashing*: thin layer of lime plaster. *Pebbledashing*: where aggregate is thrown at the wet plastered wall for a textured effect. *Roughcast*: plaster mixed with a coarse aggregate such as gravel. *Stucco*: fine lime plaster worked to a smooth surface. *Cement rendering*: a cheaper substitute for stucco, usually with a grainy texture.

REPOUSSÉ: relief designs in metalwork, formed by beating it from the back.

REREDORTER (*lit.* behind the dormitory): latrines in a medieval religious house.

REREDOS: painted and/or sculptured screen behind and above an altar. Cf. Retable.

RESPOND: half-pier or half-column bonded into a wall and carrying one end of an arch. It usually terminates an arcade.

RETABLE: painted or carved panel standing on or at the back of an altar, usually attached to it.

RETROCHOIR: in a major church, the area between the high altar and E chapel.

REVEAL: the plane of a jamb, between the wall and the frame of a door or window.

RIB-VAULT: *see* Vault and 2c.

RINCEAU: classical ornament of leafy scrolls (4b).

RISER: vertical face of a step (6c).

ROACH: a rough-textured form of Portland stone, with small cavities and fossil shells.

ROCK-FACED: masonry cleft to produce a rugged appearance.

ROCOCO: style current *c.* 1720 and *c.* 1760, characterized by a serpentine line and playful, scrolled decoration.

ROLL MOULDING: medieval moulding of part-circular section (1a).

ROMANESQUE: style current in the C11 and C12. In England often called Norman. *See also* Saxo-Norman.

ROOD: crucifix flanked by the Virgin and St John, usually over the entry into the chancel, on a beam (*rood beam*) or painted on the wall. The *rood screen* below often had a walkway (*rood loft*) along the top, reached by a *rood stair* in the side wall.

ROOFS: Shape. For the main external shapes (hipped, mansard, etc.) *see* 8a. *Helm* and *Saddleback*: *see* 1c. *Lean-to*: single sloping roof built against a vertical wall; lean-to is also applied to the part of the building beneath.

Construction. *See* 7.

Single-framed roof: with no main trusses. The rafters may be fixed to the wall-plate or ridge, or longitudinal timber may be absent altogether.

Double-framed roof: with longitudinal members, such as purlins, and usually divided into bays by principals and principal rafters. Other types are named after their main structural components, e.g. *hammerbeam*, *crown-post* (*see* Elements below and 7).

Elements. *See* 7.

Ashlar piece: a short vertical timber connecting inner wall-plate or timber pad to a rafter.

Braces: subsidiary timbers set diagonally to strengthen the frame. *Arched braces*: curved pair forming an arch, connecting wall or post below with tie- or collarbeam above. *Passing braces*: long straight braces passing across other members of the truss. *Scissor braces*: pair crossing diagonally between pairs of rafters or principals. *Wind-braces*: short, usually curved braces connecting side purlins with principals; sometimes decorated with cusping.

Collar or *collar-beam*: horizontal transverse timber connecting a pair of rafter or cruck blades (q.v.), set between apex and the wall-plate.

Crown-post: a vertical timber set centrally on a tie-beam and supporting a collar purlin braced to it longitudinally. In an open truss lateral braces may rise to the collar-beam; in a closed truss they may descend to the tie-beam.

Hammerbeams: horizontal brackets projecting at wall-plate level like an interrupted tie-beam; the inner ends carry *hammerposts*, vertical timbers which support a purlin and are braced to a collar-beam above.

Kingpost: vertical timber set centrally on a tie- or collar-beam, rising to the apex of the roof to support a ridge-piece (cf. Strut).

Plate: longitudinal timber set square to the ground. *Wall-plate*: plate along the top of a wall which receives the ends of the rafters; cf. Purlin.

Principals: pair of inclined lateral timbers of a truss. Usually they support side purlins and mark the main bay divisions.

Purlin: horizontal longitudinal timber. *Collar purlin* or *crown plate*: central timber which carries collar-beams and is supported by crown-posts. *Side purlins*: pairs of timbers placed some way up the slope of the roof, which carry common rafters. *Butt* or *tenoned purlins* are tenoned into either side of the principals. *Through purlins* pass through or past the principal; they include *clasped purlins*, which rest on queenposts or are carried in the angle between principals and collar, and *trenched purlins* trenched into the backs of principals.

Queen-strut: paired vertical, or near-vertical, timbers placed symmetrically on a tie-beam to support side purlins.

Rafters: inclined lateral timbers supporting the roof covering. *Common rafters*: regularly spaced uniform rafters placed along the length of a roof or between principals. *Principal rafters*: rafters which also act as principals.

Ridge, ridge-piece: horizontal longitudinal timber at the apex supporting the ends of the rafters.

Sprocket: short timber placed on the back and at the foot of a rafter to form projecting eaves.

Strut: vertical or oblique timber between two members of a truss,

not directly supporting longitudinal timbers.

Tie-beam: main horizontal transverse timber which carries the feet of the principals at wall level.

Truss: rigid framework of timbers at bay intervals, carrying the longitudinal roof timbers which support the common rafters.

Closed truss: with the spaces between the timbers filled, to form an internal partition.

See also Cruck, Wagon roof.

ROPE MOULDING: *see* Cable moulding.

ROSE WINDOW: circular window with tracery radiating from the centre. Cf. Wheel window.

ROTUNDA: building or room circular in plan.

ROUGHCAST: *see* Rendering.

ROVING BRIDGE: *see* Canals.

RUBBED BRICKWORK: *see* Gauged brickwork.

RUBBLE: masonry whose stones are wholly or partly in a rough state. *Coursed*: coursed stones with rough faces. *Random*: uncoursed stones in a random pattern. *Snecked*: with courses broken by smaller stones (snecks).

RUSTICATION: *see* 6d. Exaggerated treatment of masonry to give an effect of strength. The joints are usually recessed by V-section chamfering or square-section channelling (*channelled rustication*). *Banded rustication* has only the horizontal joints emphasized. The faces may be flat, but can be *diamond-faced*, like shallow pyramids, *vermiculated*, with a stylized texture like worm-casts, and *glacial* (frost-work), like icicles or stalactites.

SACRISTY: room in a church for sacred vessels and vestments.

SADDLEBACK ROOF: *see* 1C.

SALTIRE CROSS: with diagonal limbs.

SANCTUARY: area around the main altar of a church. Cf. Presbytery.

SANGHA: residence of Buddhist monks or nuns.

SARCOPHAGUS: coffin of stone or other durable material.

SAXO-NORMAN: transitional Romanesque style combining Anglo-Saxon and Norman features, current *c.* 1060–1100.

SCAGLIOLA: composition imitating marble.

SCALLOPED CAPITAL: *see* 1a.

SCOTIA: a hollow classical moulding, especially between tori (q.v.) on a column base (3b, 3f).

SCREEN: in a medieval church, usually at the entry to the chancel; *see* Rood (screen) and Pulpitum. A *parclose screen* separates a chapel from the rest of the church.

SCREENS or SCREENS PASSAGE: screened-off entrance passage between great hall and service rooms.

SECTION: two-dimensional representation of a building, moulding, etc., revealed by cutting across it.

SEDILIA (singular: sedile): seats for the priests (usually three) on the s side of the chancel.

SET-OFF: *see* Weathering.

SETTS: squared stones, usually of granite, used for paving or flooring.

SGRAFFITO: decoration scratched, often in plaster, to reveal a pattern in another colour beneath. *Graffiti*: scratched drawing or writing.

SHAFT: vertical member of round or polygonal section (1a, 3a). *Shaft-ring*: at the junction of shafts set *en delit* (q.v.) or attached to a pier or wall (1a).

SHEILA-NA-GIG: female fertility figure, usually with legs apart.

SHELL: thin, self-supporting roofing membrane of timber or concrete.

SHOULDERED ARCHITRAVE: *see* 4b.

SHUTTERING: *see* Concrete.

SILL: horizontal member at the bottom of a window or door frame; or at the base of a timber-framed wall into which posts and studs are tenoned (7).

SLAB BLOCK: *see* Multi-storey.

SLATE-HANGING: covering of overlapping slates on a wall. *Tile-hanging* is similar.

SLYPE: covered way or passage leading E from the cloisters between transept and chapter house.

SNECKED: *see* Rubble.

SOFFIT (*lit.* ceiling): underside of an arch (also called *intrados*), lintel, etc. *Soffit roll*: medieval roll moulding on a soffit.

SOLAR: private upper chamber in a medieval house, accessible from the high end of the great hall.

SOPRAPORTA: *see* Overdoor.

SOUNDING-BOARD: *see* Tester.

SPANDRELS: roughly triangular spaces between an arch and its containing rectangle, or between adjacent arches (5c). Also non-structural panels under the windows in a curtain-walled building.

SPERE: a fixed structure screening the lower end of the great hall from the screens passage. *Spere-truss*: roof truss incorporated in the spere.

SPIRE: tall pyramidal or conical feature crowning a tower or turret. *Broach*: starting from a square base, then carried into an octagonal section by means of triangular faces; and *splayed-foot*: variation of the broach form, found principally in the south-east, in which the four cardinal faces are splayed out near their base, to cover the corners, while oblique (or intermediate) faces taper away to a point (1c). *Needle spire*: thin spire rising from the centre of a tower roof, well inside the parapet: when of timber and lead often called a *spike*.

SPIRELET: *see* Flèche.

SPLAY: of an opening when it is wider on one face of a wall than the other.

SPRING or SPRINGING: level at which an arch or vault rises from its supports. *Springers*: the first stones of an arch or vaulting rib above the spring (2c).

SQUINCH: arch or series of arches thrown across an interior angle of a square or rectangular structure to support a circular or polygonal superstructure, especially a dome or spire (5a).

SQUINT: an aperture in a wall or through a pier usually to allow a view of an altar.

STAIRS: *see* 6c. *Dog-leg stair*: parallel flights rising alternately in opposite directions, without an open well. *Flying stair*: cantilevered from the walls of a stairwell, without newels; sometimes called a *Geometric* stair when the inner edge describes a curve. *Newel stair*: ascending round a central supporting newel (q.v.); called a *spiral stair* or *vice* when in a circular shaft, a *winder* when in a rectangular compartment. (Winder also applies to the steps on the turn.) *Well stair*: with flights round a square open well framed by newel posts. *See also* Perron.

STALL: fixed seat in the choir or chancel for the clergy or choir (cf. Pew). Usually with arm rests, and often framed together.

STANCHION: upright structural member, of iron, steel or reinforced concrete.

STANDPIPE TOWER: *see* Manometer.

STEAM ENGINES: *Atmospheric*: worked by the vacuum created when low-pressure steam is condensed in the cylinder, as developed by Thomas Newcomen. *Beam engine*: with a large pivoted beam moved in an oscillating fashion by the piston. It may drive a flywheel or be *non-rotative*. *Watt* and *Cornish*: single-cylinder; *compound*: two cylinders; *triple expansion*: three cylinders.

STEEPLE: tower together with a spire, lantern, or belfry.

STIFF-LEAF: type of E.E. foliage decoration. *Stiff-leaf capital see* 1b.

STOP: plain or decorated terminal to mouldings or chamfers, or at the end of hoodmoulds and labels (*label stop*), or stringcourses (5b, 6a); *see also* Headstop.

STOUP: vessel for holy water, usually near a door.

STRAINER: *see* Arch.

STRAPWORK: late C16 and C17 decoration, like interlaced leather straps.

STRETCHER: *see* Bond and 6e.

STRING: *see* 6c. Sloping member holding the ends of the treads and risers of a staircase. *Closed string*: a broad string covering the ends of the treads and risers. *Open string*: cut into the shape of the treads and risers.

STRINGCOURSE: horizontal course or moulding projecting from the surface of a wall (6d).

STUCCO: *see* Rendering.

STUDS: subsidiary vertical timbers of a timber-framed wall or partition (7).

STUPA: Buddhist shrine, circular in plan.

STYLOBATE: top of the solid platform on which a colonnade stands (3a).

SUSPENSION BRIDGE: *see* Bridge.

SWAG: like a festoon (q.v.), but representing cloth.

SYSTEM BUILDING: *see* Industrialized building.

TABERNACLE: canopied structure to contain the reserved sacrament or a relic; or architectural frame for an image or statue.

TABLE TOMB: memorial slab raised on free-standing legs.

TAS-DE-CHARGE: the lower courses of a vault or arch which are laid horizontally (2c).

TERM: pedestal or pilaster tapering downward, usually with the upper part of a human figure growing out of it.

TERRACOTTA: moulded and fired clay ornament or cladding.

TESSELLATED PAVEMENT: mosaic flooring, particularly Roman, made of *tesserae*, i.e. cubes of glass, stone, or brick.

TESTER: flat canopy over a tomb or pulpit, where it is also called a *sounding-board*.

TESTER TOMB: tomb-chest with effigies beneath a tester, either free-standing (tester with four or more columns), or attached to a wall (*half-tester*) with columns on one side only.

TETRASTYLE: *see* Portico.

THERMAL WINDOW: *see* Diocletian window.

THREE-DECKER PULPIT: *see* Pulpit.

TIDAL GATES: *see* Canals.

TIE-BEAM: *see* Roofs and 7.

TIERCERON: *see* Vault and 2c.

TILE-HANGING: *see* Slate-hanging.

TIMBER-FRAMING: *see* 7. Method of construction where the structural frame is built of interlocking timbers. The spaces are filled with non-structural material, e.g. *infill* of wattle and daub, lath and plaster, brickwork (known as *nogging*), etc. and may be covered by plaster, weatherboarding (q.v.), or tiles.

TOMB-CHEST: chest-shaped tomb, usually of stone. Cf. Table tomb, Tester tomb.

TORUS (plural: tori): large convex moulding usually used on a column base (3b, 3f).

TOUCH: soft black marble quarried near Tournai.

TOURELLE: turret corbelled out from the wall.

TOWER BLOCK: see Multi-storey.

TRABEATED: depends structurally on the use of the post and lintel. Cf. Arcuated.

TRACERY: openwork pattern of masonry or timber in the upper part of an opening. *Blind tracery* is tracery applied to a solid wall. *Plate tracery*, introduced c. 1200, is the earliest form, in which shapes are cut through solid masonry (2a). *Bar tracery* was introduced into England c. 1250. The pattern is formed by intersecting moulded ribwork continued from the mullions. It was especially elaborate during the Decorated period (q.v.). Tracery shapes can include circles, *daggers* (elongated ogee-ended lozenges), *mouchettes* (like daggers but with curved sides) and upright rectangular *panels*. They often have *cusps*, projecting points defining lobes or *foils* (q.v.) within the main shape: *Kentish* or *split-cusps* are forked (2b). Types of bar tracery (see 2b) include *geometric(al)*: c. 1250– 1310, chiefly circles, often foiled; *Y-tracery*: c. 1300, with mullions branching into a Y-shape; *inter-secting*: c. 1300, formed by inter-locking mullions; *reticulated*: early C14, net-like pattern of ogee-ended lozenges; *curvilinear*: C14, with uninterrupted flowing curves; *panel*: Perp, with straight-sided panels, often cusped at the top and bottom.

TRANSEPT: transverse portion of a church.

TRANSITIONAL: generally used for the phase between Romanesque and Early English (c. 1175– c. 1200).

TRANSOM: horizontal member separating window lights (2b).

TREAD: horizontal part of a step. The *tread end* may be carved on a staircase (6c).

TREFOIL: see Foil.

TRIFORIUM: middle storey of a church treated as an arcaded wall passage or blind arcade, its height corresponding to that of the aisle roof.

TRIGLYPHS (*lit.* three-grooved tab-lets): stylized beam-ends in the Doric frieze, with metopes be-tween (3b).

TRIUMPHAL ARCH: influential type of Imperial Roman monument.

TROPHY: sculptured or painted group of arms or armour.

TRUMEAU: central stone mullion supporting the tympanum of a wide doorway. *Trumeau figure*: carved figure attached to it (cf. Column figure).

TRUMPET CAPITAL: see 1b.

TRUSS: braced framework, spanning between supports. See also Roofs and 7.

TUMBLING or TUMBLING-IN: courses of brickwork laid at right-angles to a slope, e.g. of a gable, forming triangles by tapering into horizontal courses (8a).

TUSCAN: see Orders and 3e.

TWO-DECKER PULPIT: see Pulpit.

TYMPANUM: the surface between a lintel and the arch above it or within a pediment (4a).

UNDERCROFT: usually describes the vaulted room(s), beneath the main room(s) of a medieval house. Cf. Crypt.

VAULT: arched stone roof (some-times imitated in timber or plas-ter). For types see 2c. *Tunnel* or *barrel vault*: continuous semicircular or pointed arch, often of rubble masonry.

Groin-vault: tunnel vaults intersecting at right angles. *Groins* are the curved lines of the intersections.

Rib-vault: masonry framework of intersecting arches (ribs) supporting *vault cells*, used in Gothic architecture. *Wall rib* or *wall arch*: between wall and vault cell. *Transverse rib*: spans between two walls to divide a vault into bays. *Quadripartite* rib-vault: each bay has two pairs of diagonal ribs dividing the vault into four triangular cells. *Sexpartite* rib-vault: most often used over paired bays, has an extra pair of ribs springing from between the bays. More elaborate vaults may include *ridge ribs* along the crown of a vault or bisecting the bays; *tiercerons*: extra decorative ribs springing from the corners of a bay; and *liernes*: short decorative ribs in the crown of a vault, not linked to any springing point. A *stellar* or *star* vault has liernes in star formation.

Fan-vault: form of barrel vault used in the Perp period, made up of halved concave masonry cones decorated with blind tracery.

VAULTING SHAFT: shaft leading up to the spring or springing (q.v.) of a vault (2c).

VENETIAN or SERLIAN WINDOW: derived from Serlio (4b). The motif is used for other openings.

VERMICULATION: *see* Rustication and 6d.

VESICA: oval with pointed ends.

VICE: *see* Stair.

VILLA: originally a Roman country house or farm. The term was revived in England in the C18 under the influence of Palladio and used especially for smaller, compact country houses. In the later C19 it was debased to describe any suburban house.

VITRIFIED: bricks or tiles fired to a darkened glassy surface.

VITRUVIAN SCROLL: classical running ornament of curly waves (4b).

VOLUTES: spiral scrolls. They occur on Ionic capitals (3c). *Angle volute*: pair of volutes, turned outwards to meet at the corner of a capital.

VOUSSOIRS: wedge-shaped stones forming an arch (5c).

WAGON ROOF: with the appearance of the inside of a wagon tilt; often ceiled. Also called *cradle roof*.

WAINSCOT: *see* Panelling.

WALL MONUMENT: attached to the wall and often standing on the floor. *Wall tablets* are smaller with the inscription as the major element.

WALL-PLATE: *see* Roofs and 7.

WALL-WALK: *see* Parapet.

WARMING ROOM: room in a religious house where a fire burned for comfort.

WATERHOLDING BASE: early Gothic base with upper and lower mouldings separated by a deep hollow.

WATERLEAF: *see* Enrichments and 3f.

WATERLEAF CAPITAL: Late Romanesque and Transitional type of capital (1b).

WATER WHEELS: described by the way water is fed on to the wheel. *Breastshot*: mid-height, falling and passing beneath. *Overshot*: over the top. *Pitchback*: on the top but falling backwards. *Undershot*: turned by the momentum of the water passing beneath. In a *water turbine*, water is fed under pressure through a vaned wheel within a casing.

WEALDEN HOUSE: type of medieval timber-framed house with a central open hall flanked by bays of two storeys, roofed in line; the end bays are jettied to the front, but the eaves are continuous (8a).

WEATHERBOARDING: wall cladding of overlapping horizontal boards.

WEATHERING or SET-OFF: inclined, projecting surface to keep water away from the wall below.

WEEPERS: figures in niches along the sides of some medieval tombs. Also called mourners.

WHEEL WINDOW: circular, with radiating shafts like spokes. Cf. Rose window.

WROUGHT IRON: *see* Cast iron.

INDEX OF ARCHITECTS, ARTISTS, PATRONS AND RESIDENTS

Names of architects and artists working in the area covered by this volume are given in *italic*. Entries for partnerships and group practices are listed after entries for a single name.

Also indexed here are names/titles of families and individuals (not of bodies or commercial firms) recorded in this volume as having commissioned architectural work or owned or lived in properties in the area. The index includes monuments to members of such families and other individuals where they are of particular interest.

INDEX OF PLACES

Principal references are in **bold** type; demolished buildings are shown in *italic*. In the Bath and Bristol entries, city centres are treated first; inner districts and outer areas are grouped together afterwards, alphabetically, under the subheading 'suburbs and districts'.